STANDARD 8:
Whole Number Computation

In grades K-4, the mathematics curriculum should develop whole number computation so that students can—

- model, explain, and develop reasonable proficiency with basic facts and algorithms;
- use a variety of mental computation and estimation techniques;
- use calculators in appropriate computational situations;
- select and use computation techniques appropriate to specific problems and determine whether the results are reasonable.

STANDARD 9:
Geometry and Spatial Sense

In grades K-4, the mathematics curriculum should include two- and three-dimensional geometry so that students can—

- describe, model, draw, and classify shapes;
- investigate and predict the results of combining, subdividing, and changing shapes;
- develop spatial sense;
- relate geometric ideas to number and measurement ideas;
- recognize and appreciate geometry in their world.

STANDARD 10:
Measurement

In grades K-4, the mathematics curriculum should include measurement so that students can—

- understand the attributes of length, capacity, weight, area, volume, time, temperature, and angle;
- develop the process of measuring and concepts related to units of measurement;
- make and use estimates of measurement;
- make and use measurements in problem and everyday situations.

STANDARD 11:
Statistics and Probability

In grades K-4, the mathematics curriculum should include experiences with data analysis and probability so that students can—

- collect, organize, and describe data;
- construct, read, and interpret displays of data;
- formulate and solve problems that involve collecting and analyzing data;
- explore concepts of chance.

STANDARD 12:
Fractions and Decimals

In grades K-4, the mathematics curriculum should include fractions and decimals so that students can—

- develop concepts of fractions, mixed numbers, and decimals;
- develop number sense for fractions and decimals;
- use models to relate fractions to decimals and to find equivalent fractions;
- use models to explore operations on fractions and decimals;
- apply fractions and decimals to problem situations.

STANDARD 13:
Patterns and Relationships

In grades K-4, the mathematics curriculum should include the study of patterns and relationships so that students can—

- recognize, describe, extend, and create a wide variety of patterns;
- represent and describe mathematical relationships;
- explore the use of variables and open sentences to express relationships.

Curriculum Standards for Grades 5-8 are listed on inside back cover

A Problem Solving Approach to

Mathematics for Elementary School Teachers

Fourth Edition

A Problem Solving Approach to
Mathematics for Elementary School Teachers
Fourth Edition

Rick Billstein
University of Montana
Missoula, Montana

Shlomo Libeskind
University of Oregon
Eugene, Oregon

Johnny W. Lott
University of Montana
Missoula, Montana

 The Benjamin/Cummings Publishing Company, Inc.
Redwood City, California • Fort Collins, Colorado • Menlo Park, California
Reading, Massachusetts • New York • Don Mills, Ontario • Wokingham, U.K.
Amsterdam • Bonn • Sydney • Singapore • Tokyo • Madrid • San Juan

Sponsoring Editor: Lisa J. Moller
Production Editor: Mary B. Shields
Production Assistant: Daniel J. Heller
Text design: Vickie Vandeventer
Cover design: Linda Seals
Copy Editor: Linda Thompson/Steven Grey
Composition: Monotype Composition

Cover photograph reprinted from GAMES Magazine, copyright © 1983 PSC Games Limited Partnership, New York. Page 150, photo by Dan McCoy/Rainbow. Page 182, chart © Scott, Foresman & Co., 1990. Page 194, photo by Vince Streano/After Image © 1982. Page 221, Calvin & Hobbes cartoon © 1987 Universal Press Syndicate, reprinted with permission, all rights reserved. Page 338, photo by James Holland/Stock, Boston. Page 489, The Far Side cartoon © 1985 Universal Press Syndicate, reprinted with permission, all rights reserved. Page 525, logo compliments of Rax® Restaurants, Inc. Page 572, 596, and 642, Mira and Mira books are available through Creative Publications, Cuisenaire Company of America, Dale Seymour Publications. Compass used throughout this text is similar to the Circle Master Compass from Creative Publications, Sunnyvale, California. Page 608, photo © Larry Lee/ West Light. Page 619, Hagar the Horrible cartoon reprinted with special permission of King Features Syndicate, Inc. Page 644, B.C. cartoon by permission of Johnny Hart and Creators Syndicate, Inc. Page 676, logos reprinted by permission of Chevrolet, the Chrysler Corporation, International Harvester, Pacific Telesis Group, and Volkswagen of America, Inc. Pages 679 and 681, prints © 1989 M.C Escher Heirs/Cordon Art Holland. Page 682, tessellation reproduced with permission of *The Computing Teacher*, November 1987, published by the International Society for Technology in Education, © 1987.

Library of Congress Cataloging-in-Publication Data

Billstein, Rick.
   A problem solving approach to mathematics for elementary school teachers/Rick Billstein, Shlomo Libeskind, Johnny W. Lott.—4th ed.

   ISBN 0-8053-0390-1
   1. Mathematics—Study and teaching (Elementary) 2. Problem solving. I. Libeskind, Shlomo. II. Lott, Johnny W. III. Title.
QA135.5.B49   1990
372.7—dc20   89-18076
                                         CIP

ISBN 0-8053-0390-1
CDEFGHIJ-D0-93210

The Benjamin/Cummings Publishing Company, Inc.
390 Bridge Parkway
Redwood City, California 94065

•*To Jane, Molly, and Karly—R.B.*

•*À Janek et Eugenie, leurs filles Brigette et Martine et leurs familles—S.L.*

•*To two superb teachers, Mildred Majors and Carolyn Lott, and the next generation, John—J.W.L.*

PREFACE

The fourth edition of *A Problem Solving Approach to Mathematics for Elementary Teachers* retains the goals of the previous editions, but extends them to meet the requests of users of the third edition as well as to meet new challenges of the 1990s.

Standards of the NCTM

In particular, we focus on the 1989 publication by the National Council of Teachers of Mathematics (NCTM), *Curriculum and Evaluation Standards of School Mathematics* (hereafter referred to as the *Standards*) which states, "Prospective teachers must be taught in a manner similar to how they are to teach—by exploring, conjecturing, communicating, reasoning, and so forth." In addition, "all teachers need an understanding of both the historical developments and current applications of mathematics. Further, they should be familiar with the power of technology."

To that end, the fourth edition allows instructors a variety of approaches to teaching and encourages "doing" as well as lecturing. We kept the elementary mathematics student of the future in mind and have produced a text which allows prospective teachers to examine, represent, transform, prove, apply, solve problems, and communicate in mathematics as they study.

Continuing Goals

In the fourth edition our goals remain:

- To present the appropriate mathematics in an intellectually honest and mathematically correct manner.

- To use the heuristics of problem solving as an integral part of mathematics.

- To approach the mathematics in a sequence which initially instills confidence, then challenges students as they complete the exercises and problem sets.

New Goals

For this edition, we had two additional goals:

- To present the topics in the context of the *Standards*.
- To significantly revise and expand the geometry coverage.

Problem Solving in the Fourth Edition

We showcase problem solving skills by:

- Devoting two chapters (1 and 15) to problem solving.

Chapter 1 has been expanded. Chapter 15 includes a long problem set that utilizes many concepts presented throughout the book.

- Beginning Chapters 1 through 14 with a preliminary problem which poses a question that students can answer with the skills they've mastered from the chapter.

We encourage teachers to introduce the problem at the beginning of the chapter, then spiral back after covering the chapter to show how the techniques therein are necessary to solve the problem.

- Using a four-step problem solving process to solve problems in each chapter.

The four steps are: Understanding the Problem, Devising a Plan, Carrying out the Plan, and Looking Back.

Features Retained in this Edition

Wherever possible, we present topics in ways that could be used in actual classrooms. Further, we have incorporated various study aids and features to facilitate learning.

Computer Corner

- Historical notes add context and humanize the mathematics.
- Cartoons teach or emphasize important material and add levity.
- Problems emphasizing computer usage are indicated by a computer symbol 💻 with special computer corners where appropriate.
- Problems emphasizing calculator usage are indicated by a calculator symbol 🖩.
- Brain Teasers, solved in the Instructor's Guide, may be assigned or used by the teacher to challenge students.
- Key terms are presented in the margins for quick review.
- Review problems are at the end of each nonoptional section.
- Questions from the Classroom have been expanded. We strongly recommend that instructors use these when building a course syllabus. Instructors

Brain Teaser

may require students to write two answers to the questions—one mathematical and one pedagogical—using student texts and professional journals for research.

● Selected Bibliographies have been updated and revised. They are in the Instructor's Guide.

● Chapter tests allow students to test themselves.

● Chapter outlines help students review the chapter.

● Optional problems are marked with an asterisk (*); more difficult problems are marked with a star (★). Problems numbered in color have answers at the back of the book.

● Definitions are either set off in text or presented as key terms in the margin for quick review.

● Color highlights key mathematical concepts.

Features New to this Edition

● van Hiele-type Laboratory Activities in each non-optional geometry section.

● Optional Logo sections in each geometry chapter.

● Problem sets are reorganized first to follow the order of the chapter and second to proceed from easy to difficult.

● Accompanying Activities book by Daniel Dolan and James Williamson parallels the chapter content from the text.

Content

The material has been rewritten and the problem sets revised so that students with diverse backgrounds will find the material accessible. Flexibility is built in for instructors who wish to adapt the text to a variety of course lengths and organizations. Sections marked with asterisks (*) are optional and may be omitted without loss of continuity.

Geometry

In this edition, special attention was paid to revising the geometry chapters:

Chapter 10: Introduces material necessary to study geometry including topological notions, and sets the stage for van Hiele-type activities.

Chapter 11: Includes various types of construction activities involving congruent and similar figures. Activities use tracing paper, paperfolding, Mira, and compass and straightedge.

Chapter 12:   Teaches a transformational approach to congruence and similarity.

Chapter 13:   Presents the rudiments of the English and metric measuring systems and their uses.

Chapter 14:   Covers Coordinate geometry and the relationship between algebra and geometry.

Appendix II: Covers basics of the Logo computer language, a tool for learning geometry. Optional sections and problems in each chapter also use Logo.

Calculator usage

As prescribed in the *Standards*, coverage of calculators is necessary and timely

Chapter 1:   Introduces use of calculators as a problem solving tool. Problems involving calculators are marked with an icon in most sections throughout the book.

Chapters 7 and 9:   Incorporate the use of calculators to investigate a variety of problems.

Numerations systems, whole numbers, and integers

Historical significance of numerations sytems and conceptual development of whole numbers and integers are highlighted.

Chapters 3 and 4:   Emphasize use of different models for presenting the mathematics. Include new sections on mental mathematics and estimation.

Sets, relations, functions, and logic

These topics provide a background for later formal development of mathematics.

Chapter 2:   Includes more problems and applications of functions.

Number theory

Number theory has long been one of the most exciting areas in mathematics.

Chapter 5:   Develops divisibility rules and presents unsolved problems.

Real numbers

Decimals, fractions, and computation with these numbers are typically among the most difficult concepts elementary teachers are required to teach.

Chapters 6 and 7: Provide necessary mathematical tools for understanding relationships among these sets of numbers.

Probability

Topics in probability are now common in elementary school texts.

Chapter 8: Now includes geometric probability and more on simulations as well as tree diagrams and Monte Carlo methods, to aid in an understanding of probability topics.

Statistics

Understanding statistics is key to becoming an educated person.

Chapter 9: Presents new and expanded material using such techniques as stem and leaf graphs, box plots, and line plots for presenting and understanding data.

The content of the book is compatible with the recommendations from the *Standards*. We strongly believe that most people learn mathematics first intuitively and then formally. However we recognize that propspective teachers must learn both the content and the methods of teaching at the same time. As a result, we present the material with motivation for what a concept is, why it is important and how it may be used. To this same end, we encourage users to incorporate the laboratory activities and to use the accompanying activities book by Dolan and Williamson.

Supplements

• Instructor's Guide includes: Answers to all problems; Solutions to problems in Chapter 15, answers for Appendices I and II; Two sample chapter tests for each chapter; Selected Bibliography for each chapter; Suggested answers to Questions from the Classroom; Solutions to Brain Teasers; Solution to the problem appearing on the cover.
• *Mathematics Activities for Elementary School Teachers: A Problem Solving Approach*, by Daniel Dolan and James Williamson.
• Computerized Test Generator contains the questions from the Instructor's Guide, and allows instructors to create the tests to fit their own needs.

Acknowledgements

Our students and users of this text from across the nation have provided us with valuable feedback in revising this text. We have welcomed and continue to welcome constructive comments concerning topics in the text. Comments have led to many positive changes in the book. Many reviewers have contributed time to helping us with the book. One person in particular whose name was omitted from the last edition, but who has taught courses using the book and who has been a friend, colleague, and critic, is Professor Don Loftsgaarden of the University of Montana. We appreciate his help along with the latest reviewers of the manuscript. We could not have succeeded without your help.

Rick Billstein
Shlomo Libeskind
Johnny W. Lott

Reviewers of this edition and previous editions

Leon J. Ablon	Barbara Moses
G. L. Alexanderson	Charles Nelson
Joann Becker	Glenn Nelson
Jim Boone	Keith Peck
Maurice Burke	Barbara Pence
Louis J. Chatterley	Glenn L. Pfeifer
Donald J. Dessart	Edward Rathnell
Marjorie Fitting	Helen R. Santiz
Glenadine Gibb	M. Geralda Schaefer
Alice Guckin	Jane Schielack
Boyd Henry	Barbara Shabell
Alan Hoffer	Gwen Shufelt
E. John Hornsby Jr.	Ron Smit
Jerry Johnson	Joe K. Smith
Wilburn C. Jones	William Sparks
Robert Kalin	Virginia Strawderman
Herbert E. Kasube	C. Ralph Verno
Sarah Kennedy	John Wagner
Steven D. Kerr	Mark F. Weiner
Leland Knauf	Grayson Wheatley
Stanley Lukawecki	Jerry L. Young

BRIEF CONTENTS

C O N T E N T S

Tools for Problem Solving

PRELIMINARY PROBLEM

Sara and David were reading the same novel. When Sara asked David what page he was reading, he replied that the product of the number of the page he was reading and the next page number was 98,282. What page was David reading? 313

Introduction

In the National Council of Teachers of Mathematics (NCTM) publication *Curriculum and Evaluation Standards for School Mathematics* (1989), called simply the *Standards* hereafter, the initial standard at each of the three levels (K–4, 5–8, and 9–12) addresses *problem solving*. For example, in Standard 1 for grades K–4, we find the following quote.

Problem solving should be the central focus of the mathematics curriculum. As such, it is a primary goal of all mathematics instruction and an integral part of all mathematical activity. Problem solving is not a distinct topic but a process that should permeate the entire program and provide the context in which concepts and skills can be learned.

What is a problem? A problem exists when the following conditions are satisfied.

1. A person has no readily available procedure for finding the solution.
2. The person accepts the challenge and makes an attempt to find a solution.

Most textbook problems are designed to give students practice with the content presented in the lesson. For many students, these types of problems are exercises involving routine procedures for finding solutions. For example, $12 \times 4 = \square$ is an exercise for most eighth graders but is a problem for most second graders. Exercises serve their purpose in mathematics, but students are not exposed to problem solving through exercises alone. In the accompanying cartoon, Peppermint Patty tries to substitute one kind of exercise for a problem.

In this chapter, we teach tools or techniques for improving problem-solving skills. A good problem solver needs to experience a variety of problem-solving situations in which the focus is on the problem-solving process rather than just on obtaining the correct answer. Problem solving may require the use of many skills or strategies.

George Polya described the experience of problem solving in his book, *How to Solve It.*

A great discovery solves a great problem but there is a grain of discovery in the solution of any problem. Your problem may be modest; but if it challenges your curiosity and brings into play your inventive facilities, and if you solve it by your own means, you may experience the tension and enjoy the triumph of discovery.

As part of his work on problem solving, Polya developed a four-step process for solving problems similar to the following.

1. Understanding the Problem
   (a) Can you state the problem in your own words?
   (b) What are you trying to find or do?
   (c) What are the unknowns?
   (d) What information do you obtain from the problem?
   (e) What information, if any, is missing or not needed?
2. Devising a Plan
   The following list of strategies, although not exhaustive, is very useful.
   (a) Look for a pattern.
   (b) Examine related problems, and determine if the same technique can be applied.
   (c) Examine a simpler or special case of the problem to gain insight into the solution of the original problem.
   (d) Make a table.
   (e) Make a diagram.
   (f) Write an equation.
   (g) Use guess and check.
   (h) Work backward.
   (i) Identify a subgoal.
3. Carrying out the Plan
   (a) Implement the strategy or strategies in step 2, and perform any necessary actions or computations.
   (b) Check each step of the plan as you proceed. This may be intuitive checking or a formal proof of each step.
   (c) Keep an accurate record of your work.
4. Looking Back
   (a) Check the results in the original problem. (In some cases, this will require a proof.)
   (b) Interpret the solution in terms of the original problem. Does your answer make sense? Is it reasonable?
   (c) Determine whether there is another method of finding the solution.
   (d) If possible, determine other related or more general problems for which the techniques will work.

H I S T O R I C A L   N O T E

George Polya (1887–1985) was born in Hungary and received his PhD in 1912 from the University of Budapest for research on geometric probability. In 1940 he came to the United States and taught at Brown University before moving to Stanford University in 1942. Polya authored over 250 articles, 10 books, and numerous monographs. His book *How to Solve It,* published in 1945, has been translated into at least 17 other languages, has sold over 1 million copies, and has never been out of print. *How to Solve It* was followed in 1954 by two volumes of *Mathematics and Plausible Reasoning* and in 1962 and 1965 by the two volumes of *Mathematical Discovery*.

We urge you to spend some time trying to analyze or solve the preliminary problem. If you do not see an immediate solution to the problem, do not give up, convinced that the problem is beyond your capabilities. If you try to solve the problem but are unable to do so, the solution is presented at the end of the chapter. If you have not solved the problem, read only enough of the solution to get a hint; then try to complete the solution on your own.

In "The Heart of Mathematics," Paul Halmos wrote, "It is the duty of all teachers, and of teachers of mathematics in particular, to expose their students to problems much more than to facts." To this end, we present a variety of problems and use the four-step problem-solving process to solve many of them. The four-step process does not ensure a solution to a problem, but it gives valuable guidelines when there is no obvious way to proceed.

One of the strategies of problem solving, looking for a pattern, is used so often that it is discussed in a separate section. In addition, a separate section is devoted to choosing and using a calculator, an indispensable tool for saving time in performing routine computations and an invaluable aid in many problem-solving situations.

Section 1-1   Exploration with Patterns

Discovering patterns is a very important strategy in problem solving. Police investigators study case files to find the modus operandi, or pattern of operation, when a series of crimes is committed. Their discovery of a pattern, sometimes by using a computer, does not necessarily find the criminal, but it may provide the necessary clues to do so. Similarly, in science and mathematics we try to find solutions to problems by studying patterns and searching for clues. The patterns may or may not provide solutions.

inductive reasoning   Reasoning based on examining a variety of cases or sets of data, discovering patterns, and forming conclusions is called **inductive reasoning.** Scientists use inductive reasoning when they perform experiments to discover various laws of nature. Statisticians use inductive reasoning when they form

conjecture

counterexample

conclusions based on collected data. Inductive reasoning may lead to a **conjecture,** a statement thought to be true but not yet proved to be either true or false. Inductive reasoning should be used cautiously because conjectures developed using inductive reasoning may be false as a **counterexample** can show. Example 1-1 shows that, based on a given set of data, more than one pattern is often possible.

EXAMPLE 1-1   Find the next three terms to complete a pattern.

1, 2, 4, _____, _____, _____

SOLUTION   The difference between the first two terms is 1, and the difference between the second two terms is 2; consequently, the difference between the next two terms might be 3, then 4, and so on. Thus, we conjecture that the completed sequence might appear as follows.

1, 2, 4, <u>7</u>, <u>11</u>, <u>16</u>

Another property that 1, 2, and 4 share is that 2 is twice 1, and 4 is twice 2. Thus, the next terms could be 8, 16, and 32. Hence, the completed sequence might appear as follows.

1, 2, 4, <u>8</u>, <u>16</u>, <u>32</u>

It is evident that more than one pattern is possible, based on the given information.

EXAMPLE 1-2   Find the next three terms to complete a pattern.

□, △, △, □, △, △, □, _____, _____, _____

SOLUTION   Notice that between any two squares there are two consecutive triangles. Based on this observation, the next three terms are two triangles followed by a square. Thus, the completed sequence might appear as follows.

□, △, △, □, △, △, □, <u>△</u>, <u>△</u>, <u>□</u>

Inductive reasoning is useful in the real world to develop conjectures. However, even though inductive reasoning, based on many laboratory tests and case studies, is used to decide if a drug is safe, the pharmaceutical world has been shaken several times when a laboratory-tested drug has later proved to be extremely harmful. Sometimes it is necessary to test a large number of cases to find that a conjectured pattern does not continue.

The following discussion illustrates the danger of making a conjecture based on a few cases. In Figure 1-1, we choose points on a circle and connect them to form distinct, nonoverlapping regions. In Figure 1-1 we see that 2 points determine 2 regions, 3 points determine 4 regions, and 4 points

FIGURE 1-1

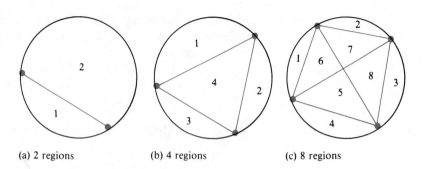

(a) 2 regions   (b) 4 regions   (c) 8 regions

determine 8 regions. What is the maximum number of regions that would be determined by 12 points and, in general, n points?

The data from Figure 1-1 are recorded in Table 1-1. It appears that each time we increase the number of points by 1, we double the number of regions. If this were true, then for 5 points we would have 16, or 2^4, regions, for 6 points we would have 32, or 2^5, regions, and so on. If we base our solution on this pattern, we would have 2^{11}, or 2048 regions for 12 points and 2^{n-1} regions for n points.

TABLE 1-1

Number of points	2	3	4	5	6	...	12	...	n
Number of regions	$2 = 2^1$	$4 = 2^2$	$8 = 2^3$				?		?

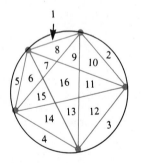

(a) 16 regions

FIGURE 1-2

Before reading on, check to see whether we obtain 16 regions for 5 points. We obtain a figure similar to Figure 1-2, and our guess of 16 regions is verified. We consider one more case to check whether the pattern continues for 6 points. If we choose the points so that they are not equally spaced and we count the regions correctly, we obtain 31 regions—and not 32 regions, as predicted. This shows that our guess of 2^{n-1} for n points is not true for all n. (Checking further will verify that it is not true for the numbers 7 through 12.) This may be shocking to most of us who put our faith in the continuation of a simple pattern once we have been fortunate enough to discover it. But it should be noted that a pattern to the sequence generated by 1, 2, 4, 8, 31, ... does exist; the nth term is given by

$$\frac{n(n-1)(n-2)(n-3)}{24} + \frac{n(n-1)}{2} + 1$$

Arithmetic Sequence

sequence In the previous examples, the terms were given in an ordered arrangement. The word **sequence** is used to describe terms given in such a way that they can be thought of as being numbered; that is, there is a first, a second, and so on. If each successive term in a sequence is obtained from the previous

difference
arithmetic sequence

term by the addition of a fixed number, the **difference,** then the sequence is an **arithmetic sequence.** Consider Example 1-3.

EXAMPLE 1-3　Find a pattern in the number of matchsticks required to continue the pattern shown in Figure 1-3. Assume that the matchsticks are arranged so that each figure has one more square than the preceding figure.

FIGURE 1-3

4　　7　　10　　13　　16　19　22

SOLUTION　The numbers of matchsticks required to make the successive figures are 4, 7, 10, and 13. As seen below, each term after the first is 3 units greater than the previous term.

Sequence　　4　7　10　13　——
Difference　　　3　3　3　3

If this pattern continues, the next three terms will be 16, 19, and 22, which indicates that the number of matchsticks in each of the next three terms will be 16, 19, and 22, respectively.

We can show that this pattern of adding 3 each time continues by observing that the addition of another square requires 3 matchsticks to be added to form the 3 sides of the square. The fourth side is determined by an existing matchstick.

The sequence in Example 1-3 is an arithmetic sequence. The difference is 3. Neither pattern in Example 1-1 illustrates an arithmetic sequence because no fixed number has been added.

It is often useful to predict the terms in a sequence. Tables are helpful problem-solving aids for finding such values. Table 1-2 shows the sequence in Example 1-3. The column headed "Number of Term" refers to the order of the term in the sequence. The column headed "Term" lists the accompa-

ellipsis　nying terms of the sequence. We use an **ellipsis,** denoted by three dots, to indicate that the sequence continues in the same manner.

TABLE 1-2

Number of Term	Term
1	4
2	$7 = 4 + 3 = 4 + 1 \cdot 3$
3	$10 = 4 + 3 + 3 = 4 + 2 \cdot 3$
4	$13 = 4 + 3 + 3 + 3 = 4 + 3 \cdot 3$
⋮	⋮

Notice that the number of 3s in each term is one less than the number of the term. If we assume that this pattern continues, the 10th term is $4 + 9 \cdot 3$, or 31, and the 100th term is $4 + 99 \cdot 3$, or 301. The general, or nth, term of a sequence enables us to find any term, given the number of the term. In the preceding sequence, the nth term is $4 + (n - 1)3$. Many students may express the pattern for the nth term as $3n + 1$. This is algebraically equivalent to $4 + (n - 1)3$. The 200th term for this sequence can be obtained by substituting 200 for n to obtain $4 + (200 - 1)3$, or $4 + (199)3$, or 601.

In the sequence in Table 1-2 the nth term is $4 + (n - 1)3$. We could use this expression to find the number of a term if we were given the value of the term. For example, suppose that we have the term 1798. We know that $4 + (n - 1)3 = 1798$. This tells us that $(n - 1)3 = 1794$, or that $n - 1 = 598$. Thus, $n = 599$.

A related problem is to generate the sequence if given the nth term.

EXAMPLE 1-4   Find the first four terms of a sequence whose nth term is given by the following.
(a) $4n + 3$
(b) $n^2 - 1$

SOLUTION   (a) To find the first term, we substitute $n = 1$ in the formula $4n + 3$ to obtain $4 \cdot 1 + 3$, or 7. Similarly, substituting $n = 2, 3, 4$, we obtain $4 \cdot 2 + 3$, or 11, $4 \cdot 3 + 3$, or 15, and $4 \cdot 4 + 3$, or 19, respectively. Hence, the first four terms of the sequence are 7, 11, 15, 19.
(b) Substituting $n = 1, 2, 3, 4$ in the formula $n^2 - 1$, we obtain $1^2 - 1$, or 0, $2^2 - 1$, or 3, $3^2 - 1$, or 8, $4^2 - 1$, or 15, respectively. Thus, the first four terms of the sequence are 0, 3, 8, 15.

It is possible to generalize our work with arithmetic sequences. Suppose that the first term in an arithmetic sequence is a and the difference is d. The strategy of *making a table* can be used to investigate the general term for the sequence $a, a + d, a + 2d, a + 3d, \ldots$, as shown in Table 1-3. We see that *the nth term of any sequence with first term a and difference d is given by $a + (n - 1)d$*. For example, in the sequence 5, 9, 13, 17, 21, 25, . . . ,

TABLE 1-3

Number of Term	Term
1	a
2	$a + d$
3	$a + 2d$
4	$a + 3d$
5	$a + 4d$
$\vdots$	$\vdots$
n	$a + (n - 1)d$

the first term is 5 and the difference is 4. Thus, the nth term is given by $a + (n - 1)d = 5 + (n - 1)4$. Simplifying algebraically, we obtain $5 + 4n - 4 = 4n + 1$.

EXAMPLE 1-5 Find the first two terms of an arithmetic sequence in which the 3rd term is 13 and the 30th term is 121.

SOLUTION The formula for the nth term in an arithmetic sequence is $a + (n - 1)d$, where a represents the 1st term and d is the difference. We construct a table similar to Table 1-3. We do not know what the 1st two terms are, but the 3rd term is 13. The 4th term is $13 + d$, and so on, as in Table 1-4.

TABLE 1-4

Number of Term	Term
1	?
2	?
3	13
4	$13 + d$
5	$13 + 2d$
6	$13 + 3d$
.	.
.	.
.	.
30	?

The 30th term is of the form $13 + \square d$. Because the 4th term is $13 + 1d$, the 5th term is $13 + 2d$ and the 6th term is $13 + 3d$ and because we have an arithmetic sequence, we see that the number of d's in each case is always 3 less than the number of the term. Therefore, the 30th term is given by $13 + 27d$. Because the 30th term is 121, we have the following.

$$13 + 27d = 121$$
$$27d = 108$$
$$d = 4$$

Now we see that the second term is $13 - 4$, or 9, and the first term is $9 - 4$, or 5.

Sometimes the fundamental idea of an arithmetic sequence is lost in the algebra. A nonalgebraic solution of Example 1-5 can be found by using a number line, as shown in Figure 1-4. Since there are 108 units between the number 13 and 121 and there are 27 gaps between the 3rd number and the 30th number in the sequence, each gap must be $108/27 = 4$ units long. Therefore, the 2nd term is $13 - 4 = 9$ and the 1st term is $9 - 4 = 5$.

FIGURE 1-4

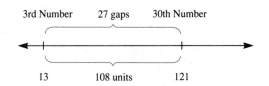

Geometric Sequence

A different type of sequence is investigated in the following discussion. A child in a family has 2 parents, 4 grandparents, 8 great-grandparents, 16 great-great-grandparents, and so on. We see that the numbers of ancestors from previous generations form the sequence 2, 4, 8, 16, 32, ... This type of sequence is called a **geometric sequence.** Each successive term of a geometric sequence is obtained from its predecessor by multiplying by a fixed number called the **ratio.** In this example, both the 1st term and the ratio are 2. To find the nth term, examine Table 1-5.

geometric sequence

ratio

TABLE 1-5

Number of Term	Term
1	$2 = 2^1$
2	$4 = 2 \cdot 2 = 2^2$
3	$8 = (2 \cdot 2) \cdot 2 = 2^3$
4	$16 = (2 \cdot 2 \cdot 2) \cdot 2 = 2^4$
5	$32 = (2 \cdot 2 \cdot 2 \cdot 2) \cdot 2 = 2^5$
.	.
.	.
.	.

● **R E M A R K**

The expression a^n, where n is a natural number, means $\underbrace{a \cdot a \cdot a \cdot a \cdots a}_{n \text{ terms}}$.

The table reveals a pattern: When the given term is written as a power of 2, the number of the term is the exponent of 2. Following this pattern, the 10th term is 2^{10}, or 1024, the 100th term is 2^{100}, and the nth term is 2^n. Thus, the number of ancestors in the nth previous generation is 2^n.

The sequence 2, 4, 8, 16, 32, . . . is a *doubling* sequence, and the nth term is 2^n. Can the nth term for the sequence 2, 6, 18, 54, . . . be obtained in a similar manner? Each term is obtained from the previous one by multiplication by 3, as shown in Table 1-6. Following this pattern, the 10th term is $2 \cdot 3^9$, the 100th term is $2 \cdot 3^{99}$, and the nth term is $2 \cdot 3^{n-1}$.

TABLE 1-6

Number of Term	Term
1	2
2	$6 = 2 \cdot 3$
3	$18 = (2 \cdot 3) \cdot 3 = 2 \cdot 3^2$
4	$54 = (2 \cdot 3^2) \cdot 3 = 2 \cdot 3^3$
.	.
.	.
.	.

Just as we could determine a formula for finding the nth term of an arithmetic sequence, we can also find the nth term of any geometric sequence by finding a relation between the number of a term and the value of the term. Making a table helped us find the terms of an arithmetic sequence, so a similar strategy might work here. An arithmetic sequence was determined by the first term and the difference. Similarly, a geometric sequence might be determined by the first term and the ratio. If the first term is a and the ratio is r, then the terms are as given in Table 1-7. We see that the nth term of any geometric sequence where the first term is a and the ratio is r is given by the formula ar^{n-1}. Notice that, for $n = 1$, we have $ar^{1-1} = ar^0$. If $r \neq 0$, then $r^0 = 1$. (This is discussed in Chapter 6.) Thus, when $n = 1$ and $r \neq 0$, we have $ar^0 = a(1) = a$. If we are given the geometric sequence 3, 12, 48, 192, . . . , the first term is 3 and the ratio is 4. Thus, the nth term is given by $ar^{n-1} = 3 \cdot 4^{n-1}$.

TABLE 1-7

Number of Term	Term
1	a
2	ar
3	ar^2
4	ar^3
5	ar^4
.	.
.	.
.	.
n	ar^{n-1}

Other Sequences

figurate numbers

Some sequences are neither arithmetic nor geometric. **Figurate numbers** provide examples of such sequences. The number 1 is the beginning of most patterns of figurate numbers, because it was felt that 1 was the beginning of all numbers. Consider the arrays in Figure 1-5, which represent the first four

square numbers

terms of a sequence of numbers known as the **square numbers** or *perfect squares*. The square numbers pictured may be written as 1^2, 2^2, 3^2, and 4^2. If each array of dots in the pattern continues in the form of a square, the number of dots in the 10th array is 10^2, the number of dots in the 100th array is 100^2, and the number of dots in the nth array is n^2.

FIGURE 1-5

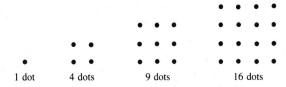

1 dot   4 dots   9 dots   16 dots

As the following diagram shows, the square numbers do not generate an arithmetic sequence, because there is no common difference.

$$1 \quad 4 \quad 9 \quad 16 \quad 25 \quad 36 \quad \underline{}$$

(1st difference) $3 \quad 5 \quad 7 \quad 9 \quad 11 \quad \underline{}$

However, the sequence of first differences, 3, 5, 7, 9, 11, . . . , does form an arithmetic sequence with common difference 2.

$$3 \quad 5 \quad 7 \quad 9 \quad 11 \quad \underline{}$$

(2nd difference) $2 \quad 2 \quad 2 \quad 2 \quad 2$

Since the 2nd differences are all 2, the next first difference is 13. Using this information, we can determine that the next term in the original sequence is 36 + 13, or 49. Additional terms in the sequence can be generated in a similar manner.

EXAMPLE 1-6   The arrays shown in Figure 1-6 represent the first four terms of a sequence of numbers called *triangular numbers*. What is the 10th term? What is the 100th term? What is the *n*th term?

FIGURE 1-6

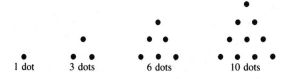

1 dot   3 dots   6 dots   10 dots

SOLUTION   Table 1-8 suggests the sequence of numbers and a pattern for finding the desired terms. From Table 1-8, we see that the 2nd term is obtained from the 1st term by adding 2, the 3rd term is obtained from the 2nd by adding 3, and so on. In general, because the *n*th triangular number has *n* dots in the *n*th row, it is equal to the sum of the dots in the previous triangular number (the $(n - 1)$th one) plus the *n* dots in the *n*th row. Following this pattern, the 10th term is $1 + 2 + 3 + 4 + 5 + 6 + 7 + 8 + 9 + 10$, or 55, the 100th term is $1 + 2 + 3 + 4 + 5 + \cdots + 99 + 100$, and the *n*th term is $1 + 2 + 3 + 4 + 5 + \cdots + (n - 1) + n$.

TABLE 1-8

Number of Term	Term
1	1
2	$3 = 1 + 2$
3	$6 = 1 + 2 + 3$
4	$10 = 1 + 2 + 3 + 4$
5	$15 = 1 + 2 + 3 + 4 + 5$
.	.
.	.
.	.
10	$55 = 1 + 2 + 3 + 4 + 5 + 6 + 7 + 8 + 9 + 10$

Example 1-6 suggests another interesting problem, namely, developing a technique for finding sums of the form $1 + 2 + 3 + \cdots + (n - 1) + n$. This problem is discussed in the next section.

Another way of looking at the sequence of triangular numbers is to consider differences, as we did for the square numbers.

$$1 \quad 3 \quad 6 \quad 10 \quad 15 \quad \underline{}$$

(1st difference) $2 \quad 3 \quad 4 \quad 5 \quad 6$

(2nd difference) $1 \quad 1 \quad 1 \quad 1$

Using the idea of differences, we see that the next triangular number after 15 is $15 + 6$, or 21.

The next example involves sequences for which it is helpful to take more than one successive difference to find a pattern.

EXAMPLE 1-7   Find the seventh term in each of the following sequences.

(a) 5, 6, 14, 29, 51, 80, . . .

(b) 2, 3, 9, 23, 48, 87, . . .

SOLUTION   (a) The pattern for the differences between successive terms is not easily recognizable.

$$5 \quad 6 \quad 14 \quad 29 \quad 51 \quad 80$$

(1st difference) $1 \quad 8 \quad 15 \quad 22 \quad 29$

To discover a pattern for the original sequence, we try to find a pattern for the sequence of differences 1, 8, 15, 22, 29, ... This sequence is an arithmetic sequence with fixed difference 7.

$$5 \quad 6 \quad 14 \quad 29 \quad 51 \quad 80$$

(1st difference) $1 \quad 8 \quad 15 \quad 22 \quad 29$

(2nd difference) $7 \quad 7 \quad 7 \quad 7$

Thus, the 6th term in the 1st-difference row is $29 + 7$, or 36, and hence the 7th term in the original sequence is $80 + 36$, or 116. What number follows 116?

(b) Since the 2nd difference is not a fixed number, we go on to the 3rd difference, as shown.

$$2 \quad 3 \quad 9 \quad 23 \quad 48 \quad 87$$

(1st difference) $1 \quad 6 \quad 14 \quad 25 \quad 39$

(2nd difference) $5 \quad 8 \quad 11 \quad 14$

(3rd difference) $3 \quad 3 \quad 3$

Since the 3rd difference is a fixed number, the 2nd difference is an arithmetic sequence. The 5th term in the 2nd-difference sequence is $14 + 3$, or 17, the

6th term in the 1st-difference sequence is $39 + 17$, or 56, and the 7th term in the original sequence is $87 + 56$, or 143.

When asked to find a pattern for a given sequence, we first look for some easily recognizable pattern. If none exists, we determine whether the sequence is either arithmetic or geometric. If a pattern is still unclear, taking successive differences may help. *It is possible that none of the methods described will reveal a pattern.*

PROBLEM SET 1-1

1. List the terms that complete a possible pattern. Then describe the pattern.
   (a) $1 \times 2, 2 \times 3, 3 \times 4, 4 \times 5,$ _____, _____, _____
   (b) □, 00, □□□, 0000, □□□□□, _____, _____, _____
   (c) 61, 57, 53, 49, _____, _____, _____
   (d) 5, 6, 8, 11, _____, _____, _____
   (e) 2, 5, 10, 17, _____, _____, _____
   (f) $X, Y, X, X, Y, X, X,$ _____, _____, _____
   (g) 1, 3, 1, 8, 1, 13, _____, _____, _____
   (h) 1, 1, 2, 3, 5, 8, 13, 21, _____, _____, _____
   (i) 1, 11, 111, 1111, 11111, _____, _____,
   (j) 1, 12, 123, 1234, 12345, _____, _____,
   (k) $1 \times 2, 2 \times 2^2, 3 \times 2^3, 4 \times 2^4, 5 \times 2^5,$ _____, _____, _____
   (l) $2, 2^2, 2^4, 2^8, 2^{16},$ _____, _____, _____
   (m) , ___, ___, ___
   (n) 5, 10, _____, 20, _____, 30, 35, _____
   (o) 0, 7, 14, _____, 28, _____, 42, _____
   (p) $0, \frac{1}{2}, 1,$ _____, 2, _____, 3, _____
   (q) 0, 22, _____, 66, _____, _____

2. In each case, list terms that complete a possible pattern. Which of the following sequences are arithmetic, which are geometric, and which are neither?
   (a) 1, 3, 5, 7, 9, _____, _____, _____
   (b) 0, 50, 100, 150, 200, _____, _____, _____
   (c) 3, 6, 12, 24, 48, _____, _____, _____
   (d) 10, 100, 1000, 10000, 100000, _____, _____, _____
   (e) $5^2, 5^3, 5^4, 5^5, 5^6,$ _____, _____, _____
   (f) 11, 22, 33, 44, 55, _____, _____, _____
   (g) $2^1, 2^3, 2^5, 2^7, 2^9,$ _____, _____, _____
   (h) 9, 13, 17, 21, 25, 29, _____, _____, _____

   (i) 1, 8, 27, 64, 125, _____, _____, _____
   (j) 2, 6, 18, 54, 162, _____, _____, _____

3. Fill in the circles by making use of the patterns in a calendar.

(a)
S	M	T	W	T	F	S
		1				
			9			○
○			17			
				25		

(b)
S	M	T	W	T	F	S
			2			
						○
	○					

4. The following geometric arrays suggest a sequence of numbers.

2   6   12   20

   (a) Find the next three terms.
   (b) Find the 100th term.
   (c) Find the nth term.

5. In the following pattern, one hexagon takes 6 toothpicks to build, two hexagons take 11 toothpicks to build, and so on. How many toothpicks would it take to build (a) 10 hexagons? (b) n hexagons?

6. The first windmill takes 5 squares to build, the second takes 9 squares to build, and the third takes 13 squares to build, as shown. How many squares will it take to build (a) the 10th windmill? (b) the nth windmill?

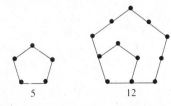

7. The school population for a certain school was predicted to increase by 50 students a year for the next 10 years. If the current enrollment is 700 students, what will the enrollment be after 10 years?

8. A tank contains 15,360 L of water. At the end of each day half of the water is removed and not replaced. How much water is left in the tank after 10 days?

9. A well driller charges $10 a foot for the first 10 feet, $10.50 a foot for the next 10 feet, $11 a foot for the next 10 feet, and so on, increasing the price by 50¢ for each 10 feet. What is the cost of drilling a 100-foot well?

10. An employee is paid $1200 at the end of the first month on the job. Each month after that, the worker is paid $20 more than in the preceding month.
    (a) What is the employee's monthly salary at the end of the second year on the job?
    (b) How much will the employee have earned after 6 months?
    (c) After how many months will the employee's monthly salary be $3240?

11. A commuter train picks up passengers at 7:30 A.M. If 1 person gets on at the first stop, 3 at the second stop, 5 at the third stop, and so on in this manner, how many people get on at the tenth stop?

12. (a) If a fixed number is added to each term of an arithmetic sequence, is the resulting sequence an arithmetic sequence? Justify your answer.
    (b) If each term of an arithmetic sequence is multiplied by a fixed number, will the resulting sequence always be an arithmetic sequence? Justify your answer.

13. Answer the questions in Problem 12 for a geometric sequence.

14. (a) Consider the following geometric arrays of pentagonal numbers. The numbers are formed by counting the dots. Find the first six numbers suggested by this sequence.
    ★(b) What is the 100th pentagonal number?

15. The first difference of a sequence is a sequence of consecutive even numbers, 2, 4, 6, 8, ... Find the first six terms of the original sequence in each of the following cases.
    (a) The first term of the original sequence is 3.
    (b) The sum of the first two terms of the original sequence is 10.
    (c) The fifth term of the original sequence is 35.

16. List the next three terms to complete a pattern in each of the following. (Finding differences may be helpful.)
    (a) 5, 6, 14, 32, 64, 115, 191, _____, _____ _____
    (b) 0, 2, 6, 12, 20, 30, 42, _____, _____, _____
    ★(c) 10, 8, 3, 0, 4, 20, 53, _____, _____, _____

17. How many terms are there in the following sequences?
    (a) 1, 2, 3, 4, . . . , 100
    (b) 51, 52, 53, 54, . . . , 151
    (c) 2, 4, 6, 8, . . . , 200
    (d) $1, 2, 2^2, 2^3, . . . , 2^{60}$
    (e) 10, 20, 30, 40, . . . , 2000

18. The following is an example of term-by-term addition of two arithmetic sequences.

    $$\begin{array}{r} 1, 3, \ \ 5, \ \ 7, \ \ 9, 11, \ldots \\ +\ 2, 4, \ \ 6, \ \ 8, 10, 12, \ldots \\ \hline 3, 7, 11, 15, 19, 23, \ldots \end{array}$$

    Notice that the resulting sequence is also arithmetic. Investigate whether this happens again, by trying two other examples.

19. Find the first five terms of the sequence whose nth term is as follows.
    (a) $n^2 + 2$ (b) $5n - 1$ (c) $10^n - 1$ (d) $3n + 2$

20. The sequence 1, 1, 2, 3, 5, 8, 13, 21, . . . , in which each term starting with the third one is the sum of the two preceding terms, is called a *Fibonacci sequence*. This sequence is named after the great Italian mathematician Leonardo Fibonacci, who lived in the twelfth and thirteenth centuries.
    (a) Write the first 12 terms of the sequence.
    (b) Notice that the sum of the first 3 terms in the sequence is one less than the 5th term of the sequence. Does a similar relationship hold for the sum of the first 4 terms, 5 terms, and 6 terms?
    (c) Guess the sum of the first 10 terms of the sequence.
    ★(d) Make a conjecture concerning the sum of the first n terms of the sequence.

21. Find the 100th term and the nth term in each of the sequences of Problem 2.

22. (a) The 10th term in an arithmetic sequence is 47 and the 20th term is 87. Find the first 3 terms.
    (b) The 4th term in an arithmetic sequence is 10 and the 10th term is 28. Find the 1st term.

23. A student claims that the sequence of first differences of every geometric sequence is itself a geometric sequence. Is the student correct? Justify your answer.

24. Consider the following two sequences.
    (a) 300, 500, 700, 900, 1100, 1300, . . .
    (b) 2, 4, 8, 16, 32, 64, . . .
    Find the number of the term in which the geometric sequence becomes greater than the arithmetic sequence.

B R A I N   T E A S E R

Find the patterns in each of the following.

(a) Find the next three terms in the following sequence.

O, T, T, F, F, S, S, E, _____, _____, _____

(b) Determine a pattern for placing letters above or below the horizontal line in the following diagram.

A		EF	HI	KLMN		T	VWXYZ
	BCD		G	J		OPQRS	U

Section 1-2   Using the Problem-Solving Process

If you follow only certain patterns in attacking problems, you may risk forming a mind set. A mind set occurs when you approach a problem in only one way. For example, consider the following children's nursery rhyme.

As I was going to St. Ives
I met a man with seven wives.
Every wife had seven sacks,
Every sack had seven cats,
Every cat had seven kits,
Kits, cats, sacks, and wives,
How many were going to St. Ives?

Without carefully reading the rhyme, you may start counting the number of wives, sacks, cats, and kits. If you do, you have a mind set. Reread the rhyme. There is only one person going to St. Ives. Could you solve the problem if the question were "How many were coming from St. Ives?"

Other common mind sets follow: Spell the word "spot" three times aloud. "S-P-O-T! S-P-O-T! S-P-O-T!" Now answer the question: "What do you do when you come to a green light?" Write your answer. If you answered "Stop," you may be guilty of forming a mind set. You do not stop at a *green* light.

Consider the following problem: "A man had 36 sheep. All but 10 died. How many lived?"

Did you answer "10"? If you did, you are catching on and are ready to try some problems. If you did not answer "10," then you did not understand the question. As was pointed out in the introduction, using the four-step process does not guarantee a solution to a problem, but it does provide a systematic means of attacking problems. We now discuss the process in more detail.

Step 1: Understanding the Problem

Understanding the Problem involves not only applying the skills necessary for literary reading but determining what is being asked, what information is known, and what information is missing or not known. Consider the following.

Bo and Jojo went to a football game. The tickets cost $4.00 each. Bo gave the cashier $10.00 and received $2.00 in change. At the concession stand, Jojo bought two cans of juice at $1.25 each and two containers of popcorn at $0.80 each. Three minutes before halftime, Bo bought a hot dog for $0.75 and a can of juice. They left the game with 4 minutes and 13 seconds left to play. How much did they spend on juice?

In this problem, the question is clear. However, there is a lot of extraneous information. The only important information is that three cans of juice were bought and each one cost $1.25, for a total of $3.75. Another example follows.

Thanksgiving was on November 24, 1983. Memorial Day was on May 28, 1984. How many days were there between the two holidays?

In this problem there is no extraneous information, but additional information is needed. We have to know how many days there are in the months of November, December, January, February, March, and April. In addition, we have to recognize that 1984 is a leap year and that February has an additional day in a leap year. Finally, we have to know what *between* means. In mathematics, *between* is not inclusive, which means that we do not count November 24 and May 28.

Step 2: Devising a Plan

Devising a Plan involves finding a strategy to aid in solving a problem. In *How to Solve It,* Polya emphasized the importance of this step when he wrote "the main achievement in the solution of a problem is to conceive the idea of a plan."

Students often ask which strategy to use for a specific problem. There is no definite answer to this question. However, being aware of general strategies for problem solving and practicing using various strategies should be helpful in determining an appropriate strategy for a particular problem. A specific strategy is learned by practicing it. Once learned, strategies are simply tools to aid in the problem-solving process. The notion here is similar to that contained in the following ancient proverb.

If you give a person a loaf of bread, you feed the person for a day;
If you teach the person to bake, you feed the person for a lifetime.

We consider several strategies in detail later in this section.

Step 3: Carrying Out the Plan

Carrying out the Plan involves attempting to solve the problem with some chosen strategy. If the chosen strategy does not work, we try to devise a new strategy. Here we also perform any necessary arithmetic or algebraic computations. An important tool for performing arithmetic operations is the calculator.

Step 4: Looking Back

The Looking Back step is where we check the solution in terms of the original problem. We begin by asking if the answer is reasonable and if it answers the required question or questions. However, there is much more than that to this step; it is here that we should consider extensions to the completed problem and other ways to solve the problem. In the problems in this text, you should try the extensions mentioned. In many cases the extension is more interesting than the original problem.

Strategies for Problem Solving

In a problem-solving situation, a student has a goal to achieve but may not have the *means* to achieve it. The student must construct the means through a process that might be hindered by unanswered questions, false starts, and dead ends. *Strategies* are tools that might be useful in discovering or constructing means to achieve a goal. For each of the strategies described, a problem is given that can be solved by using that strategy. Read each problem, and try to solve it before reading the solution. If you need a hint, read only enough of the solution to help you get started. After you have solved the problem, compare your solution with the one in the text.

Strategy—Look for a Pattern

The strategy of looking for a pattern was examined in the previous section, where we concentrated on sequences of numbers. We continue that investigation here.

PROBLEM 1

When the famous German mathematician Karl Gauss was a child, his teacher required the students to find the sum of the first 100 natural numbers. The teacher expected this problem to keep the class occupied for some time. Gauss gave the answer almost immediately. Can you?

natural numbers   **Understanding the Problem.**   The **natural numbers** are 1, 2, 3, 4, ... Thus, the problem is to find the sum $1 + 2 + 3 + 4 + \cdots + 100$.

Devising a Plan.   One possible strategy is that of *looking for a pattern*. By considering $1 + 100, 2 + 99, 3 + 98, \ldots, 50 + 51$, it is evident that there are 50 pairs of numbers, each with a sum of 101, as shown in Figure 1-7.

FIGURE 1-7

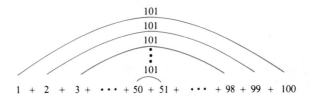

Carrying Out the Plan.   There are 50 pairs, each with the sum 101. Thus, the total sum is 50(101), or 5050.

Looking Back.   The method is mathematically correct because addition can be performed in any order, and multiplication is repeated addition. A more general problem is to find the sum of the first n numbers, $1 + 2 + 3 + 4 + 5 + \cdots + n$, where n is any natural number. We use the same plan as before and notice the relationship in Figure 1-8. If n is an even natural number, there are $n/2$ pairs of numbers. The sum of each pair is $n + 1$. Therefore, the sum $1 + 2 + 3 + \cdots + n$ is given by $(n/2)(n + 1)$. Does the same formula work if n is odd?

FIGURE 1-8

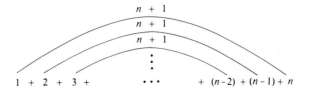

A different strategy to finding the sum $1 + 2 + 3 + \cdots + n$ involves thinking of the sum geometrically as a stack of blocks. To find the sum, we might consider the stack in Figure 1-9(a) and a stack of the same size placed differently, as in Figure 1-9(b). The total number of blocks in the stack in Figure 1-9(b) is $n(n + 1)$, which is twice the desired sum. Thus, the desired sum is $n(n + 1)/2$.

FIGURE 1-9

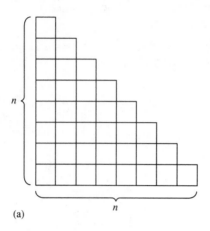

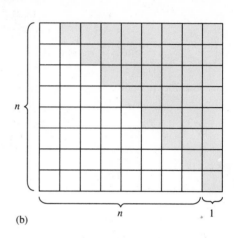

(a)

(b)

H I S T O R I C A L   N O T E

Karl Gauss (1777–1855) is regarded as the greatest mathematician of the nineteenth century and one of the greatest mathematicians of all time. Born to humble parents in Brunswick, Germany, he was an infant prodigy who, it is said, at age 3 corrected an arithmetic error in his father's bookkeeping. Gauss used to claim that he could figure before he could talk.

Gauss made contributions in the areas of astronomy, geodesy, and electricity. After his death, the King of Hanover ordered a commemorative medal prepared in his honor. On the medal was an inscription referring to Gauss as the "Prince of Mathematics," a title that has stayed with his name.

Strategy—Make a Table

The next strategy that we consider is that of making a table. A table can be used to summarize data or to help us see a pattern, and it also helps us consider all possible cases in a given problem.

PROBLEM 2

How many ways are there to make change for a quarter, using only dimes, nickels, and pennies?

Understanding the Problem. There are no special limits on the number of coins that may be used to make change for a quarter. Nickels, dimes, and pennies need not all be used; that is, 25 pennies is an acceptable answer, as is 2 dimes and 1 nickel.

Devising a Plan. In this problem the strategy of *making a table* is used to keep a record of all possibilities as they are examined.

Carrying Out the Plan. First, consider the possibilities when the number of nickels and dimes is zero and the number of pennies is 25. Continue the chart by trading nickels for pennies, as shown in Table 1-9. Are there other combinations? What about dimes? To finish the problem, consider all possibilities using dimes. Start with combinations using one dime. With one dime, the greatest number of pennies possible is 15. Next, trade nickels for pennies, as shown in Table 1-10. The last case to consider is possibilities with 2 dimes. Proceeding as before, we obtain Table 1-11. Thus, there are $6 + 4 + 2 = 12$ ways to make change for a quarter using only dimes, nickels, and pennies.

TABLE 1-9

D	N	P
0	0	25
0	1	20
0	2	15
0	3	10
0	4	5
0	5	0

(6 ways using 0 dimes)

TABLE 1-10

D	N	P
1	0	15
1	1	10
1	2	5
1	3	0

(4 ways using 1 dime)

TABLE 1-11

D	N	P
2	0	5
2	1	0

(2 ways using 2 dimes)

Looking Back. Check each row of each table to confirm that it shows change for a quarter. The systematic listing used in the tables shows that all cases have been considered. The problem can be extended easily by starting with an initial amount other than one quarter.

Another interesting, related problem is as follows. Given the number of coins it takes to make change for a quarter, is it possible to determine exactly which coins they are? (*Hint:* Look at the tables listing the 12 different combinations. Is the number of coins in each combination different?) If you think you know the answer, try it with a friend to see if it works.

Strategy—Examine a Simpler Case
Because of the complexity of many situations, it is often easier to start by considering a simpler case of the problem and then build to the original problem.

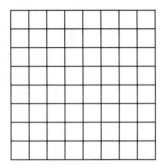

FIGURE 1-10

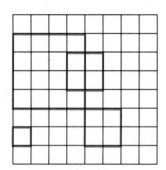

FIGURE 1-11

PROBLEM 3
Using the existing lines on the checkerboard shown in Figure 1-10, how many different squares are there?

Understanding the Problem. Before proceeding, we must be clear about what is meant by square and also what is meant by "different squares." A square is a four-sided figure with four right angles whose sides are line segments of equal length. Two squares are different if they have either different dimensions or different locations. For example, the colored lines in Figure 1-11 show four different squares.

Devising a Plan. The strategy of *examining simpler cases* is one of the most important strategies in problem solving and will be used repeatedly in this text. This strategy appears to be appropriate here. The simplest case to consider is given in Figure 1-12(a). We see that there is only one 1×1 square in this grid. Now consider the 2×2 grid in Figure 1-12(b). There are four 1×1 squares and one 2×2 square, for a total of 5 squares. In a 3×3 grid, as in Figure 1-12(c), there are nine 1×1 squares, four 2×2 squares, and one 3×3 square, for a total of 14 squares. How many squares are there in Figure 1-12(d)? The problem now becomes more involved. The information obtained from Figure 1-12 is recorded in Table 1-12.

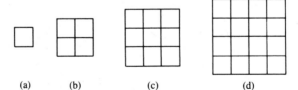

FIGURE 1-12   (a)   (b)   (c)   (d)

TABLE 1-12

Grid Size	1×1 Squares	2×2 Squares	3×3 Squares	4×4 Squares	Total Squares
1×1	1, or 1^2				1
2×2	4, or 2^2	1, or 1^2			5
3×3	9, or 3^2	4, or 2^2	1, or 1^2		14
4×4	16, or 4^2	9, or 3^2	4, or 2^2	1, or 1^2	30

Notice that each total is a sum of perfect squares and that the total of 30 is obtained by finding $1^2 + 2^2 + 3^2 + 4^2$. The table reveals a pattern that, if true, is very helpful for counting squares with larger grids. If the pattern continues in a 5×5 grid, the total should be given by $1^2 + 2^2 + 3^2 + 4^2 + 5^2$; in a 6×6 grid, the total should be $1^2 + 2^2 + 3^2 + 4^2 + 5^2 + 6^2$; and in an 8×8 checkerboard, the total should be $1^2 + 2^2 + 3^2 + 4^2 + 5^2 + 6^2 + 7^2 + 8^2$.

Carrying Out the Plan. The only computation involved is finding $1^2 + 2^2 + 3^2 + 4^2 + 5^2 + 6^2 + 7^2 + 8^2$, which equals 204.

Looking Back. To see that the number of squares is really the sum shown, we could count the squares in an 8×8 square systematically, by covering them with squares of the appropriate sizes, as demonstrated in Figure 1-13. In the same manner we can show that the number of squares in an $n \times n$ grid is $1^2 + 2^2 + 3^2 + 4^2 + \cdots + n^2$.

FIGURE 1-13

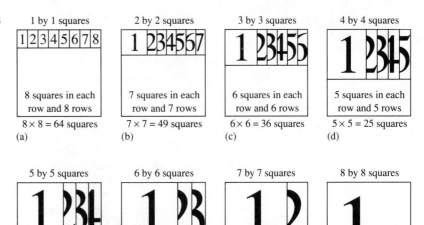

1 by 1 squares
8 squares in each row and 8 rows
$8 \times 8 = 64$ squares
(a)

2 by 2 squares
7 squares in each row and 7 rows
$7 \times 7 = 49$ squares
(b)

3 by 3 squares
6 squares in each row and 6 rows
$6 \times 6 = 36$ squares
(c)

4 by 4 squares
5 squares in each row and 5 rows
$5 \times 5 = 25$ squares
(d)

5 by 5 squares
4 squares in each row and 4 rows
$4 \times 4 = 16$ squares
(e)

6 by 6 squares
3 squares in each row and 3 rows
$3 \times 3 = 9$ squares
(f)

7 by 7 squares
2 rows of 2 squares
$2 \times 2 = 4$ squares
(g)

8 by 8 squares
1 square
$1 \times 1 = 1$ square
(h)

As problem solvers learn more mathematics, they become able to complete proofs. *Observing a pattern from a few cases does not constitute a proof.* This problem is discussed in detail in the article "Checkerboard Mathematics" by Billstein.

Questions related to Problem 3 include the following.

1. If the size of the checkerboard is doubled, is the number of different squares doubled?
2. What if we counted different rectangles instead of different squares on the checkerboard?
3. What if we counted the number of different squares on a rectangular checkerboard?
4. What if we count only nonoverlapping squares on the checkerboard?

The problem-solving strategies discussed in this text are used in elementary schools. On page 25 is an example of how the strategy of examining a simpler problem is used in *Addison-Wesley Mathematics,* 1989, Grade 5. Also notice the importance of drawing pictures or diagrams to solve this problem. Work through the restaurant problem, and then try the two problems on the bottom of the student page.

Strategy—Identify a Subgoal
In an attempt to devise a plan for solving some problems, it may become apparent that the problem could be solved if the solution to a somewhat easier or more familiar problem could be found. In such a case, the solution to the easier problem may become a subgoal of the primary goal of solving the original problem. An example of this is seen in Problem 4.

PROBLEM 4

Nora was playing with her calculator and multiplying consecutive natural numbers. She noticed that, when she multiplied $1 \times 2 \times 3 \times 4 \times 5$, the display showed 120, which has one zero at the end of the product. When she multiplied $1 \times 2 \times 3 \times 4 \times 5 \times 6 \times 7 \times 8 \times 9 \times 10$, the display showed 3628800, which has two zeros at the end of the product. She wondered how many zeros would be at the end of the number if she multiplied the first 100 natural numbers—that is, $1 \times 2 \times 3 \times 4 \times 5 \times \cdots \times 98 \times 99 \times 100$. (This number, called 100 *factorial,* can be written as 100!.) Because the product became too big for her calculator, Nora had to solve the problem without actually multiplying the numbers. Can you solve the problem?

Understanding the Problem. The product $1 \times 2 \times 3 \times 4 \times 5 \times \cdots \times 98 \times 99 \times 100$ or (100!) is to be computed. We want to know the number of zeros on the end of the number.

Problem-Solving Strategy:
Solve a Simpler Problem

Sometimes an answer to a problem can be found by solving a problem like it that has smaller numbers. This strategy is called

SOLVE A SIMPLER PROBLEM

Try This A restaurant has 30 small square tables to be used for a banquet. Each table can seat only one person on each side. If the tables are pushed together to make a long table, how many people can sit at the table?

I don't want to draw a picture for 30 tables. I'll solve simpler problems with 2, 3, and 4 tables and look for a way to solve the more difficult problem.

6 people   8 people

I see! Two people can sit at each of the 30 tables. Then I can add 2 more people for the ends.

10 people

$2 \times 30 = 60, \quad 60 + 2 = 62$

62 people could sit at the long banquet table.

Solve.

1. Jessie bought an old wagon wheel at the flea market. There are 20 spokes in the wheel. How many spaces are between the spokes? Hint: Try 3 spokes.

2. Thalia is planning a business meeting. She wants to use 36 small square tables to make 1 large square table. If each small table can seat only one person on a side, how many people can be seated at the large table? Hint: Try 4 small tables, then 9.

Devising a Plan. Notice that $1 \times 2 \times 3 \times 4 \times 5$ can be written as $1 \times 3 \times 4 \times (2 \times 5) = 1 \times 3 \times 4 \times (10) = 120$; it has one factor of 10 and one zero at the end. Likewise, $1 \times 2 \times 3 \times 4 \times 5 \times \cdots \times 9 \times 10 = (1 \times 3 \times 4 \times 6 \times 7 \times 8) \times (2 \times 5 \times 10) = 36,288 \times (10^2) = 3,628,800$, which has two factors of 10 and two zeros at the end. In general, it seems that the number of zeros at the end of a product is equal to the number of factors of 10 in the product. Because $10 = 2 \times 5$, we need to know how many 2s and 5s appear as factors of 100!. If, for example, in some product there are exactly ten 2s and three 5s, how many 10s are there? Each 10 is the product of a 2 and a 5. Because there are only three 5s, we can pair only three 5s with three 2s to form three 10s. (The other seven 2s do not contribute to the creation of 10s.) Because more 2s than 5s will appear in the product in question (why?), it is sufficient to determine the number of 5s that appear as factors of 100!. This becomes our *subgoal*. If we can achieve this subgoal, then we can solve our problem.

Carrying Out the Plan. To determine the number of factors of 5 that appear in 100!, we first count the multiples of 5 that are contained in 100!, namely, 5, 10, 15, 20, 25, 30, 35, 40, 45, 50, 55, 60, 65, 70, 75, 80, 85, 90, 95, and 100. Does this imply that there are only twenty factors of 5? Not quite, because numbers such as 25 have two factors of 5. The numbers that have two factors of 5 are 25, 50, 75, and 100. Thus, we pick up an additional four factors of 5, for a total of twenty-four. Because $5^3 = 125$, numbers containing at least three factors of 5 are greater than 125. Thus, none of the numbers in 100! contain more than two factors of 5, and it follows that there are exactly twenty-four factors of 5 in the product. Consequently, there are twenty-four factors of 10 in 100!, and 100! has 24 zeros at the end of it.

Looking Back. We can check to see if our reasoning is correct by trying it out with smaller numbers, using a calculator. We could also extend the problem by asking for the number of zeros at the end of 1000!. A related problem is to determine the number of zeros at the end of the product of the first 100 even numbers or the first 100 odd numbers.

Strategy—Examine a Related Problem

Sometimes in attempting to solve a problem, you will discover that it is very similar to a problem you have previously considered. In such a case, you may solve the new problem in a manner almost identical to the one used to solve the previous problem. An example of this is seen in Problem 5.

PROBLEM 5

Ryan was building matchstick square sequences, as shown in Figure 1-14. He used 67 matchsticks to form the last figure in his sequence. How many matchsticks did he use for the entire project?

FIGURE 1-14

Understanding the Problem. From our experience with patterns in Example 1-3, we recognize the sequence generated by the matchsticks as 4, 7, 10, 13, . . . , 67. The last number is 67, because Ryan used 67 matchsticks to form the last figure in the sequence. This is an arithmetic sequence with difference 3. We are to find the sum of the numbers in this sequence.

Devising a Plan. A *related problem* is Gauss's problem of finding the sum 1 + 2 + 3 + 4 + $\cdots$ + 100. In that problem, we paired 1 with 100, 2 with 99, 3 with 98, and so on, and observed that there were 50 pairs of numbers, each with a sum of 101. A similar approach in the present problem yields a sum of 71. To find the total, we need to know the number of pairs in Figure 1-15.

FIGURE 1-15

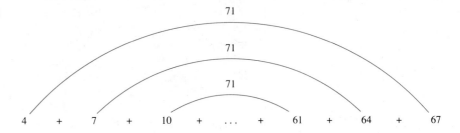

To find the number of pairs, we need the number of terms in the sequence. Thus, we have identified a *subgoal,* which is to find the number of terms in the sequence. In Example 1-3, we found the nth term of this sequence to be $3n + 1$. To find the number of the term corresponding to 67, we solve the equation $3n + 1 = 67$ and obtain $n = 22$. Thus, there are 22 terms in the given sequence.

Carrying Out the Plan. Because the number of terms is 22, we have 11 pairs of matchstick figures whose sum is 71 matchsticks each. Therefore, the total is 11 $\times$ 71, or 781 matchsticks.

Looking Back. Using the outlined procedure, we should be able to find the sum of any arithmetic sequence in which we know the first two terms and the last term.

Strategy—Work Backward

In some problems, it is easier to start with what might be considered the final result and to work backward. This is seen in Problem 6.

PROBLEM 6

Charles and Cynthia play a game called NIM. Each has a box of matchsticks. They take turns putting 1, 2, or 3 matchsticks in a common pile. The person who is able to add a number of matchsticks to the pile to make a total of 24 wins the game. What should be Charles' strategy to be sure he wins the game?

Understanding the Problem.   Each of the players chooses 1, 2, or 3 matchsticks to place in the pile. If Charles puts 3 matchsticks in the pile, Cynthia may put 1, 2, or 3 matchsticks in the pile, which makes a total of 4, 5, or 6. It is now Charles' turn. Whoever makes a total of 24 wins the game.

Devising a Plan.   Here the strategy of *working backward* can be used. If there are 21, 22, or 23 matchsticks in the pile, Charles would like it to be his turn because he can win by adding 3, 2, or 1 matchsticks, respectively. However, if there are 20 matchsticks in the pile, Charles would like for it to be Cynthia's turn because she must add 1, 2, or 3, which would give a total of 21, 22, or 23. A *subgoal* for Charles is to reach 20 matchsticks, which forces Cynthia's total to be 21, 22, or 23. The subgoal of 20 matchsticks can be reached if there are 17, 18, or 19 matchsticks in the pile when Cynthia has completed her turn. For this to happen, there should be 16 matchsticks in the pile when Charles has completed his turn. Hence, a new subgoal for Charles is to reach 16 matchsticks. By similar reasoning, we see that Charles's additional subgoals are to reach 12, 8, and 4 matchsticks.

Carrying Out the Plan.   Using the reasoning developed in Devising a Plan, we see that the winning strategy for Charles is to be the person who creates a total of 4 matchsticks and then makes the totals of 8, 12, 16, 20, and 24 on successive turns. To do this, Charles should play second; if Cynthia puts 1, 2, or 3 matchsticks in the pile, Charles should add 3, 2, or 1, respectively, to make a total of 4. The totals 8, 12, 16, 20, and 24 can be achieved in a similar fashion.

Looking Back.   A related problem is to solve the game in which the person who reaches 24 or more matchsticks loses. Now what is the winning strategy? Other related games can be examined in which different numbers are used as goals or different numbers of matchsticks are allowed to be added. For example, suppose that the goal is 21 and that 1, 3, or 5 matchsticks can be added each time.

Strategy—Write an Equation

A problem-solving strategy commonly used in algebra consists of writing an equation. We discuss how to write equations and solve them in Chapter 4. Here we discuss the strategy for problems in which the solutions to the corresponding equations require little or no algebra.

PROBLEM 7

Mary left from her home and averaged 16 km/hr riding her bicycle on an uphill trip to Larry's house. On the return trip over the same route, she averaged 20 km/hr. If it took her 4 hours to make the return trip, how much cycling time did the entire trip take?

Understanding the Problem. Mary averaged 16 km/hr on an uphill trip, as illustrated in Figure 1-16(a). She averaged 20 km/hr on a return trip along the same route, as illustrated in Figure 1-16(b). Thus, we know that the distance traveled in each direction is the same. The return trip took 4 hours, and we are asked to determine the amount of time it took to complete the entire trip.

FIGURE 1-16

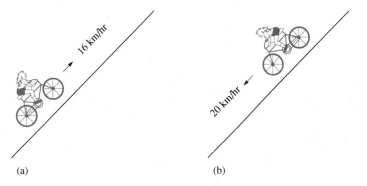

(a)   (b)

Devising a Plan. The fact that the distance in each direction is the same is the basis for *writing an equation*. We let the time that it took Mary to go uphill be t. Because Mary went uphill at a rate of 16 km/hr for t hours, she covered a distance of $16t$ km. Traveling downhill, Mary's rate was 20 km/hr for 4 hours. Therefore, she traveled $20 \times 4 = 80$ km. Thus, we have $16t = 80$. If we solve this equation for t, we can find the time required for the first half of the trip and, subsequently, the time required for the entire trip.

Carrying Out the Plan. To solve the equation $16t = 80$, we divide each side of the equation by 16. Therefore, $t = 80/16$, or 5, so it took 5 hours for the initial trip. This is not the final answer, since the problem asked for the total time for the trip. This figure is $5 + 4 = 9$ hours.

Looking Back. It is important to check the solution in terms of the original problem. In doing so, we notice that $16 \times 5 = 20 \times 4$. Without performing this step of checking the original problem, many students would report 5 hours as the final answer. A related problem is to suppose that Mary and Larry both leave their own houses and start to bicycle toward each other at exactly 12:00 noon. If Mary is traveling at 16 km/hr and Larry is traveling at 20 km/hr, at what time will they meet? Remember, we know the distance between the houses from the preceding problem.

Strategy—Draw a Diagram

It has often been said that a picture is worth a thousand words. This is particularly true in problem solving. In geometry, drawing a picture often provides the insight necessary to solve a problem. A nongeometric problem that can be solved by using a picture is seen in Problem 8.

PROBLEM 8

On the first day of math class, 20 people are present in the room. To become acquainted with one another, each person shakes hands just once with everyone else. How many handshakes take place?

Understanding the Problem. There are 20 people in the room, and each person shakes hands with each other person only once. It takes 2 people for 1 handshake; that is, if Maria shakes hands with John and John shakes hands with Maria, this counts as 1 handshake, not 2. The problem is to find the number of handshakes that take place.

Devising a Plan. One plan that would certainly work is to take 20 people and actually count the handshakes. Although this plan provides a solution, it would be nice to find a less elaborate one. One way of investigating this problem is to use the strategy of *drawing diagrams*. A diagram showing a handshake between persons A and B can be indicated by a line segment connecting A and B.

Diagrams showing handshakes for 3, 4, and 5 people are given in Figure 1-17. From the diagrams, we see that the problem becomes one of counting the different line segments needed to connect various numbers of points. In looking at the problem for 5 people [Figure 1-17(c)], we see that A shakes hands with persons B, C, D, and E (4 handshakes). Also, B shakes hands with A, C, D, and E (4 handshakes). In fact, each person shakes hands with 4 other people. Therefore, it appears that there are $5 \cdot 4$, or 20, handshakes. However, notice that the handshake between A and B has been counted

FIGURE 1-17

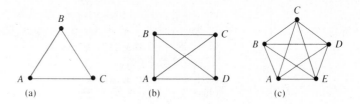

(a)   (b)   (c)

twice. This dual counting occurs for all 5 people. Consequently, each handshake was counted twice; thus, to obtain the answer, we must divide by 2. The answer is $(5 \cdot 4)/2$, or 10. This approach can be generalized for any number of people.

Carrying Out the Plan. Using the outlined strategy, we see that with 20 people there are $(20 \cdot 19)/2$, or 190, handshakes.

Looking Back. Our answer can be checked by solving the problem by means of a different strategy. We try the strategy of *looking at a simpler problem.* With one person in the room, there are no handshakes. If a second person enters the room, there is 1 handshake (remember, 2 people shaking hands counts as 1 handshake). If a third person enters the room, he or she shakes hands with each of the other persons present, so there are 2 additional handshakes, for a total of $1 + 2$. If a fourth person enters the room, he or she shakes hands with each of the other three members present, so there is an addition of 3 shakes for a total of $1 + 2 + 3$. If a fifth person enters the room, an additional 4 shakes take place.

TABLE 1-13

Number of People	Number of Handshakes
1	0
2	1
3	$3 = 1 + 2$
4	$6 = 1 + 2 + 3$
5	$10 = 1 + 2 + 3 + 4$

In Table 1-13, we record the number of handshakes. Notice that the last number in the expression $1 + 2 + 3 + 4$ is one less than the number of people shaking hands. Following this pattern, the answer for 20 people is given by $1 + 2 + 3 + 4 + \cdots + 19$. The technique used by Gauss (Problem 1) to find sums of consecutive natural numbers is very useful in completing the problem. Applying this technique, we have the following.

$$1 + 2 + 3 + \cdots + 19 = \frac{19(20)}{2} = 190$$

Strategy—Guess and Check

In the strategy of guess and check, we first attempt to guess at a solution, using as reasonable a guess as possible. Once the guess is made, we check to see if the guess is the actual solution. If the guess is not a solution, the next step is to learn as much as possible about the solution based on the guess before we make the next guess. This strategy is somewhat akin to trial and error, but, unlike trial and error, this strategy assumes that we are not using random guesses. The guess and check strategy is seen in Problem 9.

PROBLEM 9

Marques, a fourth grader, said to Mr. Treacher, "I'm thinking of a number less than or equal to 1000. Can you guess my number?"

Mr. Treacher replied, "Not only can I guess your number, but I can guess it in no more than ten questions, provided that your answers to my questions are yes or no and are truthful."

How could Mr. Treacher have been so positive about the maximum number of questions he would have to ask?

Understanding the Problem. To guarantee that Mr. Treacher could make good his statement, we need to know that Marques is thinking of a natural number. There are 1000 possibilities for the number. What types of questions could Mr. Treacher ask? Suppose he asked "Is the number 47?" With this type of question, it seems impossible to determine Marques' number in ten or fewer guesses. He needs to ask questions of a form such that he learns information about more than one number each time he receives Marques' answer to that question. For example, if he asked if the number is even, then no matter what Marques answered, Mr. Treacher would have only 500 numbers left to worry about with his next question. In other words, he would reduce the number of possibilities for his next question.

Devising a Plan. As discussed above, the primary concern is what type of questions Mr. Treacher should ask. A strategy that he should use here is guess and check, where each successive guess is based on the information learned from Marques's previous answer. In his questions, Mr. Treacher should try not only to narrow the number of numbers left to choose from but also to determine how far apart they are—that is, to find the range of the numbers. For example, if Mr. Treacher's first question is, "Is the number less than 500?" and Marques answers affirmatively, his number is in the range from 1 to 499. If he answers negatively, then his number is in the range from 500 to 1000. An equally good question is, "Is the number greater than 500?" Questions like this are better than, "Is it an even number?" because if the answer to "Is it even?" is yes, then there are 500 numbers left, but the range is from 2 to 1000. By successively asking questions such as, "Is the number less than 500?", where each question determines the range for the next question, Mr. Treacher successively halves both the field of numbers and the range in which the number lies.

Carrying Out the Plan. Suppose Marques chose 38 for his number. The questions and answers might be as follows.

Mr. Treacher's Questions	Marques's Answers
Is the number less than 500?	Yes
Is the number less than 250?	Yes
Is the number less than 125?	Yes
Is the number less than 62?	Yes
Is the number less than 31?	No
Is the number less than 46?	Yes
Is the number less than 38?	No
Is the number less than 42?	Yes
Is the number less than 40?	Yes
Is the number less than 39?	Yes

Consequently, Marques's number is 38.

Looking Back. Using the guess and check strategy, in which we utilize the information gleaned from a guess to determine the next guess, appears to be the most efficient way to attack the problem. We could change the range for Marques's number in order to change the problem. We could also use a calculator to find the values to ask about in the questions. If Marques's number were between 1 and 1,000,000, what would be the maximum number of questions that Mr. Treacher would have to ask to determine the number? If Mr. Treacher could ask 30 questions, what would be the largest allowable range for Marques's number within which Mr. Treacher could determine the chosen number?

TIME OUT

Before you attempt the problems in the problem set, try the following puzzles. These puzzles have been around in one form or another for many years. They should help you begin to think and to understand what is really being asked in a problem.

1. How much dirt is in a hole 2 feet long, 3 feet wide, and 2 feet deep?
2. Two U.S. coins have a total value of 55¢. One coin is not a nickel. What are the two coins?
3. Walter had a dozen apples in his office. He ate all but 4. How many were left?

4. Sal owns 20 blue and 20 brown socks, which he keeps in a drawer in complete disorder. What is the minimum number of socks that he must pull out of the drawer on a dark morning to be sure he has a matching pair?

5. A heavy smoker wakes up in the middle of the night and finds herself out of cigarettes. The stores are closed, so she looks through all the ashtrays for butts. She figures that with 5 butts she can make one new cigarette. She finds 25 butts and decides they will last her till morning if she smokes only 1 cigarette every hour. How long does her supply last?

6. You have 8 sticks. Four of them are exactly half the length of the other 4. Enclose exactly 3 squares of equal size with them.

7. Suppose that you have only one 5-L container and one 3-L container. How can you measure exactly 4 L of water if neither container is marked for measuring?

8. It takes 1 hour 20 minutes to drive to the airport, yet the return trip takes only 80 minutes using the same route and driving at what seems to be the same speed. How can this be?

9. What is the minimum number of pitches possible for a pitcher to make in a major league baseball game, assuming that he plays the entire 9-inning game and it is not called prior to completion?

10. Consider the following banking transaction. Deposit $50 and withdraw it as follows.

withdraw $20	leaving $30
withdraw 15	leaving 15
withdraw 9	leaving 6
withdraw 6	leaving 0
$50	$51

Where did the extra dollar come from? To whom does it belong?

11. A businessperson bought four pieces of solid-gold chain, each consisting of three links.

He wanted to keep them as an investment, but his wife felt that, joined together, the pieces would make a lovely necklace. A jeweler charges $10.50 to break a link and $10.50 to melt it together again. What is the minimum charge possible to form a necklace using all the pieces?

12. Two people played checkers. They played 5 games. Each person won 3 games. How is that possible?

13. How many animals of each species did Adam take with him on the ark?

14. The perimeter of a rectangle is 68 feet, and the length of the rectangle is 4 feet more than twice the width. Find the perimeter of the rectangle.

15. There are four volumes of Shakespeare's collected works on a shelf. The volumes are in order from left to right. The pages of each volume are exactly 2 inches thick. The covers are each $\frac{1}{8}$ inch thick. A bookworm started eating at page 1 of Volume I and ate through to the last page of Volume IV. What is the distance the bookworm traveled?

16. Six normal drinking glasses are standing in a row. The first three are full of water and the following three are empty. By handling only one glass, can you change the arrangement so that no full glass is next to another full glass and no empty glass is next to an empty glass and we still have three full glasses and three empty glasses?

PROBLEM SET 1-2

1. An alternate version of the story of Gauss computing $1 + 2 + 3 + \cdots + 100$ reports that he simply listed the numbers in the following way to discover the sum.

$$
\begin{array}{ccccccccc}
1+ & 2+ & 3+ & 4+ & 5+\cdots+ & 98+ & 99+ & 100 \\
100+ & 99+ & 98+ & 97+ & 96+\cdots+ & 3+ & 2+ & 1 \\
\hline
101+ & 101+ & 101+ & 101+ & 101+\cdots+ & 101+ & 101+ & 101
\end{array}
$$

Does this method give the same answer? Discuss the advantages of this method over the one described in the text.

2. How many different squares are in the following figure?

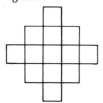

3. What is the largest sum of money—all in coins and no silver dollars—that I could have in my pocket without being able to give change for a dollar, a half-dollar, a quarter, a dime, or a nickel?

4. Arrange the numbers 1 through 9 into a square arranged like the one shown so that the sums of every row, column, and diagonal are the same. (The result is called a *magic square*.)

5. Molly is building a staircase out of blocks in the pattern shown. How many blocks will it take to build a staircase that is 25 blocks high?

6. How can you cook an egg for exactly 15 minutes if all you have are a 7-minute and an 11-minute timer?

7. How many different ways can you make change for a $50 bill using $5, $10, and $20 bills?

8. How many four-digit numbers have the same digits as 1989?

9. Tony lives at point T, and the school is located at point S. How many different routes along the grid are there from T to S if Tony walks a minimum distance each day?

10. Looking out in the backyard one day, I saw an assortment of boys and dogs. Counting heads, I got 22. Counting feet, I got 68. How many boys and how many dogs were in the yard?

11. A compass and a ruler together cost $4. The compass costs 90¢ more than the ruler. How much does the compass cost?

12. A cat is at the bottom of an 18-foot well. Each day it climbs up 3 feet, and each night it slides back 2 feet. How long will it take the cat to get out of the well?

13. You are standing on the middle rung of a ladder. If you first move up 3 rungs, then move down 5 rungs, and then climb up 10 rungs to get onto the roof, how many rungs are on the ladder?
14. In a horse race:
    (a) Fast Jack finished a length ahead of Lookout.
    (b) Lookout did not finish in last place.
    (c) Null Set finished 7 lengths ahead of Bent Leg.
    (d) Fast Jack finished 7 lengths behind Applejack.
    (e) Bent Leg finished 3 lengths behind Fast Jack.
    What was the finishing position of each horse?
15. Eight marbles look alike, but one is slightly heavier than the others. Using a balance scale, how can you determine the heavier one in exactly:
    (a) 3 weighings?   (b) 2 weighings?
16. Marc went to the store with exactly $1.00 in change. He had at least one of each coin less than a half-dollar, but he did not have a half-dollar coin.
    (a) What is the least number of coins he could have?
    (b) What is the greatest number of coins he could have?
17. A farmer needs to fence a rectangular piece of land. She wants the length of the field to be 80 feet longer than the width. If she has 1080 feet of fencing material, what should the length and the width of the field be?
18. You are given a checkerboard with the two squares on opposite corners removed and a set of dominoes such that each domino can cover two squares on the board. Can the dominoes be arranged in such a way that all of the 62 remaining squares on the board can be covered? If not, why not?

19. How many terms are there in the following sequences?
    (a) 1, 3, 5, 7, 9, . . . , 2001
    (b) 2, 5, 8, 11, 14, . . . , 899
    (c) 5, 9, 13, 17, 21, . . . , 601
20. Find the following sums.
    (a) $2 + 4 + 6 + 8 + 10 + \cdots + 1020$
    (b) $1 + 6 + 11 + 16 + 21 + \cdots + 1001$
    (c) $3 + 7 + 11 + 15 + 19 + \cdots + 403$
21. There were 20 people at a round table for dinner who shook hands with the people on their immediate right and left. At the end of the dinner, each person got up and shook hands with everybody except with the people who sat to the immediate right or left at dinner. Find the number of handshakes that took place after dinner.
22. A student has a sheet of 8½- by 11-inch paper. She needs to measure exactly 6 inches. Can she do it using the sheet of paper?
23. In the game of Life, José had to pay $1500 when he was married; then he lost half of the money that he had left. Next, he paid half of the money that he had for a house. Then the game was stopped, and he had $3000 left. With how much money did he start?
★24. Ten women are fishing all in a row in a boat. One seat in the center of the boat is empty. The five women in the front of the boat want to change seats with the five women in the back of the boat. A person can move from her seat to the next empty seat or she can step over one person without capsizing the boat. What is the minimum number of moves needed for the five women in front to change places with the five in back?

Review Problems

25. List the terms to complete a possible pattern.
    (a) 3, 6, 9, 12, 15, 18, ____, ____, ____
    (b) 1, 2, 3, 2, 9, 2, 27, 2, 81, 2, ____, ____, ____
26. Find the nth term for the sequence 22, 32, 42, 52, ...
27. How many terms are in the following sequence? 3, 7, 11, 15, 19, . . . , 83
28. Find the sums of the terms in the sequence in Problem 27.

B R A I N   T E A S E R
What day follows the day before yesterday if 2 days from now it will be Sunday?

LABORATORY ACTIVITY

Place a half-dollar, a quarter, and a nickel in position A, as shown in the figure. Try to move these coins, one at a time, to position C. At no time may a larger coin be placed on a smaller coin. Coins may be placed in position B. How many moves does it take? Now, add a penny to the pile and see how many moves it takes. This is a simple case of the famous Tower of Hanoi problem, in which ancient Brahman priests were required to move a pile of 64 disks of decreasing size, after which the world would end. How long would this take at a rate of one move per second?

Section 1-3 Using a Calculator as a Problem-Solving Tool

The *Standards* has as an assumption that a calculator with features similar to the scientific calculator described next will be available at all times for all students in grades 4–8. At the K–4 level, the *Standards* makes the following points.

The K–4 curriculum should make appropriate and ongoing use of calculators and computers. Calculators must be accepted at the K–4 level as valuable tools for learning mathematics. Calculators enable children to explore number ideas and patterns, to have valuable concept-development experiences, to focus on problem-solving processes, and to investigate realistic applications. The thoughtful use of calculators can increase the quality of the curriculum as well as the quality of children's learning.

Calculators do not replace the need to learn basic facts, to compute mentally, or to do reasonable paper-and-pencil computation. Classroom experience indicates that young children take a commonsense view about calculators and recognize the importance of not relying on them when it is more appropriate to compute in other ways. The availability of calculators means, however, that educators must develop a broader view of the various ways computation can be carried out and must place less emphasis on complex paper-and-pencil computation. Calculators also highlight the importance of teaching children to recognize whether computed results are reasonable.

In this section we discuss features of calculators and give some examples and problems appropriate for calculator use.

Recommended Features for Elementary School Calculators

At the upper elementary level, calculators should be able to do more than the basic four operations. For these grades and for this text, more advanced calculators, called *scientific calculators*, should be used. Scientific calculators differ greatly in the range of keys available, but we recommend that they have the following keys: $\boxed{y^x}$ (power), $\boxed{\sqrt{}}$ (square root), $\boxed{x!}$ (factorial), $\boxed{+/-}$ (change of sign), $\boxed{\pi}$ (pi), and $\boxed{1/x}$ (reciprocal). Further, they should be able to handle scientific notation and the correct order of operations, and they should have memory keys. We also recommend using solar-powered calculators so that batteries are not a problem.

The calculator should have an easily accessible on-off switch. The position of the keys on the keyboard may vary, but the keys should be adequately spaced and large enough that the user's finger will press no more than one key at a time. Separate $\boxed{\text{CLEAR}}$ and $\boxed{\text{CLEAR ENTRY}}$ keys are desirable.

Type of Logic

The type of logic built into a calculator determines how a computation is entered into the calculator. With different types of logic, entering a computation as it is written may or may not produce the correct result. The order in which operations are done in mathematics is very important, and you must be familiar with how your calculator works if you are to compute correctly.

On some calculators with algebraic logic, operations are processed in the order in which they are entered. For example,

$\boxed{2}\boxed{+}\boxed{4}\boxed{\times}\boxed{5}\boxed{-}\boxed{4}\boxed{\div}\boxed{2}\boxed{=}$

would be evaluated as

$6 \cdot 5 - 4 \div 2$

then as

$30 - 4 \div 2$

and finally as

$26 \div 2 = 13$

However, multiplications and divisions should be done in order from left to right before additions and subtractions, and thus the correct solution to the problem $2 + 4 \cdot 5 - 4 \div 2$ is $2 + 20 - 2 = 22 - 2 = 20$. Algebraic logic is especially disturbing when we try to perform a computation like $\frac{1}{2} + \frac{1}{4}$ by pressing the keys in the order given—that is, $\boxed{1}\boxed{\div}\boxed{2}\boxed{+}\boxed{1}\boxed{\div}\boxed{4}\boxed{=}$. A calculator with this type of logic will evaluate $\frac{1}{2} + \frac{1}{4}$ as 0.375 rather than as 0.75. (Do you see why?)

algebraic operating system   Many calculators include a desirable feature called an **algebraic operating system.** It evaluates expressions inside parentheses first, then multiplications and divisions, and then additions and subtractions. For example, in the computation $2 + 4 \cdot 5 - 4 \div 2$, if $\boxed{2}\ \boxed{+}\ \boxed{4}$ is entered, the calculator will not perform the addition. If $\boxed{2}\ \boxed{+}\ \boxed{4}\ \boxed{\times}$ is entered, no calculations will be completed. After $\boxed{2}\ \boxed{+}\ \boxed{4}\ \boxed{\times}\ \boxed{5}\ \boxed{-}$ is entered, the display will show 22. In other words, the calculator performs 4×5 before adding 2. A calculator with the algebraic operating system feature will complete the original problem $2 + 4 \cdot 5 - 4 \div 2$ and give the desired answer of 20 if the computation is entered in the order in which it is written and the $\boxed{=}$ key is pressed. If the calculator has parentheses, these keys can be used to ensure that the operations are performed in the desired order.

Decimal Notation

The calculator should have a floating decimal point or a method of allowing the user to input the number of decimal places in a computation. For example, when $\boxed{1}\ \boxed{\div}\ \boxed{3}\ \boxed{=}$ is entered, the display should show 0.3333333 rather than 0.33, as some displays do on fixed-point machines. Be aware of how a calculator rounds decimals, if it does. For example, in $\boxed{2}\ \boxed{\div}\ \boxed{3}\ \boxed{=}$, the display with a floating decimal may show 0.6666666 or 0.6666667. If the display shows 0.6666667, the round-off is apparent. If it shows 0.6666666, then we can multiply by 3 and observe the result, which may be either 1.9999998, 1.9999999, or 2. If 1.9999998 appears, there is a truncation, rather than round-off, by the calculator. If 1.9999999 or 2 appears, there is an internal round-off.

Also, when considering decimal notation, we should determine whether or not the calculator uses scientific notation and, if so, how it works. In scientific notation, a number like 238,000 is written as a product of a number greater than or equal to 1 but less than 10 times a power of 10. Thus, $238,000 = 2.38 \times 10^5$. The owner's manual should be consulted to see how scientific notation is displayed.

Error Indicator

There should be some signal on the calculator to indicate when an "illegal" operation is entered. For example, $\boxed{1}\ \boxed{\div}\ \boxed{0}\ \boxed{=}$ should cause the display to show an error. This indicator should also show when the computing limit of the calculator has been exceeded.

Special Keys

Several special keys are convenient. The first of these is the constant key, $\boxed{\text{K}}$, which allows an operation to be repeated without pressing all the keys each time. For example, the calculator might be designed so that if $\boxed{7}\ \boxed{+}\ \boxed{\text{K}}$ is entered, then 7 is added to whatever appears on the display each time $\boxed{=}$ is pressed. Some machines have automatic constants built into them, rather than a separate constant key.

For example, if the machine has an automatic constant, we simply enter $\boxed{2}\boxed{+}\boxed{=}\boxed{=}\boxed{=}$ ... and the multiples of 2 are displayed. Some models require that you press the operation key twice to activate the constant feature. You should also check to see if the other basic operations can be used with the constant feature. If you experience difficulties with the constant feature, consult the owner's manual.

Another special key is the change-of-sign key, $\boxed{+/-}$. This allows for the entry of negative numbers. Normally, each number entered into a calculator is positive. Pressing $\boxed{3}\ \boxed{+/-}$ changes 3 to $^-3$. It is desirable that the negative sign immediately precede a number to denote a negative number, rather than leaving a space between the sign and the number, as is done on some calculators.

Still another special key is the percent key, $\boxed{\%}$. This key may operate in a variety of ways, depending on the calculator. It may change a percent to a decimal. For example, pressing $\boxed{6}\boxed{\%}$ may give 0.06 on the display. On other machines, pressing $\boxed{2}\boxed{\times}\boxed{3}\boxed{\%}$ may yield 0.06 without your using the $\boxed{=}$ key. If the $\boxed{=}$ key is used, the display might show 2.06, which is 2 + 2(3%). You should carefully check how the $\boxed{\%}$ key operates on your calculator.

For work in this text, the y-to-the-x-power key, $\boxed{y^x}$, is very important. It raises y to the power of x. For example, pressing $\boxed{2}\boxed{y^x}\boxed{1}\boxed{0}\ \boxed{=}$ yields 1024, which is 2^{10}. To perform 2^{-3}, we key $\boxed{2}\boxed{y^x}\boxed{3}\boxed{+/-}\boxed{=}$.

Other keys that may be convenient are $\boxed{\sqrt{\ }}$, the square-root key, and $\boxed{x^2}$, the squaring key. Numerous other keys are available for very little cost and may be useful, depending on individual needs.

PROBLEM 10

Would you rather work for a month (31 days) and get $1,000,000 or be paid 1¢ the first day, 2¢ the second day, 4¢ the third day, and so on, but be allowed to keep only the amount that would be paid on the 31st day?

Understanding the Problem. Because we know that the wages are $1,000,000 for 31 days' work under the first option, we must compute the amount of pay under the second option. If 1¢ is paid for the first day, 2¢ for the second day, 4¢ for the third day, and so on, we need to find the amount paid on the 31st day. Then we can determine the better plan.

Devising a Plan. One strategy is to build a table and look for a pattern for the amount of pay for each day. Table 1-14 shows a pattern for the second pay plan. From Table 1-14, we see that the pay for consecutive days generates a geometric sequence with ratio 2. The exponent in each case is one less than the number of the day. Thus, the amount of money for the 31st day is

TABLE 1-14

Day	Amount of Pay in Cents
1	1
2	$2 = 2^1$
3	$4 = 2^2$
4	$8 = 2^3$
5	$16 = 2^4$
6	$32 = 2^5$
:	:
:	:
31	?

2^{30} cents. To see how great a number 2^{30} is, we could use a calculator. Then we could convert this number into dollars and compare it with $1,000,000 to determine which is greater.

Carrying Out the Plan. Determining the value of 2^{30} can be done in various ways on a calculator. If the calculator has a $\boxed{y^x}$ key, which allows the user to raise numbers to powers, then 2^{30} could be determined by pressing $\boxed{2}\boxed{y^x}$ $\boxed{3}\boxed{0}\boxed{=}$. If the $\boxed{y^x}$ key is not present and the calculator has a constant feature, then the latter feature could be used. Another approach is to use the calculator to compute $2^{10} = 1024$ and then compute $2^{30} = 2^{10} \cdot 2^{10} \cdot 2^{10} = 1024 \cdot 1024 \cdot 1024 = 1,073,741,824$. Depending on the calculator, this result may be displayed in scientific notation; for example, the calculator might read 1.0737 09, which means $1.0737 \cdot 10^9$, or 1,073,700,000. Notice that numbers in scientific notation are rounded. To convert this number of cents into dollars, we divide by 100 and see that the rounded amount received on the 31st day is much greater than $1,000,000; hence, the second option is better.

Looking Back. An alternate problem might be to consider which option is better if we keep only the money on the 25th day. How many days are needed before the second option is more attractive than $1,000,000? What if we are allowed to keep all the money from each day? How do the preceding answers change?

PROBLEM SET 1-3

1. (a) Place the digits 1, 2, 4, 5, and 7 in the boxes so that in (i) the greatest product is obtained and in (ii) the greatest quotient is obtained.

   (i) ☐☐☐
      × ☐☐

   (ii) ☐☐)☐☐☐

   (b) Use the same digits as in (a) to obtain (i) the least product and (ii) the least quotient.

2. Which of the following savings plans yields the greatest amount of money?
   (a) $10 a day for a year
   (b) $120 a week for a year
   (c) 25¢ an hour for a year
   (d) 1¢ a minute for a year

3. Vera spent $16.33 for three of the following items. Which three did she buy?

   $5.77, $3.99, $4.33, $5.87, $6.47

4. Pick your favorite single-digit number greater than zero. Multiply it by 259. Now multiply your result by 429. What is your answer? Try it with other numbers. Why does it work?

5. Use your calculator's constant feature, if it has one, to count the number of terms in the following sequence.

   1, 8, 15, 22, . . . , 113

6. If 0.2 ounce of catsup is used on each of 22 billion hamburgers, how many 16-ounce bottles are needed?

7. How many natural numbers that are evenly divisible by 5,230,010 can be displayed on your calculator without using scientific notation?

8. Suppose that the $\boxed{7}$, $\boxed{8}$, $\boxed{9}$, and $\boxed{\div}$ keys on your calculator do not work. Devise ways to perform the following computations on your calculator.
   (a) 756 + 183   (b) 155 ÷ 31

9. Suppose that your $\boxed{7}$, $\boxed{8}$, and $\boxed{+}$ keys are broken; how could you make your calculator display 73?

10. Suppose that you could spend $10 every minute, night and day. How much could you spend in a year? (Assume that there are 365 days in a year.)

11. How many times does your heart beat in each of the following?
    (a) One minute   (b) One hour
    (c) One day   (d) One week
    (e) One year (365¼ days)

12. Suppose that a number is entered on the calculator. Then it is divided by 25, 18 is subtracted from it, and it is multiplied by 37. If the answer is 259, what is the original number?

13. The number 5! (read "five factorial") is defined to be $5 \cdot 4 \cdot 3 \cdot 2 \cdot 1$, and $4! = 4 \cdot 3 \cdot 2 \cdot 1$. Evaluate 10!. If your calculator has a factorial key, $\boxed{x!}$, work the exercise with and without using the key.

14. (a) Multiply several two-digit numbers by 99 and study the products. What do you notice?
    (b) Multiply several two-digit numbers by 999. What do you notice?

15. If your calculator displays 0.3333333 when 1 is divided by 3, what other division could be performed to yield a display of 0.0333333?

16. The distance around the world is approximately 40,000 kilometers. Approximately how many people holding hands would it take to stretch around the world?

17. The following is one version of a game called NIM. Two players and one calculator are needed. Player 1 presses $\boxed{1}$ or $\boxed{2}$ and $\boxed{+}$. Player 2 presses $\boxed{1}$ or $\boxed{2}$ and $\boxed{+}$. The players take turns until the target number of 21 is reached. The first player to make the display read 21 is the winner. Determine a strategy for deciding who always wins.

18. Try a game of NIM (see Problem 17), using the digits 1, 2, 3, and 4, with a target number of 104. The first player to reach 104 wins. What is the winning strategy?

19. Try a game of NIM, using the digits 3, 5, and 7, with target number 73. The first player to exceed 73 loses. What is the winning strategy?

20. In the game of NIM in Problem 17, two players and one calculator are needed. Player 1 presses $\boxed{1}$ or $\boxed{2}$ and $\boxed{+}$. Player 2 presses $\boxed{1}$ or $\boxed{2}$ and $\boxed{+}$, and both try to reach the target number of 21. Now play Reverse NIM. Instead of $\boxed{+}$, use $\boxed{-}$. Put 21 on the display. Let the new target number be 0. Determine a strategy for winning Reverse NIM.

21. Try Reverse NIM, using the digits 1, 2, and 3, and starting with 24 on the display. (See Problem 20.) The target number is 0. What is the winning strategy?

22. Try Reverse NIM, using the digits 3, 5, and 7, and starting with 73 on the display. The first player to display a negative number loses. What is the winning strategy?

Review Problems

23. List the terms to complete a possible pattern.
    (a) 7, 14, 21, 28, _____, _____, _____
    (b) 4, 1, 8, 1, 12, _____, _____, _____

24. Find the nth term for the sequence

    12, 32, 52, 72, . . .

25. How many terms are in the following sequence?

    6, 10, 14, 18, . . . , 86

26. In how many ways can you make change for $.21?

CALCULATOR TIME OUT

Many words can be formed when the calculator display is turned upside down. For example, to become better acquainted with your calculator, press 0.7734 and turn the calculator upside down. The digits and the letters they represent are given next.

$0 \rightarrow O$ $3 \rightarrow E$ $7 \rightarrow L$
$1 \rightarrow I$ $4 \rightarrow H$ $8 \rightarrow B$
$2 \rightarrow Z$ $5 \rightarrow S$ $9 \rightarrow G$

A small vocabulary list follows.

37818 → BIBLE	3781937 → LEGIBLE
379908 → BOGGLE	35007 → LOOSE
37819173 → ELIGIBLE	35380 → OBESE
35339 → GEESE	372215 → SIZZLE
5379919 → GIGGLES	491375 → SLEIGH
378809 → GOBBLE	45075 → SLOSH

It is possible to make up word problems to make your calculator talk. Three examples are given. Make up three new words and three new word problems.

1. Is 13,632 greater than or less than 19,169? Work the following problem, turn the calculator upside down, and read the display.

   $19,169 - 13,632 =$

2. In the Winter Olympics, one of the most dangerous events is the _____ race. Complete the following problem, turn the calculator upside down, and read the display.

   $144 \times 349,832 =$

3. The fire in the burning building reached 418 degrees; 128 firemen showed up to battle the blaze but were not successful because they forgot their _____. Multiply these numbers and turn your calculator upside down to find out what they forgot.

B R A I N   T E A S E R

What holiday is suggested by the following array?

A	B	C	D	E
F	G	H	I	J
K	M	N	O	P
Q	R	S	T	U
V	W	X	Y	Z

SOLUTION TO THE PRELIMINARY PROBLEM

Understanding the Problem.   We know that the product of the page number of the page David was reading and the next page number is 98,282. We are asked to find the number of the page David was reading.

Devising a Plan.   Adjacent pages must have consecutive numbers. If we denote the page number David was on by x, then the next page number is $x + 1$. The product of these page numbers is 98,282, so we *write the equation* as $x(x + 1) = 98{,}282$. To solve the equation, we use the *guess and check* strategy. A calculator is used as a tool to multiply various consecutive numbers, trying to obtain the product 98,282. Each new guess should be based on the information obtained from previous trials.

Carrying Out the Plan.   Table 1-15 shows a series of guesses. From Table 1-15, we see that the desired page number must be closer to 300 than to 400. Checking $x = 310$ yields $310 \cdot 311 = 96{,}410$, which shows that 310 is too small for the solution. Successive trials reveal that $313 \cdot 314 = 98{,}282$, so David was reading page 313.

TABLE 1-15

x	$x + 1$	$x \cdot (x + 1)$
100	101	$100 \cdot 101$, or 10,100
200	201	$200 \cdot 201$, or 40,200
300	301	$300 \cdot 301$, or 90,300
400	401	$400 \cdot 401$, or 160,400

Looking Back.   An alternate solution involves using the concept of square root. The desired page number is close to the number that, when multiplied by itself, yields the product 98,282. This number is called the *square root* 98,282. Using a calculator, we press the keys $\boxed{9}\,\boxed{8}\,\boxed{2}\,\boxed{8}\,\boxed{2}\,\boxed{\sqrt{}}$. This yields 313.4996. Thus, a good guess for the desired page number is 313.

CHAPTER OUTLINE

I. Mathematical patterns
  A. Patterns are an important part of problem solving.
  B. Patterns are used in **inductive reasoning** to form conjectures. A **conjecture** is a statement that is thought to be true but has not yet been proved.
  C. A **sequence** is a group of terms in a definite order.
    1. **Arithmetic sequence:** Each successive term is obtained from the previous one by the addition of a fixed number called the **difference.** The nth term is given by $a + (n - 1)d$, where a is the first term and d is the difference.
    2. **Geometric sequence:** Each successive term is obtained from its predecessor by multiplying it by a fixed number called the **ratio.** The nth term is given by ar^{n-1}, where a is the first term and r is the ratio.

3. $a^n = \underbrace{a \cdot a \cdot a \cdot a \cdot a \cdots a}_{n \text{ terms}}$

4. $a^0 = 1$, where a is a natural number.
5. Finding differences for a sequence is one technique for finding the next terms.

II. Problem Solving
  A. Problem solving should be guided by the following four-step process:
    1. Understanding the Problem
    2. Devising a Plan
    3. Carrying Out the Plan
    4. Looking Back
  B. Important problem-solving strategies include:
    1. Look for a pattern.
    2. Examine related problems and determine if the same technique can be applied.
    3. Examine a simpler or special case of the problem to gain insight into the solution of the original problem.

4. Make a table.
5. Make a diagram.
6. Write an equation.
7. Use guess and check.
8. Work backward.
9. Identify a subgoal.

  C. Beware of mind sets!

III. Features of calculators
  A. Types of logic
    1. Without algebraic operating system
    2. With algebraic operating system
  B. Special keys
    1. Constant key
    2. Change-of-sign key
    3. Parentheses keys
    4. Percent key
    5. Power key
    6. Square-root key
    7. Memory keys

CHAPTER TEST

1. List the terms that complete a possible pattern in each of the following.
  (a) 0, 1, 3, 6, 10, _____, _____, _____
  (b) 52, 47, 42, 37, _____, _____, _____
  (c) 6400, 3200, 1600, 800, _____, _____, _____
  (d) 1, 2, 3, 5, 8, 13, _____, _____, _____
  (e) 2, 5, 8, 11, 14, _____, _____, _____
  (f) 1, 4, 16, 64, _____, _____, _____
  (g) 1, _____, _____, 125
  (h) 0, 4, 8, 12, _____, _____, _____
  (i) 1, 8, 27, 64, _____, _____, _____

2. Classify each of the sequences in Problem 1 as arithmetic, geometric, or neither.

3. Find the nth term in each of the following.
  (a) 5, 8, 11, 14, ...   (b) 1, 8, 27, 64, ...
  (c) 3, 9, 27, 81, 243, ...

4. Find the first five terms of the sequences whose nth term is given as follows.
  (a) $3n + 2$ (b) $n^2 + n$ (c) $4n - 1$

5. Find the following sums.
  (a) $2 + 4 + 6 + 8 + 10 + \cdots + 200$
  (b) $51 + 52 + 53 + 54 + \cdots + 151$

6. Complete the following magic square; that is, complete the square so that the sum in each row, column, and diagonal is the same.

16	3	2	13
	10		
9		7	12
4		14	

7. How many years are there between the fifth day of the year 45 B.C. and the fifth day of the year A.D. 45?

8. A worm is at the bottom of a glass that is 20 cm deep. Each day the worm crawls up 3 cm and each night it slides back 1 cm. How long will it take the worm to climb out of the glass?

9. How many people can be seated at 12 square tables lined up end to end if each table used individually holds four persons?

10. A shirt and a tie sell for $9.50. The shirt costs $5.50 more than the tie. What is the cost of the tie?

11. If fence posts are to be placed in a row 5 m apart, how many posts are needed for 100 m of fence?

12. A total of 129 players entered a single-elimination handball tournament. In the first round of play, the

top-seeded player received a bye, and the remaining 128 players played in 64 matches; thus, 65 players entered the second round of play. How many matches must be played to determine the tournament champion?

13. Given the six numbers 3, 5, 7, 9, 11, and 13, pick five of them that, when multiplied, give 19,305.

14. If a complete turn of a car tire moves a car forward 6 feet, how many turns of a tire occur before a tire goes off its 50,000-mile warranty?

15. The members of Mrs. Grant's class are standing in a circle; they are evenly spaced and are numbered in order. The student with number 7 is standing directly across from the student with number 17. How many students are in the class?

16. A carpenter has three separate large boxes. Inside each large box are two medium-sized boxes. Inside each medium-sized box are five separate small boxes. How many boxes are there altogether?

17. How many different triangles are there in the following figure?

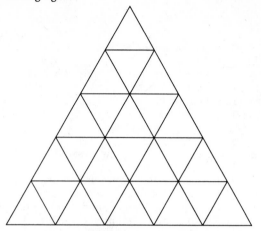

Sets,
Functions,
and Logic

PRELIMINARY PROBLEM

A pollster interviewed 500 university seniors who owned credit cards. She reported that 240 owned Goldcard, 290 had Supercard, and 270 had Thriftcard. Of these seniors, the report said that 80 owned only a Goldcard and a Supercard, 70 owned only a Goldcard and a Thriftcard, 60 owned only a Supercard and a Thriftcard, and 50 owned all three cards. When the report was submitted for publication in the local campus newspaper, the editor refused to publish it, claiming that the poll was not accurate. Was the editor right? Why or why not?

Introduction

Georg Cantor, in the years 1871–1884, created a new and special area of mathematics called *set theory*. His theories have had a profound effect on mathematical research and on the teaching of mathematics.

H I S T O R I C A L   N O T E

Georg Cantor, 1845–1918, a German mathematician, was born of Danish parents at St. Petersburg (now Leningrad), Russia. His family moved to Frankfurt when he was 11. Against his father's advice, Cantor pursued a career in mathematics and obtained his doctorate in Berlin at age 22. Most of his academic work was spent at the University of Halle (now in East Germany). His hope of becoming professor at the University of Berlin did not materialize, as his work gained little recognition during his lifetime.

Cantor suffered from nervous breakdowns and died in a mental hospital. His work on set theory and transfinite arithmetic was later praised by a prominent 20th-century mathematician, David Hilbert, as an "astonishing product of mathematical thought, one of the most beautiful realizations of human activity . . . ."

The language of set theory was introduced into elementary schools in the 1960s in the post-Sputnik era. It contained words such as *set, subset, union,* and *intersection.* In the 1970s, numerous people felt that the new language and symbolism caused confusion for children, as well as for teachers and other adults. The cartoon illustrates the feelings of many of these people.

However, the basic set concepts clarify many mathematical ideas and are used in elementary school texts.

In this chapter we discuss set notation, relations between sets, and set operations and their properties. We also use the concept of a set to define relations and functions. In the last two optional sections, we introduce the fundamentals of logic.

Section 2-1   Describing Sets

set

elements / members

In mathematics, a **set** is any collection or group of objects. The individual objects in a set are **elements,** or **members,** of the set. If we consider the set of letters in the English alphabet, each letter is an element of that set. We use braces to enclose the elements of the set and label the set with a capital letter. The set of letters of the English alphabet can be written as

$$A = \{a, b, c, d, e, f, g, h, i, j, k, l, m, n, o, p, q, r, s, t, u, v, w, x, y, z\}$$

The order in which the elements are written makes no difference, and *each element is listed only once.* For example, the set of letters in the word *book* could be written as $\{b, o, k\}$, $\{o, b, k\}$, or $\{k, o, b\}$.

We symbolize an element belonging to a set by using the symbol $\in$. For example $b \in A$. The fact that A does not contain α or that α does not belong to A is written as $\alpha \notin A$.

well defined

For a given set to be useful in mathematics, it must be **well defined.** This means that, if we are given a set and some particular object, the object does or does not belong to the set. For example, the set of all citizens of Portland, Oregon, who ate rice on January 1, 1990, is well defined. We may not know if a particular resident of Portland ate rice or not, but we do know that person either did or did not. On the other hand, the set of all large numbers is not well defined because we do not know which particular numbers qualify as large numbers.

natural numbers

counting numbers

We may use sets to define mathematical terms. For example, the set of **natural,** or **counting, numbers** is defined by the following.

$$N = \{1, 2, 3, 4, \ldots\}$$

set-builder notation

Sometimes the individual elements of a set are not known or they are too numerous to list. In these cases, the elements are indicated by using **set-builder notation.** The set of animals in the San Diego Zoo can be written as

$$Z = \{x \mid x \text{ is an animal in the San Diego Zoo}\}$$

This is read "Z is the set of all elements x such that x is an animal in the San Diego Zoo." The vertical line is read "such that."

EXAMPLE 2-1   Write the following sets using set-builder notation.
(a) $\{51, 52, 53, 54, \ldots, 498, 499\}$ (b) $\{2, 4, 6, 8, 10, \ldots\}$
(c) $\{1, 3, 5, 7, \ldots\}$ (d) $\{1^2, 2^2, 3^2, 4^2, \ldots\}$

SOLUTION   (a) $\{x \mid x$ is a natural number greater than 50 and less than 500$\}$ (b) $\{x \mid x$ is an even natural number$\}$, or $\{x \mid x = 2n, n \in N\}$
(c) $\{x \mid x$ is an odd natural number$\}$, or $\{x \mid x = 2n - 1, n \in N\}$ (d) $\{x \mid x$ is a square of a natural number$\}$ or $\{x \mid x = n^2, n \in N\}$

equal sets

Two sets are **equal** if and only if they contain exactly the same elements. (An alternate definition of set equality is introduced later in this section.) The order in which the elements are listed does not matter. If A and B are equal, written $A = B$, then every element of A is an element of B, and every element of B is an element of A. If A does not equal B, we write $A \neq B$. Consider sets $D = \{1, 2, 3\}$, $E = \{2, 5, 1\}$, and $F = \{1, 2, 5\}$. Sets D and E are not equal. Sets E and F are equal.

One-to-one Correspondence

Consider the set of people $P = \{$Tomas, Dick, Mari$\}$ and the set of numbers $S = \{1, 2, 3\}$. Suppose that each person in P is to receive a number from S so that no two people receive the same number. One possible way to show that each person receives a number is to pair the elements of the two sets.

one-to-one correspondence

Such a pairing is a **one-to-one correspondence.** One way to exhibit a one-to-one correspondence is: Thomas $\leftrightarrow$ 1, Dick $\leftrightarrow$ 2, Mari $\leftrightarrow$ 3. Another way is shown in Figure 2-1.

FIGURE 2-1

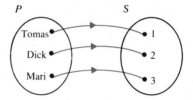

Other possible one-to-one correspondences exist between the sets P and S given in Figure 2-1. There are several schemes for exhibiting them. For example, all six possible one-to-one correspondences for sets P and S can be listed as follows.

(1) Tomas $\leftrightarrow$ 1
    Dick $\leftrightarrow$ 2
    Mari $\leftrightarrow$ 3
	(2) Tomas $\leftrightarrow$ 1
	    Dick $\leftrightarrow$ 3
	    Mari $\leftrightarrow$ 2
		(3) Tomas $\leftrightarrow$ 2
		    Dick $\leftrightarrow$ 1
		    Mari $\leftrightarrow$ 3

(4) Tomas $\leftrightarrow$ 2
    Dick $\leftrightarrow$ 3
    Mari $\leftrightarrow$ 1
	(5) Tomas $\leftrightarrow$ 3
	    Dick $\leftrightarrow$ 1
	    Mari $\leftrightarrow$ 2
		(6) Tomas $\leftrightarrow$ 3
		    Dick $\leftrightarrow$ 2
		    Mari $\leftrightarrow$ 1

● **D E F I N I T I O N**

If the elements of sets P and S can be paired so that for each element of P there is exactly one element of S and for each element of S there is exactly one element of P, then the two sets P and S are said to be in **one-to-one correspondence** (or matched).

equivalent sets

Suppose a room contains 20 chairs and one student is sitting in each chair with no one standing. There is a one-to-one correspondence between the set of chairs and the set of students in the room. In this case, the set of chairs and the set of students are **equivalent sets.**

● D E F I N I T I O N

Two sets A and B are **equivalent,** written $A \sim B$, if and only if there exists a one-to-one correspondence between the sets.

The term *equivalent* should not be confused with *equal*. The difference should be made clear by the following example.

EXAMPLE 2-2   Let

$$A = \{1, 2, 3, 4, 5\}, \qquad B = \{a, b, c\}, \qquad C = \{x, y, z\}, \qquad D = \{b, a, c\}$$

Compare the sets, using the terms *equal* and *equivalent*.

SOLUTION   Sets A and B are not equivalent ($A \nsim B$) and not equal ($A \neq B$).
Sets A and C are not equivalent ($A \nsim C$) and not equal ($A \neq C$).
Sets A and D are not equivalent ($A \nsim D$) and not equal ($A \neq D$).
Sets B and C are equivalent ($B \sim C$), but not equal ($B \neq C$).
Sets B and D are equivalent ($B \sim D$) and equal ($B = D$).
Sets C and D are equivalent ($C \sim D$), but not equal ($C \neq D$).

● R E M A R K

Note that, if two sets are equal, they are equivalent; however, if two sets are equivalent, they are not necessarily equal.

Cardinal Numbers

cardinal number

The five sets $\{a, b\}$, $\{1, 2\}$, $\{x, y\}$, $\{b, a\}$, and $\{*, \#\}$ are equivalent to one another. In fact, they are equivalent in a special way; they share the property of "twoness." In mathematics, we say that these sets have the same cardinal number, namely, 2. The **cardinal number** of a set X, denoted by $n(X)$, indicates the number of elements in the set X. If $D = \{a, b, c\}$, the cardinal number of D is 3, and we write $n(D) = 3$.

Note that, if A is equivalent to B, then A and B have the same cardinal number; that is, $n(A) = n(B)$. Also, if $n(A) = n(B)$, the two sets are equivalent, but not necessarily equal. Furthermore, if $A = B$, then $A \sim B$ and $n(A) = n(B)$.

finite set

A set is a **finite set** if the number of elements in the set is zero or a natural number. For example, the set of letters in the English alphabet is a finite set because it contains exactly 26 elements. Another way to think of this is that the set of letters in the English alphabet can be put into a one-to-one correspondence with the set {1, 2, 3, . . . , 26}. The entire set of natural numbers N is an example of an infinite set. An **infinite set** is a set that is not finite. A more formal definition of an infinite set is given in Problem 24 of Problem Set 2-1.

infinite set

Ordinal Numbers

ordinal number

Cardinal numbers answer the question, How many? **Ordinal numbers** describe the relative position an element can occupy in an ordered set, rather than the number of elements in the set. For example, we say that Carla sits in the *fourth* row and she is reading page 87 of this book. These are examples of ordinal numbers, rather than cardinal numbers, because they refer to position or order. Ordinal numbers answer the question, Which one?

More About Sets

empty set
null set

A set that contains no elements has cardinal number 0 and is called an **empty set, or null set.** The empty set is designated by the symbol $\varnothing$ or { }. The empty set is often incorrectly recorded as {$\varnothing$}. This set is not empty. It contains one element, namely, $\varnothing$. Likewise, {0} does not represent the empty set; it contains one element, namely, 0.

Two examples of sets with no elements are the following.

$C = \{x \mid x \text{ was a state of the United States before 1200}\}$

$D = \{x \mid x \text{ is a natural number less than 1}\}$

universal set / universe

The **universal set,** or the **universe,** is the set that contains all elements being considered in a given discussion. The universal set is denoted by U. The universal set may vary from one discussion to another. For this reason, you should be aware of what the universal set is in any given problem. Suppose $U = \{x \mid x \text{ is a person living in California}\}$ and $F = \{x \mid x \text{ is a female living in California}\}$. The universal set and set F can be represented by a diagram. The universal set is usually indicated by a large rectangle, and particular sets are indicated by geometric figures inside the rectangle, as shown in Figure 2.2(a). This figure is an example of a **Venn diagram,** named after the Englishman John Venn, who used such diagrams to illustrate ideas in logic. The set of elements in the universe that are not in F is the set of males living in California and is the **complement** of F. It is represented by the shaded region in Figure 2.2(b).

Venn diagram

complement

FIGURE 2-2

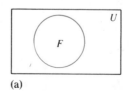

(a)

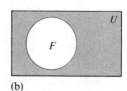

(b)

• D E F I N I T I O N

The **complement** of a set F, written $\overline{F}$, is the set of all elements in the universal set U that are not in F. $\overline{F} = \{x \mid x \in U \text{ and } x \notin F\}$.

EXAMPLE 2-3
(a) If $U = \{a, b, c, d\}$ and $B = \{c, d\}$, find: (i) $\overline{B}$; (ii) $\overline{U}$; (iii) $\overline{\varnothing}$.
(b) If $U = \{x \mid x$ is an animal in the zoo$\}$ and $S = \{x \mid x$ is a snake in the zoo$\}$, find $\overline{S}$.

SOLUTION
(a) (i) $\overline{B} = \{a, b\}$ (ii) $\overline{U} = \varnothing$ (iii) $\overline{\varnothing} = U$.
(b) Because the individual animals in the zoo are not known, $\overline{S}$ must be described using set-builder notation.

$$\overline{S} = \{x \mid x \text{ is an animal in the zoo that is not a snake}\}$$

Subsets

Consider the sets $U = \{1, 2, 3, 4, 5, 6, 7, 8, 9, 10\}$, $A = \{1, 2, 3, 4, 5, 6\}$, and $B = \{2, 4, 6\}$. Notice that all the elements of B are contained in A. B is a **subset** of A, and we write $B \subseteq A$. In general, we have the following definition.

subset

• D E F I N I T I O N

B is a **subset** of A, written $B \subseteq A$, if and only if every element of B is also an element of A.

This definition allows B to be equal to A. The definition is written with the phrase "if and only if," which means "if B is a subset of A, then every element of B is also an element of A, and if every element of B is also an element of A, then B is a subset of A." If both $A \subseteq B$ and $B \subseteq A$, then $A = B$.

proper subset

If B is a subset of A and B is not equal to A, then B is a **proper subset** of A, written $B \subset A$. This means that every element of B is contained in A and there exists at least one element of A that is not in B.

EXAMPLE 2-4
Given that $U = \{1, 2, 3, 4, 5\}$, $D = \{1, 3, 5\}$, and $E = \{1, 3\}$:
(a) Which sets are subsets of each other?
(b) Which sets are proper subsets of each other?

SOLUTION
(a) $D \subseteq U$, $E \subseteq U$, $E \subseteq D$, $D \subseteq D$, $E \subseteq E$, and $U \subseteq U$.
(b) $D \subset U$, $E \subset U$, and $E \subset D$.

When a set A is not a subset of another set B, we write $A \not\subseteq B$. To show that $A \not\subseteq B$, we must find at least one element of A that is not in B. If $A = \{1, 3, 5\}$ and $B = \{1, 2, 3\}$, then A is not a subset of B because there is an element—namely, 5—belonging to A but not to B. Likewise, $B \not\subseteq A$ because there exists an element—namely, 2—belonging to B but not to A. Subsets and elements of sets are often confused. We say that $2 \in \{1, 2, 3\}$. But because 2 is not a set, we cannot substitute the symbol $\subset$ for $\in$. However, $\{2\} \subseteq \{1, 2, 3\}$ and $\{2\} \subset \{1, 2, 3\}$.

Conversely, the symbol $\in$ should not be used between $\{2\}$ and $\{1, 2, 3\}$. Suppose that $A \subset B$. Can you always conclude that $A \subseteq B$? If $A \subseteq B$, does it follow that $A \subset B$? These and related questions are explored in the problem set.

Inequalities

The notion of a proper subset can be used to define the concept of "less than" among natural numbers. The set $\{a, b, c\}$ has *fewer* elements than the set $\{x, y, z, w\}$ because, when we try to pair the elements of the two sets, as in

$$\{a, \ b, \ c\}$$
$$| \quad | \quad |$$
$$\{x, \ y, \ z, \ w\}$$

we see that there is an element of the second set that is not paired with any element of the first set. The set $\{a, b, c\}$ is equivalent to a proper subset of the set $\{x, y, z, w\}$. In general, if A and B are finite sets, we say that A has fewer elements than B; that is, $n(A) < n(B)$ if A is equivalent to a proper subset of B. This leads us to the following definition of **less than** for natural numbers.

less than

● D E F I N I T I O N

For natural numbers a and b, a is **less than** b, written $a < b$, if and only if, for sets A and B with $n(A) = a$ and $n(B) = b$, there exists a proper subset of B equivalent to A.

We say that a is greater than b, written $a > b$, if and only if $b < a$. Defining the concept of "less than or equal" in a similar way is explored in the problem set. Notice that a person could use this definition (without the symbolism) to determine which of two given sets has fewer elements, by trying to pair the elements of one set with the elements of the other set. For example, a person entering a classroom and observing that all the students present are seated and that some empty seats still remain could conclude, without counting, that there are fewer students than chairs or, equivalently, more chairs than students.

PROBLEM 1

Of which sets, if any, is the empty set a subset?

Understanding the Problem. It is not clear how the empty set fits the definition of a subset because no elements in the empty set are elements of another set. The next question then might be, Does the empty set's being a subset of a set violate the definition of a subset?

Devising a Plan. To investigate this problem, we use the strategy of *looking at a special case*. For example, for the set $\{1, 2\}$, either $\varnothing \subseteq \{1, 2\}$ or $\varnothing \not\subseteq \{1, 2\}$. Suppose that $\varnothing \not\subseteq \{1, 2\}$. Then there must be some element in $\varnothing$ that is not in $\{1, 2\}$. Because the empty set has no elements, there cannot be an element in the empty set that is not in $\{1, 2\}$. Consequently, $\varnothing \not\subseteq \{1, 2\}$ is false, and therefore $\varnothing \subseteq \{1, 2\}$ is true. The same reasoning can be applied in the case of the empty set and any other set.

Carrying Out the Plan. Suppose that A is any set. To show that $\varnothing \not\subseteq A$, we must produce an element of $\varnothing$ that does not belong to A. Because the empty set has no elements, there can be no element in the empty set that is not in A. Therefore, it is false that $\varnothing \not\subseteq A$; hence, the empty set is a subset of any set A.

Looking Back. In particular, we note that the empty set is a subset of itself and a proper subset of any set other than itself. Using this fact, we can apply the definition of *less than* to show that 0 is less than any natural number. For example, to show that $0 < 2$, we consider the empty set whose cardinal number is 0 and the set $\{a, b\}$ with cardinal number 2. The empty set is equivalent to a proper subset of $\{a, b\}$ because the empty set is a proper subset of $\{a, b\}$ and is equivalent to itself.

PROBLEM 2

A committee of senators consists of Abel, Baro, Carni, and Davis. Suppose that each member of the committee has exactly one vote, and a simple majority is needed either to pass any measure or to reject any measure. If a measure is neither passed nor rejected, it is considered to be blocked and will be voted on again. Determine the number of ways that a measure could be passed or rejected and the number of ways that a measure could be blocked.

Understanding the Problem. A committee of the Senate consisting of four members—Abel, Baro, Carni, and Davis—requires a simple majority of votes either to pass or reject a measure. We are asked to determine how many ways the committee could pass or reject a proposal and how many ways the committee could block a proposal. To pass or reject a proposal, there must be a winning coalition of senators—that is, a group of people that can pass or reject the proposal, regardless of what the others, if any, do. To block a proposal, there must be a blocking coalition—that is, a group that can prevent any proposal from passing but at the same time does not have enough votes to reject the measure.

Devising a Plan. What is needed to solve the problem is to make a list of subsets of the set of senators. Any subset of the set of senators with three or four members will form a winning coalition. Any subset of the set of senators that contains exactly two members will form a blocking coalition.

Carrying Out the Plan. To solve the problem, we must find all subsets of the set $S = \{\text{Abel, Baro, Carni, Davis}\}$ that have at least three elements and all subsets that have exactly two elements. For ease, we identify the members as follows: A—Abel, B—Baro, C—Carni, D—Davis. All the subsets are given below.

$\varnothing$	$\{A, B\}$	$\{A, B, C\}$	$\{A, B, C, D\}$
$\{A\}$	$\{A, C\}$	$\{A, B, D\}$	
$\{B\}$	$\{A, D\}$	$\{A, C, D\}$	
$\{C\}$	$\{B, C\}$	$\{B, C, D\}$	
$\{D\}$	$\{B, D\}$		
	$\{C, D\}$		

Thus, we see that there are five subsets with at least three members that can form a winning coalition and pass or reject a measure and six subsets with exactly two members that can block a measure.

Looking Back. From the preceding, we know that there are five winning coalitions and six blocking coalitions. Other questions that might be considered include the following.

1. How many minimal winning coalitions are there; that is, how many subsets are there of which no proper subset could pass a measure?
2. Devise a method to solve this problem without listing all subsets.
3. Solve the problem if the committee had six members.

Problem 2 suggests the general problem of finding the number of subsets that a set containing n elements has. To obtain a general formula, we try some simple cases first.

1. If $B = \{a\}$, then B has 2 subsets, $\varnothing$ and $\{a\}$.
2. If $C = \{a, b\}$, then C has 4 subsets, $\varnothing$, $\{a\}$, $\{b\}$, and $\{a, b\}$.
3. If $D = \{a, b, c\}$, then D has 8 subsets, $\varnothing$, $\{a\}$, $\{b\}$, $\{c\}$, $\{a, b\}$, $\{a, c\}$, $\{b, c\}$, and $\{a, b, c\}$.

Using the information from these cases, we make a table and search for a pattern, as seen in Table 2-1.

TABLE 2-1

Number of Elements	Number of Subsets
1	2, or 2^1
2	4, or 2^2
3	8, or 2^3
⋮	⋮

Table 2-1 suggests that for 4 elements, there are 2^4, or 16, subsets. Is this guess correct? If $E = \{a, b, c, d\}$, then all the subsets of $D = \{a, b, c\}$ are also subsets of E. Eight new subsets are also formed by adjoining the element d to each of the 8 subsets of D. The 8 new subsets are $\{d\}$, $\{a, d\}$, $\{b, d\}$, $\{c, d\}$, $\{a, b, d\}$, $\{a, c, d\}$, $\{b, c, d\}$, and $\{a, b, c, d\}$. Thus, there are twice as many subsets of set E (with 4 elements) as there are of set D (with 3 elements). Consequently, there are indeed 16, or 2^4, subsets of a set with 4 elements. In a similar way, we can argue that there are $2^4 + 2^4$—that is, $2 \cdot 2^4$ or 2^5—subsets of a set with 5 elements. Notice that in each case the number of elements and the power of 2 used to obtain the number of subsets match exactly. In general it can be shown that, *if there are n elements in a set, there are 2^n subsets that can be formed.* This result can also be justified by using the Fundamental Counting Principle, which is discussed in Chapter 8.

The formula 2^n for the number of subsets of a set with n elements is based on the observation that adding one more element to a set doubles the number of possible subsets of the new set. If we apply this formula to the empty set—that is, when $n = 0$—then we have $2^0 = 1$ because the empty set has only one subset, itself. The fact that $a^0 = 1$, where a is a natural number, is investigated in Chapter 6.

B R A I N   T E A S E R

A soldier, Joe, was ordered to shave those soldiers, and only those soldiers, of his platoon who did not shave themselves. Let $A = \{x \mid x$ is a soldier who shaves himself$\}$ and $B = \{x \mid x$ is a soldier who does not shave himself$\}$. Notice that every soldier must belong to one set or the other. To which set does Joe belong?

PROBLEM SET 2-1

1. Which of the following sets are well defined?
   (a) The set of wealthy school teachers.
   (b) The set of great books.
   (c) The set of natural numbers greater than 100.
2. Write the following sets by listing the members or using set-builder notation.
   (a) The set of letters in the word *mathematics*.

(b) The set of pink elephants taking this class.
(c) The set of months whose names begin with J.
(d) The set of natural numbers greater than 20.
(e) The set of states in the United States.
(f) The set of days in a week starting with the letter P.
(g) The set of states in the United States that border the Pacific Ocean.

3. Rewrite the following statements using mathematical symbols.
   (a) B is equal to the set whose elements are x, y, z, and w.
   (b) 3 is not an element of set B.
   (c) The set consisting of the elements 1 and 2 is a proper subset of the set consisting of the elements 1, 2, 3, and 4.
   (d) The set D is not a subset of set E.
   (e) The set A is not a proper subset of set B.
   (f) A equals the set of natural numbers less than 5.
   (g) 0 is not an element of the empty set.
   (h) The set whose only element is 0 is not equal to the empty set.

4. Describe three sets of which you are a member.

5. Describe three sets that have no members.

6. Which of the following pairs of sets can be placed in one-to-one correspondence?
   (a) $\{1, 2, 3, 4, 5\}$ and $\{m, n, o, p, q\}$
   (b) $\{m, a, t, h\}$ and $\{f, u, n\}$
   (c) $\{a, b, c, d, e, f, \ldots, m\}$ and $\{1, 2, 3, 4, 5, 6, \ldots, 13\}$
   (d) $\{x | x$ is a letter in the word *mathematics*$\}$ and $\{1, 2, 3, 4, \ldots, 11\}$
   (e) $\{\bigcirc, \triangle\}$ and $\{2\}$

7. Show all possible one-to-one correspondences between the sets A and B if $A = \{1, 2\}$ and $B = \{a, b\}$.

8. How many different one-to-one correspondences are there between two sets with
   (a) four elements each
   (b) five elements each
   (c) n elements each

9. Indicate whether a cardinal number or an ordinal number is used in each of the following cases.
   (a) The book had 562 pages.
   (b) Christmas falls on December 25.
   (c) Turn to page 125.
   (d) She paid $15 for the book.

10. Find the set of all subsets of $\{x, y, z\}$.

11. Which of the following represent equal sets?

    $A = \{a, b, c, d\}$
    $B = \{x, y, z, w\}$
    $C = \{c, d, a, b\}$
    $D = \{x | x$ is one of the first four letters of the English alphabet$\}$
    $E = \varnothing$
    $F = \{\varnothing\}$
    $G = \{0\}$
    $H = \{\ \}$

12. If U is the set of all college students and A is the set of all college students with a straight-A average, describe $\overline{A}$.

13. If $B \subset C$, what is the least possible number of elements in C? Why?

14. If $C \subseteq D$ and $D \subseteq C$, what other relationship exists between C and D?

15. Is $\varnothing$ a proper subset of every set? Why?

16. Indicate which symbol, $\in$ or $\notin$, makes each of the following statements true.
    (a) 3 _____ $\{1, 2, 3\}$
    (b) 2 _____ $\{2\}$
    (c) 0 _____ $\varnothing$
    (d) a _____ $\varnothing$
    (e) $\{1\}$ _____ $\{1, 2\}$
    (f) $\varnothing$ _____ 1
    (g) $\varnothing$ _____ $\varnothing$
    (h) $\{1, 2\}$ _____ $\{1, 2\}$
    (i) $\{1\}$ _____ $\{\{1\}, \varnothing\}$
    (j) $\{1, 2\}$ _____ $\{1\}$

17. Indicate which symbol, $\subseteq$ or $\nsubseteq$, makes each part of Problem 16 true.

18. Is it always true that $A \nsubseteq B$ implies $B \subseteq A$? Why?

19. Classify each of the following as true or false. If you answer "false," tell why.
    (a) If $A = B$, then $A \subseteq B$.
    (b) If $A \subseteq B$, then $A \subset B$.
    (c) If $A \subset B$, then $A \subseteq B$.
    (d) If $A \subseteq B$, then $A = B$.

20. Use the definition of *less than* to show each of the following.
    (a) $2 < 4$
    (b) $3 < 100$
    (c) $0 < 3$

21. Define *less than or equal to* in a way similar to the definition of *less than*.

22. (a) If $A = \{a, b, c, d, e, f\}$, how many subsets does A have? How many proper subsets does A have?
    (b) If a set B has n elements where n is some natural number, how many proper subsets does B have?

$\star$23. On a certain Senate committee there are seven senators: Abel, Brooke, Cox, Dean, Eggers, Funk, and Gage. Three of these members are to be appointed to a subcommittee. How many possible subcommittees are there?

$\star$24. Georg Cantor defined a set to be **infinite** if and only if it can be put into a one-to-one correspondence with a proper subset of itself. For example, the one-to-one correspondence that follows shows that N is an infinite set.

$$N = \{\ 1,\ 2,\ 3,\ 4,\ 5, \ldots,\ \ n, \ldots\ \}$$
$$\updownarrow \ \updownarrow \ \updownarrow \ \updownarrow \ \updownarrow \qquad \updownarrow$$
$$E = \{\ 2,\ 4,\ 6,\ 8,\ 10, \ldots,\ 2n, \ldots\}$$

Use this definition to show that the following sets are infinite.
(a) $\{1, 3, 5, 7, 9, \ldots\}$
(b) $\{100, 101, 102, 103, \ldots\}$

Section 2-2 Other Set Operations and Their Properties

Finding the complement of a set is an operation that acts on only one set at a time. In this section, we consider operations on two sets.

Set Intersection

intersection

Suppose that, during the fall quarter, one college wants to mail a survey to all students who are enrolled in both art and biology classes. To do this, the school officials must identify the students who are taking both classes. If A is the set of students taking art courses during the fall quarter and B is the set of students taking biology courses during the fall quarter, then the desired set of students for the survey is the **intersection** of A and B.

● D E F I N I T I O N

The **intersection** of two sets A and B, written $A \cap B$, is the set of all elements common to both A and B. $A \cap B = \{x \mid x \in A \text{ and } x \in B\}$.

The key word in the definition of *intersection* is the word *and*. In everyday language, as in mathematics, *and* implies that both conditions must be met. For example, if the registrar wanted to survey those students majoring in both art and biology, then the desired set of students could be designated as the set $A \cap B$, where A is the set of art majors and B is the set of biology majors. In other words, the desired set is the set of those students with double majors in art and biology.

disjoint sets

If sets such as A and B have no elements in common, we call them **disjoint sets.** In other words, two sets A and B are disjoint if and only if $A \cap B = \varnothing$. For example, the sets $A = \{0, 2, 4\}$ and $B = \{1, 3, 5\}$ are disjoint.

Set Union

union

We can form a new set from two given sets by using an operation called **union.** For example, if A is the set of students taking art courses during the fall quarter and B is the set of students taking biology courses during the fall quarter, then the set of students taking art or biology or both is the union of sets A and B.

● D E F I N I T I O N

The **union** of two sets A and B, written $A \cup B$, is the set of all elements in A or in B or in both A and B. $A \cup B = \{x \mid x \in A \text{ or } x \in B\}$.

The key word in the definition of union is *or*. In mathematics, *or* usually means "one or the other or both." This usage is known as the *inclusive or*.

Venn diagrams showing the intersection and union of sets A and B are given in Figure 2-3(a) and (b), respectively.

FIGURE 2-3

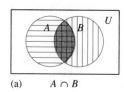

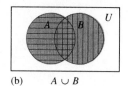

(a) $A \cap B$ (b) $A \cup B$

Set Difference

complement of A relative to B / set difference

If A is the set of students taking art classes during the fall quarter and B is the set of students taking biology classes, then the set of all students taking biology classes but not art classes is called the **complement of A relative to B** or the **set difference** of B and A.

● DEFINITION

The **complement of A relative to B**, written $B - A$, is the set of all elements in B that are not in A. $B - A = \{x \mid x \in B \text{ and } x \notin A\}$.

A Venn diagram representing $B - A$ is shown in Figure 2-4(a). A Venn diagram for $B \cap \overline{A}$ is given in Figure 2-4(b). These diagrams imply $B - A = B \cap \overline{A}$. Observe that Venn diagrams can be used to demonstrate set equality.

FIGURE 2-4

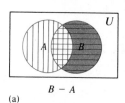

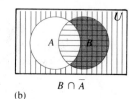

$B - A$ $B \cap \overline{A}$
(a)   (b)

EXAMPLE 2-5   If $U = \{a, b, c, d, e, f, g\}$, $A = \{d, e, f\}$, and $B = \{a, b, c, d, e\}$, find each of the following.

(a) $A \cup B$ (b) $A \cap B$ (c) $A - B$
(d) $B - A$ (e) $B \cup A$ (f) $B \cap A$

SOLUTION   (a) $A \cup B = \{a, b, c, d, e, f\}$
(b) $A \cap B = \{d, e\}$
(c) $A - B = \{f\}$
(d) $B - A = \{a, b, c\}$
(e) $B \cup A = \{a, b, c, d, e, f\}$
(f) $B \cap A = \{d, e\}$

Properties of Set Operations

From Example 2-5(a) and (e), we see that $A \cup B$ is equal to $B \cup A$. This is an example of the commutative property of set union; that is, it does not matter in which order we write the sets when the union of two sets is involved. Also, from Example 2-5(b) and (f), we see that $A \cap B = B \cap A$. This is an example of the commutative property of set intersection. Both of these properties are true for any two sets.

Other properties of set operations can be discovered by considering special cases and then trying to generalize. From Example 2-5(c) and (d), we see that set difference is not a commutative operation. That is, it matters whether we write $A - B$ or $B - A$.

When more than one operation is given, does it matter in which order the operations are done? For example, do we evaluate $A \cup B \cup C$ by first finding $B \cup C$ and then finding the union of set A and the set $B \cup C$, or by first finding the set $A \cup B$ and then finding the union of that set and C; in other words, is it true that $(A \cup B) \cup C = A \cup (B \cup C)$? We leave it as an exercise for you to verify that it does not matter which operation is done first. This and other set properties are summarized below.

● **P R O P E R T I E S**
1. **Commutative Properties** For all sets A and B:
   (a) $A \cup B = B \cup A$ Commutative property of set union.
   (b) $A \cap B = B \cap A$ Commutative property of set intersection.
2. **Associative Properties** For all sets A, B, and C:
   (a) $(A \cap B) \cap C = A \cap (B \cap C)$ Associative property of set intersection.
   (b) $(A \cup B) \cup C = A \cup (B \cup C)$ Associative property of set union.
3. **Identity Properties** For every set A and universe U:
   (a) $A \cap U = U \cap A = A$ U is the identity for set intersection.
   (b) $A \cup \varnothing = \varnothing \cup A = A$ $\varnothing$ is the identity for set union.
4. **Complement Properties** For every set A and universe U:
   (a) $\overline{U} = \varnothing$ (b) $\overline{\varnothing} = U$ (c) $A \cap \overline{A} = \varnothing$
   (d) $A \cup \overline{A} = U$ (e) $\overline{\overline{A}} = A$

Is grouping important when two different set operations are involved? For example, is it true that $A \cap (B \cup C) = (A \cap B) \cup C$? To investigate this, let $A = \{a, b, c, d\}$, $B = \{c, d, e\}$, and $C = \{d, e, f, g\}$.

$$A \cap (B \cup C) = \{a, b, c, d\} \cap (\{c, d, e\} \cup \{d, e, f, g\})$$
$$= \{a, b, c, d\} \cap \{c, d, e, f, g\}$$
$$= \{c, d\}$$

$$(A \cap B) \cup C = (\{a, b, c, d\} \cap \{c, d, e\}) \cup \{d, e, f, g\}$$
$$= \{c, d\} \cup \{d, e, f, g\}$$
$$= \{c, d, e, f, g\}$$

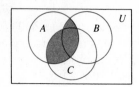

FIGURE 2-5

In this case, $A \cap (B \cup C) \neq (A \cap B) \cup C$. We have found what is called a counterexample in mathematics—that is, an example that illustrates that a general statement is not always true. One counterexample is enough to make a conjecture false. Thus, in general, $A \cap (B \cup C) \neq (A \cap B) \cup C$. Drawing Venn diagrams to show that $A \cap (B \cup C) \neq (A \cap B) \cup C$ and $A \cup (B \cap C) \neq (A \cup B) \cap C$ is left as an exercise.

To discover an expression that is equal to $A \cap (B \cup C)$, consider the Venn diagram for $A \cap (B \cup C)$ shown by the shaded region in Figure 2-5. According to the figure, two regions, $A \cap C$ and $A \cap B$, are parts (subsets) of the shaded region. The union of these two regions is the entire shaded region of the figure. Thus, this shaded region can be identified as $(A \cap C) \cup (A \cap B)$. Consequently, $A \cap (B \cup C) = (A \cap B) \cup (A \cap C)$. A similar approach illustrates that $A \cup (B \cap C) = (A \cup B) \cap (A \cup C)$. These properties that relate intersection and union are called **distributive properties.**

distributive properties

• **P R O P E R T I E S**
Distributive Properties   For all sets A, B, and C:

1. **Distributive property of set intersection over union.**

   $A \cap (B \cup C) = (A \cap B) \cup (A \cap C)$

2. **Distributive property of set union over intersection.**

   $A \cup (B \cap C) = (A \cup B) \cap (A \cup C)$

EXAMPLE 2-6   If $A = \{a, b, c\}$, $B = \{b, c, d\}$, and $C = \{d, e, f, g\}$, check the distributive property of intersection over union for these sets.

SOLUTION
$$A \cap (B \cup C) = \{a, b, c\} \cap (\{b, c, d\} \cup \{d, e, f, g\})$$
$$= \{a, b, c\} \cap \{b, c, d, e, f, g\}$$
$$= \{b, c\}$$
$$(A \cap B) \cup (A \cap C) = (\{a, b, c\} \cap \{b, c, d\}) \cup (\{a, b, c\} \cap \{d, e, f, g\})$$
$$= \{b, c\} \cup \varnothing$$
$$= \{b, c\}$$

Thus, $A \cap (B \cup C) = (A \cap B) \cup (A \cap C)$.

Using Venn Diagrams as a Problem-Solving Tool
Venn diagrams can be used as a problem-solving tool for modeling information, as seen in this section.

EXAMPLE 2-7   Use set notation to describe the shaded portions of the Venn diagrams in Figure 2-6(a) and (b).

FIGURE 2-6

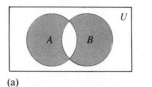
(a)

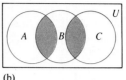
(b)

SOLUTION   The solutions can be described in many different, but equivalent, forms. The following are possible answers:
(a) $(A \cup B) \cap \overline{(A \cap B)}$, or $(A \cup B) - (A \cap B)$
(b) $(A \cap B) \cup (B \cap C)$, or $B \cap (A \cup C)$

EXAMPLE 2-8   Suppose that M is the set of all students taking mathematics and E is the set of all students taking English. Identify the students described by each region in Figure 2-7.

FIGURE 2-7

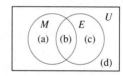

SOLUTION   Region (a) contains all students taking mathematics but not English.
Region (b) contains all students taking both mathematics and English.
Region (c) contains all students taking English but not mathematics.
Region (d) contains all students taking neither mathematics nor English.

EXAMPLE 2-9   Suppose that a survey was taken of college freshmen to determine something about their high school backgrounds. The following information was gathered from interviews with 110 students:

25 took physics
45 took biology
48 took mathematics
10 took physics and mathematics
 8 took biology and mathematics
 6 took physics and biology
 5 took all three subjects

How many students took biology, but neither physics nor mathematics?
How many did not take any of the three subjects?

SOLUTION To solve this problem, we build a model using sets. Because there are three distinct subjects, three circles should be used. The maximum number of regions of a Venn diagram determined by three circles is 8. In Figure 2-8, P is the set of students taking physics, B is the set taking biology, and M is the set taking mathematics. The shaded region represents the 5 students who took all three subjects. The lined region represents the students who took physics and mathematics, but who did not take biology.

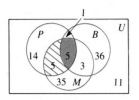

FIGURE 2-8

One mind set to beware of in this problem is thinking that the 25 who took physics, for example, took only physics. That is not necessarily the case. If those students had been taking only physics, then we should have been told so.

Because a total of 10 students took physics and mathematics, and because 5 of those also took biology, $10 - 5$, or 5, students took physics and math, but not biology. The other numbers in the diagram were derived by means of similar reasoning. After completing the diagram, we interpret the results. Of all the students, 36 took biology, but neither physics nor mathematics; 11 did not take any of the three subjects.

Cartesian Products

Cartesian product   Another way to produce a set from two given sets is by forming the **Cartesian product.** Forming the Cartesian product involves pairing the elements of one set with the elements of another set. For example, suppose that a person has three pairs of pants, $P = \{$blue, white, green$\}$, and two shirts, $S = \{$blue, red$\}$. The possible different pant-and-shirt pairs follow, with the color of pants listed first and the color of shirt listed second.

blue—blue	white—blue	green—blue
blue—red	white—red	green—red

Six pairs are possible. The pairs of pants and shirts form a set of all possible pairs in which the first member of the pair is an element of set P and the second member is an element of set S. The set of all possible pairs is

{(blue, blue), (blue, red), (white, blue), (white, red), (green, blue), (green, red)}

Another way of obtaining a Cartesian product is through a *tree diagram.* A tree diagram for this experiment is given in Figure 2-9. The elements of the Cartesian product are formed by following each of the branches of the tree. Because the first component in each pair represents pants and the second component in each pair represents shirts, *the order in which the components are written is important.* Thus, (green, blue) represents green pants and a blue shirt, whereas (blue, green) represents blue pants and a green shirt. Therefore, the two pairs represent different outfits. Because the

ordered pairs   order in each pair is important, the pairs are called **ordered pairs.** The positions that the ordered pairs occupy within the set of outfits is immaterial.

components   Only the order of the **components** within each pair is significant.

FIGURE 2-9

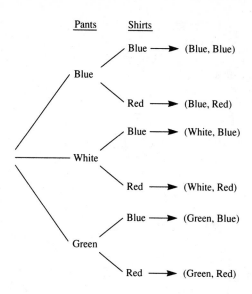

A set consisting of ordered pairs such as the ones in the pants-and-shirt example is the Cartesian product of the set of pants and the set of shirts.

● **D E F I N I T I O N**

For any sets A and B, the **Cartesian product** of A and B, written $A \times B$, is the set of all ordered pairs such that the first element of each pair is an element of A and the second element of each pair is an element of B.

$$A \times B = \{(x, y) | x \in A \text{ and } y \in B\}$$

● **R E M A R K**

$A \times B$ is commonly read as "A cross B."

By definition of equality between ordered pairs, $(x, y) = (m, n)$ if and only if $x = m$ and $y = n$.

EXAMPLE 2-10   If $A = \{a, b, c\}$ and $B = \{1, 2, 3\}$, find each of the following.
(a) $A \times B$ (b) $B \times A$ (c) $A \times A$

SOLUTION   (a) $A \times B = \{(a, 1), (a, 2), (a, 3), (b, 1), (b, 2), (b, 3), (c, 1), (c, 2), (c, 3)\}$
(b) $B \times A = \{(1, a), (1, b), (1, c), (2, a), (2, b), (2, c), (3, a), (3, b), (3, c)\}$
(c) $A \times A = \{(a, a), (a, b), (a, c), (b, a), (b, b), (b, c), (c, a), (c, b), (c, c)\}$

It is possible to form a Cartesian product involving the null set. Suppose that $A = \{1, 2\}$. Because there are no elements in $\varnothing$, no ordered pairs (x, y) with $x \in A$ and $y \in \varnothing$ are possible, so $A \times \varnothing = \varnothing$. This is true for all sets A. Similarly, $\varnothing \times A = \varnothing$ for all sets A.

PROBLEM SET 2-2

1. Suppose $U = \{e, q, u, a, l, i, t, y\}$, $A = \{l, i, t, e\}$, $B = \{t, i, e\}$, and $C = \{q, u, e\}$. Decide whether the following pairs of sets are equal.
   (a) $A \cap B$ and $B \cap A$
   (b) $A \cup B$ and $B \cup A$
   (c) $A \cup (B \cup C)$ and $(A \cup B) \cup C$
   (d) $A \cup \emptyset$ and A
   (e) $(A \cap A)$ and $(A \cap \emptyset)$
   (f) $\bar{\bar{C}}$ and C

2. Tell whether each of the following is true or false. If false, give a counterexample.
   (a) For all sets A, $A \cup \emptyset = A$.
   (b) For all sets A and B, $A - B = B - A$.
   (c) For all sets A, $A \cup A = A$.
   (d) For all sets A and B, $\overline{A \cap B} = \bar{A} \cap \bar{B}$.
   (e) For all sets A and B, $A \cap B = B \cap A$.
   (f) For all sets A, B, and C, $(A \cup B) \cup C = A \cup (B \cup C)$.
   (g) For all sets A, $A - \emptyset = A$.

3. If $B \subseteq A$, find a simpler expression for each.
   (a) $A \cap B$ (b) $A \cup B$

4. For each of the following, indicate the portion of the Venn diagram that illustrates the set.
   (a) $A \cup B$ (b) $A \cap \bar{B}$
   (c) $\overline{A \cap B}$ (d) $(A \cap B) \cup (A \cap C)$
   (e) $A \cap B$ (f) $(A \cup B) \cap \bar{C}$
   (g) $(A \cap B) \cup C$ (h) $(\bar{A} \cap B) \cup C$

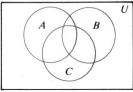

5. If S is a subset of the universe U, find each of the following.
   (a) $S \cup \bar{S}$ (b) $S \cup U$ (c) $\emptyset \cup S$
   (d) $\bar{U}$ (e) $S \cap U$ (f) $\bar{\emptyset}$
   (g) $S \cap \bar{S}$ (h) $S - \bar{S}$ (i) $U \cap \bar{S}$
   (j) $\bar{\bar{S}}$ (k) $\emptyset \cap S$ (l) $U - S$

6. Answer each of the following, and justify your answer.
   (a) If $a \in A \cap B$, is it true that $a \in A \cup B$?
   (b) If $a \in A \cup B$, is it true that $a \in A \cap B$?

7. For each of the following conditions, find $A - B$.
   (a) $A \cap B = \emptyset$ (b) $B = U$
   (c) $A = B$ (d) $A \subseteq B$

8. For each of the following, draw a Venn diagram so that sets A, B, and C satisfy the given conditions.
   (a) $A \cap B \neq \emptyset$, $C \subset (A \cap B)$
   (b) $A \cap C \neq \emptyset$, $B \cap C \neq \emptyset$, $A \cap B = \emptyset$
   (c) $A \subset B$, $C \cap B \neq \emptyset$, $A \cap C = \emptyset$

9. Use set notation to identify each of the following shaded regions.

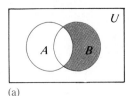

(a)   (b)

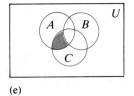

(c)   (d)

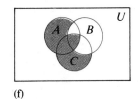

(e)   (f)

10. Shade the portion of the diagram that represents the given sets.

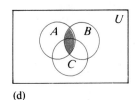

(a) $A \cap \bar{B}$ (b) $\overline{A \cup B}$

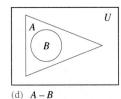

(c) $(A \cap B) \cup \bar{A}$ (d) $A - B$

11. Use Venn diagrams to determine if each of the following is true.
    (a) $A \cup (B \cap C) = (A \cup B) \cap C$
    (b) $A \cap (B \cup C) = (A \cap B) \cup C$

12. (a) If A has 3 elements and B has 2 elements, what is the greatest number of elements possible in (i) $A \cup B$? (ii) $A \cap B$?
    (b) If A has n elements and B has m elements, what is the greatest number of elements in (i) $A \cup B$? (ii) $A \cap B$?

13. Use Venn diagrams to verify the associative property of union; that is, show $A \cup (B \cup C) = (A \cup B) \cup C$.

14. Investigate the following properties of the set difference operation.
    (a) Is it commutative; that is, does $A - B = B - A$?
    (b) Is it associative; that is, does $A - (B - C) = (A - B) - C$?
    (c) Does the distributive property of set difference over union hold; that is, does $A - (B \cup C) = (A - B) \cup (A - C)$?

15. The equations $\overline{A \cup B} = \overline{A} \cap \overline{B}$ and $\overline{A \cap B} = \overline{A} \cup \overline{B}$ are referred to as *DeMorgan's Laws* in honor of the famous British mathematician who first discovered them. Use Venn diagrams to show each of the following.
    (a) $\overline{A \cup B} = \overline{A} \cap \overline{B}$ 　　　(b) $\overline{A \cap B} = \overline{A} \cup \overline{B}$
    (c) Verify (a) and (b) for specific sets A and B.

16. If $A \cap B = A \cup B$, how are A and B related?

17. Given that the universe is the set of all humans, $B = \{x \,|\, x$ is a college basketball player$\}$, and $S = \{x \,|\, x$ is a college student more than 200 cm tall$\}$, describe each of the following in words.
    (a) $B \cap S$ 　　(b) $\overline{S}$ 　　　　(c) $B \cup S$
    (d) $\overline{B \cup S}$ 　(e) $\overline{B} \cap S$ 　　(f) $B \cap \overline{S}$

18. Suppose that P is the set of all eighth-grade students at the Paxson school, with B the set of all students in the band and C the set of all students in the choir. Identify in words the students described by each region of the diagram.

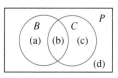

19. Of the eighth graders at the Paxson school, there were 7 who played basketball, 9 who played volleyball, 10 who played soccer, 1 who played basketball and volleyball only, 1 who played basketball and soccer only, 2 who played volleyball and soccer only, and 2 who played volleyball, basketball, and soccer. How many played one or more of the three sports?

20. In a fraternity with 30 members, 18 take mathematics, 5 take both mathematics and biology, and 8 take neither mathematics nor biology. How many take biology but not mathematics?

21. Three types of antigens are looked for in blood tests: they are A, B, and Rh. Whenever the antigen A or B is present, it is listed, but if both these antigens are absent, the blood is said to be type O. If the Rh antigen is present, the blood is said to be positive; otherwise it is negative. Thus, the main blood types are as follows.

$$\{A^+, A^-, B^+, B^-, AB^+, AB^-, O^+, O^-\}$$

A Venn diagram for blood types is shown.

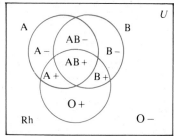

(a) Indicate the area representing the people who react positively to the A antigen but not the B antigen nor the Rh antigen.
(b) Suppose a laboratory technician reports the following results after testing the blood samples of 100 people. How many of the 100 people were classified as O negative?

Number of Samples	Antigens in Blood
40	A
18	B
82	Rh
5	A and B
31	A and Rh
11	B and Rh
4	A, B, and Rh

22. In Paul's bicycle shop, 40 bicycles are inspected. If 20 needed new tires and 30 needed their gears fixed, answer the following.
    (a) What is the greatest number of bikes that could have needed both?
    (b) What is the least number of bikes that could have needed both?
    (c) What is the greatest number of bikes that could have needed neither?

23. Classify the following as true or false. If false, give a counterexample.
    (a) If $n(A) = n(B)$, then $A = B$.
    (b) If $A \sim B$, then $A \cup B$ is not equivalent to B.
    (c) If $A - B = \varnothing$, then $A = B$.
    (d) If $B - A = \varnothing$, then $B \subseteq A$.
    (e) If $A \subset B$, then $n(A) < n(B)$.
    (f) If $n(A) < n(B)$, then $A \subset B$.

24. Howie, O. J., and Frank each tried to predict the winners of Sunday's professional football games. The only team not picked that is playing Sunday was the Giants. The choices for each person were as follows.

Howie: Cowboys, Steelers, Vikings, Bills
O. J.: Steelers, Packers, Cowboys, Redskins
Frank: Redskins, Vikings, Jets, Cowboys

If the only teams playing Sunday are those just mentioned, which teams will play which other teams?

25. Let $A = \{x, y\}$, $B = \{a, b, c\}$, and $C = \{0\}$. Find each of the following.
(a) $A \times B$　　　　　(b) $C \times B$
(c) $B \times A$　　　　　(d) $B \times \varnothing$
(e) $C \times C$　　　　　(f) $\varnothing \times C$
(g) $(A \times C) \cup (B \times C)$　(h) $(A \cup B) \times C$
(i) $A \times (B \cap C)$　　(j) $(A \times B) \cap (A \times C)$

26. For each of the following, the Cartesian product $C \times D$ is given by the following sets. Find C and D.
(a) $\{(a, b), (a, c), (a, d), (a, e)\}$
(b) $\{(1, 1), (1, 2), (1, 3), (2, 1), (2, 2), (2, 3)\}$
(c) $\{(0, 1), (0, 0), (1, 1), (1, 0)\}$

27. Answer each of the following.
(a) If A has 3 elements and B has 1 element, how many elements are in $A \times B$?
(b) If A has 3 elements and B has 2 elements, how many elements are in $A \times B$?
(c) If A has 3 elements and B has 3 elements, how many elements are in $A \times B$?
(d) If A has 5 elements and B has 4 elements, how many elements are in $A \times B$?
(e) If A has m elements and B has n elements, how many elements are in $A \times B$?
(f) If A has m elements, B has n elements, and C has p elements, how many elements are in $(A \times B) \times C$?

28. If $A = \{1, 2, 3\}$, $B = \{0\}$, and $C = \varnothing$, find the number of elements in each of the following.
(a) $A \times B$
(b) $A \times C$
(c) $B \times C$

29. If the number of elements in set B is 3 and the number of elements in $(A \cup B) \times B$ is 24, what is the number of elements in A if $A \cap B = \varnothing$?

30. If A and B are nonempty sets such that $A \times B = B \times A$, does $A = B$?

31. If there are 6 teams in the Alpha league and 5 teams in the Beta league and if each team from one league plays each team from the other league exactly once, how many games are played?

32. José has 4 pairs of slacks, 5 shirts, and 3 sweaters. From how many different combinations can he choose if he chooses a pair of slacks, a shirt, and a sweater each time?

33. (a) Is the operation of forming Cartesian products commutative?
(b) Is the operation of forming Cartesian products associative?

★34. At the end of a tour of the Grand Canyon, several guides were talking about the people on the latest British-American tour. The guides could not remember the total number in the group; however, together they compiled the following statistics about the group. It contained 26 British females, 17 American women, 17 American males, 29 girls, 44 British citizens, 29 women, and 24 British adults. Find the total number of people in the group.

★35. Using set notation, describe the shaded region shown.

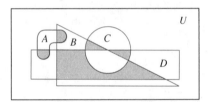

Review Problems

36. List all the subsets of $A = \{a, b, c\}$.

37. Are the following two sets equal?

$\{2, 4, 6, 8, 10, \ldots\}$
$\{x \mid x = 2n, n \in N\}$

38. Given $B = \{p, q, r, s\}$, list the nonempty, proper subsets of B.

39. Write the set of states of the United States that begin with the letter M by:
(a) listing them
(b) using set-builder notation

B R A I N　T E A S E R

Every doodad is a doohickey. Half of all thingamajigs are doohickeys. Half of all doohickeys are doodads. There are 30 thingamajigs and 20 doodads. No thingamajig is a doodad. How many doohickeys are neither doodads nor thingamajigs?

LABORATORY ACTIVITY

A set of attribute blocks consists of 32 blocks. Each block is identified by its own shape, size, and color. The four shapes in a set are square, triangle, rhombus, and circle; the four colors are red, yellow, blue, and green; the two sizes are large and small. In addition to the blocks, each set contains a group of 20 cards. Ten of the cards specify one of the attributes of the blocks—for example, red, large, square. The other 10 cards are negation cards and specify the lack of an attribute, for example, not green, not circle. Many set-type problems can be studied with these blocks. For example, let A be the set of all green blocks and B be the set of all large blocks. Using the set of all blocks as the universal set, verify that the following properties are true.

1. $A \cup B = B \cup A$
2. $\overline{A \cup B} = \overline{A} \cap \overline{B}$
3. $\overline{A \cap B} = \overline{A} \cup \overline{B}$
4. $A - B = A \cap \overline{B}$

Section 2-3   Relations and Functions

Relations

relation   A subset of a Cartesian product is called a **relation.** Before formally examining this mathematical concept, let us examine some relations. The word *relations* brings to mind members of a family—parents, brothers, sisters, grandfathers, aunts, and so on. If we say Billy is the brother of Jimmy, "is the brother of" expresses the relation between Billy and Jimmy.

Other familiar relations occur in everyday life. For example, 344-0835 is the telephone number of Karen. "Is the telephone number of" expresses the relation between the number and Karen. Other examples of relations include the following.

"Is the daughter of"   "Is the hometown of"
"Is the same color as"   "Is the author of"
"Sits in the same row as"   "Is the social security number of"

Examples of relations in mathematics are

"Is less than"   "Is three more than"
"Is parallel to"   "Is the area of"

To illustrate relations, a diagram like Figure 2-10, as seen on page 70, is useful.

Suppose that each point in Figure 2-10 represents a child on a playground, the letters represent their names, and an arrow going from I to J means that I "is the sister of" J.

FIGURE 2-10

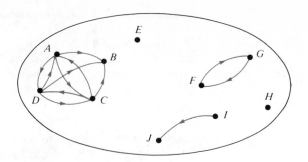

If all sister relationships are indicated in Figure 2-10, can you tell which of the children are boys and which are girls? Try to answer this question before reading further.

The information in Figure 2-10 indicates that A, C, D, F, G, and I are definitely girls and that B and J are definitely boys. Why? It also indicates that H and E have no sisters on the playground, but it does not indicate the gender of H and E.

Another way to exhibit the relation "is a sister of" is by using the same set twice, with arrows, as in Figure 2-11.

FIGURE 2-11

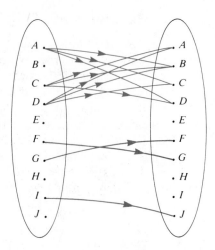

Still another way to show the relation "is a sister of" is to write the relation "A is a sister of B" as an ordered pair (A, B). Notice that (B, A) means that B is a sister of A. Using this method, the relation "is a sister of" can be described for the children on the playground as the set

{(A, B), (A, C), (A, D), (C, A), (C, B), (C, D), (D, A), (D, B), (D, C), (F, G), (G, F), (I, J)}

Observe that this set is a subset of {A, B, C, D, E, F, G, H, I, J} $\times$ {A, B, C, D, E, F, G, H, I, J}.

EXAMPLE 2-11   The pairs (Helena, Montana), (Denver, Colorado), (Springfield, Illinois), and (Juneau, Alaska) are included in some relation. Give a rule that describes the relation.

SOLUTION   One possible rule is that the ordered pair (x, y) indicates that x is the capital of y.

A relation is a pairing of elements of two sets according to some criterion. In Example 2-11, the first components of the ordered pairs are state capitals; the second components are states of the United States. Each ordered pair in the example is an element of the Cartesian product $A \times B$, where A is the set of state capitals and B is the set of states in the United States.

● **D E F I N I T I O N**
Given any two sets A and B, a **relation** from A to B is a subset of $A \times B$; that is, if R is a relation, then $R \subseteq A \times B$.

In the definition, the phrase "from A to B" means that the first components in the ordered pairs are elements of A and the second components *relation on A*   are elements of B. If $A = B$, we say that the **relation is on A.**

Properties of Relations

Figure 2-12 represents a set of children in a small group. They have drawn all possible arrows representing the relation "has the same first letter in his or her name as." Notice that the children were very careful to observe that each child in the group has the same first initial as himself or herself. Three properties of relations are illustrated in Figure 2-12.

FIGURE 2-12

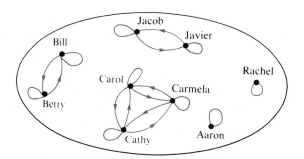

- **P R O P E R T Y**
The Reflexive Property   A relation R on a set X is reflexive if and only if, for every element $a \in X$, a is related to a. That is, for every $a \in X$, $(a, a) \in R$.

In terms of the diagram, there is a loop at every point. For example, Rachel has the same first initial as herself, namely, R. A relation such as "is taller than" is not reflexive because people cannot be taller than themselves.

- **P R O P E R T Y**
The Symmetric Property   A relation R on a set X is symmetric if and only if, for all elements a and b in X, whenever a is related to b, then b also is related to a. That is, if $(a, b) \in R$, then $(b, a) \in R$.

In terms of the diagram, every pair of points that has an arrow headed in one direction also has a return arrow.

For example, if Bill has the same first initial as Betty, then Betty has the same first initial as Bill. A relation such as "is a brother of" is not symmetric, since Dick can be a brother of Jane, but Jane cannot be a brother of Dick.

- **P R O P E R T Y**
The Transitive Property   A relation R on a set X is transitive if and only if, for all elements a, b, and c of X, whenever a is related to b and b is related to c, then a is related to c. That is, if $(a, b) \in R$ and $(b, c) \in R$, then $(a, c) \in R$.

- **R E M A R K**
a, b, and c do not have to be different. Three symbols are used to allow for difference.

In terms of the diagram in Figure 2-12, every connected portion satisfies the transitive property. For example, if Carol has the same first initial as Carmela, and Carmela has the same first initial as Cathy, then Carol has the same first initial as Cathy. A relation such as "is the father of" is not transitive since, if Tom Jones, Sr., is the father of Tom Jones, Jr., and Tom Jones, Jr., is the father of Joe Jones, then Tom Jones, Sr., is not the father of Joe Jones. He is instead the grandfather.

The relation "is the same color as" is reflexive, symmetric, and transitive. The common relation "is equal to" also satisfies all three properties. In *equivalence relations* general, relations that satisfy all three properties are called **equivalence relations.**

• **D E F I N I T I O N**

An **equivalence relation** on a set A is any relation R on A that satisfies the reflexive, symmetric, and transitive properties.

The most natural equivalence relation encountered in elementary school is "is equal to" on the set of all numbers.

  Suppose that *P* is the set consisting of all persons attending Mu University and consider the relation "is the same sex as." This relation is an equivalence relation. The relation partitions the persons at Mu University into two classes, females and males. Any equivalence relation defined on a set has the effect *equivalence classes* of partitioning the set into disjoint subsets, called **equivalence classes.** In this example, the class of females can be described as the set of all students who are the same sex as Jane, a student at M.U., and the set can be called Jane's equivalence class. This class also can be called Mary's equivalence class as long as Mary is a student at M.U. An equivalence class can be named after any of its members.

EXAMPLE 2-12 Tell whether or not the following relations are reflexive, symmetric, or transitive on the set of all people.

(a) "Is older than"
(b) "Sits in the same row as"
(c) "Is heavier than"

SOLUTION The answers are given in the form of a table.

Relation	Reflexive	Symmetric	Transitive
(a) "Is older than"	No	No	Yes
(b) "Sits in the same row as"	Yes	Yes	Yes
(c) "Is heavier than"	No	No	Yes

Note that "sits in the same row as" is an equivalence relation.

Functions

The following is an example of a game called "guess my rule." The game is *function* one way in which a special kind of relation, called a **function,** is often introduced in elementary school.

When Tom said 2, Noah said 5. When Dick said 4, Noah said 7. When Mary said 10, Noah said 13. When Liz said 6, what did Noah say? What is Noah's rule?

  The answer to the first question may be 9, and the rule could be "Take the original number and add 3"; that is, for any number *n*, Noah's answer is $n + 3$.

EXAMPLE 2-13 Guess the teacher's rule for the following responses.

(a) You	Teacher		(b) You	Teacher		(c) You	Teacher
1	3		2	5		2	0
0	0		3	7		4	0
4	12		5	11		7	1
10	30		10	21		21	1

SOLUTION

(a) The teacher's rule could be "Multiply the given number n by 3," that is, $3n$.

(b) The teacher's rule could be "Double the original number n and add 1," that is, $2n + 1$.

(c) The teacher's rule could be "If the number n is even, answer 0; if the number is odd, answer 1."

H I S T O R I C A L   N O T E

The Babylonians (ca. 2000 B.C.) probably had a working idea of what a function was. To them, it was a table or a correspondence. René Descartes (1637), Gottfried Wilhelm von Leibnitz (1692), Johann Bernoulli (1718), Leonhard Euler (1750), Joseph Louis Lagrange (1800) and Jean Joseph Fourier (1822) were among the mathematicians contributing to the notion of function. Leonhard Euler in 1734 first used the notation $f(x)$. The modern definition began to be used in the late 1800s by Georg Cantor and later by others.

---

domain
range

Another way to prepare students for the formal idea of a function is by using a "function machine," consisting of an input set, called the **domain,** a processing unit (normally a rule), and an output set, called the **range.** The function machine is sometimes pictured as in Figure 2-13. The processing unit normally consists of some rule to assign a value from the domain to a value of the range.

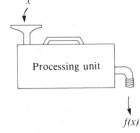

FIGURE 2-13

Function machine

In a function machine, for any input element x there is an output element denoted by $f(x)$, read "f of x." A function machine is a machine that associates *exactly one output with each input* according to some rule. That is, if you enter some number x as input and obtain some number $f(x)$ as output, then *every* time you enter that same x as input, you will obtain that same $f(x)$ as output.

EXAMPLE 2-14   Consider the function machine shown.

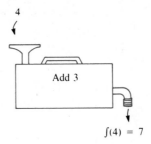

$f(4) = 7$

What will happen if the numbers 0, 1, 3, and 6 are entered?

SOLUTION   If the numbers output are denoted by $f(x)$, the corresponding values can be described using Table 2-2.

TABLE 2-2

x	$f(x)$
0	3
1	4
3	6
6	9

We can write an equation to depict the rule in Example 2-14 as follows. If the input is x, the output is $x + 3$; that is, $f(x) = x + 3$. Note that the output values can be obtained by substituting the values 0, 1, 3, 4, and 6 for x in $f(x) = x + 3$, as shown.

$f(0) = 0 + 3 = 3$
$f(1) = 1 + 3 = 4$
$f(3) = 3 + 3 = 6$
$f(4) = 4 + 3 = 7$
$f(6) = 6 + 3 = 9$

Normally, if no domain is given to describe a function, then the domain is assumed to be the largest set for which the rule is meaningful. For example, if the domain were not pictured, it would be assumed to be the entire set of natural numbers. (If students know about rational, real, or complex numbers, then any of those sets could be considered as acceptable domains.)

The idea of a function machine associating exactly one output with each input according to some rule leads us to the following definition.

● **D E F I N I T I O N**

A **function** from A to B is a relation from A to B in which each element of A is paired with one *and only one* element of B.

• R E M A R K

If a function is represented as a set of ordered pairs, then the set of all first components is the domain, and the set of the second components is the range.

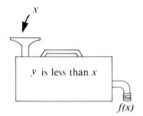

FIGURE 2-14

A calculator is a function machine. For example, suppose that a student enters $\boxed{9}\,\boxed{\times}\,\boxed{K}$ on the calculator, using the constant key, $\boxed{K}$. The student then presses $\boxed{0}$ and hands the calculator to another student. The other student is to determine the rule by entering various numbers followed by the $\boxed{=}$ key. Machines with an automatic constant feature can also be used.

Are all input-output machines function machines? Consider the machine in Figure 2-14. For any natural-number input x, the machine outputs a number that is less than x.

If, for example, you input the number 10, the machine may output 9, since 9 is less than 10. If you input 10 again, the machine may output 3, since 3 is less than 10. This clearly violates the definition of a function, since 10 can be paired with more than one element. The machine is not a function machine.

Consider the relations described in Figure 2-15. Do they illustrate functions?

FIGURE 2-15

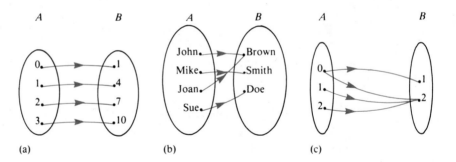

(a)   (b)   (c)

In Figure 2-15(a), for every element belonging to the domain A, there is one and only one element belonging to B. Thus, this relation is a function from A to B. A diagram, then, shows a function from A to B if there is one and only one arrow leaving each element of the domain and pointing to an element of B. Figure 2-15(b) illustrates a function, since there is only one arrow leaving each element in A. It does not matter that an element of set B, Brown, has two arrows pointing to it. Figure 2-15(c) does not define a function because 0 is paired with more than one element.

EXAMPLE 2-15   Which, if any, of the following three diagrams exhibits a function from A to B?

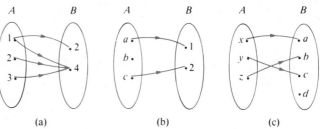

(a)   (b)   (c)

SOLUTION   (a) This diagram does not define a function from A to B, since the element 1 is paired with both 2 and 4.

(b) This diagram does not define a function from A to B, since the element b is not paired with any element of B. (It is a function from a subset of A to B.)

(c) This diagram does define a function from A to B, since there is one and only one arrow leaving each element of A. The fact that d, an element of B, is not paired with any element in the domain does not violate the definition.

EXAMPLE 2-16   Determine whether the following relations are functions from the set of first components to the set of second components.

(a) $\{(1, 2), (2, 5), (3, 7), (1, 4), (4, 8)\}$

(b) $\{(1, 2), (2, 2), (3, 2), (4, 2)\}$

SOLUTION   (a) This is not a function, since the first component, 1, is associated with two different second components, namely, 2 and 4.

(b) This is a function from $\{1, 2, 3, 4\}$ to $\{2\}$, since each first component is associated with exactly one second component. The fact that the second component, 2, is associated with more than one first component does not violate the definition of a function.

Operations on Functions

Consider the two function machines in Figure 2-16, on the top of page 78. If 2 is entered in the top machine in Figure 2-16(a), then $f(2) = 2 + 4 = 6$. Six is then entered in the second machine and $g(6) = 2 \cdot 6 = 12$. The functions in Figure 2-16 illustrate the **composition of two functions**. In the composition of two functions, the range of the first function becomes the domain of the second function.

composition of two functions

If the first function f is followed by a second function g, as in Figure 2-16(a) then we symbolize the composition of the functions as $g \circ f$. If we input 3 in the function machines of Figure 2-16(a), then the output is

FIGURE 2-16

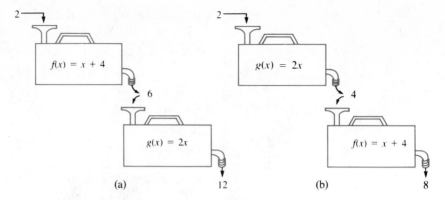

symbolized by $(g \circ f)(3)$. Because f acts first on 3, to compute $(g \circ f)(3)$, we find $f(3) = 3 + 4 = 7$ and then $g(7) = 2 \cdot 7 = 14$. Hence, $(g \circ f)(3) = 14$. Notice that $(g \circ f)(3) = g(f(3))$.

In Figure 2-16(b), the function g is followed by f. Hence, we symbolize the composition of the functions by $f \circ g$. When the input is 2, the output by $f \circ g$ in Figure 2-16(b) is shown to be 8; that is, $(f \circ g)(2) = 8$. Comparing the results in Figure 2-16(a) and (b), we see that $(g \circ f)(2) \neq (f \circ g)(2)$. Consequently $g \circ f \neq f \circ g$. This is true in general, and therefore composition of functions is not commutative.

EXAMPLE 2-17 If $f(x) = 2x + 3$ and $g(x) = x - 3$, find the following:
(a) $(f \circ g)(3)$
(b) $(g \circ f)(3)$

SOLUTION (a) $(f \circ g)(3) = f(0) = 2 \cdot 0 + 3 = 3$
(b) $(g \circ f)(3) = g(9) = 9 - 3 = 6$

EXAMPLE 2-18 Find the range of $g \circ f$ for each of the following where the domain of $g \circ f$ is the set $\{1, 2, 3\}$.
(a) $f(x) = 2x;\ g(x) = 3x$
(b) $f(x) = x + 2;\ g(x) = x - 2$

SOLUTION (a) The composition may be pictured as follows.

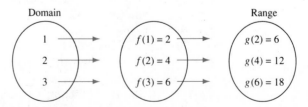

Thus, the range of $g \circ f$ is the set $\{6, 12, 18\}$.

(b) The composition may be pictured as follows.

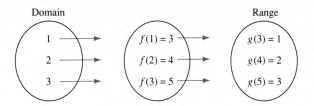

Thus, the range of $g \circ f$ is the set $\{1, 2, 3\}$.

identity function

Notice that under the function $g \circ f$ in Example 2-18(b), the image of every element in the domain is the element itself, that is $(g \circ f)(1) = 1$, $(g \circ f)(2) = 2$ and $(g \circ f)(3) = 3$. Such a function is called an **identity function.** In general we have the following definition.

● **D E F I N I T I O N**
A function I from A to A such that $I(x) = x$ for every $x \in A$ is called an **identity function.**

Identity Functions and Inverse Functions

inverse function

Example 2-18(b) showed two functions f and g, that are considered to be **inverses** of each other. That is, g "undoes" what f does. Consider, for example, finding the inverse of function f given by $f(x) = 2x$ whose domain is the set $\{1, 2, 3\}$. If the input is 3, the output is 6. The "inverse machine" should take 6 as an input and output 3, as pictured in Figure 2-17. The inverse machine needs to halve every output of f. Such a function g is given by $g(x) = x/2$.

FIGURE 2-17

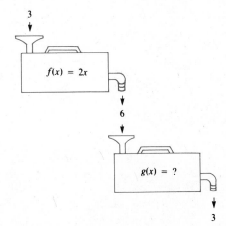

When trying to find the inverse of a function it is important to keep in mind that to "undo" addition, we use subtraction, and vice versa. To undo multiplication, we use division, and vice versa.

EXAMPLE 2-19 Describe the inverses of each of the following functions.

(a) $f(x) = 3x - 7$

(b) $f(x) = \dfrac{x}{2} + 5$

SOLUTION (a) Consider how $f(x)$ is found. We first multiply 3 times x and then subtract 7. To find the inverse of the function f, we undo what has been done. That is, we add 7 and then divide the result obtained at this stage by 3. Therefore, $g(x) = \dfrac{x + 7}{3}$.

(b) To find the inverse of f, we first subtract 5 and then multiply by 2. The inverse function might be written as $g(x) = (x - 5) \cdot 2$.

Applications of Functions

The concept of a function appears in many real-life applications. For example, on direct-dial, long-distance calls, you pay only for the minutes you talk. The initial rate period is 1 minute. Suppose the weekday rate for a long-distance phone call from Missoula, Montana, to Butte, Montana, is 50¢ for the first minute and 30¢ for each additional minute or part of a minute. We have seen that one way to describe a function is by writing an equation. Before reading on, try to express the cost C of the call in cents as a function of time t, the length of the call in minutes (see Table 2-3). Based on the information in Table 2-3, the equation relating time to cost is $C = 50 + (t - 1)30$. This could also be written as $f(t) = 50 + 30(t - 1)$, where $f(t)$ is the cost of the call. If we restrict the time in minutes to the first five natural numbers, the function can be described as the set of ordered pairs {(1, 50), (2, 80), (3, 110), (4, 140), (5, 170)}.

TABLE 2-3

Number of Minutes Talked	Total Cost in Cents
1	50
2	$50 + 1 \cdot 30 = 80$
3	$50 + 2 \cdot 30 = 110$
4	$50 + 3 \cdot 30 = 140$
5	$50 + 4 \cdot 30 = 170$
$\vdots$	$\vdots$
t	$50 + (t - 1) \cdot 30$

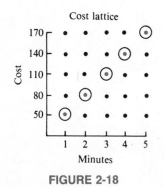

FIGURE 2-18

The information in the first five rows in Table 2-3 might also be shown on a *lattice graph*, as in Figure 2-18. The lattice graph is formed by taking the Cartesian product of the sets {1, 2, 3, 4, 5} and {50, 80, 110, 140, 170} and plotting points corresponding to the ordered pairs. If (*a*, *b*) is in the Cartesian product, then the corresponding point in the lattice is found by starting at the lower left corner and moving first horizontally *a* units, and then vertically *b* units. Functions and their graphs are frequently used in the business world, as illustrated in the following example.

EXAMPLE 2-20   In Figure 2-19, the black graph shows the cost *C* in dollars of producing a given number of widgets. The colored graph shows the revenue *R* in dollars from selling any number of widgets.

FIGURE 2-19

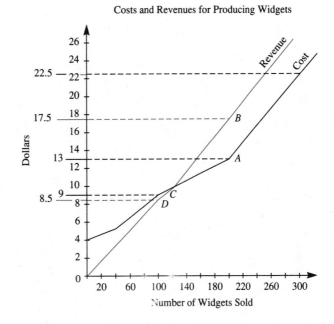

Costs and Revenues for Producing Widgets

The graphs should be a collection of disconnected points because a factory produces only a whole number of widgets. However, for visual effect, it is customary to connect the points to produce continuous segments. Based on the information in the graphs, find the following:
(a) The cost of producing the first 300 widgets
(b) The revenue from the sale of the first 200 widgets
(c) The profit or loss if the first 200 widgets are produced and sold
(d) The profit or loss if the first 100 widgets are produced and sold
(e) The break-even point; that is, the number of items that must be produced and sold in order for the net profit to be $0.

SOLUTION   (a) From the black graph in Figure 2-19, we see that the cost corresponding to 300 widgets is $22.50.

(b) From the revenue graph, we see that the revenue from the sale of the first 200 widgets is $17.50.

(c) The cost of producing 200 widgets is $13. Because the profit is the difference between the cost and the revenue, we find that the profit in this case is $17.50 − $13, or $4.50.

(d) For 100 widgets the cost is $9. The revenue is $8.50. Because the cost is higher than the revenue, the loss is $9 − $8.50, or $0.50.

(e) The break-even point is at point C, where the graphs intersect. At that point the cost and the revenue are the same. The number of widgets corresponding to point C is 120.

Elementary school math texts sometimes introduce functions as simple formulas, as seen on the student page from *Addison-Wesley Mathematics,* 1989, Grade 7, shown on page 83.

PROBLEM SET 2-3

1. Each of the following gives pairs that are included in some relation. Give a rule or phrase that could describe each relation, and list two more pairs that could be included in the relation.
   (a) (1, 1), (2, 4), (3, 9), (4, 16)
   (b) (Blondie, Dagwood), (Martha, George), (Rosalyn, Jimmy), (Flo, Andy), (Scarlett, Rhett), (Barbara, George)
   (c) (*a, A*), (*b, B*), (*c, C*), (*d, D*)
   (d) (3 candies, 10¢), (6 candies, 20¢)

2. Let $X = \{a, b, c\}$ and $Y = \{m, n\}$, and suppose X and Y represent two sets of students. The students in X point to the shorter students in Y. The following diagrams list two possibilities. Tell as much as you can about the students in each diagram.

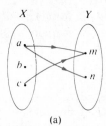
(a)

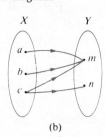
(b)

3. Write three ordered pairs that satisfy the relation "is owned by," from a set of cats to a set of people.

4. The following are the ages of the children in a family: Bill, 17; Becky, 14; John, 9; Abby, 3; Karly, 1. Draw an arrow diagram showing the names of the children and the relation "is younger than."

5. Tell whether each of the following is reflexive, symmetric, or transitive on the set of all people. Which are equivalence relations?
   (a) "Is a parent of"
   (b) "Is the same age as"
   (c) "Has the same last name as"
   (d) "Is a brother or sister of"
   (e) "Is the same height as"
   (f) "Is married to"
   (g) "Lives within 10 miles of"
   (h) "Is older than"

6. Tell whether each of the following is reflexive, symmetric, or transitive on the set of subsets of a nonempty set. Which are equivalence relations?
   (a) "Is equal to"   (b) "Is a proper subset of"
   (c) "Is not equal to"

7. Consider the set S such that $S = \{$Abe, George, Laura, Ben, Sue, Betty, Dax, Zachary, Doug, Mike, Mary, Carolyn, Anna$\}$. Identify the equivalence classes formed by each of the following relations.
   (a) "Has the same first letter in his or her name as"
   (b) "Has the same last letter in his or her name as"
   (c) "Has the same number of letters in his or her name as"

Continued on page 84

PROBLEM SOLVING: Using a Formula

QUESTION
DATA
PLAN
ANSWER
CHECK

Ronald typed 285 words in 5 minutes. He made 6 errors. For each error made, 10 words are subtracted from the total. What is his typing speed?

The formula for finding typing speed is

$$S = \frac{W - (10 \cdot e)}{n}$$

Each letter represents a number.

S = typing speed e = number of errors
W = number of words n = number of minutes

Step 1: List the value for each letter in the formula.

$W = 285$ $e = 6$ $n = 5$

Step 2: Substitute the numbers for the letters in the formula.

$$S = \frac{285 - (10 \cdot 6)}{5}$$

Remember, this bar means divide.

Step 3: Perform the operations in the formula.

$$S = \frac{285 - 60}{5} = \frac{225}{5} = 45$$

Ronald's typing speed is 45 words per minute.

Use the formula to find these typing speeds.

1. Dave typed 380 words in 5 minutes with 7 errors.

2. Lamar typed 886 words in 9 minutes. He made 13 errors.

3. A legal secretary typed 2,450 words in 20 minutes with 17 errors.

4. Vicky typed 554 words in 12 minutes and made 11 errors.

5. **DATA HUNT** What is your typing speed? Have another person watch the time while you type for 5 minutes. Use the formula to find your speed.

6. **Strategy Practice** Ann typed 5 more words per minute than Jeff. Together they typed 73 words in one minute. How many words did each person type in one minute?

8. For each of the following, guess the teacher's rule.

(a)

You	Teacher
3	8
4	11
5	14
10	29

(b)

You	Teacher
0	1
3	10
5	26
8	65

(c)

You	Teacher
6	42
0	0
8	72
2	6

9. The following sets of ordered pairs are functions. Give a rule that describes each function.
   (a) {(2, 4), (3, 6), (9, 18), (12, 24)}
   (b) {(5, 3), (7, 5), (11, 9), (14, 12)}
   (c) {(2, 8), (5, 11), (7, 13), (4, 10)}
   (d) {(2, 5), (3, 10), (4, 17), (5, 26)}

10. Following are five relations from the set {1, 2, 3} to the set {a, b, c, d}. Which are functions? If the relation is not a function, tell why it is not.
    (a) {(1, a), (2, b), (3, c), (1, d)}
    (b) {(1, c), (3, d)}
    (c) {(1, a), (2, b), (3, a)}
    (d) {(1, a), (1, b), (1, c)}

11. Does the diagram define a function from A to B? Why or why not?

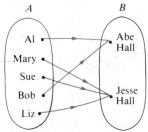

12. If g(x) = 3x + 5, find each value.
    (a) g(0)   (b) g(2)   (c) g(10)   (d) g(a)

13. Draw a diagram of a function with domain {1, 2, 3, 4, 5} and range {a, b}. (There are many possibilities.)

14. Tell which of the relations shown are functions and why.

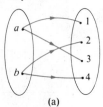

(a)

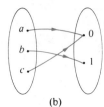

(b)

15. Suppose that f(x) = 2x + 1 and the domain is {0, 1, 2, 3, 4}. Describe the function in the following ways.
    (a) Draw an arrow diagram involving two sets.
    (b) Use ordered pairs.
    (c) Make a table.
    (d) Draw a lattice graph to depict the function.

16. Consider two function machines that are placed as shown.

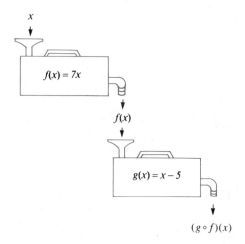

Find the final output for each of the following inputs.
    (a) 0   (b) 3   (c) 10

17. (a) Find the inverse of the function f in Problem 16.
    (b) Find the inverse of the function g in Problem 16.
    (c) Find the inverse of f(x) = 3x + 5.

18. The rule for computing the cost of a first-class letter is a function of its weight. Suppose that the first ounce costs 20¢ and each additional ounce up to 13 ounces costs 15¢.
    (a) What is the cost of an 11-ounce letter?
    (b) Find the equation relating the cost C of the letter to its weight W.

19. According to wildlife experts, the rate at which crickets chirp is a function of the temperature; that is, C = T − 40, where C is the number of chirps every 15 seconds and T is the temperature in degrees Fahrenheit.
    (a) How many chirps does the cricket make per second if the temperature is 70°F?
    (b) What is the temperature if the cricket chirps 40 times in 1 minute?

20. If taxi fares are 95¢ for the first ½ mile and 40¢ for each additional ¼ mile, what is the fare for a 2-mile trip?

21. The following graphs plot the cost and the revenue functions, in dollars, for producing widgets. From the graphs, estimate the following.

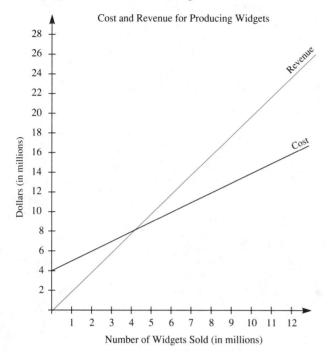

Cost and Revenue for Producing Widgets

(a) The break-even point, or the number of units that must be sold to meet expenses exactly.
(b) The profit or loss on the first million widgets produced and sold.
(c) The number of units that must be sold to yield a $5 million profit.

22. Find a rule for each of the following sequences, whose domains are the natural numbers.
    (a) {3, 8, 13, 18, 23, . . .}
    (b) {3, 9, 27, 81, 243, . . .}
    (c) {2, 4, 6, 8, 10, . . .}
23. (a) Is the rule "has as mother" a function whose domain is the set of all people?
    (b) Is the relation "has as brother" a function on the set of all boys?

Review Problems

24. Draw Venn diagrams to verify the following.
    (a) $A - (B \cup C) = (A - B) \cap (A - C)$
    (b) If $A \subseteq B$, then $A \cup B = B$.
25. Is the set of all rich men well defined? Why or why not?
26. Suppose U is the set of natural numbers, {1, 2, 3, 4, . . .}. Write each of the following, using set-builder notation.
    (a) The set of even numbers greater than 12.
    (b) The set of numbers less than 14.
27. If $U = \{a, b, c, d\}$, $A = \{a, b, c\}$, $B = \{b, c\}$, and $C = \{d\}$, find each of the following.
    (a) $A \cup \overline{B}$ (b) $\overline{A \cap B}$ (c) $A \cap \varnothing$
    (d) $B \cap C$ (e) $B - A$
28. Write two sets with three elements each and establish a one-to-one correspondence between them.
29. Write a set that is equivalent, but not equal, to the set {5, 6, 7, 8}.
30. (a) How many different one-to-one correspondences are possible between $A = \{a, b, c\}$ and $B = \{1, 2, 3\}$?
    (b) How many elements are there in $A \times B$?
31. Illustrate the associative property of set union with the sets $U = \{h, e, l, p, m, n, o, w\}$, $A = \{h, e, l, p\}$, $B = \{m, e\}$, and $C = \{n, o, w\}$.

B R A I N   T E A S E R
Only 10 rooms were vacant in the Village Hotel. Eleven men went into the hotel at the same time, each wanting a separate room. The clerk, settling the argument, said, "I'll tell you what I'll do. I'll put two men in Room 1 with the understanding that I will come back and get one of them a few minutes later." The men agreed to this. The clerk continued, "I will put the rest of you men in rooms as follows: the 3rd man in Room 2, the 4th man in Room 3, the 5th man in Room 4, the 6th man in Room 5, the 7th man in Room 6, the 8th man in Room 7, the 9th man in Room 8, and the 10th man in Room 9." Then the clerk went back and got the extra man he had left in Room 1 and put him in Room 10. Everybody was happy. What is wrong with this plan?

*Section 2-4   Logic: An Introduction

statement

Logic deals with reasoning and is a tool used in mathematical thinking and problem solving. In logic, a **statement** *is a sentence that is either true or false, but not both.*

Expressions such as "2 + 3," "Close the door," or "How tall are you?" are not statements, since they cannot be classified as true or false. The following expressions also are not statements, since their truth value cannot be determined without more information.

1. She has blue eyes.
2. $x + 7 = 18$
3. $2y + 7 > 1$

Each of the preceding expressions becomes a statement if, for (1), "she" is identified, and for (2) and (3), values are assigned to x and y, respectively. However, an expression involving *he* or *she* or x or y may already be a statement. For example, "If he is over 210 cm tall, then he is over 2 m tall," and "$2(x + y) = 2x + 2y$" are both statements, since they are true no matter who *he* is or what the values of x and y are.

negation

From a given statement, it is possible to create a new statement by forming a **negation.** The negation of a statement is a statement with the opposite truth value of the given statement; that is, if the statement is true, its negation is false, and if the statement is false, its negation is true. Consider the statement "It is snowing." The negation of this statement is "It is not true that it is snowing." Stated in a simpler form, the negation is "It is not snowing."

EXAMPLE 2-21   Negate each of the following statements.

(a) $2 + 3 = 5$
(b) A hexagon has six sides.
(c) Today is not Monday.

SOLUTION   (a) $2 + 3 \neq 5$
(b) A hexagon does not have six sides.
(c) Today is Monday.

Are the statements "The shirt is blue" and "The shirt is green" negations of each other? To check, we recall that a statement and its negation must have opposite truth values. If the shirt is actually red, then both of the statements are false and, hence, cannot be negations of each other. However, the statements "The shirt is blue" and "The shirt is not blue" are negations of each other, since they have opposite truth values no matter what color the shirt really is.

quantifiers

Some statements involve **quantifiers** and are more complicated to negate. Quantifiers include words such as *all, some, every,* and *there exists.*

universal quantifiers

existential quantifiers

The quantifiers *all*, *every*, and *no* refer to each and every element in a set and are **universal quantifiers.** The quantifiers *some* and *there exists at least one* refer to one or more, or possibly all, of the elements in a set. *Some* and *there exists* are called **existential quantifiers.** Examples with universal and existential quantifiers follow.

1. All roses are red. [universal]
2. Every student is important. [universal]
3. For each counting number x, $x + 0 = x$. [universal]
4. Some roses are red. [existential]
5. There exists at least one even counting number less than 3. [existential]
6. There exist women who are taller than 200 cm. [existential]

Venn diagrams can be used to picture statements involving quantifiers. For example, Figure 2-20(a) and (b) picture statements (1) and (4). The x in Figure 2-20(b) can be used to show that there must be at least one element of the set of roses that is red.

FIGURE 2-20

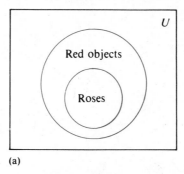
(a)

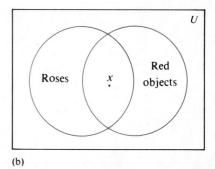
(b)

Consider the following statement involving the existential quantifier *some.* "Some professors at Paxson University have blue eyes." This means that at least one professor at Paxson University has blue eyes. It does not rule out the possibilities that all the Paxson professors have blue eyes or that some of the Paxson professors do not have blue eyes. Since the negation of a true statement is false, neither "Some professors at Paxson University do not have blue eyes" nor "All professors at Paxson have blue eyes" are negations of the original statement. One possible negation of the original statement is "No professors at Paxson University have blue eyes."

To discover if one statement is a negation of another, we use arguments similar to the preceding one to determine if they have opposite truth values in all possible cases. Some general forms of quantified statements with their negations follow.

Statement	Negation
Some *a* are *b*.	No *a* is *b*.
Some *a* are not *b*.	All *a* are *b*.
All *a* are *b*.	Some *a* are not *b*.
No *a* is *b*.	Some *a* are *b*.

EXAMPLE 2-22 Negate each of the following statements.

(a) All students like hamburgers.
(b) Some people like mathematics.
(c) There exists a counting number x such that $3x = 6$.
(d) For all counting numbers, $3x = 3x$.

SOLUTION (a) Some students do not like hamburgers.
(b) No people like mathematics.
(c) For all counting numbers x, $3x \neq 6$.
(d) There exists a counting number x such that $3x \neq 3x$.

There is a symbolic system defined to help in the study of logic. If p represents a statement, the negation of the statement p is denoted by $\sim p$. *truth table* **Truth tables** are often used to show all possible true-false patterns for statements. Table 2-4 summarizes the truth tables for p and $\sim p$.

TABLE 2-4

Statement p	Negation $\sim p$
T	F
F	T

Observe that p and $\sim p$ are analogous to sets P and $\overline{P}$. If x is an element of P, then x is not an element of $\overline{P}$.

Compound Statements

compound statement From two given statements it is possible to create a new, **compound statement** by using a connective such as *and*. For example, "It is snowing" and "The ski run is open" together with *and* give "It is snowing and the ski run is open." Other compound statements can be obtained by using the connective *or*. For example, "It is snowing or the ski run is open."

p	q	Conjunction $p \wedge q$
T	T	T
T	F	F
F	T	F
F	F	F

TABLE 2-5

The symbols $\wedge$ and $\vee$ are used to represent the connectives *and* and *or*, respectively. For example, if p represents "It is snowing," and if q represents "The ski run is open," then "It is snowing and the ski run is open" is denoted by $p \wedge q$. Similarly, "It is snowing or the ski run is open" is denoted by $p \vee q$.

The truth value of any compound statement, such as $p \wedge q$, is defined using the truth table of each of the simple statements. Since each of the statements p and q may be either true or false, there are four distinct possibilities for the truth of $p \wedge q$, as shown in Table 2-5. The compound *conjunction* statement $p \wedge q$ is the **conjunction** of p and q and is defined to be true if and only if both p and q are true. Otherwise, it is false.

P	Q	$P \cap Q$
$\in$	$\in$	$\in$
$\in$	$\notin$	$\notin$
$\notin$	$\in$	$\notin$
$\notin$	$\notin$	$\notin$

TABLE 2-6

disjunction

p	q	Disjunction $p \vee q$
T	T	T
T	F	T
F	T	T
F	F	F

TABLE 2-7

We can find similarities between conjunction and set intersection. Consider Table 2-6, which shows all possibilities of whether or not an element is a member of sets, P, Q, and $P \cap Q$.

If we consider $\in$ analogous to T and $\notin$ analogous to F, we see that Tables 2-5 and 2-6 are equivalent. The language involving set intersection and the language involving *and* in logic should be equivalent. Thus, for every property involving set intersection, there should be an equivalent property involving *and*. For example, *and* should be *commutative and associative*.

The compound statement $p \vee q$ (that is, *p or q*) is a **disjunction**. In everyday language, *or* is not always interpreted in the same way. In logic, we use an *inclusive or*. The statement "I will go to a movie or I will read a book" means that I will either go to a movie, or read a book, or do both. Hence, in logic, *p or q*, symbolized as $p \vee q$, is defined to be false if both p and q are false, and true in all other cases. This is summarized in Table 2-7.

Just as *set intersection* and *and* are analogous, so are *set union* and *or*. And in a similar way, for all properties involving set union, *there are corresponding properties involving* or, *such as the commutative and associative properties*. Expressions involving statements inside parentheses are treated similarly to expressions involving set unions and intersections.

EXAMPLE 2-23 Given the following statements, classify each of the conjunctions and disjunctions as true or false.

p: $2 + 3 = 5$ r: $5 + 3 = 9$
q: $2 \cdot 3 = 6$ s: $2 \cdot 4 = 9$

(a) $p \wedge q$ (b) $p \wedge r$ (c) $s \wedge q$ (d) $r \wedge s$
(e) $\sim p \wedge q$ (f) $\sim(p \wedge q)$ (g) $p \vee q$ (h) $p \vee r$
(i) $s \vee q$ (j) $r \vee s$ (k) $\sim p \vee q$ (l) $\sim(p \vee q)$

SOLUTION (a) p is true and q is true, so $p \wedge q$ is true.
(b) p is true and r is false, so $p \wedge r$ is false.
(c) s is false and q is true, so $s \wedge q$ is false.
(d) r is false and s is false, so $r \wedge s$ is false.
(e) $\sim p$ is false and q is true, so $\sim p \wedge q$ is false.
(f) $p \wedge q$ is true [part (a)], so $\sim(p \wedge q)$ is false.
(g) p is true and q is true, so $p \vee q$ is true.
(h) p is true and r is false, so $p \vee r$ is true.
(i) s is false and q is true, so $s \vee q$ is true.
(j) r is false and s is false, so $r \vee s$ is false.
(k) $\sim p$ is false and q is true, so $\sim p \vee q$ is true.
(l) $p \vee q$ is true [part (g)], so $\sim(p \vee q)$ is false.

Not only are truth tables used to summarize the truth values of compound statements, they are also used to determine if two statements are *logically equivalent*. Two statements are **logically equivalent** if and only if they have the same truth values. For example, we could show that $p \wedge q$ is logically equivalent to $q \wedge p$ by using truth tables as in Table 2-8.

TABLE 2-8

p	q	$p \wedge q$	$q \wedge p$
T	T	T	T
T	F	F	F
F	T	F	F
F	F	F	F

Table 2-8 shows that *and* is commutative. A summary of properties of *and* and *or* is given below.

● **P R O P E R T I E S**

1. **Commutative Properties**
   (a) $p \wedge q$ is logically equivalent to $q \wedge p$.
   (b) $p \vee q$ is logically equivalent to $q \vee p$.
2. **Associative Properties**
   (a) $(p \wedge q) \wedge r$ is logically equivalent to $p \wedge (q \wedge r)$.
   (b) $(p \vee q) \vee r$ is logically equivalent to $p \vee (q \wedge r)$.
3. **Distributive Properties**
   (a) $p \wedge (q \vee r)$ is logically equivalent to $(p \wedge q) \vee (p \wedge r)$.
   (b) $p \vee (q \wedge r)$ is logically equivalent to $(p \vee q) \wedge (p \vee r)$.

As another example, consider $\sim p \vee \sim q$ and $\sim(p \wedge q)$. Table 2-9 shows headings and the four distinct possibilities for p and q. In the column headed $\sim p$, we write the negations of the p column. In the $\sim q$ column, we write the negation of the q column. Next, we use the values in the $\sim p$ and the $\sim q$ columns to construct the $\sim p \vee \sim q$ column. To find the truth values for $\sim(p \wedge q)$, we use the p and q columns to find the truth value for $p \wedge q$ and then negate $p \wedge q$.

TABLE 2-9

p	q	$\sim p$	$\sim q$	$\sim p \vee \sim q$	$p \wedge q$	$\sim(p \wedge q)$
T	T	F	F	F	T	F
T	F	F	T	T	F	T
F	T	T	F	T	F	T
F	F	T	T	T	F	T

DeMorgan's Laws

Note that $\sim p \vee \sim q$ has the same truth values as $\sim(p \wedge q)$. Thus, the statements are logically equivalent. The equivalence between $\sim p \vee \sim q$ and $\sim(p \wedge q)$, along with the equivalence between $\sim(p \vee q)$ and $\sim p \wedge \sim q$, are referred to as **DeMorgan's Laws.** Find the set theory analogue to DeMorgan's Laws, and check your answer with Problem 15 of Problem Set 2-2.

PROBLEM SET 2-4

1. Determine which of the following are statements, and then classify each statement as true or false.
   - (a) $2 + 4 = 8$
   - (b) Shut the window.
   - (c) Los Angeles is a state.
   - (d) He is in town.
   - (e) What time is it?
   - (f) $5x = 15$
   - (g) $3 \cdot 2 = 6$
   - (h) $2x^2 > x$
   - (i) This statement is false.

2. Use quantifiers to make each of the following true where x is a natural number.
   - (a) $x + 8 = 11$
   - (b) $x + 0 = x$
   - (c) $x^2 = 4$
   - (d) $x + 1 = x + 2$

3. Use quantifiers to make each equation in Problem 2 false.

4. Write the negation for each of the following statements.
   - (a) The book has 500 pages.
   - (b) Six is less than eight.
   - (c) Johnny is not thin.
   - (d) $3 \cdot 5 = 15$
   - (e) Some people have blond hair.
   - (f) All dogs have four legs.
   - (g) Some cats do not have nine lives.
   - (h) No dogs can fly.
   - (i) All squares are rectangles.
   - (j) Not all rectangles are squares.
   - (k) For all natural numbers x, $x + 3 = 3 + x$.
   - (l) There exists a natural number x such that $3 \cdot (x + 2) = 12$.
   - (m) Every counting number is divisible by itself and 1.
   - (n) Not all natural numbers are divisible by 2.
   - (o) For all natural numbers x, $5x + 4x = 9x$.

5. Complete each of the following truth tables.

   (a)

p	$\sim p$	$\sim(\sim p)$
T		
F		

   (b)

p	$\sim p$	$p \vee \sim p$	$p \wedge \sim p$
T			
F			

6. If q stands for "This course is easy" and r stands for "Lazy students do not study," write each of the following in symbolic form.
   - (a) This course is easy and lazy students do not study.
   - (b) Lazy students do not study or this course is not easy.
   - (c) It is false that both this course is easy and lazy students do not study.
   - (d) This course is not easy.

7. If p is false and q is true, find the truth values for each of the following.
   - (a) $p \wedge q$
   - (b) $p \vee q$
   - (c) $\sim p$
   - (d) $\sim q$
   - (e) $\sim(\sim p)$
   - (f) $\sim p \vee q$
   - (g) $p \wedge \sim q$
   - (h) $\sim(p \vee q)$
   - (i) $\sim(\sim p \wedge q)$
   - (j) $\sim q \wedge \sim p$

   - (c) Based on part (a), is p logically equivalent to $\sim(\sim p)$?
   - (d) Based on part (b), is $p \vee \sim p$ logically equivalent to $p \wedge \sim p$?

8. Find the truth value for each statement in Problem 7 if p is false and q is false.

9. For each of the following, is the pair of statements logically equivalent?
   - (a) $\sim(p \vee q)$ and $\sim p \vee \sim q$
   - (b) $\sim(p \vee q)$ and $\sim p \wedge \sim q$
   - (c) $\sim(p \wedge q)$ and $\sim p \wedge \sim q$
   - (d) $\sim(p \wedge q)$ and $\sim p \vee \sim q$

10. Complete the following truth table.

p	q	$\sim p$	$\sim q$	$\sim p \vee q$
T	T			
T	F			
F	T			
F	F			

11. Apply DeMorgan's Laws to restate the following in a logically equivalent form.
    - (a) It is not true that both today is Wednesday and the month is June.
    - (b) It is not true that yesterday I both ate breakfast and watched television.
    - (c) It is not raining or it is not July.

B R A I N   T E A S E R

An explorer landed on an island inhabited by two tribes, the Abes and the Babes. Abes always tell the truth and Babes always lie. The explorer met three natives on the shore. He asked the first native to name his tribe and the native responded in his native tongue, which the explorer did not understand. The second native stated that the first native said that he was an Abe. The third native then stated that the first native had said he was a Babe. To what tribes do the second and third natives belong?

*Section 2-5 Conditionals and Biconditionals

conditionals
implications
hypothesis
conclusion

Statements expressed in the form "if p, then q" are called **conditionals,** or **implications,** and are denoted by $p \rightarrow q$. Such statements can also be read "p implies q." The "if" part of a conditional is called the **hypothesis** of the implication and the "then" part is called the **conclusion.**

Many types of statements can be put in "if-then" form; an example follows.

Statement: All first-graders are 6 years old.
If-then form: If a child is a first-grader, then the child is 6 years old.

An implication may also be thought of as a promise. Suppose Betty makes the promise, "If I get a raise, then I will take you to dinner." If Betty keeps her promise, the implication is true; if Betty breaks her promise, the implication is false. Consider the following four possibilities.

	p	q	
(1)	T	T	Betty gets the raise; she takes you to dinner.
(2)	T	F	Betty gets the raise; she does not take you to dinner.
(3)	F	T	Betty does not get the raise; she takes you to dinner.
(4)	F	F	Betty does not get the raise; she does not take you to dinner.

The only case in which Betty breaks her promise is when she gets her raise and fails to take you to dinner, case (2). If she does not get the raise, she can either take you to dinner or not without breaking her promise. The definition of implication is summarized in Table 2-10. Observe that the only case for which the implication is false is when p is true and q is false.

An implication may be worded in several equivalent ways:

1. If the sun shines, then the swimming pool is open. (If p, then q.)
2. If the sun shines, the swimming pool is open. (If p, q.)
3. The swimming pool is open if the sun shines. (q if p.)
4. The sun shines implies the swimming pool is open. (p implies q.)
5. The sun is shining only if the pool is open. (p only if q.)
6. The sun's shining is a sufficient condition for the swimming pool to be open. (p is a sufficient condition for q.)
7. The swimming pool's being open is a necessary condition for the sun to be shining. (q is a necessary condition for p.)

p	q	Implication $p \rightarrow q$
T	T	T
T	F	F
F	T	T
F	F	T

TABLE 2-10

Any implication $p \to q$ has three related implication statements:

Statement:	If p, then q.	$p \to q$
Converse:	If q, then p.	$q \to p$
Inverse:	If not p, then not q.	$\sim p \to \sim q$
Contrapositive:	If not q, then not p.	$\sim q \to \sim p$

EXAMPLE 2-24 Write the converse, the inverse, and the contrapositive for each of the following statements.
(a) If $2x = 6$, then $x = 3$.
(b) If I am in San Francisco, then I am in California.

SOLUTION (a) *Converse:* If $x = 3$, then $2x = 6$.
Inverse: If $2x \neq 6$, then $x \neq 3$.
Contrapositive: If $x \neq 3$, then $2x \neq 6$.
(b) *Converse:* If I am in California, then I am in San Francisco.
Inverse: If I am not in San Francisco, then I am not in California.
Contrapositive: If I am not in California, then I am not in San Francisco.

Table 2-11 shows that an implication and its converse do not always have the same truth value. However, an implication and its contrapositive do always have the same truth value. Also, the converse and inverse of a conditional statement are logically equivalent. (Note that the converse and the inverse are contrapositives of each other.)

TABLE 2-11

p	q	$\sim p$	$\sim q$	Implication $p \to q$	Converse $q \to p$	Inverse $\sim p \to \sim q$	Contrapositive $\sim q \to \sim p$
T	T	F	F	T	T	T	T
T	F	F	T	F	T	T	F
F	T	T	F	T	F	F	T
F	F	T	T	T	T	T	T

Connecting a statement and its converse with the connective *and* gives $(p \to q) \land (q \to p)$. This compound statement can be written as $p \leftrightarrow q$ and usually is read "p if and only if q." The statement "p if and only if q" is a

biconditional **biconditional.** A truth table for $p \leftrightarrow q$ is given in Table 2-12. Observe that $p \leftrightarrow q$ is true if and only if p and q have the same truth values—that is, if and only if both statements are true or both are false. Observe that p is a necessary and sufficient condition for q, and vice versa.

TABLE 2-12

p	q	$p \to q$	$q \to p$	Biconditional $(p \to q) \land (q \to p)$ or $p \leftrightarrow q$
T	T	T	T	T
T	F	F	T	F
F	T	T	F	F
F	F	T	T	T

EXAMPLE 2-25 Given the following statements, classify each of the biconditionals as true or false.

p: $2 = 2$ r: $2 = 1$
q: $2 \neq 1$ s: $2 + 3 = 1 + 3$

(a) $p \leftrightarrow q$ (b) $p \leftrightarrow r$ (c) $s \leftrightarrow q$ (d) $r \leftrightarrow s$

SOLUTION (a) $p \rightarrow q$ is true and $q \rightarrow p$ is true, so $p \leftrightarrow q$ is true.
(b) $p \rightarrow r$ is false and $r \rightarrow p$ is true, so $p \leftrightarrow r$ is false.
(c) $s \rightarrow q$ is true and $q \rightarrow s$ is false, so $s \leftrightarrow q$ is false.
(d) $r \rightarrow s$ is true and $s \rightarrow r$ is true, so $r \leftrightarrow s$ is true.

In the previous section we discussed analogies between the conjunction $p \wedge q$ and set intersection and between the disjunction $p \vee q$ and set union. Similar analogies exist for implication. Consider the implication "If a flower is a violet, then it is blue." The set of violets is a subset of the set of blue objects. In general, the implication $p \rightarrow q$ is analogous to $P \subseteq Q$. In fact, the definition of $P \subseteq Q$ tells us that $x \in P \rightarrow x \in Q$. Thus, for every property involving set inclusion, we should have a corresponding property involving implications. For example, we have seen that $p \rightarrow q$ and $\sim q \rightarrow \sim p$ are logically equivalent. By analogy $P \subseteq Q$ if and only if $\overline{Q} \subseteq \overline{P}$.

Now consider the following statement.

It is raining or it is not raining.

tautology This statement can be modeled as $p \vee (\sim p)$ and has the truth table shown in Table 2-13. Observe that $p \vee (\sim p)$ is always true. A statement that is always true is called a **tautology**. One way to make a tautology is to take two logically equivalent statements such as $p \rightarrow q$ and $\sim q \rightarrow \sim p$ (from Table 2-11) and form them into a biconditional as follows.

$$(p \rightarrow q) \leftrightarrow (\sim q \rightarrow \sim p)$$

Both $p \rightarrow q$ and $\sim q \rightarrow \sim p$ have the same truth values, so $(p \rightarrow q) \leftrightarrow (\sim q \rightarrow \sim p)$ is a tautology.

p	$\sim p$	$p \vee (\sim p)$
T	F	T
F	T	T

TABLE 2-13

Valid Reasoning

valid reasoning In problem solving, the reasoning used is said to be **valid** if the conclusion follows unavoidably from the hypotheses. Consider the following example.

Hypotheses: All roses are red.
             This flower is a rose.
Conclusion: Therefore, this flower is red.

The statement "All roses are red" can be written as the implication "If a flower is a rose, then it is red" and pictured with the Venn diagram in Figure 2-21(a).

FIGURE 2-21

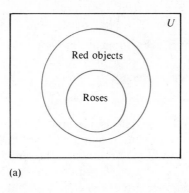 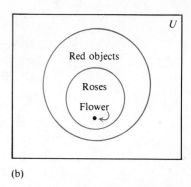

(a)   (b)

The information "This flower is a rose" implies that this flower must belong to the circle containing roses, as pictured in Figure 2-21(b). This flower must also belong to the circle containing red objects. Thus, the reasoning is valid because it is impossible to draw a picture satisfying the hypotheses and contradicting the conclusion.

Consider the following argument.

Hypotheses: All elementary school teachers are rich.
                     Some rich people are not thin.
Conclusion: Therefore, no elementary school teacher is thin.

Let E be the set of elementary school teachers, R be the set of rich people, and T be the set of thin people. Then the statement "All elementary school teachers are rich" can be pictured as in Figure 2-22(a). The statement "Some rich people are not thin" can be pictured in several ways. Three of these are illustrated in Figure 2-22(b)–(d).

FIGURE 2-22

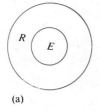 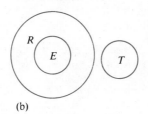 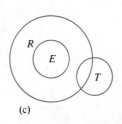 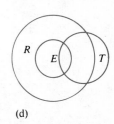

(a)   (b)   (c)   (d)

According to Figure 2-22(d), it is possible that some elementary school teachers are thin, and yet the given statements are satisfied. Therefore, the conclusion that "No elementary school teacher is thin" does not follow from the given hypotheses. Hence, the reasoning is not valid.

If a single picture can be drawn to satisfy the hypotheses of an argument and contradict the conclusion, the argument is not valid. However, to show that an argument is valid, *all* possible pictures must be considered to show that there are no contradictions; that is, that there is no way to satisfy the hypotheses and contradict the conclusion.

EXAMPLE 2-26   Determine if the following argument is valid.

Hypotheses: In Appia all chimney sweeps wear black hats.
              No one in Appia over 6 feet tall wears a black hat.
Conclusion: Persons over 6 feet tall are not chimney sweeps in Appia.

SOLUTION   The first hypothesis is pictured as shown in Figure 2-23(a). The second hypothesis is pictured along with the first in Figure 2-23(b). Because people over 6 feet tall (*T*) are outside the circle representing black-hat wearers (*B*) and chimney sweeps (*S*) are inside the circle *B*, the conclusion is valid and no person over 6 feet tall can be a chimney sweep in Appia.

FIGURE 2-23

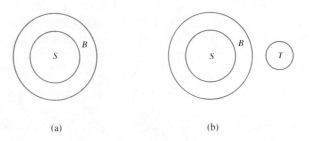

(a)   (b)

direct reasoning   A different method for determining if an argument is valid uses **direct**
Modus Ponens **reasoning** and a form of argument called the Law of Detachment (or **Modus Ponens**). For example, consider the following true statements.

If the sun is shining, then we shall take a trip.
The sun is shining.

Law of Detachment   Using these two statements, we can conclude that we shall take a trip. In general, the **Law of Detachment** is stated as follows:

If a statement is in the form "if p, then q" is true, and p is true, then q must also be true.

The Law of Detachment is sometimes described schematically as follows, where all statements above the horizontal line are true, and the statements below the horizontal line is the conclusion.

$$p \rightarrow q$$
$$\underline{p\qquad\quad}$$
$$q$$

The Law of Detachment follows from the truth table for $p \rightarrow q$ given in Table 2-10. The only case in which both p and $p \rightarrow q$ are true is when q is true (line 1 in the table).

EXAMPLE 2-27 Determine if each of the following arguments is valid.
(a) Hypotheses: If you eat spinach, then you will be strong.
You eat spinach.
Conclusion: Therefore, you will be strong.
(b) Hypotheses: If Claude goes skiing, he will break his leg.
If Claude breaks his leg, he cannot enter the dance contest.
Claude goes skiing.
Conclusion: Therefore, Claude cannot enter the dance contest.

SOLUTION (a) Using the Law of Detachment, we see that the conclusion is valid.
(b) By using the Law of Detachment twice, we see that the conclusion is valid.

indirect reasoning
Modus Tollens

A different type of reasoning, **indirect reasoning,** uses a form of argument called **Modus Tollens.** For example, consider the following true statements.

If Chicken Little had been hit by a jumping frog, he would have thought the earth was rising.
Chicken Little did not think the earth was rising.

What is the conclusion? The conclusion is that Chicken Little did not get hit by a jumping frog. This leads us to the general form of Modus Tollens:

If we have a conditional accepted as true, and we know the conclusion is false, then the hypothesis must be false.

Modus Tollens is sometimes schematically described as follows:

$$p \rightarrow q$$
$$\sim q$$
$$\overline{\qquad\qquad}$$
$$\sim p$$

The validity of Modus Tollens also follows from the truth table for $p \rightarrow q$ given in Table 2-10. The only case in which both $p \rightarrow q$ is true and q is false is when p is false (line 4 in the table). The validity of Modus Tollens can also be established from the fact that an implication and its contrapositive are equivalent (see Table 2-11).

EXAMPLE 2-28 Determine conclusions for each of the following sets of true statements.
(a) If an old woman lives in a shoe, then she does not know what to do.
Mrs. Pumpkin Eater, an old woman, knows what to do.
(b) If Jack is nimble, he will not get burned.
Jack was burned.

SOLUTION (a) Mrs. Pumpkin Eater does not live in a shoe.
(b) Jack was not nimble.

Chain Rule The final reasoning argument to be considered here involves the **Chain Rule.** Consider the following statements.

If my wife works, I will retire early.
If I retire early, I will become lazy.

What is the conclusion? The conclusion is that if my wife works, I will become lazy. In general, the Chain Rule can be stated as follows:

If "if p, then q" and "if q, then r" are true, then "if p, then r" is true.

The Chain Rule is sometimes schematically described as follows:

$$p \rightarrow q$$
$$\underline{q \rightarrow r}$$
$$p \rightarrow r$$

Notice that the chain rule shows that implication is a transitive relation.

People often make invalid conclusions based on advertising or other information. Consider, for example, the statement "Healthy people eat Super-Bran cereal." Are the following conclusions valid?

If a person eats Super-Bran cereal, then the person is healthy.
If a person is not healthy, the person does not eat Super-Bran cereal.

If the original statement is denoted by $p \rightarrow q$, where p is "a person is healthy" and q is "a person eats Super-Bran cereal," then the first conclusion is the converse of $p \rightarrow q$—that is, $q \rightarrow p$—and the second conclusion is the inverse of $p \rightarrow q$—that is, $\sim p \rightarrow \sim q$. Table 2-11 points out that neither the converse nor the inverse are logically equivalent to the original statement, and consequently the conclusions are not necessarily true.

EXAMPLE 2-29 Determine conclusions for each of the following sets of true statements.
(a) If Alice follows the White Rabbit, she falls into a hole. If she falls into a hole, she goes to a tea party.
(b) If Chicken Little is hit by an acorn, we think the sky is falling. If we think the sky is falling, we will go to a fallout shelter. If we go to a fallout shelter, we will stay there a month.

SOLUTION (a) If Alice follows the White Rabbit, she goes to a tea party.
(b) If Chicken Little is hit by an acorn, we will stay in a fallout shelter for a month.

• R E M A R K
Note that, in Example 2-29(b), the Chain Rule can be extended to contain several implications.

EXAMPLE 2-30 Determine the validity of the following argument, and then use the truth table for $p \rightarrow q$ to explain your answer.
If it is raining in the park, then the slides are wet.
The slides are wet.
Therefore, it is raining in the park.

SOLUTION Even though the first two statements are true, the last statement might be false because the lawn sprinklers might be the cause of the wet slides. Hence the argument is invalid.

  The third statement might be true, but its truth would not be the logical consequence of the first two statements. Representing the first statement as $p \rightarrow q$ and the second statement as q, we see from Table 2-10 that $p \rightarrow q$ and q are true in two cases (lines 1 and 3 in the table). Thus, from the truth table we see that the truth of p or the falsity of p are both consistent with $p \rightarrow q$ and q being true.

PROBLEM SET 2-5

1. Write each of the following in symbolic form if p is the statement "It is raining" and q is the statement "The grass is wet."
   (a) If it is raining, then the grass is wet.
   (b) If it is not raining, then the grass is wet.
   (c) If it is raining, then the grass is not wet.
   (d) The grass is wet if it is raining.
   (e) The grass is not wet implies that it is not raining.
   (f) The grass is wet if and only if it is raining.

2. For each of the following implications, state the converse, inverse, and contrapositive.
   (a) If you eat Meaties, then you are good in sports.
   (b) If you do not like this book, then you do not like mathematics.
   (c) If you do not use Ultra Brush toothpaste, then you have cavities.
   (d) If you are good at logic, then your grades are high.

3. Construct a truth table for each of the following.
   (a) $p \rightarrow (p \vee q)$ (b) $(p \wedge q) \rightarrow q$
   (c) $p \leftrightarrow \sim(\sim p)$ (d) $\sim(p \rightarrow q)$

4. If p is true and q is false, find the truth values for each of the following.
   (a) $\sim p \rightarrow \sim q$ (b) $\sim(p \rightarrow q)$
   (c) $(p \vee q) \rightarrow (p \wedge q)$ (d) $p \rightarrow \sim p$
   (e) $(p \vee \sim p) \rightarrow p$ (f) $(p \vee q) \leftrightarrow (p \wedge q)$

5. If p is false and q is false, find the truth values for each of the statements in Problem 4.

6. Can an implication and its converse both be false? Explain your answer.

7. Iris makes the true statement, "If it rains, then I am going to the movies." Does it follow logically that, if it does not rain, then Iris does not go to the movies?

8. Consider the statement "If every digit of a number is 6, then the number is divisible by 3." Which of the following is logically equivalent to the statement?
   (a) If every digit of a number is not 6, then the number is not divisible by 3.
   (b) If a number is not divisible by 3, then every digit of the number is not 6.
   (c) If a number is divisible by 3, then every digit of the number is 6.

9. Write a statement logically equivalent to the statement "If a number is a multiple of 8, then it is a multiple of 4."

10. Use truth tables to prove that the following are tautologies.
    (a) $(p \rightarrow q) \rightarrow [(p \wedge r) \rightarrow q]$ Law of Added Hypothesis
    (b) $[(p \rightarrow q) \wedge p] \rightarrow q$ Law of Detachment
    (c) $[(p \rightarrow q) \wedge (\sim q)] \rightarrow \sim p$ Modus Tollens
    (d) $[(p \rightarrow q) \wedge (q \rightarrow r)] \rightarrow (p \rightarrow r)$ Chain Rule

11. (a) If $p \rightarrow q$ is true but $q \rightarrow p$ is false, what is the analogous relation between sets?
    (b) Suppose that $p \rightarrow q$ and $q \rightarrow p$ are true. What is the analogous relation between sets?
    (c) Suppose that $A \subseteq B$ and $\overline{A} \subseteq \overline{B}$. What are the analogous statements in logic? What can you conclude about A and B?

12. (a) Suppose that $p \to q$, $q \to r$, and $r \to s$ are all true, but s is false. What can you conclude about the truth value of p?
    (b) Suppose that $(p \wedge q) \to r$ is true, r is false, and q is true. What can you conclude about the truth value of p?
    (c) Suppose that $p \to q$ is true and $q \to p$ is false. Can q be true? Why or why not?

13. Translate the following statements into symbolic form. Give the meanings of the symbols that you use.
    (a) If Mary's little lamb follows her to school, then it will break the rules and Mary will be sent home.
    (b) If it is not the case that Jack is nimble and quick, then Jack will not make it over the candlestick.
    (c) If the apple had not hit Isaac Newton on the head, then the laws of gravity would not have been discovered.

14. Investigate the validity of each of the following arguments.
    (a) All men are mortal.
        Socrates was a man.
        Therefore, Socrates was mortal.
    (b) All squares are quadrilaterals.
        All quadrilaterals are polygons.
        Therefore, all squares are polygons.
    (c) All teachers are intelligent.
        Some teachers are rich.
        Therefore, some intelligent people are rich.
    (d) All x's are y's.
        Some z's are x's.
        Therefore, all z's are y's.
    (e) If a student is a freshman, then she takes mathematics.
        Jane is a sophomore.
        Therefore, Jane does not take mathematics.
    (f) If A, then not B.
        If not B, then C.
        Therefore, if A, then C.

15. For each of the following, form a conclusion that follows logically from the given statements.
    (a) All college students are poor.
        Helen is a college student.
    (b) Some freshmen like mathematics.
        All people who like mathematics are intelligent.
    (c) If I study for the final, then I will pass the final.
        If I pass the final, then I will pass the course.
        If I pass the course, then I will look for a teaching job.
    (d) Every eagle can fly.
        Some pigs cannot fly.
    (e) Every equilateral triangle is isosceles.
        There exist triangles that are isosceles.

16. Write the following in if-then form.
    (a) Every figure that is a square is a rectangle.
    (b) All integers are rational numbers.
    (c) Figures with exactly three sides may be triangles.
    (d) It only rains if it is cloudy.

17. Determine the validity of the following argument, and then use the truth table for $p \to q$ to explain your answer.

    If it is raining in the park, then the slides are wet.
    It is not raining in the park.
    Therefore, the slides are not wet.

SOLUTION TO THE PRELIMINARY PROBLEM

Understanding the Problem. The problem is to determine whether the editor of a newspaper was right in claiming the reported poll was not accurate. The pollster interviewed 500 seniors who owned only Goldcards, Supercards, or Thriftcards and reported that 240 owned a Goldcard, 290 owned a Supercard, and 270 had a Thriftcard. It was also reported that of these seniors, 80 owned a Goldcard and a Supercard and no other cards, 70 had a Goldcard and a Thriftcard and no other cards, 60 owned a Supercard and a Thriftcard and no other cards, and 50 owned all three cards.

One of the ways to ascertain the validity of the editor's claim is to determine whether the numbers given by the pollster are consistent throughout. If we can conclude that the total number of students polled is not 500, then the editor is correct.

Devising a Plan. The Venn diagram, introduced in this chapter, can be used as a tool for classifying and sorting the given information. We use three circles because there are three different subjects. From the given information, we can determine the number of students in each of the seven regions formed by the circles and the universal set and consequently the total number of students who participated in the poll. This number should be 500, as reported. If it is not, the poll was not accurate.

Carrying Out the Plan. Using the given information, we show the number of students in some of the regions in the Venn diagram in Figure 2-24(a). To find the total number of students, we need to find the number of students in the three remaining regions. Students owning only a Goldcard are those who own a Goldcard but not a Supercard or a Thriftcard. Thus from 240, we subtract 80 (the number of students who own just a Goldcard and a Supercard), then subtract 70 (the number of students who own just a Goldcard and a Thriftcard), and finally subtract 50 (the number of students who own all three cards). We have $240 - 80 - 70 - 50 = 40$. Similarly, the number of students who own only a Supercard is $290 - 80 - 50 - 60 = 100$, and the number of students who own only a Thriftcard is $270 - 70 - 50 - 60 = 90$. This information is summarized in Figure 2-24(b). From this information, we can calculate that the total number of seniors polled should have been $40 + 70 + 50 + 80 + 100 + 60 + 90 = 490$. Because the number of polled students was reported to be 500, the report was not accurate.

FIGURE 2-24

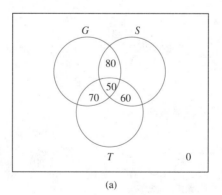

(a)

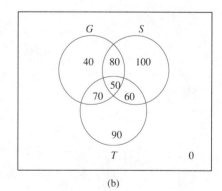

(b)

Looking Back. Another way to approach the problem is to use the fact that 500 seniors were polled and then use the rest of the data to find the number of students in one of the given regions with a known number of students in Figure 2-24(a). If the number found does not agree with the reported number, the poll is not accurate. For example, we could find the number of seniors owning all three cards, by using information in Figure 2-24(b)—adding the number of students in all the regions except the one where all three circles intersect and subtracting that number from 500. This gives $500 - (40 + 80 + 100 + 60 + 90 + 70) = 60$, which does not agree with the reported 50.

Still another approach is to find the total number of students in regions G, S, and T in Figure 2-24(b), subtract all the duplications, and see if the result is 500. Because the 70, 60, and 80 students are counted twice in the sum, we subtract these numbers only once. However, because the 50 seniors who owned all three cards are counted three times, we subtract 50 twice. We have

$$(240 + 290 + 270) - 80 - 70 - 60 - 2 \cdot 50 = 490$$

Because the result is not equal to 500, the number of interviewed students reported in the poll is inaccurate.

QUESTIONS FROM THE CLASSROOM

1. A student argues that $\{\varnothing\}$ is the proper notation for the empty set. What is your response?
2. A student asks, "If $A = \{a, b, c\}$ and $B = \{b, c, d\}$, why isn't it true that $A \cup B = \{a, b, c, b, c, d\}$?" What is your response?
3. A student asks, "How can I tell if a set is infinite?" What is your response?
4. A student says that she can show that, if $A \cap B = A \cap C$, then it is not necessarily true that $B = C$; but she thinks that, whenever $A \cap B = A \cap C$ and $A \cup B = A \cup C$, then $B = C$. What is your response?
5. A student claims that a finite set of numbers is any set that has a largest element. Do you agree?
6. A student claims that the complement bar can be broken over the operation of intersection; that is, $\overline{A \cap B} = \overline{A} \cap \overline{B}$. What is your response?
7. A student claims that $\overline{A} \cap \overline{B}$ includes all elements that are not in A. What is your response?
8. A student asks whether a formula and a function are the same. What is your response?
9. A student states that either $A \subseteq B$ or $B \subseteq A$. Is the student correct?
10. A student is asked to find all one-to-one correspondences between two given sets. He finds the Cartesian product of the sets and claims that his answer is correct because it includes all possible pairings between the elements of the sets. How do you respond?
11. A student claims that the study of sets is worthwhile because it helps in understanding the mathematical concepts studied in elementary school. Do you agree? Why?

CHAPTER OUTLINE

I. Set definitions and notation
  A. A **set** can be described as any collection of objects.
  B. Sets should be **well defined;** that is, it must be true that an object either does or does not belong to the set.
  C. An **element** is any **member** of a set; for example, $a \in \{a, b\}$.
  D. Sets can be specified by either listing all the elements or using **set-builder notation.**
  E. The **empty set,** written $\varnothing$, contains no elements.
  F. The **universal set** contains all the elements being discussed.

II. Relationships and operations on sets
  A. Two sets are **equal** if and only if they have exactly the same elements.
  B. Two sets A and B are in **one-to-one correspondence** if and only if each element of A can be paired with exactly one element of B and each element of B can be paired with exactly one element of A.
  C. Two sets are **equivalent** if and only if their elements can be placed into one-to-one correspondence (written $A \sim B$).
  D. Set A is a **subset** of set B if and only if every element of A is an element of B (written $A \subseteq B$).

E. Set A is a **proper subset** of set B if and only if every element of A is an element of B and there is at least one element of B that is not in A (written $A \subset B$).

F. The **union** of two sets A and B is the set of all elements in A, in B, or in both A and B (written $A \cup B$).

G. The **intersection** of two sets A and B is the set of all elements belonging to both A and B (written $A \cap B$).

H. The **cardinal number** of a set indicates the number of elements in the set.

I. **Ordinal numbers** are used to describe the relative position an element can occupy in an ordered set.

J. A set is **finite** if the number of elements in the set is zero or a natural number.

K. A set is **infinite** if it is not finite.

L. Two sets A and B are **disjoint** if they have no elements in common.

M. The **complement** of a set A is the set consisting of the elements of the universal set not in A (written $\overline{A}$).

N. The **complement of set A relative to set B** (set difference) is the set of all elements in B that are not in A (written $B - A$).

O. The **Cartesian product** of sets A and B is the set of all ordered pairs such that the first element of each pair is an element of A and the second element of each pair is an element of B (written $A \times B$).

III. Properties of set operations

For all sets A, B, C, and universal set U, the following properties hold:

A. $A \cap B = B \cap A$; **commutative property of set intersection**

B. $A \cup B = B \cup A$; **commutative property of set union**

C. $(A \cap B) \cap C = A \cap (B \cap C)$; **associative property of set intersection**

D. $(A \cup B) \cup C = A \cup (B \cup C)$; **associative property of set union**

E. $A \cap (B \cup C) = (A \cap B) \cup (A \cap C)$; **distributive property of set intersection over union**

F. $A \cup (B \cap C) = (A \cup B) \cap (A \cup C)$; **distributive property of set union over intersection**

G. $A \cap U = U \cap A = A$; U is the **identity for set intersection**

H. $A \cup \varnothing = \varnothing \cup A = A$; $\varnothing$ is the **identity for set union**

I. $\overline{U} = \varnothing$; $\overline{\varnothing} = U$; $A \cap \overline{A} = \varnothing$; $A \cup \overline{A} = U$; $A = \overline{\overline{A}}$; **complement properties**

IV. Relations and functions

A. A **relation** R from set A to set B is a subset of $A \times B$; that is, if R is a relation, then $R \subseteq A \times B$.

B. Properties of relations

1. A relation R on a set X is **reflexive** if and only if, for every element a of X, a is related to a.

2. A relation R on a set X is **symmetric** if and only if, for all elements a and b of X, whenever a is related to b, then b is related to a.

3. A relation R on a set X is **transitive** if and only if, for all elements a, b, and c of X, whenever a is related to b and b is related to c, then a is related to c.

C. An **equivalence relation** is any relation R that satisfies the reflexive, symmetric, and transitive properties.

D. A **function** from set A to set B is a relation from A to B in which each element of A is paired with one and only one element of B.

1. The set of all first components of a function, all the elements of A, is called the **domain** of the function.

2. The set of all second components of a function, a subset of B, is called the **range** of the function.

*V. Logic

A. A **statement** is a sentence that is either true or false, but not both.

B. The **negation** of a statement is a statement with the opposite truth value of the given statement.

C. **Universal quantifiers** refer to each and every element in a set.

D. **Existential quantifiers** refer to one or more, or possibly all, of the elements in a set.

E. The **compound statement** $p \wedge q$ is called the **conjunction** of p and q and is defined to be true if and only if both p and q are true.

F. The compound statement $p \vee q$ is called the **disjunction** of p and q and is true if either p or q or both are true.

G. Statements of the form "if p, then q" are called **conditionals** or **implications** and are false only if p is true and q is false.

H. Given the conditional $p \rightarrow q$, the following can be found:

1. **Converse:** $q \rightarrow p$

2. **Inverse:** $\sim p \rightarrow \sim q$

3. **Contrapositive:** $\sim q \rightarrow \sim p$

I. Two statements are **logically equivalent** if and only if they have the same truth value.

J. The statement "*p* if and only if *q*" is called a **biconditional**. It is true only if *p* and *q* have the same truth values.

K. A **tautology** is a statement that is always true.

L. Laws to determine the validity of arguments include the **Law of Detachment, Modus Tollens,** and the **Chain Rule.**

CHAPTER TEST

1. Write the set of letters of the English alphabet, using set-builder notation.

2. List all the subsets of {*m, a, t, h*}.

3. Let

   $U = \{x \mid x$ is a person living in Montana$\}$
   $A = \{x \mid x$ is a person 30 years or older$\}$
   $B = \{x \mid x$ is a person less than 30 years old$\}$
   $C = \{x \mid x$ is a person who owns a gun$\}$

   Describe in words a member of each of the following sets.

   (a) $\overline{A}$ (b) $A \cap C$ (c) $A \cup B$
   (d) $\overline{C}$ (e) $\overline{A \cap C}$ (f) $A - C$

4. Let

   $U = \{u, n, i, v, e, r, s, a, l\}$
   $A = \{r, a, v, e\}$ $C\{l, i, n, e\}$
   $B = \{a, r, e\}$ $D = \{s, a, l, e\}$

   Find each of the following.

   (a) $A \cup B$ (b) $C \cap D$
   (c) $\overline{D}$ (d) $A \cap \overline{D}$
   (e) $\overline{B \cup C}$ (f) $(B \cup C) \cap D$
   (g) $(\overline{A} \cup B) \cap (C \cap \overline{D})$ (h) $(C \cap D) \cap A$
   (i) $n(\overline{C})$ (j) $n(C \times D)$

5. Indicate the following sets by shading.

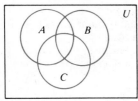

   (a) $A \cap (B \cup C)$

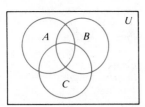

   (b) $(\overline{A \cup B}) \cap C$

6. Let $A = \{s, e, t\}$ and $B = \{i, d, e, a\}$. Find each of the following.

   (a) $B \times A$ (b) $A \times A$
   (c) $n(A \times \varnothing)$ (d) $n(B - A)$

7. If $C = \{e, q, u, a, l, s\}$, how many proper subsets does C have?

8. Show one possible one-to-one correspondence between sets D and E if $D = \{t, h, e\}$ and $E = \{e, n, d\}$. How many different one-to-one correspondences between sets D and E are possible? Explain.

9. Use a Venn diagram to determine whether $A \cap (B \cup C) = (A \cap B) \cup C$ for all sets A, B, and C.

10. Describe, using symbols, the shaded portion in each of the following.

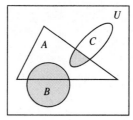 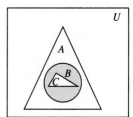

11. If $A = \{1, 2, 3\}$, $B = \{2, 3, 4, 5\}$, and $C = \{3, 4, 5, 6, 7\}$, illustrate the associative property of intersection of sets. Using sets A and B, illustrate the commutative property of union of sets.

12. Classify each of the following as true or false. If false, tell why.

    (a) For all sets A and B, either $A \subseteq B$ or $B \subseteq A$.
    (b) The empty set is a proper subset of every set.
    (c) For all sets A and B, if $A \sim B$, then $A = B$.
    (d) The set {5, 10, 15, 20, . . .} is a finite set.
    (e) No set is equivalent to a proper subset of itself.
    (f) If A is an infinite set and $B \subseteq A$, then B also is an infinite set.
    (g) For all finite sets A and B, if $A \cap B \neq \varnothing$, then $n(A \cup B) \neq n(A) + n(B)$.
    (h) If A and B are sets such that $A \cap B = \varnothing$, then $A = \varnothing$ or $B = \varnothing$.
    (i) $\varnothing \in \varnothing$

13. In a student survey, it was found that 16 students liked history, 19 liked English, 18 liked mathematics, 8 liked mathematics and English, 5 liked history and

English, 7 liked history and mathematics, 3 liked all three subjects, and every student liked at least one of the subjects. Draw a Venn diagram describing this information and answer the following questions.

(a) How many students were in the survey?

(b) How many students liked only mathematics?

(c) How many students liked English and mathematics but not history?

14. Which of the following relations are functions from the set of first components to the set of second components?

(a) $\{(a, b), (c, d), (e, a), (f, g)\}$

(b) $\{(a, b), (a, c), (b, b), (b, c)\}$

(c) $\{(a, b), (b, a)\}$

15. If $f(x) = 3x + 7$, find each of the following.

(a) $f(0)$ (b) $f(8)$ (c) $f(10)$

16. The following graph shows the cost and revenue functions in dollars for producing guided missiles. From the graph estimate the following.

(a) The break-even point—that is, the number of missiles that must be sold to meet expenses exactly.

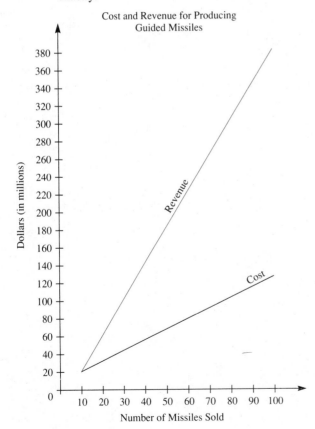

Cost and Revenue for Producing Guided Missiles

(b) The profit or loss on the first 100 missiles produced and sold.

(c) The number of units that must be sold to gain a $70 million profit.

17. Given the following function rules and the domains, find the associated ranges.

(a) $f(x) = x + 3$ domain $= \{0, 1, 2, 3\}$

(b) $f(x) = 3x - 1$ domain $= \{5, 10, 15, 20\}$

(c) $f(x) = x^2$ domain $= \{0, 1, 2, 3, 4\}$

(d) $f(x) = x^2 + 3x + 5$ domain $= \{0, 1, 2\}$

18. Find the inverses of the following functions.

(a) $f(x) = x + 1$

(b) $f(x) = -2x$

(c) $f(x) = -2x + 1$

(d) $f(x) = -2(x + 1)$

19. What properties do each of the following relations, defined on the set of all people, have?

(a) Belongs to the same book club as.

(b) Is thinner than.

(c) Is married to.

(d) Is the father of.

*20. Which of the following are statements?

(a) The moon is inhabited.

(b) $3 + 5 = 8$

(c) $x + 7 = 15$

(d) Some women smoke.

(e) How much is that doggie in the window?

*21. Negate each of the following.

(a) Some women smoke.

(b) $3 + 5 = 8$

(c) All heavy metal rock is loud.

(d) Beethoven wrote only classical music.

*22. Write truth tables for each of the following.

(a) $[p \lor (\sim q)] \land p$

(b) $[p \to (\sim q)] \lor q$

(c) $[p \to (\sim q)] \land [(\sim q) \to p]$

(d) $[(\sim p) \lor (\sim q)] \to (q \land p)$

*23. Decide whether or not the following are equivalent.

(a) $p \land (q \lor r)$; $(p \land q) \lor (p \land r)$

(b) $p \to q$; $q \to p$

*24. Write the converse, inverse, and contrapositive of the following: If we have a rock concert, someone will faint.

*25. Find valid conclusions for the following arguments.

(a) All Americans love Mom and apple pie.
Joe Czernyu is an American.

(b) Steel eventually rusts.
The Statue of Liberty has a steel structure.

(c) Albertina will pass Math 100 or be a dropout.
Albertina is not a dropout.

★26. Write the following argument symbolically and then determine its validity.

> If you are fair-skinned, you will sunburn.
> If you sunburn, you will not go to the dance.
> If you do not go to the dance, your parents will want to know why you didn't go to the dance.
> Your parents do not want to know why you didn't go to the dance.
> Therefore, you are not fair-skinned.

★27. Determine whether each of the following arguments is valid.

(a) All diets are ridiculous.
All diets are degrading.
Therefore, all ridiculous diets are degrading.

(b) No professors are stupid.
All stupid people are rich.
Therefore, no professors are rich.

(c) Blondes have more fun.
Some blondes are really brunettes.
Therefore, some brunettes have more fun.

(d) If Gloria goes fishing, she does not use flies.
If Gloria does not use flies, then she is not a real fisherwoman.
Gloria goes fishing.
Therefore, Gloria is not a real fisherwoman.

Numeration Systems and Whole Numbers

PRELIMINARY PROBLEM

A wise man performed a great service for a wealthy king. As a reward, the king announced that he would grant the man any wish. The wise man simply requested the amount of wheat that would be required to cover a checkerboard beginning by placing one grain on the first square, two grains on the second square, four grains on the third square, eight grains on the fourth square, and so on, always doubling the number of grains. The king quickly agreed to such a modest-sounding request. How many grains of wheat did the wise man request?

Introduction

With the coming of civilization, people invented numeration systems to handle numbers. Such systems did not come readily but developed over centuries. In this chapter, we examine several different *numeration systems*—logically structured methods of denoting numbers. After investigating early systems, we examine the base-ten system we use today. Algorithms for the operations of addition, subtraction, multiplication, and division of whole numbers are considered. Finally, properties and algorithms in number bases other than ten are discussed as a mechanism for developing a more generalized understanding of our present system.

Section 3-1   Numeration Systems

Early methods of "writing down" numbers included making notches or strokes on stone or wood and tying knots in a cord. The recorded symbols usually represented numbers of animals. Since that time, numerals have changed extensively. *Numerals* are written symbols used to represent quantities or numbers.

Table 3-1 shows some ways that numbers have been recorded. The Babylonians used wedge-shaped marks pressed in wet clay. The Egyptians used papyrus and ink-filled brushes, basing their system on tally marks. The

TABLE 3-1

Babylonian		▼	▼▼	▼▼▼	▼▼▼▼	▼▼▼/▼▼	▼▼▼/▼▼▼	▼▼▼▼/▼▼▼	▼▼▼▼/▼▼▼▼	▼▼▼▼▼/▼▼▼▼	⟨
Egyptian		I	II	III	IIII	III/II	III/III	IIII/III	IIII/IIII	III/III/III	∩
Mayan	⊙	•	••	•••	••••	—	•/—	••/—	•••/—	••••/—	═
Greek		A	B	Γ	Δ	E	F	Z	H	Θ	I
Chinese		一	二	三	四	五	六	七	八	九	十
Roman		I	II	III	IV	V	VI	VII	VIII	IX	X
Hindu	0	1	ح	ح	8	؟	ص	∧	8	٩	
Arabic	•	١	٢	٣	٤	٥	٦	٧	٨	٩	
modern	0	1	2	3	4	5	6	7	8	9	10

Mayans introduced a symbol for zero. The numerals we use today are called *Hindu-Arabic* numerals; they replaced the Roman numerals after Europeans studied the work of Arab mathematicians in the eleventh to thirteenth centuries. Different symbols can be used to represent the same quantity. For example, in Table 3-1 we see that 3 and III represent the quantity we call *three*.

Egyptian Numeration System

Some early numeration systems, such as the Egyptian system, which dates back to about 3400 B.C., were based on tally marks. Tally marks are scratches or marks that represent the items being counted. One tally mark is used for each object being counted, so that a one-to-one correspondence exists between tally marks and the objects. Later improvements on the tally-mark system led to new numerals for certain groupings. This use of symbols to stand for groupings was a major development. The Egyptians drew on their environment for their symbols. For example, the Egyptians used a heel bone symbol, ∩, to stand for a grouping of ten tally marks.

||||||||| ⟶ ∩

Other numerals that the Egyptians used in their system are given in Table 3-2.

TABLE 3-2

Egyptian Numeral	Description	Hindu-Arabic Equivalent
		Vertical staff	1
∩	Heel bone	10
9	Scroll	100
↿	Lotus flower	1000
⌀	Pointing finger	10,000
⌀	Polliwog or burbot	100,000
⍤	Astonished man	1,000,000

additive property   The Egyptian system involved an **additive property;** that is, the value of a number was the sum of the values of the numerals. An example is as follows.

⌀	represents	100,000	
999	represents	300	(100 + 100 + 100)
∩∩	represents	20	(10 + 10)
||	represents	2	(1 + 1)

⌀999∩∩|| represents 100,322

In the Egyptian system, the order of the numerals made no difference. However, the Egyptians customarily wrote the numerals in decreasing order from left to right.

Babylonian Numeration System

The Babylonian system was developed at about the same time as the Egyptian system. The symbols shown in Table 3-3 were made using a stylus either vertically or horizontally.

TABLE 3-3

Babylonian Numeral	Hindu-Arabic Equivalent
▼	1
<	10

The Babylonian numerals 1 through 59 were similar to the Egyptian numerals, but the staff and the heel bone were replaced by the symbols in Table 3-3.

place value

For example, << ▼▼ represented 22. For numbers greater than 59, the Babylonians used **place value.** The value of a symbol in a given numeral depended on the placement of the symbol with respect to other symbols in the numeral. Numbers greater than 59 were represented by repeated groupings of sixty, much as we use groupings of ten today. For example, ▼▼ << represented 2 · 60 + 20, or 140. The space indicates that ▼▼ represents 2 · 60 rather than 2. In the number ▼▼ <<, the *place value* of ▼▼ is 60 and the *face value* of ▼▼ is 2, which tells how many groupings of 60 are indicated.

The initial Babylonian system contained inadequacies. For example, the symbol ▼▼ could have represented 2 or 2 · 60, because the Babylonian system lacked a symbol for zero until after 300 B.C.

Numerals to the left of a second space have a value 60 · 60 times their face value, and so on.

$$<< \quad ▼ \qquad \text{represents} \quad 20 \cdot 60 + 1, \text{ or } 1201$$
$$<▼ \quad <▼ \quad ▼ \qquad \text{represents} \quad 11 \cdot 60 \cdot 60 + 11 \cdot 60 + 1, \text{ or } 40{,}261$$
$$▼ \quad <▼ \quad <▼ \quad ▼ \qquad \text{represents} \quad 1 \cdot 60 \cdot 60 \cdot 60 + 11 \cdot 60 \cdot 60 + 11 \cdot 60 + 1,$$
$$\text{or } 256{,}261$$

expanded form

factor

The representation of <▼ <▼ ▼ as $11 \cdot 60 \cdot 60 + 11 \cdot 60 + 1$ is called the **expanded form** of the number. The expanded form consists of the sum of the products resulting from multiplying face values by place values. Using exponents, a product such as $60 \cdot 60$ can be written as 60^2, in which case 60 is called a **factor** of the product. Thus, <▼ <▼ ▼ can be written in expanded form using exponents as $11 \cdot 60^2 + 11 \cdot 60 + 1$. The notion of exponents can be generalized as follows.

● **D E F I N I T I O N**

If a is any number and n is any natural number, then a^n is defined by the following equation.

$$a^n = \underbrace{a \cdot a \cdot a \cdots a}_{n \text{ factors}}$$

nth power of a
exponent / base

Here, a^n is the **nth power of a**; n is the **exponent;** and a is the **base.**

In Chapter 6 the definitions and properties of exponents are discussed in detail. It is shown there why it is useful to define a^0 as 1 if $a \neq 0$.

Computations involving exponents can be made using a calculator. If the calculator has a constant key, the following steps will compute $5^4 = 625$.

| 5 | × | K | = | = | = |

On a calculator with an automatic constant, the same type of computation is possible. Some calculators have an exponential key such as $\boxed{y^x}$. This function computes the xth power of y. For example, to compute 5^4, we press $\boxed{5}\;\boxed{y^x}\;\boxed{4}\;\boxed{=}$.

Mayan Numeration System

At some point in numeration history, people began using parts of their bodies to count. Fingers could be matched to objects to stand for one, two, three, four, or five objects. Two hands could then stand for a set of ten objects. In warmer climates where people went barefoot, people may have used their toes as well as their fingers for counting. The Mayans introduced a new attribute that was present neither in the Egyptian nor in the Babylonian systems, namely, a symbol for zero. The Mayan system used only three symbols: a dot for 1, a horizontal bar for 5, and an egg-shaped symbol for 0, as seen in Table 3-4.

TABLE 3-4

Mayan Numeral	Hindu-Arabic Equivalent
•	1
—	5
⬬	0

The symbols for the first ten numerals are shown in Table 3-1. Notice the groupings of five in Table 3-1, where each horizontal bar represents a group of five. Thus, the symbol for 19 was ☰, or 3 fives and 4 ones. The symbol for 20 was ⬬, which represents 1 group of twenty plus 0 ones. The Mayans used base twenty and wrote numbers vertically with the greatest value on top. Several examples of the Mayan system, using units and twenties, are given next. In Figure 3-1(a) we have $2 \cdot 5 + 3 \cdot 1$, or 13 groups of twenty plus $2 \cdot 5 + 1 \cdot 1$, or 11 ones, for a total of 271. In Figure 3-1(b) we have $3 \cdot 5 + 1 \cdot 1$, or 16 groups of twenty and 0 ones, for a total of 320.

FIGURE 3-1

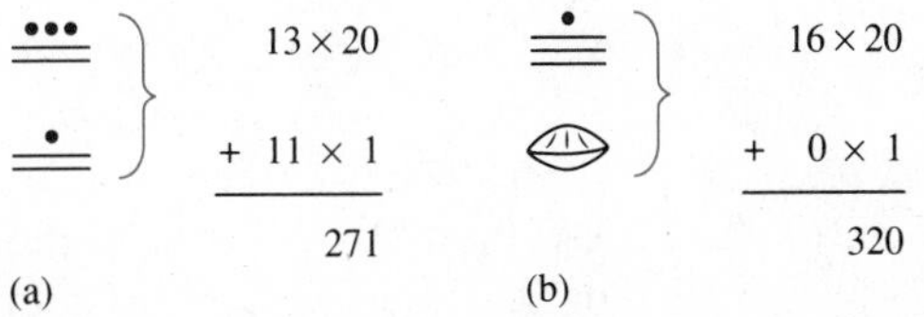

(a)   (b)

In a true base-twenty system, the value of the symbols in the third position vertically from the bottom should be 20^2, or 400. However, it is conjectured that the Mayans used $20 \cdot 18$, or 360, instead of 400. (The number 360 is an approximation of the length of a calendar year, which consisted of 18 months of 20 days each, plus 5 "unlucky" days.) Thus, instead of place values of 1, 20, 20^2, 20^3, 20^4, and so on, the Mayans used 1, 20, $20 \cdot 18$, $20^2 \cdot 18$, $20^3 \cdot 18$, and so on. For example, in Figure 3-2(a) we have $5 + 1$ (or 6) groups of 360, plus $5 + 5 + 2$ (or 12) groups of 20, plus $5 + 4$ (or 9) groups of 1, for a total of 2409. In Figure 3-2(b), we have $2 \cdot 5$ (or 10) groups of 360, plus 0 groups of 20, plus 2 ones, for a total of 3602. Spacing is important in the Mayan system. For example, if two horizontal bars are placed close together, as in $=$, the symbols represent $5 + 5 = 10$. If the bars are spaced apart, as in $=$, then the value is $5 \cdot 20 + 5 \cdot 1 = 105$.

FIGURE 3-2

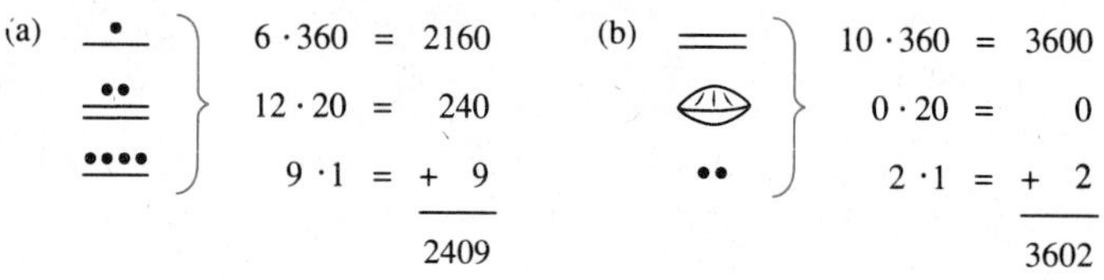

(a)
$$6 \cdot 360 = 2160$$
$$12 \cdot 20 = 240$$
$$9 \cdot 1 = + \ 9$$
$$\overline{2409}$$

(b)
$$10 \cdot 360 = 3600$$
$$0 \cdot 20 = 0$$
$$2 \cdot 1 = + \ 2$$
$$\overline{3602}$$

Roman Numeration System

The Roman numeration system remains in use today, as seen on cornerstones, on the opening pages of books, and on the faces of clocks. The basic Roman numerals are pictured in Table 3-5.

TABLE 3-5

Roman Numeral	Hindu-Arabic Equivalent
I	1
V	5
X	10
L	50
C	100
D	500
M	1000

Roman numerals can be combined by using an additive property. For example, MDCLXVI represents $1000 + 500 + 100 + 50 + 10 + 5 + 1 = 1666$, CCCXXVIII represents 328, and VI represents 6.

subtractive property   To avoid repeating a symbol more than three times, as in IIII, a **subtractive property** was introduced in the middle ages. For example, I is less than V, so if it is to the left of V, it is subtracted. Thus, IV has a value of $5 - 1$, or 4, and XC represents $100 - 10$, or 90.

Some extensions of the subtractive property could lead to ambiguous results. For example, IXC could be 91 or 89. By custom, 91 is written XCI, and 89 is written LXXXIX. In general, only one smaller number symbol can be to the left of a larger number symbol, and the pair must be one of those listed in Table 3-6.

TABLE 3-6

Roman Numeral	Hindu-Arabic Equivalent
IV	5 − 1, or 4
IX	10 − 1, or 9
XL	50 − 10, or 40
XC	100 − 10, or 90
CD	500 − 100, or 400
CM	1000 − 100, or 900

multiplicative property

The Romans adopted the use of bars to write large numbers. The use of bars is based on a **multiplicative property.** A bar over a symbol or symbols indicates that the value is multiplied by 1000. For example, $\overline{V}$ represents 5 · 1000, or 5000, and $\overline{CDX}$ represents 410 · 1000, or 410,000. To indicate even greater numbers, more bars appear. For example, $\overline{\overline{V}}$ represents (5 · 1000) · 1000, or 5,000,000; $\overline{\overline{CXI}}$ represents 111 · 1000³, or 111,000,000,000; and $\overline{CXI}$ represents 110 · 1000 + 1, or 110,001.

Hindu-Arabic Numeration System

The properties of numeration systems illustrated in this section are not definitive, but several of them are used in the Hindu-Arabic system. The Hindu-Arabic numeration system we use today has ten basic symbols, called *digits* **digits:** 0, 1, 2, 3, 4, 5, 6, 7, 8, 9. Each place in a Hindu-Arabic numeral *decimal system* represents a power of 10. Thus, the system is a **decimal system,** after the Latin word *decem* for ten.

The Hindu-Arabic system has the following important characteristics.

1. All numerals are constructed from the ten basic digits.
2. The system uses place value based on repeated grouping of ten.
3. There is a symbol for zero.

Each digit in a numeral has two functions:

1. Its position in the numeral names its *place value.*
2. The digit itself names its *face value;* that is, it tells how many groupings of ten are indicated.

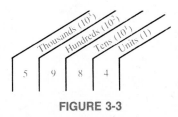

FIGURE 3-3

For example, in the numeral 5984, the 5 has place value "thousands," the 9 has place value "hundreds," the 8 has place value "tens," and the 4 has place value "units," as shown in Figure 3-3. Hence, we can write 5984 in expanded form as 5 · 1000 + 9 · 100 + 8 · 10 + 4 · 1, or 5 · 10³ + 9 · 10² + 8 · 10 + 4 · 1.

PROBLEM SET 3-1

1. For each of the following, tell which numeral represents the greater number and why.
   (a) $\overline{\text{MCDXXIV}}$ and $\overline{\text{MCDXXIV}}$
   (b) 4632 and 46,032
   (c) ＜▼▼ and ＜ ▼▼
   (d) 999∩∩⋂I and 𐃟∩I
   (e) ⋮ and ⬠

2. For each of the following, name both the succeeding and preceding numerals (one more and one less).
   (a) MCMXLIX   (b) $\overline{\text{MI}}$ (c) CMXCIX
   (d) ＜＜ ＜▼   (e) 𐃟99   (f) ⋮

3. For each of the following systems, discuss how you might add 245 and 989.
   (a) Babylonian   (b) Egyptian

4. How might you perform the following subtraction problem using Egyptian numerals?

   ⬅∩∩III
   −∩∩∩∩IIIII

5. Write each of the following in Roman symbols.
   (a) 121   (b) 42   (c) 89   (d) 5282

6. Write each of the following in Egyptian symbols.
   (a) 52   (b) 103   (c) 100,003   (d) 38

7. Complete the following table, which compares symbols for numbers in different numeration systems.

Hindu-Arabic	Babylonian	Egyptian	Roman	Mayan
72				
	＜ ▼▼			
		𐃟99∩∩III		
			DCLXVII	
				⊡

8. (a) Create a numeration system of your own with unique symbols, and write a paragraph explaining the properties of your system.
   (b) Complete the table using your system.

Hindu-Arabic Numeral	Your System Numeral	Hindu-Arabic Numeral	Your System Numeral
1		100	
5		5,000	
10		10,000	
50		15,280	

9. For each of the following decimal numerals, give the place value of the underlined numeral.
   (a) 827,367   (b) 8,421,000
   (c) 97,998   (d) 810,485

10. Rewrite each of the following as a base-ten numeral.
    (a) $3 \cdot 10^6 + 4 \cdot 10^3 + 5$
    (b) $2 \cdot 10^4 + 1$
    (c) $3 \cdot 10^3 + 5 \cdot 10^2 + 6 \cdot 10$
    (d) $9 \cdot 10^6 + 9 \cdot 10 + 9$

11. Study the counting frame shown next. In the frame, the value of each dot is represented by the number in the box below the dot. For example, the following figure represents the number 154.

••	•••	••
64	8	1

What numbers are represented in the frames in (a) and (b)?

(a)
• ••	••	•
25	5	1

(b)
	•		•	•
8	4	2	1

12. A certain 3-digit whole number has the following properties: the hundreds digit is greater than 7; the tens digit is an odd number; and the sum of the digits is 10. What is the number?

13. Use the constant feature on a calculator to determine the value of $9 \cdot 9 \cdot 9 \cdot 9 \cdot 9 \cdot 9 \cdot 9$, or 9^7.

14. Use only the keys ①, ②, ③, ④, ⑤, ⑥, ⑦, ⑧, and ⑨, for each of the following.
    (a) Fill the display to show the greatest number possible; each key may be used only once.
    (b) Fill the display to show the least number possible; each key may be used only once.
    (c) Fill the display to show the greatest number possible if a key may be used more than once.
    (d) Fill the display to show the least number possible if a key may be used more than once.

15. In a game called WIPEOUT, we are to "wipe out" digits from the calculator display without changing any of the other digits. "Wipeout" in this case means replace the chosen digit(s) with a 0. For example, if the initial number is 54321 and we are to wipe out the 4, we could subtract 4000 to obtain 50321. Complete the following two problems and then try other numbers or challenge another person to wipe out a number from the number you have placed on the screen.
    (a) Wipe out the 2s from 32420.
    (b) Wipe out the 5 from 67357.

There are 3 nickels and 3 dimes concealed inside three boxes. Two coins are placed in each of the boxes, which are labeled 10¢, 15¢, and 20¢. The coins are placed in such a way that no box contains the amount of money showing on its label; for example, the box labeled 10¢ does not really have a total of 10¢ in it. What is the minimum number of coins that you would have to remove from a box, and from which box or boxes, to determine which coins are in which boxes?

Section 3-2   Addition and Subtraction of Whole Numbers

whole numbers

Zero is important in the evolution of numeration systems. In terms of set theory, zero can be defined as the cardinal number of the empty set: $n(\varnothing) = 0$. When zero is joined with the set of natural numbers, $N = \{1, 2, 3, 4, 5, \ldots\}$, we have the set of numbers called **whole numbers,** denoted by $W = \{0, 1, 2, 3, 4, 5, \ldots\}$. Another way of defining a whole number is to define it as the cardinal number of a finite set.

Addition of Whole Numbers

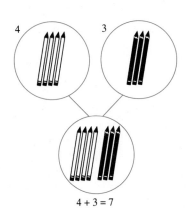

4 + 3 = 7

FIGURE 3-4

Addition is a *binary operation*—that is, a function that involves using two numbers at a time to produce a single number. (The domain of this function is the set $W \times W$, and the range is W.) The addition of whole numbers can be modeled in several ways. We present the set model and the number-line model.

Set Model   The concept of addition of whole numbers is normally introduced to children through the notion of "combining." Suppose that Jane has 4 pencils in one pile and 3 pencils in another. If she combines the two groups of pencils, how many pencils are there in the combined group? Figure 3-4 shows the solution as it might appear in an elementary school text. The combined set of pencils is the union of the set of 4 pencils and the set of 3 pencils. This leads to the following definition.

● D E F I N I T I O N
Let A and B be two disjoint finite sets. If $n(A) = a$ and $n(B) = b$, then $a + b = n(A \cup B)$.

addends
sum

The numbers a and b in this definition are the **addends;** and $(a + b)$ is the **sum.**

H I S T O R I C A L   N O T E

The symbol "+" first appeared in a 1417 manuscript and was a short way of writing the Latin word *et*, which means "and." However, Johann Widmann wrote a book in 1498 that made use of the + and − symbols for addition and subtraction. The word *minus* means "less" in Latin; at first it was written as an *m*, which was later shortened to a horizontal bar.

Number-line Model   A number line may be used to model whole number addition. Any line marked with two fundamental points, one representing 0 and the other representing 1, can be turned into a number line. The points *unit segment* representing 0 and 1 mark the ends of a **unit segment.** Other points may be marked and labeled as shown in Figure 3-5. Any two consecutive points in Figure 3-5 mark the ends of a segment that has the same length as the unit segment.

FIGURE 3-5

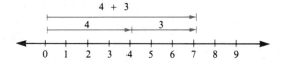

Using directed arrows on the number line, it is possible to model addition problems. For example, the sum of 4 + 3 is shown in Figure 3-5. Arrows representing the addends, 4 and 3, are combined into one arrow representing the sum.

Greater-Than and Less-Than Relations

greater-than / less-than   A number line can also be used to describe **greater-than** and **less-than** relations on the set of whole numbers. For example, in Figure 3-5, notice that 4 is to the left of 7 on the number line. We say, "four is less than seven," and we write $4 < 7$. We can also say "seven is greater than four" and write $7 > 4$. Since 4 is to the left of 7, there is a natural number that can be added to 4 to get 7, namely, 3. Thus, $4 < 7$, since $4 + 3 = 7$. (We can generalize this discussion to form a definition for *greater than*.)

● D E F I N I T I O N

For any whole numbers *a* and *b*, *a* is **less than** *b*, written $a < b$, if and only if there exists a natural number *k* such that $a + k = b$.

● R E M A R K

Recall that another method of defining *less than*, using set theory, was discussed in Chapter 2.

greater than or equal to
less than or equal to

Sometimes equality is combined with the inequalities greater than and less than to give the relations **greater than or equal to** and **less than or equal to,** denoted by $\geq$ and $\leq$. The emphasis with respect to these symbols has to be on the *or*. Observe that "$3 < 5$ or $3 = 5$" is a true statement, so $3 \leq 5$ is true. Note also that $5 \geq 3$ and $3 \geq 3$ are both true statements.

Whole-Number Addition Properties

We now examine properties of whole-number addition. These properties will be used to develop algorithms for more complicated addition. Since addition is a function from $W \times W$ to W, the result when two whole numbers are added is a unique whole number. This property is the *closure property of addition of whole numbers,* and we say, "The set of whole numbers is closed under addition."

● P R O P E R T Y
Closure Property of Addition of Whole Numbers   If a and b are any whole numbers, then $a + b$ is a unique whole number.

Note that this property guarantees both the existence and the uniqueness of the sum. With some sets, the addition of two numbers from the set results in a number that does not belong to the set. In this case, we say the set is *not closed* under addition. For example, the set $\{0, 1, 2, 3\}$ is not closed under addition because a sum such as $2 + 3$ is not an element of the set.

EXAMPLE 3-1   Which of these sets are closed under addition?
(a) $\{0, 1\}$ (b) $\{0\}$ (c) $\{1, 3, 5, 7, 9, \ldots\}$

SOLUTION   (a) This set is not closed under addition. Although the sum of two different numbers such as 0 and 1 belongs to the set $\{0, 1\}$, it is not true for all sums involving numbers from the set. For example, $1 + 1 \notin \{0, 1\}$.
(b) This set is closed under addition because $0 + 0$ belongs to the set.
(c) This set is not closed under addition because, for example, $5 + 3$ is not an element of the original set.

If $a \in W$ and $b \in W$, then, by the closure property of addition, $a + b \in W$. If $c \in W$, it follows that $(a + b) + c \in W$. This reasoning can be extended to more than three whole numbers.

Figure 3-6 on page 118 shows two additions. Pictured above the number line is $3 + 5$, and below the number line is $5 + 3$. The sums are exactly the same. This demonstrates that $3 + 5 = 5 + 3$. This idea that two whole numbers can be added in either order is true for any two whole numbers a and b. (This can be seen by using the definition of addition of whole numbers

FIGURE 3-6

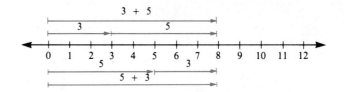

and the fact that $A \cup B = B \cup A$.) This property is called the *commutative property of addition of whole numbers*, and we say, "Addition of whole numbers is commutative."

● P R O P E R T Y

Commutative Property of Addition of Whole Numbers   If a and b are any whole numbers, then $a + b = b + a$.

The commutative property of addition of whole numbers is not obvious to many young children. They may be able to find the sum $9 + 2$ and not be able to find the sum $2 + 9$. This is because one of the techniques used to teach addition is *counting on*. Using this technique, $9 + 2$ can be computed by starting at 9 and then counting on two more, as "ten" and "eleven." To compute $2 + 9$, the *counting on* is more involved. Students need to understand that $2 + 9$ is another name for $9 + 2$.

When adding three or more numbers, it is necessary to select the order in which to add the numbers. For example, consider $24 + 8 + 2$. One person might group the 24 and the 8 together and do the computation as $(24 + 8) + 2 = 32 + 2 = 34$. The parentheses indicate that the first two numbers are grouped together. Another person might recognize that it is easy to add any number to 10 and compute it as $24 + (8 + 2) = 24 + 10 = 34$. Thus, we see that $24 + 8 + 2 = (24 + 8) + 2 = 24 + (8 + 2)$. This example illustrates the *associative property of addition of whole numbers*, and we say, "Addition of whole numbers is associative." In many elementary school texts in the lower grades, this property is referred to as the *grouping property for addition*.

● P R O P E R T Y

Associative Property of Addition of Whole Numbers   If a, b, and c are any whole numbers, then $(a + b) + c = a + (b + c)$.

When several numbers are being added, the parentheses are usually omitted, since the grouping does not alter the result. The commutative and associative properties for addition are often used together. For example, to find the sum $20 + 5 + 60 + 4$, we group the addends as $(20 + 60) + (5 + 4)$ to obtain $80 + 9$, or 89.

Another property of addition of whole numbers is seen when one addend is 0. In Figure 3-7, set A has 5 blocks and set B has 0 blocks. The union of sets A and B has only 5 blocks.

FIGURE 3-7

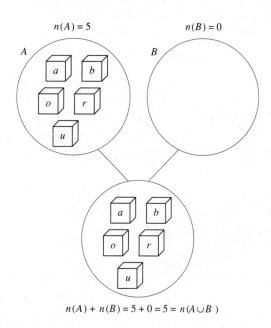

$n(A) = 5$ $n(B) = 0$

$n(A) + n(B) = 5 + 0 = 5 = n(A \cup B)$

This example illustrates the following property of whole numbers.

● **P R O P E R T Y**
Identity Property of Addition of Whole Numbers There is a unique whole number 0, called the **additive identity**, such that, for any whole number a, $a + 0 = a = 0 + a$.

● **R E M A R K**
The identity property can be justified by using set theory, since $0 = n(\varnothing)$ and, if $a = n(A)$, then $a + 0 = n(A) + n(\varnothing) = n(A \cup \varnothing) = n(A) = a$. A similar argument shows that $0 + a = a$.

EXAMPLE 3-2 Which properties justify each of the following?
(a) $5 + 7 = 7 + 5$
(b) $1001 + 733$ is a whole number.
(c) $(3 + 5) + 7 = (5 + 3) + 7$
(d) $(8 + 5) + 2 = 8 + (5 + 2)$
(e) $(10 + 5) + (10 + 3) = (10 + 10) + (5 + 3)$

SOLUTION   (a) Commutative property of addition
(b) Closure property of addition
(c) Commutative property of addition
(d) Associative property of addition
(e) Commutative and associative properties of addition

Mastering Basic Addition Facts

Certain mathematical facts are called *basic addition facts*. Basic addition facts are those involving a single digit plus a single digit. One method of learning the basic facts is to organize them according to different strategies. The strategy of *counting on* from the *greater* of the addends is usually used when the other addend is 1, 2, or 3. For example, 5 + 3 can be computed by starting at 5 and then counting on 6, 7, and 8. Likewise, 2 + 8 would be computed by starting at 8 and then counting 9 and 10.

The next strategy considered involves the use of *doubles*. Doubles such as 4 + 4 and 6 + 6 receive special attention with students. After doubles are mastered, *doubles + 1* and *doubles + 2* can be easily learned. For example, if a student knows 6 + 6 = 12, then 6 + 7 is (6 + 6) + 1, or one more than the double of 6—that is, 13. Likewise, 7 + 9 is (7 + 7) + 2, or two more than the double of 7—that is, 16.

Another strategy is that of *making 10* and then adding any leftover. For example, we could think of 8 + 5 as shown in Figure 3-8. Notice that we are really using the associative property of addition.

FIGURE 3-8

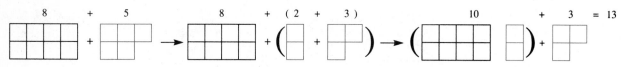

Many basic facts might be classified under more than one strategy. For example, 9 + 8 could be found using *making 10* as 9 + (1 + 7) = (9 + 1) + 7 = 10 + 7 = 17, or it could be found using a *double plus 1* as (8 + 8) + 1.

Subtraction of Whole Numbers

Subtraction of whole numbers can be modeled in several ways: the take-away model, the missing-addend model, the comparison model, and the number-line model.

Take-away Model One way to think about subtraction is this: Instead of imagining a second set of objects as being joined to a first set (as in addition), consider the second set as being *taken away* from a first set. For example, suppose that we have 8 blocks and we take away 3 of them, as shown in Figure 3-9. We record this process as $8 - 3 = 5$.

FIGURE 3-9

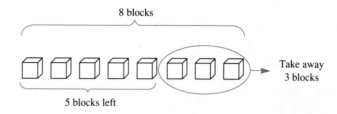

Missing-addend Model A second model for subtraction, the *missing-addend* model, relates subtraction and addition. Recall that in Figure 3-9, $8 - 3$ is pictured with blocks as 8 blocks "take away" 3 blocks. The number of blocks left is the number $8 - 3$, or 5. This can also be thought of as the number of blocks that could be added to 3 blocks in order to get 8 blocks; that is,

$$\boxed{8 - 3} + 3 = 8$$

Thus, $8 - 3$ can be thought of as the number that can be added to 3 to obtain 8. The number $8 - 3$, or 5, is called the **missing addend** in the equation

missing addend

$$\square + 3 = 8$$

Cashiers often use this method. For example, if the bill for a movie is \$8 and you pay \$10, the cashier might say "eight and two is ten." This idea can be generalized for whole numbers a and b, as shown next.

● **DEFINITION**
For any whole numbers a and b, $a - b$ is the unique whole number c such that $a = b + c$.

● **REMARK**

minuend

subtrahend / difference

The notation $a - b$ is read "a minus b." The number a is called the **minuend;** b is called the **subtrahend;** c is called the **difference.**

Comparison Model A third way to consider subtraction is by using a *comparison* model. Suppose that we have 8 blocks and 3 balls and we would like to know how many more blocks we have than balls. We can pair the blocks and balls, as shown in Figure 3-10, and determine that there are 5 more blocks than balls. We also write this as 8 − 3 = 5.

FIGURE 3-10

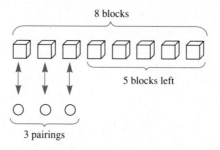

Subtraction can also be defined in terms of set theory. This will be investigated in Problem 13 of Problem Set 3-2.

Number-line Model We can also model subtraction by using a number line. For example, 5 − 3 is shown on a number line in Figure 3-11. Observe that an arrow extends 5 units to the right from 0. Because the operation is subtraction, the second arrow extends 3 units to the left from the end of the first arrow. Thus, we see that 5 − 3 = 2.

FIGURE 3-11

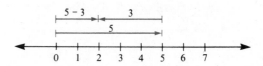

An alternate way to find 5 − 3 by using a number line is to determine the missing addend that must be added to 3 to obtain the sum of 5. In Figure 3-12, the missing addend is 2, and we have 5 − 3 = 2.

FIGURE 3-12

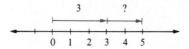

Many elementary school texts refer to the relationship between addition and subtraction in terms of "fact families." Notice the fact family on the student page below from *Addison-Wesley Mathematics*, 1989, Grade 4. Also notice that at the fourth-grade level, the commutative property of addition is referred to as the *order property of addition*.

Addition and Subtraction

Addition and subtraction are related. For two different addends and their sum, there are two addition facts and two subtraction facts.

The fact family helps us see a special property of addition.

Addend	Addend	Sum
8	6	14

Fact Family

8 + 6 = 14
6 + 8 = 14
14 − 6 = 8
14 − 8 = 6

Order Property +

When the order of the addends is changed, the sum stays the same.

Properties of Subtraction

Consider the difference $3 - 5$. Using the definition of subtraction, $3 - 5 = c$ means $c + 5 = 3$. Since there is no whole number c that satisfies the equation, the solution for $3 - 5$ cannot be found in the set of whole numbers. This means that the set of whole numbers is *not* closed under subtraction. We also see that, for whole numbers a and b, $a - b$ is meaningful if and only if $a - b$ is a whole number—that is, if a is greater than or equal to b. Later, we consider the set of integers, which is closed under subtraction. Showing that subtraction of whole numbers is not commutative, not associative, and has no identity property is left as an exercise.

PROBLEM SET 3-2

1. Explain why $5 < 7$ and why $6 > 3$ by finding natural numbers k such that each is true.
   (a) $5 + k = 7$ (b) $6 = 3 + k$

2. In the definition of *less than*, can the natural number k be replaced by the whole number k? Why or why not?

3. Give an example to show why, in the definition of addition, sets A and B must be disjoint.

4. Use the number-line model to illustrate.
   (a) $6 + 3 = 9$ (b) $11 - 3 = 8$

5. For each of the following, find whole numbers to make the statements true, if possible.
   (a) $2 + \Box = 7$ (b) $\Box + 4 = 6$
   (c) $3 + \Box \le 5$ (d) $\Box + 6 \ge 9$

6. For each of the following, find whole numbers to make the statements true, if possible, where $a \in W$.
   (a) $8 - 5 = \Box$ (b) $\Box - 4 = 9$
   (c) $a - 0 = \Box$ (d) $a - \Box = a$
   (e) $\Box - 3 \le 6$ (f) $\Box - 3 > 6$

7. Tell whether or not the following sets are closed under addition. If not, give a counterexample.
   (a) $B = \{0\}$
   (b) $T = \{0, 3, 6, 9, 12, \ldots\}$
   (c) $N = \{1, 2, 3, 4, 5, \ldots\}$
   (d) $V = \{3, 5, 7\}$
   (e) $\{x \mid x \in W, x > 10\}$

8. Rewrite each of the following subtraction problems as an equivalent addition problem.
   (a) $x - 119 = 213$
   (b) $213 - x = 119$
   (c) $213 - 119 = x$

9. Each of the following is an example of one of the properties for addition of whole numbers. Identify the property illustrated.
   (a) $6 + 3 = 3 + 6$
   (b) $(6 + 3) + 5 = 6 + (3 + 5)$
   (c) $(6 + 3) + 5 = (3 + 6) + 5$

10. Angelo read 6 pages of *Black Beauty* on Monday. He had read a total of 15 pages before Wednesday. How many pages did he read on Tuesday?

11. Find the next three terms in each of the following sequences.
   (a) $8, 13, 18, 23, 28,$ _____, _____, _____
   (b) $98, 91, 84, 77, 70, 63,$ _____, _____, _____

12. Illustrate $9 - 2$, using each of the following models.
   (a) Take-away model
   (b) Comparison model
   (c) Missing-addend model
   (d) Number-line model

13. Suppose that $A \subseteq B$. If $n(A) = a$ and $n(B) = b$, then $b - a$ could be defined as $n(B - A)$. Choose two sets A and B, and illustrate this definition.

14. Give a counterexample to show that each of the following is false in the set of whole numbers.
   (a) $a - b = b - a$
   (b) $(a - b) - c = a - (b - c)$
   (c) $a - 0 = 0 - a = a$

15. For each of the following, determine possible whole numbers a, b, and c for which the statement is true.
   (a) $a - b = b - a$

(b) $(a - b) - c = a - (b - c)$
(c) $a - 0 = 0 - a = a$
(d) $a(b - c) = ab - ac$

16. Find the total of the terms in the fiftieth row in the following figure.

1	1st row
$1 - 1$	2nd row
$1 - 1 + 1$	3rd row
$1 - 1 + 1 - 1$	4th row
$1 - 1 + 1 - 1 + 1$	5th row

17. A magic square is an array of numbers in which the sum of every row, column, and diagonal is the same. Make each of the following a magic square.

(a)
	1	6
	5	7
4		2

(b)
17	10	
		14
13	18	

18. Place whole numbers in the four squares so that each pair has the sum shown. Note that one diagonal sum must be 20 and the other diagonal sum must be 7.

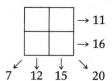

→ 11
→ 16

7   12   15   20

19. Switch two numbers in the squares below so that each row and column will sum to 15.

1	5	3
6	7	2
8	9	4

20. Place the numbers 1, 2, 3, 4, 5, 6, and 7 in the seven boxes so that the sum along each line segment is 13; that is, the three sets of connected boxes should all sum to 13.

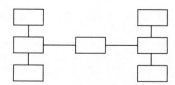

21. (a) Place the numbers 1, 2, 3, 4, 5, and 6 in the boxes so that no square has a number greater than the one directly below it or directly to the right of it.

(b) Can you find more than one way to place the numbers?

22. A domino set contains all number pairs from double-zero to double-six, with each number pair occurring only once; that is, the following domino counts as two-four and four-two. How many dominoes are in the set?

23. The cost of a soft drink at the math booth at the school fair is determined by the following clues.
   (i) You can buy one, two, or three drinks with exactly 6 coins.
   (ii) You can use pennies, nickels, dimes, or quarters, and the cost is between 20¢ and 29¢.
   What is the cost of the soft drink?

24. Millie and Samantha began saving money at the same time. Millie plans to save $3 a month, and Samantha plans to save $5 a month. After how many months will Samantha have exactly $10 more than Millie?

25. String art is formed by connecting evenly spaced nails on the vertical and horizontal axes by line segments. Connect the nail farthest from the origin on the vertical axis with the nail closest to the origin on the horizontal axis. Continue until all nails are connected, as shown below. How many intersection points are created with 10 nails on each axis?

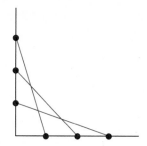

3 nails per axis
3 intersections

26. At a certain party, when the doorbell rang the first time, one guest arrived. On each successive ring, the number of arriving guests was 2 more than the number that had arrived on the previous ring. After 20 rings, how many guests had arrived?

27. Make a calculator display numbers that have the following values.
   (a) Seven tens
   (b) Nine thousands
   (c) Eleven hundreds
   (d) Fifty-six tens
   (e) Three hundred forty-seven tens

28. Make a calculator count to 100. (Use a constant operation if available.)
   (a) By ones   (b) By twos   (c) By fives

29. Make a calculator count backward to 0 from 27. (Use a constant operation if possible.)
   (a) By ones   (b) By threes   (c) By nines

30. If a calculator is made to count by twos starting at 2, what is the thirteenth number in the sequence?

Review Problems

31. Write the number that precedes each of the following.
   (a) CMLX   (b) XXXIX

32. What are the advantages of the Babylonian system over the Egyptian system?

33. Write 5286 in expanded form.

B R A I N   T E A S E R
Design an unmagic square; that is, use each of the digits 1, 2, 3, 4, 5, 6, 7, 8, and 9 exactly once so that every column, row, and diagonal adds to a different sum.

Section 3-3 Multiplication and Division of Whole Numbers

Multiplication of Whole Numbers

In this section, we use three models to discuss multiplication: the repeated-addition model, the array model, and the Cartesian-product model.

FIGURE 3-13

Repeated Addition Model Suppose that we have a classroom with 5 rows of 4 chairs each, as shown in Figure 3-13. How many chairs are there altogether?

The 5 rows of 4 suggest the following addition:

$$\underbrace{4 + 4 + 4 + 4 + 4}_{\text{five 4s}} = 20$$

Instead of writing the sum of 4s just shown, we use the notation 5×4, or $5 \cdot 4$, to mean that five 4s are added. Thus, multiplication can be defined in terms of repeated addition.

● **D E F I N I T I O N**

For any whole numbers a and $n \neq 0$,

$$n \cdot a = \underbrace{a + a + a + \cdots + a}_{n \text{ terms}}$$

If $n = 0$, then $0 \cdot a$ means that no a's are added; that is, $0 \cdot a = 0$.

● **R E M A R K**

In terms of set theory, $n \cdot a$ can be thought of as the union of n equivalent, disjoint sets, each with a elements.

H I S T O R I C A L   N O T E

William Oughtred (1575–1660), an English mathematician, placed emphasis on mathematical symbols. He first introduced the use of "St. Andrew's cross" as the symbol for multiplication. This symbol was not readily adopted because, as Gottfried Wilhelm von Leibnitz (1646–1716) objected, it was too easily confused with the letter x. Leibnitz adopted the use of the dot ($\cdot$) for multiplication, which then became prominently used.

Repeated addition can be modeled on a number line. For example, the number line for $5 \cdot 4$ is shown in Figure 3-14.

FIGURE 3-14

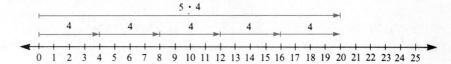

Array Model Another model that is useful in exploring multiplication of whole numbers is the *array model*. We introduce this model by crossing sticks to create intersection points, forming an array. For example, to show $2 \cdot 3$, we place three sticks side by side and then cross them with two sticks, as shown in Figure 3-15(a). The product of $2 \cdot 3$ is the number of intersection points. The product of $4 \cdot 3$ is modeled in Figure 3-15(b). In Figure 3-15(c), we see that the product of $2 \cdot 0$ is 0 because there are no intersection points.

FIGURE 3-15

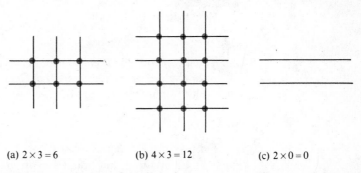

(a) $2 \times 3 = 6$ (b) $4 \times 3 = 12$ (c) $2 \times 0 = 0$

Cartesian-Product Model Suppose that you can order a soyburger on light or dark bread with one of the following: mustard, mayonnaise, or horseradish. To show the number of different soyburger orders that a waiter could call out to the cook when you order, we can use a model called a *tree diagram*. All the possible ways of ordering the soyburger are listed in Figure 3-16, where the bread is chosen from the set $B = \{$light, dark$\}$ and the condiment is chosen from the set $C = \{$mustard, mayonnaise, horseradish$\}$.

FIGURE 3-16

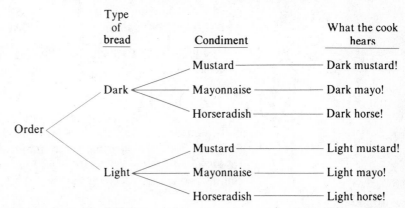

What was ordered could be written as ordered pairs—for example, (dark, mustard). The entire set of ordered pairs formed is the Cartesian product, $B \times C$. The number of ordered pairs in $B \times C$ is the number of orders the cook could have heard. Because the tree shows $2 \cdot 3$ orders, we see that $2 \cdot 3 = n(B) \cdot n(C) = n(B \times C)$.

The preceding discussion demonstrates how multiplication can be defined in terms of Cartesian products. This alternate definition is as follows.

● A L T E R N A T E   D E F I N I T I O N
For finite sets A and B, if $n(A) = a$ and $n(B) = b$, then $a \cdot b = n(A \times B)$.

● R E M A R K
Note that, in this definition, sets A and B do not have to be disjoint.

product / factors   The expression $a \cdot b$ is the **product** of a and $b,$ and a and b are **factors.** Also, note that $A \times B$ indicates the Cartesian product, not multiplication. We multiply numbers, not sets.

Properties of Whole-Number Multiplication

As with addition, multiplication on the set of whole numbers has the closure, commutative, associative, and identity properties.

● P R O P E R T I E S
Closure Property of Multiplication of Whole Numbers   For any whole numbers a and $b,$ $a \cdot b$ is a unique whole number.
Commutative Property of Multiplication of Whole Numbers   For any whole numbers a and $b,$ $a \cdot b = b \cdot a.$
Associative Property of Multiplication of Whole Numbers   For any whole numbers $a,$ $b,$ and $c,$ $(a \cdot b) \cdot c = a \cdot (b \cdot c).$
Identity Property of Multiplication of Whole Numbers   There is a unique whole number 1 such that for any whole number $a,$ $a \cdot 1 = a = 1 \cdot a.$

The commutative property for multiplication of whole numbers is easily illustrated by building a 3×5 grid and then turning it sideways, as shown in Figure 3-17. We see that the number of 1×1 squares present in either case is 15—that is, $3 \cdot 5 = 15 = 5 \cdot 3.$ In general, the commutative property can be verified by recalling that $n(A \times B) = n(B \times A).$

FIGURE 3-17

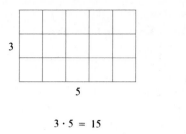

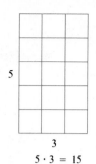

$3 \cdot 5 = 15$

$5 \cdot 3 = 15$

The associative property of multiplication of whole numbers can be illustrated as follows. Suppose that $a = 3$, $b = 5$, and $c = 4$. In Figure 3-18(a), we see a picture of $3 \cdot (5 \cdot 4)$ blocks. In Figure 3-18(b), we see the same blocks, this time arranged as $(3 \cdot 5) \cdot 4$. Because both sets of blocks in Figure 3-18(a) and (b) compress to the set shown in Figure 3-18(c), we see that $3 \cdot (5 \cdot 4) = (3 \cdot 5) \cdot 4$. The associative property is useful in computations such as the following.

$$3 \cdot 40 = 3 \cdot (4 \cdot 10) = (3 \cdot 4) \cdot 10 = 12 \cdot 10 = 120$$

FIGURE 3-18

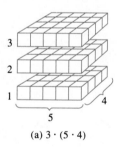 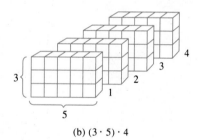 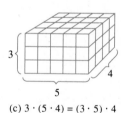

(a) $3 \cdot (5 \cdot 4)$ (b) $(3 \cdot 5) \cdot 4$ (c) $3 \cdot (5 \cdot 4) = (3 \cdot 5) \cdot 4$

multiplicative identity

The **multiplicative identity** for whole numbers is 1. For example, $3 \cdot 1 = 1 + 1 + 1 = 3$. In general, for any whole number a,

$$a \cdot 1 = \underbrace{1 + 1 + 1 + \cdots + 1}_{a \text{ terms}} = a$$

Thus, $a \cdot 1 = a$, which—along with the commutative property for multiplication—implies that $a \cdot 1 = a = 1 \cdot a$. Cartesian products can also be used to show that $a \cdot 1 = a = 1 \cdot a$.

Next, consider multiplication involving 0. For example, $6 \cdot 0 = 0 + 0 + 0 + 0 + 0 + 0 = 0$. Thus, we see that multiplying 0 by 6 yields a product of 0 and, by commutativity, $0 \cdot 6 = 0$. This is true in general and can be stated as follows.

• P R O P E R T Y

Zero Multiplication Property of Whole Numbers For any whole number a, $a \cdot 0 = 0 = 0 \cdot a$.

The zero multiplication property of whole numbers can also be verified by using the definition of multiplication in terms of Cartesian products. Let A be any set such that $n(A) = a$. Then, $a \cdot 0 = n(A \times \varnothing) = n(\varnothing) = 0$. Similarly, we can show that $0 \cdot a = 0$.

The Distributive Property of Multiplication Over Addition

The next property that we investigate is the basis for understanding multiplication algorithms. In Figure 3-19, $5 \cdot (3 + 4) = (5 \cdot 3) + (5 \cdot 4)$.

FIGURE 3-19

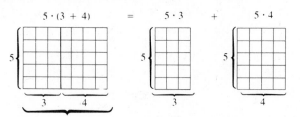

The properties of addition and multiplication also can be used to justify this result.

$$5 \cdot (3 + 4) = \underbrace{(3 + 4) + (3 + 4) + (3 + 4) + (3 + 4) + (3 + 4)}_{5 \text{ terms}}$$

                                  Definition of multiplication

$$= (3 + 3 + 3 + 3 + 3) + (4 + 4 + 4 + 4 + 4)$$

                                  Commutative and associative properties of addition

$$= 5 \cdot 3 + 5 \cdot 4$$

                                  Definition of multiplication

This example illustrates the *distributive property of multiplication over addition* for whole numbers, which is stated in general as follows.

• P R O P E R T Y

Distributive Property of Multiplication over Addition for Whole Numbers For any whole numbers a, b, and c.

$$a \cdot (b + c) = a \cdot b + a \cdot c$$

Because the commutative property of multiplication of whole numbers holds, the distributive property of multiplication over addition can be rewritten as $(b + c) \cdot a = b \cdot a + c \cdot a$. The distributive property can be generalized to any finite number of terms. For example, $a \cdot (b + c + d) = a \cdot b + a \cdot c + a \cdot d$.

Students find the distributive property of multiplication over addition useful when doing *mental arithmetic*. For example,

$$11 \cdot 17 = (10 + 1) \cdot 17 = 10 \cdot 17 + 1 \cdot 17 = 170 + 17 = 187$$

The distributive property is used to combine like terms when we work with variables; for example, $3ab + 2ab = (3 + 2) \cdot ab = 5ab$.

EXAMPLE 3-3   Rename each of the following, using the distributive property.
(a) $3 \cdot (x + y)$ (b) $(x + 1) \cdot x$
(c) $3 \cdot (2x + y + 3)$ (d) $a \cdot x + a \cdot y$
(e) $a \cdot x + a$ (f) $(x + 2) \cdot 5 + (x + 2) \cdot a$

SOLUTION   (a) $3 \cdot (x + y) = 3 \cdot x + 3 \cdot y = 3x + 3y$
(b) $(x + 1) \cdot x = x \cdot x + 1 \cdot x = x^2 + x$
(c) $3 \cdot (2x + y + 3) = 3 \cdot (2x) + 3 \cdot y + 3 \cdot 3 = (3 \cdot 2) \cdot x + 3 \cdot y + 9$
$= 6x + 3y + 9$
(d) $a \cdot x + a \cdot y = a \cdot (x + y) = a(x + y)$
(e) $a \cdot x + a = a \cdot x + a \cdot 1 = a \cdot (x + 1) = a(x + 1)$
(f) $(x + 2) \cdot 5 + (x + 2) \cdot a = (x + 2) \cdot (5 + a) = (x + 2)(5 + a)$

EXAMPLE 3-4   If $a \in W$ and $b \in W$, use the distributive property to write $(a + b)^2$ as a sum without parentheses.

SOLUTION   By the definition of exponents, $(a + b)^2 = (a + b)(a + b)$. We consider the first term, $(a + b)$, as a single whole number and apply the distributive property. Then, applying the commutative, associative, and distributive properties, we obtain the following.

$$\begin{aligned}
(a + b)(a + b) &= (a + b)a + (a + b)b \\
&= (aa + ba) + (ab + bb) \\
&= (a^2 + ba) + (ab + b^2) \\
&= a^2 + (ba + ab) + b^2 \\
&= a^2 + (ab + ab) + b^2 \\
&= a^2 + (1 \cdot ab + 1 \cdot ab) + b^2 \\
&= a^2 + (1 + 1)ab + b^2 \\
&= a^2 + 2ab + b^2
\end{aligned}$$

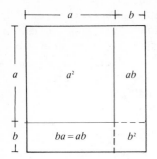

FIGURE 3-20

The result in Example 3-4 can be demonstrated geometrically by using the fact that the area A of a rectangle is given by $A = l \cdot w$, where l is the length of the rectangle and w is the width. If we build a square of length $(a + b)$ units, as shown in Figure 3-20, then it has area $(a + b)^2$. Notice that this figure is divided into four disjoint regions that make up the large square. From the figure we see that $(a + b)^2 = a^2 + ab + ab + b^2 = a^2 + 2ab + b^2$. Students often mistakenly think that $(a + b)^2 = a^2 + b^2$. From Figure 3-20 we see that this is not the case.

Order of Operations

Difficulties involving the order of arithmetic operations sometimes arise. For example, many students will treat $2 + 3 \cdot 6$ as $(2 + 3) \cdot 6$, while others will treat it as $2 + (3 \cdot 6)$. In the first case, the value is 30. In the second case, the value is 20. In order to avoid confusion, mathematicians agree that, when no parentheses are present, multiplications are performed *before* additions. Thus, $2 + 3 \cdot 6 = 2 + 18 = 20$. This order of operations is not built into calculators that display an incorrect answer of 30.

Division of Whole Numbers

We discuss division using three models: the *partition* model, the *missing-factor* model, and the *repeated-subtraction* model.

Partition Model   Suppose that we have 18 cookies and want to give an equal number of cookies to each of three friends, Bob, Dean, and Charlie. How many should each person receive? If we draw a picture, we see that we can divide (or partition) the 18 cookies into three sets, with an equal number of cookies in each set. Figure 3-21 shows that each friend received 6 cookies.

FIGURE 3-21

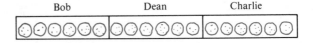

The answer may be symbolized as $18 \div 3 = 6$. Thus, $18 \div 3$ is the number of cookies in each of three disjoint sets whose union is 18 cookies. In this approach to division, we partition a set into a number of equivalent subsets.

Missing-Factor Model   Another strategy for dividing 18 cookies among 3 friends is to use the *missing-factor* model. If each friend receives c cookies, then the three friends receive $3 \cdot c$ cookies, or 18 cookies. Hence, $3 \cdot c = 18$. Since $3 \cdot 6 = 18$, then $c = 6$. We have answered the division computation by using multiplication. This leads us to the following definition of division of whole numbers.

● D E F I N I T I O N

For any whole numbers a and b, with $b \neq 0$, $a \div b = c$ if and only if c is the unique whole number such that $b \cdot c = a$.

dividend / divisor
quotient

The number a is the **dividend,** b is the **divisor,** and c is the **quotient.** Note that $a \div b$ can also be written as $\dfrac{a}{b}$ or $b\overline{)a}$.

Repeated-Subtraction Model Suppose that we have 18 cookies and want to package them in cookie boxes that hold 6 cookies each. How many boxes are needed? We could reason that, if one box is filled, then we would have 18 − 6 (or 12) cookies left. If one more box is filled, then there are 12 − 6 (or 6) cookies left. Finally, we could place the last 6 cookies in a third box. This discussion can be summarized by writing 18 − 6 − 6 − 6 = 0. We have found that 18 ÷ 6 = 3, by repeated subtraction.

Calculators can be used to show that division of whole numbers can be thought of as repeated subtraction. For example, consider 135 ÷ 15. If the calculator has a constant key, press $\boxed{1}\,\boxed{5}\,\boxed{-}\,\boxed{\text{K}}\,\boxed{1}\,\boxed{3}\,\boxed{5}\,\boxed{=}$ ..., and then count how many times you must press the $\boxed{=}$ key in order to make the display read 0. (Calculators with a different constant feature may require a different sequence of entries.) Compare your answer with the one achieved by pressing this sequence of keys.

$\boxed{1}\,\boxed{3}\,\boxed{5}\,\boxed{\div}\,\boxed{1}\,\boxed{5}\,\boxed{=}$

Division Algorithm

Just as subtraction of whole numbers is not always meaningful, division of whole numbers is not always meaningful. For example, to find 383 ÷ 57, we look for a whole number c such that

$$57 \cdot c = 383$$

Table 3-7 shows several products of whole numbers times 57. Since 383 is between 342 and 399, there is no whole number c such that $57 \cdot c = 383$. Because no whole number c satisfies this equation, we see that 383 ÷ 57 has no meaning in the set of whole numbers. Thus, the set of whole numbers is not closed under division.

TABLE 3-7

$57 \cdot 1$	$57 \cdot 2$	$57 \cdot 3$	$57 \cdot 4$	$57 \cdot 5$	$57 \cdot 6$	$57 \cdot 7$
57	114	171	228	285	342	399

However, if 383 apples were to be divided among 57 students, each student would receive 6 apples, and 41 apples would remain. The number *remainder* 41 is the **remainder.** Thus, 383 contains six 57s with a remainder of 41. Observe that the remainder is a whole number less than 57. The concept *division algorithm* illustrated is the **division algorithm.**

● **D I V I S I O N   A L G O R I T H M**

Given any whole numbers a and b with $b \neq 0$, there exist unique whole numbers q (quotient) and r (remainder) such that

$$a = b \cdot q + r \quad \text{with} \quad 0 \leq r < b$$

● **R E M A R K**

The quotient q is the greatest whole number of b's in a.

EXAMPLE 3-5   If 123 is divided by a number and the remainder is 13, what are the possible divisors?

SOLUTION   From the division algorithm, we have

$$123 = b \cdot q + 13 \quad \text{and} \quad b > 13$$

1	110
2	55
5	22
10	11

TABLE 3-8

Using the definition of subtraction, we have $bq = 123 - 13$, and hence $110 = b \cdot q$. Now we are looking for two numbers whose product is 110, where one number is greater than 13. Table 3-8 shows the pairs of factors of 110.

We see that 110, 55, and 22 are possible divisors, because each is greater than 13. The numbers 1, 2, 5, 10, and 11 cannot be divisors.

Division by 0 and 1

The whole numbers 0 and 1 deserve special attention with respect to division of whole numbers. Before reading on, try to find the values of the following three expressions:

1. $3 \div 0$
2. $0 \div 3$
3. $0 \div 0$

Consider the following explanations:

1. By definition, $3 \div 0 = c$ if there is a unique number c such that $0 \cdot c = 3$. Since the zero property of multiplication states that $0 \cdot c = 0$ for any whole number c, there is no whole number c such that $0 \cdot c = 3$. Thus, $3 \div 0$ is undefined because there is no answer to the equivalent multiplication problem.

2. By definition, $0 \div 3 = c$ if there exists a unique number c such that $3 \cdot c = 0$. The zero property of multiplication states that any number times 0 is 0. Since $3 \cdot 0 = 0$, then $c = 0$ and $0 \div 3 = 0$. Note that $c = 0$ is the only number that satisfies $3 \cdot c = 0$.

3. By definition, $0 \div 0 = c$ if there is a unique whole number c such that $0 \cdot c = 0$. Notice that, for *any* c, $0 \cdot c = 0$. According to the definition of division, c must be unique. Since there is no *unique* number c such that $0 \cdot c = 0$, it follows that $0 \div 0$ is indeterminate, or undefined.

Division involving 0 may be summarized as follows.
Let n be any natural number. Then:

1. $n \div 0$ is undefined:
2. $0 \div n = 0$;
3. $0 \div 0$ is indeterminate, or undefined.

Recall that $n \cdot 1 = n$ for any whole number n. Thus, by the definition of division, $n \div 1 = n$. For example, $3 \div 1 = 3$, $1 \div 1 = 1$, and $0 \div 1 = 0$.

PROBLEM SET 3-3

1. Use the number-line model to illustrate why $3 \cdot 5 = 15$.

2. Each ticket to the band concert costs $2.00. Each ticket to the football game costs $5.00. Jim bought 5 tickets to each event. What was his total bill?

3. Tell whether or not the following sets are closed under multiplication. If not, give a counterexample.
   (a) $\{0, 1\}$ (b) $\{0\}$
   (c) $\{2, 4, 6, 8, 10, \ldots\}$ (d) $\{1, 3, 5, 7, 9, \ldots\}$
   (e) $\{1, 4, 7, 10, 13, \ldots\}$ (f) $\{0, 1, 2\}$

4. Use the distributive property to describe how you might find the product $8 \cdot 3$ if you know only the addition table and the 2 and 6 multiplication facts.

5. Identify the property being illustrated in each of the following.
   (a) $3 \cdot 2 = 2 \cdot 3$ (b) $3(2 \cdot 4) = (3 \cdot 2)4$
   (c) $3(2 + 3) = 3(3 + 2)$ (d) $8 \cdot 0 = 0 = 0 \cdot 8$
   (e) $1 \cdot 8 = 8 = 8 \cdot 1$ (f) $6(3 + 5) = (3 + 5)6$
   (g) $6(3 + 5) = 6 \cdot 3 + 6 \cdot 5$
   (h) $(3 + 5)6 = 3 \cdot 6 + 5 \cdot 6$

6. For each of the following, find—if possible—the whole numbers that make the equations true.
   (a) $3 \cdot \square = 15$ (b) $18 = 6 + 3 \cdot \square$
   (c) $\square \cdot \square = 25$ (d) $\square \cdot (5 + 6) = \square \cdot 5 + \square \cdot 6$

7. Rename each of the following, using the distributive property for multiplication over addition so that there are no parentheses in the final answer.
   (a) $(a + b)(c + d)$ (b) $3(x + y + 5)$
   (c) $\square(\triangle + \bigcirc)$ (d) $(x + y)(x + y + z)$

8. Perform each of the following computations.
   (a) $2 \cdot 3 + 5$ (b) $2(3 + 5)$
   (c) $2 \cdot 3 + 2 \cdot 5$ (d) $3 + 2 \cdot 5$

9. The generalized distributive property for three terms states that, for any whole numbers a, b, c, and d, $a(b + c + d) = ab + ac + ad$. Justify this property, using the distributive property for two terms.

10. Which of the following, if any, are true?
    (a) $(3 \cdot 5) \cdot 7 = 3 \cdot (5 \cdot 7)$
    (b) $3 \cdot (7 + 8) = (3 \cdot 7) + 8$
    (c) $3 \cdot (7 + 5) = 3 \cdot 7 + 5$
    (d) $5 \cdot (3 \cdot 7) = (5 \cdot 3) \cdot (5 \cdot 7)$

11. The FOIL method is often used as a shortcut to multiply expressions like $(m + n)(x + y)$.

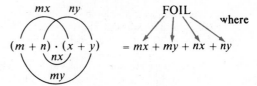

where F stands for product of the *first* terms, mx
O stands for product of the *outer* terms, my
I stands for product of the *inner* terms, nx
L stands for product of the *last* terms, ny
    (a) Use the FOIL method on each of the following.
        (i) $(a + b)(a + b)$ (ii) $(50 + 8)(20 + 6)$
    (b) Use the distributive property to show why the FOIL method works.

12. For each of the following, find whole numbers to make the statement true, if possible.
    (a) $18 \div 3 = \square$
    (b) $\square \div 76 = 0$
    (c) $28 \div \square = 7$

13. Illustrate geometrically each of the following, using the concept of area.
    (a) $a \cdot (b + c) = ab + ac$
    (b) $(a + b) \cdot (c + d) = ac + ad + bc + bd$

14. Rewrite each of the following division problems as a multiplication problem.
    (a) $40 \div 8 = 5$ (b) $326 \div 2 = x$
    (c) $48 \div x = 16$ (d) $x \div 5 = 17$
    (e) $a \div b = c$ (f) $(48 - 36) \div 6 = x$

15. Show that, in general, each of the following is false if a, b, and c are whole numbers.
    (a) $a \div b = b \div a$
    (b) $(a \div b) \div c = a \div (b \div c)$
    (c) $a \div (b + c) = (a \div b) + (a \div c)$
    (d) $a \div b$ is a whole number.

16. Because the Jones' water meter was stuck, they were billed the same amount for water each month for 5 months. If they paid $160, what was the monthly bill?

17. Use the definition of division to justify that, for any whole numbers a and b, where $b \neq 0$, $(ab) \div b = a$.

18. There were 17 sandwiches for 7 people on a picnic. How many whole sandwiches were there for each person if they were divided equally? How many were left over?

19. If it takes 1 minute per cut, how long will it take to cut a 10-foot log into 10 equal pieces?

20. For each of the following, name all the possible pairs of replacements for $\square$ and $\triangle$.
    (a) $34 = \square \cdot 8 + \triangle$
    (b) $\triangle = 4 \cdot 16 + 2$
    (c) $28 = \square \cdot \triangle + 3$

21. Find all the pairs of whole numbers whose product is 36.

22. A new model of a car is available in 4 different exterior colors and 3 different interior colors. How many different color schemes are possible for the car?

23. Tony has 5 ways to get from his home to the park. He has 6 ways to get from the park to the school. How many ways can Tony get from his home to school by way of the park?

24. Students were divided into 8 teams with 9 on each team. Later the same students were divided into teams with 6 on each team. How many teams were there then?

★25. The binary operation $\odot$ is defined on the set $S = \{a, b, c\}$, as shown in the following table. For example, $a \odot b = b$ and $b \odot a = b$.

$\odot$	a	b	c
a	a	b	c
b	b	a	c
c	c	c	c

(a) Is S closed with respect to $\odot$?
(b) Is $\odot$ commutative on S?
(c) Is there an identity for $\odot$ on S? If yes, what is it?
(d) Is $\odot$ associative on S?

26. To find $7 \div 5$ on the calculator, press $\boxed{7}\ \boxed{\div}\ \boxed{5}\ \boxed{=}$, which yields 1.4. To find the whole-number remainder, ignore the decimal portion of 1.4, multiply $5 \cdot 1$, and subtract this product from 7. The result is the remainder. Use a calculator to find the whole-number remainder for each of the following divisions.
    (a) $28 \div 5$ (b) $32 \div 10$ (c) $29 \div 3$
    (d) $41 \div 7$ (e) $49,382 \div 14$

27. In the problems that follow, use only the designated number keys. Use any function keys on the calculator.
    (a) Use the keys $\boxed{1}$, $\boxed{9}$, and $\boxed{7}$ exactly once each in any order, and use any operations available to write as many of the whole numbers as possible from 1 to 20. For example, $9 - 7 - 1 = 1$ and $1 \cdot 9 - 7 = 2$.
    (b) Use the $\boxed{4}$ key as many times as desired with any operations to display 13.
    (c) Use the $\boxed{2}$ key three times with any operations to display 24.
    (d) Use the $\boxed{1}$ key five times with any operations to display 100.

Review Problems

28. Write 75, using Egyptian, Roman, Mayan, and Babylonian numerals.
29. Write 35,206 in expanded form.
30. Give a set that is not closed under addition.
31. Are the whole numbers commutative under subtraction? If not, give a counterexample.
32. Illustrate $11 - 3$, using a number-line model.

B R A I N   T E A S E R

Rosalie bought a bike for $50 and sold it for $60. Then she bought it back for $70 and sold it for $80. What is the financial outcome of these transactions?

LABORATORY ACTIVITY

Enter a number less than 20 on the calculator. If the number is even, divide it by 2; if it is odd, multiply it by 3 and add 1. Next, use the number on the display. Follow the given directions. Repeat the process again:

1. Will the display eventually reach 1?
2. Which number less than 20 takes the most steps before reaching 1?
3. Do even or odd numbers reach 1 more quickly?
4. Investigate what happens with numbers greater than 20.

Section 3-4   Algorithms for Whole-Number Addition and Subtraction

Because of recent advances in technology, it is neither necessary nor advisable to devote large portions of instructional time to paper-and-pencil computation. Less time may be spent on instruction involving calculations with many digits, because calculators are available. Computational ability is still important, but the role of technology, mental mathematics, and estimation must be considered. Knowledge of basic facts is still necessary; for example, students still need to know that $9 + 8 = 17$ in order to compute $900 + 800$ mentally or to estimate $889 + 797$. When computing taxes, however, a person should probably use a calculator or computer. In determining a tip in a restaurant, mental mathematics is appropriate. If you need to find the total number of students in four sixth-grade classes, pencil and paper might be the most appropriate method.

In previous sections, the definitions of addition and subtraction were introduced. These definitions, along with a knowledge of basic facts and properties, are necessary to perform more complex additions and subtractions. More complex operations are commonly done by applying various algorithms.

algorithm   An **algorithm** (named for the ninth-century Arabian mathematician Mohammed al-Khowârizmî) is a step-by-step systematic procedure used to accomplish an operation. It is valuable for every prospective elementary school teacher to know more than one algorithm for doing operations. Not all students learn in the same manner, and the shortest, most efficient algorithms may not be the best for every individual.

Addition Algorithms

Paper-and-pencil algorithms need to be taught developmentally; that is, they must proceed from the concrete stage to the abstract stage at appropriate times. The use of concrete teaching aids—such as chips, bean sticks, an abacus, or base-ten blocks—helps provide insight into the creation of algorithms for addition. A set of base-ten blocks, shown in Figure 3-22, consists of *units, longs, flats,* and *blocks,* representing 1, 10, 100, and 1000, respectively.

FIGURE 3-22

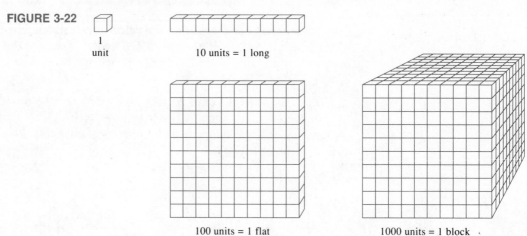

1
unit   10 units = 1 long

100 units = 1 flat   1000 units = 1 block

Students trade blocks by regrouping; that is, they take a set of base-ten blocks representing a number and trade them until they have the fewest possible pieces representing the same number. For example, suppose that you have 58 units and want to trade them. What pieces do you have if you have the smallest number of pieces you can receive in a fair exchange? The units can be grouped into tens to form longs. Five sets of 10 units each can be traded for 5 longs. Thus, 58 units can be traded for 5 longs and 8 units. In terms of numbers, this is analogous to rewriting 58 as $5 \cdot 10 + 8$. In this case, you cannot receive flats or blocks.

EXAMPLE 3-6   Suppose you have 11 flats, 17 longs, and 16 units. What pieces do you have if you have the smallest number of pieces you can receive in a fair exchange?

SOLUTION   The 16 units can be traded for 1 long and 6 units.

11 flats	17 longs	16 units	(16 units = 1 long and 6 units)
	1 long	6 units	(Trade)
11 flats	18 longs	6 units	(After the first trade)
11 flats	18 longs	6 units	(18 longs = 1 flat and 8 longs)
1 flat	8 longs		(Trade)
12 flats	8 longs	6 units	(After the second trade)

	12 flats	8 longs	6 units	(12 flats = 1 block and 2 flats)
1 block	2 flats			(Trade)
1 block	2 flats	8 longs	6 units	(After the third trade)

In terms of numbers, this is analogous to rewriting $11 \cdot 10^2 + 17 \cdot 10 + 16$ as $1 \cdot 10^3 + 2 \cdot 10^2 + 8 \cdot 10 + 6$, which implies that there are 1286 units.

We now use base-ten blocks to help develop an algorithm for whole-number addition. Suppose that we wish to add $14 + 23$. We show this computation with a concrete model in Figure 3-23(a), with an introductory algorithm in Figure 3-23(b), and with the familiar algorithm in Figure 3-23(c).

FIGURE 3-23   (a)

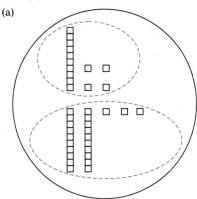

Concrete model

(b)

Tens	Ones
1	4
+2	3
3	7

Introductory
algorithm

(c)
$$\begin{array}{r} 14 \\ +23 \\ \hline 37 \end{array}$$

Familiar
algorithm

A more formal justification for this addition is the following.

$14 + 23$	$= (1 \cdot 10 + 4) + (2 \cdot 10 + 3)$	Expanded form
	$= (1 \cdot 10 + 2 \cdot 10) + (4 + 3)$	Commutative and associative properties of addition
	$= (1 + 2) \cdot 10 + (4 + 3)$	Distributive property of multiplication over addition
	$= 3 \cdot 10 + 7$	Single-digit addition facts
	$= 37$	Place value

● **R E M A R K**

In some texts, the partial sums in the computation are shown as follows.

$$\begin{array}{r} 14 \\ +23 \\ \hline 7 \\ 30 \\ \hline 37 \end{array}$$

Although this mathematical justification is not usually presented in the elementary school, the ideas and properties shown are necessary to understand why the algorithm works. Some problems are more involved than this one because they involve "regrouping" or "carrying," in which students trade by regrouping. This is described in terms of the base-ten blocks on the student page from *Addison-Wesley Mathematics,* 1989, Grade 4.

Adding: Two or More Trades

Nina and Bert are circus elephants.
One night Nina ate 196 kg of hay and Bert ate 227 kg.
How many kilograms of hay did they eat together?

Since we want the total amount, we add.

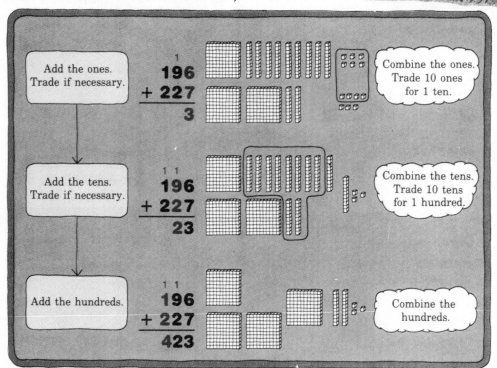

Nina and Bert ate 423 kg of hay that night.

After using concrete aids, children are ready to complete a computation such as 28 + 34. Figure 3-24(a) and (b) show introductory algorithms, whereas Figure 3-24(c) shows the traditional algorithm.

FIGURE 3-24

(a)

Tens	Ones	
2	8	
+3	4	
5	$\not{1}$2	(Add)
+1	2	Regroup
6	2	

(b)
$$\begin{array}{r} 2\;\;8 \\ +3\;\;4 \\ \hline 1\;\;2 \\ +5\;\;0 \\ \hline 6\;\;2 \end{array}$$

(c)
$$\begin{array}{r} ^1 \\ 28 \\ +34 \\ \hline 62 \end{array}$$

Scratch Addition

scratch addition   A low-stress algorithm for addition called **scratch addition** is shown for 87 + 65 + 49. This algorithm allows students to do complicated additions by doing a series of additions involving only two single digits.

1. 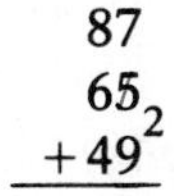
$$\begin{array}{r} 87 \\ 65_2 \\ +49^2 \\ \hline \end{array}$$
Add the numbers in the units place starting at the top. When the sum is 10 or more, record this sum by scratching a line through the last digit added and writing the number of units next to the scratched digit. For example, since 7 + 5 = 12, the "scratch" represents 10 and the 2 represents the units.

2. 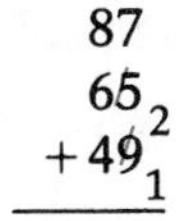
$$\begin{array}{r} 87 \\ 65_2 \\ +49^2_{\;1} \\ \hline \end{array}$$
Continue adding the units, including any new digits written down. When the addition again results in a sum of 10 or more, as with 2 + 9 = 11, repeat the process described in (1).

3. 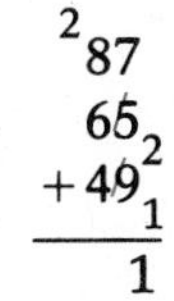
$$\begin{array}{r} ^2 87 \\ 65_2 \\ +49^2_{\;1} \\ \hline 1 \end{array}$$
When the first column of additions is completed, write the number of units, 1, below the addition line. Count the number of scratches, 2, and add this number to the second column.

4. 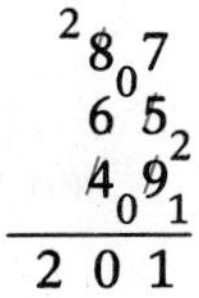
$$\begin{array}{r} ^2 8_0 7 \\ 6\,5_2 \\ 4_0 9^2_{\;1} \\ \hline 2\;\;0\;\;1 \end{array}$$
Repeat the procedure for each successive column.

EXAMPLE 3-7 Compute the following additions using the scratch algorithm.

(a)   296   (b)   1369
        840   4813
    + 27   5879
                 +6183

SOLUTION

(a)

$$\begin{array}{cccc} {}^{1}2 & {}^{1}9_{0} & 6 \\ 8_{1} & 4 & 0 \\ + & 2 & 7_{3} \\ \hline 1 \quad 1 & 6 & 3 \end{array}$$

(b)

$$\begin{array}{cccc} {}^{2}1 & {}^{2}3 & {}^{2}6 & 9 \\ 4 & 8_{3} & 1 & 3_{2} \\ 5_{2} & 8_{1} & 7_{6} & 9_{1}^{2} \\ + \quad 6^{2} & 1 & 8_{4} & 3^{1} \\ \hline 1 \quad 8 & 2 & 4 & 4 \end{array}$$

Mental Addition

Mental mathematics is an important tool in the elementary schools, as is emphasized in the *Standards*. *Mental mathematics* is the process of producing an exact answer to a computation without using external computational aids. Three commonly mentioned benefits of mental math are the following.

1. Mental math is useful in everyday life.
2. Mental math can make written computation easier and faster.
3. Mental math can help develop a better understanding of mathematical operations and properties.

Several examples involving mental mathematics are given next.

1. *Adding from the left*

(a)   67
   +36

    60 + 30 = 90   Add the tens.
      7 + 6 = 13   Add the units.
    90 + 13 = 103   Add the two sums.

(b)   36
   +36

    30 + 30 = 60   Double 30.
      6 + 6 = 12   Double 6.
    60 + 12 = 72   Add the doubles.

2. *Breaking up and bridging*

    67
   +36

    67 + 30 = 97   Add the first number to the tens in the
    97 + 6 = 103   second number.
                       Add this sum to the units in the second
                       number.

3. *Trading off*

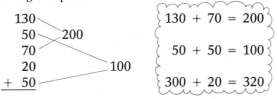

(a)
$$\begin{array}{r} 67 \\ +36 \end{array}$$

$67 + 3 = 70$
$36 - 3 = 33$
$70 + 33 = 103$

Add 3 to make a multiple of 10.
Subtract 3 to compensate for the 3 that was added.
Add the two numbers.

(b)
$$\begin{array}{r} 67 \\ +29 \end{array}$$

$67 + 30 = 97$
$97 - 1 = 96$

Add 30 (next multiple of 10 greater than 29.
Subtract 1 to compensate for the extra 1 that was added.

4. *Using compatible numbers*

$$\begin{array}{r} 130 \\ 50 \\ 70 \\ 20 \\ +\ 50 \end{array}$$

200

100

$130 + 70 = 200$
$50 + 50 = 100$
$300 + 20 = 320$

5. *Making compatible numbers*

$$\begin{array}{r} 25 \\ +79 \end{array}$$

$25 + 75 = 100$
$100 + 4 = 104$

$25 + 75$ adds to 100.
Add 4 more units.

PROBLEM 1

Each letter in the following addition represents one and only one of the digits 0 through 9. What digit does each letter represent? Is there more than one solution?

$$\begin{array}{r} MA \\ MA \\ +MA \\ \hline EEL \end{array}$$

Understanding the Problem. We are to determine which digit each letter represents in the preceding addition. Also, we are to determine if our solution is unique. We can tell that $A \neq 0$ because $A + A + A$ has L as the units digit in its sum, and $0 + 0 + 0 = 0$.

Devising a Plan. We know that the greatest possible value of $A + A + A$, or 3A, is $3 \cdot 9$, or 27, so if there is a carry from the units column to the tens column, it must be either 1 or 2. Because $M + M + M$, or 3M, plus the carry from the units column, if any, must be a two-digit number, then M cannot equal 0, 1, or 2. (Why?) These conditions imply that there are only three possibilities that must be considered to determine values for M. These possibilities are given below.

Case 1:   3M = EE   (no carry)
Case 2:   3M + 1 = EE   (carry of 1)
Case 3:   3M + 2 = EE   (carry of 2)

Because M must equal one of the numbers 3, 4, 5, 6, 7, 8, or 9, we consider the possibilities in Table 3-9.

TABLE 3-9

M	3	4	5	6	7	8	9
3M	9	12	15	18	21	24	27

Because none of these products is in the form of a two-digit number with identical digits, case 1 cannot yield a solution. Thus, if a solution exists, M and E must satisfy the equations in case 2 or case 3. If we analyze these cases in a manner similar to the preceding one, we should be able to determine a solution.

Carrying Out the Plan.   We now consider case 2, in Table 3-10.

TABLE 3-10

M	3	4	5	6	7	8	9
3M + 1	10	13	16	19	22	25	28

Hence, $3 \cdot 7 + 1$ yields the desired form, and a possibility for M is 7, in which case E must be equal to 2. At this point we have the following.

```
   7A
   7A
 + 7A
 ─────
  22L
```

Because there is a carry of 1 to the tens column, it follows that

$$A + A + A = 1 \cdot 10 + L$$

Because 3A is a two-digit number, A cannot be equal to 0, 1, 2, or 3. If A = 4, then $3A = 3 \cdot 4 = 12$ and L = 2, which cannot happen because E = 2, and each letter represents a different numeral. If A = 5, then $3A = 3 \cdot 5 = 15$ and L = 5, which cannot happen because A = 5. If A = 6, then $3A = 3 \cdot 6 = 18$ and L = 8. This causes no contradiction, and we have the following.

```
   MA          76
   MA   ⟶      76
 + MA        + 76
 ─────       ─────
  EEL          228
```

To determine if this is the only solution for case 2, we continue with the remaining possibilities. We know that A $\neq$ 7 because M = 7. Also, A $\neq$ 8 and A $\neq$ 9 because 3 $\cdot$ 8 = 24 and 3 $\cdot$ 9 = 27, which would result in a carry of 2.

The only remaining possibility of other solutions is from case 3—that is, 3M + 2 = EE. We consider the possibilities in Table 3-11.

TABLE 3-11

M	3	4	5	6	7	8	9
3M + 2	11	14	17	20	23	26	29

Thus, 3 $\cdot$ 3 + 2 yields the desired form, and a possibility for M is 3, in which case E must equal 1. Because there is a carry of 2 to the tens column, it follows that

$$3A = 2 \cdot 10 + L$$

Because 3A is a two-digit number, A cannot be 0, 1, 2, or 3. Because there must be a carry of 2, A cannot be equal to 4, 5, or 6. If A = 7, then 3A = 3 $\cdot$ 7 = 21 and L = 1, which cannot happen because E = 1. If A = 8, then 3A = 3 $\cdot$ 8 = 24 and L = 4. If A = 9, then 3A = 3 $\cdot$ 9 = 27 and L = 7. Thus, there are two more solutions, as follows.

```
  38      39
  38      39
+ 38    + 39
─────   ─────
 114     117
```

Looking Back. We have checked that our solutions are correct by performing the required additions. We have also checked all possible cases to determine all possible solutions. Related problems such as the following could also be considered.

```
(1)    HE      (2)    WRONG      (3)    HOCUS
     + EE           + WRONG           + POCUS
     ─────          ───────           ───────
      BOO            RIGHT             PRESTO
```

Other Looking Back activities might include making up your own problems and trying them with a friend or trying some problems involving an operation other than addition.

Subtraction Algorithms

As with addition, the use of base-ten blocks can provide a concrete model for subtraction. Consider 36 − 24. We do this computation in Figure 3-25(a), using base-ten blocks; in Figure 3-25(b), using an introductory algorithm

FIGURE 3-25

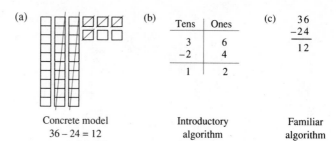

Tens	Ones
3	6
−2	4
1	2

$$\begin{array}{r} 36 \\ -24 \\ \hline 12 \end{array}$$

(a) Concrete model
36 − 24 = 12

(b) Introductory algorithm

(c) Familiar algorithm

based on the blocks; and finally in Figure 3-25(c), using the familiar algorithm. The slashes through the blocks in the concrete model indicate that these blocks are taken away. For the slashes to be used, it must be obvious that no trading has to be done.

Notice that this subtraction problem can be checked by using the definition of subtraction: 36 − 24 = 12, because 12 + 24 = 36.

Subtractions become more involved when renaming is necessary, as in 56 − 29. In the concrete model, 9 units cannot be taken from 6 units so 1 long must be traded for 10 units, giving a total of 16. The three stages for working this problem are shown in Figure 3-26.

FIGURE 3-26

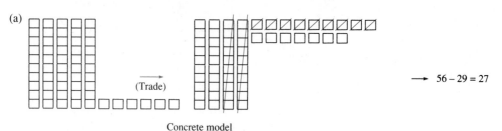

(a) (Trade)

Concrete model

56 − 29 = 27

(b)

Tens	Ones
5	6
−2	9

→

Tens	Ones
4	16
−2	9
2	7

Introductory algorithm

(c)
$$\begin{array}{r} {}^{4\,1} \\ \not{5}6 \\ -29 \\ \hline 27 \end{array}$$

Familiar algorithm

Mental Subtractions

1. *Subtracting in parts*

$$\begin{array}{r} 67 \\ -36 \end{array}$$ $\left\{ \begin{array}{l} 67 - 30 = 37 \\ 37 - 6 = 31 \end{array} \right\}$ Subtract the tens in the second number from the first number.
Subtract the units in the second number from the difference.

2. *Making an easier problem*

$$
\begin{array}{r}
71 \\
-39
\end{array}
\quad
\left\{
\begin{array}{l}
(71 + 1) = 72; \ (39 + 1) = 40 \\
(72 - 40) = 32
\end{array}
\right.
$$

Add 1 to both numbers. Perform the subtraction, which is easier than the original problem.

(Notice that adding 1 to both numbers does not change the answer. Why?)

3. *Drop the zeros*

$$
\begin{array}{r}
8700 \\
- \ 500
\end{array}
\quad
\left\{
\begin{array}{l}
87 - 5 = 82 \\
82 \rightarrow 8200
\end{array}
\right.
$$

Notice that there are two zeros in each number. Drop these zeros and perform the computation. Then replace the two zeros to obtain proper place value.

Another mental mathematics technique for subtraction is called "adding up." This method is based on the *missing addend* approach and is sometimes referred to as the "cashier's algorithm." An example of the cashier's algorithm follows.

EXAMPLE 3-8   Noah owed $11 for his groceries. He used a $50 check to pay the bill. While handing Noah the change, the cashier said, "$11, $12, $13, $14, $15, $20, $30, $50." How much change did Noah receive?

SOLUTION   Table 3-12 shows what the cashier said and how much money Noah received each time. Since $11 plus $1 is $12, Noah must have received $1 when the cashier said $12. The same reasoning follows for $13, $14, and so on. Thus, the total amount of change that Noah received is given by $1 + $1 + $1 + $1 + $5 + $10 + $20 = $39. In other words, $50 − $11 = $39 because $39 + $11 = $50.

TABLE 3-12

What the cashier said	$11	$12	$13	$14	$15	$20	$30	$50
Amount of money Noah received each time	0	$1	$1	$1	$1	$5	$10	$20

Computational Estimation

According to the *Standards,* "An ongoing emphasis on estimation helps children develop insights into concepts and procedures, encourages flexibility in working with numbers, contributes to the development of problem-solving processes, and develops an awareness of whether results are reasonable." In this section we confine ourselves to *computational estimation*, which is the process of forming an approximate answer to a numerical problem. Computational estimation is useful in determining whether an answer is reasonable when the computation is done on a calculator.

Two computational estimation strategies, *rounding* and using *front-end* numbers, are demonstrated on page 149, which is a student page from *Addison-Wesley Mathematics*, 1989, Grade 8. Study this page to see how the techniques work, and then try the estimations on the bottom of the student page.

A summary of some of the common estimation strategies is given next.

1. *Front-end strategy*
   Suppose that we are to add the following column of figures. To obtain an estimate, we focus on the "front-end," or leftmost, digits, which are the most significant. Front-end estimation is a two-step process.

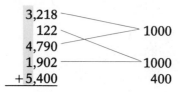

1. Find the total of the most important lead digits, and use place value.

   $$3 + 4 + 1 + 5 = 13$$

   Place value gives 13,000.
2. Adjust the estimate: 218 + 790 is about 1000; 122 + 902 is about 1000; plus 400, so about 2400.

Hence, an estimate would be 13,000 + 2400, or 15,400.

2. *Grouping to nice numbers strategy*
   The strategy used to obtain the adjustment in the preceding example is the *grouping to nice numbers* strategy, which means that numbers that "nicely" fit together are grouped. Another example is given here.

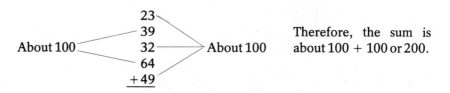

Therefore, the sum is about 100 + 100 or 200.

3. *Clustering strategy*
   Clustering is used when a group of numbers cluster around a common value. In the next example, the numbers seem to cluster around 6000.

   6200
   5842
   6512
   5521
   +6319

   1. Estimate the "average"—about 6000
   2. Multiply the "average" by the number of values.

      $$5 \cdot 6000 = 30,000$$

Although this strategy is limited to certain kinds of computations, it may be useful in many cases.

Estimating Sums and Differences

Oceans and seas cover over two-thirds of the earth's surface. Estimate the combined area of the Atlantic and Pacific oceans.

To estimate the total area you can **round** each number to the same place, then add.

$$
\begin{array}{rcl}
165,760,000 & \to & 170,000,000 \\
+\ 82,527,000 & \to & +\ 80,000,000 \\
\hline
\text{Estimate} & \to & 250,000,000
\end{array}
$$

The combined area of the Atlantic and Pacific oceans is about 250,000,000 square kilometers (km^2).

You can also use **front-end** numbers to estimate sums or differences.

Oceans

	Area (km^2)	Greatest depth (m)
Pacific	165,760,000	11,516
Atlantic	82,527,000	9,219
Indian	65,440,000	7,455
Arctic	14,090,000	5,025

Add the front-end digits.

$$
\begin{array}{r}
9,333 \\
1,157 \\
+\ 3,628 \\
\hline
13,000
\end{array}
$$

Look at the rest.

$$
\begin{array}{r}
333 \\
157 \\
+\ 628 \\
\hline
\end{array}
$$

About 1,000

Improve the estimate.

About 14,000

Subtract the front-end digits.

$$
\begin{array}{r}
11,516 \\
-\ 9,329 \\
\hline
2,000
\end{array}
$$

$11 - 9 = 2$

Look at the rest.

$$
\begin{array}{r}
516 \\
-\ 329 \\
\hline
\end{array}
$$

About 200

Improve the estimate.

About 2,200

Warm Up

Estimate each sum or difference by rounding to the nearest thousand.

1. $6,827 + 3,374$ **2.** $12,838 - 6,704$ **3.** $24,402 - 15,211$ **4.** $\$4,019 + \$2,845$

Estimate each sum or difference by using front-end estimation.

5.
$$
\begin{array}{r}
624 \\
198 \\
+\ 593 \\
\hline
\end{array}
$$

6.
$$
\begin{array}{r}
6,724 \\
-\ 2,349 \\
\hline
\end{array}
$$

7.
$$
\begin{array}{r}
9,843 \\
3,761 \\
+\ 4,508 \\
\hline
\end{array}
$$

8.
$$
\begin{array}{r}
47,069 \\
-\ 44,518 \\
\hline
\end{array}
$$

4. *Rounding strategy*

Rounding is a way of cleaning up numbers so that they are easier to handle. Rounding enables us to find approximate answers to calculations, as follows.

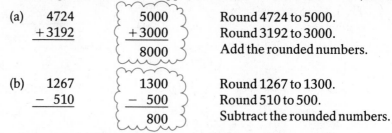

(a) 4724   5000   Round 4724 to 5000.
    +3192   +3000   Round 3192 to 3000.
                 8000   Add the rounded numbers.

(b) 1267   1300   Round 1267 to 1300.
    − 510   − 500   Round 510 to 500.
                  800   Subtract the rounded numbers.

Performing estimations requires a knowledge of place value and rounding skills. We illustrate a rounding procedure that can be generalized to all rounding situations. For example, suppose that we wish to round 4724 to the nearest thousand. We may proceed in four steps (see also Figure 3-27).

1. Determine which two consecutive thousands the number lies between.
2. Determine the midpoint between the thousands.
3. Determine which thousand the number is closer to, by observing whether it is greater than or less than the midpoint.
4. If the number to be rounded is greater than or equal to the midpoint, round the given number to the greater thousand; otherwise, round to the lesser thousand. In this case, we round 4724 to 5000.

FIGURE 3-27

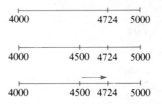

• R E M A R K

Not all texts use the same rule for rounding when a number falls at a midpoint.

Estimations are very useful when working with calculators. They can be used to determine if the answer obtained on the calculator is reasonable or not. For example, consider how estimations are used on the following student page from *Addison-Wesley Mathematics,* 1989, Grade 7.

Estimating Sums and Differences

Tim Griffin manages a large record store. On Friday the store sold 376 records. On Saturday, 519 records were sold. Tim uses a calculator to add the two numbers.

First try	Second try

Which sum seems more reasonable? We can make an **estimate** of the sum by rounding each addend to the nearest hundred.

376 + 519 $\quad$ 400 + 500 = 900
estimate

The estimate 900 is close to 895, so 895 seems more reasonable.

Estimates may vary because of the way the numbers are rounded.

Estimate the difference. 2,261 − 914

Round to the nearest thousand.

2,261 − 914   2,000 − 1,000 = 1,000
estimate

Round to the nearest hundred.

2,261 − 914   2,300 − 900 = 1,400
estimate

B R A I N   T E A S E R

The number on a license plate consists of five digits. When the license plate is looked at upside down, you can still read it, but the value of the upside down number is 78,633 greater than the real license number. What is the license number?

PROBLEM SET 3-4

1. Perform the following additions, using both the scratch and conventional algorithms. Use estimations to determine if your answers are reasonable.

   (a) 3789
       9296
     +6843

   (b) 3004
     + 987

   (c) 524
      328
      567
    +135

2. Explain why the scratch addition algorithm works.

3. An addition algorithm from an elementary school text follows. Explain why it works.

```
   2 | 7
  +6 | 8
   1 | 5
   8 |
   9 | 5
```

4. Find the missing numbers in each of the following.

   (a) _ _ 1
     + 4 2 _
     _ 4 0 2

   (b) _ 0 2 5
     1 1 _ 6
    +3 1 4 8
    6 _ 6 _

   (c) 1 _ 6 9
     2 _ 9 4
     9 5 4 6
     9 _ _ 3
    + 7 _ 6 4
    2 8 7 7 6

   (d) 2 _ 1
     4 5 _
    + _ 8 4
    1 3 2 6

5. Find the missing numbers in each of the following.

   (a) 8 7 6 9 3
     − _ _ _ _ _
     4 1 2 7 9

   (b) 8 1 3 5
     −4 6 8 2
     _ _ _ _

   (c) 3 _ _
     −1 5 9
     _ 2 4

   (d) 1 _ _ _ 6
     − 8 3 0 9
     4 9 8 7

6. Place the digits 7, 6, 8, 3, 5, and 2 in the boxes to obtain: (a) the greatest sum; (b) the least sum.

   □□□
   +□□□

7. Place the digits 7, 6, 8, 3, 5, and 2 in the boxes to obtain: (a) the greatest difference; (b) the least difference.

   □□□
   −□□□

8. At the beginning of the year, the library had 15,282 books. During fall quarter, 125 books were added; during winter quarter, 137 were added; and during spring quarter, 238 were added. How many books did the library have at the end of the school year?

9. Find the next three numbers in each of the sequences given below.
   (a) 9, 14, 19, 24, 29, _____, _____, _____
   (b) 97, 94, 91, 88, 85, _____, _____, _____

10. Maria goes into a store with 87¢. If she buys a granola bar for 25¢, a balloon for 15¢, and a comb for 17¢, how much money does she have left?

11. Tom's diet allows only 1500 calories per day. For breakfast, Tom had skim milk (90 calories), a waffle with no syrup (120 calories), and a banana (119 calories). For lunch, he had ½ cup of salad (185 calories) with mayonnaise (110 calories), tea (0 calories), and then he "blew it" with pecan pie (570 calories). Can he have dinner consisting of steak (250 calories), a salad with no mayonnaise, and tea?

12. With three girls on a large scale, the scale read 170 pounds. When Molly stepped off, the scale read 115 pounds. When Karly stepped off, leaving only Samantha, the scale read 65 pounds. What is the weight of each of the three girls?

13. Wally the waiter kept track of last week's money transactions. His salary was $150 plus $54 in overtime and $260 in tips. His transportation expenses were $22, his food expenses were $60, his laundry was $15, his entertainment expenditures amounted to $58, and he paid $185 in rent. Did he save any money last week? If so, how much?

14. If a package is 80 cm long, 60 cm wide, and 15 cm high and is wrapped as shown, what is the minimum amount of ribbon that can be used?

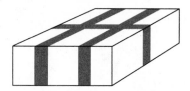

15. (a) Would the clustering strategy of estimation be a good one to use in each of the following cases? Why or why not?

   (i) 474
     1467
       64
    +2445

   (ii) 483
     475
     530
     503
    +528

   (b) Estimate each part of 15(a), using:
     (i) The front-end method.
     (ii) Grouping to nice numbers.
     (iii) Rounding.

16. Dana obtained the following results for boxes of Girl Scout cookies sold for the week. She estimated total sales at 400 boxes. Do you think her estimate is too high or too low? Why?

Monday	38
Tuesday	92
Wednesday	74
Thursday	17
Friday	130

★17. It has been reported that the Japanese mathematician Seki Kowa discovered the following magic circle over 300 years ago. Answer these questions about the circle.

(a) The sum of all the numbers on the innermost circle is 265. Find the sums of the numbers on each of the other circles. What do you notice?

(b) Add the ten numbers on each of the diameters shown, but do not include the number 1; for example, 21 + 20 + 19 + 18 + 17 + 36 + 35 + 34 + 33 + 32. What did you notice?

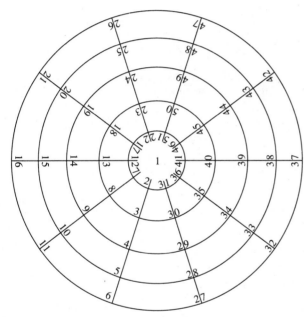

(c) In this magic circle, the numbers 1–51 were used. Complete a similar magic circle, using the numbers 1–21.

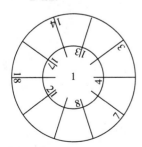

18. A palindrome is any number that reads the same backward and forward—for example, 121 and 2332. Try the following. Begin with any number. Is it a palindrome? If not, reverse the digits and add this new number to the original number. Is this a palindrome? If not, repeat the above procedure until a palindrome is obtained. For example, start with 78. Because 78 is not a palindrome, we add: 78 + 87 = 165. Because 165 is not a palindrome, we add: 165 + 561 = 726. Again, 726 is not a palindrome, so we add 726 + 627 to obtain 1353. Finally, 1353 + 3531 yields 4884, which is a palindrome.

(a) Try this method with the following numbers.
   (i) 93   (ii) 588   (iii) 2003

(b) Find a number for which the procedure described takes more than five steps to form a palindrome.

19. Given the following addition problem, replace nine digits with 0s so that the sum of the numbers is 1111.

```
 999
 777
 555
 333
 111
```

20. Arrange eight 8s so that the sum is 1000.

21. (a) Place the numbers 24 through 32 in the following circles so that the sums are the same in each direction.

(b) How many different numbers can be placed in the middle to obtain a solution?

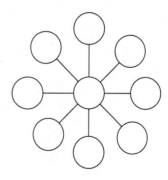

22. Andrew's calculator was not functioning properly. When he pressed ⑧ ⊕ ⑥ ⊜, the numeral 20 appeared on the display. When he pressed ⑤ ⊕ ④ ⊜, 13 was displayed. When he pressed ① ⑤ ⊖ ③ ⊜, 9 was displayed. What do you think Andrew's calculator was doing?

23. The following is a supermagic square taken from an engraving called *Melancholia* by Dürer (1514).

16	3	2	13
5	10	11	8
9	6	7	12
4	15	14	1

(a) Find the sum of each row, the sum of each column, and the sum of each diagonal.
(b) Find the sum of the four numbers in the center.
(c) Find the sum of the four numbers in each corner.
(d) Add 11 to each number in the square. Is the square still a magic square? Explain your answer.
(e) Subtract 11 from each number in the square. Is the square still a magic square?

Review Problems

24. Write 5280 in expanded form.
25. Give an example of the associative property of addition for whole numbers.
26. Illustrate 11 + 8 using a number-line model.
27. What is the value of $\overline{\text{MCDX}}$ in Hindu-Arabic numerals?
28. Rename the following using the distributive property of multiplication over addition.
   (a) $ax + a$ (b) $3(x + y) + a(x + y)$
29. Jim has 5 new shirts and 3 new pairs of pants. How many combinations of new shirts and pants does he have?

LABORATORY ACTIVITY

1. For each of the following, subtract the numbers in each row and column, as shown in Figure 3-28. Investigate why this works.

(a)

16	3	
8	1	

(b)

28	7	
15	12	

12	7	5
5	4	1
7	3	4

FIGURE 3-28

2. The Chinese abacus, *suan pan* (see Figure 3-29), is still in use today. A bar separates two sets of bead counters. Each counter above the bar represents five times the counter below the bar. Numbers are illustrated by moving the counter toward the bar. The number 7362 is pictured. Practice demonstrating numbers and adding on the *suan pan*.

FIGURE 3-29

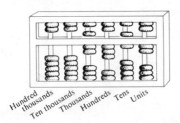

Hundred thousands | Ten thousands | Thousands | Hundreds | Tens | Units

Section 3-5 Algorithms for Whole-number Multiplication and Division

Multiplication Algorithms

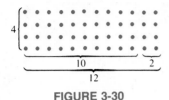

FIGURE 3-30

To aid in developing algorithms for multiplying multidigit whole numbers, we use the strategy of examining simpler computations first. Consider $4 \cdot 12$. This computation could be pictured as in Figure 3-30—that is, as 4 rows of 12 dots, or 48 dots.

The dots in Figure 3-30 can also be partitioned to show that $4 \cdot 12 = 4 \cdot (10 + 2) = 4 \cdot 10 + 4 \cdot 2$. The numbers $4 \cdot 10$ and $4 \cdot 2$ are *partial products*. Since $4 \cdot 2 = 8$ and $4 \cdot 10 = 40$, we have $4 \cdot 10 + 4 \cdot 2 = 40 + 8 = 48$. Thus, $4 \cdot 12 = 48$.

Figure 3-30 illustrates the distributive property of multiplication over addition on the set of whole numbers. The process leading to an algorithm for multiplying $4 \cdot 12$ is as follows.

Tens	Ones
1	2
×	4

$$
\begin{array}{r} 10 + 2 \\ \times \qquad 4 \\ \hline 40 + 8 \end{array}
\longrightarrow
\begin{array}{r} 12 \\ \times\ 4 \\ \hline 8 \\ 40 \\ \hline 48 \end{array}
\longrightarrow
\begin{array}{r} 12 \\ \times\ 4 \\ \hline 48 \end{array}
$$

To compute products involving powers of 10, such as $3 \cdot 200$, we proceed as follows.

$$
\begin{aligned}
3 \cdot 200 &= 3 \cdot (2 \cdot 10^2) \\
&= (3 \cdot 2) \cdot 10^2 \\
&= 6 \cdot 10^2 \\
&= 6 \cdot 10^2 + 0 \cdot 10^1 + 0 \cdot 1 \\
&= 600
\end{aligned}
$$

We see that $6 \cdot 10^2 = 600$; that is, multiplication of 6 by 10^2 resulted in annexing two zeros to 6. This idea can be generalized to the statement that *multiplication of any natural number by 10^n, where n is a natural number, results in annexing n zeros to the number.*

When multiplying powers of 10, an extension of the definition of exponents is used. For example, $10^2 \cdot 10^1 = (10 \cdot 10) \cdot 10 = 10^3$. Observe that $10^3 = 10^{2+1}$. In general, where a is a natural number and m and n are whole numbers, $a^m \cdot a^n$ is given by the following.

$$
a^m \cdot a^n = \underbrace{(a \cdot a \cdot a \cdots a)}_{m \text{ factors}} \cdot \underbrace{(a \cdot a \cdot a \cdots a)}_{n \text{ factors}}
$$

$$
= \underbrace{a \cdot a \cdot a \cdots a}_{m + n \text{ factors}} = a^{m+n}
$$

Consequently, $a^m \cdot a^n = a^{m+n}$.

EXAMPLE 3-9 Find each of the following products.

(a) $10^5 \cdot 36$ (b) $10^3 \cdot 279$ (c) $10^{13} \cdot 10^8$ (d) $7 \cdot 200$

SOLUTION (a) $10^5 \cdot 36 = 3,600,000$
(b) $10^3 \cdot 279 = 279,000$
(c) $10^{13} \cdot 10^8 = 10^{13+8} = 10^{21}$
(d) $7 \cdot 200 = 7 \cdot (2 \cdot 10^2) = (7 \cdot 2) \cdot 10^2 = 14 \cdot 10^2 = 1400$

Next we consider computations with two-digit factors, such as $14 \cdot 23$. One possibility is to use the distributive property of multiplication over addition to write out all the partial products and add, as shown.

$$
\begin{array}{r}
14 \\
\times 23 \\
\hline
12 \\
30 \\
80 \\
+200 \\
\hline
322
\end{array}
\quad
\begin{array}{l}
(3 \times 4) \\
(3 \times 10) \\
(20 \times 4) \\
(20 \times 10)
\end{array}
$$

Another approach is to write 14 as $10 + 4$ and use the distributive property of multiplication over addition, as follows.

$$
\begin{aligned}
14 \cdot 23 &= (10 + 4) \cdot 23 \\
&= 10 \cdot 23 + 4 \cdot 23 \\
&= 230 + 92
\end{aligned}
$$

This last approach leads to an algorithm for multiplication.

$$
\begin{array}{r}
23 \\
\times 14 \\
\hline
92 \\
230 \\
\hline
322
\end{array}
\quad
\begin{array}{l}
10 + 4 \\
(4 \cdot 23) \\
(10 \cdot 23)
\end{array}
\quad \text{or} \quad
\begin{array}{r}
23 \\
\times 14 \\
\hline
92 \\
23 \\
\hline
322
\end{array}
$$

We are accustomed to seeing the partial product 230 written without the zero, as 23. The placement of 23 with 3 in the tens column obviates having to write the 0 in the units column. When children first learn multiplication algorithms, however, they should be encouraged to include the zero, in order to avoid errors and promote better understanding. Children should also be encouraged to estimate whether their answers are reasonable. In this exercise, we know that the answer must be between $10 \cdot 20 = 200$ and $20 \cdot 30 = 600$ because $10 < 14 < 20$ and $20 < 23 < 30$. Because 322 is between 200 and 600, the answer is reasonable.

Lattice Multiplication

lattice multiplication An algorithm called **lattice multiplication** for multiplying 14 and 23 follows. (Determining the reasons why lattice multiplication works is left as an exercise.)

This computation is $4 \cdot 3$. The tens go above the diagonal and the units below. Continue this procedure for all the blocks.

Once the multiplication is complete, add along the diagonals. It is necessary in this example to "carry" 1 to the hundreds diagonal.

Mental Multiplication

As in cases involving addition and subtraction, mental mathematics is useful in doing multiplication. Several examples are given next.

1. *Front-end multiplying*

$$\begin{array}{r} 64 \\ \times\ 5 \\ \hline \end{array} \qquad \begin{array}{l} 60 \times 5 = 300 \\ 4 \times 5 = 20 \\ 300 + 20 = 320 \end{array}$$

Multiply the number of tens in the first number by 5.
Multiply the number of units in the first number by 5.
Add the two products.

2. *Compatible number multiplication*

$2 \times 9 \times 5 \times 20 \times 5$ Rearrange as $9 \times (2 \times 5) \times (20 \times 5) = 9 \times 10 \times 100 = 9000$

3. *Thinking money*

(a) $\begin{array}{r} 64 \\ \times\ 5 \\ \hline \end{array}$ Think of the product as 64 nickels, which can be thought of 32 dimes, which is $32 \times 10 = 320$ cents.

(b) $\begin{array}{r} 64 \\ \times 50 \\ \hline \end{array}$ Think of the product as 64 half-dollars, which is 32 dollars, or 3200 cents.

(c) $\begin{array}{r} 64 \\ \times 25 \\ \hline \end{array}$ Think of the product as 64 quarters, which is 32 half-dollars, or 16 dollars. Thus, we have 1600 cents.

Division Algorithms

Algorithms for division can be developed by using repeated subtraction. Consider the following:

A shopkeeper is packaging juice in cartons that hold 6 bottles each. She has 726 bottles. How many cartons does she need?

We might reason that if 1 carton holds 6 bottles, then 10 cartons hold 60 bottles and 100 cartons hold 600 bottles. If 100 cartons are filled, there are $726 - 100 \cdot 6$, or 126, bottles remaining. If 10 more cartons are filled, then $126 - 10 \cdot 6$, or 66, bottles remain. Similarly, if 10 more cartons are filled, $66 - 10 \cdot 6$, or 6, bottles remain. Finally, 1 carton will hold the remaining 6 bottles. The total number of cartons necessary is $100 + 10 + 10 + 1$, or 121. This procedure is summarized in Figure 3-31(a). A more efficient way to determine the number of cartons is shown in Figure 3-31(b).

FIGURE 3-31

(a)
```
6)726
-600     100 sixes
 126
 -60      10 sixes
  66
 -60      10 sixes
   6
  -6       1 six
   0     121 sixes
```

(b)
```
6)726
-600     100 sixes
 126
-120      20 sixes
   6
  -6       1 six
   0     121 sixes
```

Divisions such as the one in Figure 3-31 are usually shown in elementary school texts in the most efficient form, as in Figure 3-32(b), in which the numbers in color in Figure 3-32(a) are omitted. The technique used in Figure 3-32(a) is often called "scaffolding" and may be used as a preliminary step to Figure 3-32(b).

FIGURE 3-32

(a)
```
      121
        1
       20
      100
   6)726
   -600
    126
   -120
      6
     -6
      0
```

(b)
```
    121
 6)726
   -6
   12
  -12
    6
   -6
    0
```

Base-ten blocks can also be used to model division. This is done by *partitioning* the number of blocks in the dividend into groups. Consider the operation $36 \div 2$, as demonstrated on the student page from *Addison-Wesley Mathematics*, 1989, Grade 3.

2-Digit Quotients

Dan has 36 blocks. He wants to put them in 2 equal sets. How many should he put in each set?

Since we want to know how many in each set, we divide.

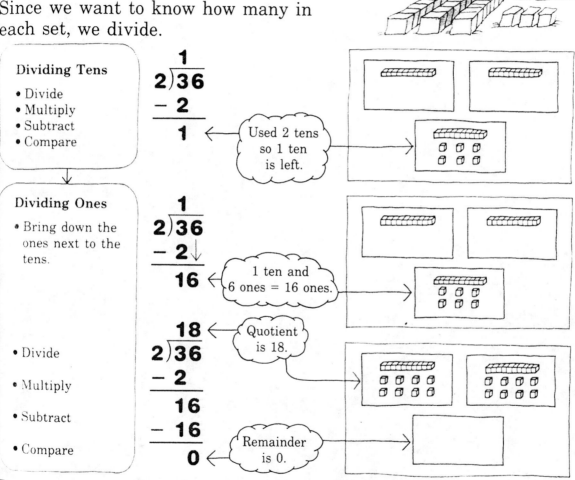

Dividing Tens
- Divide
- Multiply
- Subtract
- Compare

$$\begin{array}{r} 1 \\ 2\overline{)36} \\ -2 \\ \hline 1 \end{array}$$

Used 2 tens so 1 ten is left.

Dividing Ones
- Bring down the ones next to the tens.

$$\begin{array}{r} 1 \\ 2\overline{)36} \\ -2\downarrow \\ \hline 16 \end{array}$$

1 ten and 6 ones = 16 ones.

- Divide
- Multiply
- Subtract
- Compare

$$\begin{array}{r} 18 \\ 2\overline{)36} \\ -2 \\ \hline 16 \\ -16 \\ \hline 0 \end{array}$$

Quotient is 18.

Remainder is 0.

Dan should put 18 blocks in each set.

2-Digit Quotients

Dan has 36 blocks. He wants to put them in 2 equal sets. How many should he put in each set?

Since we want to know how many in each set, we divide.

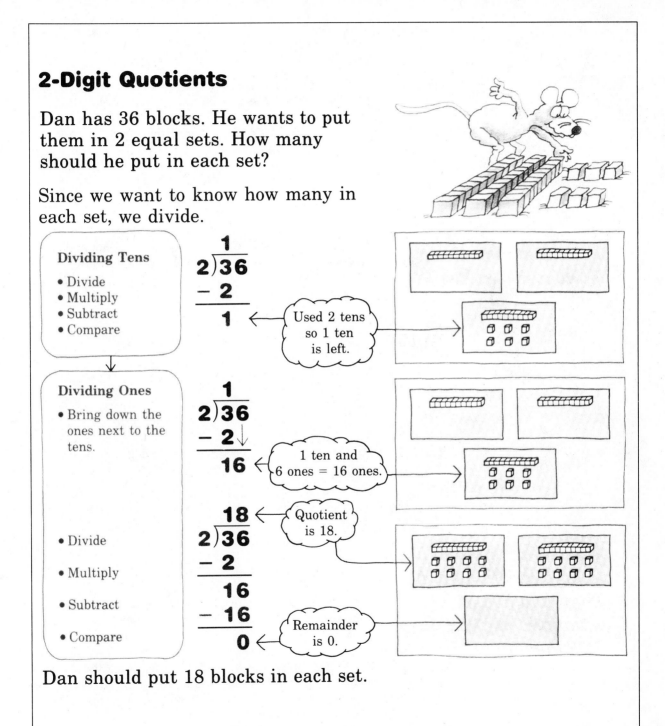

Dividing Tens

- Divide
- Multiply
- Subtract
- Compare

$$2\overline{)36}$$

Used 2 tens so 1 ten is left.

Dividing Ones

- Bring down the ones next to the tens.

1 ten and 6 ones = 16 ones.

- Divide
- Multiply
- Subtract
- Compare

Quotient is 18.

Remainder is 0.

Dan should put 18 blocks in each set.

An example of division by a divisor of more than one digit is given next.

1. Estimate the quotient in $32\overline{)2618}$. Because $1 \cdot 32 = 32$, $10 \cdot 32 = 320$, $100 \cdot 32 = 3200$, we see that the quotient is between 10 and 100.
2. Find the number of tens in the quotient. Because $26 \div 3$ is approximately 8, then 26 hundreds divided by 3 tens is approximately 8 tens. We then write the 8 in the tens place, as shown.

$$
\begin{array}{r}
80 \\
32\overline{)2618} \\
-2560 \quad (32 \cdot 80) \\
\hline
58
\end{array}
$$

3. Find the number of units in the quotient. Because $5 \div 3$ is approximately 1, then 5 tens divided by 3 tens is approximately 1. We have the following.

$$
\begin{array}{r}
81 \\
1 \\
80 \\
32\overline{)2618} \\
-2560 \\
\hline
58 \\
-32 \quad (32 \cdot 1) \\
\hline
26
\end{array}
$$

4. Check: $32 \cdot 81 + 26 = 2618$.

Normally, in grade-school books we see the following format, with the remainder written by the quotient:

$$
\begin{array}{r}
81 \text{ R26} \\
32\overline{)2618} \\
-256 \\
\hline
58 \\
-32 \\
\hline
26
\end{array}
$$

Because of the advent of calculators, many mathematics educators are suggesting that division by divisors of more than two digits should not be taught. What do you think?

The process just described is usually referred to as "long" division. Another technique, called "short" division, can be used when the divisor is a one-digit number and most of the work is done mentally. An example of short division is given on the student page below from *Addison-Wesley Mathematics*, 1989, Grade 6.

Short Division

A company paid \$2,850 for 6 minutes of prime time advertising on radio. How much did the company pay per minute?

Since we want to separate the total into equal amounts, we divide.

Decide where to start.	Divide the hundreds. Write the remainder by the tens.	Divide the tens. Write the remainder by the ones.	Divide the ones.

$$\begin{array}{r} 4 \\ 6{\overline{\smash{\big)}\,2{,}8\,5\,0}} \end{array}$$

Not enough thousands 6 < 28 Divide the hundreds.

$$\begin{array}{r} 4 \\ 6{\overline{\smash{\big)}\,2{,}8\,^45\,0}} \end{array}$$

28 ÷ 6 = 4, R4

$$\begin{array}{r} 4\,7 \\ 6{\overline{\smash{\big)}\,2{,}8\,^45\,^30}} \end{array}$$

45 ÷ 6 = 7, R3

$$\begin{array}{r} 4\,7\,5 \\ 6{\overline{\smash{\big)}\,2{,}8\,^45\,^30}} \end{array}$$

30 ÷ 6 = 5, R0

The company paid \$475 per minute for the advertising.

Mental Division

1. *Breaking up the dividend*

$7\overline{)4256}$ $7\overline{)42|56}$ Break up the dividend into parts.

$\phantom{7\overline{)4200}}600 + 8$
$7\overline{)4200 + 56}$ Divide both parts by 7.

$600 + 8 = 608$ Add the answers together.

2. *Compatible numbers in division*

   (a) $3\overline{)105}$ $105 = 90 + 15$ Look for numbers that you recognize as divisible by 3 and having a sum of 105.

   $\phantom{3\overline{)90}}30 + 5 = 35$
   $3\overline{)90 + 15}$ Divide both parts and add the answers.

   (b) $8\overline{)232}$ $232 = 240 - 8$ Look for numbers that are easily divisible by 8 and whose difference is 232.

   $\phantom{8\overline{)240}}30 - 1 = 29$
   $8\overline{)240 - 8}$ Divide both parts and take the difference.

Multiplication and Division Estimation

Examples of estimation strategies for multiplication and division are given next.

1. *Front-end estimation*

   $\begin{array}{r} 524 \\ \times\ \ 8 \end{array}$ 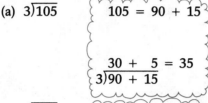 $500 \times 8 = 4000$ Start multiplying at the front to obtain a first estimate.

   $20 \times 8 = 160$ Multiply 8 times the next important digit.

   $4000 + 160 = 4160$ Adjust the first estimate by adding the two numbers.

2. *Compatible numbers*

   $5\overline{)4163}$ $5\overline{)4000}$ Change 4163 to a number close to it that you know is divisible by 5.

   $\phantom{5\overline{)4000}}800$
   $5\overline{)4000}$ Carry out the division and obtain the first estimate of 800. Various techniques can be used to adjust the first estimate.

PROBLEM SET 3-5

1. Perform the following multiplications, using both the conventional and the lattice multiplication algorithms.

   (a)   728
      × 94

   (b)   306
      × 24

2. Explain why the lattice multiplication algorithm works.

3. Fill in the missing numbers in each of the following.

   (a)   4_6
      ×783
      ────
      1_78
      3408
      _982
      ─────
      3335_8

   (b)   327
      ×9_1
      ────
      327
      1_08
      _9_3
      ──────
      30__07

4. The following chart gives average water usage for one person for one day.

Use	Average Amount
Taking bath	110 L (liters)
Taking shower	75 L
Flushing toilet	22 L
Washing hands, face	7 L
Getting a drink	1 L
Brushing teeth	1 L
Doing dishes (one meal)	30 L
Cooking (one meal)	18 L

   (a) Use the chart to calculate how much water you use each day.
   (b) The average American uses approximately 200 L of water per day. Are you average?
   (c) If there are 215,000,000 people in the United States, approximately how much water is used in the United States per day?

5. Simplify each of the following, using properties of exponents. Leave answers as powers.

   (a) $5^7 \cdot 5^{12}$
   (b) $6^{10} \cdot 6^2 \cdot 6^3$
   (c) $10^{296} \cdot 10^{17}$
   (d) $2^7 \cdot 10^5 \cdot 5^7$

6. (a) Which is greater, $2^{80} + 2^{80}$ or 2^{100}? Why?
   (b) Which is the greatest, 2^{101}, $3 \cdot 2^{100}$, or 2^{102}?

7. How many seconds are in a day? A week? A year?

8. The given model illustrates that $23 \cdot 14 = (20 + 3) \cdot (10 + 4)$ or $20 \cdot 10 + 20 \cdot 4 + 3 \cdot 10 + 3 \cdot 4$.
   Draw similar models illustrating each of the following.

   (a) $6 \cdot 23$ (b) $18 \cdot 25$

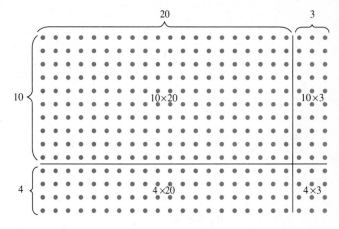

9. Consider the following.

   $$\begin{array}{r} 476 \\ \times 293 \\ \hline 952 \\ 4284 \\ 1428 \\ \hline 139468 \end{array}$$

952	$(2 \cdot 476)$
4284	$(9 \cdot 476)$
1428	$(3 \cdot 476)$

   (a) Show, by using the conventional algorithm, that the answer is correct.
   (b) Explain why the algorithm works.
   (c) Try the method to multiply 84×363.

10. The Russian peasant algorithm for multiplying 27×68 follows. (Disregard remainders when halving.)

Halves		Doubles	
	⟶ 27 ×	⑥⑧	
Halve 27 ⟶	13	⟨136⟩	Double 68.
Halve 13	6	272	Double 136.
Halve 6 ⟶	3	⟨544⟩	Double 272.
Halve 3 ⟶	1	⟨1088⟩	Double 544.

    In the "Halves" column, choose the odd numbers. In the "Doubles" column, circle the numbers paired with the odds from the "Halves" column. Add the circled numbers.

    ```
      68
     136
     544
    1088
    ────
    1836   This is the product 27 · 68.
    ```

    Try this algorithm for $17 \cdot 63$ and other numbers.

11. Find the two-digit number that, when added to its reverse, is closest to each of the following (for example, $12 + 21 = 33$).
    (a) 50   (b) 100

12. Find the greatest possible whole-number value of n such that
    (a) $14n < 300$ (b) $21n \leq 7459$
    (c) $7n \leq 2134$ (d) $483n < 79485$

13. Find the least possible whole number such that
    (a) $14n > 300$ (b) $23n \geq 4369$
    (c) $123n > 782$ (d) $222n > 8654$

14. Use the distributive property of multiplication over addition or subtraction to compute mentally each of the following.
    (a) $15 \cdot 12$ (b) $14 \cdot 102$ (c) $30 \cdot 99$

15. Compute $6 \cdot 411$, showing the mathematical justification for each step.

16. Complete the following table.

a	b	$a \cdot b$	$a + b$
	56	3752	
32			110
		270	33

17. Answer the following questions based on the activity chart given next.

Activity	Calories Burned per Hour
Playing tennis	462
Snowshoeing	708
Cross-country skiing	444
Playing volleyball	198

    (a) How many calories are burned during 3 hours of cross-country skiing?
    (b) Jane played tennis for 2 hours while Carolyn played volleyball for 3 hours. Who burned more calories, and how many more?
    (c) Lyle went snowshoeing for 3 hours and Maurice went cross-country skiing for 5 hours. Who burned more calories, and how many more?

18. On a 14-day vacation, Glenn increased his caloric intake by 1500 calories per day. He also worked out more than usual by swimming 2 hours a day. Swimming burns 666 calories per hour, and a net gain of 3500 calories adds 1 pound of weight. Did Glenn gain at least 1 pound during his vacation?

19. Sue purchased a $30,000 life-insurance policy at the price of $24 for each $1000 of coverage. If she pays the premium in 12 monthly installments, how much is each installment?

20. I am thinking of a number. If I multiply it by 2, subtract 3, and add 11, I get 18. What is my number?

21. There are five containers of apples. Each container holds 36 apples. Jim reported that 23 apples were damaged. How many apples were not damaged?

22. Perform each of the following divisions, using both the repeated-subtraction and familiar algorithms.
    (a) $8\overline{)623}$ (b) $36\overline{)298}$ (c) $391\overline{)4001}$

23. Place the digits 7, 6, 8, and 3 in the boxes to obtain:
    (a) the greatest quotient; (b) the least quotient.

    □)□□□

24. Rudy is buying a new car that costs $8600. The car salesman said that Rudy could pay cash or pay $1500 down and $450 a month for 2 years.
    (a) Which option is more expensive?
    (b) How much more expensive?

25. Jill's book is 668 pages long. She has read 324 pages. If she reads 32 pages a day, how long will it take her to finish the book?

26. A 1K computer memory chip can store 1024 bits of information. How many bits of information can be stored in a 64K chip?

27. Using a calculator, Ralph multiplied by 10 when he should have divided by 10. The display read 300. What should the correct answer be?

28. Twenty members of the band plan to attend a festival. The band members washed 245 cars at $2 per car to help cover expenses. The school will match every dollar that the band raises with a dollar from the school budget. The cost of renting the bus to take the band is 72¢ per mile and the round trip is 350 miles. The band members can stay in the dorm for 2 nights at $5 per person per night. Meals for the trip will cost $28 per person. Has the band raised enough money yet? If not, how many more cars do they have to wash?

29. The following figure shows four function machines. The output from one machine becomes the input for the one below it. Complete the accompanying chart.

Input	Output
2	11
4	
0	
	19
	31

Choose three different digits.
(a) Form six different two-digit numbers from the numbers you chose. Each number can be used only once.
(b) Add the six numbers.
(c) Add the three digits you chose.
(d) Divide the answer in (b) by the answer in (c).
(e) Repeat (a)–(d) with three different numbers.
(f) Is the final result always the same? Why?

31. Consider the following multiplications. Notice that when the digits in the factors are reversed, the products are the same.

$$
\begin{array}{cc}
36 & 63 \\
\times 42 & \times 24 \\
\hline
1512 & 1512
\end{array}
$$

(a) Find other multiplications where this procedure works.
(b) Find a pattern for the numbers that work in this way.

32. In a certain book, 2981 digits were used to print the page numbers. How many pages are in the book?

33. Place the digits 7, 6, 8, and 3 in the boxes to obtain: (a) the greatest product; (b) the least product.

34. Place the digits 7, 6, 8, 3, and 2 in the boxes to obtain: (a) the greatest product; (b) the least product.

35. If a cow produces 700 pounds of hamburger and there are 4 Quarter Pounders to a pound, how many cows would it take to produce 21 billion Quarter Pounders?

36. Use a calculator to find the missing numbers.

(a)
$$
\begin{array}{r}
37 \\
\times 43 \\
\hline
\_\_\_ \\
\_\_\_\_ \\
\hline
\_591
\end{array}
$$

(b)
$$
\begin{array}{r}
\_\_ \\
\times 36 \\
\hline
558 \\
2790 \\
\hline
\_\_\_\_
\end{array}
$$

(c)
$$
\begin{array}{r}
\overline{)123} \\
-9 \\
\hline
33 \\
-27 \\
\hline
6
\end{array}
$$

37. Find the products of the following, and describe the pattern that emerges.

(a)   1 × 1
        11 × 11
        111 × 111
        1111 × 1111

(b)   99 × 99
        999 × 999
        9999 × 9999

38. Suppose that a person can spend $1 per second. How much can that person spend in a minute? An hour? A day? A week? A month? A year? Twenty years?

39. Suppose that a friend chooses a number between 250,000 and 1,000,000. What is the least number of questions you must ask in order to guess the number if the friend answers only "yes" or "no" to the questions?

Review Problems

40. Write the number succeeding 673 in Egyptian numerals.

41. Write $3 \cdot 10^5 + 2 \cdot 10^2 + 6 \cdot 10$ as a Hindu-Arabic numeral.

42. Illustrate the identity property of addition for whole numbers.

43. Rename each of the following, using the distributive property of multiplication over addition.
(a) $ax + bx + 2x$
(b) $3(a + b) + x(a + b)$

44. At the beginning of a trip, the odometer registered 52,281. At the end of the trip, the odometer registered 59,260. How many miles were traveled on this trip?

45. The registration for the computer conference was 192 people on Thursday, 215 on Friday, and 317 on Saturday. What was the total registration?

B R A I N   T E A S E R

For each of the following, replace the letters with digits in such a way that the computation is correct. Each letter may represent only one digit.

$$
\begin{array}{r}
\text{LYNDON} \\
\times B \\
\hline
\text{JOHNSON}
\end{array}
$$

LABORATORY ACTIVITY

Finger multiplication has long been popular in many parts of the world. Multiplication of single digits by 9 is very simple using the following steps.
1. Place your hands next to each other as shown.

Second finger bent

2. To multiply 2 by 9, bend down the second finger from the left. The remaining fingers show the product.
3. Similarly, to multiply 3 by 9, bend down the third finger from the left. The remaining fingers will show the product $3 \times 9 = 27$. Try this procedure with other multiplications by 9.

*Section 3-6   Other Number Bases

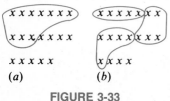

FIGURE 3-33

The Babylonian numeration system was based on 60 and the digital computer is based on 2, while the Hindu-Arabic system is based on 10. Mathematical historians believe that one reason the majority of the world uses the base-ten system, with the ten digits 0 through 9, is that most people have ten fingers. When you count with two hands and reach the last finger, you begin using two-digit numbers. Suppose you can use only one hand and the digits available for counting are 0, 1, 2, 3, and 4. In the "one-hand system," you count 1, 2, 3, 4, 10, where 10 represents one hand and no fingers. The one-hand system is a base-five system. Counting is in groups of five rather than in groups of ten. In Figure 3-33(a), x's are grouped into tens, and in Figure 3-33(b), they are grouped into fives. In Figure 3-33(a), the grouping shows 1 set of ten x's and 9 other x's. This is written as 19_{ten}, or just 19. *When the number base is not indicated, it is understood to be base ten.*

Figure 3-33(b) shows 3 groups of five x's and 4 other x's. This is written as 34_{five}. Thus, $19_{ten} = 34_{five}$. We write the small "five" below the numeral as a reminder that the number is written in base five. Counting in base five proceeds as shown in Figure 3-34.

What number follows 44_{five}? There are no more two-digit numbers in the system after 44_{five}. In base ten, the same situation occurs at 99. We use 100 to represent ten tens or one hundred. In the base-five system, we need a symbol to represent five fives. To continue the analogy with base ten, we use 100_{five} to represent 1 group of five fives, 0 groups of five, and 0 units. To distinguish from "one hundred" in base ten, the name for 100_{five} is "one-zero-zero base five." The number 100_{ten} means $(1 \cdot 10^2 + 0 \cdot 10^1 + 0)_{ten}$, whereas the number 100_{five} means $(1 \cdot 10^2 + 0 \cdot 10^1 + 0)_{five}$, or $(1 \cdot 5^2 + 0 \cdot 5^1 + 0)_{ten}$ or 25.

FIGURE 3-34

Base-Five Symbol	Base-Five Grouping	One-Hand System
0_{five}		0 fingers
1_{five}	x	1 finger
2_{five}	xx	2 fingers
3_{five}	xxx	3 fingers
4_{five}	xxxx	4 fingers
10_{five}	(xxxxx)	1 hand and 0 fingers
11_{five}	(xxxxx) x	1 hand and 1 finger
12_{five}	(xxxxx) xx	1 hand and 2 fingers
13_{five}	(xxxxx) xxx	1 hand and 3 fingers
14_{five}	(xxxxx) xxxx	1 hand and 4 fingers
20_{five}	(xxxxx) (xxxxx)	2 hands and 0 fingers
21_{five}	(xxxxx) (xxxxx) x	2 hands and 1 finger

EXAMPLE 3-10 Convert 11244_{five} to base ten.

SOLUTION
$$\begin{aligned}
11244_{five} &= 1 \cdot 5^4 + 1 \cdot 5^3 + 2 \cdot 5^2 + 4 \cdot 5 + 4 \cdot 1 \\
&= 1 \cdot 625 + 1 \cdot 125 + 2 \cdot 25 + 4 \cdot 5 + 4 \cdot 1 \\
&= 625 + 125 + 50 + 20 + 4 \\
&= 824
\end{aligned}$$

Example 3-10 also suggests a method for changing a base-ten number to a base-five number. Notice that the conversion involves powers of five. To convert 824 to base five, we divide by the successive powers of five: 5^1, or 5; 5^2, or 25; 5^3, or 125; 5^4, or 625; 5^5, or 3125; and so on. For example, the greatest power of 5 contained in 824 is 5^4, or 625. There is $1 \cdot 5^4$, with 199 left over. Thus,

$$824 = 1 \cdot 5^4 + 199$$

The greatest power of 5 contained in 199 is 5^3. There is $1 \cdot 5^3$, with 74 left over, in 199. Thus,

$$824 = 1 \cdot 5^4 + 1 \cdot 5^3 + 74$$

The greatest power of 5 contained in 74 is 5^2. There are $2 \cdot 5^2$, with 24 left over, in 74.

$$824 = 1 \cdot 5^4 + 1 \cdot 5^3 + 2 \cdot 5^2 + 24$$

Finally, the greatest power of 5 in 24 is 5^1. There are $4 \cdot 5^1$, with 4 left, in 24, and there are 4 ones in 4. Thus,

$$824 = 1 \cdot 5^4 + 1 \cdot 5^3 + 2 \cdot 5^2 + 4 \cdot 5 + 4 = 11244_{\text{five}}$$

Thus, changing from base ten to base five can be accomplished by dividing by successive powers of five. A shorthand method for illustrating this conversion follows.

625	824	1	How many groups of 625 in 824?
	-625		
125	199	1	How many groups of 125 in 199?
	-125		
25	74	2	How many groups of 25 in 74?
	-50		
5	24	4	How many groups of 5 in 24?
	-20		
1	4	4	How many 1s in 4?
	-4		
	0		

Thus, $824 = 11244_{\text{five}}$.

A different method of converting 824 to base five is shown next. This method uses successive divisions by 5. The quotient in each case is placed below the dividend and the remainder is placed on the right-hand side, on the same line with the quotient. Study this method and compare it to the method given before. Why does it work?

5	824	
	164	4
	32	4
	6	2
	1	1

The answer is read from bottom to top—that is, as 11244_{five}.

Historians tell of early tribes that used base two. Some Australian tribes still count "one, two, two and one, two twos, two twos and one, ..." *binary system* Because base two has only two digits, it is called the **binary system.** Base two is especially important because of its use in computers. One of the two digits may be represented by the presence of an electrical signal and the other by the absence of an electrical signal. Although base two works well for computers, it is inefficient for everyday use because multidigit numbers are reached very rapidly in counting in this system.

Conversions from base two to base ten, and vice versa, may be accomplished in a manner similar to that used for base-five conversions.

EXAMPLE 3-11 (a) Convert 10111_{two} to base ten.
(b) Convert 27 to base two.

SOLUTION (a) $10111_{two} = 1 \cdot 2^4 + 0 \cdot 2^3 + 1 \cdot 2^2 + 1 \cdot 2^1 + 1$
$$= 16 + 0 + 4 + 2 + 1$$
$$= 23$$

(b)

| 16 | 27 | 1 | How many groups of 16 in 27? |

-16

| 8 | 11 | 1 | How many groups of 8 in 11? |

-8

| 4 | 3 | 0 | How many groups of 4 in 3? |

-0

| 2 | 3 | 1 | How many groups of 2 in 3? |

-2

| 1 | 1 | 1 | How many 1s in 1? |

-1

0

ALTERNATE SOLUTION

2	27	
2	13	1
2	6	1
2	3	0
	1	1

Reading from the bottom, the answer is 11011_{two}.
Thus, 27 is equivalent to 11011_{two}.

Another commonly used number base system is the base-twelve, or duodecimal, system, known popularly as the "dozens" system. Eggs are bought by the dozens, and pencils are bought by the gross (a dozen dozens). In base twelve, there are twelve digits, just as there are ten digits in base ten, five digits in base five, and two digits in base two. In base twelve, new symbols are needed to represent the following groups of x's.

$$
\overbrace{x\,x\,x\,x\,x\,x\,x\,x\,x\,x}^{10\ x's}\quad\text{and}\quad\overbrace{x\,x\,x\,x\,x\,x\,x\,x\,x\,x\,x}^{11\ x's}
$$

The new symbols chosen are T and E, respectively, so that the base-twelve digits are 0, 1, 2, 3, 4, 5, 6, 7, 8, 9, T, E. Thus, in base twelve you count "1, 2, 3, 4, 5, 6, 7, 8, 9, T, E, 10, 11, 12, . . . , 17, 18, 19, $1T$, $1E$, 20, 21, 22, . . . , 28, 29, $2T$, $2E$, 30, ..." Notice that T_{twelve} is another way of writing 10_{ten} and E_{twelve} is another way of writing 11_{ten}. Also, $10_{\text{twelve}} = 12_{\text{ten}}$.

EXAMPLE 3-12   (a) Convert $E2T_{\text{twelve}}$ to base ten.   (b) Convert 1277 to base twelve.

SOLUTION   (a) $E2T_{\text{twelve}} = 11 \cdot 12^2 + 2 \cdot 12^1 + 10$
$\qquad\qquad\qquad = 11 \cdot 144 + 24 + 10$
$\qquad\qquad\qquad = 1584 + 24 + 10$
$\qquad\qquad\qquad = 1618$

(b)

| 144 | 1277 | 8 | How many groups of 144 in 1277?

$\qquad\qquad -1152$

| 12 | 125 | T | How many groups of 12 in 125?

$\qquad\qquad -120$

| 1 | 5 | 5 | How many 1s in 5?

$\qquad\qquad\ -5$
$\qquad\qquad\ \ \ 0$

Thus, $1277 = 8T5_{\text{twelve}}$.

Addition and Subtraction in Different Bases

One reason for studying computations in different number bases is to enhance our understanding of base-ten computations. Recall that, before studying algorithms in base ten, you had to assume a knowledge of the basic addition and multiplication facts. The same is true for other bases.

Using a number line such as the one pictured in Figure 3-35, which illustrates $4_{\text{five}} + 3_{\text{five}} = 12_{\text{five}}$, we could construct the base-five addition table shown in Table 3-13.

FIGURE 3-35

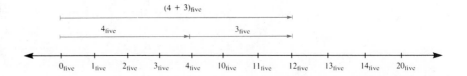

TABLE 3-13
Addition Table
(Base Five)

+	0	1	2	3	4
0	0	1	2	3	4
1	1	2	3	4	10
2	2	3	4	10	11
3	3	4	10	11	12
4	4	10	11	12	13

Using the addition facts in Table 3-13, we can begin to develop algorithms for base-five addition similar to those for base-ten addition. Concrete teaching aids, such as multibase blocks, chip trading, and bean sticks, can be used to develop these algorithms.

Suppose that we wish to add $12_{five} + 31_{five}$. We show the computation using a concrete model in Figure 3-36(a), using an introductory algorithm in Figure 3-36(b), and using the familiar algorithm in Figure 3-36(c). Additions in other number bases can be handled similarly.

FIGURE 3-36

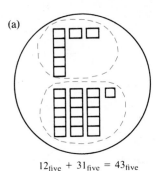

(a)

$12_{five} + 31_{five} = 43_{five}$

(b) Fives	Ones
1	2
3	1
4	3

(c) 12_{five}
$+31_{five}$
———
43_{five}

Subtraction such as $12_{five} - 4_{five}$ can be modeled using a number line, as shown in Figure 3-37. Thus, we see that $12_{five} - 4_{five} = 3_{five}$. The subtraction

FIGURE 3-37

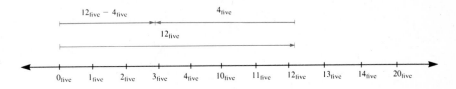

facts for base five can also be derived from the addition-facts table, by using the definition of subtraction. For example, to find $(12 - 4)_{five}$, recall that $(12 - 4)_{five} = c_{five}$ if and only if $(c + 4)_{five} = 12_{five}$. From Table 3-13, we see that $c = 3_{five}$. More involved subtraction problems can be performed by applying the same ideas developed for base ten.

An example of subtraction involving regrouping, $32_{five} - 14_{five}$, is developed in Figure 3-38 on page 172.

FIGURE 3-38

(a)

$$32_{five} - 14_{five} = 13_{five}$$

(b)

Fives	Ones
3	2
−1	4

→

Fives	Ones
2	12
−1	4
1	3

(c)
$$\overset{2\,1}{\cancel{3}2}_{five}$$
$$\underline{-14_{five}}$$
$$13_{five}$$

Addition and subtraction in other number bases can be handled similarly, as shown in Example 3-13.

EXAMPLE 3-13 (a) Add:

$$101_{two}$$
$$111_{two}$$
$$\underline{+110_{two}}$$

(b) Subtract:

$$1010_{two}$$
$$\underline{-\ 111_{two}}$$

SOLUTION (a)

$$\overset{1\,1}{101}_{two}$$
$$111_{two}$$
$$\underline{+\ 110_{two}}$$
$$10010_{two}$$

(b)

$$1010_{two}$$
$$\underline{-\ 111_{two}}$$
$$11_{two}$$

Multiplication and Division in Different Bases

As with addition and subtraction, we need to identify the basic facts of multiplication before we can use algorithms. The multiplication facts for base five are given in Table 3-14. These facts can be derived by using repeated addition.

TABLE 3-14
Multiplication Table
(Base Five)

×	0	1	2	3	4
0	0	0	0	0	0
1	0	1	2	3	4
2	0	2	4	11	13
3	0	3	11	14	22
4	0	4	13	22	31

There are various ways to do the multiplication $21_{five} \cdot 3_{five}$.

Five	Ones
2	1
×	3

→

$$(20 + 1)_{five}$$
$$\underline{\times \qquad\quad 3_{five}}$$
$$(110 + 3)_{five}$$

→

$$21_{five}$$
$$\underline{\times \quad 3_{five}}$$
$$3$$
$$\underline{110}$$
$$113_{five}$$

→

$$21_{five}$$
$$\underline{\times \quad 3_{five}}$$
$$113_{five}$$

The multiplication of a two-digit number by a two-digit number is developed next.

$$
\begin{array}{r}
23_{\text{five}} \\
\times\ 14_{\text{five}} \\
\hline
22 \\
130 \\
30 \\
200 \\
\hline
432_{\text{five}}
\end{array}
\qquad
\begin{array}{l}
(10 + 4)_{\text{five}} \\
(4 \cdot 3)_{\text{five}} \\
(4 \cdot 20)_{\text{five}} \\
(10 \cdot 3)_{\text{five}} \\
(10 \cdot 20)_{\text{five}}
\end{array}
\qquad
\begin{array}{r}
23_{\text{five}} \\
\times\ 14_{\text{five}} \\
\hline
202 \\
230 \\
\hline
432_{\text{five}}
\end{array}
$$

Lattice multiplication can also be used to multiply numbers in various number bases. This will be explored in Problem 31 of Problem Set 3-6.

Division in different bases can be performed using the multiplication facts and the definition of division. For example, $22_{\text{five}} \div 3_{\text{five}} = c$ if and only if $c \cdot 3_{\text{five}} = 22_{\text{five}}$. From Table 3-14, we see that $c = 4_{\text{five}}$. As in base ten, computing multidigit divisions efficiently in different bases requires practice. The ideas behind the algorithms for division can be developed by using repeated subtraction, just as they were for base ten. For example, $3241_{\text{five}} \div 43_{\text{five}}$ is computed by means of the repeated-subtraction technique in Figure 3-39(a) and by means of the conventional algorithm in Figure 3-39(b). Thus, $3241_{\text{five}} \div 43_{\text{five}} = 34_{\text{five}}$ with remainder 14_{five}.

FIGURE 3-39

$$
\begin{array}{lll}
\text{(a)} & 43_{\text{five}} \overline{)\, 3241_{\text{five}}} & \\
& \underline{-\ 430} & (10 \cdot 43)_{\text{five}} \\
& 2311 & \\
& \underline{-\ 430} & (10 \cdot 43)_{\text{five}} \\
& 1331 & \\
& \underline{-\ 430} & (10 \cdot 43)_{\text{five}} \\
& 401 & \\
& \underline{-\ 141} & (2 \cdot 43)_{\text{five}} \\
& 210 & \\
& \underline{-\ 141} & (2 \cdot 43)_{\text{five}} \\
& 14 & (34 \cdot 43)_{\text{five}}
\end{array}
\qquad
\begin{array}{ll}
 & \quad\quad 34_{\text{five}} \\
\text{(b)} & 43_{\text{five}} \overline{)\, 3241_{\text{five}}} \\
& \underline{-\ 234} \\
& 401 \\
& \underline{-\ 332} \\
& 14
\end{array}
$$

Multiplication and division involving base two is demonstrated in Example 3-14.

EXAMPLE 3-14 Multiply: Divide:

(a) $\quad 101_{\text{two}}$ (b) $101_{\text{two}} \overline{)\, 110110_{\text{two}}}$

$\quad\quad \times\ 11_{\text{two}}$

SOLUTION

(a)
$$
\begin{array}{r}
101_{\text{two}} \\
\times\ 11_{\text{two}} \\
\hline
101 \\
101 \\
\hline
1111_{\text{two}}
\end{array}
$$

(b)
$$
\begin{array}{r}
1010_{\text{two}} \\
101_{\text{two}} \overline{)\, 110110_{\text{two}}} \\
-\ 101 \quad\quad \\
\hline
111 \quad\quad \\
-\ 101 \quad\quad \\
\hline
100 \quad\quad
\end{array}
$$

PROBLEM SET 3-6

1. Write the first 15 counting numbers for each of the following bases.
   (a) Base two   (b) Base three
   (c) Base four   (d) Base eight

2. How many different digits are needed for base twenty?

3. Write 2032_{four} in expanded base-four notation.

4. What is the greatest three-digit number in each base?
   (a) Base two   (b) Base six
   (c) Base ten   (d) Base twelve

5. Find the numbers preceding and succeeding each of the following.
   (a) $EE0_{twelve}$ (b) 100000_{two} (c) 555_{six}
   (d) 100_{seven} (e) 1000_{five} (f) 110_{two}

6. What, if anything, is wrong with the numerals below?
   (a) 204_{four} (b) 607_{five} (c) $T12_{three}$

7. Convert each of the following base-ten numbers to numbers in the indicated bases.
   (a) 432 to base five   (b) 1963 to base twelve
   (c) 404 to base four   (d) 37 to base two
   (e) $3 \cdot 10^4 + 2 \cdot 10^2 + 4$ to base five
   (f) $4 \cdot 10^4 + 3 \cdot 10^2$ to base twelve
   (g) $9 \cdot 12^5 + 11 \cdot 12$ to base twelve

8. Change 42_{eight} to base two.

9. Write each of the following numbers in base ten.
   (a) 432_{five} (b) 101101_{two} (c) $92E_{twelve}$
   (d) $T0E_{twelve}$ (e) 111_{twelve} (f) 346_{seven}
   (g) 551_{six} (h) 3002_{four}

10. Suppose you have two quarters, four nickels, and two pennies. What is the value of your money in cents? Write a base-five representation to indicate the value of your fortune.

11. You are asked to distribute $900 in prize money. The dollar amounts for the prizes are $625, $125, $25, $5, and $1. How should this $900 be distributed in order to give the fewest number of prizes?

12. What is the minimum number of quarters, nickels, and pennies necessary to make 97¢?

13. Convert each of the following.
    (a) 58 days to weeks and days
    (b) 54 months to years and months
    (c) 29 hours to days and hours
    (d) 68 inches to feet and inches

14. A bookstore ordered 11 gross, 6 dozen, and 6 pencils. Express the number of pencils in base twelve and in base ten.

15. For each of the following, find b.
    (a) $b2_{seven} = 44_{ten}$ (b) $5b2_{twelve} = 734_{ten}$
    (c) $23_{ten} = 25_b$

16. George is cooking an elaborate meal for Thanksgiving. He can only cook one thing at a time in his microwave oven. His turkey takes 75 minutes; the pumpkin pie takes 18 minutes; rolls take 45 seconds; and a cup of coffee takes 30 seconds to heat. How much time does he need to cook the meal?

17. An inspector of weights and measures uses a special set of weights to check the accuracy of scales. Various weights are placed on a scale to check accuracy of any amount from 1 ounce through 15 ounces. What is the least number of weights that the inspector needs? What weights are needed to check the accuracy of scales from 1 ounce through 15 ounces? From 1 through 31 ounces?

18. Anna's bank contains only pennies, nickels, and quarters. What is the minimum number of coins she could trade for 117 pennies? If she trades 2 quarters, 4 nickels, and 3 pennies for pennies, how many pennies will she have?

19. Perform each of the following operations, using the bases shown.
    (a) $43_{five} + 23_{five}$ (b) $43_{five} - 23_{five}$
    (c) $432_{five} + 23_{five}$ (d) $42_{five} - 23_{five}$
    (e) $110_{two} + 11_{two}$ (f) $10001_{two} - 111_{two}$

20. Construct addition and multiplication tables for base eight.

21. Perform each of the following operations.
    (a)   3 hours 36 minutes 58 seconds
        $+$5 hours 56 minutes 27 seconds

    (b)   5 hours 36 minutes 38 seconds
        $-$3 hours 56 minutes 58 seconds

22. Perform each of the following operations (2 cups = 1 pint, 2 pints = 1 quart, 4 quarts = 1 gallon).
    (a)   1 quart 1 pint 1 cup   (b)   1 quart 1 cup
        $+$ 1 pint 1 cup $-$ 1 pint 1 cup

    (c)   1 gallon 3 quarts 1 cup
        $-$ 4 quarts 2 cups

23. Use scratch addition to perform the following.

    32_{five}
    13_{five}
    22_{five}
    43_{five}
    23_{five}
    $+12_{five}$

24. Perform each of the following operations.
    (a)   4 gross 4 dozen 6 ones
        $-$ 5 dozen 9 ones

    (b)   2 gross 9 dozen 7 ones
        $+$3 gross 5 dozen 9 ones

25. In a small rural community, the elementary school had no refrigerators. Through a federally financed program, the school provided 1 cup of milk per day for each student. Milk for the day was purchased at the local store each morning and the school bought the exact amount necessary. The milk was available in gallons, half-gallons, quarts, pints, or cups, and the larger containers were better buys.
    (a) If 1 gallon, 1 quart, and 1 pint of milk were purchased on Tuesday, how many students were at school that day?
    (b) On Wednesday, 31 students were at school. How much milk was purchased that day to make the best buy?

26. A *score* is equal to 20. Indicate each of the following as a base-ten number.
    (a) Three score and ten
    (b) Four score and seven

27. What is wrong with the following?

    $$22_{\text{five}}$$
    $$+\,33_{\text{five}}$$
    $$\overline{55_{\text{five}}}$$

28. Fill in the missing numbers in each of the following.
    (a) $\quad 2\_\_{}_{\text{five}}$
        $\quad +\ 2\,2_{\text{five}}$
        $\quad \overline{\_\,0\,3_{\text{five}}}$
    (b) $\quad 2\,0\,0\,1\,0_{\text{three}}$
        $\quad -\ 2\_2\_{}_{\text{three}}$
        $\quad \overline{1\_2\_1_{\text{three}}}$

29. Perform each of the following operations using the bases shown.
    (a) $32_{\text{five}} \cdot 4_{\text{five}}$
    (b) $32_{\text{five}} \div 4_{\text{five}}$
    (c) $43_{\text{five}} \cdot 23_{\text{five}}$
    (d) $143_{\text{five}} \div 3_{\text{five}}$
    (e) $13_{\text{eight}} \cdot 5_{\text{eight}}$
    (f) $67_{\text{eight}} \div 4_{\text{eight}}$
    (g) $10010_{\text{two}} \div 11_{\text{two}}$
    (h) $10110_{\text{two}} \cdot 101_{\text{two}}$

30. For what possible bases are each of the following computations correct?
    (a) $\quad 213$
        $\quad +308$
        $\quad \overline{\ 522}$
    (b) $\quad 322$
        $\quad -233$
        $\quad \overline{\ \ 23}$
    (c) $\quad 213$
        $\quad \times\ 32$
        $\quad \overline{\ 430}$
        $\quad \underline{1043}$
        $\quad 11300$
    (d) $\quad\quad 101$
        $\quad 11\overline{)1111}$
        $\quad \underline{-11}$
        $\quad\quad\ 11$
        $\quad\quad \underline{-11}$
        $\quad\quad\quad\ 0$

31. Use lattice multiplication to compute $(323_{\text{five}}) \cdot (42_{\text{five}})$.

32. (a) Write $12^6 + 4 \cdot 12^3 + 120$ in base twelve.
    (b) Write $12^5 \cdot (8 \cdot 12 + 4)$ in base twelve.

LABORATORY ACTIVITY

1. Messages can be coded on paper tape in base two. A hole in the tape represents 1, while a space represents 0. The value of each hole depends on its position; from left to right, 16, 8, 4, 2, 1 (all powers of 2). Letters of the alphabet may be coded in base two according to their position in the alphabet. For example, G is the seventh letter. Since $7 = 1 \cdot 4 + 1 \cdot 2 + 1$, the holes appear as they do in the following figure.

		○	○	○
16	8	4	2	1

(a) Decode the following message.
(b) Write your name on a tape, using base two.

2. The following number game uses base-two arithmetic.

Card E		Card D		Card C		Card B		Card A	
16	24	8	24	4	20	2	18	1	17
17	25	9	25	5	21	3	19	3	19
18	26	10	26	6	22	6	22	5	21
19	27	11	27	7	23	7	23	7	23
20	28	12	28	12	28	10	26	9	25
21	29	13	29	13	29	11	27	11	27
22	30	14	30	14	30	14	30	13	29
23	31	15	31	15	31	15	31	15	31

(a) Suppose that a person's age appears on cards E, C, and B. Then, the person is 22. Can you discover how this works and why?

(b) Design card F so that the numbers 1–63 can be used in the game. Note that cards A–E must also be changed.

SOLUTION TO THE PRELIMINARY PROBLEM

Understanding the Problem. We are to determine the total number of grains of wheat obtained by placing 1 grain on the first square of a checkerboard, 2 grains on the second square, 4 grains on the third square, and so on, doubling the number of grains each time, until all 64 squares on the checkerboard have been accounted for.

Devising a Plan. Rather than attempting the more difficult problem, we reduce the problem to some simpler cases of boards with 4 and 9 squares, as shown in Figure 3-40. From these simpler cases, we hope to gain insight into how to solve the more difficult problem.

FIGURE 3-40

The 2 × 2 board holds $1 + 2 + 2^2 + 2^3 = 15$ grains, and the 3 × 3 board holds $1 + 2 + 2^2 + 2^3 + 2^4 + 2^5 + 2^6 + 2^7 + 2^8 = 511$ grains. We notice that 15 is one less than 16 (or 2^4) and 511 is one less than 512 (or 2^9). Thus, we conjecture that the number of grains on the 8 × 8 checkerboard is $1 + 2 + 2^2 + 2^3 + 2^4 + \cdots + 2^{63} = 2^{64} - 1$.

Carrying Out the Plan. The number of grains of wheat to be calculated is $1 + 2 + 2^2 + 2^3 + 2^4 + \cdots + 2^{63}$. It has been conjectured that this sum is given by $2^{64} - 1$. A justification for this conjecture follows. Let

$$S = 1 + 2 + 2^2 + 2^3 + \cdots + 2^{62} + 2^{63}$$

Multiply both sides of this equation by 2 to obtain

$$2S = 2 + 2^2 + 2^3 + 2^4 + \cdots + 2^{63} + 2^{64}$$

Subtracting S from $2S$, we obtain the following.

$$\begin{aligned} 2S - S &= (2 + 2^2 + 2^3 + \cdots + 2^{64}) - (1 + 2 + 2^2 + \cdots + 2^{63}) \\ &= (2 - 2) + (2^2 - 2^2) + (2^3 - 2^3) + \cdots + (2^{63} - 2^{63}) + 2^{64} - 1 \\ &= 2^{64} - 1 \end{aligned}$$

Do you have a feeling for how large a number this is? For estimating purposes, a useful fact is that $2^{10} = 1024$, or approximately 1000. Therefore, $2^{64} = 2^4 \cdot 2^{60} = 2^4 \cdot (2^{10})^6$, which is approximately $2^4 \cdot (10^3)^6$, or $16 \cdot 10^{18}$, which is 16 billion billion, or 16 quintillion. On a calculator, if we find 2^{64} using the $\boxed{y^x}$ key, the value $\boxed{1.8447 \quad 19}$ is displayed. Remember, this number is in scientific notation and represents $1.8447 \cdot 10^{19}$ or $18,447,000,000,000,000,000$. The exact value of 2^{64} is $18,446,744,073,709,551,616$. Notice that we are obtaining only an approximation on the calculator. It has been estimated that it would take the United States approximately 14,000 years to produce the amount of wheat necessary to place on the last square.

Looking Back. An alternate proof showing that $1 + 2 + 2^2 + 2^3 + 2^4 + \cdots + 2^{63} = 2^{64} - 1$ makes use of base two. Recall that $11111_{\text{two}} = 1 \cdot 2^4 + 1 \cdot 2^3 + 1 \cdot 2^2 + 1 \cdot 2 + 1$, and notice the following pattern.

$$\begin{aligned} 1_{\text{two}} + 1_{\text{two}} &= 10_{\text{two}} = 2^1 = 2 \\ 11_{\text{two}} + 1_{\text{two}} &= 100_{\text{two}} = 2^2 = 4 \\ 111_{\text{two}} + 1_{\text{two}} &= 1000_{\text{two}} = 2^3 = 8 \\ 1111_{\text{two}} + 1_{\text{two}} &= 10000_{\text{two}} = 2^4 = 16 \end{aligned}$$

Therefore,

$$1 + 2 + 2^2 + 2^3 = 1111_{\text{two}} = 10000_{\text{two}} - 1_{\text{two}} = 2^4 - 1$$

and

$$\begin{aligned} 1 + 2 + 2^2 + 2^3 + 2^4 + 2^5 + 2^6 + 2^7 + 2^8 \\ = 111111111_{\text{two}} = 1000000000_{\text{two}} - 1_{\text{two}} = 2^9 - 1 \end{aligned}$$

If we proceed in this manner, we see that

$$1 + 2 + 2^2 + 2^3 + 2^4 + \cdots + 2^{63} = 2^{64} - 1$$

The size of the checkerboard could be varied to introduce more problems. Questions concerning the length of time required to count the grains or the amount of storage space required to store the grain could also be asked. We might also compute the number of grains if each square contains three times as many grains as the previous square or, in general, n times as many as the previous square, where n is a positive integer.

QUESTIONS FROM THE CLASSROOM

1. A student asks, "Does $2 \cdot (3 \cdot 4)$ equal $(2 \cdot 3) \cdot (2 \cdot 4)$?" Is there a distributive property of multiplication over multiplication?

2. Since $39 + 41 = 40 + 40$, is it true that $39 \cdot 41 = 40 \cdot 40$?

3. The division algorithm, $a = bq + r$, holds for $a > b$; $a, b, q, r \in W$ and $b \neq 0$. Does the algorithm hold when $a < b$?

4. A student asks if 5 times 4 is the same as 5 multiplied by 4. How do you respond?

5. Can we define $0 \div 0$ as 1? Why or why not?

6. A student divides as follows. How do you help?

$$
\begin{array}{r}
15 \\
6\overline{)36} \\
\underline{6} \\
30 \\
\underline{30}
\end{array}
$$

7. When using Roman numerals, a student asks whether or not it is correct to write $\overline{\text{II}}$, as well as MI, for 1001. How do you respond?

8. A student says that $(x + 7) \div 7 = x + 1$. What is that student doing wrong?

9. A student says $x \div x$ is always 1. Is the student correct?

10. A student claims that the expressions $(2^3)^2$ and $2^{(3^2)}$ are equal. How do you respond?

11. A student asks if division on the set of whole numbers is distributive over subtraction. How do you respond?

12. A student says that 0 is the identity for subtraction. How do you respond?

13. A student asks if zero is the same as nothing. What is your answer?

14. A student claims that, on the following number line, the arrow doesn't really represent 3 because the end of the arrow does not start at 0. How do you respond?

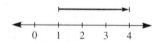

CHAPTER OUTLINE

I. Numeration systems
A. Properties of numeration systems give basic structure to the systems.
  1. Additive property
  2. Place-value property
  3. Subtractive property
  4. Multiplicative property

II. Exponents
A. For any whole number a and any natural number n,

$$a^n = \underbrace{(a \cdot a \cdot a \cdots a)}_{n \text{ factors}}$$

where a is the **base** and n is the **exponent**.

B. $a^0 = 1$, $a \in N$
C. For any natural number a, with whole numbers m and n, $a^m \cdot a^n = a^{m+n}$.

III. Whole numbers
A. The set of **whole numbers** W is $\{0, 1, 2, 3, \ldots\}$.
B. The basic operations for whole numbers are addition, subtraction, multiplication, and division.
  1. Addition: If $n(A) = a$ and $n(B) = b$, where $A \cap B = \varnothing$, then $a + b = n(A \cup B)$. The numbers a and b are **addends** and $a + b$ is the **sum.**
  2. Subtraction: If a and b are any whole numbers, then $a - b$ is the unique whole number c such that $a = b + c$. The number a is the **minuend,** b is the **subtrahend,** and c is the **difference.**
  3. Multiplication: If a and b are any whole numbers,

$$a \cdot b = \underbrace{b + b + b + \cdots + b}_{a \text{ terms}}$$

a and b are called **factors** and $a \cdot b$ is the **product.**

4. Multiplication: If A and B are sets such that $n(A) = a$ and $n(B) = b$, then $a \cdot b = n(A \times B)$.
5. Division: If a and b are any whole numbers with $b \neq 0$, $a \div b$ is the unique whole number c such that $b \cdot c = a$. The number a is the **dividend,** b is the **divisor,** and c is the **quotient.**
6. **Division algorithm:** Given any whole numbers a and b, with $b \neq 0$, there exist unique whole numbers q and r such that $a = b \cdot q + r$, with $0 \leq r < b$.
C. Properties of addition and multiplication of whole numbers.
   1. Closure: If $a, b \in W$, then $a + b \in W$ and $a \cdot b \in W$.

2. Commutative: If $a, b \in W$, then $a + b = b + a$ and $a \cdot b = b \cdot a$.
3. Associative: If $a, b, c \in W$, then $(a + b) + c = a + (b + c)$ and $a \cdot (b \cdot c) = (a \cdot b) \cdot c$.
4. Identity: 0 is the unique identity element for addition of whole numbers; 1 is the unique identity element for multiplication.
5. Distributive property of multiplication over addition: If $a, b, c \in W$, then $a \cdot (b + c) = a \cdot b + a \cdot c$.

D. Relations on whole numbers
   1. $a < b$ if and only if there is a natural number c such that $a + c = b$.
   2. $a > b$ if and only if $b < a$.

CHAPTER TEST

1. Convert each of the following to base ten.
   (a) $\overline{\text{CDXLIV}}$ *(b) 432_{five} *(c) $ET0_{\text{twelve}}$
   *(d) 1011_{two} *(e) 4136_{seven}
2. Convert each of the following numbers to numbers in the indicated system.
   (a) 999 to Roman
   (b) 86 to Egyptian
   (c) 123 to Mayan
   *(d) 346_{ten} to base five
   *(e) 1728_{ten} to base twelve
   *(f) 27_{ten} to base two
   *(g) 928_{ten} to base nine
   *(h) 13_{eight} to base two
3. Simplify each of the following, if possible. Write your answers in exponential form, a^b.
   (a) $3^4 \cdot 3^7 \cdot 3^6$ (b) $2^{10} \cdot 2^{11}$
   (c) $3^4 + 2 \cdot 3^4$ (d) $2^{80} + 3 \cdot 2^{80}$
4. For each of the following, identify the properties of the operation(s) for whole numbers illustrated.
   (a) $3 \cdot (a + b) = 3 \cdot a + 3 \cdot b$
   (b) $2 + a = a + 2$
   (c) $16 \cdot 1 = 1 \cdot 16 = 16$
   (d) $6 \cdot (12 + 3) = 6 \cdot 12 + 6 \cdot 3$
   (e) $3 \cdot (a \cdot 2) = 3 \cdot (2 \cdot a)$
   (f) $3 \cdot (2 \cdot a) = (3 \cdot 2) \cdot a$
5. Using the definitions of less than or greater than, prove that each of the following inequalities is true.
   (a) $3 < 13$ (b) $12 > 9$
6. Explain why the product of $1000 \cdot 483$, namely, 483,000, has 0 for the hundreds, tens, and units digits.

7. Use both the scratch and the traditional algorithms to perform each of the following.
   (a) $\begin{array}{r} 316 \\ 712 \\ + \ 91 \end{array}$ *(b) $\begin{array}{r} 316_{\text{twelve}} \\ 712_{\text{twelve}} \\ + 913_{\text{twelve}} \end{array}$
8. Use both the traditional and the lattice multiplication algorithms to perform each of the following.
   (a) $\begin{array}{r} 613 \\ \times \ 98 \end{array}$ *(b) $\begin{array}{r} 216_{\text{eight}} \\ \times \ 54_{\text{eight}} \end{array}$
9. Use both the repeated-subtraction and the conventional algorithms to perform each of the following.
   (a) $912 \overline{)4803}$ (b) $11 \overline{)1011}$
   *(c) $23_{\text{five}} \overline{)3312_{\text{five}}}$ *(d) $11_{\text{two}} \overline{)1011_{\text{two}}}$
10. Use the division algorithm to check your answers in Problem 9.
11. For each of the following base-ten numbers, tell the place value for each of the circled digits.
   (a) $4\textcircled{3}2$ (b) $\textcircled{3}432$ (c) $19\textcircled{3}24$
12. For each of the following, find all possible whole-number replacements that make the following statements true.
   (a) $4 \cdot \square - 37 < 27$ (b) $398 = \square \cdot 37 + 28$
   (c) $\square \cdot (3 + 4) = \square \cdot 3 + \square \cdot 4$
   (d) $42 - \square \geq 16$
13. Use a number line to perform each of the following operations.
   (a) $27 - 15$ (b) $17 + 2$
   *(c) $3_{\text{five}} + 11_{\text{five}}$ *(d) $12_{\text{three}} + 2_{\text{three}}$

14. Use the distributive property of multiplication and addition facts, if possible, to rename each of the following.
    (a) $3a + 7a + 5a$ (b) $3x^2 + 7x^2 - 5x^2$
    (c) $x(a + b + y)$ (d) $(x + 5)3 + (x + 5)y$
15. Solve each of the following.
    (a) Mary had 5 apples, 14 oranges, and 6 raisins. How many fruits did she have?
    (b) Carlos had 32 apricots and 4 friends. If he wished to give each friend an equal number of apricots, how many did each receive?
    (c) Joe had 6 books, each with 12 chapters. How many chapters were there in all?
    (d) Jerry paid $24 for a shirt with a $50 bill. How much change did he receive?
16. You had a balance in your checking account of $720 before writing checks for $162, $158, and $33 and making a deposit of $28. What is your new balance?
17. Jim was paid $320 a month for 6 months and $410 a month for 6 months. What were his total earnings for the year?
18. A soft drink manufacturer produces 15,600 cans of his product each hour. Cans are packed 24 to a case. How many cases are produced in 4 hours?
19. A limited partnership of 120 investors sold a piece of land for $461,040. How much did each investor receive?
20. (a) Use each of the digits 1 through 9 to obtain a correct sum.
    (b) Is only one correct answer possible?

$$\begin{array}{c}\square\square\square \\ +\square\square\square \\ \hline \square\square\square\end{array}$$

21. Merle took a 2040-mile trip, which took 10 days. Each day he drove 30 miles more than he had the day before. How many miles did he cover on the first day?
22. How many 12-ounce cans of juice would it take to give 60 people one 8-ounce serving each?
23. Heidi has a brown and a gray pair of slacks; a brown, a yellow, and a white blouse; and a blue and a white sweater. How many different outfits does she have if she wears slacks, a blouse, and a sweater?
24. Complete the following base-ten addition table.

+			9
8		15	
	16		
	26		30

25. I am thinking of a whole number. If I divide it by 13, then multiply the answer by 12, then subtract 20, and then add 89, I end up with 93. What was my original number?
26. Apples normally sell for 32¢ each. They go on sale for 3 for 69¢. How much money is saved if we purchase 2 dozen apples?
27. A ski resort offers a weekend ski package for $80 per person or $6000 for a group of 80 people. Which would be the cheaper option for a group of 80?
28. The owner of a bicycle shop reported his inventory of bicycles and tricycles in an unusual way. He said he counted 126 wheels and 108 pedals. How many bikes and how many trikes did he have?
*29. Write $9 \cdot 12^7 + 11 \cdot 12^4 + 10$ as a base-twelve numeral.

The
Integers

PRELIMINARY PROBLEM

A sailor went to three casinos on the same night. At the Tropicana, he doubled his money and then lost $30; he took his remaining money and went to Caesar's Palace. There, he tripled the money with which he entered and then lost $54. At that point, he took his remaining money and went to Aladdin's. There he quadrupled the money with which he entered but then spent $72. He spent no more money, and when he returned to his room he had $48 left. How much money did he have before he went to the casinos?

Introduction

Negative numbers serve useful purposes in everyday life. Uses of positive numbers, zero, and negative numbers are seen in the following chart, taken from the University of Chicago School Mathematics Project, *Transition Mathematics*, Grade 7, 1990.

Situation	Negative	Zero	Positive
savings account	withdrawal	no change	deposit
time	before	now	after
games	behind	even	ahead
business	loss	break even	profit
elevation	below sea level	sea level	above sea level

In mathematics, the need for negative numbers arises because subtractions cannot always be performed using only the set of whole numbers. The cartoon depicts Linus attempting a subtraction using only whole numbers.

To compute $4 - 6$ in accordance with the definition of subtraction for whole numbers, a whole number a must be found such that $6 + a = 4$. Because there is no whole number a such that $6 + a = 4$, Linus's subtraction is not possible using only whole numbers. In order to perform the computation in the cartoon, a new number must be invented. This new number is called a *negative integer*. This chapter deals with the creation of negative integers, with operations involving integers, and with properties of integers.

The last section of the chapter deals with prealgebra and algebra skills, including word problems that can be solved with algebraic equations. This section should help prepare teachers to meet the recommendations of the *Standards,* which states that students in grades 5–8 should be able to "apply algebraic methods to examine and solve a variety of real-world and mathematical problems" and that students should be able to "develop confidence in solving linear equations using concrete, informal, and formal methods" and to "investigate inequalities and nonlinear equations informally."

H I S T O R I C A L   N O T E
The Chinese used red rods for positive numbers and black rods for negative numbers in calculations possibly as early as 500 B.C. Brahmagupta, a seventh-century Hindu mathematician, wrote, "Positive divided by positive, or negative by negative, is affirmative." The Italian mathematician Girolamo Cardano (1501–1576) provided the first significant treatment of negative numbers (which he called "false numbers"). However, as late as the eighteenth century, some mathematicians worried whether two negative numbers could be multiplied and many textbooks categorically denied the possibility of multiplying two negative numbers.

Section 4-1 Integers and the Operations of Addition and Subtraction

If we attempt to subtract $4 - 6$ on a horizontal number line, as we did with whole numbers, we see that it is necessary to draw intervals to the left of 0. On the extended number line in Figure 4-1, $4 - 6$ is pictured as an arrow that starts at 0 and ends 2 units to the left of 0. The name we give to the new number that corresponds to a point 2 units to the left of 0 is *negative two,* which is symbolized by $^-2$. Other numbers to the left of 0 are created similarly. The new set of numbers, $\{^-1, \ ^-2, \ ^-3, \ ^-4, \ ^-5, \ldots\}$ is called the set

negative integers of **negative integers.**

FIGURE 4-1

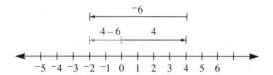

Unfortunately, the symbol " $-$ " is used to indicate both a subtraction and a negative sign. To reduce confusion between the uses of this symbol, it is customary initially to use a raised " $-$ " sign for negative numbers, as in $^-2$, in contrast to the ordinary minus sign for subtraction. To emphasize that an integer is positive, some people use a raised plus sign, as in $^+3$. In this text, we use the plus sign for addition only and write $^+3$ simply as 3.

integers   The union of the set $\{^-1, \ ^-2, \ ^-3, \ ^-4, \ ^-5, \ldots\}$ and the set of whole numbers, $\{0, 1, 2, 3, \ldots\}$, is called the set of **integers.** The set of integers is denoted by I:

$$I = \{\ldots, \ ^-5, \ ^-4, \ ^-3, \ ^-2, \ ^-1, 0, 1, 2, 3, 4, 5, \ldots\}$$

Frequently, it is convenient to partition the set of integers into the three subsets $\{1, 2, 3, 4, \ldots\}$, $\{0\}$, and $\{^-1, \ ^-2, \ ^-3, \ ^-4, \ldots\}$. The elements of the three subsets are the *positive integers, zero,* and the *negative integers,* respectively. *Zero is neither a positive nor a negative number.*

In Figure 4-1, the negative integers can be described as mirror images of the positive integers. For example, the mirror image of 5 is $^-5$, and the

opposite

mirror image of 0 is 0. Similarly, the positive integers can be described as mirror images of the negative integers. For example, 4 is the mirror image of ⁻4. Another term for "mirror image of" is "**opposite** of." Thus, the opposite of 4 is denoted by ⁻4, and the opposite of ⁻4 can be denoted by ⁻(⁻4), or 4. In general, we have the following definition.

● **D E F I N I T I O N**
If n is an integer, then the unique integer ^-n is called the **opposite** of n if $n + (^-n) = 0 = (^-n) + n$.

H I S T O R I C A L   N O T E

The dash has not always been used for both the subtraction operation and the negative sign. Other notations were developed but never adopted. One such notation was used by Mohammed al-Khowârizmî (ca. 825), who indicated a negative number by placing a small circle over it. For example, ⁻4 was recorded as 4̊. The Hindus denoted a negative number by enclosing it in a circle; for example, ⁻4 was recorded as ④. The symbols + and − first appeared in print in European mathematics in the late fifteenth century. The symbols referred not to addition or subtraction or to positive or negative numbers, but to surpluses and deficits in business problems.

EXAMPLE 4-1

For each of the following, find the opposite of x.
(a) $x = 3$ (b) $x = ^-5$ (c) $x = 0$

SOLUTION

(a) $^-x = ^-3$ (b) $^-x = ^-(^-5) = 5$ (c) $^-x = ^-0 = 0$

Notice that ^-x does not necessarily represent a negative integer. For example, the value of ^-x in Example 4-1(b) is 5. In other words, x is a variable that can be replaced by some number, either positive, zero, or negative.

Representations of Integers

There are many ways to represent the same integer. For example, on a number line, ⁻2 may be pictured by any of the arrows in Figure 4-2, where each points to the left and is two units long.

FIGURE 4-2

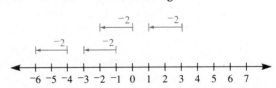

Absolute Value

Because 4 and ⁻4 are opposites of each other, they are on opposite sides of 0 on the number line and are the same distance—4 units—from 0, as shown in Figure 4-3.

FIGURE 4-3

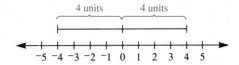

absolute value   Distance is always a positive number or zero. The distance between the points corresponding to an integer and 0 is called the **absolute value** of the integer. Thus, the absolute value of both 4 and ⁻4 is 4, written as $|4| = 4$ and $|^-4| = 4$, respectively. (A more formal definition of absolute value as a function is given in Problem Set 4-1.)

EXAMPLE 4-2   Evaluate each of the following.
(a) $|20|$ (b) $|^-5|$ (c) $|0|$ (d) $^-|^-3|$ (e) $|2 - 5|$

SOLUTION   (a) $|20| = 20$ (b) $|^-5| = 5$ (c) $|0| = 0$ (d) $^-|^-3| = ^-3$
(e) $|2 - 5| = |^-3| = 3$

EXAMPLE 4-3   Solve each of the following for x, where x is an integer.
(a) $|x| = 4$ (b) $|^-x| = 4$ (c) $|x - 3| = 4$ (d) $^-|^-x| = 4$

SOLUTION   (a) The only two points on the number line at a distance of 4 away from 0 are 4 and ⁻4. Thus, $x = 4$ or $x = ^-4$.
(b) If $|^-x| = 4$, then the only two points on the number line at a distance 4 from 0 are 4 and ⁻4. Therefore, $^-x = 4$ or $^-x = ^-4$. Thus, $x = ^-4$ or $x = 4$.
(c) Since both 4 and ⁻4 are at a distance 4 from 0, we have $x - 3 = 4$ or $x - 3 = ^-4$. Thus, $x = 7$ or $x = ^-1$.
(d) Since $^-|^-x| = 4$, then $|^-x| = ^-4$. Because the absolute value of every number is either 0 or a positive number, this equation has no solution, or the solution set is the empty set.

Integer Addition

Absolute value can be used to define addition of integers, but we consider more informal approaches first.

Charged-field Model. One model for integer addition utilizes positive and negative charges. To make use of this model, we consider a field with 0 charge, that is, a field with the same number of positive (+) and negative (−) charges, as in Figure 4-4(a). The number of pairs of charges in Figure 4-4(a) may vary as long as the net charge is 0.

FIGURE 4-4

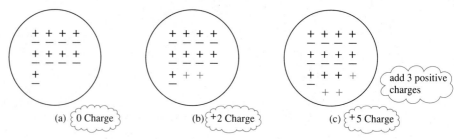

To show 2 + 3 in this model, we first place two positive charges in the field, to give it a charge of ⁺2, as in Figure 4-4(b). We then add three additional positive charges, as in Figure 4-4(c). The resulting charge on the field is ⁺5, since there are 5 more positive than negative charges present. In a similar manner, we can compute 3 + ⁻5, as in Figure 4-5. Hence, 3 + ⁻5 = ⁻2. In a similar manner, we can compute addition of all combinations of integers—positive, negative, and zero.

FIGURE 4-5

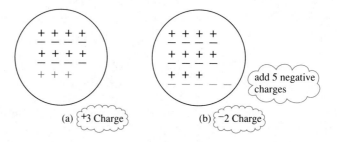

On page 187 is a different type of model that involves the use of colored chips, as seen on this student page from *Addison-Wesley Mathematics*, 1989, Grade 7.

Stock-market Model. The following model from the stock market illustrates integer addition based on gains and losses:

1. A stock gains 7 points on Monday and 6 points on Tuesday. Interpreting both gains as positive numbers, we can write the net gain as 7 + 6 = 13.
2. A stock drops 10 points on Monday and then drops an additional 15 points on Tuesday. We think about the total loss in points as ⁻10 + ⁻15. Because the total loss is 25 points, we record this as ⁻10 + ⁻15 = ⁻25.

Combining Integer Quantities

Kevin and Juan decided to use chips to learn more about integers. They let black chips represent positive integers and red chips represent negative integers.

Four black chips represent $^+4$. What do 3 red chips represent?

A set of 2 black chips and 3 red chips represents $^-1$. What does a set of 2 reds and 3 blacks represent?

Work with a partner.
You will need some red chips and some black chips.

Part 1

Kevin and Juan each selected some chips, and each recorded the value of the set he selected. Then they combined their sets and recorded the total value in a chart like the one shown.

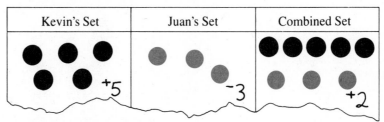

Kevin's Set	Juan's Set	Combined Set
$^+5$	$^-3$	$^+2$

1. In each of the following 4 activities, you and your partner will select a set of chips. Then you will combine the two sets and record your results on a chart like Kevin and Juan's. Repeat each activity, using different numbers of chips.

   • Activity 1: Each partner selects some black chips.
   • Activity 2: Each partner selects some red chips.
   • Activity 3: One selects some red chips and the other selects some black chips.
   • Activity 4: Each selects a set of chips using both reds and blacks.

2. Discuss with your partner what happens when sets that contain only one color are combined. How can you know whether the total value of combined sets will be positive, negative, or zero?

3. A stock drops 10 points on Monday and then gains 10 points on Tuesday. The net gain is 0. Thus, $^-10 + 10 = 0$.

4. A stock gains 3 points on Monday and drops 5 points on Tuesday. The net gain can be written as $3 + ^-5$. The net gain can also be thought of as $3 - 5$, or $^-2$. Hence, $3 + ^-5 = 3 - 5$.

5. A stock gains 10 points on Monday and then drops 25 points on Tuesday. We think of the total loss in points as $10 + ^-25$. Because the total loss is 15 points, we record this as $10 + ^-25 = ^-15$. Because $25 - 10 = 15$, we see that $10 + ^-25 = ^-(25 - 10)$.

Number-line Model. Another model for addition of integers involves a number line. The number-line model of Figure 4-6 is sometimes used with a toy car to model integer addition. In the addition model, the car starts at 0, facing in a positive direction (to the right). To represent a positive integer, the car is moved forward, and to represent a negative integer, the car is moved in reverse. For example, Figure 4–6(a)–(d) illustrates four different additions.

FIGURE 4-6

(a)
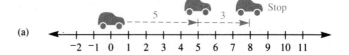

5 + 3 is seen as moving the car forward 5 units and then 3 units, for a net move of 8 units to the right from 0. Thus, 5 + 3 = 8.

(b)
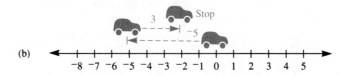

$^-5 + 3$ is seen as moving the car 5 units in reverse and then moving it forward 3 units, for a net move of 2 units to the left from 0. Thus, $^-5 + 3 = ^-2$.

(c)
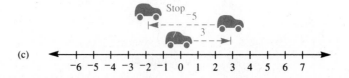

$3 + ^-5$ is seen as moving the car 3 units forward and then moving it 5 units in reverse, for a net move of 2 units to the left from 0. Thus, $3 + ^-5 = ^-2$.

$^-3 + {}^-5$ is seen as moving the car 3 units in reverse and 5 units in reverse, for a net move of 8 units to the left from 0. Thus, $^-3 + {}^-5 = {}^-8$.

In an analogous manner (but without the car), $^-3 + {}^-5$ can be pictured as in Figure 4-7.

FIGURE 4-7

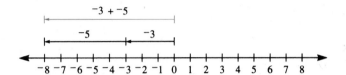

Figure 4-8 similarly depicts integer addition of $3 + {}^-5$.

FIGURE 4-8

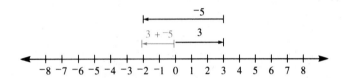

In Figure 4-8, we see that $3 + {}^-5 = {}^-2$. From the gain-loss model, we saw that $3 + {}^-5$ is $3 - 5$, or $^-2$. In both models, a difference involving the whole numbers 3 and 5 was found. Because 3 and 5 are absolute values of 3 and $^-5$, respectively, the pattern appears to be one of finding the difference of the absolute values of these integers. In fact, this pattern is true and is summarized in general as follows:

To add integers with unlike signs, subtract the lesser of the two absolute values of the integers from the greater. The sum has the same sign as the integer with the greater absolute value. If the two integers with unlike signs have equal absolute values, their sum is 0.

The pattern for addition of integers with like signs can also be summarized using absolute values:

To add integers with like signs, add the absolute values of the integers. The sum has the same sign as the integers.

EXAMPLE 4-4   Find each of the following sums.
(a) $9 + {}^-4$ (b) $^-5 + {}^-8$ (c) $^-5 + 5$ (d) $3 + {}^-10$

SOLUTION   (a) $9 + {}^-4 = 5$ (b) $^-5 + {}^-8 = {}^-13$
(c) $^-5 + 5 = 0$ (d) $3 + {}^-10 = {}^-7$

Example 4-5 involves a thermometer with a scale in the form of a vertical number line.

EXAMPLE 4-5 The temperature was ⁻4°C. In an hour, it rose 10°C. What is the new temperature?

SOLUTION Figure 4-9 shows that the new temperature is 6°C and that ⁻4 + 10 = 6.

FIGURE 4-9

Properties of Integer Addition
Integer addition has all the properties of whole-number addition. These properties are summarized next.

● **P R O P E R T I E S**
Given integers a, b, and c:

Closure Property of Addition of Integers $a + b$ is a unique integer.
Commutative Property of Addition of Integers $a + b = b + a$
Associative Property of Addition of Integers $(a + b) + c = a + (b + c)$
Identity Element of Addition of Integers 0 is the unique integer such that, for all integers a, $0 + a = a = a + 0$.

An additional property that we acquire when we expand from the set of whole numbers to the set of integers is that each member of the set of integers has an opposite. This opposite is also called the **additive inverse.** The fact that the set of integers has an additive inverse for each element in the set is recorded in the following property.

additive inverse

● **P R O P E R T Y**
Additive Inverse Property For every integer a, there exists a unique integer ⁻a, called the *additive inverse* of a, such that $a + {}^-a = 0 = {}^-a + a$.

Observe that the additive inverse of ^-a can be written as $^-(^-a)$, or a. Because the additive inverse of ^-a must be unique, we have $^-(^-a) = a$.

The additive inverse property and other properties of integer addition makes it possible to prove the following property.

● P R O P E R T Y
Property of Integer Addition

For any integers, a and b:

$^-a + ^-b = ^-(a + b)$

EXAMPLE 4-6   Find the additive inverse of each of the following.
(a) $^-(3 + x)$ (b) $(a + ^-4)$ (c) $^-3 + (^-x)$

SOLUTION   (a) $3 + x$
(b) $^-(a + ^-4)$, which can be written as $^-(a) + ^-(^-4)$, or $^-a + 4$.
(c) $^-[^-3 + (^-x)]$, which can be written as $^-(^-3) + ^-(^-x)$, or $3 + x$.

Integer Subtraction

As with integer addition, we explore several models for integer subtraction.

Patterns Model.   We may find the difference of two integers by considering the following patterns, where we start with subtractions that we already know how to do. Both the pattern on the left and the pattern on the right start with $3 - 2 = 1$.

$3 - 2 = 1$	$3 - 2 = 1$
$3 - 3 = 0$	$3 - 1 = 2$
$3 - 4 = ?$	$3 - 0 = 3$
$3 - 5 = ?$	$3 - ^-1 = ?$

In the pattern on the left, the difference decreases by 1. If we continue the pattern, we have $3 - 4 = ^-1$ and $3 - 5 = ^-2$. In the pattern on the right, the difference increases by 1. If we continue the pattern, we have $3 - ^-1 = 4$ and $3 - ^-2 = 5$.

Charged-field Model.   Integer subtraction can be modeled with a charged field. For example, consider Figure 4-10, where $^-3 - ^-5$ is modeled. We start with a 0 charge, as in Figure 4-10(a). To model the integer $^-3$, we place 3 negative charges in the 0-charged field, as shown in Figure 4-10(b). Finally, we take away 5 negative charges from the charges in Figure 4-10(b), giving the result of a positive 2 charge on the field, as shown in Figure 4-10(c). Thus, $^-3 - ^-5 = 2$.

FIGURE 4-10

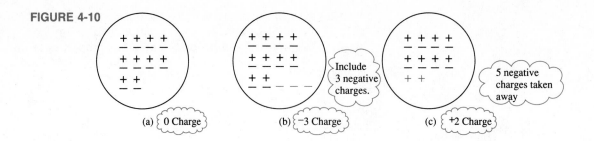

(a) 0 Charge   (b) ⁻3 Charge   (c) ⁺2 Charge

Number-line Model. The number-line model used for integer addition may also be used to model integer subtraction. In Figure 4-11, the car starts at 0 and is pointed in a positive direction.

FIGURE 4-11

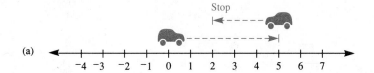

(a)

5 – 3 first involves moving the car forward 5 units; then the minus sign for the subtraction operation tells us to face the car in the negative direction, finally moving it forward 3 units, for a net move of 2 units to the right from 0. Thus, 5 – 3 = 2.

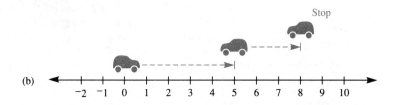

(b)

5 – ⁻3 involves moving the car forward 5 units and then facing it in a negative direction and moving it in reverse 3 units. The net move is 8 units to the right of 0. Thus, 5 – ⁻3 = 8.

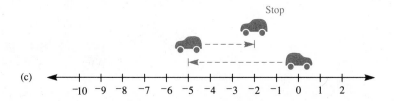

(c)

⁻5 – ⁻3 involves moving the car 5 units in reverse and then facing it in a negative direction and moving it in reverse 3 units. The net move is 2 units to the left of 0. Thus, ⁻5 – ⁻3 = ⁻2.

Subtraction as the Inverse of Addition

Subtraction of integers, like subtraction of whole numbers, can be defined in terms of addition. Recall that $5 - 3$ can be computed by finding a whole number n as follows.

$$5 - 3 = n \quad \text{if and only if} \quad 5 = 3 + n$$

Because $3 + 2 = 5$, then $n = 2$.

Similarly, we compute $3 - 5$ as follows.

$$3 - 5 = n \quad \text{if and only if} \quad 3 = 5 + n$$

Because $5 + {}^-2 = 3$, then $n = {}^-2$. In general, for integers a and b, we have the following definition of *subtraction*.

- **D E F I N I T I O N**
  For integers a and b, $a - b$ is the unique integer n such that $a = b + n$.

From our previous work with addition of integers, we know that $3 + {}^-5 = {}^-2$ and $3 - 5 = {}^-2$. Hence, $3 - 5 = 3 + {}^-5$. In general, the following is true.

- **P R O P E R T Y**
  For all integers a and b, $a - b = a + ({}^-b)$.

EXAMPLE 4-7 Use the definition of subtraction to compute the following.
(a) $3 - 10$ (b) ${}^-2 - 10$

SOLUTION (a) Let $3 - 10 = n$. Then $10 + n = 3$, so $n = {}^-7$. Therefore, $3 - 10 = {}^-7$.
(b) Let ${}^-2 - 10 = n$. Then $10 + n = {}^-2$, so $n = {}^-12$. Therefore, ${}^-2 - 10 = {}^-12$.

Many calculators have a change-of-sign key, either $\boxed{\text{CHS}}$ or $\boxed{+/-}$, that allows computation with integers. For example, to compute $8 - ({}^-3)$, we would press $\boxed{8}\boxed{-}\boxed{3}\boxed{+/-}\boxed{=}$.

Subtraction of integers is developed on the following student page from *Addison-Wesley Mathematics*, 1989, Grade 7. This student page uses the missing-addend approach, as well as the addition-of-the-opposite approach.

Subtracting Integers

The air temperature outside a plane was
⁻10°C at an altitude of 1,500 m. The
temperature at ground level was 2°C. What is
the difference between the ground level
temperature and the temperature at 1,500 m?

To find the difference, we subtract.

$2 - {}^- 10$ ⟨ What number added to ⁻10 equals 2? ⟩

Since $12 + {}^- 10 = 2$, then $2 - {}^- 10 = 12$.

The difference in the temperature is 12°C.

To *subtract* any integer, we *add* its
opposite.

$$2 - {}^- 10 = 2 + 10 = 12$$
opposites

$$3 - 8 = 3 + {}^- 8 = {}^- 5$$
opposites

Other Examples

$$0 - {}^- 6 = 0 + 6 = 6$$
opposites

$$3 - 5 = 3 + {}^- 5 = {}^- 2$$
opposites

$${}^- 1 - {}^- 3 = {}^- 1 + 3 = 2$$
opposites

EXAMPLE 4-8 Compute each of the following, using the fact that $a - b = a + (^-b)$.
(a) $2 - 8$ (b) $2 - (^-8)$ (c) $^-12 - (^-5)$ (d) $^-12 - 5$

SOLUTION (a) $2 - 8 = 2 + {}^-8 = {}^-6$
(b) $2 - (^-8) = 2 + {}^-(^-8) = 2 + 8 = 10$
(c) $^-12 - (^-5) = {}^-12 + {}^-(^-5) = {}^-12 + 5 = {}^-7$
(d) $^-12 - 5 = {}^-12 + {}^-5 = {}^-17$

EXAMPLE 4-9 Write an expression equal to $^-(b + {}^-c)$ that contains no parentheses.

SOLUTION $^-(b + {}^-c) = {}^-b + {}^-(^-c) = {}^-b + c$

EXAMPLE 4-10 Simplify each of the following.
(a) $2 - (5 - x)$ (b) $5 - (x - 3)$ (c) $^-(x - y) - y$

SOLUTION (a) $2 - (5 - x) = 2 + {}^-(5 + {}^-x)$
$= 2 + {}^-5 + {}^-(^-x)$
$= 2 + {}^-5 + x$
$= {}^-3 + x$
(b) $5 - (x - 3) = 5 + {}^-(x + {}^-3)$
$= 5 + {}^-x + {}^-(^-3)$
$= 5 + {}^-x + 3$
$= 8 + {}^-x$
$= 8 - x$
(c) $^-(x - y) - y = (^-x + y) - y$
$= (^-x + y) + {}^-y$
$= {}^-x + (y + {}^-y)$
$= {}^-x + 0$
$= {}^-x$

Order of Operations

Subtraction on the set of integers is neither commutative nor associative, as illustrated in these counterexamples.

$$5 - 3 \neq 3 - 5 \quad \text{because} \quad 2 \neq {}^-2$$
$$(3 - 15) - 8 \neq 3 - (15 - 8) \quad \text{because} \quad {}^-20 \neq {}^-4$$

Remember, if parentheses are present in an arithmetic expression, any computations within parentheses must be completed before other computations.

An expression such as $3 - 15 - 8$ is ambiguous unless there is agreement about the order in which subtractions are performed. Mathematicians agree that $3 - 15 - 8$ means $(3 - 15) - 8$; that is, the subtractions in $3 - 15 - 8$ are performed in the order of their appearance from left to right. Similarly, $3 - 4 + 5$ means $(3 - 4) + 5$ and not $3 - (4 + 5)$. Thus, $(a - b) - c$ may be written without parentheses as $a - b - c$.

EXAMPLE 4-11 Compute each of the following.
(a) $2 - 5 - 5$ (b) $3 - 7 + 3$ (c) $3 - (7 - 3)$

SOLUTION   (a) $2 - 5 - 5 = {}^-3 - 5 = {}^-8$
(b) $3 - 7 + 3 = {}^-4 + 3 = {}^-1$
(c) $3 - (7 - 3) = 3 - 4 = {}^-1$

PROBLEM SET 4-1

1. Find the opposite of each of the following integers. Write your answer in the simplest possible form.
   (a) 2   (b) $^-5$ (c) m
   (d) 0   (e) ^-m (f) $a + b$

2. Simplify each of the following.
   (a) $^-(^-2)$ (b) $^-(^-m)$ (c) $^-0$

3. Evaluate each of the following.
   (a) $|^-5|$ (b) $|10|$ (c) $^-|^-5|$ (d) $^-|5|$

4. Demonstrate each of the following additions, using the charged-field model.
   (a) $5 + {}^-3$ (b) $^-2 + 3$ (c) $^-3 + 2$
   (d) $^-3 + {}^-2$

5. Demonstrate each of the additions in Problem 4, using the colored-chips model.

6. Demonstrate each of the additions in Problem 4, using a number-line model.

7. Add each of the following.
   (a) $10 + {}^-3$ (b) $10 + {}^-12$
   (c) $10 + {}^-10$ (d) $^-10 + 10$
   (e) $^-2 + {}^-8$ (f) $(^-2 + {}^-3) + 7$
   (g) $^-2 + (^-3 + 7)$

8. Write an addition fact corresponding to each of the following sentences, and then answer the question.
   (a) A certain stock dropped 17 points and the following day gained 10 points. What was the net change in the stock's worth?
   (b) The temperature was $^-10°C$ and then it rose by $8°C$. What is the new temperature?
   (c) The plane was at 5000 feet and dropped 100 feet. What is the new altitude of the plane?
   (d) A visitor in a Las Vegas casino lost $200, won $100, and then lost $50. What was the change in the gambler's net worth?
   (e) In four downs, the football team lost 2 yards, gained 7 yards, gained 0 yards, and lost 8 yards. What was the total gain or loss?

9. On January 1, Jane's bank balance was $300. During the month, she wrote checks for $45, $55, $165, $35, and $100 and made deposits of $75, $25, and $400.

   (a) If a check is represented by a negative integer and a deposit by a positive integer, express Jane's transactions as a sum of positive and negative integers.
   (b) What was the balance in Jane's account at the end of the month?

10. Use the charged-field model to show each of the following.
    (a) $3 - {}^-2 = 5$ (b) $^-3 - 2 = {}^-5$
    (c) $^-3 - {}^-2 = {}^-1$

11. Use the car model to find the following.
    (a) $^-4 - {}^-1$ (b) $^-4 - {}^-3$

12. Use patterns to show the following.
    (a) $^-4 - {}^-1 = {}^-3$ (b) $^-2 - 1 = {}^-3$

13. Evaluate each of the following, using the definition of subtraction.
    (a) $2 - 11$ (b) $^-3 - 7$
    (c) $5 - (^-8)$ (d) $0 - 4$

14. Perform each of the following.
    (a) $^-2 + (3 - 10)$ (b) $[8 - (^-5)] - 10$
    (c) $(^-2 - 7) + 10$ (d) $^-2 - (7 + 10)$
    (e) $8 - 11 - 10$ (f) $^-2 - 7 + 3$

15. Consider the expressions $(x + y) - (z + w)$ and $(x - z) + (y - w)$.
    (a) Are the expressions equal if $x = 30$, $y = 4$, $z = 10$, and $w = 7$?
    (b) Are the expressions equal if $x = {}^-4$, $y = 5$, $z = {}^-9$, and $w = 7$?

16. Simplify each of the following as much as possible
    (a) $3 - (2 - 4x)$ (b) $x - (^-x - y)$
    (c) $4x - 2 - 3x$

17. Find all integers x such that the following are true.
    (a) ^-x is positive.
    (b) ^-x is negative.
    (c) $^-x - 1$ is positive.
    (d) $|x| = 2$
    (e) $^-|x| = 2$
    (f) $^-|x|$ is negative.
    (g) $^-|^-x|$ is positive.

18. Columbus discovered America in 1492. Rome was founded 2,275 years before that. When was Rome founded?

19. Let W stand for the set of whole numbers, I the set of integers, I^+ the set of positive integers, and I^- the set of negative integers. Find each of the following.
    (a) $W \cup I$ (b) $W \cap I$ (c) $I^+ \cup I^-$
    (d) $I^+ \cap I^-$ (e) $W - I$ (f) $I - W$
    (g) $W - I^+$ (h) $W - I^-$ (i) $I \cap I$

20. Complete the magic square, using the following integers: $^-13$, $^-10$, $^-7$, $^-4$, 2, 5, 8, 11.

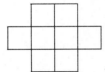

21. Place the integers 1 through 8 in the following boxes so that no two consecutive integers are in boxes that share a common side or vertex (corner).

22. Donna picked the Knicks basketball team to win by 12 points. Instead, they lost by 21. By how many points did Donna misjudge the score?

23. Answer each of the following.
    (a) In a game of Triominoes, Jack's scores in five successive turns were 17, $^-8$, $^-9$, 14, and 45. What was his total at the end of five turns?
    (b) The largest bubble chamber in the world is 15 feet in diameter and contains 7259 gallons of liquid hydrogen at a temperature of $^-247°C$. If the temperature is dropped by 11°C per hour for 2 consecutive hours, what is the new temperature?
    (c) The greatest recorded temperature ranges in the world are around the Siberian "cold pole" in the USSR. Temperatures in Verkhoyansk have varied from $^-94°F$ to 98°F. What is the difference between the high and low temperatures in Verkhoyansk?

(d) A turnpike driver had car trouble. He knew that he had driven 12 miles from milepost 68 before the trouble. If he is confused and disoriented when he calls on his CB for help, what are his possible locations?

24. Let $f(x) = {}^-x - 1$. Find the following.
    (a) $f(^-1)$ (b) $f(100)$ (c) $f(^-2)$
    (d) For which values of x will the output be 3?

25. Let $f(x) = |1 - x|$. Find the following.
    (a) $f(10)$ (b) $f(^-1)$
    (c) all the inputs for which the output is 1.
    (d) The range.

26. The following is the definition for the absolute value function, where the domain is the set of integers.

    If x is a positive integer or 0, then $|x| = x$.
    If x is a negative integer, then $|x| = {}^-x$.

    (a) What is the range of this function?
    (b) Use the definition to evaluate each of the following.
        (i) $|5|$ (ii) $|^-5|$
        (iii) $|0|$ (iv) $^-|^-7|$

27. Find the opposites for each of the following, using the $\boxed{+/-}$ key on a calculator.
    (a) 14   (b) 24   (c) $^-2$ (d) $^-5$

28. Complete each of the following integer arithmetic problems on the calculator, making use of the $\boxed{+/-}$ key. For example, to find $^-5 + {}^-4$, press $\boxed{5}\boxed{+/-}$ $\boxed{+}\boxed{4}\boxed{+/-}\boxed{=}$.
    (a) $^-12 + {}^-6$ (b) $^-7 + {}^-99$
    (c) $^-12 + 6$ (d) $27 + {}^-5$
    (e) $3 + {}^-14$ (f) $^-7 - {}^-9$
    (g) $^-12 - 6$ (h) $16 - {}^-7$

★29. Classify each of the following as true or false. If false, give a counterexample.
    (a) $|^-x| = |x|$
    (b) $|x - y| = |y - x|$
    (c) $|^-x + {}^-y| = |x + y|$
    (d) $|x^2| = x^2$
    (e) $|x^3| = x^3$
    (f) $|x^3| = x^2|x|$

B R A I N   T E A S E R

If the digits 1 through 9 are written in order, it is possible to place plus and minus signs between the numbers or to use no operation symbol at all to obtain a total of 100. For example,

$$1 + 2 + 3 + {}^-4 + 5 + 6 + 78 + 9 = 100$$

Can you obtain a total of 100 using fewer plus or minus signs than in the given example? Notice that digits, such as 7 and 8, may be combined.

Section 4-2   Multiplication and Division of Integers

Multiplication of integers can be approached through a variety of models.

Patterns Model. We may approach multiplication of integers by using repeated addition. For example, if E. T. Simpson lost 2 yards on each of three carries in a football game, then he had a net loss of ⁻2 + ⁻2 + ⁻2, or ⁻6, yards. Since ⁻2 + ⁻2 + ⁻2 can be written as $3 \cdot (⁻2)$, using repeated addition, we have $3 \cdot (⁻2) = ⁻6$.

Consider a product such as $(⁻2) \cdot 3$. It is meaningless to say that there are ⁻2 threes in a sum. To develop a feeling for what $(⁻2) \cdot 3$ should be, consider this pattern.

$$4 \cdot 3 = 12$$
$$3 \cdot 3 = 9$$
$$2 \cdot 3 = 6$$
$$1 \cdot 3 = 3$$
$$0 \cdot 3 = 0$$
$$⁻1 \cdot 3 = ?$$
$$⁻2 \cdot 3 = ?$$

The first five products, 12, 9, 6, 3, and 0, are terms of an arithmetic sequence with fixed difference ⁻3. If the pattern continues, the next two terms in the sequence are ⁻3 and ⁻6. Thus, it appears that $(⁻2) \cdot 3 = ⁻6$. Recall that $3 \cdot (⁻2)$ also equals ⁻6. Hence, if $(⁻2) \cdot 3 = ⁻6$, we have $(⁻2) \cdot 3 = 3 \cdot (⁻2)$. This result is consistent with the commutative property of multiplication developed for whole numbers.

Next, consider the product $(⁻2) \cdot (⁻3)$. Using the previous results, the following pattern can be developed.

$$(^-2) \cdot 3 = {}^-6$$
$$(^-2) \cdot 2 = {}^-4$$
$$(-2) \cdot 1 = {}^-2$$
$$(^-2) \cdot 0 = 0$$
$$(^-2) \cdot (^-1) = ?$$
$$(^-2) \cdot (^-2) = ?$$
$$(^-2) \cdot (^-3) = ?$$

The first four products, $^-6$, $^-4$, $^-2$, and 0, are terms in an arithmetic sequence with fixed difference 2. If the pattern continues, the next three terms in the sequence are 2, 4, and 6. Thus, it appears that $(^-2) \cdot (^-3) = 6$.

Charged-field Model. The charged-field model can be used to illustrate multiplication of integers, although an interpretation must be given to the signs. Consider Figures 4-12 and 4-13, where $3 \cdot (^-2)$ and $-3 \cdot (^-2)$, respectively, are pictured.

FIGURE 4-12

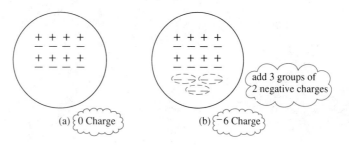

The result is a charge of $^-6$, so $3 \cdot (-2) = {}^-6$.

FIGURE 4-13

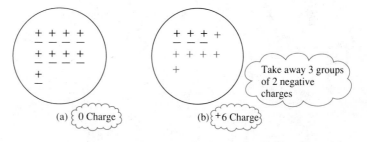

The result is a charge of positive 6, so $^-3 \cdot (^-2) = 6$.

Number Line Model. One model involves imagining a car moving along a number line. The rules for moving along the number line are as follows.

1. Traveling to the left (west) means moving in the negative direction, and traveling to the right (east) means moving in the positive direction.
2. Time in the future is denoted by a positive value, and time in the past is denoted by a negative value.

Consider the number line shown in Figure 4-14. Various cases using this number line are given next.

FIGURE 4-14

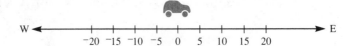

1. If you are now at 0 and move east at 50 km/hr, where will you be 3 hrs from now?

$$50 \times 3 = 150$$

Move east at 50 km/hr.   3 hrs from now   You will be 150 km east of 0.

2. If you are now at 0, moving east at 50 km/hr, where were you 3 hrs ago?

$$50 \times {}^-3 = {}^-150$$

Moving east at 50 km/hr.   3 hrs ago   You were 150 km west of 0.

3. If you are now at 0 and move west at 50 km/hr, where will you be 3 hrs from now?

$${}^-50 \times 3 = {}^-150$$

Move west at 50 km/hr.   3 hrs from now   You will be 150 km west of 0.

4. If you are now at 0, moving west at 50 km/hr, where were you 3 hrs ago?

$${}^-50 \times {}^-3 = 150$$

Moving west at 50 km/hr.   3 hrs ago   You were 150 km east of 0.

These models illustrate the following definition of *multiplication of integers*.

• **D E F I N I T I O N**
For any whole numbers a and b:

1. $ab = n(A \times B)$, where $a = n(A)$ and $b = n(B)$, for sets A and B.
2. $({}^-a)({}^-b) = ab$
3. $({}^-a)b = b({}^-a) = {}^-(ab)$

H I S T O R I C A L   N O T E
Leonard Euler, in his book *Anleitung zur Algebra* (1770), was one of the first mathematicians to attempt to prove that $({}^-1) \cdot ({}^-1) = 1$. He reasoned that the product must be either 1 or $^-1$. It was already known that $(1) \cdot ({}^-1) = {}^-1$, so he reasoned that $({}^-1) \cdot ({}^-1) = 1$. Do you agree with this reasoning?

Properties of Integer Multiplication

The set of integers has properties under multiplication analogous to those of the set of whole numbers under multiplication. These properties are summarized next.

● P R O P E R T I E S

The set of integers I satisfies the following properties of multiplication for all integers $a, b, c \in I$.

Closure Property of Multiplication of Integers ab is a unique integer.
Commutative Property of Multiplication of Integers $ab = ba$.
Associative Property of Multiplication of Integers $(ab)c = a(bc)$
Identity Element of Multiplication of Integers   1 is the unique integer such that for all integers a, $1 \cdot a = a = a \cdot 1$.
Distributive Properties of Multiplication over Addition for Integers $a(b + c) = ab + ac$ and $(b + c)a = ba + ca$
Zero Multiplication Property of Integers   0 is the unique integer such that, for all integers a, $a \cdot 0 = 0 = 0 \cdot a$

A mathematical approach to showing that $(^-2) \cdot 3 = {^-}(2 \cdot 3)$ uses the uniqueness property of additive inverses. If we can show that $(^-2) \cdot 3$ and $^-(2 \cdot 3)$ are additive inverses of the same number, then they must be equal. By definition, the additive inverse of $(2 \cdot 3)$ is $^-(2 \cdot 3)$. That $(^-2) \cdot 3$ is also the additive inverse of $2 \cdot 3$ can be proved by showing that $(^-2) \cdot 3 + 2 \cdot 3 = 0$. The proof follows.

$(^-2) \cdot 3 + 2 \cdot 3 = (^-2 + 2) \cdot 3$ Distributive property of multiplication over addition

$\qquad\qquad = 0 \cdot 3$ Additive inverse

$\qquad\qquad = 0$ Zero multiplication

Because $(^-2) \cdot 3$ and $^-(2 \cdot 3)$ are both additive inverses of $(2 \cdot 3)$ and because the additive inverse must be unique, $(^-2) \cdot 3 = {^-}(2 \cdot 3)$.

The preceding proof holds for any integers a and b.

● P R O P E R T Y

For any integers a and b, $(^-a)b = {^-}(ab)$.

Similarly, we can prove the following.

● P R O P E R T Y

For any integers a and b, $(^-a)(^-b) = ab$.

Note that there is no restriction that a must be positive or that ^-a must be negative.

EXAMPLE 4-12   Find each of the following.
(a) $(^-3) \cdot (^-15)$ (b) $(^-5) \cdot 7$ (c) $0 \cdot (^-3)$
(d) $0 \cdot (^-n), n \in W$ (e) $(^-5)^4$

SOLUTION   (a) $(^-3) \cdot (^-15) = 45$ (b) $(^-5) \cdot 7 = ^-35$
(c) $0 \cdot (^-3) = 0$ (d) $0 \cdot (^-n) = 0$
(e) $(^-5)^4 = (^-5) \cdot (^-5) \cdot (^-5) \cdot (^-5) = 625$

Another property that can be developed using the distributive property of multiplication over addition is the distributive property of multiplication over subtraction. Consider the following.

$$a(b - c) = a(b + {}^-c)$$
$$= ab + a(^-c)$$
$$= ab + {}^-(ac)$$
$$= ab - ac$$

Consequently, $a(b - c) = ab - ac$. Similarly, it can be shown that $(b - c)a = ba - ca$.

● P R O P E R T Y
Distributive Property of Multiplication over Subtraction for Integers   For any integers a, b, and c,
$$a(b - c) = ab - ac$$
$$(b - c)a = ba - ca$$

EXAMPLE 4-13   Simplify each of the following so that there are no parentheses in the final answer.
(a) $(^-3)(x - 2)$ (b) $(a + b)(a - b)$

SOLUTION   (a) $(^-3)(x - 2) = (^-3)x - (^-3)(2) = {}^-3x - (^-6) = {}^-3x + 6$
(b) $(a + b)(a - b) = (a + b)a - (a + b)b$
$$= (a^2 + ba) - (ab + b^2)$$
$$= a^2 + ab - ab - b^2$$
$$= a^2 - b^2$$
Thus, $(a + b)(a - b) = a^2 - b^2$.

The result $(a + b)(a - b) = a^2 - b^2$ in Example 4-13(b) generally is called *difference of squares*   the **difference-of-squares** formula.

EXAMPLE 4-14 Use the difference-of-squares formula to aid in simplifying the following.
(a) $22 \cdot 18$ (b) $(4 + b)(4 - b)$ (c) $(^-4 + b)(^-4 - b)$ (d) $24 \cdot 26$

SOLUTION (a) $22 \cdot 18 = (20 + 2)(20 - 2) = 20^2 - 2^2 = 400 - 4 = 396$
(b) $(4 + b)(4 - b) = 4^2 - b^2 = 16 - b^2$
(c) $(^-4 + b)(^-4 - b) = (^-4)^2 - b^2 = 16 - b^2$
(d) $24 \cdot 26 = (25 - 1)(25 + 1) = (25)^2 - 1^2 = 625 - 1 = 624$

Both the difference-of-squares formula and the distributive properties of multiplication over addition and subtraction can be used for factoring.

EXAMPLE 4-15 Factor each of the following completely.
(a) $x^2 - 9$ (b) $(x + y)^2 - z^2$ (c) $^-3x + 5xy$ (d) $3x - 6$

SOLUTION (a) $x^2 - 9 = x^2 - 3^2 = (x + 3)(x - 3)$
(b) $(x + y)^2 - z^2 = (x + y + z)(x + y - z)$
(c) $^-3x + 5xy = x(^-3 + 5y)$
(d) $3x - 6 = 3(x - 2)$

Integer Division

Division is the last operation on integers to be considered. Recall that, on the set of whole numbers, $a \div b$, where $b \neq 0$, is defined to be the unique whole number c such that $a = bc$. If such a whole number c does not exist, then $a \div b$ is undefined. Division on the set of integers is defined analogously.

- **D E F I N I T I O N**
  If a and b are any integers, with $b \neq 0$, then $a \div b$ is the unique integer c, if it exists, such that $a = bc$.

EXAMPLE 4-16 Use the definition of division to evaluate each of the following.
(a) $12 \div (^-4)$ (b) $^-12 \div 4$ (c) $^-12 \div (^-4)$ (d) $^-12 \div 5$

SOLUTION (a) Let $12 \div (^-4) = c$. Then, $12 = ^-4c$, and consequently, $c = ^-3$. Thus, $12 \div (^-4) = ^-3$.
(b) Let $^-12 \div 4 = c$. Then, $^-12 = 4c$, and therefore, $c = ^-3$. Thus, $^-12 \div 4 = ^-3$.
(c) Let $^-12 \div (^-4) = c$. Then, $^-12 = ^-4c$, and consequently, $c = 3$. Thus, $^-12 \div (^-4) = 3$.
(d) Let $^-12 \div 5 = c$. Then, $^-12 = 5c$. Because no integer c exists to satisfy this equation, $^-12 \div 5$ is undefined.

Example 4-16 suggests that, *if it exists, the quotient of two negative integers is a positive integer and, if it exists, the quotient of a positive and a negative integer or of a negative and a positive integer is negative.*

Order of Operations on Integers

The following rules apply to the order in which arithmetic operations are performed. Recall that, when addition and multiplication appear in a problem without parentheses, multiplication is done first.

When addition, subtraction, multiplication, and division appear without parentheses, multiplications and divisions are done first, in the order of their appearance from left to right, and then additions and subtractions are done, in the order of their appearance from left to right. Any arithmetic operation appearing inside parentheses must be done first.

EXAMPLE 4-17   Evaluate each of the following.
(a) $2 - 5 \cdot 4 + 1$ (b) $(2 - 5) \cdot 4 + 1$
(c) $2 - 3 \cdot 4 + 5 \cdot 2 - 1 + 5$ (d) $2 + 16 \div 4 \cdot 2 + 8$
(e) $(^-3)^4$ (f) $^-3^4$

SOLUTION   (a) $2 - 5 \cdot 4 + 1 = 2 - 20 + 1 = {}^-18 + 1 = {}^-17$
(b) $(2 - 5) \cdot 4 + 1 = {}^-3 \cdot 4 + 1 = {}^-12 + 1 = {}^-11$
(c) $2 - 3 \cdot 4 + 5 \cdot 2 - 1 + 5 = 2 - 12 + 10 - 1 + 5 = 4$
(d) $2 + 16 \div 4 \cdot 2 + 8 = 2 + 4 \cdot 2 + 8 = 2 + 8 + 8 = 10 + 8 = 18$
(e) $(^-3)^4 = (^-3)(^-3)(^-3)(^-3) = 81$
(f) $^-3^4 = {}^-(3^4) = {}^-(81) = {}^-81$

● **R E M A R K**
Notice that, from Example 4-17(e) and (f), we have $(^-3)^4 \neq {}^-3^4$.

That $(^-3)^4$ means $(^-3)(^-3)(^-3)(^-3)$ and that $^-3^4$ means $^-(3^4)$, or $^-(3 \cdot 3 \cdot 3 \cdot 3)$ follow from a convention that, in an arithmetic operation involving exponents, the raising of powers should be done first, followed by any operations inside of parentheses, followed by the normal arithmetic operations.

B R A I N   T E A S E R
Express each of the numbers from 1 through 10 using four 4s and any operations. For example,

$1 = 44 \div 44$ or
$1 = (4 \div 4)^{44}$ or
$1 = {}^-4 + 4 + (4 \div 4)$

PROBLEM SET 4-2

1. Use patterns to show that $(^-1)(^-1) = 1$.
2. Use the charged-field model to show that $(^-4)(^-2) = 8$.
3. Use the number-line model to show that $(^-4) \cdot 2 = {}^-8$.

4. Evaluate each of the following.
    (a) $^-3(^-4)$ (b) $3(^-5)$
    (c) $(^-5) \cdot 3$ (d) $^-5 \cdot 0$
    (e) $^-2(^-3 \cdot 5)$ (f) $[^-2(^-5)](^-3)$
    (g) $(^-4 + 4)(^-3)$ (h) $(^-5 - {}^-3)(^-5 - 3)$

5. Use the definition of division to find each quotient (if possible). If a quotient is not defined, explain why.
   (a) $^-40 \div ^-8$
   (b) $143 \div (^-11)$
   (c) $^-143 \div 13$
   (d) $0 \div (^-5)$
   (e) $^-5 \div 0$
   (f) $0 \div 0$

6. Evaluate each of the following (if possible).
   (a) $(^-10 \div ^-2)(^-2)$
   (b) $(^-40 \div 8)8$
   (c) $(a \div b)b$
   (d) $(^-10 \cdot 5) \div 5$
   (e) $(ab) \div b$
   (f) $(^-8 \div ^-2)(^-8)$
   (g) $(^-6 + ^-14) \div 4$
   (h) $(^-8 + 8) \div 8$
   (i) $^-8 \div (^-8 + 8)$
   (j) $(^-23 - ^-7) \div 4$
   (k) $(^-6 + 6) \div (^-2 + 2)$
   (l) $^-13 \div (^-1)$
   (m) $(^-36 \div 12) \div 3$
   (n) $|^-24| \div (3 - 15)$

7. (a) On each of four consecutive plays in a football game, Foo University lost 11 yards. If lost yardage is interpreted as a negative integer, write the information as a product of integers and determine the total number of yards lost.
   (b) If Jack Jones lost a total of 66 yards in 11 plays, how many yards, on the average, did he lose on each play?

8. The temperature has been rising by 6°C each hour. If the temperature is 9°C now, what was it 4 hours ago?

9. In 1979, it was predicted that the farmland acreage lost to family dwellings over the next 9 years would be 12,000 acres per year. If this prediction were true, and if this pattern were to continue, how much acreage would be lost to homes by the end of 1990?

10. Consider the distributive property of multiplication over addition, $a(b + c) = ab + ac$. Show that this property is true for each of the following values of a, b, and c.
    (a) $a = ^-1, b = ^-5, c = ^-2$
    (b) $a = ^-3, b = ^-3, c = 2$
    (c) $a = ^-5, b = 2, c = ^-6$

11. Show that $a \div (b + c) \neq (a \div b) + (a \div c)$ for each of the following values of a, b, and c.
    (a) $a = 12, b = ^-2, c = 4$
    (b) $a = ^-20, b = 4, c = ^-5$
    (c) $a = ^-10, b = 1, c = 1$

12. Consider the statement $(a + b) \div c = (a \div c) + (b \div c)$. Is this statement true for each of the following values of a, b, and c?
    (a) $a = ^-9, b = 21, c = 3$
    (b) $a = ^-9, b = ^-21, c = ^-3$
    (c) $a = 9, b = ^-21, c = ^-3$
    (d) $a = ^-50, b = 25, c = ^-25$

13. Compute each of the following.
    (a) $(^-2)^3$
    (b) $(^-2)^4$
    (c) $(^-10)^5 \div (^-10)^2$
    (d) $(^-3)^5 \div (^-3)$
    (e) $(^-1)^{10}$
    (f) $(^-1)^{15}$
    (g) $(^-1)^{50}$
    (h) $(^-1)^{151}$

14. Compute each of the following.
    (a) $^-2 + 3 \cdot 5 - 1$
    (b) $10 - 3 \cdot 7 - 4(^-2) + 3$
    (c) $10 - 3 - 12$
    (d) $10 - (3 - 12)$
    (e) $(^-3)^2$
    (f) $^-3^2$
    (g) $^-5^2 + 3(^-2)^2$
    (h) $^-2^3$
    (i) $(^-2)^5$
    (j) $^-2^4$

15. If x is an integer and $x \neq 0$, which of the following are always positive and which are always negative?
    (a) $^-x^2$
    (b) x^2
    (c) $(^-x)^2$
    (d) $^-x^3$
    (e) $(^-x)^3$
    (f) $^-x^4$
    (g) $(^-x)^4$
    (h) x^4
    (i) x
    (j) ^-x

16. Which of the expressions in Problem 15 are equal to each other for all values of x except 0?

17. Simplify each of the following expressions by removing parentheses to write an equivalent expression.
    (a) $(^-x)(^-y)$
    (b) $^-2x(^-y)$
    (c) $^-(x + y) + x + y$
    (d) $^-1 \cdot x$
    (e) $x - 2(^-y)$
    (f) $a - (a - b)$
    (g) $y - (y - x)$
    (h) $^-(x - y) + x$

18. Find a pattern for each of the following, and write the next three terms.
    (a) $7, 3, ^-1, ^-5, ^-9, \underline{\quad}, \underline{\quad}, \underline{\quad}$
    (b) $^-2, ^-4, ^-6, ^-8, ^-10, \underline{\quad}, \underline{\quad}, \underline{\quad}$
    (c) $2187, ^-729, 243, ^-81, 27, \underline{\quad}, \underline{\quad}, \underline{\quad}$
    (d) $^-20, ^-17, ^-14, ^-11, ^-8, \underline{\quad}, \underline{\quad}, \underline{\quad}$

19. For each of the following, find all integers x (if possible) that make the following true.
    (a) $^-3x = 6$
    (b) $^-3x = ^-6$
    (c) $^-2x = 0$
    (d) $5x = ^-30$
    (e) $x \div 3 = ^-12$
    (f) $x \div (^-3) = ^-2$
    (g) $x \div (^-x) = ^-1$
    (h) $0 \div x = 0$
    (i) $x \div 0 = 1$
    (j) $x^2 = 9$
    (k) $x^2 = ^-9$
    (l) $^-x \div ^-x = 1$
    (m) $^-x^2$ is negative.
    (n) $^-(1 - x) = x - 1$
    (o) $x - 3x = ^-2x$

20. Multiply each of the following.
    (a) $^-2(x - 1)$
    (b) $^-2(x - y)$
    (c) $x(x - y)$
    (d) $^-x(x - y)$
    (e) $^-2(x + y - z)$
    (f) $^-x(x - y - 3)$
    (g) $(^-5 - x)(5 + x)$
    (h) $(x - y - 1)(x + y + 1)$
    (i) $(^-x^2 + 2)(x^2 - 1)$

21. Use the difference-of-squares formula to simplify each of the following, if possible.
    (a) $52 \cdot 48$
    (b) $(5 - 100)(5 + 100)$
    (c) $(^-x - y)(^-x + y)$
    (d) $(2 + 3x)(2 - 3x)$
    (e) $(x - 1)(1 + x)$
    (f) $213^2 - 13^2$

22. Can $(^-x - y)(x + y)$ be multiplied by using the difference-of-squares formula? Explain why or why not.

23. Factor each of the following expressions completely and then simplify, if possible.
    (a) $3x + 5x$ (b) $ax + 2x$
    (c) $xy + x$ (d) $ax - 2x$
    (e) $x^2 + xy$ (f) $3x - 4x + 7x$
    (g) $3xy + 2x - xz$ (h) $3x^2 + xy - x$
    (i) $abc + ab - a$
    (j) $(a + b)(c + 1) - (a + b)$
    (k) $16 - a^2$ (l) $x^2 - 9y^2$
    (m) $4x^2 - 25y^2$ (n) $(x^2 - y^2) + x + y$

24. Identify the property of integers being illustrated in each of the following.
    (a) $(^-3) \cdot (4 + 5) = (4 + 5) \cdot (^-3)$
    (b) $^-4 + \; ^-7 \in I$
    (c) $5 \cdot [4 \cdot (^-3)] = (5 \cdot 4) \cdot (^-3)$
    (d) $(^-9) \cdot [5 + (^-8)] = (^-9) \cdot 5 + (^-9) \cdot (^-8)$

25. If x is positive and $y = \; ^-x$, then which of the following statements is false?
    (a) $x^2y > 0$ (b) $x + y = 0$
    (c) xy is negative   (d) xy^2 is positive.

26. (a) Given a calendar for any month of the year, such as the one shown, pick several 3×3 groups of numbers and find the sum of these numbers. How are the obtained sums related to the middle number?

    JULY
S	M	T	W	T	F	S
		1	2	3	4	5
6	7	8	9	10	11	12
13	14	15	16	17	18	19
20	21	22	23	24	25	26
27	28	29	30	31		

    ★(b) Prove that the sum of any 9 digits in any 3×3 set of numbers selected from a monthly calendar will always be equal to 9 times the middle number.

★27. Use the properties of integers to justify each of the following.
    (a) $(^-a)b = \; ^-(ab)$
    (b) $(^-a)(^-b) = ab$
    (c) $^-(a + b) = \; ^-a + \; ^-b$

28. Use the $\boxed{+/-}$ key on the calculator to compute each of the following.
    (a) $^-27 \times 3$ (b) $^-46 \times \; ^-4$
    (c) $^-26 \div 13$ (d) $^-26 \div \; ^-13$

Review Problems

29. Compute each of the following.
    (a) $3 - 6$ (b) $8 + \; ^-7$
    (c) $5 - \; ^-8$ (d) $^-5 - \; ^-8$
    (e) $^-8 + 5$ (f) $^-8 + \; ^-5$

30. Illustrate $^-8 + \; ^-5$ on a number line.

31. Find the opposite of each of the following.
    (a) $^-5$ (b) 7 (c) 0

32. Compute each of the following.
    (a) $|^-14|$ (b) $|^-14| + 7$
    (c) $8 - |^-12|$ (d) $|11| + |^-11|$

33. In the 1400s, European merchants used positive and negative numbers to label barrels of flour. For example, a barrel labeled $^+3$ meant that the barrel was 3 pounds overweight, whereas a barrel labeled $^-5$ meant that the barrel was 5 pounds underweight. If the following numbers were found on 100-pound barrels, what was the total weight of the barrels?

  $+4$ $^-3$ $+5$ $^-6$

B R A I N T E A S E R

If $a, \ldots, z$ are integers, find the product

$$(x - a)(x - b)(x - c) \cdots (x - z)$$

Section 4-3   Solving Equations and Inequalities

The topic of this section is writing and solving equations and inequalities.

Properties of Equations

To solve equations, we need several properties of equality. Many of these can be discovered by children using a balance scale. For example, consider two weights of amounts a and b on the balances, as in Figure 4-15(a). If the balance is level, then we can conclude that $a = b$. When we add an equal amount of weight c to both sides, the balance is still level, as in Figure 4-15(b)

FIGURE 4-15

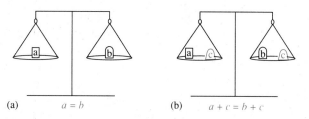

(a) $a = b$ (b) $a + c = b + c$

This demonstrates that, if $a = b$, then $a + c = b + c$.

Similarly, if we have the scale balanced with amounts a and b, as in Figure 4-16(a), and we put some additional a's on one side and an equal number of b's on the other side, the scale remains level, as in Figure 4-16(b).

FIGURE 4-16

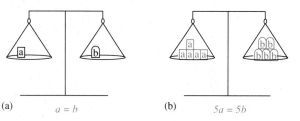

(a) $a = b$ (b) $5a = 5b$

The principle demonstrated is that, if $a = b$, then $ac = bc$. The properties illustrated in Figures 4-15 and 4-16 are given next.

● P R O P E R T I E S

The Addition Property of Equality   For any integers a, b, and c, if $a = b$, then $a + c = b + c$.

The Multiplication Property of Equality   For any integers a, b, and c, if $a = b$, then $ac = bc$.

According to the addition property of equality, it is possible to add the same integer to both sides of an equation without affecting the equality. According to the multiplication property of equality, it is possible to multiply both sides of an equation by the same integer without affecting the equality. (Multiplication of both sides by zero is rarely used.)

substitution property

Also using the balance scale, it follows that any quantity may be substituted for a quantity of equal weight. This demonstrates that it is valid to substitute a number for its equal. This property is referred to as the **substitution property.** Examples of substitution follow:

1. If $a + b = c + d$ and $d = 5$, then $a + b = c + 5$.
2. If $a + b = c + d$, if $b = e$, and if $d = f$, then $a + e = c + f$.

The addition property of equality was formulated as follows. For any integers, a, b, and c, if $a = b$, then $a + c = b + c$. A new statement results from reversing the order of the *if* and *then* parts of this addition property. This new statement is called the *converse* of the original statement. In the case of the addition property, the converse is a true statement. The converse of the multiplication property of equality is also true when $c \neq 0$. These properties are as follows.

● **P R O P E R T Y**
The Subtraction and Division Properties of Equality:

1. For any integers a, b, and c, if $a + c = b + c$, then $a = b$.
2. For any integers a, b, and c, with $c \neq 0$, if $ac = bc$, then $a = b$.

Properties of Inequalities

Before we consider solving equations and inequalities, we have to develop additional properties of inequalities for integers. As with whole numbers, greater-than and less-than relations can be defined for integers.

● **D E F I N I T I O N**
For any integers a and b, a is **greater than** b, written $a > b$, if and only if there exists a positive integer k such that $a = b + k$. Also, b is **less than** a, written $b < a$, if and only if $a > b$.

By the definition of *greater than*, $a > b$ if and only if there exists a positive integer k such that $a = b + k$. By the definition of subtraction, $a = b + k$ if and only if $a - b = k$. Thus, because k is positive, $a - b > 0$. We summarize this discussion as follows.

For any two integers a and b, $a > b$ if and only if $a - b > 0$; that is, $a > b$ if and only if $a - b$ is positive.

Table 4-1 compares the properties of the inequality relations with the properties of the equality relation. Assume that a, b, and c represent integers. It is possible to combine properties of equality and inequality by using the $\geq$ or $\leq$ symbols.

TABLE 4-1

Property	Equality	Inequality
Addition	$a = b$ implies $a + c = b + c$	$a > b$ implies $a + c > b + c$ $a < b$ implies $a + c < b + c$
Multiplication	$a = b$ implies $ac = bc$	$a > b$ and $c > 0$ implies $ac > bc$ $a > b$ and $c < 0$ implies $ac < bc$ $a < b$ and $c > 0$ implies $ac < bc$ $a < b$ and $c < 0$ implies $ac > bc$

Examples of the addition property of greater than follow.

$$5 > 2 \quad \text{implies} \quad 5 + 10 > 2 + 10$$
$$^-2 > {}^-5 \quad \text{implies} \quad {}^-2 + 2 > {}^-5 + 2$$
$$x > 3 \quad \text{implies} \quad x + 2 > 3 + 2$$
$$x - 3 > 5 \quad \text{implies} \quad x - 3 + 3 > 5 + 3$$

The following are examples of the multiplication property.

$$5 > 3 \quad \text{implies} \quad 5 \cdot 2 > 3 \cdot 2, \text{ but } 5(^-2) < 3(^-2)$$
$$^-3 > {}^-5 \quad \text{implies} \quad (^-3)2 > (^-5)2, \text{ but } (^-3)(^-2) < (^-5)(^-2)$$
$$x > 3 \quad \text{implies} \quad 2x > 2 \cdot 3, \text{ but } {}^-2x < {}^-2 \cdot 3$$

The preceding examples suggest that the multiplication properties of greater than and less than summarized in Table 4-1 are true. In general, it is possible to prove the following.

When both sides of an inequality are multiplied by a positive integer, the direction of inequality is preserved, but if both sides of an inequality are multiplied by a negative integer, the direction of inequality is reversed.

Properties for subtraction and division of inequalities follow from the addition and multiplication properties of inequality.

● **P R O P E R T I E S**
Subtraction and Division Properties of Inequalities:
If a, b, and c are any integers, then:
1. $a > b$ implies $a - c > b - c$;
2. $a > b$ and $c > 0$ implies $a \div c > b \div c$, provided that the divisions are defined;
3. $a > b$ and $c < 0$ implies $a \div c < b \div c$, provided that the divisions are defined.

EXAMPLE 4-18 Justify each of the following.

(a) $^-2 > {}^-5$ implies $^-7 > {}^-10$.
(b) $10 > 6$ implies $5 > 3$.
(c) $10 > 6$ implies $^-5 < {}^-3$.
(d) $2x > 6$ implies $x > 3$.
(e) $^-2x > {}^-6$ implies $x < 3$.

SOLUTION   (a) By the subtraction property of inequality, $^-2 > {}^-5$ implies
$^-2 - 5 > {}^-5 - 5$; that is, $^-7 > {}^-10$.

(b) By the division property of inequality, $10 > 6$ implies
$10 \div 2 > 6 \div 2$; that is, $5 > 3$.

(c) By the division property of inequality, $10 > 6$ implies
$10 \div {}^-2 < 6 \div {}^-2$; that is, $^-5 < {}^-3$.

(d) By the division property of inequality, $2x > 6$ implies
$2x/2 > 6/2$; that is, $x > 3$.

(e) By the division property of inequality, $^-2x > {}^-6$ implies
$^-2x/({}^-2) < {}^-6/({}^-2)$; that is $x < 3$.

Developing Prealgebra Skills

To apply algebra in solving problems, we frequently need to translate given information into a symbolic expression involving quantities designated by letters. Consider the following.

A teacher told her class to do the following computations.
"Take any number and add 15 to it. Now multiply that sum by 4. Next subtract 8, and divide the difference by 4. If you now subtract 12 from the quotient and tell me the number, I will tell you the number you started with."

To analyze the problem and to see how the teacher was able to tell the original number, we translate the information into an algebraic form.

Instructions	Discussion	Symbols
Take any number.	Since any number is used, we need a variable to represent the number. Let n be that variable.	n
Add 15 to it.	We are told to add 15 to "it." "It" refers to the variable n.	$n + 15$
Multiply that sum by 4.	We are told to multiply "that sum" by 4. "That sum" is $n + 15$.	$4(n + 15)$
Subtract 8.	Now we subtract 8 from the product.	$4(n + 15) - 8$
Divide the difference by 4.	The difference is $4(n + 15) - 8$. We divide by 4.	$\dfrac{4(n + 15) - 8}{4}$
Subtract 12 from the quotient, and tell me the answer.	We subtract 12 from the quotient.	$\dfrac{4(n + 15) - 8}{4} - 12$

It is left as an exercise to determine why the teacher was able to give the original number.

Some common English phrases used in word problems, together with their symbolic translations, are given in Table 4-2, where n and a represent variables.

TABLE 4-2

Greater than n by a	$n + a$
Less than n by a	$n - a$
a times n	an
The difference of n and a	$n - a$
The sum of n and a	$n + a$
The square of a subtracted from the square of n	$n^2 - a^2$
The square of the difference of a and n	$(a - n)^2$

• **R E M A R K**
It should be noted that the difference of n and a could also be written as $a - n$. The context is frequently the only guide as to which is intended.

Solving Equations

Part of the study of algebra involves operations on numbers and other elements represented by symbols. Finding solutions to equations and inequalities is one part of algebra.

H I S T O R I C A L   N O T E
The word "algebra" comes from the Arabic book *Al-jabr wa'l muqabalah* written by Mohammed al-Khowârizmî (ca. 825). *Al-jabr* means restoring the balance in an equation by putting on one side of an equation a term that has been removed from the other side. Algebra was introduced in Europe in the thirteenth and fourteenth centuries by Leonardo of Pisa (also called Fibonacci). Algebra was occasionally referred to as *Ars Magna*, "the great art." Both Diophantus (ca. A.D. 250) and Francois Viete (1540–1603) have been called "fathers of algebra." About Diophantus, a Greek, little is known except that he is supposed to have lived to be 84 years old and that he was the author of *Arithmetica,* a treatise originally in 13 books. Viete was a French lawyer who devoted his leisure time to mathematics. Not liking the word *algebra,* he referred to the subject as "the analytic art." Mary Fairfax Somerville (1780–1872) was born in Scotland of upper-class parents. Her introduction to algebra came while looking at a fashion magazine. She was not allowed to study mathematics formally, but at age 27, widowed and with two children, she bought and studied a set of mathematics books. At 92, she read and worked problems in higher algebra for 4 or 5 hours each morning.

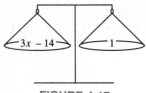

FIGURE 4-17

In order to solve equations, we may use the properties of equality developed earlier. We can use a balance scale to solve the equation $3x - 14 = 1$. We first put the equal expressions on the opposite pans of the balance scale. Since the expressions are equal, the pans should be level, as in Figure 4-17.

To solve for x, we use the properties of equality to manipulate the expressions on the scale in such a way that, after each successive move, the scale remains level and such that, at the final step, only an x remains on one side of the scale. The number on the other side of the scale represents the solution to the original equation. To find a possible value for x in the equation of Figure 4-17, consider the scales pictured in successive steps in Figure 4-18. In Figure 4-18, each successive scale represents an equation that is equivalent to the original equation; that is, each has the same solution as the original. Because the last scale determines the equation $x = 5$, it follows that 5 is the only potential solution to the original equation. To check that $x = 5$ is the correct solution, we substitute 5 into the original equation for x. We obtain $3 \cdot 5 - 14 = 1$; this is a true statement, and hence 5 is the solution to the original equation.

FIGURE 4-18

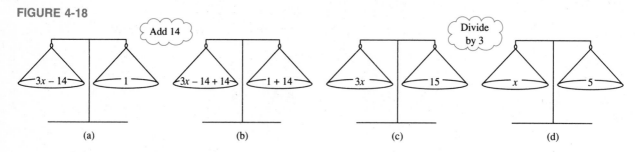

(a) (b) (c) (d)

EXAMPLE 4-19   Solve each of the following for x, where x is an integer.
(a) $x + 4 = {}^-6$ (b) $x + 4 > {}^-6$
(c) ${}^-x - 5 = 8$ (d) ${}^-x - 5 \geq 8$
(e) ${}^-2x + 3 = {}^-11$ (f) ${}^-2x + 3 > {}^-11$

SOLUTION   (a)
$$x + 4 = {}^-6$$
$$(x + 4) + {}^-4 = {}^-6 + {}^-4$$
$$x + (4 + {}^-4) = {}^-6 + {}^-4$$
$$x + 0 = {}^-10$$
$$x = {}^-10$$

(b)
$$x + 4 > {}^-6$$
$$(x + 4) + {}^-4 > {}^-6 + {}^-4$$
$$x + (4 + {}^-4) > {}^-6 + {}^-4$$
$$x + 0 > {}^-10$$
$$x > {}^-10, \quad x \in I$$

(c)
$${}^-x - 5 = 8$$
$$({}^-x - 5) + 5 = 8 + 5$$
$${}^-x = 13$$
$$({}^-x)({}^-1) = 13({}^-1)$$
$$x = {}^-13$$

(d)
$${}^-x - 5 \geq 8$$
$$({}^-x - 5) + 5 \geq 8 + 5$$
$${}^-x \geq 13$$
$$({}^-x)({}^-1) \leq 13({}^-1)$$
$$x \leq {}^-13, \quad x \in I$$

$$(e) \qquad {}^-2x + 3 = {}^-11$$
$$({}^-2x + 3) + {}^-3 = {}^-11 + {}^-3$$
$${}^-2x = {}^-14$$
$$({}^-2x) \div {}^-2 = {}^-14 \div {}^-2$$
$$x = 7$$

$$(f) \qquad {}^-2x + 3 > {}^-11$$
$$({}^-2x + 3) + {}^-3 > {}^-11 + {}^-3$$
$${}^-2x > {}^-14$$
$$({}^-2x) \div {}^-2 < ({}^-14) \div {}^-2$$
$$x < 7, \quad x \in I$$

Algebra can be used to solve many types of problems. Naturally, the types of problems we attempt in the elementary school are not the complex problems involved with topics such as world economics or space travel, but they can help develop competence in problem solving. Students need to practice problem solving at a low level before they can attempt higher-order problems. The following simple model demonstrates a method for solving word problems: Formulate the word problem as a mathematical problem, solve the mathematical problem, and then interpret the solution in terms of the original problem.

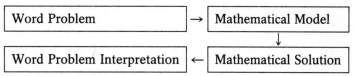

At the third-grade level, an example of this model appears as follows.

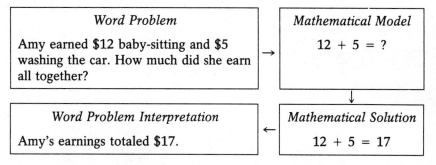

Polya's four-step problem-solving process can be applied to solving word problems in which the use of algebra is appropriate.

In the first step of Polya's four-step process, Understanding the Problem, we identify what is given and what is to be found. In the second step, Devising a Plan, we assign letters to the unknown quantities and translate the information in the problem into a model involving equations or inequalities. In the third step, Carrying Out the Plan, we solve the equations or inequalities. In the fourth step, Looking Back, we interpret the solution in terms of the original problem and check the solution to be sure the original problem is answered. This process is demonstrated on page 214, which is a student page from *Addison-Wesley Mathematics*, 1988, Grade 8, and in the following problems. Work through the problems at the bottom of the student page.

PROBLEM SOLVING: Writing and Solving Equations

QUESTION
DATA
PLAN
ANSWER
CHECK

Ken and May Yamamoto bought living room furniture. The total cost with tax and interest was $2,250. They made a down payment of $450. The balance was to be paid in 8 equal payments. How much was each payment?

To solve the problem, you can write and solve a two-step equation.

Let p = the amount of each payment.

$8p$ = amount for 8 payments

$8p + 450$ = total cost

Equation: $8p + 450 = 2,250$

$$8p + 450 - 450 = 2,250 - 450$$

$$8p = 1,800$$

$$\frac{8p}{8} = \frac{1,800}{8}$$

$$p = 225$$

Check: $8 \times 225 + 450 = 1,800 + 450 = 2,250$

Each payment was $225.

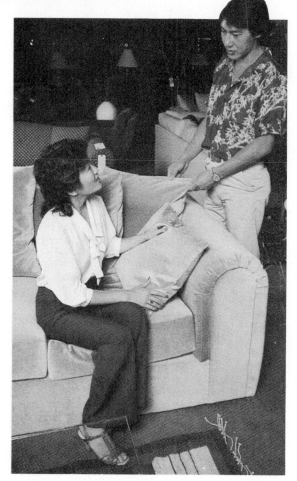

Write and solve an equation for each problem.

1. A certain number is divided by 6 and 17 is added to the quotient. The result is 21. What is the number?

Let n = the number.

2. If 15 is subtracted from 8 times a certain number, the difference is 57. What is the number?

Let n = the number.

3. A number is multiplied by 7 and then 36 is added to the product. The sum is 106. What is the number?

4. A number is divided by 4 and then 19 is subtracted from the quotient. The difference is 2. What is the number?

PROBLEM 1

David is thinking of a number. If he multiplies that number by $^-3$ and then adds 6, he has $^-4$ times his original number. What is David's original number?

Understanding the Problem. The problem asks us to find David's number. We are given that the number times $^-3$, plus 6, equals $^-4$ times the number.

Devising a Plan. Let n represent David's number. Now, we translate the information from the problem into mathematical symbols and solve the resulting equation.

Information	*Mathematical Translation*
David is thinking of a number.	n
He multiplies that number by $^-3$.	^-3n
He adds 6.	$^-3n + 6$
He has $^-4$ times his original number.	$^-3n + 6 = {}^-4n$

Carrying Out the Plan. Solve the equation.

$$^-3n + 6 = {}^-4n$$
$$4n + {}^-3n + 6 = 4n + {}^-4n$$
$$n + 6 = 0$$
$$n = {}^-6$$

Thus, the number David is thinking about is $^-6$.

Looking Back. To check that $^-6$ is the correct solution, follow the written information, using $^-6$ as David's number. The number, $^-6$, times $^-3$, is 18. Next, 18 plus 6 is 24. Also, $^-4$ times the number, $^-6$, is 24. So the answer is correct.

PROBLEM 2

Beans that cost 75¢ per pound are mixed with beans that cost 95¢ per pound to produce a 20-pound mixture that costs 80¢ per pound. How many pounds of the beans costing 75¢ per pound are used?

Understanding the Problem. The problem asks how many pounds of beans costing 75¢ per pound are necessary to make 20 pounds of a mixture costing 80¢ per pound. To make the 20-pound mixture, beans costing 95¢ per pound are mixed with beans costing 75¢ per pound. Thus, the number of pounds of beans costing 95¢ per pound is 20 minus the number of pounds of beans costing 75¢ per pound. Also, the total cost of the beans costing 75¢ per pound and the beans costing 95¢ per pound must be the cost of 20 pounds of beans costing 80¢ per pound.

Devising a Plan. Let x stand for the number of pounds of beans costing 75¢ per pound. Using this symbolism, we know that the number of pounds of beans costing 95¢ per pound is $20 - x$ pounds. Since the rest of the given information involves cost, we need the cost of each type of beans. The cost of x pounds of beans costing 75¢ per pound is $75x$ (in cents). Similarly, the cost of $20 - x$ pounds of beans costing 95¢ per pound is $95(20 - x)$ (in cents). The total mixture, 20 pounds, costs 80¢ per pound or $80 \cdot 20$ cents. We use this information to write the following equation.

$$75x + 95(20 - x) = 80 \cdot 20$$

Carrying Out the Plan.

We must solve the equation for x. This will give the number of pounds of beans costing 75¢ per pound.

$$
\begin{aligned}
75x + 95(20 - x) &= 80 \cdot 20 \\
75x + 1900 - 95x &= 1600 \\
^-20x + 1900 &= 1600 \\
^-20x &= {}^-300 \\
x &= 15
\end{aligned}
$$

Thus, 15 pounds of beans costing 75¢ per pound are required. Because there are 20 pounds of the final mixture, of which 15 pounds consist of beans costing 75¢ per pound, $20 - 15$, or 5, pounds of beans costing 95¢ per pound are used.

Looking Back. The solution should be checked in the original problem. The cost of 15 pounds of beans costing 75¢ per pound is $15 \cdot 75$¢, or \$11.25. The cost of 5 pounds of beans costing 95¢ per pound is $5 \cdot 95$¢, or \$4.75. The cost of 20 pounds of the final mixture at 80¢ per pound is $20 \cdot 80$¢, or \$16.00. The conditions of the problem are satisfied because \$11.25 + \$4.75 = \$16.00.

A different method of solving the problem involves using two unknowns. We let x stand for the number of pounds of 75¢ beans and y stand for the number of pounds of 95¢ beans. Next, we translate the information from the problem into mathematical statements. There are 20 pounds in the blend, so we have $x + y = 20$. The remaining information tells us about the cost per pound of each type of bean. To produce an equation using this information, notice that the value of beans costing 75¢ per pound plus the value of beans costing 95¢ per pound equals the value of the 20-pound mixture of beans.

Cost of 75¢ per pound beans plus cost of 95¢ per pound beans = cost of mixture

$$75x \qquad + \qquad 95y \qquad = \qquad 80 \cdot 20$$

The two equations obtained are as follows.

$$
\begin{aligned}
x + y &= 20 \\
75x + 95y &= 80 \cdot 20
\end{aligned}
$$

We know how to solve equations with one unknown, so we try to combine these two equations into one equation with one unknown. This can be achieved by solving one of the equations for y and then substituting the expression for y in the other equation. Because $x + y = 20$ implies $y = 20 - x$, we substitute $20 - x$ for y in the second equation and solve for x. We then use the value of x obtained to find the value of y.

PROBLEM 3

In a certain factory, machine A produces three times as many bolts as machine B. Machine C produces 13 more bolts than machine A. If the total production is 4997 bolts per day, how many bolts does each machine produce in a day?

Understanding the Problem.   The problem asks for the number of bolts that each of machine A, machine B, and machine C produces in 1 day. The problem gives information that compares the production of A to B and of C to A.

Devising a Plan.   Let a, b, and c be the number of bolts produced by machines A, B, and C, respectively. We translate the given problem into equations as follows.

Machine A produces 3 times as many bolts as B: $a = 3b$
Machine C produces 13 more bolts than A: $c = a + 13$
Total production is 4997: $a + b + c = 4997$

In order to reduce the number of variables, we substitute $3b$ for a in the second and third equations.

$c = a + 13$ becomes $c = 3b + 13$
$a + b + c = 4997$ becomes $3b + b + c = 4997$

Next, we make an equation in one variable, b, by substituting $3b + 13$ for c in the equation $3b + b + c = 4997$, solve for b, and then find a and c.

Carrying Out the Plan.

$$3b + b + 3b + 13 = 4997$$
$$7b + 13 = 4997$$
$$7b = 4984$$
$$b = 712$$

Thus, $a = 3b = 3 \cdot 712 = 2136$. Also, $c = a + 13 = 2136 + 13 = 2149$. Machine A produces 2136 bolts, machine B produces 712 bolts, and machine C produces 2149 bolts.

Looking Back. To check the answers, we follow the original information, using $a = 2136$, $b = 712$, and $c = 2149$. The information in the first sentence, "Machine A produces 3 times as many bolts as machine B," checks, since $2136 = 3 \cdot 712$. The second sentence, "Machine C produces 13 more bolts than machine A," is true because $2149 = 13 + 2136$. The information in the last sentence, "The total production was 4997 bolts," checks, since $2136 + 712 + 2149 = 4997$.

An alternate solution to Problem 3 is as follows. Let x be the number of bolts produced by machine B. Then, we express the number of bolts that machines A and C produce in terms of x.

Information	Mathematical Translation
The number of items that machine B produces.	x
Machine A produces three times as many items as machine B.	$3x$
Machine C produces 13 more items than machine A.	$3x + 13$
The total production is 4997.	$x + 3x + (3x + 13) = 4997$

Solve the equation.

$$x + 3x + (3x + 13) = 4997$$
$$7x + 13 = 4997$$
$$7x = 4984$$
$$x = 712$$

Hence, machine B produces 712 bolts. Because $3x = 3 \cdot 712 = 2136$, machine A produces 2136 bolts; $3x + 13 = 2136 + 13 = 2149$, so machine C produces 2149 bolts.

If we had let x be the number of bolts that machine A produces, the problem would have been more complicated to solve, because machine B then produces $x \div 3$ bolts.

PROBLEM 4

Mary, a 10-year-old calculator genius, announced a discovery to her classmates one day. She said, "I have found a special five-digit number I call *abcde*. If I enter 1 and then the number on my calculator and then multiply by 3, the result is the number with 1 on the end!" Can you find her number?

Understanding the Problem. Mary found a five-digit number called *abcde*, for which three times the display

1	a	b	c	d	e

gives the display

a	b	c	d	e	1

on the calculator.

It will help us to understand the problem if we guess any five-digit number and see if our guess is correct. Suppose that we guess 34,578. With 1 after it, it becomes 345,781. With 1 before it, it becomes 134,578. But since $3 \cdot 134{,}578 \neq 345{,}781$, our guess is incorrect.

Devising a Plan. We know that three times $1abcde$ is $abcde1$. This can be translated to an equation by letting the unknown number on the display $abcde$ be n and using place value. Note that $1abcde$ equals $1 \cdot 10^5 + n$, or $100{,}000 + n$, and $abcde1$ equals $n \cdot 10 + 1$, or $10n + 1$. Thus, Mary's computation tells us that

$$3(100{,}000 + n) = 10n + 1$$

Now all we have to do to solve the problem is to solve this equation for n.

Carrying Out the Plan. We use properties of equality to solve the equation for n.

$$
\begin{aligned}
3(100{,}000 + n) &= 10n + 1 \\
300{,}000 + 3n &= 10n + 1 \\
299{,}999 &= 7n \\
42{,}857 &= n
\end{aligned}
$$

Consequently, the five-digit number is 42,857.

Looking Back. To check the answer, we compute $3 \cdot 142{,}857 = 428{,}571$ and see that the solution is correct. Similar problems can be investigated by asking analogous questions for six-, seven-, or eight-digit numbers. Another generalization is to find a five-digit number n such that $k(100{,}000 + n) = 10n + 1$, where k is different from 3.

An alternate solution to this problem can be found by considering the multiplication one digit at a time. For example, in Figure 4-19(a), we see that $3 \cdot e$ has a 1 in the units digit of the product. Because e is a single digit and 7 is the only single digit that can be multiplied by 3 to yield a product with units digit 1, then e must be 7. If we substitute 7 for e, as shown in Figure 4-19(b), we see that $3 \cdot d + 2$ has 7 as a units digit, or—equivalently— that $3 \cdot d$ has 5 as units digit. Because d is a single digit and 5 is the only single digit that can be multiplied by 3 to yield a product with a units digit 5, we know that $d = 5$. Similarly, each of the digits a, b, and c can also be found.

FIGURE 4-19

$$
\begin{array}{r}
1abcde \\
\times \quad 3 \\
\hline
abcde1
\end{array}
\qquad
\begin{array}{r}
\overset{2}{1abcd7} \\
\times \quad 3 \\
\hline
abcd71
\end{array}
$$

(a)   (b)

B R A I N   T E A S E R

The following is an argument showing that an ant weighs as much as an elephant. What is wrong?

Let e be the weight of the elephant and a the weight of the ant. Let $e - a = d$. Consequently, $e = a + d$. Multiply each side of $e = a + d$ by $e - a$. Then simplify.

$$e(e - a) = (a + d)(e - a)$$
$$e^2 - ea = ae + de - a^2 - da$$
$$e^2 - ea - de = ae - a^2 - da$$
$$e(e - a - d) = a(e - a - d)$$
$$e = a$$

Thus, the weight of the elephant equals the weight of the ant.

PROBLEM SET 4-3

1. Write each of the following lists of numbers in increasing order.
   (a) $^-13, ^-20, ^-5, 0, 4, ^-3$
   (b) $^-5, ^-6, 5, 6, 0$
   (c) $^-20, ^-15, ^-100, 0, ^-13$
   (d) $13, ^-2, ^-3, 5$
2. Show that each of the following is true.
   (a) $^-3 > ^-5$ (b) $^-6 < 0$
   (c) $^-8 > ^-10$ (d) $^-5 < 4$
3. Solve each of the following if x is an integer.
   (a) $x + 3 = ^-15$ (b) $x + 3 > ^-15$
   (c) $3 - x = ^-15$ (d) $^-x + 3 > ^-15$
   (e) $^-x - 3 = 15$ (f) $^-x - 3 \geq 15$
   (g) $3x + 5 = ^-16$ (h) $3x + 5 < ^-16$
   (i) $^-3x + 5 = 11$ (j) $^-3x + 5 \leq 11$
   (k) $5x - 3 = 7x - 1$ (l) $5x - 3 > 7x - 1$
   (m) $3(x + 5) = ^-4(x + 5) + 21$
   (n) $^-5(x + 3) > 0$
4. Which of the following are true for all possible integer values of x?
   (a) $3(x + 1) = 3x + 3$ (b) $x - 3 = 3 - x$
   (c) $x + 3 = 3 + x$.
   (d) $2(x - 1) + 2 = 3x - x$
   (e) $x^2 + 1 > 0$
   (f) $3x > 4x - x$
5. For each of the following, which elements of the given set, if any, satisfy the equation or inequality?
   (a) $x^3 + x^2 = 2x$, $\{1, ^-1, ^-2, 0\}$
   (b) $3x - 3 = 24$, $\{^-9, 9\}$
   (c) $^-x \geq 5$, $\{6, ^-6, 7, ^-7, 2\}$
   (d) $x^2 < 16$, $\{^-4, ^-3, ^-2, ^-1, 0, 1, 2, 3, 4\}$
6. Solve each of the following equations. Check your answers by substituting in the given equation. Assume that x, y, and z represent integers.

   (a) $^-2x + ^-11 = 3x + 4$ (b) $5(^-x + 1) = 5$
   (c) $^-3y + 4 = y$ (d) $^-3(z - 1) = 8z + 3$
7. Translate each of the following expressions into symbolic expressions, where n represents the unknown number.
   (a) The difference of 6 and another number.
   (b) The sum of a number and 14.
   (c) Seven less than four times n.
   (d) Eight greater than three times n.
   (e) The number increased by 10.
   (f) The number multiplied by 4.
   (g) Thirteen decreased by the number.
   (h) The number less four.
8. The area of Asia is 982,000 square miles more than twice that of North America. The area of North America exceeds that of South America by 1,186,000 square miles and exceeds that of Europe by 4,383,000 square miles. The total area of the four continents is 35,692,000 square miles. Find the area of each.
9. If you multiply Tom's age by 3 and add 4, the result is more than 37. What can you tell about Tom's age?
10. If you multiply a number by $^-6$ and then add 20 to the product, the result is 50. What is the number?
11. David has three times as much money as Rick. Together, they have $400. How much does each have?
12. Ran is 4 years older than Nureet. Six years ago Ran was twice as old as Nureet was then. How old are they now?
13. Help Calvin in the cartoon by translating the information in the first panel of the cartoon into symbols. Assume that A, B, and C lie in a straight line.

Calvin and **Hobbes** by Bill Watterson

14. Factory A produces twice as many cars per day as factory B. Factory C produces 300 cars more per day than factory A. If the total production in the three factories is 7300 cars per day, how many cars per day are produced in each factory?

15. Tea that costs 60¢ per pound is mixed with tea that costs 45¢ per pound to produce a 100-pound blend that costs 51¢ per pound. How much of each kind of tea is used?

16. For a certain event, 812 tickets were sold, totaling $1912. If students paid $2 per ticket and non-students paid $3 per ticket, how many student tickets were sold?

17. The sum of three consecutive integers is 237. Find the three integers.

18. The sum of three consecutive even integers is 240. Find the three integers.

19. The sum of two integers is 21. The first number is twice the second number. Find the integers.

20. A man left an estate of $64,000 to three children. The eldest child received three times as much as the youngest. The middle child received $14,000 more than the youngest. How much did each child receive?

★21. (a) Is it always true that, for any integers x and y, $x^2 + y^2 \geq 2xy$? Prove your answer.
(b) For which integers x and y is $x^2 + y^2 = 2xy$?

★**22.** If $0 < a < b$, where a and b are integers, prove that $a^2 < b^2$.

★23. If $a < b$, where a and b are integers, is it always true that $a^2 < b^2$?

★**24.** If $a < b$, where a and b are integers, prove that $c - b < c - a$, if c is an integer.

★25. For each of the following, find all integers x such that the statement is true.
(a) $x + 1 < 3$ and $^-x + 1 < 5$
(b) $2x < {}^-6$ or $1 + x < 0$

Review Problems

26. Find the additive inverse of each of the following.
(a) $^-7$ (b) 5
(c) $^-(^-3)$ (d) $3 - (^-7)$

27. Compute each of the following.
(a) $^-3 + {}^-7$ (b) $^-3 - {}^-7$
(c) $3 + {}^-7$ (d) $3 - {}^-7$
(e) $^-3 \cdot 7$ (f) $^-3 \cdot {}^-7$
(g) $3 - 7$ (h) $^-21 \div 7$
(i) $^-21 \div {}^-7$ (j) $7 - 3 - 8$
(k) $8 + 2 \cdot 3 - 7$ (l) $^-8 - 7 - 2 \cdot 3$
(m) $|^-7| \cdot |^-3|$ (n) $|^-7| \cdot |^-8|$
(o) $|^-7| + 8$ (p) $|^-7| - |^-8|$

28. Compute $^-7 + (^-3)$, using a number line.

SOLUTION TO THE PRELIMINARY PROBLEM

Understanding the Problem. The problem is to find the amount of money that a sailor had before he went to three casinos. We know that at the first casino he doubled his money and then lost $30; at the second, he tripled his money but then lost $54; and, finally, at the third, he quadrupled his money but spent $72, at which time he had $48 left.

Devising a Plan.   We could work backward, since we know how much money the sailor had after his casino visits. Another approach is to write and solve an equation. We examine the strategy writing an equation in Carrying Out the Plan, and then we consider the working backward strategy in Looking Back.

Carrying out the Plan.   If we let a be the amount of money with which the sailor started, then we may make the following translations.

Doubled his money	$2a$
Lost $30	$2a - 30$
Tripled his money	$3(2a - 30)$
Lost $54	$3(2a - 30) - 54$
Quadrupled his money	$4[3(2a - 30) - 54]$
Spent $72	$4[3(2a - 30) - 54] - 72$
He was left with $48	$4[3(2a - 30) - 54] - 72 = 48$

Now we have to solve the equation and then check to see if the answer is reasonable. We determine a possible solution set as follows.

$$4[3(2a - 30) - 54] - 72 = 48$$
$$4[3(2a - 30) - 54] - 72 + 72 = 48 + 72$$
$$4[3(2a - 30) - 54] = 120$$
$$4[6a - 90 - 54] = 120$$
$$4[6a - 144] = 120$$
$$6a - 144 = 30$$
$$6a = 174$$
$$a = 29$$

Thus, the sailor started with $29.

Looking Back.   We substitute 29 for a in our original equation to see if it checks. This will simply check the algebra involved, without guaranteeing that 29 is the correct solution to the problem. Substituting, we find the following.

$$4[3(2\cdot29 - 30) - 54] - 72 = 4[3(58 - 30) - 54] - 72 = 4[3\cdot28 - 54] - 72$$
$$= 4[84 - 54] - 72$$
$$= 4\cdot30 - 72 = 120 - 72 = 48$$

Therefore, if our original equation is correct, the final answer is correct.

   Instead of checking the answer in the original problem, we now try our other strategy of solving the problem by working backward. If the sailor had $48 when he left Aladdin's, then he must have had $48 + $72, or $120, immediately before leaving. This was after he had quadrupled his money, so he must have had $120/4, or $30, when he arrived at Aladdin's. This means he had $30 + $54, or $84, before he lost the $54 at Caesar's Palace. Thus, he had $84/3, or $28, before he tripled his money there. Since he left the Tropicana with $28, he had $28 + $30, or $58, just after he doubled his original amount at the Tropicana. Therefore, he had $58/2, or $29 when he started.

To extend the original problem, we could ask: "When should the sailor have quit gambling and spending in order to have had the most money at the end of the evening?"

QUESTIONS FROM THE CLASSROOM

1. A fourth-grade student devised the following subtraction algorithm for subtracting 84 − 27.
   Four minus seven equals negative three.

   $$\begin{array}{r} 84 \\ -27 \\ \hline ^-3 \end{array}$$

   Eighty minus twenty equals sixty.

   $$\begin{array}{r} 84 \\ -27 \\ \hline ^-3 \\ 60 \end{array}$$

   Sixty plus negative three equals fifty-seven.

   $$\begin{array}{r} 84 \\ -27 \\ \hline ^-3 \\ +60 \\ \hline 57 \end{array}$$

   Thus, the answer is 57. What is your response as a teacher?

2. A seventh-grade student does not believe that $^-5 < {}^-2$. The student argues that a debt of $5 is greater than a debt of $2. How do you respond?

3. An eighth-grade student claims she can prove that subtraction of integers is commutative. She points out that if a and b are integers, then $a - b =$ $a + {}^-b$. Since addition is commutative, so is subtraction. What is your response?

4. A student claims that, since $(a \cdot b)^2 = a^2 \cdot b^2$, it must also be true that $(a + b)^2 = a^2 + b^2$. How do you respond?

5. A student solves $1 - 2x > x - 5$, where x is an integer, and reports the solution as $x < 2$. The student asks if it is possible to check the answer in a way similar to the method of substitution for equations. What is your response?

6. A student computes $^-8 - 2(^-3)$ by writing $^-10(^-3)$ $= 30$. How would you help this student?

7. A student says that his father showed him a very simple method for dealing with expressions like $^-(a - b + 1)$ and $x - (2x - 3)$. The rule is: If there is a negative sign before the parentheses, change the signs of the expressions inside the parentheses. Thus, $^-(a - b + 1) = {}^-a + b - 1$ and $x - (2x - 3) = x - 2x + 3$. What is your response?

8. A student solving word problems always checks her solutions by substituting in equations rather than by following the written information. Is this an accurate check for the word problem?

9. A student shows you the following proof that $(^-1)(^-1) = 1$: There are two possibilities, either $(^-1)(^-1) = 1$ or $(^-1)(^-1) = {}^-1$. Suppose $(^-1)(^-1) = {}^-1$. Since $^-1 = (^-1) \cdot 1$, then $(^-1)(^-1) = {}^-1$ can be written as $(^-1)(^-1) = (^-1) \cdot 1$. By the cancellation property of multiplication, it follows that $^-1 = 1$, which is impossible. Hence, $(^-1)(^-1)$ cannot equal $^-1$ and must, therefore, equal 1. What is your reaction?

CHAPTER OUTLINE

I. Basic concepts of integers
   A. The set of **integers**, I, is $\{\ldots, {}^{-}3, {}^{-}2, {}^{-}1, 0, 1, 2, 3, \ldots\}$.
   B. The distance from any integer to 0 is called the **absolute value** of the integer. The absolute value of an integer x is denoted $|x|$.
   C. Operations with integers
      1. **Addition:** For any integers a and b:
      $${}^{-}a + {}^{-}b = {}^{-}(a + b)$$
      2. **Subtraction:**
         (a) If a and b are any integers, then
         $$a - b = n \quad \text{if and only if} \quad a = b + n$$
         (b) For all integers a and b,
         $$a - b = a + {}^{-}b$$
      3. **Multiplication:** For any whole numbers a and b:
         (a) $a \cdot b = n(A \times B)$, where $a = n(A)$ and $b = n(B)$, for sets A and B.
         (b) $({}^{-}a) \cdot ({}^{-}b) = ab$
         (c) $({}^{-}a) \cdot b = b \cdot ({}^{-}a) = {}^{-}(ab)$
      4. **Division:** If a and b are any integers with $b \neq 0$, then $a \div b$ is the unique integer c, if it exists, such that $a = bc$.
      5. **Order of operations:** When addition, subtraction, multiplication, and division appear without parentheses, multiplications and divisions are done first, in the order of their appearance from left to right, and then additions and subtractions are done, in the order of their appearance from left to right. Any arithmetic in parentheses is done first.

II. The system of integers
   A. The set of integers, $I = \{\ldots, {}^{-}3, {}^{-}2, {}^{-}1, 0, 1, 2, 3, \ldots\}$, along with the operations of addition and multiplication, satisfy the following properties.

Property	+	×
Closure	Yes	Yes
Commutative	Yes	Yes
Associative	Yes	Yes
Identity	Yes, 0	Yes, 1
Inverse	Yes	No
Distributive property of multiplication over addition		

B. **Zero multiplication property of integers**
$$a \cdot 0 = 0 = 0 \cdot a$$

C. **Addition property of equality:** For any integers a, b, and c, if $a = b$, then $a + c = b + c$.
D. **Multiplication property of equality:** For any integers a, b and c, if $a = b$, then $ac = bc$.
E. **Substitution property:** Any number may be substituted for its equal.
F. **Subtraction and division properties of equality:**
   (a) For any integers a, b, and c, if $a + c = b + c$, then $a = b$.
   (b) For any integers a, b, and c, if $c \neq 0$ and $ac = bc$, then $a = b$.
G. For all integers a, b, and c:
   1. ${}^{-}({}^{-}a) = a$
   2. $a - (b - c) = a - b + c$
   3. $(a + b)(a - b) = a^2 - b^2$ **(Difference-of-squares formula)**

III. Inequalities
   A. $a > b$ if and only if there exists a positive integer k such that $a = b + k$. $b < a$ if and only if $a > b$.
   B. Let a and b be any two integers. Then, $a > b$ if and only if $a - b > 0$.
   C. Properties of inequalities:
      1. **Addition property:** If $a > b$ and c is any integer, then $a + c > b + c$.
      2. **Multiplication properties:**
         (a) If $a > b$ and $c > 0$, then $ac > bc$.
         (b) If $a > b$ and $c < 0$, then $ac < bc$.

IV. Solving word problems
   A. Solving word problems involves each of the following.
      1. **Understanding the Problem:** Identify what is given and what is to be found.
      2. **Devising a Plan:** Assign letters to the unknown quantities, and translate the data into equations or inequalities.
      3. **Carrying Out the Plan:** Solve the equations or inequalities.
      4. **Looking Back:** Check and interpret the solution in terms of the situation given in the problem.

CHAPTER TEST

1. Find the additive inverse of each of the following.
   - (a) 3
   - (b) ^-a
   - (c) 0
   - (d) $x + y$
   - (e) $^-x + y$
   - (f) $(^-2)^5$
   - (g) $^-2^5$

2. Perform each of the following operations.
   - (a) $(^-2 + ^-8) + 3$
   - (b) $^-2 - (^-5) + 5$
   - (c) $^-3(^-2) + 2$
   - (d) $^-3(^-5 + 5)$
   - (e) $^-40 \div (^-5)$
   - (f) $(^-25 \div 5)(^-3)$

3. For each of the following, find all integer values of x (if there are any) that make the given equation true.
   - (a) $^-x + 3 = 0$
   - (b) $^-2x = 10$
   - (c) $0 \div (^-x) = 0$
   - (d) $^-x \div 0 = ^-1$
   - (e) $3x - 1 = ^-124$
   - (f) $^-2x + 3x = x$

4. Use a pattern approach to show that $(^-2)(^-3) = 6$.

5. (a) Show that $(x - y)(x + y) = x^2 - y^2$.
   (b) Use the result in (a) to compute
   $$(^-2 - x)(^-2 + x).$$

6. Simplify each of the following expressions.
   - (a) ^-1x
   - (b) $(^-1)(x - y)$
   - (c) $2x - (1 - x)$
   - (d) $(^-x)^2 + x^2$
   - (e) $(^-x)^3 + x^3$
   - (f) $(^-3 - x)(3 + x)$

7. Factor each of the following expressions and then simplify, if possible.
   - (a) $x - 3x$
   - (b) $x^2 + x$
   - (c) $x^2 - 36$
   - (d) $81y^6 - 16x^4$
   - (e) $5 + 5x$
   - (f) $(x - y)(x + 1) - (x - y)$

8. Solve each of the following for x, if x is an integer.
   - (a) $^-3x + 7 = ^-x + 11$
   - (b) $|x| = 5$
   - (c) $^-2x + 1 < 0$
   - (d) $^-2(^-3x + 7) < ^-2(^-x + 11)$

9. Classify each of the following as true or false (all letters represent integers).
   - (a) $|x|$ always is positive.
   - (b) For all x and y, $|x + y| = |x| + |y|$.
   - (c) If $a < ^-b$, then $a < 0$.
   - (d) For all x and y, $(x - y)^2 = (y - x)^2$.
   - (e) $(^-a)(^-b)$ is the additive inverse of ab.

10. Find a counterexample to disprove each of the properties on the set of integers.
    - (a) Commutative property of division
    - (b) Associative property of subtraction
    - (c) Closure property for division
    - (d) Distributive property of division over subtraction

11. Use the car model to illustrate each of the following computations.
    - (a) $^-3 - ^-4$
    - (b) $^-3 + ^-4$
    - (c) $^-3(^-4)$

12. If the temperature was $^-16°C$ and it rose by $9°C$, what is the new temperature?

13. Twice Molly's weight added to 50 pounds is equal to 78 pounds. Find Molly's weight.

14. A truck contains 150 small packages, some weighing 1 kg each and some weighing 2 kg each. How many packages of each weight are in the truck if the total weight of the packages is 265 kg?

15. John has a collection of nickels and dimes. He has three more dimes than twice the number of nickels. If he has $2.05, how many of each type of coin does he have?

16. A certain college has 5715 undergraduates. There are 115 more seniors than juniors. The number of sophomores is twice the number of seniors, and the number of freshmen is twice the number of juniors. How many freshmen, sophomores, juniors, and seniors attend the college?

17. Two kegs contain equal quantities of beer. From one keg 37 gallons are drawn, and from the other 7 gallons are drawn. The quantity now remaining in one keg is 7 times that remaining in the other. How much did each keg contain at first?

Number Theory

PRELIMINARY PROBLEM

When his students asked Mr. Factor what his children's ages were, he said, "I have three children. The product of their ages is 72 and the sum of their ages is the number of this room." The children then asked for the door to be opened to verify the room number. Then, Sonja, the class math whiz, told the teacher that she needed more information to solve the problem. Mr. Factor said, "My oldest child is good at chess." Then, Sonja announced the correct ages of Mr. Factor's children. What are the ages of Mr. Factor's children?

Introduction

Number theory, which is concerned primarily with relationships among integers, is associated with names like Pythagoras (500 B.C.), Euclid (300 B.C.), and Diophantus (A.D. 250). As a field of study, number theory began to flourish in the seventeenth century, with the work of Pierre de Fermat, the father of number theory. Many topics from number theory are incorporated in the elementary mathematics curriculum. Such topics include multiples, factors, divisibility tests, prime numbers, prime factorizations, greatest common divisors, and least common multiples. A major use of topics in number theory arises in operations on rational numbers written as fractions in the form a/b, where a and b are integers and $b \neq 0$. The *Standards* offers the following remarks:

Number theory provides rich opportunities for explorations that are interesting, enjoyable, and useful. The fruits of these explorations have payoffs in problem solving, in understanding and developing other mathematical concepts, and in illustrating the beauty of mathematics.

Section 5-1   Divisibility

In a division such as $12 \div 3 = 4$, we can make any of the statements given in the left-hand column below. In general, if $a \div b = c$, where a, b, and c are integers, then the statements in the right-hand column are true.

Example	*General Statement*
12 is divisible by 3.	a is divisible by b.
3 is a divisor of 12.	b is a divisor of a.
12 is a multiple of 3.	a is a multiple of b.
3 is a factor of 12.	b is a factor of a.
3 divides 12.	b divides a.

Each statement in the left-hand column can be written as $3|12$, and each statement in the right-hand column can be written as $b|a$. The expression $b|a$ is usually read "b **divides** a." If $b|a$, then b is a **factor,** or a **divisor,** of a, and a is a **multiple** of b.

divides / factor / divisor
multiple

● **D E F I N I T I O N**

If a and b are any integers, then b divides a, written $b|a$, if and only if there is an integer c such that $a = cb$.

Do not confuse $b|a$ with b/a, which is interpreted as $b \div a$. The former, a relation, is either true or false. The latter, an operation, has a numerical value. To compare $0 \div 0$ and $0|0$, recall that $0 \div 0$ is undefined. However, $0|0$ is a true statement because $0 \cdot a = 0$ for all integers a.

H I S T O R I C A L   N O T E

Pierre de Fermat (1601–1665) was a lawyer and a magistrate who served in the provincial parliament in Toulouse, France. He devoted his leisure time to mathematics—a subject in which he had no formal training. His greatest contribution was to number theory, although during his lifetime he was better known for his research in coordinate geometry, calculus, and probability.

It seems that, through reading Diophantus' *Arithmetica*, Fermat became interested in number theory.

After Fermat's death, his son decided to publish a new edition of *Arithmetica* with Fermat's notes. One of the notes in the margin of Fermat's copy asserted that the equation $x^n + y^n = z^n$ has no positive integer solutions if n is an integer greater than 2 and commented, "I have found an admirable proof of this, but the margin is too narrow to contain it." Many great mathematicians spent years trying to prove Fermat's assertion, now called "Fermat's Last Theorem." With the help of a computer, Fermat's Last Theorem has been proved for all exponents up to 125,000. In 1983, a 29-year-old West German mathematician, Gerd Falting, made major progress toward the solution of the problem, for which he received the Field's Medal in Mathematics (equivalent to the Nobel Prize). However, the original Fermat's Last Theorem, which is now more than 300 years old, remains unproved.

To symbolize that 12 is not divisible by 5, or 5 does not divide 12, we write $5 \nmid 12$. The notation $5 \nmid 12$ is also used to indicate that 12 is not a multiple of 5 and 5 is not a factor of 12.

EXAMPLE 5-1 Classify each of the following as true or false. Explain your answer.
(a) $^-3 \mid 12$ (b) $0 \mid 3$ (c) $3 \mid 0$ (d) $8 \nmid 2$
(e) For all integers, a, $1 \mid a$ (f) For all integers a, $^-1 \mid a$

SOLUTION (a) $^-3 \mid 12$ is true because $12 = {}^-4(^-3)$.
(b) $0 \mid 3$ is false because there is no integer c such that $3 = c \cdot 0$.
(c) $3 \mid 0$ is true because $0 = 0 \cdot 3$.
(d) $8 \nmid 2$ is true because there is no integer c such that $2 = c \cdot 8$.
(e) $1 \mid a$ is true for all integers a because $a = a \cdot 1$.
(f) $^-1 \mid a$ is true for all integers a because $a = (^-a)(^-1)$.

To obtain multiples of any integer, we need only multiply the integer by other integers. We now use multiples of 3 to investigate some properties of divisibility. Consider two bags of apples. Suppose that the number of apples in each bag can be equally divided among three students; that is, the number of apples in each bag is a multiple of 3. If all the apples are put in one large bag, it is still possible to divide the apples equally among the three students. Consequently, if the number of apples in the first bag is a and the number of apples in the second bag is b, then we can record the preceding discussion as follows: if $3|a$ and $3|b$, then $3|(a + b)$. If the number of apples in one bag cannot be divided among three students, then the total number of apples cannot be equally divided among three students. That is, if $3|a$ and $3 \nmid b$, then $3 \nmid (a + b)$. These ideas may be generalized in the following theorem.

● T H E O R E M   5-1
For any integers a, b, and d,
(a) If $d|a$ and $d|b$, then $d|(a + b)$.
(b) If $d|a$ and $d \nmid b$, then $d \nmid (a + b)$.

Since subtraction is defined in terms of addition, a similar theorem holds for subtraction.

● T H E O R E M   5-2
For any integers a, b, and d,
(a) If $d|a$ and $d|b$, then $d|(a - b)$.
(b) If $d|a$ and $d \nmid b$, then $d \nmid (a - b)$.

The proofs of most theorems in this section are left as exercises, but the proof of Theorem 5-1(a) is given as an illustration.

Proof. To show that $d|(a + b)$, we must show that $(a + b) = d \cdot k$, for some $k \in I$. To do this, we proceed as follows.

$d|a$ implies $a = m \cdot d, \quad m \in I$
$d|b$ implies $b = n \cdot d, \quad n \in I$

Substituting, we obtain

$a + b = md + nd$
$\qquad = (m + n)d$

Thus, $a + b = (m + n)d$.

Because $m \in I$ and $n \in I$ and the set of integers is closed under addition, $(m + n) \in I$. Therefore, $m + n = k$, where $k \in I$, and thus $d|(a + b)$.

Another result can be obtained using the definition of divides. If d divides a, then $a = dn$ where $n \in I$. To obtain a multiple of a, we multiply a by an integer k. Since $a = dn$, then $ka = d(kn)$ and we have the result in Theorem 5-3.

● **T H E O R E M   5-3**

For any integers a and d, if $d \mid a$ and k is any integer, then $d \mid ka$.

EXAMPLE 5-2   Classify each of the following as true or false, where x, y, and z are integers. If a statement is true, prove it. If a statement is false, provide a counterexample.

(a) If $3 \mid x$ and $3 \mid y$, then $3 \mid xy$.

(b) If $3 \mid (x + y)$, then $3 \mid x$ and $3 \mid y$.

(c) If $9 \nmid a$, then $3 \nmid a$.

SOLUTION   (a) True. By Theorem 5-3, if $3 \mid x$, then, for any integer k, $3 \mid kx$. If $k = y$, then $3 \mid yx$ or $3 \mid xy$. (Notice that $3 \mid xy$ regardless of whether $3 \mid y$ or $3 \nmid y$.)

(b) False. For example, $3 \mid (7 + 2)$ but $3 \nmid 7$ and $3 \nmid 2$. [How does this compare with Theorem 5-1(a)?]

(c) False. For example, $9 \nmid 21$, but $3 \mid 21$.

EXAMPLE 5-3   Five students found a padlocked money box, which had a deposit slip attached to it. The deposit slip was water-spotted, so the currency total appeared as shown in Figure 5-1. One student remarked that if the money listed on the deposit slip was in the box, it could easily be divided equally among the five students without using coins. How did the student know this?

FIGURE 5-1

SOLUTION   Because the units digit of the amount of the currency is zero, the solution to the problem becomes one of determining whether any natural number whose units digit is 0 is divisible by 5. One method for attacking this problem is to look for a pattern. Natural numbers whose units digit is zero form a pattern—that is, 10, 20, 30, 40, 50, ... These numbers are multiples of 10. We are to determine whether 5 divides all multiples of 10.

We know that the amount of money in the box is a multiple of 10. Since $5 \mid 10$, by Theorem 5-3, 5 divides any multiple of 10. Hence, 5 divides the amount of money in the box, and the student is correct.

Divisibility Rules

Without actually dividing, consider whether 1734 is divisible by 17. Because $17 \mid 1700$ and $17 \mid 34$, Theorem 5-1(a) implies that $17 \mid (1700 + 34)$ and hence that $17 \mid 1734$. Does 17 divide 1735? Because $1735 = 1700 + 35$ and $17 \mid 1700$

but $17 \nmid 35$, Theorem 5-1(b) tells us that $17 \nmid (1700 + 35)$, or $17 \nmid 1735$. The approach in these two examples is the basis for divisibility tests. To determine whether a given integer n is divisible by another integer d, we write n as a sum or difference of two numbers, where we can tell whether or not d divides these numbers. If it is not possible to determine two numbers of this type, we try to choose two numbers such that one of them is as close as possible to n and we can determine its divisibility by d. Then we can check the divisibility of the other number (which is relatively small) manually, if necessary. For example, let us investigate divisibility by 2. Consider the number 358, whose expanded form is $3 \cdot 10^2 + 5 \cdot 10 + 8$. Since $2 | 10$, then $2 | 10^2$ and $2 | (5 \cdot 10)$. Likewise, $2 | 10^2$ implies that $2 | (3 \cdot 10^2)$. Hence, $2 | (3 \cdot 10^2 + 5 \cdot 10)$. Now, since $358 = (3 \cdot 10^2 + 5 \cdot 10) + 8$ and $2 | 8$, it follows that 2 divides the sum $[(3 \cdot 10^2 + 5 \cdot 10) + 8]$; that is, $2 | 358$. The same argument holds if the units digit is any even number. A similar argument shows that 2 does not divide a number whose units digit is odd. For example, consider 357, or $3 \cdot 10^2 + 5 \cdot 10 + 7$. Since $2 | (3 \cdot 10^2 + 5 \cdot 10)$ and $2 \nmid 7$, it follows that $2 \nmid (3 \cdot 10^2 + 5 \cdot 10 + 7)$; that is, $2 \nmid 357$. In general, the following divisibility test holds.

● **DIVISIBILITY TEST FOR 2**
An integer is divisible by 2 if and only if its units digit is divisible by 2.

There are similar tests for divisibility by 5 and 10. The tests follow from the fact that the only positive integers other than 1 and 2 that divide 10 are 5 and 10.

● **DIVISIBILITY TEST FOR 5**
An integer is divisible by 5 if and only if its units digit is divisible by 5—that is, if and only if the units digit is 0 or 5.

● **DIVISIBILITY TEST FOR 10**
An integer is divisible by 10 if and only if its units digit is divisible by 10—that is, if and only if the units digit is 0.

Because both 4 and 8 divide certain powers of 10, there exist divisibility rules for 4 and 8. We first develop a divisibility rule for 4. Consider any four-digit number n such that $n = a \cdot 10^3 + b \cdot 10^2 + c \cdot 10 + d$. The first step is to write the given number as a sum of two numbers, one of which is as great as possible and divisible by 4. We know that $4 \nmid 10$, but $4 | 10^2$ because $10^2 = 4 \cdot 25$. Consequently, $4 | 10 \cdot 10^2$; that is, $4 | 10^3$. Now, $4 | 10^2$

implies $4|b \cdot 10^2$, and $4|10^3$ implies $4|a \cdot 10^3$. Finally, $4|a \cdot 10^3$ and $4|b \cdot 10^2$ imply $4|(a \cdot 10^3 + b \cdot 10^2)$. Since $4|(a \cdot 10^3 + b \cdot 10^2)$, the divisibility of $a \cdot 10^3 + b \cdot 10^2 + c \cdot 10 + d$ by 4 depends on the divisibility of $(c \cdot 10 + d)$ by 4. If $4|(c \cdot 10 + d)$, then 4 divides the given number n. If $4 \nmid (c \cdot 10 + d)$, then 4 does not divide the given number n. Notice that $c \cdot 10 + d$ is the number represented by the last two digits in the given number n. We summarize this in the following test.

● **DIVISIBILITY TEST FOR 4**
An integer is divisible by 4 if and only if the last two digits of the integer represent a number divisible by 4.

To investigate divisibility by 8, we note that the least positive power of 10 divisible by 8 is 10^3 since $10^3 = 8 \cdot 125$. Consequently, all integral powers of 10 greater than 10^3 also are divisible by 8. Hence, the following is a divisibility test for 8.

● **DIVISIBILITY TEST FOR 8**
An integer is divisible by 8 if and only if the last three digits of the integer represent a number divisible by 8.

EXAMPLE 5-4   (a) Determine whether 97,128 is divisible by 2, 4, and 8.
(b) Determine whether 83,026 is divisible by 2, 4, and 8.

SOLUTION   (a) $2|97,128$ because $2|8$.   (b) $2|83,026$ because $2|6$.
$4|97,128$ because $4|28$. $4 \nmid 83,026$ because $4 \nmid 26$.
$8|97,128$ because $8|128$. $8 \nmid 83,026$ because $8 \nmid 026$.

● R E M A R K
Notice, in Example 5-4(a), that it would have been sufficient to check that the given number is divisible by 8, because, if $8|a$, then $2|a$ and $4|a$. (Why?) However, if $8 \nmid a$, we cannot conclude from this that $4 \nmid a$ or $2 \nmid a$. (Why?)

Next, we consider a divisibility test for 3. We illustrate the procedure on the number 5721, that is, $5 \cdot 10^3 + 7 \cdot 10^2 + 2 \cdot 10 + 1$. No power of 10 is divisible by 3, but there are numbers close to powers of 10 that are divisible by 3. The numbers 9, or 99, or 999, or others of this type are such numbers. To determine whether 5721, or $5 \cdot 10^3 + 7 \cdot 10^2 + 2 \cdot 10 + 1$, is divisible by 3, we see that the number $5 \cdot 999 + 7 \cdot 99 + 2 \cdot 9$ is close to

5721 and is divisible by 3. (Why?) Next, look for a number x to make the following equation true.

$$5721 = 5 \cdot 10^3 + 7 \cdot 10^2 + 2 \cdot 10 + 1 = (5 \cdot 999 + 7 \cdot 99 + 2 \cdot 9) + x$$

What must be added to $5 \cdot 999$ to obtain $5 \cdot 10^3$? Because $5 \cdot 10^3 = 5 \cdot 1000 = 5(999 + 1) = 5 \cdot 999 + 5 \cdot 1$, the answer is 5. Similarly, $7 \cdot 10^2 = 7 \cdot 100 = 7(99 + 1) = 7 \cdot 99 + 7 \cdot 1$, and $2 \cdot 10 = 2(9 + 1) = 2 \cdot 9 + 2 \cdot 1$. Thus, the number x is $5 \cdot 1 + 7 \cdot 1 + 2 \cdot 1 + 1$, or $5 + 7 + 2 + 1$. Consequently,

$$5721 = 5 \cdot 10^3 + 7 \cdot 10^2 + 2 \cdot 10 + 1$$
$$= (5 \cdot 999 + 7 \cdot 99 + 2 \cdot 9) + (5 + 7 + 2 + 1)$$

The sum in the first set of parentheses is divisible by 3, so the divisibility of 5721 by 3 depends on the sum in the second set of parentheses. In this case, $5 + 7 + 2 + 1 = 15$ and $3|15$, so $3|5721$. Hence, to test 5721 for divisibility by 3, simply test $5 + 7 + 2 + 1$ for divisibility by 3. Notice that $5 + 7 + 2 + 1$ is the sum of the digits of 5721. The example suggests the following test for divisibility by 3.

● **DIVISIBILITY TEST FOR 3**
An integer is divisible by 3 if and only if the sum of its digits is divisible by 3.

An argument similar to the one used to demonstrate that $3|5721$ can be used to prove the test for divisibility by 3 on an integer with any number of digits and in particular for any four-digit number $n = a \cdot 10^3 + b \cdot 10^2 + c \cdot 10 + d$. Even though $a \cdot 10^3 + b \cdot 10^2 + c \cdot 10 + d$ is not necessarily divisible by 3, the number $a \cdot 999 + b \cdot 99 + c \cdot 9$ is close to n and *is* divisible by 3. We have

$$a \cdot 10^3 = a \cdot 1000 = a(999 + 1) = a \cdot 999 + a \cdot 1$$
$$b \cdot 10^2 = b \cdot 100 = b(99 + 1) = b \cdot 99 + b \cdot 1$$
$$c \cdot 10^1 = c \cdot 10 = c(9 + 1) = c \cdot 9 + c \cdot 1$$

Thus, $n = a \cdot 10^3 + b \cdot 10^2 + c \cdot 10 + d = (a \cdot 999 + b \cdot 99 + c \cdot 9) + (a + b + c + d)$. Because $3|9$, $3|99$, and $3|999$, it follows that $3|(a \cdot 999 + b \cdot 99 + c \cdot 9)$. If $3|(a + b + c + d)$, then $3|[(a \cdot 999 + b \cdot 99 + c \cdot 9) + (a + b + c + d)]$; that is, $3|n$. If, on the other hand, $3 \nmid (a + b + c + d)$, it follows from Theorem 5-1(b) that $3 \nmid n$.

Since $9|9$, $9|99$, $9|999$, and so on, a test similar to that for divisibility by 3 applies to divisibility by 9. (Why?)

● **DIVISIBILITY TEST FOR 9**
An integer is divisible by 9 if and only if the sum of the digits of the integer is divisible by 9.

EXAMPLE 5-5   Use divisibility tests to determine whether each of the following numbers is divisible by 3 and divisible by 9.
(a) 1002   (b) 14,238

SOLUTION   (a) Because $1 + 0 + 0 + 2 = 3$ and $3|3$, it follows that $3|1002$. Because $9 \nmid 3$, it follows that $9 \nmid 1002$.
(b) Because $1 + 4 + 2 + 3 + 8 = 18$ and $3|18$, it follows that $3|14{,}238$. Because $9|18$, it follows that $9|14{,}238$.

Divisibility tests can be devised for 7 and 11. We state such tests but omit the proofs.

- **DIVISIBILITY TEST FOR 7**
An integer is divisible by 7 if and only if the integer represented without its units digit, minus twice the units digit of the original integer, is divisible by 7.

- **DIVISIBILITY TEST FOR 11**
An integer is divisible by 11 if and only if the sum of the digits in the places that are even powers of 10 minus the sum of the digits in the places that are odd powers of 10 is divisible by 11.

For example, to test whether 8,471,986 is divisible by 11, we check whether 11 divides the difference $(6 + 9 + 7 + 8) - (8 + 1 + 4)$, or 17. Because $11 \nmid 17$, it follows from the divisibility test for 11 that $11 \nmid 8{,}471{,}986$.

At this point, the only number less than 11 for which we have no divisibility test is 6. The divisibility test for 6 depends on the divisibility tests for 2 and 3. If $6|n$, then $n = 6k$, or $n = 2 \cdot 3k$ for some integer k. Consequently, 2 and 3 are factors of n. Thus $2|n$ and $3|n$. In Section 5-2, it will be shown that the converse statement is also true; that is, if $2|n$ and $3|n$, then $2 \cdot 3|n$. Consequently, the following divisibility test is true.

- **DIVISIBILITY TEST FOR 6**
An integer is divisible by 6 if and only if the integer is divisible by both 2 and 3.

EXAMPLE 5-6   Test each of the following numbers for divisibility by: (i) 7; (ii) 11; (iii) 6.
(a) 462   (b) 964,194

SOLUTION   (a) (i) $7|(46 - 2 \cdot 2)$, so $7|462$.
(ii) $11|(2 + 4 - 6)$, so $11|462$.
(iii) $2|462$ and $3|462$, so $6|462$.

(b) (i) To determine whether or not 7 divides 964,194, we use the process several times.

$$7 \mid 964{,}194 \quad \text{if and only if} \quad 7 \mid (96{,}419 - 2 \cdot 4), \text{ or } 7 \mid 96{,}411$$
$$7 \mid 96{,}411 \quad \text{if and only if} \quad 7 \mid (9641 - 2 \cdot 1), \text{ or } 7 \mid 9639$$
$$7 \mid 9639 \quad \text{if and only if} \quad 7 \mid (963 - 2 \cdot 9) \text{ or } 7 \mid 945$$
$$7 \mid 945 \quad \text{if and only if} \quad 7 \mid (94 - 2 \cdot 5), \text{ or } 7 \mid 84$$

Because $7 \mid 84$ is true, it follows that $7 \mid 964{,}194$.

(ii) $11 \mid [(4 + 1 + 6) - (9 + 4 + 9)]$, so $11 \mid 964{,}194$.

(iii) $2 \mid 964{,}194$ and $3 \mid 964{,}194$, so $6 \mid 964{,}194$.

● **R E M A R K**

A calculator can often be used to determine divisibility. On a calculator $a \mid b$ if and only if the display for $b \div a$ is an integer—that is, if and only if it has no decimal part. This approach is practical only if the number of digits of b does not exceed the maximum number of display digits on your calculator.

PROBLEM 1

A class from Washington School visited a neighborhood cannery warehouse. The warehouse manager told the class that there were 11,368 cans of juice in the inventory and that the cans were packed in boxes of 6 or 24, depending on the size of the can. One of the students, Sam, thought for a moment and announced that there was a mistake in the inventory. Is Sam's announcement correct? Why or why not?

Understanding the Problem. The problem is to determine whether the manager's inventory of 11,368 cans was correct. To solve the problem, we must assume that there are no partial boxes of cans; that is, a box must contain exactly 6 or exactly 24 cans of juice.

Devising a Plan. We know that the boxes contain either 6 cans or 24 cans, but we do not know how many boxes of each type there are. One strategy for solving this problem is to find an equation that involves the total number of cans in all the boxes.

The total number of cans, 11,368, equals the number of cans in all the 6-can boxes plus the number of cans in all the 24-can boxes. If there are n boxes containing 6 cans each, there are $6n$ cans altogether in those boxes. Similarly, if there are m boxes with 24 cans each, these boxes contain a total of $24m$ cans. Because the total was reported to be 11,368 cans, we have the equation $6n + 24m = 11{,}368$. Sam claimed that $6n + 24m \neq 11{,}368$.

One way to show that $6n + 24m \neq 11{,}368$ is to show that $6n + 24m$ and 11,368 do not have the same divisors. Both $6n$ and $24m$ are divisible by 6, which implies that $6n + 24m$ must be divisible by 6. If 11,368 is not divisible by 6, then Sam is correct.

Carrying Out the Plan. The divisibility test for 6 states that a number is divisible by 6 if and only if the number is divisible by both 2 and 3. Because 11,368 is an even number, it is divisible by 2. Is it divisible by 3?

The divisibility test for 3 states that a number is divisible by 3 if and only if the sum of the digits in the number is divisible by three. We see that $1 + 1 + 3 + 6 + 8 = 19$, which is not divisible by 3, so 11,368 is not divisible by 3. Hence, Sam is correct.

Looking Back. Suppose 11,368 had been divisible by 6. Would that have implied that the manager was correct? The answer is no; it would have implied only that we would have to change our approach to the problem.

As a further Looking Back activity, suppose that, given different data, the manager is correct. Can we determine values for m and n? This, in fact, can be done, and if a computer is available, a program can be written to determine all possible natural-number values of m and n.

Equations involving only integers, like the one in Problem 1, are called *Diophantine equations* in honor of the Greek mathematician Diophantus, who lived in Alexandria in the third century A.D. The solution of various Diophantine equations has been the center of research in number theory from antiquity to the present. The equation $6n + 24m = 11,368$ of Problem 1 is a special case of the Diophantine equation $ax + by = c$, where a, b, and c are given integers and where integer solutions x and y are desired. As in Problem 1, if some integer divides both a and b but does not divide c, the equation has no solution.

PROBLEM SET 5-1

1. Classify each of the following as true or false.
   (a) 6 is a factor of 30.   (b) 6 is a divisor of 30.
   (c) $6 | 30$ (d) 30 is divisible by 6.
   (e) 30 is a multiple of 6.   (f) 6 is a multiple of 30.

2. Use Theorem 5-1(a) to complete each of the following sentences. Simplify your answers, if possible.
   (a) If $7 | 14$ and $7 | 21$, then _____.
   (b) If $d | (213 - 57)$ and $d | 57$, then _____.
   (c) If $d | (a - b)$ and $d | b$, then _____.

3. Use Theorem 5-2(a) to complete each of the following sentences. Simplify your answers, if possible.
   (a) If $7 | 231$ and $7 | 14$, then _____.
   (b) If $d | (213 + 57)$ and $d | 57$, then _____.
   (c) If $d | (a + b)$ and $d | b$, then _____.

4. There are 1379 children signed up to play Little League baseball. If exactly 9 players are assigned to each team, will any teams be short of players?

5. A forester has 43,682 seedlings to be planted. Can these be planted in an equal number of rows with 11 seedlings in each row?

6. For each of the following, state the theorems that justify the given statements, assuming that a, b, and c are integers. If a statement cannot be justified by one of the theorems in this section, answer "none."
   (a) $4 | 20$ implies $4 | 113 \cdot 20$.
   (b) $4 | 100$ and $4 \nmid 13$ imply $4 \nmid (100 + 13)$.
   (c) $4 | 100$ and $4 \nmid 13$ imply $4 \nmid 1300$.
   (d) $3 | (a + b)$ and $3 \nmid c$ imply $3 \nmid (a + b + c)$.
   (e) $3 | a$ implies $3 | a^2$.

7. Without actually dividing, determine each of the following (justify your answers).
   (a) Is 34,015 divisible by 17?
   (b) Is 34,051 divisible by 17?
   (c) Is 19,031 divisible by 19?
   (d) Is 19,031 divisible by 31?
   (e) Is $2^{64} + 1$ divisible by 2^{14}?
   (f) Is $2 \cdot 3 \cdot 5 \cdot 7 \cdot 13 \cdot 17 + 1$ divisible by 2, 3, 5, 7, 13, or 17?

8. Classify each of the following as true or false, assuming that a, b, c and d are integers. If a statement is false, give a counterexample.
   (a) If $d|(a + b)$, then $d|a$ and $d|b$.
   (b) If $d|(a + b)$, then $d|a$ or $d|b$.
   (c) If $d|a$ and $d|b$, then $d|ab$.
   (d) If $d|ab$, then $d|a$ or $d|b$.
   (e) If $ab|c$, $a \neq 0$ and $b \neq 0$, then $a|c$ and $b|c$.
   (f) $1|a$
   (g) $d|0$
   (h) If $a|b$ and $b|a$, then $a = b$.
   (i) If $d|a$ and $d|b$, then $d|(ax + by)$, for any integers x and y.
   (j) If $d \nmid a$ and $d \nmid b$, then $d \nmid (a + b)$.
   (k) If $d|a^2$, then $d|a$.
   (l) If $d \nmid a$, then $d \nmid a^2$.
   (m) If $d \nmid a^2$, then $d \nmid a$.

9. (a) If we multiply any odd number by 5, what is the units digit of the product?
   (b) If we multiply any even whole number by 5, what is the units digit of the product?

10. Classify each of the following as true or false.
    (a) If every digit of a number is divisible by 3, the number itself is divisible by 3.
    (b) If a number is divisible by 3, then every digit of the number is divisible by 3.
    (c) A number is divisible by 3 if and only if every digit of the number is divisible by 3.
    (d) If a number is divisible by 6, then it is divisible by 2 and by 3.
    (e) If a number is divisible by 2 and 3, then it is divisible by 6.
    (f) If a number is divisible by 2 and 4, then it is divisible by 8.
    (g) If a number is divisible by 8, then it is divisible by 2 and 4.

11. Classify each of the statements in Problem 10 as "sometimes," "always," or "never."

12. Devise a test for divisibility by each given number.
    (a) 16   (b) 25

13. Conjecture divisibility tests for 12 and 15.

14. Jack owes $7812 on a new car. Can this be paid in 12 equal monthly installments?

15. A group of people ordered No-Cal candy bars. The bill was $2.09. If the original price of each was 12¢

but the price has been inflated, how much does each cost?

16. When the two missing digits in the given number are replaced, the number is divisible by 99. What is the number?

    85__1

17. Test each of the following numbers for divisibility by 2, 3, 4, 5, 6, 7, 8, 9, 10, 11, 12, and 15. Use a calculator to check your answers.
    (a) 746,988   (b) 81,342   (c) 15,810
    (d) 183,324   (e) 901,815   (f) 4,201,012
    (g) 1001   (h) 10,001   (i) 30,860

18. Answer each of the following, and justify your answer.
    (a) If a number is not divisible by 5, can it be divisible by 10?
    (b) If a number is not divisible by 10, can it be divisible by 5?

19. Fill each blank with the greatest digit that makes the statement true.
    (a) $3|74\_$ (b) $9|83\_45$ (c) $11|6\_55$

20. A number in which each digit except 0 appears exactly three times is divisible by 3. For example, 777,555,222 and 414,143,313 are divisible by 3. Explain why this statement is true.

★21. Prove the following theorem: For any integers a, b, and c, with $a \neq 0$ and $b \neq 0$, if $a|b$ and $b|c$, then $a|c$.

22. Leap years occur in years that are divisible by 4. However, if the year ends in two zeros, in order for the year to be a leap year, it must be divisible by 400. Determine which of the following are leap years.
    (a) 1776   (b) 1986   (c) 2000   (d) 2024

23. A palindrome is a number that reads the same forward and backward.
    (a) Check the following four-digit palindromes for divisibility by 11.
        (i) 4554   (ii) 9339   (iii) 2002
        (iv) 2222
    ★(b) Prove that any four-digit palindrome is divisible by 11.
    (c) Is every five-digit palindrome divisible by 11? Why or why not?
    (d) Is every six-digit palindrome divisible by 11? Why or why not?

24. (a) Choose a two-digit number such that the number in the tens place is one greater than the number in the units place. Reverse the digits in your number, and subtract this number from your original number; for example, 87 − 78 = 9. Make a conjecture concerning the results of performing these kinds of operations.

(b) Choose any two-digit number such that the number in the tens place is two greater than the number in the units place. Reverse the digits in your number, and subtract this number from your original number; for example, $31 - 13 = 18$. Make a conjecture concerning the results of performing these kinds of operations.

★(c) Prove that, for any two-digit number, if the digits are reversed and the numbers subtracted, the difference is a multiple of 9.

(d) Investigate what happens whenever two-digit numbers with equal digit sums are subtracted: for example, $62 - 35 = 27$.

25. A customer wants to mail a package. The postal clerk determines the cost of the package as $2.86, but only 6¢ and 15¢ stamps are available. Can the available stamps be used for the exact amount of postage for the package? Why or why not?

26. Which of the following Diophantine equations can be shown not to have solutions? Explain your reasoning.

(a) $18x + 27y = 3111$ (b) $2x + 6y = 113$
(c) $10x + 25y = 1007$ (d) $4x + y = 108$
(e) $8x + 108y = 4001$ (f) $5x + 12y = 606$

27. (a) Use the division algorithm from Chapter 3 to explain why, among any three consecutive integers, there is always one that is divisible by 3.

(b) Generalize the statement in (a) to any n consecutive integers.

★28. Prove each of the following.
(a) Theorem 5-1(b)   (b) Theorem 5-2(a) and (b).

★29. Prove the test for divisibility by 9 for any five-digit number.

📱 30. Enter any three-digit number on the calculator; for example, enter 243. Repeat it: 243,243. Divide by 7. Divide by 11. Divide by 13. What is the answer? Try it again with any other three-digit number. Will this always work? Why?

📱 31. A traveler wishes to purchase $610 worth of travelers checks. The checks are available only in denominations of $20 and $50. How many of each denomination should the traveler buy? Is the answer unique?

B R A I N   T E A S E R
Dee finds that she has an extraordinary social security number. Its nine digits contain all the numbers from 1 through 9. They also form a number with the following characteristics: when read from left to right, its first two digits form a number divisible by 2, its first three digits form a number divisible by 3, its first four digits form a number divisible by 4, and so on, until the complete number is divisible by 9. What is Dee's social security number?

Section 5-2   Prime and Composite Numbers

In Section 5-1, we discussed divisors of numbers. For example, the number 12 has six divisors: 1, 2, 3, 4, 6, and 12. The number 7 has only two divisors: 1 and 7. To introduce the next concept, we construct Table 5-1. Below each number listed across the top, we identify numbers less than or equal to 37 that have that number of positive divisors. For example, 12 is in the 6 column because it has six divisors, and 7 is in the 2 column because it has only two divisors.

Do you see any patterns forming in the table? Do you see why there will be no other entries in the 1 column? What is the next number in the 3 column? The numbers in the 2 column are of particular importance. Notice that they have exactly two divisors, namely, 1 and themselves. Any positive

TABLE 5-1

1	2	3	4	5	6	7	8	More than 8
1	2	4	6	16	12		24	36
	3	9	8		18		30	
	5	25	10		20			
	7		14		28			
	11		15		32			
	13		21					
	17		22					
	19		26					
	23		27					
	29		33					
	31		34					
	37		35					

prime
composite

integer with exactly two distinct, positive divisors is called a *prime number,* or a **prime.** Any integer greater than 1 that has a positive factor other than 1 and itself is called a *composite number,* or a **composite.** For example, 4, 6, and 16 are composites because they have positive factors other than 1 and themselves. The number 1 has only one positive factor, so it is neither prime nor composite.

From the 2 column in Table 5-1, we see that the first twelve primes are 2, 3, 5, 7, 11, 13, 17, 19, 23, 29, 31, and 37. Other patterns in the table are explored in the problem set.

EXAMPLE 5-7

Show that the following numbers are composite.

(a) 1564   (b) 2781   (c) 1001

SOLUTION

(a) Since $2|4$, 1564 is divisible by 2.
(b) Since $3|(2 + 7 + 8 + 1)$, 2781 is divisible by 3.
(c) Since $11|[(1 + 0) - (0 + 1)]$, 1001 is divisible by 11.

---

factorization
prime factorization

Composite numbers can be expressed as products of two or more whole numbers greater than 1. For example, $18 = 2 \cdot 9$, $18 = 3 \cdot 6$, or $18 = 2 \cdot 3 \cdot 3$. Each expression of 18 as a product of factors is called a **factorization.** A factorization containing only prime numbers is called a **prime factorization.** To find a prime factorization of a given composite number, first rewrite the number as a product of two smaller numbers. Continue the process, factoring the lesser numbers until all factors are primes. For example, consider 260.

$$260 = 26 \cdot 10 = 2 \cdot 13 \cdot 2 \cdot 5 = 2 \cdot 2 \cdot 5 \cdot 13 = 2^2 \cdot 5 \cdot 13$$

factor tree

The procedure for finding a prime factorization of a number can be organized by using a model called a **factor tree.** A factor tree is demonstrated in Figure 5-2(a). Notice that the last branches of the trees display the prime factors of 260.

The factorization of 260 or other composite numbers can be started in different ways. A second way to factor 260 is shown in Figure 5-2(b). The two trees produce the same prime factorization, expect for the order in which the primes appear in the products.

FIGURE 5-2

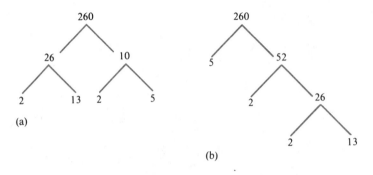

(a)

(b)

In general, if order is disregarded, the prime factorization of a number is unique. The *Fundamental Theorem of Arithmetic,* sometimes called the *Unique Factorization Theorem,* states this fact.

● **T H E O R E M   5-4**
Fundamental Theorem of Arithmetic   Each composite number can be written as a product of primes in one and only one way, aside from variation in the order of the prime factors.

The Fundamental Theorem of Arithmetic has many uses, some of which we will encounter in our discussion of terminating decimals and rational numbers.

$$2\,\underline{|\,260}$$
$$130$$
(a)

$$2\,\underline{|\,260}$$
$$2\,\underline{|\,130}$$
$$65$$
(b)

$$2\,\underline{|\,260}$$
$$2\,\underline{|\,130}$$
$$5\,\underline{|\,65}$$
$$13\,\underline{|\,13}$$
$$1$$
(c)

FIGURE 5-3

The Fundamental Theorem of Arithmetic is a basis for a more algorithmic approach to finding the prime factorization of a number. We start with the smallest prime and check to see if it divides the number. If not, we try the next greater prime and check for divisibility by this prime. Once we find a prime that divides the number in question, we must find the quotient of the number divided by the prime. This step in the prime factorization of 260 using the Fundamental Theorem is shown in Figure 5-3(a). Next we check if the prime divides the quotient. If so, we repeat the process; if not, we try the next greater prime and check to see if it divides the quotient. We see that 260 divided by 2 yields 130, as shown in Figure 5-3(b). We continue the procedure, using greater primes, until a quotient of 1 is reached. The original number is the product of all the prime divisors used. The complete procedure for 260 is shown in Figure 5-3(c).

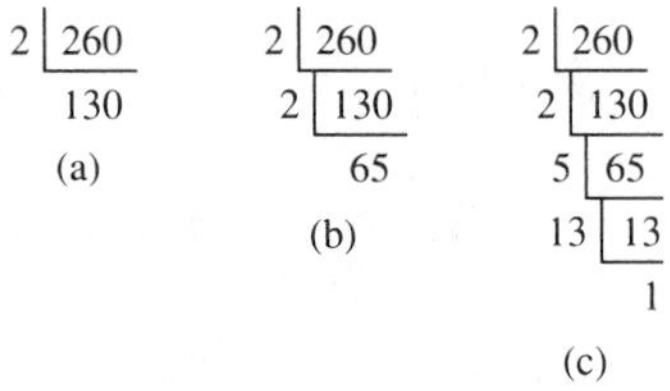

Normally, the primes in the prime factorization of a number are listed in increasing order from left to right; if a prime appears in a product more than once, exponential notation is used. Thus, the factorization of 260 is written as $2^2 \cdot 5 \cdot 13$.

In determining the factorization of a number such as 8127, observe that $9|8127$, or $8127 = 9k$, where k is an integer. Because $8127 = 9k$, then k is a factor of 8127 and $k = \frac{8127}{9}$. Theorem 5-5 states the general case.

● **T H E O R E M   5-5**

If d is a factor of n, where $n \neq 0$ and $d \neq 0$, then $\frac{n}{d}$ is a factor of n.

● **R E M A R K**

Sometimes we do not obtain a different factor when using this process. This occurs when $\frac{n}{d} = d$. For example, 7 is a factor of 49 and so is $\frac{49}{7}$, or 7.

Suppose that p is the *least* prime factor of the number n. If n is prime, then $p = n$; but if n is composite, we have $p \leq \frac{n}{p}$, because $\frac{n}{p}$ is also a factor of n and p is the least factor of n. Thus $p^2 \leq n$. This idea is summarized in the following theorem.

● **T H E O R E M   5-6**
If n is composite, then n has a prime factor p such that $p^2 \leq n$.

Theorem 5-6 can be used to help determine whether a given number is prime or composite. Consider, for example, the number 109. If 109 is composite, it must have a prime divisor p such that $p^2 \leq 109$. The primes whose squares do not exceed 109 are 2, 3, 5, and 7. Checking for divisibility by these primes reveals that $2 \nmid 109$, $3 \nmid 109$, $5 \nmid 109$, and $7 \nmid 109$. Hence, 109 is prime. The argument used leads to the following theorem.

● **T H E O R E M   5-7**
In n is an integer greater than 1 such that n is not divisible by any prime p, where $p^2 \leq n$, then n is prime.

EXAMPLE 5-8   Is 397 composite or prime?

SOLUTION   The possible primes p such that $p^2 \leq 397$ are 2, 3, 5, 7, 11, 13, 17, and 19. Because $2 \nmid 397$, $3 \nmid 397$, $5 \nmid 397$, $7 \nmid 397$, $11 \nmid 397$, $13 \nmid 397$, $17 \nmid 397$, and $19 \nmid 397$, the number 397 is prime.

PROBLEM 2

In the central prison of Ilusia, there were 1000 cells numbered from 1 to 1000. Each cell was occupied by a single prisoner, and each had a separate guard. The guards were ordered to free certain prisoners based on the following scheme. The guards are to walk through the prison one at a time. The first guard opens all 1000 cells. The second guard follows immediately and closes all the cells with even numbers. The third guard follows and changes every third cell, starting with cell 3—closing the open cells and opening the closed cells. Similarly, the fourth guard starts at cell 4 and changes every fourth cell. This process continues until the 1000th guard passes through the prison, at which point the prisoners whose cells are open are freed. How many prisoners are freed?

Understanding the Problem.   In a prison, 1000 cells are numbered 1 through 1000. Each cell contains a single prisoner. Guard 1 opens every cell, starting at cell 1. Guard 2 follows and closes every second cell starting at cell 2. Guard 3 follows and changes the state of every third cell, starting with cell 3; that is, if the cell is open, he closes it, and if it is closed, he opens it. The remaining guards pass through in a similar manner. We are to determine how many cells are open after all 1000 guards have passed through.

Divising a Plan.   We use the strategy of examining a simpler problem in order to gain insight into the solution of the original problem. Suppose that there are only 20 cells. If we denote an open cell by o and a closed cell by c, we can record the state of each cell changed by the guards as in Table 5-2. For example, the fourth guard opens cell 4, opens cell 8, closes cell 12, opens cell 16, and closes cell 20, and so on.

The table shows that after 20 guards pass through, the only open cells are 1, 4, 9, and 16. Each of these numbers is a perfect square. We must determine if this pattern will continue for 1000 cells and 1000 guards. If it does, we must count the number of perfect squares that are less than 1000.

Carrying Out the Plan.   To determine if the pattern determined above continues, consider cell 25. The cell is opened by guard 1, closed by guard 5, and opened by guard 25. This suggests that the pattern is correct. (Note

Cell Number

Guard Number	1	2	3	4	5	6	7	8	9	10	11	12	13	14	15	16	17	18	19	20
1	o	o	o	o	o	o	o	o	o	o	o	o	o	o	o	o	o	o	o	o
2		c		c		c		c		c		c		c		c		c		c
3			c			o			c			o			c			o		
4				o				o				c				o				o
5					c					o					o					c
6						c						o						c		
7							c							o						
8								c								c				
9									o									o		
10										c										o
11											c									
12												c								
13													c							
14														c						
15															c					
16																o				
17																	c			
18																		c		
19																			c	
20																				c

TABLE 5-2

that 1, 5, and 25 are the only positive divisors of 25.) What happens with a cell number such as 26, which is not a square? Cell 26 is opened by guard 1, closed by guard 2, opened by guard 13, and closed by guard 26, and, hence, remains closed. In general, we observe that a cell is changed only by guards whose numbers divide the cell number.

For the final state of a cell to be open, it must be opened one more time than it is closed; that is, the state must be changed an odd number of times. For this to happen, the number of the cell must have an odd number of divisors. We can show that the open cells have numbers that are perfect squares by showing that only perfect squares have an odd number of divisors.

Recall that the divisors of a number appear in pairs. For example, the pairs of divisors of 80 and 81 are given by the following.

$80 = 1 \cdot 80 = 2 \cdot 40 = 4 \cdot 20 = 5 \cdot 16 = 10 \cdot 8$
$81 = 1 \cdot 81 = 3 \cdot 27 = 9 \cdot 9$

Thus, 80 has ten distinct divisors, or five pairs. On the other hand, the perfect square 81 has five distinct divisors: the pairs 1 and 81 and 3 and 27, and a single divisor, 9, which is paired with itself. In this chapter we have seen that, if d is a divisor of n, then n/d is a divisor of n. Consequently, for all divisors d of n, if $d \neq n/d$, then each divisor can be paired with a different divisor, and n must have an even number of positive divisors. If for some divisor d, $d = n/d$, then $n = d^2$, and all the divisors of n, except d, are paired with a different divisor. Hence, the number of divisors of n is odd. Because $d = n/d$ occurs only when $n = d^2$, it follows that n has an odd number of divisors if and only if n is a perfect square. As a result, the freed prisoners leave the cells with numbers that are perfect squares less than 1000, namely, $1^2, 2^2, 3^2, 4^2, 5^2, 6^2, \ldots, 31^2$. Thus, 31 prisoners are freed.

Looking Back   This problem suggests the following questions.

1. Which guards will open or close only one cell?
2. How many times will a cell with a prime number be opened or closed?
3. Determine a method of finding the number of factors a number has, without actually listing all the factors. (*Hint:* Consider prime factorizations.)

More About Primes

One way to find all the primes less than a given number is to use the Sieve of Eratosthenes, named after the Greek mathematician Eratosthenes (276–194 or 192 B.C.). If all the natural numbers greater than 1 are considered (or placed in the sieve), the numbers that are not prime are methodically crossed out (or drop through the holes of the sieve). The remaining numbers are prime. The following procedure illustrates this process.

1. In Figure 5-4, we cross out 1 because 1 is not prime.
2. Circle 2 because 2 is prime.
3. Cross out other multiples of 2; they are not prime.
4. Circle 3 because 3 is prime.
5. Cross out other multiples of 3.
6. Circle 5 and 7 because they are primes; cross out their multiples.
7. In Figure 5-4, we stop after step 6 because 7 is the greatest prime whose square, 49, is less than 100. All the numbers remaining in the list and not crossed out are prime.

FIGURE 5-4

1	2	3	4	5	6	7	8	9	10
11	12	13	14	15	16	17	18	19	20
21	22	23	24	25	26	27	28	29	30
31	32	33	34	35	36	37	38	39	40
41	42	43	44	45	46	47	48	49	50
51	52	53	54	55	56	57	58	59	60
61	62	63	64	65	66	67	68	69	70
71	72	73	74	75	76	77	78	79	80
81	82	83	84	85	86	87	88	89	90
91	92	93	94	95	96	97	98	99	100

Theorem 5-7, discussed earlier, can be used to explain why, after we have crossed out all the multiples of 2, 3, 5, and 7, the remaining numbers in the sieve are prime. The details of the argument are left as an exercise.

There are infinitely many whole numbers, infinitely many odd numbers, and infinitely many even numbers. Are there infinitely many primes? Because prime numbers do not appear in any known pattern, the answer to this question is not obvious. Euclid was the first to prove that there are infinitely many primes (see Problem Set 5-2, Problem 26).

PROBLEM 3

Although Euclid proved that there are infinitely many primes, it has been shown that there are strings of as many consecutive composite numbers as desired. Find 1000 consecutive natural numbers that are composite.

Understanding the Problem. The goal is to find 1000 consecutive natural numbers that are not prime. Because the numbers must be consecutive, they can be written in the form $n, n + 1, n + 2, n + 3, \ldots, n + 999$, where n is some natural number. Also, since each of the numbers is to be composite, each must have at least one divisor other than 1 and itself.

Devising a Plan. To find a set of 1000 consecutive composite natural numbers using the Sieve of Eratosthenes would seem to require a large list of numbers. In the sieve in Figure 5-4, we can find no more than seven consecutive composites, namely, 90, 91, 92, 93, 94, 95 and 96. Constructing a large sieve and counting the number of composites would be very time-consuming, so we try other alternatives.

A possible strategy is to look at a simpler problem. For example, we might consider finding a string of ten consecutive composites, which we can label n, $n + 1$, $n + 2$, ..., $n + 9$. We want to choose n so that these ten numbers are composite. The greatest number in the list, $n + 9$, will be composite if n is a multiple of 9. Similarly, $n + 8$ will be composite if n is a multiple of 8. Continuing in this way, the numbers, $n + 7$, $n + 6$, ..., $n + 2$ will be composite if n is a multiple of 7, 6, ..., 2, respectively. This process reveals little about $n + 1$, but the process can be used to create the number n. Because n is to be a multiple of 9, 8, 7, 6, ..., 2, perhaps the simplest value for n is $9 \cdot 8 \cdot 7 \cdot 6 \cdots 3 \cdot 2$.

With $n = 9 \cdot 8 \cdot 7 \cdot 6 \cdots 3 \cdot 2$, we have $n + 9$, $n + 8$, $n + 7$, ..., $n + 2$ as composite numbers. Notice that this process yields eight consecutive composite numbers, rather than ten. Also, observe that to obtain eight consecutive composites, we used $n + 9$ as the greatest number. Similarly, to obtain ten consecutive composites, we choose $n + 11$ as the greatest composite, with $n = 11 \cdot 10 \cdot 9 \cdot 8 \cdots 3 \cdot 2$; to obtain 1000 consecutive composites, we use $n + 1001$, with $n = 1001 \cdot 1000 \cdot 999 \cdots 3 \cdot 2$.

Carrying Out the Plan. Using the process just developed, we consider the 1000 consecutive natural numbers $n + 2$, $n + 3$, ..., $n + 1000$, $n + 1001$. We choose $n = 2 \cdot 3 \cdot 4 \cdots 1001$. With this choice of n, the 1000 consecutive natural numbers we have just described are composite.

Looking Back. In a similar manner, we can find as many consecutive composite numbers as desired. Though there are infinitely many primes, we can find a million, a billion, or a trillion consecutive composite numbers and, in general, as many as we want.

For centuries, mathematicians have looked for a formula that produces only primes, but no one has ever found one. One such attempt resulted in the expression $n^2 - n + 41$, where n is a whole number. Substituting 0, 1, 2, 3, ..., 40 for n in the expression always results in a prime number. However, substituting 41 for n gives $41^2 - 41 + 41$, or 41^2, a composite number.

In 1971, the largest known prime was $2^{19,937} - 1$, found by Bryant Tuckerman of IBM. In 1978, two high school students—Laura Nickel and Curt Noll, from Hayward, California—found a larger prime, $2^{23,209} - 1$, using a computer. Other larger primes have since been discovered, one of the latest being $2^{132,049} - 1$. It too was discovered with the help of a computer, in 1983. Subsequently, the number $2^{216,091} - 1$, which has 65,050 digits, was discovered to be a prime.

In the 1970s, determining large primes became extremely useful in coding and decoding secret messages. In all coding and decoding, the letters of an alphabet correspond in some way to nonnegative integers. A safe coding system is one in which messages are unintelligible to everyone except the intended receiver. Such a system was devised by three MIT (Massachusetts

Institute of Technology) scientists—Ronald Rivast, Adi Shamir, and Leonard Adleman—and is referred to by their initials, as the RSA system. The secret deciphering key consists of two large prime numbers chosen by the user. (It is relatively easy with the help of a computer to generate primes of approximately 50 digits.) The enciphering key is the product of these two primes. Because it is extremely difficult and time-consuming—even for a computer—to factor large numbers, it was practically impossible to recover the deciphering key from a known enciphering key. In 1982 new methods for factoring large numbers were invented, which resulted in the use of even greater primes to prevent the breaking of decoding keys.

There are many interesting problems concerning primes. For example, Christian Goldbach (1690–1764) asserted in a letter to Euler that every even integer greater than 2 is the sum of two primes. This statement is known as *Goldbach's conjecture* **Goldbach's conjecture.** For example, $4 = 2 + 2, 6 = 3 + 3, 8 = 3 + 5$, $10 = 3 + 7, 12 = 5 + 7$, and $14 = 3 + 11$. In spite of the simplicity of the statement, no one knows for sure whether or not the statement is true.

PROBLEM 4

A woman with a basket of eggs finds that, if she removes the eggs from the basket 2, 3, 4, 5, or 6 at a time, there is always 1 egg left. However, if she removes the eggs 7 at a time, there are no eggs left. If the basket holds up to 500 eggs, how many eggs does the woman have?

Understanding the Problem.   When a woman removes eggs from the basket 2, 3, 4, 5, or 6 at a time, there is always 1 egg left. That means that if the number of eggs is divided by 2, 3, 4, 5, or 6, the remainder is always 1. We also know that when she removes the eggs 7 at a time, there are no eggs left; that is, the number of eggs is a multiple of 7. Finally, we know that the basket holds up to 500 eggs. We have to find the number of eggs in the basket.

Devising a Plan.   One way to solve the problem is to write all the multiples of 7 between 7 and 500 and check which ones have a remainder of 1 when divided by 2, 3, 4, 5, or 6. Since this method is tedious, we look for a different approach. Let the number of eggs be n. Then, if n is divided by 2, the remainder is 1. Consequently, $n - 1$ will be divisible by 2. Similarly, 3, 4, 5, and 6 divide $n - 1$.

Since 2 and 3 divide $n - 1$, the primes 2 and 3 appear in the prime factorization of $n - 1$. Note that $4 | (n - 1)$ implies that $2 | (n - 1)$, and hence, from the information $2 | (n - 1)$ and $4 | (n - 1)$, we can conclude only that 2^2 appears in the prime factorization of $n - 1$. Since $5 | (n - 1)$, 5 appears in the prime factorization of $n - 1$. The fact that $6 | (n - 1)$ does not provide any new information, since it only implies that 2 and 3 are prime factors of $n - 1$, which we already know. Now, $n - 1$ may also have other prime factors. Denoting the product of these other prime factors by k, we have $n - 1 = 2^2 \cdot 3 \cdot 5 \cdot k = 60k$, where k is some natural number, and so $n = 60k + 1$. We now find all possible values for n in the form $60k + 1$ less than 500 and determine which ones are divisible by 7.

Carrying Out the Plan. Because $n = 60k + 1$ and k is any natural number, we substitute $k = 1, 2, 3, \ldots$ to obtain the following possible values for n that are less than 500:

61, 121, 181, 241, 301, 361, 421, 481

Among these values, only 301 is divisible by 7; hence, 301 is the only possible answer to the problem.

Looking Back. In the preceding situation, we still had to test eight numbers for divisibility by 7. Is it possible to reduce the computations further? We know that $n = 60k + 1$ and that the possible values for k are $k = 1, 2, 3, 4, 5, 6, 7, 8$. We also know that $7 | n$; that is, $7|(60k + 1)$. The problem is to find for which of the above values of k, $7|(60k + 1)$. The question would have been easier to answer if, instead of $60k + 1$, we had a smaller number. We know that the least multiple of k closest to $60k$ that is divisible by 7 is $56k$. Since $7|(60k + 1)$ and $7|56k$, we conclude that $7|(60k + 1 - 56k)$; that is, $7|(4k + 1)$. We now see that $7|(60k + 1)$, if and only if $7|(4k + 1)$. The only value of k between 1 and 8 that makes $4k + 1$ divisible by 7 is 5. Consequently, $7|(60 \cdot 5 + 1)$, and 301 is the solution to the problem.

PROBLEM SET 5-2

1. Use a factor tree to find the prime factorization for each of the following.
   (a) 504   (b) 2475   (c) 11,250
2. Which of the following numbers are primes?
   (a) 149   (b) 923   (c) 433
   (d) 101   (e) 463   (f) 897
3. What is the greatest prime you must consider to test whether or not 5669 is prime?
4. Explain why, in the Sieve of Eratosthenes in Figure 5-4, after we cross out all the multiples of 2, 3, 5, and 7, the remaining numbers are primes.
5. Extend the Sieve of Eratosthenes to find all primes less than 200.
6. Factors of a locker number are 2, 5, and 9. If there are exactly nine other factors, what is the locker number?
7. (a) When the United States flag had 48 stars, the stars were arranged in a 6 × 8 rectangular array. In what other rectangular arrays could they have been arranged?

   (b) How many different rectangular arrays of stars could there be if there were only 47 states?
8. If the Spanish Armada had consisted of 177 galleons, could it have gone to sea in an equal number of small flotillas? If so, how many ships would have been in each?
9. Suppose that the 435 members of the House of Representatives are placed on committees consisting of more than 2 members but less than 30 members. Each committee is to have an equal number of members and each member is to be on only one committee.
   (a) What size committees are possible?
   (b) How many committees are there of each size?
10. Mr. Arboreta wants to set out fruit trees in a rectangular array. For each of the following numbers of trees, find all possible numbers of rows if each row is to have the same number of trees.
    (a) 36   (b) 28   (c) 17   (d) 144
11. What is the smallest number that has exactly seven positive factors?

12. (a) Find a composite number different from 41^2 that is of the form $n^2 - n + 41$.

★(b) Prove that there are infinitely many composite numbers of the form $n^2 - n + 41$.

13. Find the least number divisible by each natural number less than or equal to 12.

14. The primes 2 and 3 are consecutive integers. Is there another pair of consecutive integers both of which are prime? Justify your answer.

15. The prime numbers 11 and 13 are called **twin primes** because they differ by 2. Find all the twin primes less than 200. (The existence of infinitely many twin primes has not been proved.)

16. (a) Use the Fundamental Theorem of Arithmetic to justify that if $2|n$ and $3|n$, then $6|n$.

(b) Is it always true that if $a|n$ and $b|n$, then $ab|n^2$? Either prove the statement or give a counter-example.

17. In order to test for divisibility by 12, one student checked to determine divisibility by 3 and 4, while another checked for divisibility by 2 and 6. Are both students using a correct approach to divisibility by 12? Why or why not?

18. (a) Is it always true that if $3|ab$, then $3|a$ or $3|b$?

(b) Is it always true that if $4|ab$, then $4|a$ or $4|b$?

19. Show that, if 1 were considered a prime, every number would have more than one prime factorization.

20. If $42|n$, what other positive integers divide n?

21. Is it possible to find positive integers x, y, and z such that $2^x \cdot 3^y = 5^z$? Why or why not?

22. Find all positive integers x and y such that $xy = 60$.

23. (a) Find all the positive divisors of 2^8.

(b) Find all the positive divisors of 3^5.

(c) How many positive divisors does $2^8 \cdot 3^5$ have?

★(d) If p and q are primes, how many divisors does $p^k q^m$ have?

24. Use Table 5-1 for each of the following.

(a) Guess the next three numbers in the 3 column. Describe a pattern for forming the numbers.

(b) Guess the next three numbers in the 5 column. Describe a pattern for forming the numbers.

★(c) Guess the next three numbers in the 4 column. Describe a pattern for forming the numbers.

25. Find the greatest four-digit number that has exactly three factors.

★**26.** Complete the details for the following proof, which shows that there are infinitely many prime numbers.

If the number of primes is finite, then there is a greatest prime denoted by p. Consider the product of all the primes, $2 \cdot 3 \cdot 5 \ldots p$, and let $N = (2 \cdot 3 \cdot 5 \ldots p) + 1$. Because $N > p$, where p is

the greatest prime, N is composite. Because N is composite, there is a prime q among the primes 2, 3, 5, $\ldots$, p such that $q|N$. However, none of the primes 2, 3, 5, $\ldots$, p divides N. (Why?)

Consequently, $q \nmid N$, which is a contradiction. Thus, the assumption that there are finitely many primes is false and the set of primes must be infinite.

27. Find the prime factorizations of each of the following.

(a) 5!

(b) 5! + 1

(c) 10!

(d) $(10!)^3$

(e) 10! − 9!

28. (a) Does any number between 2 and 100 (inclusive) divide 100! + 1? Why or why not?

(b) If p is a prime, show that no prime less than or equal to p divides $p! + 1$.

(c) 12! was found to be 479,0■1,600, but one of the digits was blotted out. Find the missing digit without multiplying out 12!.

(d) How many zeros are there at the end of 100! when it is multiplied out? (Notice that a calculator cannot handle this problem.)

29. It is not known whether there are infinitely many primes in the infinite sequence consisting only of ones: 1, 11, 111, 1111, $\ldots$. Find infinitely many composite numbers in the sequence.

30. Find infinitely many composite numbers in the sequence whose nth term is $3n + 1$.

31. One formula yielding several primes is $n^2 + n + 17$. Substitute $n = 1, 2, 3, \ldots$, 17 in the formula and find which of the resulting numbers are primes and which are composites.

Review Problems

32. Classify each of the following as true or false.

(a) 11 is a factor of 189.

(b) 1001 is a multiple of 13.

(c) $7|1001$ and $7 \nmid 12$ imply $7 \nmid (1001 - 12)$.

(d) If a number is divisible by both 7 and 11, then its prime factorization contains 7 and 11.

33. Test each of the following for divisibility by 2, 3, 4, 5, 6, 7, 8, 9, 10, and 11.

(a) 438,162   (b) 2,345,678,910

34. Prove that, if a number is divisible by 12, then it is divisible by 3.

35. Could \$3376 be divided exactly among either 7 or 8 people?

C O M P U T E R　　C O R N E R

The following BASIC program will determine if a positive integer N is prime. Type it into your computer.

```
 10 PRINT "THIS PROGRAM DETERMINES IF A POSITIVE INTEGER IS"
 15 PRINT "PRIME."
 20 PRINT "AFTER THE QUESTION MARK, TYPE A POSITIVE INTEGER."
 30 INPUT N
 40 IF N = 1 GOTO 90
 50 IF N = 2 GOTO 120
 60 FOR K = 2 TO SQR(N)
 70 IF N/K = INT(N/K) THEN 90
 80 GOTO 110
 90 PRINT N; " IS NOT PRIME."
100 GOTO 130
110 NEXT K
120 PRINT N; " IS PRIME."
130 PRINT "IF YOU WANT TO CHECK ANOTHER NUMBER, TYPE 1. IF"
135 PRINT "NOT TYPE 0."
140 INPUT V
150 IF V = 1 GOTO 20
160 END
```

Run this program, using different values for N.

Section 5-3　Greatest Common Divisor and Least Common Multiple

Greatest Common Divisor

greatest common divisor (GCD)　The **greatest common divisor (GCD)** of two whole numbers is the greatest divisor or factor that the two numbers have in common. The concept of GCD is used in Chapter 6 to reduce fractions to lowest terms. In what follows, we present several ways to find the GCD of two or more numbers.

The Intersection-of-Sets Method.　In the intersection-of-sets method, we list all members of the set of positive divisors of the two numbers, then find the set of all *common divisors*, and, finally, pick the *greatest* element in that set. For example, to find the GCD of 20 and 32, denote the sets of divisors of 20 and 32 by D_{20} and D_{32}, respectively.

$D_{20} = \{1, 2, 4, 5, 10, 20\}$
$D_{32} = \{1, 2, 4, 8, 16, 32\}$

The set of all common positive divisors of 20 and 32 is

$D_{20} \cap D_{32} = \{1, 2, 4\}$

Because the greatest number in the set of common positive divisors is 4, the GCD of 20 and 32 is 4, written GCD(20, 32) = 4.

The Prime Factorization Method. The intersection-of-sets method is rather time-consuming and tedious if the numbers have many divisors. Another, more efficient, method is the *prime factorization method*. To find GCD(180, 168), first notice that

$$180 = 2 \cdot 2 \cdot 3 \cdot 3 \cdot 5$$
$$\text{and} \quad \updownarrow \ \updownarrow \quad \updownarrow$$
$$168 = 2 \cdot 2 \cdot 2 \cdot 3 \cdot 7$$

Prime factorization shows that 180 and 168 have two factors of 2 and one of 3 in common. These common primes divide both 180 and 168. In fact, the only numbers other than 1 that divide both 180 and 168 must have no more than two 2s and one 3 and no other prime factors in their prime factorizations. The possible common divisors are 1, 2, 2^2, 3, $2 \cdot 3$, and $2^2 \cdot 3$. Hence, the greatest common divisor of 180 and 168 is $2^2 \cdot 3$. The procedure for finding the GCD of two or more numbers by using the prime factorization method is summarized as follows.

To find the GCD of two or more numbers, first find the prime factorizations of the given numbers, then take each common prime factor of the given numbers; the GCD is the product of these common factors, each raised to the lowest power of that prime that occurs in either of the prime factorizations.

EXAMPLE 5-9   Find each of the following.
(a) GCD(108, 72)
(b) GCD (x, y) is $x = 2^3 \cdot 7^2 \cdot 11 \cdot 13$ and $y = 2 \cdot 7^3 \cdot 13 \cdot 17$
(c) GCD(x, y, z) is $z = 2^2 \cdot 7$, using x and y from part (b)

SOLUTION   (a) Since $108 = 2^2 \cdot 3^3$ and $72 = 2^3 \cdot 3^2$, it follows that GCD(108, 72) = $2^2 \cdot 3^2 = 36$.
(b) GCD$(x, y) = 2 \cdot 7^2 \cdot 13 = 1274$.
(c) Because $x = 2^3 \cdot 7^2 \cdot 11 \cdot 13$, $y = 2 \cdot 7^3 \cdot 13 \cdot 17$, and $z = 2^2 \cdot 7$, then GCD$(x, y, z) = 2 \cdot 7 = 14$. Notice that GCD$(x, y, z)$ can also be obtained by finding the GCD of z and 1274—the answer from part (b).

If we apply the prime factorization technique to finding GCD(4, 9), we see that 4 and 9 have no common prime factors. Consequently, 1 is the only common divisor, so GCD(4, 9) = 1. Numbers such as 4 and 9, whose GCD

relatively prime   is 1, are called **relatively prime.**

Euclidean Algorithm Method. Some numbers are hard to factor. For these numbers, another method is more efficient for finding the GCD. For example, suppose that we want to find GCD(676, 221). If we could find two smaller numbers whose GCD is the same as GCD(676, 221), our task would be easier. From Theorem 5-2(a), every divisor of 676 and 221 is also a divisor of $676 - 221$ and 221. Conversely, every divisor of $676 - 221$ and 221 is also a divisor of 676 and 221. Thus, the set of all the common divisors of 676 and 221 is the same as the set of all common divisors of 676 − 221 and 221. Consequently, GCD(676, 221) = GCD(676 − 221, 221). This argument holds in general, and we have the following theorem.

● **T H E O R E M   5-8**
If a and b are any whole numbers and $a \geq b$, then GCD(a, b) = GCD($a − b$, b)

Using Theorem 5-8 repeatedly, we can find the GCD of any two numbers; for example, consider GCD(676, 221). By using Theorem 5-8 several times, we have

GCD(676, 221) = GCD(676 − 221, 221)
    = GCD(455, 221)   Because 676 − 221 = 455
    = GCD(234, 221)   Because 455 − 221 = 234
    = GCD(13, 221)   Because 234 − 221 = 13

Notice that we have actually subtracted $3 \cdot 221$ from 676, and the difference is $676 − 3 \cdot 221 = 13$. Because division can be thought of as repeated subtraction, the three subtractions could have been achieved by dividing 676 by 221 and recording the remainder, as follows.

$$
\begin{array}{r}
3 \\
221\overline{)676} \\
663 \\
\hline
13
\end{array}
$$

It follows that GCD(676, 221) = GCD(13, 221). Since the only divisors of 13 are 1 and 13, the only possible values for GCD(13, 221) are 1 and 13. Because $221 = 17 \cdot 13$, we know that $13 \mid 221$, and we have GCD(13, 221) = 13. This implies that GCD(676, 221) = 13.

  We could have continued to use Theorem 5-8 to calculate GCD(13, 221). Because GCD(13, 221) = GCD(221, 13), we can subtract 13 from 221 as many times as needed. If 13 is subtracted from 221 seventeen times, we conclude that GCD(221, 13) = GCD(0, 13). Every integer divides 0, so GCD(0, 13) = 13. Thus, GCD(221, 13) = 13. Notice that GCD(221, 13) could also have been found through division rather than through repeated subtraction:

$$
\begin{array}{r}
17 \\
13\overline{)221} \\
13 \\
\hline
91 \\
91 \\
\hline
0
\end{array}
$$

Because the remainder in the division is 0, GCD(221, 13) = GCD(0, 13) = 13. The process of repeated division ends when we obtain a zero remainder in some division. Because each remainder is smaller than the remainder in a preceding division, we must eventually obtain a remainder of 0.

Based on this development, Theorem 5-8 can be generalized as follows.

● T H E O R E M 5-9

If a and b are any whole numbers and $a \geq b$, then GCD (a, b) = GCD(r, b), where r is the remainder when a is divided by b.

Euclidean algorithm

Finding the GCD of two numbers by repeatedly using Theorem 5-9 until the remainder 0 is reached is referred to as the **Euclidean algorithm.**

EXAMPLE 5-10 Use the Euclidean algorithm to find GCD(10764, 2300).

SOLUTION

$$
\begin{array}{r}
4 \\
2300\overline{)10{,}764} \\
9{,}200 \\
\hline
1{,}564
\end{array}
$$
Thus, GCD(10764, 2300) = GCD(2300, 1564).

$$
\begin{array}{r}
1 \\
1564\overline{)2300} \\
1564 \\
\hline
736
\end{array}
$$
Thus, GCD(2300, 1564) = GCD(1564, 736).

$$
\begin{array}{r}
2 \\
736\overline{)1564} \\
1472 \\
\hline
92
\end{array}
$$
Thus, GCD(1564, 736) = GCD(736, 92).

$$
\begin{array}{r}
8 \\
92\overline{)736} \\
736 \\
\hline
0
\end{array}
$$
Thus, GCD(736, 92) = GCD(92, 0).

Because GCD(92, 0) = 92, it follows that GCD(10764, 2300) = 92.

● R E M A R K

The procedure for finding the GCD by using the Euclidean algorithm can be stopped at any step at which the GCD is obvious.

Least Common Multiple

least common multiple (LCM)

Another useful concept in number theory is that of least common multiple. This concept is useful for determining the least common denominator of two fractions. The **least common multiple (LCM)** of two natural numbers is the least positive multiple that the two numbers have in common. There are various methods for finding the LCM of two given natural numbers.

The Intersection-of-Sets Method. In the intersection-of-sets method, we first find the set of all positive *multiples* of both the first and second numbers, then find the set of all *common multiples* of both numbers, and finally pick the *least* element in that set. For example, to find the LCM of 8 and 12, denote the sets of positive multiples of 8 and 12 by M_8 and M_{12}, respectively.

$M_8 = \{8, 16, 24, 32, 40, 48, 56, 64, 72, \ldots\}$
$M_{12} = \{12, 24, 36, 48, 60, 72, 84, 96, 108, \ldots\}$

The set of common multiples is

$M_8 \cap M_{12} = \{24, 48, 72, \ldots\}$

Because the least number in $M_8 \cap M_{12}$ is 24, the LCM of 8 and 12 is 24, written LCM(8, 12) = 24.

The Prime Factorization Method. The intersection-of-sets method for finding the LCM is often lengthy, especially when it is used to find the LCM of three or more natural numbers. Another, more efficient method for finding the LCM of several numbers is the *prime factorization method*. For example, to find LCM(40, 12), first find the prime factorizations of 40 and 12, namely, $2^3 \cdot 5$ and $2^2 \cdot 3$, respectively.

Next, let $m = \text{LCM}(40, 12)$. Because m is a multiple of 40, it must contain both 2^3 and 5 as factors. Also, m is a multiple of 12, so it must contain 2^2 and 3 as factors. Since 2^3 is a multiple of 2^2, then $m = 2^3 \cdot 5 \cdot 3 = 120$. In general, we have the following.

To find the LCM of two natural numbers, first find the prime factorization of each number. Then take each of the primes that are factors of either of the given numbers. The LCM is the product of these primes, each raised to the greatest power of the prime that occurs in either of the prime factorizations.

EXAMPLE 5-11   Find the LCM of 2520 and 10,530.

SOLUTION
$$2520 = 2^3 \cdot 3^2 \cdot 5 \cdot 7$$
$$10{,}530 = 2 \cdot 3^4 \cdot 5 \cdot 13$$
$$\text{LCM}(2520, 10530) = 2^3 \cdot 3^4 \cdot 5 \cdot 7 \cdot 13$$

The Euclidean Algorithm Method. The similarity between the prime factorization algorithms for GCD and LCM suggests a connection. Consider the GCD and LCM of 6 and 9. Because $6 = 2 \cdot 3$ and $9 = 3^2$, it follows that GCD(6, 9) = 3 and LCM(6, 9) = 18. Notice that GCD(6, 9) $\cdot$ LCM(6, 9) = $3 \cdot 18 = 54$. Observe that 54 is also the product of the original numbers 6 and 9. In general, for any two natural numbers a and b, the connection between their GCD and LCM is given by Theorem 5-10.

● T H E O R E M   5-10
For any two natural numbers a and b,

$$\text{GCD}(a, b) \cdot \text{LCM}(a, b) = ab$$

This result is useful for finding the LCM of two numbers a and b when their prime factorizations are not easy to find. GCD(a, b) can be found by the Euclidean algorithm, the product ab can be found by simple multiplication, and LCM(a, b) can be found by division.

EXAMPLE 5-12   Find LCM(731, 952).

SOLUTION   By the Euclidean algorithm, GCD(731, 952) = 17. By Theorem 5-10, $17 \cdot$ LCM(731, 952) = $731 \cdot 952$. Consequently,

$$\text{LCM}(731, 952) = \frac{731 \cdot 952}{17} = 40{,}936$$

Although Theorem 5-10 cannot be used to find the LCM of more than two numbers, it is possible to find the LCM for three or more numbers. For example, to find LCM(12, 108, 120), we can use the prime factorization method.

$$12 = 2^2 \cdot 3$$
$$108 = 2^2 \cdot 3^3$$
$$120 = 2^3 \cdot 3 \cdot 5$$

Then, LCM(12, 108, 120) = $2^3 \cdot 3^3 \cdot 5 = 1080$.

The Division-by-Primes Method. Another procedure for finding the LCM of several natural numbers involves division by primes. For example, to find LCM(12, 75, 120), we start with the least prime that divides at least one of the given numbers and divide as follows.

$$2 \, \lfloor \underline{12, \, 75, \, 120}$$
$$6, \, 75, \quad 60$$

Because 2 does not divide 75, simply bring down the 75. In order to obtain the LCM using this procedure, continue the division process until the row of answers consists of relatively prime numbers.

$$
\begin{array}{r|r}
2 & 12,\ 75,\ 120 \\
2 & 6,\ 75,\ \ 60 \\
2 & 3,\ 75,\ \ 30 \\
3 & 3,\ 75,\ \ 15 \\
5 & 1,\ 25,\ \ \ 5 \\
& 1,\ \ 5,\ \ \ 1
\end{array}
$$

Thus, LCM(12, 75, 120) $= 2 \cdot 2 \cdot 2 \cdot 3 \cdot 5 \cdot 1 \cdot 5 \cdot 1 = 2^3 \cdot 3 \cdot 5^2 = 600$.

PROBLEM SET 5-3

1. Find the GCD and the LCM for each of the following, using the intersection-of-sets method.
   (a) 18 and 10   (b) 24 and 36
   (c) 8, 24, and 52
2. Find the GCD and the LCM for each of the following using the prime factorization method.
   (a) 132 and 504   (b) 65 and 1690
   (c) 900, 96, and 630   (d) 108 and 360
   (e) 63 and 147   (f) 625, 750, and 1000
3. Find the GCD for each of the following, using the Euclidean algorithm.
   (a) 220 and 2924   (b) 14,595 and 10,856
   (c) 122,368 and 123,152
4. Find the LCM for each of the following, using any method.
   (a) 24 and 36   (b) 72 and 90 and 96
   (c) 90 and 105 and 315
5. Find the LCM for each of the following pairs of numbers, using Theorem 5-10 and the answers from Problem 3.
   (a) 220 and 2924   (b) 14,595 and 10,856
   (c) 122,368 and 123,152
6. Find each of the following, using any method.
   (a) GCD(56, 72)   (b) GCD(84, 92)
   (c) GCD(1804, 328)   (d) LCM(56, 72)
   (e) LCM(24, 82)   (f) LCM(963, 657)
7. Midas has 120 gold coins and 144 silver coins. He wants to place his gold coins and his silver coins in stacks so that there are the same number of coins in each stack. What is the greatest number of coins that he can place in each stack?
8. Bill and Sue both work at night. Bill has every sixth night off and Sue has every eighth night off. If they are both off tonight, how many nights will it be before they are both off again?
9. By selling cookies at 24¢ each, José made enough money to buy several cans of pop costing 45¢ per can. If he had no money left over after buying the

pop, what is the least number of cookies he could have sold?
10. Bijous I and II start their movies at 7:00 P.M. The movie at Bijou I takes 75 minutes, while the movie at Bijou II takes 90 minutes. If the shows run continuously, when will they start at the same time again?
11. Two bike riders ride around in a circular path. The first rider completes one round in 12 minutes and the second rider completes it in 18 minutes. If they both start at the same place and the same time and go in the same direction, after how many minutes will they meet again at the starting place?
12. Assume that a and b are any natural numbers, and answer each of the following.
    (a) If GCD(a, b) = 1, find LCM(a, b).
    (b) Find GCD(a, a) and LCM(a, a).
    (c) Find GCD(a^2, a) and LCM(a^2, a).
    (d) If $a \mid b$, find GCD(a, b) and LCM(a, b).
    (e) If a and b are two different primes, find GCD(a, b) and LCM(a, b).
    (f) What is the relationship between a and b if GCD(a, b) = a?
    (g) What is the relationship between a and b if LCM(a, b) = a?
13. Classify each of the following as true or false. Justify your answers.
    (a) If GCD(a, b) = 1, then a and b cannot both be even.
    (b) If GCD(a, b) = 2, then both a and b are even.
    (c) If a and b are even, then GCD(a, b) = 2.
    (d) For all natural numbers a and b, LCM(a, b)$\mid$GCD(a, b).
    (e) For all natural numbers a and b, LCM(a, b)$\mid ab$.
    (f) GCD(a, b) $\leq a$
    (g) LCM(a, b) $\geq a$
14. To find GCD(24, 20, 12), it is possible to find GCD(24, 20), which is 4, and then find GCD(4, 12), which is 4. Use this approach and the Euclidean algorithm to find GCD(120, 75, 105).

15. Is it true that GCD(a, b, c) · LCM(a, b, c) = abc? Justify your answer.

16. (a) Show that 97,219,988,751 and 4 are relatively prime.

(b) Show that 181,345,913 and 11 are relatively prime.

(c) Show that 181,345,913 and 33 are relatively prime.

17. Find all natural numbers x such that GCD(25, x) = 1 and $1 \leq x \leq 25$.

18. One use of GCD is to reduce fractions to lowest terms (see Chapter 6). For example, $\frac{12}{54}$ can be reduced to $\frac{2}{9}$ by dividing both 12 and 54 by GCD(12, 54), or 6. Use the GCD to reduce each of the following.

(a) $\frac{28}{48}$ (b) $\frac{63}{99}$ (c) $\frac{117}{288}$ (d) $\frac{65}{260}$

19. (a) A number is called *perfect* if it is equal to the sum of its proper divisors—that is, to the sum of all its divisors except the number itself. For example, because 6 = 1 + 2 + 3, it is perfect. Find another perfect number less than 30.

(b) Two numbers are said to be *amicable* if each is the sum of the proper divisors of the other. Show that 220 and 284 are amicable.

20. Is it always true that if d|GCD(a, b), then d|a and d|b? Why or why not?

21. Find two integers x and y such that $x \cdot y$ = 1,000,000 and neither x nor y contains any zeros as digits.

Review Problems

22. Fill each blank space with a single digit that makes the corresponding statement true. Find all possible answers.

(a) 3|83 __ 51   (b) 11|8 __ 691

(c) 23|103 __ 6

23. Is 3111 a prime? Prove your answer.

24. Find a number that has exactly six prime factors.

25. Produce the least positive number that is divisible by 2, 3, 4, 5, 6, 7, 8, 9, 10, and 11.

26. What is the greatest prime that must be used to determine if 2089 is prime?

C O M P U T E R   C O R N E R

1. Type the following Logo procedure for finding the GCD of two positive integers into your computer, and then use the procedure to find the GCD of the given numbers.

```
TO GCD :A :B
  IF :B=0 OUTPUT :A
  OUTPUT GCD :B (REMAINDER :A :B)
END
```

(In Apple Logo II, replace IF :B=0 OUTPUT :A with IF :B=0 [OUTPUT :A].)

(a) GCD (676, 221)

(b) GCD (10764, 2300)

2. Use Theorem 5-10 and the preceding GCD procedure to write a procedure LCM for finding the LCM of any two positive integers, :A and :B.

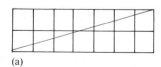

B R A I N   T E A S E R

For any $n \times m$ rectangle such that GCD(n, m) = 1, find a rule for determining the number of unit squares (1 × 1) that a diagonal passes through. For example, in Figure 5-5(a) and (b), the diagonal passes through 8 and 6 squares, respectively.

FIGURE 5-5   (a)   (b)

*Section 5-4 Clock and Modular Arithmetic

Clock Arithmetic

The book *Disquisitiones Arithmeticae* is among Karl Friedrich Gauss's great mathematical works. In this book, Gauss introduced a new topic, the theory of congruences, which very rapidly gained general acceptance and has since become a foundation for number theory. The basics of the theory of congruences can be understood in elementary school and can provide enrichment for students.

FIGURE 5-6

One type of enrichment activity involving congruences uses the arithmetic of a 12-hour clock. For example, if it is 9 o'clock, what time will it be 8 hours later? It is possible to use the clock in Figure 5-6 to determine that 8 hours after 9 o'clock is 5 o'clock. We record this as $9 \oplus 8 = 5$, where $\oplus$ denotes clock addition.

The answer, $9 \oplus 8 = 5$, can also be obtained by performing the regular addition $9 + 8 = 17$ and then subtracting 12 (or by dividing 17 by 12 and taking the remainder). Thus, whenever the sum of two digits on a 12-hour clock under regular addition exceeds 12, add the numbers in the regular way and then subtract 12 to obtain the answer for clock addition.

It is possible to perform other operations on the clock. For example, $2 \ominus 9$ on the clock, where $\ominus$ denotes clock subtraction, could be interpreted as the time 9 hours before 2 o'clock. Counting backward (counterclockwise) 9 units from 2 reveals that $2 \ominus 9 = 5$. If subtraction on the clock is defined in terms of addition, we have $2 \ominus 9 = x$, if and only if $2 = 9 \oplus x$. Consequently, $x = 5$.

EXAMPLE 5-13 Perform each of the following computations on a 12-hour clock.

(a) $8 \oplus 8$ (b) $4 \ominus 12$ (c) $4 \ominus 4$ (d) $4 \ominus 8$

SOLUTION
(a) $8 + 8 - 12 = 4$. Hence, $8 \oplus 8 = 4$.
(b) $4 \ominus 12 = 4$, since, by counting forward or backward 12 hours, you arrive at the original position.
(c) $4 \ominus 4 = 12$. This should be clear from looking at the clock, but it can also be found by using the definition of subtraction in terms of addition.
(d) $4 \ominus 8 = 4 - 8 + 12 = 8$

As with whole numbers, clock multiplication can be defined using repeated addition. For example, $2 \otimes 8 = 8 \oplus 8 = 4$, where $\otimes$ denotes clock multiplication. Similarly, $3 \otimes 5 = (5 \oplus 5) \oplus 5 = 10 \oplus 5 = 3$. Notice that $3 \otimes 5$ can also be found as follows:

$$3 \otimes 5 = 3 \cdot 5 - 12 = 3$$

Similarly,

$$8 \otimes 11 = 8 \cdot 11 - 7 \cdot 12 = 4$$

As with whole numbers, clock division can be defined in terms of multiplication. For example, $8 \ominus 5 = x$, where $\ominus$ denotes clock division, if and only if $8 = 5 \otimes x$, for a unique x in the set $\{1, 2, 3, \ldots, 12\}$. Because $5 \otimes 4 = 8$, then $8 \ominus 5 = 4$.

EXAMPLE 5-14   Perform the following operations on a 12-hour clock, if possible.

(a) $3 \otimes 11$ (b) $2 \ominus 7$ (c) $3 \ominus 2$ (d) $5 \ominus 12$

SOLUTION   (a) $3 \otimes 11 = (11 \oplus 11) \oplus 11 = 10 \oplus 11 = 9$
(b) $2 \ominus 7 = x$ if and only if $2 = 7 \otimes x$. Consequently, $x = 2$.
(c) $3 \ominus 2 = x$ if and only if $3 = 2 \otimes x$. Multiplying each of the numbers 1, 2, 3, 4, . . . , 12 by 2 shows that none of the multiplications yields 3. Thus, the equation $3 = 2 \otimes x$ has no solution, and consequently, $3 \ominus 2$ is undefined.
(d) $5 \ominus 12 = x$ if and only if $5 = 12 \otimes x$. However, $12 \otimes x = 12$ for every x in the set $\{1, 3, 4, \ldots, 12\}$. Thus, $5 = 12 \otimes x$ has no solution on the clock; and therefore, $5 \ominus 12$ is undefined.

We have seen that, on a 12-hour clock, adding or subtracting 12 does not change the result. Thus, on a 12-hour clock, 12 behaves as 0 does in a base-ten addition or subtraction and is the additive identity for addition on the 12-hour clock. Similarly, on a 5-hour clock, 5 behaves as 0 does.

On a 12-hour clock, addition, subtraction, and multiplication can be performed for any two numbers, but as shown in Example 5-14, not all divisions can be performed. Division by 12, the additive identity, on a 12-hour clock either can never be performed or is not meaningful, since it does not yield a unique answer. However, there are clocks on which all divisions can be performed, except by the corresponding additive identities. One such clock is a 5-hour clock, shown in Figure 5-7.

FIGURE 5-7

On this clock, $3 \oplus 4 = 2$, $2 \ominus 3 = 4$, $2 \otimes 4 = 3$, and $3 \ominus 4 = 2$. Since adding 5 to any number yields the original number, 5 is the additive identity for this 5-hour clock, as seen in Table 5-3(a). Consequently, you might suspect that division by 5 is not possible on a 5-hour clock. To determine which divisions are possible, consider Table 5-3(b), a multiplication table for 5-hour clock arithmetic. To find $1 \ominus 2$, we write $1 \ominus 2 = x$, which

TABLE 5-3

(a)

$\oplus$	1	2	3	4	5
1	2	3	4	5	1
2	3	4	5	1	2
3	4	5	1	2	3
4	5	1	2	3	4
5	1	2	3	4	5

(b)

$\otimes$	1	2	3	4	5
1	1	2	3	4	5
2	2	4	1	3	5
3	3	1	4	2	5
4	4	3	2	1	5
5	5	5	5	5	5

is equivalent to $1 = 2 \otimes x$. The second row of part (b) of the table shows that $2 \otimes 1 = 2$, $2 \otimes 2 = 4$, $2 \otimes 3 = 1$, $2 \otimes 4 = 3$, and $2 \otimes 5 = 5$. The solution of $1 = 2 \otimes x$ is $x = 3$, so $1 \oplus 2 = 3$. The information given in the second row of the table can be used to determine the following divisions.

$$2 \oplus 2 = 1 \quad \text{because} \quad 2 = 2 \otimes 1$$
$$3 \oplus 2 = 4 \quad \text{because} \quad 3 = 2 \otimes 4$$
$$4 \oplus 2 = 2 \quad \text{because} \quad 4 = 2 \otimes 2$$
$$5 \oplus 2 = 5 \quad \text{because} \quad 5 = 2 \otimes 5$$

According to the table, division by 2 is always possible, because every element occurs in the second row. Similarly, division by all other numbers, except 5, is always possible. In the problem set, you are asked to perform arithmetic on different clocks and to investigate for which clocks all computations, except division by the additive identity, can be performed.

Modular Arithmetic

April

S	M	T	W	T	F	S
1	2	3	4	5	6	7
8	9	10	11	12	13	14
15	16	17	18	19	20	21
22	23	24	25	26	27	28
29	30					

FIGURE 5-8

Many of the concepts for clock arithmetic can be used to work problems involving a calendar. On the calendar in Figure 5-8, the five Sundays have dates 1, 8, 15, 22, and 29. Any two of these dates for Sunday differ by a multiple of 7. The same property is true for any other day of the week. If the second day of the month falls on Monday, then 7 days later the day will be Monday again. In fact, it will be Monday after any multiple of 7 days. For example, the second and thirtieth days fall on the same day, since $30 - 2 = 28$ and 28 is a multiple of 7. We say that 30 is congruent to 2, modulo 7, and we write $30 \equiv 2 \pmod 7$. Similarly, because 18 and 6 differ by a multiple of 12, we write $18 \equiv 6 \pmod{12}$. This leads to the following definition.

● **D E F I N I T I O N**

For integers a and b, **a is congruent to b modulo m**, written $a \equiv b \pmod m$, if and only if $a - b$ is a multiple of m, where m is a positive integer greater than 1.

EXAMPLE 5-15   Tell why each of the following is true.

(a) $23 \equiv 3 \pmod{10}$
(b) $23 \equiv 3 \pmod 4$
(c) $23 \not\equiv 3 \pmod 7$
(d) $10 \equiv {}^-1 \pmod{11}$
(e) $25 \equiv 5 \pmod 5$

SOLUTION   (a) $23 \equiv 3 \pmod{10}$, because $23 - 3$ is a multiple of 10.
(b) $23 \equiv 3 \pmod 4$, because $23 - 3$ is a multiple of 4.
(c) $23 \not\equiv 3 \pmod 7$, because $23 - 3$ is not a multiple of 7.
(d) $10 \equiv {}^-1 \pmod{11}$, because $10 - ({}^-1) = 11$ is a multiple of 11.
(e) $25 \equiv 5 \pmod 5$, because $25 - 5 = 20$ is a multiple of 5.

EXAMPLE 5-16   Find all integers x such that $x \equiv 1 \pmod{10}$.

SOLUTION $x \equiv 1 \pmod{10}$ if and only if $x - 1 = 10k$, where k is any integer. Consequently, $x = 10k + 1$. Letting $k = 0, 1, 2, 3, \ldots$ yields the sequence 1, 11, 21, 31, 41, ... Also, letting $k = {}^-1, {}^-2, {}^-3, {}^-4, \ldots$ yields the negative integers $^-9, {}^-19, {}^-29, {}^-39, \ldots$. The two sequences can be combined to give the solution set

$$\{\ldots, {}^-39, {}^-29, {}^-19, {}^-9, 1, 11, 21, 31, 41, 51, \ldots\}$$

In Example 5-16, the positive integers obtained, 1, 11, 21, 31, 41, 51, ..., differ from each other by a multiple of 10; hence, they are congruent to each other modulo 10. Notice that each of the numbers 1, 11, 21, 31, 41, 51, ... has a remainder of 1 when divided by 10. In general, *two whole numbers are congruent modulo m if and only if their remainders, on division by m, are the same.*

Many properties of congruence are similar to properties for equality. Several of these are listed below.

● **P R O P E R T I E S**
For all integers a, b, and c:

1. $a \equiv a \pmod{m}$.
2. If $a \equiv b \pmod{m}$, then $b \equiv a \pmod{m}$.
3. If $a \equiv b \pmod{m}$ and $b \equiv c \pmod{m}$, then $a \equiv c \pmod{m}$.
4. If $a \equiv b \pmod{m}$, then $a + c \equiv b + c \pmod{m}$.
5. If $a \equiv b \pmod{m}$, then $ac \equiv bc \pmod{m}$.
6. If $a \equiv b \pmod{m}$ and $c \equiv d \pmod{m}$, then $ac \equiv bd \pmod{m}$.
7. If $a \equiv b \pmod{m}$ and k is a natural number, then $a^k \equiv b^k \pmod{m}$.

With these properties, it is possible to solve a variety of problems, such as the following.

PROBLEM 5
Find the remainder when 3^{100} is divided by 5.

Understanding the Problem. No calculator will accurately find 3^{100}, and thus we cannot actually divide 3^{100} by 5 to find the remainder. We do know that the remainder when a number is divided by 5 should be 0, 1, 2, 3, or 4.

Devising a Plan. Since use of a calculator will not work, we have to look for an alternate plan. The use of modular arithmetic may help. If we can find small integers that are equivalent to powers of 3, then we can use properties (5) and (7) to build up 3^{100} and find the mod 5 equivalent.

Carrying Out the Plan. We know that $3^2 \equiv 4 \pmod 5$
Thus,

$3^3 \equiv 3 \cdot 4 \equiv 2 \pmod 5$
$3^4 \equiv 3 \cdot 2 \equiv 1 \pmod 5$

Using property (7), we see that $(3^4)^{25} \equiv 1^{25} \pmod 5$ or $3^{100} \equiv 1 \pmod 5$. It follows that 3^{100} and 1 have the same remainder when divided by 5. Thus, 3^{100} has remainder 1 when divided by 5.

This type of problem can be changed to find the remainders when dividing by different numbers or to find the units digit of numbers such as 2^{96}.

EXAMPLE 5-17 (a) If it is now Monday, October 14, on what day of the week will October 14 fall next year, if next year is not a leap year?
(b) If Christmas falls on Thursday this year, on what day of the week will Christmas fall next year, if next year is a leap year?

SOLUTION (a) Because next year is not a leap year, we have 365 days in the year. Because $365 = 52 \cdot 7 + 1$, we have $365 \equiv 1 \pmod 7$. Thus, 365 days after October 14 will be 52 weeks and one day later. Thus, October 14 will be on a Tuesday.
(b) Because there are 366 days in a leap year, we have $366 \equiv 2 \pmod 7$. Thus, Christmas will be two days after Thursday, or Saturday.

PROBLEM SET 5-4

1. Perform each of the following operations on a 12-hour clock, if possible.
   (a) $7 \oplus 8$ (b) $4 \oplus 10$ (c) $3 \ominus 9$
   (d) $4 \ominus 8$ (e) $3 \otimes 9$ (f) $4 \otimes 4$
   (g) $1 \oslash 3$ (h) $2 \oslash 5$

2. Perform each of the following operations on a 5-hour clock.
   (a) $3 \oplus 4$ (b) $3 \oplus 3$ (c) $3 \otimes 4$
   (d) $1 \otimes 4$ (e) $3 \otimes 4$ (f) $2 \otimes 3$
   (g) $3 \oslash 4$ (h) $1 \oslash 4$

3. (a) Construct an addition table for a 7-hour clock.
   (b) Using the addition table in (a), find $5 \ominus 6$ and $2 \ominus 5$.
   (c) Using the addition table in (a), show that sub-

traction can always be performed on a 7-hour clock.

4. (a) Construct a multiplication table for a 7-hour clock.
   (b) Use the multiplication table in (a) to find $3 \oslash 5$ and $4 \oslash 6$.
   (c) Use the multiplication table to find whether division by numbers different from 7 is always possible.

5. (a) Construct the multiplication tables for 3-, 4-, 6-, and 11-hour clocks.
   (b) On which of the clocks in part (a) can divisions by numbers other than the additive identity always be performed?

(c) How do the multiplication tables of clocks for which division can always be performed (except by an additive identity) differ from the multiplication tables of clocks for which division is not always meaningful?

6. On a 12-hour clock, find each of the following.
   (a) Additive inverse of 2   (b) Additive inverse of 3
   (c) $(^-2) \oplus (^-3)$ (d) $^-(2 \oplus 3)$
   (e) $(^-2) \ominus (^-3)$ (f) $(^-2) \otimes (^-3)$

7. If September 3 falls on Monday, on what day of the week will it fall next year, if next year is a leap year?

8. Fill in each blank so that the answer is nonnegative and the least possible number.
   (a) $29 \equiv$ _____ (mod 5)
   (b) $3498 \equiv$ _____ (mod 3)
   (c) $3498 \equiv$ _____ (mod 11)
   (d) $^-23 \equiv$ _____ (mod 10)

9. Show that each of the following statements is true.
   (a) $81 \equiv 1$ (mod 8)
   (b) $81 \equiv 1$ (mod 10)
   (c) $1000 \equiv ^-1$ (mod 13)
   (d) $10^{84} \equiv 1$ (mod 9)
   (e) $10^{100} \equiv 1$ (mod 11)
   (f) $937 \equiv 37$ (mod 100)

10. Show that $a \equiv 0$ (mod m), if and only if $m|a$.

11. Translate each of the following statements into the language of congruences.
    (a) $8|24$ (b) $3|^-90$
    (c) Any integer n divides itself.

12. (a) Find all x such that $x \equiv 0$ (mod 2).
    (b) Find all x such that $x \equiv 1$ (mod 2).
    (c) Find all x such that $x \equiv 3$ (mod 5).

13. Find the remainder for each of the following.
    (a) 5^{100} is divided by 6.
    (b) 5^{101} is divided by 6.
    (c) 10^{99} is divided by 11.
    (d) 10^{100} is divided by 11.

★14. (a) Find a negative integer value for x such that $10^3 \equiv x$ (mod 13) and $|x|$ is the least possible.
     (b) Find the remainder when 10^{99} is divided by 13.

★15. Use the fact that $100 \equiv 0$ (mod 4) to find and prove a test for divisibility by 4.

★16. (a) Show that, in general, the cancellation property for multiplication does not hold for congruences; that is, show that $ac \equiv bc$ (mod m) does not always imply $a \equiv b$ (mod m).
     (b) Show that, in general, $a^k \equiv b^k$ (mod m) does not imply $a \equiv b$ (mod m).

★17. Prove each of the properties of congruences mentioned in this section.

B R A I N   T E A S E R
How many primes are in the following sequence?

9, 98, 987, 9876, . . . , 987654321, 9876543219, 98765432198, . . .

SOLUTION TO THE PRELIMINARY PROBLEM

Understanding the Problem.   Mr. Factor has three children, and the product of their ages is 72. When Sonja was given the sum of the ages, she concluded that Mr. Factor did not provide enough information to determine the ages of the three children. After Mr. Factor announced that his oldest child is good at chess, Sonja was able to find the ages of the children. We are to determine the children's ages. From the given information, it seems that the fact that Mr. Factor has an oldest child is significant.

Devising a Plan.   To find the possible ages, we need to find three positive integers whose product is 72. We can do this systematically by listing the possible ages if there is a 1-year-old child in the family, then listing all the possible ages; if there is a 2-year-old in the family; and so on. Because $1 \cdot 2 \cdot 36 = 72$, the combination (1, 2, 36) is a possibility. However, because it does not matter in what order we list the ages, the combination (2, 1, 36) is the same as (1, 2, 36). Knowing that $72 = 2^3 \cdot 3^2$ can help us to list all the possible combinations, along with the corresponding sums, in a table. After examining the table, we hope to be able to determine how the additional information can be used to solve the problem.

Carrying Out the Plan. Table 5-4 shows all the possible ages whose product is 72, along with the corresponding sums. Notice that all the sums other than 14 appear only once in Table 5-4. Sonja knew the sum of the ages but could not determine the ages. The only logical reason for this is that the classroom's number (the sum of the ages) must have been 14. There are two possible combinations that give the sum 14, (2, 6, 6) and (3, 3, 8). When Sonja was told that the oldest child was good at chess, she knew that (2, 6, 6) could not be a possible combination because, if the children were 2, 6, and 6 years old, there would not be an oldest among them. Thus, she concluded that the children's ages were 3, 3, and 8.

TABLE 5-4

Age	Age	Age	Sum of the ages
1	1	72	74
1	2	36	39
1	3	24	28
1	4	18	23
1	6	12	19
2	2	18	22
2	3	12	17
2	4	9	15
2	6	6	14
1	8	9	18
3	4	6	13
3	3	8	14

Looking Back. Is it possible to substitute another integer for 72 and solve the corresponding problem? If we choose the product of the ages to be 12, what similar problem can we pose? The possible triples are then (1, 1, 12), (1, 2, 6), (1, 3, 4), and (2, 2, 3), and the corresponding sums are 14, 9, 8, and 7. Given one of these numbers as a sum, we would be able to determine the triple—that is, the ages. But suppose that Mr. Factor said, "The youngest does not like spinach." We would know then that the first and the last triple are not possible as they do not determine a youngest child. To determine which of the triples (1, 2, 6), and (1, 3, 4) represents the ages of his children, Mr. Factor could say, "The middle child is a year older than the youngest." We would know then that the ages of his children are 1, 2, and 6.

QUESTIONS FROM THE CLASSROOM

1. A student claims that $a|a$ and $a|a$ implies $a|(a - a)$, and hence, $a|0$. Is the student correct?

2. A student argues that $0|0$, since $0 = k \cdot 0$ for any integer k. How do you respond?

3. A student writes, "If $d \nmid a$ and $d \nmid b$, then $d \nmid (a + b)$." How do you respond?

4. Your seventh-grade class has just completed a unit on divisibility rules. One of the better students asks why divisibility by numbers other than 3 and 9 cannot be tested by dividing the sum of the digits by the tested number. How should you respond?

5. A student claims that a number with an even number of digits is divisible by 7 if and only if each of the numbers formed by pairing the digits into groups of two is divisible by 7. For example, 49,562,107 is divisible by 7, since each of the numbers 49, 56, 21, and 07 is divisible by 7. Is this true?

6. A sixth-grade student argues that there are infinitely many primes because "there is no end to numbers." How do you respond?

7. A student claims that a number is divisible by 21 if and only if it is divisible by 3 and by 7, and, in general, a number is divisible by $a \cdot b$ if and only if it is divisible by a and by b. What is your response?

8. A student claims that, for any two integers a and b, $GCD(a, b)$ divides $LCM(a, b)$ and, hence, $GCD(a, b) < LCM(a, b)$. Is the student correct? Why or why not?

9. A student claims that there are infinitely many triples of positive integers x and y, z that make the equation $x^2 + y^2 = z^2$ true. How do you respond?

CHAPTER OUTLINE

I. Divisibility
  A. If a and b are any integers, then b **divides** a, denoted by $b|a$, if and only if there is an integer c such that $a = cb$.
  B. The following are basic divisibility theorems for integers a, b, and d.
    1. If $d|a$ and $d|b$, then $d|(a + b)$.
    2. If $d|a$ and $d \nmid b$, then $d \nmid (a + b)$.
    3. If $d|a$ and $d|b$, then $d|(a - b)$.
    4. if $d|a$ and $d \nmid b$, then $d \nmid (a - b)$.
    5. If $d|a$ and k is any integer, then $d|ka$.
  C. Divisibility tests
    1. An integer is divisible by 2, 5, or 10 if and only if its units digit is divisible by 2, 5, or 10, respectively.
    2. An integer is divisible by 4 if and only if the last two digits of the integer represent a number divisible by 4.
    3. An integer is divisible by 8 if and only if the last three digits of the integer represent a number divisible by 8.
    4. An integer is divisible by 3 or by 9 if and only if the sum of its digits is divisible by 3 or 9, respectively.
    5. An integer is divisible by 7 if and only if the integer represented without its units digit minus twice the units digit of the original number is divisible by 7.
    6. An integer is divisible by 11 if and only if the sum of the digits in the places that are even powers of 10 minus the sum of the digits in the places that are odd powers of 10 is divisible by 11.
    7. An integer is divisible by 6 if and only if the integer is divisible by both 2 and 3.

II. Prime and composite numbers
  A. Positive integers that have exactly two positive divisors—namely, 1 and themselves—are called **primes**. Integers greater than 1 that are not primes are called **composites**.
  B. **Fundamental Theorem of Arithmetic:** Every composite number has one and only one prime factorization.
  C. Criterion for determining if a given number n is prime: *If n is not divisible by any prime p such that $p^2 \le n$, then n is prime.*

III. Greatest common divisor and least common multiple
  A. The **greatest common divisor (GCD)** of two or more natural numbers is the greatest divisor, or factor, that the numbers have in common.
  B. The **least common multiple (LCM)** of two or more natural numbers is the least positive multiple that the numbers have in common.
  C. **Euclidean algorithm:** If a and b are whole numbers and $a \ge b$, then $GCD(a, b) = GCD(b, r)$, where r is the remainder when a is divided by b. The procedure of finding the GCD of two numbers a and b by using the above result repeatedly is called the *Euclidean algorithm*.
  D. $GCD(a, b) \cdot LCM(a, b) = ab$.

*IV. Modular arithmetic.

A. For any integers a and b, **a is congruent to b modulo m** if and only if $a - b$ is a multiple of m, where m is a positive integer greater than 1.

B. Two integers are congruent modulo m if and only if their remainders upon division by m are the same.

CHAPTER TEST

1. Classify each of the following as true or false.
   (a) $8 \mid 4$ (b) $0 \mid 4$ (c) $4 \mid 0$
   (d) If a number is divisible by 4 and by 6, then it is divisible by 24.
   (e) If a number is not divisible by 12, then it is not divisible by 3.

2. Classify each of the following as true or false. If false, show a counterexample.
   (a) If $7 \mid x$ and $7 \nmid y$, then $7 \nmid xy$.
   (b) If $d \nmid (a + b)$, then $d \nmid a$ and $d \nmid b$.
   (c) If $16 \mid 10^4$, then $16 \mid 10^6$.
   (d) If $d \mid (a + b)$ and $d \nmid a$, then $d \nmid b$.
   (e) If $d \mid (x + y)$ and $d \mid x$, then $d \mid y$.
   (f) If $4 \nmid x$ and $4 \nmid y$, then $4 \nmid xy$.

3. Test each of the following numbers for divisibility by 2, 3, 4, 5, 6, 7, 8, 9, and 11.
   (a) 83,160   (b) 83,193

4. Assume that 10,007 is prime. Without actually dividing 10,024 by 17, prove that 10,024 is not divisible by 17.

5. Fill each blank with one digit to make each of the following true. (Find all the possible answers.)
   (a) $6 \mid 87\_4$
   (b) $24 \mid 4\_856$
   (c) $29 \mid 87\_\_4$

6. Determine whether each of the following numbers is prime or composite.
   (a) 143   (b) 223

7. How can you tell if a number is divisible by 24? Check 4152 for divisibility by 24.

8. Find the GCD for each of the following.
   (a) 24 and 52   (b) 5767 and 4453

9. Find the LCM for each of the following.
   (a) $2^3 \cdot 5^2 \cdot 7^3$, $2 \cdot 5^3 \cdot 7^2 \cdot 13$, and $2^4 \cdot 5 \cdot 7^4 \cdot 29$
   (b) 278 and 279

10. Construct a number that has exactly five divisors.

11. Find all divisors of 144.

12. Find the prime factorization of each of the following.
    (a) 172   (b) 288   (c) 260   (d) 111

13. Jane and Ramon are running laps on a track. If they start at the same time and place and go in the same direction, with Jane running a lap in 5 minutes and Ramon running a lap in 3 minutes, how long will it take for them to be at the starting place at the same time, if they continue to run at the same pace?

14. Candy bars priced at 50¢ each were not selling, so the price was reduced. Then they all sold in one day for a total of $31.93. What was the reduced price for each candy bar?

15. Two bells ring at 8:00 A.M. For the remainder of the day, one bell rings every half hour and the other bell rings every 45 minutes. What time will it be when the bells ring together again?

★16. Prove the test for divisibility by 9, using a three-digit number n such that $n = a \cdot 10^2 + b \cdot 10 + c$.

*17. Find the remainder for each of the following.
    (a) 7^{100} is divided by 16.
    (b) 7^{100} is divided by 17.
    (c) 13^{1937} is divided by 10.

Rational Numbers as Fractions

PRELIMINARY PROBLEM

When the lights in her house went out, Julia remembered having two tall, cylindrical candles of equal diameter, one of which was $1\frac{1}{2}$ inches shorter than the other. She lit the longer candle at 7 P.M. At 8:30 P.M. Julia decided to light the second candle as well. At 10:30 P.M., both candles were of equal height. At 11:30 P.M., the candle that had originally been shorter burned out, and at midnight the other candle burned out. Assuming that each of the candles burned at a constant rate, how tall was each candle initially?

Introduction

Rational numbers can be developed as integers were. Recall that, because the equation $x + a = 0$ had no solution in the set of whole numbers, we devised a new number, denoted by $-a$, that is the unique solution of the equation. Similarly, the need for rational numbers arises from the need to have a unique solution to an equation like $6x = 5$. We make up a number denoted by $\frac{5}{6}$ that is the unique solution of the equation. Thus, $\frac{5}{6}$ can be thought of as a number such that $6 \cdot \frac{5}{6} = 5$. In general, the unique solution for x in the equation $b \cdot x = a$, where $b \neq 0$, is denoted by $\frac{a}{b}$. Thus, $\frac{a}{b}$ can

fraction be thought of as a number such that $b \cdot \frac{a}{b} = a$. A **fraction** is a number of the form $\frac{a}{b}$, where a and b are any numbers ($b \neq 0$), not necessarily integers. In Chapter 7, we will see fractions in which a and b are not integers $\left(\text{for example, } \frac{\sqrt{2}}{2} \right)$.

In most grade-school textbooks, only fractions of the form $\frac{a}{b}$, where a and b are integers, are discussed. Such fractions are rational numbers. The set of rational numbers is a subset of the set of fractions. Table 6-1 shows several different ways in which we use rational numbers.

TABLE 6-1

Use	Example
Division problem or solution to a multiplication problem	The solution to $2x = 3$ is $\frac{3}{2}$.
Partition, or part, of a whole	Joe received one half of Mary's salary each month for alimony.
Ratio	The ratio of Republicans to Democrats in the Senate is three to five.
Probability	When you toss a coin, the probability of getting heads is $\frac{1}{2}$.

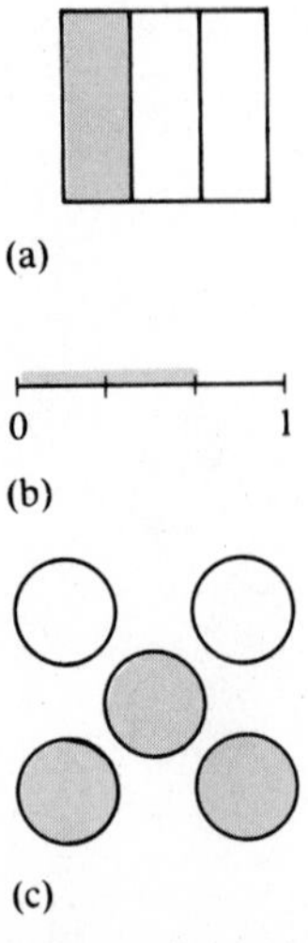

(a)

(b)

(c)

FIGURE 6-1

Figure 6-1 illustrates the use of rational numbers as part of a whole and as part of a given set. For example, in Figure 6-1(a), one part out of three congruent parts, or $\frac{1}{3}$ of the largest rectangle, is shaded. In Figure 6-1(b), two parts out of three parts, or $\frac{2}{3}$ of the unit segment, are shaded. In Figure 6-1(c), three circles out of five circles, or $\frac{3}{5}$ of the circles, are shaded.

In this chapter we discuss addition, subtraction, multiplication, and division of rational numbers, as well as solutions of equations and inequalities involving these numbers. The use of rationals as ratios and as negative exponents is discussed in the last two sections of this chapter. Throughout the chapter we emphasize estimation. According to the *Standards*, "From children's earliest experiences with mathematics, estimation needs to be an ongoing part of their study of numbers, computation and measurement."

H I S T O R I C A L   N O T E

The early Egyptian numeration system had symbols for fractions with numerators of 1. Most fractions with numerators other than 1 were expressed as a sum of different fractions with numerators of 1, for example, $\frac{7}{12} = \frac{1}{3} + \frac{1}{4}$.

Fractions with denominator 60 or powers of 60 were common in ancient Babylon about 2000 B.C., where 12,35 meant $12 + \frac{35}{60}$. The method was later adopted by the Greek astronomer Ptolemy (approximately A.D. 125). The same method was also used in Islamic and European countries and is presently used in the measurements of angles, where $13°19'47''$ means $13 + \frac{19}{60} + \frac{47}{60^2}$.

The modern notation for fractions with a bar between numerator and denominator is of Hindu origin. It came into general use in Europe in sixteenth-century books.

Section 6-1

The Set of Rational Numbers

Our early exposure to fractions usually takes the form of oral descriptions rather than mathematical notations. We hear phrases such as "one half of a pizza," "one third of a cake," or "three fourths of a pie." Later, fractions are introduced as parts of a whole and bar notation is used, as in $\frac{2}{3}$ or 2/3 for two thirds. We also encounter such division problems as "If two identical fruit bars are equally divided among three friends, how much does each get?" The answer is that each receives $\frac{2}{3}$ of a bar. The *Standards* recommends introducing useful fractions that can be easily modeled and applied in problem situations in grades K–4.

rational numbers

Numbers represented by fractions such as $\frac{1}{3}$, $\frac{3}{5}$, and $\frac{2}{3}$ belong to the set of rational numbers. The set of **rational numbers,** denoted by Q, can be written as follows.

$$Q = \left\{ \frac{a}{b} \,\middle|\, a \text{ and } b \text{ are integers and } b \neq 0 \right\}$$

numerator / denominator

In the rational number $\frac{a}{b}$, a is the **numerator** and b is the **denominator.** The rational number $\frac{a}{b}$ may also be represented as a/b or as $a \div b$.

If we use the division representation of a rational number, then $a \div 1 = \frac{a}{1}$. Since $a \div 1 = a$, every integer a can be represented by $\frac{a}{1}$. This and the fact that not every rational number is an integer show that the set of integers is a proper subset of the set of rational numbers; that is, $I \subset Q$.

Rational numbers, like integers, can be represented on a number line. Once the integers 0 and 1 are assigned to points on a line, every other rational number is assigned to a specific point. For example, to represent $\frac{3}{4}$ on the number line, we divide the segment from 0 to 1 into 4 segments of equal length. Then, starting from 0, we count 3 of these segments and stop at the mark corresponding to the right endpoint of the third segment the rational number $\frac{3}{4}$. Figure 6-2 shows the points that correspond to $\frac{3}{4}$, $\frac{5}{4}$, 1, 2, $^-\frac{3}{4}$, $^-1$, $^-\frac{5}{4}$ and $^-2$.

FIGURE 6-2

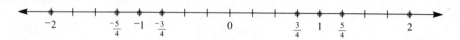

Equivalent Fractions

In higher mathematics, rational numbers are often introduced as a collection of disjoint sets called equivalence classes. For example, the fractions in the set

$$\left\{ \ldots, \frac{^-3}{^-9}, \frac{^-2}{^-6}, \frac{^-1}{^-3}, \frac{1}{3}, \frac{2}{6}, \frac{3}{9}, \ldots \right\}$$

equivalent fractions   are **equivalent fractions,** and the set is an *equivalence class of fractions.* This particular class is typically represented by $\frac{1}{3}$.

One way to find equivalent fractions is shown in Figure 6-3. In Figure 6-3(a), one of three congruent parts, or $\frac{1}{3}$, is shaded. Also, in Figure 6-3(a), two of six congruent parts, or $\frac{2}{6}$, are shaded. Thus, both $\frac{1}{3}$ and $\frac{2}{6}$ represent exactly the same shaded portion. Although the symbols $\frac{1}{3}$ and $\frac{2}{6}$ do not look alike, they represent the same rational number. Strictly speaking, $\frac{1}{3}$ and $\frac{2}{6}$ are equivalent fractions. However, because they represent equal amounts, we write $\frac{1}{3} = \frac{2}{6}$ and say that $\frac{1}{3}$ equals $\frac{2}{6}$.

FIGURE 6-3

(a)

(b)

Figure 6-3(b) shows the rectangle subdivided into 12 parts, with 4 parts shaded. Thus, $\frac{1}{3}$ is equal to $\frac{4}{12}$ because the same portion of the model is covered. Similarly, we could illustrate that $\frac{1}{3}$, $\frac{2}{6}$, $\frac{3}{9}$, $\frac{4}{12}$, $\frac{5}{15}$, . . . are equal. In other words, there are infinitely many ways of naming the rational number $\frac{1}{3}$. Similarly, there are infinitely many ways of naming any rational number.

This process of generating fractions equal to $\frac{1}{3}$ can be thought of as follows: If each of 3 equal-sized parts of a whole are halved, there must be twice as many of the smaller pieces. Hence, $\frac{1}{3} = \frac{2}{6}$. Similarly, $\frac{1}{3} = \frac{4}{12}$ because if each of three equal-sized parts of a whole are divided into four equal-sized parts, then there must be four times as many of the smaller pieces. In general, we have the following property of fractions, called the *Fundamental Law of Fractions.*

● P R O P E R T Y

Fundamental Law of Fractions   For any fraction $\dfrac{a}{b}$ and any number $c \neq 0$,

$$\frac{a}{b} = \frac{ac}{bc}$$

The Fundamental Law of Fractions may be stated in words as follows: *The value of a fraction does not change if its numerator and denominator are multiplied by the same nonzero number.* However, the Fundamental Law of Fractions does not imply that adding the same nonzero number to the numerator and the denominator results in an equivalent fraction. For example,

$$\frac{1}{2} \neq \frac{1 + 2}{2 + 2} = \frac{3}{4}$$

From the Fundamental Law of Fractions, $\dfrac{7}{^-15} = \dfrac{^-7}{15}$ because $\dfrac{7}{^-15} = \dfrac{7 \cdot (^-1)}{^-15 \cdot (^-1)} = \dfrac{^-7}{15}$. Similarly, $\dfrac{a}{^-b} = \dfrac{^-a}{b}$. The form $\dfrac{^-a}{b}$ is usually the preferred one. The Fundamental Law of Fractions and equivalent fractions are illustrated on the page below, which is from *Heath Mathematics,* 1986, Grade 5.

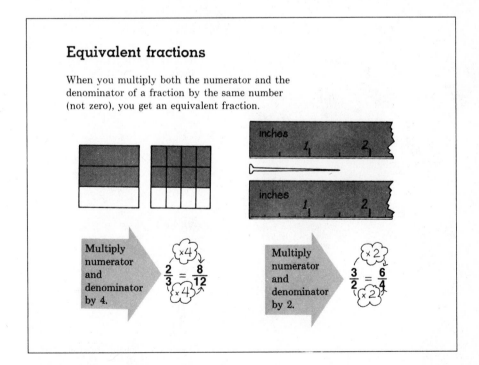

The Fundamental Law of Fractions can be used to solve algebraic equations, as seen in the following example.

EXAMPLE 6-1 Find a value for x so that $\dfrac{12}{42} = \dfrac{x}{210}$.

SOLUTION We try to find a fraction with denominator 210 equivalent to $\frac{12}{42}$. By the Fundamental Law of Fractions, $\dfrac{12}{42} = \dfrac{12 \cdot 5}{42 \cdot 5} = \dfrac{60}{210}$. Hence, $\dfrac{x}{210} = \dfrac{60}{210}$, and $x = 60$.

Simplifying Fractions

simplifying fractions   The Fundamental Law of Fractions justifies a process called **simplifying fractions.** Consider the following.

$$\frac{60}{210} = \frac{6 \cdot 10}{21 \cdot 10} = \frac{6}{21}$$

Also,

$$\frac{6}{21} = \frac{2 \cdot 3}{7 \cdot 3} = \frac{2}{7}$$

We can simplify $\frac{60}{210}$ because the numerator and denominator have a common factor of 10. Also, we can simplify $\frac{6}{21}$ because 6 and 21 have a common factor of 3. However, we cannot simplify $\frac{2}{7}$ because 2 and 7 have no common *simplest form*   factors other than 1. The fraction $\frac{2}{7}$ is called the **simplest form** of $\frac{60}{210}$.

Finding the simplest form of $\frac{60}{210}$ can be achieved with fewer steps by writing

$$\frac{60}{210} = \frac{2 \cdot 30}{7 \cdot 30} = \frac{2}{7}$$

The number 30 is the GCD of 60 and 210. This process amounts to dividing 60 and 210 by their greatest common divisor, 30.

In general, *a fraction $\dfrac{a}{b}$ is in simplest form if a and b have no common factor greater than 1, that is, if a and b are relatively prime. To write a fraction $\dfrac{a}{b}$ in simplest form, we divide both, a and b by GCD(a, b).*

EXAMPLE 6-2 Write each of the following in simplest form.

(a) $\dfrac{45}{60}$ (b) $\dfrac{35}{17}$

SOLUTION (a) GCD(45, 60) = 15, so $\dfrac{45}{60} = \dfrac{3 \cdot 15}{4 \cdot 15} = \dfrac{3}{4}$.

(b) GCD(35, 17) = 1, so $\frac{35}{17}$ is in simplest form.

• R E M A R K

Another method for writing the fraction in simplest form is to find the prime factorization of the numerator and denominator and then divide both numerator and denominator by common primes.

$$\frac{45}{60} = \frac{3 \cdot 3 \cdot 5}{2 \cdot 2 \cdot 3 \cdot 5} = \frac{3 \cdot 3}{2 \cdot 2 \cdot 3} = \frac{3}{2 \cdot 2} = \frac{3}{4}$$

It is often possible to write an algebraic fraction—that is, a fraction involving variables—in its simplest form. For example,

$$\frac{a^2b}{ab^2} = \frac{a \cdot (ab)}{b \cdot (ab)} = \frac{a}{b}$$

EXAMPLE 6-3 Write each of the following in simplest form.

(a) $\dfrac{28ab^2}{42a^2b^2}$ (b) $\dfrac{(a + b)^2}{3a + 3b}$ (c) $\dfrac{x^2 + x}{x + 1}$ (d) $\dfrac{3 + x^2}{3x}$ (e) $\dfrac{3 + 3x^2}{3x}$

SOLUTION (a) $\dfrac{28ab^2}{42a^2b^2} = \dfrac{2(14ab^2)}{3a(14ab^2)} = \dfrac{2}{3a}$

(b) $\dfrac{(a + b)^2}{3a + 3b} = \dfrac{(a + b) \cdot (a + b)}{3(a + b)} = \dfrac{a + b}{3}$

(c) $\dfrac{x^2 + x}{x + 1} = \dfrac{x(x + 1)}{x + 1} = \dfrac{x(x + 1)}{1(x + 1)} = \dfrac{x}{1} = x$

(d) $\dfrac{3 + x^2}{3x}$ cannot be further reduced because $3 + x^2$ and $3x$ have no factors in common except 1.

(e) $\dfrac{3 + 3x^2}{3x} = \dfrac{3 \cdot (1 + x^2)}{3 \cdot x} = \dfrac{1 + x^2}{x}$

Two fractions such as $\frac{12}{42}$ and $\frac{10}{35}$ can be shown to be equal by several methods.

1. Reduce both fractions to the same simplest form.

$$\frac{12}{42} = \frac{2^2 \cdot 3}{2 \cdot 3 \cdot 7} = \frac{2}{7} \quad \text{and} \quad \frac{10}{35} = \frac{5 \cdot 2}{5 \cdot 7} = \frac{2}{7}$$

Thus,

$$\frac{12}{42} = \frac{10}{35}$$

2. Rewrite both fractions with the same least common denominator. Since LCM(42, 35) = 210, then

$$\frac{12}{42} = \frac{60}{210} \quad \text{and} \quad \frac{10}{35} = \frac{60}{210}$$

Thus,

$$\frac{12}{42} = \frac{10}{35}$$

3. Rewrite both fractions with a common denominator (not necessarily the least). A common multiple of 42 and 35 may be found by finding the product 42 · 35 or 1470. Now,

$$\frac{12}{42} = \frac{420}{1470} \quad \text{and} \quad \frac{10}{35} = \frac{420}{1470}$$

Hence,

$$\frac{12}{42} = \frac{10}{35}$$

The third method suggests a general algorithm for determining if two fractions $\frac{a}{b}$ and $\frac{c}{d}$ are equal. Rewrite both fractions with common denominator bd. That is,

$$\frac{a}{b} = \frac{ad}{bd} \quad \text{and} \quad \frac{c}{d} = \frac{bc}{bd}$$

Because the denominators are the same, $\frac{ad}{bd} = \frac{bc}{bd}$ if and only if $ad = bc$.

For example, $\frac{24}{36} = \frac{6}{9}$ because $24 \cdot 9 = 216 = 36 \cdot 6$. In general, the following property results.

• P R O P E R T Y

Two fractions $\frac{a}{b}$ and $\frac{c}{d}$ are equal if and only if $ad = bc$.

Using a calculator, we may determine if two fractions are equal by using the property that $\frac{a}{b} = \frac{c}{d}$ if and only if $ad = bc$. We see that $\frac{2}{4} = \frac{1098}{2196}$, since both $\boxed{2} \boxed{\times} \boxed{2} \boxed{1} \boxed{9} \boxed{6} \boxed{=}$ and $\boxed{4} \boxed{\times} \boxed{1} \boxed{0} \boxed{9} \boxed{8} \boxed{=}$ yield a display of 4392.

PROBLEM SET 6-1

1. Write a sentence illustrating the use of $\frac{7}{8}$ in each of the following ways.
   (a) As a division problem
   (b) As part of a whole
   (c) As a ratio

2. For each of the following, write a fraction to represent the shaded portion.

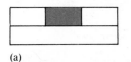

(a)   (b)

(c)   (d)

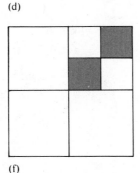

(e)

                             (f)

3. For each of the following four squares, write a fraction to represent the shaded portion. What property of fractions does the diagram illustrate?

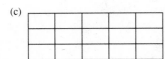

(a)   (b)   (c)   (d)

4. Complete each figure so that it shows $\frac{3}{5}$.

(a)    (b)

          0   1

(c)

(d)

(e)   (f)

5. Represent each of the following as a fraction.
   (a) The dots inside the circle as a part of all the dots in the figure
   (b) The dots inside the rectangle as a part of all the dots in the figure
   (c) The dots in the intersection of the rectangle and the circle as a part of all the dots in the figure
   (d) The dots outside the circle but inside the rectangle as a part of all the dots in the figure

6. For each of the following, write three fractions equal to the given fraction.
   (a) $\frac{2}{9}$ (b) $\frac{-2}{5}$ (c) $\frac{0}{3}$ (d) $\frac{a}{2}$

7. Find the simplest form for each of the following fractions.
   (a) $\frac{156}{93}$ (b) $\frac{27}{45}$ (c) $\frac{-65}{91}$
   (d) $\frac{0}{68}$ (e) $\frac{84^2}{91^2}$ (f) $\frac{6629}{70,395}$

8. Mr. Gonzales and Ms. Price gave the same test to their fifth-grade classes. In Mr. Gonzales' class, 20 out of 25 students passed the test, and in Ms. Price's class, 24 out of 30 students passed the test. One of Ms. Price's students heard about the results of the tests and claimed that the classes did equally well. Is the student right? Explain.

9. Choose the expression in parentheses that equals or best describes the given fraction.
   (a) $\frac{0}{0}$ (1, undefined, 0)
   (b) $\frac{5}{0}$ (undefined, 5, 0)
   (c) $\frac{0}{5}$ (undefined, 5, 0)

(d) $\dfrac{2 + a}{a}$ (2, 3, cannot be simplified)

(e) $\dfrac{15 + x}{3x}$ $\left(\dfrac{5 + x}{x},\ 5,\ \text{cannot be simplified}\right)$

(f) $\dfrac{2^6 + 2^5}{2^4 + 2^7}$ $\left(1, \dfrac{2}{3},\ \text{cannot be simplified}\right)$

(g) $\dfrac{2^{100} + 2^{98}}{2^{100} - 2^{98}}$ $\left(2^{196}, \dfrac{5}{3},\ \text{too large to simplify}\right)$

10. Find the simplest form for each of the following fractions.

(a) $\dfrac{x}{x}$ (b) $\dfrac{14x^2y}{63xy^2}$ (c) $\dfrac{a^2 + ab}{a + b}$

(d) $\dfrac{a^3 + 1}{a^3b}$ (e) $\dfrac{a}{3a + ab}$ (f) $\dfrac{a}{3a + b}$

11. Determine if the following pairs are equal by writing each in simplest form.

(a) $\dfrac{3}{8}$ and $\dfrac{375}{1000}$ (b) $\dfrac{18}{54}$ and $\dfrac{23}{69}$

(c) $\dfrac{6}{10}$ and $\dfrac{600}{1000}$ (d) $\dfrac{17}{27}$ and $\dfrac{25}{45}$

(e) $\dfrac{24}{36}$ and $\dfrac{6}{9}$ (f) $\dfrac{^-7}{49}$ and $\dfrac{^-14}{98}$

12. Determine if the following pairs are equal by changing both to the same denominator.

(a) $\dfrac{10}{16}$ and $\dfrac{12}{18}$ (b) $\dfrac{3}{12}$ and $\dfrac{41}{154}$

(c) $\dfrac{3}{^-12}$ and $\dfrac{^-36}{144}$ (d) $\dfrac{^-21}{86}$ and $\dfrac{^-51}{215}$

(e) $\dfrac{6}{10}$ and $\dfrac{6000}{10{,}000}$ (f) $\dfrac{^-a}{b}$ and $\dfrac{a}{^-b}$

13. Solve for x in each of the following.

(a) $\dfrac{2}{3} = \dfrac{x}{16}$ (b) $\dfrac{3}{4} = \dfrac{^-27}{x}$ (c) $\dfrac{3}{x} = \dfrac{3x}{x^2}$

14. (a) If $\dfrac{a}{c} = \dfrac{b}{c}$, what must be true?

    (b) If $\dfrac{a}{b} = \dfrac{a}{c}$, what must be true?

15. Let W be the set of whole numbers, I be the set of integers, and Q be the set of rational numbers. Classify each of the following as true or false.

(a) $W \subseteq Q$

(b) $(I \cup W) \subset Q$

(c) If Q is the universal set, $\bar{I} = W$.

(d) $Q \cap I = W$

(e) $Q \cap W = W$

16. Use a calculator to check whether each of the following pairs of fractions are equal.

(a) $\dfrac{24}{31}$ and $\dfrac{23}{30}$ (b) $\dfrac{86}{75}$ and $\dfrac{85}{74}$

(c) $\dfrac{1513}{1691}$ and $\dfrac{1581}{1767}$

Section 6-2   Addition and Subtraction of Rational Numbers

Addition of Rational Numbers with Like Denominators

Suppose that a pizza is divided into five parts of equal size. If one person ate one piece of the pizza and another person ate two pieces of the pizza, then they ate $\frac{1}{5}$ and $\frac{2}{5}$ of the pizza, respectively, as shown in Figure 6-4.

We see from the figure that $\frac{3}{5}$ of the pizza was eaten. That is, $\frac{1}{5} + \frac{2}{5} = \frac{3}{5}$, or

$$\frac{1}{5} + \frac{2}{5} = \frac{1 + 2}{5} = \frac{3}{5}$$

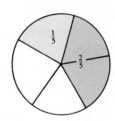

FIGURE 6-4

In general, we have the following definition for addition of rational numbers with like denominators.

• D E F I N I T I O N

If $\dfrac{a}{b}$ and $\dfrac{c}{b}$ are rational numbers, then $\dfrac{a}{b} + \dfrac{c}{b} = \dfrac{a + c}{b}$.

The sum of two rational numbers can also be found using a number line. For example, to compute $\frac{1}{5} + \frac{2}{5}$, we use a number line with one unit divided into fifths, as shown in Figure 6-5.

FIGURE 6-5

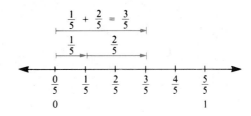

Addition of Rational Numbers with Unlike Denominators

To determine how to add fractions with unequal denominators, we use the strategy of changing the problem into an equivalent problem that we already know how to do. We know how to add fractions with the same denominators, so to add $\frac{3}{8} + \frac{1}{6}$, we rewrite $\frac{3}{8}$ and $\frac{1}{6}$ with the same denominators and add. A common denominator for the two fractions is $8 \cdot 6$. Hence,

$$\frac{3}{8} = \frac{3 \cdot 6}{8 \cdot 6} \quad \text{and} \quad \frac{1}{6} = \frac{8 \cdot 1}{8 \cdot 6}$$

Thus,

$$\frac{3}{8} + \frac{1}{6} = \frac{3 \cdot 6}{8 \cdot 6} + \frac{8 \cdot 1}{8 \cdot 6} = \frac{3 \cdot 6 + 8 \cdot 1}{8 \cdot 6} = \frac{18 + 8}{48} = \frac{26}{48}, \text{ or } \frac{13}{24}$$

In general, given two rational numbers $\frac{a}{b}$ and $\frac{c}{d}$, we may add the fractions as follows.

$$\frac{a}{b} + \frac{c}{d} = \frac{a \cdot d}{b \cdot d} + \frac{b \cdot c}{b \cdot d} = \frac{ad + bc}{bd}$$

We summarize this result in the following.

● P R O P E R T Y

If $\frac{a}{b}$ and $\frac{c}{d}$ are any two rational numbers, then $\frac{a}{b} + \frac{c}{d} = \frac{ad + bc}{bd}$.

EXAMPLE 6-4   Find each of the following sums.

(a) $\dfrac{2}{15} + \dfrac{4}{21}$ (b) $\dfrac{2}{-3} + \dfrac{1}{5}$ (c) $\left(\dfrac{3}{4} + \dfrac{1}{5}\right) + \dfrac{1}{6}$

SOLUTION

(a) $\dfrac{2}{15} + \dfrac{4}{21} = \dfrac{2 \cdot 21 + 15 \cdot 4}{15 \cdot 21} = \dfrac{102}{315}$, or $\dfrac{34}{105}$

(b) $\dfrac{2}{-3} + \dfrac{1}{5} = \dfrac{(2)(5) + (^-3)(1)}{(^-3)(5)} = \dfrac{10 + {}^-3}{-15} = \dfrac{7}{-15}$

(c) $\dfrac{3}{4} + \dfrac{1}{5} = \dfrac{3 \cdot 5 + 4 \cdot 1}{4 \cdot 5} = \dfrac{19}{20}$. Hence, $\left(\dfrac{3}{4} + \dfrac{1}{5}\right) + \dfrac{1}{6} = \dfrac{19}{20} + \dfrac{1}{6} =$

$\dfrac{19 \cdot 6 + 20 \cdot 1}{20 \cdot 6} = \dfrac{134}{120}$ or $\dfrac{67}{60}$.

In Example 6-4(a), we used the product of the denominators as a common denominator to add the fractions $\frac{2}{15}$ and $\frac{4}{21}$. We also could find LCM(15, 21), which is the *least common denominator* for these two fractions. Because LCM(15, 21) = 105, we have the following.

$$\dfrac{2}{15} + \dfrac{4}{21} = \dfrac{14}{105} + \dfrac{20}{105} = \dfrac{34}{105}$$

Mixed Numbers

mixed numbers

The sum of an integer and a rational number is often written as a **mixed number.** For example, $1 + \frac{3}{4}$ can be written as $1\frac{3}{4}$. It is sometimes inferred that $1\frac{3}{4}$ means 1 times $\frac{3}{4}$, since yx means $y \cdot x$. This is not the case; $1\frac{3}{4}$ means $1 + \frac{3}{4}$. Also, the number $^-4\frac{3}{4}$ means $^-(4 + \frac{3}{4})$, not $^-4 + \frac{3}{4}$.

A mixed number is a rational number, and therefore it can always be written in the form $\dfrac{a}{b}$. For example,

$$1\dfrac{3}{4} = 1 + \dfrac{3}{4} = \dfrac{1}{1} + \dfrac{3}{4} = \dfrac{1 \cdot 4 + 1 \cdot 3}{1 \cdot 4} = \dfrac{4 + 3}{4} = \dfrac{7}{4}$$

proper fraction

A fraction $\dfrac{a}{b}$, where $0 \le |a| < |b|$, is called a **proper fraction.** For example, $\frac{4}{7}$ is a proper fraction, but $\frac{7}{4}$ and $\frac{4}{4}$ are not proper fractions.

EXAMPLE 6-5

Change each of the following mixed numbers to the form $\dfrac{a}{b}$, where a and b are integers.

(a) $4\dfrac{1}{3}$ (b) $^-3\dfrac{2}{5}$

SOLUTION

(a) $4\dfrac{1}{3} = 4 + \dfrac{1}{3} = \dfrac{4}{1} + \dfrac{1}{3} = \dfrac{4 \cdot 3 + 1 \cdot 1}{1 \cdot 3} = \dfrac{12 + 1}{3} = \dfrac{13}{3}$

(b) $^-3\dfrac{2}{5} = {}^-\left(3 + \dfrac{2}{5}\right) = {}^-\left(\dfrac{3}{1} + \dfrac{2}{5}\right) = {}^-\left(\dfrac{3 \cdot 5 + 1 \cdot 2}{1 \cdot 5}\right) = \dfrac{^-17}{5}$

EXAMPLE 6-6   Change $\frac{29}{5}$ to a mixed number.

SOLUTION $\dfrac{29}{5} = \dfrac{5 \cdot 5 + 4}{5} = \dfrac{5 \cdot 5}{5} + \dfrac{4}{5} = 5 + \dfrac{4}{5} = 5\dfrac{4}{5}$

• **R E M A R K**
In elementary schools, problems like Example 6-6 are usually solved using division.

$$5\overline{)29} \quad \begin{array}{r} 5 \\ \hline 29 \\ 25 \\ \hline 4 \end{array}$$

Hence, $\frac{29}{5} = 5 + \frac{4}{5} = 5\frac{4}{5}$.

EXAMPLE 6-7   Find $2\frac{4}{5} + 3\frac{5}{6}$.

SOLUTION   The problem is solved in two ways, for comparison.

Add the fractional parts and the integers of the mixed numbers separately.	Change each mixed number into a rational number in the form $\dfrac{a}{b}$ and then add.

$$\begin{array}{r} 2\dfrac{4}{5} = \quad 2\dfrac{24}{30} \\[2mm] +3\dfrac{5}{6} = +3\dfrac{25}{30} \\[2mm] \hline 5\dfrac{49}{30} \end{array}$$

But,

$$\dfrac{49}{30} = 1\dfrac{19}{30}$$

so

$$5\dfrac{49}{30} = 5 + \dfrac{49}{30} = 5 + 1\dfrac{19}{30} = 6\dfrac{19}{30}$$

$$\begin{aligned} 2\dfrac{4}{5} + 3\dfrac{5}{6} &= \dfrac{14}{5} + \dfrac{23}{6} \\[2mm] &= \dfrac{14 \cdot 6 + 5 \cdot 23}{5 \cdot 6} \\[2mm] &= \dfrac{84 + 115}{30} \\[2mm] &= \dfrac{199}{30} \\[2mm] &= 6\dfrac{19}{30} \end{aligned}$$

Properties of Addition for Rational Numbers

As with integers, rational numbers have the following properties for addition: closure property, commutative property, associative property, additive identity property, and additive inverse property. To emphasize the additive inverse property of rational numbers, we state it explicitly.

● **P R O P E R T Y**

Additive Inverse Property of Rational Numbers For any rational number $\frac{a}{b}$, there exists a unique rational number $-\frac{a}{b}$, called the additive inverse of $\frac{a}{b}$, such that

$$\frac{a}{b} + \left(-\frac{a}{b}\right) = 0 = \left(-\frac{a}{b}\right) + \frac{a}{b}.$$

Another form of $-\frac{a}{b}$ can be found by considering the sum $\frac{a}{b} + \frac{^-a}{b}$. Because

$$\frac{a}{b} + \frac{^-a}{b} = \frac{a + {^-a}}{b} = \frac{0}{b} = 0$$

it follows that $-\frac{a}{b}$ and $\frac{^-a}{b}$ are both additive inverses of $\frac{a}{b}$, so $-\frac{a}{b} = \frac{^-a}{b}$.

EXAMPLE 6-8 Find the additive inverses for each of the following.

(a) $\frac{3}{5}$ (b) $\frac{^-5}{11}$ (c) $4\frac{1}{2}$

SOLUTION (a) $\frac{^-3}{5}$ or $-\frac{3}{5}$ (b) $-\left(\frac{^-5}{11}\right)$ or $\frac{5}{11}$ (c) $^-4\frac{1}{2}$

Properties of the additive inverse for rational numbers are analogous to those of the additive inverse for integers, as shown in Table 6-2. As with the set of integers, the set of rational numbers also has the addition property of equality.

TABLE 6-2
Properties of
Additive Inverse

Integers	Rational Numbers
1. $^-(^-a) = a$	1. $-\left(-\frac{a}{b}\right) = \frac{a}{b}$
2. $^-(a + b) = {^-a} + {^-b}$	2. $-\left(\frac{a}{b} + \frac{c}{d}\right) = \frac{^-a}{b} + \frac{^-c}{d}$

● **P R O P E R T Y**

Addition Property of Equality If $\frac{a}{b}$ and $\frac{c}{d}$ are any rational numbers such that $\frac{a}{b} = \frac{c}{d}$, and if $\frac{e}{f}$ is any rational number, then $\frac{a}{b} + \frac{e}{f} = \frac{c}{d} + \frac{e}{f}$.

Subtraction of Rational Numbers

In elementary school, subtraction of national numbers is usually introduced by using a take-away model. If we have $\frac{6}{7}$ of a pizza, and $\frac{2}{7}$ of the original pizza is taken away, $\frac{4}{7}$ of the pizza remains—that is, $\dfrac{6}{7} - \dfrac{2}{7} = \dfrac{6-2}{7} = \dfrac{4}{7}$.

In general, subtraction of rational numbers with like denominators is determined as follows.

$$\frac{a}{b} - \frac{c}{b} = \frac{a-c}{b}$$

Subtraction of rational numbers, like subtraction of integers, can be defined in terms of addition as follows.

● **D E F I N I T I O N**
Subtraction of Rational Numbers   If $\dfrac{a}{b}$ and $\dfrac{c}{d}$ are any rational numbers, then

$$\frac{a}{b} - \frac{c}{d} = \frac{e}{f} \text{ if and only if } \frac{a}{b} = \frac{c}{d} + \frac{e}{f}.$$

As with integers, it can be shown that subtraction of rational numbers can be performed by adding the additive inverses. This is stated in the following theorem.

● **T H E O R E M   6-1**
If $\dfrac{a}{b}$ and $\dfrac{c}{d}$ are any rational numbers, then $\dfrac{a}{b} - \dfrac{c}{d} = \dfrac{a}{b} + \dfrac{^{-}c}{d}$.

Now, using the definition of addition of rational numbers, we obtain the following.

$$\frac{a}{b} - \frac{c}{d} = \frac{a}{b} + \frac{^{-}c}{d}$$

$$= \frac{ad + b(^{-}c)}{bd}$$

$$= \frac{ad - bc}{bd}$$

We summarize this result in the following theorem.

● **T H E O R E M   6-2**
If $\dfrac{a}{b}$ and $\dfrac{c}{d}$ are any rational numbers, then $\dfrac{a}{b} - \dfrac{c}{d} = \dfrac{ad - bc}{bd}$.

EXAMPLE 6-9 Find each difference.

(a) $\dfrac{5}{8} - \dfrac{1}{4}$ (b) $5\dfrac{1}{3} - 2\dfrac{3}{4}$

SOLUTION (a) $\dfrac{5}{8} - \dfrac{1}{4} = \dfrac{5\cdot 4 - 8\cdot 1}{8\cdot 4} = \dfrac{5\cdot 4 - 8\cdot 1}{32} = \dfrac{12}{32}\ \text{or}\ \dfrac{3}{8}$

An alternative and often more efficient approach is first to find the least common denominator for the fractions. Because LCM(8, 4) = 8, we have

$$\dfrac{5}{8} - \dfrac{1}{4} = \dfrac{5}{8} - \dfrac{2}{8} = \dfrac{3}{8}$$

(b) Two methods of solution are given.

$$5\dfrac{1}{3} = 5\dfrac{4}{12} = 4 + 1\dfrac{4}{12} = 4\dfrac{16}{12}$$
$$-2\dfrac{3}{4} = -2\dfrac{9}{12} = -2\dfrac{9}{12} \qquad = -2\dfrac{9}{12}$$
$$\underline{\hspace{4cm}}$$
$$2\dfrac{7}{12}$$

$$5\dfrac{1}{3} - 2\dfrac{3}{4} = \dfrac{16}{3} - \dfrac{11}{4}$$
$$= \dfrac{16\cdot 4 - 3\cdot 11}{3\cdot 4}$$
$$= \dfrac{64 - 33}{12}$$
$$= \dfrac{31}{12}\ \text{or}\ 2\dfrac{7}{12}$$

Estimation with Rational Numbers

Standards for grades 5–8 lists "Computation and Estimation" as one of 13 standards, commenting, *"Estimation is a powerful idea to be used both in solving problems and in checking the reasonableness of a result."* Consider for example, a student who added $\frac{3}{4}$ and $\frac{1}{2}$ and obtained $\frac{4}{6}$ (most likely, the student confused the procedure with the procedure for multiplying fractions and added the numerators and then the denominators.) An estimation of $\frac{3}{4} + \frac{1}{2}$ as a number greater than $\frac{1}{2} + \frac{1}{2}$ shows that the answer should be greater than 1 and hence that $\frac{4}{6}$ is unreasonable.

Sometimes it is desirable to round fractions to a convenient fraction, such as $\frac{1}{2}$, $\frac{1}{3}$, $\frac{1}{4}$, $\frac{1}{5}$, $\frac{2}{3}$, $\frac{3}{4}$, or 1. For example, if a student had 59 correct answers out of 80 questions, the student answered $\frac{59}{80}$ of the questions correctly, which is approximately $\frac{60}{80}$, or $\frac{3}{4}$. Intuitively, $\frac{60}{80}$ is greater than $\frac{59}{80}$. On a number line, the greater fraction is to the right of the lesser. (The concepts of greater than and less than are dealt with in more detail in Section 6-4.) The estimate $\frac{3}{4}$ for $\frac{59}{80}$ is a high estimate. This fact is often denoted by $(\frac{3}{4})^-$, the minus sign showing that the actual answer is less then $\frac{3}{4}$. In a similar way, we can estimate $\frac{31}{90}$ by $\frac{30}{90}$, or $\frac{1}{3}$. In this case we write the estimate as $(\frac{1}{3})^+$ to show that the actual answer is greater than the estimate, $\frac{1}{3}$. As pointed out by the *Standards* (p. 36), estimations such as the ones presented here *"enhance the abilities of children to deal with everyday quantitative situations."*

EXAMPLE 6-10 Estimate each of the following:

(a) $\dfrac{9}{17} + \dfrac{9}{10} + \dfrac{1}{30} + \dfrac{21}{40}$ (b) $1\dfrac{3}{20} + 3\dfrac{4}{9} + 5\dfrac{9}{10}$

SOLUTION (a) $\dfrac{1}{2} + 1 + 0 + \dfrac{1}{2} = 2$ (b) $(1 + 3 + 5) + \left(0 + \dfrac{1}{2} + 1\right) = 10\dfrac{1}{2}$

EXAMPLE 6-11 Estimate each of the following, indicating if the actual answer is greater than $(+)$ or less than $(-)$ the estimate.

(a) $\dfrac{27}{13} + \dfrac{10}{9}$ (b) $3\dfrac{9}{10} + 2\dfrac{7}{8} + \dfrac{11}{12}$

SOLUTION (a) Because $\frac{27}{13}$ is more than 2 and $\frac{10}{9}$ is more than 1, an estimate is 3^{+}.
(b) We first add the whole parts and obtain $3 + 2$, or 5. Because each of the fractions, $\frac{9}{10}$, $\frac{7}{8}$ and $\frac{11}{12}$, is less than 1, their sum is less than 3. The approximate answer to the problem can be written as 8^{-}.

PROBLEM SET 6-2

1. Use a number line to find $\frac{1}{5} + \frac{2}{3}$.

2. In each case, perform the computation by using the least common denominator.

(a) $\dfrac{3}{16} + \dfrac{7}{-8}$ (b) $\dfrac{4}{12} - \dfrac{2}{3}$

(c) $\dfrac{5}{6} + \dfrac{-4}{9} + \dfrac{2}{3}$ (d) $\dfrac{2}{21} - \dfrac{3}{14}$

3. Use the definition of addition of rational numbers to find each of the following.

(a) $\dfrac{6}{5} + \dfrac{-11}{4}$ (b) $\dfrac{4}{5} + \dfrac{6}{7}$

(c) $\dfrac{-7}{8} + \dfrac{2}{5}$ (d) $\dfrac{5}{x} + \dfrac{-3}{y}$

4. Add the following rational numbers. Write your answers in simplest form.

(a) $\dfrac{6}{7} + \dfrac{3}{14}$ (b) $\dfrac{-2}{3} + \dfrac{-4}{7} + \dfrac{3}{21}$

(c) $\dfrac{-3}{2x} + \dfrac{3}{2y} + \dfrac{-1}{4xy}$ (d) $\dfrac{-3}{2x^2y} + \dfrac{5}{6xy^2} + \dfrac{7}{x^2}$

5. Change each of the following fractions to mixed numbers.

(a) $\dfrac{56}{3}$ (b) $\dfrac{14}{5}$

(c) $-\dfrac{293}{100}$ (d) $-\dfrac{47}{8}$

6. Change each of the following mixed numbers to fractions in the form $\dfrac{a}{b}$, where a and b are integers.

(a) $6\dfrac{3}{4}$ (b) $7\dfrac{1}{2}$

(c) $^{-}3\dfrac{5}{8}$ (d) $^{-}4\dfrac{2}{3}$

7. Compute the following.

(a) $2\dfrac{1}{3} - 1\dfrac{3}{4}$ (b) $2\dfrac{1}{3} + 1\dfrac{3}{4}$

(c) $\dfrac{5}{6} + 2\dfrac{1}{8}$ (d) $^{-}4\dfrac{1}{2} - 3\dfrac{1}{6}$

(e) $\dfrac{5}{2^4 \cdot 3^2} - \dfrac{1}{2^3 \cdot 3^4}$ (f) $11 - \left(\dfrac{3}{5} + \dfrac{-4}{45}\right)$

8. Compute the following.

   (a) $3\dfrac{5}{6} - 2\dfrac{1}{8}$

   (b) $^-4\dfrac{3}{4} + 2\dfrac{5}{6}$

   (c) $\dfrac{11}{2^3 \cdot 5^4 \cdot 7^5} + \dfrac{3}{2^4 \cdot 5^3 \cdot 7}$

   (d) $\dfrac{3}{4} - \left(2\dfrac{3}{4} - 1\dfrac{1}{2}\right)$

   (e) $134\dfrac{13}{16} - 131\dfrac{1}{4}$

9. Approximate each of the following situations with a convenient fraction, and explain your reasoning. If the correct answer is greater than the estimate, indicate this by a plus sign. If it is less than the estimate, indicate this by a minus sign.
   (a) Giorgio had 15 base hits out of 46 times at bat.
   (b) Ruth made 7 goals out of 41 shots.
   (c) Laura answered 62 problems correctly out of 80.
   (d) Jonathan made 9 baskets out of 19.

10. Use the information in the table to answer each of the following questions.

Team	Games Played	Games Won
Ducks	22	10
Beavers	19	10
Tigers	28	9
Bears	23	8
Lions	27	7
Wildcats	25	6
Badgers	21	5

   (a) Which team won just over half of its games?
   (b) Which team won just under half its games?
   (c) Which team won just over $\frac{1}{3}$ of its games?
   (d) Which team won just under $\frac{1}{3}$ of its games?
   (e) Which team won just over $\frac{1}{4}$ of its games?
   (f) Which team won just under $\frac{1}{4}$ of its games?

11. Approximate each of the following fractions by 0, $\frac{1}{4}$, $\frac{1}{2}$, $\frac{3}{4}$, or 1. Use a plus or minus sign to indicate if the correct answer is higher or lower, respectively, than the estimate.

   (a) $\dfrac{19}{39}$ (b) $\dfrac{19}{37}$ (c) $\dfrac{3}{197}$ (d) $\dfrac{150}{201}$

   (e) $\dfrac{8}{9}$ (f) $\dfrac{9}{8}$ (g) $\dfrac{113}{110}$ (h) $\dfrac{-2}{117}$

   (i) $\dfrac{150}{198}$ (j) $\dfrac{110}{200}$ (k) $\dfrac{999}{2000}$ (l) $\dfrac{100}{99}$

   (m) $\dfrac{99}{100}$

12. Without actually finding the exact answer, state which of the numbers given in parentheses is the best approximation for the given sum or difference.
   (a) $\frac{6}{13} + \frac{7}{15} + \frac{11}{23} + \frac{17}{35}$ $(1, 2, 3, 3\frac{1}{2})$
   (b) $\frac{30}{41} + \frac{1}{1000} + \frac{3}{2000}$ $(\frac{3}{8}, \frac{3}{4}, 1, 2)$
   (c) $\frac{103}{300} + \frac{203}{601} - \frac{602}{897}$ $(1, \frac{1}{3}, \frac{2}{3}, 0)$
   (d) $\frac{1}{100} - \frac{1}{101} + \frac{1}{102} - \frac{1}{103}$ $(\frac{1}{200}, \frac{1}{2}, 1, 0)$

13. Find the best estimate you can for each of the following, indicating a high estimate by + and a low estimate by −.

   (a) $4\dfrac{9}{10} + 1\dfrac{17}{18} + 3$

   (b) $3\dfrac{1}{9} + 5\dfrac{1}{10} + 4\dfrac{3}{10} - 12\dfrac{1}{2}$

   (c) $5\dfrac{4}{9} + 3\dfrac{5}{11} + 4\dfrac{1}{100}$ (d) $148\dfrac{3}{4} + 2\dfrac{1}{5}$

14. Use estimation to answer each of the following.
   (a) Juan needs to make $11\frac{1}{4}$ pounds of breakfast cereal. He bought $4\frac{7}{8}$ pounds of oats, $3\frac{1}{4}$ pounds cracked wheat and $2\frac{15}{16}$ pounds of triticale. Does Juan have enough grain?
   (b) Jill expected to drive from Eugene to Seattle in less than 5 hours. It took her $1\frac{3}{4}$ hours to get from Eugene to Portland and $3\frac{5}{12}$ hours to get from Portland to Seattle. Did Jill make the trip in less than 5 hours?

15. Compute each of the following mentally.

   (a) $1 - \dfrac{3}{4}$ (b) $6 - \dfrac{7}{8}$

   (c) $3\dfrac{3}{8} + 2\dfrac{1}{4} - 5\dfrac{5}{8}$ (d) $2\dfrac{3}{5} + 4\dfrac{1}{10} + 3\dfrac{3}{10}$

16. Perform the indicated operations, and write your answers in simplest form.

   (a) $\dfrac{d}{bc} - \dfrac{a}{bc}$ (b) $\dfrac{7}{a-b} + \dfrac{5}{a+b}$

   (c) $\dfrac{a^2 b}{c} - \dfrac{bc}{ad}$

17. Perform the indicated operations, and write your answers in simplest form.

   (a) $\dfrac{d}{b} + \dfrac{a}{bc}$ (b) $\dfrac{a}{a-b} + \dfrac{b}{a+b}$

   (c) $\dfrac{a}{a^2 - b^2} - \dfrac{b}{a-b}$

18. What, if anything, is wrong with each of the following?

   (a) $2 = \dfrac{6}{3} = \dfrac{3+3}{3} = \dfrac{3}{3} + 3 = 1 + 3 = 4$

   (b) $1 = \dfrac{4}{2+2} = \dfrac{4}{2} + \dfrac{4}{2} = 2 + 2 = 4$

(c) $\dfrac{ab + c}{a} = \dfrac{\cancel{a}b + c}{\cancel{a}} = b + c$

(d) $\dfrac{a^2 - b^2}{a - b} = \dfrac{a \cdot \cancel{a} - b \cdot \cancel{b}}{\cancel{a} - \cancel{b}} = a - b$

(e) $\dfrac{a + c}{b + c} = \dfrac{a + \cancel{c}}{b + \cancel{c}} = \dfrac{a}{b}$

19. A class is $\frac{2}{5}$ freshmen, $\frac{1}{4}$ sophomores, and $\frac{1}{10}$ juniors; the rest are seniors. What fraction of the class is seniors?

20. Laura, who lives in New York, spends $\frac{9}{20}$ of her income on housing, $\frac{2}{3}$ on food and clothing, and $\frac{1}{10}$ on entertainment. If she saves the rest, what fraction of her income does she save?

21. Joe lives $\frac{4}{10}$ mile from the university, and Mary lives $\frac{1}{6}$ mile away from it. How much further from the university does Joe live than Mary?

22. A clerk sold three pieces of ribbon. One piece was $\frac{1}{3}$ yard long, another piece was $2\frac{3}{4}$ yards long, and the third was $3\frac{1}{2}$ yards long. What was the total length of ribbon sold?

23. In a certain Swiss city, each resident speaks only one language: $\frac{3}{4}$ speak German, $\frac{1}{8}$ speak French, and $\frac{1}{16}$ speak Italian. What fraction of the residents do not speak German, French, or Italian?

24. A recipe requires $3\frac{1}{4}$ cups of flour. Dan has $1\frac{3}{8}$ cups of flour. How much more flour does he need?

25. A recipe requires $3\frac{1}{2}$ cups of milk. Ran put in $\frac{3}{4}$ cup and then another cup. How much more milk does he need to put in?

26. Joel worked $9\frac{1}{2}$ hours one week grading math assignments and $11\frac{2}{3}$ hours the next week. How many more hours did he work the second week than the first?

27. Martine bought $8\frac{3}{4}$ yards of fabric. If she wants to make a skirt using $1\frac{7}{8}$ yards, pants using $2\frac{3}{8}$ yards, and a vest using $1\frac{2}{3}$ yards, how much fabric will be left over?

28. A plywood board $15\frac{3}{4}$ inches long is cut from a $38\frac{1}{4}$-inch board. The saw cut takes $\frac{3}{8}$ inch. How long is the piece of board left after cutting?

29. Make up a word problem that can be solved by finding each of the following.

(a) $10\dfrac{3}{4} - 6\dfrac{7}{8}$ (b) $\left(2\dfrac{1}{2} + 3\dfrac{1}{4}\right) - 5$

(c) $12\dfrac{1}{4} - \left(\dfrac{3}{8} + \dfrac{5}{12}\right)$ (d) $\dfrac{5}{12} + \dfrac{7}{8} - \left(\dfrac{1}{4} + \dfrac{3}{12}\right)$

30. Demonstrate by example that each of the following properties of rational numbers holds.
    (a) Closure property of addition
    (b) Commutative property of addition
    (c) Addition property of equality
    (d) Associative property of addition

31. Does each of the following properties hold for subtraction of rational numbers? Justify your answer.
    (a) Closure   (b) Commutative
    (c) Associative   (d) Identity
    (e) Inverse
    (f) Subtraction property of equality

32. For each of the following sequences, discover a pattern and write three more terms of the sequence if the pattern continues. Which of the sequences are arithmetic, and which are not? Justify your answers.

(a) $\dfrac{1}{4}, \dfrac{1}{2}, \dfrac{3}{4}, 1, \dfrac{5}{4}, \dots$ (b) $\dfrac{1}{2}, \dfrac{2}{3}, \dfrac{3}{4}, \dfrac{4}{5}, \dfrac{5}{6}, \dots$

(c) $\dfrac{2}{3}, \dfrac{5}{3}, \dfrac{8}{3}, \dfrac{11}{3}, \dfrac{14}{3}, \dots$ (d) $\dfrac{1}{2}, \dfrac{1}{3}, \dfrac{1}{4}, \dfrac{1}{5}, \dfrac{1}{6}, \dots$

(e) $\dfrac{5}{4}, \dfrac{3}{4}, \dfrac{1}{4}, \dfrac{-1}{4}, \dfrac{-3}{4}, \dots$

33. Find the nth term in each of the sequences in Problem 32.

34. Insert five fractions between the numbers 1 and 2 so that the seven numbers (including 1 and 2) constitute an arithmetic sequence.

35. Let $f(x) = x + \frac{3}{4}$.
    (a) Find the outputs if the inputs are:

    (i) 0   (ii) $\dfrac{4}{3}$ (iii) $\dfrac{-3}{4}$

    (b) For which inputs will the outputs be:

    (i) 1   (ii) $^-1$ (iii) $\dfrac{1}{2}$

36. Let $f(x) = \dfrac{x + 2}{x - 1}$, and let the domain of the function be the set of all integers except 1. Find the following.
    (a) $f(0)$ (b) $f(^-2)$ (c) $f(^-5)$ (d) $f(5)$

37. (a) Check that each of the following is true.

$\dfrac{1}{3} = \dfrac{1}{4} + \dfrac{1}{3 \cdot 4}$ $\dfrac{1}{4} = \dfrac{1}{5} + \dfrac{1}{4 \cdot 5}$

$\dfrac{1}{5} = \dfrac{1}{6} + \dfrac{1}{5 \cdot 6}$

(b) Based on the examples in (a), write $\dfrac{1}{n}$ as a sum of two unit fractions—that is, as a sum of fractions with numerator 1.

★(c) Prove your answer in (b).

Review Problems

38. Write each of the following fractions in simplest form.

(a) $\dfrac{14}{21}$ (b) $\dfrac{117}{153}$ (c) $\dfrac{5^2}{7^2}$ (d) $\dfrac{a^2 + a}{1 + a}$ (e) $\dfrac{a^2 + 1}{a + 1}$

39. Determine if each of the following pairs of fractions is equal.

(a) $\dfrac{3}{17}$ and $\dfrac{69}{391}$ (b) $\dfrac{^-145}{261}$ and $\dfrac{^-155}{279}$

(c) $\dfrac{a^2}{b}$ and $\dfrac{a^2b^2}{b^3}$ (d) $\dfrac{377}{400}$ and $\dfrac{378}{401}$

(e) $\dfrac{0}{10}$ and $\dfrac{0}{^-10}$ (f) $\dfrac{a}{b}$ and $\dfrac{a+1}{b+1}$, where $a \neq b$

C O M P U T E R   C O R N E R

The following is a BASIC program for adding two rational numbers and obtaining the result in the simplest form. The program may be used as a drill for addition of fractions. Type this program into your computer and run it to add the following:

(a) $\dfrac{2}{5} + \dfrac{8}{10}$ (b) $\dfrac{3}{4} + \dfrac{1}{3}$

```
 10 REM ADDITION OF FRACTIONS
 15 PRINT "THIS PROGRAM IS AN ADDITION OF FRACTIONS DRILL."
 20 PRINT "ENTER THE NUMERATOR AND DENOMINATOR OF"
 30 PRINT "THE FIRST FRACTION SEPARATED BY A COMMA."
 40 INPUT A, B
 50 PRINT "ENTER THE NUMERATOR AND DENOMINATOR OF"
 60 PRINT "THE SECOND FRACTION SEPARATED BY A COMMA."
 70 INPUT C, D
 80 LET N = D * A + B * C
 90 LET E = B * D
100 REM REDUCE THE FRACTION N/E
110 IF N < E THEN M = N
115 IF N > = E THEN M = E
120 FOR I = M TO 1 STEP -1
130 IF N/I = INT (N/I) AND E/I = INT (E/I) THEN 150
140 NEXT I
150 REM GCD = I
160 LET N = N/I
170 LET E = E/I
180 PRINT
190 PRINT "ENTER NUMERATOR AND DENOMINATOR OF THE"
200 PRINT "SUM IN LOWEST TERMS"
210 INPUT X, Y
220 IF X = N AND Y = E THEN PRINT "CORRECT" GOTO 240
230 PRINT "NO, THAT IS WRONG."
240 PRINT "DO YOU WANT TO ADD OTHER FRACTIONS (YES OR NO)"
250 INPUT Q$
260 IF Q$ = "YES" THEN 20
270 END
```

When Professor Sum was asked by Mr. Little how many students were in his classes, he answered, "All of them study either languages, physics, or not at all. One half of them study languages only, one fourth of them study French, one seventh of them study physics only, and there are 20 who do not study at all." How many students does Professor Sum have?

Section 6-3 Multiplication and Division of Rational Numbers

Multiplication of Rational Numbers

To motivate the definition of multiplication of rational numbers, we use the interpretation of multiplication as repeated addition. Using repeated addition, $8 \cdot \frac{1}{4}$ can be interpreted as follows.

$$8 \cdot \frac{1}{4} = \frac{1}{4} + \frac{1}{4} + \frac{1}{4} + \frac{1}{4} + \frac{1}{4} + \frac{1}{4} + \frac{1}{4} + \frac{1}{4} = \frac{8}{4} = 2$$

If the commutative property of multiplication for rational numbers is to be true, then $8 \cdot \frac{1}{4} = \frac{1}{4} \cdot 8 = 2$. The product $\frac{1}{4} \cdot 8$ may be thought of as $\frac{1}{4}$ of 8, because one of the four equal parts of 8 is equal to 2. Similarly, we can interpret $\frac{1}{4} \cdot \frac{1}{3}$ as $\frac{1}{4}$ of $\frac{1}{3}$—that is, as one part when $\frac{1}{3}$ is divided into four equal parts.

Figure 6-6(a) shows a one-unit rectangle separated into fifths, with $\frac{2}{5}$ shaded. Figure 6-6(b) shows the rectangle further separated into thirds, with $\frac{2}{3}$ shaded. The crosshatched portion represents $\frac{2}{3}$ of $\frac{2}{5}$. In order to find $\frac{2}{3}$ of $\frac{2}{5}$, we could divide just the shaded portion of the rectangle in Figure 6-6(a) into 3 equal parts and take 2 of those parts. The result would be the crosshatched portion of 6-6(b). However, the crosshatched portion represents 4 parts out of 15, or $\frac{4}{15}$, of the one-unit rectangle. Thus,

$$\frac{2}{3} \cdot \frac{2}{5} = \frac{4}{15} = \frac{2 \cdot 2}{3 \cdot 5}$$

FIGURE 6-6

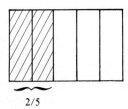

(a)

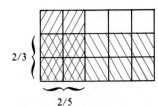

(b)

This discussion leads to the following definition of multiplication for rational numbers.

● **D E F I N I T I O N**

If $\dfrac{a}{b}$ and $\dfrac{c}{d}$ are any rational numbers, then $\dfrac{a}{b} \cdot \dfrac{c}{d} = \dfrac{a \cdot c}{b \cdot d}$.

EXAMPLE 6-12 Find each of the following products.

(a) $\dfrac{5}{6} \cdot \dfrac{7}{11}$ (b) $6 \cdot \dfrac{1}{5}$ (c) $2\dfrac{1}{3} \cdot 3\dfrac{1}{5}$

SOLUTION (a) $\dfrac{5}{6} \cdot \dfrac{7}{11} = \dfrac{5 \cdot 7}{6 \cdot 11} = \dfrac{35}{66}$

(b) $6 \cdot \dfrac{1}{5} = \dfrac{6}{1} \cdot \dfrac{1}{5} = \dfrac{6 \cdot 1}{1 \cdot 5} = \dfrac{6}{5}$

(c) $2\dfrac{1}{3} \cdot 3\dfrac{1}{5} = \dfrac{7}{3} \cdot \dfrac{16}{5} = \dfrac{7 \cdot 16}{3 \cdot 5} = \dfrac{112}{15} = 7\dfrac{7}{15}$

H I S T O R I C A L   N O T E

In the Middle Ages, mathematical skill was admired and supported by the monarchs. Leonardo of Pisa (1170–1230), known as Fibonacci, was the most prominent of the medieval mathematicians. In 1225, Fibonacci participated in a mathematical tournament before the Roman Emperor Frederic II, who came to Pisa with a group of mathematicians to test Fibonacci's immense reputation. One of the questions was to find a rational number that is a square ($\frac{4}{9} = (\frac{2}{3})^2$ and hence is a square) and that remains a square if it is decreased or increased by 5. Fibonacci found the number: $\frac{1,681}{144}$, or $(\frac{41}{12})^2$. When 5 is subtracted, it remains a square because $\frac{1,681}{144} - 5 = \frac{961}{144} = (\frac{31}{12})^2$, and when 5 is added, it remains a square because $\frac{1,681}{144} + 5 = \frac{2,401}{144} = (\frac{49}{12})^2$.

Properties of Multiplication for Rational Numbers

Multiplication of rational numbers has properties analogous to the properties of addition of rational numbers. These include the following properties for multiplication: closure property, commutative property, associative property, multiplicative identity, and multiplicative inverse. For emphasis, we list the last two properties.

• **P R O P E R T I E S**

Multiplicative Identity of Rational Numbers   The number 1 is the unique number such that for every rational number $\frac{a}{b}$,

$$1 \cdot \left(\frac{a}{b}\right) = \frac{a}{b} = \left(\frac{a}{b}\right) \cdot 1$$

Multiplicative Inverse of Rational Numbers   For any nonzero rational number $\frac{a}{b}$, $\frac{b}{a}$ is the unique rational number such that $\frac{a}{b} \cdot \frac{b}{a} = 1 = \frac{b}{a} \cdot \frac{a}{b}$. The multiplicative

reciprocal   inverse of $\frac{a}{b}$ is also called the **reciprocal** of $\frac{a}{b}$.

EXAMPLE 6-13   Find the multiplicative inverse of each of the following rational numbers.

(a) $\frac{2}{3}$ (b) $\frac{-2}{5}$ (c) 4   (d) 0   (e) $6\frac{1}{2}$

SOLUTION   (a) $\frac{3}{2}$

(b) $\frac{5}{-2}$, or $\frac{-5}{2}$

(c) Because $4 = \frac{4}{1}$, the multiplicative inverse of 4 is $\frac{1}{4}$.

(d) Even though $0 = \frac{0}{1}$, $\frac{1}{0}$ is undefined, so there is no multiplicative inverse of 0.

(e) Because $6\frac{1}{2} = \frac{13}{2}$, the multiplicative inverse of $6\frac{1}{2}$ is $\frac{2}{13}$.

As with integers, multiplication and addition are connected through the distributive property of multiplication over addition.

• **P R O P E R T I E S**

Distributive Property of Multiplication over Addition for Rational Numbers   If $\frac{a}{b}$, $\frac{c}{d}$, and $\frac{e}{f}$ are any rational numbers, then

$$\frac{a}{b}\left(\frac{c}{d} + \frac{e}{f}\right) = \left(\frac{a}{b} \cdot \frac{c}{d}\right) + \left(\frac{a}{b} \cdot \frac{e}{f}\right)$$

Multiplication Property of Equality for Rational Numbers   If $\frac{a}{b}$ and $\frac{c}{d}$ are any rational numbers such that $\frac{a}{b} = \frac{c}{d}$, and $\frac{e}{f}$ is any rational number, then $\frac{a}{b} \cdot \frac{e}{f} = \frac{c}{d} \cdot \frac{e}{f}$.

Multiplication Property of Zero for Rational Numbers   If $\frac{a}{b}$ is any rational number, then $\frac{a}{b} \cdot 0 = 0 = 0 \cdot \frac{a}{b}$.

The properties of rational numbers are used to solve equations, as shown in the following examples.

EXAMPLE 6-14   Solve for x.

(a) $\dfrac{3}{2}x = \dfrac{3}{4}$ (b) $\dfrac{2}{3}x - \dfrac{1}{5} = \dfrac{3}{4}$

SOLUTION   (a) $\dfrac{3}{2}x = \dfrac{3}{4}$

To obtain $1x$, or x, we multiply both sides of the equation by $\frac{2}{3}$.

$$\frac{2}{3} \cdot \frac{3}{2}x = \frac{2}{3} \cdot \frac{3}{4}$$

$$1 \cdot x = \frac{2 \cdot 3}{3 \cdot 4}$$

$$x = \frac{2}{4}, \text{ or } \frac{1}{2}$$

(b) To isolate x, we would like to eliminate $-\frac{1}{5}$ from the left side of the equation. To achieve this goal, we add $\frac{1}{5}$ to both sides of the equation and proceed by using the technique of part (a).

$$\frac{2}{3}x - \frac{1}{5} = \frac{3}{4}$$

$$\frac{2}{3}x - \frac{1}{5} + \frac{1}{5} = \frac{3}{4} + \frac{1}{5}$$

$$\frac{2}{3}x = \frac{19}{20}$$

$$\frac{3}{2} \cdot \frac{2}{3}x = \frac{3}{2} \cdot \frac{19}{20}$$

$$x = \frac{57}{40}$$

● **R E M A R K**

In Example 6-14(a), $\dfrac{3}{2}x$ can be treated as $\dfrac{3}{2} \cdot \dfrac{x}{1}$, or $\dfrac{3 \cdot x}{2 \cdot 1} = \dfrac{3x}{2}$. Hence, $\dfrac{3}{2}x = \dfrac{3x}{2}$.

EXAMPLE 6-15 A bicycle is on sale at $\frac{3}{4}$ of its original price. If the sale price is \$330, what was the original price?

SOLUTION Let x be the original price. Then $\frac{3}{4}$ of the original price is $\frac{3}{4}x$. Because the sale price is \$330, we have $\frac{3}{4}x = 330$. Solving for x gives

$$\frac{4}{3} \cdot \frac{3}{4} x = \frac{4}{3} \cdot 330$$

$$1 \cdot x = 440$$

$$x = 440$$

Thus, the original price was \$440.

An alternate approach, which does not use algebra, is as follows: Because $\frac{3}{4}$ of the original price is \$330, $\frac{1}{4}$ of the original price is $\frac{1}{3} \cdot 330$, or \$110; thus $4 \cdot \frac{1}{4}$ of the original price is $4 \cdot 110$, or \$440.

EXAMPLE 6-16 At the end of the month, when Devora was paid for her paper route, she spent \$50 on records and then $\frac{2}{5}$ of the remaining money on books. With $\frac{1}{3}$ of the remaining amount, she bought presents; she was left with \$48. How much was she paid at the end of the month?

SOLUTION Let x denote Devora's earnings in dollars from her paper route. After spending \$50, she had $x - 50$ dollars left. Since she spent $\frac{2}{5}$ of that on books, she was left with $\frac{3}{5}$ of $x - 50$, that is, $\frac{3}{5}(x - 50)$. Because she spent $\frac{1}{3}$ of this amount on presents, she was left with $\frac{2}{3}$ of the last amount—that is $\frac{2}{3} \cdot \frac{3}{5} \cdot (x - 50)$. Because she was finally left with \$48, we have

$$\frac{2}{3} \cdot \frac{3}{5}(x - 50) = 48$$

$$\frac{2}{5}(x - 50) = 48$$

$$\frac{5}{2} \cdot \frac{2}{5}(x - 50) = \frac{5}{2} \cdot 48$$

$$x - 50 = 120$$

$$x = 170$$

Consequently, Devora earned \$170 from her paper route.

PROBLEM 1

Madame Castafiore, a famous opera singer, had a large collection of jewels. One day all her precious stones disappeared. The investigating detectives wanted to know how many emeralds she owned and how many jewels she had altogether. She did not remember either number, but she did know that one fourth of her jewels were diamonds, three tenths were pieces of jade, one fifth were rubies, and one tenth were sapphires. She also remembered that she had six fewer emeralds than diamonds. If Mme. Castafiore's entire jewel collection consisted of diamonds, jade, rubies, sapphires, and emeralds, how large was her jewel collection and how many emeralds did she own?

Understanding the Problem.   To understand the problem, suppose that the collection consisted of 40 precious stones. (We try 40 because $\frac{1}{4}$ of 40, $\frac{3}{10}$ of 40, and $\frac{1}{5}$ of 40 are all integers. Twenty also would have been a good number to try.) In this case, the number of diamonds is $\frac{1}{4} \cdot 40$, or 10; the number of pieces of jade is $\frac{3}{10} \cdot 40$, or 12; the number of rubies is $\frac{1}{5} \cdot 40$, or 8; and the number of sapphires is $\frac{1}{10} \cdot 40$, or 4. The number of emeralds could be found by subtracting the total number of all the other precious stones from 40; that is, $40 - (10 + 12 + 8 + 4)$, or 6. Could 40 be the correct answer to the original problem? To see whether this is the case, we must determine if the condition that Mme. Castafiore had 6 fewer emeralds than diamonds is satisfied. Because 6 is 4 less than 10, not 6 less, 40 is an incorrect solution.

   Part of the information given in the problem is summarized in Table 6-3. In addition, we know that the number of emeralds is 6 less than the number of diamonds.

TABLE 6-3

Devising a Plan.

Type of Stone	Information about the Jewel Collection
Diamonds	$\frac{1}{4}$ of the collection
Jades	$\frac{3}{10}$ of the collection
Rubies	$\frac{1}{5}$ of the collection
Sapphires	$\frac{1}{10}$ of the collection

Devising a Plan.   Because the total number of jewels is not known, we designate it by x and try to set up an equation involving x. From Table 6-3 and the fact that the number of emeralds is 6 less than the number of diamonds, we find the number of corresponding stones in terms of x, as follows.

Diamonds, $\dfrac{1}{4} x$, Jades, $\dfrac{3}{10} x$, Rubies, $\dfrac{1}{5} x$, Sapphires, $\dfrac{1}{10} x$,

Emeralds, $\dfrac{1}{4} x - 6$

Because the total number of stones is x, we have the following equation.

$$\frac{1}{4}x + \frac{3}{10}x + \frac{1}{5}x + \frac{1}{10}x + \left(\frac{1}{4}x - 6\right) = x$$

Carrying Out the Plan. We solve the preceding equation for x. One approach is as follows.

$$\left(\frac{1}{4}x + \frac{1}{4}x\right) + \left(\frac{3}{10}x + \frac{1}{10}x + \frac{1}{5}x\right) - x = 6$$

$$\frac{1}{2}x + \frac{3}{5}x - x = 6$$

$$\left(\frac{1}{2} + \frac{3}{5} - 1\right)x = 6$$

$$\frac{1}{10}x = 6$$

$$x = 60$$

Thus, there are 60 precious stones altogether. Because the emeralds are $\frac{1}{4}x - 6$ of the collection, the number of emeralds is $\frac{1}{4} \cdot 60 - 6$, or 9.

Looking Back. Another way to approach the problem is to note that the emeralds are $1 - (\frac{1}{4} + \frac{3}{10} + \frac{1}{5} + \frac{1}{10})$, or $\frac{3}{20}$, of the total collection. Because the diamonds are $\frac{1}{4}$ of the collection and the emeralds are $\frac{3}{20}$ of the collection and because the difference between the diamonds and the emeralds is 6, we have ($\frac{1}{4}$ of the collection) $-$ ($\frac{3}{20}$ of the collection) $= 6$. Because $\frac{1}{4} - \frac{3}{20} = \frac{5}{20} - \frac{3}{20} = \frac{2}{20} = \frac{1}{10}$, we have that $\frac{1}{10}$ of the collection is 6. Consequently the collection consists of 60 precious stones. Still another approach involves using the guess and check strategy. We may reduce the guessing by realizing that the number of jewels must be divisible by 4 and 5. Hence the number of jewels must be a multiple of 20—that is, one of the numbers 20, 2 · 20, 3 · 20, ...

Division of Rational Numbers

The following examples provide concrete experience with division of rational numbers.

EXAMPLE 6-17   The fraction $2\frac{1}{4}$ is modeled in Figure 6-7(a), where a unit consists of four of the smaller squares. How many of the pieces shown in Figure 6-7(b) are there in the $2\frac{1}{4}$ piece?

FIGURE 6-7

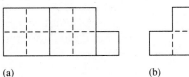

(a)   (b)

SOLUTION   Figure 6-7(b) represents $\frac{3}{4}$. To determine $2\frac{1}{4} \div \frac{3}{4}$, we may find how many $\frac{3}{4}$ pieces would fit in the $2\frac{1}{4}$ piece. In Figure 6-8, we see that exactly three of the $\frac{3}{4}$ pieces fit in the $2\frac{1}{4}$ piece.

FIGURE 6-8

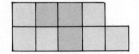

EXAMPLE 6-18   An empty swimming pool is to be filled until it is $\frac{9}{10}$ full. If it takes half an hour to fill $\frac{3}{10}$ of the pool, how long will it take to fill $\frac{9}{10}$ of the pool?

SOLUTION   We need to find how many $\frac{3}{10}$s there are in $\frac{9}{10}$; that is, we need to solve the division problem $\frac{9}{10} \div \frac{3}{10}$. Because $3 \cdot \frac{3}{10} = \frac{9}{10}$, the answer is 3. Thus, it would take 3 half hours, or $1\frac{1}{2}$ hours, to fill the pool.

Formally, we define division for rational numbers in terms of multiplication in the same way as we define division for integers.

- **DEFINITION**

  If $\frac{a}{b}$ and $\frac{c}{d}$ are any rational numbers and $\frac{c}{d}$ is not zero, then $\frac{a}{b} \div \frac{c}{d} = \frac{e}{f}$ if and only if $\frac{e}{f}$ is the unique rational number such that $\frac{c}{d} \cdot \frac{e}{f} = \frac{a}{b}$.

- **REMARK**

  In the definition of division, $\frac{c}{d}$ is not zero because division by zero is impossible.

  Also, $\frac{c}{d} \neq 0$ implies that $c \neq 0$.

Algorithm for Division of Rational Numbers

Recall that the set of integers is not closed under division. However, the set of rational numbers is closed under division as long as we do not divide by 0. To find an algorithm for rational-number division, examine the following examples.

EXAMPLE 6-19 Find $1 \div \frac{2}{3}$.

SOLUTION By definition, $1 \div \frac{2}{3} = x$ if and only if $\frac{2}{3} \cdot x = 1$. Since $\frac{2}{3}$ and x must be multiplicative inverses of each other, $x = \frac{3}{2}$. Thus, $1 \div \frac{2}{3} = \frac{3}{2}$.

EXAMPLE 6-20 Find $\frac{2}{3} \div \frac{5}{7}$.

SOLUTION Let $\frac{2}{3} \div \frac{5}{7} = x$. Then, $\frac{5}{7} \cdot x = \frac{2}{3}$. To solve for x, multiply both sides of the equation by the reciprocal of $\frac{5}{7}$, namely, $\frac{7}{5}$. Thus,

$$\frac{7}{5}\left(\frac{5}{7}x\right) = \frac{7}{5} \cdot \frac{2}{3}$$

Hence,

$$x = \frac{7}{5} \cdot \frac{2}{3} = \frac{14}{15}$$

The procedures in Examples 6-19 and 6-20 suggest using an extension of the Fundamental Law of Fractions, $\dfrac{a}{b} = \dfrac{ac}{bc}$, where a, b, and c are all fractions.

$$\frac{2}{3} \div \frac{5}{7} = \frac{\frac{2}{3}}{\frac{5}{7}} = \frac{\frac{2}{3}}{\frac{5}{7}} \cdot \frac{\frac{7}{5}}{\frac{7}{5}} = \frac{\frac{2}{3} \cdot \frac{7}{5}}{\frac{5}{7} \cdot \frac{7}{5}} = \frac{\frac{2}{3} \cdot \frac{7}{5}}{1} = \frac{2}{3} \cdot \frac{7}{5}$$

Thus,

$$\frac{2}{3} \div \frac{5}{7} = \frac{2}{3} \cdot \frac{7}{5}$$

The preceding equations illustrate the standard algorithm, "invert and multiply," that is taught in elementary school.

- **ALGORITHM FOR DIVISION OF FRACTIONS**

  $\dfrac{a}{b} \div \dfrac{c}{d} = \dfrac{a}{b} \cdot \dfrac{d}{c}$, where $\dfrac{c}{d} \neq 0$.

An example of this algorithm is given on the accompanying student page from *Addison-Wesley Mathematics*, 1989, Grade 6.

• R E M A R K

An alternative approach for developing an algorithm for division of fractions can be found by first dividing fractions with equal denominators. For example, $\frac{9}{10} \div \frac{3}{10} = 9 \div 3$ and $\frac{15}{23} \div \frac{5}{23} = 15 \div 5$. These examples suggest that, when two fractions with the same denominators are divided, the result can be obtained by dividing the numerator of the first fraction by the numerator of the second. To divide fractions with different denominators, we rename the fractions so that the denominators are equal. Thus,

$$\frac{a}{b} \div \frac{c}{d} = \frac{ad}{bd} \div \frac{bc}{bd} = ad \div bc = \frac{ad}{bc}$$

Dividing Fractions

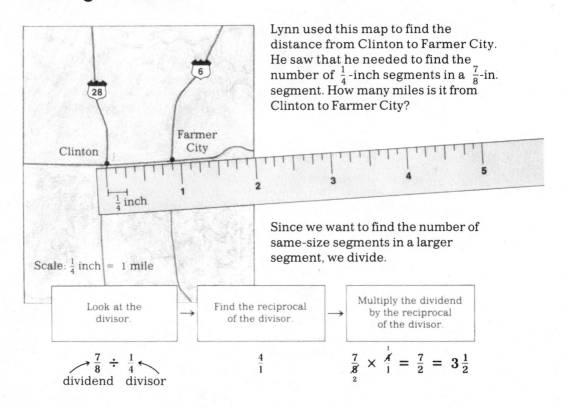

Lynn used this map to find the distance from Clinton to Farmer City. He saw that he needed to find the number of $\frac{1}{4}$-inch segments in a $\frac{7}{8}$-in. segment. How many miles is it from Clinton to Farmer City?

Scale: $\frac{1}{4}$ inch = 1 mile

Since we want to find the number of same-size segments in a larger segment, we divide.

Look at the divisor.	→	Find the reciprocal of the divisor.	→	Multiply the dividend by the reciprocal of the divisor.

$$\frac{7}{8} \div \frac{1}{4}$$
dividend   divisor

$$\frac{4}{1}$$

$$\frac{7}{\underset{2}{8}} \times \frac{\overset{1}{4}}{1} = \frac{7}{2} = 3\frac{1}{2}$$

The distance from Clinton to Farmer City is $3\frac{1}{2}$ mi.

• R E M A R K

Observe on the student page that the author has taken a shortcut in multiplying $\frac{7}{8} \cdot \frac{4}{1}$ by dividing the numerator and the denominator by 4, or "canceling."

EXAMPLE 6-21 Perform each of the following divisions and write your answers in simplest form.

(a) $\dfrac{{}^-5}{6} \div \dfrac{{}^-3}{8}$ (b) $5\dfrac{1}{6} \div 4\dfrac{2}{3}$ (c) $\dfrac{\frac{1}{4} + \frac{{}^-3}{2}}{\frac{5}{6} + \frac{7}{8}}$

SOLUTION (a) $\dfrac{{}^-5}{6} \div \dfrac{{}^-3}{8} = \dfrac{{}^-5}{6} \cdot \dfrac{8}{{}^-3} = \dfrac{{}^-40}{{}^-18} = \dfrac{20}{9}$

(b) $5\dfrac{1}{6} \div 4\dfrac{2}{3} = \dfrac{31}{6} \div \dfrac{14}{3} = \dfrac{31}{6} \cdot \dfrac{3}{14} = \dfrac{93}{84} = \dfrac{31}{28}$, or $1\dfrac{3}{28}$

(c) We first perform the additions and then do the division.

$$\dfrac{1}{4} + \dfrac{{}^-3}{2} = \dfrac{1}{4} + \dfrac{{}^-6}{4} = \dfrac{{}^-5}{4}$$

$$\dfrac{5}{6} + \dfrac{7}{8} = \dfrac{20}{24} + \dfrac{21}{24} = \dfrac{41}{24}$$

Hence,

$$\dfrac{\frac{1}{4} + \frac{{}^-3}{2}}{\frac{5}{6} + \frac{7}{8}} = \dfrac{\frac{{}^-5}{4}}{\frac{41}{24}} = \dfrac{{}^-5}{4} \cdot \dfrac{24}{41} = \dfrac{{}^-30}{41}$$

Another method for dividing the two fractions in Example 6-21(c) is based on multiplying each fraction by the LCM of the two fractions' denominators. Thus,

$$\dfrac{\frac{{}^-5}{4}}{\frac{41}{24}} = \dfrac{\frac{{}^-5}{4} \cdot 24}{\frac{41}{24} \cdot 24} = \dfrac{{}^-5 \cdot 6}{41} = \dfrac{{}^-30}{41}$$

EXAMPLE 6-22 A person has $35\frac{1}{2}$ yards of material available to make shirts. Each shirt requires $\frac{3}{8}$ of a yard of material.
(a) How many shirts can be made?
(b) How much material will be left over?

SOLUTION (a) We need to find the integer part of the answer to $35\frac{1}{2} \div \frac{3}{8}$. We have

$$35\dfrac{1}{2} \div \dfrac{3}{8} = \dfrac{71}{2} \cdot \dfrac{8}{3} = \dfrac{284}{3} = 94\dfrac{2}{3}$$

Thus 94 shirts can be made.
(b) Because the division in part (a) was by $\frac{3}{8}$, the amount of material left over is $\frac{2}{3}$ of $\frac{3}{8}$, or $\frac{2}{3} \cdot \frac{3}{8}$, or $\frac{1}{4}$ yard.

B R A I N   T E A S E R

A castle in the faraway land of Aluossim was surrounded by four moats. One day, the castle was attacked and captured by a fierce tribe from the north. Guards were stationed at each bridge. Prince Juanaricmo was allowed to take a number of bags of gold from the castle as he went into exile. However, the guard at the first bridge demanded half the bags of gold plus one more bag. Prince Juanaricmo met this demand and proceeded to the next bridge. The guards at the second, third, and fourth bridges made identical demands, all of which the prince met. When the prince finally crossed all the bridges, he had a single bag of gold left. With how many bags did he start?

PROBLEM SET 6-3

1. In the following figures, a unit rectangle is used to illustrate the product of two fractions. Name the fractions and their product.

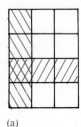 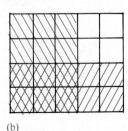

(a)   (b)

2. Use a rectangular region to illustrate each of the following products.

   (a) $\dfrac{3}{4} \cdot \dfrac{1}{3}$ (b) $\dfrac{1}{5} \cdot \dfrac{2}{3}$ (c) $\dfrac{2}{5} \cdot \dfrac{1}{3}$

3. Find each product. Write your answers in simplest form.

   (a) $\dfrac{10}{9} \cdot \dfrac{27}{40}$ (b) $\dfrac{^-3}{5} \cdot \dfrac{^-15}{24}$

   (c) $\dfrac{2a}{3b} \cdot \dfrac{^-5ab}{2ab}$ (d) $^-5\dfrac{1}{6} \cdot 4\dfrac{1}{2}$

4. Find each product. Write your answers in simplest form.

   (a) $\dfrac{49}{65} \cdot \dfrac{26}{98}$ (b) $\dfrac{a}{b} \cdot \dfrac{b^2}{a^2}$ (c) $\dfrac{xy}{z} \cdot \dfrac{z^2a}{x^3y^2}$

   (d) $2\dfrac{1}{3} \cdot 3\dfrac{3}{4}$ (e) $\dfrac{22}{7} \cdot 4\dfrac{2}{3}$ (f) $\dfrac{^-5}{2} \cdot 2\dfrac{1}{2}$

5. Use the distributive property to find each product.

   (a) $4\dfrac{1}{2} \cdot 2\dfrac{1}{3}$ $\left[\text{Hint: } \left(4 + \dfrac{1}{2}\right) \cdot \left(2 + \dfrac{1}{3}\right).\right]$

   (b) $3\dfrac{1}{3} \cdot 2\dfrac{1}{2}$ (c) $248\dfrac{2}{5} \cdot 100\dfrac{1}{8}$

6. Find the multiplicative inverse for each of the following.

   (a) $\dfrac{^-1}{3}$ (b) $\dfrac{3}{5}$

   (c) $\dfrac{14}{7}$ (d) $3\dfrac{1}{3}$

   (e) $\dfrac{x}{y}$, if $x \neq 0$ and $y \neq 0$ (f) $^-7$

7. Perform each of the following divisions, and write your answers in simplest form.

   (a) $3 \div \dfrac{1}{9}$ (b) $\dfrac{2}{3} \div \dfrac{7}{12}$ (c) $\dfrac{^-3}{4} \div \dfrac{7}{8}$

   (d) $\dfrac{x}{y} \div \dfrac{x^2}{y^2}$, where $x, y \neq 0$

   (e) $\dfrac{\frac{3}{16}}{\frac{4}{9}}$ (f) $\dfrac{\frac{3}{16}}{\frac{9}{4}}$ (g) $\dfrac{\frac{8}{7}}{\frac{3}{4}}$

   (h) $\dfrac{\frac{^-3}{5}}{\frac{^-6}{7}}$ (i) $\dfrac{^-3}{1\frac{1}{14}}$

8. Express each of the following in simplest form.

   (a) $\dfrac{2\frac{3}{4}}{1\frac{1}{4}}$ (b) $2\dfrac{3}{4} \cdot 1\dfrac{4}{3}$

(c) $\left(3\dfrac{2}{5} + 1\right)\left(4\dfrac{1}{3} - 2\dfrac{2}{3}\right)$ (d) $1\dfrac{1}{2} \cdot 1\dfrac{1}{3} \cdot 1\dfrac{1}{4}$

(e) $\dfrac{\frac{1}{2} + \frac{1}{3}}{\frac{1}{2} - \frac{1}{3}}$ (f) $\dfrac{\frac{1}{4} + \frac{3}{2}}{\frac{5}{6} + \frac{-7}{8}}$

(g) $\dfrac{1\frac{1}{2} - 2\frac{3}{4}}{\frac{1}{4} + \frac{-7}{8}}$ (h) $\dfrac{x}{y} \div \dfrac{x}{z}$

(i) $\dfrac{x}{y} \cdot \dfrac{yz}{x}$ (j) $x \cdot \dfrac{5}{xy} \cdot \dfrac{y}{x}$ (k) $\dfrac{x^2 y^3}{z^3} \cdot \dfrac{z^2}{xy^2}$

9. Choose the number from among the numbers in parentheses that best approximates each of the following.

(a) $3\dfrac{11}{12} \cdot 5\dfrac{3}{100}$ (8, 20, 15, 16)

(b) $2\dfrac{1}{10} \cdot 7\dfrac{7}{8}$ (16, 14, 4, 3)

(c) $20\dfrac{2}{3} \div 9\dfrac{7}{8}$ $\left(2, 180, \dfrac{1}{2}, 10\right)$

(d) $\dfrac{1}{101} \div \dfrac{1}{103}$ $\left(0, 1, \dfrac{1}{2}, \dfrac{1}{4}\right)$

10. Estimate by rounding the fractions.
(a) $5\frac{4}{5} \cdot 3\frac{1}{10}$ (b) $4\frac{10}{11} \cdot 5\frac{1}{8}$

(c) $\dfrac{20\frac{8}{9}}{3\frac{1}{12}}$ (d) $\dfrac{12\frac{1}{3}}{1\frac{7}{8}}$

11. Without actually doing the computations, choose the number in parentheses that correctly describes each of the following.

(a) $\dfrac{13}{14} \cdot \dfrac{17}{19}$ (greater than 1, less than 1)

(b) $3\dfrac{2}{7} \div 5\dfrac{1}{9}$ (greater than 1, less than 1)

(c) $4\dfrac{1}{3} \div 2\dfrac{3}{100}$ (greater than 2, less than 2)

(d) $16 \div 4\dfrac{3}{18}$ (greater than 4, less than 4)

(e) $16 \div 3\dfrac{8}{9}$ (greater than 4, less than 4)

(f) $15\dfrac{7}{8} \div 4\dfrac{3}{17}$ (greater than 4, less than 4)

(g) $16\dfrac{1}{10} \div 3\dfrac{8}{9}$ (greater than 4, less than 4)

12. Estimate by rounding the appropriate fractions. Use a plus or minus sign to indicate whether the actual answer is greater than the estimate or less than the estimate.

(a) $5\dfrac{2}{3} \cdot 7\dfrac{8}{9}$ (b) $4\dfrac{1}{8} \cdot 3\dfrac{3}{14}$

(c) $4\dfrac{7}{8} \cdot 8\dfrac{10}{11}$ (d) $3\dfrac{1}{9} \cdot 4\dfrac{1}{10}$

13. Multiply mentally. Find the exact answer.

(a) $3\dfrac{1}{4} \cdot 8$ (b) $7\dfrac{1}{2} \cdot 4$

(c) $9\dfrac{1}{5} \cdot 10$ (d) $8 \cdot 2\dfrac{1}{4}$

14. Divide mentally. Find the exact answer.

(a) $3 \div \dfrac{1}{2}$ (b) $3\dfrac{1}{2} \div \dfrac{1}{2}$

(c) $3 \div \dfrac{1}{3}$ (d) $4\dfrac{1}{2} \div 2$

15. Solve each of the following for x, and write your answers in simplest form.

(a) $\dfrac{1}{3} x = \dfrac{7}{8}$ (b) $\dfrac{1}{5} = \dfrac{7}{3} x$

(c) $\dfrac{1}{2} x - 7 = \dfrac{3}{4} x$ (d) $\dfrac{2}{3}\left(\dfrac{1}{2} x - 7\right) = \dfrac{3}{4} x$

(e) $\dfrac{2}{5} \cdot \dfrac{3}{6} = x$ (f) $x \div \dfrac{3}{4} = \dfrac{5}{8}$

(g) $2\dfrac{1}{3} x + 7 = 3\dfrac{1}{4}$ (h) $\dfrac{-2}{5}(10x + 1) = 1 - x$

(i) $\dfrac{1}{x} + \dfrac{1}{3} = \dfrac{1}{5}$

16. Find two consecutive integers, x and $x + 1$, such that one half of the greater integer exceeds one third of the lesser integer by 9.

17. Di Paloma University had a faculty reduction and lost one fifth of its faculty. If 320 faculty members were left after the reduction, how many members were there originally?

18. Alberto owns five ninths of the stock in the North West Tofu Company. His sister, Renatta, owns half as much stock as Alberto. What part of the stock is owned by neither Alberto nor Renatta?

19. A person has $29\frac{1}{2}$ yards of material available to make uniforms. Each uniform requires $\frac{3}{4}$ yard of material.
(a) How many uniforms can be made?
(b) How much material will be left over?

20. Create a problem that has the same structure as each of the following, using whole numbers if possible (if not, use simpler fractions such as $\frac{1}{2}$ or $\frac{1}{4}$), so that the answer will be a whole number. Solve your problem, and then solve the original problem.
    (a) Four students share three pizzas equally. How much pizza does each student get?
    (b) If a pizza had $\frac{5}{8}$ pound of cheese uniformly distributed on it, and John ate $\frac{2}{3}$ of the pizza, how much cheese did John eat?
    (c) John ate $\frac{3}{8}$ pound of sausage while eating $\frac{2}{3}$ of a pizza. If the sausage was uniformly distributed over the pizza, how much sausage was on the whole pizza?
    (d) Michael can paint $\frac{2}{5}$ of a house in one day. If he continues working at this rate, how many days will it take him to paint the whole house?
    (e) If Nora spent $\frac{3}{10}$ of her salary on presents for friends and $\frac{2}{5}$ of her salary on presents for family this month, what part of her salary did she spend on presents?
    (f) On a scale drawing of a house, the caption read, "$\frac{7}{16}$ inch represents 1 foot." How long is the living room in reality if it is $10\frac{1}{2}$ inches long on the drawing?
    (g) Joanna is entitled to $\frac{2}{5}$ of her parents' estate, which is valued at $\frac{3}{4}$ million dollars. How much should Joanna receive?

21. Show that the following properties do *not* hold for division of rational numbers.
    (a) Commutative (b) Associative
    (c) Identity   (d) Inverse

22. When you multiply a certain number by 3 and then subtract $\frac{7}{18}$, you get the same result as when you multiply the number by 2 and add $\frac{5}{12}$. What is the number?

23. Five eighths of the students at Salem State College live in dormitories. If 6000 students at the college live in the dormitories, how many students are there in the college?

24. A suit is on sale for $200. What was the original price of the suit if the discount was one fourth of the original price?

25. If every employee's salary at the Sunrise Software Company increases each year by $\frac{1}{10}$ of that person's salary the previous year, answer the following.
    (a) If Martha's present annual salary is $100,000, what will her salary be in 2 years?
    (b) If Aaron's present salary is $99,000, what was his salary 1 year ago?
    (c) If Juanita's present salary is $363,000, what was her salary 2 years ago?

26. At a certain company, three times as many men as women apply for work. If $\frac{1}{10}$ of the applicants are hired and $\frac{1}{20}$ of the men who apply are hired, what fraction of the women who apply are hired?

27. Rachel had a certain number of marbles. One day she got 30 marbles from Tara and decided to take $\frac{5}{8}$ of the new number of marbles to school. In school, she noticed that she brought with her as many marbles as she had originally. How many marbles did Rachel have originally?

28. John took out all his money from his bank savings account. He spent $50 on a radio and $\frac{3}{5}$ of what remained on presents. Half of what was left he put back in his checking account, and the remaining $35 he donated to charity. How much money did John originally have in his savings account?

29. Three children got a bag of marbles, which they divided equally among themselves. Later each lost 4 marbles. The total number of remaining marbles was equal to the number each had before losing some of the marbles. How many marbles were in the bag originally?

30. Peppermint Patty is frustrated by a problem. Help her solve it.

31. For each of the following sequences, (a) find a pattern and (b) write two more terms of the sequence, assuming that the pattern continues. (c) Which of the sequences are geometric and which are not? Justify your answers.
    (i) $1, \frac{1}{2}, \frac{1}{4}, \frac{1}{8}, \frac{1}{16}, \cdots$
    (ii) $1, \frac{-1}{2}, \frac{1}{4}, \frac{-1}{8}, \frac{1}{16}, \cdots$
    (iii) $\frac{4}{3}, 1, \frac{3}{4}, \frac{9}{16}, \frac{27}{64}, \cdots$
    (iv) $\frac{1}{3}, \frac{2}{3^2}, \frac{3}{3^3}, \frac{4}{3^4}, \cdots$

32. There is a simple method for squaring any number that consists of a whole number and $\frac{1}{2}$. For example $(3\frac{1}{2})^2 = 3 \cdot 4 + (\frac{1}{2})^2 = 12\frac{1}{4}$; $(4\frac{1}{2})^2 = 4 \cdot 5 + (\frac{1}{2})^2 = 20\frac{1}{4}$; $(5\frac{1}{2})^2 = 5 \cdot 6 + (\frac{1}{2})^2 = 30\frac{1}{4}$.
    (a) Write a statement for $(n + \frac{1}{2})^2$ that generalizes these examples, where n is a whole number.
    ★(b) Justify this procedure.

33. Let $f(x) = (\frac{3}{4})x + \frac{1}{2}$, where the domain is all rational numbers.
    (a) Find the outputs if the inputs are:
       (i) 0   (ii) $\frac{2}{5}$ (iii) $\frac{-2}{5}$
    (b) For which inputs will the outputs be:
       (i) 0   (ii) 1   (iii) $\frac{-1}{2}$

34. Let $f(x) = \dfrac{3x + 4}{4x - 5}$, where the domain is all rational numbers for which the function has a value.
    (a) Find the outputs if the inputs are:
       (i) 0   (ii) $\frac{2}{5}$ (iii) $\frac{-2}{5}$
    (b) For which inputs will the outputs be:
       (i) 0   (ii) $\frac{2}{5}$ (iii) $\frac{-1}{2}$
    (c) What value for x is not in the domain of the function?

35. Consider these products.

    First product: $\left(1 + \dfrac{1}{1}\right)\left(1 + \dfrac{1}{2}\right)$

    Second product: $\left(1 + \dfrac{1}{1}\right)\left(1 + \dfrac{1}{2}\right)\left(1 + \dfrac{1}{3}\right)$

    Third product: $\left(1 + \dfrac{1}{1}\right)\left(1 + \dfrac{1}{2}\right)\left(1 + \dfrac{1}{3}\right)\left(1 + \dfrac{1}{4}\right)$

    (a) Calculate the value of each product. Based on the pattern in your answers, guess the value of the fourth product; then check to determine if your guess is correct.
    (b) Guess the value of the 100th product.
    (c) Find as simple an expression as possible for the nth product.

★36. Investigate under what conditions, if any,
$$\frac{a}{b} = \frac{a + c}{b + c}$$

★37. Let $S = \dfrac{1}{2} + \dfrac{1}{2^2} + \dfrac{1}{2^3} + \cdots + \dfrac{1}{2^{64}}$.
    (a) Use the distributive property of multiplication over addition to find an expression for $2S$.
    (b) Show that $2S - S = S = 1 - (\frac{1}{2})^{64}$.
    (c) Find a simple expression for the sum
$$\frac{1}{2} + \frac{1}{2^2} + \frac{1}{2^3} + \cdots + \frac{1}{2^n}$$

★38. Find the sum of the first 100 terms of the arithmetic sequence
$$\frac{1}{4}, 1, \frac{7}{4}, \frac{5}{2}, \frac{13}{4}, \cdots$$

★39. In an arithmetic sequence, the 1st term is 1 and the 100th term is 2. Find the following.
    (a) The 50th term
    (b) The sum of the first 50 terms

Review Problems

40. Perform each of the following computations. Leave your answers in simplest form.
    (a) $\dfrac{-3}{16} + \dfrac{7}{4}$ (b) $\dfrac{1}{6} + \dfrac{-4}{9} + \dfrac{5}{3}$
    (c) $\dfrac{-5}{2^3 \cdot 3^2} - \dfrac{-5}{2 \cdot 3^3}$ (d) $3\dfrac{4}{5} + 4\dfrac{5}{6}$
    (e) $5\dfrac{1}{6} - 3\dfrac{5}{8}$ (f) $-4\dfrac{1}{3} - 5\dfrac{5}{12}$

41. Each student at Sussex Elementary School takes one foreign language. Two thirds of the students take Spanish, $\frac{1}{9}$ take French, $\frac{1}{18}$ take German, and the rest take some other foreign language. If there are 720 students in the school, how many do not take Spanish, French, or German?

42. Perform the indicated operations, and write your answers in simplest form.
    (a) $\dfrac{-3}{5x} + \dfrac{1}{x} - \dfrac{-2}{3x}$ (b) $\dfrac{-2}{2xy^2} + \dfrac{3}{x^2y} - \dfrac{1}{xy}$

A woman's will decreed that her cats be shared among her three daughters as follows: $\frac{1}{2}$ of the cats to the eldest daughter, $\frac{1}{3}$ of the cats to the middle daughter, and $\frac{1}{9}$ of the cats to the youngest daughter. Since the woman had 17 cats, the daughters decided that they could not carry out their mother's wishes. The judge who held the will agreed to lend the daughters a cat so they could share the cats as their mother wished. Now, $\frac{1}{2}$ of 18 is 9; $\frac{1}{3}$ of 18 is 6; and $\frac{1}{9}$ of 18 is 2. Since $9 + 6 + 2 = 17$, the daughters were able to divide the 17 cats and return the borrowed cat. They obviously did not need the extra cat to carry out their mother's bequest, but they could not divide 17 into halves, thirds, and ninths. Has the woman's will really been followed?

Section 6-4   Some Properties of Rational Numbers

Ordering of Rational Numbers

We saw in Section 6-1 that one rational number is greater than another if the first is to the right of the second on the number line. Thus, $\frac{7}{8} > \frac{5}{8}$ because $\frac{7}{8}$ is to the right of $\frac{5}{8}$ on the number line. Children know than $\frac{7}{8} > \frac{5}{8}$ because, if a pizza is divided into 8 parts, then 7 parts of a pizza is more than 5 parts. Similarly, $\frac{3}{7} < \frac{4}{7}$. Thus, given two fractions with common positive denominators, the one with the greater numerator is the greater fraction. This can be written as follows.

- T H E O R E M   6-3

  If a, b, and c are integers and $b > 0$, then $\dfrac{a}{b} > \dfrac{c}{b}$ if and only if $a > c$.

- R E M A R K

  The condition $b > 0$ is essential in the property. Check to see that, if $b < 0$, the theorem is not necessarily true. Theorem 6-3 can be deduced from the definition that follows.

The greater-than and less-than relations for rational numbers are defined in such a way that the previously given definitions of these relations are still true.

- D E F I N I T I O N

  If $\dfrac{a}{b}$ and $\dfrac{c}{d}$ are rational numbers, then $\dfrac{a}{b} > \dfrac{c}{d}$ if and only if there is a positive

  rational number k such that $\dfrac{c}{d} + k = \dfrac{a}{b}$, or equivalently, if and only if $\dfrac{a}{b} - \dfrac{c}{d}$ is positive.

To determine the greater of two fractions that do not have common denominators, consider $\frac{6}{7}$ and $\frac{8}{11}$. Suppose we have two pizzas of equal size, one cut into 7 pieces and the other cut into 11 pieces. Is there more pizza in 6 slices of the first than there is in 8 slices of the second? To answer this, we need to divide a whole into equal parts in such a way that $\frac{6}{7}$ and $\frac{8}{11}$ will be easily comparable. This can be accomplished by finding fractions equal to $\frac{6}{7}$ and $\frac{8}{11}$ with common denominators. We have $\frac{6}{7} = \frac{6 \cdot 11}{7 \cdot 11} = \frac{66}{77}$ and $\frac{8}{11} = \frac{7 \cdot 8}{7 \cdot 11} = \frac{56}{77}$. Because $66 > 56$, it follows that $\frac{66}{77} > \frac{56}{77}$, so $\frac{6}{7} > \frac{8}{11}$. Similarly, to compare $\frac{-5}{12}$ and $\frac{1}{-2}$, we first write them with common denominators, as follows.

$$\frac{1}{-2} = \frac{1 \cdot (^-6)}{-2 \cdot (^-6)} = \frac{^-6}{12}$$

Because $^-5 > ^-6$, $\frac{^-5}{12} > \frac{^-6}{12}$; therefore, $\frac{^-5}{12} > \frac{1}{-2}$.

A general criterion for the greater-than relation on rational numbers can be developed for the case in which the denominators are positive. Using the common denominator bd, the fractions $\frac{a}{b}$ and $\frac{c}{d}$ can be written as $\frac{ad}{bd}$ and $\frac{bc}{bd}$. Because $b > 0$ and $d > 0$, $bd > 0$, we apply theorem 6-3 to realize that $\frac{ad}{bd} > \frac{bc}{bd}$ if and only if $ad > bc$.

EXAMPLE 6-23   Prove that the following order relations are true.

(a) $\dfrac{8}{9} > \dfrac{16}{19}$ (b) $\dfrac{^-7}{8} < \dfrac{14}{15}$ (c) $\dfrac{1}{^-4} < \dfrac{2}{11}$ (d) $\dfrac{1}{^-4} > \dfrac{^-1}{2}$

SOLUTION   (a) We write the fractions with the common denominator $9 \cdot 19$. We have $\dfrac{8}{9} > \dfrac{16}{19}$ is equivalent to $\dfrac{8 \cdot 19}{9 \cdot 19} > \dfrac{9 \cdot 16}{9 \cdot 19}$. The last inequality is true because $8 \cdot 19 > 9 \cdot 16$ (or $152 > 144$).

(b) $\dfrac{^-7}{8} < \dfrac{14}{15}$ because a negative number is less than a positive number.

(c) $\dfrac{1}{^-4} < \dfrac{2}{11}$ because a negative number is less than a positive number.

(d) We write the fractions with common positive denominators.

$$\frac{1}{^-4} = \frac{^-1}{4} \quad \text{and} \quad \frac{^-1}{2} = \frac{^-1 \cdot 2}{2 \cdot 2} = \frac{^-2}{4}$$

$$\frac{^-1}{4} > \frac{^-2}{4} \text{ because } ^-1 > ^-2.$$

As in Example 6-23(b) and (c), we can often compare the size of fractions by inspection and common sense. Such approaches should be strongly encouraged. Consider which is greater, $\frac{3}{4}$ or $\frac{4}{5}$. Three fourths of a pizza is a pizza with $\frac{1}{4}$ cut out, while $\frac{4}{5}$ of a pizza is a pizza with $\frac{1}{5}$ cut out. Can you find a similar way to determine which of the fractions $\frac{6}{5}$ and $\frac{7}{6}$ is greater? How about $\frac{134}{137}$ and $\frac{131}{130}$?

The proofs of the following theorems of the greater-than relation on rational numbers are similar to those involving integers and are left as exercises. Similar properties hold for $<$, $\le$, and $\ge$.

- **T H E O R E M 6-4**

  Transitive Property of Greater Than For any rational numbers $\frac{a}{b}$, $\frac{c}{d}$, and $\frac{e}{f}$,

  if $\frac{a}{b} > \frac{c}{d}$ and $\frac{c}{d} > \frac{e}{f}$, then $\frac{a}{b} > \frac{e}{f}$.

- **T H E O R E M 6-5**

  Addition Property of Greater Than For any rational numbers, $\frac{a}{b}$, $\frac{c}{d}$, and $\frac{e}{f}$,

  if $\frac{a}{b} > \frac{c}{d}$, then $\frac{a}{b} + \frac{e}{f} > \frac{c}{d} + \frac{e}{f}$.

- **T H E O R E M 6-6**

  Multiplication Property of Greater Than For any rational numbers $\frac{a}{b}$, $\frac{c}{d}$, and $\frac{e}{f}$.

  1. If $\frac{a}{b} > \frac{c}{d}$ and $\frac{e}{f} > 0$, then $\frac{a}{b} \cdot \frac{e}{f} > \frac{c}{d} \cdot \frac{e}{f}$.

  2. If $\frac{a}{b} > \frac{c}{d}$ and $\frac{e}{f} < 0$, then $\frac{a}{b} \cdot \frac{e}{f} < \frac{c}{d} \cdot \frac{e}{f}$.

Solutions to Algebraic Inequalities

The preceding theorems can be used to aid in solving algebraic inequalities, as shown in the following example.

EXAMPLE 6-24 Solve for x, where x is a rational number.

(a) $\frac{3}{2}x < \frac{3}{4}$

(b) $\frac{1}{4}x + \frac{1}{5} \ge \frac{3}{8}x - \frac{1}{10}$

SOLUTION (a)

$$\frac{3}{2}x < \frac{3}{4}$$

$$\left(\frac{2}{3}\right)\left(\frac{3}{2}x\right) < \left(\frac{2}{3}\right)\left(\frac{3}{4}\right)$$

$$x < \frac{6}{12}, \text{ or } x < \frac{1}{2}$$

(b)

$$\frac{1}{4}x + \frac{1}{5} \geq \frac{3}{8}x - \frac{1}{10}$$

$$\frac{1}{4}x + \frac{1}{5} + \frac{^-1}{5} \geq \frac{3}{8}x - \frac{1}{10} + \frac{^-1}{5}$$

$$\frac{1}{4}x \geq \frac{3}{8}x - \frac{3}{10}$$

$$\frac{^-3}{8}x + \frac{1}{4}x \geq \frac{^-3}{8}x + \frac{3}{8}x - \frac{3}{10}$$

$$\left(\frac{^-3}{8} + \frac{1}{4}\right)x \geq \frac{^-3}{10}$$

$$-\frac{1}{8}x \geq \frac{^-3}{10}$$

$$^-8\left(\frac{^-1}{8}x\right) \leq {^-8}\left(\frac{^-3}{10}\right)$$

$$x \leq \frac{24}{10}, \text{ or } 2\frac{2}{5}$$

Often there is more than one way to solve an inequality. Two alternate methods for solving Example 6-24(b) follow.

1. First, add the fractions on each side of the inequality. Then, solve the resulting inequality.

$$\frac{1}{4}x + \frac{1}{5} \geq \frac{3}{8}x - \frac{1}{10}$$

$$\frac{5x + 4}{20} \geq \frac{15x - 4}{40}$$

$$40(5x + 4) \geq 20(15x - 4)$$

$$200x + 160 \geq 300x - 80$$

$$^-100x \geq {^-240}$$

$$\left(\frac{^-1}{100}\right)(^-100x) \leq \frac{^-1}{100}(^-240)$$

$$x \leq \frac{240}{100}$$

$$x \leq \frac{12}{5}, \text{ or } 2\frac{2}{5}$$

2. First, multiply both sides of the inequality by the LCM of all the denominators. (This gives an inequality that does not involve fractions.) Then, solve the resulting inequality.

$$\frac{1}{4}x + \frac{1}{5} \geq \frac{3}{8}x - \frac{1}{10}$$

Since LCM(4, 5, 8, 10) = 40,

$$40\left(\frac{1}{4}x + \frac{1}{5}\right) \geq 40\left(\frac{3}{8}x - \frac{1}{10}\right)$$

$$10x + 8 \geq 15x - 4$$

$$^{-}5x \geq ^{-}12$$

$$x \leq \frac{^{-}12}{^{-}5}$$

$$x \leq \frac{12}{5}, \quad \text{or } 2\frac{2}{5}$$

Estimations with Order

Properties of greater-than or less-than relations sometimes can be used to estimate the answers to problems. For example, to find the number of curtains requiring $5\frac{3}{8}$ yards of cloth that can be prepared from a bolt that contains $19\frac{3}{4}$ yards, we could compute $\dfrac{19\frac{3}{4}}{5\frac{3}{8}}$. However, because $19\frac{3}{4}$ is approximately 20, and $5\frac{3}{8}$ is close to 5, we estimate that the answer should be approximately $\frac{20}{5}$, or 4. Is the actual answer greater than or less than 4? To answer that question, notice that, if two positive fractions have equal denominators, the one with the greater numerator is greater, and if two positive fractions have equal numerators, the one with the greater denominator is smaller. (Do you see intuitively why this is so?) Hence $\dfrac{19\frac{3}{4}}{5\frac{3}{8}} < \dfrac{20}{5\frac{3}{8}} < \dfrac{20}{5}$. Thus (by Theorem 6-4), $\dfrac{19\frac{3}{4}}{5\frac{3}{8}} < \dfrac{20}{5}$. Similarly, it is possible to show that $\dfrac{19\frac{3}{8}}{5\frac{3}{8}} > \dfrac{18}{5\frac{3}{8}} > \dfrac{18}{6}$. Because $\dfrac{19\frac{3}{4}}{5\frac{3}{8}}$ is between 3 and 4, we can conclude that only 3 curtains can be prepared.

EXAMPLE 6-25 In each of the following, estimate the answer by finding two integers, one smaller than the answer and one greater than the answer.

(a) $9\frac{3}{4} \cdot 14\frac{5}{9}$ (b) $35\frac{1}{3} \div 6\frac{3}{5}$

SOLUTION (a) $9 \cdot 14 < 9\frac{3}{4} \cdot 14\frac{5}{9} < 10 \cdot 15$

Hence,

$$126 < 9\frac{3}{4} \cdot 14\frac{5}{9} < 150$$

(b) $\dfrac{35\frac{1}{3}}{6\frac{3}{5}} < \dfrac{36}{6\frac{3}{5}} < \dfrac{36}{6}$

Hence,

$$\dfrac{35\frac{1}{3}}{6\frac{3}{5}} < 6$$

Similarly,

$$\dfrac{35\frac{1}{3}}{6\frac{3}{5}} > 5$$

Thus,

$$5 < \dfrac{35\frac{1}{3}}{6\frac{3}{5}} < 6$$

EXAMPLE 6-26 In each of the following, use estimation techniques to determine which is a correct description of the answer.

(a) $\dfrac{1}{2} + 1\dfrac{2}{3}$

between: (i) 1 and $1\dfrac{1}{2}$

(ii) $1\dfrac{1}{2}$ and 2

(iii) 2 and $2\dfrac{1}{2}$

(b) $\dfrac{8}{9} + \dfrac{17}{18} + \dfrac{29}{30}$

between: (i) 2 and $2\dfrac{1}{2}$

(ii) $2\dfrac{1}{2}$ and 3

(iii) 3 and $3\dfrac{1}{2}$

(c) $\dfrac{1}{2} \cdot \left(3\dfrac{9}{10}\right)$

between: (i) $\dfrac{1}{2}$ and 1

(ii) 1 and $1\dfrac{1}{2}$

(iii) $1\dfrac{1}{2}$ and 2

SOLUTION Each of the following can be done mentally.

(a) $\dfrac{1}{2} + 1\dfrac{2}{3} > \dfrac{1}{2} + 1\dfrac{1}{2} = 2$. Also $\dfrac{1}{2} + 1\dfrac{2}{3} < \dfrac{1}{2} + 2 = 2\dfrac{1}{2}$. Hence, (iii) is correct.

(b) Each fraction is quite close to 1 but less than 1. Hence, (ii) is correct.

(c) This product is quite close to $\frac{1}{2} \cdot 4$ because $3\frac{9}{10}$ is close to 4. Hence, (iii) seems to be correct. A more precise approach is as follows.

$$\dfrac{1}{2} \cdot 3 < \dfrac{1}{2} \cdot \left(3\dfrac{9}{10}\right) < \dfrac{1}{2} \cdot 4 \quad \text{or} \quad 1\dfrac{1}{2} < \dfrac{1}{2} \cdot \left(3\dfrac{9}{10}\right) < 2$$

EXAMPLE 6-27   Without actually performing the computations, arrange the following in increasing order, from least to greatest.

(a) $\dfrac{41}{80}, \dfrac{29}{60}, \dfrac{3}{4}, \dfrac{19}{17}, \dfrac{9}{10}, 0, \dfrac{1}{10}, \dfrac{^-3}{4}$

(b) $1\dfrac{5}{8} \cdot 6\dfrac{3}{5}, \; 2\dfrac{7}{19} \cdot 6\dfrac{3}{5}, \; \dfrac{1}{2} \cdot 5\dfrac{9}{19}, \; \dfrac{9}{10} \cdot 5\dfrac{1}{19}$

SOLUTION   (a) Because a negative number is less than 0 or a positive number, $^-\dfrac{3}{4}$ is the least number. 0 is the next larger number. Notice that $\dfrac{41}{80}$ is $\dfrac{1}{80}$ more than $\dfrac{1}{2}$ and that $\dfrac{29}{60}$ is $\dfrac{1}{60}$ less than $\dfrac{1}{2}$. Also, $\dfrac{9}{10}$ is close to 1 but less than 1, and $\dfrac{19}{17} > 1$. The fraction $\dfrac{1}{10}$ is much less than $\dfrac{1}{2}$. These observations enable us to order the numbers as follows.

$$\dfrac{^-3}{4} < 0 < \dfrac{1}{10} < \dfrac{29}{60} < \dfrac{41}{80} < \dfrac{3}{4} < \dfrac{9}{10} < \dfrac{19}{17}$$

(b) Notice that each of the last two products is smaller than the first or the second product. The second product is greater than the first, and the fourth is greater than the third. Hence,

$$\dfrac{1}{2} \cdot 5\dfrac{9}{19} < \dfrac{9}{10} \cdot 5\dfrac{1}{19} < 1\dfrac{5}{8} \cdot 6\dfrac{3}{5} < 2\dfrac{7}{19} \cdot 6\dfrac{3}{5}$$

Inequalities are useful in many applications of mathematics. Following are examples of problems that can be solved with inequalities.

PROBLEM 2

A plane increased its normal speed by 60 miles per hour and traveled a distance of less than 2860 miles in $5\frac{1}{2}$ hours. When the plane decreased its normal speed by 100 miles per hour, it covered a distance that was greater than 2720 miles in 8 hours. The pilot claimed that the plane's normal speed was less than 500 miles per hour. Was the pilot correct?

Devising a Plan. Table 6-4 outlines the given information. We know that distance = rate × time, where rate is another name for speed. If we denote the normal speed by x miles per hour, we can write the distance traveled during the $5\frac{1}{2}$ hours and during the 8 hours in terms of x. From the information about the distances, we will have two inequalities involving x. The solution of these inequalities should give us more information about x.

TABLE 6-4

Speed (in miles per hour)	Time (in hours)	Distance (in miles)
Normal + 60 Normal − 100	$5\frac{1}{2}$ 8	Less than 2860 Greater than 2720

Carrying Out the Plan. The outlined procedure for finding the distances is shown in Table 6-5.

TABLE 6-5

Normal Speed (in miles per hour)	New Speed (in miles per hour)	Time (in hours)	Distance (in miles, in terms of x)
x	$x + 60$	$5\frac{1}{2}$	$5\frac{1}{2}(x + 60)$
x	$x - 100$	8	$8(x - 100)$

Because we know that the first distance is less than 2860 and the second is greater than 2720, we have the following inequalities.

$5\frac{1}{2}(x + 60) < 2860$ and $8(x - 100) > 2720$

These inequalities are equivalent to each of the following pairs of inequalities.

$$5\frac{1}{2}(x + 60) < 2860 \qquad \text{and} \qquad 8(x - 100) > 2720$$

$$\frac{2}{11} \cdot \frac{11}{2}(x + 60) < \frac{2}{11} \cdot 2860 \quad \text{and} \quad \frac{1}{8} \cdot 8(x - 100) > \frac{1}{8} \cdot 2720$$

$$x + 60 < 520 \qquad \text{and} \qquad x - 100 > 340$$

$$x < 460 \qquad \text{and} \qquad x > 440$$

Consequently, $440 < x < 460$. Hence, the plane's normal speed is between 440 and 460 miles per hour, and the pilot's claim was correct.

Looking Back. Even though we could not find the exact speed, the data in the question enabled us to find a fairly narrow range for the possible normal speeds.

Suppose we knew that the speed was a whole number. Could you make a change in numbers in the question (without changing any words) that would enable you to find the exact value of x?

Denseness Property

denseness property
The set of rational numbers has a very special property called the **denseness property.** Neither the set of whole numbers nor the set of integers has this property. *Given any two rational numbers $\frac{a}{b}$ and $\frac{c}{d}$, there is another rational number between these two.* Also, between $\frac{a}{b}$ and the new rational number, there is another rational number. Continuing this process shows that, between any two rational numbers $\frac{a}{b}$ and $\frac{c}{d}$, there are infinitely many other rational numbers. For example, consider $\frac{1}{2}$ and $\frac{2}{3}$. To find a rational number between $\frac{1}{2}$ and $\frac{2}{3}$, we first rewrite the fractions with a common denominator, as $\frac{3}{6}$ and $\frac{4}{6}$. Because there is no whole number between the numerators 3 and 4, we next find two fractions equivalent to $\frac{1}{2}$ and $\frac{2}{3}$ with greater denominators. For example, $\frac{1}{2} = \frac{6}{12}$ and $\frac{2}{3} = \frac{8}{12}$, and $\frac{7}{12}$ is between the two fractions $\frac{6}{12}$ and $\frac{8}{12}$. So $\frac{7}{12}$ is between $\frac{1}{2}$ and $\frac{2}{3}$.

Another way to find a rational number between two given rationals $\frac{a}{b}$ and $\frac{c}{d}$ is to find the arithmetic mean of the two numbers. For example, the arithmetic mean of $\frac{1}{2}$ and $\frac{2}{3}$ is $\frac{1}{2}(\frac{1}{2} + \frac{2}{3})$, or $\frac{7}{12}$. The proof that the arithmetic mean of two given rational numbers always is between them is left as an exercise.

EXAMPLE 6-28 Find two fractions between $\frac{1}{2}$ and $\frac{7}{18}$.

SOLUTION We rewrite the fractions with common denominators. We have $\frac{1}{2} = \frac{1 \cdot 9}{2 \cdot 9} = \frac{9}{18}$. We see that $\frac{8}{18}$, or $\frac{4}{9}$, is between $\frac{7}{18}$ and $\frac{9}{18}$. To find another fraction between the given fractions, we find two fractions equivalent to $\frac{7}{18}$ and $\frac{9}{18}$, but with greater denominators. For example, $\frac{7}{18} = \frac{14}{36}$ and $\frac{9}{18} = \frac{18}{36}$.

We now see that $\frac{15}{36}$, $\frac{16}{36}$, and $\frac{17}{36}$ are all between $\frac{14}{36}$ and $\frac{18}{36}$.

B R A I N   T E A S E R
Two cyclists, David and Sara, started riding their bikes at 9:00 A.M. at City Hall. They followed the local bike trail and returned to City Hall at the same time. However, David rode three times as long as Sara rested on her trip and Sara rode four times as long as David rested on his trip. Assuming that each cyclist rode at a constant speed, who rode faster?

PROBLEM SET 6-4

1. For each of the following pairs of fractions, replace the comma with the correct symbol ($<$, $=$, $>$) to make a true statement.

   (a) $\dfrac{7}{8}, \dfrac{5}{6}$ (b) $2\dfrac{4}{5}, 2\dfrac{3}{6}$ (c) $\dfrac{-7}{8}, \dfrac{-4}{5}$

   (d) $\dfrac{1}{-7}, \dfrac{1}{-8}$ (e) $\dfrac{2}{5}, \dfrac{4}{10}$ (f) $\dfrac{0}{7}, \dfrac{0}{17}$

2. Illustrate each of the following fractions on a number line.

   $-2\dfrac{1}{4}, -1\dfrac{3}{8}, -\dfrac{1}{2}, 1\dfrac{1}{8}, 2\dfrac{5}{8}$

3. Arrange each of the following in decreasing order.

   (a) $\dfrac{11}{22}, \dfrac{11}{16}, \dfrac{11}{13}$ (b) $\dfrac{33}{16}, \dfrac{23}{16}, 3$

   (c) $\dfrac{-1}{5}, \dfrac{-19}{36}, \dfrac{-17}{30}$

4. Solve for x in each of the following.

   (a) $\dfrac{2}{3}x - \dfrac{7}{8} \le \dfrac{1}{4}$

   (b) $x - \dfrac{1}{3} < \dfrac{2}{3}x + \dfrac{4}{5}$

   (c) $\dfrac{1}{5}x - 7 \ge \dfrac{2}{3}$

   (d) $5 - \dfrac{2}{3}x \le \dfrac{1}{4}x - \dfrac{7}{8}$

5. (a) If $b < 0$ and $d > 0$, is it true that $\dfrac{a}{b} > \dfrac{c}{d}$ if and only if $ad > bc$? Explain your answer.

   (b) If $b < 0$ and $d < 0$, is it true that $\dfrac{a}{b} > \dfrac{c}{d}$ if and only if $ad > bc$? Explain your answer.

6. Estimate each of the following; then perform the multiplications to see how good your estimates are.

   (a) $19\dfrac{8}{9} \cdot 20\dfrac{1}{9}$ (b) $19\dfrac{8}{9} \cdot 9\dfrac{1}{10}$ (c) $3\dfrac{9}{10} \cdot \dfrac{81}{82}$

7. In each of the following, choose the better estimate from the pair of estimates in parentheses.

   (a) $4\dfrac{5}{8} + 2\dfrac{5}{9}$ (under 7, over 7)

   (b) $7\dfrac{1}{10} + 5\dfrac{6}{11}$ (under 13, over 13)

   (c) $8\dfrac{1}{3} \div 8\dfrac{2}{3}$ (under 1, over 1)

   (d) $6\dfrac{1}{10} \div \dfrac{11}{12}$ (under 6, over 6)

   (e) $10 - 3\dfrac{4}{5}$ (under 6, over 6)

8. In each of the following, use estimation techniques to determine which of the corresponding statements is true.

   (a) $4 \cdot 5\dfrac{1}{16}$ between: 20 and $20\dfrac{1}{2}$, $20\dfrac{1}{2}$ and 21, 21 and $21\dfrac{1}{2}$

   (b) $3\dfrac{1}{2} + 2\dfrac{1}{3}$ between: 5 and $5\dfrac{1}{2}$, $5\dfrac{1}{2}$ and 6, 6 and $6\dfrac{1}{2}$

   (c) $10\dfrac{19}{20} \div 2\dfrac{1}{25}$ between: 5 and $5\dfrac{1}{2}$, $5\dfrac{1}{2}$ and 6, 6 and $6\dfrac{1}{2}$

   (d) $13\dfrac{1}{8} - 3\dfrac{1}{44}$ between: 10 and $10\dfrac{1}{2}$, $10\dfrac{1}{2}$ and 11, 11 and $11\dfrac{1}{2}$

9. In each of the following, estimate the answer.

   (a) $19\dfrac{8}{9} \cdot 9\dfrac{1}{10}$ (b) $80\dfrac{3}{4} \cdot 9\dfrac{1}{8}$ (c) $77\dfrac{3}{5} \cdot 6\dfrac{1}{4}$

   (d) $\dfrac{48\frac{2}{3}}{8\frac{4}{9}}$ (e) $\dfrac{5\frac{2}{3}}{2\frac{1}{17}}$

10. Estimate the number of $11\frac{3}{4}$-ounce birdseed packages that can be produced from a supply of 21 pounds of birdseed.

11. (a) Choose several positive proper fractions. Square each of the fractions, and compare the size of the original fraction and its square. Make a conjecture concerning a fraction and its square.

    ★(b) Justify your conjecture in (a).

    (c) If a fraction is greater than 1, make a conjecture concerning which is greater—the fraction or its square.

    ★(d) Justify your conjecture in (c).

12. If $\dfrac{a}{b} < 1$ and $\dfrac{c}{d} > 0$, compare $\dfrac{c}{d}$ with $\dfrac{a}{b} \cdot \dfrac{c}{d}$. Which is lesser?

13. If x and y are two rational numbers such that $x > 1$ and $y > 0$, which is greater: xy or y? Justify your answer.

14. Show that the sequence $\frac{1}{2}, \frac{2}{3}, \frac{3}{4}, \frac{4}{5}, \frac{5}{6}, \frac{6}{7}, \ldots$ is an increasing sequence; that is, show that each term in the sequence is greater than the preceding one.

15. Find an infinite, decreasing sequence (each term is smaller than the preceding one) of positive, rational numbers such that all the terms are greater than 1.

16. (a) Explain why the system of whole numbers does not have the denseness property.
    (b) Explain why the system of integers does not have the denseness property.

17. For each of the following, find two rational numbers between the given fractions.
    (a) $\dfrac{3}{7}$ and $\dfrac{4}{7}$ (b) $\dfrac{^-7}{9}$ and $\dfrac{^-8}{9}$
    (c) $\dfrac{5}{6}$ and $\dfrac{83}{100}$ (d) $\dfrac{^-1}{3}$ and $\dfrac{3}{4}$

18. Find the greatest integer x, if one exists, satisfying each of the following.
    (a) $3x < 100$ (b) $\dfrac{3}{4}x < 100$
    (c) $\dfrac{3}{4}x < {}^-x + 1$ (d) $\dfrac{3}{8} < 2x - 13$

19. Find the least integer x, if one exists, satisfying each of the following.
    (a) $4x > 110$ (b) $\dfrac{^-4}{3}x > 400$
    (c) $\dfrac{4}{5}(x - 1) > 1 - \dfrac{x}{10}$ (d) $\dfrac{1}{x} < 3$

★20. Show that the arithmetic mean of two rational numbers is between the two numbers; that is, for
    $0 < \dfrac{a}{b} < \dfrac{c}{d}$, prove that $0 < \dfrac{a}{b} < \dfrac{1}{2}\left(\dfrac{a}{b} + \dfrac{c}{d}\right) < \dfrac{c}{d}$

★21. If the same positive number is added to the numerator and denominator of a positive proper fraction, is the new fraction greater than, less than, or equal to the original fraction? Justify your answer.

Review Problems

22. Write each of the following in simplest form.
    (a) $3\dfrac{5}{8}$ (b) $3\dfrac{5}{8} \div 2\dfrac{5}{6}$
    (c) $\dfrac{^-5}{12} \div \dfrac{^-12}{5}$ (d) $\dfrac{(x - y)^2}{x^2 - y^2} \cdot \dfrac{x + y}{x - y}$

23. The distance from Albertson to Florance is $28\frac{3}{4}$ miles. Roberto walks at the rate of $4\frac{1}{2}$ miles per hour. How long will it take him to walk from Albertson to Florance?

24. Solve each of the following for x and write your answer in simplest form.
    (a) $\dfrac{^-3}{4}x = 1$ (b) $^-x - \dfrac{3}{4} = \dfrac{5}{8}$
    (c) $\dfrac{3}{4}x = \dfrac{^-2}{3}x + 2$ (d) $\dfrac{3}{4}\left(1 - \dfrac{2}{3}x\right) = \dfrac{^-3}{4}x$

25. A team practiced three times a week for 5 weeks. Each practice lasted $1\frac{3}{4}$ hours. How many hours did the team practice in the 5 weeks?

26. Estimate the following by finding two integers such that the answers are between the integers.
    (a) $\dfrac{8}{9} + 1\dfrac{19}{20} + \dfrac{14}{13}$ (b) $\dfrac{7}{15} \cdot \left(16\dfrac{2}{9} - 6\dfrac{1}{10}\right)$

Section 6-5   Ratio and Proportion

One common use of fractions is as ratios. For example, there may be a two-to-three ratio of Democrats to Republicans on a certain legislative committee, a friend may be given a speeding ticket for driving 63 miles per hour, or *ratio* eggs may cost 98¢ per dozen. Each of these illustrates a **ratio**. A 1-to-2 ratio of males to females means that the number of males is $\frac{1}{2}$ the number of females, or that there is 1 male for every 2 females. The ratio 1 to 2 can be written as $\frac{1}{2}$ or 1:2. In general, a ratio is denoted by $\dfrac{a}{b}$ or $a:b$, where $b \neq 0$.

EXAMPLE 6-29   There were 7 males and 12 females in the Dew Drop Inn on Monday evening. In the Game Room, next door, there were 14 males and 24 females.

(a) Express the number of males to females at the Inn as a ratio.
(b) Express the number of males to females at the Game Room as a ratio.

SOLUTION   (a) The ratio is $\frac{7}{12}$.   (b) The ratio is $\frac{14}{24}$.

proportional
proportion

In Example 6-29 the ratios $\frac{7}{12}$ and $\frac{14}{24}$ are equal and proportional to each other. In general, two ratios are **proportional** if and only if the fractions representing them are equal. Two equal ratios form a **proportion.** We know that, for rational numbers, $\frac{a}{b} = \frac{c}{d}$ if and only if $ad = bc$. Thus, $\frac{a}{b} = \frac{c}{d}$ is a proportion if and only if $ad = bc$. For example, $\frac{14}{24} = \frac{7}{12}$ is a proportion, because $14 \cdot 12 = 24 \cdot 7$.

Frequently, one term in a proportion is missing, as in

$$\frac{3}{8} = \frac{x}{16}$$

We know that this equation is a proportion if and only if

$$3 \cdot 16 = 8 \cdot x$$
$$48 = 8 \cdot x$$
$$6 = x$$

Another way to solve the equation is to multiply both sides by 16, as follows.

$$\frac{3}{8} \cdot 16 = \frac{x}{16} \cdot 16$$
$$3 \cdot 2 = x$$
$$x = 6$$

It is important to remember that, in the ratio $a \div b$, a and b do not have to be integers. For example, if in Eugene, Oregon, $\frac{7}{10}$ of the population exercises regularly, then $\frac{3}{10}$ of the population does not exercise regularly, and the ratio of those who do exercise regularly to those who do not is $\frac{7}{10} \div \frac{3}{10}$, or $\frac{7}{3}$.

The following are examples of problems utilizing ratio and proportion.

EXAMPLE 6-30 If there should be 3 calculators for every 4 students in an elementary school class, how many calculators are needed for 44 students?

SOLUTION Set up a table (Table 6-6).
TABLE 6-6

Number of calculators	3	x
Number of students	4	44

The ratio of calculators to students should always be the same.

$$\frac{3}{4} = \frac{x}{44}$$
$$3 \cdot 44 = 4 \cdot x$$
$$132 = 4x$$
$$33 = x$$

Thus, 33 calculators are needed.

EXAMPLE 6-31   Kai, Paulus, and Judy made $2520 for painting a house. Kai worked 30 hours, Paulus worked 50 hours, and Judy worked 60 hours. They divided the money in proportion to the number of hours worked. How much did each earn?

SOLUTION   The ratio of hours worked is 30:50:60, or 3:5:6. If we denote the amount of money that Kai received by $3x$, then the amount of money that Paulus received must be $5x$, because then and only then will the ratios of the amounts $3x:5x$ be the same as 3:5, as required. Similarly, Judy received $6x$. Because the total amount of money received is $3x + 5x + 6x$, we have

$$3x + 5x + 6x = 2520$$
$$14x = 2520$$
$$x = 180$$

Hence

Kai received $3x = 3 \cdot 180$, or $540
Paulus received $5x = 5 \cdot 180$, or $900
Judy received $6x = 6 \cdot 180$, or $1080

To verify that the answers are correct, we find that

$$540 + 900 + 1080 = 2520$$

and that $540:900:1080$ is equivalent to $\frac{540}{180}:\frac{900}{180}:\frac{1080}{180}$, or 3:5:6.

Properties of Proportions

Consider the proportion $\frac{15}{30} = \frac{3}{6}$. Because the ratios in the proportion are equal fractions and because equal nonzero fractions have equal reciprocals, it follows that $\frac{30}{15} = \frac{6}{3}$.

● **THEOREM 6-7**

For any rational numbers $\frac{a}{b}$ and $\frac{c}{d}$, with $a \neq 0$ and $c \neq 0$, $\frac{a}{b} = \frac{c}{d}$ if and only if $\frac{b}{a} = \frac{d}{c}$.

Suppose that Jaffa oranges sell at 7 for $1 in one store and 21 for $3 in another. Which store has a better buy? We see that the price of one orange is $1/7 in the first store and $3/21 in the second. Because $\frac{1}{7} = \frac{3}{21}$, each store charges the same price per orange. Another way to see this is to observe that if 7 oranges cost $1, then 3 times that many oranges should cost 3 times that much. Using ratios, we see that the ratio of the numbers of oranges is the same as the ratio of the prices; that is, $\frac{7}{21} = \frac{1}{3}$. This is true in general and is summarized in the following theorem, whose proof is left as an exercise.

● T H E O R E M   6-8

For any rational numbers $\frac{a}{b}$ and $\frac{c}{d}$, with $c \neq 0$, $\frac{a}{b} = \frac{c}{d}$ if and only if $\frac{a}{c} = \frac{b}{d}$.

● R E M A R K

In the preceding theorem, it was not necessary to stipulate that $b \neq 0$ and $d \neq 0$, since these are inherent in the definition of rational numbers.

It is important to notice units of measure when working with proportions. For example, if a turtle travels 5 inches every 10 seconds, how many feet does it travel in 50 seconds? If units of measure are ignored, the following proportion might be set up.

$$\frac{5 \text{ inches}}{10 \text{ seconds}} = \frac{x \text{ feet}}{50 \text{ seconds}}$$

This statement is incorrect. A correct statement must involve the same units in each ratio. We may write the following:

$$\frac{5 \text{ inches}}{10 \text{ seconds}} = \frac{x \text{ inches}}{50 \text{ seconds}}$$

This implies that $x = 25$ inches. Consequently, since 12 inches = 1 foot, the turtle travels $\frac{25}{12}$ feet, or $2\frac{1}{12}$ feet.

Sometimes a proportion is not immediately apparent, as can be seen in the following problem.

PROBLEM 4

In the Klysler auto factory, robots assemble cars. If 3 robots can assemble 17 cars in 10 minutes, how many cars can 14 robots assemble in 45 minutes if all robots work at the same rate all the time?

Understanding the Problem.   Knowing that the robots work at the same rate, we are to determine the number of cars that 14 robots can assemble in 45 minutes given that 3 robots can assemble 17 cars in 10 minutes. If we knew how many cars one robot could assemble in 45 minutes or how many cars one robot could assemble in 1 minute, we could solve the problem.

Devising a Plan. Let x be the number of cars that 14 robots assemble in 45 minutes. Because the robots work at the same rate, we can express this rate by taking the information that 3 robots assemble 17 cars in 10 minutes and equating it with the information that 14 robots assemble x cars in 45 minutes. The rate would be the number of cars (or parts of a car) that 1 robot can assemble in 1 minute. Thus, we first need to find the number of cars that 1 robot can assemble in 1 minute. Then, we need to write and solve the desired equation to solve the problem.

Carrying Out the Plan. If 3 robots assemble 17 cars in 10 minutes, then the 3 robots assemble $\frac{17}{10}$ cars in 1 minute. Consequently, 1 robot assembles $\frac{1}{3} \cdot \frac{17}{10}$, or $\frac{17}{30}$, of a car in 1 minute. Similarly, if 14 robots assemble x cars in 45 minutes, then the 14 robots assemble $\dfrac{x}{45}$ cars in 1 minute. Thus, 1 robot assembles $\dfrac{1}{14} \cdot \dfrac{x}{45}$, or $\dfrac{x}{14 \cdot 45}$, of a car in 1 minute. Because the rates are equal, we have the proportion $\dfrac{x}{14 \cdot 45} = \dfrac{17}{30}$. Solving this equation, we obtain $x = 357$, or 357 cars.

Looking Back. The problem can be solved without writing any equations, as follows. Because 1 robot assembles $\frac{17}{30}$ of a car in 1 minute, 14 robots assemble $14 \cdot \frac{17}{30}$ cars in 1 minute. Thus, in 45 minutes, 14 robots assemble $45 \cdot 14 \cdot \frac{17}{30}$, or 357, cars.

The problem can be varied by changing the data or by considering two kinds of robots, each kind working at a different rate. Similar problems can be constructed concerning other jobs such as painting houses or washing cars.

PROBLEM SET 6-5

1. If there are 18 poodles and 12 cocker spaniels in a dog show, what is the ratio of poodles to cockers?

2. If a 4-ounce can of pepper costs 98¢, what is the cost per ounce?

3. Solve for x in each proportion.

    (a) $\dfrac{12}{x} = \dfrac{18}{45}$ (b) $\dfrac{x}{7} = \dfrac{^-10}{21}$

    (c) $\dfrac{5}{7} = \dfrac{3x}{98}$ (d) $3\frac{1}{2}$ is to 5 as x is to 15.

4. If a new car is 8 feet long and $4\frac{1}{2}$ feet high, what is the ratio of length to height?

5. There are five adult drivers to each teenage driver in Aluossim. If there are 12,345 adult drivers in Aluossim, how many teenage drivers are there?

6. If 3 grapefruits sell for 79¢, how much do 18 grapefruits cost?

7. On a map, $\frac{1}{3}$ inch represents 5 miles. If New York and Aluossim are 18 inches apart on the map, what is the actual distance between them?

8. David read 40 pages of a book in 50 minutes. How many pages should he be able to read in 80 minutes if he reads at a constant rate?

9. A candle is 30 inches long. After burning for 12 minutes, the candle is 25 inches long. How long would the whole candle burn?

10. Two numbers are in the ratio 3:4. Find the numbers if:
    (a) Their sum is 98.   (b) Their product is 768.

11. A rectangular yard has width-to-length ratio of 5:9. If the distance around the yard is 2800 feet, what are the dimensions of the yard?

12. Gary, Bill, and Carmella invested in a corporation in the ratio of 2:4:5. If they divide the profit of $82,000 proportionally to their investment, how much will each receive?

13. Sheila and Dora worked $3\frac{1}{2}$ hours and $4\frac{1}{2}$ hours, respectively, on a programming project. They were paid $176 for the project. How much did each earn?

14. Vonna scored 75 goals in her soccer practice. If her success-to-failure rate is 5 to 4, how many times did she attempt a goal?

15. Three painters can paint 4 houses in 5 days. How long would it take 7 painters to paint 18 houses if all work was done at the same rate all the time?

16. Suppose that a 10-inch pizza costs $4. To find the price x of a 14-inch pizza, is it correct to set up the proportion $\frac{x}{4} = \frac{14}{10}$? Why or why not?

17. (a) If the ratio of boys to girls in a class is 2:3, what is the ratio of boys to all the students in the class? Why?
    (b) If the ratio of boys to girls in a class is $m:n$, what is the ratio of boys to all the students in the class?

★18. If Sherwin can paint the house in 2 days working by himself and William can paint the house in 4 days working by himself, how many days should it take Sherwin and William working together?

★19. If Mary and Carter can paint a house in 5 hours and Mary alone can do the same job in 8 hours, how long would it take Carter working alone?

★20. Prove: For any rational numbers $\frac{a}{b}$ and $\frac{c}{d}$, if $\frac{a}{b} = \frac{c}{d}$, where $a \neq 0$ and $c \neq 0$, then $\frac{b}{a} = \frac{d}{c}$.

★21 Prove that the product of two proper fractions greater than 0 is less than either of the fractions.

22. (a) In Room A of the University Center there are one man and two women; in Room B there are two men and four women; and in Room C there are five men and ten women. If all the people in Rooms B and C go to Room A, what will be the ratio of men to women in Room A?
    ★(b) Prove the following generalization of the proportions used in (a).

$$\text{If } \frac{a}{b} = \frac{c}{d} = \frac{e}{f}, \text{ then } \frac{a}{b} = \frac{c}{d} = \frac{e}{f} = \frac{a+c+e}{b+d+f}.$$

★23. Prove that, if $\frac{a}{b} = \frac{c}{d}$, then
    (a) $\frac{a+b}{b} = \frac{c+d}{d}$ $\left(Hint: \frac{a}{b} + 1 = \frac{c}{d} + 1\right)$
    (b) $\frac{a}{a+b} = \frac{c}{c+d}$
    (c) $\frac{a-b}{a+b} = \frac{c-d}{c+d}$

★24. Tom can beat Dick by $\frac{1}{10}$ mile in a 5-mile race. Dick can beat Harry by $\frac{1}{5}$ mile in a 5-mile race. By how far can Tom beat Harry in a 5-mile race?

Review Problems

25. Arrange each of the following in increasing order.
    (a) $\frac{-2}{5}, \frac{-3}{5}, 0, \frac{1}{5}, \frac{2}{5}$ (b) $\frac{7}{12}, \frac{13}{18}, \frac{13}{24}$

26. Find the solution sets for each of the following.
    (a) $\frac{3}{4}x - \frac{5}{8} \geq \frac{1}{2}$ (b) $\frac{-x}{5} + \frac{1}{10} < \frac{-1}{2}$
    (c) $\frac{-2}{5}(10x + 1) < 1 - x$
    (d) $\frac{2}{3}\left(\frac{1}{2}x - 7\right) \geq \frac{3}{4}x$

27. For each of the following, find three rational numbers between the given fractions.
    (a) $\frac{1}{3}$ and $\frac{2}{3}$ (b) $\frac{-5}{12}$ and $\frac{-1}{18}$

B R A I N   T E A S E R

Janna walks from her home to a friend's house at the same speed every day. One day, without stopping, she walked to her friend's house and back to her own house and then another $\frac{3}{8}$ mile. She found that this took her exactly the same time as it took on another day to walk from her house to the friend's house and then another $\frac{5}{12}$ mile. What is the distance between the houses?

Section 6-6 Exponents Revisited

Recall that, for whole numbers a, m, and n, with $a \neq 0$, the following properties hold.

1. $a^m = \underbrace{a \cdot a \cdot a \cdots a}_{m \text{ factors}}$

2. $a^m \cdot a^n = a^{m+n}$
3. $a^0 = 1$, where $a \neq 0$

Property 3 follows from property 2, if we assume that property 2 holds for $m = 0$. If $m = 0$, then $a^m \cdot a^n = a^{m+n}$ becomes $a^0 \cdot a^n = a^{0+n} = a^n$; and 1 is the only number that, on multiplying by a^n, gives a^n. The above notions can be extended for rational-number values of a. For example, consider the following.

$$\left(\frac{2}{3}\right)^4 = \frac{2}{3} \cdot \frac{2}{3} \cdot \frac{2}{3} \cdot \frac{2}{3}$$

$$\left(\frac{2}{3}\right)^2 \cdot \left(\frac{2}{3}\right)^3 = \left(\frac{2}{3} \cdot \frac{2}{3}\right) \cdot \left(\frac{2}{3} \cdot \frac{2}{3} \cdot \frac{2}{3}\right) = \left(\frac{2}{3}\right)^{2+3} = \left(\frac{2}{3}\right)^5$$

Also, $\left(\frac{2}{3}\right)^0 = 1$, and in general, for any nonzero rational number, we have $\left(\frac{a}{b}\right)^0 = 1$.

Exponents can also be extended to negative integers. Notice that as the exponents decrease by 1, the numbers on the right are divided by 10. Thus, the pattern might be continued.

$10^3 = 10 \cdot 10 \cdot 10$
$10^2 = 10 \cdot 10$
$10^1 = 10$
$10^0 = 1$

$$10^{-1} = \frac{1}{10} = \frac{1}{10^1}$$

$$10^{-2} = \frac{1}{10} \cdot \frac{1}{10} = \frac{1}{10^2}$$

$$10^{-3} = \frac{1}{10^2} \cdot \frac{1}{10} = \frac{1}{10^3}$$

If the pattern is extended, then we would predict that $10^{-n} = \dfrac{1}{10^n}$. This is true; and in general, for any nonzero number a, $a^{-n} = \dfrac{1}{a^n}$.

• **R E M A R K**
Another explanation for the definition of a^{-n} is as follows. If the property $a^m \cdot a^n = a^{m+n}$ is to hold for all integer exponents, then $a^{-n} \cdot a^n = a^{-n+n} = a^0 = 1$. Thus, a^{-n} is the multiplicative inverse of a^n, and consequently, $a^{-n} = \dfrac{1}{a^n}$.

Consider whether the property $a^m \cdot a^n = a^{m+n}$ can be extended to include all powers of a, where the exponents are integers. For example, is it true that $2^4 \cdot 2^{-3} = 2^{4 + \, -3} = 2^1$? The definitions of 2^{-3} and the properties of nonnegative exponents ensure that this is true, as shown next.

$$2^4 \cdot 2^{-3} = 2^4 \cdot \frac{1}{2^3} = \frac{2^4}{2^3} = \frac{2^1 \cdot 2^3}{2^3} = 2^1$$

Also, $2^{-4} \cdot 2^{-3} = 2^{-4 + \, -3} = 2^{-7}$ is true, because

$$2^{-4} \cdot 2^{-3} = \frac{1}{2^4} \cdot \frac{1}{2^3} = \frac{1 \cdot 1}{2^4 \cdot 2^3} = \frac{1}{2^{4+3}} = \frac{1}{2^7} = 2^{-7}$$

In general, with integer exponents, the following property holds.

• **P R O P E R T Y**
For any nonzero rational number a and any integers m and n, $a^m \cdot a^n = a^{m+n}$

Other properties of exponents can be developed by using the properties of rational numbers. For example,

$$\frac{2^5}{2^3} = \frac{2^3 \cdot 2^2}{2^3} = 2^2 = 2^{5-3} \qquad \frac{2^5}{2^8} = \frac{2^5}{2^5 \cdot 2^3} = \frac{1}{2^3} = 2^{-3} = 2^{5-8}$$

In general with integer exponents, the following property holds.

• **P R O P E R T Y**
For any rational number a such that $a \neq 0$ and for any integers m and n, $\dfrac{a^m}{a^n} = a^{m-n}$.

Suppose that a is a nonzero rational number and m and n are positive integers.

$$(a^m)^n = \underbrace{a^m \cdot a^m \cdot a^m \cdots a^m}_{n \text{ factors}} = a^{\overbrace{m+m+\cdots+m}^{n \text{ terms}}} = a^{nm} = a^{mn}$$

Thus, $(a^m)^n = a^{mn}$. For example, $(2^3)^4 = 2^{3\cdot 4} = 2^{12}$.

Does this property hold for negative-integer exponents? For example, does $(2^3)^{-4} = 2^{(3)(-4)} = 2^{-12}$? The answer is yes, because $(2^3)^{-4} = \dfrac{1}{(2^3)^4} = \dfrac{1}{2^{12}} = 2^{-12}$. Also, $(2^{-3})^4 = \left(\dfrac{1}{2^3}\right)^4 = \dfrac{1}{2^3} \cdot \dfrac{1}{2^3} \cdot \dfrac{1}{2^3} \cdot \dfrac{1}{2^3} = \dfrac{1^4}{(2^3)^4} = \dfrac{1}{2^{12}} = 2^{-12}$.

• **P R O P E R T Y**

For any rational number $a \neq 0$ and any integers m and n, $(a^m)^n = a^{mn}$.

Using the definitions and properties developed, we can derive additional properties. Notice, for example, that

$$\left(\frac{2}{3}\right)^4 = \frac{2}{3} \cdot \frac{2}{3} \cdot \frac{2}{3} \cdot \frac{2}{3} = \frac{2 \cdot 2 \cdot 2 \cdot 2}{3 \cdot 3 \cdot 3 \cdot 3} = \frac{2^4}{3^4}$$

This can be generalized as follows.

• **P R O P E R T Y**

For any nonzero rational number $\dfrac{a}{b}$ and any integer m,

$$\left(\frac{a}{b}\right)^m = \frac{a^m}{b^m}$$

Note that, from the definition of negative exponents, the above property, and division of fractions, we have

$$\left(\frac{a}{b}\right)^{-m} = \frac{1}{\left(\dfrac{a}{b}\right)^m} = \frac{1}{\dfrac{a^m}{b^m}} = \frac{b^m}{a^m} = \left(\frac{b}{a}\right)^m$$

Consequently, $\left(\dfrac{a}{b}\right)^{-m} = \left(\dfrac{b}{a}\right)^m$.

A property similar to this holds for multiplication. For example,

$$(2 \cdot 3)^{-3} = \frac{1}{(2 \cdot 3)^3} = \frac{1}{2^3 \cdot 3^3} = \left(\frac{1}{2^3}\right) \cdot \left(\frac{1}{3^3}\right) = 2^{-3} \cdot 3^{-3}$$

and in general, it is true that $(a \cdot b)^m = a^m \cdot b^m$ if a and b are rational numbers and m is an integer.

The definitions and properties of exponents are summarized in the following list.

● **P R O P E R T I E S**
Properties of Exponents

1. $a^m = \underbrace{a \cdot a \cdot a \cdots a,}_{m \text{ factors}}$ where m is a positive integer

2. $a^0 = 1$, where $a \neq 0$

3. $a^{-m} = \dfrac{1}{a^m}$, where $a \neq 0$

4. $a^m \cdot a^n = a^{m+n}$

5. $\dfrac{a^m}{a^n} = a^{m-n}$, where $a \neq 0$

6. $(a^m)^n = a^{mn}$

7. $\left(\dfrac{a}{b}\right)^m = \dfrac{a^m}{b^m}$, where $b \neq 0$

8. $(ab)^m = a^m \cdot b^m$

9. $\left(\dfrac{a}{b}\right)^{-m} = \left(\dfrac{b}{a}\right)^m$

Observe that all the properties of exponents refer to powers with either the same base or the same exponent. Hence, to evaluate expressions using exponents where different bases or powers are used, perform all the computations or rewrite the expressions in either the same base or the same exponent if possible. For example, $\dfrac{27^4}{81^3}$ can be rewritten as $\dfrac{27^4}{81^3} = \dfrac{(3^3)^4}{(3^4)^3} = \dfrac{3^{12}}{3^{12}} = 1$.

EXAMPLE 6-32   Write each of the following in simplest form, using positive exponents in the final answer.

(a) $16^2 \cdot 8^{-3}$
(b) $20^2 \div 2^4$
(c) $(3x)^3 + 2y^2x^0 + 5y^2 + x^2 \cdot x$, where $x \neq 0$
(d) $(a^{-3} + b^{-3})^{-1}$

SOLUTION   (a) $16^2 \cdot 8^{-3} = (2^4)^2 \cdot (2^3)^{-3} = 2^8 \cdot 2^{-9} = 2^{8+-9} = 2^{-1} = \dfrac{1}{2}$

(b) $\dfrac{20^2}{2^4} = \dfrac{(2^2 \cdot 5)^2}{2^4} = \dfrac{2^4 \cdot 5^2}{2^4} = 5^2$

(c) $(3x)^3 + 2y^2x^0 + 5y^2 + x^2 \cdot x = 27x^3 + 2y^2 \cdot 1 + 5y^2 + x^3$
$$= (27x^3 + x^3) + (2y^2 + 5y^2)$$
$$= 28x^3 + 7y^2$$

(d) $(a^{-3} + b^{-3})^{-1} = \left(\dfrac{1}{a^3} + \dfrac{1}{b^3}\right)^{-1} = \left(\dfrac{b^3 + a^3}{a^3b^3}\right)^{-1} = \dfrac{1}{\dfrac{a^3 + b^3}{a^3b^3}} = \dfrac{a^3b^3}{a^3 + b^3}$

PROBLEM SET 6-6

1. Write each of the following in simplest form, with positive exponents in the final answer.
   (a) $3^{-7} \cdot 3^{-6}$ (b) $3^7 \cdot 3^6$
   (c) $5^{15} \div 5^4$ (d) $5^{15} \div 5^{-4}$
   (e) $(-5)^{-2}$ (f) $\dfrac{a^2}{a^{-3}}$, where $a \neq 0$
   (g) $\dfrac{a}{a^{-1}}$, where $a \neq 0$ (h) $\dfrac{a^{-3}}{a^{-2}}$, where $a \neq 0$

2. Write each of the following in simplest form, using positive exponents in the final answer.
   (a) $\left(\dfrac{1}{2}\right)^3 \cdot \left(\dfrac{1}{2}\right)^7$ (b) $\left(\dfrac{1}{2}\right)^9 \div \left(\dfrac{1}{2}\right)^6$
   (c) $\left(\dfrac{2}{3}\right)^5 \cdot \left(\dfrac{4}{9}\right)^2$ (d) $\left(\dfrac{3}{5}\right)^7 \div \left(\dfrac{3}{5}\right)^7$
   (e) $\left(\dfrac{3}{5}\right)^{-7} \div \left(\dfrac{5}{3}\right)^4$ (f) $\left[\left(\dfrac{5}{6}\right)^7\right]^3$

3. If a and b are rational numbers, with $a \neq 0$ and $b \neq 0$, and if m and n are integers, which of the following are true and which are false? Justify your answer.
   (a) $a^m \cdot b^n = (ab)^{m+n}$ (b) $a^m \cdot b^n = (ab)^{mn}$
   (c) $a^m \cdot b^m = (ab)^{2m}$ (d) $a^0 = 0$
   (e) $(a + b)^m = a^m + b^m$ (f) $(a + b)^{-m} = \dfrac{1}{a^m} + \dfrac{1}{b^m}$
   (g) $a^{mn} = a^m \cdot a^n$ (h) $\left(\dfrac{a}{b}\right)^{-1} = \dfrac{b}{a}$

4. Solve for the integer n in each of the following.
   (a) $2^n = 32$ (b) $n^2 = 36$
   (c) $2^n \cdot 2^7 = 2^5$ (d) $2^n \cdot 2^7 = 8^-$
   (e) $(2 + n)^2 = 2^2 + n^2$ (f) $3^n = 27^5$

5. A human has approximately 25 trillion ($25 \cdot 10^{12}$) red blood cells, each with an average radius of $4 \cdot 10^{-3}$ mm (millimeters). If these cells were placed end to end in a line, how long would the line be, in millimeters? If 1 km is 10^6 mm, how long would the line be, in kilometers?

6. Solve each of the following inequalities for x, where x is an integer.
   (a) $3^x \leq 81$ (b) $4^x < 8$
   (c) $3^{2x} > 27$ (d) $2^x > 1$

7. Rewrite the following expressions, using positive exponents and expressing all fractions in simplest form.
   (a) $x^{-1} - x$ (b) $x^2 - y^{-2}$
   (c) $2x^2 + (2x)^2 + 2^2x$ (d) $y^{-3} + y^3$
   (e) $\dfrac{3a - b}{(3a - b)^{-1}}$ (f) $\dfrac{a^{-1}}{a^{-1} + b^{-1}}$

8. Which of the fractions in each pair is greater?
   (a) $\left(\dfrac{1}{2}\right)^3$ or $\left(\dfrac{1}{2}\right)^4$ (b) $\left(\dfrac{3}{4}\right)^{10}$ or $\left(\dfrac{3}{4}\right)^8$
   (c) $\left(\dfrac{4}{3}\right)^{10}$ or $\left(\dfrac{4}{3}\right)^8$ (d) $\left(\dfrac{3}{4}\right)^{10}$ or $\left(\dfrac{4}{5}\right)^{10}$
   (e) $\left(\dfrac{4}{3}\right)^{10}$ or $\left(\dfrac{5}{4}\right)^{10}$ (f) $\left(\dfrac{3}{4}\right)^{100}$ or $\left(\dfrac{3}{4} \cdot \dfrac{9}{10}\right)^{100}$

9. Suppose that the amount of bacteria in a certain culture is given as a function of time by $Q(t) = 10^{10}(\frac{6}{5})^t$, where t is the time in seconds and $Q(t)$ is the amount of bacteria after t seconds. Find the following.
   (a) The initial number of bacteria—that is, the number of bacteria at $t = 0$.
   (b) The number of bacteria after 2 seconds.

10. If the nth term of a sequence is given by $a_n = 3 \cdot 2^{-n}$, answer the following.
    Find the first 5 terms.
    Show that the first 5 terms are in a geometric sequence.
    (c) Find the first term that is less than $\frac{3}{1000}$.

11. If $f(n) = \frac{3}{4} \cdot 2^n$, find the following
    (a) $f(0)$ (b) $f(5)$ (c) $f(^-5)$
    (d) The greatest integer value of n for which
    $f(n) < \frac{3}{400}$

📱 12. (a) Which number is greater, 4^{300} or 3^{400}?
    (b) Justify your answer to part (a).
    (c) What happens when you try to evaluate these numbers on a calculator using the $\boxed{y^x}$ key?

13. Which number is greater?
    (a) 32^{50} or 4^{100}
    (b) $(^-27)^{-15}$ or $(^-3)^{-75}$

Review Problems

14. If a machine produces 6 items every 5 seconds, how many items can the machine produce in 3 minutes?

15. If 3 out of every 80 items are defective, how many defective items are there among 720 items?

16. Find the simplest form for each of the following.
    (a) $\dfrac{24}{84}$ (b) $\dfrac{12 \cdot 180}{18 \cdot 9}$ (c) $\dfrac{8^4}{24^4}$

    (d) $\dfrac{13 \cdot 4}{40 \cdot 130}$ (e) $\dfrac{4}{3} \cdot \dfrac{27}{16}$ (f) $\dfrac{10^4 \cdot 7^8}{10^6 \cdot 7^6}$

    (g) $\dfrac{3}{4} \div \dfrac{4}{3}$ (h) $\dfrac{x^3}{x^3 + x^2 y}$

17. Solve for x in each of the following.
    (a) $\dfrac{^-3}{4} x = 1$ (b) $\dfrac{2}{3} x = \dfrac{^-3}{5}$

    (c) $\dfrac{1}{3} x - 5 = \dfrac{^-3}{4} x$ (d) $\dfrac{x}{3} = \dfrac{^-3}{4}$

    (e) $\dfrac{x}{3} = \dfrac{27}{x}$ (f) $\dfrac{x+1}{3} = \dfrac{3}{4} x$

18. If Rachel can paint $\frac{5}{8}$ of a house in 1 day, how long will it take her to paint the whole house?

19. If the ratio of boys to girls in a class is 3 to 8, will the ratio of boys to girls change, become greater, or become lesser if 2 new boys and 2 new girls join the class? Justify your answer.

20. Arrange the following in increasing order:
    $\frac{^-2}{3}, \frac{^-3}{4}, \frac{^-6}{7}, \frac{^-1}{2}, 0, \frac{4}{5}, \frac{6}{7}, \frac{7}{9}, \frac{9}{7}$.

SOLUTION TO THE PRELIMINARY PROBLEM

Understanding the Problem. Julia had two candles, one of which was $1\frac{1}{2}$ inches shorter than the other. The taller candle was lit at 7 P.M and went out at midnight; the shorter candle was lit at 8:30 P.M. and went out at 11:30 P.M. At 10:30 P.M., both candles were of equal height. We are supposed to find the initial height of each candle. We know that the longer candle burned from 7 P.M. to midnight—that is, for 5 hours—and the shorter from 8:30 P.M. to 11:30 P.M.—that is, for 3 hours.

Devising a Plan. If we let x be the height in inches of the longer candle, then $x - 1\frac{1}{2}$ is the height of the shorter candle. We know that at 10:30 P.M. the candles were of equal height. If we could express the height of each candle at 10:30 P.M. in terms of x, we would have an equation. Solving the equation for x, we could then find x and $x - 1\frac{1}{2}$. At 10:30 P.M. the longer candle had burned for $3\frac{1}{2}$ hours, whereas the shorter had burned for 2 hours. To find the height of each candle in terms of x, it would be sufficient to know how many inches per hour each candle burns. The first candle burns x inches in 5 hours; thus, it burns $x/5$ inches per hour. Similarly, the second candle burns $\dfrac{x - 1\frac{1}{2}}{3}$ inches per hour. Thus, at 10:30 the longer candle had burned $3\frac{1}{2} \cdot \dfrac{x}{5}$ inches and was, therefore, $x - 3\frac{1}{2} \cdot \dfrac{x}{5}$ inches tall. Meanwhile, the shorter candle had burned $2\left(\dfrac{x - 1\frac{1}{2}}{3}\right)$ inches and therefore was

$(x - 1\frac{1}{2}) - 2\left(\dfrac{x - 1\frac{1}{2}}{3}\right)$ inches tall. Since the candles were the same height at 10:30, we have the following equation.

$$x - 3\frac{1}{2} \cdot \frac{x}{5} = (x - 1\frac{1}{2}) - 2\left(\frac{x - 1\frac{1}{2}}{3}\right)$$

Carrying Out the Plan. The equation obtained is equivalent to each of the following.

$$x - 3\frac{1}{2} \cdot \frac{x}{5} = \left(x - 1\frac{1}{2}\right) - 2\left(\frac{x - 1\frac{1}{2}}{3}\right)$$

$$1 \cdot x - \frac{7}{2} \cdot \frac{x}{5} = 1 \cdot \left(x - \frac{3}{2}\right) - \frac{2}{3}\left(x - \frac{3}{2}\right)$$

$$\left(1 - \frac{7}{2} \cdot \frac{1}{5}\right)x = \left(1 - \frac{2}{3}\right)\left(x - \frac{3}{2}\right)$$

$$\frac{3}{10}x = \frac{1}{3}\left(x - \frac{3}{2}\right)$$

$$\frac{3}{10}x = \frac{1}{3}x - \frac{1}{2}$$

$$\frac{1}{2} = \frac{1}{3}x - \frac{3}{10}x$$

$$\frac{1}{2} = \frac{1}{30}x$$

$$15 = x$$

Thus, the longer candle was 15 inches long, and the shorter one was $15 - 1\frac{1}{2}$, or $13\frac{1}{2}$, inches long.

Looking Back. We can check whether our solution is correct. Because $x = 15$, the longer candle burns at the rate of $\frac{15}{5}$, or 3, inches per hour. The shorter candle burns at the rate $\dfrac{13\frac{1}{2}}{3}$, or $4\frac{1}{2}$, inches per hour. At 10:30 the longer candle had burned $3\frac{1}{2} \cdot 3$, or $10\frac{1}{2}$, inches and therefore was $15 - 10\frac{1}{2}$, or $4\frac{1}{2}$, inches tall. At 10:30, the shorter candle had burned $2 \cdot 4\frac{1}{2}$, or 9, inches and hence was $13\frac{1}{2} - 9$, or $4\frac{1}{2}$, inches tall. Because each candle was $4\frac{1}{2}$ inches tall at 10:30, our solution implies that the candles had the same height. Consequently, our solution is correct. The problem can be varied by giving the heights of the candles and the times when they were lit and went out and asking for the time when the heights were the same. We could also ask whether at any time one candle was twice as tall as the other.

QUESTIONS FROM THE CLASSROOM

1. A student wrote the solution set to the equation $\frac{x}{7} - 2 < {}^{-}3$ as $\{{}^{-}8, {}^{-}9, {}^{-}10, {}^{-}11, \ldots\}$. Is the student correct?

2. A student simplified the fraction $\frac{m + n}{p + n}$ to $\frac{m}{p}$. Is that student correct?

3. Without thinking, one student argued that a pizza cut into 12 pieces was more than a pizza cut into 6 pieces. How would you respond?

4. When working on the problem of simplifying $\frac{3}{4} \cdot \frac{1}{2} \cdot \frac{2}{3}$, a student did the following.

$$\frac{3}{4} \cdot \frac{1}{2} \cdot \frac{2}{3} = \left(\frac{3 \cdot 1}{4 \cdot 2}\right)\left(\frac{3 \cdot 2}{4 \cdot 3}\right) = \frac{3}{8} \cdot \frac{6}{12} = \frac{18}{96}$$

What was the error?

5. A student asks, "If the ratio of boys to girls in the class is $\frac{2}{3}$ and 4 boys and 6 girls join the class, then the new ratio is $\frac{2 + 4}{3 + 6}$, or $\frac{6}{9}$. Since $\frac{2}{3} + \frac{4}{6} = \frac{2 + 4}{3 + 6}$, can all fractions be added in the same way?"

6. When the teacher asked the class to solve the equation $\frac{1}{4} + \frac{7}{4}(x + \frac{1}{5}) = x + \frac{6}{5}$, Nat wrote $(\frac{1}{4} + \frac{7}{4})(x + \frac{1}{5}) = x + \frac{6}{5}$, solved the equation, and got the answer $x = \frac{4}{5}$, which is the correct answer to the original equation. The teacher told Nat that he had obtained the correct answer by using an incorrect method. Nat in turn responded that his method will also work for the equation $\frac{3}{8} + \frac{1}{4}(x - 1) = x - \frac{11}{8}$ and for the equation $1 + \frac{1}{2}(x - \frac{1}{4}) = x + \frac{1}{4}$. How would you respond now if you were the teacher?

7. Is $\frac{0}{6}$ in simplest form? Why or why not?

8. A student says that taking one half of a number is the same as dividing the number by one half. Is this correct?

9. A student writes $\frac{15}{53} < \frac{1}{3}$ because $3 \cdot 15 < 53 \cdot 1$. Another student writes $\frac{18}{53} = \frac{1}{3}$. Where is the fallacy?

10. On a test, a student wrote the following.

$$\frac{x}{7} - 2 < {}^{-}3$$
$$\frac{x}{7} < {}^{-}1$$
$$x > {}^{-}7$$

What is the error?

11. A student claims that each of the following is an arithmetic sequence. Is the student right?
    (a) $\frac{1}{2}, \frac{2}{3}, \frac{3}{4}, \frac{4}{5}, \frac{5}{6}, \frac{6}{7}, \frac{7}{8}, \ldots$
    (b) $\frac{1}{2}, \left(\frac{1}{2}\right)^{-2}, \left(\frac{1}{2}\right)^{-5}, \left(\frac{1}{2}\right)^{-8}, \left(\frac{1}{2}\right)^{-11}, \ldots$

12. A student claims that she found a new way to obtain a fraction between two positive fractions: If $\frac{a}{b}$ and $\frac{c}{d}$ are two positive fractions, then $\frac{a + c}{b + d}$ is between these fractions. Is she right?

13. A student claims that, if $\frac{a}{b} = \frac{c}{d}$, then $\frac{a + c}{b + d} = \frac{a}{b} = \frac{c}{d}$. Is he right?

14. A student claims that $\frac{1}{x} < \frac{1}{y}$ if and only if $x > y$. Is this correct?

15. A student claims that if x is positive, then $\frac{1}{x} < x$. What is your response?

CHAPTER OUTLINE

I. Rational numbers

  A. Numbers of the form $\frac{a}{b}$, where a and b are integers and $b \neq 0$, are called **rational numbers.**

  B. A rational number can be used as:

1. A division problem or the solution to a multiplication problem.
2. A partition, or part, of a whole.
3. A ratio.
4. A probability.

C. **Fundamental Law of Fractions:** For any fractions $\dfrac{a}{b}$ and any number $c \neq 0$, $\dfrac{a}{b} = \dfrac{ac}{bc}$.

D. Two fractions $\dfrac{a}{b}$ and $\dfrac{c}{d}$ are **equal** if and only if $ad = bc$.

E. If $\text{GCD}(a, b) = 1$, then $\dfrac{a}{b}$ is said to be in **simplest form.**

F. If $0 < |a| < |b|$, then $\dfrac{a}{b}$ is called a **proper fraction.**

II. Operations on rational numbers

A. $\dfrac{a}{b} + \dfrac{c}{b} = \dfrac{a + c}{b}$

B. $\dfrac{a}{b} + \dfrac{c}{d} = \dfrac{ad + bc}{bd}$

C. $\dfrac{a}{b} - \dfrac{c}{d} = \dfrac{ad - bc}{bd}$

D. $\dfrac{a}{b} \cdot \dfrac{c}{d} = \dfrac{ac}{bd}$

E. $\dfrac{a}{b} \div \dfrac{c}{d} = \dfrac{a}{b} \cdot \dfrac{d}{c} = \dfrac{ad}{bc}$, where $c \neq 0$

III. Properties of rational numbers

A.

	Addition	Subtraction	Multiplication	Division
Closure	Yes	Yes	Yes	Yes, except for division by 0
Commutative	Yes	No	Yes	No
Associative	Yes	No	Yes	No
Identity	Yes	No	Yes	No
Inverse	Yes	No	Yes, except 0	No

B. **Distributive property of multiplication over addition** for rational numbers x, y, and z:

$$x(y + z) = xy + xz$$

C. **Denseness property:** Between any two rational numbers, there is another rational number.

IV. Ratio and proportion

A. A quotient $a \div b$ is a **ratio.**

B. A **proportion** is an equation of two ratios.

C. Properties of proportions

1. If $\dfrac{a}{b} = \dfrac{c}{d}$, then $\dfrac{b}{a} = \dfrac{d}{c}$, where $a \neq 0$ and $c \neq 0$.

2. If $\dfrac{a}{b} = \dfrac{c}{d}$, then $\dfrac{a}{c} = \dfrac{b}{d}$, where $c \neq 0$.

V. Exponents

A. $a^m = \underbrace{a \cdot a \cdot a \cdots a}_{m \text{ factors}}$, where m is a positive integer and a is a rational number.

B. Properties of exponents involving rational numbers

1. $a^0 = 1$, where $a \neq 0$

2. $a^{-m} = \dfrac{1}{a^m}$, where $a \neq 0$

3. $a^m \cdot a^n = a^{m+n}$

4. $\dfrac{a^m}{a^n} = a^{m-n}$, where $a \neq 0$

5. $(a^m)^n = a^{mn}$

6. $\left(\dfrac{a}{b}\right)^m = \dfrac{a^m}{b^m}$, where $b \neq 0$

7. $(ab)^m = a^m \cdot b^m$

8. $\left(\dfrac{a}{b}\right)^{-m} = \left(\dfrac{b}{a}\right)^m$

CHAPTER TEST

1. For each of the following, draw a diagram illustrating the fraction.

    (a) $\dfrac{3}{4}$ (b) $\dfrac{2}{3}$

2. Write three rational numbers equal to $\frac{5}{6}$.

3. Reduce each of the following rational numbers to simplest form.

    (a) $\dfrac{24}{28}$ (b) $\dfrac{ax^2}{bx}$ (c) $\dfrac{0}{17}$

    (d) $\dfrac{45}{81}$ (e) $\dfrac{b^2 + bx}{b + x}$ (f) $\dfrac{16}{216}$

4. Replace the comma with $>$, $<$, or $=$ in each of the following pairs to make a true statement.

    (a) $\dfrac{6}{10}, \dfrac{120}{200}$ (b) $\dfrac{-3}{4}, \dfrac{-5}{6}$

    (c) $\left(\dfrac{4}{5}\right)^{10}, \left(\dfrac{4}{5}\right)^{20}$ (d) $\left(1 + \dfrac{1}{3}\right)^2, \left(1 + \dfrac{1}{3}\right)^3$

5. Perform each of the following computations.

    (a) $\dfrac{5}{6} + \dfrac{4}{15}$ (b) $\dfrac{4}{25} - \dfrac{3}{35}$

    (c) $\dfrac{5}{6} \cdot \dfrac{12}{13}$ (d) $\dfrac{5}{6} \div \dfrac{12}{15}$

    (e) $\left(5\dfrac{1}{6} + 7\dfrac{1}{3}\right) \div 2\dfrac{1}{4}$ (f) $\left(-5\dfrac{1}{6} + 7\dfrac{1}{3}\right) \div \dfrac{-9}{4}$

6. Find the additive and multiplicative inverses for each of the following.

    (a) 3   (b) $3\dfrac{1}{7}$ (c) $\dfrac{5}{6}$ (d) $-\dfrac{3}{4}$

7. Order the following numbers from least to greatest.

    $-1\dfrac{7}{8}, \ 0, \ -2\dfrac{1}{3}, \ \dfrac{69}{140}, \ \dfrac{71}{140}, \ \left(\dfrac{71}{140}\right)^{300}, \ \dfrac{1}{2}, \ \left(\dfrac{74}{73}\right)^{300}$

8. Simplify each of the following. Write your answer in the form $\dfrac{a}{b}$, where a and b are integers and $b \neq 0$.

    (a) $\dfrac{\frac{1}{2} - \frac{3}{4}}{\frac{5}{6} - \frac{7}{8}}$ (b) $\dfrac{\frac{3}{4} \cdot \frac{5}{6}}{\frac{1}{2}}$ (c) $\dfrac{(\frac{1}{2})^2 - (\frac{3}{4})^2}{\frac{1}{2} + \frac{3}{4}}$

9. Solve each of the following for x, where x is a rational number.

    (a) $\dfrac{1}{4}x - \dfrac{3}{5} \leq \dfrac{1}{2}(3 - 2x)$

    (b) $\dfrac{x}{3} - \dfrac{x}{2} \geq \dfrac{-1}{4}$

    (c) $\dfrac{2}{3}\left(\dfrac{3}{4}x - 1\right) = \dfrac{2}{3} - x$

    (d) $\dfrac{5}{6} = \dfrac{4 - x}{3}$

10. Justify the invert-and-multiply algorithm for division of rational numbers.

11. If the ratio of boys to girls in Mr. Good's class is 3 to 5, the ratio of boys to girls in Ms. Garcia's is the same, and you know that there are 15 girls in Ms. Garcia's class, how many boys are in her class?

12. Write each of the following in simplest form, with nonnegative exponents in the final answer.

    (a) $\left(\dfrac{1}{2}\right)^4 \left(\dfrac{1}{2}\right)^7$ (b) $5^{-16} \div 5^4$

    (c) $\left[\left(\dfrac{2}{3}\right)^7\right]^{-4}$ (d) $3^{16} \cdot 3^2$

13. John has $54\frac{1}{4}$ yards of material. If he needs to cut the cloth into pieces that are $3\frac{1}{12}$ yards long, how many pieces can be cut? How much material will be left over?

14. Without actually performing the given operations, choose the most appropriate estimation (among the numbers in parentheses) for the given expression.

    (a) $\dfrac{30\frac{3}{8}}{4\frac{1}{9}} \cdot \dfrac{8\frac{1}{3}}{3\frac{8}{9}}$ (15, 20, 8)

    (b) $\left(\dfrac{3}{800} + \dfrac{4}{5000} + \dfrac{15}{6}\right) \cdot 6$ (15, 0, 132)

    (c) $\dfrac{1}{407} \div \dfrac{1}{1609}$ ($\frac{1}{4}$, 4, 0)

15. Find two rational numbers between $\frac{3}{4}$ and $\frac{4}{5}$.

16. Rosa spent $10 of her savings on a record and $\frac{3}{5}$ of what remained on cloth. One fourth of what was left she put back in the bank account and was left with $18. What were Rosa's initial savings?

Decimals

PRELIMINARY PROBLEM
A watermelon weighing 100 pounds was found to be 99% water. After it sat in the sunlight all day, some of the water evaporated, leaving the melon 98% water. How much did the melon weigh after the evaporation occurred?

Introduction

Although the Hindu-Arabic numeration system discussed in Chapter 3 was perfected around the sixth century, the extension of the system to decimals did not take place until about a thousand years later. Suggestions for decimals were recorded long before the Dutch scientist Simon Stevin was credited for their invention. The only significant improvement in the system since Stevin's time has been in notation. Even today there is no universally accepted form of writing a decimal point. For example, in the United States we write 6.75; in England this number is written as 6·75; and in Germany and France it is written 6,75.

Today, the use of calculators and computers makes a knowledge of decimals indispensable. The *Standards* states that students should

understand, represent, and use numbers in a variety of equivalent forms (integer,
*   fraction, decimal, percent, exponential, and scientific notation) in real-world and*
*   mathematical problem situations*
investigate relationships among fractions, decimals, and percents
understand and apply ratios, proportions, and percents in a wide variety of situations.

Section 7-1   Decimals and Decimal Operations

The word *decimal* comes from the Latin *decem*, which means ten. Most people first see decimals when dealing with our notation for money. For example, a sign that says that a doll costs $9.95 means that the cost is nine whole dollars and some part of a dollar. The dot in $9.95 is called the **decimal point.** The digits to the left of the dot form the integer part of the decimal. The digits to the right represent the sum of the elements of a set of rational numbers whose numerators are the given digits and whose denominators are successive natural-number powers of 10, starting with 10^1. For example, 12.61843 represents

decimal point

$$12 + \frac{6}{10^1} + \frac{1}{10^2} + \frac{8}{10^3} + \frac{4}{10^4} + \frac{3}{10^5} \quad \text{or} \quad 12\,\frac{61,843}{100,000}$$

The decimal 12.61843 is read "twelve and sixty-one thousand eight hundred forty-three hundred-thousandths." (The decimal point is read as "and.") Each place to the right of a decimal point may be named by its power of 10. For example, the places of 12.61843 can be named as shown in Table 7-1.

TABLE 7-1

1	2	.	6	1	8	4	3
Tens	Units	And	Tenths	Hundredths	Thousandths	Ten-thousandths	Hundred-thousandths

In 1584, Simon Stevin (1548–1620) wrote *La Disme,* a work that gave rules for computing with decimals. He recognized the need to shorten work with fractions. He not only stated the rules for decimal computations, but also suggested practical applications for decimals and recommended that his government adopt the decimal system. Stevin's other achievements include being a quartermaster general for the Dutch army; his contributions in physics to statics and hydrostatics; his work with military engineering; and his invention of a carriage that carried 28 people and that was propelled by sails and ran along the seashore.

Table 7-2 shows other examples of decimals, their fractional notation, and their common fractional forms.

TABLE 7-2

Decimal	Fractional Notation	Common Fraction
5.3	$5 + \dfrac{3}{10}$	$5\dfrac{3}{10}$, or $\dfrac{53}{10}$
0.02	$0 + \dfrac{0}{10} + \dfrac{2}{100}$	$\dfrac{2}{100}$
2.0103	$2 + \dfrac{0}{10} + \dfrac{1}{100} + \dfrac{0}{1000} + \dfrac{3}{10,000}$	$2\dfrac{103}{10,000}$, or $\dfrac{20,103}{10,000}$
-3.6	$-\left(3 + \dfrac{6}{10}\right)$	$-3\dfrac{6}{10}$, or $-\dfrac{36}{10}$

We can write every decimal in expanded form by using place value and negative exponents. Thus, we can write 12.61843 as $1 \cdot 10^1 + 2 \cdot 10^0 + 6 \cdot 10^{-1} + 1 \cdot 10^{-2} + 8 \cdot 10^{-3} + 4 \cdot 10^{-4} + 3 \cdot 10^{-5}$. However, to avoid negative exponents, most elementary school texts use fractional notation, as in Table 7-2.

Example 7-1 shows how to convert rational numbers, whose denominators are powers of 10, to decimals.

EXAMPLE 7-1   Convert each of the following to decimals.

(a) $\dfrac{56}{100}$ (b) $\dfrac{205}{10,000}$

SOLUTION   (a) $\dfrac{56}{100} = \dfrac{5 \cdot 10 + 6}{10^2} = \dfrac{5 \cdot 10}{10^2} + \dfrac{6}{10^2} = \dfrac{5}{10} + \dfrac{6}{10^2} = 0.56$

(b) $\dfrac{205}{10,000} = \dfrac{2 \cdot 10^2 + 0 \cdot 10 + 5}{10^4} = \dfrac{2 \cdot 10^2}{10^4} + \dfrac{0 \cdot 10}{10^4} + \dfrac{5}{10^4}$

$= \dfrac{2}{10^2} + \dfrac{0}{10^3} + \dfrac{5}{10^4} = \dfrac{0}{10^1} + \dfrac{2}{10^2} + \dfrac{0}{10^3} + \dfrac{5}{10^4} = 0.0205$

The ideas in Example 7-1 can be reinforced through use of a calculator. For example, in part (a), press $\boxed{5}\,\boxed{6}\,\boxed{\div}\,\boxed{1}\,\boxed{0}\,\boxed{0}\,\boxed{=}$ and watch the display. Divide by 10 again, and look at the new placement of the decimal point. Once more, divide by 10 (which amounts to dividing the original number, 56, by 10,000), and note the placement of the decimal point. This leads to the following general rule for dividing an integer by a power of 10.

To divide an integer by 10^n, count n digits from right to left, annexing zeros if necessary, and insert the decimal point to the left of the nth digit.

The fractions in Example 7-1 are easy to convert to decimals because the denominators are powers of 10. If the denominator of a fraction is not a power of 10, then the conversion to a decimal requires more work. For example, to write $\frac{3}{5}$ as a decimal, we use the problem-solving strategy of converting the problem to one we already know how to do. We know how to convert fractions in which the denominators are powers of 10 to decimals. Hence, we first change $\frac{3}{5}$ to a fraction in which the denominator is a power of 10, and then we convert it to a decimal.

$$\frac{3}{5} = \frac{3\cdot 2}{5\cdot 2} = \frac{6}{10} = 0.6$$

The reason for multiplying the numerator and the denominator by 2 is apparent when we observe that, in the denominator, $10 = 2\cdot 5$. Because $10^n = (2\cdot 5)^n = 2^n\cdot 5^n$, the prime factorization of the denominator must be $2^n\cdot 5^n$, in order for the denominator of a rational number to be 10^n. We use these ideas to write each fraction in Example 7-2 as a decimal.

EXAMPLE 7-2 Express each of the following as decimals.

(a) $\dfrac{7}{2^6}$ (b) $\dfrac{1}{2^3\cdot 5^4}$ (c) $\dfrac{1}{125}$ (d) $\dfrac{7}{250}$

SOLUTION (a) $\dfrac{7}{2^6} = \dfrac{7\cdot 5^6}{2^6\cdot 5^6} = \dfrac{7\cdot 15{,}625}{(2\cdot 5)^6} = \dfrac{109{,}375}{10^6} = 0.109375$

(b) $\dfrac{1}{2^3\cdot 5^4} = \dfrac{1\cdot 2^1}{2^3\cdot 5^4\cdot 2^1} = \dfrac{2}{2^4\cdot 5^4} = \dfrac{2}{(2\cdot 5)^4} = \dfrac{2}{10^4} = 0.0002$

(c) $\dfrac{1}{125} = \dfrac{1}{5^3} = \dfrac{1\cdot 2^3}{5^3\cdot 2^3} = \dfrac{8}{(5\cdot 2)^3} = \dfrac{8}{10^3} = 0.008$

(d) $\dfrac{7}{250} = \dfrac{7}{2\cdot 5^3} = \dfrac{7\cdot 2^2}{(2\cdot 5^3)2^2} = \dfrac{28}{(2\cdot 5)^3} = \dfrac{28}{10^3} = 0.028$

terminating decimals The answers in Example 7-2 are illustrations of **terminating decimals**— *decimals that can be written with only a finite number of places to the right of the decimal point.* If we attempt to rewrite $\frac{2}{11}$ as a terminating decimal, using the method just developed, we first try to find a natural number b such that the following holds.

$$\frac{2}{11} = \frac{2b}{11b}, \qquad \text{where } 11b \text{ is a power of } 10$$

By the Fundamental Theorem of Arithmetic (discussed in Chapter 5), the only prime factors of a power of 10 are 2 and 5. Because $11b$ has 11 as a factor, we cannot write $11b$ as a power of 10, and therefore $\frac{2}{11}$ cannot be written as a terminating decimal. A similar argument using the Fundamental Theorem of Arithmetic holds in general, so we have the following result.

● **THEOREM 7-1**

A rational number $\frac{a}{b}$ in simplest form can be written as a terminating decimal if and only if the prime factorization of the denominator contains no primes other than 2 or 5.

EXAMPLE 7-3 Which of the following fractions can be written as terminating decimals?

(a) $\frac{7}{8}$ (b) $\frac{6}{125}$ (c) $\frac{21}{28}$ (d) $\frac{37}{768}$

SOLUTION (a) $\frac{7}{8} = \frac{7}{2^3}$. Because the denominator is 2^3, $\frac{7}{8}$ can be written as a terminating decimal.

(b) $\frac{6}{125} = \frac{6}{5^3}$. The denominator is 5^3, so $\frac{6}{125}$ can be written as a terminating decimal.

(c) $\frac{21}{28} = \frac{21}{2^2 \cdot 7} = \frac{3}{2^2}$. The denominator of the fraction in simplest form is 2^2, so $\frac{21}{28}$ can be written as a terminating decimal.

(d) $\frac{37}{768} = \frac{37}{2^8 \cdot 3}$. This fraction is in simplest form and the denominator contains a factor of 3, so $\frac{37}{768}$ cannot be written as a terminating decimal.

● **REMARK**

As shown in Example 7-3(c), to determine whether a rational number $\frac{a}{b}$ can be represented as a terminating decimal, we consider the prime factorization of the denominator *only* if the fraction is in simplest form.

Adding and Subtracting Decimals

To develop an algorithm for addition of terminating decimals, consider the sum 3.26 + 14.7. We can compute the sum by changing it to a problem we already know how to solve—that is, to a sum involving fractions. We then use the commutative and associative properties of addition to complete the computation.

$$3.26 + 14.7 = \left(3 + \frac{2}{10} + \frac{6}{100}\right) + \left(14 + \frac{7}{10}\right)$$

$$= (3 + 14) + \left(\frac{2}{10} + \frac{7}{10}\right) + \left(\frac{6}{100}\right)$$

$$= 17 + \frac{9}{10} + \frac{6}{100}$$

$$= 17.96$$

This addition, using fractions, was accomplished by grouping the integers, the tenths, and the hundredths, and adding. Because $14.7 = 14 + \frac{7}{10} = 14 + \frac{7}{10} + \frac{0}{100} = 14.70$, the addition 3.26 + 14.7 can be accomplished by lining up the decimal points and adding as with whole numbers.

$$
\begin{array}{r}
3.26 \\
+\,14.70 \\
\hline
17.96
\end{array}
$$

The algorithm for adding terminating decimals is a three-step process:

1. *List the numbers vertically, lining up the decimal points. (Append zeros if necessary.)*
2. *Add the numbers as though they were whole numbers.*
3. *Insert the decimal point in the sum directly below the decimal points in the numbers being added.*

Subtraction of terminating decimals also can be accomplished by lining up the decimal points and subtracting as with whole numbers. The justification of the method is left as an exercise.

EXAMPLE 7-4 Compute each of the following.

(a) 14.36 + 5.2 + 0.036   (b) 17.013 − 2.98
(c) 17.01 − 2.938

SOLUTION

(a)
$$
\begin{array}{r}
14.360 \\
5.200 \\
+\,0.036 \\
\hline
19.596
\end{array}
$$

(b)
$$
\begin{array}{r}
17.013 \\
-\,2.980 \\
\hline
14.033
\end{array}
$$

(c)
$$
\begin{array}{r}
17.010 \\
-\,2.938 \\
\hline
14.072
\end{array}
$$

Multiplying Decimals

Algorithms for multiplication of terminating decimals can be found by multiplying the corresponding fractions, each in the form $\dfrac{a}{b}$, where a and b are integers, $b \neq 0$. Consider the product $(4.62)(2.4)$.

$$(4.62)(2.4) = \frac{462}{100} \cdot \frac{24}{10} = \frac{462}{10^2} \cdot \frac{24}{10^1} = \frac{462 \cdot 24}{10^2 \cdot 10^1} = \frac{11{,}088}{10^3} = 11.088$$

Notice that the answer to this computation was obtained by multiplying the whole numbers 462 and 24 and then dividing the result by 10^3.

The algorithm for multiplying decimals can be stated as follows.

If there are n digits to the right of the decimal point in one number and m digits to the right of the decimal point in a second number, multiply the two numbers, ignoring the decimals, and then place the decimal point so that there are n + m digits to the right of the decimal point in the product.

● **R E M A R K**
There are $n + m$ digits to the right of the decimal point in the product because $10^n \cdot 10^m = 10^{n+m}$.

EXAMPLE 7-5 Compute each of the following.
(a) $(6.2)(1.43)$ (b) $(0.02)(0.013)$ (c) $(1000)(3.6)$

SOLUTION (a)
$$\begin{array}{r} 1.4\,3 \\ \times \quad\; 6.2 \\ \hline 2\,8\,6 \\ 8\,5\,8 \\ \hline 8.8\,6\,6 \end{array}$$
(2 digits after the decimal point)
(1 digit after the decimal point)

(3 digits after the decimal point)

(b)
$$\begin{array}{r} 0.0\,1\,3 \\ \times \quad\;\; 0.0\,2 \\ \hline 0.0\,0\,0\,2\,6 \end{array}$$

(c)
$$\begin{array}{r} 3.6 \\ \times \quad 1\,0\,0\,0 \\ \hline 3\,6\,0\,0.0 \end{array}$$

● **R E M A R K**
Example 7-5(c) suggests that multiplication by 10^n, where n is a positive integer, results in moving the decimal point in the multiplicand n places to the right.

Dividing Decimals

To develop an algorithm for dividing terminating decimals, we first consider the case of dividing a terminating decimal by a whole number. Consider

$0.96 \div 3$. This division can be approached by rewriting the decimal as a fraction and then dividing.

$$0.96 \div 3 = \frac{96}{100} \div \frac{3}{1} = \frac{96}{100} \cdot \frac{1}{3} = \frac{96 \cdot 1}{100 \cdot 3} = \frac{96}{3} \cdot \frac{1}{100}$$

$$= 32\left(\frac{1}{100}\right) = \frac{32}{100} = 0.32$$

The computation can also be accomplished by means of the following procedure.

$$
\begin{array}{r}
0.32 \\
3\overline{)0.96} \\
\underline{9} \\
6 \\
\underline{6} \\
0
\end{array}
$$

When the divisor is a whole number, we see that the division can be handled as with whole numbers and the decimal point can be placed directly over the decimal point in the dividend. When the divisor is not a whole number, we try to change the division problem to an equivalent division in which the divisor is a whole number. For example, consider $1.2032 \div 0.32$. To obtain a whole-number divisor in the problem, we express the quotient as a fraction and then multiply the numerator and denominator of the fraction by 100.

$$\frac{1.2032}{0.32} = \frac{1.2032 \cdot 100}{0.32 \cdot 100} = \frac{120.32}{32}$$

This corresponds to rewriting the division problem in form (a) as an equivalent problem in form (b).

(a) $0.32\overline{)1.2032}$ (b) $32\overline{)120.32}$

In elementary school texts, this process is usually described as "moving" the decimal point two places to the right in both the dividend and the divisor. This process is usually indicated with arrows, as shown next.

$$
\begin{array}{r}
3.7\,6 \\
0.3\,2\,\overline{)1.2\,0\,3\,2} \\
\underline{9\,6} \\
2\,4\,3 \\
\underline{2\,2\,4} \\
1\,9\,2 \\
\underline{1\,9\,2} \\
0
\end{array}
$$

Multiply divisor and dividend by 100.

EXAMPLE 7-6 Compute each of the following.
(a) $13.169 \div 0.13$ (b) $9 \div 0.75$

SOLUTION (a)

$$
\begin{array}{r}
1\,0\,1.3 \\
0.1\,3\,\overline{)1\,3.1\,6\,9} \\
\underline{1\,3} \\
1\,6 \\
\underline{1\,3} \\
3\,9 \\
\underline{3\,9} \\
0
\end{array}
$$

(b)

$$
\begin{array}{r}
1\,2 \\
0.7\,5\,\overline{)9.0\,0} \\
\underline{7\,5} \\
1\,5\,0 \\
\underline{1\,5\,0} \\
0
\end{array}
$$

Notice that, in Example 7-6(b), we annexed two zeros in the dividend because $9/0.75 = (9 \cdot 100)/(0.75 \cdot 100) = \frac{900}{75}$.

EXAMPLE 7-7 An owner of a gasoline station must collect a gasoline tax of $0.11 on each gallon of gasoline sold. One week the owner paid $1595 in gasoline taxes. The pump price of a gallon of gas that week was $1.35.
(a) How many gallons of gas were sold during the week?
(b) What was the revenue after taxes for the week?

SOLUTION (a) To find the number of gallons of gas sold during the week, we must divide the total gas tax bill by the amount of the tax per gallon.

$$\frac{1595}{0.11} = 14,500$$

Thus, 14,500 gallons were sold.

(b) To obtain the revenue after taxes, we must first determine the revenue before taxes, which we do by multiplying the number of gallons sold times the cost per gallon.

$(14,500)(\$1.35) = \$19,575$

We then subtract the cost remitted in gasoline taxes from the total revenue.

$\$19,575 - \$1595 = \$17,980$

Thus, the revenue after gasoline taxes is $17,980.

Mental Computation
We can use some of the same tools we used for mental computations with whole numbers to perform mental computations with decimals.

1. *Breaking and bridging*

   1.5 + 3.7 + 4.48

   = 4.5 + 0.7 + 4.48

   = 5.2 + 4.48

   = 9.2 + 0.48 = 9.68

   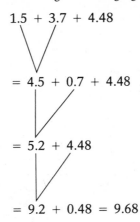

   1.5 + 3

   4.5 + 0.7

   5.2 + 4

   9.2 + 0.48

2. *Using compatible numbers*
   (Decimal numbers are compatible when they add to a whole number.)

   7.91
   3.85   12
   4.09   +4
   +0.15   16

   7.91 + 4.09

   3.85 + 0.15

   12 + 4

3. *Making compatible numbers*

   $$\begin{array}{r} 9.27 = \quad 9.25 + 0.02 \\ +3.79 = \quad 3.75 + 0.04 \\ \hline 13.00 + 0.06 = 13.06 \end{array}$$

4. *Balancing with decimals in subtraction*

   $$\begin{array}{r} 4.63 = \quad 4.63 + 0.03 = \quad 4.66 \\ -1.97 = -(1.97 + 0.03) = -2.00 \\ \hline 2.66 \end{array}$$

5. *Balancing with decimals in division*

   $0.25\overline{)8}$

   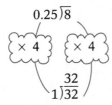

   $\times\,4$ $\times\,4$

   $\dfrac{32}{1\overline{)32}}$

● R E M A R K

Balancing with decimals in division uses the property $\dfrac{a}{b} = \dfrac{a \cdot c}{b \cdot c}$.

Another technique for doing mental division involves dividing by powers of 10, as shown on the following student page from *Addison-Wesley Mathematics*, 1989, Grade 7.

Dividing Decimals: Mental Math

Lele ran a 10-kilometer race in 56.4 minutes (min). At this rate, how long did it take her to run 1 km?

Since we know the time for 10 km, we divide to find the time for 1 km.

```
        5.6 4
1 0 ) 5 6.4 0
      5 0
        6 4
        6 0
          4 0
          4 0
             0
```

It took Lele 5.64 min to run 1 km.

Study the division pattern. Look for a shortcut for dividing a decimal by 10, 100, or 1,000.

56.4 ÷ 10 = 5.64	shift 1 place left
56.4 ÷ 100 = 0.564	shift 2 places left
56.4 ÷ 1,000 = 0.0564	shift 3 places left

Other Examples

1,950 ÷ 10 = 195.0	32.6 ÷ 10 = 3.26	0.25 ÷ 10 = 0.025
1,950 ÷ 100 = 19.50	32.6 ÷ 100 = 0.326	0.25 ÷ 100 = 0.0025
1,950 ÷ 1,000 = 1.950	32.6 ÷ 1,000 = 0.0326	0.25 ÷ 1,000 = 0.00025

PROBLEM 1

Big Save Airlines allows each passenger to carry x pounds of luggage free of charge, with an additional charge for each extra pound. The combined weight of luggage for Mr. and Mrs. Byrd was 105 pounds. Mr. Byrd and Mrs. Byrd had to pay $1.00 and $1.50, respectively, for extra weight. They then noticed that a third passenger also had 105 pounds of luggage and was charged $6.50 for the number of pounds over the x-pound limit. How many pounds are allowed for each passenger without a charge?

Understanding the Problem. We are to determine the number of pounds that are allowed free for each passenger. We know that, if each passenger is allowed x pounds, Mr. and Mrs. Byrd were allowed $x + x$, or $2x$ pounds together. Since their luggage weight of 105 pounds was overweight, then the amount the weight was over is $105 - 2x$ pounds. In addition, since the third passenger's luggage weight of 105 pounds was also overweight, the amount of excess weight in that person's luggage is $105 - x$.

Devising a Plan. Because Mr. and Mrs. Byrd are each allowed x pounds of luggage free, they must pay for $(105 - 2x)$ pounds of luggage, whereas the third passenger must pay for $(105 - x)$ pounds. Assuming that the airline charges the same rate for each pound over the allowed limit for each person, we can express the rate per pound for Mr. and Mrs. Byrd and for the third passenger, equate the rates, and obtain an equation in terms of x. If we solve the equation for x, then we should obtain the number of pounds allowed for each passenger free of charge.

Carrying Out the Plan. Because Mr. and Mrs. Byrd paid $2.50 on their overweight $(105 - 2x)$ pounds of luggage, the price per pound on their excess luggage was $2.50/(105 - 2x)$. Because the third passenger paid $6.50 for his $(105 - x)$ pounds of excess luggage, the airline charged him $6.50/(105 - x)$ dollars per pound. Equating the rates per pound, we obtain the following proportion.

$$\frac{2.50}{105 - 2x} = \frac{6.50}{105 - x}$$

We solve the equation for x as follows.

$$2.50(105 - x) = 6.50(105 - 2x)$$
$$262.5 - 2.5x = 682.5 - 13x$$
$$10.5x = 420$$
$$x = 40$$

This shows that the number of pounds allowed for each passenger free of charge is 40.

Looking Back. Checking the value for $x = 40$, we find that Mr. and Mrs. Byrd's luggage is $(105 - 2 \cdot 40)$, or 25, pounds overweight. Because they were charged $2.50, we see that the charge is 10¢ per pound for each pound over 40 pounds. Checking that this ratio applies to the third passenger, we see that his luggage is $(105 - 40)$, or 65, pounds overweight. At 10¢ per pound, this agrees with the airline charge of $6.50. Luggage weights and/or charges can also be varied to create new problems.

Calculator Computations

All the computations in this section can be carried out with a calculator. The *Standards* recommends that students "select and use the most appropriate tool," and it adds that they should be prepared to "select and use appropriate mental, paper-and-pencil, calculator, and computer methods."

For example, if a car has been driven 462.8 miles and it takes 11.7 gallons of gas to fill the tank, we can compute the number of miles per gallon the car has been driven. To do this, the following division must be completed.

$$11.7\overline{)462.8}$$

This is a multidigit division of terminating decimals that can be done faster with a calculator than with pencil and paper.

A different type of computation is necessary when a person needs to multiply a 1990 governmental budget of $14,329,846,537 by 6 to project the minimum cost of the budget for the coming 6 years. This computation is given to show how to use a calculator to handle large numbers where accuracy is important. Most calculators have only an 8-digit display, but the budget contains 11 digits. This problem can be overcome with a combination of calculator and pencil-and-paper computation. Recognizing that $14,329,846,537 = 14,329,000,000 + 846,537$, we have the following.

$$
\begin{aligned}
6 \times 14,329,846,537 &= 6(14,329,000,000 + 846,537) \\
&= 6 \cdot 14,329,000,000 + 6 \cdot 846,537 \\
&= 6 \cdot 14,329 \cdot 1,000,000 + 6 \cdot 846,537 \\
&= 85,974 \cdot 1,000,000 + 5,079,222
\end{aligned}
$$

Therefore, we could write the computation, using place value, as follows.

$$
\begin{array}{r}
14,329,846,537 \\
\times 6 \\
\hline
5\,079\,222 \\
+85\,974 \\
\hline
85,979,079,222
\end{array}
$$

We see that the distributive property of multiplication over addition and the associative property of multiplication can be used for the multiplication of numbers with more digits than the calculator can accommodate. Similar computations are left as exercises.

PROBLEM SET 7-1

1. Write each of the following in expanded form.
   (a) 0.023   (b) 206.06
   (c) 312.0103   (d) 0.000132

2. Rewrite each of the following as decimals.
   (a) $4 \cdot 10^3 + 3 \cdot 10^2 + 5 \cdot 10 + 6 + 7 \cdot 10^{-1} + 8 \cdot 10^{-2}$
   (b) $4 \cdot 10^3 + 6 \cdot 10^{-1} + 8 \cdot 10^{-3}$
   (c) $4 \cdot 10^4 + 3 \cdot 10^{-2}$
   (d) $2 \cdot 10^{-1} + 4 \cdot 10^{-4} + 7 \cdot 10^{-7}$

3. Write each of the following as numerals.
   (a) Five hundred thirty-six and seventy-six ten-thousandths
   (b) Three and eight thousandths
   (c) Four hundred thirty-six millionths
   (d) Five million and two tenths

4. Write each of the following terminating decimals as fractions.
   (a) 0.436   (b) 25.16   (c) $^-$316.027
   (d) 28.1902   (e) $^-$4.3   (f) $^-$62.01

5. Without performing the actual divisions, determine which of the following represent terminating decimals.
   (a) $\dfrac{4}{5}$ (b) $\dfrac{61}{2^2 \cdot 5}$ (c) $\dfrac{3}{6}$ (d) $\dfrac{1}{2^5}$ (e) $\dfrac{36}{5^5}$
   (f) $\dfrac{133}{625}$ (g) $\dfrac{1}{3}$ (h) $\dfrac{2}{25}$ (i) $\dfrac{1}{13}$

6. Where possible, write each of the numbers in Problem 5 as terminating decimals.

7. Compute each of the following.
   (a) 36.812 + 0.43 + 1.96
   (b) 200.01 − 32.007   (c) $^-$4.612 − 386.0193
   (d) (3.61)(0.413)   (e) ($^-$2.6)(4)
   (f) 10.7663 ÷ 2.3

8. Calculate the following by converting each decimal to a fraction, performing the computation, and then converting the fraction answer to a decimal.
   (a) 13.62 + 4.082   (b) 12.62 − 4.082
   (c) (1.36)(0.02)   (d) 1.36 ÷ 0.02

9. If Maura went to the store and bought a chair for $17.95, a lawn rake for $13.59, a spade for $14.86, a lawn mower for $179.98, and two six-packs of mineral water for $2.43 each, what was the bill?

10. If the rainfall was 1.9 inches in March and 2.7 inches in April, how much more rain was there in April than in March?

11. Explain why subtraction of terminating decimals can be accomplished by lining up the decimal points, subtracting as if the numbers were whole numbers, and then placing the decimal point in the difference.

12. Multiply each of the following by 10^8.
    (a) 4.63   (b) 0.04   (c) 46.3
    (d) 463.0   (e) 0.00463   (f) 0.0000000463

13. Multiply each of the following by 10^{-4}.
    (a) 4.63   (b) 0.04   (c) 46.3   (d) 0.0000463

14. Divide each of the following by 10^{-4}.
    (a) 4.63   (b) 0.04   (c) 46.3   (d) 0.0000463

15. Which of the following divisions are equivalent to 18 ÷ 2?
    (a) $20\overline{)180}$ (b) $0.2\overline{)0.18}$
    (c) $0.002\overline{)0.018}$ (d) $20\overline{)1800}$
    (e) $0.0002\overline{)0.00018}$ (f) $0.2\overline{)1.8}$

16. If 0.8 inch of rain fell during 7 hours, what was the average amount of rain per hour?

17. If the average for common stocks rose 8.395 points during 5 days of trading, what was the average gain per day?

18. (a) Find the product of 0.22 and 0.35 on the calculator. How does the placement of the decimal point in the answer on the calculator compare with the placement of the decimal point using the rule in this chapter? Explain.
    (b) In a similar manner, investigate placement of the decimal point in the quotient obtained by performing the division 0.2436 ÷ 0.0006.

19. The following are answers to various types of computations. Write an exercise for each answer.
    (a) 86.04 as an addition of two numbers
    (b) 353.76 as an addition of four numbers
    (c) 96.72 as a subtraction of two numbers
    (d) 0.0138 as a multiplication of two numbers
    (e) 0.12 as a subtraction of two numbers
    (f) 2.03 as a division of two numbers.

20. At 60°F, 1 quart of water weighs 2.082 pounds. One cubic foot of water is 29.922 quarts. What is the weight of a cubic foot of water, to the nearest thousandth of a pound?

21. Complete the following magic square; that is, make the sum of every row, column, and diagonal the same.

8.2		
3.7	5.5	
	9.1	2.8

22. Keith bought 30 pounds of nuts at $3.00 per pound and 20 pounds of nuts at $5.00 per pound. If he wanted to buy 10 more pounds of a different kind of nut to make the average price per pound equal to $4.50, what price should he pay for the additional 10 pounds?

23. Continue the decimal patterns shown below. (Assume each sequence is either arithmetic or geometric.)
    (a) 0.9, 1.8, 2.7, 3.6, 4.5, ____, ____, ____
    (b) 0.3, 0.5, 0.7, 0.9, 1.1, ____, ____, ____
    (c) 1, 0.5, 0.25, 0.125, ____, ____, ____
    (d) 0.2, 1.5, 2.8, 4.1, 5.4, ____, ____, ____

24. In doing a calculator addition, a person pressed 42095 as an addend instead of 42.095. Using only one arithmetic operation, how could the person correct this error?

25. Describe how the following might be computed on a calculator: If a satellite flies at the rate of 1565 miles per hour, how long would it take to reach the surface of the sun, which is 93,000,000 miles away?

26. Compute each of the following.
    (a) 123,456.7894 + 90,876,543.3212
    (b) 123,456.7894 − 90,876,543.3212
    (c) 4,234,567.891 × 36.56
    (d) 123,456,789.51432 ÷ 0.0012

27. At a local bank, two different systems are available for charging for checking accounts. System A is a "dime-a-time" plan, as there is no monthly service charge and the charge is 10¢ per check written. System B is a plan with a service charge of 75¢ per month plus 7¢ per check written during that month.
    (a) Which plan is the more economical if an average of 12 checks per month is written?
    (b) Which system is the more economical if an average of 52 checks per month is written?

    (c) What is the "break-even point" for the number of checks written (that is, the number of checks for which the costs of the two plans are as close as possible)?

28. A bank statement from a local bank shows that a checking account has a balance of $83.62. The balance recorded in the checkbook shows only $21.69. After checking the canceled checks against the record of these checks, the customer finds that the bank has not yet recorded six checks in the amounts of $3.21, $14.56, $12.44, $6.98, $9.51, $7.49. Is the bank record correct? (Assume the person's checkbook records *are* correct.)

29. The winner of the big sweepstakes has 15 minutes to decide whether to receive $1,000,000 cash immediately or to receive 1¢ on the first day of the month, 2¢ on the second day, 4¢ on the third, and so on, each day receiving double the previous day's amount, until the end of a 30-day month. However, only the amount received on that last day may be kept and all the rest of the month's "allowance" must be returned. Use a calculator to find which of these two options is more profitable, and determine how much more profitable one way is than the other.

★30. Given any reduced rational $\frac{a}{b}$ with $0 < a < b$, where b is of the form $2^m \cdot 5^n$ (m and n are whole numbers), determine a relationship between m and/or n and the number of digits in the terminating decimal.

B R A I N   T E A S E R
Arrange four 7s, using any operations and decimal points needed to obtain a value of 100.

Section 7-2   More About Decimals and Their Properties

The division processes described in Section 7-1 can be used to develop a procedure for converting any rational number to a decimal. Recall that $\frac{7}{8}$ can be written as a terminating decimal because it is in simplest form and the denominator contains only factors of 2.

$$\frac{7}{8} = \frac{7}{2^3} = \frac{7 \cdot 5^3}{2^3 \cdot 5^3} = \frac{875}{1000} = 0.875$$

The decimal for $\frac{7}{8}$ can also be found by division, as follows.

$$
\begin{array}{r}
0.875 \\
8\overline{)7.000} \\
\underline{6\ 4} \\
60 \\
\underline{56} \\
40 \\
\underline{40}
\end{array}
$$

In a similar way, nonterminating decimals can be obtained for other rational numbers. For example, to find a decimal representation for $\frac{2}{11}$, consider the following division.

$$
\begin{array}{r}
0.18 \\
11\overline{)2.00} \\
\underline{1\ 1} \\
90 \\
\underline{88} \\
2
\end{array}
$$

repeating decimal
repetend

At this point, if the division is continued, the division pattern repeats. Thus, the quotient is 0.181818 . . . . A decimal of this type is called a **repeating decimal,** and the repeating block of digits is called the **repetend.** The repeating decimal is written as $0.\overline{18}$, where the bar indicates that the block of digits underneath is repeated infinitely.

EXAMPLE 7-8   Convert $\frac{1}{7}$ to a decimal.

SOLUTION

$$
\begin{array}{r}
0.142857 \\
7\overline{)1.000000} \\
\underline{7} \\
30 \\
\underline{28} \\
20 \\
\underline{14} \\
60 \\
\underline{56} \\
40 \\
\underline{35} \\
50 \\
\underline{49} \\
1
\end{array}
$$

If the division process is continued at this point, the division pattern repeats; thus, $\frac{1}{7} = 0.\overline{142857}$.

In Example 7-8, the remainders obtained in the division are 3, 2, 6, 4, 5, and 1. These are all the possible nonzero remainders that can be obtained when dividing by 7. (If a remainder of 0 had been obtained, the decimal would terminate.) If $\frac{a}{b}$ is any rational number in simplest form with $b > a$ and it does not represent a terminating decimal, then the possible remainders on division by b are 1, 2, 3, 4, ..., $b - 1$. Thus, after b or fewer divisions, at least one remainder appears twice. When this happens, a block of at most $b - 1$ digits in the quotient repeats. Therefore, *a rational number may always be represented either as a terminating decimal or as a repeating decimal.*

EXAMPLE 7-9 Use a calculator to convert $\frac{1}{17}$ to a repeating decimal.

SOLUTION In using a calculator, if we press $\boxed{1}\ \boxed{\div}\ \boxed{1}\ \boxed{7}\ \boxed{=}$, we obtain the following, shown as part of a division problem.

$$
\begin{array}{r}
0.0588235 \\
17\overline{)1}
\end{array}
$$

Without knowing whether or not the calculator has an internal round-off and with an 8-digit display, the greatest number of digits to be trusted in the quotient is 6 following the decimal. (Why?) If we use those 6 places and multiply 0.058823 times 17, we may continue the operation as follows.

$$\boxed{.}\,\boxed{0}\,\boxed{5}\,\boxed{8}\,\boxed{8}\,\boxed{2}\,\boxed{3}\,\boxed{\times}\,\boxed{1}\,\boxed{7}\,\boxed{=}$$

We then obtain 0.999991, which we may place in the preceding division.

$$
\begin{array}{r}
0.058823 \\
17\overline{)1.000000} \\
\underline{999991} \\
9
\end{array}
$$

We now divide $9 \div 17$ to obtain 0.5294118. Again ignoring the rightmost digit, we continue as before, completing the division as follows, where the repeating pattern is apparent.

$$
\begin{array}{r}
0.0588235294117647 0588235 \\
17\overline{)1.0000000000000000000000000} \\
\underline{999991} \\
9000000 \\
\underline{8999987} \\
13000000 \\
\underline{12999985} \\
15
\end{array}
$$

Thus, $\frac{1}{17} = 0.\overline{0588235294117647}$, and the repetend is 16 digits long.

We have already considered how to write terminating decimals in the form $\frac{a}{b}$, where $a, b \in I$, $b \neq 0$. For example,

$$0.55 = \frac{55}{10^2} = \frac{55}{100}$$

To write $0.\overline{5}$ in a similar way, we may try the same method. We see that, because the repeating decimal has infinitely many digits, there is no single power of 10 that can be placed in the denominator. To overcome this difficulty, we must somehow eliminate the infinitely repeating part of the decimal. Suppose that $n = 0.\overline{5}$. It can be shown that $10(0.555 \ldots) = 5.555 \ldots = 5.\overline{5}$. Hence, $10n = 5.\overline{5}$. Using this information, we subtract to obtain an equation whose solution can be written as a rational number in the form a/b, where a and b are integers and $b \neq 0$.

$$
\begin{array}{rcl}
10n &=& 5.\overline{5} \\
-n &=& -0.\overline{5} \\
\hline
9n &=& 5 \\
n &=& \dfrac{5}{9}
\end{array}
$$

Thus, $0.\overline{5} = \frac{5}{9}$. This result can be checked by performing the division $5 \div 9$. Notice that performing the subtraction gives an equation containing only integers. (The repeating blocks "cancel" each other.)

Suppose that a decimal has a repetend of more than one digit, such as $0.\overline{235}$. In order to write it in the form $\frac{a}{b}$, it is reasonable to multiply by 10^3, since there is a three-digit repetend. Let $n = 0.\overline{235}$. Then,

$$
\begin{array}{rcl}
1000n &=& 235.\overline{235} \\
-n &=& -0.\overline{235} \\
\hline
999n &=& 235 \\
n &=& \dfrac{235}{999}
\end{array}
$$

Hence, $0.\overline{235} = \frac{235}{999}$.

Notice that $0.\overline{5}$ repeats in blocks of one digit, and therefore, to write it in the form $\frac{a}{b}$, we first multiply by 10^1; $0.\overline{235}$ repeats in blocks of three digits, and therefore we first multiply by 10^3. In general, *if the repetend is immediately to the right of the decimal point, first multiply by 10^n, where n is the number of digits in the repetend, and then continue as in the preceding cases.*

Now, suppose that the repeating block does *not* occur immediately after the decimal point. For example, let $n = 2.3\overline{45}$. A strategy for solving this problem is to change it to a problem we already know how to do—that is, change it to a problem where the repeating block immediately follows the decimal point. To do this, we multiply both sides by 10.

$$n = 2.3\overline{45}$$
$$10n = 23.\overline{45}$$

We now proceed as with previous problems. Since $10n = 23.\overline{45}$ and since the number of digits in the repetend is 2, we multiply by 10^2 as follows.

$$100(10n) = 2345.\overline{45}$$

Thus,

$$1000n = 2345.\overline{45}$$
$$-10n = -23.\overline{45}$$
$$\overline{990n = 2322}$$

$$n = \frac{2322}{990}, \text{ or } \frac{387}{165}$$

Hence, $2.3\overline{45} = \frac{2322}{990}$, or $\frac{387}{165}$.

To find the $\frac{a}{b}$ form of $0.\overline{9}$, we proceed as follows:

(1) $n = 0.\overline{9}$
(2) $10n = 9.\overline{9}$ (Multiply both sides of equation (1) by 10.)
(3) $9n = 9$ (Subtract equation (1) from equation (2).)
         $n = 9/9$, or 1   (Solve equation (3) for n.)

Hence, $0.\overline{9} = 1$. This approach to the problem may not be convincing. Another approach to show that $0.\overline{9}$ is really another name for 1 is shown next.

(1) $\frac{1}{3} = 0.33333333\ldots$

(2) $\frac{2}{3} = 0.66666666\ldots$

Adding equations (1) and (2), we have $1 = 0.99999999\ldots$, or $0.\overline{9}$. Can you show that $4.\overline{9} = 5$? Deciding whether or not $0.\overline{9} = 1$ hinges on understanding the meaning of the decimal $0.\overline{9}$. This decimal represents the infinite sum $\frac{9}{10} + \frac{9}{10^2} + \frac{9}{10^3} + \ldots$. Such sums are defined as the limits of finite sums in more advanced mathematics courses.

Ordering Decimals

Since rational numbers can be written as either terminating or repeating decimals and vice versa, decimals of this type have all the properties of rational numbers. However, some students have trouble ordering decimals.

They incorrectly reason that $0.36 > 0.9$ because $36 > 9$. One way to see that this is not true is to convert both decimals to fractions and then compare the fractions. For example, because $0.36 = \frac{36}{100}$ and $0.9 = \frac{9}{10} = \frac{90}{100}$ and $\frac{36}{100} < \frac{90}{100}$, then it follows that $0.36 < 0.9$. Decimals can also be ordered without conversion to fractions. For example, because $0.9 = 0.90$, we can line up the decimal points as follows.

0.36
0.90

The digit in the tenths place of 0.36 is less than the tenths digit in 0.90, so $0.36 < 0.90$. A similar procedure works for repeating decimals.

For example, to compare repeating decimals, such as $1.3\overline{478}$ and $1.34\overline{7821}$, we write the decimals one under the other, in their equivalent forms without the bars, and line up the decimal points.

1.34783478 . . .
1.34782178 . . .

The digits to the left of the decimal points and the first four digits after the decimal points are the same in each of the numbers. However, since the digit in the hundred-thousandths place of the top number, which is 3, is greater than the digit 2 in the hundred-thousandths place of the bottom number, $1.3\overline{478}$ is greater than $1.34\overline{7821}$.

It is easy to compare two fractions, such as $\frac{21}{43}$ and $\frac{37}{75}$, using a calculator. We convert each to a decimal and then compare the decimals.

$\boxed{2}\,\boxed{1}\,\boxed{\div}\,\boxed{4}\,\boxed{3}\,\boxed{=} \longrightarrow 0.4883721$
$\boxed{3}\,\boxed{7}\,\boxed{\div}\,\boxed{7}\,\boxed{5}\,\boxed{=} \longrightarrow 0.4933333$

Examining the digits in the hundredths place, we see that $\frac{37}{75} > \frac{21}{43}$.

EXAMPLE 7-10 Find a rational number in decimal form between $0.\overline{35}$ and $0.3\overline{51}$.

SOLUTION First, line up the decimals.

0.353535 . . .
0.351351 . . .

To find a decimal between these two, observe that, starting from the left, the first place at which the two numbers differ is the thousandths place. Clearly, one decimal between these two is 0.352. Others include 0.3514, $0.35\overline{15}$, and 0.35136. In fact, there are infinitely many others.

Rounding Decimals

Frequently, it is not necessary to know the exact numerical answer to a question. For example, if we ask a person's age, we usually are not interested in an exact answer. Also, we do not know exactly how far it is to the moon or how many people live in New York City. However, we do know approximately how old we are, and we can find that it is approximately 239,000 miles to the moon and that there are approximately 7,772,000 people who live in New York City.

In order to approximate numbers, we adopt rules for rounding. The rounding rules given in the following flowchart are those used in most elementary schools and thus are the ones used in this text. As an example, directly below the flowchart, 0.867 is rounded to the nearest tenth.

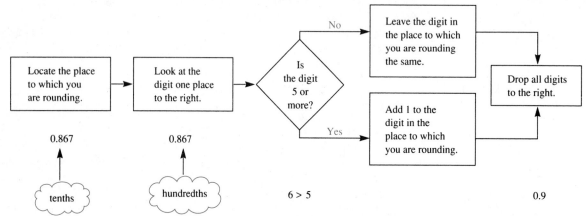

Therefore, 0.867 rounded to the nearest tenth is 0.9, and we write 0.867 $\doteq$ 0.9 to symbolize the approximation. Rounding rules often vary at the high school and college levels when the digit to the right of the last digit to be retained is 5. The following rules, although *not* used in this text, are frequently used elsewhere. If the digit to the right of the last digit to be retained is 5, then increase by 1 the last digit to be retained when there is at least one nonzero digit to the right of the 5; when there is no nonzero digit to the right of the 5, increase by 1 the last digit to be retained only if the last digit is odd.

EXAMPLE 7-11 Round each of the following numbers.

(a) 7.456 to the nearest hundredth
(b) 7.456 to the nearest tenth
(c) 7.456 to the nearest unit
(d) 7456 to the nearest thousand
(e) 745 to the nearest ten
(f) 74.56 to the nearest ten

SOLUTION (a) 7.456 $\doteq$ 7.46   (b) 7.456 $\doteq$ 7.5   (c) 7.456 $\doteq$ 7
(d) 7456 $\doteq$ 7000   (e) 745 $\doteq$ 750   (f) 74.56 $\doteq$ 70

Estimating in Decimal Computations

Rounded numbers can be useful for estimating answers to computations. For example, consider each of the following.

1. Karly goes to the grocery store to buy items that cost the following amounts. She can estimate the total cost by rounding each amount to the nearest dollar and adding the rounded numbers.

$$
\begin{array}{rcr}
\$2.39 & \longrightarrow & \$2 \\
0.89 & \longrightarrow & 1 \\
6.13 & \longrightarrow & 6 \\
4.75 & \longrightarrow & 5 \\
+\ 5.05 & \longrightarrow & \underline{5} \\
& & \$19
\end{array}
$$

Thus, Karly's estimate for her grocery bill is $19.

2. Karly's bill for car repairs was $72.80 and she had a coupon for $17.50 off. She can estimate her total cost by rounding each amount to the nearest ten dollars and subtracting.

$$
\begin{array}{rr}
\$72.80 & \$70 \\
-\ 17.50 & -\ 20 \\
& \$50
\end{array}
$$

Thus, an estimate for the repair bill is $50.

3. Karly sees a flash of lightning and hears the thunder 3.2 seconds later. She knows that sound travels at 0.33 km per second. She may estimate the distance she is from the lightning by rounding the time to the nearest unit and the speed to the nearest tenth and multiplying.

$$
\begin{array}{rcr}
0.33 & \longrightarrow & 0.3 \\
\times\ 3.2 & \longrightarrow & \times\ 3 \\
& & 0.9
\end{array}
$$

Thus, Karly estimates that she is approximately 0.9 km from the lightning. An alternate approach is to recognize that $0.33 \doteq \frac{1}{3}$ and 3.2 is close to 3.3, so an approximation using compatible numbers is $(\frac{1}{3}) \cdot 3.3$, or 1.1, km.

4. Karly wants to estimate the cost per kilogram of a frozen turkey that sells for $17.94 and weighs 6.42 kg. She rounds and divides as follows.

$$
6.42\overline{)17.94} \longrightarrow 6\overline{)18.00} \;\; \overset{3.00}{}
$$

Thus, the turkey sells for approximately $3.00 per kilogram.

An example of estimating sums and differences by using rounding and also *front-end estimation* is shown on the following student page from *Addison-Wesley Mathematics*, 1989, Grade 8.

Estimating Sums and Differences with Decimals

Jon Stein needed some supplies for his home computer system. He made this list of prices from a catalog. Then he made an estimate of the total cost. What is his estimate of the total?

Floppy disc	$ 3.15
Printer ribbon	6.95
Print wheel	9.67
Printer paper	8.09

To estimate the total we can **round** the numbers or we can use **front-end** estimation.

Rounding

$3.15	⟶	$3.00
6.95	⟶	7.00
9.67	⟶	10.00
+ 8.09	⟶	+ 8.00
Estimate	⟶	**$28.00**

His estimate is $28.00.

Front-end

$ 3.15		$0.15
6.95	Look at the rest	0.95
9.67		0.65
+ 8.09		+ 0.09
$26.00	About $2.00 more	About $28.00

Improved estimate:

Other Examples

0.0813	⟶	0.08
− 0.0324	⟶	− 0.03
Estimate	⟶	**0.05**

0.718	⟶	0.7
0.893	⟶	0.9
+ 0.415	⟶	+ 0.4
Estimate	⟶	**2.0**

● **R E M A R K**

Front-end estimation depends on the accurate use of place value.

Scientific Notation

scientific notation

In disciplines such as chemistry, microbiology, and physics, where either very large or very small numbers are used, a special notation called scientific notation is used to help handle such numbers. In **scientific notation,** *a positive number is written as the product of a number greater than or equal to 1 and less than 10, and an integral power of 10.* For example, "the sun is 93,000,000 miles from Earth" is expressed as "the sun is $9.3 \cdot 10^7$ miles from Earth." A micrometer, a metric unit of measure that is 0.000001 m (meter), is written as $1 \cdot 10^{-6}$ m.

EXAMPLE 7-12   Write each of the following in scientific notation.
(a) 413,682,000   (b) 0.0000231
(c) 83.7   (d) 10,000,000

SOLUTION   (a) $413,682,000 = 4.13682 \cdot 10^8$ (b) $0.0000231 = 2.31 \cdot 10^{-5}$
(c) $8.37 \cdot 10^1$ (d) $1 \cdot 10^7$

EXAMPLE 7-13   Convert each of the following to standard numerals.
(a) $6.84 \cdot 10^{-5}$ (b) $3.12 \cdot 10^7$

SOLUTION   (a) $6.84 \cdot 10^{-5} = 6.84 \cdot \left(\dfrac{1}{10^5}\right) = 0.0000684$

(b) $3.12 \cdot 10^7 = 31,200,000$

---

significant digits

In Example 7.13(a), the number $6.84 \cdot 10^{-5}$ is in scientific notation. The digits in 6.84 are called **significant digits.** Notice that, if the number $6.84 \cdot 10^{-5}$ were written out in standard form, it would be 0.0000684. Even though there are 8 digits in the number in standard form, only 3 are considered significant. Also consider the number 684,000. Written in scientific notation, this number is $6.84 \cdot 10^5$, and it too has only 3 significant digits. As a final example, consider 604.3 in scientific notation, which is $6.043 \cdot 10^2$. This number has 4 significant digits.

It is possible to perform computations involving numbers in scientific notation by using the laws of exponents. For example, $(5.6 \cdot 10^5) \cdot (6 \cdot 10^4)$ can be rewritten as $(5.6 \cdot 6) \cdot (10^5 \cdot 10^4) = 33.6 \cdot 10^9$, which is $3.36 \cdot 10^{10}$ in scientific notation. Also,

$$(2.35 \cdot 10^{-15}) \cdot (2 \cdot 10^8) = (2.35 \cdot 2) \cdot (10^{-15} \cdot 10^8) = 4.7 \cdot 10^{-7}.$$

To investigate how your calculator handles scientific notation, consider the computation $41,368,200 \times 1000$. The answer is 41,368,200,000, or $4.13682 \cdot 10^{10}$. On a calculator, perform the following computation.

$\boxed{4}\boxed{1}\boxed{3}\boxed{6}\boxed{8}\boxed{2}\boxed{0}\boxed{0}\boxed{\times}\boxed{1}\boxed{0}\boxed{0}\boxed{0}\boxed{=}$

On many calculators, the display will read

$\boxed{4.1368 \quad 10}$

The number to the right of the space is the power to which 10 is raised when the number is written in scientific notation.

Calculators with an $\boxed{\text{EE}}$ key can be used to represent numbers in scientific notation. For example, to represent $5.2 \cdot 10^{16}$, we press

$\boxed{5}\boxed{.}\boxed{2}\boxed{\text{EE}}\boxed{1}\boxed{6}$.

PROBLEM SET 7-2

1. Find the decimal representation for each of the following.

   (a) $\dfrac{4}{9}$ (b) $\dfrac{2}{7}$ (c) $\dfrac{3}{11}$ (d) $\dfrac{1}{15}$

   (e) $\dfrac{2}{75}$ (f) $\dfrac{1}{99}$ (g) $\dfrac{5}{6}$ (h) $\dfrac{1}{13}$

2. This group of exercises concentrates on finding repeating decimals.
   (a) Use a calculator to find decimals for each of the following.

   (i) $\dfrac{1}{7}$

   (ii) $\dfrac{2}{7}$

   (iii) $\dfrac{3}{7}$

   (iv) $\dfrac{4}{7}$

   (v) $\dfrac{5}{7}$

   (vi) $\dfrac{6}{7}$

   (b) How many places were used before each decimal repeated?
   (c) Do you see any relationship among your answers in (i)–(vi) of (a)?

3. Using the answers obtained in Problem 2, add the numbers in the first half of each repetend to the numbers in the last half of each repetend. For example, $\frac{1}{7} = 0.\overline{142857}$, so we add $142 + 857$.
   (a) What do you discover?
   (b) Try the same experiment with $\frac{5}{13}$. Do you obtain the same type of result?
   (c) Make a conjecture about the sums of numbers formed by the halves of the repetend of a repeating decimal.
   (d) Will this conjecture work on the repeating decimal for $\frac{1}{3}$?

4. Find repeating decimals for each of the following.

   (a) $\dfrac{1}{13}$ (b) $\dfrac{1}{21}$ (c) $\dfrac{3}{19}$

5. Convert each of the following repeating decimals to fractions.

   (a) $2.4\overline{5}$ (b) $2.\overline{45}$ (c) $2.4\overline{54}$
   (d) $0.2\overline{45}$ (e) $0.02\overline{45}$ (f) $^-24.\overline{54}$
   (g) $0.\overline{4}$ (h) $0.\overline{6}$ (i) $0.5\overline{5}$
   (j) $0.3\overline{4}$ (k) $^-2.\overline{34}$ (l) $^-0.\overline{02}$

6. Order each of the following sets of decimals from greatest to least.
   (a) $\{3.2,\ 3.\overline{22},\ 3.\overline{23},\ 3.2\overline{3},\ 3.23\}$
   (b) $\{^-1.454,\ ^-1.45\overline{4},\ ^-1.45,\ ^-1.4\overline{54},\ ^-1.\overline{454}\}$

7. Find a decimal between each of the following pairs of decimals.
   (a) 3.2 and 3.3   (b) 462.24 and 462.25
   (c) $462.2\overline{4}$ and $462.\overline{24}$ (d) 0.003 and 0.03

8. Find the decimal halfway between the two given decimals.
   (a) 3.2 and 3.3   (b) 462.24 and 462.25
   (c) 0.0003 and 0.03   ★(d) $462.2\overline{4}$ and $462.\overline{24}$

9. Some digits in the number shown below have been covered by squares. If each of the digits 1 through 9 is used exactly once in the number, what is the number in each of the following cases?

$$4\ \square\ \square\ 3\ \square\ .\ \square\ \square\ 8\ \square$$

   (a) The number is as great as possible.
   (b) The number is the least possible.

10. Round each of the following numbers as specified.
    (a) 203.651 to the nearest hundred
    (b) 203.651 to the nearest ten
    (c) 203.651 to the nearest unit
    (d) 203.651 to the nearest tenth
    (e) 203.651 to the nearest hundredth

11. Jane's car travels 224 miles on 12 gallons of gas. How many miles to the gallon does her car get, rounded to the nearest mile?

12. Sooner or later, most people are faced with the task of buying a number of items at the store, knowing that they have just barely enough money to cover the needed items. In order to avoid the embarrassment of coming up short and having to put some of the items back, they must use their estimating or rounding skills. For each of the following sets of items, estimate the cost. If you are short of funds, tell what must be returned to come just under the allotted amount to be spent. Use your calculator to check your answers.
    (a) Amount on hand—$2.98

      2 packs of gum at 24¢ each
      3 suckers at 10¢ each
      1 licorice at 4 for 20¢
      1 soft drink at 35¢
      1 pack dental floss at 99¢

(b) Amount on hand—$20.00

> 7 gallons of gas at $1.089 per gallon
> 2 quarts of oil at $1.05 per quart
> a car wash at $1.99
> flashlight batteries at $3.39
> air in a tire at 0¢ per pound
> air freshener at 99¢
> starter fluid at 99¢
> parking ticket at $1.00
> windshield wiper at $1.59
> soft drink for your date at 35¢

13. Audrey wants to buy some camera equipment to take pictures on her daughter's birthday. To estimate the total cost, she rounds each price to the nearest dollar and adds the rounded prices. What is her estimate for the items listed?

Camera	$24.95
Film	$3.50
Case	$7.85

14. Estimate the sum or difference in each of the following by using (i) rounding and (ii) front-end estimation. (Front-end estimation is demonstrated on the student page in this section.) Then perform the computations to see how close your estimates are to the actual answers.

(a) 65.84
     24.29
     12.18
    +19.75

(b) 89.47
    −32.16

(c) 5.85
     6.13
     9.10
    +4.32

(d) 223.75
    − 87.60

▤ 15. It is estimated that it would take the United States approximately 14,000 years to produce the amount of wheat that should be placed on the last square of a checkerboard if one grain were placed on the first square, two grains were placed on the second square, and so on, doubling the amount of wheat each time. At this rate, approximately how many years would it take the United States to produce the amount of wheat required to cover all the squares?

16. Express each of the following numbers in scientific notation.
    (a) 3325   (b) 46.32
    (c) 0.00013   (d) 930,146

17. Convert each of the following numbers to standard numerals.
    (a) $3.2 \cdot 10^{-9}$ (b) $3.2 \cdot 10^9$
    (c) $4.2 \cdot 10^{-1}$ (d) $6.2 \cdot 10^5$

18. Write the numerals in each of the following sentences in scientific notation.
    (a) The diameter of the earth is about 12,700,000 m.
    (b) The distance from Pluto to the sun is 5,797,000 km.
    (c) Each year, about 50,000,000 cans are discarded in the United States.

19. Write the numerals in each sentence in standard form.
    (a) A computer requires $4.4 \cdot 10^{-6}$ seconds to do an addition problem.
    (b) There are about $1.99 \cdot 10^4$ km of coastline in the United States.
    (c) The earth has existed for approximately $3 \cdot 10^9$ years.

20. Write the results of each of the following in scientific notation.
    (a) $(8 \cdot 10^{12}) \cdot (6 \cdot 10^{15})$
    (b) $(16 \cdot 10^{12}) \div (4 \cdot 10^5)$
    (c) $(5 \cdot 10^8) \cdot (6 \cdot 10^9) \div (15 \cdot 10^{15})$

21. Which of the following numbers is the greatest? $100,000^3$; 1000^5; $100,000^2$

▤ 22. Use a calculator to find $\frac{26}{99}$ and $\frac{78}{99}$. Can you predict a decimal value for $\frac{51}{99}$? Will the technique used in your prediction always work? Why or why not?

23. Continue the following decimal patterns.
    (a) $0, 0.\overline{3}, 0.\overline{6}, 1, 1.\overline{3},$ _____, _____, _____
    (b) $0, 0.5, 0.\overline{6}. 0.75, 0.8, 0.8\overline{3},$ _____, _____, _____

★24. Suppose that $a = 0.\overline{32}$ and $b = 0.\overline{123}$.
    (a) Find $a + b$ by adding from left to right. How many digits are in the repetend of the sum?
    (b) Find $a + b$ if $a = 1.2\overline{34}$ and $b = 0.\overline{1234}$. Is the answer a rational number? How many digits are in the repetend?

Review Problems

25. (a) Human bones make up 0.18 of a person's total body weight. How much do the bones of a 120-pound person weigh?
    (b) Muscles make up about 0.4 of a person's body weight. How much do the muscles of a 120-pound person weigh?

26. John is a payroll clerk for a small company. Last month, the employees' gross earnings (earnings before deductions) totaled $27,849.50. He then deducted $1520.63 for social security, $723.30 for unemployment insurance, and $2843.62 for federal income tax. What was the employees' net pay (their earnings after deductions)?

27. How can you tell whether a fraction will represent a terminating decimal without performing the actual division?

28. Write each of the following decimals as fractions.
    (a) 16.72
    (b) 0.003
    (c) ⁻5.07
    (d) 0.123

C O M P U T E R   C O R N E R

The following BASIC program rounds decimals to a given number of places. See if it gives the same results as the rules identified in this chapter.

```
 10 PRINT "THIS PROGRAM ROUNDS DECIMALS."
 20 PRINT
 30 PRINT "ENTER YOUR DECIMAL AND PRESS RETURN."
 40 INPUT D
 50 PRINT "HOW MANY DIGITS WOULD YOU LIKE TO THE "
 55 PRINT "RIGHT OF THE DECIMAL POINT?"
 60 INPUT N
 70 LET S = INT (D * 10 ^ N + .5)
 80 LET R = S / (10 ^ N)
 90 PRINT
100 PRINT D ; " ROUNDS TO "; R
110 PRINT
120 PRINT "TO ENTER ANOTHER DECIMAL: TYPE RUN."
130 END
```

Section 7-3   Percents

Percents are very useful in conveying information. People hear that there is a 60 percent chance of rain or that their savings accounts are drawing 6 percent interest. Many become familiar with the sales tax when they make *percent* a purchase. The word **percent** comes from the Latin phrase *per centum*, which can be translated as *per hundred*. For example, a bank that pays 6 percent simple interest on a savings account pays $6 for each $100 in the account for one year; that is, it pays $\frac{6}{100}$ of whatever amount is in the account for one year. We use the symbol % to indicate percent and, for example, write 6% for $\frac{6}{100}$.

In general, we have the following definition.

● D E F I N I T I O N

$$n\% = \frac{n}{100}$$

FIGURE 7-1

Percents can be illustrated by using a hundreds grid. For example, what percent of the squares are shaded in Figure 7-1? Because 30 out of the 100, or $\frac{30}{100}$, of the squares are shaded, we say that 30% of the grid is shaded.

We can convert any number to a percent by first writing the number as a fraction with denominator 100. For instance, consider the example in the cartoon that follows. Obviously, the adult is incorrect.

The child in the cartoon missed 6 questions out of 10 and hence had 4 correct answers; therefore, $\frac{4}{10}$ of the answers were correct. Because $\frac{4}{10} = \frac{40}{100}$, the child had 40%, not 90%, correct answers.

From the definition of percent, $n\% = n/100$, it follows that $n = 100 \cdot n\%$. Using this equality, we can convert a number to a percent by multiplying it by 100. For example,

$$0.0002 = 100 \cdot 0.0002\% = 0.02\%$$

$$\frac{3}{4} = 100 \cdot \frac{3}{4}\% = \frac{300}{4}\% = 75\%$$

EXAMPLE 7-14 Write each of the following as a percent.

(a) 0.03   (b) $0.\overline{3}$ (c) 1.2   (d) 0.00042

(e) 1   (f) $\frac{3}{5}$ (g) $\frac{2}{3}$ (h) $2\frac{1}{7}$

SOLUTION (a) $0.03 = 100 \cdot 0.03\% = 3\%$

(b) $0.\overline{3} = 100 \cdot 0.\overline{3}\% = 33.\overline{3}\%$

(c) $1.2 = 100 \cdot 1.2\% = 120\%$

(d) $0.00042 = 100 \cdot 0.00042\% = 0.042\%$

(e) $1 = 100 \cdot 1\% = 100\%$

(f) $\dfrac{3}{5} = 100 \cdot \dfrac{3}{5}\% = \dfrac{300}{5}\% = 60\%$

(g) $\dfrac{2}{3} = 100 \cdot \dfrac{2}{3}\% = \dfrac{200}{3}\% = 66.\overline{6}\%$

(h) $2\dfrac{1}{7} = 100 \cdot 2\dfrac{1}{7}\% = \dfrac{1500}{7}\% = 214\dfrac{1}{7}\%$

A number can also be converted to a percent by using a *proportion*. For example, to write $\frac{3}{5}$ as a percent, we need only find the value of n in the following proportion.

$$\frac{3}{5} = \frac{n}{100}$$

Solving the proportion, we obtain $(\frac{3}{5}) \cdot 100 = n$, or $n = 60$. Hence, the answer is 60%.

In doing computations, it is sometimes useful to convert percents to decimals. This can be done by writing the percent as a fraction and then converting the fraction to a decimal.

EXAMPLE 7-15   Write each percent as a decimal.

(a) 5%   (b) 6.3%   (c) 100%
(d) 250%   (e) $\frac{1}{3}$%   (f) $33\frac{1}{3}$%

SOLUTION

(a) $5\% = \dfrac{5}{100} = 0.05$

(b) $6.3\% = \dfrac{6.3}{100} = 0.063$

(c) $100\% = \dfrac{100}{100} = 1$

(d) $250\% = \dfrac{250}{100} = 2.50$

(e) $\dfrac{1}{3}\% = \dfrac{\frac{1}{3}}{100} = \dfrac{0.\overline{3}}{100} = 0.00\overline{3}$

(f) $33\dfrac{1}{3}\% = \dfrac{33\frac{1}{3}}{100} = \dfrac{33.\overline{3}}{100} = 0.\overline{3}$

Example 7-15 may be used to discover an algorithm for converting percents to decimals: *To change a percent to a decimal, drop the percent sign and divide by* 100. A percent key on a calculator may perform this algorithm. For example, if the keys $\boxed{3}\,\boxed{4}\,\boxed{.}\,\boxed{5}\,\boxed{\%}$ are pressed in the order given, many calculators will display 0.345. You should investigate how your calculator handles percents.

Application problems involving percents usually take one of the following forms:

1. Finding a percent of a number.
2. Finding what percent one number is of another.
3. Finding a number when a percent of that number is known.

Before considering examples illustrating these forms, recall what it means to find a fraction "of" a number. For example, $\frac{2}{3}$ of 70 means $\frac{2}{3} \cdot 70$. Similarly, to find 40% of 70, we have $\frac{40}{100}$ of 70, which means $\frac{40}{100} \cdot 70$, or $0.40 \cdot 70 = 28$.

EXAMPLE 7-16   A house that sells for $72,000 requires a 20% down payment. What is the amount of the down payment?

SOLUTION   The down payment is 20% of $72,000, or $0.20 \cdot \$72,000 = \$14,400$. Hence, the amount of the down payment is $14,400.

EXAMPLE 7-17   If Alberto has 45 correct answers on an 80-question test, what percent of his answers are correct?

SOLUTION   Alberto has $\frac{45}{80}$ of the answers correct. To find the percent of correct answers, we need to convert $\frac{45}{80}$ to a percent. This can be done by writing an equation as follows.

$$\frac{45}{80} = 100 \cdot \frac{45}{80}\% = \frac{4500}{80}\% = 56.25\%$$

Thus, 56.25% of the answers are correct.

An alternate solution can be found by using a proportion. Let n be the percent of correct answers. Hence, we have the following.

$$\frac{45}{80} = \frac{n}{100}$$

$$\frac{45}{80} \cdot 100 = n$$

$$n = \frac{4500}{80} = 56.25$$

EXAMPLE 7-18 Forty-two percent of the parents of the school children in the Paxson School District are employed at Di Paloma University. If the number of parents employed by D.P.U. is 168, how many parents are in the school district?

SOLUTION If we let n be the number of parents in the school district, then we know that 42% of n is 168. We translate this information into an equation and solve for n.

$$42\% \text{ of } n = 168$$
$$\frac{42}{100} \cdot n = 168$$
$$0.42 \cdot n = 168$$
$$n = \frac{168}{0.42} = 400$$

Hence, there are 400 parents in the school district.

     The problem can be solved using a proportion. We know that 42%, or $\frac{42}{100}$, of the parents are employed at D.P.U. If n is the total number of parents, then $168/n$ also represents the fraction of parents employed at D.P.U. Thus,

$$\frac{42}{100} = \frac{168}{n}$$
$$42n = 100 \cdot 168$$
$$n = \frac{16,800}{42} = 400$$

     The problem can also be solved as follows.

$$42\% \text{ of } n \text{ is } 168$$
$$1\% \text{ of } n \text{ is } \frac{168}{42}$$
$$100\% \text{ of } n \text{ is } 100\left(\frac{168}{42}\right)$$

Therefore, n is $100\left(\frac{168}{42}\right)$ or 400.

EXAMPLE 7-19 Mike bought a bicycle and then sold it for 20% more than he paid for it. If he sold the bike for $144, what did he pay for it?

SOLUTION We are looking for the original price P that Mike paid for the bike. We know that he sold the bike for $144 and that this included a 20% profit. Thus, we can write the following equation.

$$\$144 = P + \text{Mike's profit}$$

Since Mike's profit is 20% of P, we proceed as follows.

$$144 = P + 20\% \cdot P$$
$$144 = P + 0.20 \cdot P$$
$$144 = (1 + 0.20)P$$
$$144 = 1.20P$$
$$\frac{144}{1.20} = P$$
$$120 = P$$

Thus, Mike originally paid $120 for the bike.

EXAMPLE 7-20   Westerner's Clothing Store advertised a suit for 10% off, for a savings of $15. Later, the manager marked the suit at 30% off the original price. What is the amount of the current discount?

SOLUTION   A 10% discount amounts to a $15 savings. This information can be used to find the original price P. Since 10% of P is $15, we have the following.

$$10\% \cdot P = \$15$$
$$0.10 \cdot P = \$15$$
$$P = \$150$$

We must now calculate 30% of $150 to find the current discount. Because $0.30 \cdot \$150 = \$45$, the amount of the 30% discount is $45.

In the Looking Back stage of problem solving, we check the answer and look for other ways to solve the problem. A different approach leads to a more efficient solution. If 10% of the price is $15, then 30% of the price is 3 times $15, or $45.

Mental Math with Percents

Mental math may be helpful when working with percents. Several techniques follow.

1. *Using fraction equivalents*

   Knowing fractional equivalents for some percents can make some computations easier. Several are given in Table 7-3. The fraction equivalents can be used in such computations as the following.

$$50\% \text{ of } \$75 = \left(\frac{1}{2}\right)75 = \$37.50$$

$$66\frac{2}{3}\% \text{ of } 48 = \frac{2}{3}(48) = 32$$

TABLE 7-3

Percent	25%	50%	75%	$33\frac{1}{3}\%$	$66\frac{2}{3}\%$	10%	1%
Fraction Equivalent	$\frac{1}{4}$	$\frac{1}{2}$	$\frac{3}{4}$	$\frac{1}{3}$	$\frac{2}{3}$	$\frac{1}{10}$	$\frac{1}{100}$

2. *Using a known percent*
Many times we may not know a percent of something, but we know a close percent of it. For example, to find 55% of 62, we might do the following.

$$50\% \text{ of } 62 = \left(\frac{1}{2}\right)(62) = 31$$

$$5\% \text{ of } 62 = \left(\frac{1}{2}\right)(10\%)(62) = \left(\frac{1}{2}\right)(6.2) = 3.1$$

Adding, we see that 55% of 62 is $31 + 3.1 = 34.1$.

Estimations with Percents

Estimations with percents can be used to determine whether answers are reasonable or not. Following are some examples.

1. To estimate 27% of 598, we see that 27% of 598 is a little more than 25% of 598, but 25% of 598 is approximately the same as 25% of 600, or $\frac{1}{4}$ of 600, or 150. Here we have adjusted 27% downward and 598 upward, so 150 should be a reasonable estimate. A better estimate might be obtained by estimating 30% of 600 and then subtracting 3% of 600 to obtain 27% of 600, giving $180 - 18$, or 162.

2. To estimate 148% of 500, we see that 148% of 500 should be slightly less than 150% of 500. 150% of 500 is $1.5(500) = 750$. Thus, 148% of 500 should be a little less than 750.

PROBLEM SET 7-3

1. Express each of the following as percents.
   (a) 7.89   (b) 0.032   (c) 193.1   (d) 0.2
   (e) $\frac{5}{6}$ (f) $\frac{3}{20}$ (g) $\frac{1}{8}$ (h) $\frac{3}{8}$
   (i) $\frac{5}{8}$ (j) $\frac{1}{6}$ (k) $\frac{4}{5}$ (l) $\frac{1}{40}$

2. Convert each of the following percents to decimals.
   (a) 16%   (b) $4\frac{1}{2}\%$ (c) $\frac{1}{5}\%$ (d) $\frac{2}{7}\%$
   (e) $13\frac{2}{3}\%$ (f) 125%   (g) $\frac{1}{3}\%$ (h) $\frac{1}{4}\%$

3. Fill in the blanks to find other expressions for 4%.
   (a) _____ for every 100
   (b) _____ for every 50
   (c) 1 for every _____
   (d) 8 for every _____
   (e) 0.5 for every _____

4. Different calculators compute percents in various ways. To investigate this, consider $5 \cdot 6\%$.
   (a) If the following sequence of keys is pressed, is the correct answer of 0.3 displayed on your calculator?

   $\boxed{5}\ \boxed{\times}\ \boxed{6}\ \boxed{\%}\ \boxed{=}$

   (b) Press $\boxed{6}\ \boxed{\%}\ \boxed{\times}\ \boxed{5}\ \boxed{=}$. Is the answer 0.3?

5. Answer each of the following.
   (a) Find 6% of 34.
   (b) 17 is what percent of 34?
   (c) 18 is 30% of what number?
   (d) Find 7% of 49.
   (e) 61.5 is what percent of 20.5?
   (f) 16 is 40% of what number?

6. Marc had 84 boxes of candy to sell. He sold 75% of the boxes. How many did he sell?

7. Gail made $16,000 last year and received a 6% raise. How much does she make now?

8. Gail received a 7% raise last year. If her salary is now $15,515, what was her salary last year?

9. A company bought a used typewriter for $350, which was 80% of the original cost. What was the original cost of the typewriter?

10. Joe sold 180 newspapers out of 200. Bill sold 85% of his 260 newspapers. Ron sold 212 newspapers, 80% of those he had.
    (a) Who sold the most newspapers? How many?
    (b) Who sold the greatest percent of his newspapers? What percent?
    (c) Who started with the greatest number of newspapers? How many?

11. If a dress that normally sells for $35 is on sale for $28, what is the "percent off"? (This could be called a *percent of decrease,* or a *discount.*)

12. A car originally cost $8000. One year later, it was worth $6800. What is the percent of depreciation?

13. On a certain day in Glacier Park, 728 eagles were counted. Five years later, 594 were counted. What was the percent of decrease in the number of eagles counted?

14. Mort bought his house in 1975 for $29,000. It was recently appraised at $55,000. What is the *percent of increase* in value?

15. Xuan weighed 9 pounds when he was born. At 6 months, he weighed 18 pounds. What was the percent of increase in Xuan's weight?

16. Sally bought a dress marked at 20% off. If the regular price was $28.00, what was the sale price?

17. What is the sale price of a softball if the regular price is $6.80 and there is a 25% discount?

18. If a $\frac{1}{4}$-cup serving of Crunchies breakfast food has 0.5% of the minimum daily requirement of Vitamin C, how many cups would you have to eat in order to obtain the minimum daily requirement of Vitamin C?

19. An airline ticket costs $320 without the tax. If the tax rate is 5%, what is the total bill for the airline ticket?

20. Bill got 52 correct answers on an 80-question test. What percent of the questions did he not answer correctly?

21. A real estate broker receives 4% of an $80,000 sale. How much does the broker receive?

22. A survey reported that $66\frac{2}{3}$% of 1800 employees favored a new insurance program. How many employees favored the new program?

23. A family has a monthly income of $2400 and makes a monthly house payment of $400. What percent of the income is the house payment?

24. A plumber's wage this year is $19.80 an hour. This is a 110% increase over last year's hourly wage. What is the dollar increase in the hourly wage over last year?

25. Ms. Price has received a 10% raise in salary in each of the last 2 years. If her annual salary this year is $100,000, what was her salary 2 years ago, rounded to the nearest penny?

26. Soda is advertised at 45¢ a can or $2.40 a six-pack. If 6 cans are to be purchased, what percent is saved by purchasing the six-pack?

27. John paid $330 for a new mountain bicycle to sell in his shop. He wants to price it so that he can offer a 10% discount and still make 20% of the price he paid for it. At what price should the bike be marked?

28. The price of a suit that sold for $100 was reduced by 25%. By what percent must the price of the suit be increased to bring the price back to $100?

29. Howard entered a store and said to the owner, "Give me as much money as I have with me and I will spend 80% of the total." After this was done, Howard repeated the operation at a second store and at a third store and was finally left with $12. With how much money did he start?

30. The car Elsie bought 1 year ago has depreciated by $1116.88, which is 12.13% of the price she paid for it. How much did she pay for the car, to the nearest cent?

31. Solve each of the following, using mental mathematics.
    (a) 15% of $22   (b) 20% of $120
    (c) 5% of $38   (d) 25% of $98

32. If we build a 10 × 10 model with blocks, as shown in the figure, and paint the entire model, what percent of the cubes will have each of the following?
    (a) Four faces painted   (b) Three faces painted
    (c) Two faces painted

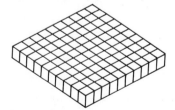

33. Answer the questions in Problem 32 for models of the following sizes.
    (a) 9 × 9   (b) 8 × 8
    (c) 7 × 7   (d) 12 × 12

34. A worker earns d dollars for each item he produces if he produces 7 or fewer items per hour. He earns 25% more for each item after the seventh.
    (a) How much does the worker make per hour if he produces 11 items per hour?
    (b) How much does he make per hour if he produces n items per hour and n is greater than 7?

Review Problems

35. A state charged a company $63.27 per day for overdue taxes. The total bill for the overdue taxes was $6137.19. How many days were the taxes overdue?
36. Write 33.21 as a fraction in simplest form.
37. Write $\frac{2}{8}$ as a decimal.

38. Write $31.0\overline{5}$ as a fraction in simplest form.
39. Write each of the following in scientific notation.
    (a) 3,250,000   (b) 0.00012
40. Round 32.015 to the indicated place.
    (a) The nearest tenth   (b) The nearest ten

B R A I N   T E A S E R

The crust of a certain pumpkin pie is 25% of the pie. By what percent should the amount of crust be reduced in order to make it constitute 20% of the pie?

---

*Section 7-4   Computing Interest

interest

principal

interest rate

simple interest

When a bank advertises a $5\frac{1}{2}\%$ interest rate on a savings account, the amount of money the bank will pay for using that money is called **interest.** If we borrow money from a bank, we must pay interest to the bank for using that money. The original amount deposited or borrowed is called the **principal.** The percent used to determine the interest is called the **interest rate.** Interest rates are given for specific periods of time, such as years, months, or days. Interest computed on the original principal is called **simple interest.** For example, suppose we borrow $5000 from a company at a simple interest rate of 12% for 1 year. The interest we owe on the loan for 1 year is 12% of $5000, or $5000 · 0.12. In general, if a principal P is invested at an annual interest rate of r, then the simple interest after 1 year is $Pr · 1$; after t years it is Prt, or Prt. *If I represents simple interest, we have*

$$I = Prt$$

amount / balance

The amount needed to pay off a $5000 loan at 12% simple interest is the $5000 borrowed plus the interest on the $5000, that is, 5000 + 5000 · 0.12, or $5600. In general, *an* **amount** (*or* **balance**) *A is equal to the principal P plus the interest I; that is, $A = P + I$, or $A = P + Prt$.* This formula can also be written as

$$A = P(1 + rt)$$

EXAMPLE 7-21   Vera opens a savings account that pays simple interest at the rate of $5\frac{1}{4}\%$ per year. If she deposits $2000 and makes no other deposits, find the interest and the final amount for the following periods of time.

(a) 1 year   (b) 90 days

SOLUTION   (a) To find the interest for 1 year, we proceed as follows.

$$I = \$2000 \cdot 5\tfrac{1}{4}\% \cdot 1 = \$2000 \cdot 0.0525 = \$105$$

Thus, her amount at the end of 1 year is

$$\$2000 + \$105 = \$2105$$

(b) When the interest rate is annual and the interest period is less than 1 year, we represent the time as a fractional part of a year by dividing the number of days by 365. Thus, to find the interest and the final amount, we perform the following computations.

$$I = \$2000 \cdot 5\tfrac{1}{4}\% \cdot \frac{90}{365}$$

$$= \$2000 \cdot 0.0525 \cdot \frac{90}{365} \doteq \$25.89$$

Hence, $A = \$2,000 + \$25.89 = \$2025.89.$

EXAMPLE 7-22   Find the annual interest rate if a principal of $10,000 increased to $10,900 at the end of 1 year.

SOLUTION   We use the strategy of writing an equation based on the relationship $I = Prt$. We need to solve for r, so we divide both sides of the equation by Pt, obtaining

$$r = \frac{I}{Pt}$$

To find the interest, we compute the difference between the balance and the principal. Thus, $I = \$10,900 - \$10,000 = \$900$. Substituting the values of I, P, and t in the preceding equation, we obtain

$$r = \frac{900}{10,000 \cdot 1} = 0.09, \text{ or } 9\%$$

Thus, the interest rate is 9%.

Compound Interest

In all our discussions thus far, we have computed simple interest—interest based only on the original principal, which stays fixed for the entire interest period. A second method of computing interest involves compound

compound interest   interest. **Compound interest** is different from simple interest in that, after the first interest calculation, the interest is added to the principal, so interest may be earned on previous interest as well as on the principal. Compound interest rates are usually given as annual rates no matter how many times the interest is compounded per year. Compounding is most commonly done annually(1 time a year), semiannually (2 times a year), quarterly (4 times a year), monthly (12 times a year), or daily (365 times a year).

If i is the interest rate for a period, r is the annual interest rate, and n is the number of compounding periods per year, then we have $i = r/n$. For example, if the annual rate is 6% compounded quarterly, then the interest rate per quarter is given by $i = r/n = 0.06/4 = 0.015$, or 1.5%.

A formula can be developed for problems involving compound interest. The amount A at the end of each period is equal to the principal P at the beginning of the period plus the interest I for the period. If the interest rate per period is i, then we have the following.

$$A = P + I = P + P \cdot i = P(1 + i)$$

For example, suppose that we have \$100 invested at 8% compounded quarterly. Since the interest rate is 8% per year, it is $\frac{1}{4}$ of 8%, or 2% per quarter. Thus, at the end of one quarter, we have

$$A = P(1 + i) = 100(1 + 0.08/4) = 100(1 + 0.02) = \$102$$

To compute the amount we have at the end of the second quarter, we treat \$102 as the principal, and we have

$$A = P(1 + i) = 102(1 + 0.02) = \$104.04$$

To compute the amount at the end of the third quarter, we treat \$104.04 as the principal, and we have

$$A = P(1 + i) = 104.04(1 + 0.02) \doteq \$106.12$$

Similarly, at the end of one year, we have

$$A = P(1 + i) = 106.12(1 + 0.02) \doteq \$108.24$$

This process is rather easy to understand but rather hard to apply, because increasing the number of compounding periods increases the number of computations required to find the balance. A formula generalizing the above discussion is given in Table 7-4. Therefore, the amount at the end of the nth period is $P(1 + i)^n$. If the formula $A = P(1 + i)^n$ is applied to the example

TABLE 7-4

Period	Initial Amount	Final Amount
1	P	$P(1 + i)$
2	$P(1 + i)$	$[P(1 + i)](1 + i)$, or $P(1 + i)^2$
3	$P(1 + i)^2$	$[P(1 + i)^2](1 + i)$, or $P(1 + i)^3$
4	$P(1 + i)^3$	$[P(1 + i)^3](1 + i)$, or $P(1 + i)^4$
$\vdots$	$\vdots$	$\vdots$
n	$p(1 + i)^{n-1}$	$[P(1 + i)^{n-1}](1 + i)$, or $P(1 + i)^n$

of finding the amount at the end of one year when $100 earns 8% compounded quarterly, we have the following.

$$A = P(1 + i)^n = \$100\left(1 + \frac{0.08}{4}\right)^4 \doteq \$108.24$$

Notice that this answer agrees with our previous result.

EXAMPLE 7-23 Suppose that we deposit $1000 in a savings account that pays 6% interest compounded quarterly.
(a) What is the balance at the end of 1 year?
(b) What is the *effective annual yield* on this investment; that is, what is the rate that would have been paid if the amount had been invested using simple interest?

SOLUTION (a) An annual interest rate of 6% earns $\frac{1}{4}$ of 6%, or an interest rate of $\frac{0.06}{4}$, in one quarter. Since there are four periods, we have the following.

$$A = 1000\left(1 + \frac{0.06}{4}\right)^4 \doteq \$1061.36$$

Thus, the balance at the end of one year is $1061.36.
(b) Because the interest earned is $1061.36 − $1000.00 = $61.36, the effective annual yield can be computed by using the simple interest formula, $I = Prt$.

$$61.36 = 1000 \cdot r \cdot 1$$

$$\frac{61.36}{1000} = r$$

$$0.06136 = r$$

$$6.136\% = r$$

Hence, the effective annual yield is 6.136%.

EXAMPLE 7-24 To save for their child's college education, a couple deposits $3000 into an account that pays 11% annual interest compounded daily. Find the amount in this account after 12 years.

SOLUTION The principal in the problem is $3000, the daily rate i is 0.11/365, and the number of compounding periods is 12 · 365, or 4380. Thus, we have

$$A = \$3000\left(1 + \frac{0.11}{365}\right)^{4380} \doteq \$11,228$$

PROBLEM SET 7-4

A calculator is needed in most of these problems.

1. Complete the following compound-interest chart.

Compounding Period	Principal	Annual Rate	Length of Time (Years)	Interest Rate Per Period	Number of Periods	Amount of Interest Paid
(a) Semiannual	$1000	6%	2			
(b) Quarterly	$1000	8%	3			
(c) Monthly	$1000	10%	5			
(d) Daily	$1000	12%	4			

2. Ms. Jackson borrowed $42,000 at 13% annual simple interest to buy her house. If she won the Irish Sweepstakes exactly 1 year later and was able to repay the loan without penalty, how much interest did she owe?

3. Carolyn went on a shopping spree with her Bankamount card and made purchases totaling $125. If the interest rate is 1.5% per month on the unpaid balance and she does not pay this debt for 1 year, how much interest will she owe at the end of the year?

4. A man collected $28,500 on a loan of $25,000 he made 4 years ago. If he charged simple interest, what was the rate he charged?

5. Burger Queen will need $50,000 in 5 years for a new addition. To meet this goal, money is deposited today in an account that pays 9% annual interest compounded quarterly. Find the amount that should be invested to total $50,000 in 5 years.

6. A company is expanding its line to include more products. To do so, it borrows $320,000 at 13.5% annual simple interest for a period of 18 months. How much interest must the company pay?

7. An amount of $3000 was deposited in a bank at a rate of 5% compounded quarterly for 3 years; the rate then increased to 8% and was compounded quarterly for the next 3 years. If no money was withdrawn, what was the balance at the end of this time period?

8. To save for their retirement, a couple deposits $4000 in an account that pays 9% interest compounded quarterly. What will be the value of their investment after 20 years?

9. A money-market fund pays 14% annual interest compounded daily. What is the value of $10,000 invested in this fund after 15 years?

10. A car company is offering car loans at a simple-interest rate of 9%. Find the interest charged to a customer who finances a car loan of $7200 for 3 years.

11. The New Age Savings Bank advertises 9% interest rates compounded daily, while the Pay More Bank pays 10.5% interest compounded annually. Which bank offers a better rate for a customer if she plans to leave her money in for exactly 1 year?

12. Johnny and Carolyn have three different savings plans, which accumulated the following amounts of interest for 1 year:
   (i)   A passbook savings account that accumulated $53.90 on a principal of $980.
   (ii) A certificate of deposit that accumulated $55.20 on a principal of $600.
   (iii) A money market certificate that accumulated $158.40 on a principal of $1200.
   Which of these accounts paid the best interest rate for the year?

13. If a hamburger costs $1.35 and if the price continues to rise at a rate of 11% a year for the next 6 years, what will the price of a hamburger be at the end of 6 years?

14. If college tuition is $2500 this year, what will it be 10 years from now, if we assume a constant inflation rate of 9% a year?

15. Sara invested money at a bank that paid 6.5% compounded quarterly. If she had $4650 at the end of 4 years, what was her initial investment?

16. A car is purchased for $15,000. If each year the car depreciates by 10% of its value the preceding year, what will its value be at the end of 3 years?

17. If Adrien and Jarrell deposit $300 on January 1 in a holiday savings account that pays 1.1% per month interest and they withdraw the money on December 1 of the same year, what is the effective annual yield?

★18. Determine the number of years (to the nearest tenth) that it would take for any amount of money deposited at a 10% interest rate compounded annually to double.

C O M P U T E R   C O R N E R

The following BASIC program will compute compound interest. Type it into the computer and compare the results with those obtained in this chapter.

```
10  PRINT "COMPOUND INTEREST PROGRAM"
20  PRINT
30  PRINT "TYPE IN THE PRINCIPAL AND PRESS RETURN."
40  INPUT P
50  PRINT "TYPE IN THE RATE AS A DECIMAL AND PRESS RETURN."
60  INPUT R
70  PRINT "TYPE IN THE NUMBER OF YEARS AND PRESS RETURN."
80  INPUT T
90  PRINT "TYPE IN THE COMPOUNDING PERIOD AND PRESS RETURN."
100 PRINT "ENTER 2 FOR SEMIANNUALLY, 4 FOR QUARTERLY, "
110 PRINT "12 FOR MONTHLY, OR 365 FOR DAILY."
120 INPUT C
130 LET N = T * C
140 LET I = R/C
150 LET A = P * ((1 + I) ^ N)
160 PRINT
170 PRINT "PRINCIPAL"; TAB(11); "RATE"; TAB (16) ;
180 PRINT "TIME"; TAB(21); "COMPOUNDED"; TAB(32) ; "AMOUNT"
190 PRINT P; TAB(11) ; R; TAB(16) ; T; TAB(21) ; C; TAB(32) ; A
200 PRINT
210 PRINT "TO ENTER ANOTHER PROBLEM TYPE RUN."
220 END
```

Section 7-5   Real Numbers

As we have seen, every rational number can be expressed either as a repeating decimal or as a terminating decimal. The ancient Greeks discovered numbers that are not rational. Such numbers must have a decimal representation that neither terminates nor repeats. To find such decimals, we focus on the characteristics they must have:

1. There must be an infinite number of nonzero digits to the right of the decimal point.
2. There cannot be a repeating block of digits (a repetend).

Does a decimal like 0.1432865 . . . have these characteristics? Because the decimal is infinite, the first characteristic is satisfied. However, without more information, there is no way to tell whether there is a repeating block of digits in the decimal.

There are several ways to construct a nonterminating, nonrepeating decimal. Perhaps the simplest is to devise a pattern of infinite digits in such a way that there will definitely be no repeated block. Consider the number 0.1010010001 . . . . If the pattern shown continues, the next groups of digits are four zeros followed by 1, five zeros followed by 1, and so on. It is possible to describe a pattern for this decimal, but there is no repeating block

irrational numbers

of digits. Because this decimal is nonterminating and nonrepeating, it cannot represent a rational number. Numbers that are not rational numbers are called **irrational numbers.**

π (pi)

In the mid-eighteenth century, it was proved that the number that is the ratio of the circumference of a circle to its diameter, symbolized by **π (pi),** is an irrational number. The numbers $\frac{22}{7}$, 3.14, or 3.14159 are rational-number approximations of π. The value of π has been computed to thousands of decimal places with no apparent pattern.

square root

principal square root

Other irrational numbers occur in the study of area. For example, to find the area of a square, we use the formula $A = s^2$, where A is the area and s is the length of a side of the square. If a side of a square is 3 cm long, then the area of the square is 9 cm^2 (square centimeters). Conversely, we can use the formula to find the length of a side of a square, given its area. If the area of a square is 25 cm^2, then $s^2 = 25$, so $s = 5$ or $^-5$. Each of these solutions is called a **square root** of 25. However, because lengths are always nonnegative, 5 is the only possible solution. The positive solution of $s^2 = 25$—namely, 5—is called the **principal square root** of 25 and is denoted by $\sqrt{25}$. Similarly, the principal square root of 2 is denoted by $\sqrt{2}$. Note that $\sqrt{16} \neq \,^-4$, because $^-4$ is not the principal square root of 16.

● **D E F I N I T I O N**

If a is any whole number, the **principal square root** of a is the nonnegative number b such that $b^2 = a$.

● **R E M A R K**

radical sign / radicand

The principal square root of a is denoted by $\sqrt{a}$, where the symbol $\sqrt{}$ is called a **radical sign** and a is called the **radicand.**

H I S T O R I C A L   N O T E

The discovery of irrational numbers by members of the Pythagorean Society (founded by Pythagoras) is one of the greatest events in the history of mathematics. This discovery was very disturbing to the Pythagoreans, who believed that everything depended on whole numbers, so they decided to keep the matter secret. One legend has it that Hippasus, a society member, was drowned because he relayed the secret to persons outside the society.

Christoff Rudolff, a German mathematician, was the first to use the symbol $\sqrt{}$, in 1525.

EXAMPLE 7-25 Find: (a) the square roots of 144;

(b) the principal square root of 144.

SOLUTION (a) The square roots of 144 are 12 and $^-12$.

(b) The principal square root of 144 is 12.

Some square roots are rational numbers. For example, $\sqrt{25}$ is 5, a rational number. Other square roots, like $\sqrt{2}$, are irrational numbers. To see this, note that $1^2 = 1$ and $2^2 = 4$, and that there is no whole number s such that $s^2 = 2$. Is there a rational number $\dfrac{a}{b}$ such that $\left(\dfrac{a}{b}\right)^2 = 2$? If we assume there is such a rational number, then the following must be true.

$$\left(\frac{a}{b}\right)^2 = 2$$
$$\frac{a^2}{b^2} = 2$$
$$a^2 = 2b^2$$

Since $a^2 = 2b^2$, the Fundamental Theorem of Arithmetic says that the prime factorizations of a^2 and $2b^2$ are the same. In particular, the prime 2 appears the same number of times in the prime factorization of a^2 as it does in the factorization of $2b^2$. Since $b^2 = b \cdot b$, then no matter how many times 2 appears in the prime factorization of b, it appears twice as many times in $b \cdot b$. Also, a^2 has an even number of 2s for the same reason that b^2 does. In $2b^2$, another factor of 2 is introduced, resulting in an odd number of 2s in the prime factorization of $2b^2$ and hence of a^2. But 2 cannot appear both an odd number of times and an even number of times in the same prime factorization of a^2. We have a contradiction. This contradiction could have been caused only by the assumption that $\sqrt{2}$ is a rational number. Consequently, $\sqrt{2}$ must be an irrational number. A similar argument can be used to show that $\sqrt{3}$ is irrational or $\sqrt{n}$ is irrational, where n is a whole number but not the square of another whole number.

EXAMPLE 7-26 Prove that $2 + \sqrt{2}$ is an irrational number.

SOLUTION Suppose that $2 + \sqrt{2} = \dfrac{a}{b}$, where $\dfrac{a}{b}$ is a rational number. Then,

$$\sqrt{2} = \frac{a}{b} - 2$$
$$\sqrt{2} = \frac{a - 2b}{b}$$

But $\dfrac{a - 2b}{b}$ is a rational number (why?), and this is a contradiction because $\sqrt{2}$ is an irrational number. Thus, $2 + \sqrt{2}$ is an irrational number.

- **R E M A R K**

  In a similar manner, we could prove $m + n\sqrt{2}$ is an irrational number for all rational numbers m and n except $n = 0$.

Many irrational numbers can be interpreted geometrically. For example, a point on a number line can be found to represent $\sqrt{2}$ by using the
Pythagorean Theorem   **Pythagorean Theorem** (see Chapter 13). That is, if a and b are the lengths of the shorter sides (legs) of a right triangle and c is the length of the longer side (hypotenuse), then $a^2 + b^2 = c^2$, as shown in Figure 7-2.

FIGURE 7-2

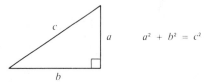

Figure 7-3 shows a segment one unit long constructed perpendicular to a number line at point P. Thus, two sides of the triangle shown are one unit long. By the Pythagorean Theorem, $1^2 + 1^2 = c^2$. Thus, $c^2 = 2$, and $c = \sqrt{2}$. Because $\sqrt{2}$ is the length of the hypotenuse, there must be some point Q on the number line such that the distance from zero to Q is $\sqrt{2}$.

FIGURE 7-3

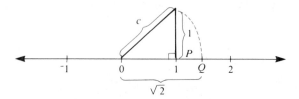

Similarly, other square roots can be constructed, as shown in Figure 7-4.

FIGURE 7-4

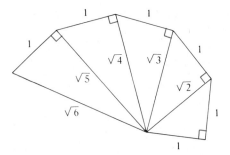

From Figure 7-3, we see that $\sqrt{2}$ must have a value between 1 and 2—that is, $1 < \sqrt{2} < 2$. To obtain a closer approximation of $\sqrt{2}$, we attempt

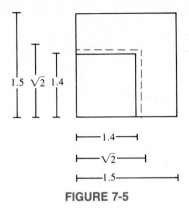

FIGURE 7-5

to "squeeze" $\sqrt{2}$ between two numbers that are between 1 and 2. Because $(1.5)^2 = 2.25$ and $(1.4)^2 = 1.96$, it follows that $1.4 < \sqrt{2} < 1.5$. Because a^2 can be interpreted as the area of a square with side of length a, this discussion can be pictured geometrically, as in Figure 7-5.

If a more accurate approximation for $\sqrt{2}$ is desired, this squeezing process can be continued. We see that $(1.4)^2$, or 1.96, is closer to 2 than is $(1.5)^2$, or 2.25, so we choose numbers closer to 1.4 in order to find the next approximation. We find the following.

$$(1.42)^2 = 2.0164$$
$$(1.41)^2 = 1.9981$$

Thus, $1.41 < \sqrt{2} < 1.42$. We can continue this process until we obtain the desired approximation. Note that, if the calculator has a square-root key, the approximation can be obtained directly.

The System of Real Numbers

real numbers The set of **real numbers** R is the union of the set of rational numbers and the set of irrational numbers. Real numbers represented as decimals can be terminating, repeating, or nonterminating and nonrepeating. The concept of fractions can now be extended to include all numbers of the form $\dfrac{a}{b}$, where a and b are real numbers with $b \neq 0$, such as $\dfrac{\sqrt{3}}{5}$. Addition, subtraction, multiplication, and division are defined on the set of real numbers in such a way that all the properties of these operations on rationals still hold. The properties are summarized next.

● **P R O P E R T I E S**

Closure Properties For real numbers a and b, $a + b$ and $a \cdot b$ are unique real numbers.

Commutative Properties For real numbers a and b, $a + b = b + a$ and $a \cdot b = b \cdot a$.

Associative Properties For real numbers a, b, and c, $a + (b + c) = (a + b) + c$ and $a \cdot (b \cdot c) = (a \cdot b) \cdot c$.

Identity Properties The number 0 is the unique additive identity and 1 is the unique multiplicative identity such that, for any real number a, $0 + a = a = a + 0$ and $1 \cdot a = a = a \cdot 1$.

Inverse Properties (1) For every real number a, ^-a is its unique additive inverse; that is, $a + {^-a} = 0 = {^-a} + a$. (2) For every nonzero real number a, $\dfrac{1}{a}$ is its unique multiplicative inverse; that is, $a \cdot \left(\dfrac{1}{a}\right) = 1 = \left(\dfrac{1}{a}\right) \cdot a$.

Distributive Property of Multiplication over Addition For real numbers a, b, and c, $a \cdot (b + c) = a \cdot b + a \cdot c$.

Denseness Property For real numbers a and b, there exists a real number c such that $a < c < b$.

Properties of equality and inequality similar to those for rational numbers hold for real numbers. Using these properties, we can solve real-number equations and inequalities. The number line can be used to picture real numbers, because every point on a number line corresponds to a real number and every real number corresponds to a point on the number line. Because such a one-to-one correspondence is possible, solution sets of real-number equations and inequalities can be graphed on a number line.

EXAMPLE 7-27 Solve each of the following, and show the solution on a number line.

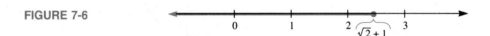

(a) $x - 3 \le \sqrt{2} + {}^-2$ (b) $\dfrac{3x^2}{2} - 4 = 5$ (c) $|x| \ge 2$

SOLUTION (a) $x - 3 \le \sqrt{2} + {}^-2$
$$x \le \sqrt{2} + 1$$

Thus, the solution is $x \le \sqrt{2} + 1$, where x is a real number, is shown in Figure 7-6.

FIGURE 7-6

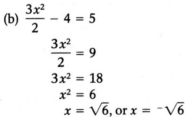

(b) $\dfrac{3x^2}{2} - 4 = 5$

$$\frac{3x^2}{2} = 9$$
$$3x^2 = 18$$
$$x^2 = 6$$
$$x = \sqrt{6}, \text{ or } x = {}^-\sqrt{6}$$

The solution is shown on the number line in Figure 7-7.

FIGURE 7-7

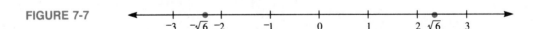

(c) To solve $|x| \ge 2$, we look for all the points on the number line whose distance from the origin is greater than or equal to 2. All such points are shown on the number line in Figure 7-8. The answer can be written as $x \le {}^-2$ or $x \ge 2$. Note that the answer could not be written as $2 \le x \le {}^-2$. Why not?

FIGURE 7-8

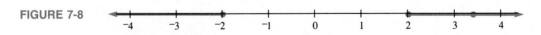

- **R E M A R K**
  If the inequality in Example 7-27(a) had been $x - 3 < \sqrt{2} + {}^-2$, then the solution would be $x < \sqrt{2} + 1$, as seen in Figure 7-9, with a hollow dot to indicate that $\sqrt{2} + 1$ is not included.

FIGURE 7-9

PROBLEM SET 7-5

1. Without using a radical sign, write an irrational number all of whose digits are 2s and 3s.
2. Arrange the following real numbers in order from least to greatest.

$$0.78, 0.7\overline{7}, 0.\overline{78}, 0.788, 0.7\overline{8}, 0.7\overline{88},$$
$$0.77, 0.787787778 \ldots$$

3. Arrange the following real numbers in order from greatest to least.

$$0.9, 0.\overline{9}, 0.\overline{98}, 0.9\overline{88}, 0.9\overline{98}, 0.\overline{898}$$

4. Which of the following represent irrational numbers?
   (a) $\sqrt{51}$ (b) $\sqrt{64}$ (c) $\sqrt{324}$
   (d) $\sqrt{325}$ (e) $2 + 3\sqrt{2}$ (f) $\sqrt{2} \div 5$
5. Find the square roots, correct to tenths, for each of the following without a calculator, if possible.
   (a) 225   (b) 251   (c) 169
   (d) 512   (e) $^-81$ (f) 625
6. Find the approximate square roots for each of the following, rounded to hundredths, by the squeezing method.
   (a) 17   (b) 7   (c) 21
   (d) 0.0120   (e) 20.3   (f) 1.64
7. Classify each of the following as true or false. If false, give a counterexample.
   (a) The sum of any rational number and any irrational number is a rational number.
   (b) The sum of any two irrational numbers is an irrational number.
   (c) The product of any two irrational numbers is an irrational number.
   (d) The difference of any two irrational numbers is an irrational number.
8. Is it true that $\sqrt{a + b} = \sqrt{a} + \sqrt{b}$? Either prove the statement or give a counterexample.
9. Find three irrational numbers between 1 and 3.
10. Find an irrational number between $0.5\overline{3}$ and $0.5\overline{4}$.
11. Pi (π) is an irrational number. Could $\pi = \frac{22}{7}$? Why or why not?

12. Without using a calculator or doing any computation, determine whether $\sqrt{13} = 3.605$? Why or why not?
13. If R is the set of real numbers, Q is the set of rational numbers, I is the set of integers, W is the set of whole numbers, and S is the set of irrational numbers, find each of the following.
    (a) $Q \cup S$ (b) $Q \cap S$ (c) $Q \cap R$
    (d) $S \cap W$ (e) $W \cup R$ (f) $Q \cup R$
14. Solve each of the following for real numbers and graph the solution.
    (a) $5x - 1 \le \frac{7}{2}x + 3$ (b) $4 + 3x \ge \sqrt{5} - 7x$
    (c) $\frac{2}{3}x + \sqrt{3} \le {}^-5x$ (d) $(2x - 1)^2 = 4$
    (e) $|x| \ge 7$ (f) $|x| \le 3$
15. If the following letters correspond to the sets listed in Problem 13, put a check mark under each set of numbers for which a solution to the problem exists. (N is the set of natural numbers.)

	N	I	Q	R
(a) $x^2 + 1 = 5$				
(b) $2x - 1 = 32$				
(c) $x^2 = 3$				
(d) $x^2 = 4$				
(e) $\sqrt{x} = {}^-1$				
(f) $\sqrt[3]{4}x = 4$				

16. For what real values of x, if any, is each statement true?
    (a) $\sqrt{x} = 8$ (b) $\sqrt{x} = {}^-8$
    (c) $\sqrt{{}^-x} = 8$ (d) $\sqrt{{}^-x} = {}^-8$
    (e) $\sqrt{x} > 0$ (f) $\sqrt{x} < 0$
17. A diagonal brace is placed in a 4-foot by 5-foot rectangular gate. What is the length of the brace to the nearest tenth of a foot? (*Hint:* Use the Pythagorean Theorem.)

18. For a simple pendulum of length l, given in centimeters (cm), the time of the period T in seconds is given by $T = 2\pi\sqrt{\dfrac{l}{g}}$, where $g = 9.8$ cm/second^2.

    Find the time T rounded to hundredths if:
    (a) $l = 20$ cm   (b) $l = 100$ cm

★19. Prove: $\sqrt{3}$ is irrational.

★20. Prove: If p is a prime number, then $\sqrt{p}$ is an irrational number.

21. (a) For what whole numbers m is $\sqrt{m}$ a rational number?

    ★(b) Prove your answer in (a).

22. (a) Show that $0.5 + \dfrac{1}{0.5} \geq 2$.

    ★(b) Prove that any positive real number x plus its reciprocal $\dfrac{1}{x}$ is greater than or equal to 2.

Review Problems

23. Write 0.00024 as a fraction in simplest form.

24. Arrange the following from least to greatest.

$$4.09, \ 4.099, \ 4.0\overline{9}, \ 4.09\overline{1}$$

25. Write $0.\overline{24}$ as a fraction in simplest form.

26. Write each of the following as a standard numeral.
    (a) $2.03 \cdot 10^5$ (b) $3.8 \cdot 10^{-4}$

27. Joan's salary this year is $18,600. If she receives a 9% raise, what is her salary next year?

28. If 800 of the 2000 students at the university are males, what percent of the university students are females?

---

*Section 7-6 Radicals and Rational Exponents

The positive solution to $x^2 = 5$ is $\sqrt{5}$. Similarly, the positive solution to $x^4 = 5$ can be denoted as $\sqrt[4]{5}$. In general, the positive solution to $x^n = 5$ is

nth root / index $\sqrt[n]{5}$ and is called the **nth root** of 5. The numeral n is called the **index**. Note that, in the expression $\sqrt{5}$, the index 2 is understood and is not expressed.

In general, the positive solution to $x^n = b$, *where b is nonnegative*, is $\sqrt[n]{b}$. Substituting $\sqrt[n]{b}$ for x in the equation $x^n = b$ gives the following.

$$(\sqrt[n]{b})^n = b$$

If b is negative, $\sqrt[n]{b}$ cannot always be defined. For example, consider $\sqrt[4]{-16}$. If $\sqrt[4]{-16} = x$, then $x^4 = {}^-16$. Since any nonzero real number raised to the fourth power is positive, there is no real-number solution to $x^4 = {}^-16$ and, therefore, $\sqrt[4]{-16}$ cannot be a real number. Similarly, it is not possible to find *any* even root of a negative number. However, the value $^-2$ satisfies the equation $x^3 = {}^-8$. Hence, $\sqrt[3]{-8} = {}^-2$. *In general, the odd root of a negative number is a negative number.*

Because $\sqrt{a}$, if it exists, is positive by definition, $\sqrt{(-3)^2} = \sqrt{9} = 3$ and not $^-3$. Many students think that $\sqrt{a^2}$ always equals a. This is true if $a \geq 0$, but false if $a < 0$. *In general, $\sqrt{a^2} = |a|$.* Similarly, $\sqrt[4]{a^4} = |a|$ and $\sqrt[6]{a^6} = |a|$, but $\sqrt[3]{a^3} = a$.

Now, consider an expression like $4^{1/2}$. What does it mean? By extending the properties of exponents previously developed for integer exponents, it must be that $4^{1/2} \cdot 4^{1/2} = 4^{1/2+1/2} = 4^1$. This implies that $(4^{1/2})^2 = 4$, or $4^{1/2}$ is a square root of 4. The number $4^{1/2}$ is assumed to be the principal square root of 4; that is, $4^{1/2} = \sqrt{4}$. In general, if x is a nonnegative real number, then $x^{1/2} = \sqrt{x}$. Similarly, $(x^{1/3})^3 = x^{(1/3)\cdot 3} = x^1$, and $x^{1/3} = \sqrt[3]{x}$. This discussion leads to the following definition.

- **DEFINITION**
  For any real number x and any positive integer n, $x^{1/n} = \sqrt[n]{x}$, where $\sqrt[n]{x}$ is meaningful.

Also, since $(x^m)^{1/n} = \sqrt[n]{x^m}$, and if $(x^m)^{1/n} = x^{m/n}$, it follows that $x^{m/n} = \sqrt[n]{x^m}$.

EXAMPLE 7-28 Simplify each of the following.
  (a) $16^{1/4}$ (b) $32^{1/6}$
  (c) $(^-8)^{1/3}$ (d) $64^{3/2}$

SOLUTION (a) $16^{1/4} = \sqrt[4]{16} = 2$ (b) $32^{1/6} = \sqrt[6]{32}$
  (c) $(^-8)^{1/3} = \sqrt[3]{^-8} = {}^-2$ (d) $64^{3/2} = (2^6)^{3/2} = 2^9 = 512$

The properties of integer exponents also hold for rational exponents. These properties are equivalent to the corresponding properties of radicals if the expressions involving radicals are meaningful.

- **PROPERTIES**
  Let r and s be any rational numbers, x and y be any real numbers, and n be any nonzero integer.

  (a) $(xy)^r = x^r \cdot y^r$ implies $(xy)^{1/n} = x^{1/n}y^{1/n}$ and $\sqrt[n]{xy} = \sqrt[n]{x} \, \sqrt[n]{y}$.

  (b) $\left(\dfrac{x}{y}\right)^r = \dfrac{x^r}{y^r}$ implies $\left(\dfrac{x}{y}\right)^{1/n} = \dfrac{x^{1/n}}{y^{1/n}}$ and $\sqrt[n]{\dfrac{x}{y}} = \dfrac{\sqrt[n]{x}}{\sqrt[n]{y}}$.

  (c) $(x^r)^s = x^{rs}$ implies $(x^{1/n})^s = x^{s/n}$ and, hence, $(\sqrt[n]{x})^s = \sqrt[n]{x^s}$.

The preceding properties can be used to simplify the square roots of many numbers. For example, $\sqrt{96} = \sqrt{16 \cdot 6} = \sqrt{16}\sqrt{6} = 4\sqrt{6}$. When $\sqrt{96}$ is written as $4\sqrt{6}$, it is said to be in *simplest form*. In general, *to write an nth root in simplest form, factor out as many nth powers as possible.* Note that $\sqrt{32} = \sqrt{4 \cdot 8} = 2\sqrt{8}$. Hence, $2\sqrt{8}$ is a simplified form, but not the simplest form. The simplest form of $\sqrt{32}$ is $\sqrt{16 \cdot 2} = \sqrt{16} \cdot \sqrt{2} = 4\sqrt{2}$.

EXAMPLE 7-29 Write each of the following in simplest form.

(a) $\sqrt{200}$ (b) $\sqrt{75}$ (c) $\sqrt[3]{240}$
(d) $\sqrt{3} \cdot \sqrt{15}$ (e) $\sqrt[3]{81} \cdot \sqrt[3]{32}$

SOLUTION (a) $\sqrt{200} = \sqrt{100 \cdot 2} = \sqrt{100}\sqrt{2} = 10\sqrt{2}$
(b) $\sqrt{75} = \sqrt{25 \cdot 3} = \sqrt{25}\sqrt{3} = 5\sqrt{3}$
(c) $\sqrt[3]{240} = \sqrt[3]{8 \cdot 30} = \sqrt[3]{8}\sqrt[3]{30} = 2\sqrt[3]{30}$
(d) $\sqrt{3} \cdot \sqrt{15} = \sqrt{3 \cdot 15} = \sqrt{45} = \sqrt{9 \cdot 5} = \sqrt{9} \cdot \sqrt{5} = 3\sqrt{5}$
(e) $\sqrt[3]{81} \cdot \sqrt[3]{32} = \sqrt[3]{81 \cdot 32} = \sqrt[3]{3^4 \cdot 2^5} = \sqrt[3]{3^3 \cdot 2^3 \cdot 3 \cdot 2^2} =$
$\sqrt[3]{3^3 \cdot 2^3} \cdot \sqrt[3]{3 \cdot 2^2} = 6\sqrt[3]{12}$

Some expressions in the form $\sqrt{x} + \sqrt{y}$ can be simplified. For example,

$$\sqrt{24} + \sqrt{54} = \sqrt{4 \cdot 6} + \sqrt{9 \cdot 6}$$
$$= \sqrt{4}\sqrt{6} + \sqrt{9}\sqrt{6}$$
$$= 2\sqrt{6} + 3\sqrt{6}$$
$$= (2 + 3)\sqrt{6}$$
$$= 5\sqrt{6}$$

Be careful! Notice that $\sqrt{9} + \sqrt{4} = 3 + 2 = 5$, but $\sqrt{9 + 4} = \sqrt{13}$. Thus, $\sqrt{9} + \sqrt{4} \neq \sqrt{9 + 4}$ and, in general, $\sqrt{x} + \sqrt{y} \neq \sqrt{x + y}$.

EXAMPLE 7-30 Write each expression in simplest form.

(a) $\sqrt{20} + \sqrt{45} - \sqrt{80}$ (b) $\sqrt{12} + \sqrt{13}$
(c) $\sqrt{49x} + \sqrt{4x}$

SOLUTION (a) $\sqrt{20} + \sqrt{45} - \sqrt{80} = 2\sqrt{5} + 3\sqrt{5} - 4\sqrt{5} = \sqrt{5}$
(b) $\sqrt{12} + \sqrt{13} = 2\sqrt{3} + \sqrt{13}$
(c) $\sqrt{49x} + \sqrt{4x} = 7\sqrt{x} + 2\sqrt{x} = 9\sqrt{x}$

PROBLEM SET 7-6

1. Write each of the following square roots in simplest form.

   (a) $\sqrt{180}$ (b) $\sqrt{529}$ (c) $\sqrt{363}$
   (d) $\sqrt{252}$ (e) $\sqrt{\dfrac{169}{196}}$ (f) $\sqrt{\dfrac{49}{196}}$

2. Write each of the following in simplest form.

   (a) $\sqrt[3]{-27}$ (b) $\sqrt[3]{96}$ (c) $\sqrt[5]{32}$
   (d) $\sqrt[3]{250}$ (e) $\sqrt[5]{-243}$ (f) $\sqrt[3]{64}$

3. Write each of the following expressions in simplest form.

   (a) $2\sqrt{3} + 3\sqrt{2} + \sqrt{180}$
   (b) $\sqrt[3]{4} \cdot \sqrt[3]{10}$
   (c) $(2\sqrt{3} + 3\sqrt{2})^2$
   (d) $\sqrt{6} \div \sqrt{12}$
   (e) $5\sqrt{72} + 2\sqrt{50} - \sqrt{288} - \sqrt{242}$
   (f) $\sqrt{8/7} \div \sqrt{4/21}$

4. Rewrite each of the following in simplest form.

   (a) $16^{1/2}$ (b) $27^{2/3}$ (c) $64^{5/6}$
   (d) $3^{1/2} \cdot 3^{3/2}$ (e) $\dfrac{(32)^{-2/5}}{(\frac{1}{16})^{-3/2}}$ (f) $9^{2/3} \cdot 27^{2/9}$
   (g) $16^{-1/2}$ (h) $27^{-2/3}$ (i) $32^{2/5}$
   (j) $8^{3/2} \cdot 4^{1/4}$ (k) $(10^{1/3} \cdot 10^{-1/6})^6$ (l) $16^{5/12} \cdot 16^{1/3}$
   (m) $64^{2/3}$ (n) $64^{-1/3}$ (o) $(2 \cdot 64^{1/2})^{1/2}$

5. Is $\sqrt{x^2 + y^2} = x + y$ for all values of x and y?

6. Answer the following as being true "sometimes," "always," or "never."

    (a) $\sqrt{a^2} = a$

    (b) $\sqrt{(-x)^2} = {}^-x$

    (c) $\sqrt{(-x)^2} = |x|$

    (d) $\sqrt{(a + b)^2} = a + b$

    (e) $\sqrt[4]{a^2} = \sqrt{a}$

7. The numbers $3^{3/4}$, 3, $3^{5/4}$, ..., 729 are in a geometric sequence. Find the number of terms in the sequence.

8. The following exponential function approximates the number of bacteria after t hours: $E(t) = 2^{10} \cdot 16^t$.

    (a) What is the initial number of bacteria—that is, the number when $t = 0$?

    (b) After $\frac{1}{4}$ hour, how many bacteria are there?

    (c) After $\frac{1}{2}$ hour, how many bacteria are there?

9. Without using a calculator, arrange the following in increasing order.

    $(4/25)^{-1/3}$, $(25/4)^{1/3}$, $(4/25)^{-1/4}$

10. Without using a calculator, determine which is greater in each of the following.

    (a) $\sqrt{3}$ or $\sqrt[3]{4}$

    (b) $\sqrt[3]{3}$ or $\sqrt{2}$

    ★(c) $\sqrt{12} + \sqrt{14}$ or $\sqrt{11} + \sqrt{15}$

11. Write $\sqrt{2\sqrt{2\sqrt{2}}}$ in the form $\sqrt[n]{2^m}$, where n and m are positive integers.

12. Solve for x, where x is a rational number.

    (a) $3^x = 81$ (b) $4^x = 8$

    (c) $128^{-x} = 16$ (d) $\left(\dfrac{4}{9}\right)^{3x} = \dfrac{32}{243}$

13. What is the value of $\sqrt[3]{(x - 2)^{-2}}$ when $x = 6$?

14. (a) For what values of n is $\sqrt[n]{a}$ meaningful when $a < 0$?

    (b) For what values of m and n is $\sqrt[n]{a^m}$ meaningful when $a < 0$?

SOLUTION TO THE PRELIMINARY PROBLEM

Understanding the Problem. A watermelon weighing 100 pounds was 99% water. After some evaporation occurred, the melon was only 98% water. We are to determine the weight of the melon when it was 98% water.

Devising a Plan. A common strategy in solving word problems is *writing an equation*. Because we have information about the amount of water that evaporated, it seems convenient to designate the amount of water that evaporated as the unknown. After finding the amount of water that evaporated, we can subtract that amount from 100 to find the new weight of the watermelon. If we let w be the weight of the water that the melon lost due to evaporation, then the new weight of the melon after evaporation is $(100 - w)$ pounds, and the new weight of the water content is 98% of $(100 - w)$ pounds. The new weight of the water content can also be computed by subtracting the number of pounds of water lost from the original weight of the water, which is 99 pounds. Thus, the new weight of the water content is $(99 - w)$ pounds. An equation can be written using this information as follows.

$$\begin{pmatrix} \text{New weight of} \\ \text{water content} \end{pmatrix} = 98\% \text{ of weight of melon after evaporation}$$
$$99 - w = 0.98 \times (100 - w)$$

To complete this problem, we solve the equation for w.

Carrying Out the Plan. The equation given above is solved for w as follows.

$$99 - w = 0.98(100 - w)$$
$$99 - w = 98 - 0.98\,w$$
$$1 = 0.02w$$
$$50 = w$$

Thus, the weight of the water that was lost due to evaporation is 50 pounds, and hence the melon weighs $(100 - 50)$, or 50, pounds after evaporation.

Looking Back. An alternate solution can be found using the fact that the amount of material other than water does not change after evaporation. Let x be the weight of the watermelon after evaporation. We know that in the original 100 pounds of watermelon, there was 99% water and hence 1%, or 1 pound, was not water. After evaporation, the watermelon's weight was x pounds and 98% of the weight was water; hence, 2% of it was not water. Because the amount of material that was not water did not change, we know that 2% of x equals 1, which implies that $x = 50$ pounds.

Another way to solve the problem is think of the question as, "2% of how much weight is equal to 1% of 100?" Because 2% of 50 is the same as 1% of 100, the answer is 50 pounds.

QUESTIONS FROM THE CLASSROOM

1. A student says that $3\frac{1}{4}\% = 0.03 + 0.25 = 0.28$. What is the error, if any?

2. Why is $\sqrt{25} \neq {}^-5$?

3. A student claims that $\sqrt{({}^-5)^2} = {}^-5$ because $\sqrt{a^2} = a$. Is this correct?

4. Another student says that $\sqrt{({}^-5)^2} = [({}^-5)^2]^{1/2} = ({}^-5)^{2/2} = ({}^-5)^1 = {}^-5$. Is this correct?

5. A student claims that the equation $\sqrt{{}^-x} = 3$ has no solution since the square root of a negative number does not exist. Why is this argument wrong?

6. On a test, a student wrote the following.

$$\frac{x^2}{7} - 2 \geq {}^-3$$
$$\frac{x^2}{7} \geq {}^-1$$
$$x^2 \geq {}^-7$$

Because $\sqrt{{}^-7}$ does not exist, there is no solution. What is the error?

7. A student reports that it is impossible to mark a product up 150% because 100% of something is all there is. What is your response?

8. A student reports that ${}^-438,\!340,\!000$ cannot be written in scientific notation. How do you respond?

9. A student multiplies $(6.5)(8.5)$ to obtain the following.

$$
\begin{array}{r}
8.5 \\
\times\ 6.5 \\
\hline
4\,2\,5 \\
5\,1\,0 \\
\hline
5\,5.2\,5
\end{array}
$$

However, when the student multiplies $8\frac{1}{2} \cdot 6\frac{1}{2}$, the following is obtained.

$$
\begin{array}{r}
8\dfrac{1}{2} \\
\times\ 6\dfrac{1}{2} \\
\hline
4\dfrac{1}{4} \quad \left(\dfrac{1}{2} \cdot 8\dfrac{1}{2}\right) \\
48 \quad (6 \cdot 8) \\
\hline
52\dfrac{1}{4}
\end{array}
$$

How is this possible?

CHAPTER OUTLINE

I. Decimals
   A. Every rational number can be represented as a terminating or repeating decimal.
   B. A rational number $\frac{a}{b}$, whose denominator is of the form $2^m \cdot 5^n$, where m and n are whole numbers, can be expressed as a **terminating decimal.**
   C. A **repeating decimal** is a decimal with a block of digits, called the **repetend,** repeated infinitely many times.
   D. A number is in **scientific notation** if it is written as the product of a number n that is greater than or equal to 1 and an integral power of 10. The number of digits in n is called the number of **significant digits** of n.
   E. An **irrational number** is represented by a non-terminating, nonrepeating decimal.
   F. **Percent** means *per hundred*. Percent is written using the % symbol; $x\% = \frac{x}{100}$.

*II. Interest
   A. **Simple interest** is computed using the formula $I = Prt$, where I is the interest, P is the principal, r is the annual interest rate, and t is the time in years.
   B. When **compound interest** is involved, we use the formula $A = P(1 + i)^n$, where A is the balance, P is the principal, i is the interest rate per period, and n is the number of periods.

III. Real numbers
   A. The set of **real numbers** is the set of all decimals, namely, the union of the set of rational numbers and the set of irrational numbers.
   B. If a is any whole number, then the **principal square root** of a, denoted by $\sqrt{a}$, is the nonnegative number b such that $b \cdot b = b^2 = a$.
   C. Square roots can be found using the **squeezing method.**

*IV. Radicals and rational exponents
   A. $\sqrt[n]{x}$, or $x^{1/n}$, is called **nth root** of x and n is called the **index.**
   B. The following properties hold for radicals if the expressions involving radicals are meaningful.
   (a) $\sqrt[n]{xy} = \sqrt[n]{x} \cdot \sqrt[n]{y}$
   (b) $\sqrt[n]{\dfrac{x}{y}} = \dfrac{\sqrt[n]{x}}{\sqrt[n]{y}}$
   (c) $(\sqrt[n]{x})^m = \sqrt[n]{x^m}$

CHAPTER TEST

1. Perform the following operations.
   (a) $3.6 + 2.007 - 6.3$ (b) $(5.2)(6.07)$
   (c) $(5.1 + 6.32)0.02$ (d) $0.12032 \div 3.76$
   (e) $0.012 - 0.109$ (f) $(0.02)^4$
2. Write each of the following in expanded form.
   (a) 32.012 (b) 0.00103
3. Give a test to determine if a fraction can be written as a terminating decimal, without actually performing the division.
4. A board is 442.4 cm long. How many shelves can be cut from it if each shelf is 55.3 cm long? (Disregard the width of the cuts.)
5. Write each of the following as a decimal.
   (a) $\frac{4}{7}$ (b) $\frac{1}{8}$ (c) $\frac{2}{3}$ (d) $\frac{5}{8}$
6. Write each of the following as a fraction in simplest form.
   (a) 0.28 (b) $0.\overline{3}$ (c) $2.0\overline{8}$

7. Round each of the following numbers as specified.
   (a) 307.625 to the nearest hundredth
   (b) 307.625 to the nearest tenth
   (c) 307.625 to the nearest unit
   (d) 307.625 to the nearest hundred
8. Solve each of the following for x, where x is a real number.
   (a) $0.2x - 0.75 \geq \frac{1}{2}(x - 3.5)$
   (b) $0.\overline{9} + x = 1$
   (c) $23\%(x) = 4600$
   (d) 10 is x percent of 50
   (e) 17 is 50% of x
   (f) $0.\overline{3} + x = 1$
9. Answer each of the following.
   (a) 6 is what percent of 24?
   (b) What is 320% of 60?
   (c) 17 is 30% of what number?
   (d) 0.2 is what percent of 1?

10. Change each of the following to percents.

    (a) $\dfrac{1}{8}$ (b) $\dfrac{3}{40}$ (c) 6.27

    (d) 0.0123   (e) $\dfrac{3}{2}$

11. Change each of the following percents to decimals.

    (a) 60%   (b) $\left(\dfrac{2}{3}\right)$%   (c) 100%

12. Answer each of the following, and explain your answers.
    (a) Is the set of irrational numbers closed under addition?
    (b) Is the set of irrational numbers closed under subtraction?
    (c) Is the set of irrational numbers closed under multiplication?
    (d) Is the set of irrational numbers closed under division?

13. Find an approximation for $\sqrt{23}$ correct to three decimal places.

14. Rewrite each of the following in scientific notation.
    (a) 426,000   (b) 0.00000237
    (c) 32   (d) 0.325

15. What is the number of significant digits in each of the numbers in Problem 14?

16. Classify each of the following as rational or irrational. (Assume the patterns shown continue.)
    (a) 2.19119911999119999119 . . .

    (b) $\dfrac{1}{\sqrt{2}}$ (c) $\dfrac{4}{9}$

    (d) 0.0011001100110011 . . .
    (e) 0.001100011000011 . . .

17. Sandy received a dividend that equals 11% of the value of her investment. If her dividend was $1020.80, how much was her investment?

18. Five computers in a shipment of 150 were found to be defective. What percent of the computers were defective?

19. On a mathematics examination, a student missed 8 of 70 questions. What percent of the questions, rounded to the nearest tenth, did the student do correctly?

20. A microcomputer system costs $3450 at present. This is 60% of the cost 4 years ago. What was the cost of the system 4 years ago?

21. If, on a purchase of one new suit, you are offered successive discounts of 5%, 10%, or 20%, in any order you wish, what order should you choose?

22. Jane bought a bicycle and sold it for 30% more than she paid for it. She sold it for $104; how much did she pay for it?

*23. A company was offered a $30,000 loan at a 12.5% annual interest rate for 4 years. Find the simple interest due on the loan at the end of 4 years.

*24. A money-market fund pays 14% annual interest compounded quarterly. What is the value of a $10,000 investment after 3 years?

*25. Find the simplest form for each of the following.

    (a) $\sqrt{242}$ (b) $\sqrt{288}$
    (c) $\sqrt{360}$ (d) $\sqrt[3]{162}$

*26. Write each of the following in simplest form, with nonnegative exponents in the final answer.

    (a) $\left(\dfrac{1}{2}\right)^{4}\left(\dfrac{1}{2}\right)^{7}$ (b) $5^{-16} \div 5^{4}$

    (c) $\left[\left(\dfrac{2}{3}\right)^{7}\right]^{-4}$ (d) $3^{16} \cdot 3^{2}$

Probability

PRELIMINARY PROBLEM

Jane has two tennis serves, a hard serve and a soft serve. Her hard serve is *in* (it is a good serve) 50% of the time, and her soft serve is in (good) 75% of the time. If her hard serve is in, she wins 75% of her points. If her soft serve is in, she wins 50% of her points. Since she is allowed to reserve one time if her first serve is out, what should be Jane's serving strategy? Should she serve hard then soft, both hard, soft then hard, or both soft?

Introduction

Many people predict what is likely to happen in the future by using probability. Probability had its roots in gambling but has developed into a branch of mathematics that is useful in many areas such as predicting sales, planning campaigns, and determining insurance premiums. Here are some examples of uses of probability found in everyday conversations:

What is the *probability* that the Braves will win the World Series?
The *odds* are 2 to 1 that Millie will win the cat show.
There is *no chance* you will get a raise.
There is a 50 percent *chance* of rain today.

Probability plays an important role in both the K–4 and the 5–8 *Standards*. The following quote from the 5–8 *Standards* shows how important the study of probability is in solving problems.

To see how the predictions we hear and see every day are based on probability, students must use their knowledge of probability to solve problems. In modeling problems, conducting simulations, and collecting, graphing, and studying data, students will come to understand how predictions can be based on data. Mathematically derived probabilities can be determined by building a table or tree diagram, creating an area model, making a list, or using simple counting procedures. Students develop an appreciation of the power of simulation and experimentation by comparing experimental results to the mathematically derived probabilities.

In this chapter, we use tree diagrams and geometric probabilities (area models) to solve problems and to analyze games involving spinners, cards, and dice. Counting techniques are introduced to aid in the solution of certain probability problems. The role of simulations in probability is also discussed. Many of the ideas in this chapter are adapted from the materials developed in the Comprehensive School Mathematics Project (CSMP).

H I S T O R I C A L   N O T E

Girolamo Cardano (1501–1576), a mathematician, physician, and astrologer, wrote one of the first books concerning probability and gambling. However, the founders of probability theory, Blaise Pascal (1623–1662) and Pierre de Fermat (1601–1665), became involved in probability as a result of questions asked of them by Chevalier de Meré, a professional gambler. In one question, he wanted to know how to divide the stakes if two players start, but fail to complete, a game in which the winner is the one who wins three matches out of five. The correspondence between Fermat and Pascal led to what is considered to be the beginning of probability theory.

Section 8.1 How Probabilities Are Determined

experiment

outcome

Probabilities are ratios that may be expressed as fractions, decimals, or percents. The ratios are determined by considering results or outcomes of experiments. An **experiment** is an activity under consideration, such as tossing a coin. Each of the possible observations in an experiment is an **outcome.** If we toss a coin and if we assume that the coin cannot land on its edge, then there are two distinct possible outcomes: heads (H) and tails (T).

sample space

outcome set

tree diagram

A set of possible outcomes for an experiment is called a **sample space,** or **outcome set,** if every possible result of the experiment corresponds to one and only one outcome in the sample space. In the case of a single coin toss, a sample space S is given by $S = \{H, T\}$. Determining a sample space for an experiment is an important step in solving a probability problem. The sample space for the coin-tossing experiment can be modeled by a **tree diagram,** as shown in Figure 8-1. Each outcome of the experiment is designated by a separate branch in the tree diagram.

FIGURE 8-1

EXAMPLE 8-1 (a) Write the sample space S for rolling a standard die.
(b) Use a tree diagram to develop the sample space for tossing a fair coin twice.
(c) Use a tree diagram to develop the sample space for an experiment consisting of tossing a fair coin and then rolling a die.

SOLUTION (a) The sample space is $S = \{1, 2, 3, 4, 5, 6\}$.
(b) The tree diagram is given in Figure 8-2.
The sample space is $S = \{HH, HT, TH, TT\}$.

FIGURE 8-2

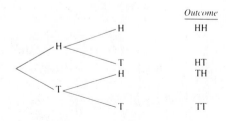

(c) The sample space for this experiment is taken from the tree diagram in Figure 8-3. The sample space is

$$S = \{H1, H2, H3, H4, H5, H6, T1, T2, T3, T4, T5, T6\}$$

FIGURE 8-3

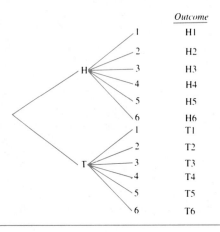

event   Any subset of a sample space is called an **event.** For example, the set of all even-numbered faces of a die {2, 4, 6} is a subset of all possible rolls of a die {1, 2, 3, 4, 5, 6}. The set of all even-numbered rolls is an event.

EXAMPLE 8-2   Suppose that an experiment consists of drawing one slip of paper from a jar containing 12 slips of paper, each with a different month of the year written on it. Find each of the following.

(a) The sample space S for the experiment
(b) The event A consisting of outcomes having a month beginning with J
(c) The event B consisting of outcomes having the name of a month that has exactly four letters
(d) The event C consisting of outcomes having a month that begins with M or N

SOLUTION   (a) $S = \{$January, February, March, April, May, June, July, August, September, October, November, December$\}$
(b) $A = \{$January, June, July$\}$
(c) $B = \{$June, July$\}$
(d) $C = \{$March, May, November$\}$

EXAMPLE 8-3 Two spinners are shown in Figure 8-4. Suppose that an experiment consists of spinning X and then spinning Y. Find each of the following.

(a) The sample space S for the experiment
(b) The event A consisting of outcomes from spinning an even number followed by an even number
(c) The event B consisting of outcomes from spinning at least one 2
(d) The event C consisting of outcomes from spinning exactly one 2

FIGURE 8-4

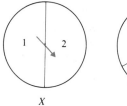 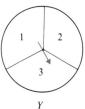

X   Y

SOLUTION (a) The sample space for this experiment can be described by using ordered pairs. The first component in each pair is the result of the first spin, and the second component is the result of the second spin.

$$S = \{(1, 1), (1, 2), (1, 3), (2, 1), (2, 2), (2, 3)\}$$

(b) $A = \{(2, 2)\}$
(c) $B = \{(1, 2), (2, 1), (2, 2), (2, 3)\}$
(d) $C = \{(1, 2), (2, 1), (2, 3)\}$

Determining Probabilities

Around 1900, the English statistician Karl Pearson tossed a coin 24,000 times. He recorded 12,012 heads. In World War II, while a prisoner of war, the English mathematician John Kerrich tossed a coin 10,000 times and recorded the results. A subset of his results is given in Table 8-1. The *relative frequency* column on the right is obtained by dividing the number of heads by the number of tosses of the coin.

TABLE 8-1

Number of Tosses	Number of Heads	Relative Frequency
10	4	0.400
50	25	0.500
100	44	0.440
500	255	0.510
1,000	502	0.502
5,000	2,533	0.507
8,000	4,034	0.504
10,000	5,067	0.507

After only 10 tosses, the data in Table 8-1 suggest that heads might occur $\frac{4}{10}$ of the time. After 50 tosses, the data in Table 8-1 suggest that we could expect heads about $\frac{25}{50}$ of the time. Notice that sometimes Kerrich tossed heads a little less than half the time and sometimes a little more than half the time; but as the number of tosses increased, he obtained heads close to half the time. The relative frequency for Pearson's 24,000 tosses gives a similar result. It is 12,012/24,000, or 0.5005.

experimentally When a probability is determined by observing outcomes of experi-
empirically ments, it is said to be determined **experimentally,** or **empirically.** The exact number of heads that occur when a fair coin is tossed a few times cannot be accurately predicted. Probabilities do not give exact answers to questions but rather suggest what will happen in the "long run." Thus, when a fair coin is tossed many times, the fraction (or proportion) of heads is near $\frac{1}{2}$. For this reason, we say that the probability of heads occurring is $\frac{1}{2}$ and write
equally likely $P(H) = \frac{1}{2}$. We also say that the two outcomes, H and T, are **equally likely;** that is, one outcome is just as likely to occur as the other.

Because a fair coin is symmetric and has two sides, we could argue that each side should appear roughly one half of the time in long strings of tosses, and hence we would again conclude that

$$P(H) = P(T) = \frac{1}{2}$$

In this case, we assume ideal conditions, and we determine the probability
theoretically **theoretically.** If an experiment is repeated a great number of times, we expect the empirical probability to approach the theoretical probability.

If a *fair* die (one that is just as likely to land on any of the numerals 1 through 6) is rolled many times, each outcome will appear about $\frac{1}{6}$ of the time. Hence, we assign to each outcome a probability of $\frac{1}{6}$ and write, for example, $P(4) = \frac{1}{6}$ for the probability of tossing a 4. Saying that $P(4) = \frac{1}{6}$ means that we expect the fraction of 4s that occur in many tosses of the die to be near $\frac{1}{6}$. Since there are six faces on a die and because the die is symmetric, we can also argue that $P(4) = \frac{1}{6}$ and that any other face should also be assigned probability $\frac{1}{6}$.

For a fair coin, the sample space is given by $S = \{H, T\}$ and $P(H) = P(T) = \frac{1}{2}$, whereas for a fair die, $S = \{1, 2, 3, 4, 5, 6\}$ and $P(1) = P(2) = P(3) = P(4) = P(5) = P(6) = \frac{1}{6}$. Notice that, in each case, the probability for each outcome is a number between 0 and 1 and the sum of the probabilities for the distinct outcomes in the sample space is equal to 1. Each of the preceding experiments has a sample space with equally likely outcomes. Not all experiments have equally likely outcomes; for example, a bent coin might yield $P(H) = 0.4$ and $P(T) = 0.6$.

For a sample space with equally likely outcomes, the probability of an event A can be defined as follows.

● **D E F I N I T I O N**

For an experiment with sample space S and equally likely outcomes, the **probability of an event** A is given by

$$P(A) = \frac{n(A)}{n(S)}$$

● **R E M A R K**

Recall that $n(A)$ means "the number of elements in A." Also, if A is an event, then $A \subseteq S$.

EXAMPLE 8-4   One number is selected at random from the numbers in the set S given by $S = \{1, 2, 3, 4, \ldots, 24, 25\}$. List the elements in each of the following events, and calculate each probability.

(a) The event A that an even number is drawn
(b) The event B that a number less than 10 and greater than 20 is drawn
(c) The event C that a number less than 26 is drawn
(d) The event D that a prime number is drawn
(e) The event E that a number both even and prime is drawn

SOLUTION

at random   The phrase **at random** means that each of the 25 numbers has an equal chance of being drawn.

(a) $A = \{2, 4, 6, 8, 10, 12, 14, 16, 18, 20, 22, 24\}$, so $n(A) = 12$. Thus,

$$P(A) = \frac{n(A)}{n(S)} = \frac{12}{25}$$

(b) $B = \varnothing$, so $n(B) = 0$. Thus, $P(B) = \frac{0}{25} = 0$.
(c) $C = S$ and $n(C) = 25$. Thus, $P(C) = \frac{25}{25} = 1$.
(d) $D = \{2, 3, 5, 7, 11, 13, 17, 19, 23\}$, so $n(D) = 9$. Thus,

$$P(D) = \frac{n(D)}{n(S)} = \frac{9}{25}$$

(e) $E = \{2\}$, so $n(E) = 1$. Thus,

$$P(E) = \frac{n(E)}{n(S)} = \frac{1}{25}$$

impossible event   In Example 8-4(b), event B is the empty set. An event such as B that has no outcomes in it is called an **impossible event.** *An impossible event always has probability* 0. Note that, if the word *and* were replaced by *or* in

Example 8-4(b), then event B would no longer be the empty set. In Example 8-4(c), event C consists of drawing a number less than 26 on a single draw. Because every number in S is less than 26, $P(C) = \frac{25}{25} = 1$. An event that has probability 1 is called a **certain event.**

certain event

No event has a probability greater than 1. For events with equally likely outcomes, the number of outcomes in an event cannot be greater than the total number of outcomes in the sample space. Likewise, no event has a probability less than 0. Consequently, if A is any event we have:

$$0 \leq P(A) \leq 1$$

We can see that this result is true in terms of sets because $\emptyset \subseteq A \subseteq S$. This implies that

$$0 = n(\emptyset) \leq n(A) \leq n(S)$$

Therefore,

$$\frac{0}{n(S)} \leq \frac{n(A)}{n(S)} \leq \frac{n(S)}{n(S)}$$

so that $0 \leq P(A) \leq 1$.

Mutually Exclusive Events

Consider one spin of the wheel shown in Figure 8-5. For this experiment, we have $S = \{0, 1, 2, 3, 4, 5, 6, 7, 8, 9\}$. If $A = \{0, 1, 2, 3, 4\}$ and $B = \{5, 7\}$, then $A \cap B = \emptyset$. Two such events are called **mutually exclusive** events. If event A occurs, then event B cannot occur, and we have the following definition.

mutually exclusive

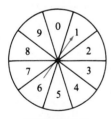

FIGURE 8-5

● D E F I N I T I O N
Events A and B are **mutually exclusive** if $A \cap B = \emptyset$.

Each outcome in the preceding sample space S is equally likely, with probability $\frac{1}{10}$. Thus, if we write the probability of A or B as $P(A \cup B)$, we have the following.

$$P(A \cup B) = \frac{n(A \cup B)}{n(S)} = \frac{7}{10} = \frac{5 + 2}{10} = \frac{5}{10} + \frac{2}{10}$$

$$= \frac{n(A)}{n(S)} + \frac{n(B)}{n(S)} = P(A) + P(B)$$

The result developed in this example is true for any mutually exclusive events. In general, we have the following.

- **P R O P E R T Y**
  If events A and B are mutually exclusive, then $P(A \cup B) = P(A) + P(B)$.

- **R E M A R K**
  This property follows immediately from the fact that, if $A \cap B = \emptyset$, then $n(A \cup B) = n(A) + n(B)$.

As an illustration of events that are not mutually exclusive, we spin the spinner in Figure 8-5 again. Let E be the event of spinning an even number, and let T be the event of spinning a number divisible by 3. Events E and T are not mutually exclusive, because

$$E = \{0, 2, 4, 6, 8\} \quad \text{and} \quad T = \{0, 3, 6, 9\} \quad \text{and} \quad E \cap T \neq \emptyset$$

To compute $P(E \cup T)$, which is the probability of E or T, using the definition of probability of any event with equally likely outcomes, we calculate as follows.

$$
\begin{aligned}
P(E \cup T) &= \frac{n(E \cup T)}{n(S)} \\
&= \frac{n(\{0, 2, 4, 6, 8, 3, 9\})}{n(\{0, 1, 2, 3, 4, 5, 6, 7, 8, 9\})} \\
&= \frac{7}{10}
\end{aligned}
$$

It can be shown that, if E and T are not mutually exclusive, then $P(E \cup T) = P(E) + P(T) - P(E \cap T)$. This is true in our illustration, as the following computations show.

$$
\begin{aligned}
P(E \cup T) &= P(E) + P(T) - P(E \cap T) \\
&= \frac{5}{10} + \frac{4}{10} - \frac{2}{10} \\
&= \frac{9}{10} - \frac{2}{10} \\
&= \frac{7}{10}
\end{aligned}
$$

Complementary Events

Two mutually exclusive events whose union is the sample space are called *complementary events.* If A is an event, the case where A fails to happen is also an event, which is the **complement of A,** written $\overline{A}$. For example, if we *complement of A* spin the spinner in Figure 8-5 once and if event A is the event that the number obtained is greater than 0, then $\overline{A} = \{0\}$. Because events are sets,

$A \cup \overline{A} = S$ and $A \cap \overline{A} = \emptyset$. Because A and $\overline{A}$ are mutually exclusive, then $P(A \cup \overline{A}) = P(A) + P(\overline{A})$. Because $A \cup \overline{A} = S$, we see that $P(A \cup \overline{A}) = 1$. Therefore,

$$P(A) + P(\overline{A}) = 1 \quad \text{or} \quad P(A) = 1 - P(\overline{A}) \quad \text{or} \quad P(\overline{A}) = 1 - P(A)$$

Thus, the probability that we spin a number greater than 0 is given by

$$P(A) = 1 - P(\overline{A}) = 1 - \frac{1}{10} = \frac{9}{10}$$

As another example, if we are given that $P(\text{sun shines}) = 0.6$, then $P(\text{sun does not shine}) = 1 - 0.6 = 0.4$.

The properties of probability discussed thus far are summarized next.

1. $P(\emptyset) = 0$ (impossible event).
2. $P(S) = 1$, where S is the sample space (certain event).
3. For any event A, $0 \leq P(A) \leq 1$.
4. If A and B are events and $A \cap B = \emptyset$, then $P(A \cup B) = P(A) + P(B)$.
5. If A and B are events and $A \cap B \neq \emptyset$, then $P(A \cup B) = P(A) + P(B) - P(A \cap B)$.
6. If A is an event, then $P(\overline{A}) = 1 - P(A)$.

EXAMPLE 8-5 A golf bag contains 2 red tees, 4 blue tees, and 5 white tees.

(a) What is the probability of the event A that a tee drawn at random is red?
(b) What is the probability of the event "not A"—that is, that a tee drawn at random is not red?
(c) What is the probability of the event that a tee drawn at random is either red or blue?

SOLUTION (a) Because the bag contains a total of $2 + 4 + 5$, or 11, tees and 2 tees are red, $P(A) = \frac{2}{11}$.
(b) The bag contains 11 tees and 9 are not red, so the probability of "not A" is $\frac{9}{11}$. Also, notice that $P(\overline{A}) = 1 - P(A) = 1 - \frac{2}{11} = \frac{9}{11}$.
(c) The bag contains 2 red tees and 4 blue tees and $R \cap B = \emptyset$, so $P(R \cup B) = \frac{2}{11} + \frac{4}{11}$, or $\frac{6}{11}$.

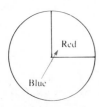

FIGURE 8-6

Probabilities of Events Without Equally Likely Outcomes

It is important to remember that the definition of probability introduced earlier applies *only to a sample space with equally likely outcomes*. Applying the definition to outcomes that are not equally likely leads to incorrect conclusions. For example, the sample space for spinning the spinner in Figure 8-6 is given by $S = \{\text{Red, Blue}\}$. However, the outcome Blue is more likely to occur than the outcome Red, and hence $P(\text{Red})$ is not equal to $\frac{1}{2}$. If the spinner were spun 100 times, it would seem reasonable to expect that about $\frac{1}{4}$, or 25, of the outcomes would be Red, while about $\frac{3}{4}$, or 75, of the outcomes would be Blue.

Next, consider tossing a loaded die in which $P(1) = P(2) = \frac{3}{10}$ and $P(3) = P(4) = P(5) = P(6) = \frac{1}{10}$. If event A consists of tossing a 2 and event B consists of tossing a 4, then events A and B are mutually exclusive, and the probability of tossing a 2 *or* a 4 is given by the following.

$$P(A \cup B) = P(A) + P(B) = P(2) + P(4) = \frac{3}{10} + \frac{1}{10} = \frac{4}{10}$$

We see that the probability of tossing a 2 or a 4 is found by adding the probabilities of events A and B. Likewise, the probability of an event C of tossing an even number, $\{2, 4, 6\}$, is given by finding the sum of $P(A \cup B)$ and $P(6)$; that is,

$$P(C) = [P(A) + P(B)] + P(6) = \left(\frac{3}{10} + \frac{1}{10}\right) + \frac{1}{10} = \frac{5}{10}$$

This leads to the following definition.

• **D E F I N I T I O N**
The probability of an event A is equal to the sum of the probabilities of all the outcomes in set A.

EXAMPLE 8-6   If a card is drawn at random from an ordinary deck of playing cards, what is the probability that it is an ace?

SOLUTION   Because the card is drawn at random, we have a sample space, S, with equally likely outcomes and $n(S) = 52$. If event A is drawing an ace, then we can use the definition of probability involving equally likely outcomes to compute the following.

$$P(A) = \frac{n(A)}{n(S)} = \frac{4}{52}$$

A different approach is to notice that, because the probability of drawing any of the four aces on a single draw is $\frac{1}{52}$, then

$$P(A) = \frac{1}{52} + \frac{1}{52} + \frac{1}{52} + \frac{1}{52} = \frac{4}{52}$$

EXAMPLE 8-7 Find the probability of rolling a sum of 7 or 11 when rolling a fair pair of dice.

SOLUTION The possible sums in rolling a pair of fair dice are 2, 3, 4, 5, . . . , 12. However, these sums are not equally likely. To solve this problem, we work with a sample space of equally likely outcomes. The outcomes of landing on the numbers 1 through 6 for each die are equally likely. If we picture the dice in two different colors, we can identify the sample space as 36 combinations of equally likely outcomes, as shown in Figure 8-7(a). Alternatively, we could represent a toss by an ordered pair, with the first component representing the number on the first die and the second component representing the number on the second die, as shown in Figure 8-7(b).

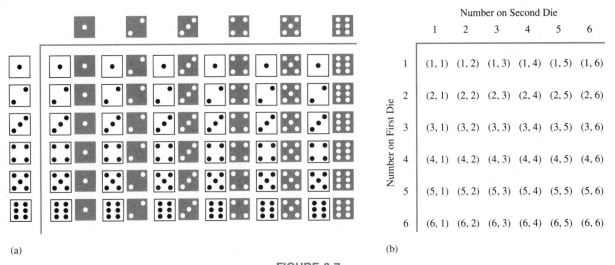

(a)

(b)

FIGURE 8-7

From Figure 8-7(b), we see that a sum of 7 can be obtained in 6 different ways, from the ordered pairs (6, 1), (5, 2), (4, 3), (3, 4), (2, 5), and (1, 6). Similarly, a sum of 11 can be obtained in two different ways from the ordered pairs (5, 6) and (6, 5). Because there are 36 different elements in the sample space, we have $P(7) = \dfrac{6}{36}$ and $P(11) = \dfrac{2}{36}$

Since the events are mutually exclusive, we have

$$P(7 \text{ or } 11) = P(7) + P(11) = \frac{6}{36} + \frac{2}{36} = \frac{8}{36}$$

PROBLEM 1

A butcher wrapped three 1-pound packages of meat in butcher paper while having a conversation with a customer. The packages contained round steak, ground beef, and sausage and were to be labeled *R*, *G*, and *S*, respectively. During the conversation, the butcher forgot which package was which, but labeled them anyway. What is the probability that each of the packages is labeled correctly?

Understanding the Problem. The packages of round steak, ground beef, and sausage were labeled *R*, *G*, and *S*. The problem of determining the probability that each of the three packages of meat is labeled correctly depends on determining the sample space, or at least how many elements are in the sample space.

Devising a Plan. To aid in the solution, we represent the contents—round steak, ground beef, and sausage—as *r*, *g*, and *s*, respectively. To construct the sample space, we use the strategy of *making a table*. The table should show all the possibilities of what could be in each package; that is, the table should show all the one-to-one correspondences between the set of labels {R, G, S} and the set of contents {r, g, s}. Once the table is completed, the probability that each package is labeled correctly can be determined.

Carrying Out the Plan. Table 8-2 is constructed by using the package labels *R*, *G*, and *S* as headings and listing all equally likely possibilities of contents *r*, *g*, and *s* underneath the headings. Case 1 is the only case out of six in which each of the packages is labeled correctly, so the probability that each package is labeled correctly is $\frac{1}{6}$.

Looking Back. Another question to consider is whether the probability of having each package labeled incorrectly is the same as the probability of having each package labeled correctly. A first guess might be that the probabilities are the same, but that is not true. Can you determine why?

Labels

		R	G	S
Cases	1	r	g	s
	2	r	s	g
	3	g	r	s
	4	g	s	r
	5	s	r	g
	6	s	g	r

TABLE 8-2

PROBLEM SET 8-1

1. Write the sample space for each of the following experiments.
   (a) Spin spinner 1 once.
   (b) Spin spinner 2 once.
   (c) Spin spinner 1 once and then spin spinner 2 once.
   (d) Spin spinner 2 once and then roll a die.
   (e) Spin spinner 1 twice.
   (f) Spin spinner 2 twice.

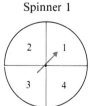

Spinner 1

Spinner 2

2. An experiment consists of selecting the last digit of a telephone number. Assume that each of the ten digits is equally likely to appear as a last digit. List each of the following.
   (a) The sample space.
   (b) The event consisting of outcomes that the digit is less than 5.
   (c) The event consisting of outcomes that the digit is odd.
   (d) The event consisting of outcomes that the digit is not 2.

3. Find the probability of each of the events (b)–(d) in Problem 2.

4. A card is selected from an ordinary bridge deck consisting of 52 cards. Find the probabilities for each of the following.
   (a) A red card
   (b) A face card
   (c) A red card or a ten
   (d) A queen
   (e) Not a queen
   (f) A face card or a club
   (g) A face card and a club
   (h) Not a face card and not a club

5. A drawer contains six black socks, four brown socks, and two green socks. Suppose that one sock is drawn from the drawer and that it is equally likely that any one of the socks is drawn. Find the probabilities for each of the following.
   (a) The sock is brown.
   (b) The sock is either black or green.
   (c) The sock is red.
   (d) The sock is not black.

6. If each letter of the alphabet is written on a separate piece of paper and placed in a box and then one piece of paper is drawn at random, what is the probability that the paper has a vowel written on it? What is the probability that the paper has a consonant written on it?

7. The questions below refer to a very popular dice game, craps, in which a player rolls two dice.
   (a) Rolling a sum of 7 or 11 on the first roll of the dice is a win. What is the probability of winning on the first roll?
   (b) Rolling a sum of 2, 3, or 12 on the first roll of the dice is a loss. What is the probability of losing on the first roll?
   (c) Rolling a sum of 4, 5, 6, 8, 9, or 10 on the first roll is neither a win nor a loss. What is the probability of neither winning nor losing on the first roll?
   (d) After rolling a sum of 4, 5, 6, 8, 9, or 10, a player must roll the same sum again before rolling a sum of 7. Which sum, 4, 5, 6, 8, 9, or 10, has the highest probability of occurring again?
   (e) What is the probability of rolling a sum of 1 on any roll of the dice?
   (f) What is the probability of rolling a sum less than 13 on any roll of the dice?
   (g) If the two dice are rolled 60 times, predict about how many times a sum of 7 will be rolled.

8. According to a weather report, there is a 30% chance that it will rain tomorrow. What is the probability that it will not rain tomorrow?

9. A roulette wheel has 38 slots around the rim. The first 36 slots are numbered from 1 to 36. Half of these 36 slots are red and the other half are black. The remaining 2 slots are numbered 0 and 00 and are colored green. As the roulette wheel is spun in one direction, a small ivory ball is rolled along the rim in the opposite direction. The ball has an equally likely chance of falling into any one of the 38 slots. Find each of the following.
   (a) The probability the ball lands in a black slot.
   (b) The probability the ball lands on 0 or 00.
   (c) The probability the ball does not land on a number from 1 through 12.
   (d) The probability the ball lands on an odd number or on a green slot.

10. If the roulette wheel in problem 9 is spun 190 times, predict about how many times the ball will land on 0 or 00.

11. Determine if each player has an equal probability of winning each of the following games.
    (a) Toss a fair coin. If heads appears, I win; if tails appears, you lose.
    (b) Toss a fair coin. If heads appears, I win; otherwise, you win.
    (c) Toss a fair die numbered 1 through 6. If 1 appears, I win; if 6 appears, you win.
    (d) Toss a fair die numbered 1 through 6. If an even number appears, I win; if an odd number appears, you win.
    (e) Toss a fair die numbered 1 through 6. If a number greater than or equal to 3 appears, I win; otherwise, you win.
    (f) Toss two fair dice numbered 1 through 6. If a 1 appears on each die, I win; if a 6 appears on each die, you win.
    (g) Toss two fair dice numbered 1 through 6. If the sum is 3, I win; if the sum is 2, you win.
    (h) Toss two dice numbered 1 through 6; one die is red and one die is white. If the number on the red die is greater than the number on the white die, I win; otherwise, you win.

12. A bowler has made 45 strikes in the last 150 frames she has bowled. What is the estimated probability that she will get a strike in the next frame she bowls?

13. Suppose that 2 coins are tossed. Find the probability for each of the following.
    (a) Exactly 1 head
    (b) At least 1 head
    (c) At most 1 head

14. If A and B are mutually exclusive and if $P(A) = 0.3$ and $P(B) = 0.4$, what is $P(A \cup B)$?

15. If $P(A) = 0.8$ and $P(B) = 0.9$, can events A and B be mutually exclusive?

16. A calculus class is composed of 35 men and 45 women. There are 20 business majors, 30 biology majors, 10 computer science majors, and 20 mathematics majors. No person has a double major. If a single student is chosen from the class, what is the probability that the student is:
    (a) Female
    (b) A computer science major
    (c) Not a mathematics major
    (d) A computer science major or a mathematics major

17. Al put 4 letters in 4 envelopes without looking at either the names on the envelopes or the names on the letters. What is the probability that no person on Al's list will receive the right letter?

LABORATORY ACTIVITY

1. Suppose that a paper cup is tossed in the air. The different ways it can land are shown below.

Top   Bottom   Side

   Toss a cup 100 times and record each result. From this information, calculate the experimental probability of each outcome. Do the outcomes appear to be equally likely? Based on experimental probabilities, how many times would you predict the cup will land on its side if tossed 200 times?

2. Toss a coin 100 times and record the results. From this information, calculate the experimental probability of getting heads on a particular toss. Does the experimental result agree with the expected theoretical probability of $\frac{1}{2}$?

3. Hold a coin upright on its edge under your forefinger on a hard surface and then spin it with your other finger so that it spins before landing. Repeat this experiment 100 times, and compare your experimental probabilities with those in activity 2.

B R A I N   T E A S E R

A Stanford University statistician, Bradley Efron, designed the following set of nonstandard dice. They are designed in such a way that if you choose a die and roll it, I can choose one and know that the probability of my roll will be greater than yours two-thirds of the time. Which die should I choose if you choose A, B, C, or D?

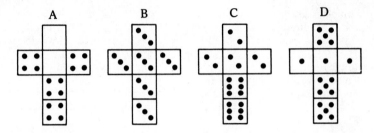

(In 1970, Martin Gardner discussed this type of dice in *Scientific American* in an article "The Paradox of the Nontransitive Dice and the Elusive Principle of Indifference."

Section 8-2   Multistage Experiments with Tree Diagrams and Geometric Probabilities

FIGURE 8-8

In Section 8-1, we considered one-stage experiments—that is, experiments that are over after one step. For example, the box in Figure 8-8 has one black ball and three white balls. Suppose that one ball is drawn at random from the box. The probability of any one particular ball being drawn from the box is $\frac{1}{4}$. Since there are three indistinguishable white balls and one black ball, the probability of drawing a white ball is $\frac{3}{4}$, and the probability of drawing a black ball is $\frac{1}{4}$. A tree diagram for this experiment is given in Figure 8-9. Notice that the sum of the probabilities of the branches coming from a single point equals one.

FIGURE 8-9

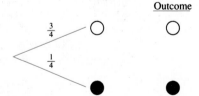

FIGURE 8-10

Next, we consider several multistage experiments. For example, the box in Figure 8-10 contains one black and two white balls. A ball is drawn at random and its color is recorded. The ball is then *replaced* and a second ball is drawn and its color is recorded. Figure 8-11 shows a tree diagram for this two-stage experiment. What probability should be assigned to each pictured outcome?

FIGURE 8-11

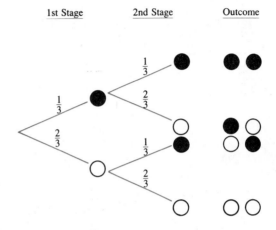

Consider the path for the outcome ● ○. In the first stage, the probability of obtaining a black ball is $\frac{1}{3}$. Then, the probability of obtaining a white ball in the second stage (second draw) is $\frac{2}{3}$. Thus, we expect to obtain a black ball on the first draw $\frac{1}{3}$ of the time and then to draw a white ball $\frac{2}{3}$ of those times that we obtained a black ball, that is, $\frac{2}{3}$ of $\frac{1}{3}$, or $\frac{2}{3} \cdot \frac{1}{3}$. Observe that this product may be obtained by multiplying the probabilities along the branches used for the path leading to ● ○, that is, $\frac{1}{3} \cdot \frac{2}{3}$, or $\frac{2}{9}$. The probabilities shown in Table 8-3 are obtained by following the paths leading to each of the four outcomes and multiplying the probabilities along the paths. This discussion yields the following property for tree diagrams.

TABLE 8-3

Outcome	● ●	● ○	○ ●	○ ○
Probability	$\frac{1}{3} \cdot \frac{1}{3}$, or $\frac{1}{9}$	$\frac{1}{3} \cdot \frac{2}{3}$, or $\frac{2}{9}$	$\frac{2}{3} \cdot \frac{1}{3}$, or $\frac{2}{9}$	$\frac{2}{3} \cdot \frac{2}{3}$, or $\frac{4}{9}$

● P R O P E R T Y

For all multistage experiments, the probability of the outcome along any path is equal to the product of all the probabilities along the path.

The sum of the probabilities on branches from any point always equals 1, and the sum of the probabilities for the possible outcomes must also be 1. Why? In Table 8-3, we see that $\frac{1}{9} + \frac{2}{9} + \frac{2}{9} + \frac{4}{9} = \frac{9}{9} = 1$.

Look at the box pictured in Figure 8-10 again. This time, suppose two balls are drawn one by one *without replacement*. A tree diagram for this experiment, along with the set of possible outcomes, is shown in Figure 8-12.

FIGURE 8-12

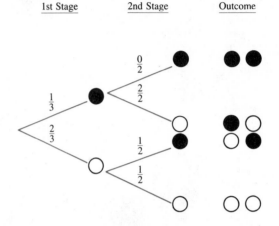

| 1st Stage | 2nd Stage | Outcome |

Notice that the denominators of the fractions along the second stage are all two. Since the draws are made without replacement, there are only two balls remaining for the second draw. The probabilities for the second stage are *conditional probabilities,* because their values depend on what happens at the first stage. Conditional probabilities are discussed further in Section 8-3. Table 8-4 gives a probability model for this example.

TABLE 8-4

Outcome	●●	●○	○●	○○
Probability	$\frac{1}{3} \cdot \frac{0}{2}$, or 0	$\frac{1}{3} \cdot \frac{2}{2}$, or $\frac{2}{6}$	$\frac{2}{3} \cdot \frac{1}{2}$, or $\frac{2}{6}$	$\frac{2}{3} \cdot \frac{1}{2}$, or $\frac{2}{6}$

Table 8-4 can be used to find the probabilities of various events. Consider event A, consisting of the outcomes for drawing exactly one black ball in the two draws without replacement. This event is given by $A = \{●○, ○●\}$. Since the outcome ●○ appears $\frac{2}{6}$ of the time, and the outcome ○● appears $\frac{2}{6}$ of the time, then either ●○ or ○● will appear $\frac{4}{6}$ of the time. Thus, $P(A) = \frac{2}{6} + \frac{2}{6} = \frac{4}{6}$.

Event B, consisting of outcomes for drawing *at least* one black ball, could be recorded as $B = \{●○, ○●, ●●\}$. Because $P(●○) = \frac{2}{6}$, $P(○●) = \frac{2}{6}$, and $P(●●) = 0$, then $P(B) = \frac{2}{6} + \frac{2}{6} + 0 = \frac{4}{6}$. Because $\overline{B} = \{○○\}$ and $P(\overline{B}) = \frac{2}{6}$, the probability of B could have been computed as follows: $P(B) = 1 - P(\overline{B}) = 1 - \frac{2}{6} = \frac{4}{6}$.

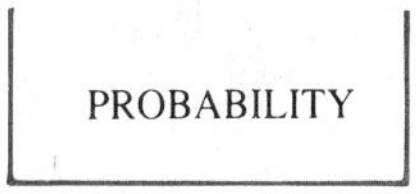

PROBABILITY

FIGURE 8-13

Figure 8-13 shows a box with 11 letters. An example of a four-stage experiment is to draw four letters at random from the box one by one *without replacement*. The probability of the outcome BABY in exactly this order may be found by using just one branch of a much larger tree diagram. Because the entire tree is not needed to find this probability, only the portion required to complete the problem is pictured in Figure 8-14. Notice that, because the experiment is performed without replacement, each successive denominator decreases by one. Also note that the probability of the first B is $\frac{2}{11}$ because there are 2 Bs out of 11 letters. The probability of the second B is $\frac{1}{9}$ because there are 9 letters left after one B and an A have been chosen. Thus, $P(\text{BABY}) = \left(\frac{2}{11}\right) \cdot \left(\frac{1}{10}\right) \cdot \left(\frac{1}{9}\right) \cdot \left(\frac{1}{8}\right)$, or $\frac{2}{7920}$.

FIGURE 8-14

$$\xrightarrow{\frac{2}{11}} B \xrightarrow{\frac{1}{10}} A \xrightarrow{\frac{1}{9}} B \xrightarrow{\frac{1}{8}} Y$$

Suppose four letters are drawn one by one from the box in Figure 8-13 and the letters are *replaced* after each drawing. In this case, the branch needed to find $P(\text{BABY})$ is pictured in Figure 8-15. Thus, $P(\text{BABY}) = \left(\frac{2}{11}\right) \cdot \left(\frac{1}{11}\right) \cdot \left(\frac{2}{11}\right) \cdot \left(\frac{1}{11}\right)$, or $\frac{4}{14,641}$.

FIGURE 8-15

$$\xrightarrow{\frac{2}{11}} B \xrightarrow{\frac{1}{11}} A \xrightarrow{\frac{2}{11}} B \xrightarrow{\frac{1}{11}} Y$$

EXAMPLE 8-8   Consider the three boxes in Figure 8-16. A letter is drawn from box 1 and placed in box 2. Then, a letter is drawn from box 2 and placed in box 3. Finally, a letter is drawn from box 3. What is the probability that the letter drawn from box 3 is B?

FIGURE 8-16

| AAB | AB | ABBB |
| 1 | 2 | 3 |

SOLUTION   A tree diagram for this experiment is given in Figure 8-17. Notice that the denominators in the second stage are 3 rather than 2 because in this stage there are now 3 letters in box 2. The denominators in the third stage are 5 because in this stage there are 5 letters in box 3. To find the probability that a B is drawn from box 3, add the probabilities for the outcomes *AAB*, *ABB*, *BAB*, and *BBB* that make up this event.

FIGURE 8-17

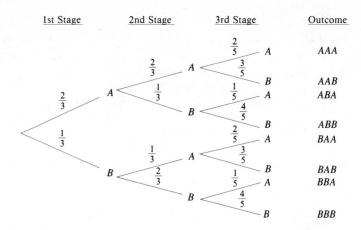

$$P(AAB) = \frac{2}{3} \cdot \frac{2}{3} \cdot \frac{3}{5} = \frac{12}{45}$$

$$P(ABB) = \frac{2}{3} \cdot \frac{1}{3} \cdot \frac{4}{5} = \frac{8}{45}$$

$$P(BAB) = \frac{1}{3} \cdot \frac{1}{3} \cdot \frac{3}{5} = \frac{3}{45}$$

$$P(BBB) = \frac{1}{3} \cdot \frac{2}{3} \cdot \frac{4}{5} = \frac{8}{45}$$

Thus, the probability of obtaining a B on the draw from box 3 in this experiment is $\frac{12}{45} + \frac{8}{45} + \frac{3}{45} + \frac{8}{45} = \frac{31}{45}$.

Modeling Games

Arthur and Bunny play the following game. There are two black marbles and one white marble in a box. Bunny mixes the marbles, and Arthur draws two marbles at random without replacement. If they match, Arthur wins. If they don't match, Bunny wins. Does each player have an equal chance of winning? How can we tell? We could play it many times and see if each player wins about the same number of times. Another way is to develop a model for analyzing the game. One possible model is a tree diagram, as shown in Figure 8-18.

FIGURE 8-18

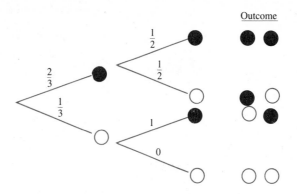

Outcome

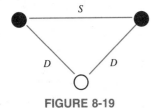

FIGURE 8-19

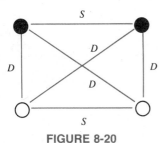

FIGURE 8-20

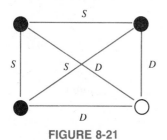

FIGURE 8-21

The probability that the marbles are the same color is $\frac{2}{3} \cdot \frac{1}{2} + \frac{1}{3} \cdot 0$, or $\frac{2}{6}$, and the probability that they are not the same color is $\frac{2}{3} \cdot \frac{1}{2} + \frac{1}{3} \cdot 1$, or $\frac{4}{6}$. Because $\frac{2}{6} \neq \frac{4}{6}$, the players do not have the same chance of winning.

An alternate model for analyzing this game is given in Figure 8-19, where the black and white marbles are shown along with the possible ways of drawing two marbles. Each line segment in the diagram represents one pair of marbles that could be drawn; S indicates that the marbles in the pair are the same color, and D indicates that the marbles are different colors. Because there are two Ds in Figure 8-19, we see that the probability of drawing two different-colored marbles is $\frac{2}{3}$. Likewise, the probability of drawing two marbles of the same color is $\frac{1}{3}$. Because $\frac{2}{3} \neq \frac{1}{3}$, the players do not have an equal chance of winning. Will adding another white marble give each player an equal chance of winning? With two white and two black marbles, we have the model in Figure 8-20. Therefore, $P(D) = \frac{4}{6}$, or $\frac{2}{3}$, and $P(S) = \frac{2}{6}$, or $\frac{1}{3}$. We see that adding another white marble does not change the probabilities.

Next, consider a game with the same rules but using three black marbles and one white marble. A model for this situation is shown in Figure 8-21.

Thus, the probability of drawing two marbles of the same color is $\frac{3}{6}$, and the probability of drawing two marbles of different colors is $\frac{3}{6}$; finally, we have a game in which each player has an equal chance of winning.

Does each player have an equal chance of winning if only one white marble and one black marble are used and the ball is replaced after the first draw? Can you find additional fair games involving different numbers of marbles? Can you find a pattern for the numbers of black and white marbles that allow each player to have an equal chance of winning?

PROBLEM 2

A person in a small foreign town applies for a marriage permit at age 18. To obtain the permit, the person is handed six strings, as shown in Figure 8-22(a). On one side the ends (top or bottom) are picked randomly, two at a time, and tied, forming three separate knots. The same procedure is then repeated for the other set of string ends, forming three more knots, as in Figure 8-22(b). If the strings form one closed ring, as in Figure 8-22(c), the person obtains the permit. If not, the person must wait another year before reapplying for a permit. What is the probability that the marriage permit will be obtained on the first try?

FIGURE 8-22

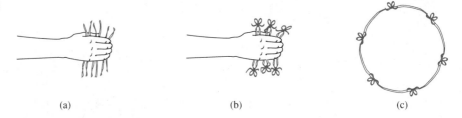

(a)　　　　　　　　(b)　　　　　　　　(c)

Understanding the Problem. The problem is to determine the probability that one closed ring will be formed. One closed ring means that all six pieces are joined end to end to form one and only one ring, as shown in Figure 8-22(c).

Devising a Plan. Figure 8-23(a) shows what happens when the ends of the strings of one set are tied in pairs at the top. Notice that no matter in what order those ends are tied, the result appears as in Figure 8-23(a).

FIGURE 8-23

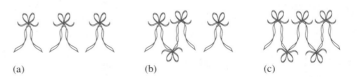

(a)　　　　　　(b)　　　　　　(c)

Then, the other ends are tied in a three-stage experiment. If we pick any string in the first stage, then there are five choices for its mate. Four of these choices are favorable choices for forming a ring. Thus, the probability of forming a favorable first tie is $\frac{4}{5}$. Figure 8-23(b) shows a favorable tie at the first stage.

For any one of the remaining four strings, there are three choices for its mate. Two of these choices are favorable ones. Thus, the probability of forming a favorable second tie is $\frac{2}{3}$. Figure 8-23(c) shows a favorable tie at the second stage.

Now, two ends remain. Since nothing can go wrong at the third stage, the probability of making a favorable tie is 1. If we use the probabilities completed at each stage and a single branch of a tree diagram, we can calculate the probability of performing three successful ties in a row and hence the probability of forming one closed ring.

Carrying Out the Plan. If we let S represent a successful tie at each stage, then the branch of the tree with which we are concerned is the one shown in Figure 8-24.

FIGURE 8-24

Thus, the probability of forming one ring is $P(\text{ring}) = \frac{4}{5} \cdot \frac{2}{3} \cdot \frac{1}{1} = \frac{8}{15} = 0.5\overline{3}$.

Looking Back. The probability that an applicant will obtain a marriage permit in any given year is $\frac{8}{15}$. The fact that this result is greater than $\frac{1}{2}$ is surprising to most people. A class might simulate this problem several times with strings to see how the fraction of successes compares with the theoretical probability of $\frac{8}{15}$.

Related problems that could be attempted include the following:

1. If a person fails to get a ring 10 years in a row, the person must remain single. What is the probability of such a streak of bad (good) luck?
2. If the number of strings is reduced to three and the rule is that an upper end must be tied to a lower end, what is the probability of a single ring?
3. If the number of strings is three, but an upper end can be tied to either an upper or a lower end, what is the probability of a single ring?
4. What is the probability of forming three rings in the original problem?
5. What is the probability of forming two rings in the original problem?

Geometric Probability

Most probability problems that we have discussed involve fractions. In dealing with fractions, it is often convenient to consider a geometric model. We begin with any geometric shape as a unit and then consider parts of that unit. In **geometric probability,** outcomes are associated with points chosen at random in a geometric region that represents the sample space. Suppose, for example, that we are throwing darts at a square target 2 units long on a side and divided into four congruent triangles, as shown in Figure 8-25. If the dart is certain to hit the target somewhere and if all spots can be hit with equal probability, what is the probability that the dart will land in the shaded region? The entire target, which has an area of 4 square units, represents the sample space—that is, all possible points where the dart can land. The shaded area, which defines the zone for a successful toss, is the event. In this case, the area of the shaded part is $\frac{1}{4}$ of the sample space. Thus, the probability of the dart's landing in the shaded region is the ratio of the area

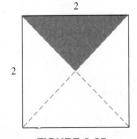

FIGURE 8-25

of the event to the area of the sample space, or $\frac{1}{4}$. This probability is based on the geometry of the figure, and it is the ratio that we would expect to obtain if we performed the experiment a great number of times. If under the conditions of the problem, 100 darts were thrown, we would expect about $\frac{1}{4}$, or 25, of them to land in the shaded area.

EXAMPLE 8-9   A square field that is 1.5 km long on a side has a large tree in each corner. A parachutist plans to jump into the field. If she lands within 50 m of a corner, her ropes will get tangled. What is the probability that she can land safely in the field?

SOLUTION   Figure 8-26 represents the field. The shaded area shows where the jumper can land safely.

FIGURE 8-26

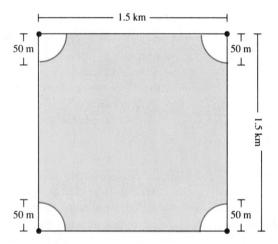

To solve this problem, we assume that the parachutist lands somewhere within the field, at a point chosen at random. To obtain the probability that she does not get caught in a tree, we compute the ratio of the shaded area to the area of the square field. If we place the four corner regions together, we can form a complete circle with radius 50 m, or 0.05 km. Using the fact that the area of a circle is πr^2, where r is the radius of the circle, we find that the area of the four corner regions, or the area of the circle, is $\pi(0.05)^2$ km^2. The area of the square region is 1.5^2, or 2.25, km^2. Thus, the area in which the parachutist can safely land is $[2.25 - \pi(0.05)^2]$ km^2. Then the probability of a safe landing is the ratio of the areas, which is $[2.25 - \pi(0.05)^2]/2.25$, or approximately 0.99. (π is approximately 3.14.)

Other geometric probability problems are investigated in the problem set. Problem 3 is solved by using both tree diagrams and a geometrical approach.

PROBLEM 3

Leah, a princess, fell in love with Ronald, a peasant. Her father, the king, found out and ordered Ronald thrown to the lions. In response to Leah's pleas, the king proposed the following compromise. He designed a maze that opened into two rooms, as shown in Figure 8-27. Leah could choose one of the rooms in which to wait, and lions would be placed in the other room. Ronald was to walk through the maze until one of the rooms was entered. If Leah was in the room, they could be married; otherwise, the lions would take care of Ronald's fate. If Ronald makes each decision in the maze at random, in which room should Leah choose to wait?

FIGURE 8-27

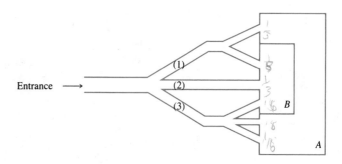

Understanding the Problem. Leah is to choose one of the rooms marked *A* or *B* in Figure 8-27. Lions are to be placed in the other room. Ronald enters the maze and makes each choice of paths at random. We are to determine in which room Leah should wait—that is, which room has the greater probability of being entered by Ronald after he walks through the maze.

Devising a Plan. One way to determine which choice Leah should make is to calculate the probability of Ronald's reaching each room and to choose the one with the greater probability. A tree diagram can be used to determine these probabilities.

Carrying Out the Plan. A tree diagram for the maze in Figure 8-27, along with the possible outcomes, is shown in Figure 8-28.

FIGURE 8-28

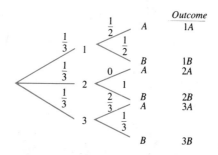

From Figure 8-28, we compute the following.

$$P(A) = \frac{1}{3} \cdot \frac{1}{2} + \frac{1}{3} \cdot 0 + \frac{1}{3} \cdot \frac{2}{3} = \frac{1}{6} + 0 + \frac{2}{9} = \frac{7}{18}$$

$$P(B) = \frac{1}{3} \cdot \frac{1}{2} + \frac{1}{3} \cdot 1 + \frac{1}{3} \cdot \frac{1}{3} = \frac{1}{6} + \frac{1}{3} + \frac{1}{9} = \frac{11}{18}$$

Thus, room B has the greater probability of being chosen, and this is the room in which Leah should wait.

Looking Back. An alternate model for this problem and for many probability problems is a geometric probability model. The rectangle in Figure 8-29 represents the first three choices that Ronald can make. Because each choice is equally likely, each is represented by an equal area. If the upper path is chosen, then rooms A and B have an equal chance of being chosen. If the middle path is chosen, then only room B can be entered. If the lower path is chosen, then room A is entered $\frac{2}{3}$ of the time. This can be expressed in terms of the area model as shown in Figure 8-30. Dividing the rectangle into pieces of equal area, we obtain the model in Figure 8-31, in which the area representing room B is shaded. Because the area representing room B is greater than the area representing room A, room B has the greater probability of being chosen. If desired, Figure 8-31 enables us to find the probability of choosing room B. Because the shaded area consists of 11 rectangles out of a total of 18 rectangles the probability of choosing room B is $\frac{11}{18}$. The problem can be varied by changing the maze or by changing the locations of the rooms.

FIGURE 8-29

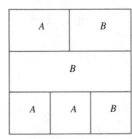

FIGURE 8-30

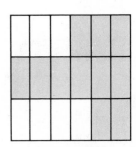

FIGURE 8-31

PROBLEM SET 8-2

1. A box contains six letters, as shown. What is the probability of the outcome DAN if three letters are drawn one by one (a) with replacement? (b) without replacement?

| RANDOM |

2. Three boxes containing letters are shown.

| MATH | | AND | | HISTORY |
| 1 | | 2 | | 3 |

Answer each of the following questions about the boxes.
   (a) From box 1, three letters are drawn one by one without replacement and recorded in order. What is the probability that the outcome is HAT?
   (b) From box 1, three letters are drawn one by one with replacement and recorded in order. What is the probability that the outcome is HAT?
   (c) One letter is drawn at random from box 1, then another from box 2, and then another from box 3, with the results recorded in order. What is the probability that the outcome is HAT?
   (d) If a box is chosen at random and then a letter is drawn at random from the box, what is the probability that the outcome is A?

3. An executive committee consisted of ten members—four women and six men. Three members were selected at random to be sent to a meeting in Hawaii. A blindfolded woman drew three of the ten names from a hat. All three names drawn were women. What was the probability of such luck?

4. Two boxes with letters follow. You are to choose a box and draw three letters at random, one by one, without replacement. If the outcome is SOS, you win a prize.

| SOS | | SOSSOS |
| 1 | | 2 |

   (a) Which box should you choose?
   (b) Which box would you choose if the letters are to be drawn with replacement?

5. Three boxes containing balls are shown. Draw a ball from box 1 and place it in box 2. Then draw a ball from box 2 and place it in box 3. Finally, draw a ball from box 3.

   (a) What is the probability that the last ball, drawn from box 3, is white?
   (b) What is the probability that the last ball drawn is black?

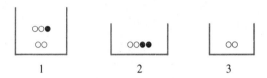

6. Carolyn will win a large prize if she wins two tennis games in a row out of three games. She is to play alternately against Billie and Bobby. She may choose to play Billie-Bobby-Billie or Bobby-Billie-Bobby. She wins against Billie 50% of the time and against Bobby 80% of the time. Which alternative should she choose, and why?

7. Two boxes with black and white balls are shown. A ball is drawn at random from box 1, and then a ball is drawn at random from box 2, and the colors are recorded in order.

Find each of the following.
   (a) The probability of two white balls
   (b) The probability of at least one black ball
   (c) The probability of at most one black ball
   (d) The probability of ● ○ or ○ ●

8. A penny, a nickel, a dime, and a quarter are tossed. What is the probability of at least three heads?

9. Assume that the probability that a child born is a boy is ½. What is the probability that, if a family is going to have four children, they will all be boys?

10. Brittany is going to ascend a 4-step staircase. At any time she is just as likely to stride up 1 step or 2 steps. Find the probabilities that she will ascend the 4 steps in:
   (a) 2 strides
   (b) 3 strides
   (c) 4 strides

11. The numbers of symbols on each of the three dials of a standard slot machine are shown in the table.

Symbol	Dial 1	Dial 2	Dial 3
Bar	1	3	1
Bell	1	3	3
Plum	5	1	5
Orange	3	6	7
Cherry	7	7	0
Lemon	3	0	4
Total	20	20	20

Find the probability for each of the following.
(a) Three plums   (b) Three oranges
(c) Three lemons   (d) No plums

12. If a person takes a five-question true-false test, what is the probability that the score is 100% correct if the person guesses on every question?

13. In a drawer containing only black and blue socks, there are 10 blue socks and 12 black socks. Suppose that it is dark and you choose 3 socks at random. What is the probability that you will choose a matching pair?

14. Rattlesnake and Paxson Colleges play four games against each other in a chess tournament. Rob Fisher, the chess whiz from Paxson, withdrew from the tournament, so the probabilities that Rattlesnake and Paxson will win each game are $\frac{2}{3}$ and $\frac{1}{3}$, respectively. What are the following probabilities?
(a) Paxson loses all four games.
(b) The match is a draw with each school winning two games.

15. The combinations on the lockers at the high school consist of three numbers, each ranging from 0 to 39. If a combination is chosen at random, what is the probability that the first two numbers are multiples of nine and the third number is a multiple of four?

16. A box contains the 11 letters shown. The letters are drawn one by one without replacement, and the results are recorded in order. Find the probability of the outcome MISSISSIPPI.

| MIIIIPPSSSS |

17. Assume that the radius in each of the corners of the field around the trees in Example 8-9 is 100 m. Now what is the probability of a safe landing?

18. Consider the following dart board. If a dart may hit any point on the board with equal probability, what is the probability that it will land in:
(a) Section A
(b) Section B
(c) Section C

(Assume that all shapes are squares and that the x's represent equal measures.)

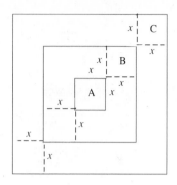

19. The following dart board is a rectangle that measures 2 inches wide and 3 inches long. The circle has a radius of $\frac{3}{4}$ inch. Assume that all darts thrown at the board land at random within the rectangle.

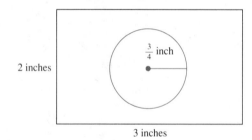

(a) What is the probability, to the nearest tenth, that a dart will land within the circle?
(b) If 50 darts are thrown, how many darts should fall within the circle?

20. The land area of the earth is approximately 57,500,000 square miles. The water area of the earth is approximately 139,600,000 square miles. If a meteor landing at random hits the earth, what is the probability, to the nearest tenth, that it will hit water?

21. An electric clock is stopped by a power failure. What is the probability that the second hand is stopped between the 3 and the 4?

22. A husband and wife discover that there is a 10% probability of passing on a hereditary disease to any one of their children. If they plan to have three children, what is the probability that at least one child will inherit the disease?

23. Let $A = \{x \mid -1 < x < 1\}$ and $B = \{x \mid -3 < x < 2\}$. If a real number is picked at random from set B, what is the probability that it will be in A?

★24. Consider the three spinners A, B, and C shown in the figure. The probabilities for the various outcomes are given below each spinner.

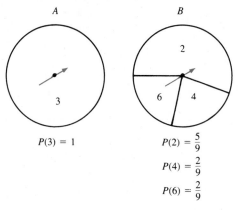

$$A \qquad\qquad B$$

$$P(3) = 1 \qquad\qquad P(2) = \frac{5}{9}$$

$$P(4) = \frac{2}{9}$$

$$P(6) = \frac{2}{9}$$

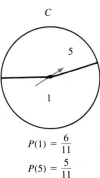

$$C$$

$$P(1) = \frac{6}{11}$$

$$P(5) = \frac{5}{11}$$

(a) Suppose that you choose a spinner and then a friend chooses a spinner, and each person spins the chosen spinner. If the person spinning the higher number wins, which spinner should you choose if you want to win?

(b) This time you are to play the same game as in (a), but two friends play. If each player chooses a spinner, would you make the same choice that you did in (a)? Why?

★25. Abe proposes the following game. He lets you choose one of the four equally likely outcomes obtained by tossing a coin twice: {HH, HT, TH, TT}. Abe then chooses one of the other outcomes. A coin is flipped until either your choice or Abe's choice appears. For example, suppose that you choose TT and Abe chooses HT. If the first two flips yield TH, then no one wins and the game continues. If, after five flips, the string THH<u>HT</u> appears, then Abe is the winner because the sequence HT finally appeared. Is this game fair? Why?

Review Problems

26. Match the phrase to the probability that describes it.
  (a) A certain event   (i) $\frac{1}{1000}$
  (b) An impossible event   (ii) $\frac{999}{1000}$
  (c) A very likely event   (iii) 0
  (d) An unlikely event   (iv) $\frac{1}{2}$
  (e) A 50% chance   (v) 1

27. A date in the month of April is chosen at random. Find the probabilities of the date's being each of the following.
  (a) April 7
  (b) April 31
  (c) Before April 20

B R A I N   T E A S E R

Suppose that n people are in a room. Two people bet on whether at least two of the people in the room have a birthday on the same date during the year (for example, October 14). Assume that a person is as likely to be born on one day as another, and ignore leap years. How many people must be in the room before the bet is even? (If $n = 366$, it is a sure bet.) Poll your class to see if two people have the same birthday. Use this information to find an experimental answer. Then find a theoretical solution. A calculator is very helpful for the computations.

*Section 8-3 Conditional Probability, Independent Events, and Simulations

conditional probability

In **conditional probability,** we are concerned about the probability that an event A will happen given that event B has already happened. We denote this as $P(A|B)$ and read this as "the probability of A, given B." To develop a formula for computing conditional probability, consider the following example. At a certain hospital, it is known that 40 patients have lung cancer (C), 30 patients smoke (S), and 25 have lung cancer and smoke. Suppose that there are 200 patients. A Venn diagram for this information is given in Figure 8-32. If $P(C)$ is the probability that a patient selected at random from the 200 patients has lung cancer, then $P(C) = \frac{40}{200}$. Similarly, $P(S) = \frac{30}{200}$, and $P(C \cap S) = \frac{25}{200}$. If a patient chosen at random is known to smoke, what is the probability that the patient has lung cancer? We would like to know the probability that a patient has lung cancer, given that the patient smokes—that is, $P(C|S)$. We see from the Venn diagram that, of the 30 smokers, there are 25 who have lung cancer. Thus, $P(C|S) = \frac{25}{30} = n(C \cap S)/n(S)$. In this case, $P(C|S) = \frac{25}{30} = (\frac{25}{200})/(\frac{30}{200})$, and we have $P(C|S) = P(C \cap S)/P(S)$. This idea can be generalized to produce the following definition.

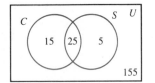

FIGURE 8-32

● **D E F I N I T I O N**
If A and B are events in a sample space, and $P(B) \neq 0$, the **conditional probability** of A, given B, denoted by $P(A|B)$, is defined as $P(A|B) = \dfrac{P(A \cap B)}{P(B)}$.

If A and B are events in a sample space, with $P(B) \neq 0$, then by multiplying both sides of the equation $P(A|B) = \dfrac{P(A \cap B)}{P(B)}$ by $P(B)$ we obtain

Multiplication Rule for Probabilities

$P(A \cap B) = P(B) \cdot P(A|B)$. This is called the **Multiplication Rule for Probabilities.**

The Multiplication Rule for Probabilities justifies multiplying probabilities on tree diagrams as we did in Section 8-2. For example, suppose that a container has three black marbles and two white marbles, and suppose that two marbles are drawn at random without replacement. What is the probability that both marbles are white? If we let W_2 represent drawing a white ball on the second draw and W_1 represent drawing a white ball on the first draw, then applying the Multiplication Rule for Probabilities we have

$$P(W_2 \cap W_1) = P(W_1) \cdot P(W_2|W_1) = \frac{2}{5} \cdot \frac{1}{4} = \frac{2}{20}$$

Therefore, the probability of obtaining two white balls is $\frac{2}{20}$.

A tree diagram for this problem is given in Figure 8-33. We see that the Multiplication Rule for Probabilities in the preceding example is represented by the bottom branch of the tree diagram.

FIGURE 8-33

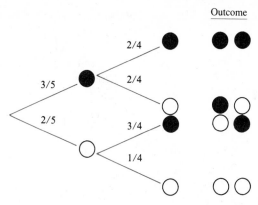

EXAMPLE 8-10   There are 40 employees in a certain firm, and it is known that 28 of these employees are males (M), 2 of these males are secretaries (S), and there are 10 secretaries employed with the firm. What is the probability that an employee chosen at random is a secretary, given that the person is a male?

SOLUTION   We would like to compute the probability of an employee's being a secretary, given that the employee is a male—that is, $P(S|M)$. From the formula given above, we have the following.

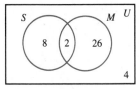

FIGURE 8-34

$$P(S|M) = \frac{P(S \cap M)}{P(M)} = \frac{\frac{2}{40}}{\frac{28}{40}} = \frac{2}{28}, \quad \text{or} \quad \frac{1}{14}$$

The Venn diagram given in Figure 8-34 could also be used to find this probability.

Independent Events

On August 18, 1913, the roulette wheel at a casino in Monte Carlo came up black 26 times in a row. Many people in the crowd at various times during the streak placed large bets on the red because they were convinced that the "law of averages" would catch up with the wheel. If the wheel was fair, what is the probability that the wheel would have shown black on the 27th spin?

The wheel does not have a memory. It does not care how many people lost money on previous spins of the wheel. If this wheel is fair, the probability of the wheel's showing red or black is the same on the 27th spin as it was on each of the previous spins, because the outcome of any spin is independent of what happened on previous spins. In general, events are called **independent** if the occurrence or nonoccurrence of one event does not affect the probability of the other.

independent   In a similar manner, if a fair coin has come up heads 9 times in a row, the probability of its coming up heads on the tenth toss is still $\frac{1}{2}$. The outcome on the 10th toss is independent of the outcomes of the previous 9 tosses. In contrast, consider the probability of tossing 10 heads in a row. In this case, the probability is $(\frac{1}{2})^{10}$, or $\frac{1}{1024}$, which is very unlikely to occur. Using the concept of conditional probability, we could say that the probability of heads on the 10th toss, given heads on the previous 9 tosses, is the same as the probability of heads on one toss of the coin at any given time. This leads to the following definition.

● D E F I N I T I O N
Two events A and B are **independent** if $P(A|B) = P(A)$.

dependent events   If $P(A|B) \neq P(A)$, then the events are called **dependent.**

In the case of independent events A and B, we may use the equation for conditional probability to obtain the following equivalent statements.

$$\frac{P(A \cap B)}{P(B)} = P(A|B) \qquad \text{[Definition of conditional probability]}$$

$$\frac{P(A \cap B)}{P(B)} = P(A) \qquad \text{[Substitute } P(A) \text{ for } P(A|B).]$$

$$P(A \cap B) = P(A) \cdot P(B) \qquad \text{[Multiply both sides by } P(B).]$$

Thus, if A and B are independent events, we have $P(A \cap B) = P(A) \cdot P(B)$.

EXAMPLE 8-11   A box contains five black balls, two red balls, and five white balls. One ball is drawn at random, its color is recorded, and it is replaced in the box. A second ball is then drawn at random. Find the probability that the first ball is red and the second is black.

SOLUTION   Let's say that R is the event of drawing a red ball on the first draw and B is the event of drawing a black ball on the second draw. The events R and B are independent, because the first ball is replaced and consequently the probability of drawing a black ball on the second draw is not influenced by the first draw. Since $P(R) = \frac{2}{12}$ and $P(B|R) = P(B) = \frac{5}{12}$, we have

$$P(R \cap B) = P(R) \cdot P(B) = \left(\frac{2}{12}\right)\left(\frac{5}{12}\right) = \frac{10}{144}, \quad \text{or} \quad \frac{5}{72}$$

If a tree diagram were used for computing this probability, the branch used in obtaining the answer would appear as shown in Figure 8-35.

FIGURE 8-35

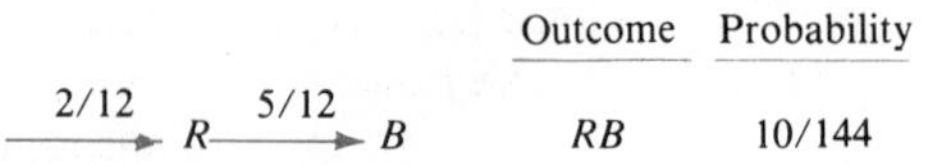

			Outcome	Probability
2/12 → R	5/12 → B		RB	10/144

● **R E M A R K**
The preceding independent events differ from the dependent events that would occur if the ball drawn on the first draw were not replaced.

PROBLEM 4

A publishing company hires two proofreaders, Al and Betsy, to read a manuscript. Al finds 48 errors and Betsy finds 42 errors. The editor finds that 30 common errors were found by the proofreaders; that is, 30 errors were found by both Al and Betsy. What is your estimate of the number of errors not yet found?

Understanding the Problem. Al found 48 errors and Betsy found 42 errors in a manuscript. Thirty errors were listed by both of them. From this information, we are to estimate the number of errors not yet detected in the manuscript. If we could estimate how efficient either Al or Betsy was at finding errors, then we could estimate the fraction of errors that he or she could be expected to find and thus be able to estimate the number of errors not yet found. This amounts to finding the probability that either Al or Betsy will find a given error.

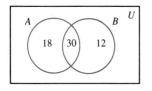

FIGURE 8-36

Devising A Plan. To find the probability that either Al or Betsy will find a given error, we draw a Venn diagram for the given information. From Figure 8-36, we see that the total number of errors found is $18 + 30 + 12$, or 60.

To compute the probability that Al will find a given error, we use the set of errors found by Betsy as a sample space. Thus, Al found $\frac{30}{42}$ of the errors in the set of 42 errors. From this information, we can estimate the number of errors in the manuscript.

Carrying Out the Plan. We have estimated that Al finds $\frac{30}{42}$ of the errors in a given sample. If we let n be the total number of errors in the manuscript, then we could set up the proportion $30/42 = 48/n$. Therefore, $30n = 42 \cdot 48$ and $n = (42 \cdot 48)/30$, which is approximately 67. Because 60 errors were found, the estimate is that $67 - 60$, or 7, errors remain undetected.

Looking Back. We might wonder what result is obtained if we use Betsy's probability of finding an error instead of Al's probability. If we use Al's 48 errors as a sample space, then Betsy found $\frac{30}{48}$ of these errors. Solving as before, we have $30/48 = 42/n$, and $n \doteq 67$. The estimate for the number of undetected errors is $67 - 60$, or 7. We see that it makes no difference which proofreader is chosen to make the estimates. Do you think it would be worthwhile to hire a third proofreader? Investigate this probability by trying various inputs for a third proofreader.

Using Simulations in Probability

Simulations can be used by students to study phenomena that are too complex to analyze by other means. If a problem is simulated many times, students can use the results to estimate probabilities rather than determining probabilities analytically. In the words of the *Standards,* "students should actively explore situations by experimenting and simulating probability models." Consider how we might simulate the problem of determining if a couple will have two girls. One way is to use a fair coin and let a toss of heads represent the birth of a girl and a toss of tails represent the birth of a boy. In this example, a success would consist of tossing two heads in two throws of the coin. An estimate for the probability that a two-child family has two girls is given by dividing the number of successes by the number of trials. The greater the number of trials that are conducted, the more accurate the estimate will become. Table 8-5 represents 50 tosses of two coins. In this simulation, we have 11 sets of two girls out of 50 trials, so we estimate that the probability of having two girls in a two-child family is $\frac{11}{50}$. Compare this with the theoretical probability of having two girls in a two-child family. Other devices, such as dice or spinners, could also be used to perform this simulation.

TABLE 8-5
Outcome of 50
Pairs of Coin Tosses

HH	HT	HT	TT	HT
HT	TH	HT	HT	TT
TT	TT	TT	HT	TH
HH	TH	HT	HT	TT
TH	TH	TH	HH	TT
TH	HT	TT	HH	HT
HH	HH	TT	HT	TT
TT	HH	TH	TH	HT
HT	TT	TH	TH	HH
HT	TT	HH	HH	HH

Random-digit tables are also used in simulations. Random-digit tables are tables of digits selected at random, often by a computer. A portion of a random-digit table is given in Table 8-6. A starting place on this table could be picked at random, and we could start reading across, letting an even digit represent the birth of a girl and an odd digit represent the birth of a boy. Use the random-digit table to simulate the probability of births in a two-child family for 50 cases, by reading pairs of numbers from it. Then compare the results with the earlier coin-tossing simulation.

**TABLE 8-6
Random Digits**

36422	93239	76046	81114	77412	86557	19549	98473	15221	87856
78496	47197	37961	67568	14861	61077	85210	51264	49975	71785
95384	59596	05081	39968	80495	00192	94679	18307	16265	48888
37957	89199	10816	24260	52302	69592	55019	94127	71721	70673
31422	27529	95051	83157	96377	33723	52902	51302	86370	50452
07443	15346	40653	84238	24430	88834	77318	07486	33950	61598
41348	86255	92715	96656	49693	99286	83447	20215	16040	41085
12398	95111	45663	55020	57159	58010	43162	98878	73337	35571
77229	92095	44305	09285	73256	02968	31129	66588	48126	52700
61175	53014	60304	13976	96312	42442	96713	43940	92516	81421
16825	27482	97858	05642	88047	68960	52991	67703	29805	42701
84656	03089	05166	67571	25545	26603	40243	55482	38341	97782
03872	31767	23729	89523	73654	24626	78393	77172	41328	95633
40488	70426	04034	46618	55102	93408	10965	69744	80766	14889
98322	25528	43808	05935	78338	77881	90139	72375	50624	91385
13366	52764	02407	14202	74172	58770	65348	24115	44277	96735
86711	27764	86789	43800	87582	09298	17880	75507	35217	08352
53886	50358	62738	91783	71944	90221	79403	75139	09102	77826
99348	21186	42266	01531	44325	61042	13453	61917	90426	12437
49985	08787	59448	82680	52929	19077	98518	06251	58451	91140
49807	32863	69984	20102	09523	47827	08374	79849	19352	62726
46569	00365	23591	44317	55054	99835	20633	66215	46668	53587
09988	44203	43532	54538	16619	45444	11957	69184	98398	96508
32916	00567	82881	59753	54761	39404	90756	91760	18698	42852
93285	32297	27254	27198	99093	97821	46277	10439	30389	45372
03222	39951	12738	50303	25017	84207	52123	88637	19369	58289
87002	61789	96250	99337	14144	00027	43542	87030	14773	73087
68840	94259	01961	42552	91843	33855	00824	48733	81297	80411
88323	28828	64765	08244	53077	50897	91937	08871	91517	19668
55170	71062	64159	79364	53088	21536	39451	95649	65256	23950

The Peanuts cartoon suggests a simulation problem concerning chocolate chip cookies.

EXAMPLE 8-12   Suppose that Lucy makes enough batter for exactly 100 chocolate chip cookies and mixes 100 chocolate chips into the batter. If the chips are distributed at random and Charlie chooses a cookie at random from the 100 cookies, estimate the probability that it will contain exactly 1 chocolate chip.

SOLUTION   A simulation can be used to estimate the probability of choosing a cookie with exactly 1 chocolate chip. We can construct a 10 × 10 grid, as shown in Figure 8-37, to represent the 100 cookies made by Lucy. Each square (cookie) can be associated with some ordered pair, where the first component is for the horizontal scale and the second component is for the vertical scale. For example, the squares (0, 2) and (5, 3) are pictured in Figure 8-37. Using the table of random digits, close your eyes, take a pencil, and point to one number to start. Look at the number and the number immediately following it. Consider these numbers as an ordered pair and continue on until 100 ordered pairs are obtained. For example, suppose we start at a 3 and the numbers following 3 are as shown.

39968   80495   00192 . . .

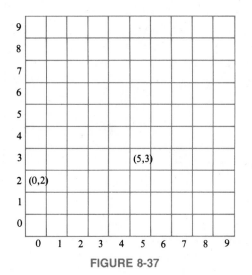

FIGURE 8-37

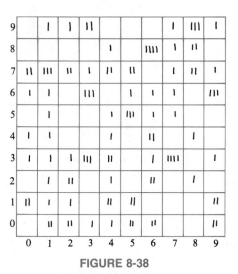

FIGURE 8-38

Then the ordered pairs would be given as (3, 9), (9, 6), (8, 8), (0, 4), and so on. Use each pair of numbers as the coordinates for the square (cookie) and place a tally on the grid to represent each chip, as shown in Figure 8-38. (Note that there are other schemes for using the random-digit table to select the 100 ordered pairs.) We estimate the probability that a cookie has exactly 1 chip by counting the number of squares with exactly one tally and dividing by 100. Table 8-7 shows the results of one simulation. Thus, the estimate for the probability of Charlie's receiving a cookie with exactly 1 chip is $\frac{34}{100}$.

TABLE 8-7

Number of Chips	Number of Cookies
0	38
1	34
2	20
3	6
≥ 4	2

Try a simulation on your own, and compare your results with the preceding ones and with the results given in Table 8-8, which we obtained by theoretical methods.

TABLE 8-8

Number of Chips	Number of Cookies
0	36.8
1	36.8
2	18.4
3	6.1
≥ 4	1.9

EXAMPLE 8-13   A baseball player, Reggie, has a batting average of 0.400; that is, his probability of getting a hit on any particular time at bat is 0.400. Estimate the probability that he will get at least one hit in his next 3 times at bat.

SOLUTION   We use a random-digit table to simulate this example. We choose a starting point, and place the random digits in groups of three. Because Reggie's probability of getting a hit on any particular time at bat is 0.400, we could use the occurrence of four particular numbers from 0 through 9 in the table to represent a hit. Suppose a hit is represented by the digits 0, 1, 2, and 3. At least one hit is obtained in three times at bat if, in any sequence of three digits, a 0, 1, 2, or 3 appears. Data for 50 trials are given below.

```
780  862  760  580  783  720  590  506  021  366
848  118  073  077  042  254  063  667  374  153
377  883  573  683  780  115  662  591  685  274
279  652  754  909  754  892  310  673  964  351
803  034  799  915  059  006  774  640  298  961
```

We see that a 0, 1, 2, or 3 appears in 42 out of the 50 trials; thus, an estimate for the probability of at least one hit in Reggie's next 3 times at bat is $\frac{42}{50}$. Try to determine the theoretical probability for this experiment.

How might we use the random-digit table to pick 5 states at random from the 50 states? One possibility is to number the states 00, 01, 02, 03, ..., 49. We now go to the table of random digits and select blocks of two digits, for example,

74   19   30   44   00   52   42   99   21   85   53 . . .

If we ignore blocks of two that have values greater than or equal to 50, we obtain the following state numbers to be selected.

19, 30, 44, 00, 42

This is a random sample of 5 states chosen from the 50 states.

From a random sample, we can deduce information about the population from which the sample was taken. To see how this can be done, consider Example 8-14.

EXAMPLE 8-14   We wish to determine the number of fish in a certain pond. Suppose that we capture 300 fish, mark them, and throw them back into the pond. Suppose that, the next day, 200 fish are caught and 20 of these are already marked. Then these 200 fish are thrown back into the pond. Estimate how many fish are in the pond.

SOLUTION   Because 20 of the 200 fish are marked, we assume that $\frac{20}{200}$, or $\frac{1}{10}$, of the fish are marked. Thus, $\frac{1}{10}$ of the population is marked. If n represents the population, then $\frac{1}{10}n = 300$, and $n = 300 \cdot 10 = 3000$. Hence, an estimate for the fish population of the pond is 3000 fish.

PROBLEM 5

Assume that Carmen Smith, a basketball player, makes free throws with 80% probability of success and is placed in a one-and-one situation. This means that Carmen is given a second foul shot only if the first shot goes through the basket. Thus, in a one-and-one situation, Carmen can score 0, 1, or 2 points. How can we simulate 25 attempts from the foul line in one-and-one situations to determine how many times we would expect Carmen to score 0 points, 1 point, and 2 points?

Understanding the Problem.   The probability that Carmen makes any given free throw is 80%. She is shooting in a one-and-one situation: If she misses the first shot, she receives 0 points; if she makes the first shot, she receives 1 point and is allowed to shoot *one* more time. Each basket made counts as 1 point. Thus, Carmen has the opportunity to score 0, 1, or 2 points. We are to determine by simulation how many times Carmen can be expected to score 0 points, 1 point, and 2 points over the course of 25 attempts at one-and-one situations.

Devising a Plan. One way to simulate the problem is to use a random-digit table. Because Carmen's probability of making any basket is 80%, we could use the occurrence of a 0, 1, 2, 3, 4, 5, 6, or 7 to simulate making the basket and the occurrence of an 8 or a 9 to simulate missing the basket. Another way to simulate the problem would be to construct a spinner with 80% of the spinner devoted to making a basket and 20% of the spinner devoted to missing the basket. This could be done by constructing the spinner with 80% of the 360 degrees—that is, 288 degrees—devoted to making the basket and 72 degrees devoted to missing the basket. A spinner for this simulation is shown in Figure 8-39.

FIGURE 8-39

Carrying Out the Plan. We use a spinner similar to the one in Figure 8-39. We spin the spinner to simulate 25 sets of one-and-one situations. If the spinner lands on "miss," 0 points are recorded for the set. If the spinner lands on "make," a second spin is taken. If the spinner shows another "make," then 2 points are recorded; otherwise, 1 point is recorded. This is repeated for 25 sets and the results are recorded. Four simulations of 25 sets are given in Table 8-9. We used four trials to obtain a better estimate than we would get from only a single trial.

TABLE 8-9

Number of Points	Trial 1	Trial 2	Trial 3	Trial 4	Total	Estimated Probability
0	4	6	5	5	20	$\frac{20}{100}$
1	2	4	5	4	15	$\frac{15}{100}$
2	19	15	15	16	65	$\frac{65}{100}$

To solve the problem, we use the estimated probability and multiply by 25 to obtain the results in Table 8-10.

TABLE 8-10

Number of Points	Expected Number of Times Points Are Scored in 25 Attempts
0	5
1	3.75
2	16.25

Looking Back. Similar problems could be attempted, using different models for the simulation. The shooting percentage for Carmen could also be raised or lowered, and the effects on the number of points scored could be compared. Could you write a computer program to perform these simulations?

It is possible to compute the theoretical probability for this experiment by using a tree diagram, as shown in Figure 8-40.

FIGURE 8-40

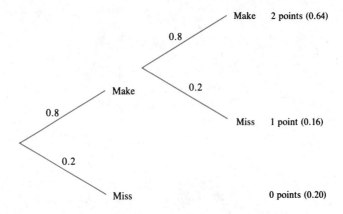

Thus, theoretical estimates for the number of points scored in 25 attempts can be computed. These estimates are given in Table 8-11. Compare these results with the experimental probability obtained previously.

TABLE 8-11

Number of Points	Expected Number of Times Points Are Scored in 25 Attempts
0	5
1	4
2	16

Geometric probability could also be used to solve this problem. We start with the 10 × 10 grid shown in Figure 8-41 to represent the sample space. We separate the sample space into two parts, with a vertical line to represent the dividing line between making 80% on the first shot and missing 20% on it; that is, 80 of the 100 squares are devoted to making the first shot, and 20 of the 100 squares are devoted to missing the first shot. If the first shot is made, a second shot is taken with an 80% probability of success. Therefore, we subdivide the "make" area from the first shot into two portions of 80% and 20%. This is done by marking off 8 of the 10 rows in the "make" area. We then assign the appropriate number of points to each of the three areas, as shown in Figure 8-42. Now we see that 64 of the 100 squares (or 64% of the sample space) are devoted to scoring 2 points, 16 of the 100 squares (or 16%) are devoted to scoring 1 point, and 20 of the 100 squares (or 20%) are devoted to scoring 0 points. These results are consistent with the results obtained by using the tree diagram.

First shot

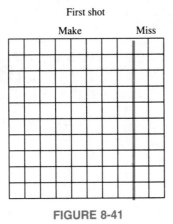

FIGURE 8-41

First shot

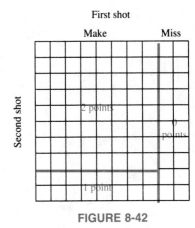

FIGURE 8-42

PROBLEM SET 8-3

1. Two standard dice are thrown.
   (a) What is the probability of a sum of 7 showing, given that the sum is an odd number?
   (b) What is the probability of a sum of 7 showing, given that one die shows a 1?

2. A penny, a nickel, and a quarter are tossed. What is the probability of obtaining three heads if it is known that the penny came up heads?

3. A family is known to have three children. What is the probability that the family has all boys if it is known that the eldest child is a boy?

4. Al and Betsy are drawing cards to determine who has to clean the house. Al draws an ace and does not replace it in the deck. Now it is Betsy's turn. What is the probability that Betsy will also draw an ace?

5. A single card is drawn from a standard deck of cards. What is the probability that it is a king, given that it is a face card?

6. An assembly line has two inspectors. The probability that the first inspector will miss a defective item is 0.05. If the defective item passes the first inspector, the probability that the second inspector will miss it is 0.01. What is the probability that a defective item will pass by both inspectors?

7. A die is rolled and a coin is tossed. Find the probability of tossing a prime number on the die and tails on the coin.

8. If 75% of a store's customers are female and 60% of the female customers have charge accounts at the store, what is the probability that a customer chosen at random is female and has a charge account?

9. A box contains three red balls, four white balls, and five blue balls. Balls are drawn at random from the box without replacement until a red ball is drawn. Find the probability that the first time that a red ball is drawn is on:
   (a) The first draw.   (b) The second draw.
   (c) The third draw.   (d) The fourth draw.

10. In a certain population of caribou, the probability of an animal's being sickly is $\frac{1}{20}$. If a caribou is sickly, the probability of its being eaten by wolves is $\frac{1}{5}$. If a caribou is not sickly, the probability of its being eaten by wolves is $\frac{1}{150}$. If a caribou is chosen at random from the herd, what is the probability that it will be eaten by wolves?

11. In a survey of 100 students, it was determined that 15 students were taking algebra, biology, and chemistry; 25 were taking algebra and biology; 30 were taking algebra and chemistry; 22 were taking biology and chemistry; 5 were taking only algebra; 4 were taking only biology; and 6 were taking only chemistry. If a student is chosen at random from the 100 students, what is the probability of each of the following?
    (a) The student is not taking any of the three subjects.
    (b) The student is taking algebra and biology, but not chemistry.
    (c) The student is taking algebra, given that he or she is taking biology.

12. In a group of 50 students, 30 are taking mathematics, 15 are taking biology, and 10 are taking both subjects. A student is chosen at random from the group. What is the probability that the student is taking biology if we know that the student is taking mathematics?

13. How might you use a table of random digits to simulate each of the following?
    (a) Tossing a single die
    (b) Choosing 3 people at random from a group of 20 people
    (c) Spinning the spinner, where the probability of each color is as shown.

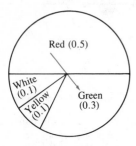

14. To estimate the fish population of a certain pond, 200 fish were caught, marked, and returned to the pond. The next day, 300 fish were caught, of which 50 had been marked the previous day. Estimate the fish population of the pond.

15. Pick a block of two digits from the random-digit table. What is the probability that the number picked is less than 30?

16. A cereal company places a coupon bearing a number from 1 to 9 in each box of cereal. If the numbers are distributed at random in the boxes of cereal, estimate the number of boxes of cereal, on the average, that would have to be purchased in order to obtain all nine numbers. Explain how the table of random digits could be used to estimate the number of coupons.

17. A school has 500 students. The principal is to pick 30 students at random from the school to go to the Rose Bowl. How can this be done by using a random-digit table?

18. In a certain city, the probability that it will rain on a certain day is 0.8 if it rained the day before. The probability that it will be dry on a certain day is 0.3 if it was dry the day before. It is now Sunday and it is raining. Use the table of random digits to simulate the weather for the rest of the week.

19. How many cards would you expect to have to turn over on the average in an ordinary bridge deck before an ace appears? Try this experiment with cards and see how close your guess is. Could you simulate this experiment with a random-digit table?

20. Suppose that, in the World Series, the two teams are evenly matched. The two teams play until one team wins 4 games, and no ties are possible.
    (a) What is the maximum number of games that could be played?
    (b) Use simulation to approximate the probabilities that the series will end in 4 games and in 7 games.

21. The probability of the home team's winning a basketball game is 80%. Describe a simulation of the probability that the home team will win 3 home games in a row.

22. It is reported that 15% of people who came into contact with a person infected with strep throat contracted the disease. Use the random-digit table to simulate the probability that at least one child in a three-child family will catch the disease, given that each of the children has come into contact with the infected person.

★23. Montana duck hunters are all perfect shots. Ten Montana hunters are in a duck blind when 10 ducks fly over. All 10 hunters pick a duck at random to shoot at, and all 10 hunters fire at the same time. How many ducks could be expected to escape, on the average, if this experiment were repeated a large number of times? How could this problem be simulated?

*Section 8-4   Odds and Expected Value

Computing Odds

odds

People often speak about the *odds in favor of* or the *odds against* a particular team in an athletic contest. For example, when we say that the **odds** in favor of the Falcons' winning a particular football game are 4 to 1, we are speaking of how likely the Falcons are to win relative to how likely they are to lose. In other words, in this example, the probability of their winning is four times the probability of their losing. Thus, if W represents the event Falcons win and L represents the event Falcons lose, then $P(W) = 4P(L)$; as a proportion,

$$\frac{P(W)}{P(L)} = \frac{4}{1}, \quad \text{or} \quad 4:1$$

Furthermore, because W and L are complements of each other, we have

$$\frac{P(W)}{P(\overline{W})} = \frac{P(W)}{1 - P(W)} = \frac{4}{1}, \quad \text{or} \quad 4:1$$

Formally, odds are defined as follows.

- **D E F I N I T I O N**

Let $P(A)$ be the probability that A occurs, and let $P(\overline{A})$ be the probability that A does not occur. Then the **odds in favor** of an event A are

$$\frac{P(A)}{P(\overline{A})} \quad \text{or} \quad \frac{P(A)}{1 - P(A)}$$

The **odds against** an event A are

$$\frac{P(\overline{A})}{P(A)} \quad \text{or} \quad \frac{1 - P(A)}{P(A)}$$

Thus, the odds against tossing a 4 on one throw of a die are $(\frac{5}{6})/(\frac{1}{6}) = \frac{5}{1}$, or 5 to 1, or 5:1. Most odds are written with a colon.

Notice that, when odds are calculated, the denominators of the probabilities divide out. Thus, alternate definitions for odds in case of *equally likely* outcomes are as follows.

$$\text{Odds in favor} = \frac{\text{Number of favorable outcomes}}{\text{Number of unfavorable outcomes}}$$

$$\text{Odds against} = \frac{\text{Number of unfavorable outcomes}}{\text{Number of favorable outcomes}}$$

When you roll a die, the number of favorable ways of rolling a four in one throw of a die is 1, and the number of unfavorable ways is 5. Thus, the odds in favor of rolling a four are 1 to 5.

This technique is demonstrated on the student page from *Addison-Wesley Mathematics,* 1989, Grade 8.

Odds

Nina is trying to draw a blue marble from the box without looking into the box.

There are **2** ways she can succeed.

There are **3** ways she can fail.

The **odds in favor** of drawing a blue marble are 2 to 3.

$$\frac{2}{3} \begin{array}{l} \leftarrow \text{ Successes} \\ \leftarrow \text{ Failures} \end{array}$$

The **odds against** drawing a blue marble are 3 to 2.

$$\frac{3}{2} \begin{array}{l} \leftarrow \text{ Failures} \\ \leftarrow \text{ Successes} \end{array}$$

Find the odds for each event.

1. Spin the spinner.

Event: Get a 2
Odds in favor = ▦
Odds against = ▦

2. Draw a marble from the box without looking.

Event: Draw a red marble
Odds in favor = ▦
Odds against = ▦

3. Toss a coin.

Event: Comes up heads
Odds in favor = ▦
Odds against = ▦

4. Spin the spinners.

Event: Sum of 6
Odds in favor = ▦
Odds against = ▦

5. Toss both coins.

Event: The coins match
Odds in favor = ▦
Odds against = ▦

6. Toss the dice.

Event: Sum of 2
Odds in favor = ▦
Odds against = ▦

EXAMPLE 8-15   For each of the following, find the odds in favor of the event's occurring.
(a) Rolling a number less than 5 on a die
(b) Tossing heads on a fair coin
(c) Drawing an ace from an ordinary 52-card deck
(d) Drawing a heart from an ordinary 52-card deck

SOLUTION   (a) Because the probability of rolling a number less than 5 is $\frac{4}{6}$ and the probability of rolling a number not less than 5 is $\frac{2}{6}$, the odds in favor of rolling a number less than 5 are $(\frac{4}{6}) \div (\frac{2}{6})$, or 4:2 or 2:1.

(b) Because $P(H) = \frac{1}{2}$ and $P(\overline{H}) = \frac{1}{2}$, the odds in favor of getting heads are $(\frac{1}{2}) \div (\frac{1}{2})$, or 1:1.

(c) Because the probability of drawing an ace is $\frac{4}{52}$ and the probability of not drawing an ace is $\frac{48}{52}$, the odds in favor of drawing an ace are $(\frac{4}{52}) \div (\frac{48}{52})$, or 4:48, or 1:12.

(d) Because the probability of drawing a heart is $\frac{13}{52}$, or $\frac{1}{4}$, and the probability of not drawing a heart is $\frac{39}{52}$, or $\frac{3}{4}$, the odds in favor of drawing a heart are $(\frac{13}{52}) \div (\frac{39}{52}) = \frac{13}{39}$, or 13:39, or 1:3.

● R E M A R K

The preceding examples could have been worked just as easily by using the alternate definition for odds. In Example 8-15(c) we could reason that, since there are 4 ways of drawing an ace (favorable outcomes) and 48 ways of not drawing an ace, (unfavorable outcomes) the odds in favor of drawing an ace are 4:48, or 1:12. Rework the other three parts of this example, using the alternate definition for odds.

Given the probability of an event, it is possible to find the odds in favor of (or against) the event. Conversely, given the odds in favor of (or against) an event, it is possible to find the probability of the event. For example, if the odds in favor of an event A are 5:1, then the following proportion holds.

$$\frac{P(A)}{1 - P(A)} = \frac{5}{1}$$
$$P(A) = 5[1 - P(A)]$$
$$6P(A) = 5$$
$$P(A) = \frac{5}{6}$$

● R E M A R K

Note that the probability $\frac{5}{6}$ is a ratio. The exact number of favorable outcomes and the exact total of all outcomes are not necessarily known.

EXAMPLE 8-16 In the cartoon, Snoopy is told that the odds are 1000 to 1 that he will end up with a broken arm if he touches Linus' blanket. What is the probability of this event E?

© 1974 United Feature Syndicate, Inc.

SOLUTION $\dfrac{P(E)}{1 - P(E)} = \dfrac{1000}{1}$, which implies $P(E) = \dfrac{1000}{1001}$.

FIGURE 8-43

Expected Value

Consider the spinner in Figure 8-43, with the payoff for each region written on the spinner. Should the owner of this spinner expect to make money over an extended period of time if the charge is $2.00 per spin? If the spinner is fair, then the following probabilities can be assigned to each region.

$$P(\$1.00) = \frac{1}{2} \qquad P(\$2.00) = \frac{1}{4} \qquad P(\$3.00) = \frac{1}{8} \qquad P(\$4.00) = \frac{1}{8}$$

To determine the average payoff over the long run, we multiply the probability of landing on the payoff by the payoff and then find the sum of the products. This computation is given by $E = (\frac{1}{2})1 + (\frac{1}{4})2 + (\frac{1}{8})3 + (\frac{1}{8})4 = 1.875$, or about 1.88. The owner can expect to pay out about $1.88 per spin, and $1.88 is less than the $2.00 charge, so the owner should make a profit on the spinner if it is used many times.

expected value

The approximate total of the products in this example, $1.88, is called the **expected value,** or *mathematical expectation,* of the experiment. The expected value is an average of winnings for the long run. Expected value can be used to predict the average result of an experiment when it is repeated many times, but an expected value cannot be used to determine the outcome of any single experiment. A general definition is given next.

• **D E F I N I T I O N**

If, in an experiment, the possible outcomes are numbers $a_1, a_2, \ldots, a_n$, occurring with probabilities $p_1, p_2, \ldots, p_n$, respectively, then the **expected value** (mathematical expectation) E is given by the equation

$$E = a_1 \cdot p_1 + a_2 \cdot p_2 + a_3 \cdot p_3 + \cdots + a_n \cdot p_n$$

Suppose that Mega-Mouth Toothpaste Company is giving away $20,000 in a contest. To win the contest, a person must send in a postcard with his or her name on it (no purchase of toothpaste is necessary). Suppose the company expects to receive 1 million postcards. Is this contest fair? *A game is considered fair if the net winnings are* $0; that is, the expected value of the game must equal the price of playing the game. The expected value is one millionth of $20,000; that is, $E = (1/1,000,000) \cdot (20,000) = \frac{2}{100} = 0.02$. Because the cost of the postcard and postage exceeds $0.02, the contest is not fair.

EXAMPLE 8-17   Suppose that you pay $5.00 to play the following game. Two coins are tossed. You receive $10 if two heads occur, $5 if exactly one head occurs, and nothing if no heads appear. Is this a fair game?

SOLUTION   Before we determine the average payoff, recall that $P(HH) = \frac{1}{4}$, $P(HT$ or $TH) = \frac{1}{2}$, and $P(TT) = \frac{1}{4}$. To find the expected value we perform the following computation.

$$E = \left(\frac{1}{4}\right) \cdot (\$10) + \left(\frac{1}{2}\right) \cdot (\$5) + \left(\frac{1}{4}\right) \cdot (0) = \$5$$

Because the price of playing is equal to the average payoff, the net winnings are 0, and this is a fair game.

EXAMPLE 8-18   Lori spends $1.00 for 1 ticket in a raffle with a $100 prize. If 200 tickets are sold, is $1.00 a fair price to pay for the ticket?

SOLUTION   The probability of winning $100 is $\frac{1}{200}$. Thus, $E = (\frac{1}{200})100$, or 0.50. Because $1.00 is greater than $0.50, $1.00 is not a fair price. If the raffle is repeated many times, Lori can expect to lose $0.50 per raffle ticket, on the average.

PROBLEM 6

Al and Betsy were playing a coin-tossing game in which a fair coin was to be tossed until a total of either three heads or three tails occurred. Al was to win when a total of three heads were tossed, and Betsy was to win when a total of three tails were tossed. Each bet $50 on the game. The coin was lost when Al had two heads and Betsy had one tail. How should the stakes be fairly split if the game is not continued?

Understanding the Problem. Al and Betsy each bet $50 on a coin-tossing game in which a fair coin was to be tossed five times. Al was to win when a total of three heads was obtained; Betsy was to win when a total of three tails was obtained. When Al had two heads and Betsy had one tail, the coin was lost. The problem is how to split the stakes fairly.

If the stakes of the game are to be split fairly, then we should agree on what this means. There could be many interpretations, but possibly the best is to agree to split the pot in proportion to the probabilities of each player's winning the game when play was halted; that is, we must calculate the expected value for each player and split the pot accordingly.

Devising a Plan. A third head would have made Al the winner, whereas Betsy would have needed two more tails to win. A tree diagram that simulates the completion of the game allows us to find the probability of each player's winning the game. Once the probabilities are found, all that is necessary is to multiply the probabilities by the amount of the pot, $100, to determine each player's fair share.

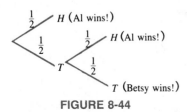

FIGURE 8-44

Carrying Out the Plan. The tree diagram in Figure 8-44 shows the possibilities for game winners if the game is completed. We can find the probabilities of each player's winning as follows:

$$P(\text{Betsy wins}) = \frac{1}{2} \cdot \frac{1}{2} = \frac{1}{4}$$

$$P(\text{Al wins}) = 1 - \frac{1}{4} = \frac{3}{4}$$

Hence, the fair way to split the stakes is for Al to receive $\frac{3}{4}$ of $100, or $75, while Betsy should receive $\frac{1}{4}$ of $100, or $25.

Looking Back. The problem could be made even more interesting by assuming that the coin is not fair so that the probability is not $\frac{1}{2}$ for each branch in the tree diagram. Other possibilities arise if the players have unequal amounts of money in the pot or if more tosses are required in order to win.

PROBLEM SET 8-4

1. What are the odds in favor of drawing a face card from an ordinary deck of playing cards? What are the odds against drawing a face card?

2. On a single roll of a pair of dice, what are the odds against rolling a sum of 7?

3. Assume that the probability of a boy's being born is ½. If a family plans to have four children, what are the odds against having all boys?

4. Diane tossed a coin nine times and got nine tails. Assume that Diane's coin is fair and answer each of the following questions.

   (a) What is the probability of tossing a tail on the tenth toss?

   (b) What is the probability of tossing ten more tails in a row?

   (c) What are the odds against tossing ten more tails in a row?

5. If the odds against Sam's winning his first prize fight are 3 to 5, what is the probability that he will win the fight?

6. What are the odds in favor of tossing at least two heads if a fair coin is tossed three times?

7. If the probability of rain for the day is 60%, what are the odds against its raining?

8. On an American roulette wheel, half of the slots numbered 1–36 are red and half are black. Two slots, numbered 0 and 00, are green. What are the odds against a red slot's coming up on any spin of the wheel?

9. A game involves tossing two coins. A player wins $1.00 if both tosses result in heads. What should you pay to play this game in order to make it a fair game?

10. Suppose that a player rolls a fair die and receives the number of dollars equal to the number of spots showing on the die. What is the expected value?

11. A punch-out card contains 500 spaces. One particular space pays $1000, five other spaces each pay $100, and the remaining spaces pay nothing. If a player chooses one space, what is the expected value of the game?

12. The following chart shows the probabilities assigned by Stu to the number of hours spent on homework on a given night.

Hours	Probability
1	0.15
2	0.20
3	0.40
4	0.10
5	0.05
6	0.10

If Stu's friend Stella calls and asks how long his homework will take, what would you expect his answer to be, based on this table?

13. Suppose five quarters, five dimes, five nickels, and ten pennies are in a box. One coin is selected at random. What is the expected value of this experiment?

14. If the odds in favor of Fast Leg's winning a horse race are 5 to 2 and the first prize is $14,000, what is the expected value of Fast Leg's winning?

15. Al and Betsy are playing a coin-tossing game in which a fair coin is tossed. Al wins when a total of ten heads are tossed, and Betsy wins when a total of ten tails are tossed.

    (a) If nine heads and eight tails have been tossed and the game is stopped, how should a pot of $100 be fairly divided?

    (b) What are the odds against Betsy's winning at the time the game was stopped in (a)?

    *(c) Suppose eight heads and five tails have been tossed when the game is stopped. How should a pot of $100 be fairly divided?

    (d) What are the odds in favor of Al's winning at the time the game was stopped in (c)?

Section 8-5 Methods of Counting

Tree diagrams can be used to list possible outcomes of experiments. For example, the tree diagram in Figure 8-45 lists the different ways three different flavors of ice cream—chocolate (c), vanilla (v), and strawberry (s)—can be arranged on a cone, with no flavor used more than once.

FIGURE 8-45

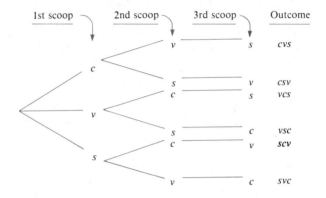

The tree starts out with three branches in the first stage, representing the three possibilities for the first scoop. For each outcome at the first stage, there are two possibilities at the second stage. Hence, there are $3 \cdot 2$ possibilities at the second stage. Then, for each outcome in the second stage, there is only one possibility at the third stage. Consequently, there are $3 \cdot 2 \cdot 1$, or 6, different arrangements.

Now, consider a double-dip ice cream cone for which there are ten flavors of ice cream and six flavors of sherbet. How many different double-dip cones can be made with ice cream on the bottom and sherbet on the top? Since for each of the ten ice cream flavors there are six flavors of sherbet, the number of all possible double-dip cones is

$$\underbrace{6 + 6 + 6 + \cdots + 6}_{10 \text{ terms}} \quad \text{or} \quad 10 \cdot 6 = 60$$

A tree diagram can be used to verify the result. The counting argument used to find the number of possible double-dip cones is an example of the Fundamental Counting Principle.

• **P R O P E R T Y**

Fundamental Counting Principle If event M can occur in m ways and, after it has occurred, event N can occur in n ways, then event M followed by event N can occur in $m \cdot n$ ways.

• **R E M A R K**

The Fundamental Counting Principle can be extended to any number of events.

EXAMPLE 8-19   Solve each of the following.
(a) If a man owns seven shirts and six pairs of pants, how many different shirt-pant combinations are possible?
(b) Sally is taking a five-item true-false test. If she guesses at every item, how many different patterns of answers are possible?
(c) Suppose that eight horses are entered in a race. In how many different ways can the first three horses finish?
(d) If automobile license plates consist of two letters followed by four digits, what is the total number of different license plates possible, assuming that numbers and letters may be repeated?

SOLUTION   (a) Because a shirt can be chosen in seven ways and a pair of pants can be chosen in six ways, there are $7 \cdot 6$, or 42, shirt-pant combinations.
(b) Because there are two ways to answer question 1 on the test, two ways to answer question 2, and so on, there are $2 \cdot 2 \cdot 2 \cdot 2 \cdot 2$, or 32, different possible patterns of answers.
(c) There are eight possible winners, leaving seven possible second places and six possible third places. Thus, there are $8 \cdot 7 \cdot 6$, or 336, ways in which the first three horses can finish the race.
(d) There are $26 \cdot 26 \cdot 10 \cdot 10 \cdot 10 \cdot 10$, or 6,760,000, different license plates possible.

Now consider how many ways the owner of an ice cream parlor can display ten ice cream flavors in a row along the front of the display case. The first position can be filled in ten ways, the second position in nine ways, the third position in eight ways, and so on. Thus, by the Fundamental Counting Principle, there are $10 \cdot 9 \cdot 8 \cdot 7 \cdot 6 \cdot 5 \cdot 4 \cdot 3 \cdot 2 \cdot 1$, or 3,628,800, ways to display the flavors. If there were 16 flavors, there would be $16 \cdot 15 \cdot 14 \cdot 13 \cdots 3 \cdot 2 \cdot 1$ ways to arrange them. In general, *if there are n objects, then the number of possible ways to arrange the objects in a row is the product of all the natural numbers from n to 1, inclusive.* This expression is called ***n* factorial** and is denoted by ***n!***, as shown next.

n factorial / n!

$$n! = n \cdot (n - 1) \cdot (n - 2) \cdots 3 \cdot 2 \cdot 1$$

For example, $5! = 5 \cdot 4 \cdot 3 \cdot 2 \cdot 1$, $3! = 3 \cdot 2 \cdot 1$, and $1! = 1$. Using factorial notation is helpful in counting and probability problems. A calculator is also very useful for finding the products in such problems. Practice problems with factorials are included in the problem set.

Permutations of Unlike Objects

The ice cream cone arrangements discussed previously were in a definite order, and no flavor could be chosen twice. A scoop of chocolate ice cream on top of a scoop of vanilla is a different arrangement from a scoop of vanilla on top of a scoop of chocolate. An arrangement of things in a definite order *permutation* with no repetitions is called a **permutation.** For example, RAT, RTA, TAR, TRA, ART, and ATR are all different arrangements of the letters R, A, and T.

Consider the set of people in a small club, {Al, Betty, Carl, Dan}. In how many ways can they elect a president and a secretary? Order is important and no repetitions are possible. Thus, this is a permutation problem. Since there are four ways of choosing a president and then three ways of choosing a secretary, by the Fundamental Counting Principle, there are $4 \cdot 3$, or 12, ways of choosing a president and a secretary. Note that an Al-Betty choice is different from a Betty-Al choice. Choosing two officers from a club of four is a permutation of four people chosen two at a time. The number of possible permutations of four objects taken two at a time is denoted by $_4P_2$. Hence, $_4P_2 = 4 \cdot 3$, or 12. In general, *if n objects are chosen r at a time, then the number of possible permutations is denoted by $_nP_r$.* Because there are n choices for the first object, $n - 1$ choices for the second object, $n - 2$ choices for the third object, and so on, then by the Fundamental Counting Principle, we have

$$_nP_r = n \cdot (n - 1) \cdot (n - 2) \cdots [n - (r - 1)]$$

or

$$_nP_r = n \cdot (n - 1) \cdot (n - 2) \cdots (n - r + 1)$$

For example, $_7P_3 = 7 \cdot 6 \cdot (7 - 3 + 1) = 7 \cdot 6 \cdot 5$.

The formula for permutations can be written in terms of factorials. This can be done by noticing the following. Because

$$_nP_r = n \cdot (n - 1) \cdot (n - 2) \cdots (n - r + 1) \quad \text{and} \quad 1 = \frac{(n - r)!}{(n - r)!} \quad \text{we have}$$

$$_nP_r = {_nP_r} \cdot 1 = {_nP_r} \cdot \frac{(n - r)!}{(n - r)!}$$

$$= n \cdot (n - 1) \cdot (n - 2) \cdots (n - r + 1) \cdot \frac{[(n - r) \cdot (n - r - 1) \cdots 3 \cdot 2 \cdot 1]}{[(n - r) \cdot (n - r - 1) \cdots 3 \cdot 2 \cdot 1]}$$

Therefore,

$$_nP_r = \frac{n!}{(n - r)!}$$

Notice that $_nP_n$ is the number of permutations of n objects chosen n at a time—that is, the number of ways of rearranging n objects in a row. We have seen that this number is $n!$. If we use the formula for $_nP_r$ to compute $_nP_n$, we obtain

$$_nP_n = \frac{n!}{(n - n)!} = \frac{n!}{0!}$$

Consequently, $n! = n!/0!$. For this equation to be true, *we must define* 0! as 1.

EXAMPLE 8-20 (a) A baseball team has nine players. Find the number of ways the manager can arrange the batting order.

(b) Find the number of ways of choosing three initials from the alphabet if none of the letters can be repeated.

SOLUTION (a) Here order is important, and this is a permutation problem. Because there are nine ways to choose the first batter, eight ways to choose the second batter, and so on, there are $9 \cdot 8 \cdot 7 \cdots 2 \cdot 1 = 9!$, or 362,880, ways of arranging the batting order. Also, using the formula for permutations we have $_9P_9 = 9! = 362,880$.

(b) Because order is important, this is a permutation problem. There are 26 ways of choosing the first letter, 25 ways of choosing the second letter, and 24 ways of choosing the third letter; hence, there are $26 \cdot 25 \cdot 24$, or 15,600, ways of choosing the three letters. Using the formula for permutations we have $_{26}P_3 = 26 \cdot 25 \cdot 24 = 15,600$.

Permutations of Like Objects

In attempting the permutations of the letters in the word *zoo,* we must adapt the rule for computing the number of permutations to accommodate the situation where items are identical. If the two *o*'s were different, such as o_1 and o_2, then we would have 3!, or 6, permutations of the letters *z,* o_1, and o_2, as shown.

$$z\ o_1\ o_2, \quad z\ o_2\ o_1, \quad o_1\ z\ o_2, \quad o_2\ z\ o_1, \quad o_1\ o_2\ z, \quad o_2\ o_1\ z$$

Because the *o*'s are not different, however, exchanging the *o*'s does not produce a different arrangement of letters. Therefore, we must eliminate the duplication. To do this, we divide the number of permutations possible with a *z* and two differentiated *o*'s by the number of ways the two *o*'s can be rearranged, which is 2!. Consequently there are 3!/2!, or 3, ways of arranging the letters in *zoo.* The arrangements are *zoo, ozo,* and *ooz.*

In a similar manner, the letters of the word *bubble* can be arranged in 6!/3!, or 120 ways. We divide by 3! because there are 3 *b*'s and 3! is the number of ways we could arrange 3 objects if they were distinguishable. If more than one letter is repeated, as in the word *statistics,* each repetition must be represented in the denominator. (Why?) For the word *statistics,* there are 3 *s*'s, 3 *t*'s, and 2 *i*'s, so there are 10!/(3! · 3! · 2!), or 50,400, different arrangements of the letters. This discussion is summarized next.

● **PERMUTATIONS OF LIKE OBJECTS**
If a set contains *n* elements, of which r_1 are of one kind, r_2 are of another kind, and so on through r_k, then the number of different arrangements of all *n* elements is equal to

$$\frac{n!}{r_1! \cdot r_2! \cdot r_3! \cdots r_k!}$$

EXAMPLE 8-21   (a) In how many ways can the letters in each of the following words be arranged? (i) GOOD (ii) MATHEMATICS

(b) In a car race there are 6 Chevrolets, 4 Fords, and 2 Dodges. In how many ways can the 12 cars finish if we consider only the makes of the cars?

SOLUTION   (a) (i) $\dfrac{4!}{2!} = 12$

(ii) $\dfrac{11!}{2! \cdot 2! \cdot 2!} = 4,989,600$

(b) We have 12 cars, of which 6 are of one kind, 4 are of another kind, and 2 are of yet another kind. The number of ways the 12 cars can finish is $12!/(6! \cdot 4! \cdot 2!) = 83,160$.

Combinations

combination

Reconsider the club {Al, Betty, Carl, Dan}. Suppose that a two-person committee is selected with no chair. In this case, order is not important. In other words, an Al-Betty choice is the same as a Betty-Al choice. An arrangement of objects in which the order does not make any difference is called a **combination**. A comparison of the results of electing a president and secretary for the club and the results of simply selecting a two-person committee are shown in Figure 8-46. From Figure 8-46, we see that the

FIGURE 8-46

Permutations (Election)	Combinations (Committee)
(A, B)	
(B, A)	$\{A, B\}$
(A, C)	
(C, A)	$\{A, C\}$
(A, D)	
(D, A)	$\{A, D\}$
(B, C)	
(C, B)	$\{B, C\}$
(B, D)	
(D, B)	$\{B, D\}$
(C, D)	
(D, C)	$\{C, D\}$

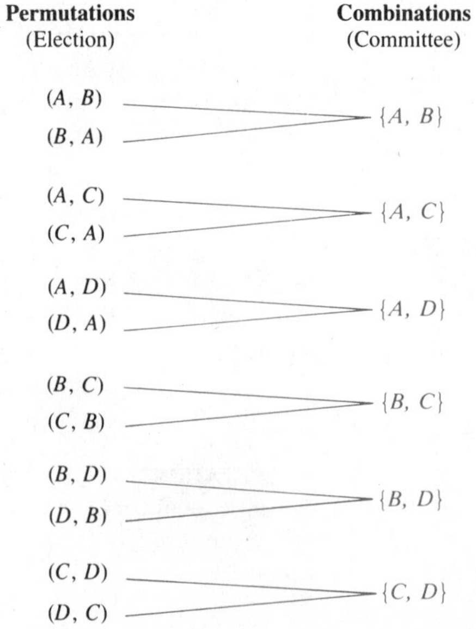

number of permutations divided by 2 is the number of combinations, $\frac{4 \cdot 3}{2}$, or 6. We divide the number of permutations by 2 because each two-person choice can be arranged in 2!, or 2, ways.

In how many ways can a committee of three people be selected from the club {Al, Betty, Carl, Dan}? To solve this problem, we first solve the problem of finding the number of three-person committees, assuming that a president, vice president and secretary are chosen. A partial list of possibilities for both problems is shown in Figure 8-47.

FIGURE 8-47

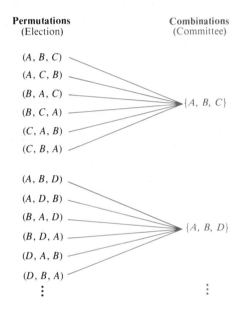

Permutations
(Election)

Combinations
(Committee)

By the Fundamental Counting Principle, the number of permutations is $4 \cdot 3 \cdot 2$, or 24. There are 3!, or 6, times as many permutations as there are combinations. Hence the number of combinations is

$$\frac{4 \cdot 3 \cdot 2}{3!} = 4$$

If we continued the listing begun in Figure 8-47, we would discover that the possible combinations are {A, B, C}, {A, B, D}, {A, C, D}, and {B, C, D}. The number of permutations is divided by 3! since each committee choice can be arranged in 3! ways. In general, we use the following rule to count combinations: *To find the number of combinations possible in a counting problem, first use the Fundamental Counting Principle to find the number of permutations, and then divide by the number of ways in which each choice can be arranged.*

Symbolically, the number of combinations of n objects taken r at a time is denoted by $_nC_r$. From the preceding rule, we develop the following formula.

$$_nC_r = \frac{_nP_r}{_rP_r} = \frac{\dfrac{n!}{(n-r)!}}{r!} = \frac{n!}{r!(n-r)!}$$

It is not necessary to memorize this formula, since we can always find the number of combinations by using the reasoning developed in the committee example. Such reasoning is used on the student page from *Addison-Wesley Mathematics*, 1989, Grade 8.

Counting Selections: Combinations

How many selections of 2 topics from the 4 topics are possible?

First we find the number of permutations of 2 topics from 4 topics.

Permutations = $4 \times 3 = 12$

The **order** of the topics is not important. Choosing A, then B, is the same as choosing B, then A. We need to divide by the number of permutations of 2 topics from 2 topics.

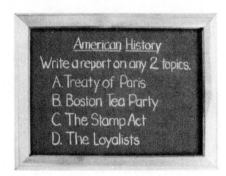

Permutations of
2 topics from 4 topics → $\dfrac{4 \times 3}{2 \times 1} = \dfrac{12}{2} = 6$
Permutations of →
2 topics from 2 topics

There are 6 possible selections.

A selection of a number of objects from a set of objects, *without regard to order*, is called a **combination** of the objects.

List of Permutations

A,B	A,C	A,D	B,C	B,D	C,D
B,A	C,A	D,A	C,B	D,B	D,C

Selections

A and B	A and D	B and D
A and C	B and C	C and D

Other Examples

How many combinations or selections of 3 topics from 5 topics are possible?

Combinations = $\dfrac{5 \times 4 \times 3}{3 \times 2 \times 1} = \dfrac{60}{6} = 10$

	Combinations of
Topics	**3 topics from 5 topics**

Topics		
A	ABC	ADE
B	ABD	BCD
C	ABE	BCE
D	ACD	BDE
E	ACE	CDE

EXAMPLE 8-22   A book-of-the-month club offers 3 free books from a list of 42 books. How many combinations are possible?

SOLUTION   By the Fundamental Counting Principle, there are $42 \cdot 41 \cdot 40$ ways to choose the 3 free books in order. The number of ways the 3 choices of books can be arranged is 3!, or 6. Therefore, the number of combinations possible for 3 books is

$$\frac{42 \cdot 41 \cdot 40}{3!} = 11,480$$

EXAMPLE 8-23   At the beginning of the second quarter of a mathematics class for elementary school teachers, each of the 25 students shook hands with each of the other students exactly once. How many handshakes took place?

SOLUTION   Since the handshake between persons A and B is the same as that between persons B and A, order is not important in this problem. This is a problem of choosing combinations of 25 people two at a time. Thus, there are

$$\frac{25 \cdot 24}{2!} = 300$$

different handshakes.

PROBLEM 7

In the cartoon, suppose that Peppermint Patty took a 6-question true-false test. If she answered each question true or false at random, what is the probability that she answered 50% of the questions correctly?

Understanding the Problem.   A score of 50% indicates that Peppermint Patty answered $\frac{1}{2}$ of the 6 questions, or 3 questions, correctly. She answered the questions true or false at random, so the probability that she answered a given question correctly is $\frac{1}{2}$. We are asked to determine the probability that Patty answered exactly 3 of the questions correctly.

Devising a Plan. We do not know which 3 questions Patty missed. She could have missed any 3 questions out of 6 on the test. Suppose that she answered questions 2, 4, and 5 incorrectly. In this case, she would have answered questions 1, 3, and 6 correctly. We can compute the probability of this set of answers by using Figure 8-48, where C represents a correct answer and I represents an incorrect answer. To find the probability for the set of answers in Figure 8-48, we multiply the probabilities along the branches. Hence, $(\frac{1}{2})^6$ is the probability of answering questions 1–6 in the following way: C I C I I C. However, there are other ways to answer exactly 3 questions correctly: for example, C C C I I I. The probability of answering questions 1–6 in this way is also $(\frac{1}{2})^6$. How many such ways are there to answer the questions? The number of such ways is simply the number of ways of arranging 3 Cs and 3 I's in a row, which is also the number of ways of choosing 3 correct questions out of 6—that is, $_6C_3$. Because all these arrangements give Patty a score of 50%, the desired probability is the sum of the probabilities for each arrangement.

FIGURE 8-48

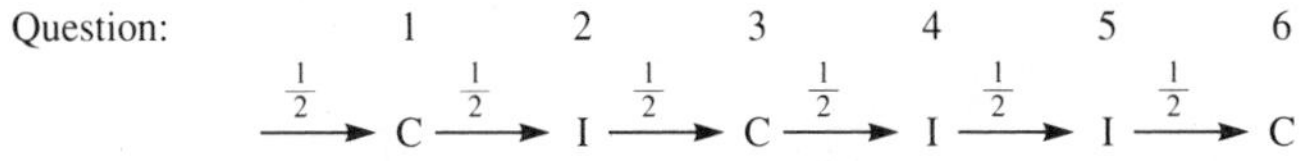

Question:

| 1 | 2 | 3 | 4 | 5 | 6 |

$\xrightarrow{\frac{1}{2}}$ C $\xrightarrow{\frac{1}{2}}$ I $\xrightarrow{\frac{1}{2}}$ C $\xrightarrow{\frac{1}{2}}$ I $\xrightarrow{\frac{1}{2}}$ I $\xrightarrow{\frac{1}{2}}$ C

Carrying Out the Plan. There are $_6C_3$, or 20, ways that the C's and I's can be arranged. Hence, there are 20 sets of answers similar to the one in Figure 8-48 with 3 correct and 3 incorrect answers. The product of the probabilities for each of these sets of answers is $(\frac{1}{2})^6$, so the sum of the probabilities for all 20 sets is $20 \cdot (\frac{1}{2})^6$, or approximately 0.3125. Thus, Peppermint Patty has a probability of 0.3125 of obtaining a score of exactly 50% on the test.

Looking Back. It seems paradoxical to learn that the probability of obtaining a score of 50% on a 6-question true-false test is not close to $\frac{1}{2}$. As an extension of the problem, suppose that a passing score is a score of at least 70%. Now what is the probability that Peppermint Patty will pass? What is the probability of her obtaining a score of at least 50% on the test? If the test is a 6-question multiple-choice test with 5 alternative answers for each question, what is the probability of obtaining a score of at least 50% by random guessing?

PROBLEM SET 8-5

1. The eighth-grade class at a grade school has 16 girls and 14 boys. How many different possible boy-girl dates can be arranged?

2. How many different three-digit numbers can be formed from the digits 1, 2, 3, 4, 5, 6, and 7? Each digit can be used only once.

3. If a coin is tossed five times, in how many different ways can the sequence of heads and tails appear?

4. The telephone prefix for a university is 243. The prefix is followed by four digits. How many telephones are possible before a new prefix is needed?

5. Radio stations in the United States have call letters that begin with either K or W. Some have a total of three letters, while others have four letters. How many sets of three-letter call letters are possible? How many sets of four-letter call letters are possible?

6. Carlin's Pizza House offers 3 kinds of salads, 15 kinds of pizza, and 4 kinds of desserts. How many different three-course meals can be ordered?

7. Decide whether each of the following is true or false.

   (a) $6! = 6 \cdot 5!$ (b) $3! + 3! = 6!$

   (c) $\dfrac{6!}{3!} = 2!$ (d) $\dfrac{6!}{3} = 2!$

   (e) $\dfrac{6!}{5!} = 6$ (f) $\dfrac{6!}{4!2!} = 15$

   (g) $n!(n + 1) = (n + 1)!$

8. In how many ways can the letters in the word SCRAMBLE be rearranged?

9. How many two-person committees can be formed from a group of six people?

10. Find the number of ways to rearrange the letters in the following words.
    (a) OHIO
    (b) ALABAMA
    (c) ILLINOIS
    (d) MISSISSIPPI
    (e) TENNESSEE

11. Assume a class has 30 members.
    (a) In how many ways can a president, vice president, and secretary be selected?
    (b) How many committees of three persons can be chosen?

12. A basketball coach was criticized in the newspaper for not trying out every combination of players. If the team roster has 12 players, how many 5-player combinations are possible?

13. Solve the problem posed by the following cartoon. (AAUGHH! is not an acceptable answer.)

© 1979 United Feature Syndicate, Inc.

14. A 5-volume numbered set of books is placed randomly on a shelf. What is the probability that the books will be numbered in the correct order from left to right?

15. Take 10 points in a plane, no 3 of them on a line. How many straight lines can be drawn if each line is drawn through a pair of points?

16. A bicycle lock has 3 reels, each of which contains the numbers 0–9. To open the lock, you must have the right combination of numbers, such as 355 or 962, where one number is chosen from each reel. How many different combinations are possible for the lock?

17. Sally has 4 red flags, 3 green flags, and 2 white flags. How many 9-flag signals can she run up a flagpole?

18. Find the number of shortest paths from point A to point B along the edges of the cubes in each of the following. (For example, in (a) one shortest path is A-C-D-B.)

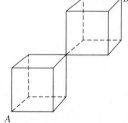

19. In a basketball conference, there are 9 teams. If each team plays each of the other teams twice, what is the total number of games played?

20. At a party, 28 handshakes took place. Each person shook hands exactly once with each of the others present. How many people were at the party?

21. A committee of 3 people is selected at random from a set consisting of 7 Americans, 5 French people, and 3 English people.
    (a) What is the probability that the committee consists of all Americans?
    (b) What is the probability that the committee has no Americans?

22. The triangular array of numbers pictured is called **Pascal's triangle.** Notice that the first and last numbers in each row are 1s. Every other number is the sum of the two numbers immediately above it. The rows are counted starting at 0.

													Row
						1							(0)
					1		1						(1)
				1		2		1					(2)
			1		3		3		1				(3)
		1		4		6		4		1			(4)
	1		5		10		10		5		1		(5)
1		6		15		20		15		6		1	(6)

It can be shown that the entries in Pascal's triangle are the numbers of combinations of n objects taken r at a time, where n is the number of the row and r is the number of the item in the row. (Note that r could be 0.) For example, in the third row we have $_3P_0 = 1$, $_3P_1 = 3$, $_3P_2 = 3$, and $_3P_3 = 1$. Use the triangle to determine the following.
    (a) $_5C_3$ (b) $_5C_5$ (c) $_6C_0$ (d) $_3C_2$

23. The probability of a basketball player's making a free throw successfully at any time in a game is $\frac{2}{3}$. If the player attempts ten free throws in a game, what is the probability that exactly six free throws are made?

★24. In how many ways can 5 couples be seated in a row of 10 chairs if no couple is separated?

★25. From a group of 6 girls and 9 boys, how many 5-member committees consisting of 3 boys and 2 girls can be formed?

★26. Solve the problem for Peppermint Patty.

© 1974 United Feature Syndicate, Inc.

Review Problems

27. A single card is drawn from an ordinary bridge deck. What is the probability of obtaining each of the following?
    (a) A club   (b) A queen and a spade
    (c) Not a queen   (d) Not a heart
    (e) A spade or a heart (f) The six of diamonds
    (g) A queen or a spade (h) Either red or black

28. From a sack containing seven red marbles, eight blue marbles, and four white marbles, marbles are drawn at random for several experiments. What is the probability of each of the following events?
    (a) One marble drawn at random is either red or blue.
    (b) The first draw is red and the second is blue, where one marble is drawn at random, its color is recorded, the marble is replaced, and another marble is drawn.
    (c) The event in (b), where the first marble is not replaced.

B R A I N   T E A S E R

An airplane can complete its flight if at least $\frac{1}{2}$ of its engines are working. If the probability that an engine fails is 0.01 and all engine failures are independent events, what is the probability of a successful flight if the plane has the given number of engines?
(a) 2 engines   (b) 4 engines

SOLUTION TO THE PRELIMINARY PROBLEM

Understanding the Problem. In tennis, a person gets two serves. If the first one is in (good), the point is played, and the server can win or lose the point. If the serve is *out* (not good), then the server gets another serve. If the second serve is in, the point is played. If the second serve is out, the server loses the point. The probability of Jane's getting her hard serve in is 50%, and the probability of her getting her soft serve in is 75%. If her hard serve is in, she wins the point 75% of the time. If her soft serve is in, she wins the point 50% of the time. We are to determine her best strategy for winning the point when serving.

Devising a Plan. The strategy of drawing tree diagrams to represent different possibilities seems appropriate. Once the tree diagrams are drawn, the appropriate probabilities can be computed, the alternatives can be compared, and the question can be answered.

Carrying Out the Plan. As a first possibility, we consider the case of a hard first serve and a soft second serve. On the first serve, the serve can be in (good), or out (no good), with probability 50%, or $\frac{1}{2}$. This can be represented by the first branch of the tree in Figure 8-49. If the first serve is in, the probability of a win is 75%, or $\frac{3}{4}$, and the probability of a loss is 25%, or $\frac{1}{4}$. If the first serve is out, then Jane serves soft with a probability of $\frac{3}{4}$ of the serve's being in and $\frac{1}{4}$ of its being out. If the serve is in, she wins $\frac{1}{2}$ of the time. If the serve is out, she loses. The complete tree diagram for this case is given in Figure 8-49. Therefore, the probability that Jane wins the point with a hard first serve and a soft second serve is $\frac{3}{8} + \frac{3}{16}$, or $\frac{9}{16}$. In a similar

FIGURE 8-49

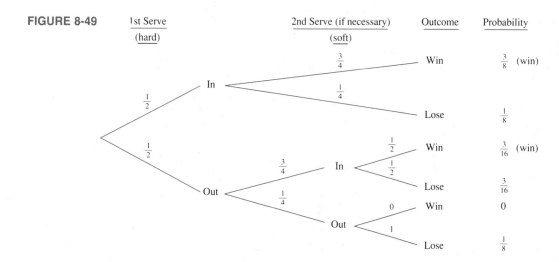

manner, the probabilities for the other three cases can be computed. The results are reported in Table 8-12.

TABLE 8-12

1st Serve	2nd Serve	Probability of Win
Hard	Soft	$\frac{9}{16}$, or 0.5625
Hard	Hard	$\frac{9}{16}$, or 0.5625
Soft	Hard	$\frac{15}{32}$, or 0.46875
Soft	Soft	$\frac{15}{32}$, or 0.46875

We see that Jane should hit her first serve hard; if that serve is not good, it makes no difference whether the second serve is hit hard or soft. On your own, verify the other cases listed.

Looking Back. This problem could also have been solved using geometric probability (area models). The results in this problem may have surprised you if your immediate impression was that the best strategy would be to serve hard the first time and then soft the second. Make up some probabilities that you think would make the choice of hard first serve and soft second serve the best strategy. What would happen if Jane's probability of getting either a hard or a soft serve in were $\frac{1}{2}$ and her probability of winning if the shot is in were $\frac{1}{2}$ for both hard and soft serves? A related problem is to determine a set of probabilities, if possible, that would make each of the four cases the best strategy.

QUESTIONS FROM THE CLASSROOM

1. A student claims that, if a fair coin is tossed and comes up heads five times in a row, then, according to the law of averages, the probability of tails on the next toss is greater than the probability of heads. What is your reply?

2. A student observes the spinner and claims that the color red has the highest probability of appearing since there are two red areas on the spinner. What is your reply?

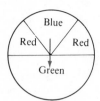

3. A student tosses a coin three times, and tails appears each time. The student concludes that the coin is not fair. What is your response?

4. An experiment consists of tossing a coin twice. The student reasons that there are three possible outcomes: two heads, one head and one tail, or two tails. Thus, $P(HH) = \frac{1}{3}$. What is your reply?

5. A student says that there is really no need to learn the formulas for combinations and permutations. How do you reply?

6. Conditional probabilities can be determined by using tree diagrams. Why is the Multiplication Rule for Probabilities necessary?

7. In response to the question "If a fair die is rolled twice, what is the probability of rolling a pair of 5s?" a student replies, "One third, because $\frac{1}{6} + \frac{1}{6} = \frac{1}{3}$." How do you respond?

8. A student wonders why probabilities cannot be negative. What is your response?

9. A student claims that "if the probability of an event is $\frac{3}{5}$, then there are 3 ways the event can occur and only 5 elements in the sample space." How do you respond?

CHAPTER OUTLINE

I. Probability
  A. Probabilities can be determined *experimentally* (*empirically*) or *theoretically*.
  B. A **sample space** is the set of all possible outcomes of an **experiment.**
  C. Sample spaces can be modeled using **tree diagrams.**
  D. An **event** is a subset of a sample space.
  E. Outcomes are **equally likely** if each outcome is as likely to occur as another.
  F. If all outcomes of an experiment are *equally likely,* the **probability of an event A** from sample space S is given by

$$P(A) = \frac{n(A)}{n(S)}$$

  G. An **impossible event** is an event with a probability of zero. An impossible event can never occur.
  H. A **certain event** is an event with a probability of one. A certain event is sure to happen.
  I. Two events are **mutually exclusive** if and only if exactly one of the events can occur at any given time—that is, if and only if the events are disjoint.
  J. The probability of the **complement of an event** is given by $P(\overline{A}) = 1 - P(A)$, where A is the event and $\overline{A}$ is its complement.
  K. For all **multistage experiments,** the probability of the outcome along any path of a tree diagram is equal to the product of all the probabilities along the path.

*II. Conditional probability, independent events, and simulations
  A. If A and B are events in a sample space and $P(B) \neq 0$, the **conditional probability of A, given B,** denoted by $P(A|B)$, is defined as $P(A|B) = P(A \cap B)/P(B)$.
  B. **Multiplication Rule for Probabilities** $P(A \cap B) = P(B) \cdot P(A|B)$
  C. Two events A and B are **independent** if $P(A|B) = P(A)$.
  D. **Simulations** can play an important part in probability. Fair coins, dice, spinners, and random-digit tables are useful in performing simulations.

*III. Odds and expected value
  A. The **odds in favor** of an event A are given by

$$\frac{P(A)}{1 - P(A)}$$

  B. The **odds against** an event A are give by

$$\frac{1 - P(A)}{P(A)}$$

  C. If, in an experiment, the possible outcomes are numbers $a_1, a_2, \ldots, a_n$, occurring with probabilities $p_1, p_2, \ldots, p_n$, respectively, then the **expected value** E is defined as

$$E = a_1 \cdot p_1 + a_2 \cdot p_2 + a_3 \cdot p_3 + \cdots + a_n \cdot p_n$$

IV. Counting principles
  A. **Fundamental Counting Principle** If an event M can occur in m ways and, after it has occurred, event N can occur in n ways, then event M followed by event N can occur in $m \cdot n$ ways.
  B. **Permutations** are arrangements in which order is important.

$$_nP_r = \frac{n!}{(n-r)!}$$

  C. The expression **$n!$,** called **n factorial,** represents the product of all the natural numbers less than or equal to n. $0!$ is defined as 1.
  D. **Permutations of like objects** If a set contains n elements, of which r_1 are of one kind, r_2 are of another kind, and so on through r_k, then the number of different arrangements of all n elements is equal to

$$\frac{n!}{r_1! \cdot r_2! \cdot r_3! \cdots r_k!}$$

  E. **Combinations** are arrangements in which order is *not* important. To find the number of combinations possible, first use the Fundamental Counting Principle to find the number of permutations, and then divide by the number of ways in which each choice can be arranged.

$$_nC_r = \frac{_nP_r}{_rP_r}$$

CHAPTER TEST

1. Suppose that the names of the days of the week are placed in a box and one name is drawn at random.
   (a) List the sample space for this experiment.
   (b) List the event consisting of outcomes that the day drawn starts with the letter T.
   (c) What is the probability of drawing a day that starts with T?

2. Complete each of the following.
   (a) If A is an impossible event, then $P(A) = $ _____.
   (b) If A is a certain event, then $P(A) = $ _____.
   (c) If A is any event, then _____ $\leq P(A) \leq$ _____.
   (d) If A is any event, then $P(\overline{A}) = $ _____.

3. A box contains three red balls, five black balls, and four white balls. Suppose that one ball is drawn at random. Find the probability of each of the following events.
   (a) A black ball is drawn.
   (b) A black or a white ball is drawn.
   (c) Neither a red nor a white ball is drawn.
   (d) A red ball is not drawn.
   (e) A black ball and a white ball are drawn.
   (f) A black or white or red ball is drawn.

4. One card is selected at random from an ordinary set of 52 cards. Find the probability of each of the following events.
   (a) A club is drawn.
   (b) A spade and a 5 are drawn.
   (c) A heart or a face card is drawn.
   (d) A jack is not drawn.

5. A box contains five black balls and four white balls. If three balls are drawn one by one, find the probability that they are all white if the draws are made as follows.
   (a) With replacement
   (b) Without replacement

6. Suppose that a three-stage rocket is launched into orbit. The probability for failure at stage one is $\frac{1}{10}$, at stage two is $\frac{1}{5}$, and at stage three is $\frac{1}{3}$. What is the probability of a successful flight?

7. Consider the two boxes in the figure. If a letter is drawn from box 1 and placed into box 2, and then a letter is drawn from box 2, what is the probability that the letter is an L?

8. Use the following boxes for a two-stage experiment. First select a box at random, and then select a letter at random from the box. What is the probability of drawing an A?

9. Consider the boxes shown. Draw a ball from box 1, and put it into box 2. Then draw a ball from box 2, and put it into box 3. Finally, draw a ball from box 3. Construct a tree diagram for this experiment, and calculate the probability that the last ball chosen is black.

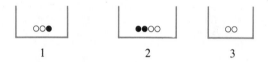

*10. What are the odds in favor of drawing a jack when one card is drawn from an ordinary deck of playing cards?

*11. A die is rolled once. What are the odds against rolling a prime number?

*12. If the odds in favor of a certain event are 3 to 5, what is the probability that the event will occur?

*13. A game consists of rolling two dice. Rolling double 1s pays $7.20. Rolling double 6s pays $3.60. Any other roll pays nothing. What is the expected value for this game?

*14. A total of 3000 tickets have been sold for a drawing. If one ticket is drawn for a single prize of $1000, what is a fair price for a ticket?

15. How many four-digit numbers can be formed if the first digit cannot be zero and the last digit must be two?

16. A club consists of ten members. In how many different ways can a group of three people be selected to go on a European trip?

17. In how many ways can the names of four candidates be listed on a ballot for an election?

18. Compute 100!/98!. (Look for shortcuts!)

19. Find the number of different ways that four flags can be displayed on a flagpole, one above the other, if ten different flags are available.

20. Five women live together in an apartment. Two of the women have blue eyes. If two of the women are chosen at random, what is the probability that they both have blue eyes?

21. Five horses—Deadbeat, Applefarm, Bandy, Cash, and Egglegs—run in a race.
    (a) In how many ways can the first-, second-, and third-place horses be determined?
    (b) Find the probability that Deadbeat finished first and Bandy finished second in the race.
    (c) Find the probability that the first-, second-, and third-place horses are Deadbeat, Egglegs, and Cash, in that order.

22. Al and Ruby each roll an ordinary die once. What is the probability that the number of Ruby's roll is greater than the number of Al's roll?

23. Amy has a quiz on which she is to answer any three of the five questions. If she is equally well versed on all questions and chooses three questions at random, what is the probability that question 1 is not chosen?

24. On a certain street there are three traffic lights. At any given time, the probability that a light is green is 0.3. What is the probability that a person will hit all three lights when they are green?

25. Simplify each of the following.
    (a) $(n - 1)! \cdot n$ (b) $\dfrac{n!}{(n - 1)!}$

*26. A three-stage rocket has the following probabilities for failure. The probability for failure at stage one is $\frac{1}{6}$; at stage two it is $\frac{1}{8}$; and at stage three it is $\frac{1}{10}$. What is the probability of a successful flight, given that the first stage was successful?

*27. Two standard dice are rolled. What is the probability that a sum of 7 is rolled, given that at least one die shows an even number?

*28. How could each of the following be simulated by using a random-digit table?
    (a) Tossing a fair die
    (b) Picking 3 months at random from the 12 months of the year

(c) Spinning the spinner shown

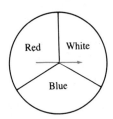

29. If a dart is thrown at the following dart board and we assume that the dart lands at random on the board, what are the probabilities of its landing in each of the following areas?
    (a) Area A
    (b) Area B
    (c) Area C

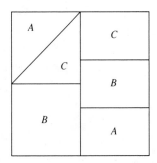

30. The points M, N, O, P, and Q represent exits on a highway. An accident occurs at random between points M and Q. What is the probability that it has occurred between N and O?

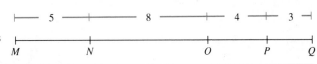

C H A P T E R   9

Statistics: An Introduction

PRELIMINARY PROBLEM

The mean age of the first seven people to arrive at Grandpa Elmer's birthday party was 21. When Jeff, who is 29, arrived at the party, the mean age increased to 22. Mary, who is also 29, arrived next. Did the mean age increase to 23 with Mary's arrival? The 10th and last person to arrive was Grandpa Elmer, and the mean age increased to 30 years. How old is Grandpa Elmer on this birthday?

Introduction

For a long time, the word *statistics* referred to numerical information about state or political territories. The word itself comes from the Latin *statisticus,* meaning "of the state." Statistics as we know it today took several centuries and many great minds to develop. John Graunt was one of the first people to record his work in the area of statistics.

Descriptive statistics is the science of organizing and summarizing numerical data. Newspapers, magazines, radio, and television all use descriptive statistics to inform and persuade us about certain courses of action. Governments and organizations use statistics to make decisions that directly affect our lives. Statistics are both used and abused. Sometimes the abuse is of little consequence and entirely unintentional. This may or may not be true in Sally's case, below. Statistics plays an important role in the *Standards*

at both the K–4 level and the 5–8 level. Following is an excerpt from the middle-school *Standards.*

In this age of information and technology, an ever-increasing need exists to understand how information is processed and translated into usable knowledge. Because of society's expanding use of data for prediction and decision making, it is important that students develop an understanding of the concepts and processes used in analyzing data. A knowledge of statistics is necessary if students are to become intelligent consumers who can make critical and informed decisions.

In grades K–4, students begin to explore basic ideas of statistics by gathering data appropriate to their grade level, organizing them in charts or graphs, and reading information from displays of data. These concepts should be expanded in the middle grades. Students in grades 5–8 have a keen interest in trends in music, movies, fashion, and sports. An investigation of how such trends are developed and communicated is an excellent motivator for the study of statistics. Students need to be actively involved in each of the steps that comprise statistics, from gathering information to communicating results.

In this chapter, we discuss various statistical graphs, measures of central tendency and variation, normal distributions, z-scores, and, finally, possible abuses of statistics.

H I S T O R I C A L   N O T E

John Graunt (1620–1674) was an English haberdasher who studied birth and death records and discovered that more boys were born than girls. He also found that, because men were more subject to death from occupational accidents, diseases, and war, the numbers of men and women of marriageable age were about equal.

In 1662, Graunt's book *Natural and Political Observations upon the Bills of Mortality* was published. His work was the first to analyze statistics and to draw conclusions on the basis of such analysis. Graunt's work led to the development of actuarial science, which is used by life insurance companies.

Section 9-1   Statistical Graphs

Visual illustrations are an important part of statistics. Such illustrations take many forms—line plots, stem-and-leaf plots, frequency tables, histograms, bar graphs, frequency polygons or line graphs, pictographs, and circle graphs or pie charts.

Line Plots

Suppose that the 30 students in Mr. Abel's first-period algebra class received the following test scores.

82 97 70 72 83 75 76 84 76 88 80 81 81 52 82
82 73 98 83 72 84 84 76 85 86 78 97 97 82 77

data
line plot

The grades in Mr. Abel's class might be referred to as *raw data*. The term **data** refers to the elements of the set under consideration. The data in this case might be more meaningful if they were summarized in a **line plot.** A line plot for Mr. Abel's class consists of a horizontal number line, on which each score is denoted by an x above the corresponding value on the number line, as shown in Figure 9-1. The number of x's above each score indicates how many times each score occurred.

FIGURE 9-1   SCORES ON MR. ABEL'S ALGEBRA TEST

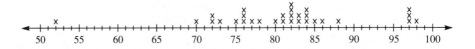

Line plots provide a quick, easy way to organize data. Line plots are typically used when the number of values is 50 or smaller. When the number of values is greater than 50, line plots become hard to read. Line plots are a useful first display of data when we have only one group and one variable.

Figure 9-1 yields information about Mr. Abel's exam. For example, we see that 3 students scored 76 and that 4 students scored greater than 90. We also see that the low score was 52, the high score was 98, and the most frequent score was 82. Several features of the data become more obvious when line plots are used. For example, outliers, clusters, and gaps are

outliers apparent. **Outliers** are data points whose values are significantly larger or smaller than other values, such as the score of 52 in Figure 9-1. Outliers will

clusters be discussed in greater detail in the next section. **Clusters** are isolated groups

gaps of points, such as the one located at scores of 97 and 98. **Gaps** are large spaces between points, such as the one between 88 and 97.

Stem-and-Leaf Plots

Mr. Abel's class's scores could be shown graphically in a different way.

stem-and-leaf plot Figure 9-2 is an example of a **stem-and-leaf plot.**

FIGURE 9-2

SCORES ON MR. ABEL'S ALGEBRA TEST

```
5 | 2
6 |
7 | 0223566678
8 | 011222233444568      9 | 7 represents 97
9 | 7778
```

stems   The numbers on the left side of the vertical line are the **stems,** and the

leaves numbers on the right side are the **leaves.** Stem-and-leaf plots were introduced by John Tukey and are discussed in his 1977 book *Exploratory Data Analysis.* A stem-and-leaf plot is a combination of a table and a graph. To understand how a stem-and-leaf plot is constructed, first look at Table 9-1, which lists the names of 35 U.S. presidents and their ages at death.

TABLE 9-1

President	Age at Death	President	Age at Death	President	Age at Death
George Washington	67	Millard Fillmore	74	Theodore Roosevelt	60
John Adams	90	Franklin Pierce	64	William Taft	72
Thomas Jefferson	83	James Buchanan	77	Woodrow Wilson	67
James Madison	85	Abraham Lincoln	56	Warren Harding	57
James Monroe	73	Andrew Johnson	66	Calvin Coolidge	60
John Q. Adams	80	Ulysses Grant	63	Herbert Hoover	90
Andrew Jackson	78	Rutherford Hayes	70	Franklin Roosevelt	63
Martin Van Buren	79	James Garfield	49	Harry Truman	88
William H. Harrison	68	Chester Arthur	57	Dwight Eisenhower	78
John Tyler	71	Grover Cleveland	71	John Kennedy	46
James K. Polk	53	Benjamin Harrison	67	Lyndon Johnson	64
Zachary Taylor	65	William McKinley	58		

We see that the presidents died in their 40s, 50s, 60s, 70s, 80s, or 90s. Thus, in this set of data, we are to concentrate on numbers from 40 to 99 or, explicitly, from 46 to 90. For our display of the data, we choose the tens digits of the numbers in the raw data as the stems. The leaves are the units digits of the numbers in the raw data. The plot itself is formed by placing the stem digits in a column from least to greatest on the left side of a vertical line, as shown in Figure 9-3(a). We write only the tens digits as stems, because the leaves (which represent the units digits of the ages) are to be given on the right side of the vertical line, in whichever row contains their stem, as shown in Figure 9-3(b).

FIGURE 9-3

Stem	Leaf
4	
5	
6	
7	
8	
9	

(a)

AGES OF PRESIDENTS AT DEATH

4	96
5	36787
6	785463707034
7	38914701128
8	3508
9	00

4 | 9 represents 49
years old

(b)

Each leaf represents one observation from the data. For example, in Figure 9-3(b), the top row has 4 as a stem and 9 and 6 as leaves. These numbers represent the ages 49 and 46, the ages at death of James Garfield and John Kennedy, respectively. Normally, the graph is titled and is accompanied by a legend telling how to interpret the symbols used in it.

In some sense, the data in Figure 9-3(b) are still not orderly, because the numbers within each leaf are not in order from least to greatest on a given row. To make an **ordered stem-and-leaf plot,** we arrange the leaves on their given rows from least to greatest, starting at the left, as in Figure 9-4.

ordered stem-and-leaf plot

FIGURE 9-4

AGES OF PRESIDENTS AT DEATH

4	69
5	36778
6	003344567778
7	01112347889
8	0358
9	00

4 | 9 represents 49
years old

There is no unique way to construct stem-and-leaf plots. Smaller numbers are usually placed at the top so that, when the plot is turned counterclockwise 90°, it resembles a histogram (discussed later in this section). Important advantages of stem-and-leaf plots are that they can be created by hand rather easily and that they do not become as unmanageable as line plots when the number of values becomes large. Moreover, no original values are lost in a stem-and-leaf plot. For example, we can still tell that the youngest age at death was 46 and that exactly two presidents died when they were 90. A disadvantage of stem-and-leaf plots is that we do lose some information; for example, we know from the plot that some president died at age 88, but we do not know which one.

Following is a summary of how to construct a stem-and-leaf plot.

1. Find the high and low values of the data.
2. Decide on the stems.
3. List the stems in a column from least to greatest.
4. Use each piece of data to create leaves to the right of the stems on the appropriate rows.
5. If the plot is to be ordered, list the leaves in order from least to greatest.
6. Add a legend identifying the values represented by the stems and leaves. For example, 5|6 represents 56.
7. Add a title explaining what the graph is about.

Example 9-1 involves constructing a stem-and-leaf plot in which the stems are not just the tens digits of the raw data.

EXAMPLE 9-1 Table 9-2 shows the Nielsen average-audience estimates of percents of households watching various television programs in November, 1985. Construct a stem-and-leaf plot depicting the data in Table 9-2.

TABLE 9-2

TV Program	Percent of Households Watching
Bill Cosby Show	32.3
Family Ties	29.3
Murder She Wrote	26.0
60 Minutes	25.7
Dynasty	23.6
Cheers	22.9
Dallas	22.9
Miami Vice	22.1
Golden Girls	21.4
Who's the Boss	20.7
Night Court	20.6
NBC Monday Night Movie	20.2
CBS NFL Football	20.0
Highway to Heaven	20.0
Facts of Life	19.9

Source: *The World Almanac and Book of Facts*, 1987. New York: Newspaper Enterprise Association, 1986.

SOLUTION To construct a stem-and-leaf plot for the data, we first note that the lowest estimate is 19.9 and the highest is 32.3. We use the whole number parts of the rating as stems and the tenths as the leaves. To do this, we start by listing the stems from 19 to 32 in intervals of 1. The ordered plot is shown in Figure 9-5.

FIGURE 9-5

NIELSEN RATINGS
NETWORK PROGRAMS (NOVEMBER, 1985)

```
19 | 9
20 | 00267
21 | 4
22 | 199
23 | 6
24 |
25 | 7
26 | 0
27 |                    29 | 3 represents 29.3%
28 |
29 | 3
30 |
31 |
32 | 3
```

If there are too many leaves per stem or if only two or three stems are required, the data can be spread out through the use of *two-line stems*. The two-line-stem approach is illustrated in Figure 9-6 for the data from Table 9-1. The first line for each stem has leaves varying from 0 to 4. The second line for each stem, indicated by an asterisk, has leaves varying from 5 to 9. For example, the fourth stem is an asterisk located beneath a 5 and above a 6. The leaves in that row stand for 56, 57, 57, and 58. Three-, four-, or five-line stems are sometimes used to spread out data even more.

FIGURE 9-6

AGES OF PRESIDENTS AT DEATH

```
4 |
* | 69
5 | 3                   4 | 6 represents 46
* | 6778                    years old
6 | 003344
* | 567778
7 | 0111234
* | 7889
8 | 03
* | 58
9 | 00
```

If two sets of data are to be compared, a *back-to-back stem-and-leaf plot* can be used. Two plots are made—one with leaves to the right, and one with leaves to the left. For example, if Mr. Abel gave the same geometry test to his two geometry classes, he might prepare a back-to-back stem-and-leaf plot, as shown in Figure 9-7. Which class do you think did better on the test? Why?

FIGURE 9-7

MR. ABEL'S GEOMETRY TEST SCORES

2nd - Period Class   5th - Period Class

0 | 5 | represents
       a score of 50

20	5	2
531	6	24
99987542	7	1257
875420	8	4456999
1	9	2457
	10	0

| 5 | 2 represents
      a score of 52

• R E M A R K

When back-to-back stem-and-leaf plots are used, both sets of data should have about the same number of data points.

EXAMPLE 9-2 Group the presidents in Table 9-1 into two groups, the first consisting of George Washington to Ulysses Grant, and the second consisting of Rutherford Hayes to Lyndon Johnson.

(a) Create back-to-back stem-and-leaf plots of the two groups and see if there appears to be a difference in ages at death between the two groups.
(b) Which group of presidents seems to have lived longer?

SOLUTION (a) Because the ages at death vary from 46 to 90, the stems vary from 4 to 9. The first 18 presidents are listed on the left, and the remaining 17 presidents are listed on the right in Figure 9-8.

FIGURE 9-8

AGES OF PRESIDENTS AT DEATH

Early Presidents   Later Presidents

3 | 8 | represents
       83 years old

	4	96
63	5	787
364587	6	707034
741983	7	0128
053	8	8
0	9	0

| 6 | 7 represents
      67 years old

(b) The early presidents seem, on average, to have lived longer, because the ages at the high end, especially in the 70s and 80s, come more often from the early presidents. The ages at the lower end come more often from the later presidents. For the stems in the 50s and 60s, the numbers of leaves are about equal.

The stem-and-leaf plot is easier to manage than a line plot when the number of pieces of data is great. When there are 50 or fewer values, the choice of a line plot or a stem-and-leaf plot is a matter of personal preference. When the number of pieces of data is between 50 and 250, the stem-and-leaf plot is more appropriate than a line plot. If there are 100 or more values, two-, three-, or four-line stems are appropriate.

A stem-and-leaf plot shows how wide a range of values the data cover, where the values are concentrated, the symmetry (if any) of the data, where gaps in the data are, and whether any data points are decidedly different from the rest of the data.

Frequency Tables

frequency table

A slightly different way to display data is to use a frequency table. A **frequency table** shows how many times a certain piece of data occurs. For example, suppose that Dan offers the following deal. He rolls a die. If any number other than 6 appears, he pays $5. If a 6 appears, you pay him $5. With a fair die, the probability of Dan's winning is $\frac{1}{6}$. Thus, Dan will not win unless the die is loaded or unless 6 appears considerably more often than could normally be expected. The data in Table 9-3 show the results of 60 rolls with Dan's die.

TABLE 9-3

Results of Dan's Die Tosses									
1	6	6	2	6	3	6	6	4	6
6	2	6	6	4	5	6	6	1	6
1	6	6	5	6	6	4	6	5	6
6	5	6	2	4	2	5	6	3	4
3	6	1	6	3	6	6	1	6	6
6	4	6	3	6	3	6	4	6	5

The results of Dan's die tosses may be summarized as shown in the frequency table in Table 9-4.

According to the frequency table, 6 appears many more times than could be expected from a fair die. (If the die were fair, the number of 6s should be closer to $\frac{1}{6} \cdot 60$, or 10.)

TABLE 9-4

Number	Tally	Frequency
1	𝍷𝍷𝍷	5
2	||||	4
3	𝍷𝍷𝍷 |	6
4	𝍷𝍷𝍷 ||	7
5	𝍷𝍷𝍷 |	6
6	𝍷𝍷𝍷 𝍷𝍷𝍷 𝍷𝍷𝍷 𝍷𝍷𝍷 𝍷𝍷𝍷 𝍷𝍷𝍷 ||	32
	Total	60

Histograms and Bar Graphs

histogram

The data from Table 9-4 may be pictured graphically. Figure 9-9 shows a **histogram** that gives a good picture of the results obtained from throwing Dan's die.

FIGURE 9-9

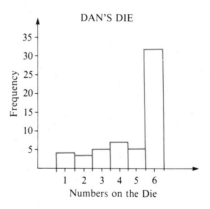

A histogram is made up of adjoining vertical rectangles, or bars. In this case the numbers on the die are shown on the horizontal axis. The numbers along the vertical axis give the scale for the frequency. The frequencies of the numbers on the die are shown by the bars, which are all the same width. The higher the bar, the greater the frequency. The scale on the vertical axis must also be of uniform interval size. In addition, all histograms should have the axes labeled and should include a title identifying the graph's content. Histograms can easily be made from single-sided stem-and-leaf plots. For example, if we take the stem-and-leaf plot in Figure 9-3(b) and enclose each row (set of leaves) in a bar, as in Figure 9-10, we have what looks like a histogram.

FIGURE 9-10

AGES OF PRESIDENTS AT DEATH

4 | 9 represents 49
years old

● **R E M A R K**

It is common to use vertical bars and to have the graph appear as in Figure 9-9 rather than as in Figure 9-10. This appearance can be obtained from a stem-and-leaf plot by rotating the plot 90° counterclockwise.

bar graph   A histogram is a particular kind of **bar graph.** A typical bar graph showing the heights in centimeters of five students is given in Figure 9-11.

FIGURE 9-11

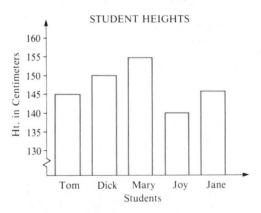

The break in the vertical axis, denoted by a squiggle, indicates that part of the scale has been omitted. Therefore, the scale is not accurate from 0 to 130. The height of each bar represents the height in centimeters of each student named on the horizontal axis. Each space between bars is usually one half the width of the bars.

Frequency Polygons (Line Graphs)

Another graphic form used in presenting the data from a frequency table is *frequency polygon / line graph* a **frequency polygon,** or **line graph.** A frequency polygon can be plotted from a frequency table, or it can be constructed from a histogram by using line segments to connect the midpoints of the tops of each of the rectangular bars. Figure 9-12(a) shows the frequency polygon (line graph) for the data from Table 9-4. Figure 9-12(b) shows how to obtain the same frequency polygon from the histogram in Figure 9-9.

FIGURE 9-12

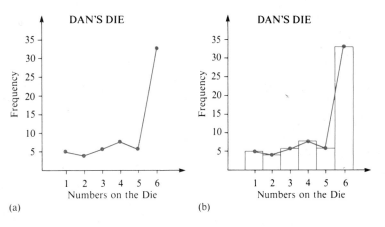

(a)   (b)

Pictographs

pictograph   A **pictograph** is a graph in which pictures or symbols are used. A pictograph uses one or more rows of identical symbols, has a key explaining the meaning of the symbol, and is frequently used in comparisons of output. Examples are shown in Figure 9-13. A major disadvantage of pictographs is evident in Figure 9-13(a). The month of September contains a smaller bundle of newspapers than the others. It is impossible to tell the weight of that bundle with any accuracy.

FIGURE 9-13

RECYCLED NEWSPAPERS

Each ⊞ represents 10 kg.

Months	
July	⊞ ⊞ ⊞ ⊞
Aug.	⊞ ⊞ ⊞ ⊞ ⊞
Sept.	⊞ ⊞ ⊞ ⊞ ⊞ ⊞ ⊞
Oct.	⊞ ⊞ ⊞ ⊞ ⊞ ⊞
Nov.	⊞ ⊞ ⊞ ⊞ ⊞ ⊞
Dec.	⊞ ⊞ ⊞

Weights of Newspapers

(a)

HILLVIEW FIFTH-GRADE
STUDENT DISTRIBUTION

Each 人 represents 5 students

Teacher	
Ames	人 人 人 人
Ball	人 人 人 人
Cox	人 人 人
Day	人 人 人 人 人
Eves	人 人 人
Fagin	人 人

Students per class

(b)

Other examples of graphs in student texts are shown on the student page from *Heath Mathematics*, 1987, Grade 7.

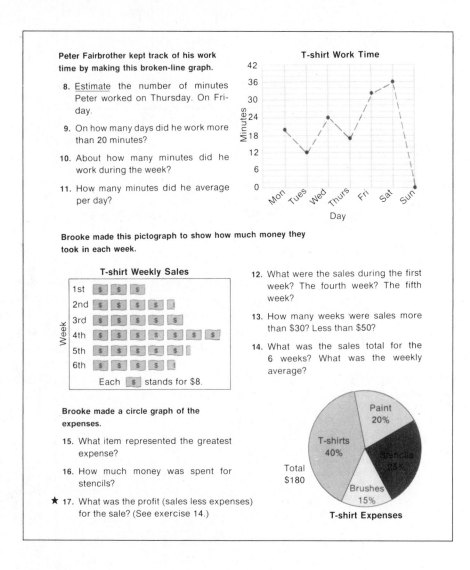

Peter Fairbrother kept track of his work time by making this broken-line graph.

8. <u>Estimate</u> the number of minutes Peter worked on Thursday. On Friday.

9. On how many days did he work more than 20 minutes?

10. About how many minutes did he work during the week?

11. How many minutes did he average per day?

T-shirt Work Time

Brooke made this pictograph to show how much money they took in each week.

T-shirt Weekly Sales

Each $ stands for $8.

12. What were the sales during the first week? The fourth week? The fifth week?

13. How many weeks were sales more than $30? Less than $50?

14. What was the sales total for the 6 weeks? What was the weekly average?

Brooke made a circle graph of the expenses.

15. What item represented the greatest expense?

16. How much money was spent for stencils?

★ 17. What was the profit (sales less expenses) for the sale? (See exercise 14.)

Paint 20%
T-shirts 40%
Stencils 25%
Brushes 15%
Total $180

T-shirt Expenses

Grouped Data

The greater the amount of data, the more difficult it becomes to construct a frequency table for individual items. In such cases, the data may be grouped. For example, consider the scores in Table 9-5. A stem-and-leaf plot for the data in Table 9-5 is shown in Figure 9-14.

TABLE 9-5

50 Student Scores									
52	56	25	56	68	73	66	64	56	100
20	39	9	50	98	54	54	40	50	96
36	44	18	97	109	65	21	60	44	54
92	49	37	94	72	88	89	35	59	34
48	32	15	53	84	72	88	16	52	60

FIGURE 9-14

STUDENT SCORES

```
 0 | 9
 1 | 856
 2 | 051
 3 | 692754
 4 | 84904
 5 | 266034460924
 6 | 856400
 7 | 232
 8 | 4898
 9 | 27486
10 | 09
```

10 | 9 represents a
score of 109

The construction of the stem-and-leaf plot leads in a natural way to a *classes* grouping of scores in intervals. The intervals are called **classes;** for the data in Figure 9-14, the following classes are used: 0–9, 10–19, 20–29, 30–39, 40–49, 50–59, 60–69, 70–79, 80–89, 90–99, 100–109. Each class has an interval size of 10; that is, ten different scores can fall within the interval 0 through 9. (Students often incorrectly report the interval size as 9 because $9 - 0 = 9$.) The **grouped frequency table** for the data in Table 9-5 with *grouped frequency table* intervals of length 10 is given in Table 9-6. Figure 9-14 contains more information than does Table 9-6, because the raw scores themselves are not available in Table 9-6. Although Table 9-6 shows that 12 scores fall in the

TABLE 9-6

Classes	Tally	Frequency
0–9	I	1
10–19	III	3
20–29	III	3
30–39	卌 I	6
40–49	卌	5
50–59	卌 卌 II	12
60–69	卌 I	6
70–79	III	3
80–89	IIII	4
90–99	卌	5
100–109	II	2

interval 50–59, it does not show the particular scores in the interval. The greater the size of the interval, the greater the amount of information lost (possibly beyond the usable point). The choice of interval size may vary. Classes should be chosen to accommodate *all* the data, and each item should fit into only one class; that is, the classes should not overlap.

A bar graph or histogram can be used to display the data from a grouped frequency table. A bar graph of the data in Table 9-6 is shown in Figure 9-15(a). To construct a histogram for the data in Table 9-6, we find the midpoint of each class in order to mark the horizontal axis, as follows: $(0 + 9)/2 = 4.5$, $(10 + 19)/2 = 14.5$, and so on. The completed histogram is given in Figure 9-15(b).

FIGURE 9-15

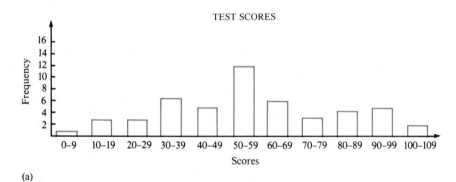

(a)

(b)

Circle Graphs (Pie Charts)

circle graph
pie chart

Another type of graph used to represent data is the circle graph. A **circle graph,** or **pie chart,** consists of a circular region partitioned into disjoint sections, with each section representing a part or percentage of the whole. A circle graph shows how parts are related to the whole. This type of picture usually is used when money is involved and various distributions of dollars are to be displayed.

Suppose that two college roommates, Kurt and Mark, kept records of their expenses and, at the end of the quarter, made Table 9-7 based on these records. Figure 9-16 shows a circle graph that depicts the same percentages listed in Table 9-7. A circle has a total of 360 degrees, written 360°. Thus, 360° represents the total expenses for the quarter, or 100% of the expenses. Since food accounts for 30% of the total expenses, 30% of 360°—that is, 0.30(360°), or 108°—is devoted to food expenses. In the same way, 0.25(360°), or 90°, is devoted to rent. The remaining sections are computed in a similar manner. A protractor is used to construct circle graphs, and a calculator is useful in determining the percentages. The circle graph is usually marked with section identifications and with the percent of the circle represented by each section.

TABLE 9-7

Item	Percent of Total
Food	30
Rent	25
Clothing	10
Books	10
Entertainment	15
Other	10

FIGURE 9-16

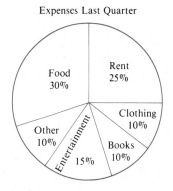

Expenses Last Quarter

EXAMPLE 9-3 Construct a circle graph for the following data, which were obtained by tossing Dan's loaded die 60 times.

Number	Frequency
1	5
2	4
3	6
4	7
5	6
6	32
	60

SOLUTION   Two computational steps are necessary in order to prepare the data for a circle graph. We need to determine the number of degrees and the percent of the circle in each section. Table 9-8 shows this information. A circle graph depicting the information is given in Figure 9-17.

TABLE 9-8

Item	Degrees	Percent
1	$\frac{5}{60} \cdot 360°$, or 30°	$\frac{5}{60} \doteq 8.3\%$
2	$\frac{4}{60} \cdot 360°$, or 24°	$\frac{4}{60} \doteq 6.7\%$
3	$\frac{6}{60} \cdot 360°$, or 36°	$\frac{6}{60} = 10\%$
4	$\frac{7}{60} \cdot 360°$, or 42°	$\frac{7}{60} \doteq 11.7\%$
5	$\frac{6}{60} \cdot 360°$, or 36°	$\frac{6}{60} = 10\%$
6	$\frac{32}{60} \cdot 360°$, or 192ᶜ	$\frac{32}{60} \doteq 53.3\%$

FIGURE 9-17

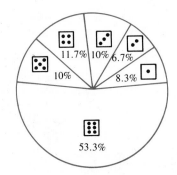

PROBLEM SET 9-1

1. The following stem-and-leaf plot gives the weights in pounds of all 15 students in the Algebra 1 class at East Junior High.

   (a) Write the weights of the 15 students.
   (b) What is the weight of the lightest student in the class?
   (c) What is the weight of the heaviest student in the class?

Weights of Students in East Junior High
Algebra 1 Class

7	24
8	112578
9	2478
10	3
11	
12	35

10 | 3 represents
103 pounds

2. Draw a histogram based on the stem-and-leaf plot given in Problem 1.
3. Toss a coin 30 times.
   (a) Construct a line plot for these data.
   (b) Draw a histogram for your data.
4. Following are the names and records of the home run leaders in the American and National Leagues from 1976 to 1988. Construct an ordered back-to-back stem-and-leaf plot for the data. Are any patterns of difference evident in comparisons of the two groups of data?

Year	National League	HR	American League	HR
1976	Mike Schmidt	38	Graig Nettles	32
1977	George Foster	52	Jim Rice	39
1978	George Foster	40	Jim Rice	46
1979	Dave Kingman	48	Gorman Thomas	45
1980	Mike Schmidt	48	Reggie Jackson, Ben Oglivie	41
1981	Mike Schmidt	31	Bobby Grich, Eddie Murray, Tony Armas, Dwight Evans	22
1982	Dave Kingman	37	Gorman Thomas, Reggie Jackson	32
1983	Mike Schmidt	40	Jim Rice	39
1984	Mike Schmidt, Dale Murphy	36	Tony Armas	43
1985	Dale Murphy	37	Darrell Evans	40
1986	Mike Schmidt	37	Jesse Barfield	40
1987	Andre Dawson	49	Mark McGuire	49
1988	Darryl Strawberry	39	José Canseco	42

5. The following are the average ages, rounded to the nearest tenth, of airline fleets as of July 1, 1988, according to Avmark, Inc. Draw an ordered back-to-back stem-and-leaf plot comparing U.S. airlines to the selected foreign airlines. Are any patterns of difference evident in comparisons of the two sets of data?

Major U.S. Airlines	Age Years	Selected Foreign Airlines	Age Years
Northwest	15.5	Air Canada	13.0
TWA	15.3	Malaysian	10.3
Eastern	15.1	British Air	10.0
United	14.9	Alitalia	9.9
Pam Am	14.6	Air France	9.6
Continental	12.1	Japan Air	9.1
American	10.8	Cathay	8.8
Piedmont	10.3	KLM	8.7
USAir	10.1	All Nippon	8.2
Delta	9.5	Lufthansa	7.7

6. The figure shows a bar graph of the rainfall in centimeters during the last school year. Answer each of the following questions.

   (a) Which month had the greatest rainfall, and how much did it have?
   (b) What were the amounts of rainfall in October, December, and January?

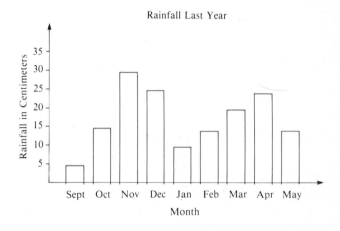

7. A list of presidents, with the number of children for each, follows.

   1. Washington, 0
   2. J. Adams, 5
   3. Jefferson, 6
   4. Madison, 0
   5. Monroe, 2
   6. J. Q. Adams, 4
   7. Jackson, 0
   8. Van Buren, 4
   9. W. H. Harrison, 10
   10. Tyler, 14
   11. Polk, 0
   12. Taylor, 6
   13. Fillmore, 2
   14. Pierce, 3
   15. Buchanan, 0
   16. Lincoln, 4
   17. A. Johnson, 5
   18. Grant, 4
   19. Hayes, 8
   20. Garfield, 7
   21. Arthur, 3
   22. Cleveland, 5
   23. B. Harrison, 3
   24. McKinley, 2
   25. T. Roosevelt, 6
   26. Taft, 3
   27. Wilson, 3
   28. Harding, 0
   29. Coolidge, 2
   30. Hoover, 2
   31. F. D. Roosevelt, 6
   32. Truman, 1
   33. Eisenhower, 2
   34. Kennedy, 3
   35. L. B. Johnson, 2
   36. Nixon, 2
   37. Ford, 4
   38. Carter, 3
   39. Reagan, 4
   40. Bush, 5

   (a) Construct a line plot for these data.
   (b) Make a frequency table for these data.
   (c) What is the most frequent number of children?

8. The given data represent total car sales for Johnson's car lot from January through June. Draw a bar graph for the data.

Month	Jan.	Feb.	Mar.	Apr.	May	June
Number of Cars Sold	90	86	92	96	90	100

9. Five coins are tossed 64 times. A distribution for the number of heads obtained is shown.

Number of Heads	0	1	2	3	4	5
Frequency	2	10	20	20	10	2

   (a) Draw a histogram for the data.
   (b) Draw a frequency polygon for the data.

10. The grade distribution for the final examination in the mathematics course for elementary teachers is shown.

Grade	Frequency
A	4
B	10
C	37
D	8
F	1

   (a) Draw a bar graph of the data.
   (b) Draw a circle graph of the data.

11. The following are the amounts (rounded to the nearest dollar) paid by 25 students for textbooks during the fall term.

35	37	53
42	37	62
33	16	30
48	23	50
45	49	39
42	62	51
50	60	40
39	58	23
41		

   (a) Draw a two-line ordered stem-and-leaf plot to illustrate the data.
   (b) Construct a grouped frequency table for the data, starting the first class at $15.00 with intervals of $5.00 each.
   (c) Draw a histogram of the data.
   (d) Draw a frequency polygon of the data.

12. Make a pictograph to represent the data, using 🥤 to represent 10 glasses of lemonade sold.

GLASSES OF LEMONADE SOLD

	Tally	Frequency
Monday	ЖЖ ЖЖ ЖЖ	15
Tuesday	ЖЖ ЖЖ ЖЖ ЖЖ	20
Wednesday	ЖЖ ЖЖ ЖЖ ЖЖ ЖЖ ЖЖ	30
Thursday	ЖЖ	5
Friday	ЖЖ ЖЖ	10

13. Give an example of a situation in which a circle graph would be preferable to either a bar graph or a line graph.

14. Give an example of a situation in which a line graph would be preferable to a bar graph.

15. The following graphs give the temperatures for a certain day. Which graph is more helpful for guessing the actual temperature at 10:00 A.M.? Why?

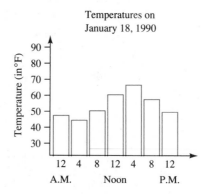

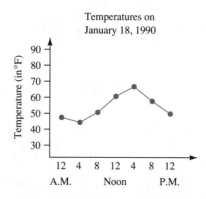

16. Give an example of a set of data for which a stem-and-leaf plot is more informative than a histogram.

Section 9-2 **Measures of Central Tendency and Variation**

In the previous section, we examined data by looking at graphs and tables involving the data. It often is convenient to describe a set of data by choosing a single number that indicates where the data in the set are centered or concentrated.

Examine the following set of data for three teachers, each of whom claims that his or her class scored better than the other two classes.

Mr. Smith: 62, 94, 95, 98, 98

Mr. Jones: 62, 62, 98, 99, 100

Ms. Leed: 40, 62, 85, 99, 99

All of these teachers are correct in their assertions, because each one has used a different number to characterize the scores in his or her particular class. In general, three different types of numbers can be used to characterize where data are centered: the arithmetic mean, the median, and the mode. In studying these numbers, *a calculator is a definite aid.*

Computing Means

arithmetic mean The number most commonly used to characterize a set of data is the **arithmetic**
average / mean **mean,** frequently called the **average,** or the **mean.** For example, suppose that three officemates make \$20,000, \$21,000, and \$25,000 annually. The mean salary is the salary that each worker would make if the total earnings in the office were divided equally among the three people—that is, (20,000 + 21,000 + 25,000)/3, or \$22,000.

To find the mean of scores for each of the teachers given above, we find the sum of the scores in each case and divide by 5, the number of scores.

$$\text{Mean (Smith):}\quad \frac{62 + 94 + 95 + 98 + 98}{5} = \frac{447}{5} = 89.4$$

$$\text{Mean (Jones):}\quad \frac{62 + 62 + 98 + 99 + 100}{5} = \frac{421}{5} = 84.2$$

$$\text{Mean (Leed):}\quad \frac{40 + 62 + 85 + 99 + 99}{5} = \frac{385}{5} = 77$$

Thus, in terms of the mean, Mr. Smith's class scored better than the other two classes. In general, we define the *arithmetic mean* as follows.

• **D E F I N I T I O N**

The **arithmetic mean** of the numbers $x_1, x_2, \ldots, x_n$, denoted by $\bar{x}$ and read "x bar," is given by

$$\bar{x} = \frac{x_1 + x_2 + x_3 + \cdots + x_n}{n}$$

Computing Medians

median   The value exactly in the middle of an ordered set of numbers is called the **median.** To find the median for the teachers' scores, we arrange each of their scores in increasing order and pick the middle score. Intuitively, we know that half the scores are greater than the median and half are less.

Median (Smith):   62, 94, ⟨95,⟩ 98, 98   median = 95

Median (Jones):   62, 62, ⟨98,⟩ 99, 100   median = 98

Median (Leed):   40, 62, ⟨85,⟩ 99, 99   median = 85

Thus, in terms of the median, Mr. Jones's class scored better than the other two classes.

With an odd number of scores, as in the present example, the median is the middle score. With an even number of scores, however, the median is defined as the mean of the middle two scores; thus, to find the median, we add the middle two scores and divide by 2. For example, the median of the scores

64, 68, | 70, 74 | 82, 90

is given by

$$\frac{70 + 74}{2}, \quad \text{or} \quad 72$$

In general, to find the median for a set of n numbers, proceed as follows.

1. Arrange the numbers in order from least to greatest.
2. (a) If n is odd, the median is the middle number.
    (b) If n is even, the median is the mean of the two middle numbers.

Finding Modes

mode   The **mode** of a set of data is the number that appears most frequently, if there is one. In some distributions no number appears more than once, and in other distributions there may be more than one mode. For example, the set of scores 64, 79, 80, 82, 90 has no mode (or five modes). The set of *bimodal*   scores 64, 75, 75, 82, 90, 90, 98 is **bimodal** (two modes), because both 75 and 90 are modes. It is possible for a set of data to have too many modes for this type of number to be useful in describing the data.

For the three classes listed earlier, if the mode is used as a criterion, Ms. Leed's class scored better than the other two classes.

Mode (Smith):   62, 94, 95, 98, 98   mode = 98

Mode (Jones):   62, 62, 98, 99, 100   mode = 62

Mode (Leed):   40, 62, 85, 99, 99   mode = 99

EXAMPLE 9-4 Find (a) the mean, (b) the median, and (c) the mode for the following collection of data.

60, 60, 70, 95, 95, 100

SOLUTION (a) $\bar{x} = \dfrac{60 + 60 + 70 + 95 + 95 + 100}{6} = \dfrac{480}{6} = 80$

(b) The median is $\dfrac{70 + 95}{6}$, or 82.5

(c) The set of data is bimodal and has both 60 and 95 as modes.

Although the mean is the number most commonly used to describe a set of data, it may not always be the best number to use. Suppose, for example, that a company employs 20 people. The president of the company earns \$200,000, the vice president earns \$75,000, and 18 employees earn \$10,000 each. The mean salary for this company is

$$\frac{\$200,000 + \$75,000 + 18(\$10,000)}{20} = \frac{\$455,000}{20} = \$22,750$$

In this case, the mean salary of \$22,750 is not representative, and either the median or mode, both of which are \$10,000, would better describe the typical salary. Notice that *the mean is affected by extreme values.*

In most cases, the median is not affected by extreme values. The median, however, can be misleading. For example, suppose that nine students make the following scores on a test: 30, 35, 40, 40, 92, 92, 93, 98, 99. From the median score of 92, one might infer that the individuals all scored very well, yet 92 is certainly not a typical score.

The mode, too, can be misleading in describing a set of data with very few items or many frequently occurring items. For example, the scores 40, 42, 50, 62, 63, 65, 98, 98 have a mode of 98, which is not a typical value.

PROBLEM 1
Lacking time to record his students' homework grades, Dr. Van Gruff asked them to keep track of their own grades. A few days later, Dr. Van Gruff asked the students to report their grades. One of the students, Eddy, had lost his papers but remembered the grades on four of six assignments—100, 82, 74, and 60. Also, according to Eddy, the mean of all six papers was 69, and the other two papers had identical grades. What were the grades on Eddy's other two homework papers?

Understanding the Problem. Eddy reported that he had scores of 100, 82, 74, and 60 on four of his six papers, that the mean of all six papers was 69, and that he had identical scores on the missing two grades. The problem is to determine the two missing grades from this information.

Devising a Plan. Because the mean is obtained by finding the sum of the scores and then dividing by the number of scores, which is six, if we let x stand for each of the two missing grades, we have

$$69 = \frac{100 + 82 + 74 + 60 + x + x}{6}$$

To find the missing grades, we solve this equation for x.

Carrying Out the Plan. We now solve the equation as follows.

$$69 = \frac{100 + 82 + 74 + 60 + x + x}{6}$$

$$69 = \frac{316 + 2x}{6}$$

$$49 = x$$

Since the solution to the equation is $x = 49$, we conclude that each of the two missing scores was 49.

Looking Back. The answer of 49 seems reasonable, since the mean of 69 is less than three of the four given scores. This can easily be checked by computing the mean of the scores 100, 82, 74, 60, 49, 49 and showing that it is indeed 69.

Measures of Dispersion

The choice of which number to use to represent a particular set of data is not always easy. In the example involving the three teachers, each teacher chose the number that best suited his or her claim. For clarity and honesty, the type of number used should always be specified. However, in many cases, no single number gives adequate information about a set of data. The need for other numbers to describe data will become apparent in the following discussion.

Suppose that Professors Abel and Babel each taught a section of a statistics course and each had six students. Both professors gave the same final exam. The results, along with the means for each group of scores, are given in Table 9-9, with stem-and-leaf plots in Figure 9-18(a) and (b), respectively. As shown in the stem-and-leaf plots the sets of data are very different. The first set of scores is more spread out, or varies more, than the second. However, each set of scores has 60 as the mean. Each median also equals 60. Although the mean and the median for these two groups are the same, the two distributions of scores are very different.

Abel	Babel
100	70
80	70
70	60
50	60
50	60
10	40
$\bar{x} = \dfrac{360}{6} = 60$	$\bar{x} = \dfrac{360}{6} = 60$

TABLE 9-9

FIGURE 9-18

PROFESSOR ABEL'S CLASS SCORES

1	0
2	
3	
4	
5	00
6	
7	0
8	0
9	
10	0

7 | 0 represents a score of 70

(a)

PROFESSOR BABEL'S CLASS SCORES

4	0
5	
6	000
7	00

7 | 0 represents a score of 70

(b)

There are several ways to measure the spread (variation) of data. The simplest way is to subtract the least number from the greatest number. This difference is called the **range.** The range for Professor Abel's class is 100 − 10, or 90. The range for Professor Babel's class is 70 − 40, or 30. Although the range is easy to calculate, it has the disadvantage of being determined by two scores. For example, the sets of scores 10, 20, 25, 30, 100 and 10, 80, 85, 90, 90, 100 both have a range of 90.

range

Several other ways to measure the spread of data are more useful than the range. The two most commonly used measures of variation are variance and standard deviation. These two measures are essentially equivalent, but the standard deviation has the same units as the original data and is particularly useful in making precise statements about the spread of data.

variance
standard deviation

The steps involved in calculating the **variance** v and **standard deviation** s of n numbers are as follows.

1. Find the mean of the numbers.
2. Subtract the mean from each number.
3. Square each difference found in step 2.
4. Find the sum of the squares in step 3.
5. Divide by n to obtain the variance.
6. Find the square root of v to obtain the standard deviation.

These six steps can be summarized for the numbers $x_1, x_2, x_3, \ldots, x_n$ as follows, where $\bar{x}$ is the mean of these numbers.

$$s = \sqrt{v} = \sqrt{\frac{(x_1 - \bar{x})^2 + (x_2 - \bar{x})^2 + (x_3 - \bar{x})^2 + \cdots + (x_n - \bar{x})^2}{n}}$$

• REMARK

In some textbooks, this formula involves division by $n - 1$ instead of by n. Division by $n - 1$ is more useful for advanced work in statistics.

The variances and standard deviations for the final exam data from the classes of Professors Abel and Babel are calculated by using Tables 9-10 and 9-11, respectively.

TABLE 9-10

Abel's Scores

x	$x - \bar{x}$	$(x - \bar{x})^2$
100	40	1600
80	20	400
70	10	100
50	-10	100
50	-10	100
10	-50	2500
Totals 360	0	4800

$$\bar{x} = \frac{360}{6} = 60$$

$$v = \frac{4800}{6} = 800$$

$$s = \sqrt{800} \doteq 28.3$$

TABLE 9-11

Babel's Scores

x	$x - \bar{x}$	$(x - \bar{x})^2$
70	10	100
70	10	100
60	0	0
60	0	0
60	0	0
40	-20	400
Totals 360	0	600

$$\bar{x} = \frac{360}{6} = 60$$

$$v = \frac{600}{6} = 100$$

$$s = \sqrt{100} = 10$$

The standard deviation is a large number when the values from a set of data are widely spread. The standard deviation is a small number (close to 0) when the data values are close together. This is further illustrated in Example 9-5.

EXAMPLE 9-5 Professor Boone gave two exams. Exam A had grades of 0, 0, 0, 100, 100, and 100, and exam B had grades of 50, 50, 50, 50, 50, and 50. Find the following for each exam.

(a) The mean   (b) The median   (c) The standard deviation

SOLUTION (a) The means for exams A and B are each 50.
(b) The medians for the exams are each 50.
(c) The standard deviations for exams A and B are as follows.

$$s_A = \sqrt{\frac{3(0 - 50)^2 + 3(100 - 50)^2}{6}} = 50$$

$$s_B = \sqrt{\frac{6(50 - 50)^2}{6}} = 0$$

EXAMPLE 9-6 Given the data 32, 41, 47, 53, 57, find each of the following.

(a) The range (b) The variance
(c) The standard deviation

SOLUTION (a) The range is $57 - 32$, or 25.
(b) The variance v is computed by using the information in Table 9-12.
(c) $s = \sqrt{78.4} \doteq 8.9$

TABLE 9-12

x	$x - \bar{x}$	$(x - \bar{x})^2$
32	$^-14$	196
41	$^-5$	25
47	1	1
53	7	49
57	11	121
Totals 230	0	392

$$\bar{x} = \frac{230}{5} = 46$$

$$v = \frac{392}{5} = 78.4$$

Box Plots

box plot A **box plot,** sometimes called a *box-and-whisker plot,* was introduced by Tukey along with the stem-and-leaf plot discussed earlier. To construct a box plot, we must find the *lower quartile* and the *upper quartile* of a given set of data. If scores are arranged from lowest to highest, the lower quartile, the median, and the upper quartile divide the data into four groups that are approximately the same size. Consider the following set of test scores.

20 25 .40 50 50 60 70 75 80 80 90 100 100

We first find the median, which is 70, and draw a line segment through it.

20 25 40 50 50 60 7|0 75 80 80 90 100 100

Next we consider only the values to the left of the segment and draw a line segment where the median of those values is located.

20 25 40 | 50 50 60

lower quartile
first quartile(Q_1)
upper quartile(Q_3)

The score of $45 = (40 + 50)/2$ is the median of the scores less than the median of all scores and therefore is the **lower quartile.** The lower quartile is often called the **first quartile** and is denoted by Q_1. Similarly, we can find the upper (or third) quartile (Q_3), which is $(80 + 90)/2$, or 85. The **upper quartile** is the median of the scores greater than the median of all scores. Thus we have divided the scores into 4 groups of 3 scores each, as shown.

20 25 40 | 50 50 60 7|0 75 80 80 | 90 100 100

interquartile range (IQR)

The **interquartile range (IQR)** is the difference between the upper quartile and the lower quartile. In this case, IQR = 85 − 45 = 40. The IQR is itself another useful measure of variation, because it represents the middle 50%, or half, of the data. The median, the lower and upper quartiles, and the lower and upper extreme scores give us five numbers that characterize a distribution reasonably well.

Box plots can be drawn vertically or horizontally. To draw a vertical box plot, we first plot the median, the quartiles, and the extreme values. The scale for the set of scores just given is shown on the left-hand side of Figure 9-19.

FIGURE 9-19

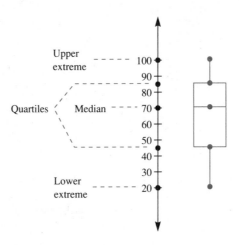

Next we draw short horizontal lines at the median and the two quartiles, and we connect them to form a *box*. We then draw segments from each end of the box to the extreme values. These segments are called *whiskers*. The result is the upright box plot shown on the right-hand side of Figure 9-19. Similarly, a box plot can be drawn lengthwise by using a horizontal scale.

The box plot gives a fairly clear picture of the spread of the data. If we look at the graph in Figure 9-19, we see that the median is 70, the maximum value is 100, the minimum value is 20, and the upper and lower quartiles are 45 and 85. The box plot is a *summary display* because it shows only certain statistics, rather than all the data.

EXAMPLE 9-7 What are the minimum and maximum values, the median, and the lower and upper quartiles of the box plot shown in Figure 9-20?

FIGURE 9-20

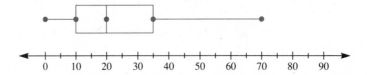

SOLUTION   The minimum value is 0, the maximum value is 70, the median is 20, the lower quartile is 10, and the upper quartile is 35.

Constructing Box Plots from Stem-and-Leaf Plots

Another way to produce a box plot is to construct it from an ordered stem-and-leaf plot. We first draw a vertical segment next to an ordered stem-and-leaf plot. Counting in from the ends of the stem-and-leaf plot, we get the quartiles and the median. In Figure 9-21(a), because there are 30 values, we count $\frac{1}{4}$ of 30, or 7.5, values from the upper extreme to find the upper quartile (third quartile), which we label as Q_3. Thus, in this instance, Q_3 has value 111.5. Then we count 7.5 values from the lower extreme to find the lower quartile (first quartile), which we label as Q_1. Here, Q_1 has value 84.50. Likewise, we can count in from either end to find the median, which is 102. From these points we can construct a box to enclose the middle half of the data and to mark the median, as shown in Figure 9-21(b). Next we draw the whiskers connecting the box to the extreme values.

FIGURE 9-21

Box Plot

Stem-and-Leaf Plot

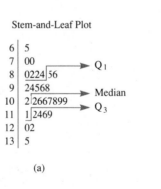

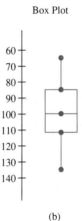

(a)

(b)

Outliers

Recall that an *outlier* is a value that is widely separated from the rest of a group of data. For example, in a set of scores such as 91, 92, 92, 93, 93, 93, 94, all data are grouped close together and no values are widely separated. However, in a set of scores such as 21, 92, 92, 93, 93, 93, 95, 150, both 21 and 150 are widely separated from the rest of the data. These values are potential outliers. The upper and lower extreme values are not necessarily outliers. In data such as 75, 90, 91, 92, 92, 93, 93, it is not easy to decide, so a rule is developed. The rule we use to determine outliers is: *An outlier is any value that is more than 1.5 interquartile ranges above the upper quartile or more than 1.5 interquartile ranges below the lower quartile.* Statisticians sometimes use values different from 1.5 to determine outliers.

It is common practice to indicate outliers with asterisks. Whiskers are then drawn to the extreme points that are *not* outliers. To investigate how this works, we use the data in Table 9-13.

TABLE 9-13

Final Medal Standings for the
Top 20 Countries—1988 Olympics

Country	Number of Medals
USSR	132
East Germany	102
United States	94
West Germany	40
Bulgaria	35
South Korea	33
China	28
Romania	24
Great Britain	24
Hungary	23
France	16
Poland	16
Italy	14
Japan	14
Australia	14
New Zealand	13
Yugoslavia	12
Sweden	11
Canada	10
Kenya	9

The extreme scores are 132 and 9, the median is 19.5, and the quartiles are 34 and 13.5, with IQR = 20.5. Outliers are scores that are greater than 34 + 1.5(20.5), or 64.75, or less than 13.5 − 1.5(20.5), or ⁻17.25. Therefore, in this data set, there are three outliers: 94, 102, and 132. A box plot is given in Figure 9-22.

FIGURE 9-22

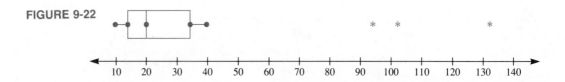

Comparing Sets of Data

Box plots are often useful in comparing two sets of data. The data given in Table 9-14 provide an illustration.

TABLE 9-14

Batting Average Champions
1978–1988

Year	National League		American League	
1978	Parker	.334	Carew	.333
1979	Hernandez	.344	Lynn	.333
1980	Buckner	.324	Brett	.390
1981	Madlock	.341	Lansford	.336
1982	Oliver	.331	Wilson	.332
1983	Madlock	.323	Boggs	.361
1984	Gwynn	.351	Mattingly	.343
1985	McGee	.353	Boggs	.368
1986	Raines	.334	Boggs	.357
1987	Gwynn	.369	Boggs	.363
1988	Gwynn	.313	Boggs	.366

Before constructing horizontal box plots, we must find the five important values for each class. These are given in Table 9-15. Next we draw the horizontal scale and construct the box plots for the American and National Leagues, as shown in Figure 9-23.

TABLE 9-15

Value	National League	American League
Maximum	.369	.390
Upper quartile	.351	.366
Median	.334	.357
Lower quartile	.324	.333
Minimum	.313	.332

FIGURE 9-23

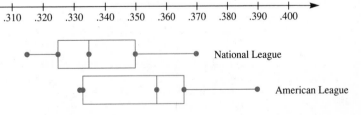

From Figure 9-23, we can see that the length of the box (IQR) for the American League is longer than the box (IQR) for the National League. This implies that the top batting averages in the American League vary more from year to year than do those in the National League. The top batting averages in the American League tend to be higher than those in the National League, since the extreme scores, median, and quartiles for the American League are all higher than those for the National League. Also, almost 75% of the top batting averages in the American League are higher than the median of the top averages in the National League.

In this example, the IQR for the National League is .351 − .324, or .027. The upper cutoff point for identifying outliers is .351 + 1.5(.027), or .3915. The lower cutoff point for outliers is .324 − 1.5(.027), or .2835. Because no top batting averages in the National League are greater than .3915 or less than .2835, there are no outliers in the National League data. For the American League, the IQR is .366 − .333 = .033. Values greater than .366 + 1.5(.033), or .4155, or less than .333 − 1.5(.033), or .2835, are outliers. Therefore, there are no outliers in the American League data, either.

Although we cannot spot clusters or gaps in box plots (as we can with stem-and-leaf or line plots), we can more easily compare data from different sets, as was evident in the last example. With box plots we do not need to have sets of data that are approximately the same size, as we did for stem-and-leaf plots. To compare data from two or more sets using their box plots, we first study the boxes to see if they are located in approximately the same places. Next we consider the lengths of the boxes to see if the variability of the data is about the same. We also check whether the median, the quartiles, and the extreme values in one set are greater than those in another set. If they are, the data in the first set are greater than those of the other set, no matter how we compare them. If they are not, we can continue to study the data for other similarities and differences.

B R A I N   T E A S E R

The speeds of racing cars were timed after 3 miles, $4\frac{1}{2}$ miles, and 6 miles. Freddy averaged 140 miles per hour (mph) for the first 3 miles, 168 mph for the next $1\frac{1}{2}$ miles, and 210 mph for the last $1\frac{1}{2}$ miles. What was his mean speed for the total 6-mile run?

PROBLEM SET 9-2

1. Calculate the mean, the median, and the mode for each of the following collections of data.
   (a) 2, 8, 7, 8, 5, 8, 10, 5
   (b) 10, 12, 12, 14, 20, 16, 12, 14, 11
   (c) 18, 22, 22, 17, 30, 18, 12
   (d) 82, 80, 63, 75, 92, 80, 92, 90, 80, 80
   (e) 5, 5, 5, 5, 5, 10

2. (a) If each of 6 students scored 80 on a test, find each of the following for the set of 6 scores.
       (i) Mean   (ii) Median   (iii) Mode
   (b) Make up another set of 6 scores that are not all the same but in which the mean, median, and mode are all 80.

3. The mean score on a set of 20 tests is 75. What is the sum of the 20 test scores?
4. The tram at a ski area has a capacity of 50 people with a load limit of 7500 pounds. What is the mean weight of the passengers if the tram is loaded to capacity?
5. The mean for a set of 28 scores is 80. Suppose 2 more students take the test and score 60 and 50. What is the new mean?
6. The names and ages for each person in a family of five follow.

Name	Dick	Jane	Kirk	Jean	Scott
Age	40	36	8	6	2

   (a) What is the mean age?
   (b) Find the mean of the ages 5 years from now.
   (c) Find the mean 10 years from now.
   (d) Describe the relationships among the means found in (a), (b), and (c).
7. Ten alumni of a state college are chosen at random and asked their annual incomes, which are $15,000, $20,000, $18,000, $28,000, $12,000, $30,000, $20,000, $14,000, $20,000, and $50,000. Find the mean, the median, and the mode for these incomes.
8. Suppose that you own a hat shop and decide to order hats in only *one* size for the coming season. To decide which size to order, you look at last year's sales figures, which are itemized according to size. Should you find the mean, median, or mode for the data?
9. A table showing Jon's fall quarter grades follows. Find his grade point average for the term ($A = 4$, $B = 3, C = 2, D = 1, F = 0$).

Course	Credits	Grades
Math	5	B
English	3	A
Physics	5	C
German	3	D
Handball	1	A

10. If the mean weight of seven linemen on a football team is 230 pounds and the mean weight of the four backfield members is 190 pounds, what is the mean weight of the eleven-man team?
11. A total of 210 people stayed at the Rancho Costa Plenty over the weekend for a total cost of $67,200. What was the mean cost per person?

12. If 99 people had a mean income of $12,000, how much is the mean income increased by the addition of a single income of $200,000?
13. The following table gives the annual salaries of the 40 players of a certain professional football team.
   (a) Find the mean annual salary for the team.
   (b) Find the median annual salary.
   (c) Find the mode.

Salary	Number of Players
$ 18,000	2
22,000	4
26,000	4
35,000	3
38,000	12
44,000	8
50,000	4
80,000	2
150,000	1

   What is the standard deviation of the heights of seven trapeze artists if their heights are 175 cm, 182 cm, 190 cm, 180 cm, 192 cm, 172 cm, and 190 cm?
15. What happens to the mean and to the standard deviation of a set of data when the same number is added to each value in the data?
16. (a) If all the numbers in a set are equal, what is the standard deviation?
   (b) If the standard deviation of a set of numbers is zero, must all the numbers in the set be equal?
17. In a Math 131 class at DiPaloma University, the grades on the first exam were as follows.

96	71	43	77	75	76	61
83	71	58	97	76	74	91
74	71	77	83	87	93	79

   (a) Find the mean.
   (b) Find the median.
   (c) Find the mode.
   (d) Find the variance of the scores.
   (e) Find the standard deviation of the scores.
18. To receive an A in a class, Willie needs at least a mean of 90 on five exams. Willie's grades on the first four exams were 84, 95, 86, and 94. What minimum score does he need on the fifth exam to receive an A in the class?
19. Ginny's median score on three tests was 90. Her mean score was 92 and her range was 6. What were her three test scores?
20. The mean of five numbers is 6. If one of the five numbers is removed, the mean becomes 7. What is the value of the number that was removed?

21. Sue drives 5 miles at 30 mph and then 5 miles at 50 mph. Is the mean speed for the trip 40 mph? Why or why not?

22. Construct a box plot for the following set of test scores. Indicate outliers, if any, with asterisks.

$$20, 95, 40, 70, 90, 70, 80, 80, 90, 95$$

23. Following are the heights in feet of the tallest ten buildings in Los Angeles and in Minneapolis.
    (a) Draw horizontal box plots to compare the data.
    (b) Are there any outliers in this data? If so, which values are they?

Los Angeles	Minneapolis
858	950
750	775
735	668
699	579
625	561
620	447
578	440
571	416
534	403
516	366

24. In a school system, teachers start at a salary of $15,200 and have a top salary of $31,800. The teacher's union is bargaining with the school district for next year's salary increment.
    (a) If every teacher is given a $1000 raise, what happens to each of the following?
       (i) Mean   (ii) Median   (iii) Extremes
       (iv) Quartiles   (v) Standard deviation
    (b) If every teacher received a 5% raise, what does this do to the following?
       (i) mean   (ii) standard deviation

25. (a) Find the mean and the median of the following arithmetic sequences.
       (i) 1, 3, 5, 7, 9
       (ii) 1, 3, 5, 7, 9, . . . , 199
       (iii) 7, 10, 13, 16, . . . , 607
    (b) Based on your answers in part (a), make a conjecture about the mean and the median of any arithmetic sequence.

★26. Show that the following formula for variance is equivalent to the one given in the text.

$$v = \frac{x_1^2 + x_2^2 + \cdots + x_n^2}{n} - \overline{x}^2$$

Review Problems

27. Raw test scores from a history test are as follows.

86	85	87	96	55
90	94	82	68	77
88	89	85	74	90
72	80	76	88	73
64	79	73	85	93

   (a) Construct an ordered stem-and-leaf plot for the given data.
   (b) Construct a grouped frequency table for these scores with intervals of 5, starting the first class at 55.
   (c) Draw a histogram of the data.
   (d) Draw a frequency polygon of the data.
   (e) If a circle graph of the grouped data in (b) were drawn, how many degrees would be in the section representing the 85–89 interval?

*Section 9-3   Normal Distributions

A histogram drawn to depict the frequencies of many sets of data may resemble the one shown in Figure 9-24. If the frequency polygon is sketched on the histogram, as in Figure 9-24, we see a mound-shaped curve. In statistics, the Empirical Rule relates mound-shaped distributions and standard deviations to the measurements being depicted.

FIGURE 9-24

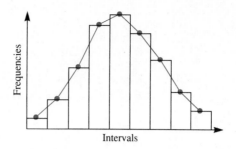

• D E F I N I T I O N

Empirical Rule   The **Empirical Rule** applies to sets of data with frequency polygons that are mound-shaped.

(a) Approximately 68% of the data will fall within one standard deviation of the mean.
(b) Approximately 95% of the data will fall within two standard deviations of the mean.
(c) Approximately 99.8% of the data will fall within three standard deviations of the mean.

normal curve   The Empirical Rule was developed from the study of a normal curve, as a rule of thumb. A **normal curve** is a smooth, bell-shaped curve that depicts frequency values distributed symmetrically about the mean. (Also, the mean, median, and mode all have the same value.) On a normal curve, about 68% of the values lie within one standard deviation of the mean, about 95% lie within two standard deviations, and about 99.8% are within three standard deviations. The percentages represent approximations of the total percent of area under the curve. The curve and the percentages are illustrated in Figure 9-25.

FIGURE 9-25

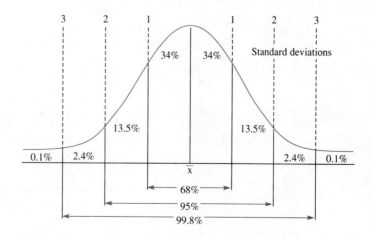

H I S T O R I C A L   N O T E
Abraham De Moivre (1667–1754), a French Huguenot, was the first to develop and study the normal curve. He was one of the first to study actuarial information, in his book *Annuities upon Lives*. He also worked in trigonometry and complex numbers. An interesting fable is told about the death of De Moivre. It is reported that he noticed that each day he required one quarter of an hour more sleep than he had on the previous day; when the arithmetic progression for sleep reached 24 hours, he died.

EXAMPLE 9-8 When a standardized test was scored, there was a mean of 500 and a standard deviation of 100. Suppose that 10,000 students took the test and their scores had a mound-shaped distribution, making it possible to use a normal curve to approximate the distribution.

(a) How many scored between 400 and 600?
(b) How many scored between 300 and 700?
(c) How many scored between 200 and 800?

SOLUTION (a) Since one standard deviation on either side of the mean is from 400 to 600, about 68% of the scores fall in this interval. Thus, 0.68(10,000), or 6800, students scored between 400 and 600.
(b) About 95% of 10,000, or 9500, students scored between 300 and 700.
(c) About 99.8% of 10,000, or 9980, students scored between 200 and 800.

● **R E M A R K**
About 0.2%, or 20, students' scores in Example 9-8 fall outside three standard deviations. About 10 of these students did very well on the test, and about 10 students did very poorly.

Suppose that a group of students asked their teacher to grade "on a curve." If the teacher gave a test to 200 students and the mean on the test was 71, with a standard deviation of 7, the graph in Figure 9-26 shows how the grades could be assigned. In Figure 9-26 the teacher has used the normal curve in grading. (The use of the normal curve presupposes that the teacher had a mound-shaped distribution of scores and also that the teacher arbitrarily decided to use the lines marking standard deviations to determine the boundaries of the As, Bs, Cs, Ds, and Fs). Thus, based on the normal curve in Figure 9-26, Table 9-16 shows the range of grades that the teacher might assign if he or she uses the rounding rules given in Chapter 7. Students who ask their teachers to grade on the curve may wish to reconsider if the normal curve is to be used.

FIGURE 9-26

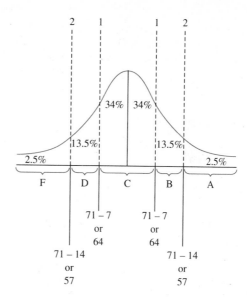

TABLE 9-16

Test Score	Grade	Number of People per Grade	Percentage Receiving Grade
85 and Above	A	5	2.5%
78–84	B	27	13.5%
64–77	C	136	68%
57–63	D	27	13.5%
Below 57	F	5	2.5%

Percentiles

Kristy and Kim were applying for a job. On the application, Kristy wrote that she finished 15th in her class. Kim reported that she finished 40th in her class. Does Kristy's class rank imply that she is a better student than Kim? Suppose that there were 50 students in Kristy's class and 400 students in Kim's class. In such a case, we need a common method of comparing their rankings. In order to make a balanced comparison, we can find Kristy's and *percentile ranks / percentile* Kim's **percentile ranks,** or **percentiles,** in their respective classes. In Kristy's class, there were $50 - 15 = 35$ students ranked below her. In terms of percents, 35/50, or 70%, of the class ranked below her, so we say that Kristy ranked at the 70th percentile. Similarly, $(400 - 40)/400 = 360/400$, or 90%, of the students ranked below Kim. We say that Kim ranked at the 90th percentile for her school. Thus, comparatively, Kim ranked higher in her class than Kristy did in hers. As the name implies, percentiles divide the set of data into 100 equal parts. For example, if Tomas reports that he scored at the 50th percentile (the median) on the SAT, he is saying that he scored *rth percentile*   better than 50% of the people taking the test. In general, the **rth percentile,** denoted by P_r, is a score such that r percent of the scores are less than P_r. In a case in which the distribution is normal, as in Figure 9-27, we see several percentages and a relationship between percentiles and standard deviations.

FIGURE 9-27

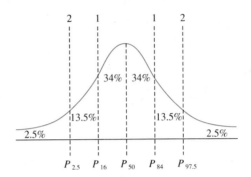

Typically, percentiles are reported only to whole-number percents such as P_1, P_2 P_3, . . . , P_{97}, P_{98}, P_{99}. However, as seen in Figure 9-27, $P_{2.5}$ and $P_{97.5}$, correspond to specific whole numbers of standard deviations and are easy to recognize and find in a set of data.

The discussion of percentiles thus far has centered on distributions that can be represented by a normal curve. Percentiles can also be found from distributions that are not mound-shaped. This can be done by constructing a frequency table, determining the number of scores less than the score for which we are trying to determine a percentile, and then dividing that number by the total number of scores in the set of data. This is investigated further in the problem set.

deciles   **Deciles** are points that divide a distribution into ten equally spaced sections. There are nine deciles, denoted D_1, D_2, . . . , D_9, and $D_1 = P_{10}$, $D_2 = P_{20}$, . . . , $D_9 = P_{90}$. Quartiles are points that divide a distribution into quarters. There are three quartiles:

$$Q_1 = P_{25} \qquad Q_2 = P_{50} \qquad Q_3 = P_{75}$$

As was noted previously, Q_3 is referred to as the *upper quartile,* and Q_1 is referred to as the *lower quartile.*

● R E M A R K
In some finite sets of test scores, a particular percentile may not be represented. This does not stop their being used with small sets of data, but it does inhibit their usefulness.

EXAMPLE 9-9   The standardized test of Example 9-8 had a mean of 500 and a standard deviation of 100. The 16th percentile, P_{16}, is 400, since 400 is one standard deviation from the mean, or better than 16% of the scores. Find each of the following.

(a) P_{50} (b) P_{84}

SOLUTION   (a) Since 500 is the mean, 50% of the distribution is less than 500. Thus, $P_{50} = 500$.

(b) Since 600 is one standard deviation to the right of the mean, 84% of the distribution is less than 600. Thus, $P_{84} = 600$.

EXAMPLE 9-10   (a) Ossie's was 25th in a class of 250. What was his percentile rank?

(b) In a class of 50, Cathy has a percentile rank of 60. What is her class standing?

SOLUTION   (a) There were $250 - 25 = 225$ students ranked below Ossie. Hence, 225/250, or 90%, of the class ranked below him. Therefore, Ossie ranked at the 90th percentile.

(b) Cathy's percentile rank is 60. Therefore, 60% of the class ranks below Cathy. Because 60% of 50 is 30, 30 students rank below Cathy. Therefore, Cathy is 20th in her class.

Comparing Scores from Different Tests

Scores by themselves may have very little meaning. For example, Wayne's receiving a score of 20 on his first math quiz does not mean much unless we know more about the possible set of points on the test and how the other students scored. However, if we knew that the quiz on which Wayne received a score of 20 had a mean of 16 and a standard deviation of 2.2, we would have enough information to determine how he scored in relation to the rest of the class. Now suppose that Wayne received a score of 52 on his second quiz, where the mean was 48 and the standard deviation was 3.1. Did Wayne do better on the first quiz or on the second quiz? We need a way to compare the scores in these two cases.

One way to deal with this problem is to translate all scores into *standard scores*. One such standard score is the *z*-score. A **z-score** gives the position of a score in relation to the remainder of the distribution, using the standard deviation as the unit of measure. Specifically, a *z*-score gives the number of standard deviations by which the score differs from the mean. It can be found by means of the following formula, where x is the score, $\bar{x}$ is the mean, and s is the standard deviation.

z-score

$$z = \frac{x - \bar{x}}{s}$$

For Wayne's two quizzes, we have the following.

$$z = \frac{20 - 16}{2.2} \doteq 1.81 \quad \text{and} \quad z = \frac{52 - 48}{3.1} \doteq 1.29$$

Therefore, we can say that Wayne did slightly better in relation to the rest of his class on the first quiz than on the second quiz. This is because he is about 1.8 standard deviations above the mean on the first quiz and only about 1.3 standard deviations above the mean on the second test. The use of z-scores thus allows us to compare different test scores.

Consider three student scores on a test with a mean of 71 and a standard deviation of 7. If the student scores are 71, 64, and 85, then the respective z-scores are as follows.

$$z = \frac{71 - 71}{7} = 0$$

$$z = \frac{64 - 71}{7} = {}^{-}1$$

$$z = \frac{85 - 71}{7} = 2$$

Figure 9-28 can be used to interpret the z-scores *if the scores in the class have a mound-shaped distribution.* A z-score of 0 indicates that the score of 71 is the mean. A z-score of $^{-}1$ indicates that the score of 64 is one standard deviation below the mean. Similarly, a z-score of 2 indicates that the score of 85 is two standard deviations above the mean.

FIGURE 9-28

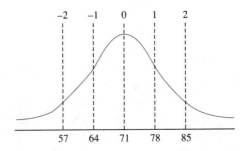

z-scores are useful in comparisons of results from various tests taken by the same reference group. Suppose that a group of students took both an English test and a mathematics test; then a comparison of the z-scores would be reasonable. If a college class and a fourth-grade class took a mathematics test, a comparison of z-scores would not be reasonable, because the reference groups are different.

EXAMPLE 9-11 For a certain group of people, the mean height is 182 cm, with a standard deviation of 11 cm. Juanita's height has a z-score of 1.4. What is her height?

SOLUTION We use the formula for z-scores, $z = \dfrac{x - \bar{x}}{s}$. We know that $z = 1.4$, $\bar{x} = 182$, and $s = 11$.

$$1.4 = \frac{x - 182}{11}$$

$$15.4 = x - 182$$

$$x = 197.4$$

Therefore, Juanita's height is 197.4 cm.

In a large group of scores, such as may be obtained on various standardized tests, we generally expect the scores to approximate a normal curve. Each test may determine a different normal curve; that is, the mean and the standard deviation may be different. However, the shapes are the same. If all scores are translated to z-scores, then with any given z-score we should be able to determine the approximate percentage of people who scored either above or below this z-score. For example, suppose a z-score on a test is 1.5. In determining the percentage of people who scored below this, we know from the graph in Figure 9-27 that the percentage is more than 84% and less than 97.5%. Table 9-17 can be used to find that percentage.

TABLE 9-17

z-score	Percentile	z-score	Percentile	z-score	Percentile
-3.0	0.13	-1.0	15.87	1.0	84.13
-2.9	0.19	-0.9	18.41	1.1	86.43
-2.8	0.26	-0.8	21.19	1.2	88.49
-2.7	0.35	-0.7	24.20	1.3	90.32
-2.6	0.47	-0.6	27.42	1.4	91.92
-2.5	0.62	-0.5	30.85	1.5	93.32
-2.4	0.82	-0.4	34.46	1.6	94.52
-2.3	1.07	-0.3	38.21	1.7	95.54
-2.2	1.39	-0.2	42.07	1.8	96.41
-2.1	1.79	-0.1	46.02	1.9	97.13
-2.0	2.27	0.0	50.00	2.0	97.73
-1.9	2.87	0.1	53.98	2.1	98.21
-1.8	3.59	0.2	57.93	2.2	98.61
-1.7	4.46	0.3	61.79	2.3	98.93
-1.6	5.48	0.4	65.54	2.4	99.18
-1.5	6.68	0.5	69.15	2.5	99.38
-1.4	8.08	0.6	72.58	2.6	99.53
-1.3	9.68	0.7	75.80	2.7	99.65
-1.2	11.51	0.8	78.81	2.8	99.74
-1.1	13.57	0.9	81.59	2.9	99.81
				3.0	99.87

Table 9-17 gives the percentiles corresponding to some z-scores for normal distributions. The percentile corresponding to any observation from a normal distribution can be found by converting the observation to a corresponding z-score and then looking in the table. In our example, we see from Table 9-17 that approximately 93.32% of the population had z-scores below 1.5. More detailed tables show z-scores carried out to more decimal places. Figure 9-29 provides a graphic representation of the type of information given in Table 9-17.

FIGURE 9-29

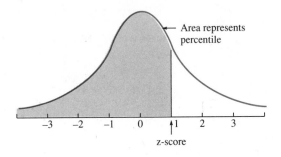

EXAMPLE 9-12   Use Table 9-17 to find the percentage of population below each of the following z-scores.

(a) 2.5   (b) $^-1.4$

SOLUTION   (a) If $z = 2.5$, then from Table 9-17 the percentage of the population below the given z-score is 99.38%.
(b) The z-score of $^-1.4$ has 8.08% of the population below it.

Suppose that the grades on a certain test are normally distributed and we want to grade an exam so that a grade of C is given to all students scoring within 1.2 standard deviations of the mean. What percent of the students should receive Cs? Table 9-17 shows that 88.49% of the population scored less than 1.2 standard deviations above the mean. We know that 50% of the population scored below the mean. Therefore, 88.49% − 50% = 38.49% of the population lies between the mean and 1.2 standard deviations. Because the normal curve is symmetric, we have the same percent on the other side of the mean, for a total of 2 · (38.49%) = 76.98%. Therefore, approximately 77% of the students should receive Cs.

PROBLEM SET 9-3

1. The mean IQ score for 1500 students is 100, with a standard deviation of 15. Assuming the scores have a normal curve:
   (a) How many have an IQ between 85 and 115?
   (b) How many have an IQ between 70 and 130?
   (c) How many have an IQ over 145?

2. Sugar Plops boxes say they hold 16 ounces. To make sure, the manufacturer fills the box to a mean weight of 16.1 ounces, with a standard deviation of 0.05 ounce. If the weights have a normal curve, what percent of the boxes actually contain 16 ounces or more?

3. For certain workers, the mean wage is $5.00 per hour, with a standard deviation of $0.50. If a worker is chosen at random, what is the probability that the worker's wage is between $4.50 and $5.50? Assume a normal distribution of wages.

4. A job-applicant test consisted of three parts: verbal, quantitative, and logical reasoning. The mean and standard deviation for each part are given below.

	Verbal	Quantitative	Logical Reasoning
$\bar{x}$	84	118	14
s	10	18	4

   (a) Holly's scores were 90 on verbal, 133 on quantitative, and 18 on logical reasoning. Determine her z-score for each part.
   (b) Use the answers in (a) to determine each of the following.
      (i) On which part did she perform relatively the highest?
      (ii) On which part did she perform relatively the lowest?
      (iii) To determine an overall composite score, we find the mean of the z-scores. What is Holly's composite score?

5. If a standardized test has a mean of 65 and a standard deviation of 12, find
   (a) Q_2 (b) P_{16} (c) P_{84}

6. In a normal distribution, how are the mean and the median related?

7. Listed in the table is a set of children's weights and the cumulative total of children.
   (a) Find the percentiles for each weight by dividing the cumulative total in each case by the total number of children.
   (b) Sketch the "cumulative" curve, in which weights are marked on a horizontal axis and percentiles are marked on a vertical axis.

(c) Should "cumulative" curves, or percentile curves, always have the shape you found in (b)? Why or why not?

Cumulative Totals and Percentiles of Children's Weights			
Weights	F	Cum	(Cum/n) · 100
90	0	0	
91	1	1	
92	0	1	
93	3	4	
94	2	6	
95	6	12	
96	5	17	
97	7	24	
98	5	29	
99	8	37	
100	2	39	
Total	39 = n		

F = Frequency
Cum = Cumulative total

8. Use Table 9-17 to find the percentages of scores below each of the following z-scores.
   (a) -2.3 (b) 1.7 (c) -2.0

9. Use Table 9-17 to find the percentage of scores between z-scores of 1.4 and 1.5.

10. Jill was 80th in a class of 200, whereas Nathan, who is in the same class, has a percentile rank of 80. Which student has the higher standing in the class?

11. In a class of 25 students, Bill has a rank of 25th. What is his percentile rank?

12. On a certain exam, the mean is 72 and the standard deviation is 9. If a grade of A is given to any student who scores at least two standard deviations above the mean, what is the lowest score that a person could receive and still get an A?

13. Assume that the heights of American women are approximately normally distributed, with a mean of 64 inches and a standard deviation of 2.5 inches. Within what range are the heights of 95% of American women?

14. A tire company tested a particular model of tire and found the tires to be normally distributed with respect to wear. The mean was 28,000 miles, and the standard deviation was 2,500 miles. If 2,000 tires are tested, about how many are likely to wear out before 23,000 miles?

15. A standardized mathematics test was given to 10,000 students, and the scores were normally distributed. The mean was 500, and the standard deviation was 60. If a student scored below 440 points, the student was considered deficient in mathematics. About how many students were rated deficient?

Review Problems

16. On the English 100 exam, the scores were as follows.

43	91	73	65
56	77	84	91
82	65	98	65

(a) Find the mean.
(b) Find the median.
(c) Find the mode.
(d) Find the variance.
(e) Find the standard deviation.
(f) Make a frequency table for the data.
(g) Draw a frequency polygon depicting the data.

17. If the mean of a set of 36 scores is 27 and two additional scores of 40 and 42 are added, what is the new mean?

18. On a certain exam, Tony corrected 10 papers and found the mean for his group to be 70. Alice corrected the remaining 20 papers and found that the mean for her group was 80. What is the mean of the combined group of 30 students?

19. Following are the men's gold-medal times for the 100-meter run in the Olympic games from 1896 to 1964. Construct an ordered two-line stem-and-leaf plot for the data.

Year	Time (in seconds)
1896	12.0
1900	11.0
1904	11.0
1908	10.8
1912	10.8
1920	10.8
1924	10.6
1928	10.8
1932	10.3
1936	10.3
1948	10.3
1952	10.4
1956	10.5
1960	10.2
1964	10.0

*Section 9-4   Abuses of Statistics

Not only are statistics frequently used, they are also frequently abused. Benjamin Disraeli (1804–1881), an English prime minister, once remarked, "There are three kinds of lies: lies, damned lies, and statistics." People sometimes deliberately use statistics to mislead others. In the past, this has been seen in advertising. More often, the misuse of statistics is the result of misinterpreting what the statistics actually mean. For example, if we were told that the average depth of water in a lily pond was 2 feet, most of us would presume that a heron could stand up in any part of the pond. That this is not necessarily the case is seen in the Far Side cartoon, shown on the right.

Now consider an advertisement in which it is reported that, of the people responding to a recent survey, 98% reported that Buffepain is the most effective pain reliever of headaches and arthritis of all those tested. To certify that the statistics are not being misused, the following information also should have been reported.

1. The number of people surveyed
2. The number of people responding
3. How the people participating in the survey were chosen
4. The number and type of pain relievers tested

THE FAR SIDE

Without the information listed, the following situations are possible, all of which could cause the advertisement to be misleading.

1. Suppose that 1,000,000 people nationwide were sent the survey, and only 50 responded. This would mean that there was only a 0.005% response, which would certainly cause us to mistrust the ad.
2. Of the 50 responding in (1), suppose that 49 responses were affirmative. The 98% claim is true, but 999,950 people did not respond at all.
3. Suppose that all the people sent the survey were chosen from a town in which the major industry was the manufacture of Buffepain. It is very doubtful that the survey would represent an unbiased sample.
4. Suppose that only two pain relievers were tested: Buffepain, whose active ingredient is 100% aspirin, and a placebo containing only powdered sugar.

This is not to say that advertisements of this type are all misleading or dishonest but simply that statistics are only as honest as their users. The next time you hear an advertisement that "After using Ultraguard toothpaste, Joseph has 40% fewer cavities," you might ask whether or not Joseph has 40% fewer teeth than an average person.

A different type of misuse of statistics involves graphs. Among the things to look for in a graph are the following. If they are not there, then the graph may be misleading.

1. Title
2. Labels on both axes of a line or bar chart and on all sections of a pie chart
3. Source of the data
4. Key in a pictograph
5. Uniform size of symbols in a pictograph
6. Scale—does it start with zero? If not, is there a break shown?
7. Scale—are the numbers evenly spaced?

As an example of a misleading use of graphs, consider how they can be used to distort data or exaggerate certain pieces of information. A frequency polygon, histogram, or bar graph can be altered by changing the scale of the graph. For example, consider the data in Table 9-18 for the number of graduates from a community college for the years 1986 to 1990.

TABLE 9-18

Year	1986	1987	1988	1989	1990
Number of graduates	140	180	200	210	160

The two graphs in Figure 9-30(a) and (b) represent the same data, but different scales are used in each. The statistics presented are the same, but these two graphs do not convey the same psychological message. Notice that, in Figure 9-30(b), the years on the horizontal axis of the graph are spread out and the numbers on the vertical axis are condensed. Both of these changes minimize the variability of the data. A college administrator might use the graph in Figure 9-30(b) to convince people that the college was not in serious enrollment trouble.

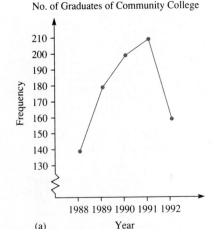

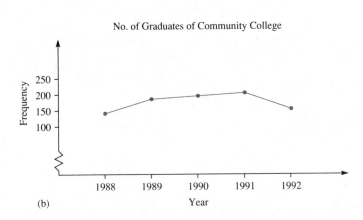

(a)

(b)

FIGURE 9-30

Other graphs can also be misleading. Suppose, for example, that the number of boxes of cereal sold by Sugar Plops last year was 2 million and the number of boxes of cereal sold by Korn Krisps was 8 million. The Korn Krisps executives prepared the graph in Figure 9-31 to demonstrate the data. The Sugar Plops people objected. Do you see why?

FIGURE 9-31

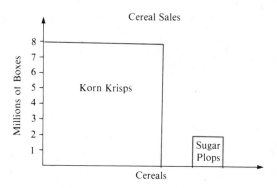

The graph in Figure 9-31 clearly distorts the data, since the figure for Korn Krisps is both 4 times as high and 4 times as wide as the bar for Sugar Plops. Thus, the area representing Korn Krisps is 16 times the area representing Sugar Plops, rather than 4 times the area, as would be justified by the original data.

Other ways to distort bar graphs include omitting the scales, as in Figure 9-32(a). The scale is given in Figure 9-32(b).

FIGURE 9-32

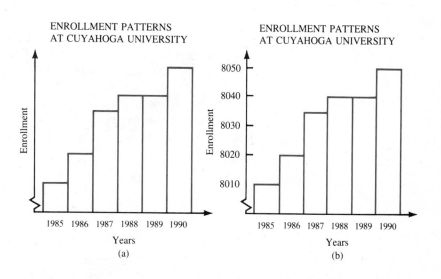

USE OF FORESTS

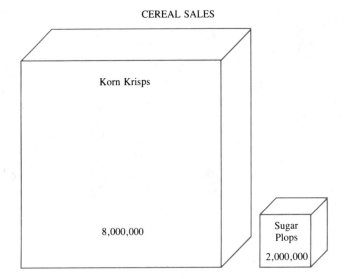

FIGURE 9-33

Circle graphs easily become distorted when attempts are made to depict them as three-dimensional. Many graphs of this type do not acknowledge either the variable thickness of the depiction or the distortion due to perspective. Observe that the 27% sector pictured in Figure 9-33 looks far greater than the 23% sector, although they should be very nearly the same size.

Figure 9-34 shows how the comparison of Sugar Plops and Korn Krisps cereals from Figure 9-31 might look if the figures were made three-dimensional. The figure for Korn Krisps has a volume 64 times the volume of the Sugar Plops figure.

CEREAL SALES

Korn Krisps

8,000,000

Sugar Plops

2,000,000

FIGURE 9-34

The final examples we discuss of the misuses of statistics involve misleading uses of mean, median, and mode. All these are "averages" and may be used to suit a person's purposes. As discussed in Section 9-2 in the example involving the teachers Smith, Jones, and Leed, each teacher had reported that his or her class had done better than the other two. Each of the teachers was using a different number to represent the test scores.

The use of statistics in this way is often misleading. For example, college administrators wishing to portray to prospective employees a rosy salary picture may find a mean salary of $38,000 for ranked professors along with deans, vice-presidents, and presidents in the schedule of salaries. At the same time, a faculty union or teachers' group that is bargaining for faculty salaries may include part-time employees and instructors along with ranked professors and may exclude all administration personnel in order to present a mean salary of $29,000 at the bargaining table. The important thing to watch for when a mean is reported is disparate cases in the reference group. If the sample is small, then a few extremely high or low scores can have a great influence on the mean.

If the median is being used as the average, then suppose that Figure 9-35 shows the salaries of both administrators and faculty members at the college. The median in this case might be $33,500, which is representative of neither major group of employees. The bimodal distribution allows the median to be nonrepresentative of the distribution.

FIGURE 9-35

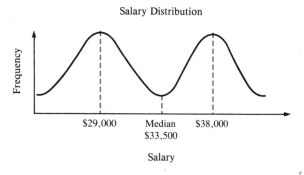

Salary Distribution

To conclude the comments on the misuse of statistics, consider this quote from Darrell Huff's book *How to Lie with Statistics* (p. 8):

So it is with much that you read and hear. Averages and relationships and trends and graphs are not always what they seem. There may be more in them than meets the eye, and there may be a great deal less.

The secret language of statistics, so appealing in a fact-minded culture, is employed to sensationalize, inflate, confuse, and oversimplify. Statistical methods and statistical terms are necessary in reporting the mass data of social and economic trends, business conditions, "opinion" polls, census. But without writers who use the words with honesty and understanding and readers who know what they mean, the result can be semantic "nonsense."

PROBLEM SET 9-4

1. Write a list of scores for which the mean and the median are not representative of the list.

2. The city of Podunk advertised that its temperature was the ideal temperature in the country because its mean temperature was 25°C. What possible misconceptions could people draw from this advertisement?

3. Jenny averaged 70 on her quizzes during the first part of the quarter and 80 on her quizzes during the second part of the quarter. When she found out that her final average for the quarter was not 75, she went to argue with her teacher. Give a possible explanation for Jenny's misunderstanding.

4. Suppose that the following circle graphs are used to illustrate the fact that the number of elementary teaching majors at teachers' colleges has doubled between 1980 and 1990, while the percentage of male elementary teaching majors has stayed the same. What is misleading about the way the graphs are constructed?

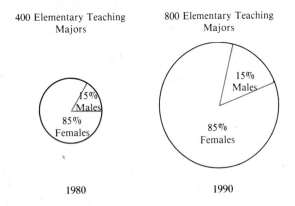

400 Elementary Teaching Majors
15% Males
85% Females
1980

800 Elementary Teaching Majors
15% Males
85% Females
1990

5. What is wrong with the line graph shown?

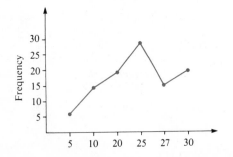

6. Make up three distributions, in each of which one of the following is not representative of the group, but the other two are.
(a) Mean   (b) Median   (c) Mode

7. Can you draw any valid conclusions about a set of data in which the mean is less than the median?

8. A student read that nine out of ten pickup trucks sold in the last 10 years are still on the road. She concluded that the average life of a pickup is around 10 years. Is she correct?

9. General Cooster once asked a person by the side of a river if it was too deep to ride his horse across. The person responded that the average depth was 2 feet. If General Cooster rode out across the river, what assumptions did he make on the basis of the person's information?

10. Doug's Dog Food Company wanted to impress the public with the magnitude of the company's growth. Sales of Doug's Dog Food had doubled from 1989 to 1990, so the company displayed the following graph, in which the radius of the base and the height of the 1990 can are double those of the 1989 can. What does the graph really show with respect to the growth of the company? (*Hint:* The volume of a cylinder is given by $V = \pi r^2 h$, where r is the radius of the base and h is the height.)

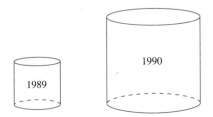

1989

1990

DOUG'S DOG FOOD SALES

SOLUTION TO THE PRELIMINARY PROBLEM

Understanding the Problem. With 7 people in the room, the mean age was 21. The arrival of Jeff, age 29, increased the mean age to 22. We are to determine if the arrival of Mary, also age 29, increased the mean age to 23. We are also to determine Grandpa Elmer's age if his age increased the mean age of the 10 people in the room to 30.

Devising a Plan Let n be the sum of the ages of the first 7 people in the room. Then because 21 is the mean, we have $n/7 = 21$, and therefore $n = 7 \cdot 21$, or 147. When Jeff, age 29, arrived, there were 8 people in the room. The mean increased to 22 because $(147 + 29)/8 = 22$.

    The sum of the ages of the 8 people in the room at that point was $147 + 29$, or 176. To find the effect of Mary's age on the mean, we add her age, 29, to the sum of the other ages in the room, 176, and divide by 9, the number of people in the room. If we continue in this manner, we can also find Grandpa Elmer's age.

Carrying Out the Plan. The mean age of the 9 people after Mary entered is given by

$$\frac{176 + 29}{9} = \frac{205}{9} \doteq 22.8$$

Therefore, Mary's age increased the mean age to approximately 22.8, not to 23.

    The sum of the ages of the 9 people then in the room was $176 + 29$, or 205 years. When Elmer entered the room, there were 10 people in the room, and the mean age became 30. If we denote Elmer's age by e, we have

$$\frac{205 + e}{10} = 30$$
$$205 + e = 300$$
$$e = 95$$

Therefore, Grandpa Elmer is 95 years old on this birthday.

Looking Back. We can check that $(7 \cdot 21 + 2 \cdot 29 + 95)/10 = 30$. The problem can be varied in many different ways. For example, suppose that there are 8 people with a mean age of 21 in the room, then 2 people of age 30 enter the room, and finally Elmer enters the room. How old is Elmer if the mean age at this point is 30?

QUESTIONS FROM THE CLASSROOM

1. A student asks, "If the average income of each of 10 people is $10,000 and one person gets a raise of $10,000, is the median, the mean, or the mode changed and, if so, by how much?"

2. A student asks for an example of when the mode is the best average. What is your response?

3. A student says that a stem-and-leaf plot is always the best way to present data. How do you respond?

4. Suppose that the class takes a test and the following averages are obtained: mean, 80; median, 90; mode, 70. Tom, who scored 80, would like to know if he did better than half the class. What is your response?

5. A student wants to know the advantages of presenting data in graphic form rather than in tabular form. What is your response? What are the disadvantages?

6. A student asks if it is possible to find the mode for data in a grouped frequency table. What is your response?

7. A student asks if she can draw any conclusions about a set of data if she knows that the mean for the data is less than the median. How do you answer?

8. A student asks if it is possible to have a standard deviation of ⁻5. How do you respond?

9. Mel's mean on 10 tests for the quarter was 89. He complained to the teacher that he should be given an A because he missed the cutoff of 90 by only a single point. Did he really miss an A by only a single point?

CHAPTER OUTLINE

I. Descriptive statistics
   A. **Descriptive statistics** is the science of organizing and summarizing numerical data.
   B. Information can be summarized in each of the following forms.
      1. **Line plots**
      2. **Stem-and-leaf plots**
      3. **Frequency tables**
      4. **Histograms** or **bar graphs**
      5. **Frequency polygons** or **line graphs**
      6. **Pictographs**
      7. **Circle graphs** or **pie charts**
      8. **Box plots**

II. Numbers used to describe data
   A. The **mean** of n given numbers is the sum of the numbers divided by n.
   B. The **median** of a set of numbers is the middle number if the numbers are arranged in numerical order; if there is no middle number, the median is the mean of the two middle numbers.
   C. The **mode** of a set of numbers is the number or numbers that occur most frequently in the set.

III. Measures of variation.
   A. The **range** is the difference between the greatest and least numbers in the set.
   B. The **variance** is found by subtracting the mean from each value, squaring each of these differences, finding the sum of these squares, and dividing by n, where n is the number of observations.
   C. The **standard deviation** is equal to the square root of the variance.

D. **Box plots** focus attention on the median, the quartiles, and the extremes and invite comparisons among them.
   1. The **lower quartile** is the median of the subset of data less than the median of all the values in the data set.
   2. The **upper quartile** is the median of the subset of data greater than the median of all the values in the data set.
   3. The **interquartile range** (IQR) is calculated as the difference between the upper quartile and the lower quartile.
   4. An **outlier** is any value more than 1.5 IQR above the upper quartile or more than 1.5 IQR below the lower quartile.

*E. In a **normal curve,** 68% of the values are within one standard deviation of the mean, 95% are within two standard deviations of the mean, and 99.8% are within three standard deviations of the mean.

*F. A **z-score** gives the position of a score in relation to the remainder of the distribution, using the standard deviation as the unit of measure.

$$z = \frac{x - \overline{x}}{s}$$

*G. The **rth percentile,** denoted by P_r, is a score such that r percent of the scores are less than P_r.

*H. **Deciles** are points that divide a distribution into ten equally spaced sections. $D_1 = P_{10}$, $D_2 = P_{20}$, ..., $D_9 = P_{90}$.

*I. **Quartiles** are points that divide a distribution into quarters. $Q_1 = P_{25}$, $Q_2 = P_{50}$, and $Q_3 = P_{75}$.

CHAPTER TEST

1. Suppose that you read that "the average family in Rattlesnake Gulch has 2.41 children." What average is being used to describe the data? Explain your answer. Suppose that the sentence had said 2.5; then what are the possibilities?

2. At Bug's Bar-B-Q restaurant, the average weekly wage for full-time workers is $150. If there are ten part-time employees whose average weekly salary is $50 and the total weekly payroll is $3950, how many full-time employees are there?

3. Find the mean, the median, and the mode for each of the following groups of data.
   (a) 10, 50, 30, 40, 10, 60, 10
   (b) 5, 8, 6, 3, 5, 4, 3, 6, 1, 9

4. Find the range, variance, and standard deviation for each set of scores in Problem 3.

5. The masses, in kilograms, of children in Ms. Rider's class follows.

40	49	43	48
42	41	42	39
46	42	49	39
47	49	44	42
41	40	45	43

   (a) Make a line plot for the data.
   (b) Make an ordered two-line stem-and-leaf plot for the data.
   (c) Make a frequency table for the data.
   (d) Make a bar graph of the data.

6. The grades on a test for 30 students follow.

96	73	61	76	77	84
78	98	98	80	67	82
61	75	79	90	73	80
85	63	86	100	94	77
86	84	91	62	77	64

   (a) Make a grouped frequency table for these scores, using four classes and starting the first class at 61.
   (b) Draw a histogram of the grouped data.
   (c) Draw a frequency polygon of the data.

7. The budget for the Wegetem Crime Company is $2,000,000. If $600,000 is spent on bribes, $400,000 is spent for legal fees, $300,000 for bail money, $300,000 for contracts, and $400,000 for public relations, draw a circle graph to indicate how the company spends its money.

8. What, if anything, is wrong with the following bar graph?

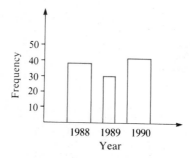

9. The mean salary of 24 people is $9000. How much will one additional salary of $80,000 increase the mean salary?

10. Holly drove 90 miles at a mean speed of 30 mph. At what speed would she have to make the return trip in order to achieve a mean speed of 50 mph for the entire trip?

11. The life expectancies at birth for males and females are given in the following table.
    (a) Draw back-to-back ordered stem-and-leaf plots to compare the data.
    (b) Draw box plots to compare the data.

Year	Male	Female
1970	67.1	74.7
1971	67.4	75.0
1972	67.4	75.1
1973	67.6	75.3
1974	68.2	75.9
1975	68.8	76.6
1976	69.1	76.8
1977	69.5	77.2
1978	69.6	77.3
1979	70.0	77.8
1980	70.0	77.5
1981	70.4	77.8
1982	70.9	78.1
1983	71.0	78.1
1984	71.2	78.2
1985	71.2	78.2
1986	71.3	78.3

12. Larry and Moe both took the same courses last quarter. Each had bet that he would receive the better grades. Their courses and grades are as follows.

Courses	Larry's Grades	Moe's Grades
Math (4 credits)	A	C
Chemistry (4 credits)	A	C
English (3 credits)	B	B
Psychology (3 credits)	C	A
Tennis (1 credit)	C	A

Moe claimed that the results constituted a tie, since both received 2 As, 1 B, and 2 Cs. Larry said that he won the bet because he had the higher grade-point average for the quarter. Who is correct? (Allow 4 points for an A, 3 points for a B, 2 points for a C, 1 point for a D, and 0 points for an F.)

13. Following are the lengths in yards of the 9 holes of the University Golf Course.

$$
\begin{array}{ccc}
160 & 360 & 330 \\
350 & 180 & 460 \\
480 & 450 & 380
\end{array}
$$

Find each of the following measures with respect to the lengths of the holes.
(a) Median   (b) Mode   (c) Mean
(d) Standard deviation

14. The speeds in mph of 30 cars were checked by radar. The data are as follows.

62 67 69 72 75 60 58 86 74 68 56 67 82 88 90
54 67 65 64 68 74 65 58 75 67 65 66 64 45 64

(a) Find the median.
(b) Find the upper and lower quartiles.
(c) Draw a box plot for the data, and indicate outliers (if any exist) with asterisks.
(d) What percent of the scores is in the interquartile range?
(e) If every person driving faster than 70 received a ticket, what percent of the drivers received speeding tickets?
(f) Is the median in the center of the box? Why or why not?

*15. The heights of 1,000 girls at East High School were measured, and the mean was found to be 64 inches, with a standard deviation of 2 inches. If the heights are approximately normally distributed, about how many of the girls are
(a) Over 68 inches tall
(b) Between 60 and 64 inches tall

*16. A standardized test has a mean of 600 and a standard deviation of 75. If 1,000 students took the test and their scores approximated a normal curve, how many scored between 600 and 750?

*17. Use the information in Problem 16 to find:
(a) P_{16} (b) D_5 (c) P_{84}

*18. If a student scored 725 on the test in problem 16, what is his or her z-score?

*19. Find the percentile for a score of 79 in the data of Problem 6.

*20. The Nielsen Television Index rating of 30 means that an estimated 30% of American televisions are tuned to the show with that rating. The ratings are based on the preferences of a scientifically selected sample of 1200 homes.
(a) Discuss possible ways in which viewers could bias this sample.
(b) How could networks attempt to bias the results?

*21. List and give examples of several ways to misuse statistics graphically.

Introductory Geometry

PRELIMINARY PROBLEM

In a connect-the-dots drawing of points around a circle, as shown, Eli decided to draw all possible segments connecting the 25 distinct points. How many segments did he draw?

Introduction

The word *geometry* comes from two Greek words, *ge* and *metria*, which might literally be translated as "earth measuring." Over the years, geometry has been adapted to serve as the first mathematics course in which students encounter logic as a deductive way to develop theorems—mathematical statements that can be proved. The proofs are based on *undefined terms* such as set, point, line, and plane and a list of basic assumptions called *axioms* or *postulates* that are considered to be true. This approach is often referred to as the *axiomatic approach.* The use of undefined terms is necessary in mathematics. Otherwise, one runs the risk of using circular definitions, as is often the case in a dictionary. For example, the mathematical definition of *line* in one dictionary is "the path of a moving point." However, the definition of *path* is "a line of movement." The axiomatic approach, developed by Euclid of Alexandria in *The Elements,* has been used for over 2,000 years as the basis of secondary-school geometry.

H I S T O R I C A L   N O T E

Euclid of Alexandria (ca. 300 B.C.) was a teacher at the Museum, a school formed by Ptolemy I of Egypt. Little is known of his life, although legend has it that he was a kindly gentleman who studied geometry for its beauty and logic. When asked by a student what use there was in the study of geometry, he requested that the student be given some money, "since he needs make gain of what he learns." Euclid is best known for *The Elements,* a work so systematic and encompassing that many earlier mathematical works were simply discarded and thus lost to all future generations. *The Elements* included not only geometry but arithmetic and topics in algebra.

Elementary-school geometry has not been as standardized as secondary-school geometry. Today, there is very little agreement worldwide about exactly what topics should be covered. According to the *Standards,* "*Students [in grades 5–8] should learn to use correct vocabulary, including common words like and, or, all, some, always, never, and if—then to reason, as well as words like parallel, perpendicular, and similar to describe.*" The *Standards* further suggest that learning of such vocabulary should be done in an investigative manner. Much research suggests that children may learn geometry along the lines of a structure for reasoning developed by Dina and Pierre van Hiele of the Netherlands in the 1950s. In the geometry chapters' Laboratory Activities, exercises demonstrating the van Hiele levels of learning are presented. Developing geometry totally along the lines of the van Hiele structure is beyond the scope of this text.

H I S T O R I C A L   N O T E

Dina van Hiele-Geldof and Pierre van Hiele were high school teachers in the Netherlands who were disturbed by the way their students learned geometry. In their 1957 and 1959 dissertations, respectively, at the University of Utrecht, they devised a structure for helping students develop insight into reasoning in geometry. The following levels were developed by Dina, who died shortly after completing her dissertation; the levels were further developed and written about by Pierre, and they were modified by Alan Hoffer in 1981.

Level 0: Students recognize figures by their global appearance. They say such words as *triangle* and *square* but do not recognize properties of these figures.

Level 1: Students analyze component parts of figures but do not interrelate figures and properties. They may know that all sides of a square are congruent and that the diagonals of a rhombus are perpendicular bisectors of each other.

Level 2: Students may relate figures and their properties, but they do not organize sequences of statements to justify their observations. They may know that all squares are rhombuses but may not be able to state why in an organized way.

Level 3: Students at this level can reason deductively within the mathematical system to justify their observations.

Level 4: Students at this level can compare different axiom systems with a high degree of rigor, even without concrete models.

It is equally important to recognize the sequence of phases the van Hieles specified to help students move from one level of learning to another. These phases are as follows:

Phase 1. *Inquiry:* Teachers and students engage in dialogue about the topic to be studied. Use of vocabulary is extremely important at this stage.

Phase 2. *Directed orientation:* Teachers sequence activities to be explored by students in such a way that students become familiar with the structures involved.

Phase 3. *Expliciting:* With little help, students build on experiences and refine their vocabulary to discuss the relations of the structures.

Phase 4. *Free orientation:* Students encounter multistep tasks to be completed in different ways. They gain experience in resolving tasks on their own and make explicit many relations among the objects of the structures being studied.

Phase 5. *Integration:* Students are able to internalize and unify relations into a new body of thought. Teachers help by giving global surveys of what students already know.

In this chapter, we consider some basic notions of Euclidean geometry and elementary *topology*. Generally we approach these topics through the use of informal methods and intuition, but at times we use deductive methods to consider specific topics in depth.

Section 10-1 Basic Notions

Points, lines, and planes are basic notions in geometry. However, these words are commonly used in daily life to represent physical objects. For example, the tip of a compass, the sharpened end of a pencil, the pointed end of a safety pin, and the tip of the Washington Monument are all thought of as points.

Points

point We represent a **point** on paper as a dot made by a pencil, and we label it with a capital letter, as in Figure 10-1.

FIGURE 10-1

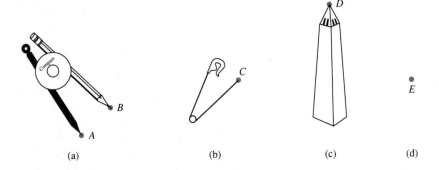

(a)   (b)   (c)   (d)

Lines

line A "straight" highway center line as in Figure 10-2(a) is considered a line in the everyday world, but it is viewed as only a representation of part of a line in mathematics. In Euclidean geometry, a **line** extends indefinitely in both directions and is considered to be "straight." We represent a line by a streak of pencil lead or ink drawn with the aid of a pencil or pen and a straightedge, as in Figure 10-2(b). Arrowheads indicate the direction of the line.

FIGURE 10-2

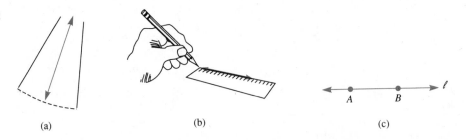

(a)   (b)   (c)

To refer to a line, we use either a single lowercase letter or two capital letters representing two dots (points) on the line. Line AB, written as $\overleftrightarrow{AB}$ or ℓ, is pictured in Figure 10-2(c).

A line is an infinite set of points, but a line is determined by any two points. Thus, points A and B are elements of $\overleftrightarrow{AB}$, and we write $A \in \overleftrightarrow{AB}$ and $B \in \overleftrightarrow{AB}$.

When discussing situations involving points and lines, we also rely on undefined relations as "contains," "belongs to," "is on," and "is between." In Figure 10-3, for example, line ℓ contains points A, B, and C but does not contain point D. Also, points A, B, and C belong to line ℓ, but point D does *collinear* not. Similarly, points A, B, and C are on line ℓ, or are **collinear**, but points B, C, and D are *noncollinear*. If three collinear points A, B, and C are arranged as in Figure 10-3, we say that B is *between* A and C. Point D is not between B and C, because B, D, and C are noncollinear. (Betweenness as a characteristic of points is discussed in more detail when distance is introduced.)

FIGURE 10-3

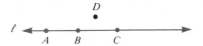

Certain subsets of a line are given separate names and symbols. Several of these are defined and illustrated in Table 10-1, with symbols shown beneath the appropriate illustration.

TABLE 10-1

Definition	Illustration
A **line segment,** or **segment,** is a subset of a line that contains two points of the line and all points between those two points.	A B $\overline{AB}$ or $\overline{BA}$
A **half-line** is a subset of a line that contains all points on the line on one side of a given point (excluding the point itself).	A B $\overrightarrow{AB}$
A **ray** is a subset of a line that contains a point and all points on the line on one side of the point.	A B $\overrightarrow{AB}$

● **R E M A R K**

$\overrightarrow{AB} \neq \overrightarrow{BA}$ because they do not have the same endpoint. They have only $\overline{AB}$ in common. Likewise, $\overset{\circ\to}{AB} \neq \overset{\circ\to}{BA}$. However, $\overline{AB} = \overline{BA}$ and $\overleftrightarrow{AB} = \overleftrightarrow{BA}$.

It is sometimes convenient to refer to other subsets of a line. A *half-open* (or *half-closed*) segment is a segment without one endpoint, symbolized, for example, by $\overline{AB}$; an open segment is a segment without either endpoint, symbolized, for example, by $\overline{AB}$. In general, the word *segment,* when used without a qualifying adjective, refers to a *closed segment*—that is, to a segment containing both endpoints.

A point separates a line into three subsets: two half-lines and the point itself. An example is shown in Figure 10-4, where point M separates line ℓ into half-lines $\overrightarrow{MN}$ and $\overrightarrow{MO}$ and point M itself.

FIGURE 10-4

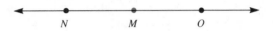

Planes

plane
A tabletop, a floor, a ceiling, a wall, or any other smooth level surface is commonly thought of as a plane. However, each of these is only part of a plane, because a plane extends indefinitely in two dimensions. A **plane** is usually represented by a parallelogram, as pictured in Figure 10-5(c), and it is commonly denoted by a lowercase Greek letter, such as alpha (α), beta (β), or gamma (γ) or by capital letters representing three noncollinear points in the plane, such as ABC. Three noncollinear points uniquely determine a plane, just as two points uniquely determine a line. That is why $\overleftrightarrow{AB}$ is used for a line and ABC is used for a plane.

FIGURE 10-5

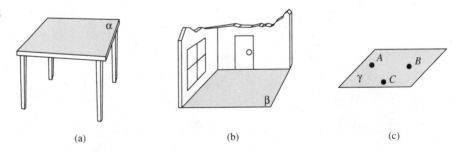

(a) (b) (c)

A plane contains infinitely many points. Because a plane is a set of points, we say that points A, B, and C belong to plane ABC, or are contained in plane ABC, or lie in plane ABC. Points that belong to the same plane are

coplanar points

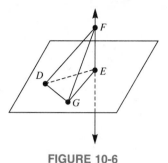

FIGURE 10-6

coplanar points. Figure 10-6 shows coplanar points *D*, *G*, and *E*; *D*, *G*, *E*, and *F* are noncoplanar points, because no single plane contains all four points. Points are *noncoplanar* if and only if no one plane can contain them.

Similarly, we can define *coplanar* and *noncoplanar lines.* In Figure 10-6, lines $\overleftrightarrow{DE}$ and $\overleftrightarrow{GE}$ are coplanar, whereas lines $\overleftrightarrow{GF}$ and $\overleftrightarrow{DE}$ are noncoplanar.

Definitions and illustrations of various types of lines are given in Table 10-2. Exercises using these definitions are given in the problem set.

Definition	Illustration
Two coplanar lines *m* and *n* are called **intersecting lines** if and only if they have exactly one point in common.	
Concurrent lines are lines that contain the same point. Concurrent lines may be either coplanar or noncoplanar.	
Two coplanar lines *m* and *n* that have no points in common are called **parallel lines.**	
Two lines that cannot be contained in the same plane are called **skew lines.** $\overleftrightarrow{AB}$ and $\overleftrightarrow{CD}$ are skew lines.	

TABLE 10-2

• R E M A R K

Skew lines cannot intersect. However, skew lines are not parallel, because no single plane can contain them.

Other Relations Among Points, Lines, and Planes

The model of two walls intersecting in a line suggests that, if two distinct planes have any points in common, then that set of points is a line, as in Figure 10-7(a). If we consider the spine of a book to be a line and each page to be a plane, as in Figure 10-7(b), we see that infinitely many planes can contain a given line. However, it is surprising to many students that three

FIGURE 10-7

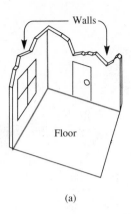

Walls

Floor

(a)

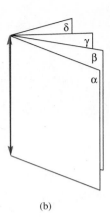

δ

γ

β

α

(b)

distinct planes may have a line in common, no common points, or just a single common point. In Figure 10-7(a), we see the walls and the floor (three distinct planes) intersecting at a single point, the corner. As we consider the drawings in Figure 10-7, other questions about the relations among points and lines may come to mind.

1. How many different lines in a plane can be drawn through two distinct points?
2. If lines were defined as lines of longitude on a globe, would the answer to Question 1 be different? Would it matter where the two points were located?
3. Why do surveyors and camera buffs include a tripod in their equipment?
4. What is the minimum number of points needed to determine a level surface or a plane?

The following set of properties summarizes some common notions about points, lines, and planes.

● **PROPERTIES OF POINTS, LINES, AND PLANES**
1. Exactly one line contains any two distinct points.
2. Exactly one plane contains any three distinct noncollinear points.
3. If two points lie in a plane, then the line containing the points lies in the plane.
4. If two distinct planes intersect, then their intersection is a line.

Property 2 gives one method of determining a plane, and implicit in this property are several other ways of determining a plane. Some of these are listed next and are illustrated in terms of the cube in Figure 10-8.

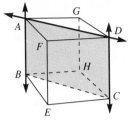

FIGURE 10-8

1. A line and a point not on the line determine a plane. (*Example:* $\overleftrightarrow{AB}$ and point C determine plane ABC.)
2. Two parallel lines determine a plane. (*Example:* $\overleftrightarrow{AB}$ and $\overleftrightarrow{CD}$ determine plane ABC.)
3. Two intersecting lines determine a plane. (*Example:* $\overleftrightarrow{AB}$ and $\overleftrightarrow{DA}$ determine plane ABD.)

• R E M A R K

Unless they are parallel, two nonintersecting lines do not determine a plane. For example, in Figure 10-8, $\overleftrightarrow{AB}$ and $\overleftrightarrow{GD}$ cannot be placed in the same plane. They are skew lines.

parallel planes

Two distinct planes either intersect in a line or are parallel. In Figure 10-9(a), the planes are **parallel** ($\alpha \| \beta$); that is, they have no points in common. Figure 10-9(b) shows two planes that intersect in $\overleftrightarrow{AB}$.

FIGURE 10-9

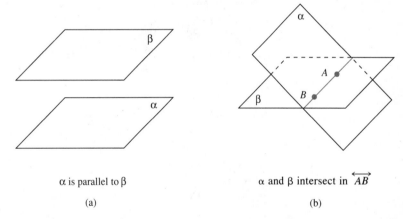

α is parallel to β

(a)

α and β intersect in $\overleftrightarrow{AB}$

(b)

A line and a plane can be related in one of three possible ways. If a line and a plane have no points in common, the line is parallel to the plane, as in Figure 10-10(a). If two points of a line are in the plane, then the entire line containing the points is contained in the plane, as in Figure 10-10(b). If a line intersects a plane but is not contained in the plane, it intersects the plane at only one point, as in Figure 10-10(c).

FIGURE 10-10

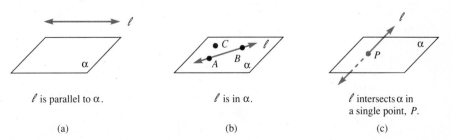

ℓ is parallel to α.

(a)

ℓ is in α.

(b)

ℓ intersects α in a single point, P.

(c)

Just as a point separates a line into two half-lines and the point itself, a line separates a plane into two half-planes and the line itself. In Figure 10-10(b), line ℓ separates plane *ABC* into two half-planes. A half-plane may be specified by the line determining the half-plane and one point in the half-plane, such as the half-plane determined by $\overleftrightarrow{AB}$ and containing point *C* in Figure 10-10(b). Line $\overleftrightarrow{AB}$ itself is not considered to be in either half-plane. A line and the two half-planes determined by the line are three disjoint subsets of a plane. Points, lines, and planes are all subsets of space. In three *space* dimensions, **space** is the set of all points. A plane separates space into two half-spaces. A plane and the two half-spaces determined by the plane are three disjoint subsets of space. The notion of a half-plane might be modeled by one side of a road on a plain. Can you think of a model for a half-space?

Angles

Euclid claimed that "A plane angle is the inclination of one another of two lines in a plane which meet one another and do not lie in a straight line." *angle* The more recent definition of an **angle** as the union of two rays with a common endpoint, as illustrated in Figure 10-11(a), is the one used in this text. (Also, in this text *angle* is used to mean a planar angle or an angle in a plane, as opposed to a dihedral angle, which is discussed later.)

FIGURE 10-11

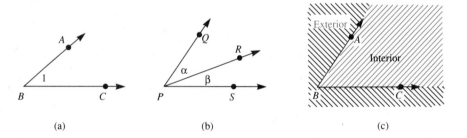

(a)   (b)   (c)

sides   The rays of an angle are called the **sides** of the angle, and the common *vertex* endpoint is called the **vertex** of the angle. An angle can be named by three different points: the vertex and a point on each ray, with the vertex always listed between the other two points. Thus, the angle in Figure 10-11(a) may be named $\angle CBA$ or $\angle ABC$. The latter is read "angle *ABC*." When there is no risk of confusion, it is customary simply to name an angle by its vertex, by a number, or (occasionally) by a lowercase Greek letter. The angle in Figure 10-11(a) can therefore be named $\angle B$ or $\angle 1$. In Figure 10-11(b), however, more than one angle has vertex *P*, namely, $\angle QPR$, $\angle RPS$, and $\angle QPS$. Thus, the notation $\angle P$ is inadequate for naming any one of the angles α, β, or $\angle QPS$.

In Figure 10-11(c), $\angle B$ separates the plane into three disjoint sets, the interior of the angle, the angle itself, and the exterior of the angle. Using the concept of the interior of an angle, we define adjacent angles, such as $\angle QPR$

adjacent angles

and $\angle RPS$ in Figure 10-11(b), as follows: **Adjacent angles** are angles that share a common vertex and a common side and have nonoverlapping interiors.

Angle Measurement

Angles are classified according to their measure. The attribute measured is the amount of "opening" between the two rays or the amount of "turning" that occurs as one of the rays moves from a position coinciding with the first ray to its fixed position as the second ray. A unit commonly used for

degree

measuring angles is the **degree.** A complete rotation about a point is an opening of 360°. One degree is then $\frac{1}{360}$ of a complete rotation.

Figure 10-12 shows that $\angle BAC$ has a measure of 30 degrees, written

protractor
minutes
seconds

$m(\angle BAC) = 30°$. The measuring device pictured is a **protractor.** A degree is subdivided into 60 equal parts called **minutes,** and each minute is further subdivided into 60 equal parts called **seconds.** The measurement 29 degrees, 47 minutes, 13 seconds is written 29°47′13″.

FIGURE 10-12

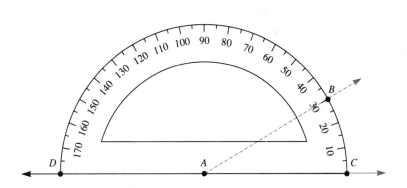

H I S T O R I C A L   N O T E

In 1634, Pierre Herigone used a symbol for an angle. It was not until 1923 that the Mathematical Association of America recommended $\angle$ as the standard symbol for angle in the United States. The use of 360° to measure angles seems to date to the Babylonian culture (4000–3000 B.C.), with minutes and seconds coming from Latin translations of Arabic translations of Babylonian sexagesimal (base 60) fractions.

EXAMPLE 10-1 (a) In Figure 10-13, find the measure of $\angle BAC$ if $m(\angle 1) = 47°45'$ and $m(\angle 2) = 27°58'$.

FIGURE 10-13

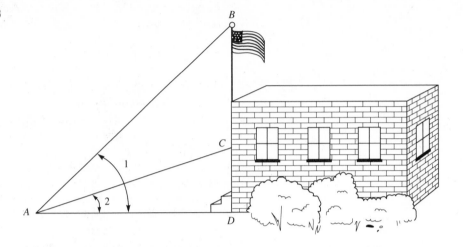

(b) Express $47°45'$ as a number of degrees.

SOLUTION (a) $m(\angle BAC) = 47°45' - 27°58'$
$= 46°(60 + 45)' - 27°58'$
$= 46°105' - 27°58'$
$= (46 - 27)° + (105 - 58)'$
$= 19°47'$

(b) $47°45' = 47\dfrac{45°}{60} = 47.75°$

• **R E M A R K**
In the solution of Example 10-1(a), we used the fact that $m(\angle BAC) = m(\angle 1) - m(\angle 2)$. In general, if C is in the interior of $\angle BAD$, then $m(\angle BAD) = m(\angle BAC) + m(\angle DAC)$. This implies $m(\angle BAD) - m(\angle BAC) = m(\angle DAC)$.

Types of Angles

Different types of angles can be seen by paperfolding. Consider the folds shown in Figure 10-14(a) and (b). A piece of paper is folded in half and then reopened. If any point on the fold line labeled ℓ is chosen as the vertex, then the measure of the angle pictured is 180°. If the paper is refolded and folded once more, as in Figure 10-14(c), and then is reopened, as in Figure 10-14(d), four angles of the same size are created. Each angle has measure

FIGURE 10-14

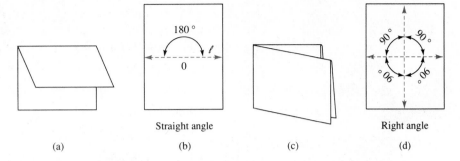

(a)   (b)   (c)   (d)

90°. If the paper is folded as shown in Figure 10-15 and reopened, then angles α and β are formed, with measures that are less than 90° and greater than 90°, respectively. (Note that β has measure less than 180°.)

FIGURE 10-15

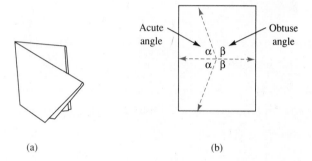

(a)   (b)

The different types of planar angles we have just discovered are listed next, along with their definitions.

straight angle   1. If the degree measure of an angle is 180°, the angle is a **straight angle.**

right angle   2. If the degree measure of an angle is 90°, the angle is a **right angle.**

   3. If the degree measure of an angle is greater than 0° and less than 90°, the

acute angle   angle is an **acute angle.**

   4. If the degree measure of an angle is greater than 90° and less than 180°,

obtuse angle   the angle is an **obtuse angle.**

Perpendicular Lines

perpendicular lines   When two lines intersect so that the angles formed are right angles, as in Figure 10-16, the lines are **perpendicular lines.** In Figure 10-16, lines m and n are perpendicular, and we write $m \perp n$. (The symbol ⌐ is used to indicate *perpendicular*

a right angle.) Two intersecting segments, two intersecting rays, or a segment and a ray that intersect are called **perpendicular** if they lie on perpendicular lines. For example, in Figure 10-16, $\overline{AB} \perp \overline{BC}$, $\overrightarrow{BA} \perp \overrightarrow{BC}$, and $\overleftrightarrow{AB} \perp \overrightarrow{BC}$.

FIGURE 10-16

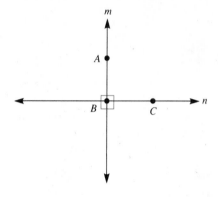

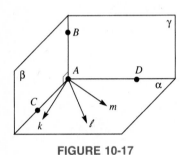

FIGURE 10-17

If a line and a plane intersect, it is possible for them to be perpendicular. For example, consider Figure 10-17, where planes β and γ represent two walls intersecting along $\overleftrightarrow{AB}$. The edge $\overleftrightarrow{AB}$ is perpendicular to the floor. Also, every line in the plane of the floor (plane α) passing through point A is perpendicular to $\overleftrightarrow{AB}$. This discussion leads to the following definition

● **D E F I N I T I O N**
A line and a plane are perpendicular if and only if they intersect and the line is perpendicular to every line in the plane that passes through the point of intersection.

● **R E M A R K**
It is possible to prove that a line is perpendicular to a plane if and only if it is perpendicular to and concurrent with two intersecting lines forming the plane.

The plane containing one wall and the plane containing the floor of a typical room, such as α and β in Figure 10-17, are perpendicular planes. Notice that β and γ contain $\overleftrightarrow{AB}$, which is perpendicular to α. In fact, any plane containing $\overleftrightarrow{AB}$ is perpendicular to plane α. Thus, β ⊥ α and γ ⊥ α.

● **D E F I N I T I O N**
Two planes are perpendicular if and only if one plane contains a line perpendicular to the other plane.

Dihedral Angles

An alternate method for determining whether two planes are perpendicular is to determine the measure of an angle formed by the intersecting planes. If the angle formed by the planes is a right angle, then the planes are perpendicular. We define an angle formed by two intersecting planes in an analogous way to the definition of a planar angle. A **dihedral angle** is the union of two half-planes and the common line defining the half-planes. The half-planes are usually referred to as the *faces* of the dihedral angle, and the common line is referred to as the *edge* of the dihedral angle. In Figure 10-18, dihedral angle O-AC-D is formed by intersecting planes α and β. Note that point O is in plane α, $\overleftrightarrow{AC}$ is the edge of the dihedral angle, and point D is in plane β. In what other ways could the dihedral angle be named?

With a given dihedral angle, we can associate a planar angle by choosing a point P on the edge of the dihedral angle and drawing two rays, one in each face, perpendicular to the edge. In Figure 10-18, $\angle OPD$ and $\angle EQF$ are planar angles associated with the dihedral angle. It can be shown that $\angle OPD$ and $\angle EQF$ are congruent and, in general, that all planar angles associated with a given dihedral angle are congruent. This property enables us to measure a dihedral angle. *We define the measure of a dihedral angle as the measure of any of the associated planar angles.*

dihedral angle

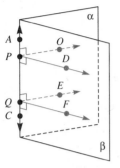

FIGURE 10-18

EXAMPLE 10-2

FIGURE 10-19

Given Figure 10-19 answer each of the following.
(a) Name two pairs of skew lines.
(b) Are $\overleftrightarrow{BD}$ and $\overleftrightarrow{FH}$ parallel, skew, or intersecting lines?
(c) Are $\overleftrightarrow{BD}$ and $\overleftrightarrow{GH}$ parallel?
(d) Find the intersection of $\overleftrightarrow{BD}$ and plane EFG.
(e) Find the intersection of $\overleftrightarrow{BH}$ and plane DCG.
(f) Name two pairs of perpendicular planes.
(g) Name two lines that are perpendicular to plane EFH.
(h) Name a planar angle that could be used to measure dihedral angle E-FH-B.
(i) What is the measure of dihedral angle D-HG-F?

SOLUTION

(a) $\overleftrightarrow{BC}$ and $\overleftrightarrow{DH}$, and $\overleftrightarrow{AE}$ and $\overleftrightarrow{BD}$. Others are possible.
(b) $\overleftrightarrow{BD}$ and $\overleftrightarrow{FH}$ are parallel.
(c) No, $\overleftrightarrow{BD}$ and $\overleftrightarrow{GH}$ are skew lines.
(d) The intersection is the empty set, because $\overleftrightarrow{BD}$ and plane EFG have no points in common.
(e) The intersection of $\overleftrightarrow{BH}$ and plane DCG is point H.
(f) Planes BFC and EFG are perpendicular, as are planes BFD and EFG.
(g) $\overleftrightarrow{BF}$ and $\overleftrightarrow{DH}$ are perpendicular to plane EFH.
(h) One possibility is $\angle EFB$.
(i) $90°$

PROBLEM SET 10-1

1. A line, a line segment, or a ray can be considered as a set of points. Given the figure, find a more concise name for each of the following.

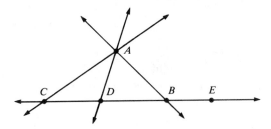

   (a) $\overleftrightarrow{AC} \cap \overleftrightarrow{BE}$ (b) $\overline{AC} \cap \overline{BE}$
   (c) $\overrightarrow{CA} \cap \overrightarrow{EB}$ (d) $\overleftrightarrow{CA} \cap \overrightarrow{BC}$
   (e) $\overline{CB} \cup \overline{BE}$ (f) $\overline{AB} \cup \overrightarrow{AB}$
   (g) $\overrightarrow{AB} \cup \overrightarrow{BA}$ (h) $\overrightarrow{AD} \cup \overrightarrow{DA}$

2. Letters on a computer monitor are formed when a series of pixels (picture elements) are lighted. The more lights used, the more distinct the letter becomes. Consider the following magnified symbol for the number 1. Is the symbol a true geometric segment?

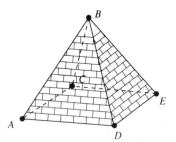

3. Use the accompanying drawing of one of the Great Pyramids of Egypt to find the following.

   (a) The intersection of $\overline{AD}$ and $\overline{CE}$
   (b) The dihedral angle formed by planes BDE and BDA

   (c) The intersection of planes ABC, ACE, and BCE
   (d) The intersection of $\overleftrightarrow{AD}$ and $\overleftrightarrow{CA}$
   (e) The intersection of $\overleftrightarrow{AD}$ and $\overleftrightarrow{CA}$
   (f) The intersection of $\overline{AD}$ and $\overrightarrow{CA}$
   (g) A pair of skew lines
   (h) A pair of parallel lines
   (i) A plane that is not determined by one of the triangular faces or by the base

4. Determine whether each of the following is true or false.
   (a) Two distinct planes either intersect in a line or are parallel.
   (b) If two points are common to a line and to a plane, then the entire line is in the plane.
   (c) It is always possible to find a plane through four given points in space.
   (d) If two distinct lines do not intersect, they are parallel.
   (e) The intersection of three planes may be a single point.
   (f) If two distinct lines intersect, one and only one plane contains the lines.
   (g) Infinitely many planes contain both of two skew lines.
   (h) If each of two parallel lines is parallel to a plane α, then the plane determined by the two parallel lines is parallel to α.
   (i) If three points are coplanar, then they must be collinear.
   (j) If two distinct lines are parallel to a third line in space, then the two lines are parallel to each other.
   (k) If a plane α contains one line ℓ, but not another line m, and ℓ is parallel to m, then α is parallel to m.
   (l) A line parallel to each of two intersecting planes is parallel to the line of intersection of the planes.

5. For every false statement in Problem 4, give an example of a physical situation that demonstrates its falsity.

6. Consider a maypole with ribbons attached at the top as shown in top left column on page 515. If each ribbon is stretched tautly and pegged to the ground along a straight line as indicated, we have a model of a line ℓ and a point A not on the line. Consider the model in answering the following questions.
   (a) How many lines intersecting ℓ may be drawn through A?
   (b) How many planes contain ℓ and A?

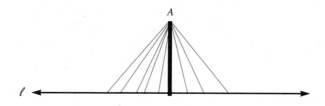

7. Consider line ℓ on the airport runway, point A on the tower light, point B at a boundary light, and point X where the airplane parks. Use these points and the line to answer the following questions.

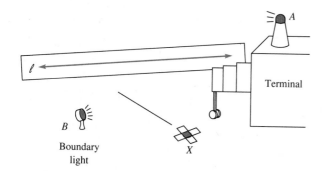

(a) How many planes contain both $\overleftrightarrow{AB}$ and line ℓ?
(b) How many planes contain B, X, and A?

8. Identify a possible physical model for each of the following?
(a) Perpendicular lines
(b) An acute angle
(c) An obtuse angle
(d) An obtuse dihedral angle
(e) An acute dihedral angle
(f) A line containing two distinct points
(g) Four noncoplanar points

9. Express each of the following in degrees, minutes, and seconds, without decimals.
(a) 0.9°   (b) 15.13°

10. (a) If two parallel planes α and β intersect a third plane γ in two lines ℓ and m, are ℓ and m necessarily parallel? Explain your answer.
(b) If two planes α and β intersect a third plane in two parallel lines, are α and β always parallel? Why?
(c) Suppose that two intersecting lines are both parallel to a plane α. Is the plane determined by these intersecting lines parallel to α? Why?

11. Use a protractor to find the measure of each of the pictured angles.

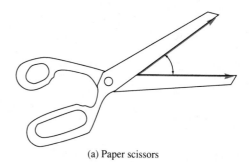

(a) Paper scissors

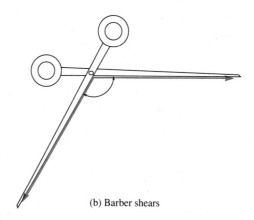

(b) Barber shears

12. Perform each of the following operations, leaving your answers in simplest form.
(a) 18°35′29″ + 22°55′41″
(b) 93°38′14″ − 13°49′27″

13. How many rays are determined by each of the following?
(a) Three collinear points
(b) Four collinear points
(c) Five collinear points
(d) n collinear points

14. (a) How many lines are determined by three non-collinear points?
(b) How many lines are determined by four points, no three of which are collinear?
(c) How many lines are determined by five points, no three of which are collinear?
(d) How many lines are determined by n points, no three of which are collinear?

15. (a) In the following table, sketch the possible intersections of the given number of lines. (Using dry spaghetti may help.) Two sketches are given for you.

Number of Intersection Points

Number of Lines	0	1	2	3	4	5	...
2		✕	Not possible	Not possible	Not possible	Not possible	
3					Not possible	Not possible	
4				✳		Not possible	
5							
6							

(b) Find a formula for determining the greatest possible number of intersection points, given n lines.

16. Explain mathematically why a three-legged stool is always stable and a four-legged stool sometimes rocks.

17. In the given figure, m is a line perpendicular to plane α. The intersection of m with α is C. Points A and B are in plane α. $D \in m$, but $D \notin \alpha$.

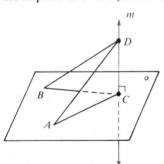

(a) Is $\angle BDC$ a right angle? Explain your answer.
(b) Is it possible to find a point P in plane α such that $\angle DPC$ is obtuse? Justify your answer.
(c) Is the plane determined by the points A, D, and C perpendicular to plane α? Why?

18. (a) Is it possible for a line to be perpendicular to one line in a plane but not to be perpendicular to the plane?
(b) Is it possible for a line to be perpendicular to two distinct lines in a plane and yet not be perpendicular to the plane?
(c) If a line not in a given plane is perpendicular to two distinct lines in the plane, is the line necessarily perpendicular to the plane?

19. Trace each of the following drawings. In your tracing, use dashed lines for segments that would not be seen, and use solid lines for segments that would be seen. (Different people may see different perspectives.)

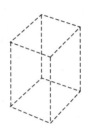

(a)

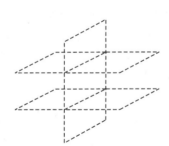

(b)

(c)

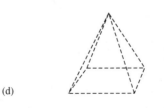

(d)

★20. Use the statement "There is one and only one plane containing three distinct, noncollinear points" to prove each of the following.
(a) A line and a point not on the line determine a plane.
(b) Two intersecting lines determine a plane.

★21. Prove that if two parallel planes are intersected by a third plane, the lines of intersection are parallel.

22. Write Logo procedures to draw each of the following.
    (a) A procedure called ANGLE with input :SIZE to draw a variable-sized angle
    (b) A procedure called SEGMENT with input :LENGTH to draw a variable-sized segment

(c) A procedure called PERPENDICULAR with inputs :LENGTH1 and :LENGTH2 to draw two variable-sized perpendicular segments
(d) A procedure called PARALLEL with inputs :LENGTH1 and :LENGTH2 to draw two variable-sized parallel segments

LABORATORY ACTIVITY

The following activities involve Level 0 of the van Hiele structure for learning geometry.

1. Within the classroom, identify a physical object with the following shapes.
   (a) Parallel lines
   (b) Parallel planes
   (c) Skew lines
   (d) Dihedral angle
   (e) Right angles

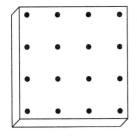

2. On a sheet of dot paper or on a geoboard, as pictured, create the following shapes.
   (a) Right angle
   (b) Acute angle
   (c) Obtuse angle
   (d) Adjacent angles
   (e) Parallel lines
   (f) Intersecting lines

Section 10-2 Polygonal Curves in a Plane

polygonal curve

simple curves

closed curves

polygon

In mathematics, curves are subsets of a plane. A careful definition of a curve requires the use of advanced mathematical concepts. Any plane curve, as in Figure 10-20, is a **polygonal curve**. The polygonal curves in Figure 10-20(a), (c), and (e) are **simple curves**—curves that do not cross themselves when traced (although the starting and stopping points may be the same). The polygonal curves in Figure 10-20(c), (d), and (e) are **closed curves**—curves that, when traced, have the same starting and stopping points but may cross themselves at individual points. **Polygons** are polygonal curves that are both simple and closed, as in Figure 10-20(c) and (e). The line segments forming

FIGURE 10-20

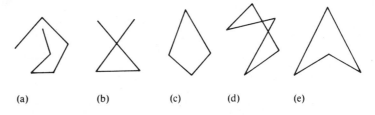

(a)   (b)   (c)   (d)   (e)

a polygon are the *sides* of the polygon. A point where two sides meet is a *vertex* of the polygon. Every simple closed polygon separates the plane into three disjoint subsets, the interior of the polygon, the exterior of the polygon, and the polygon itself. This is illustrated in Figure 10-21(a). Together a polygon and its interior form a *polygonal region*.

FIGURE 10-21

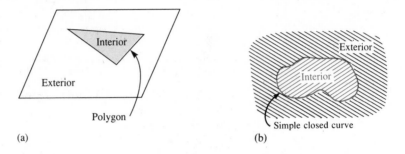

(a)　　　　　　　　　　　　　　　　　(b)

Jordan Curve Theorem　　　Figure 10-21(a) shows a special case of the **Jordan Curve Theorem,** which states that *any simple closed curve separates a plane into three disjoint sets, the exterior, the interior, and the curve itself.* Another example is shown in Figure 10-21(b). Deciding whether a point is inside or outside a curve is investigated in Problem 1.

PROBLEM 1

Determine whether point X is inside or outside the simple closed curve of Figure 10-22.

FIGURE 10-22

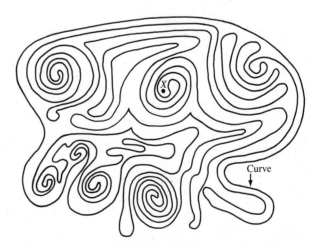

Understanding the Problem. We must determine whether point X is inside the curve in Figure 10-22; that is, does point X belong to the exterior or to the interior of the curve?

Devising a Plan. One approach to this problem is to start shading the area surrounding point X. If we do this and stay between the lines, we should be able to decide eventually whether the shaded area is inside or outside the curve.

Carrying Out the Plan. If we shade the area around point X and stay within the boundaries, we obtain a drawing similar to Figure 10-23. The shaded area of Figure 10-23 indicates that point X is located outside the curve.

FIGURE 10-23

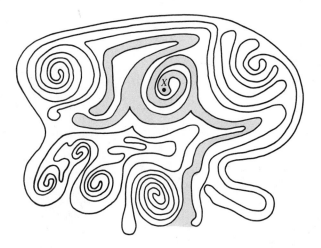

Looking Back. Another strategy is explored in Figure 10-24(a) and (b), in which point X is connected with any point Y, where point Y is definitely outside the curve. How many times does the dashed segment cross the curve in each of these cases? Try different locations for point Y outside the curve in Figure 10-24(a) and (b). What is your conjecture?

FIGURE 10-24

(a)   (b)

More about Polygons

convex polygon

The polygon in Figure 10-25(a) is a convex polygon whereas the polygon in Figure 10-25(b) is *concave*. Intuitively, we can tell that a convex polygon has no indentations. Mathematically, if the segment connecting any two points of the polygonal region is a subset of the polygonal region, then the polygon is a **convex polygon.** For example, in Figure 10-25(a), no matter what two points of the hexagonal region are chosen as the endpoints of a segment, the entire segment lies in the hexagonal region. This is not the case in Figure 10-25(b), where it is possible to draw a segment between two points of the polygonal region such that part of the segment lies outside the region.

FIGURE 10-25

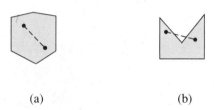

(a)   (b)

Polygons are classified according to the number of sides or vertices they have. For example, consider the polygons listed in Table 10-3.

TABLE 10-3

Polygon	Number of Sides or Vertices
Triangle	3
Quadrilateral	4
Pentagon	5
Hexagon	6
Heptagon	7
Octagon	8
Nonagon	9
Decagon	10
n-gon	n

interior angle, or
angle, of a polygon
exterior angle of a polygon

Polygons could also be named by the number of angles they have, because the number of angles in a polygon is the same as the number of sides. Strictly speaking, a polygon contains no angles because an angle is a union of two rays with a common endpoint, and a polygon contains no rays. However, any two sides of a polygon having a common vertex determine an **interior angle,** or **angle, of the polygon,** such as $\angle 1$ of polygon $ABCD$ in Figure 10-26(a). An **exterior angle of a polygon** is determined by a side of the polygon and the extension of a contiguous side of the polygon. An example is $\angle 2$ in Figure 10-26(b).

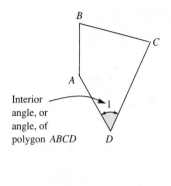

Interior angle, or angle, of polygon *ABCD*

(a)

(b)

Exterior angle of polygon *ABCD*

FIGURE 10-26

diagonal

Any line segment connecting nonconsecutive vertices of a polygon is a **diagonal.** Thus, in Figure 10-27(a), segments $\overline{AC}$, $\overline{AD}$, $\overline{BE}$, $\overline{BD}$, and $\overline{CE}$ are diagonals of the given pentagon. In Figure 10-27(b), segments $\overline{QS}$ and $\overline{PR}$ are the diagonals of the quadrilateral *PQRS*. Notice that, in Figure 10-27(a), the diagonals (except for their endpoints) of the pentagon lie in the interior of the pentagon. In contrast, the quadrilateral in Figure 10-27(b) has a diagonal that, except for its endpoints, lies in the exterior of the quadrilateral. What type of polygon must have a diagonal such that a part of the diagonal falls outside the polygon?

String art is often constructed on the basis of polygons and their diagonals. Problem 2 investigates the number of diagonals in such a polygon.

FIGURE 10-27

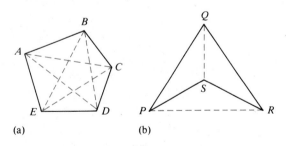

(a)

(b)

PROBLEM 2

How many diagonals does the 24-gon pictured in Figure 10-28 have?

FIGURE 10-28

Understanding the Problem. We are given a polygon with 24 sides, and we are asked to determine how many different diagonals can be drawn by connecting the 24 vertices of the polygon in all possible ways.

Devising a Plan. We use the strategy of examining related simple cases of the problem in order to develop a pattern for the original problem. Figure 10-29 shows that a triangle has no diagonals, a square has two diagonals, a pentagon has five diagonals, and a hexagon has nine diagonals.

FIGURE 10-29

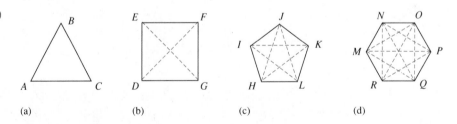

(a)   (b)   (c)   (d)

Examining Figure 10-29(c), we see that, if we choose any vertex, we can draw only two diagonals from that vertex. In general, we cannot draw a diagonal from a chosen vertex to itself or from a chosen vertex to either of the two adjacent vertices. Thus, in Figure 10-29(d), the number of diagonals that can be drawn from any one vertex is three less than the total number of vertices—that is, 6 − 3, or 3. Similarly, in a polygon with 24 sides, the number of diagonals that can be drawn from any one vertex is three less than the number of vertices—that is, 24 − 3, or 21. From each of the 24 vertices of the 24-gon, 21 diagonals can be drawn. We can use this information to determine the total number of diagonals.

Carrying Out the Plan. From the preceding information, it appears that we have 24(21), or 504, diagonals in a 24-gon. However, based on this notion, we should also have $6(6 - 3)$, or 18, diagonals in a hexagon. This result does not agree with the actual number of 9. This is because each diagonal is determined by two vertices; and when we counted the number of diagonals from each vertex, we counted each diagonal twice. Hence, in a 24-gon, there must be 24(21)/2, or 252 diagonals.

Looking Back. Based on this reasoning, the number of diagonals in an n-gon is $n(n - 3)/2$. This formula gives results consistent with the number of diagonals pictured in Figure 10-29. An alternate solution to this problem uses the notion of combinations developed in Chapter 8. The number of ways that all the vertices in an n-gon can be connected two at a time is the number of combinations of n vertices chosen two at a time—that is, $_nC_2$, or $\dfrac{n(n - 1)}{2}$. This number of segments includes both the number of diagonals and the number of sides. If we subtract the number of sides n from $\dfrac{n(n - 1)}{2}$, we find that the number of diagonals is $n(n - 1)/2 - n$. This expression can be simplified to $n(n - 3)/2$.

Congruent Segments and Angles

congruent parts   Most modern industries operate on the notion of creating **congruent parts**— parts that are of the same size and shape. For example, the basic specifications for all cars of a particular model are the same, and calibrationists' jobs are to make sure that machines are tooled to a very fine accuracy so that all parts produced for that model are basically "the same." Most frequently, when we discuss congruent figures, we are discussing figures in a plane. For *congruent segments*   example, two line **segments** are described as **congruent** if and only if they have the same length. (Length is discussed in Chapter 13.) In the case of line segments, having the same length means that a tracing of one line segment can be fitted exactly on top of the other. If $\overline{AB}$ is congruent to $\overline{CD}$, we write $\overline{AB} \cong \overline{CD}$. The symbol $\cong$ is read "is congruent to." In a similar manner, we *congruent angles*   say that two **angles** are **congruent** to each other if and only if they have the same measure. Congruent segments and congruent angles are shown in Figure 10-30(a) and (b), respectively.

FIGURE 10-30

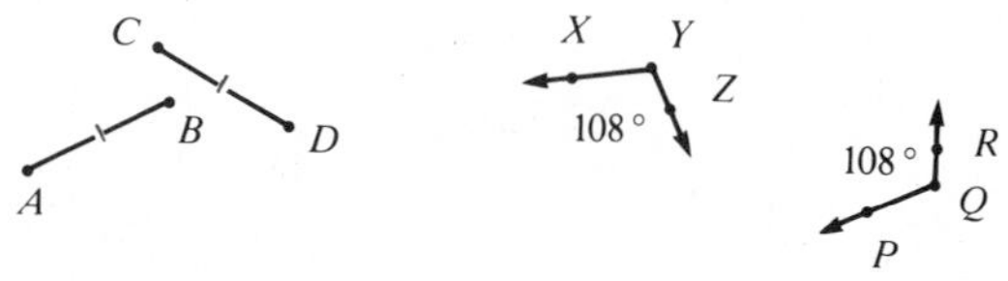

$\overline{AB} \cong \overline{CD}$

(a)

$\angle ZYX \cong \angle RQP$

(b)

Regular Polygons

regular polygons

Polygons in which all the angles are congruent and all the sides are congruent are called **regular polygons.** We say that a regular polygon is both *equiangular* and *equilateral*. A regular triangle is an equilateral triangle. A regular pentagon and a regular hexagon are illustrated in Figure 10-31. The congruent sides and congruent angles are marked.

FIGURE 10-31

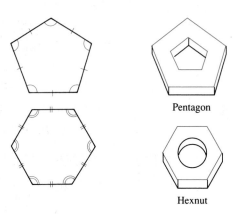

Pentagon

Hexnut

Triangles and Quadrilaterals

Triangles may be classified according to their angle measures, as shown in Table 10-4. Triangles and quadrilaterals may also be classified as shown in Table 10-5.

TABLE 10-4

Definition	Illustration	Example
A triangle containing a right angle is a **right triangle.**		
A triangle in which all the angles are acute is an **acute triangle.**		YIELD
A triangle containing an obtuse angle is an **obtuse triangle.**		

TABLE 10-5

Definition	Illustration	Example
A triangle with no sides congruent is a **scalene triangle.**		
A triangle with at least two sides congruent is an **isosceles triangle.**		
A triangle with three sides congruent is an **equilateral triangle.**		
A **trapezoid** is a quadrilateral with at least one pair of parallel sides.		
A **kite** is a quadrilateral with two distinct pairs of consecutive sides congruent.		
An **isosceles trapezoid** is a trapezoid with a pair of base angles congruent.		
A **parallelogram** is a quadrilateral in which each pair of opposite sides is parallel.		
A **rectangle** is a parallelogram with a right angle.		
A **rhombus** is a parallelogram with all sides congruent.		
A **square** is a rectangle with all sides congruent.		

• **R E M A R K**
Some texts give different definitions for a trapezoid and an isosceles trapezoid. Many elementary texts define a trapezoid as a quadrilateral with exactly one pair of parallel sides.

Notice that every triangle is a polygon and every equilateral triangle is also isosceles. However, not every isosceles triangle is equilateral. Using set concepts, we can say that the set of all triangles is a proper subset of the set of all polygons; also, the set of all equilateral triangles is a proper subset of the set of all isosceles triangles. This hierarchy is shown in Figure 10-32, where more general terms appear above more specific ones.

FIGURE 10-32

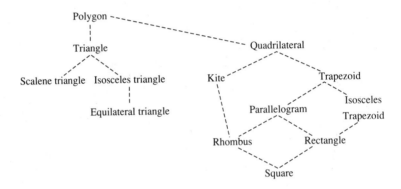

Using the definitions in Tables 10-4 and 10-5, we can prove many properties of both triangles and quadrilaterals. Among these properties are the following.

1. An equilateral triangle is isosceles.
2. A square is a regular quadrilateral.
3. A square is a rhombus with a right angle.
4. A rectangle is an isosceles trapezoid.
5. Some isosceles trapezoids are kites.

Circles

circle

center

In Figure 10-33, the regular 24-gon resembles a circle. The more sides a regular n-gon has, the closer it resembles a circle. (This type of thinking has led to a procedure in Logo for drawing a turtle-type circle.) A **circle** is defined as the set of all points in a plane that lie the same distance from a given point, called the **center**. Circles are simple closed curves and are discussed in more detail in Chapter 11.

FIGURE 10-33

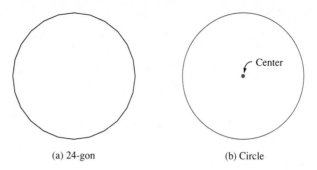

(a) 24-gon   (b) Circle

PROBLEM SET 10-2

1. For each of the following, which figures labeled (1)–(12) can be classified under the given term?

   (a) Polygonal curve
   (b) Simple polygonal curve
   (c) Simple closed polygonal curve
   (d) Polygon
   (e) Convex polygon
   (f) Concave polygon

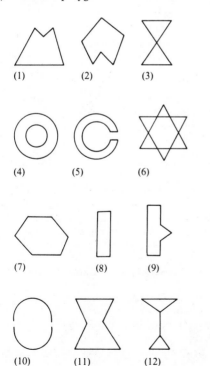

(1)   (2)   (3)

(4)   (5)   (6)

(7)   (8)   (9)

(10)   (11)   (12)

2. Find a path out of each of the following mazes, starting at point X.

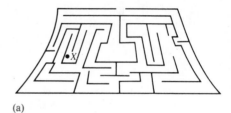

(a)

(b)

3. In each of the following diagams, determine whether point *X* is inside or outside the curve.

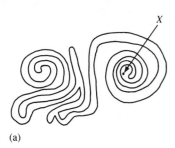

(a)

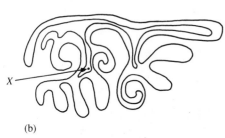

(b)

4. For each of the following figures, determine if it is possible to connect like numerals by curves that do not cross each other or any other curves in the figure.

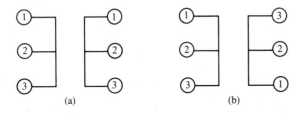

(a)   (b)

5. Use the given drawing to find each of the following.
   (a) $\ell \cap$ (polygon *ABCD*)
   (b) $\ell \cap$ (interior of polygon *ABCD*)
   (c) $\ell \cap$ (exterior of polygon *ABCD*)
   (d) $\ell \cap \overleftrightarrow{AC}$

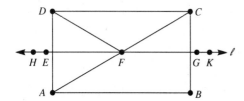

6. What is the maximum number of intersection points between a quadrilateral and a triangle (where no sides of the polygons are on the same line)?

7. Which of the following figures are convex, and which are concave?

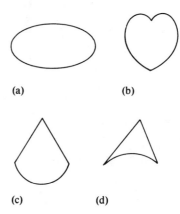

(a)   (b)

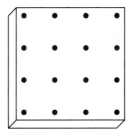

(c)   (d)

8. On a geoboard, construct each of the following.
   (a) A scalene triangle
   (b) A square
   (c) A trapezoid
   (d) A convex hexagon
   (e) A concave quadrilateral
   (f) A parallelogram

9. If possible, draw the following triangles. If it is not possible to do so, state why.
   (a) An obtuse scalene triangle
   (b) An acute scalene triangle
   (c) A right scalene triangle
   (d) An obtuse equilateral triangle
   (e) An acute equilateral triangle
   (f) A right equilateral triangle
   (g) An obtuse isosceles triangle
   (h) An acute isosceles triangle
   (i) A right isosceles triangle

10. How many diagonals does each of the following have?
    (a) Decagon   (b) 20-gon   (c) 100-gon

11. Find the number of triangles in each of the following figures.

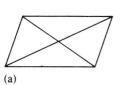

(a) (b)

12. Identify each of the following triangles as scalene, isosceles, or equilateral.

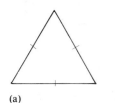 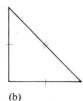

(a) (b)

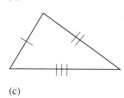

(c) (d)

13. In the following design, how many triangles are there?

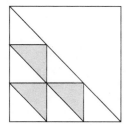

Birds in the air
quilt pattern

14. Find illustrations of each named figure in Tables 10-4 and 10-5 from your everyday surroundings.

15. Tell whether each of the following is true or false. If the statement is false, explain why.
(a) Every isosceles triangle is equilateral.
(b) All equilateral triangles are isosceles.
(c) All squares are rectangles.

(d) Some rectangles are rhombuses.
(e) All parallelograms are quadrilaterals.
(f) Every rhombus is a regular quadrilateral.
(g) Every parallelogram is a trapezoid.
(h) Every equilateral triangle is a scalene triangle.
(i) Every square is a kite.
(j) Some rectangles are squares.
(k) No square is a rectangle.
(l) No trapezoid is a parallelogram.
(m) Some right triangles are isosceles.
(n) An isosceles trapezoid may not be a kite.
(o) No parallelogram is an isosceles trapezoid.

16. Write Logo procedures to draw each of the following.
(a) A simple polygonal curve
(b) A closed polygonal curve
(c) A nonsimple nonclosed polygonal curve
(d) A simple closed polygonal curve

17. Write a Logo program to draw each of the following.
(a) A square
(b) A rectangle

Review Problems

18. If three distinct rays with the same vertex are drawn as shown, then three different angles are formed: $\angle AOB$, $\angle AOC$, and $\angle BOC$.
(a) How many different angles are formed by using ten distinct noncollinear rays with the same vertex?
(b) How many different angles are formed by using n distinct noncollinear rays with the same vertex?

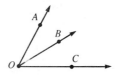

19. Use the accompanying figure to solve each of the following.

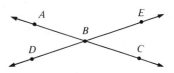

(a) Name at least four different angles.
(b) Find $\angle ABE \cap \angle EBC$.
(c) Find $\angle EBA \cap \angle DBC$.
(d) Find $\angle EBC \cap \angle CBE$.
(e) Is it true that $\angle ABE \cup \angle EBC = \angle ABC$?

20. What are the possible intersection sets of a line and an angle?
21. Find each of the following in the given figure.

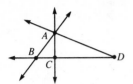

    (a) $\overleftrightarrow{AC} \cap \overline{BC}$
    (b) $\overline{BD} \cup \overline{CD}$
    (c) Three line segments containing point A
    (d) $\overleftrightarrow{DC} \cap \overrightarrow{DA}$

22. Classify the following as true or false. If false, tell why.
    (a) A ray has two endpoints.
    (b) For any points M and N, $\overleftrightarrow{MN} = \overleftrightarrow{NM}$.
    (c) Skew lines are coplanar.
    (d) $\overrightarrow{MN} = \overrightarrow{NM}$
    (e) A line segment contains an infinite number of points.
    (f) If two distinct planes intersect, their intersection is a line segment.
23. Draw two line segments $\overline{AB}$ and $\overline{CD}$ such that $\overline{AB} \cap \overline{CD} = \varnothing$ and $\overleftrightarrow{AB} \cup \overleftrightarrow{CD}$ is a single line.

B R A I N　　T E A S E R

Given three buildings A, B, and C, as shown, and three utility centers for electricity (E), gas (G), and water (W), is it possible to connect each of the three buildings to each of the three utility centers without crossing lines?

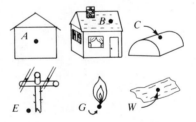

LABORATORY ACTIVITY

The following van Hiele Level 1 activity consists of using cutouts of different quadrilaterals. Sort the shapes according to the following attributes.
(a) Number of parallel sides
(b) Number of right angles
(c) Number of congruent sides
(d) Polygons with congruent diagonals

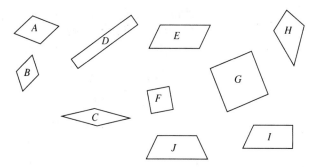

2. Use the cutouts to identify properties that are characteristic of different classes of figures. For example, "Congruent opposite sides describe a parallelogram."
3. For the following van Hiele Level 2 activity, work with a partner. One of you should construct a figure on a geoboard. Do not show the figure to your partner, but tell your partner the properties of the figure you constructed. Have your partner try to identify the figure you constructed. Try this with each of the figures named.

    (a) Scalene triangle   (b) Isosceles triangle
    (c) Square   (d) Parallelogram
    (e) Trapezoid   (f) Rectangle
    (g) Kite   (h) Rhombus

Section 10-3 More About Angles

Two intersecting lines form four nonstraight angles in the plane. In Figure 10-34, the four angles are $\angle 1$, $\angle 2$, $\angle 3$, and $\angle 4$.

FIGURE 10-34

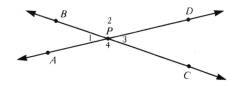

vertical angles

Angles formed by two intersecting lines, such as $\angle 1$ and $\angle 3$ in Figure 10-34, are **vertical angles.** Another pair of vertical angles in Figure 10-34 is $\angle 2$ and $\angle 4$.

supplementary angles

Figure 10-34 also illustrates pairs of supplementary angles. Two angles are **supplementary angles** if the sum of their measures is 180°. Each is a *supplement* of the other. Angles 1 and 2, 1 and 4, 2 and 3, and 3 and 4 are pairs of supplementary angles in Figure 10-34.

complementary angles   Two angles are **complementary angles** if the sum of their measures is 90°. Each is a *complement* of the other. Figure 10-35 shows examples of supplementary and complementary angles.

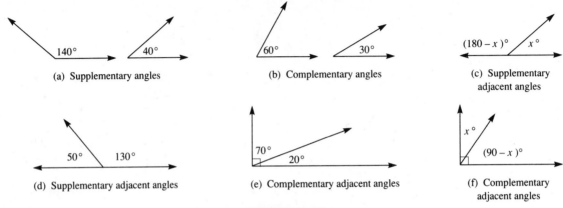

(a) Supplementary angles (b) Complementary angles (c) Supplementary adjacent angles

(d) Supplementary adjacent angles (e) Complementary adjacent angles (f) Complementary adjacent angles

FIGURE 10-35

Using the notion of congruence of angles, we can derive the following theorems involving supplementary and complementary angles.

● **T H E O R E M   10-1**
(a) Supplements of the same angle, or of congruent angles, are congruent.
(b) Complements of the same angle, or of congruent angles, are congruent.

Using Theorem 10-1(a), we can easily prove that vertical angles are congruent. Look at Figure 10-36.

FIGURE 10-36

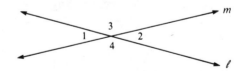

Because ℓ is a straight line, $\angle 1$ is a supplement of $\angle 4$. Because m is a straight line, $\angle 2$ is a supplement of $\angle 4$. As $\angle 1$ and $\angle 2$ are the supplements of the same angle, $\angle 4$, they are congruent and equal in measure. Similarly, $\angle 3$ and $\angle 4$ are supplements of $\angle 1$ and, therefore, are congruent. Thus, vertical angles are congruent. We summarize the preceding result in the following theorem.

● **T H E O R E M   10-2**
Vertical angles formed by intersecting lines are congruent.

Theorem 10-1(b) can also be used to deduce congruence relationships among certain angles, a shown in Example 10-3.

EXAMPLE 10-3   In Figure 10-37, suppose $\angle APC$ and $\angle BPD$ are right angles. Why are $\angle 1$ and $\angle 3$ congruent?

FIGURE 10-37

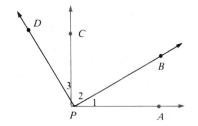

SOLUTION   Because $\angle APC$ is a right angle, $\angle 1$ is a complement of $\angle 2$. Because $\angle BPD$ is a right angle, $\angle 3$ is also a complement of $\angle 2$. Thus, $\angle 1$ and $\angle 3$ are complements of the same angle and hence are congruent.

---

transversal   We have seen that vertical angles are formed by two intersecting lines. Angles are also formed when a line intersects two distinct lines. Any line that intersects a pair of lines is called a **transversal** of those lines. In Figure 10-38(a), line p is a transversal of lines m and n. Angles formed by these lines are named according to their placement in relation to the transversal and the two given lines. Various types of angles, together with examples of each in Figure 10-38, are listed next.

FIGURE 10-38

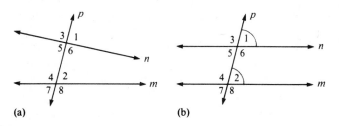

(a)   (b)

interior angles   **Interior angles:** $\angle 2$, $\angle 4$, $\angle 5$, $\angle 6$
exterior angles   **Exterior angles:** $\angle 3$, $\angle 1$, $\angle 7$, $\angle 8$
alternate interior angles   **Alternate interior angles:** $\angle 5$ and $\angle 2$, $\angle 4$ and $\angle 6$
alternate exterior angles   **Alternate exterior angles:** $\angle 1$ and $\angle 7$, $\angle 3$ and $\angle 8$
corresponding angles   **Corresponding angles:** $\angle 3$ and $\angle 4$, $\angle 5$ and $\angle 7$, $\angle 1$ and $\angle 2$, $\angle 6$ and $\angle 8$

If corresponding angles, such as $\angle 1$ and $\angle 2$, are congruent, as in Figure 10-38(b), it can be shown that each pair of corresponding angles, alternate interior angles, and alternate exterior angles are congruent.

If we further examine Figure 10-38(b), we see that lines m and n appear to be parallel when $\angle 1$ is congruent to $\angle 2$. The converse of this observation can be used to show that, if the lines are parallel, the sets of angles mentioned previously are congruent. The preceding discussion leads to the following theorem.

● **T H E O R E M   10-3**
If any two distinct lines are cut by a transversal, then a pair of corresponding angles, alternate interior angles, or alternate exterior angles are congruent if and only if the lines are parallel.

EXAMPLE 10-4   (a) If one angle of a parallelogram is 50°, what are the measures of the other angles?
(b) Find x, the measure of $\angle Q$ in Figure 10-39, where $\overrightarrow{AB} \parallel \overrightarrow{CD}$.

FIGURE 10-39

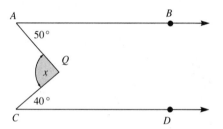

SOLUTION   (a) In Figure 10-40, we draw the lines containing the sides of parallelogram $ABCD$. Since $\angle 4$ and the angle with measure 50° are corresponding angles formed by parallel lines $\overleftrightarrow{AB}$ and $\overleftrightarrow{CD}$ cut by transversal $\overleftrightarrow{AD}$, then $m(\angle 4) = 50°$. Because $\angle 1$ and $\angle 4$ are supplementary, $m(\angle 1) = 180° - 50° = 130°$. Using similar reasoning, we find that $m(\angle 2) = 50°$ and $m(\angle 3) = 130°$.

FIGURE 10-40

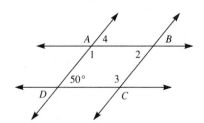

(b) In Figure 10-41, we draw $\overleftrightarrow{QR}$ through point Q parallel to $\overleftrightarrow{AB}$ and $\overleftrightarrow{CD}$. We also draw rays $\overrightarrow{CQ}$ and $\overrightarrow{AQ}$.

FIGURE 10-41

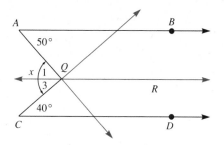

Using alternate interior angles formed by transversal $\overleftrightarrow{AQ}$ cutting parallel lines $\overrightarrow{AB}$ and $\overrightarrow{QR}$, we see that $m(\angle 1) = 50°$. Similarly, $m(\angle 3) = 40°$. Since $x = m(\angle 1) + m(\angle 3)$ (why?), we find that $x = 90°$.

The Sum of the Measures of the Angles of a Triangle

The sum of the measures of the angles in a triangle can intuitively be shown to be 180° by using a torn triangle, as in Figure 10-42. Angles 1, 2, and 3 of triangle ABC in Figure 10-42(a) are torn as pictured and then placed along line ℓ, as shown in Figure 10-42(b). Because the sum of the measures of the angles equals the measure of a straight angle, the sum of the measures of the angles of triangle ABC is 180°.

FIGURE 10-42

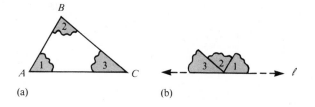

(a)   (b)

Another demonstration to confirm the discovery that the sum of the angles in a triangle is 180° is summarized in Figure 10-43. If we start in Figure 10-43(a) at A facing B, walk all the way around the triangle, and end

FIGURE 10-43

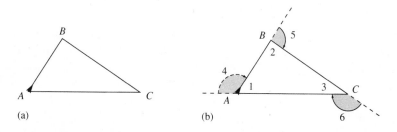

(a)   (b)

up in the same position and pointed in the same direction as we started, then we turned 360°. The 360° we turned is the sum of the shaded exterior angles of the triangle. Since an exterior angle and its adjacent interior angle are supplementary, the sum of all the interior and exterior angles is $3 \cdot 180°$, or 540°. By performing the subtraction $540° - 360°$, we see that the sum of the interior angles of the triangle is 180°.

The amount of turning that takes place in walking around the triangle in Figure 10-43(b) and returning to the original position and heading is equal to the amount of turning in a complete circle. This concept can be expressed in generalized form in a statement often referred to in Logo as the Total Turtle Trip Theorem.

● **TOTAL TURTLE TRIP THEOREM**
Any convex polygon can be drawn with a total turning of 360°.

The Total Turtle Trip Theorem leads to the following theorem concerning the sum of the exterior angles of any convex polygon.

● **T H E O R E M   10-4**
The sum of the exterior angles of any convex polygon is 360°.

A more general case of the Total Turtle Trip Theorem is the Closed Path Theorem.

● **CLOSED PATH THEOREM**
The total turning around any closed path is a multiple of 360°.

● **R E M A R K**
In the Closed Path Theorem, the curve may or may not be polygonal and does not have to be simple.

For a proof that the sum of the measures of the angles of a triangle is 180°, consider triangle ABC in Figure 10-44(a). We want to show that $m(\angle 1) + m(\angle 2) + m(\angle 3) = 180°$. To prove this assertion, we show that the sum of the measures of the three angles of the triangle is the same as the measure of a straight angle. This can be accomplished by drawing line ℓ

FIGURE 10-44

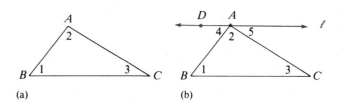

(a)   (b)

parallel to $\overleftrightarrow{BC}$ through vertex A, as shown in Figure 10-44(b). Because ℓ and $\overleftrightarrow{BC}$ are parallel, with transversals $\overleftrightarrow{AB}$ and $\overleftrightarrow{AC}$, it follows that alternate interior angles are congruent. Consequently, $m(\angle 1) = m(\angle 4)$ and $m(\angle 3) = m(\angle 5)$. Thus, $m(\angle 1) + m(\angle 2) + m(\angle 3) = m(\angle 4) + m(\angle 2) + m(\angle 5) = 180°$. So, $m(\angle 1) + m(\angle 2) + m(\angle 3) = 180°$. From the preceding proof, we obtain the following theorem.

- **T H E O R E M   10-5**
  The sum of the measures of the interior angles of a triangle is 180°.

EXAMPLE 10-5   (a) In Figure 10-45(a), $m(\angle D) = 90°$ and $m(\angle E) = 25°$. Find $m(\angle A)$.
(b) In Figure 10-45(b), the measures of $\angle A$ and $\angle B$ are twice the measure of $\angle C$. Find the measures of each of the angles in the triangle.
(c) In Figure 10-45(c), $m(\angle A) = 70°$ and $m(\angle B) = 30°$. Find $m(\angle 1)$.

FIGURE 10-45

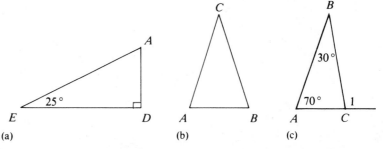

(a)   (b)   (c)

SOLUTION   (a) The sum of the measures of the angles in a triangle is 180°. Thus, $m(\angle A) + 90° + 25° = 180°$, and, consequently, $m(\angle A) = 65°$.
(b) Suppose that $m(\angle C) = x$. Then $m(\angle A) = 2x$ and $m(\angle B) = 2x$. Thus, $x + 2x + 2x = 180°$. Consequently, $5x = 180°$ and $x = 36°$. Because $2x = 72°$, we see that $m(\angle C) = 36°$, $m(\angle A) = 72°$, and $m(\angle B) = 72°$.
(c) The sum of the measures of the angles of a triangle is 180°. Thus, $m(\angle BCA) = 180° - (30° + 70°)$, or 80°. Now, $m(\angle BCA) + m(\angle 1) = 180°$, so $m(\angle 1) = 180° - 80°$, or 100°.

EXAMPLE 10-6 Find the sum of the measures of the interior angles of a convex n-gon.

SOLUTION Any n-gon has n interior angles and n exterior angles. Since the sum of every interior angle and its adjacent exterior angle is 180°, the sum of all the interior and exterior angles is $180n$. We know that the sum of the exterior angles of any convex n-gon is 360°, so the sum of the interior angles is $180n - 360°$, or $(n - 2)180°$.

Example 10-6 provides the key to determining the measure of a single angle of a regular n-gon. In a regular n-gon, all n angles are congruent, and the sum of their measures is $(n - 2)180°$, so the measure of a single angle is $(n - 2)180°/n$.

The major results from the preceding discussion are summarized in the following theorem.

● **T H E O R E M   10-6**
(a) The sum of the measures of the interior angles of any convex polygon with n sides is $(n - 2)180°$.
(b) The measure of a single interior angle of a regular n-gon is $(n - 2)180°/n$.

EXAMPLE 10-7 (a) Find the measure of each angle of a regular decagon.
(b) Find the number of sides of a regular polygon, each of whose angles has a measure of 175°.

SOLUTION (a) The sum of the measures of the angles in any n-gon is $(n - 2)180°$, and a decagon has ten sides. Thus, the sum of the measures of the angles of a decagon is $(10 - 2)180°$, or 1440°. A regular decagon has ten angles, all of which are congruent, so each one has a measure of $\dfrac{1440°}{10}$, or 144°.

(b) Each interior angle of the regular polygon is 175°. Thus, the measure of each exterior angle of the polygon is $180° - 175°$, or 5°. Because the sum of the measures of all exterior angles of a convex polygon is 360°, the number of exterior angles is $\frac{360°}{5}$, or 72. Hence, the number of sides is 72.

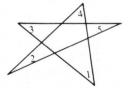

B R A I N   T E A S E R
Find the sum of the measures of $\angle 1$, $\angle 2$, $\angle 3$, $\angle 4$, and $\angle 5$ in any five-pointed star like the one in the accompanying figure. What is the sum of the measures of the angles in any seven-pointed star? What is the sum of the measures of the angles in any odd-pointed star, no vertex of which is in the interior of any angle of the star?

PROBLEM SET 10-3

1. For each of the given figures, which pairs of angles marked are adjacent and which are vertical?

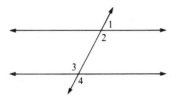

(a)

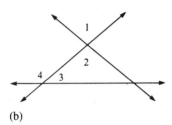

(b)

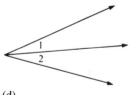

(c)

(d)

2. If $m(\angle 1) = 50°$ in the given figure, find each of the following.
   (a) $m(\angle 2)$
   (b) $m(\angle 3)$
   (c) $m(\angle 4)$

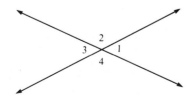

3. Explain how you might find the measure of the angle of inclination of a staircase.

4. For each of the following, sketch a pair of angles whose intersection is given.
   (a) The empty set
   (b) Exactly two points
   (c) Exactly three points
   (d) Exactly four points
   (e) More than four points

5. If five lines all meet in a single point, how many pairs of vertical angles are formed?

6. How many pairs of adjacent angles are there in the figure?

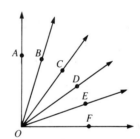

7. Find the measure of the third angle in each of the following triangles.

(a)   (b)

(c)   (d)

8. In each of the pictured cases, are *m* and *n* parallel lines? Justify your answer.

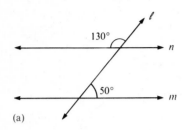

(a)

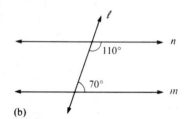

(b)

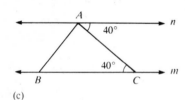

(c)

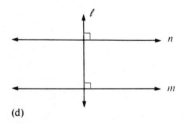

(d)

9. (a) If one of the angles in a triangle is obtuse, can another angle be obtuse? Why?
   (b) If one of the angles in a triangle is acute, can the other two angles be acute? Why?
   (c) Can a triangle have two right angles? Why?
   (d) If a triangle has one acute angle, is the triangle necessarily acute? Why?

10. In the following figure, $\overleftrightarrow{DE} \parallel \overleftrightarrow{BC}$, $\overleftrightarrow{EF} \parallel \overleftrightarrow{AB}$, and $\overleftrightarrow{DF} \parallel \overleftrightarrow{AC}$.

    Also, $m(\angle 1) = 45°$ and $m(\angle 2) = 65°$. Find each value.
    (a) $m(\angle 3)$ (b) $m(\angle D)$
    (c) $m(\angle E)$ (d) $m(\angle F)$

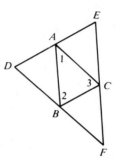

11. In each figure, find the measures of the angles marked *x* and *y*.

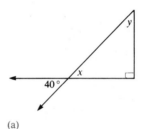

(a)

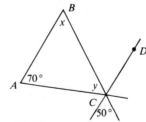

(b) $\overline{AB} \parallel \overline{CD}$

12. What is the measure of an angle whose measure is twice that of its complement?

13. If two angles of a triangle are complementary, what is the measure of the third angle?

14. If the measures of the three angles of a triangle are $(3x + 15)°$, $(5x - 15)°$, and $(2x + 30)°$, what is the measure of each angle?

15. Find the sum of the measures of the marked angles in each of the following.

(a)

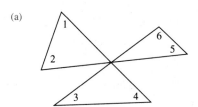

(b)

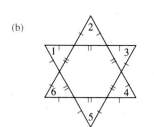

(c)

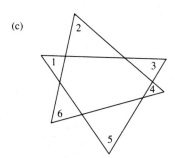

16. In the figure, A is a point not on line ℓ. Why is it impossible to have two distinct perpendicular segments from A to ℓ?

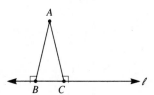

17. (a) In a regular polygon, the measure of each angle is 162°. How many sides does the polygon have?
    (b) Find the measure of each of the angles of a regular dodecagon.

18. (a) Show how to find the sum of the measures of the angles of any convex pentagon by choosing any point P in the interior and constructing triangles as shown in the figure.

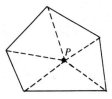

    (b) Using the method suggested by the diagram in (a), find the sum of the measures of the angles of any convex n-gon. Is your answer the same as the one already obtained in this section—that is, $(n - 2)180°$?

19. (a) Show how to find the sum of the measures of the angles of any convex pentagon by drawing all diagonals of the pentagon from one vertex, as shown in the figure.

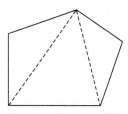

    (b) Using the method suggested by the diagram in (a), find the sum of the measures of the angles of any convex n-gon.

20. Classify each of the following as true or false.
    (a) All angles in a regular polygon are congruent.
    (b) Any polygon with congruent sides must have congruent angles.
    (c) Any polygon with congruent angles must have congruent sides.
    (d) The sum of the measures of the interior angles of any obtuse triangle is 180°.
    (e) The interior angles of a triangle are supplementary, since the sum of their measures is 180°.
    (f) Two angles of a right triangle are always complementary.

21. (a) In the figure, what is the relationship between $m(\angle 4)$ and $[m(\angle 1) + m(\angle 2)]$?

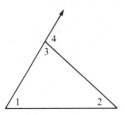

  (b) Justify your conjecture in (a).
22. Calculate the measure of each angle of a pentagon, where the measures of the angles form an arithmetic sequence and the least measure is 60°.
★23. Prove Theorem 10-1(a) and (b).
★24. Prove that two distinct coplanar lines perpendicular to the same line are parallel.
★25. Suppose that the polygon *ABCD* shown is a parallelogram. Prove each of the following.

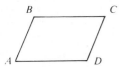

  (a) $m(\angle A) + m(\angle B) = 180°$
  (b) $m(\angle A) = m(\angle C)$ and $m(\angle B) = m(\angle D)$
★26. Use the definition of a rectangle and properties of parallel lines to show that all the angles in a rectangle are right angles.
★27. Prove that, if the opposite pairs of angles in a quadrilateral are congruent, then the quadrilateral is a parallelogram.
★28. What is the measure of the angle between the hands of the clock at exactly 4:37?
 29. (a) Study the accompanying figure, and notice that a parallelogram can be determined by knowing the length of two sides :L and :W and the measure of one angle :A. Write a procedure called PARALLELOGRAM with inputs :L, :A, and :W that draws such a parallelogram.

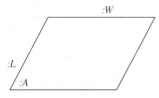

(b) Write a procedure called RECTANGLE that calls the PARALLELOGRAM procedure to draw a rectangle.
(c) Write a procedure called RHOMBUS that calls the PARALLELOGRAM procedure to draw a rhombus.
(d) How could a square of size 50 be generated by the PARALLELOGRAM procedure?
(e) How could a square of size 50 be generated by the RHOMBUS procedure?

Review Problems

30. If four distinct lines lie in a plane, what is the maximum number of intersection points of the four lines?
31. Is it possible for the union of two rays to be a line segment? Explain your answer.
32. Draw a polygonal curve that is closed but not simple.
33. Sketch two angles whose intersection is exactly one line segment.
34. Describe how you might determine the dihedral angle *A-BC-D* formed on the hip roof of a house.

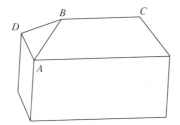

35. If a cube, as pictured, intersects with a plane, what possible figures can be obtained by the intersection. Sketch the planes and figures obtained in each case.

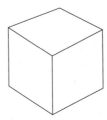

36. Name the geometric figure suggested by each of the following.
  (a) A stop sign
  (b) A school crossing sign
  (c) A railroad crossing sign
  (d) A speed limit sign
  (e) A deer crossing sign

37. In each of the following, find the required properties. If it is not possible to find the indicated properties, explain why.

(a) Two properties that hold true for all rectangles but not for all rhombuses

(b) Two properties that hold true for all squares but not for all isosceles trapezoids

(c) Two properties that hold true for all parallelograms but not for all squares

---

LABORATORY ACTIVITY

As a van Hiele Level 2 activity, prepare a set of cards labeled with the following names of quadrilaterals: rectangle, parallelogram, square, trapezoid, rhombus, quadrilateral. Use colored strings and develop a Venn diagram arranging the cards in their proper places as subsets of the Venn diagram, if possible.

Section 10-4 Geometry in Three Dimensions

Simple Closed Surfaces

A visit to the grocery store exposes us to many three-dimensional objects that possess simple closed surfaces. Examples are shown in Figure 10-46.

FIGURE 10-46

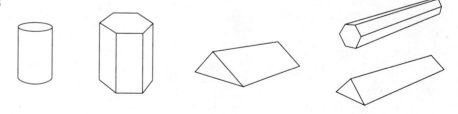

Simple closed surfaces
sphere
center

Simple closed surfaces have no holes and are hollow. Perhaps the most simple example is a sphere. A **sphere** is defined as the set of all points at a given distance from a given point, the **center**. As with the relation of a polygon to the plane containing it, a simple closed surface partitions space into three disjoint sets: points outside the surface, points belonging to the surface, and points inside the surface. The union of all points on a simple

solid
polyhedron

closed surface and all interior points is referred to as a **solid.** Figure 10-47(a), (b), (c), and (d) are examples of simple closed surfaces; (e) and (f) are not. A **polyhedron** is a simple closed surface formed entirely by polygonal regions. Figure 10-47(a) and (b) are examples of polyhedra, but (c), (d), (e), and (f) are not.

FIGURE 10-47

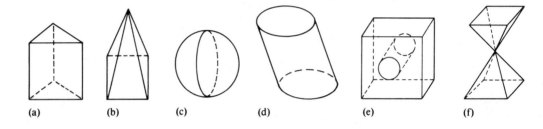

(a) (b) (c) (d) (e) (f)

face
vertices
edges
prism

bases

Each of the polygonal regions of a polyhedron is called a **face.** The vertices of the polygonal regions are called the **vertices** of the polyhedron, and the sides of each polygonal region are called the **edges** of the polyhedron.

A **prism** is a polyhedron in which two congruent polygonal faces lie in parallel planes, and the other faces are bounded by parallelograms. Figure 10-48 shows four different prisms. The upper and lower parallel faces of a prism, like the faces *ABC* and *DEF* at the bottom and top of the prism in Figure 10-48(a), are called the **bases** of the prism. A prism usually is named after its bases, as the figure suggests.

FIGURE 10-48

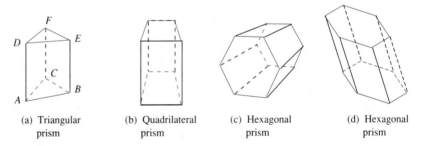

(a) Triangular prism (b) Quadrilateral prism (c) Hexagonal prism (d) Hexagonal prism

lateral faces

right prism
oblique prism

pyramid

The **lateral faces** of a prism, the faces other than the bases, are bounded by parallelograms. If the lateral faces of a prism are all bounded by rectangles, the prism is called a **right prism.** The first three prisms in Figure 10-48 are right prisms. Figure 10-48(d) is called an **oblique prism** because all its lateral edges are *not* perpendicular to the bases, and, therefore, its faces are *not* bounded by rectangles.

A **pyramid** is a polyhedron determined by a simple closed polygonal region, a point not in the plane of the region, and triangular regions determined by the point and each pair of consecutive vertices of the polygonal region.

base
apex / lateral faces
The polygonal region is called the **base** of the pyramid, and the point is called the **apex.** The faces other than the base are called **lateral faces.** Pyramids are classified according to their bases, as shown in Figure 10-49.

FIGURE 10-49

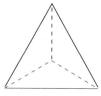

Triangular pyramid   Square pyramid   Pentagonal pyramid

convex polyhedron
A polyhedron is a **convex polyhedron** if and only if the segment connecting any two points in the interior of the polyhedron is itself in the interior. Figure 10-50 shows a concave polyhedron (one that is caved in).

FIGURE 10-50

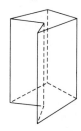

Regular Polyhedra

regular polyhedron
A **regular polyhedron** is a convex polyhedron whose faces are congruent regular polygonal regions such that the number of edges that meet at each vertex is the same for all the vertices of the polyhedron.

H I S T O R I C A L   N O T E

The regular solid polyhedra are called the **Platonic solids,** after the Greek philosopher Plato (fourth century B.C.). Plato attached a mystical significance to the five regular polyhedra, associating them with what he believed were the four elements—earth, air, fire, water—and the universe. Plato suggested that the smallest particles of earth have the form of a cube, those of air look like an octahedron, those of fire have a tetrahedral shape, those of water are shaped like an icosahedron, and those of the universe have the shape of a dodecahedron.

Regular polyhedra have fascinated mathematicians for centuries. At least three of them were identified by the Pythagoreans (ca. 500 B.C.). Two others were known to the followers of Plato (ca. 350 B.C.). Three of the five polyhedra occur in nature in the form of crystals of sodium sulphantimoniate, sodium chloride (common salt), and chrome alum, respectively as seen in Figure 10-51. The other two do not occur in crystalline form but have been observed as skeletons of microscopic sea animals called radiolaria.

FIGURE 10-51

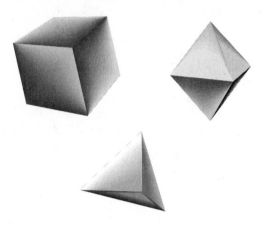

PROBLEM

How many regular polyhedra are there?

Understanding the Problem. We are asked to find the number of different types of regular polyhedra. We know that each face on a given regular polyhedron is congruent to each of the other faces on that polyhedron. This means that the measures of all the exterior angles on the faces are the same and the lengths of all the sides are the same.

Devising a Plan. We know that the sum of the measures of all the angles at a vertex of a regular polyhedron must be less than 360°. (Do you see intuitively why this is true?) We next examine the measures of the interior angles of regular polygons to determine which of the polygons could be faces of a regular polyhedron, and then we will try to determine how many types of polyhedra there are.

Carrying Out the Plan. Theorem 10-6(b) states that the measure of an interior angle of a regular n-gon is $(n - 2)180°/n$. We use this formula to determine the size of an angle of some regular polygons in Table 10-6. Could a regular heptagon be a face of a regular polyhedron? At least three figures must fit together at a vertex to make a polyhedron (why?). If three angles of a regular heptagon were together at one vertex, then the sum of the measures of these angles would be $\dfrac{3 \cdot 900°}{7}$, or $\dfrac{2700°}{7}$, which is greater than 360°. Similarly,

TABLE 10-6

Polygon	Measure of an Interior Angle
Triangle	60°
Square	90°
Pentagon	108°
Hexagon	120°
Heptagon	$\left(\dfrac{900}{7}\right)^{\circ}$

more than three angles cannot be used at a vertex. Thus, a heptagon cannot be used to make a regular polyhedron.

Because the measure of an interior angle of a regular polygon increases as the number of sides of the polygon increases (why?), any polygon with more than six sides will have an interior angle greater than 120°. Hence, if three angles were to fit together at a vertex, the sum of the measures of the angles would be greater than 360°. Thus, the only polygons that might be used to make regular polyhedra are equilateral triangles, squares, regular pentagons, and regular hexagons. Consider the possibilities in Table 10-7.

TABLE 10-7

Polygon	Measure of an Interior Angle	Number of Polygons at a Vertex	Sum of the Angles at the Vertex	Polyhedron Formed	Model
Triangle	60°	3	180°	**Tetrahedron**	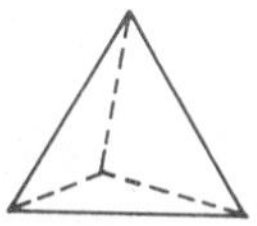
Triangle	60°	4	240°	**Octahedron**	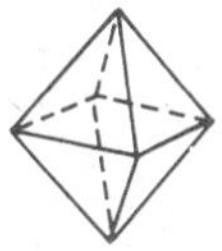
Triangle	60°	5	300°	**Icosahedron**	
Square	90°	3	270°	**Cube**	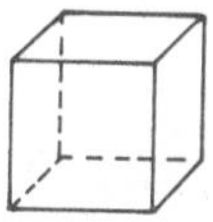
Pentagon	108°	3	324°	**Dodecahedron**	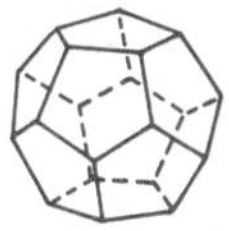

Notice that we were not able to use six equilateral triangles to make a polyhedron, because 6(60°) = 360° and the triangles would lie in a plane. Similarly, we could not use four squares or any hexagons. We also could not use more than three pentagons, because if we did the sum of the angles would be more than 360°.

semiregular polyhedra

Looking Back. Interested readers may want to investigate **semiregular polyhedra.** These are also formed by using regular polygons as faces, but the regular polygons used need not have the same number of sides. For example, a semiregular polyhedron might have squares and regular octagons as its faces.

The patterns in Figure 10-52 may be used to construct the five regular polyhedra. It is left as an exercise to determine other patterns for constructing the regular polyhedra.

FIGURE 10-52

Cube   Tetrahedron   Octahedron

 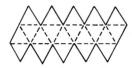

Dodecahedron   Icosahedron

Euler's Formula

A simple relationship among the number of faces, the number of edges, and the number of vertices of any polyhedron was discovered by the French mathematician and philosopher René Descartes (1596–1650) and rediscovered by the Swiss mathematician Leonhard Euler (1707–1783). Table 10-8 suggests a relationship among the numbers of vertices (V), edges (E), and *Euler's formula* faces (F). In each case, $V + F - E = 2$. This result is known as **Euler's formula.** Prisms, pyramids, and Euler's formula are investigated in the problem set.

TABLE 10-8

Name	V	F	E
Tetrahedron	4	4	6
Cube	8	6	12
Octahedron	6	8	12
Dodecahedron	20	12	30
Icosahedron	12	20	30

Cylinders and Cones

A cylinder is an example of a simple closed surface that is not a polyhedron. Consider a line segment $\overline{AB}$ and a line ℓ as shown in Figure 10-53. When $\overline{AB}$ moves so that it always remains parallel to a given line ℓ and points A and B trace simple closed planar curves other than polygons, the surface generated by $\overline{AB}$, along with the simple closed curves and their interiors, *cylinder* forms a **cylinder.** The simple closed curves traced by A and B along with *bases* their interiors are the **bases** of the cylinder and the remaining points constitute the *lateral surface of the cylinder.* Three different cylinders are pictured in Figure 10-53.

FIGURE 10-53

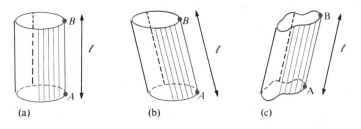

(a)　　　　(b)　　　　(c)

circular cylinder　　　　If a base of a cylinder is a circular region, the cylinder is a **circular cylinder.** If the line segment forming a cylinder is perpendicular to a base, *right cylinder* the cylinder is a **right cylinder.** Cylinders that are not right cylinders are *oblique cylinder* **oblique cylinders.** The cylinder in Figure 10-53(a) is a right cylinder; those in Figure 10-53(b) and (c) are oblique cylinders.

Suppose that we have a simple closed curve, other than a polygon, in a plane and a point P not in the plane of the curve. The union of the set of line segments connecting point P to each point of a simple closed curve and *cone* the simple closed curve and its interior is a **cone.** Cones are pictured in *vertex* Figure 10-54. Point P is the **vertex** of the cone. The points of the cone that are not in the base constitute the *lateral surface of the cone.* A line segment *altitude* from the vertex P perpendicular to the plane of the base is the **altitude.** A *right circular cone* **right circular cone,** such as the one in Figure 10-54(a), is a cone whose altitude intersects the base (a circular region) at the center of the circle. Figure 10-54(b) illustrates an oblique cone, and Figure 10-54(c) illustrates an *oblique circular cone* **oblique circular cone.**

FIGURE 10-54

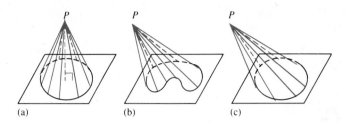

(a)　　　　　(b)　　　　　(c)

H I S T O R I C A L   N O T E

Leonhard Euler went blind in 1766 and for the remaining 17 years of his life continued to do mathematics by dictating to a secretary and by writing formulas in chalk on a slate for his secretary to copy down. He published 530 papers in his lifetime and left enough work to supply the *Proceedings of the St. Petersburg Academy* for the next 47 years.

PROBLEM SET 10-4

1. Identify each of the following polyhedra. If a polyhedron can be described in more than one way, give as many names as possible.

 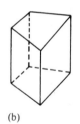 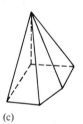

(a)　　　　　(b)　　　　　(c)

2. Given the following tetrahedron, name the following.
   (a) Vertices　　(b) Edges　　(c) Faces
   (d) Intersection of face *DRW* and edge *RA*

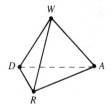

3. Identify five different shapes of containers that can be found in the grocery store.

4. For each of the following, what is the minimum number of faces possible?
   (a) Prism　　(b) Pyramid　　(c) Polyhedron

5. Classify each of the following as true or false.
   (a) If the lateral faces of a prism are rectangles, it is a right prism.
   (b) Every pyramid is a prism.
   (c) Every pyramid is a polyhedron.
   (d) The bases of a prism lie in perpendicular planes.
   (e) The bases of all cones are circles.
   (f) A cylinder has only one base.
   (g) All lateral faces of an oblique prism are rectangular regions.
   (h) All regular polyhedra are convex.

6. How many possible pairs of bases does a rectangular prism have? Explain.

7. For each of the following, draw a prism and a pyramid that have the given region as a base.
   (a) Triangle　　(b) Pentagon
   (c) Regular hexagon

8. It has been said that any three segments that are concurrent at an endpoint, as shown next, can be used to sketch a rectangular prism. Do you believe this? Make sketches to illustrate your answer.

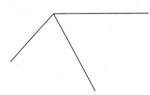

9. If possible, sketch each of the following.
   (a) An oblique square prism
   (b) An oblique square pyramid
   (c) A noncircular right cone
   (d) A noncircular cone that is not right

10. Consider a jar with a lid, as illustrated. The jar is half filled with water. In each of the marked drawings, sketch the water.

(a)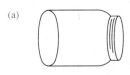

(b)

(c)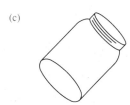

11. On the left is a pattern for a three-dimensional object. On the right are several objects. Which object will the pattern fold to make?

(a)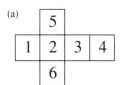

   (1)   (2)   (3)   (4)

(b)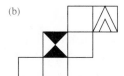

   (1)   (2)   (3)   (4)

12. Sketch the intersection of each of the following.

(a)

Cube

(b)

Remainder of unseen figure completes the cube

(c)

Sphere

(d)

Right pentagonal prism

(e)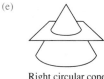

Right circular cone
(plane parallel to base)

(f)

Right circular cylinder
(plane not parallel to base)

13. The diagrams in Figure 10-52 are called *nets* for the various polyhedra. A **net** is a pattern that can be folded into a polyhedron. Find at least two other nets for each of the regular polyhedra.

14. Verify Euler's formula for each of the polyhedra in Problem 1.

15. Answer each of the following questions about a pyramid and a prism, each having an *n*-gon as a base.
    (a) How many faces does each have?
    (b) How many vertices does each have?
    (c) How many edges does each have?
    (d) Use your answers to (a), (b), and (c) to verify Euler's formula for all pyramids and all prisms.

16. Complete the table for each of the polyhedra described in the table.

Polyhedron	Vertices	Faces	Edges
(a)		8	12
(b)	20	30	
(c)	6		15

17. A circle may be considered a "many-sided" polygon. Use this notion to describe the relationship between each of the following.
    (a) A pyramid and a cone
    (b) A prism and a cylinder.

18. Check whether Euler's formula holds for each figure.

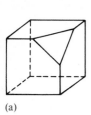

(a)

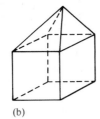

(b)

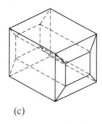

(c)

Review Problems

19. In the cube, $\overline{BF}$ and $\overline{AE}$ are diagonals of the upper and lower faces, respectively.

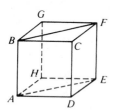

(a) Is quadrilateral *ABFE* a parallelogram? Is it a rectangle? Explain.
(b) Find six planes perpendicular to the plane containing square *ADEH*.
(c) Is $\overleftrightarrow{CD}$ parallel to the plane containing quadrilateral *ABFE*? Why?

20. Triangles *ABC* and *CDE* are equilateral triangles. Find the measure of $\angle BCD$.

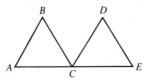

21. What is the measure of each angle in a regular nonagon?
22. Classify the following as true or false. If false, tell why.
    (a) Every rhombus is a parallelogram.
    (b) Every polygon has at least three sides.
    (c) Triangles can have at most two acute angles.
23. (a) If two angles of a triangle are complementary, what type of triangle is it?
    (b) Justify your answer.
24. If two lines are intersected by a third line in such a way that the sum of the measures of two interior angles formed by the transversal (the third line) is less than 180°, what can be said about the two original lines?
25. If a toilet-tissue roll is cut along the seams, what is the shape obtained?

B R A I N   T E A S E R

A rectangular region can be rolled to form the lateral surface of a right circular cylinder. What shape of paper is needed to make an oblique circular cylinder? (See "Making a Better Beer Glass" by A. Hoffer.)

LABORATORY ACTIVITY

1. As a van Hiele Level O activity, use isometric dot paper, as shown, to construct two-dimensional representations of three-dimensional figures. In this case, the letter O is pictured.

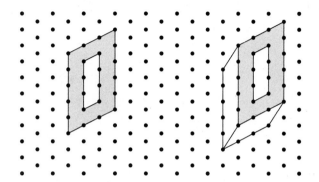

   Use similar dot paper to make three-dimensional models of the following letters.

   (a) *A*   (b) *X*   (c) *Z*   (d) *B*

2. As a van Hiele Level 1 activity, consider the front view, side view looking from the right, and top view of a structure made of cubes. Build the structure.

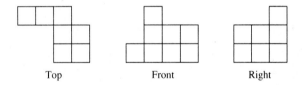

Top   Front   Right

*Section 10-5 Networks and Topological Equivalence

In the following Think Math section from *Addison-Wesley Mathematics*, 1989, Grade 7, we are introduced to a network problem.

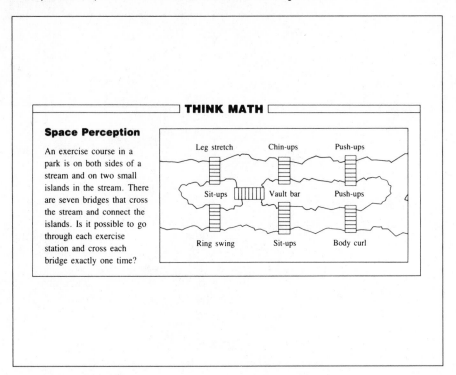

This problem is a variation on a famous problem, known as the Königsberg Bridge Problem, introduced by Leonhard Euler in 1735. The old German city of Königsberg contained a river, two islands, and seven bridges, as shown in Figure 10-55. The problem is to determine if a person can take a walk around the city in such a way that each bridge is crossed exactly once. A person can start at any land area and end at the same or a different land area. The person may visit any part of the city more than once. We designate the land areas *A*, *B*, *C*, and *D* by points, and we identify a path between land areas by drawing a curve connecting the appropriate points.

FIGURE 10-55

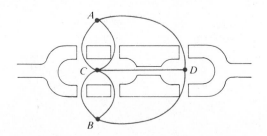

network
vertices / arcs

The colored diagram in Figure 10-55 is an example of a **network.** The points are **vertices,** and the curves are **arcs.** Using a network diagram, we can restate the Königsberg bridge problem as follows: Is there a path through the network beginning at some vertex and ending at the same or another vertex such that each arc is traversed exactly once? A network having such

traversable

a path is **traversable;** that is, each arc is passed through exactly once.

A traversable network is the type of network, or route, that a highway inspector would like to have if given the responsibility of checking out all the roads in a highway system. The inspector needs to traverse each road (arc) in the system but would save time by not having to make any repeat journeys during any inspection tour. It would be feasible for the inspector to go through any town (vertex) more than once on the route. Consider the networks in Figure 10-56. Is it possible for the highway inspector to do the job with these networks without traversing any road twice?

FIGURE 10-56

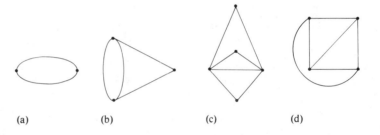

(a)   (b)   (c)   (d)

even vertex
odd vertex

The first three networks, (a), (b), and (c), are traversable; the fourth network, (d), is not. Notice that the number of arcs meeting at each vertex in networks (a) and (c) is even. Any such vertex is an **even vertex.** If the number of arcs meeting at a vertex is odd, it is an **odd vertex.** In network (b), only the odd vertices will work as starting or stopping points. In network (d), which is not traversable, all the vertices are odd. If a network is traversable, each arrival at a vertex other than a starting or a stopping point requires a departure. Thus, each vertex that is not a starting or stopping point must be even. The starting and stopping vertices in a traversable network may be even or odd, as seen in Figure 10-56(a) and (b), respectively.

In general, networks have the following properties.

1. *If a network has all even vertices, it is traversable. Any vertex can be a starting point, and the same vertex must be the stopping point.*
2. *If a network has two odd vertices, it is traversable. One odd vertex must be the starting point, and the other odd vertex must be the stopping point.*
3. *If a network has more than two odd vertices, it is not traversable.*
4. *There is no network with exactly one odd vertex.*

EXAMPLE 10-8   Which of the networks in Figure 10-57 are traversable?

FIGURE 10-57

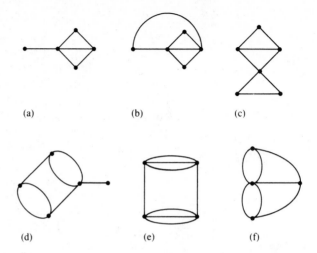

(a)   (b)   (c)

(d)   (e)   (f)

SOLUTION   Networks in (b) and (e) have all even vertices and therefore are traversable. Networks in (a) and (c) have exactly two odd vertices and are traversable. Networks in (d) and (f) have four odd vertices and are not traversable.

The network in Figure 10-57(f) represents the Königsberg bridge problem. The network has four odd vertices, and consequently is not traversable; hence, no walk is possible to complete the problem.

A problem similar to the highway inspector problem involves a traveling salesperson. Such a person might have to travel networks comparable to those of the highway inspector; however, the salesperson is interested only in visiting each town (vertex) once—and not necessarily in following each road. It is not known for which networks this can be accomplished. Can you find a route for the traveling salesperson for each network in Figure 10-57?

A different type of application of network problems is discussed in Example 10-9.

EXAMPLE 10-9   Look at the floor plan of the house shown in Figure 10-58. Is it possible to go through all the rooms of the house and pass through each door exactly once?

FIGURE 10-58

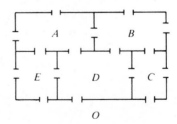

SOLUTION   Represent the floor plan as a network, as in Figure 10-59. Designate the rooms and the outside as vertices, and the paths through the doors as arcs. The network has more than two odd vertices, namely, A, B, D, and O. Thus, the network is not traversable, and it is impossible to go through all the rooms and pass through each door exactly once.

FIGURE 10-59

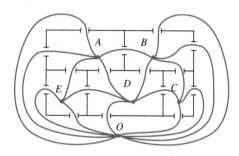

Topological Equivalence in a Plane

topology
topologically equivalent

The study of **topology** has been referred to as "rubber-sheet" geometry. In topology, one figure is **topologically equivalent** to another figure as long as one figure can be deformed into the other by simply stretching or shrinking. No cutting or tearing is allowed. As suggested in Figure 10-60, a circle may be deformed in many ways into different figures that are topologically equivalent.

FIGURE 10-60

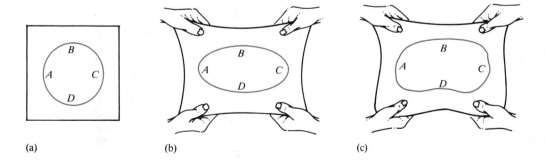

(a)   (b)   (c)

In general, any simple closed curve is topologically equivalent to a circle.

EXAMPLE 10-10 Which of the figures in Figure 10-61 are topologically equivalent to each other?

FIGURE 10-61

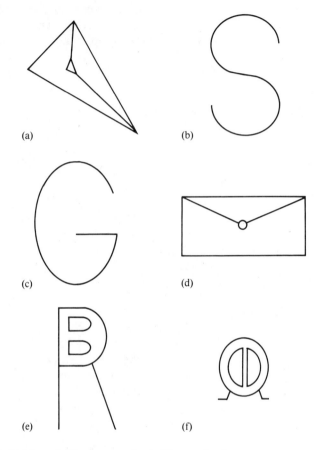

(a)

(b)

(c)

(d)

(e)

(f)

SOLUTION Figure 10-61(a) and (d) are topologically equivalent.
Figure 10-61(b) and (c) are topologically equivalent.
Figure 10-61(e) and (f) are topologically equivalent.

Topological Equivalence in Three Dimensions

In a manner similar to the one used to determine topological equivalence in a plane, objects in three dimensions can be considered topologically equivalent if one object can be deformed into another by stretching or shrinking but without cutting, tearing, or puncturing. For example, in Figure 10-62(a), the beach ball is topologically equivalent to the slightly deflated beach ball; in Figure 10-62(b), the doughnut is topologically equivalent to the coffee cup because the doughnut mass can be reshaped into the coffee cup (the hole becomes the hole for the handle); and in Figure 10-62(c), the sugar bowl is topologically equivalent to the two-handled satchel.

FIGURE 10-62

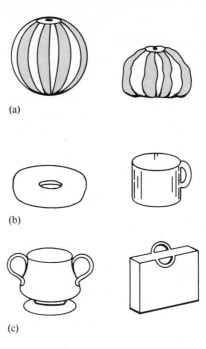

(a)

(b)

(c)

Intuitively speaking, we can say that the objects in Figure 10-62(a) are topologically equivalent because they have no holes; the objects in Figure 10-62(b) are topologically equivalent because they have one hole, and the objects in Figure 10-62(c) are topologically equivalent because they have two holes. In each of the equivalences, the number of holes remained unchanged although the shapes were altered.

PROBLEM SET 10-5

1. Which of the following networks are traversable? If the network is traversable, draw an appropriate path through it, labeling the starting and stopping vertices.

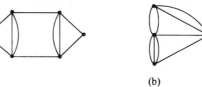

(a)

(b)

(c)

(d)

(e)

(f)

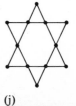

(g)

(h)

(i)

(j)

2. Which of the networks in Problem 1 can be efficiently traveled by the traveling salesperson, with no vertex visited more than once?

3. A city contains a river, three islands, and ten bridges, as shown in the accompanying figure. Is it possible to take a walk around the city by starting at any land area and returning after visiting every part of the city and crossing each bridge exactly once? If so, show such a path both on the original figure and on the corresponding network.

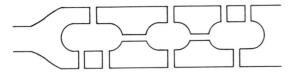

4. Use the accompanying floor plans for each of the following.
   (a) Draw a network that corresponds to each floor plan.
   (b) Determine if it is possible to pass through each room of each house by passing through each door exactly once. If it is possible, draw such a trip.

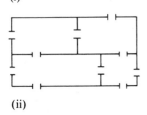

(i)

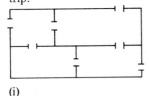

(ii)

5. Can a person walk through each door once and only once and also go through both of the following houses in a single path? If it is possible, draw such a path.

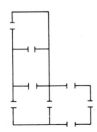
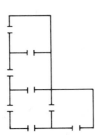

6. The following drawing represents the floor plan of an art museum. All tours begin and end at the entry. If possible, design a tour route that will allow a person to see every room but not go through any room twice.

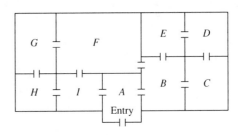

7. Each of the networks in Problem 1 separate the plane into several subsets. If R is the number of interior and exterior regions of the plane, Y is the number of vertices, A is the number of arcs, complete the following chart using each of the networks. (The first one is done for you.)

Network	R	Y	A	Y+F−A
(a)	6	6	10	2

8. Molly is making her first trip to the United States and would like to tour the eight states pictured. She would like to plan her trip so that she can cross each border between neighboring states exactly once—that is, the Washington-Oregon border, the Washington-Idaho border, and so on. Is such a trip possible? If so, does it make any difference in which state she starts her trip?

9. Which of the following pairs of figures are topologically equivalent?

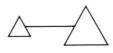
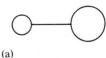

(a)

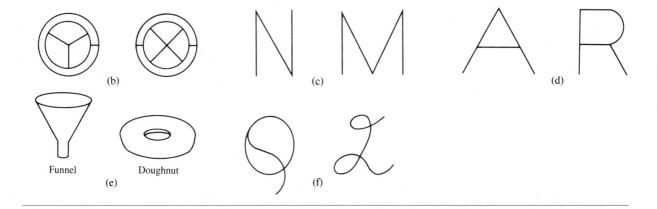

(b)   (c)   (d)

Funnel   Doughnut

(e)   (f)

LABORATORY ACTIVITY

1. Take a strip of paper like the one shown in the figure. Give one end a half-twist and join the ends by taping them. The surface obtained is called a Möbius strip.

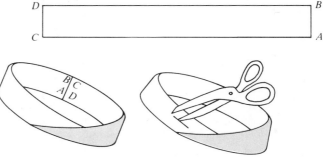

(a) Use a pencil to shade one side of a Möbius strip. What do you discover?

(b) Imagine cutting a Möbius strip all around midway between the edges. What do you predict will happen? Now do the actual cutting. What is the result?

(c) Imagine cutting a Möbius strip one third of the way from an edge and parallel to the edge all the way through until you return to the starting point. Predict the result. Then actually do the cutting. Was your prediction correct?

(d) Imagine cutting around a Möbius strip one fourth of the way from an edge. Predict the result. Then actually do the cutting. How does the result compare with the result of experiment (c)?

2. (a) Take a strip of paper and give it two half-twists (one full twist). Then join the ends together. Answer the questions in part 1.

(b) Repeat the experiment in (a), using three half-twists.

(c) Repeat the experiment in (a), using four half-twists. What do you find for odd-numbered twists? Even-numbered twists?

*Section 10-6   Introducing Logo as a Tool in Geometry

Appendix II on Logo should be completed before this section is begun. In this section, we show some examples of how Logo might be used as a problem-solving tool in helping teach and learn geometrical topics.

Logo Quadrilaterals

In Appendix II, you will find the following procedures for drawing variable-sized squares and rectangles.

```
TO SQUARE :SIDE
 REPEAT 4 [FORWARD :SIDE RIGHT 90]
END

TO RECTANGLE :HEIGHT :WIDTH
 REPEAT 2 [FORWARD :HEIGHT RIGHT 90 FORWARD
      :WIDTH RIGHT 90]
END
```

The procedures for a square and rectangle just presented are natural procedures to develop and execute. However, because a square is a special type of rectangle whose length and width are the same, we should be able to use the RECTANGLE procedure to draw a square as follows.

```
TO SQUARE :SIDE
 RECTANGLE :SIDE :SIDE
END
```

With a view toward designing other procedures for quadrilaterals, consider the diagram in Figure 10-63. Since rhombuses, rectangles, and squares are parallelograms, we first write a PARALLELOGRAM procedure so that it can be used to write the RHOMBUS and RECTANGLE procedures. Consider Figure 10-64, which depicts two parallelograms made out of tagboard and brads. The lengths of the sides are the same, but the parallelograms are very different.

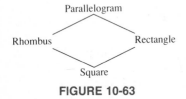

FIGURE 10-63

FIGURE 10-64

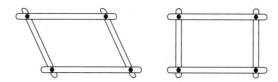

Therefore, it is necessary to specify lengths of sides and the measure of an angle when a parallelogram is to be constructed. If we specify the measure of one angle of the parallelogram, then the measures of the other angles follow, as seen in Figure 10-65.

FIGURE 10-65

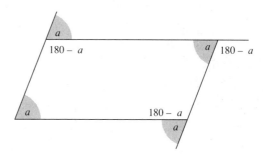

Thus, a possible procedure for drawing a parallelogram is as follows.

```
TO PARALLELOGRAM :SIDE1 :SIDE2 :ANGLE
  REPEAT 2 [FORWARD :SIDE1 RIGHT :ANGLE FORWARD
    :SIDE2 RIGHT 180-:ANGLE]
END
```

It is left as an exercise to use the PARALLELOGRAM procedure to write procedures for drawing a rectangle and a rhombus. Use of the developed rhombus procedure can also yield a different procedure for drawing a square.

Other Logo Geometry and Problem-Solving Notions

The Total Turtle Trip Theorem can be used to write procedures to draw regular polygons. For example, to constitute a regular pentagon (five sides), each of the five angles must have measure $\frac{1}{5}$ of the total turning involved in walking around the regular pentagon. Thus, each turn angle must have measure 360°/5, or 72°.

To draw a five-pointed star, we recall from the Closed Path Theorem that the total turning must be a multiple of 360°. Thus, we could write the following STARS procedure, when :N is the number of sides, :SIZE is the length of each side, and :MULT is an integer we multiply times 360 to give multiples of 360.

```
TO STARS :N :SIZE :MULT
  REPEAT :N [FD :SIZE RT 360*:MULT*:N]
END
```

STARS 5 50 1 gives a pentagon; STARS 5 50 2 gives the desired star, and hence the turning angle is $(360° \cdot 2)/5$, or $144°$.

What results can you obtain with other inputs? Could you draw a seven-pointed star by using the STARS procedure? Is only one seven-pointed star possible? How about a six-pointed star?

PROBLEM SET 10-6

1. Use the PARALLELOGRAM procedure of this section to write procedures to draw quadrilaterals for the figures named by the following procedures.
   (a) RECTANGLE   (b) RHOMBUS
2. Use the RHOMBUS procedure developed in Problem 1 to write a new SQUARE procedure.
3. Use the RHOMBUS procedure from Problem 1 to write a CUBE procedure to draw the following. (Do you see a cube?)

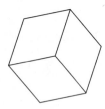

4. How many degrees should the turn be at each angle to produce a drawing of each of the following?
   (a) A regular hexagon (6 sides)
   (b) A regular heptagon (7 sides)
   (c) A regular octagon (8 sides)
   (d) A regular dodecagon (12 sides)
5. Predict the results of executing each of the following, and then use the computer to check your predictions.
   (a) STARS 5 50 3
   (b) STARS 5 50 4
   (c) STARS 5 50 5
   (d) STARS 5 50 6
   (e) STARS 5 50 7
6. Is it possible to draw a six-pointed star by using the methods developed in this section? Why or why not?

7. Write procedures for drawing each of the following.

(a)   (b)

8. Write a procedure called THIRTY that draws a $30°$ angle.
9. (a) Write a procedure called SEG that draws a segment of length 100 steps, with midpoint at home and heading of 45.
   (b) Write a procedure called PAR to draw a segment of length 100 steps that is parallel to the segment drawn in (a).
★10. Write a procedure called COUNT.ANGLES to count the number of angles formed by n concurrent rays with the same endpoint. An example is pictured next, where six angles are formed by four rays.

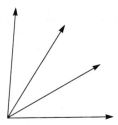

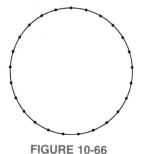

FIGURE 10-66

SOLUTION TO THE PRELIMINARY PROBLEM

Understanding the Problem. In the Preliminary Problem we are asked to determine how many segments could be drawn connecting 25 distinct points around a circle, as in Figure 10-66. If the points lie around a circle, then we know that no more than two can be collinear. (Why?) We also know that a segment can be drawn with any two distinct points as endpoints.

Devising a Plan. One strategy might be to draw several simple examples, make a table, and see if we can determine a pattern. Figure 10-67 shows the first five cases. From Figure 10-67, we see that, when one new point is added, the new point must be connected to every other point already given.

FIGURE 10-67

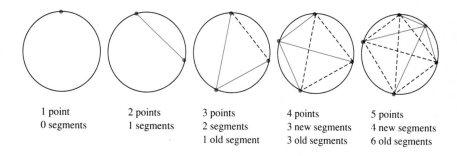

1 point	2 points	3 points	4 points	5 points
0 segments	1 segments	2 segments	3 new segments	4 new segments
		1 old segment	3 old segments	6 old segments

Thus, when a fifth point is added, it must be connected to the four given points, adding four new segments to the six already given. These results are summarized in Table 10-9. Thus to find the number of segments to be drawn, given 25 points, we must compute the sum

$$1 + 2 + 3 + 4 + \cdots + 24$$

TABLE 10-9

Number of Points	Number of Segments to Be Drawn
1	0
2	1
3	$3 = 1 + 2$
4	$6 = (1 + 2) + 3$
5	$10 = [(1 + 2) + 3] + 4$
.	.
.	.
.	.
25	$? = 1 + 2 + 3 + 4 + \cdots + 24$

Carrying Out the Plan. From Gauss's approach to computing the sum of n consecutive numbers (given in Chapter 1), we know the following.

$$1 + 2 + 3 + 4 + \cdots + n = \frac{n(n+1)}{2}$$

When $n = 24$, we have

$$1 + 2 + 3 + 4 + \cdots + 24 = \frac{24(24+1)}{2}, \quad \text{or} \quad 300$$

Therefore, there are 300 segments to be drawn.

Looking Back. It should be observed that, if we want to find the nth term for the pattern in Table 10-9, the answer is not $n(n+1)/2$. When $n = 25$, we find the sum $1 + 2 + \cdots + 24$. In general, the sum of the first $n - 1$ numbers is $(n - 1)(n - 1 + 1)/2$, or $(n - 1)n/2$. Thus, given n points on a circle, there are $(n - 1)n/2$ possible segments.

Another approach to the original problem is based on the fact that each segment is determined by two points. Consequently, the number of segments is equal to the number of ways we can choose 2 points out of 25 possible points with no regard to the order in which they are chosen—that is, a combination of 25 points taken 2 at a time. By applying the formula for combinations developed in Chapter 8, we have the following.

$$_{25}C_2 = \frac{25!}{2!(25-2)!} = \frac{25!}{2!23!} = \frac{25 \cdot 24}{2 \cdot 1} = 300$$

Still another approach is to count how many segments originate from a given point. Because every point can be connected to 24 other points and because there are 25 points, it may seem that there are $25 \cdot 24$ segments. However, in this way each segment is counted twice, once for each of its endpoints. Therefore, there are $25 \cdot 24/2$ segments. Similarly, there are $n(n-1)/2$ segments connecting n points around a circle.

QUESTIONS FROM THE CLASSROOM

1. A student claims that, if any two planes that do not intersect are parallel, then any two lines that do not intersect should also be parallel. How do you respond?

2. A student says that it is actually impossible to measure an angle, since each angle is the union of two rays that extend infinitely and, therefore, continue forever. What is your response?

3. A student asks whether a polygon whose sides are congruent is necessarily a regular polygon and whether a polygon with all angles congruent is necessarily a regular polygon. How do you answer?

4. A student thinks that a square is the only regular polygon with all right angles. The student asks if this is true and if so, why. How do you answer?

5. A student says that a line is parallel to itself. How do you reply?

6. A student says that a line in the plane of the classroom ceiling cannot be parallel to a line in the plane of the classroom floor because the lines are not in the same plane. Is this student correct? Why?

7. "If a line were a great circle, as on a globe, would there be any parallel lines?" asks one student. What is your answer?

8. One student says, "My sister's high school geometry book talked about equal angles. Why don't we use equal angles instead of congruent angles?" How do you reply?

9. A student says that there can only be 360 different rays emanating from a point since there are only 360 degrees in a circle. How do you respond?

CHAPTER OUTLINE

I. Basic geometric notions
  A. Points, lines, and planes
    1. **Points, lines,** and **planes** are basic, but undefined, terms.
    2. **Collinear points** are points that belong to the same line.
    3. Important subsets of lines are **segments, half-lines,** and **rays.**
    4. **Coplanar points** are points that lie in the same plane. **Coplanar lines** are defined similarly.
    5. Two coplanar lines with exactly one point in common are **intersecting lines.**
    6. **Concurrent lines** are lines that contain a common point.
    7. Two coplanar lines with no points in common are **parallel.**
    8. **Skew lines** are lines that cannot be contained in the same plane.
    9. An **angle** is the union of two rays with a common endpoint.
    10. Angles are classified according to size as **acute, obtuse, right,** or **straight.**
    11. Two lines that meet to form a right angle are **perpendicular.**
    12. **Parallel planes** are planes with no points in common.
    13. A **dihedral angle** is the union of two half-planes and the common line defining the half-planes.
    14. **Space** is the set of all points.
  B. Plane figures
    1. A **simple curve** is a curve that does not cross itself when traced, except that it is possible for the starting and stopping points to be the same.
    2. A **closed curve** is a curve that, when traced, has the same starting and stopping points and may cross itself at individual points.
    3. **Jordan Curve Theorem:** A simple closed curve separates the plane into three disjoint subsets: the interior of the curve, the exterior of the curve, and the curve itself.
    4. A **polygon** is a simple closed polygonal curve.
      (a) A **diagonal** is any line segment connecting two nonconsecutive vertices of a polygon.
      (b) A **convex polygon** is one such that, if any two points of the polygonal region are connected by a segment, the segment is a subset of the polygonal region.
      (c) A **concave polygon** is a nonconvex polygon.
      (d) A **regular polygon** is a polygon in which all the angles are congruent and all the sides are congruent.
    5. A **polygonal region** is the union of a polygon and its interior.
    6. **Congruent figures** are figures with the same size and shape.
    7. Triangles are classified according to the lengths of their sides as **scalene, isosceles,** or **equilateral,** and according to the measures of their angles as **acute, obtuse,** or **right.**
    8. Quadrilaterals with special properties are **trapezoids, parallelograms, rectangles, kites, isosceles trapezoids, rhombuses,** and **squares.**
    9. A **circle** is a set of points in a plane that lie at the same distance from a given point, called the **center.**
II. Theorems involving angles
  A. **Supplements** of the same angle, or of congruent angles, are congruent.
  B. **Complements** of the same angle, or of congruent angles, are congruent.
  C. **Vertical angles** formed by intersecting lines are congruent.
  D. If any two distinct lines are cut by a transversal, then a pair of **corresponding angles, alternate interior angles,** *or* **alternate exterior angles** are congruent if and only if the lines are parallel.
  E. The sum of the measures of the angles of a triangle is $180°$.
  F. The sum of the measures of the interior angles of any convex polygon with n sides is $(n - 2)180°$. One angle of a regular polygon has measure $(n - 2)\,180°/n$.
  G. The sum of the measures of the exterior angles of any convex polygon is $360°$.

H. **Total Turtle Trip Theorem:** Any convex polygon can be drawn with a total turning of 360°.

I. **Closed Path Theorem:** The total turning around any closed path is a multiple of 360°.

III. Three-dimensional figures
  A. A **polyhedron** is a simple closed surface formed by polygonal regions.
  B. Three-dimensional figures with special properties are **prisms, pyramids, regular polyhedra, cylinders, cones,** and **spheres.**
  C. **Euler's formula,** $V + F - E = 2$, holds for polyhedra, where V, E, and F represent the number of vertices, the number of edges, and the number of faces of a polyhedron, respectively.

*IV. Network and topology
  A. A **network** is a collection of points called **vertices** and a collection of curves called **arcs.**
  B. A vertex of a network is called an **even vertex** if the number of arcs meeting at the vertex is even.

A vertex is called an **odd vertex** if the number of arcs meeting at a vertex is odd.

C. A network is called **traversable** if there is a path through the network such that each arc is passed through exactly once.
  1. If all the vertices of a network are even, then the network is traversable. Any vertex can be a starting point and the same vertex must be the stopping point.
  2. If a network has two odd vertices, it is traversable. One odd vertex must be the starting point and the other odd vertex must be the stopping point.
  3. If a network has more than two odd vertices, it is not traversable.
  4. No network has exactly one odd vertex.

D. A figure is **topologically equivalent** to another when the first can be deformed into the other as a result of stretching or shrinking. No cutting or tearing is allowed.

CHAPTER TEST

1. Sketch diagrams such that each of the following is true.
   (a) The intersection of two segments is a segment.
   (b) The intersection of two rays is a ray.
   (c) The intersection of two rays is a segment.
   (d) The intersection of two angles is an angle.
   (e) The intersection of two angles is a segment.

2. (a) List three different names for line m.

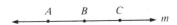

   (b) Name two different rays on m that have endpoint B.
   (c) Find a simpler name for $\overrightarrow{AB} \cap \overrightarrow{BA}$.
   (d) Find a simpler name for $\overrightarrow{AB} \cap \overleftrightarrow{BC}$.
   (e) Find a simpler name for $\overrightarrow{BA} \cap \overrightarrow{AC}$.

3. In the figure, $\overleftrightarrow{PQ}$ is perpendicular to α.

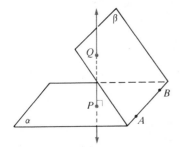

   (a) Name a pair of skew lines.
   (b) Using only the letters in the figure, name as many planes as possible that are each perpendicular to α.
   (c) What is the intersection of planes APQ and β?
   (d) Is there a single plane containing A, B, P, and Q? Explain your answer.

4. For each of the following, sketch two parallelograms, if possible, that satisfy the given conditions.
   (a) Their intersection is a single point.
   (b) Their intersection is exactly two points.
   (c) Their intersection is exactly three points.
   (d) Their intersection is exactly one line segment.

5. Draw each of the following curves.
   (a) A simple closed curve
   (b) A closed curve that is not simple
   (c) A concave hexagon
   (d) A convex decagon

6. (a) Can a triangle have two obtuse angles? Justify your answer.
   (b) Can a parallelogram have four acute angles? Justify your answer.

7. In a certain triangle, the measure of one angle is twice the measure of the smallest angle. The measure of the third angle is seven times greater than the measure of the smallest angle. Find the measures of each of the angles in the triangle.

8. (a) Explain how to derive an expression for the sum of the measures of the angles in a convex n-gon.

(b) In a certain regular polygon, the measure of each angle is 176°. How many sides does the polygon have?

9. (a) Sketch a convex polyhedron with at least ten vertices.
   (b) Count the number of vertices, edges, and faces for the polyhedron in (a) and determine if Euler's formula holds for this polyhedron.

10. Sketch each of the following.
    (a) Three planes that intersect in a point
    (b) A plane and a cone that intersect in a circle
    (c) A plane and a cylinder that intersect in a segment
    (d) Two pyramids that intersect in a triangle

11. Sketch drawings to illustrate all possible intersections of a square pyramid and a plane.

12. If $3x°$ and $(6x - 18)°$ are measures of corresponding angles formed by two parallel lines and a transversal, what is the value of x?

13. Find $6°48'59'' + 28°19'36''$. Write your answer in simplest terms.

14. In the figure, ℓ is parallel to m, and $m(\angle 1) = 60°$. Find each of the following.

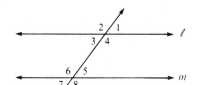

(a) $m(\angle 3)$ (b) $m(\angle 6)$ (c) $m(\angle 8)$

15. If a pyramid has an octagon for a base, how many lateral faces does it have?

16. If ABC is a right triangle and $m(\angle A) = 42°$, what is the measure of the other acute angle?

*17. (a) Which of the following networks are traversable?
     (b) Find a corresponding path for the networks that are traversable.

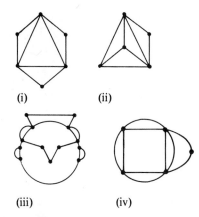

(i)   (ii)

(iii)   (iv)

*18. Write a Logo program to construct two perpendicular segments.

*19. Write a Logo program to draw a variable-sized isosceles triangle.

C H A P T E R   11

Constructions,
Congruence,
and Similarity

PRELIMINARY PROBLEM

A building was to be built on a triangular piece of property. The architect was given the measurements of the angles of the triangular lot as approximately 54°, 39°, and 87° and the lengths of two of the sides as 100 m and 80 m. When the architect began the design on drafting paper, she drew a triangle to scale with the corresponding measures and found that the lot was considerably smaller than she had been led to believe. It appeared that the proposed building would not fit. The surveyor was called; he confirmed each of the measurements and could not see any problem with the size. Neither could understand the reason for the other's opinion. Determine the reason for the miscommunication, and suggest a way to provide an accurate description of the lot.

Introduction

In the *Standards*, it is recommended that "students examine and discover relationships and develop spatial sense by constructing, drawing, measuring, visualizing, comparing, transforming, and classifying geometric figures." In this chapter, we introduce the concepts of congruence and similarity and investigate properties of congruent triangles through compass-and-straightedge constructions. The restriction to straightedge and compass goes back to antiquity. The straight line and circle were considered the basic geometric figures by the Greeks and the straightedge and compass are their physical analogues. It is also believed that the Greek philosopher Plato (427–347 B.C.) rejected the use of other mechanical devices for geometric constructions because they emphasized practicality rather than "ideas," which he regarded as more important. Constructions are also done in this chapter by means of paper folding and through use of a plastic device called a Mira.

Throughout the chapter, we use linear measurement and the notion of length, although a formal discussion of measurement is postponed until Chapter 13.

Section 11-1 Congruence Through Constructions

In mathematics, the word *congruent* is used to describe objects that have the same size and shape. In elementary schools tracing is a method for determining congruence. For example, the squares in Figure 11-1 are congruent because a tracing of one square can be made to match the other. We say that square *ABCD* is congruent to square *EFGH*, and we write *ABCD* ≅ *EFGH*.

FIGURE 11-1

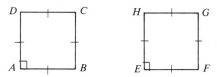

Any two line segments have the same shape, so *two line segments are congruent if they have the same size (length). The length of the line segment* $\overline{AB}$ *is denoted by AB.* In a similar way, two angles are congruent if and only if their measures are the same.

$\overline{AB} \cong \overline{CD}$ if and only if $AB = CD$
$\angle ABC \cong \angle DEF$ if and only if $m(\angle ABC) = m(\angle DEF)$

The congruence relation has the reflexive, symmetric, and transitive properties.

The three most famous compass-and-ruler construction problems of antiquity are:

1. Constructing a square equal in area to a given circle (often referred to as "squaring the circle")
2. Constructing the edge of a cube whose volume is double that of a cube of a given edge
3. Trisecting any angle

For generations, mathematicians endeavored to solve these problems, but their efforts were unsuccessful. In the nineteenth century, as a result of the work of the French mathematician Evariste Galois (1811–1832), it was proved that these constructions cannot be done using only a compass and a straightedge.

Geometric Constructions

Completing a geometric construction is a task in which, given some geometric elements such as points, segments, angles, or circles, we derive other elements by using certain well-defined instruments. Besides asking how a particular problem can be solved with given instruments, geometers are interested in knowing which problems can and which cannot be solved with the given instruments.

Ancient Greek mathematicians constructed geometric figures with a staightedge (no markings on it) and a collapsible compass. Figure 11-2 shows a modern compass. It can be used to mark off and duplicate lengths and to construct circles or arcs with a radius of a given measure.

FIGURE 11-2
Construct a circle given its radius.

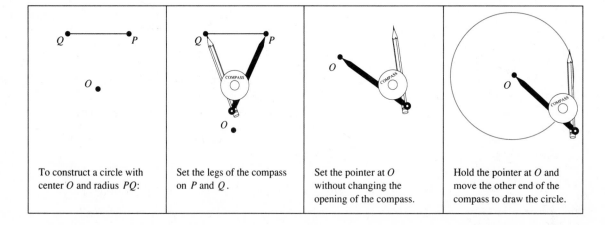

| To construct a circle with center O and radius PQ: | Set the legs of the compass on P and Q. | Set the pointer at O without changing the opening of the compass. | Hold the pointer at O and move the other end of the compass to draw the circle. |

To draw a circle when given the radius *PQ* of a circle, we follow the steps illustrated in Figure 11-2. The figure formed is a circle with center *O*.

A circle with center *O* is called circle *O*. Any other circle is congruent to circle *O* if the radii are congruent. In general, *two circles are congruent if their radii are congruent.*

arc   An **arc** of a circle can be thought of as any part of the circle that can be drawn without lifting a pencil. An arc is either a part of a circle or the

center of an arc   entire circle. The **center of an arc** is the center of the circle containing the arc.

Two points on a circle determine two different arcs. To avoid this ambiguity, an arc is normally named by three letters, such as arc *ACB* in Figure 11-3. Arc *ACB* is denoted by $\overparen{ACB}$. In this notation, the first and last letters indicate the endpoints of the arc, and the middle letter indicates which of two possible arcs is intended. If there is no danger of ambiguity in a discussion, we use two letters to name the arc formed. In Figure 11-3, $\overparen{ACB}$,

minor arc / major arc   is a **minor arc,** and $\overparen{ADB}$ is a **major arc.** If the major arc and the minor arc

semicircle   of a circle are the same size, each is a **semicircle.**

FIGURE 11-3

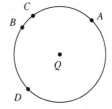

Constructing Segments

There are many ways to construct a segment congruent to a given segment $\overline{AB}$. A natural approach is to use a ruler, measure $\overline{AB}$, and then draw a

FIGURE 11-4

Construct a line segment congruent to a given segment.

congruent segment. A different way is to trace $\overline{AB}$ onto a piece of paper. A third method is to use a straightedge and a compass (see Figure 11-4).

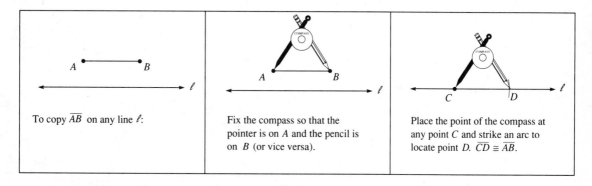

| To copy $\overline{AB}$ on any line ℓ: | Fix the compass so that the pointer is on *A* and the pencil is on *B* (or vice versa). | Place the point of the compass at any point *C* and strike an arc to locate point *D*. $\overline{CD} \cong \overline{AB}$. |

Triangle Congruence

We use the concept of congruence for segments and angles as the basis for determining whether polygons, specifically triangles, are congruent. Consider the two triangles shown in Figure 11-5. *If triangle ABC is congruent to triangle A'B'C', written* $\triangle ABC \cong \triangle A'B'C'$, *then the congruency establishes a one-to-one correspondence between vertices of one triangle and the vertices of the other triangle such that A corresponds to A', B to B', and C to C'.*

$$\angle A \cong \angle A', \quad \angle B \cong \angle B' \quad \text{and} \quad \angle C \cong \angle C'$$
$$\overline{AB} \cong \overline{A'B'}, \quad \overline{BC} \cong \overline{B'C'} \quad \text{and} \quad \overline{AC} \cong \overline{A'C'}$$

FIGURE 11-5

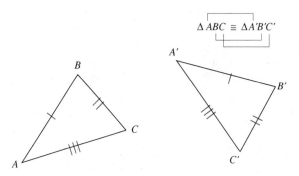

If $\triangle ABC \cong \triangle A'B'C'$, as in Figure 11-5, then any rearrangement of the letters ABC and the corresponding rearrangement of $A'B'C'$ results in another symbolic representation of the same congruence. For example, $\triangle BCA \cong \triangle B'C'A'$.

Because there are $3 \cdot 2 \cdot 1$, or 6, ways to rearrange the letters A, B, and C, each pair of congruent triangles can be symbolized in six ways. However, each of the six symbolic representations gives the same information about the triangles.

EXAMPLE 11-1 Assume that each of the pairs of triangles in Figure 11-6 is congruent, and write an appropriate symbolic congruence in each case.

FIGURE 11-6

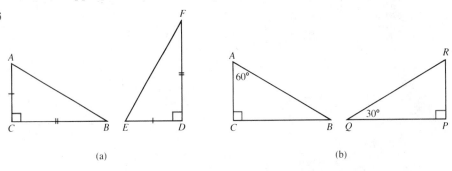

(a) (b)

SOLUTION   (a) Vertex C corresponds to D because the angles at C and D are right angles. Also, $\overline{CB} \cong \overline{DF}$ and C corresponds to D, so B corresponds to F. Consequently, the remaining vertices must correspond; that is, A corresponds to E. Thus, one possible symbolic congruence is $\triangle ABC \cong \triangle EFD$.

(b) Vertex C corresponds to P because the angles at C and P are both right angles. To establish the other correspondences, we first find the missing angles in the triangles. We see that $m(\angle B) = 90° - 60° = 30°$ and $m(\angle R) = 90° - 30° = 60°$. Consequently, A corresponds to R because $m(\angle A) = m(\angle R) = 60°$, and B corresponds to Q because $m(\angle B) = m(\angle Q) = 30°$. Thus, one possible symbolic congruence is $\triangle ABC \cong \triangle RQP$.

Side, Side, Side Property (SSS)

In an automotive assembly line, the entire production process is designed in such a way that the same model cars are congruent to each other. (Outside paint and different colors of upholstery fabric and interiors provide individual differences for customers.) Calibration experts have worked to ensure that car parts are interchangeable, so the same part fits on all basic models of the same car. To ensure that the cars are congruent, the parts must be congruent. In considering congruence of figures in geometry we supply the same process. To establish that two triangles are congruent, we must determine the congruency of segments and angles that make up the triangles. In the assembly line of automotive production, decisions have to be made about the minimal set of items to consider for eventual congruency; similar decisions must be made in triangle congruency.

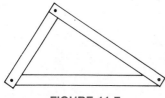

FIGURE 11-7

Consider the triangle formed by attaching three segments, as in Figure 11-7. Such a triangle is *rigid.* Its size and shape cannot be changed. Because of this property, a manufacturer can make duplicates if the lengths of the sides are known.

Because a triangle is completely determined by its three sides, we have the following property.

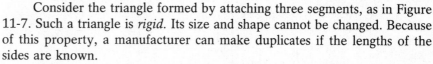

● **P R O P E R T Y**
Side, Side, Side (SSS)   If the three sides of one triangle are congruent, respectively, to the three sides of a second triangle, then the triangles are congruent.

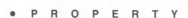

● **R E M A R K**
The fact that two triangles are congruent by SSS implies that all six parts—the corresponding sides and the corresponding angles—of the triangles are congruent. The statement, *"Corresponding parts of congruent triangles are congruent,"* is *sometimes abbreviated CPCTC.*

EXAMPLE 11-2 For each of the parts in Figure 11-8, use SSS to explain why the given pair(s) of triangles are congruent.

FIGURE 11-8

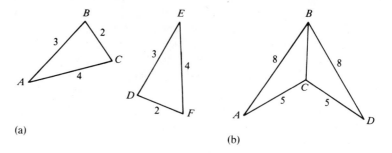

(a)

(b)

SOLUTION (a) $\triangle ABC \cong \triangle EDF$ by SSS because $\overline{AB} \cong \overline{ED}$, $\overline{BC} \cong \overline{DF}$, and $\overline{AC} \cong \overline{EF}$.
(b) $\triangle ABC \cong \triangle DBC$ by SSS because $\overline{AB} \cong \overline{DB}$, $\overline{AC} \cong \overline{DC}$, and $\overline{BC} \cong \overline{BC}$.

Using the SSS property, we can construct a duplicate triangle if given a triangle or construct a triangle if given the lengths of the three sides. For example, using only segments of lengths AB, BC, and AC, as shown in Figure 11-9, we can construct $\triangle A'B'C'$ congruent to $\triangle ABC$.

FIGURE 11-9

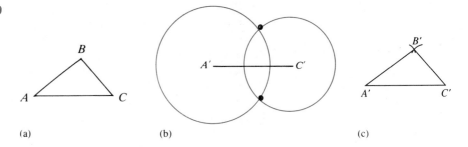

(a)

(b)

(c)

First, we construct a segment congruent to one of the three segments. For example, we may construct $\overline{A'C'}$ so that it is congruent to $\overline{AC}$. To complete the triangle construction, the other vertex, B', must be located. The distance from A' to B' is AB. All points at a distance AB from A' are on a circle with center at A' and radius of length AB. Similarly, B' must be on a circle with center C' and radius of length BC. Figure 11-9(b) shows the two circles. The only possible locations for B' are at the points where the two circles intersect. Either point is acceptable. Usually, a picture of the construction shows only one possibility, and the construction uses only arcs, as pictured in Figure 11-9(c).

● **R E M A R K**
Starting the construction with a segment $\overline{A'B'}$ congruent to $\overline{AB}$ or with $\overline{B'C'}$ congruent to $\overline{BC}$ would also result in triangles congruent to $\triangle ABC$.

From the preceding construction, it may seem that, given any three segments, it is possible to construct a triangle whose sides are congruent to the given segments. However, this is not the case. For example, consider the segments in Figure 11-10(a), whose measures are p, q, and r. If we choose the base of the triangle to be a side of length p and attempt to find the third vertex by intersecting arcs, as in Figure 11-10(b), we find that the arcs do not intersect. Because no intersection occurs, a triangle is not determined.

FIGURE 11-10

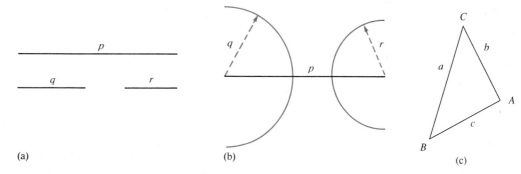

(a)　　　　　　　　　　　　　　　(b)　　　　　　　　　　　　　　　(c)

In Figure 11-10(c), we see that the path from B to A along $\overline{BC}$ and then $\overline{CA}$ is longer than the path from B to A along $\overline{AB}$. Thus, $a + b > c$. Therefore, *the sum of the measures of any two sides of a triangle must be greater than the measure of the third side.* This property is called the **Triangle Inequality.** For example, segments of length 3 cm, 5 cm, and 9 cm do not determine a triangle, because $3 + 5$ is not greater than 9.

Triangle Inequality

Constructing Congruent Angles

We use the SSS notion of congruent triangles to construct an angle congruent to a given angle $\angle B$ by making $\angle B$ a part of an isosceles triangle and then reproducing this triangle, as in Figure 11-11.

FIGURE 11-11
Copy an angle.

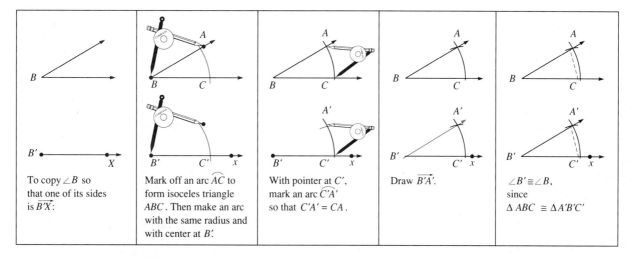

| To copy $\angle B$ so that one of its sides is $\overrightarrow{B'X}$: | Mark off an arc $\overset{\frown}{AC}$ to form isoceles triangle ABC. Then make an arc with the same radius and with center at B'. | With pointer at C', mark an arc $\overset{\frown}{C'A'}$ so that $C'A' = CA$. | Draw $\overrightarrow{B'A'}$. | $\angle B' \cong \angle B$, since $\triangle ABC \cong \triangle A'B'C'$ |

We have seen that, given three segments, no more than one triangle can be constructed. Could more than one triangle be constructed from only two segments? Consider Figure 11-12(b), which shows three different triangles with sides congruent to the segments given in Figure 11-12(a). The length of the third side depends on the measure of the angle between the other two sides, the **included angle.**

included angle

FIGURE 11-12

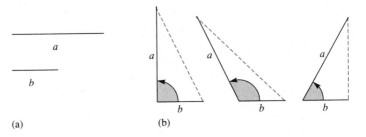

(a)

(b)

Side, Angle, Side Property (SAS)

It appears that, if we knew the lengths of two sides and the measure of the angle included between these two sides, we could construct a unique triangle. This is true; and we can express the rule as the **Side, Angle, Side (SAS)** property.

● **P R O P E R T Y**
Side, Angle, Side (SAS) If two sides and the included angle of one triangle are congruent to two sides and the included angle of another triangle, respectively, then the two triangles are congruent.

● **R E M A R K**
When *A* is written between *S* and *S*, as in *SAS*, it is assumed to be the included angle; otherwise, the property may not hold.

EXAMPLE 11-3 For each part of Figure 11-13, use SAS to show that the given pair of triangles is congruent.

FIGURE 11-13

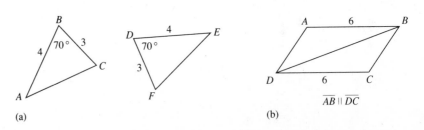

(a)

$\overline{AB} \parallel \overline{DC}$

(b)

SOLUTION (a) $\triangle ABC \cong \triangle EDF$ by SAS because $\overline{AB} \cong \overline{ED}$, $\angle B \cong \angle D$, and $\overline{BC} \cong \overline{DF}$.
(b) Because $\overline{AB} \cong \overline{CD}$ and $\overline{DB} \cong \overline{BD}$, we need either another side or another angle to show that the triangles are congruent. We know nothing about the sides except that $\overline{AB} \parallel \overline{DC}$. Since parallel segments $\overline{AB}$ and $\overline{DC}$ are cut by transversal $\overline{BD}$, we have alternate interior angles $\angle ABD$ and $\angle BDC$ congruent. Now $\triangle ABD \cong \triangle CBD$ by SAS.

EXAMPLE 11-4 Given isosceles triangle ABC with $\overline{AB} \cong \overline{AC}$ and $\overrightarrow{AD}$ the bisector of $\angle A$, as shown in Figure 11-14, show that $\angle B \cong \angle C$.

FIGURE 11-14

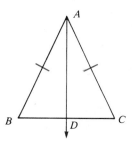

SOLUTION Because $\overrightarrow{AD}$ is the bisector of $\angle A$, then $\angle BAD \cong \angle CAD$. Also, $\overline{AD} \cong \overline{AD}$ and $\overline{AB} \cong \overline{AC}$, so $\triangle BAD \cong \triangle CAD$ by SAS. Therefore, $\angle B \cong \angle C$ because the angles are corresponding parts of congruent triangles.

Example 11-4 proves the following theorem.

● **T H E O R E M 11-1**
If two sides of a triangle are congruent, then the angles opposite these sides are congruent.

Constructions Involving Two Sides and an Angle of a Triangle

Figure 11-15 shows how to construct a triangle congruent to $\triangle ABC$ by using two sides $\overline{AB}$ and $\overline{AC}$ and the *included angle*, $\angle A$, formed by these sides. First, a ray with an arbitrary endpoint A' is drawn, and $\overline{A'C'}$ is constructed congruent to $\overline{AC}$. Then, $\angle A'$ is constructed so that $\angle A' \cong \angle A$, and B' is marked on the side of $\angle A'$ not containing C' so that $\overline{A'B'} \cong \overline{AB}$. Connecting B' and C' completes $\triangle A'B'C'$ so that $\triangle A'B'C' \cong \triangle ABC$.

FIGURE 11-15

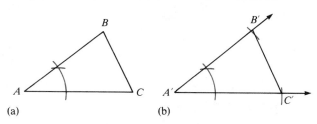

(a) (b)

If, in two triangles, two sides and an angle not included between these sides are congruent, respectively, the information is not sufficient to guarantee congruent triangles. For example, we use $\overline{AB}$, $\overline{AC}$, and $\angle C$ of Figure 11-16(a). By making $\overline{A'C'} \cong \overline{AC}$, reproducing $\angle C$ as $\angle C'$, and finding the set of all points at a distance AB from A', it is possible to construct two noncongruent triangles, as shown in Figure 11-16(b) and (c). In certain special cases, if the arc formed by the circle with center A' and radius AB intersects the side of $\angle C'$ at exactly one point, only one triangle can be formed. (For what kind of triangles does this happen? For what cases is no triangle formed?)

FIGURE 11-16

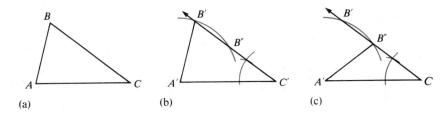

(a) (b) (c)

PROBLEM SET 11-1

1. (a) Draw any triangle ABC in which the measure $\angle A$ is greater than the measure of $\angle B$. Compare BC and AC. What did you find?
   (b) Draw any triangle ABC in which BC is greater than AC. Measure the angles opposite $\overline{BC}$ and $\overline{AC}$. Compare the angle measures. What did you find?
   (c) Based on your findings in (a) and (b), make a conjecture concerning the lengths of sides and the measures of angles of a triangle.

2. Using a ruler, protractor, compass, or tracing paper, construct each of the following, if possible.
   (a) A segment congruent to $\overline{AB}$ and an angle congruent to $\angle CAB$

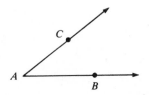

   (b) A triangle with sides of lengths 2 cm, 3 cm, and 4 cm
   (c) A triangle with sides of lengths 4 cm, 3 cm, and 5 cm (What kind of triangle is it?)
   (d) A triangle with sides 4 cm, 5 cm, and 10 cm
   (e) An equilateral triangle with sides 5 cm
   (f) A triangle with sides 6 cm and 7 cm and an included angle of measure 75°
   (g) A triangle with sides 6 cm and 7 cm and a nonincluded angle of measure 40°
   (h) A triangle with sides 6 cm and 6 cm and a nonincluded angle of measure 40°
   (i) A right triangle with legs 4 cm and 8 cm (The legs include the right angle.)

3. For each of the conditions in Problem 2(b)–(h), does the given information determine a unique triangle? Explain why or why not.

4. Given segments of integer length from 1 through 10, inclusive, how many different triangles can be constructed if for each triangle exactly three segments must be used and duplicates of segments are allowed?

5. For each of the following, determine whether the given conditions are sufficient to prove that $\triangle PQR \cong \triangle MNO$. Justify your answers.

   (a) $\overline{PQ} \cong \overline{MN}$, $\overline{PR} \cong \overline{MO}$, $\angle P \cong \angle M$
   (b) $\overline{PQ} \cong \overline{MN}$, $\overline{PR} \cong \overline{MO}$, $\overline{QR} \cong \overline{NO}$
   (c) $\overline{PQ} \cong \overline{MN}$, $\overline{PR} \cong \overline{MO}$, $\angle Q \cong \angle N$

6. For each of the following, determine from the given information if it is possible to conclude that triangles (1) and (2) are congruent. Justify your answers.

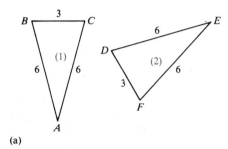

(a)

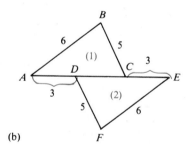

(b)

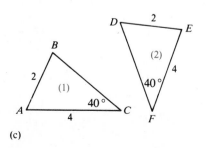

(c)

7. In each of the following, find and identify two congruent triangles.

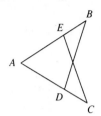

(a) $\overline{AB} \cong \overline{AC}$
     $\overline{AE} \cong \overline{AD}$

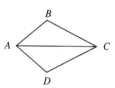

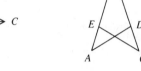

(b) $\overline{AB} \cong \overline{AD}$
     $\overline{BC} \cong \overline{DC}$

(c) $\overline{BE} \cong \overline{BD}$, $\overline{EC} \cong \overline{DA}$
     $\angle BDA \cong \angle BEC$

8. A rancher designed a wooden gate as shown. Explain the purpose of the diagonal boards on the gate.

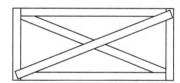

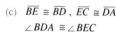

9. A rural homeowner had his television antenna held in place by three guy wires, as shown below. If the distances to each of the stakes from the base of the antenna are the same, what is true about the lengths of the wires? Why?

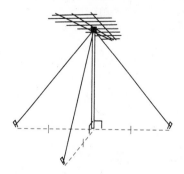

10. A group of students on a hiking trip wants to find the distance AB across a pond. One student suggests choosing any point C, connecting it with B, and then finding point D such that $\angle DCB \cong \angle ACB$ and $\overline{DC} \cong \overline{AC}$. How and why does this help in finding the distance AB?

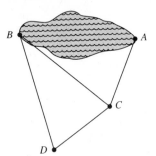

11. Using only a compass and a straightedge, perform each of the following.
    (a) Reproduce $\angle A$.

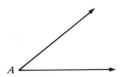

(b) Construct an equilateral triangle with side $\overline{AB}$.

(c) Construct a 60° angle.
(d) Construct an isosceles triangle with $\angle A$ as the angle included between the two congruent sides.

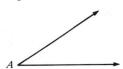

12. Using only a compass and a straightedge, perform each of the following.
    (a) Construct $\angle C$ so that $m(\angle C) = m(\angle A) + m(\angle B)$.

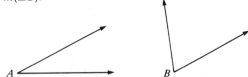

(b) Using the angles in (a), construct $\angle C$ so that $m(\angle C) = m(\angle B) - m(\angle A)$.

13. An equilateral triangle ABC is congruent to itself.
    (a) Write all possible true correspondences between the triangle and itself.
    (b) Use one of your answers in (a) to show that an equilateral triangular is also equiangular.

14. In the accompanying drawing, $\overrightarrow{BD}$ bisects $\angle ABC$ of isosceles triangle ABC with $\overline{AB} \cong \overline{CB}$.

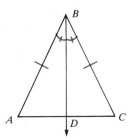

(a) Make a conjecture about a relation between $\overline{AD}$ and $\overline{CD}$.
★(b) Prove or disprove your conjecture in (a).
(c) What are the measures of $\angle ADB$ and $\angle CDB$?
★(d) Prove your answer in (c).

15. Suppose that polygon $ABCD$ is any square.
    (a) What is the relationship between point F and the diagonals $\overline{BD}$ and $\overline{AC}$?
    (b) Justify your answer in (a).
    (c) What are the measures of $\angle BFA$ and $\angle AFD$?
    (d) Justify your answer in (c).

16. The diagonals of a quadrilateral bisect each other (that is, each diagonal is divided by the point of intersection into two congruent segments).
    (a) What kind of quadrilateral must it be?
    (b) Justify your answer in (a).

17. Construct several noncongruent rhombuses and several noncongruent parallelograms that are not rhombuses. In each case, construct the diagonals.
    (a) Based on your observations, what is true about the angles formed by the diagonals of a rhombus that is not necessarily true about the angles formed by the diagonals of a parallelogram that is not a rhombus?
    (b) Justify your conjecture in (a).

18. (a) What kind of figure is a quadrilateral in which both pairs of opposite sides are congruent?
    (b) Justify your answer in (a).

★19. The theorem stating that the base angles of an isosceles triangle are congruent followed from Example 11-4, where the angle bisector $\overrightarrow{AD}$ was drawn. It is also possible to justify this theorem without drawing an angle bisector. Show that $\triangle BAC \cong \triangle CAB$ by using one of the congruence properties, and hence conclude the theorem.

20. Write a Logo procedure to draw a variable-sized equilateral triangle.

21. Logo programs can be used to construct triangles based on parts of a triangle. Type the accompanying program into your computer and then run the following.
    (a) SAS 50 75 83
    (b) SAS 60 120 60

```
TO SAS :SIDE1 :ANGLE :SIDE2
   DRAW
   FORWARD :SIDE1
   RIGHT 180 - :ANGLE
   FORWARD :SIDE2
   HOME
END
```

(*In Apple Logo II, replace DRAW with CLEARSCREEN.*)

22. Following is a different procedure for constructing a triangle when given two sides and an included angle. Compare this procedure to the one in Problem 21.

```
TO SAS1 :SIDE1 :ANGLE :SIDE2
   DRAW
   BACK :SIDE1
   RIGHT :ANGLE
   FORWARD :SIDE2
   HOME
END
```

(*In Apple Logo II, replace DRAW with CLEARSCREEN.*)

23. (a) In Problem 21, if SAS 50 190 60 is executed, what is the result?
    (b) Is it possible in reality to draw a triangle with sides of 50 and 60 units and an included angle of 190°? Why?
    (c) What line could be added to the procedure in Problem 21 to correct the "bug" you encountered in (b)?

LABORATORY ACTIVITY

In this van Hiele Level 3 activity, you are given the name of a shape. (i) List sufficient properties to define that shape. For example, if given the words *isosceles triangle*, you might say that it is a triangle with at least two sides congruent. (ii) Now derive other properties of the shape, based upon your answer in (i). For example, you could show that the base angles are congruent in the isosceles triangle.

(a) Parallelogram
(b) Rectangle
(c) Kite
(d) Rhombus
(e) Square

Section 11-2 Other Congruence Properties

Angle, Side, Angle Property (ASA)

We have seen that triangles can be determined to be congruent by SSS and SAS. Can a triangle be constructed congruent to a given triangle by using two angles and a side? There are two possibilities: one with the side included between the angles, and one with the side not included between the angles. Figure 11-17 shows the construction of a triangle $A'B'C'$ such that $\overline{A'C'} \cong \overline{AC}$, $\angle A' \cong \angle A$, and $\angle C' \cong \angle C$. It seems that $\triangle A'B'C' \cong \triangle ABC$. This construction illustrates a property of congruence called **Angle, Side, Angle,** abbreviated **ASA.**

Angle, Side, Angle (ASA)

FIGURE 11-17

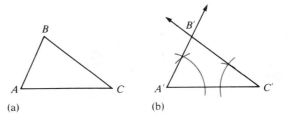

(a)   (b)

- **P R O P E R T Y**

Angle, Side, Angle (ASA) If two angles and the included side of one triangle are congruent to two angles and the included side of another triangle, respectively, then the triangles are congruent.

Is there another congruence property involving two angles and a side of two respective triangles? Consider the noncongruent triangles ABC and DEF in Figure 11-18.

FIGURE 11-18

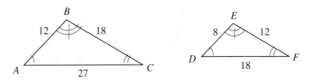

We see that $\overline{AB} \cong \overline{EF}$, $\overline{BC} \cong \overline{DF}$, $\angle B \cong \angle E$, $\angle A \cong \angle D$, and $\angle C \cong \angle F$. Thus, as the figure shows, we can have five parts of one triangle congruent to five parts of another triangle and yet be left with triangles that are not congruent. Specifically, we can have two angles and a side of one triangle congruent to two angles and a side of another triangle and yet not have two congruent triangles. In Figure 11-19, however, $\triangle ABC$ and $\triangle DEF$ have two

FIGURE 11-19

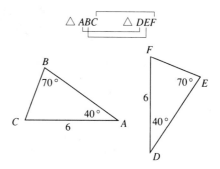

pairs of angles congruent and a pair of sides congruent. If $\angle A \cong \angle D$ and $\angle B \cong \angle E$, we can deduce that $\angle C \cong \angle F$ because both are equal to $180°$ − $(70 + 40)°$. Then, since $\overline{AC} \cong \overline{DF}$, we have $\triangle ABC \cong \triangle DEF$ by ASA. In general, by using the ASA property, we can justify the following property.

● **P R O P E R T Y**
Angle, Angle, Side (AAS)   If two angles and a corresponding side of one triangle are congruent to two angles and a corresponding side of another triangle, respectively, then the two triangles are congruent.

EXAMPLE 11-5   Show that each of the given pairs of triangles in Figure 11-20 is congruent.

FIGURE 11-20

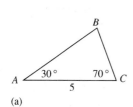

(a)

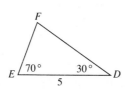

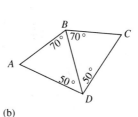

(b)

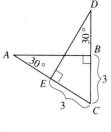

(c) $\triangle ABC$ and $\triangle DEC$

SOLUTION   (a) $\angle A \cong \angle D$, $\overline{AC} \cong \overline{DE}$, and $\angle C \cong \angle E$. Consequently, by ASA, $\triangle ABC \cong \triangle DFE$.

(b) $\angle ABD \cong \angle CBD$, $\overline{BD} \cong \overline{BD}$, and $\angle ADB \cong \angle CDB$. Consequently, by ASA, $\triangle ABD \cong \triangle CBD$.

(c) $\angle A \cong \angle D$, $\angle ABC \cong \angle DEC$, and $\overline{BC} \cong \overline{EC}$. Consequently, by AAS, $\triangle ABC \cong \triangle DEC$.

In Figure 11-21, the angles of one triangle are congruent to corresponding angles in another triangle, and the triangles are not congruent. Thus, an AAA property for congruency does not exist. (The triangles are *similar*, a concept discussed later in this chapter.)

FIGURE 11-21

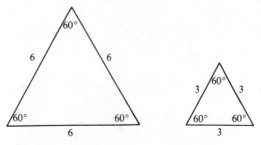

Using properties of congruent triangles, we can deduce various properties of quadrilaterals. Table 11-1 summarizes the definitions and lists some properties of four quadrilaterals. These and other properties of quadrilaterals are further investigated in the problem set.

Congruent Polygons

Determining congruency conditions for polygons other than triangles is not an easy task. For example, the SSS property for congruent triangles has no analogy for quadrilaterals. The quadrilaterals in Figure 11-22 do not have the same shape, despite having four congruent sides. *One way to be sure that two polygons are congruent is to know that all corresponding sides and angles of the polygons are congruent.* This may be done by "moving" one figure to see if it "fits" exactly on top of the other figure.

FIGURE 11-22

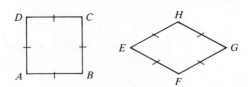

TABLE 11-1

Quadrilateral and Its Definition	Properties of the Quadrilateral
 Parallelogram: A quadrilateral in which each pair of opposite sides is parallel	(a) Opposite sides are congruent. (b) Opposite angles are congruent. (c) Diagonals bisect each other.
 Rectangle: A parallelogram with a right angle	(a) A rectangle has all the properties of a parallelogram. (b) All the angles of a rectangle are right angles. (c) A quadrilateral in which all the angles are right angles is a rectangle.
 Kite: A quadrilateral with two distinct pairs of consecutive sides congruent	(a) Lines containing the diagonals are perpendicular to each other. (b) A line containing one diagonal is a bisector of the other. (c) A line containing one diagonal bisects nonconsecutive angles.
 Rhombus: A parallelogram with all sides congruent	(a) A rhombus has all the properties of a parallelogram. (b) A quadrilateral in which all the sides are congruent is a rhombus. (c) The diagonals of a rhombus are perpendicular to each other. (d) Diagonals bisect opposite angles. (e) Diagonals are bisectors of each other.
 Square: A rectangle with all sides congruent	A square has all the properties of a parallelogram, a rectangle, and a rhombus.

PROBLEM SET 11-2

1. Use a ruler, protractor, and compass to construct each of the following, if possible.
   (a) A triangle with angles of 60° and 70° and an included side of 8 inches.
   (b) A triangle with angles of 60° and 70° and a nonincluded side of 8 cm on a side of the 60° angle.
   (c) A right triangle with one acute angle of 75° and a leg of 5 cm on a side of the 75° angle.
   (d) A triangle with angles of 30°, 70°, and 80°.

2. For each of the conditions in Problem 1(a)–(d), is it possible to construct two noncongruent triangles? Explain why or why not.

3. For each of the following, determine whether the given conditions are sufficient to prove that $\triangle PQR \cong \triangle MNO$. Justify your answers.
   (a) $\angle Q \cong \angle N, \angle P \cong \angle M, \overline{PQ} \cong \overline{MN}$
   (b) $\angle R \cong \angle O, \angle P \cong \angle M, \overline{QR} \cong \overline{NO}$
   (c) $\overline{PQ} \cong \overline{MN}, \overline{PR} \cong \overline{MO}, \angle N \cong \angle Q$
   (d) $\angle P \cong \angle M, \angle Q \cong \angle N, \angle R \cong \angle O$

4. Determine whether each of the following pairs of triangles, (1) and (2), is congruent. Justify your answers.

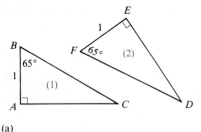

(a)

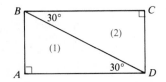

(b)

5. In the symbol used by Chrysler Corporation on its cars (a regular pentagon), what is true about the triangles pictured? Justify your answer.

6. In each of the following, if possible, fill in the blank by choosing one of the words *parallelogram, rectangle, rhombus,* or *square* so that the resulting sentence is true. If none of the words makes the sentence true, answer "none" and justify your answer.
   (a) A quadrilateral is a _____ if and only if its diagonals bisect each other.
   (b) A quadrilateral is a _____ if and only if its diagonals are congruent.
   (c) A quadrilateral is a _____ if and only if its diagonals are perpendicular to each other.
   (d) A quadrilateral is a _____ if and only if its diagonals are congruent and bisect each other.
   (e) A quadrilateral is a _____ if and only if its diagonals are perpendicular to each other and bisect each other.
   (f) A quadrilateral is a _____ if and only if its diagonals are congruent, perpendicular to each other, and bisect each other.
   (g) A quadrilateral is a _____ if and only if a pair of opposite sides is parallel and congruent.

7. Classify each of the following statements as either true or false. If the statement is false, provide a counterexample.
   (a) The diagonals of a square are perpendicular bisectors of each other.
   (b) If all sides of a quadrilateral are congruent, the quadrilateral is a rhombus.
   (c) If a rhombus is a square, it must also be a rectangle.
   (d) An isosceles trapezoid can be a rectangle.
   (e) A square is a trapezoid.
   (f) A trapezoid is a parallelogram.
   (g) A parallelogram is a trapezoid.
   (h) No rectangle is a rhombus.
   (i) No trapezoid is a square.
   (j) Some squares are trapezoids.

8. (a) Construct quadrilaterals having exactly one, two, and four right angles.
   (b) Why can a quadrilateral not have exactly three right angles?
   (c) Can a parallelogram have exactly two right angles?

9. In parallelogram *ABCD*, suppose that we connect *P*, a point on $\overline{DC}$, to *O* and extend $\overline{PO}$ until it intersects $\overline{AB}$ at *Q*.
   (a) How are $\overline{OP}$ and $\overline{QO}$ related?
   (b) Justify your answer in (a).

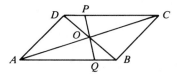

10. Figure *ABCD* is a kite.

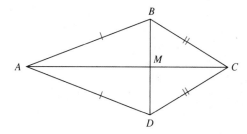

   (a) Argue that $\overline{AC}$ bisects $\angle A$ and $\angle C$.
   (b) Let *M* be the point where the diagonals of kite *ABCD* intersect. Measure $\angle AMD$, and make a conjecture concerning the angle between the diagonals of a kite. Justify your conjecture.
   (c) Show that $\overline{BM} \cong \overline{MD}$.

11. (a) If *ABCDE* is a regular pentagon, how are $\overline{AC}$, $\overline{CE}$, $\overline{BE}$, $\overline{BD}$, and $\overline{DA}$ related?
   (b) Justify your answer in (a).

12. (a) In an isosceles trapezoid, make a conjecture concerning the lengths of the sides opposite the congruent angles.
   (b) Make a conjecture concerning the diagonals of an isosceles trapezoid.
   (c) Justify your conjectures in (a) and (b).

13. (a) What type of figure is formed by joining the midpoints of a rectangle?

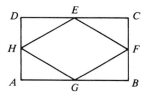

   ★(b) Prove your answer in (a).
   (c) What type of figure is formed by joining the midpoints of the sides of a parallelogram?
   ★(d) Prove your answer in (c).
   (e) Make a conjecture concerning the type of figure that is formed by joining the midpoints of any quadrilateral.

★14. Suppose that polygon *ABCD* is any parallelogram. Use congruent triangles to justify each of the following.
   (a) $\angle A \cong \angle C$ and $\angle B \cong \angle D$ (opposite angles are congruent).
   (b) $\overline{BC} \cong \overline{AD}$ and $\overline{AB} \cong \overline{CD}$ (opposite sides are congruent).
   (c) $\overline{BF} \cong \overline{DF}$ and $\overline{AF} \cong \overline{CF}$ (the diagonals bisect each other).
   (d) $\angle DAB$ and $\angle ABC$ are supplementary.

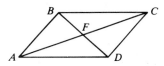

15. Suppose that polygon *ABCD* is a rectangle. Justify each of the following.

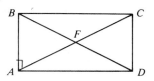

   (a) $\overline{AC}$ and $\overline{BD}$ bisect each other (the diagonals bisect each other).
   (b) $\overline{AC} \cong \overline{BD}$

16. Joachim is cutting a pane of glass to replace a rectangular window. What measures must he use to cut the glass to ensure that it will fit the window?

17. What information is needed to determine congruency for each of the following?
    (a) Two squares
    (b) Two rectangles
    (c) Two parallelograms

 18. (a) Logo programs can be used to construct triangles, using the ASA property. Type the given procedures into your computer and then run the following.
    (i)   ASA 60 50 70
    (ii) ASA 80 50 60
    (iii) AAS 60 50 70
    (iv) AAS 130 20 50

```
TO ASA :ANGLE1 :SIDE :ANGLE2
   DRAW
   FORWARD 120
   BACK 120
   LEFT :ANGLE1
   FORWARD :SIDE
   RIGHT (180 - :ANGLE2)
   FORWARD 120
END
TO AAS :ANGLE1 :ANGLE2 :SIDE
   ASA :ANGLE1 :SIDE 180 -
     (:ANGLE1 + :ANGLE2)
END
```

(In Apple Logo II, replace DRAW with CLEARSCREEN.)

(b) Predict the outcomes when the following are executed.
    (i) AAS 130 50 100   (ii) AAS 90 45 120
(c) Add a line to the ASA procedure so that inputs for angles that are impossible in a triangle are not allowed.
(d) The following ASA procedure is written with the turtle starting at home. Enter it into your computer, and execute the following.
    (i)   ASA 60 50 70
    (ii) ASA 60 40 60
    (iii) ASA 20 50 90

```
TO ASA :ANGLE1 :SIDE :ANGLE2
   DRAW
   IF NOT (:ANGLE1 + :ANGLE2 <
    180) STOP
   BACK :SIDE
   RIGHT :ANGLE1
   CHECKHEAD :ANGLE1 :ANGLE2
   HOME
END
```

(In Apple Logo II, replace DRAW with CLEARSCREEN and IF NOT (:ANGLE1 + :ANGLE2 < 180) STOP with IF NOT (:ANGLE1 + :ANGLE2 < 180) [STOP].)

```
TO CHECKHEAD :ANGLE1 :ANGLE2
   SETHEADING TOWARDS 0 0
   IF ABS (HEADING - (360 -
    :ANGLE2)) < 2 STOP
   SETHEADING :ANGLE1
   FORWARD 1
   CHECKHEAD :ANGLE1 :ANGLE2
END
```

(In Apple Logo II, replace SETHEADING TOWARDS 0 0 with SETHEADING TOWARDS [0 0] and IF ABS (HEADING - (360 - :ANGLE2)) < 2 STOP with IF (ABS HEADING - (360 - :ANGLE2)) < 2 [STOP].)

```
TO ABS :VALUE
   IF :VALUE < 0 OUTPUT
    -:VALUE ELSE OUTPUT :VALUE
END
```

(In Apple Logo II, replace IF :VALUE < 0 OUTPUT - :VALUE ELSE OUTPUT :VALUE with IF (:VALUE < 0) [OUTPUT -:VALUE] [OUTPUT:VALUE].)

 19. (a) Write a Logo procedure called RHOMBUS with inputs :SIDE and :ANGLE in which the first variable is the length of the side of the rhombus and the second is the measure of an interior angle of the rhombus.
(b) Execute RHOMBUS 80 50 and RHOMBUS 80 130. What is the relationship between the two figures? Why?
(c) Write a Logo procedure called SQ.RHOM with inputs :SIDE and :ANGLE that will draw a square by calling on the RHOMBUS procedure.

Review Problems

20. If possible, construct a triangle having the following three segments a, b, and c as its sides.

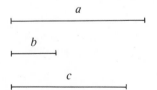

21. Construct an equilateral triangle whose sides are congruent to the following segment.

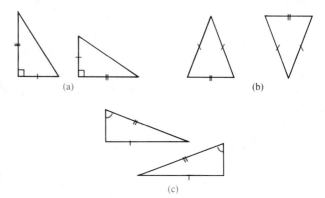

(a)

(b)

22. For each pair of triangles shown, determine whether the given conditions are sufficient to show that the triangles are congruent. If the triangles are congruent, tell which property can be used to verify this fact.

(c)

B R A I N   T E A S E R

A treasure map, shown in the accompanying figure, floated ashore in a bottle. It showed Shipwreck Island, where a treasure was buried. According to the directions on the map, the treasure is equidistant from two roads, one joining Bluebeard's Cove with Bottle O'Rum Inn and the other joining Long John's Bay with Bottle O'Rum Inn. Also, the treasure is equidistant from Long John's Bay and Bottle O'Rum Inn. Can you find the treasure?

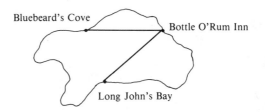

Bluebeard's Cove

Bottle O'Rum Inn

Long John's Bay

LABORATORY ACTIVITY

As a van Hiele Level 3 activity, consider the statements "If a quadrilateral has opposite sides congruent, then it is a parallelogram," and "If one pair of sides of a quadrilateral are congruent and parallel, then the quadrilateral is a parallelogram." Show that, if one statement is true, then the other must also be true.

Section 11-3   Other Constructions

We use the following properties of a rhombus (given in Section 11-2) to accomplish basic compass-and-straightedge constructions.

1. A rhombus has all the properties of a parallelogram.
2. A rhombus is a quadrilateral in which all the sides are congruent.
3. The diagonals of a rhombus are perpendicular to each other.
4. The diagonals of a rhombus bisect the opposite angles.
5. The diagonals of a rhombus are bisectors of each other.

Constructing Parallel Lines

To construct a line parallel to a given line through a point P not on ℓ, as in the leftmost panel of Figure 11-23, our strategy is to construct a rhombus with one of its vertices at P and one of its sides on line ℓ. Because the opposite sides of a rhombus are parallel, one of the sides through P will be parallel to ℓ. This construction is shown in Figure 11-23.

FIGURE 11-23
Constructing parallel lines (rhombus method).

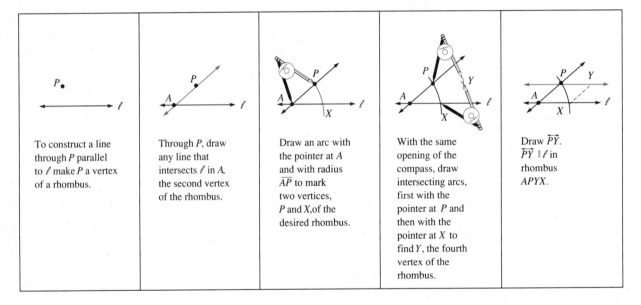

| To construct a line through P parallel to ℓ make P a vertex of a rhombus. | Through P, draw any line that intersects ℓ in A, the second vertex of the rhombus. | Draw an arc with the pointer at A and with radius $\overline{AP}$ to mark two vertices, P and X, of the desired rhombus. | With the same opening of the compass, draw intersecting arcs, first with the pointer at P and then with the pointer at X to find Y, the fourth vertex of the rhombus. | Draw $\overrightarrow{PY}$. $\overrightarrow{PY} \parallel \ell$ in rhombus $APYX$. |

Figure 11-24 shows another way to do the construction. If congruent corresponding angles are formed by a transversal cutting two lines, then the lines are parallel. Thus, the first step is to draw a transversal through P that intersects ℓ. The angle marked α is formed by the transversal and line ℓ. By constructing an angle with a vertex at P congruent to α, we create congruent corresponding angles; therefore, $m \parallel \ell$. Two more ways to construct parallel lines use congruent alternate interior or alternate exterior angles. (These constructions are left as exercises.)

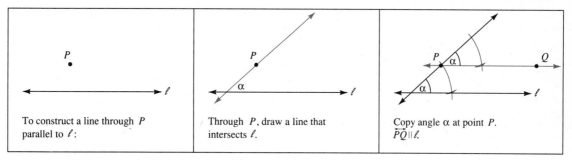

FIGURE 11-24
Constructing parallel lines (corresponding angle method).

Constructing Angle Bisectors

angle bisector

Another construction based on a property of a rhombus is the construction
of an **angle bisector,** a ray that separates an angle into two congruent angles.
The diagonal of a rhombus with vertex A bisects $\angle A$, as shown in Figure
11-25.

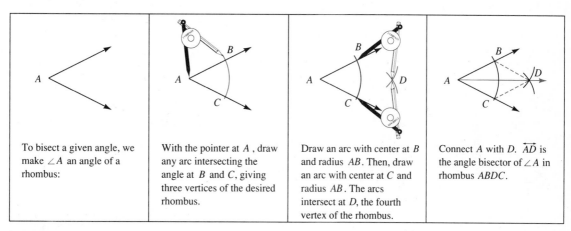

FIGURE 11-25
Bisecting an angle.

Constructing Perpendicular Lines

In order to construct a line through P perpendicular to line ℓ, where P is not
a point on ℓ, as in Figure 11-26, recall that the diagonals of a rhombus are
perpendicular to each other. If we construct a rhombus with a vertex at P
and two vertices A and B on ℓ, as in Figure 11-26, the segment connecting
the fourth vertex Q to P is perpendicular to ℓ because $\overline{AB}$ and $\overline{PQ}$ are
diagonals of the rhombus.

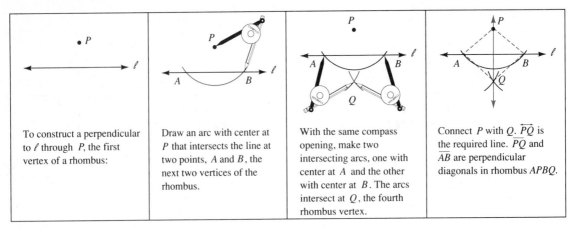

FIGURE 11-26
Constructing a perpendicular to
a line from a point not on a line.

perpendicular bisector   The line perpendicular to a segment at its midpoint is the **perpendicular bisector** of the segment. To construct the perpendicular bisector of a line segment, as in Figure 11-27, we use the fact that the diagonals of a rhombus are perpendicular bisectors of each other. The construction yields a rhombus such that the original segment is one of the diagonals of the rhombus and the other diagonal is the perpendicular bisector, as in Figure 11-27.

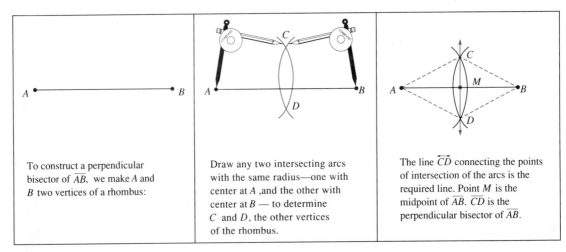

FIGURE 11-27
Bisecting a line segment.

Constructing a perpendicular to a line ℓ at a point M on ℓ is based on the same property of a rhombus just used. That is, the diagonals of a rhombus are perpendicular bisectors of each other. Observe in Figure 11-27 that $\overline{CD}$

is a perpendicular to $\overline{AB}$ through M. Thus, we construct a rhombus whose diagonals intersect at point M, as in Figure 11-28.

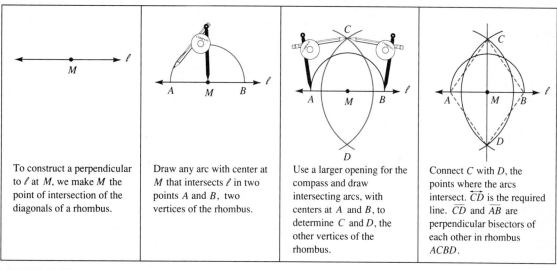

| To construct a perpendicular to ℓ at M, we make M the point of intersection of the diagonals of a rhombus. | Draw any arc with center at M that intersects ℓ in two points A and B, two vertices of the rhombus. | Use a larger opening for the compass and draw intersecting arcs, with centers at A and B, to determine C and D, the other vertices of the rhombus. | Connect C with D, the points where the arcs intersect. $\overleftrightarrow{CD}$ is the required line. $\overleftrightarrow{CD}$ and $\overline{AB}$ are perpendicular bisectors of each other in rhombus $ACBD$. |

FIGURE 11-28
Constructing a perpendicular to
a line from a point on the line.

Constructing perpendiculars is useful in locating altitudes of a triangle. *altitude* An **altitude** of a triangle is the perpendicular segment from a vertex of the triangle to the line containing the opposite side of the triangle. The construction of altitudes is described in Example 11-6.

EXAMPLE 11-6   Given triangle ABC, construct an altitude from vertex A in each part of Figure 11-29.

FIGURE 11-29

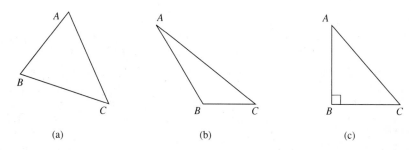

(a)   (b)   (c)

SOLUTION   (a) Since an altitude is the perpendicular from a vertex to the line containing the opposite side of a triangle, we need to construct a perpendicular from point A to the line containing $\overline{BC}$. Such a construction is shown in Figure 11-30. $\overline{AD}$ is the required altitude.

FIGURE 11-30

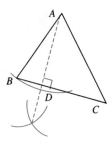

(b) The construction of the altitude from vertex A is shown in Figure 11-31. Notice that the required altitude $\overline{AD}$ does not intersect the interior of $\triangle ABC$.

FIGURE 11-31

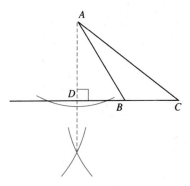

(c) Triangle ABC is a right triangle. The altitude from vertex A is the side $\overline{AB}$. No construction is required.

Paper Folding and Mira Constructions

Perpendicularity constructions can also be completed by means of paper folding or by using a Mira. A Mira is a plastic device that acts as a reflector so that the image of an object can be seen behind the Mira. The drawing edge of the Mira acts as a folding line on paper. In fact, any construction demonstrated in this text that uses paper folding can also be done by using a Mira.

To use paper folding to construct a perpendicular to a given line ℓ at a point P on the line, we fold the line onto itself, as in Figure 11-32(a). The fold line is perpendicular to ℓ. To perform the construction with a Mira, we place the Mira with the drawing edge on P, as in Figure 11-32(b), so that ℓ

is reflected onto itself. The line along the drawing edge is the required perpendicular.

FIGURE 11-32

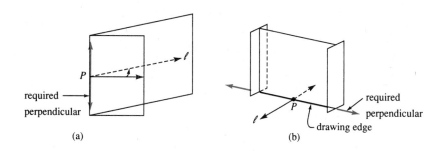

(a)   (b)

To construct the bisector of an angle with a Mira, we place the drawing edge of the Mira on the vertex of the angle and reflect one side of the angle onto the other. Similarly, we can bisect an angle by folding a line through the vertex so that one side of the angle folds onto the other side. For example, in Figure 11-33, to bisect $\angle ABC$, we fold and crease the paper through the vertex, B, so that $\overrightarrow{BA}$ coincides with $\overrightarrow{BC}$.

FIGURE 11-33

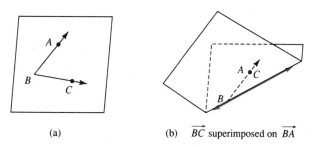

(a)   (b) $\overrightarrow{BC}$ superimposed on $\overrightarrow{BA}$

Properties of Angle Bisectors and Perpendicular Bisectors

Consider the angle bisector in Figure 11-34. It seems that any point P on the angle bisector is equidistant from the sides of the angle; that is, $PD = PE$. (The distance from a point to a line is the length of the perpendicular from the point to the line.)

To justify this, we find two congruent triangles that have these segments as corresponding sides. The only triangles pictured are $\triangle ADP$ and $\triangle AEP$. Because $\overrightarrow{AP}$ is the angle bisector, $\angle DAP \cong \angle EAP$. Also, $\angle PDA$ and $\angle PEA$ are right angles and are thus congruent. Because $\overline{AP}$ is congruent to itself, $\triangle PDA \cong \triangle PEA$ by AAS. Thus, $\overline{PD} \cong \overline{PE}$ because they are corresponding parts of congruent triangles PDA and PEA. Consequently, we have the following theorem.

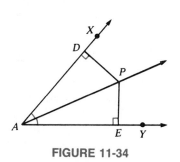

FIGURE 11-34

- **T H E O R E M   11-2**
  Any point *P* on an angle bisector is equidistant from the sides of the angle.

- **R E M A R K**
  It can also be shown that, if a point is in the interior of the angle and is equidistant from the sides of the angle, it must be on the angle bisector of that angle.

Next, consider the perpendicular bisector of a segment. In Figure 11-35(a), ℓ is the perpendicular bisector of $\overline{AB}$. Consider some point *P* on ℓ. It appears that *P* is equidistant from points *A* and *B*; that is, $\overline{PA} \cong \overline{PB}$. To show this, we find two congruent triangles with sides $\overline{PA}$ and $\overline{PB}$. Triangles *PCA* and *PCB*, as shown in Figure 11-35(b), appear to be such triangles.

FIGURE 11-35

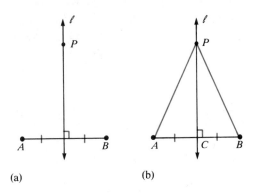

(a)   (b)

To justify that $\triangle PCA \cong \triangle PCB$, we notice that, because ℓ is the perpendicular bisector of $\overline{AB}$, $\overline{AC} \cong \overline{BC}$ and $\angle PCA$ and $\angle PCB$ are congruent right angles. Also, $\overline{PC} \cong \overline{PC}$, so $\triangle PCA \cong \triangle PCB$ by SAS. Hence, $\overline{PA} \cong \overline{PB}$ because the line segments are corresponding sides of congruent triangles. Because *P* is an arbitrary point, we have the following theorem.

- **T H E O R E M   11-3**
  Any point on the perpendicular bisector of a line segment is equidistant from the endpoints of the bisected segment.

- **R E M A R K**
  It can also be proved that a point equidistant from the endpoints of a segment must be on a perpendicular bisector of the segment.

PROBLEM SET 11-3

1. Use a compass and a straightedge to construct a line m through P parallel to ℓ, using each of the following.
(a) Alternate interior angles
(b) Alternate exterior angles

$P \bullet$

 ℓ

2. Construct each of the following, using paper folding.
(a) Bisector of $\angle A$

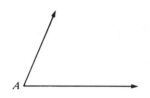

(b) Perpendicular bisector of $\overline{AB}$

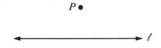

(c) Perpendicular from P to ℓ

$P \bullet$

 ℓ

3. Complete the constructions in Problem 2, using a compass and straightedge.
4. Complete the constructions in Problem 2, using a Mira, if one is available.
5. Construct the three altitudes of each of the following types of triangles, using any method.
(a) Acute triangle

(b) Right triangle   (c) Obtuse triangle

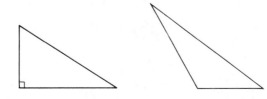

(d) Make a conjecture about the lines containing the three altitudes of an acute triangle.
(e) Make a conjecture about the lines containing the three altitudes of a right triangle.
(f) Make a conjecture about the lines containing the three altitudes of an obtuse triangle.
6. Construct the perpendicular bisectors of each of the triangles in Problem 5.
(a) Make a conjecture about the perpendicular bisectors of an acute triangle.
(b) Make a conjecture about the perpendicular bisectors of a right triangle.
(c) Make a conjecture about the perpendicular bisectors of an obtuse triangle.
7. A planning committee for a new tri-city airport wants to locate the airport an equal distance from each city. A map of the three cities is shown next. How can the location of the airport be found?

8. A **chord** of a circle is a segment with endpoints on the circle.
(a) Construct a circle, several chords, and a perpendicular bisector of each chord. Make a conjecture concerning the perpendicular bisector of a chord and the center of the circle.
(b) Justify your conjecture in (a).
(c) Given a circle with an unmarked center, find the center of the circle.
9. A **median** of a triangle is a segment from a vertex of the triangle to the midpoint of the opposite side. Construct the three medians of each triangle in Problem 5. Their point of intersection is the **centroid,** the center of gravity of the triangle.
10. Construct a square with $\overline{AB}$ as a side.

11. Using a compass and a straightedge, construct a parallelogram with A, B, and C as vertices.

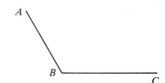

12. In the concave quadrilateral $APBQ$, $\overline{PQ}$ and $\overline{AB}$ are the diagonals; $\overline{AP} \cong \overline{BP}$, $\overline{AQ} \cong \overline{BQ}$, and $\overline{PQ}$ has been extended until it intersects $\overline{AB}$ at C.
    (a) Make a conjecture concerning $\overline{PQ}$ and $\overline{AB}$.
    (b) Justify your conjecture in (a).
        Make conjectures concerning the relationships between $\overrightarrow{PQ}$ and $\angle APB$ and between $\overrightarrow{QC}$ and $\angle AQB$.
    (d) Justify your conjectures in (c).

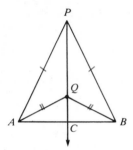

13. Construct each of the following, if possible. If the construction is not possible, explain why.
    (a) A square, given one side
    (b) A square, given one diagonal
    (c) A rectangle, given one diagonal
    (d) A parallelogram, given two of its adjacent sides
    (e) A rhombus, given two of its diagonals
    (f) A triangle with two obtuse angles
    (g) A parallelogram with exactly three right angles
    (h) A kite with two right angles
    (i) A kite with three right angles
    ★(j) An isosceles triangle, given its base and the angle opposite the base
    ★(k) A trapezoid, given four of its sides
14. Using only a compass and a straightedge, construct angles with each of the following measures.
    (a) 30°   (b) 15°   (c) 45°
    (d) 75°   (e) 105°
15. An alternate set of constructions for each of the following uses properties of a kite that is not a rhombus. Use a kite to construct each of the following.
    (a) Angle bisector
    (b) A line parallel to a given line ℓ and passing through a point P not on ℓ
16. Given $\overline{AB}$ in the following figure, use a compass and a straightedge to construct the perpendicular bisector of $\overline{AB}$. You are not allowed to put any marks below $\overline{AB}$.

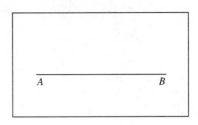

17. Write a Logo procedure to draw an equilateral triangle and three segments containing the altitudes of the triangle, as shown in the figure.

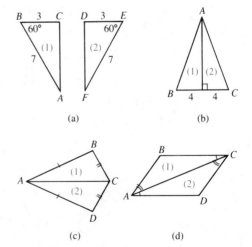

18. Use variables to write a Logo procedure to draw each of the following.
    (a) The angle bisector of a variable-sized angle
    (b) The perpendicular bisector of a variable-sized segment
    (c) A set of two variable-sized parallel segments

Review Problems

19. For each of the following, determine whether the two triangles (1) and (2) are congruent. Justify your answers.

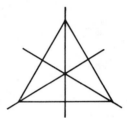

20. Given that $\overleftrightarrow{AB} \parallel \overleftrightarrow{ED}$ and $\overline{BC} \cong \overline{CE}$, why is $\overline{AC} \cong \overline{CD}$?

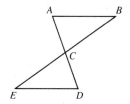

21. Draw $\triangle ABC$; then construct $\triangle PQR$ congruent to $\triangle ABC$, using each of the following combinations.
    (a) Two sides of $\triangle ABC$ and an angle included between these sides
    (b) The three sides of $\triangle ABC$
    (c) Two angles and a side included between these angles

LABORATORY ACTIVITY

As a van Hiele Level 1 activity, consider the following drawing.

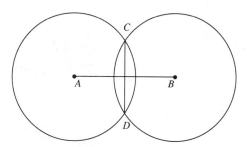

In this drawing the circles have congruent radii. Use a marked ruler and protractor to find the relationship between segments $\overline{AB}$ and $\overline{CD}$. Explain why the measured relationship is true.

Section 11-4   Circles and Spheres

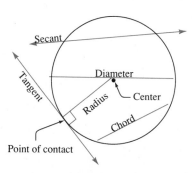

FIGURE 11-36

A circle is a set of points in a plane that are equidistant from a given point in the plane called the *center*, as shown in Figure 11-36. The radius is the length of any segment connecting the center with a point on the circle. Any segment with both endpoints on the circle is a **chord**. A line that contains a chord is a **secant**. A chord that passes through the center of the circle is a **diameter**. A diameter is the longest chord of the circle, and its length equals twice the length of the radius.

A line that intersects the circle at exactly one point and is perpendicular to a radius at that point of intersection is a **tangent**. The point of intersection is the **point of contact,** or **point of tangency.**

The symbol for a fallout shelter, pictured in Figure 11-37(a), contains three equilateral triangles with a vertex at the center of the circle. It suggests that congruent chords in a circle intersect the circle to form congruent arcs. In Figure 11-37(b), we have congruent chords $\overline{AB}$ and $\overline{CD}$. Triangles AOB and COD are formed by connecting the endpoints of the chords to the center of the circle, O. These triangles are congruent, giving us congruent angles *central angles* $\angle AOB$ and $\angle COD$. (Why?) These angles are **central angles** because their shared vertex is the center of the circle. In general, *congruent chords determine congruent central angles and congruent arcs of the circle.* Conversely, it can be shown that *congruent central angles determine congruent chords and congruent arcs of a circle.*

FIGURE 11-37

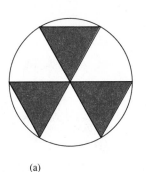
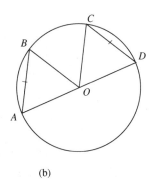

(a) (b)

Inscribing Polygons in a Circle

inscribed polygon
When all the vertices of a polygon are points of a given circle, the polygon is called an **inscribed polygon.** A regular hexagon inscribed in a circle is shown in Figure 11-38(a). All sides of a regular hexagon are congruent, so the corresponding arcs are congruent and the six corresponding central angles are congruent. Because the sum of the measures of these angles is 360°, the measure of each central angle is 60°. This fact is sufficient to inscribe a hexagon in a given circle, using a protractor. A compass-and-straightedge construction can also be accomplished. Look at $\triangle AOB$. Because $\overline{OA} \cong \overline{OB}$,

FIGURE 11-38

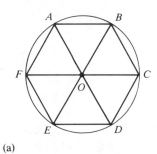

(a)

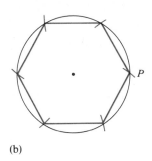

(b)

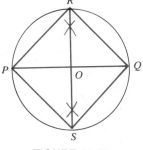

FIGURE 11-39

the triangle is isosceles, and the base angles $\angle BAO$ and $\angle ABO$ are congruent. The central angle is 60°, so $m(\angle BAO) + m(\angle ABO) = 120°$. Consequently, $m(\angle BAO) = m(\angle ABO) = 60°$, and the triangle is equiangular and equilateral. Thus, $\overline{AB}$ is congruent to a radius of the circle. As a result, to inscribe a regular hexagon in a circle, we pick any point P on the circle and mark off chords congruent to the radius. Figure 11-38(b) shows such a construction.

   To inscribe a square in a circle, we determine four congruent central angles. The central angles must be right angles because the sum of their measures is 360°. Hence, we need only construct two perpendicular diameters of the circle. Figure 11-39 shows the construction. First, we draw any diameter $\overline{PQ}$. Then, we construct a perpendicular to $\overline{PQ}$ at O and thus determine points R and S. Quadrilateral $PRQS$ is the required square.

H I S T O R I C A L   N O T E

Determining which polygons can and which cannot be inscribed in a circle, using only a compass and a straightedge, has intrigued mathematicians for centuries. At age 19, Karl Friedrich Gauss proved that a regular 17-gon could be inscribed in a circle with these tools. He considered it one of his master achievements and wanted a replica of his construction placed on his tombstone. Later he proved that a regular n-gon can be constructed with compass and straightedge, if and only if, either (1) n is a prime number of the form $2^{2k} + 1$, or a product of distinct primes of this form (2) n is a power of 2, or (3) n is a product of numbers satisfying conditions (1) and (2). Thus, a regular septagon cannot be inscribed in a circle with a compass and a straightedge because 7 is not of the form $2^{2k} + 1$. However, because the only factors of 17 are 1 and 17 and $2^{2^2} + 1 = 2^4 + 1 = 17$, it follows from Gauss's Theorem that a 17-gon can be inscribed in a circle with the aid of only a compass and a straightedge. On the basis of these notions, it has been shown that regular polygons with 257 and 65,537 sides can also be constructed. In 1832 F. J. Richelot published a study of the regular polygon of 257 sides, and, reportedly, a professor from Lingen, Germany, named Hermes spent 10 years of his life trying to construct a regular polygon of 65,537 sides.

Circumscribing Circles About Triangles

We can inscribe a triangle in a circle by connecting any three points of the circle with line segments. Conversely, given three vertices of any triangle, we can draw a circle that contains the vertices. This process is called *circumscribing* **circumscribing** a circle about a triangle. For example, in Figure 11-40, circle O is circumscribed about $\triangle ABC$. Such a circle must contain $\overline{AB}$, $\overline{BC}$, and $\overline{AC}$ as chords. Also, it must have $\overline{OA} \cong \overline{OB} \cong \overline{OC}$, since they are all radii. Hence, O must be equidistant from A and B and, consequently, O must be on the perpendicular bisector of $\overline{AB}$. Similarly, O is on the perpendicular bisectors of $\overline{BC}$ and $\overline{AC}$. Hence, to find the center of the circle, we construct perpendicular bisectors of any two chords. The point of intersection of the chords is the center of the circle. Segments connecting O with A, B, and C are the radii of the circle.

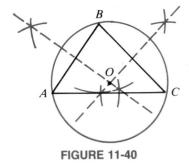

FIGURE 11-40

Inscribing Circles in Triangles

Recall that a tangent was defined as being perpendicular to a radius drawn to the point of contact. Thus, to construct a tangent to a given circle at any point on the circle, we construct a perpendicular to the radius at that point.

inscribed   A circle is **inscribed** in a triangle if it is tangent to the three sides of the triangle. For example, in Figure 11-41(a), circle O is inscribed in $\triangle DEF$ and A, B, and C are the points of contact. Because $\overline{OA}$, $\overline{OB}$, and $\overline{OC}$ are radii, they all have the same length, and they are perpendicular to the three sides of the triangle they each intersect. Thus, O is equidistant from the sides, so it lies on the bisectors of $\angle 1$, $\angle 2$, and $\angle 3$ (see Section 11-3).

FIGURE 11-41

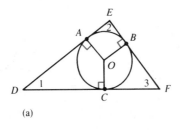

(a)

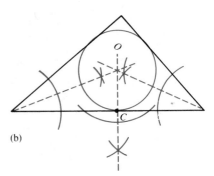

(b)

To inscribe a circle in a triangle, we first construct the bisectors of two of the angles. Their intersection point O is the center of the inscribed circle. The radius of the circle can be determined by constructing a perpendicular from O to a side of the triangle. Figure 11-41(b) shows the construction. The circle with center O and radius $\overline{OC}$ is the required circle.

Spheres

A sphere is the three-dimensional analogue of a circle. The definitions of chord, secant, and tangent apply to spheres as well as to circles. A plane is tangent to a sphere if it intersects the sphere at exactly one point.

If a plane intersects a sphere at more than one point, then the intersection is a circle, as shown in Figure 11-42(a).

FIGURE 11-42

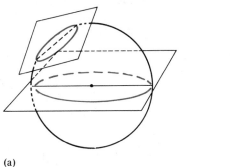

(a)

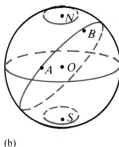

(b)

great circle

circles of latitude

circles of longitude

The largest of all such circles, a circle that contains a diameter of a sphere, is called a **great circle.** Any plane containing the center of the sphere intersects the sphere in a great circle. On the globe, the equator is a great circle. If the globe is cut by a plane parallel to the equator, the circles obtained are called **circles of latitude.** They become smaller the farther they are from the equator, and they become very small near the North and South Poles, as shown in Figure 11-42(b). Any circle passing through the North and South Poles is called a **circle of longitude.** Each circle of longitude is a great circle. (Why?)

In a plane, the shortest route between two points is the segment connecting the points. What is the shortest distance between two points A and B on a sphere? It is possible to prove that the shortest route between two points on a sphere is the minor arc $\widehat{AB}$ of the great circle obtained by cutting the sphere with a plane through A, B, and the center of the sphere. For that reason, if you take a nonstop flight between Seattle and London, it is likely that you will pass over Greenland.

● R E M A R K

Note that, when the two points A and B are relatively close, the distance along the minor arc $\widehat{AB}$ is close to the length of the segment $\overline{AB}$.

PROBLEM SET 11-4

1. What is the relation between a diameter of a circle and any chord that is not a diameter?

2. If a triangle is drawn in a circle so that one vertex is at the center and the other two vertices are on the circle, what type of triangle must it be? Why?

3. If one side of a triangle is a diameter of a circle and the third vertex is a point on the circle, what type of triangle must it be? Measure the angles of several such triangles to decide.

4. In the following figure, $\overline{AB}$ is a diameter of the circle. What is $m(\angle ACB)$ for each value of $m(\angle CAB)$?
(a) 30° (b) 50° (c) 71°
(d) Based on your answers in (a)–(c), make a conjecture.
(e) Justify your conjecture.

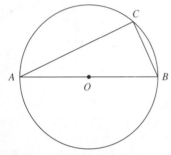

5. Draw a circle on a piece of paper, and use paper folding (or a Mira) to determine the center of the circle.

6. **Concentric circles** are circles that have the same center. Can you construct a common tangent to two distinct concentric circles? Why?

7. Inscribe a regular dodecagon (12-gon) in a circle by first inscribing a regular hexagon in the circle and then bisecting the six central angles of the hexagon.

8. Inscribe an equilateral triangle in a circle.

9. Inscribe a regular octagon in a circle.

10. Draw a circle.
(a) Inscribe several quadrilaterals.
(b) Measure the angles of the quadrilaterals from (a), and find the sums of the measures of pairs of opposite angles.
(c) What seems to be true about the relationships among the angles?

11. Inscribe a circle in the given square, using only a compass and a straightedge.

12. Is it possible to inscribe a circle in every quadrilateral? Explain.

13. Construct a circle with center O that is tangent to ℓ, using only a compass and a straightedge.

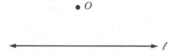

14. Construct a circle that is tangent to lines ℓ, m, and n, where $\ell \parallel m$.

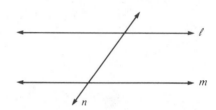

15. In the accompanying figure, $\overline{AC}$ is a diameter of circle O and $\overline{CB}$ is a chord of the circle.
(a) What type of triangle is $\triangle OCB$?
(b) Find a relationship between $m(\angle 1) + m(\angle 2)$ and $m(\angle 3)$.
(c) Find a relationship between $m(\angle 1)$ and $m(\angle 3)$.

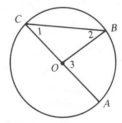

(d) Use your answer in (c) to find a relationship between angle measures α and β in each of the accompanying figures. (O is the center of the circle in each figure.)

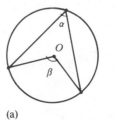

(a)

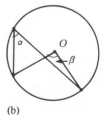

(b)

(e) Find the relationships among the measures of angles 1, 2, and 3, where the points P_1, P_2, and P_3 are arbitrary points on the major arc $\overset{\frown}{AB}$.

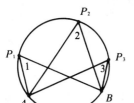

20. Write a Logo procedure to draw a circle and a segment containing one of its diameters.

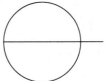

16. (a) In how many points can a line intersect a sphere?
(b) In how many points can a plane intersect a sphere?

★**17.** Show that congruent chords in a circle are the same distance from the center.

★**18.** Construct a circle that contains point P and is tangent to the two given parallel lines ℓ and m.

P •

19. Write a Logo procedure called FILL.CIRCLE with variable :RADIUS to shade the interior of a circle of a given radius.

Review Problems

21. In $\triangle ABC$, what is the *included side* between angles $\angle ABC$ and $\angle CAB$?

22. In $\triangle ABC$, what is the *included angle* between sides $\overline{AB}$ and $\overline{BC}$?

23. In two right triangles, $\triangle ABC$ and $\triangle DEF$, if $\angle A$ and $\angle D$ are congruent and $\overline{AC}$ and $\overline{DF}$ are congruent, what do we know about the two triangles? Why?

24. Draw any obtuse angle. Use a compass and a straightedge to construct the angle bisector.
(a) If the sides of the original angle and the bisector are extended in both directions, what is the relation of the angle bisector constructed and the angle opposite the original (that is, the other vertical angle)?
(b) Do you think this is true in general? Justify your answer.

LABORATORY ACTIVITY

As a van Hiele Level 0 activity on a geoboard, construct right triangles, squares, rectangles, and other polygons. Which of the following, if any, can you construct?

(a) Pentagon
(b) Hexagon
(c) Equilateral triangle
(d) Circle

Section 11-5 Similar Triangles and Similar Figures

When a germ is examined through a microscope, when a slide is projected on a screen, or when a wet wool sweater shrinks in a clothes dryer, the shapes in each case remain the same, but the sizes are altered. In mathematics we say that *two figures that have the same shape but not necessarily the same size are* **similar.**

similar

scale factor

For example, on the student page of *Addison-Wesley Mathematics,* 1989, Grade 7, we see a photograph reduced from the original size of 25 cm in width to 10 cm in width. The ratio of these corresponding sides, 25/10, or $\frac{5}{2}$, is called the **scale factor.** Also, the ratio of the length of the larger picture to the length of the smaller picture is 20/8, or $\frac{5}{2}$. In fact, it seems that, in any such reduction (or enlargement, for that matter), the results will be similar; that is, the corresponding angle measures remain the same, and the corresponding sides are proportional.

Similar Figures

A photograph for use in a book is 25 cm wide and 20 cm in height. A lithographer must make a reduced photograph that will be only 10 cm wide to fit the space in the book. What will be the height of the reduced photograph?

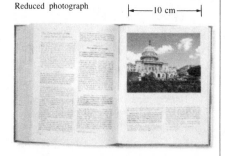

Original photograph

20 cm

25 cm

Reduced photograph   10 cm

The two photographs are examples of a pair of **similar figures**. Similar figures have the same shape.

The lengths of the corresponding sides of similar figures have equal ratios. We can use these ratios to form a proportion.

Let h = the height of the reduced photograph.

$$\text{Original} \rightarrow \frac{25}{10} = \frac{20}{h} \leftarrow \text{Reduced}$$

$$25 \cdot h = 200$$
$$h = 8$$

The reduced photograph will have a height of 8 cm.

In general, we have the following definition of similar triangles.

- **DEFINITION**
  $\triangle ABC$ is similar to $\triangle DEF$, written $\triangle ABC \sim \triangle DEF$, if and only if $\angle A \cong \angle D$,
  $\angle B \cong \angle E$, $\angle C \cong \angle F$, and $\dfrac{AB}{DE} = \dfrac{AC}{DF} = \dfrac{BC}{EF}$.

- **REMARK**
  Note that the one-to-one correspondence in similar triangles is analogous to that in congruent triangles.

EXAMPLE 11-7 Given the pairs of similar triangles in Figure 11-43, find a one-to-one correspondence among the vertices of the triangles such that the corresponding angles are congruent. Then write the proportion for the corresponding sides that follows from the definition.

FIGURE 11-43

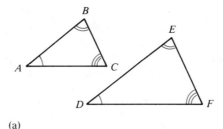

(a)

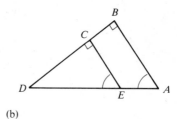

(b)

SOLUTION (a) $\triangle ABC \sim \triangle DEF$

$$\frac{AB}{DE} = \frac{BC}{EF} = \frac{AC}{DF}$$

(b) $\triangle ABD \sim \triangle ECD$

$$\frac{AB}{EC} = \frac{BD}{CD} = \frac{AD}{ED}$$

Angle, Angle, Angle Property (AAA)

As with congruent triangles, minimal conditions may be used to determine when two triangles are similar. For example, suppose that two triangles each have angles with measures of 50°, 30°, and 100°, but the side opposite the 100° angle is 5 units long in one of the triangles and 1 unit long in the other.

The triangles appear to have the same shape, as shown in Figure 11-44. The figure suggests that if the angles of the two triangles are congruent, then the sides are proportional and the triangles are similar. There is no easy proof of this statement, but it is true in general. It is called the **Angle, Angle, Angle** property of similarity for triangles, abbreviated **AAA**.

Ange, Angle, Angle (AAA)

FIGURE 11-44

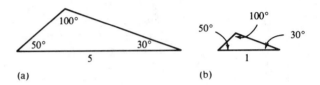

(a)   (b)

• **P R O P E R T Y**
Angle, Angle, Angle (AAA)   If three angles of one triangle are congruent to the three angles of a second triangle, then the triangles are similar.

Given the measures of any two angles of a triangle, the measure of the third angle can be found. Hence, if two angles in one triangle are congruent to two angles in another triangle, then the third angles must also be congruent. Consequently, the AAA condition may be reduced to **Angle, Angle (AA)**.

Angle, Angle (AA)

EXAMPLE 11-8   For each part of Figure 11-45, find a pair of similar triangles.

FIGURE 11-45

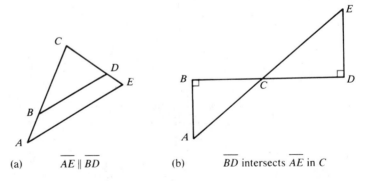

(a) $\overline{AE} \parallel \overline{BD}$ (b) $\overline{BD}$ intersects $\overline{AE}$ in C

SOLUTION   (a) Because $\overline{AE} \parallel \overline{BD}$, congruent corresponding angles are formed by a transversal cutting the parallel segments. Thus, $\angle CBD \cong \angle CAE$, and $\angle CDB \cong \angle CEA$. Also, $\angle C \cong \angle C$, so $\triangle CBD \sim \triangle CAE$ by AAA.

(b) $\angle B \cong \angle D$ because both are right triangles. Also, $\angle ACB \cong \angle ECD$ because they are vertical angles. Thus, $\triangle ACB \sim \triangle ECD$ by AA.

In general, knowing that the corresponding angles are congruent is not sufficient to determine similarity for any two polygons. For example, in a square of side 4 cm and a rectangle 2 cm by 4 cm, all of the angles are congruent, but the two figures are not similar. In fact, *two* **polygons** *are* **similar** *if and only if the corresponding angles are congruent and the corresponding sides are proportional.*

EXAMPLE 11-9   In each pair of similar triangles in Figure 11-46, find x.

FIGURE 11-46

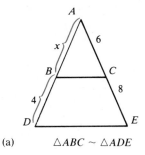

(a) $\triangle ABC \sim \triangle ADE$

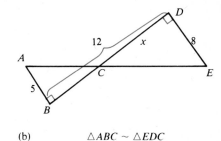

(b) $\triangle ABC \sim \triangle EDC$

SOLUTION   (a) $\triangle ABC \sim \triangle ADE$, so

$$\frac{AB}{AD} = \frac{AC}{AE} = \frac{BC}{DE}$$

Now, $AB = x$, $AD = x + 4$, $AC = 6$, and $AE = 6 + 8 = 14$. Thus,

$$\frac{x}{x + 4} = \frac{6}{14}$$

$$14x = 6(x + 4)$$

$$14x = 6x + 24$$

$$8x = 24$$

$$x = 3$$

(b) $\triangle ABC \sim \triangle EDC$, so

$$\frac{AB}{ED} = \frac{AC}{EC} = \frac{BC}{DC}$$

Now, $AB = 5$, $ED = 8$, and $CD = x$, so that $BC = 12 - x$. Thus,

$$\frac{5}{8} = \frac{12 - x}{x}$$

$$5x = 8(12 - x)$$

$$5x = 96 - 8x$$

$$13x = 96$$

$$x = \frac{96}{13}$$

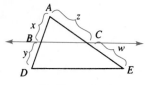

FIGURE 11-47

Properties of Proportion

Similar triangles give rise to various properties involving proportions. For example, in Figure 11-47, if $\overline{BC}\|\overline{DE}$, then $\dfrac{AB}{BD} = \dfrac{AC}{CE}$. This can be justified as follows: $\overline{BC}\|\overline{DE}$, so $\triangle ADE \sim \triangle ABC$. (Why?) Consequently, $\dfrac{AD}{AB} = \dfrac{AE}{AC}$, which may be written as follows.

$$\frac{x+y}{x} = \frac{z+w}{z}$$

$$\frac{x}{x} + \frac{y}{x} = \frac{z}{z} + \frac{w}{z}$$

$$1 + \frac{y}{x} = 1 + \frac{w}{z}$$

$$\frac{y}{x} = \frac{w}{z}$$

$$\frac{x}{y} = \frac{z}{w}$$

This result is summarized in the following theorem.

● T H E O R E M 11-4

If a line parallel to one side of a triangle intersects the other sides, then it divides those sides into proportional segments.

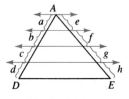

FIGURE 11-48

In Figure 11-47, if B is the midpoint of $\overline{AD}$, then $x = y$. Consequently, $\dfrac{x}{y} = 1$. Because $\dfrac{x}{y} = \dfrac{z}{w}$, it follows that $\dfrac{z}{w} = 1$ and, hence, that $z = w$. That is, if B is the midpoint of $\overline{AD}$ and $\overline{BC}\|\overline{DE}$, then C is the midpoint of $\overline{AE}$. Similarly, if parallel lines intersect $\triangle ADE$, as shown in Figure 11-48, so that $a = b = c = d$, it can be shown that $e = f = g = h$. This result is stated in the following theorem.

● T H E O R E M 11-5

If parallel lines cut off congruent segments on one transversal, then they cut off congruent segments on any transversal.

Theorem 11-5 can be used to divide a given segment into any number of congruent parts. For example, using only a compass and a straightedge, we can divide segment $\overline{AB}$ in Figure 11-49 into three congruent parts by making the construction resemble Figure 11-48.

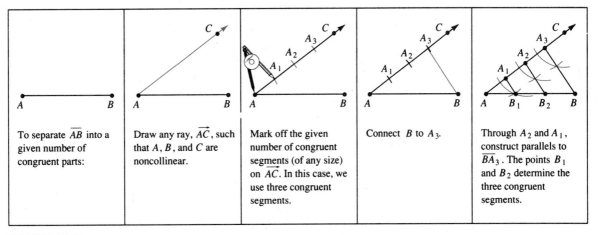

To separate $\overline{AB}$ into a given number of congruent parts:	Draw any ray, $\overrightarrow{AC}$, such that A, B, and C are noncollinear.	Mark off the given number of congruent segments (of any size) on $\overrightarrow{AC}$. In this case, we use three congruent segments.	Connect B to A_3.	Through A_2 and A_1, construct parallels to $\overline{BA_3}$. The points B_1 and B_2 determine the three congruent segments.

FIGURE 11-49

- **R E M A R K**
  It is necessary to construct only $\overline{A_2B_2}$. We can then use a compass to mark off point B_1, making $B_1B_2 = BB_2$, as in Figure 11-50.

FIGURE 11-50

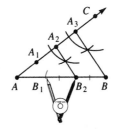

Indirect Measurements

Similar triangles have also been used to make indirect measurements since the time of Thales of Miletus (ca. 600 B.C.), who is believed to have determined the height of the Great Pyramid of Egypt. Most likely, he used ratios involving shadows, similar to those in Figure 11-51. The sun is so far

FIGURE 11-51

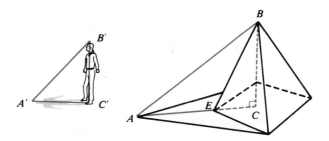

away that it should make approximately congruent angles at B and B'. Because the angles at C and C' are right angles, $\triangle ABC \sim \triangle A'B'C'$. Hence,

$$\frac{AC}{A'C'} = \frac{BC}{B'C'}$$

And because $AC = AE + EC$, the following proportion is obtained.

$$\frac{AE + EC}{A'C'} = \frac{BC}{B'C'}$$

The person's height and shadow can be measured. Also, the length of the shadow of the pyramid AE can be measured, and EC can be found because the base of the pyramid is a square. Each term of the proportion except the height of the pyramid is known. Thus, the height of the pyramid can be found by solving the proportion.

EXAMPLE 11-10 On a sunny day, a tall tree casts a 40-m shadow. At the same time, a meter stick held vertically casts a 2.5-m shadow. How tall is the tree?

SOLUTION Look at Figure 11-52. The pictured triangles are similar by AA because the tree and the stick both meet the ground at right angles, and the angles formed by the sun's rays are congruent (because the shadows are measured at the same time).

FIGURE 11-52

$$\frac{x}{40} = \frac{1}{2.5}$$

$$2.5x = 40$$

$$x = 16$$

The tree is 16 m tall.

PROBLEM 1

Two neighbors, Smith and Wesson, planned to erect flagpoles in their yards. Smith wanted a 10-foot pole, and Wesson wanted a 15-foot pole. In order to keep the poles straight while the concrete bases hardened, they agreed to tie guy wires from the tops of the flagpoles to a fence post on the property lines and to the bases of the flagpoles, as shown in Figure 11-53. How high should the fence post be and how far apart should they erect flagpoles for this scheme to work?

FIGURE 11-53

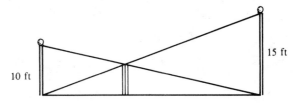

10 ft

15 ft

Understanding the Problem. In Figure 11-54, $AB = 10$ feet and $DC = 15$ feet; we need to find EF and AC. We know that $\overline{AB}$, $\overline{EF}$, and $\overline{DC}$ are perpendicular to $\overline{AC}$ and are therefore parallel.

FIGURE 11-54

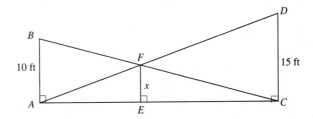

Devising a Plan. $\overline{EF}$ is a side in $\triangle EFC$. Because $\triangle EFC$ and $\triangle ABC$ are right triangles and share $\angle BCA$, it follows by AA that $\triangle EFC \sim \triangle ABC$. $\overline{EF}$ is also a side in $\triangle AFE$, and we have $\triangle AFE \sim \triangle ADC$. (Why?) From the two pairs of similar triangles, we will have proportions containing the unknown FE. The distance AC between the poles will appear in those proportions as well. We will then attempt to find FE and AC by solving the equations.

Carrying Out the Plan. Let $FE = x$. Then, from $\triangle EFC \sim \triangle ABC$ and $\triangle AFE \sim \triangle ADC$, we have

$$\frac{x}{10} = \frac{EC}{AC}$$

$$\frac{x}{15} = \frac{AE}{AC}$$

We also know that $EC + AE = AC$. This suggests adding the proportions.

$$\frac{x}{10} + \frac{x}{15} = \frac{EC}{AC} + \frac{AE}{AC}$$

or

$$\frac{x}{10} + \frac{x}{15} = \frac{EC + AE}{AC} = \frac{AC}{AC} = 1$$

Thus, $\dfrac{x}{10} + \dfrac{x}{15} = 1$. We may solve this equation as follows.

$$\left(\frac{1}{10} + \frac{1}{15}\right)x = 1$$

$$\frac{5}{30}x = 1$$

$$\frac{1}{6}x = 1$$

$$x = 6$$

Thus, the fence post should be 6 feet high. Notice that, when finding the height of the fence post, we did not have to know how far apart the poles are. This means that, if the poles are placed farther apart, we would have the same height for the fence post. Thus, the poles could be any distance apart.

Looking Back. We could solve the problem for flagpoles of any length. If $AB = a$ and $CD = b$, then we would have $\dfrac{x}{a} + \dfrac{x}{b} = 1$ (why?) and, hence,

$$\left(\frac{1}{a} + \frac{1}{b}\right)x = 1 \quad \text{or} \quad \frac{a+b}{ab} \cdot x = 1 \quad \text{or} \quad x = \frac{ab}{a+b}$$

PROBLEM SET 11-5

1. Which of the following triangles is not similar to the other three?

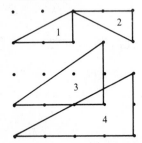

2. Which of the following are always similar? Why?
   (a) Any two equilateral triangles
   (b) Any two squares
   (c) Any two rectangles
   (d) Any two rhombuses
   (e) Any two circles
   (f) Any two regular polygons
   (g) Any two regular polygons with the same number of sides

3. Use grid paper to draw figures that have sides three times as large as the given ones.

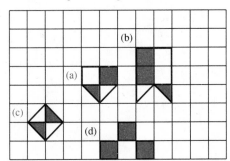

4. Are congruent triangles similar? Why?

5. (a) Construct a triangle with sides of lengths 4 cm, 6 cm, and 8 cm.
   (b) Construct another triangle with sides of lengths 2 cm, 3 cm, and 4 cm.
   (c) Make a conjecture about the similarity of triangles that have proportional sides only.

6. (a) Construct a triangle with sides of lengths 4 cm and 6 cm and an included angle of 60°.
   (b) Construct a triangle with sides of lengths 2 cm and 3 cm and an included angle of 60°.
   (c) Make a conjecture about the similarity of triangles that have two sides proportional and congruent included angles.

7. (a) Sketch two nonsimilar polygons for which corresponding angles are congruent.
   (b) Sketch two nonsimilar polygons for which corresponding sides are proportional.

8. Examine several examples of similar polygons, and make a conjecture concerning the ratio of their perimeters.

9. (a) Which of the following pairs of triangles are similar? If they are similar, explain why.
   (b) For each pair of similar triangles, find the scale factor of the sides of the triangles.

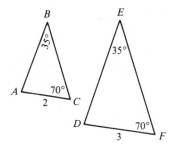

(i)

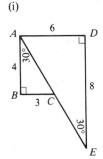

(ii)

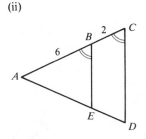

(iii)

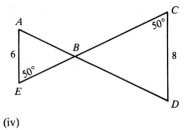

(iv)

10. Assume that the triangles in each part are similar, and find the measures of the unknown sides.

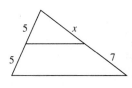

(a)

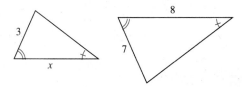

(b)

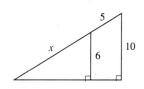

(c)

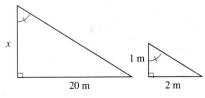

(d)

11. For each of the following, find x.

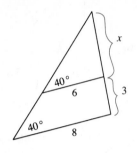

(a)

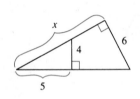

(b)

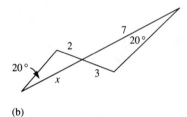

(c)

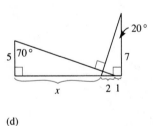

(d)

12. Use a compass and a straightedge to separate $\overline{AB}$ into five congruent pieces.

A B

13. Polly claims that each of the following pairs of triangles is similar. In each part, determine whether Polly is right or wrong. Explain why.

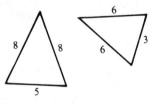

(a)

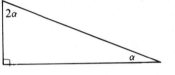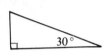

(b)

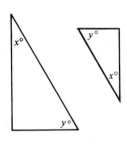

(c)

14. In right triangle ABC, we have $\overline{CD} \perp \overline{AB}$.

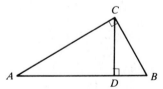

(a) Find three pairs of similar triangles. Justify your answers.

(b) Write the corresponding proportions for each set of similar triangles.

15. In the cartoon on the top of the next page, if a smaller map were obtained and its scale was half the size of the original map, would the distance to be traveled be any different? Why?

16. Construct a square and then construct another square with a side two-thirds the length of the first square.

17. Find the distance AB across the pond using the similar triangles shown.

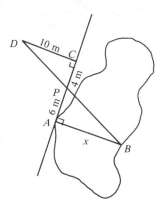

18. To find the height of a tree, a group of Girl Scouts devised the following method. A girl walks away from the tree along its shadow until the shadow of the top of her head coincides with the shadow of the top of the tree. If the girl is 150 cm tall, her distance to the foot of the tree is 1500 cm, and the length of her shadow is 300 cm, how tall is the tree?

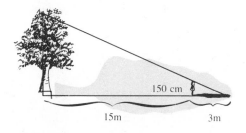

19. In the isosceles triangle ABC, $m(\angle A) = 36°$, $\overrightarrow{BD}$ bisects $\angle ABC$, and $\overline{AB} \cong \overline{AC}$.
  (a) Find two similar triangles in the figure.
  (b) Why are the triangles in (a) similar?

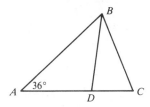

20. If $ABCD$ is a parallelogram, show that $\triangle BFE \sim \triangle CDE$.

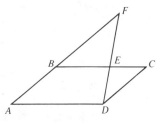

21. In the figure, $DEFG$ is a square and $m(\angle ACB) = 90°$.
  (a) Show that $\triangle ADG \sim \triangle GCF$.
  (b) Is it true that $\triangle ADG \cong \triangle GCF$? Justify your answer.

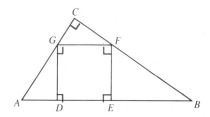

★**22.** A toy maker wants to cut the following plastic rectangle *EFGH* into four right triangles and a rectangle. Given the measurements shown, how long is $\overline{CE}$?

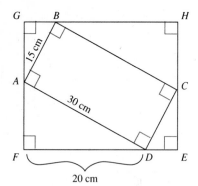

23. (a) Write a procedure called RECTANGLE that draws a rectangle of variable size with inputs :LEN and :WID; then write a procedure called SIM.RECT that draws a rectangle whose sides measure twice as large as those of the rectangle drawn by RECTANGLE when the same inputs are used for :LEN and :WID.

(b) Write a procedure called SIM.RECTANGLE that draws a rectangle similar to the one drawn by RECTANGLE, with a scale factor called :SCALE that affects the size of the rectangle.

(c) Write a procedure called PARALLELOGRAM that draws a parallelogram of variable size with inputs :LEN, :WID, and :ANGLE; then write a procedure called SIM.PAR that generates similar parallelograms.

24. (a) Write a Logo procedure called TRISECT that draws a line segment of length determined by input :LEN and has the turtle divide it into three congruent parts.

(b) Write a procedure called PARTITION that draws a line segment of length determined by input :LEN and has the turtle divide it into :NUM parts, where :NUM is also an input.

Review Problems

25. If a person holds a mirror at arm's length and looks into it, is the image seen congruent to the original? Why or why not?

26. Given the length of the base of an isosceles triangle and the length of the altitude to that base, construct the triangle.

_____

Base

_____

Altitude

B R A I N   T E A S E R

Poles $\overline{AB}$, $\overline{CF}$, and $\overline{DE}$ are constructed perpendicular to the ground in such a way that, when B, C, D, and F are connected by wires, BCDF is a rectangle. If $\overline{AB}$ is 9 m long and $\overline{DE}$ is 4 m long, how long is $\overline{CF}$ and how far apart are $\overline{AB}$ and $\overline{DE}$?

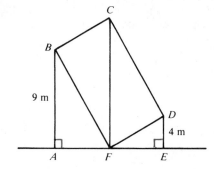

*Section 11-6   More on Geometry and Logo

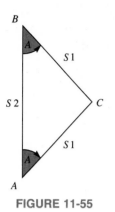

FIGURE 11-55

In the exercises of this chapter, we have investigated several Logo procedures for constructing triangles. In this section we consider the construction of isosceles triangles. In the general case, an isosceles triangle can be assumed to have only two sides congruent. In Figure 11-55, we see an isosceles triangle with sides S_1 and S_2 and base angles with measure A. This implies that the measure of the other angle of the triangle is $180 - 2A$. Thus, if the length of any side and the measure of one angle is given, we should be able to construct the triangle by ASA.

In the process of writing a Logo procedure for drawing isosceles triangles, we exhibit the use of recursive procedures for geometric purposes. It is likely that the following procedures require a deeper understanding than most elementary students have, but they may be simply given to the students as a piece of useful software.

We begin our Logo procedures by assuming that the length of the two congruent sides and the measure of one of the two base angles are given, as in Figure 11-56. If we start the turtle at home with a heading of 0, we might first draw the length of the known side :S1, turn the turtle right 2*:A (why?), move forward the length of the known side :S1, and then send the turtle home. This procedure follows.

FIGURE 11-56

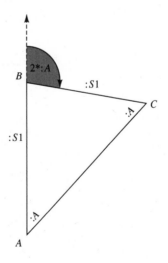

```
TO ISOSCELES1 :S1 :A
    DRAW
    FORWARD :S1
    RIGHT 2*:A
    FORWARD :S1
    HOME
END
```

(In Apple Logo II, replace DRAW with CLEARSCREEN.)

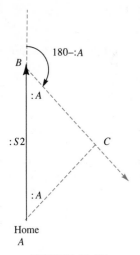

FIGURE 11-57

A different procedure for drawing △*ABC* (Figure 11-57) is required if we are given the length of the base, :S2, and the measure of a base angle, :A. Again suppose that the turtle starts at home with a heading of 0 and that we draw the length of the known side, :S2, first. In Figure 11-57, this would leave the turtle at point *B* with a heading of 0. We might then turn the turtle 180 − :A in order to draw $\overline{BC}$. We do not know how far the turtle should move to reach point *C*, but we want the turtle to move along $\overleftrightarrow{BC}$ until point *C* is located, and then we want it to return HOME to complete the triangle. To have the turtle do this, we might consider programming it to check many points along $\overleftrightarrow{BC}$ until it has the desired heading when pointed in the direction of *A*. In Figure 11-58(a), if the turtle were at point *A* (HOME) and pointed toward point *C*, it would have a heading of :A. However, if it were at point *C* and pointed toward point *A*, as in Figure 11-58(b), what would its heading be?

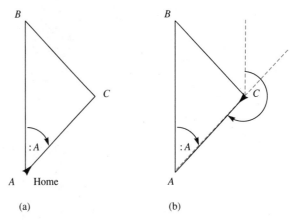

FIGURE 11-58

(a)   (b)

Since the two directions are on the same line but in opposite directions, the headings differ by 180°. Thus, the heading at point *C* toward point *A* is 180 + :A, as shown in Figure 11-58(b).

With this in mind, we move the turtle along $\overleftrightarrow{BC}$, stopping it at intervals to turn toward point *A* to check whether it has the desired heading. Suppose that a procedure called CHECKHEAD is written to accomplish this. If it were, then the ISOSCELES2 procedure might be the following.

```
TO ISOSCELES2 :S2 :A
    DRAW
    FORWARD :S2
    RIGHT 180 - :A
    CHECKHEAD :A
    HOME
END
```

(In Apple Logo II, replace DRAW with CLEARSCREEN.)

In the CHECKHEAD procedure, we want the turtle to move a bit along $\overleftrightarrow{BC}$, stop, turn toward point A, see if its heading is 180 + :A, and, if it is, stop checking. If the heading is not 180 + :A, then we want the turtle to turn back along $\overleftrightarrow{BC}$ with its original heading, move forward a bit more, and repeat the process. Because we do not know how many times the process has to be repeated, we use a recursive procedure. A first draft of the procedure might be the following.

```
DRAFT
TO CHECKHEAD :A
    FORWARD 1
    SETHEADING TOWARDS 0 0
    IF HEADING = 180 + :A THEN STOP ELSE
        SETHEADING 180 - :A CHECKHEAD :A
END
```

(In Apple Logo II, replace SETHEADING TOWARDS 0 0 with SETHEADING TOWARDS [0 0]. Also replace IF HEADING = 180 + :A THEN STOP ELSE SETHEADING 180 − :A CHECKHEAD :A with IF (HEADING = 180 + :A) [STOP] [SETHEADING 180 − :A CHECKHEAD :A].)

This draft is a good idea, but if you try it, it may not do what you want. One reason for this is that all measurements on the computer are approximations, and the exact heading may never be reached. If it cannot be reached, you have to decide how close an approximation to demand. This issue is entirely up to you. Suppose that you decide that being within 2° is acceptable. If so, you will want to know whether or not the absolute value of the difference of the heading and 180 + :A is less than 2°. As was mentioned earlier, Logo does not have an absolute value procedure. Here is the one written earlier.

```
TO ABS :VALUE
    IF :VALUE < 0 OUTPUT - :VALUE ELSE OUTPUT :VALUE
END
```

(In Apple Logo, replace IF :VALUE < 0 OUTPUT − :VALUE ELSE OUTPUT :VALUE with IF :VALUE < 0 [OUTPUT − :VALUE] [OUTPUT :VALUE].)

With this discussion in mind, the CHECKHEAD procedure might be as follows.

```
TO CHECKHEAD :A
    FORWARD 1
    SETHEADING TOWARDS 0 0
    IF ABS (HEADING - (180 + :A)) < 2 THEN STOP ELSE
        SETHEADING 180 - :A CHECKHEAD :A
END
```

(In Apple Logo, replace SETHEADING TOWARDS 0 0 with SETHEADING TOWARDS [0 0]. Also replace IF (ABS HEADING − (180 + :A)) < 2 THEN STOP ELSE SETHEADING 180 − :A CHECKHEAD :A with IF (ABS HEADING − (180 + :A)) < 2 [STOP] [SETHEADING 180 − :A CHECKHEAD :A].)

Other Logo geometry procedures are investigated in the exercises.

PROBLEM SET 11-6

1. Write a procedure called SIMSQS to draw two similar squares when given the length of a side :SIDE of one of the squares and the scale factor :K.

2. Write a procedure called RTISOS to draw an isosceles right triangle when given the length of the hypotenuse, :HYPOT.

3. A 30°-60°-90° triangle is formed by drawing an altitude of an equilateral triangle. Use this hint to write a procedure called TRI30 to draw a 30°-60°-90° triangle if given the length of the hypotenuse, :HYPOT.

4. Write a procedure called STAR to draw a regular hexagon for which, on each side of the hexagon, there is an equilateral triangle with congruent sides of length :SIDE, where :SIDE is the length of a side of the hexagon.

★5. Write a procedure called ISOSCELES3 to draw an isosceles triangle when given the measure of one base angle, :ANGLE, and the height, :HEIGHT.

SOLUTION TO THE PRELIMINARY PROBLEM

Understanding the Problem. The problem involves determining why an architect and a surveyor are apparently miscommunicating about a triangular piece of property with angles of measures approximately 54°, 39°, and 87° and two sides of lengths 80 m and 100 m. With the same set of measurements, the architect seems to think that the lot is smaller than does the surveyor. We must explore whether the five measurements can determine two different triangles. In most of the construction problems in this chapter involving triangles, three measurements have been enough to determine the triangle, as in SSS, SAS, ASA, and AAS.

Devising a Plan. Perhaps the most straightforward approach to this problem is to attempt several constructions in order to determine if two different triangles are possible. Since we are sure that both the architect and the surveyor had the measures of all three angles and of two sides of the triangle, it appears that we should be able to use the SAS, ASA, or AAS constructions of this chapter. If two different triangles are determined by the measurements, the different triangles must be similar by the AA property.

Carrying Out the Plan. If we call the known angles A, B, and C, with measures of 54°, 87°, and 39°, respectively, how should we label the two sides of lengths 80 m and 100 m? Suppose that the segment of length 80 m is $\overline{AB}$, and the segment of length 100 m is $\overline{BC}$. Using a protractor, we construct an 87° angle, label the vertex B, and use a ruler to scale the sides of 80 m and 100 m. We then connect the two endpoints to obtain $\overline{AC}$. Such a drawing is shown in Figure 11-59(a).

As a second trial, suppose that we use a protractor to draw a 39° angle, labeling it C'. On its sides, we make $A'C'$ be 100 m and $B'C'$ be 80 m, using the same scale as in Figure 11-59(a). The result is shown in Figure 11-59(b). Obviously, the triangles are not the same size, but they do have similar

FIGURE 11-59

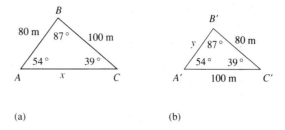

(a)   (b)

shape. Hence, the surveyor and the architect could both have been correct in their conclusions. Hence, one way for them to avoid their confusion is to specify which sides are opposite which angles.

Looking Back. Since the triangles of Figure 11-59 are similar, we could discern several other bits of information. For example, the ratio of the triangles' corresponding sides is $\frac{80}{100}$, or $\frac{4}{5}$. Furthermore, we could find the lengths of the sides labeled x and y, as follows.

$$\frac{80}{100} = \frac{100}{x} \qquad\qquad \frac{y}{80} = \frac{80}{100}$$

$$80x = 10{,}000 \qquad 100y = 6400$$

$$x = 125 \text{ m} \qquad\quad y = 64 \text{ m}$$

Since the primary source of confusion in this problem seems to have been that the surveyor and the architect did not have the corresponding parts of the triangles labeled in the same way, a question should arise about what types of triangles can have five parts of one congruent to five parts of another and yet not be congruent. These are called 5-con triangles; a general discussion of such triangles is provided in "5-Con Triangles" by R. Pawley.

QUESTIONS FROM THE CLASSROOM

1. On a test, a student wrote $AB \cong CD$ instead of $\overline{AB} \cong \overline{CD}$. Is this answer correct?

2. A student asks if there are any constructions that cannot be done with a compass and a straightedge. How do you answer?

3. A student asks for a mathematical definition of congruence that holds for all figures. How do you respond? Is your response the same for similarity?

4. One student claims that by trisecting $\overline{AB}$ and drawing $\overrightarrow{CD}$ and $\overrightarrow{CE}$ as shown, she has trisected $\angle ACB$.

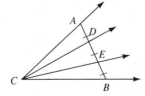

How do you convince her that her construction is wrong?

5. In the following drawing, a student claims that polygon $ABCD$ is a parallelogram if $\angle 1 \cong \angle 2$. Is he correct?

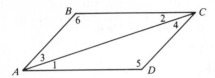

6. A student claims that, when the midpoints of the sides of any polygon are connected, a polygon similar to the original results. Is this true?

7. A student asks why $\cong$ rather than $=$ is used to discuss triangles that have the same size and shape. What do you say?

8. A student draws the following figure and claims that, because every triangle is congruent to itself, we can write $\triangle ABC \cong \triangle BCA$. What is your response?

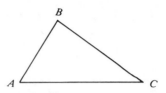

9. A student says that, since every circle can have a quadrilateral inscribed in it, we should be able to inscribe a circle in every quadrilateral. How do you respond?

CHAPTER OUTLINE

I. Congruence
- A. Two geometric figures are **congruent** if and only if they have the same size and shape.
- B. Two triangles are congruent if they satisfy any of the following properties.
  1. **Side, Side, Side (SSS)**
  2. **Side, Angle, Side (SAS)**
  3. **Angle, Side, Angle (ASA)**
  4. **Angle, Angle, Side (AAS)**
- C. **Triangle Inequality:** The sum of the measures of any two sides of a triangle must be greater than the measure of the third side.

II. Circles and spheres
- A. A **circle** is a set of points in a plane that are the same distance (radius) from a given point (center).
- B. An **arc** of a circle is any part of the circle that can be drawn without lifting a pencil. The **center of the arc** is the center of the circle containing the arc.
- C. A **chord** is a segment whose endpoints lie on a circle.
- D. A **secant** is a line that contains a chord of a circle.
- E. A **tangent** is a line that intersects a circle at exactly one point and is perpendicular to a radius drawn at that point.
- F. A **sphere** is a set of points in space that are the same distance (radius) from a given point (center).
- G. A **central angle** is an angle whose vertex is at the center of the circle in which it is defined.

III. Similar figures
- A. Two polygons are **similar** if and only if their corresponding angles are congruent and their corresponding sides are proportional.
- B. **AAA or AA:** If three (two) angles of one triangle are congruent to three (two) angles of a second triangle, the triangles are **similar.**

IV. Proportion
- A. If a line parallel to one side of a triangle intersects the other sides, it divides those sides into proportional segments.
- B. If parallel lines cut off congruent segments on one transversal, they cut off congruent segments on any transversal.

V. Constructions that can be accomplished using a compass and a straightedge
- A. Copy a line segment.
- B. Copy a circle.
- C. Copy an angle.
- D. Bisect a segment.
- E. Bisect an angle.
- F. Construct a perpendicular from a point to a line.
- G. Construct a perpendicular bisector of a segment.
- H. Construct a perpendicular to a line through a point on the line.
- I. Construct a parallel to a line through a point not on the line.
- J. Divide a segment into congruent parts.
- K. Inscribe regular polygons in a circle.
- L. Circumscribe a circle about a triangle.
- M. Inscribe a circle in a triangle.

CHAPTER TEST

1. Each of the following figures contains at least one pair of congruent triangles. Identify them and tell why they are congruent.

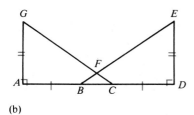

(a)

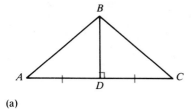

(b)

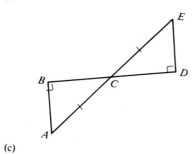

(c)

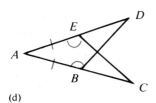

(d)

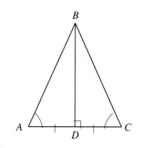

(e)

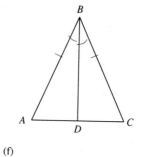

(f)

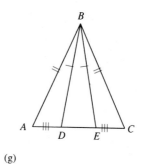

(g)

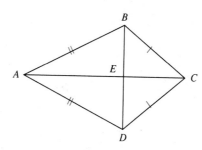

(h)

2. In the figure, *ABCD* is a square and $\overline{DE} \cong \overline{BF}$. What kind of figure is *AECF*? Justify your answer.

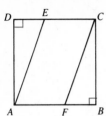

3. Construct each of the following by using (a) compass and straightedge; (b) paper folding.

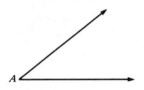

(a) Bisector of ∠*A*

(b) Perpendicular to ℓ at *B*

• *B*

(c) Perpendicular to ℓ from *B*

• *P*

(d) Parallel to ℓ through *P*

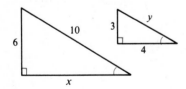

(e) Perpendicular bisector of $\overline{AB}$

4. For each of the following pairs of similar triangles, find the missing measures.

(a)

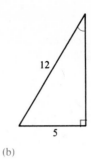

(b)

5. Divide the given segment into five congruent parts.

$\overline{}$
A   *B*

6. If *ABCD* is a trapezoid, $\overline{EF} \| \overline{AD}$, and $\overline{AC}$ is a diagonal. What is the relationship between $\dfrac{a}{b}$ and $\dfrac{c}{d}$? Why?

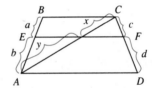

7. Construct a circle that contains *A* and *B* and has its center on ℓ.

8. For each of the following, show that appropriate triangles are similar, and find *x* and *y*.

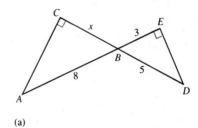

(a)

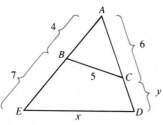

(b) Given: ∠ABC ≅ ∠ADE

9. Determine whether each of the following is true or false. If false, explain why.
   (a) A radius of a circle is a chord of the circle.
   (b) A diameter of a circle may be a tangent of the circle.
   (c) If a radius bisects a chord of a circle, then it is perpendicular to the chord.
   (d) Two spheres may intersect at exactly one point.
   (e) Two spheres may intersect in a circle.
10. A person 2 m tall casts a shadow 1 m long when a building has a 6-m shadow. How high is the building?
11. (a) Which of the following polygons can be inscribed in a circle? Assume that all sides of each polygon are congruent and that all the angles of polygons (iii) and (iv) are congruent.
    (b) Based on your answer in (a), make a conjecture about what kinds of polygons can be inscribed in a circle.

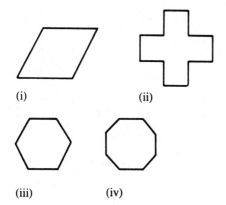

(i)

(ii)

(iii)

(iv)

12. What is the vertical height of the playground slide shown?

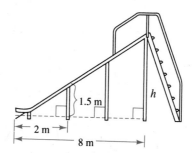

13. Find the distance across the river shown.

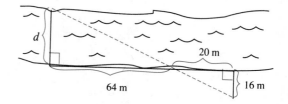

C H A P T E R   12

Motion Geometry
and Tessellations

PRELIMINARY PROBLEM

A farmer wanted to place three scarecrows in a garden in such a way that one would be in each of the furrows indicated below and so that each was the same distance from the other. Where could the scarecrows have been placed?

_____

_____

_____

Introduction

Euclid envisioned moving one geometric figure in a plane and placing it on top of another to determine if the two figures were congruent. Intuitively, this can be done by making a tracing of one figure, shifting, turning, or flipping the tracing, and placing it back down atop the other figure. Elementary school students seem to be able to identify congruences by this type of predeductive activity. The *Standards* supports this approach: "Explorations of flips, slides, turns, stretchers, and shrinkers will illuminate the concepts of congruence and similarity."

One of the first projects in the United States for elementary students involving moving figures resulted in the 1969 publication of the four-book series *Motion Geometry* by the University of Illinois Committee on School Mathematics. The concepts presented there had been introduced at a much higher level in Germany by Felix Klein in 1872.

The notions of motion geometry are introduced in this chapter, along with coverage of *tessellations* of a plane—the filling of a plane with repetitions of a figure in such a way that no figures overlap and there are no gaps. In the process of examining tessellations, we will consider some of the work of the Dutch artist M. C. Escher and investigate tessellations with Logo.

H I S T O R I C A L   N O T E

In 1872, at age 23, Felix Klein (1849–1925) was appointed to a chair at the University of Erlangen, Germany. His inaugural address, referred to as the *Erlanger Programm*, described geometry as the study of properties of figures that do not change under a particular set of transformations. Specifically, Euclidean geometry was described as the study of such properties of figures as area and lengths, which remain unchanged under a set of transformations, called *isometries*. It was not until 1975 that a secondary-school text was introduced in the United States that utilized Klein's ideas in a major way.

Section 12-1   Translations and Rotations

Translations

Plane figures can be moved from one position to another by different motions. One such motion is described in Figure 12-1, where a child moves down a slide without any accompanying twisting or turning. This type of motion is

translation / slide called a **translation,** or a **slide.**

FIGURE 12-1

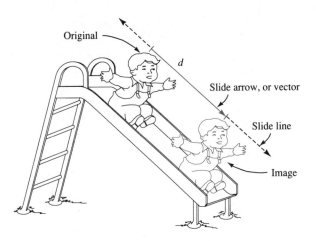

Notice that, in Figure 12-1, the child has moved a certain distance in a certain direction along a line. The distance and direction the original figure is moved are marked with a **slide arrow,** or **vector,** along a **slide line** to obtain the **image.** As another example of this type of motion, consider Figure 12-2(a), where figures in plane α are traced on plane α'. The tracing is then slid without twisting or turning along the slide arrow so that point P falls on point Q. Once the sliding is completed, we punch holes in α' to mark points A', B', and C'—and hence, the image of the figure in plane α determined by points A, B, and C—and complete the drawing, as in Figure 12-2(b). In Figure 12-2(b), $AA' = d$ and $\overline{AA'}$ is parallel to $\overline{PQ}$. Similarly, $BB' = d$ and $\overline{BB'}$ is parallel to $\overline{PQ}$. In this example, we have a one-to-one correspondence between the plane and itself. Any one-to-one correspondence between a plane and itself is a **transformation** of the plane. A transformation is determined if it is possible to find the image of every point in the plane. A translation is a special type of transformation, as defined next.

slide arrow / vector
slide line / image

transformation

FIGURE 12-2

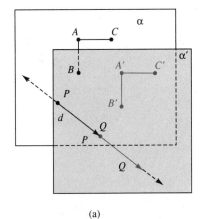

(a)

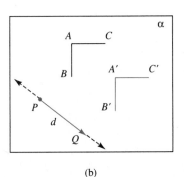

(b)

- **D E F I N I T I O N**
A **translation** is a transformation of a plane that moves every point of the plane a specified distance in a specified direction along a straight line.

Figure 12-3 shows a translation that takes $\triangle ABC$ to $\triangle A'B'C'$. The translation is determined by the slide arrow, or vector, from M to N. The vector determines the image of any point in the plane in the following way: The image of a point A in the plane is the point A' obtained by sliding A along a line parallel to $\overleftrightarrow{MN}$ in the direction from M to N by the distance MN. (MN is denoted by d in Figure 12-3.) Dashed segments have been used to connect the vertices of $\triangle ABC$ with their respective images under the translation. Notice the $AA' = BB' = CC' = d$ and $\overline{AA'} \parallel \overline{BB'} \parallel \overline{CC'}$. It appears that, under the translation, figures do not change their shapes or sizes. This is true in general, and we say that a translation preserves both length and angle size (and hence, the congruence) of figures.

FIGURE 12-3

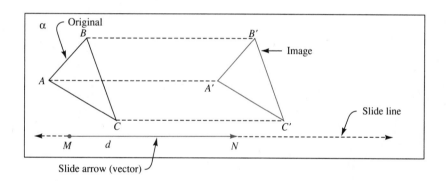

In Figure 12-3, the translation is determined by the slide arrow connecting M with N. One way to symbolize the translation from M to N is as T_{MN}.

We have seen that a translation preserves distance; that is, the distance between two points is the same as the distance between their images. Any *isometry* transformation that preserves distance is called an **isometry** (derived from *rigid motion* Greek and meaning "equal measure"), or a **rigid motion.** Thus, a translation is an isometry.

More Constructions of Translations
As just seen, the image of a figure *under a translation* (or *by a translation* or *in a translation*) can be constructed with tracing paper. We can also

construct a translation image of a figure by using only a compass and a straightedge. To construct such an image, we first need to know how to find the image of a given point, since geometric figures are made of points. Given a translation determined by the slide arrow from M to N in Figure 12-4(a), A', the image of A under this translation, must be such that $\overline{AA'}$ is parallel to $\overline{MN}$ and $AA' = MN$. From the definitions of quadrilaterals in Chapter 10 and the properties of quadrilaterals in Chapter 11, we know that $AA'NM$ is a parallelogram. Hence, to find A', we construct parallelogram $AA'NM$, where we are given A, N, and M. For an efficient construction of the parallelogram, recall that a quadrilateral in which each pair of opposite sides is congruent is a parallelogram. Thus, we construct vertex A' by making $AA' = MN$ and $NA' = MA$. This is shown in Figure 12-4(b).

FIGURE 12-4

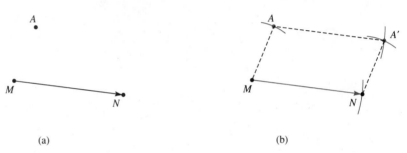

(a)   (b)

● **R E M A R K**
There exist two parallelograms with vertices A, M, and N, but only one, as indicated in Figure 12-4(b), takes A to A' in the direction of the arrow $\overrightarrow{MN}$.

To find the image of a triangle under a translation, we find the images of the three vertices by a process similar to that used in Figure 12-4 and connect these images with segments to form the triangle's image.

On a geoboard or a grid, it is often possible to find an image of a point, as the following example shows.

EXAMPLE 12-1 Find the image of $\overline{AB}$ under the translation $T_{XX'}$ pictured on the dot paper in Figure 12-5.

FIGURE 12-5

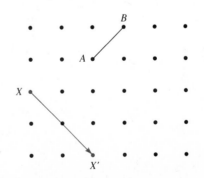

SOLUTION   To find the image of $\overline{AB}$, we first find the images of A and B by using tracing paper. The result is shown in Figure 12-6.

FIGURE 12-6

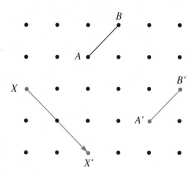

• R E M A R K

The image could have been found without tracing by noticing that the image of each point can be determined by shifting each point down two units and then shifting it two units to the right.

Rotations

rotation / turn   A **rotation,** or **turn,** is another kind of isometry. Figure 12-7 illustrates congruent figures resulting from a rotation about point Q. A rotation can be constructed by using tracing paper, as in Figure 12-8. In Figure 12-8(a), $\triangle ABC$ and point O are traced on tracing paper. Holding point O fixed, we can turn the tracing paper to obtain an image, $\triangle A'B'C'$, as shown in Figure

turn center / turn angle   12-8(b). Point O is the **turn center,** and $\angle COC'$ is the **turn angle.**

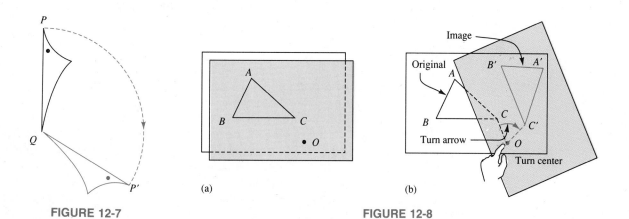

FIGURE 12-7

(a)   (b)

FIGURE 12-8

In order to determine a rotation, we must be given three things: the turn center; the direction of the turn, either clockwise or counterclockwise; and the amount of the turn. The amount and the direction of the turn can be illustrated by a **turn arrow**, or it can be specified as a number of degrees.

turn arrow

The rotation pictured in Figure 12-8 might be symbolized by using the turn center O and the turn angle $\angle COC'$. However, such symbolism may cause confusion, since the rotation could have been either clockwise or counterclockwise. To eliminate the ambiguity, it is necessary to adopt some conventions concerning the direction of the rotation. Mathematicians typically use an amount turned in a counterclockwise direction as a positive number and an amount turned in a clockwise direction as a negative number. If $m(\angle COC') = \alpha$, then the symbol for the rotation in Figure 12-8 is $R_{O,-\alpha}$, where O is the turn center.

The amount of turning in a rotation could be any real number of degrees. In Figure 12-8, by holding point O fixed, we can turn the tracing paper any number of times in either direction. Sometimes, when it is convenient, we refer to the *angle* of a rotation, but what we are talking about is the *amount* of a rotation.

This discussion leads us to the following definition.

- **D E F I N I T I O N**
A **rotation** is a transformation of the plane determined by holding one point, the center, fixed and rotating the plane about this point by a certain amount in a certain direction.

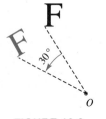

FIGURE 12-9

Another example of a rotation about point O through 30° in a counterclockwise direction, written as $R_{O,30°}$, is shown in Figure 12-9. In Figure 12-9, it is clear that point O is its own image, and we could write $R_{O,30°}(O) = O$. In any rotation, the center of the rotation is its own image.

More Constructions of Rotations

The definition of a rotation can be used to find the image of any point of the plane under a rotation with center O and through a specified amount, as pictured in Figure 12-10(a). Consider what must be done to find the image of any point P in the plane. We need to draw a circle with center O and radius OP, as in Figure 12-10(b), and then, starting at P, we need to move along the circle—counterclockwise if $\alpha > 0$, and clockwise if $\alpha < 0$—until we locate the point P' such that $m(\angle POP') = \alpha$. Using a compass and a straightedge, we can find the location of P' by constructing $\angle POP'$ congruent to the angle of rotation so that P' will be drawn in the desired direction indicated by the amount of the rotation, or the turn angle. This is illustrated in Figure 12-10(b).

FIGURE 12-10

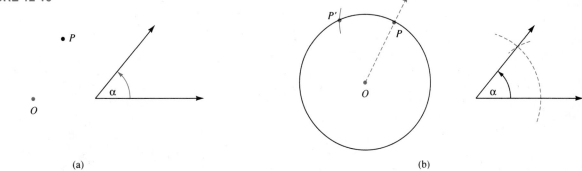

(a)   (b)

Because a rotation is an isometry, the image of a figure under a rotation is congruent to the original figure. Thus, under a rotation as under a translation, the image of a line is a line, the image of a circle is a circle, and the images of parallel lines are parallel.

Because we know how to use a compass and a straightedge to find the image of a point under a rotation about a given point by a given amount, we can also find the images of various geometric figures. Suppose that we want to find the image of $\overline{PQ}$ under a counterclockwise rotation by α about point O, as shown in Figure 12-11(a). Because the image of a segment is a segment, we find the images of the endpoints of the segments by using the procedure in Figure 12-10. The results are pictured in Figure 12-11(b).

FIGURE 12-11

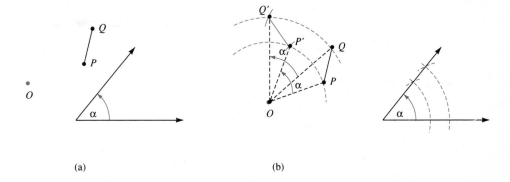

(a)   (b)

Using a compass and a straightedge, we can find the images of many figures under a rotation by an arbitrary amount about a given point.

EXAMPLE 12-2   Find the image of line ℓ in Figure 12-12 under a rotation of 45° counter-clockwise about point O.

FIGURE 12-12

SOLUTION   Because a line is determined by two points and because the image of a line is a line, it is sufficient for us to pick any two points on ℓ and find the images of these points under the given rotation. We pick two arbitrary points A and B on ℓ and find their images A' and B' by constructing $\angle AOA'$ and $\angle BOB'$ so that $m(\angle AOA')$ and $m(\angle BOB') = 45°$. The line ℓ' connecting A' with B' is the image of ℓ under the rotation. A summary of the construction without all arcs drawn is given in Figure 12-13.

FIGURE 12-13

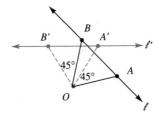

Rotations may be constructed on dot paper, as demonstrated in Example 12-3.

EXAMPLE 12-3   Find the image of $\triangle ABC$ under the rotation with center O in Figure 12-14.

FIGURE 12-14

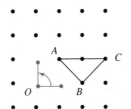

SOLUTION   We use tracing paper to find $\triangle A'B'C'$, the image of $\triangle ABC$, as shown in Figure 12-15.

FIGURE 12-15

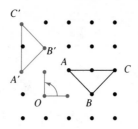

A rotation of 360° will transform any figure onto itself. A rotation of 180° about a point is also of particular interest. Such a rotation is called a *half-turn* **half-turn.** Because a half-turn is a rotation, it has all the properties of rotations. Figure 12-16 shows some shapes and their images under a half-turn about point O.

FIGURE 12-16

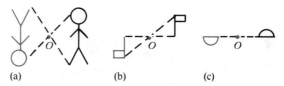

     (a)   (b)   (c)

EXAMPLE 12-4

Use a compass and a straightedge to find the image of a line ℓ under a half-turn about point O in Figure 12-17.

FIGURE 12-17

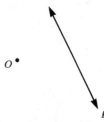

SOLUTION

Because a line is determined by two points and the image of a line is a line, it is sufficient for us to pick any two points on ℓ and find the images of these points under the half-turn. In Figure 12-18, we pick two arbitrary points A and B on ℓ and find their images A' and B' by drawing $\overrightarrow{AO}$ and marking off $OA' = OA$ so that of O is the mid-point of $\overline{AA'}$. We find B' similarly. The line connecting A' and B' is the image of ℓ. The result is illustrated in Figure 12-18.

FIGURE 12-18

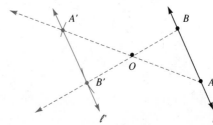

EXAMPLE 12-5 Find $\overline{AB}$ in Figure 12-19 such that A is on circle O, B is on line m, and P is the midpoint of $\overline{AB}$.

FIGURE 12-19

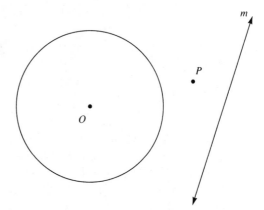

SOLUTION If we find points A on circle O and B on line m such that P is the midpoint of $\overline{AB}$, then we have a drawing similar to that in Figure 12-20. We do not know the location of either A or B. However, we do know that A is on the circle and that it is the image of some point on line m under the half-turn in P. Since we do not know the point on m whose image will be on the circle, we find the images of all the points on m and see which ones (if any) lie on the circle. This can be accomplished by finding the image m' of m under a half-turn in P. Since m' intersects circle O in two points, A_1 and A_2, as shown in Figure 12-21, either could be labeled A. The point on m whose image is A_1 is labeled B_1, and the point on m whose image is A_2 is labeled B_2. Thus, both $\overline{A_1B_1}$ and $\overline{A_2B_2}$ are possible solutions.

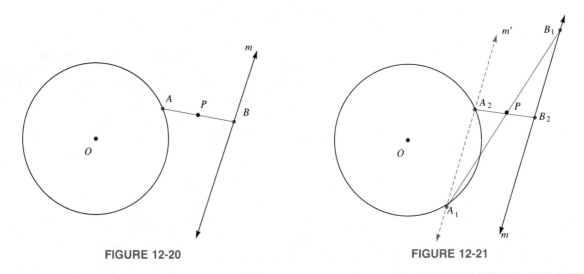

FIGURE 12-20   **FIGURE 12-21**

• R E M A R K

We also could have found the solution in Example 12-5 by finding the image of circle *O* under a half-turn in *P* and then finding where this image circle intersects line *m* in a half-turn in point *P*.

PROBLEM SET 12-1

1. What type of motion is involved in each of the following?
   (a) A skier skiing straight down a slope
   (b) A leaf floating down a stream
2. For each of the following, find the image of the given quadrilateral under a translation from *A* to *B*.

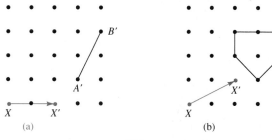

3. Find the figure whose image is given in each of the following under a translation from *X* to *X'*.

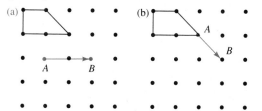

4. Construct the image of $\overline{BC}$ under the translation pictured, using the following.
   (a) Tracing paper
   (b) Compass and straightedge

5. Draw a slide arrow and a circle. Find the image of the circle under the translation indicated by the slide arrow.

6. Name three everyday examples of rotations.
7. Find the image of the given quadrilateral in a 90° counterclockwise rotation about *O*.

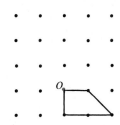

8. The images of segment $\overline{AB}$ under various rotations are given in the accompanying drawings. Find $\overline{AB}$ in each case.

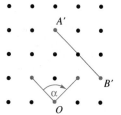
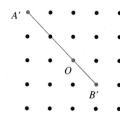

(a) A rotation with center *O* through α

(b) A half-turn through *O*

9. Find the rotation image of $\overline{AB}$ by the given angle about *O* using the following.
   (a) Tracing paper
   (b) Compass and straightedge.

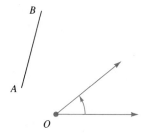

10. Use a compass and a straightedge to find the image of the circle *M* under a half-turn about *O*.

11. In each of the following, find the image of the circle *M* under a 120° counterclockwise rotation about *O*.

(a)

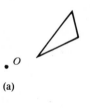

(b)

12. In each of the following figures, find the image of the figure under a half-turn about *O*.

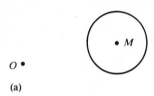

(a)

(b)

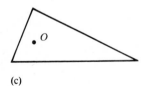

(c)

13. Draw three arbitrary points *P*, *P′*, and *Q*. If *P′* is the image of *P* under a half-turn, construct the image of *Q* under that half-turn.

14. Through point *P*, construct a segment $\overline{AB}$ that is bisected by point *P*, where point *A* is on line *ℓ* and point *B* is on line *m*.

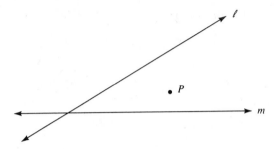

15. (a) In succession, perform the two rotations, each with center *O*, in the figure.

(b) What is the result of the two rotations?

(c) Is the order of the rotations important?

(d) Could the result have been accomplished in one rotation?

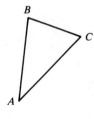

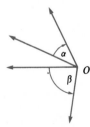

16. Given two circles and point P, as follows, find $\overline{AB}$ such that $\overline{AP} = \overline{PB}$, A is on circle O, and B is on circle Q.

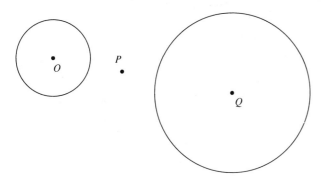

★17. Construct an equilateral triangle such that there is exactly one vertex on each of the concentric circles shown.

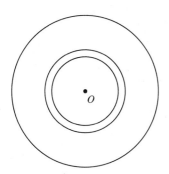

18. (a) Translations may be explored in Logo by using a figure called an EE. Type the given programs into your computer and then run the following, with the turtle starting at home with heading 0.
    (i) SLIDE 40 45
    (ii) SLIDE 200 57
    (iii) SLIDE (−50) (−75)

```
TO SLIDE :DIRECTION :DISTANCE
  EE
  PENUP
  SETHEADING :DIRECTION
  FORWARD :DISTANCE
  PENDOWN
  SETHEADING 0
  EE
END
```

```
TO EE
  FORWARD 50 RIGHT 90
  FORWARD 25 BACK 25
  LEFT 90 BACK 25
  RIGHT 90 FORWARD 10
  BACK 10 LEFT 90
  BACK 25 RIGHT 90
  FORWARD 25 BACK 25
  LEFT 90
END
```

(b) Edit the SLIDE procedure in (a) so that it will slide an equilateral triangle.

19. Write a Logo procedure called ROTATE that will draw a square and produce the image of the square when the square is rotated by an arbitrary angle :A about one of its vertices.

20. Write a Logo procedure called TURN.CIRCLE that will draw a circle passing through the home of the turtle and produce the image of the circle under the following transformations.
    (a) A half-turn about the turtle's home
    (b) A 90° counterclockwise rotation about the turtle's home

LABORATORY ACTIVITY

1. As a van Hiele Level 1 activity, look around your classroom and find and list the following.
   (a) Congruent objects such that a translation will take one object to another
   (b) Congruent objects such that a rotation will take one object to another
2. As a van Hiele Level 3 activity, use a compass and a straightedge in the following drawing to construct two chords of equal length through points P and Q that are perpendicular to each other.

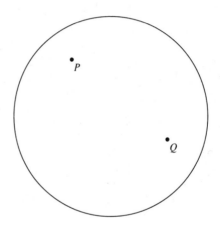

Section 12-2 Reflections and Glide Reflections

Reflections

reflection / flip Another isometry is a **reflection,** or a **flip.** One example of a reflection often encountered in our daily lives is a mirror image. Figure 12-22 shows a figure with its mirror image. Another reflection is shown in the B.C. cartoon.

FIGURE 12-22

B.C.

In a plane, we can simulate reflections in various ways. Consider the half tree shown in Figure 12-23(a). Folding the paper along the **reflecting line** and drawing the image gives the **mirror image,** or *image,* of the half tree. In Figure 12-23(b), the paper is unfolded. The total figure obtained is symmetric about the fold line in much the same way that a mirror gives symmetry in space. Another way to simulate a reflection in a line involves using a Mira and is illustrated in Figure 12-23(c).

reflecting line
mirror image

FIGURE 12-23

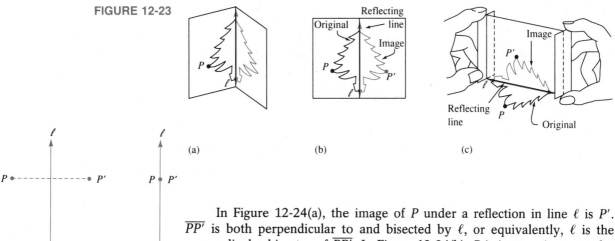

(a)   (b)   (c)

FIGURE 12-24

In Figure 12-24(a), the image of P under a reflection in line ℓ is P'. $\overline{PP'}$ is both perpendicular to and bisected by ℓ, or equivalently, ℓ is the perpendicular bisector of $\overline{PP'}$. In Figure 12-24(b), P is its own image under the reflection in line ℓ. If ℓ were a mirror, then P' would be the mirror image of P. We use M_ℓ to denote a reflection in line ℓ. This leads us to the following definition of a reflection.

● D E F I N I T I O N

A **reflection** in a line ℓ is a transformation of a plane that pairs each point P of the plane with a point P' in such a way that ℓ is the perpendicular bisector of $\overline{PP'}$, as long as P is not on ℓ. If P is on ℓ, then $P = P'$.

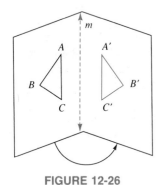

FIGURE 12-25

In Figure 12-25, we see another property of a reflection. Observe that, in the original triangle, if we walk clockwise around the vertices, starting at vertex A, we see the vertices in the order A-B-C. However, in the reflection image of triangle ABC, if we start at A' (the image of A) and walk clockwise, we see the vertices in the following order: A'-C'-B'. Thus, a reflection does something that neither a translation nor a rotation does; it reverses the orientation of the original figure. There are many methods of constructing a reflection image. We illustrate such constructions with paper folding, tracing paper, a Mira, and compass and straightedge.

Constructing a Reflection by Paper Folding. To find the image of $\triangle ABC$ in Figure 12-26, we fold the paper along reflecting line m and mark the image of the triangle. This may require punching holes in the paper or indenting the vertices heavily with a pencil so that they are visible.

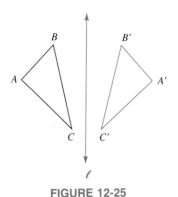

FIGURE 12-26

Constructing a Reflection Using Tracing Paper. Another method of constructing the image of an original under a reflection involves using tracing paper or an acetate sheet. Figure 12-27(a) shows the use of tracing paper. We trace the original figure, the reflecting line, and a point on the reflecting line, which we use as a reference point. When we flip the tracing paper over to perform the reflection, we align the reflecting line and the reference point, as in Figure 12-27(b). Aligning the reference point ensures that no translating occurs along the reflecting line when the reflection is performed. If we wish the image to be on the paper with the original, we may indent the tracing paper or acetate sheet to mark the images of the original vertices.

FIGURE 12-27

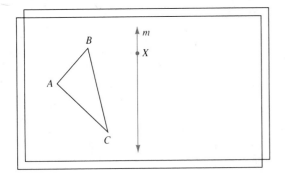

(a)

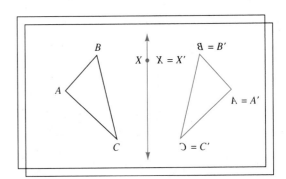

(b)

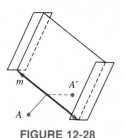

FIGURE 12-28

Constructing a Reflection with a Mira. To construct the image of an original under a reflection in line m by using a Mira, as in Figure 12-28, we align the drawing edge of the Mira along line m and mark the image of the original.

Constructing a Reflection with Compass and Straightedge. To construct the image of a figure under a reflection with a compass and a straightedge, first recall that the reflecting line m is the perpendicular bisector of the segment connecting any point P and its image P'. Thus, given point P and reflecting line m, as in Figure 12-29(a), we construct the image of P in two stages. First we construct a perpendicular ray from P to m, as in Figure 12-29(b), that intersects m in point X. Then we find P' on $\overrightarrow{PX}$ such that $XP' = PX$. If the compass setting is not changed in the construction, then P' is found automatically, as in Figure 12-29(b). (Why?)

FIGURE 12-29

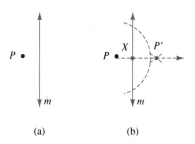

(a)   (b)

EXAMPLE 12-6 Use a compass and a straightedge to construct the image of $\overleftrightarrow{AB}$ under a reflection in line m in Figure 12-30.

FIGURE 12-30

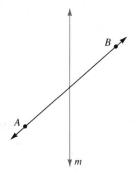

SOLUTION Under a reflection, the image of a line is a line. Thus, to find the image of $\overleftrightarrow{AB}$, it is sufficient to choose any two points on the line and find their images. The images determine the line that is the image of $\overleftrightarrow{AB}$. We choose two points whose images are easy to find. Point X, the intersection of $\overleftrightarrow{AB}$ and m, is its own image. If we choose point A and use the compass and straightedge method explained earlier, we produce the construction shown in Figure 12-31.

FIGURE 12-31

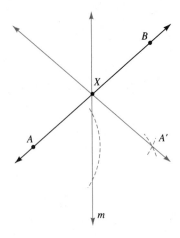

●   R E M A R K
We could have used the compass and straightedge to find the images of both A and B, in order to complete the construction.

Tracing paper and dot paper or geoboards may be used to find the images of figures under a reflection, as described in Example 12-7.

EXAMPLE 12-7   Find the image of $\triangle ABC$ under a reflection in line m, as in Figure 12-32.

FIGURE 12-32

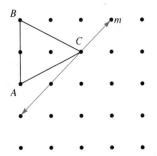

SOLUTION   We can use tracing paper to find the image of the reflection. The result is shown in Figure 12-33. Note that C is the image of itself and that the images of vertices A and B are A' and B' such that m is the perpendicular bisector of $\overline{AA'}$ and $\overline{BB'}$.

FIGURE 12-33

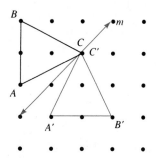

It is possible to find the reflecting line, given an original figure and its reflection image. An example of this is provided in Example 12-8.

EXAMPLE 12-8   Given the $\triangle ABC$ and its reflection image $\triangle A'B'C'$, as shown in Figure 12-34, find the line of reflection.

FIGURE 12-34

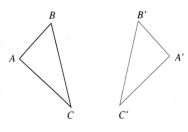

SOLUTION   Since the reflecting line m is the perpendicular bisector of all segments connecting points and their images, it is sufficient to find the perpendicular bisector of $\overline{AA'}$. This is shown in Figure 12-35.

FIGURE 12-35

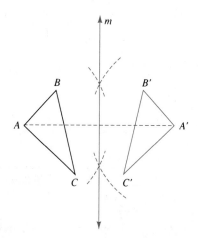

● **R E M A R K**
Any vertex other than A could also have been used. Another technique is to fold $\triangle ABC$ onto $\triangle A'B'C'$ and crease the fold line. The fold line is the reflecting line.

PROBLEM 1
The hiker in Figure 12-36, carrying a bucket, sees that his tent is on fire. To what point on the bank of the river should the hiker run to fill his bucket in order to make his trip to the tent as short as possible?

FIGURE 12-36

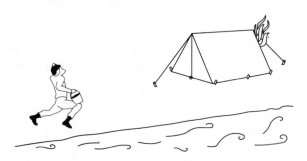

Understanding the Problem.   To understand the problem better, we first draw a diagram, as seen in Figure 12-37. We label the hiker H, the tent T, and the river r. The hiker needs to find point P on the bank of the river so that the distance $HP + PT$ is as short as possible.

FIGURE 12-37

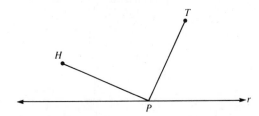

Devising a Plan.   From the properties of reflections, we know that, if T' is the reflection of the tent T in line r, then r is the perpendicular bisector of $\overline{TT'}$, as shown in Figure 12-38(a). Hence, any point on r is equidistant from T and T'. Thus, $PT = PT'$. Therefore, the hiker may solve the problem by finding a point P on r such that the path from H to P and then to T' is as short as possible. The shortest path connecting H and T' is a segment. The intersection of $\overline{HT'}$ and r determines the point on the river toward which the hiker should run.

3. (a) Find the image of △ABC under a reflection in line ℓ.

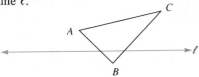

   (b) Is it possible to find the image of △ABC in (a) without first finding the image of B? If so, explain how.

4. Draw a line and a circle whose center is not on the line. Find the image of the circle under a reflection in the line.

5. Which of the following figures have a reflecting line such that the image of the figure under the reflecting line is the figure itself? In each case, find as many such reflecting lines as possible, sketching appropriate drawings.
   - (a) Circle
   - (b) Segment
   - (c) Ray
   - (d) Square
   - (e) Rectangle
   - (f) Scalene triangle
   - (g) Isosceles triangle
   - (h) Equilateral triangle
   - (i) Trapezoid whose base angles are not congruent
   - (j) Isosceles trapezoid
   - (k) Arc
   - (l) Kite
   - (m) Rhombus
   - (n) Regular hexagon
   - (o) Regular *n*-gon

6. Justify your answers in problem 5 by paper folding.

7. Use any construction method to find the image of △ABC if it is reflected in ℓ to obtain △A'B'C' and then △A'B'C' is reflected in *m* to obtain △A"B"C". (Lines ℓ and *m* are parallel.)

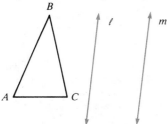

8. What is the result of performing two successive reflections in line ℓ in the figure?

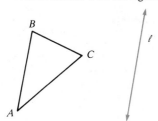

9. Suppose that lines ℓ and *m* are parallel and △ABC is reflected in ℓ and then *m*. How does the final image compare with the final image after reflecting first in *m* and then in ℓ? Are the images ever the same?

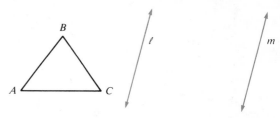

10. For the following, use any construction methods to find the image of △ABC if △ABC is reflected in ℓ to obtain △A'B'C' and then △A'B'C' is reflected in *m* to obtain △A"B"C" (ℓ and *m* intersect at O).

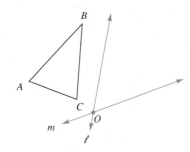

11. Suppose that lines ℓ and *m* intersect and triangle ABC is reflected first in ℓ and then in *m*. How does the final image compare with the final image after reflecting first in *m* and then in ℓ?

12. Find the image of the footprint in the glide reflection that is the result of a translation from *M* to *N* followed by a reflection in ℓ.

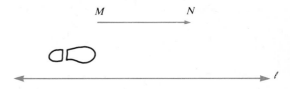

13. A glide reflection was defined as a translation followed by a reflection in appropriate lines.
   (a) Use the drawing in Problem 12 to determine whether the same final image is obtained if the reflection is followed by the translation.
   (b) Based on your answer in part (a), are the reflection and translation involved in the glide reflection commutative?

14. For the given figure numbered 1, decide whether a reflection, a translation, a rotation, or a glide reflection will transform the figure into each of the other numbered figures. (There may be more than one possible answer.)

*15. If a Mira is available, use it to investigate Problems 2, 3, 7, 8, 9, and 10.

★16. When a billiard ball bounces off a side of a pool table, the angle of incidence is usually congruent to the angle of reflection; that is, $\angle 1 \cong \angle 2$. If a cue ball is at point A, show how the player should aim to hit three sides of the table and then the ball at B.

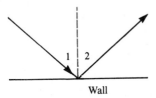

Wall

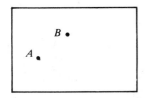

★17. Two cities, represented by points A and B, are located near two perpendicular roads as shown. The cities' mayors found it necessary to build another road connecting A with a point P on road 1, then connecting P with a point Q on road 2, and finally connecting Q with B. How should the road $APQB$ be constructed if it is to be as short as possible? Copy

the figure shown and use a straightedge and a compass, a Mira, or paper folding to construct the shortest possible path.

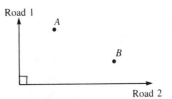

18. Enter the given procedures into your computer, and then describe the transformations illustrated in each of the following.

```
TO SQ
  REPEAT 4 [FD 40 RT 90]
END

TO FSQ
  REPEAT 4 [FD 40 LT 90]
END
```

(a)
```
TO MOVE1
  SQ
  RT 150
  SQ
END
```

(b)
```
TO MOVE2
  SQ
  FSQ
END
```

(c)
```
TO MOVE3
  SQ
  PU RT 45 FD 60 PD
  SQ
END
```

19. (a) Write a simple Logo procedure called FIG1, using FD, BK, RT, and LT several times. Run your procedure.

(b) Write a new procedure, FIG2, in which you replace every FD in your FIG1 procedure with BK and every BK with FD. How does the drawing made with FIG2 compare to the drawing made with FIG1?

(c) Write a new procedure, FIG3, in which you replace every RT in your FIG1 procedure with LT and every LT with RT. How does the drawing made with FIG3 compare with the drawings made with FIG1 and FIG2?

20. (a) Write a Logo procedure called EQTRI to draw a variable-sized equilateral triangle.
   (b) Now write a procedure called EQTRI2, in which all the RIGHTs in EQTRI have been replaced with LEFTs, and vice versa.
   (c) Execute EQTRI and EQTRI2 on the same screen, without erasing anything. What single transformation could produce the same result on the original triangle drawn by EQTRI?
   (d) Execute EQTRI 50 and then EQTRI −50. What single transformation could produce the same result on the original triangle drawn by EQTRI 50?

Review Exercises

21. Which capital printed letters of the English alphabet are their own images under a rotation?
22. Which capital letters of the English alphabet are their own images under a half-turn?
23. MOW is an example of a word that could be transformed into itself by which isometry?
24. (a) Find all possible rotations that transform a circle into itself.
   (b) By what other kinds of transformations can a circle be transformed into itself?

B R A I N   T E A S E R

Two cities are on opposite sides of a river, as shown. The cities' engineers want to build a bridge across the river that is perpendicular to the banks of the river, as well as access roads to the bridge, so that the total distance between the cities is as short as possible. Where should the bridge and the roads be built?

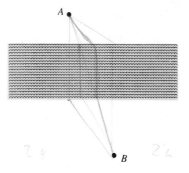

LABORATORY ACTIVITY

As a van Hiele Level 1 activity, take a 1-ft by 1-ft square of linoleum tile and carve a pattern in the tile comparable to the one shown.

Now spread ink over the uncarved surface and press a piece of paper onto the ink, being careful not to let it slide across the tile. Next remove the paper and consider the printed impression made on the paper. How are the printed paper and the original carved tile related to one another?

*Section 12-3 Composition and Inverses of Isometries and Similarities

A glide reflection is a translation followed by a reflection. This is an example of the composition of two transformations, or isometries. The composition of any two isometries must be an isometry. (Why?) We now begin an investigation of whether the composition of isometries discussed thus far results in a different type of isometry. To investigate the composition of other isometries, we examine the orientation of figures under different isometries.

We know that a reflection and a glide reflection are isometries that reverse orientation, whereas translations and rotations do not. It should also be evident that, if two reflections were performed in succession, any final image would have the same orientation as its original, but if three reflections were performed on the same original, the orientation would be reversed. (Why?) If this type of pattern is true and if translations and rotations are related to reflections, then we might be led to believe that both translations and rotations could be performed by executing an even number of reflections. Let us consider two special cases of an even number of reflections: two reflections in parallel lines, and two reflections in intersecting lines.

Reflecting in Two Parallel Lines

In Figure 12-44, suppose that $\triangle ABC$ is reflected in line m and then the image obtained is reflected in line n, where $m \| n$.

FIGURE 12-44

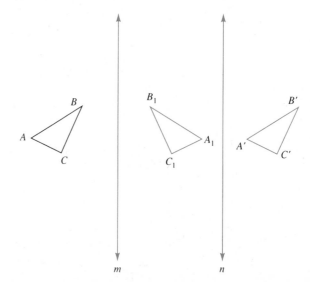

It appears that, in Figure 12-44, $\triangle A'B'C'$ could have been obtained by translating $\triangle ABC$ to the right some distance. Let us determine if that is the case by considering the distances from A to A', from B to B', and from C to C' in Figure 12-45.

FIGURE 12-45

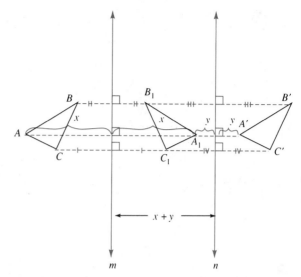

Comparing these distances with a marked ruler or a compass, we observe that $AA' = BB' = CC'$, and each distance is twice as long as the distance between the parallel lines m and n. To justify this, note that m is the perpendicular bisector of $\overline{AA_1}$, $\overline{BB_1}$, and $\overline{CC_1}$. Similarly, we know that n is the perpendicular bisector of $\overline{A_1A'}$, $\overline{B_1B'}$, and $\overline{C_1C'}$. In addition, all segments mentioned are parallel to each other. (Why?) Denoting the distance between the points and the lines, as marked in Figure 12-45, $AA' = AA_1 + A_1A' = 2x + 2y = 2(x + y)$. Because $x + y$ is the distance between m and n, it follows that AA' is twice the distance between the parallel lines. Similarly, we find that $BB' = CC' = 2(x + y)$. In general, the distance between any point and its image is twice the distance between the two parallel reflecting lines. Hence, every point in $\triangle ABC$ has moved the same distance and in the same direction along a line parallel to the mentioned segments. Thus, *the transformation obtained by reflecting in two parallel lines is a translation along a line perpendicular to the parallel lines and twice the distance between the two lines and in the direction from the first line to the second.* Conversely, *the distance between reflecting lines is one-half the length of the slide arrow.* The following example shows one method of finding reflecting lines that produce a given translation.

EXAMPLE 12-10   Find two reflecting lines that produce the same results as the translation pictured in Figure 12-46.

FIGURE 12-46

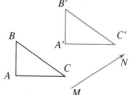

SOLUTION

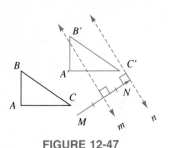

FIGURE 12-47

As has been explained, the desired reflecting lines must be perpendicular to the slide arrow and the distance between the two desired reflecting lines must be half the length of the slide arrow. (Why?) Because the reflecting lines must be half the length of the slide arrow apart and perpendicular to it, one natural line to use is the perpendicular bisector of the slide arrow. Two other natural lines to use are the perpendiculars to the slide arrow at the ends of it. It is irrelevant which of these is used, but the order in which the reflections is done is important. (This is investigated in the exercises.) We use the perpendicular at the end of the arrow in Figure 12-47. Thus, our reflecting lines are m and n, and they must be used in that order.

● R E M A R K
There are infinitely many pairs of parallel lines that accomplish the translation called for in Example 12-10. One line can be chosen anywhere, but once that line is fixed, there is exactly one choice for the other line.

In an exercise, we investigate the possibility that other reflecting lines might be used to produce the same result as in Example 12-10.

Reflecting in Two Intersecting Lines
We now consider the case in which the reflecting lines intersect each other. In Figure 12-48, we have $\triangle ABC$ reflected in line m to obtain $\triangle A_1B_1C_1$; then $\triangle A_1B_1C_1$ is reflected in line n, where m and n are two intersecting lines. If we use tracing paper, we observe that it looks as though $\triangle ABC$ might have been rotated through some angle to obtain $\triangle A'B'C'$. It appears that the center of that rotation might be O, the point of intersection of the two lines.

FIGURE 12-48

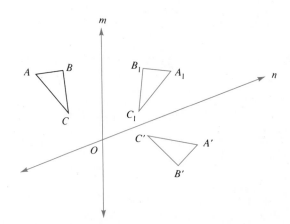

To prove that $\triangle A'B'C'$ can be obtained from $\triangle ABC$ by a rotation about O, we need to show that each point and its image are on the same circle with center O and that each point is rotated by the same amount. In Figure 12-49, we need to show that $AO = A'O$, $BO = B'O$, and $CO = C'O$ and that each point was rotated by the same amount.

FIGURE 12-49

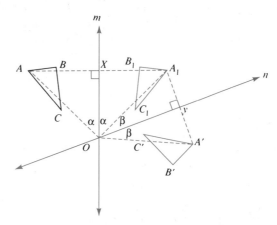

Since m is the perpendicular bisector of all segments connecting points and their images in triangles ABC and $A_1B_1C_1$, respectively, we see that $\angle AOX \cong \angle A_1OX$; and we denote their measure by α. Similarly, $m(\angle A_1OY) = m(\angle A'OY) = \beta$. Therefore, point A is turned through $\angle AOA'$ with measure $m(\angle AOA_1) + m(\angle A_1OA') = 2\alpha + 2\beta$, or $2(\alpha + \beta)$. Note that $\alpha + \beta$ is the measure of the angle between m and n. Hence, $m(\angle AOA')$ is twice the measure of the angle between lines m and n. By the same procedure, we could show that all points of $\triangle ABC$ are rotated through an angle of measure $2(\alpha + \beta)$, where the center of the rotation is O. Therefore, reflecting in two intersecting lines yields a rotation whose center is the point of intersection of the two lines and whose amount of rotation is twice the measure of an angle formed by the two lines and in the direction from the first line to the second.

Conversely, given any rotation, it is possible to find two reflecting lines such that, when the reflections are performed in succession, the rotation results. This is seen in the following example.

EXAMPLE 12-11   Given the rotation of 60° counterclockwise with center O, as shown in Figure 12-50, find two reflecting lines that can be used to accomplish the rotation, and determine which reflecting line must be used first.

FIGURE 12-50

SOLUTION Since we are to find two reflecting lines that determine the pictured rotation, we need two intersecting lines that intersect at point O. To find these we may draw any line $\overleftrightarrow{OX}$ through point O, bisect the 60° angle pictured, and copy the 30° angle obtained, using $\overrightarrow{OX}$ as one of its sides. (There are two such 30° angles, one in each half-plane determined by $\overleftrightarrow{OX}$. We use the 30° angle above $\overleftrightarrow{OX}$.) This result is shown in Figure 12-51. Lines ℓ and m are two such required reflecting lines, and they must be used in that order.

FIGURE 12-51

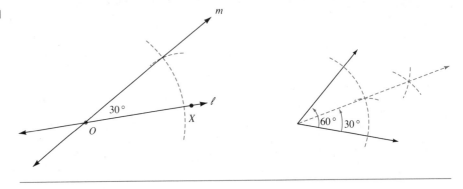

• **R E M A R K**
If we had found m in the half plane below $\overrightarrow{OX}$, then the reflecting lines would have been m and ℓ, in that order.

As with a translation, infinitely many pairs of lines can be used to accomplish a given rotation. However, all of these lines are concurrent at the center of the turn, and if the first line through the center of the turn is chosen at random, then there is only one choice in the placement of the second line.

We have seen that a translation and a rotation can be accomplished by using two reflections. Because a glide reflection is the composition of a translation and a reflection, it can be accomplished by three reflections (two from the translation and one from the reflection). Thus, each of the isometries discussed thus far can be accomplished by utilizing no more than three reflections. It can be shown that every isometry can be accomplished by a composition of at most three reflections. It can also be proved that there are no other isometries besides the ones introduced here. This result is investigated in the exercises and is stated here in the following theorem.

• **T H E O R E M** 12-1
Classification Theorem for Isometries of the Plane. Every isometry of the plane is a translation, a rotation, a reflection, or a glide reflection.

Using Theorem 12-1, if we are given any triangle in the plane and its image under some isometry, we should be able to find no more than three reflecting lines that will take the triangle to its image. To see how this might be done, consider the properties of isometries discussed earlier and now summarized in Table 12-1.

TABLE 12-1

Isometry	Perpendicular Bisectors of Segments Connecting Points and Their Images	Orientation
Translation	They are parallel.	Stays the same
Rotation	They intersect at the center	Stays the same
Reflection	There is only one.	Reverses
Glide reflection	Midpoints of segments are collinear and on the reflecting line.	Reverses

The information in Table 12-1 is helpful in finding three reflecting lines so that successive reflections in these lines will take any triangle to a congruent triangle in the plane. An example is given next.

EXAMPLE 12-12   In Figure 12-52, $\triangle ABC$ is congruent to $\triangle A'B'C'$. Find no more than three reflecting lines that can be used to take $\triangle ABC$ to $\triangle A'B'C'$.

FIGURE 12-52

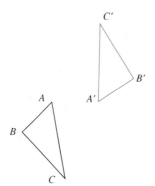

SOLUTION   The orientation of the figure has not changed under the isometry. This tells us that the transformation involved is either a translation or a rotation. Table 12-1 suggests that we consider the perpendicular bisectors of $\overline{AA'}$, $\overline{BB'}$, and $\overline{CC'}$, as shown in Figure 12-53 on the next page.

FIGURE 12-53

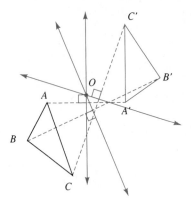

Since the perpendicular bisectors of these segments are concurrent and the orientation is not changed, the isometry is a rotation with center at the point of intersection of the perpendicular bisectors. A rotation is determined by two intersecting reflecting lines. Since the two lines sought form an angle of half the amount of rotation, then one possible set of reflecting lines is $\overleftrightarrow{OA}$ and the angle bisector of $\angle AOA'$, as in Figure 12-54. (Why?)

FIGURE 12-54

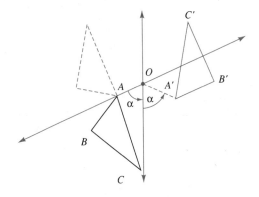

Other examples similar to that of Example 12-12 are investigated in the exercises.

Size Transformations

Since all congruences in a plane can be accomplished by using no more than three reflections, it is reasonable to ask if similar figures can be transformed into each other. Since isometries preserve distance and similar figures are not necessarily the same size, no isometry will transform one figure into another noncongruent similar figure. We first consider a special case of similar triangles, illustrated in Figure 12-55, where $\overline{AB} \parallel \overline{A'B'}$ and $\triangle ABC \sim \triangle A'B'C'$, with scale factor $AB/A'B'$. (Why?)

FIGURE 12-55

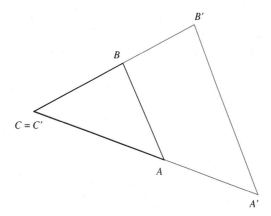

If we could define a transformation that has $\triangle A'B'C'$ as the image of $\triangle ABC$, then we might be able to determine whether there is a type of transformation that takes similar figures to each other in general. In Figure 12-55, consider what such a transformation would do. Since C would be in both triangles, we probably would want C to be its own image. Such a transformation would take $\overline{AB}$ to $\overline{A'B'}$, where $\overline{AB}$ and $\overline{A'B'}$ are parallel. We call the transformation sought a **size transformation,** for which we have the following definition.

size transformation

● D E F I N I T I O N

A **size transformation** S from the plane to the plane takes some point O, called the *center* of the size transformation, to itself; and for any other point Q, its image Q' is such that $OQ/OQ' = r$, where r is a real number greater than 0 and O, Q, and Q' are collinear.

The number r is the *scale factor,* as defined in similar triangles. It is possible to show that the image of a triangle under a size transformation is a similar triangle.

EXAMPLE 12-13   Find the image of $\triangle ABC$ in Figure 12-56 under the size transformation, with center O and scale factor 2.

FIGURE 12-56

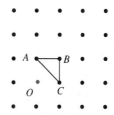

SOLUTION   The image of $\triangle ABC$ is $\triangle A'B'C'$, as pictured in Figure 12-57.

FIGURE 12-57

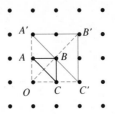

If two similar triangles are given, as pictured in Figure 12-58(a), then a size transformation as just defined is not sufficient to transform one into the other. However, we may first use an isometry to transform $\triangle ABC$ into $\triangle A_1B_1C_1$, as in Figure 12-58(b). Then we can find a size transformation that will transform $\triangle A_1B_1C_1$ into $\triangle A'B'C'$. The composition of transformations *similarity* in Figure 12-58 is an example of a **similarity.**

• D E F I N I T I O N
A **similarity** is the composition of an isometry and a size transformation.

FIGURE 12-58

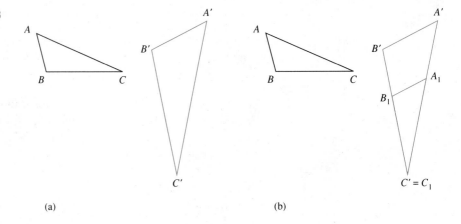

(a)   (b)

PROBLEM SET 12-3

1. In each of the following drawings, reflect the original triangle in line ℓ, and then reflect the image found in line m. After that, start again—this time first reflecting the original triangle in line m and then reflecting the image found in line ℓ. Is the final image in both cases the same?

(a)

(b)

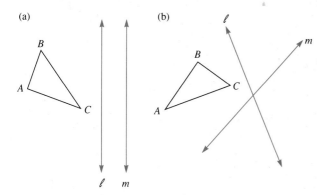

2. Describe a transformation that would "undo" each of the following.
   (a) A translation determined by slide arrow *MN*
   (b) A rotation of 75° with center *O* in a clockwise direction
   (c) A rotation of 45° with center *A* in a counter-clockwise direction
   (d) A glide reflection that is the composition of a reflection in line *m* and a translation that takes *A* to *B*
   (e) A reflection in line *n*

3. If possible, find a single transformation that accomplishes the following.
   (a) The composition of reflections in two perpendicular lines
   (b) The composition of two rotations, one 40° clockwise and the other 60° clockwise, where each has the same center
   (c) The composition of two rotations, one 40° clockwise and the other 90° counterclockwise, where each has the same center
   (d) The composition of two translations, one of 5 cm and the other of 10 cm, along the same line and in the same direction
   (e) The composition of two translations, one of 5 cm and the other of 10 cm, along the same line but in opposite directions
   (f) The composition of three reflections in parallel lines
   (g) The composition of three reflections in concurrent lines

4. Given the following triangles and their images, find reflecting lines that will take one triangle to the other.
   (a)

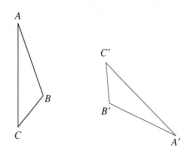

   (b)

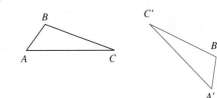

   (c)

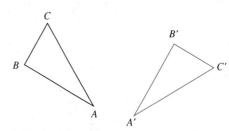

5. Draw three noncollinear points *A*, *B*, and *C*.
   (a) Find the image of point *C* under the composition of a half-turn in *A* and then a half-turn in *B*.
   (b) Find the image of point *C* under the composition of a half-turn in *B* and then a half-turn in *A*.
   (c) What is the relation of the images you found in (a) and (b)?

6. A half-turn is sometimes called a *reflection in a point*. Let △*ABC* be any triangle. Pick any point *P*, either on the triangle or not.
   (a) What is the final image of point *P* when it is reflected in *A*, *B*, *C*, *A*, *B*, and *C* in the order given?
   (b) Pick another point *Q* and find its final image under the same set of reflections.
   (c) Make a conjecture about what the combined set of reflections always does.

7. In the following drawing, a coin is shown atop another coin. Suppose that the top coin is rotated around the circumference of the bottom coin until it rests directly below the bottom coin. Will the head be straight up or upside down? Why?

8. Use the following drawing to explain how a periscope works.

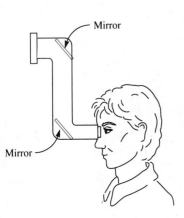

9. Which of the following sets of transformations are closed under the operation of composition?
   (a) All translations south
   (b) All translations east or west
   (c) All reflections
   (d) All isometries

10. In the following coordinate plane, find the images of each of the given points in the transformation that is the composition of a reflection in line m followed by a reflection in line n.
    (a) (4, 3)   (b) (0, 1)   (c) (⁻1, 0)   (d) (0, 0)

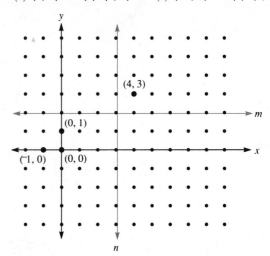

11. In the following drawing, find the image of $\triangle ABC$ under the size transformation with center O and scale factor $\frac{1}{2}$.

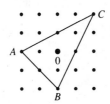

12. Describe a similarity that will take quadrilateral $ABCD$ to quadrilateral $A'B'C'D'$.

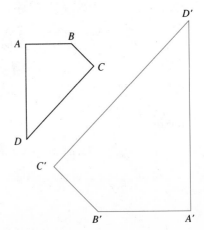

13. In each of the following drawings, find transformations that will take $\triangle ABC$ to its image, $\triangle A'B'C'$, which is similar.

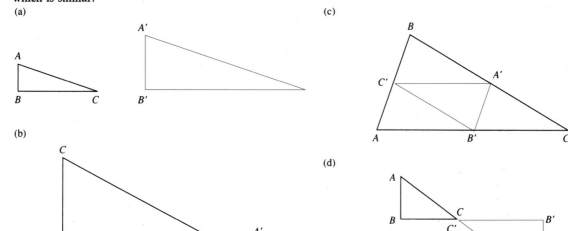

(a)

(c)

(b)

(d)

LABORATORY ACTIVITY

As a van Hiele Level 3 activity, consider $\triangle ABC$ and its image after being reflected in lines m, n, and p in order. Find a single line q that could be used to reflect the original $\triangle ABC$ onto the final image. Explain why it is always possible to find such a line.

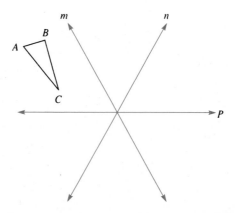

Section 12-4   Symmetries

Line Symmetries

The concept of a reflection can be used to identify line symmetries of a figure. All the drawings in Figure 12-59 have symmetries about the dashed lines.

FIGURE 12-59

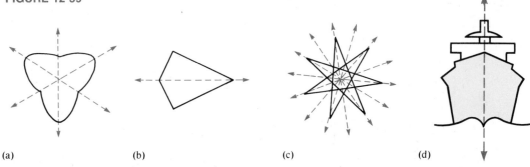

(a)   (b)   (c)   (d)

line of symmetry   Mathematically, a geometrical figure is said to have **a line of symmetry** if it is its own image under a reflection in line ℓ. A method of creating a symmetrical figure is seen in Example 12-14.

EXAMPLE 12-14   In Figure 12-60, we are given a figure and a line m. Do the minimum amount of drawing to create a figure from the given figure so that the result is symmetric about line m.

FIGURE 12-60

SOLUTION   In order for the resulting figure both to be symmetric about line m and to incorporate the existing figure, we need to reflect the existing figure about line m. The desired result of doing that is the combination of the original and the image. The resulting figure is shown in Figure 12-61.

FIGURE 12-61

• R E M A R K

The type of problem shown in Example 12-14 is much easier to do with a Mira.

EXAMPLE 12-15 How many lines of symmetry does each of the drawings in Figure 12-62 have?

FIGURE 12-62

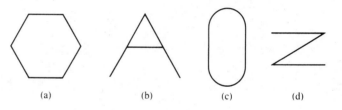

(a)   (b)   (c)   (d)

SOLUTION (a) 6   (b) 1   (c) 2   (d) 0

PROBLEM 2

At the site of an ancient settlement, archaeologists found a fragment of a saucer, as shown in Figure 12-63. To restore the saucer, the archaeologists had to determine the radius of the original saucer. How can they find the radius?

Understanding the Problem. The border of the shard shown in Figure 12-63 was part of a circle. In order to reconstruct the saucer, we are to determine the radius of the circle of which the shard is a part.

FIGURE 12-63

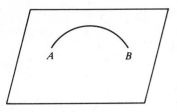

FIGURE 12-64

Devising a Plan. A model can be used to determine the radius. We trace an outline of the circular edge of the three-dimensional shard on a piece of paper. The result is an arc of a two-dimensional circle, as shown in Figure 12-64. To determine the radius, find the center O. A circle has infinitely many lines of symmetry, and each line passes through the center of the circle, where all the lines of symmetry intersect.

Carrying Out the Plan. To find a line of symmetry, fold the paper containing $\overarc{AB}$ so that a portion of the arc is folded onto itself. Then unfold the paper and draw the line of symmetry on the fold mark, as shown in Figure 12-65(a). By refolding the paper in Figure 12-65(a) so that a different portion of the arc $\overarc{AB}$ is folded onto itself, determine a second line of symmetry, as shown in Figure 12-65(b). The two dotted lines of symmetry intersect at O, the center of the circle of which $\overarc{AB}$ is an arc. To complete the problem, measure the length of either $\overline{OB}$ or $\overline{OA}$. (They should be the same.)

FIGURE 12-65

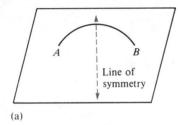 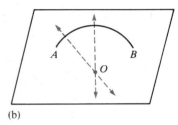

(a)   (b)

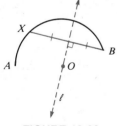

FIGURE 12-66

Looking Back. In the first fold, endpoint B of the arc was folded onto another point of the arc. Label this other point X. The result is shown in Figure 12-66. Because the fold line ℓ is a line of symmetry of the circle containing $\overarc{AB}$, it must be the perpendicular bisector of $\overline{XB}$ and it must contain the center of the circle. This is the property proved in Section 11-3, which states that the center of the circle lies on the perpendicular bisector of a chord. We could have used this property to determine the center of the circle by choosing two chords on the arc and finding the point where the perpendicular bisectors of the chords intersect. Alternatively, we could have used a compass and a straightedge.

A related problem is: What would happen if the piece of pottery had been part of a sphere? Would the same ideas still work?

Rotational (Turn) Symmetries

rotational symmetry   A figure has **rotational symmetry,** or **turn symmetry,** when the traced figure
turn symmetry   can be rotated less than 360° about some point so that it matches the original figure. Note that the condition "less than 360°" is necessary because any

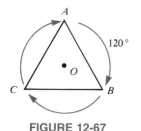

FIGURE 12-67

figure will coincide with itself after being rotated 360°. In Figure 12-67, the equilateral triangle coincides with itself after a rotation of 120° about point O. Hence, we say that the triangle has 120° rotational symmetry. In addition, in Figure 12-67, if we rotated the triangle another 120°, we would find that it again matches the original, so we can say that the triangle also has 240° rotational symmetry.

Other examples of figures that have rotational symmetry are shown in Figure 12-68. In Figure 12-68, (a), (b), (c), and (d) have 72°, 90°, 180°, and 180° rotational symmetries, respectively. [Parts (a) and (b) also have other rotational symmetries.]

FIGURE 12-68

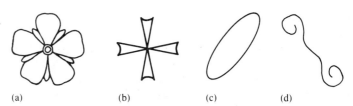

(a) (b) (c) (d)

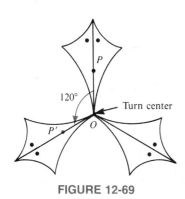

FIGURE 12-69

In general, we can determine whether a figure has rotational symmetry by tracing it and turning the tracing about a point (the center of the figure) to see if it aligns on the figure before the tracing has turned in a complete circle, or 360°. The amount of the rotation can be determined by measuring the angle, $\angle POP'$, through which a point P is rotated around a point O to match another point P' when the figures align. Such an angle, $\angle POP'$, is labeled with points P, O, and P' of Figure 12-69 and has measure 120°. Point O, the point held fixed when the tracing is turned, is the *turn center*.

EXAMPLE 12-16 Determine the amount of the turn for the rotational symmetries of each figure in Figure 12-70.

FIGURE 12-70

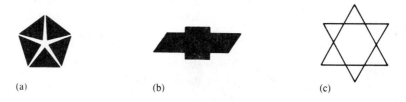

(a) (b) (c)

SOLUTION (a) The amounts of the turns are $\frac{360°}{5}$ or 72°, 144°, 216°, and 288°.
(b) The amount of the turn is 180°.
(c) The amounts of the turns are 60°, 120°, 180°, 240°, and 300°.

The rotation in Figure 12-70(b) exemplifies yet another type of symmetry, namely, point symmetry.

Point Symmetry

point symmetry Any figure that has 180° rotational symmetry is said to have **point symmetry** about the turn center. Figures with point symmetry are shown in Figure 12-71.

FIGURE 12-71

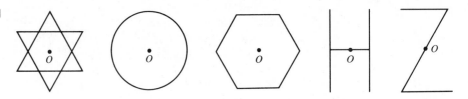

Suppose that P is any point of a figure with point symmetry, such as in Figure 12-72(a). If the figure is rotated 180° about its center, point O, there is a corresponding point P', as shown in part (b) of the figure. Points P, O, and P' are on the same line, and O divides the segment connecting points P and P' into two parts of equal length; that is, O is the midpoint of $\overline{PP'}$.

FIGURE 12-72

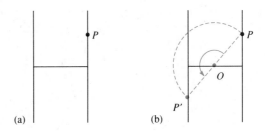

(a)　(b)

Plane Symmetry

plane of symmetry A three-dimensional figure has a **plane of symmetry** when every point of the figure on one side of the plane has a mirror image on the other side of the plane. Examples of figures with plane symmetry are shown in Figure 12-73. Solids can also have point symmetry, line symmetry, and turn symmetry. These symmetries are analogous to the two-dimensional symmetries and are investigated in the exercises.

FIGURE 12-73

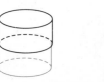 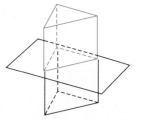

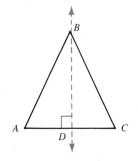

FIGURE 12-74

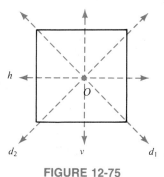

FIGURE 12-75

Applications of Symmetries in Geometry

Geometric figures in a plane can be classified according to the number of symmetries they have. Consider a triangle described as having exactly one line of symmetry and no turn symmetries at all. What could the triangle look like? The only possibility is a triangle in which two sides are congruent—that is, an isosceles triangle. The line of symmetry passes through a vertex, as shown in Figure 12-74.

Just as we used the number of lines of symmetry to describe an isosceles triangle, we can describe equilateral and scalene triangles in terms of the number of lines of symmetry they have. This is left as an exercise.

A square, as in Figure 12-75, can be defined as a four-sided figure with four lines of symmetry—d_1, d_2, h, and v—and three turn symmetries about point O. In fact, we can use lines of symmetry and turn symmetries to define various types of quadrilaterals normally used in geometry, as seen on the student page from *Heath Mathematics*, 1987, Grade 7. It is left as an exercise to see how these definitions differ from those in Chapter 10.

Quadrilaterals

We can use points of symmetry and lines of symmetry to study properties of some special **quadrilaterals** (4-sided figures).

A quadrilateral with a point of symmetry is a **parallelogram.**

A quadrilateral with a point of symmetry and two lines of symmetry through opposite vertices is a **rhombus.**

A quadrilateral with a point of symmetry and two lines of symmetry through opposite sides is a **rectangle.**

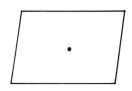

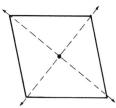

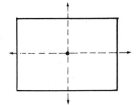

A quadrilateral with a point of symmetry and four lines of symmetry is a **square.**

A quadrilateral with one line of symmetry through opposite sides is an **isosceles trapezoid.**

A quadrilateral with one line of symmetry through opposite vertices is a **kite.**

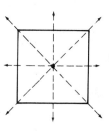

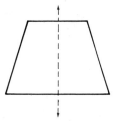

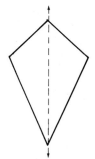

PROBLEM SET 12-4

1. Various international signs have symmetries. Determine which of the following have (i) line symmetry; (ii) rotational symmetry; (iii) point symmetry.

(a)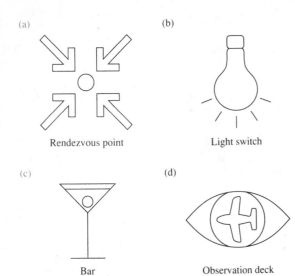

Rendezvous point

(b)

Light switch

(c)

Bar

(d)

Observation deck

2. Design symbols that have each of the following symmetries, if possible.
   (a) Line symmetry but not rotational symmetry
   (b) Rotational symmetry but not point symmetry
   (c) Rotational symmetry but not line symmetry

3. In each of the following, complete the sketches so that they have line symmetry about ℓ.

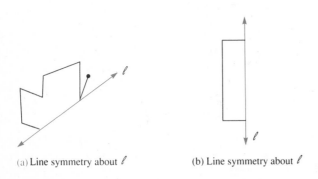

(a) Line symmetry about ℓ

(b) Line symmetry about ℓ

4. (a) Determine the number of lines of symmetry in each of the following flags.
   (b) Sketch the lines of symmetry for each flag.

(i)   Switzerland

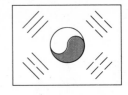

(ii)   South Korea

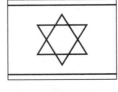

(iii)   Israel

(iv)   Barbados

5. Find the lines of symmetry, if any, for each of the following trademarks.

(a) The Bell System

(b) The Yellow Pages

(c) Chevrolet

(d) Volkswagen of America

(e)   Chrysler Corporation

(f) International Harvester

6. If possible, sketch a triangle that satisfies each of the following.
   (a) It has no lines of symmetry.
   (b) It has exactly one line of symmetry.
   (c) It has exactly two lines of symmetry.
   (d) It has exactly three lines of symmetry.

7. Sketch a figure that has point symmetry but no line symmetry.

8. Answer each of the following. If your answer is no, provide a counterexample.
   (a) If a figure has point symmetry, must it have rotational symmetry? Why?
   (b) If a figure has rotational symmetry, must it have point symmetry? Why?
   (c) Can a figure have point, line, and rotational symmetry? If so, sketch a figure with these properties.
   (d) If a figure has point symmetry, must it have line symmetry? Is the converse true?
   (e) If a figure has both point and line symmetry, must it have rotational symmetry? Why?

9. In each of the following, complete the sketches so that they have the indicated symmetry.

(a)

(b)

Point symmetry about *O*   60° rotational symmetry about *O*

10. How many planes of symmetry, if any, do each of the following three-dimensional vehicle controls have?

(a)

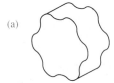

Army vehicle
fuel system

(b)

Aircraft
RPM

(c)

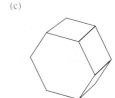

Army vehicle
special-purpose
equipment

(d)

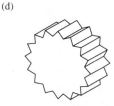

Automotive
finger-operated
continuous
multiturn

11. How do the definitions from the Heath student page of this section differ from the quadrilateral definitions given in Chapter 10?

12. Write a Logo procedure that draws a square and produces a figure with rotational symmetry of (a) 60°; (b) 120°; (c) 180°; (d) 240°; (e) 300°.

13. Write a Logo procedure that draws an equilateral triangle and produces a figure with rotational symmetry of (a) 60°; (b) 120°; (c) 240°; (d) 300°.

Review Problems

14. For each case, find the image of the given figure, using paper folding.

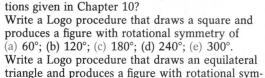

Reflection about *l*
(a)

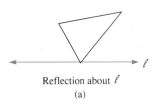

Reflection about *l*
(b)

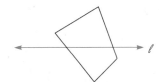

A translation from *A* to *B*
(c)

15. Construct each of the images in Problem 14, using a compass and a straightedge.

LABORATORY ACTIVITY

As a van Hiele Level 1 activity, consider the following figure.

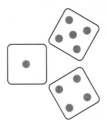

If this figure is reflected and then rotated, which of the following is a possible result?

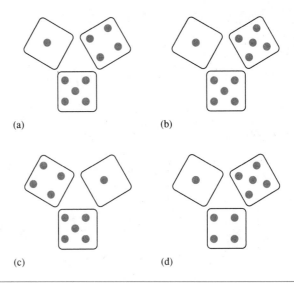

(a) (b)

(c) (d)

Section 12-5 Tessellations of the Plane

tessellation A **tessellation** of a plane is the filling of the plane with repetitions of a figure in such a way that no figures overlap and there are no gaps. The tiling of a floor and various mosaics are examples of tessellations. Maurits C. Escher, born in the Netherlands in 1902, was a master of tessellations. Many of his drawings have fascinated mathematicians for decades. An example of his work, *Study of Regular Division of the Plane with Reptiles,* pen, ink, and watercolor, 1939, contains an exhibit of a tessellation of the plane by a lizardlike shape, as shown in Figure 12-76.

FIGURE 12-76

At the heart of the tessellation in Figure 12-76, we see a regular hexagon, but perhaps the simplest tessellation of the plane can be achieved with squares. Figure 12-77 shows two different tessellations of the plane with squares.

FIGURE 12-77

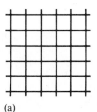

(a)

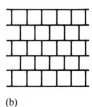

(b)

Regular Tessellations

Tessellations with regular polygons are appealing and interesting because of their simplicity. Figure 12-78 shows portions of tessellations with equilateral triangles and with regular hexagons. What other regular polygons tessellate the plane? To answer this question, we investigate the possible size of the interior angle of a tessellating polygon. If n is the number of sides of a regular polygon, then because the sum of the measures of the exterior angles is 360°

FIGURE 12-78

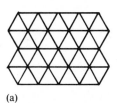

(a)

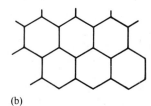

(b)

(see Theorem 10-4), the measure of an exterior angle is $360°/n$. Hence, the measure of an interior angle is $180° - 360°/n$. Table 12-2 gives some values of n, the type of regular polygon related to each, and the angle measure of an interior angle found by using the expression $180° - 360°/n$. If a regular polygon tessellates the plane, the sum of the congruent angles of the polygons around every vertex must be 360°. Thus, 360 divided by the angle measure gives the number of angles around a vertex and hence must be an integer. If we divide 360 by each of the angle measures in the table, we find that of these measures only 60, 90, and 120 divide 360; hence only an equilateral triangle, a square, and a regular hexagon can tessellate the plane. Can other regular polygons tessellate the plane? Notice that $\frac{360}{120} = 3$, and hence 360 divided by a number greater than 120 is smaller than 3; however, the number of sides of a polygon cannot be less than 3. Because a polygon with more than six sides has an interior angle greater than 120°, it is actually not necessary to consider polygons with more than six sides.

TABLE 12-2

Number of Sides	Regular Polygon	Measure of Interior Angle
3	Triangle	60°
4	Square	90°
5	Pentagon	108°
6	Hexagon	120°
7	Heptagon	900/7°
8	Octagon	135°
9	Nonagon	140°
10	Decagon	144°

To determine whether some nonregular polygons can tessellate the plane, we cut a scalene triangle out of cardboard, produce several congruent triangles, and try to tessellate a part of the plane with these triangles.

Next we consider tessellating the plane with arbitrary convex quadrilaterals. Before reading on, you may wish to investigate the problem yourself, with the help of cardboard quadrilaterals. Figure 12-79 shows an arbitrary

FIGURE 12-79

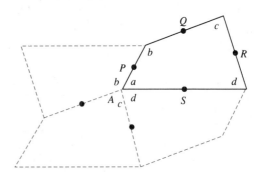

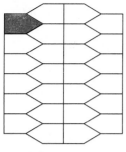

FIGURE 12-80

convex quadrilateral and a way to tessellate the plane with the quadrilateral. Successive 180° turns of the quadrilateral about the midpoints P, Q, R, and S of its sides will produce four congruent quadrilaterals around a common vertex. Notice that the sum of the measures of the angles around vertex A is $a + b + c + d$, which is the sum of the measures of the interior angles of the quadrilateral, or 360°. As we have seen earlier, a regular pentagon does not tessellate the plane. However, one type of nonregular pentagon does tessellate the plane. Such a pentagon, along with a tessellation of the plane by the pentagon, is shown in Figure 12-80.

Other tessellations involving irregular figures are possible by using rotations and reflections. Consider the *Study of Regular Division of the Plane with Birds*, india ink and watercolor, 1955, by M. C. Escher in Figure 12-81. There are various ways to construct the basic figure in Figure 12-81. One is suggested in *Creating Escher-type Drawings* by Ranucci and Teeters. Another

FIGURE 12-81

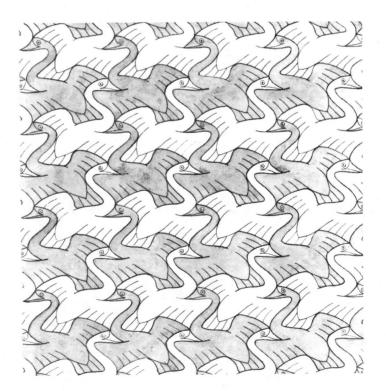

is presented in Figure 12-82, which utilizes graph paper, semicircles, translations, and rotations. This figure can be used to form the basis of a tessellation drawn with Logo procedures, as seen in "Escher-like Logo-type Tessellations" by Lott.

FIGURE 12-82

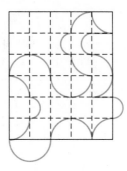

PROBLEM SET 12-5

1. On dot paper, draw a tessellation of the plane using the given figures.

(a)

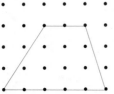

(b)

2. (a) Tessellate the plane with the quadrilateral shown.

(b) Is it possible to tessellate the plane with any quadrilateral?

3. On square-dot paper, use each of the following four pentominoes, one at a time, to make a tessellation of the plane, if possible. (A pentomino is a polygon composed of five congruent, nonoverlapping squares.) Which of the pentominoes tessellate the plane?

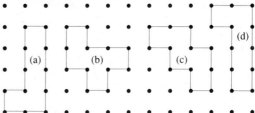

4. The **dual of a tessellation** is the tessellation obtained by connecting the centers of the polygons in the original tessellation that share a common side. The dual of the tessellation of equilateral triangles is the tessellation of regular hexagons (shown in color).

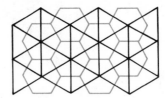

Describe and show the dual of each of the following.

(a) The regular tessellation of squares shown in Figure 12-77(a)

(b) The tessellation of squares shown in Figure 12-77(b)

(c) A tessellation of hexagons

5. We have seen that equilateral triangles, squares, and regular hexagons are the only regular polygons that will tessellate the plane by themselves. However, there are many ways to tessellate the plane by using combinations of these and other regular polygons, as shown in the figure. Try to produce other such tessellations, using the following.
(a) Only equilateral triangles, squares, and regular hexagons
(b) Regular octagons (8-gons) and squares

 6. Write Logo procedures to draw partial tessellations of the following figures. Have each tessellation appear on the screen in the form of two vertical strips.
(a) Squares
(b) Equilateral triangles
(c) Regular hexagons

7. A sidewalk is made of tiles of the type shown in the figure. Each tile is made of three regular hexagons from which three sides have been removed. Write a Logo procedure to draw a partial tessellation composed of four such figures.

LABORATORY ACTIVITY

As a van Hiele Level 0 activity, use pattern blocks to construct tessellations, using each of the following types of pieces.
1. Squares
2. Equilateral triangles
3. Octagons and squares
4. Rhombuses

---

*Section 12-6 Escher-like Logo-type Tessellations

Logo, with recursion and turtle graphics, provides a natural environment in which to create Escher-like tessellations. A monitor screen can be tessellated with an equilateral triangle, a square, and a regular hexagon, as mentioned in Section 12-5. Specifically, the set of procedures given here will tessellate the screen with squares, using -120 and 120 as boundaries for x-coordinates of the squares and -100 and 100 as boundaries for the y-coordinates of the squares. The main procedure is WALL, which requires inputs for the coordinates of the point at which the first square is to have a lower left vertex, as well as an input for the length of a side of that square. First the WALL procedure calls the SETUP procedure, which moves the turtle to the proper position at the lower left of the screen to begin the drawing. It then calls WALLPAPER, which does the drawing of the tessellation. The plan is to draw a strip of vertical squares, move over to the right side of the first square drawn, and repeat the process. This should continue until the screen is filled with squares. Figure 12-83(a) shows the start of the procedure. Figure 12-83(b) shows a printout when WALL −60 (−60) 30 is executed.

FIGURE 12-83

(a)

WALL –60 (–60) 30

(b)

The procedures for tessellating with a square are given next.

```
TO WALL :XPT :YPT :SIDE          TO SQUARE :SIDE
  DRAW
  SETUP :XPT :YPT                  REPEAT 4[FORWARD
  WALLPAPER :YPT :SIDE              :SIDE RIGHT 90]
END                              END

TO SETUP :XPT :YPT
  PENUP
  SETXY :XPT :YPT
  PENDOWN
END
```

(In Apple Logo II, replace DRAW with CLEARSCREEN and SETXY :XPT :YPT with SETPOS (LIST :XPT :YPT).)

```
TO WALLPAPER :YPT :SIDE
  SQUARESTRIP :SIDE
  PENUP
  SETUP (XCOR + :SIDE) :YPT
  PENDOWN
  WALLPAPER :YPT :SIDE
END

TO SQUARESTRIP :SIDE
  IF XCOR + :SIDE > 120 TOPLEVEL
  IF (ANYOF (XCOR - :SIDE < -120)(XCOR + :SIDE >
   120)(YCOR - :SIDE < -100)(YCOR + :SIDE > 100)) STOP
  SQUARE :SIDE
  FORWARD :SIDE
  SQUARESTRIP :SIDE
END
```

(In Apple Logo II, replace IF XCOR + :SIDE > 120 TOPLEVEL with IF XCOR + :SIDE > 120 [THROW "TOPLEVEL]. Also replace IF (ANYOF (XCOR − :SIDE < −120)(XCOR + :SIDE > 120)(YCOR − :SIDE < −100)(YCOR + :SIDE > 100)) STOP with IF (OR (XCOR − :SIDE < −120)(XCOR + :SIDE > 120)(YCOR − :SIDE < − 100)(YCOR + :SIDE > 100)) [STOP].)

To create Escher-like tessellations using Logo, one possibility is to create a tessellation using deformations of sides of a regular polygon and a translation to complete the drawing. We simply determine how to deform the sides of the squares in such a way that they will fit when translated. Consider Figure 12-84(a), where a square is drawn; Figure 12-84(b), where one side of the square is deformed; and Figure 12-84(c), where the deformation is translated to the side of the square parallel to the one where the original deformation took place and is attached to that side, as shown.

FIGURE 12-84

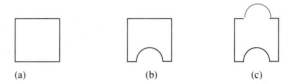

(a) (b) (c)

In order to write a set of procedures for a tessellation based on the drawing in Figure 12-84(c), we use the SETUP procedure, edit other procedures just presented, and use arc procedures listed next from the ARCS file of the MIT Terrapin Logo Utilities disk.

```
TO WALL1 :XPT :YPT :SIDE
 DRAW
 SETUP :XPT :YPT
 WALLPAPER1 :YPT :SIDE
END
```

(In Apple Logo II, replace DRAW with CLEARSCREEN.)

```
TO WALLPAPER1 :YPT :SIDE
 SQUARARCSTRIP :SIDE
 PENUP
 SETUP (XCOR + :SIDE) :YPT
 PENDOWN
 WALLPAPER1 :YPT :SIDE
END

TO SQUARARCSTRIP :SIDE
 IF XCOR + :SIDE > 120 TOPLEVEL
 IF (ANYOF (XCOR - :SIDE < -120)(XCOR + :SIDE >
  120)(YCOR - :SIDE < -100)(YCOR + :SIDE > 100))
  STOP
 SQARC :SIDE
 FORWARD :SIDE
 SQUARARCSTRIP :SIDE
END
```

(In Apple Logo II, replace IF XCOR + :SIDE > 120 TOPLEVEL with IF XCOR + :SIDE > 120 [THROW "TOPLEVEL] and replace IF (ANYOF (XCOR − :SIDE < −120)(XCOR + :SIDE > 120)(YCOR − :SIDE < −100)(YCOR + :SIDE > 100)) STOP with IF (OR (XCOR − :SIDE < −120)(XCOR + :SIDE > 120)(YCOR − :SIDE < −100)(YCOR + :SIDE > 100)) [STOP].)

```
TO SQARC :SIDE
 FORWARD :SIDE RIGHT 90
 FORWARD :SIDE/4 LEFT 90
 RARC :SIDE/4 180
 LEFT 90 FORWARD :SIDE/4
 RIGHT 90 FORWARD :SIDE
 RIGHT 90 FORWARD :SIDE/4 RIGHT 90 LARC :SIDE/4 180
 RIGHT 90 FORWARD :SIDE/4
 RIGHT 90
END
```

(In Apple Logo II, replace RARC with ARCR and replace LARC with ARCL. Both ARCR and ARCL are loaded into the computer when you boot Apple Logo without inserting your own disk. You do not need any of the Terrapin procedures listed next.)

```
TO RARC :RADIUS :DEGREES
 RIGHT 2.5
 RARC1 RADIUS*0.0174532 :DEGREES
 LEFT 2.5
END

TO RARC1 :SIZE :DEGREES
 REPEAT QUOTIENT :DEGREES 5 [FORWARD :SIZE*5 RIGHT 5]
   CORRECTARCR :SIZE (REMAINDER :DEGREES 10)
END

TO CORRECTARCR :SIZE :AMOUNT
 FORWARD :SIZE*:AMOUNT
 RIGHT :AMOUNT
END

TO LARC :RADIUS :DEGREES
 LEFT 2.5
 LARC1 :RADIUS*0.0174532 :DEGREES
 RIGHT 2.5
END

TO LARC1 :SIZE :DEGREES
 REPEAT QUOTIENT :DEGREES 5 [FORWARD :SIZE*5 LEFT 5]
 CORRECTARCL :SIZE (REMAINDER :DEGREES 10)
END

TO CORRECTARCL :SIZE :AMOUNT
 FORWARD :SIZE * :AMOUNT
 LEFT :AMOUNT
END
```

Using these procedures, we obtain a tessellation similar to the one shown in Figure 12-85.

FIGURE 12-85

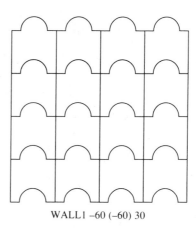

WALL1 –60 (–60) 30

One method of using an equilateral triangle to create a different tessellation is to change the triangle's shape by altering a side and rotating the changed side about a vertex to form the third side and a new figure with which to tessellate. Figure 12-86 shows how this might be done.

FIGURE 12-86

The set of procedures for drawing a tessellation with this shape are more like a tessellation drawn with a regular hexagon. Depending on where the starting and stopping points are, there will appear to be gaps in the tessellation. The interested reader should try these procedures to establish that this is not the case. The entire set of procedures for creating the tessellation are given next. SETUP is used, as before.

```
TO WALL2 :XPT :YPT :SIDE
 DRAW
 SETUP :XPT :YPT
 WALLPAPER2 :YPT :SIDE
END
```

(In Apple Logo II, replace DRAW with CLEARSCREEN.)

```
TO WALLPAPER2 :YPT :SIDE
 MAKE "X XCOR
 RTRISTRIP :SIDE
 PENUP
 SETUP (:X + :SIDE*SQRT 3) :YPT
 PENDOWN
 WALLPAPER2 :YPT :SIDE
END
```

```
TO RTRISTRIP :SIDE
 IF XCOR + :SIDE > 120 TOPLEVEL
 IF (ANYOF (XCOR < -120)(XCOR + :SIDE *SQRT 3 >
  120)(YCOR < -100)(YCOR + :SIDE *3 > 100)) STOP
 REPEAT 3 [RTRIANGLE :SIDE RIGHT 120]
 PENUP
 FORWARD :SIDE
 RIGHT 60
 FORWARD :SIDE LEFT 60
 PENDOWN
 RTRISTRIP :SIDE
END
```

*(In Apple Logo II, replace IF XCOR + :SIDE > 120 TOPLEVEL with IF XCOR + :SIDE > 120 [THROW "TOPLEVEL]. Also replace IF (ANYOF (XCOR< -120)(XCOR + :SIDE *SQRT3 > 120)(YCOR< -100)(YCOR + :SIDE*3 > 100)) STOP with IF (OR (XCOR < -120)(XCOR + :SIDE*SQRT 3 > 120)(YCOR < -100)(YCOR + :SIDE *3 > 100)) [STOP].)*

```
TO RTRIANGLE :SIDE
 FORWARD :SIDE RIGHT 150
 LARC :SIDE 60
 RIGHT 120
 RARC :SIDE 60
 RIGHT 90
END
```

(In Apple Logo II, replace LARC and RARC with ARCL and ARCR, respectively.)

It is left as an exercise to determine why the conditions are as they are in the inputs to ANYOF. *(Use OR if in Apple Logo II.)* A tessellation drawn using these procedures is given in Figure 12-87. The tessellation in Figure 12-87 makes use of the altered triangle to draw many figures and also uses what might be called the negative space to complete the picture. This means that not every altered triangle in the final picture is traced around. This technique is sometimes helpful, especially if the figure to be used to tessellate is complicated and takes some time to draw.

FIGURE 12-87

WALL2 –60 (–60) 30

The tessellations given here are but a start and should be used only as ideas for creating your own. It is a good idea to use graph paper to help in the creation of design.

PROBLEM SET 12-6

1. Write a set of procedures to tessellate the screen with an equilateral triangle.

2. Why are the inputs to ANYOF *(OR in Apple Logo II)* in the RTRISTRIP procedure as they are?

3. Write a set of procedures to tessellate the screen with a regular hexagon. (*Hint:* The "width" of a hexagon is $\sqrt{3}$ times the length of a side.)

4. (a) Draw any figure that you wish.
   (b) Write a procedure to draw a vertical strip of these figures. Will they necessarily fit one atop the other?

5. Will any set of figures that will fit between two parallel lines tessellate the plane? Explain your answer.

6. Write a set of procedures to tessellate the screen with a rectangle.

7. Edit the first set of procedures in this section to tessellate the screen with the following figure.

SOLUTION TO THE PRELIMINARY PROBLEM

Understanding the Problem. To place the scarecrows at equal distances from each other, we seek an equilateral triangle with one vertex on each of three parallel segments. In Figure 12-88, we have three parallel segments at different distances apart. We do not know how long to make the sides of the equilateral triangle, nor are we given any other information about the desired triangle. We do know that an equilateral triangle has three congruent sides and three congruent angles. In addition, we know that an equilateral triangle has three rotational symmetries and three lines of symmetry.

FIGURE 12-88

_____

_____

_____

Devising a Plan. We assume that the construction is completed and see if we can deduce any properties of the triangle that will let us discover how to accomplish the original construction. In Figure 12-89, $\triangle ABC$ has one vertex on each of the segments, as required.

FIGURE 12-89

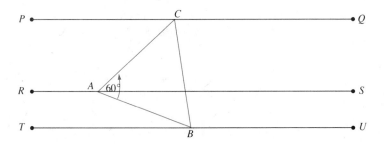

Carrying Out the Plan. It seems that $\triangle ABC$ might not be the only triangle satisfying the conditions of the problem. For example, it seems that $\triangle A_1B_1C_1$ in Figure 12-90 also satisfies the conditions. In fact, it seems that, if we find one solution and translate this triangle along the parallel segments, an infinite number of solutions are possible. Therefore, we should be able to choose vertex A anywhere on $\overline{RS}$. To find another vertex, notice that C is the image of B under a rotation of 60° counterclockwise about center A. We do not know which points on $\overline{TU}$ have the property that their images under a 60° rotation about A are on $\overline{PQ}$. Therefore, we rotate all points of $\overline{TU}$ 60° about

FIGURE 12-90

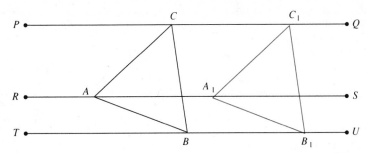

A and see which images appear on $\overline{PQ}$. To rotate all points on $\overline{TU}$, we use methods from Section 12-1. The intersection of the image of $\overline{TU}$ and $\overline{PQ}$ should give us point *C*. Then we can rotate point *C* using a 60° clockwise rotation about point *A* as center to find point *B*. A possible location of the scarecrows is shown in Figure 12-91.

FIGURE 12-91

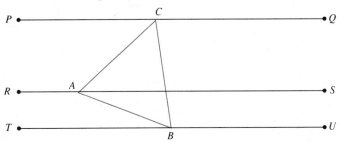

Looking Back. This problem required that we consider the properties and definition of an equilateral triangle and the properties of a rotation in order to complete the construction. Finding point *B* could also be based on the fact that it lies on the perpendicular bisector of $\overline{AC}$, since the triangle is symmetric about that line.

The problem could be varied by giving one of the vertices at the outset. How many solutions would there be then? It could also be set up to require us to construct an equilateral triangle on three lines that are not all parallel or on three concentric circles.

QUESTIONS FROM THE CLASSROOM

1. A student asks, "If I have a point and its image, is that enough to determine whether the image was found using a translation, reflection, rotation, or glide reflection?" How do you respond?

2. Another student asks a question similar to Question 1 but is concerned about a segment and its image. How do you respond to this student?

3. A student claims that a kite has no lines of symmetry. How do you respond?

4. A student says that every three-dimensional figure that has plane symmetry automatically has line symmetry. Do you agree?

5. A student claims that anything that can be accomplished by a rotation can also be accomplished by a reflection in a line. She claims that if *A'* is the image of *A* under a rotation about point *O* by some amount, then *A'* can also be obtained from *A* by a reflection in the perpendicular bisector of $\overline{AA'}$. Hence, a reflection and a rotation are the same. How do you respond?

*6. A student says that, in a size transformation where the scale factor is 0, we do not have a transformation. Is that true?

CHAPTER OUTLINE

I. Transformations
  A. **Isometries** are transformations that preserve distance.
    1. A **translation,** or **slide,** is a transformation of a plane that moves every point a specified distance in a specified direction along a straight line.
    2. A **rotation** is a transformation of the plane determined by holding one point (the center) fixed and rotating the plane about this point by a certain amount in a certain direction.
    3. A **half-turn** is a rotation of 180°.
    4. A **reflection** in a line m is a transformation among points of the plane that pairs each point P of the plane with a point P' in such a way that m is the perpendicular bisector of $\overline{PP'}$, as long as P is not on m. If P is on m, then $P = P'$.
    5. A **glide reflection** is the composition of a translation and a reflection in a line parallel to the slide arrow of the translation.
  *B. **Classification Theorem for Isometries of the Plane:** Every isometry of the plane is a translation, a rotation, a reflection, or a glide reflection.
  *C. A **size transformation** S from the plane to the plane has the following properties: The image of some point O, the center of the size transformation, is its own image. For any other point Q of the plane, its image Q' is such that $OQ/OQ' = r$, where r is a positive real number, and O, Q, and Q' are collinear.
  *D. A **similarity** is the composition of an isometry and a size transformation.

II. Symmetries
  A. A figure has **line symmetry** if it is its own image under a reflection.
  B. A figure has **rotational symmetry** if it is its own image under a rotation of less than 360° about its center.
  C. A figure that has 180° rotational symmetry is said to have **point symmetry.**
  D. A three-dimensional figure has a **plane of symmetry** when every point of the figure on one side of the plane has a mirror image on the other side of the plane.

*III. Tessellations
  A. A **tessellation** of a plane is the filling of the plane with repetitions of a figure in such a way that no figures overlap and there are no gaps.
  B. Tessellations may be drawn with Logo procedures.

CHAPTER TEST

1. Complete each of the following motions.

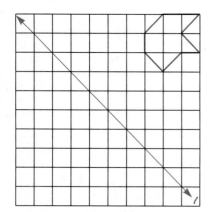

(a) A reflection in ℓ

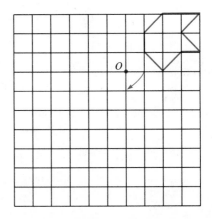

(b) A rotation in O through the given arc

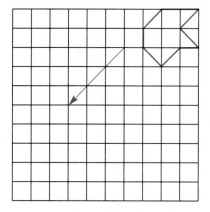

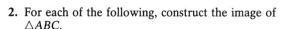

(c) A translation, as pictured

2. For each of the following, construct the image of △*ABC*.

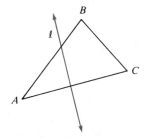

(a) Through a reflection in ℓ

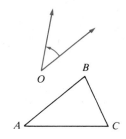

(b) Through the given rotation in *O*

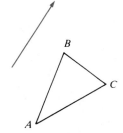

(c) Through the translation pictured

3. How many lines of symmetry, if any, does each of the following figures have?

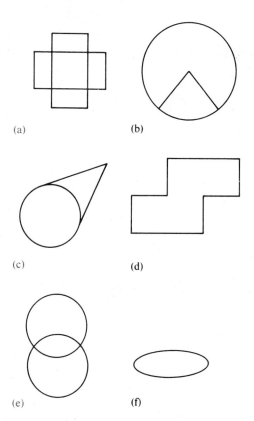

(a)   (b)

(c)   (d)

(e)   (f)

4. For each of the following, identify the types of symmetry (line, rotational, or point) possessed by the given figure.

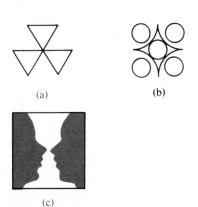

(a)   (b)

(c)

5. How many planes of symmetry does each of the following have?
   (a) A ball
   (b) A right cylindrical water pipe
   (c) A box that is a right rectangular prism but not a cube
   (d) A cube
6. For each of the following pairs of figures, determine which transformation might take one figure to the other.

7. Find the minimum number of reflecting lines that can be used to accomplish each of the isometries in Problem 6.
8. What type of symmetries (line, rotational, or point) does each of the lowercase letters of the printed English alphabet have?
9. Describe a single figure that can be transformed into a congruent figure by each of a reflection, translation, rotation, and glide reflection.
10. Given points A and B and circle O, find point C on circle O such that $\triangle ABC$ is isosceles.

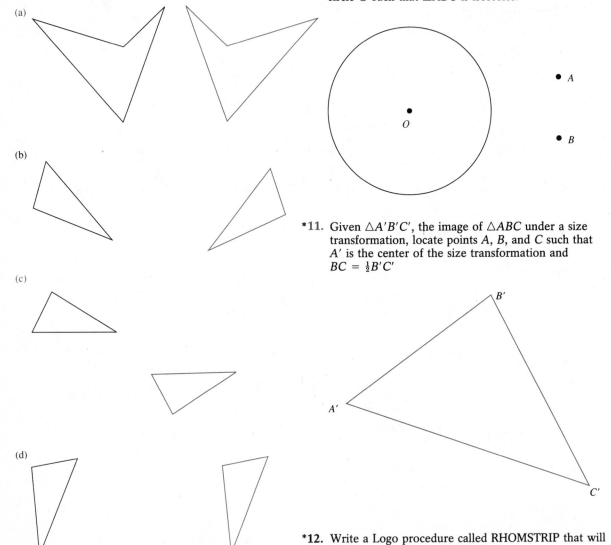

(a)

(b)

(c)

(d)

*11. Given $\triangle A'B'C'$, the image of $\triangle ABC$ under a size transformation, locate points A, B, and C such that A' is the center of the size transformation and $BC = \frac{1}{2}B'C'$

*12. Write a Logo procedure called RHOMSTRIP that will draw a vertical strip of rhombuses.

CONCEPTS OF MEASUREMENT

PRELIMINARY PROBLEM

Each student in a class is given a rectangular sheet of paper 10 inches by 17 inches and some tape. The students are to roll the paper into a circular cylinder, tape the edges together, and make the cylinder stand on the desk so that it will hold popcorn. How should students roll the sheets of paper in order for the resulting cylinders to hold the maximum amount of popcorn?

Introduction

In this chapter, we develop the metric and English systems of measurement for length, area, volume, mass, and temperature with the philosophy that students should learn to think within a measurement system. Consequently, conversions among units of measure in the metric and the English systems are not considered. In measuring geometric objects, our goal is to describe the size of the object relative to a given standard object of fixed size and shape. The standard figure is referred to as a *unit of measure*. Once a unit of measure is chosen, we can determine the measure of a given object by finding how many congruent unit objects are necessary to cover the object.

We develop formulas for the areas of plane figures and for surface areas and volumes of solids. We also use the concept of area in discussing the Pythagorean Theorem. The *Standards* for grades 5–8 states that "The curriculum should focus on the development of understanding, not the rote memorization of formulas." In that regard we attempt to show how area and volume formulas can be developed through exercises that show different developmental techniques, as well as applications of the formulas.

Section 13-1   Units of Length

Three fundamental quantities of measure are length, mass, and time. Early attempts at measurement lacked a standard unit object and used hands, arms, and feet as units of measure. These early crude measurements were eventually refined and standardized by the English into a very complicated system. The English system of weights and measures has been used in many countries and is still used in the United States.

The English System

In the English system, the yard was the distance from the tip of the nose to the end of an outstretched arm of an adult person, and the foot was the length of a human foot. In 1893, the United States defined the yard and other units in terms of metric units. The various units of length in the English system and relationships among them are summarized in Table 13-1.

TABLE 13-1

Unit	Equivalent in Other Units
yard (yd)	3 ft.
foot (ft)	12 in.
mile (mi)	1760 yd., or 5280 ft.

EXAMPLE 13-1   Convert each of the following.

(a) 218 ft. = _____ yd.   (b) 8432 yd. = _____ mi.
(c) 0.2 mi. = _____ ft.   (d) 64 in. = _____ yd.

SOLUTION   (a) Because 1 ft. = $\frac{1}{3}$ yd., 218 ft. = 218 · $\frac{1}{3}$ yd. = 72.66 yd.

(b) Because 1 yd. = $\frac{1}{1760}$ mi., 8432 yd. = 8432 · $\frac{1}{1760}$ mi. $\doteq$ 4.79 mi.

(c) 1 mi. = 5280 ft. Hence, 0.2 mi. = 0.2 · 5280 ft. = 1056 ft.

(d) We first find a connection between yards and inches. We have 1 yd. = 3 ft. and 1 ft. = 12 in. Hence, 1 yd. = 3 ft. = 3 · 12 in. = 36 in. Hence, 1 in. = $\frac{1}{36}$ yd.; therefore, 64 in. = 64 · $\frac{1}{36}$ yd. $\doteq$ 1.78 yd.

The Metric System

The metric system, a decimal system, was proposed in France in 1670 by Gabriel Mouton. However, not until the French Revolution in 1790 did the French Academy of Sciences bring various groups together to develop the new system. The academy recognized the need for a standard base unit of linear measurement. The members chose $\frac{1}{10,000,000}$ of the distance from the equator to the North Pole, on a meridian through Paris, as the base unit of length and called it the *meter*. Later, the meter was redefined in terms of krypton 86 wavelengths. Recently the meter has been defined as the distance traveled by light in a vacuum during $\frac{1}{299,792,458}$ second.

The scientific definition of meter is not very meaningful in everyday life. If you turn your head away from your outstretched arm, the distance from your nose to your fingertip is about 1 meter. Also, 1 meter is about the distance from a doorknob to the floor; and 1 meter is about 39 inches, slightly longer than 1 yard.

Different units of length in the metric system are obtained by combining an appropriate prefix with the base unit, the meter. The prefixes, the multiplication factors they indicate, and their symbols are given in Table 13-2.

TABLE 13-2

Prefix	Factor		Symbol
kilo	1000	(one thousand)	k
hecto	100	(one hundred)	h
deka	10	(ten)	da
deci	0.1	(one tenth)	d
centi	0.01	(one hundredth)	c
milli	0.001	(one thousandth)	m

• R E M A R K

Hecto, deka, and deci are not common prefixes and have limited use. These should not be stressed when teaching the metric system. Kilo, hecto, and deka are Greek prefixes, whereas deci, centi, and milli are Latin prefixes.

Using the metric prefixes along with the base unit meter gives the names for different units of length. Table 13-3 gives these units, their relationship to the meter, and the symbol for each.

TABLE 13-3

Unit	Symbol	Relationship to Base Unit
kilometer	km	1000 meters
*hectometer	hm	100 meters
*dekameter	dam	10 meters
meter	**m**	**base unit**
*decimeter	dm	0.1 meter
centimeter	cm	0.01 meter
millimeter	mm	0.001 meter

* Not commonly used, although some educators recommend the use of decimeter in elementary school (see Lindquist and Dana, "The Neglected Decimeter").

The relationships among metric units of length are based on powers of ten, as reflected by the prefixes in the names of the units. For example, 1 centimeter is 0.01 meter, because "centi" means one-hundredth. We write this as 1 cm = 0.01 m. Consequently, when 1 meter is divided into 100 congruent parts, each part is 1 centimeter long. Hence, 1 m = 100 cm. One centimeter is about the width of your little finger, the diameter of the head of a thumbtack, or the width of a white Cuisenaire rod. A unit smaller than a centimeter is found by dividing 1 meter into 1000 congruent parts or by dividing 1 centimeter into 10 congruent parts. Thus, 1 mm = 0.1 cm = 0.001 m, or 1000 mm = 100 cm = 1 m.

Some additional estimations for a meter, a decimeter, a centimeter, and a millimeter are shown in Figure 13-1.

FIGURE 13-1

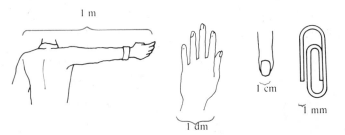

The units decimeter, dekameter, and hectometer represent 0.1 m, 10 m, and 100 m, respectively, but (as indicated in Table 13-3) they are not commonly used. The kilometer is commonly used for measuring long distances. Because "kilo" stands for 1000, 1 km = 1000 m. Nine football fields, including end zones, laid end to end are approximately 1 kilometer long.

Because metric units of length are based on powers of ten, the conversion from one metric unit to another is easy. As with money, we simply move the decimal point to the left or right, depending on the units. For example,

0.123 km = 1.23 hm = 12.3 dam = 123 m = 1230 dm = 12,300 cm
        = 123,000 mm

It is possible to convert units by using the chart in Figure 13-2. We count the number of steps from one unit to the other and move the decimal point that many steps in the same direction.

FIGURE 13-2

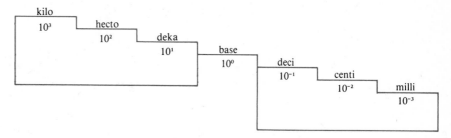

EXAMPLE 13-2   Convert each of the following.

(a) 1.4 km = _____ m   (b) 285 mm = _____ m

SOLUTION   (a) Since 1 km = 1000 m, we know that, to change from kilometers to meters, we must multiply by 1000. Therefore, we move the decimal point three places to the right. Hence, 1.4 km = 1400 m.

(b) Since 1 mm = 0.001 m, we know that, to change from millimeters to meters, we must multiply by 0.001. Therefore, we move the decimal point three places to the left. Thus, 285 mm = 0.285 m.

In geometry, units of length are usually used to measure distances along lines and thus are called *linear measure*. Recall that, in the development of the number line (Chapter 3), we chose a point on the line to represent 0 and a second point to represent 1. If we select the points so that the distance between 0 and 1 is 1 centimeter and we develop the number line accordingly, then the number line can be used to measure lengths of segments in centimeters. Figure 13-3 shows part of a centimeter ruler. By making the distance between 0 and 1 an inch, a meter, a foot, and so on, we can develop other rulers for measuring lengths in a similar fashion.

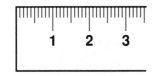

FIGURE 13-3

Following are three basic properties of distance.

Properties of Distance
1. The distance between any two points A and B is greater than or equal to 0, written $AB \geq 0$.
2. The distance between any two points A and B is the same as the distance between B and A, written $AB = BA$.
3. For any three points A, B, and C, the distance between A and B plus the distance between B and C is greater than or equal to the distance between A and C, written $AB + BC \geq AC$.

●   R E M A R K
Notice that, as shown in Figure 13-4(a), $AB + BC = AC$ if and only if A, B, and C are collinear and B is between A and C. If A, B, and C are not collinear, as in Figure 13-4(b), then $AB + BC > AC$. The inequality $AB + BC \geq AC$ is the Triangle Inequality discussed in Chapter 11.

FIGURE 13-4

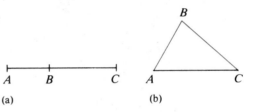

(a)   (b)

Distance Around a Plane Figure

perimeter   The **perimeter** of a simple closed curve is the length of the curve—that is, the distance around the figure. If a figure is a polygon, its perimeter is the sum of the lengths of the sides. Perimeter is always expressed in linear measure.

EXAMPLE 13-3   Find the perimeter of each of the shapes in Figure 13-5.

FIGURE 13-5

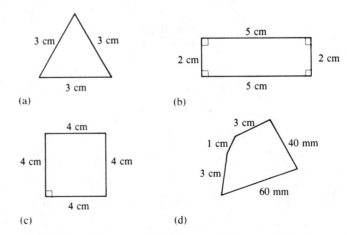

SOLUTION
(a) The perimeter is 3(3) = 9, or 9 cm.
(b) The perimeter is 2(2) + 2(5) = 14, or 14 cm.
(c) The perimeter is 4(4) = 16, or 16 cm.
(d) Because 40 mm = 4 cm and 60 mm = 6 cm, the perimeter is 1 + 3 + 4 + 6 + 3 = 17, or 17 cm.

Circumference of a Circle

circumference The distance around a circle is called its **circumference.** The ancient Greeks discovered that, if they divided the circumference of a circle by the length of its diameter, they always obtained approximately the same number, regardless of the size of the circle. The value of the number is approximately 3.14 (see the Laboratory Activity at the end of this section). Today, the ratio
pi of circumference C to diameter d is symbolized as π **(pi).** In the late eighteenth century, mathematicians proved that this ratio $\dfrac{C}{d}$, or π, is not a terminating or repeating decimal but an irrational number.

The relationship $\dfrac{C}{d} = \pi$ gives a formula for finding the circumference of a circle. Usually, it is written as $C = \pi d$ or $C = 2\pi r$ because the length of diameter d is twice the radius of the circle. *For most practical purposes, π is approximated by $\frac{22}{7}$, $3\frac{1}{7}$, or 3.14. These values are only approximations and are not exact values of π.* If you are asked for the exact circumference of a circle with diameter 6 cm, the answer is 6π cm. Circumference is always expressed in linear measure.

H I S T O R I C A L   N O T E

$\pi = 3.14159$
26535
89793
23846
26433
83279
50288
41971
69399
37510
58209
$\cdot$
$\cdot$
$\cdot$

Archimedes (b. 287 B.C.) found an approximation for π given by the inequality $3\frac{10}{71} < \pi < 3\frac{10}{70}$. A Chinese astronomer thought that $\pi = \frac{355}{113}$. Ludolph van Ceulen (1540–1610), a German mathematician, calculated π to 35 decimal places. The approximation was engraved on his tombstone. With help of a computer π has been found to more than 30,000,000 decimal places. Leonhard Euler adopted the symbol π in 1737 and caused its wide usage. In 1761, Johann Lambert, an Alsatian mathematician, proved that π is an irrational number.

Arc Length

The length of an arc depends on the radius of the circle and the central angle determining the arc. If the angle has a measure of 180°, as in Figure 13-6(a), the arc is often referred to as a **semicircle.** The length of a semicircle is $\frac{1}{2} \cdot 2\pi r$, or πr. The length of an arc whose central angle is θ degrees can be developed as in Figure 13-6(b). Since a circle has 360 degrees, an angle of θ degrees determines θ/360 of a circle. Because the circumference of a circle is $2\pi r$, an arc of θ degrees has length $\dfrac{\theta}{360} \cdot 2\pi r$ or $\dfrac{\pi r\theta}{180}$.

semicircle

FIGURE 13-6

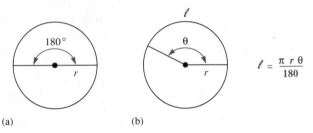

(a) (b)

$$\ell = \frac{\pi r \theta}{180}$$

EXAMPLE 13-4 Find each of the following.

(a) The circumference of a circle if the radius is 2 m
(b) The radius of a circle if the circumference is 15π m
(c) The length of a 25° arc of a circle of radius 10 cm

SOLUTION
(a) $C = 2\pi(2) = 4\pi$; thus, the circumference is 4π m.
(b) $C = 2\pi r$ implies $15\pi = 2\pi r$. Hence, $r = \frac{15}{2}$. Thus, the radius is $\frac{15}{2}$ m.
(c) The arc length is $\dfrac{\pi r\theta}{180} = \dfrac{\pi \cdot 10 \cdot 25}{180}$ cm, or $\dfrac{25\pi}{18}$ cm, or approximately 4.36 cm.

LABORATORY ACTIVITY

To approximate the value of π, you need several different-sized round tin cans or jars, string, and a marked ruler. Pick a can and wrap the string tightly around the can. Use a pen to mark a point on the string where the beginning of the string meets the string again. Unwrap the string and measure its length. Next, determine the diameter of the can by tracing the bottom of the can on a piece of paper. Fold the circle onto itself to find a line of symmetry. The chord determined by the line is a diameter of the circle. Measure the diameter and determine the ratio of the circumference to the diameter. (Use the same units in all of your measurements.) Repeat the experiment with at least three cans, and find the average of the corresponding ratios.

PROBLEM SET 13-1

1. A millimeter is the smallest distance pictured on the metric ruler in the following figure. Starting from the left end of the ruler, the distance from the end to *A* is 1 mm, and the distance from the end to *B* is 10 mm, or 1 cm. The distance from the end to *J* is 100 mm, 10 cm, or 1 dm.

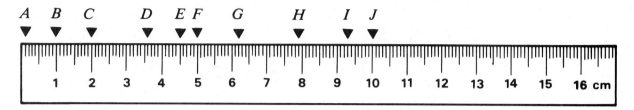

Use the ruler to answer each of the following.
(a) *C* points to _____ mm or _____ cm
(b) *D* points to _____ mm or _____ cm
(c) *E* points to _____ mm or _____ cm
(d) *F* points to _____ cm or _____ mm
(e) *G* points to _____ cm or _____ mm
(f) *H* points to _____ cm or _____ mm
(g) *I* points to _____ mm or _____ cm

2. Convert each of the following.
(a)   100 in. = _____ yd.
(b)   400 yd. = _____ in.
(c)   300 ft. = _____ yd.
(d)   843 yd. = _____ mi.
(e)   372 in. = _____ ft.
(f)   238 mi. = _____ yd.

3. Draw segments that you estimate to be of the following lengths. Then, using a metric ruler, check the estimates.
(a) 10 mm   (b) 100 mm   (c) 1 cm
(d) 10 cm   (e) 0.01 m   (f) 15 cm
(g) 0.1 m   (h) 27 mm

4. Estimate the length of the following segment and then measure it. Express the measurement in each of the following units.

|—————————————————————————|

(a) Millimeters   (b) Centimeters

5. Choose an appropriate metric unit, and estimate each of the following. Measure, if possible, to check the estimate.
(a) The length of a pencil
(b) The diameter of a nickel
(c) The width of the top of a desk
(d) The thickness of the top of a desk
(e) The length of this sheet of paper
(f) The height of a door
(g) Your height
(h) Your hand span

6. Redo Problem 5, using English measures.

7. Complete the following table.

	Item	m	cm	mm
(a)	Length of a piece of paper		35	
(b)	Height of a woman	1.63		
(c)	Width of a filmstrip			35
(d)	Length of a cigarette			100
(e)	Length of two meter sticks laid end to end	2		

8. For each of the following, place a decimal point in the number to make the sentence reasonable.
(a) A stack of ten dimes is 1000 mm high.
(b) The desk is 770 m high.
(c) It is 100 m across the street.
(d) A dollar bill is 155 cm long.
(e) The basketball player is 1950 cm tall.
(f) A new piece of chalk is about 8100 cm long.
(g) The speed limit in town was 400 km/hour.

9. List the following in decreasing order.
8 cm, 5218 mm, 245 cm, 91 mm, 6 m, 700 mm

10. Complete each of the following.
(a) 17 m + 24 cm = _____ cm
(b) 1 m + 40 mm + 2 cm = _____ cm
(c) 3 m + 130 mm + 3 cm = _____ cm

11. Guess the perimeter of each figure in centimeters, and then check the estimates using a ruler.

(a)    (b)

(c) 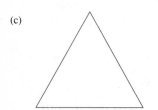   (d)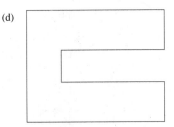

12. Complete each of the following.
(a) 10 mm = _____ cm
(b) 17 cm = _____ m
(c) 262 m = _____ km
(d) 3 km = _____ m
(e) 30 mm = _____ m
(f) 0.17 km = _____ m
(g) 35 m = _____ cm
(h) 359 mm = _____ m
(i) 1 mm = _____ cm
(j) 647 mm = _____ cm
(k) 0.1 cm = _____ mm
(l) 5 km = _____ m
(m) 51.3 m = _____ cm

13. Draw a triangle ABC. Measure the length of each of its sides in millimeters. For each of the following, tell which is greater and by how much.
(a) $AB + BC$ or AC (b) $BC + CA$ or AB
(c) $AB + CA$ or BC

14. Which of the following cannot be the lengths of the sides of a triangle?
(a) 23 cm, 50 cm, 60 cm
(b) 10 cm, 40 cm, 50 cm
(c) 410 mm, 260 mm, 14 cm

15. Find the perimeter of each of the following.

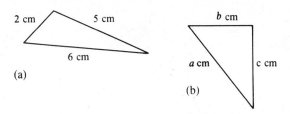

(a)

(b)

(c) An equilateral triangle with a side of length s
(d) A square with a side of length s
(e) A rectangle with one side of length ℓ and another side of length w
(f) A regular polygon with n sides, each of which has length s

16. The following figure made of 6 unit squares has a perimeter of 12 units.
(a) Add more squares to the figure so that the perimeter of the new figure is 18.
(b) What is the minimum number of squares required to make a figure of perimeter 18?
(c) What is the maximum number of squares that can be used to make a figure of perimeter 18? The figure is made in such a way that any two squares share a common side or a common vertex or have no points in common and each square shares an edge with another.

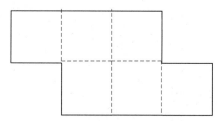

17. For each of the following circumferences, find the length of the radius of the circle.
(a) 12π cm   (b) 6 m   (c) 0.67 m   (d) 92π cm

18. For each of the following, if a circle has the dimensions given, what is its circumference?
(a) 6 cm diameter   (b) 3 cm radius
(c) $\dfrac{2}{\pi}$ cm radius   (d) 6π cm diameter

19. What happens to the circumference of a circle if the length of the radius is doubled?

20. The following figure is a circle whose radius is *r* units. The diameters of the two semicircular regions inside the large circle are both *r* units as well. Compute the length of the curve that separates the shaded and white regions.

21. A student has a can containing three tennis balls. To the student's surprise, the perimeter of the top of the can is longer than the height of the can. The student wants to know if this fact can be explained without performing any measurements. Can you help?

22. (a) If, in two similar triangles, the ratio between the lengths of the corresponding sides is 2:1, what is the ratio between their perimeters?
    (b) Make a conjecture concerning the relationship between the ratio of the perimeters of two similar triangles and the ratio of the corresponding sides.
    (c) Justify your conjecture in part (b).

23. (a) Astronomers use a unit of distance called a light year, which is the distance that light travels in one year. If the speed of light is 300,000 km per second, how long is one light year, in kilometers?
    (b) The nearest star (other than the sun), Alpha Centauri, is 4.34 light years away from earth. How far is that in kilometers?
    (c) How long will it take a rocket traveling 60,000 km/hr to reach Alpha Centauri?
    (d) How long will it take the rocket in part (c) to travel to the sun, if it takes approximately 8 minutes 19 seconds for light from the sun to reach the Earth?

24. Since jet planes can exceed the speed of sound, a new measurement called *Mach number* was invented to measure the speed of such planes. Mach 2 is twice the speed of sound. (Mach number is a number indicating the ratio of the speed of an object through a medium to the speed of sound in the medium.) The speed of sound in air is approximately 344 m/sec.
    (a) Express Mach 2.5 in kilometers per hour.
    (b) Express Mach 3 in meters per second.
    (c) Express the speed of 5000 km/hr as a Mach number.

B R A I N T E A S E R

Suppose that a wire is stretched tightly around the Earth. (The radius of the Earth is approximately 6400 km.) If the wire is cut, its length is increased by 20 m, and the wire is then placed back around the earth so that the wire is the same distance from the Earth at every point, could you walk under the wire?

LABORATORY ACTIVITY

1. As a van Hiele Level 1 activity, use a metric ruler to find the perimeter of each of the following figures in millimeters.

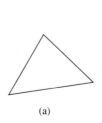

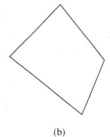

(a)   (b)   (c)

2. As a van Hiele Level 1 activity, use an English ruler to measure the indicated part of each of the given figures in inches.

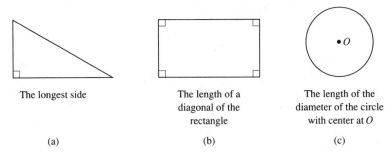

The longest side	The length of a diagonal of the rectangle	The length of the diameter of the circle with center at O
(a)	(b)	(c)

Section 13-2   Areas of Polygons and Circles

area   The term **area** refers to a number assigned to the amount of surface in the interior region determined by a figure. Using a square as the basic unit of area, we see that the area of a region is the number of square units required to cover the region without overlapping the squares and without allowing any gaps.

A square measuring 1 inch on each side has area of 1 square inch, denoted by 1 in.^{2} A square measuring 1 cm on each side has an area of 1 square centimeter, denoted by 1 cm^2. A square measuring 1 m on each side has an area of 1 square meter, denoted by 1 m^2. *The measure of area is always expressed in square units.* Recall that perimeters and circumferences are measured using linear units.

To determine how many square centimeters are in a square meter, look at Figure 13-7(a). There are 100 cm in 1 m, so each side of the square meter has a measure of 100 cm. Thus, it takes 100 rows of 100 square centimeters each to fill a square meter—that is, $100 \cdot 100$, or 10,000 cm^2. In general, the area A of a square that is s units on a side is s^2, as shown in Figure 13-7(b).

FIGURE 13-7

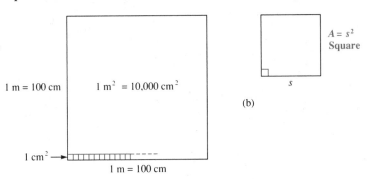

$1 \text{ m} = 100 \text{ cm}$ $1 \text{ m}^2 = 10,000 \text{ cm}^2$

$A = s^2$
Square

s

(b)

$1 \text{ cm}^2 \longrightarrow$

$1 \text{ m} = 100 \text{ cm}$

(a)

Other metric conversions of area measure can be developed by using the formula for the area of a square. For example, Figure 13-8(a) shows that $1 \text{ m}^2 = 10{,}000 \text{ cm}^2 = 1{,}000{,}000 \text{ mm}^2$. Likewise, Figure 13-8(b) shows that $1 \text{ m}^2 = 0.000001 \text{ km}^2$. Similarly, $1 \text{ cm}^2 = 100 \text{ mm}^2$ and $1 \text{ km}^2 = 1{,}000{,}000 \text{ m}^2$.

FIGURE 13-8

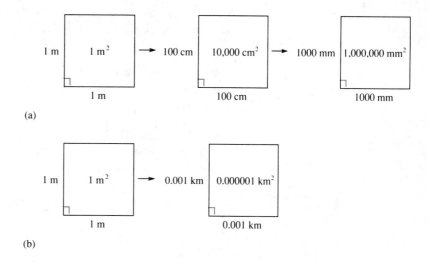

(a)

(b)

Table 13-4 shows the symbols for metric units of area and their relationship to the square meter.

TABLE 13-4

Unit	Symbol	Relationship to Square Meter
square kilometer	km²	1,000,000 m²
*square hectometer	hm²	10,000 m²
*square dekameter	dam²	100 m²
square meter	**m²**	**1 m²**
*square decimeter	dm²	0.01 m²
square centimeter	cm²	0.0001 m²
square millimeter	mm²	0.000001 m²

      * Not commonly used.

● R E M A R K

Students sometimes confuse the area of 5 cm^2 with the area of a square 5 cm on each side. The area of a square 5 cm on each side is $(5 \text{ cm})^2$, or 25 cm^2. Five squares each 1 cm by 1 cm have the area of 5 cm^2. Thus, $5 \text{ cm}^2 \neq (5 \text{ cm})^2$.

EXAMPLE 13-5   Convert each of the following.

(a) 5 cm² = _____ mm²   (b) 124,000,000 m² = _____ km²

SOLUTION   (a) 1 cm² = 100 mm² implies 5 cm² = 5 · 1 cm² = 5 · 100 mm² = 500 mm².

(b) 1 m² = 0.000001 km² implies 124,000,000 m² = 124,000,000 · 1 m² = 124,000,000 · 0.000001 km² = 124 km².

Based on the relationship among units of length in the English system, it is possible to convert one square unit to another. For example, because 1 yd. = 3 ft., it follows that (1 yd.)² = 1 yd. · 1 yd. = 3 ft. · 3 ft. = 9 ft.² Similarly, because 1 ft. = 12 in., (1 ft.)² = 1 ft. · 1 ft. = 12 in. · 12 in. = 144 in². Table 13-5 summarizes various relationships among units of area in the English system. You should verify these relationships.

TABLE 13-5

Unit of area	Equivalent in Other Units
1 ft.²	$\frac{1}{9}$ yd.², or 144 in.²
1 yd.²	9 ft.²
1 mi.²	27,878,400 ft.², or 3,097,600 yd.²
1 a. (acre)	4840 yd.²
1 mi.²	640 a.

Land Measure

One of the most common applications of area today is in land measure. Old deeds in the United States include land measures in terms of chains, poles, rods, acres, sections, lots, and townships. In the metric system, small land *are* areas are measured in terms of a square unit 10 m on a side, called an **are** (pronounced "air") and denoted by **a**. Thus, 1 a = 10 m · 10 m, or 100 m². Larger land areas (currently measured in acres in the English system) are *hectares* measured in **hectares**. A hectare is 100 a. A hectare, denoted by **ha**, is the amount of land whose area is 100 m · 100 m, or 10,000 m², about 2½ acres. It follows that one hectare is the area of a square that is 100 m on a side. *square kilometer* For very large land measures, the **square kilometer,** denoted by km², is used. One square kilometer is the area of a square with a side 1 km, or 1000 m, *acre* long. A unit of land measure in the English system is the **acre.** As shown in Table 13-5, 1 acre equals 4840 square yards. For very large land measures *square mile* in the English system, the **square mile** is used.

EXAMPLE 13-6 (a) A square field has a side of 400 m. Find the area of the field in hectares.
(b) A square field has a side of 400 yds. Find the area of the field in acres.

SOLUTION (a) $A = (400 \text{ m})^2 = 160,000 \text{ m}^2 = \dfrac{160,000}{10,000} \text{ ha.} = 16 \text{ ha.}$

(b) $A = (400 \text{ yd.})^2 = 160,000 \text{ yd}^2 = \dfrac{160,000}{4840} \text{ acre} \doteq 33.06 \text{ acre}$

Area of a Rectangle

One way to measure area is to count the number of units of area contained in any given region. For example, suppose that the square in Figure 13-9(a) represents one square unit. Then, the rectangle $ABCD$ in Figure 13-9(b) contains $3 \cdot 4$ or 12, square units.

FIGURE 13-9

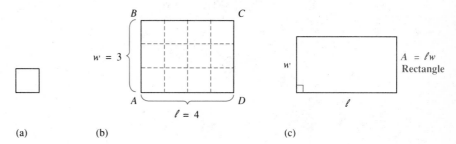

(a)   (b)   (c)

Hence, the area of rectangle $ABCD$ is 12 square units. If the unit is 1 cm², then the area of rectangle $ABCD$ is 12 cm². In general, the area A of any rectangle may be found by multiplying the lengths of two adjacent sides ℓ and w, or $A = \ell w$, as given in Figure 13-9(c).

EXAMPLE 13-7 Find the area of each rectangle in Figure 13-10.

FIGURE 13-10

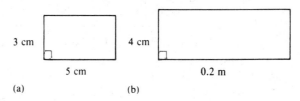

(a)   (b)

SOLUTION (a) $A = (3 \text{ cm})(5 \text{ cm}) = 15 \text{ cm}^2$
(b) First, write the lengths of the sides in the same unit of length. Because 0.2 m = 20 cm, $A = (4 \text{ cm})(20 \text{ cm}) = 80 \text{ cm}^2$. Alternatively, 4 cm = 0.04 m, so $A = (0.04 \text{ m})(0.2 \text{ m}) = 0.008 \text{ m}^2$.

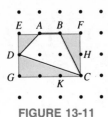

FIGURE 13-11

Areas on a Geoboard

Activities that foster an intuitive grasp of the concept of area should precede the teaching of formulas for finding the areas of different figures. Such activities involving area can be successfully accomplished on a geoboard. In Figure 13-11, the distance between two adjacent nails in a row or column is one unit, so, to find the area of the shaded quadrilateral $ABCD$, we construct the colored rectangle $EFCG$ around the quadrilateral and then subtract the areas of the three shaded triangles. The area of the rectangle $EFCG$ is 6 square units. The area of $\triangle EAD$ is $\frac{1}{2}$ square unit, and the area of $\triangle BFC$ is half the area of rectangle $BFCK$, or $\frac{1}{2}$ of 2, or 1, square unit. Similarly, the area of $\triangle DGC$ is half the area of rectangle $DHCG$, that is, $\frac{1}{2} \cdot 3$, or $\frac{3}{2}$, square unit. Consequently, the area of $ABCD$ is $6 - (\frac{1}{2} + 1 + \frac{3}{2})$, or 3, square units.

EXAMPLE 13-8 Using a geoboard, find the areas of each of the figures shown in Figure 13-12.

FIGURE 13-12

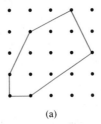
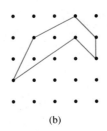

(a)   (b)

SOLUTION

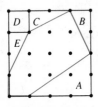

FIGURE 13-13

(a) We construct a square around the hexagon, and then subtract the areas of regions A, B, C, D, E from the area of this square, as shown in Figure 13-13. Therefore, the area of the quadrilateral is $16 - (3 + 1 + 1 + 1 + 1)$, or 9, square units.

(b) The area of the hexagon equals the area of the surrounding rectangle shown in Figure 13-14 minus the sum of the area of figures A, B, C, D, E, F, and G. Thus, the area of the hexagon is $12 - (3 + 1 + \frac{1}{2} + \frac{1}{2} + 1 + 1 + 1)$, or 4, square units.

FIGURE 13-14

Area of a Parallelogram

Formulas for areas of various polygons follow from the formula for the area of a rectangle. Consider, for example, the parallelogram $ABCD$ in Figure 13-15(a). The parallelogram can be separated into two parts. The shaded triangle can be translated, or slid, to the right of the parallelogram, as in Figure 13-15(b), to obtain a rectangle with length b and width h. This can

FIGURE 13-15

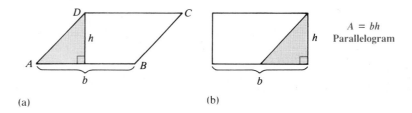

$$A = bh$$
Parallelogram

(a)   (b)

be achieved by sliding the shaded triangle in the direction from D to C along $\overleftrightarrow{DC}$ by a distance of DC. The parallelogram and the rectangle have the same area. (Why?) Because the area of the rectangle is bh, the area of the original parallelogram $ABCD$ is also bh. In general, any side of a parallelogram can be designated as a **base,** with measure b. The **height** is the distance between the bases. Thus, the height h is always the length of a segment perpendicular to the line containing the base. Any side of a parallelogram can be used as a base, along with its corresponding height. In Figure 13-16, $EB = g$, and g is the height that corresponds to the bases $\overline{AD}$ and $\overline{BC}$, each of which has measure a. Consequently, the area of the parallelogram is also ag. Therefore, $A = ag = bh$.

base / height

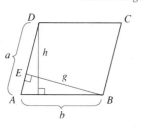

FIGURE 13-16

Area of a Triangle

A formula for the area of a triangle follows from the formula for the area of a parallelogram. In Figure 13-17(a), $\triangle BAC$ has base b and height h. Let $\triangle BAC'$ be the image of $\triangle BAC$ when $\triangle BAC$ is rotated about M, the midpoint of $\overline{AB}$, as in Figure 13-17(b). It can be proved that quadrilateral $BCAC'$ is a parallelogram. The area of parallelogram $BCAC'$ is bh, so the area of $\triangle ABC$ is $\frac{1}{2}bh$. Thus, the area of a triangle is equal to half the product of the length of a side and the altitude to that side or to the line containing that side. As with a parallelogram, any side of a triangle can be chosen as a base. Because a triangle has three bases, it has three corresponding altitudes. In finding the area of a triangle, we always multiply $\frac{1}{2}$ times the length of a base times the length of the corresponding altitude.

FIGURE 13-17

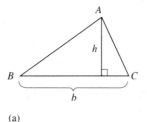

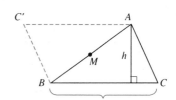

$$A = \frac{1}{2}bh$$
Triangle

(a)   (b)

In Figure 13-18, $\overline{BC}$ is a base of $\triangle ABC$, and the corresponding height h_1, or AE, is the distance from the opposite vertex A to the line containing $\overline{BC}$. Similarly, $\overline{AC}$ can be chosen as a base. Then h_2, or BG, the distance from the opposite vertex B to the line containing $\overline{AC}$, is the corresponding height. If AB is chosen as a base, then the corresponding height is h_3, or FC. Thus, the area A of $\triangle ABC$ is

$$A = \frac{bh_1}{2} = \frac{ah_2}{2} = \frac{ch_3}{2}$$

FIGURE 13-18

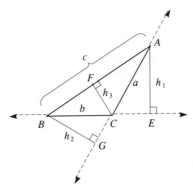

EXAMPLE 13-9 Find the area of each drawing in Figure 13-19. Assume that the quadrilaterals in (a) and (b) are parallelograms.

FIGURE 13-19

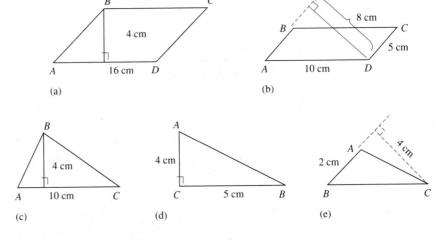

(a)

(b)

(c)

(d)

(e)

SOLUTION
(a) $A = bh = (16 \text{ cm})(4 \text{ cm}) = 64 \text{ cm}^2$
(b) $A = bh = (5 \text{ cm})(8 \text{ cm}) = 40 \text{ cm}^2$
(c) $A = \frac{1}{2}bh = \frac{1}{2}(10 \text{ cm})(4 \text{ cm}) = 20 \text{ cm}^2$
(d) $A = \frac{1}{2}bh = \frac{1}{2}(5 \text{ cm})(4 \text{ cm}) = 10 \text{ cm}^2$
(e) $A = \frac{1}{2}bh = \frac{1}{2}(2 \text{ cm})(4 \text{ cm}) = 4 \text{ cm}^2$

Area of a Trapezoid

Areas of other polygons can be found by partitioning the polygons into triangles. Trapezoid $ABCD$ in Figure 13-20(a) has bases b_1 and b_2 and height h. By drawing diagonal $\overline{BD}$ (or $\overline{AC}$), as in Figure 13-20(b), we create two triangles: one with base $\overline{AB}$ and height DE, and the other with base $\overline{CD}$ and height BF. Because $\overline{DE} \cong \overline{BF}$, each has height h. Thus, the areas of triangles ADB and DCB are $\frac{1}{2}(b_1 h)$ and $\frac{1}{2}(b_2 h)$, respectively. Hence, the area of trapezoid $ABCD$ is $\frac{1}{2}(b_1 h) + \frac{1}{2}(b_2 h)$, or $\frac{1}{2}h(b_1 + b_2)$. That is, the area of a trapezoid is equal to half the height times the sum of the lengths of the bases.

FIGURE 13-20

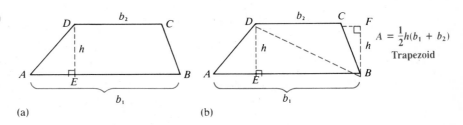

(a)   (b)

EXAMPLE 13-10 Find the areas of the trapezoids in Figure 13-21.

FIGURE 13-21

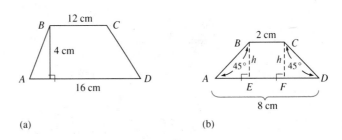

(a)   (b)

SOLUTION (a) $A = \frac{1}{2}h(b_1 + b_2) = \frac{1}{2}(4 \text{ cm})(12 \text{ cm} + 16 \text{ cm}) = 56 \text{ cm}^2$

(b) To find the area, we need to find h, the height of the trapezoid. In Figure 13-21(b), $BE = CF = h$. Also, $\overline{BE}$ is a side of $\triangle ABE$, which has angles with measures of 45° and 90°. Consequently, the third angle in triangle ABE is $180 - (45 + 90)$, or 45°. Therefore, $\triangle ABE$ is isosceles and $AE = BE = h$. Similarly, it follows that $FD = h$. Because $AD = 8 = h + EF + h$, if we knew the value of EF, we could find h. From Figure 13-21(b), $EF = BC = 2$. This is true because $BCFE$ is a rectangle (why?) and opposite sides of a rectangle are congruent. Hence, we have $h + EF + h = h + 2 + h = 8$. Thus, $h = 3$ cm and the area of the trapezoid is $A = \frac{1}{2}(3 \text{ cm})(2 \text{ cm} + 8 \text{ cm})$, or 15 cm².

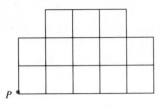

FIGURE 13-22

PROBLEM 1

Rancher Larry purchased a plot of land surrounded by a fence. The former owner had marked off 13 squares of equal size to subdivide the land, as shown in Figure 13-22. Larry wants to divide the land into two plots of equal area. To divide the property, he wishes to build a single, straight fence beginning at the far left corner (point P on the drawing). Is such a fence possible? Is so, where should it be?

Understanding the Problem. We wish to divide the land in Figure 13-22 into two plots of equal area, by means of a straight fence starting at point P. Because the area of the entire plot is 13 square units, the area of each part formed by the fence must be $6\frac{1}{2}$ square units.

Devising a Plan. In order to find an approximate location for the fence, consider a fence connecting P with point A, as shown in Figure 13-23. The area of the land below the fence $\overline{PA}$ can be found as the sum of the areas of $\triangle APD$ and the rectangle $DAFE$. The area of $\triangle APD$ is 4 and the area of rectangle $DAFE$ is 2. Hence, the desired area below the fence $\overline{PA}$ is $4 + 2$, or 6, square units. Because the area is supposed to be $6\frac{1}{2}$ square units, this does not allow enough area below the fence. Consequently, the other end of the fence should be above A.

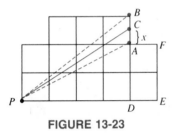

FIGURE 13-23

A similar argument shows that the area below $\overline{PB}$ is 8 square units and, hence, that the end of the fence should be below B. It follows that the other end of the fence should be at a point C between A and B. To find the exact location of the fence, we need to find CA. To do this, we designate CA by x, write an equation for x by finding the area below $\overline{PC}$ in terms of x, make it equal to $6\frac{1}{2}$, or $\frac{13}{2}$, and solve for x.

Carrying Out the Plan. The area below $\overline{PC}$ equals the area of $\triangle PCD$ plus the area of the rectangle $DAFE$. The area of $\triangle PCD$ is

$$\frac{PD \cdot DC}{2} = \frac{4(2 + x)}{2} = 2(2 + x)$$

Thus, the total area below $\overline{PC}$ is $2(2 + x) + 2$. This area should equal half the area of the plot, that is $\frac{13}{2}$. Consequently, we have the following.

$$2(2 + x) + 2 = \frac{13}{2}$$

$$4 + 2x + 2 = \frac{13}{2}$$

$$2x = \frac{1}{2}$$

$$x = \frac{1}{4}$$

Therefore, the fence should be built along the line connecting point P to the point C, which is $\frac{1}{4}$ unit directly above point A.

Looking Back. The point C can be found by dividing $\overline{AB}$ into four equal parts. We can also check that the solution is correct by finding the area above $\overline{PC}$. To find the area above $\overline{PC}$, we consider the area of the polygon $PCBGHI$ in Figure 13-24(a).

FIGURE 13-24

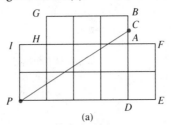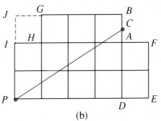

(a)   (b)

One way to find the area of the polygon is to make it into a trapezoid $PCBJP$ by adding one square, as shown in Figure 13-24(b). Hence, to find the required area we may find the area of the trapezoid and then subtract the area of square $HGJI$. The area of trapezoid $BCPJ$ in Figure 13-24(b) is $\frac{1}{2}(BC + JP)JB = \frac{1}{2}(\frac{3}{4} + 3) \cdot 4 = 7\frac{1}{2}$. Hence, the area above the fence $\overline{PC}$ is $7\frac{1}{2} - 1$, or $6\frac{1}{2}$, square units, as required.

Area of a Regular Polygon

The area of a triangle can also be used to find the area of any regular polygon. For example, consider the regular hexagon pictured in Figure 13-25(a). The hexagon can be separated into six congruent triangles, each with a vertex at the center, with side s and height a. (The height of such a triangle of a regular polygon is called the *apothem* and is denoted by a.) The area of each triangle is $\frac{1}{2}as$. Since six triangles make up the hexagon, the area of the hexagon is $6(\frac{1}{2}as)$, or $\frac{1}{2}a(6s)$. However, $6s$ is the perimeter p of the hexagon, so the area of the hexagon is $\frac{1}{2}ap$. The same process can be used to develop the formula for the area of any regular polygon. That is, the area of any regular polygon is $\frac{1}{2}ap$, where a is the height of one of the triangles involved and p is the perimeter of the polygon, as shown in Figure 13-25(b).

FIGURE 13-25

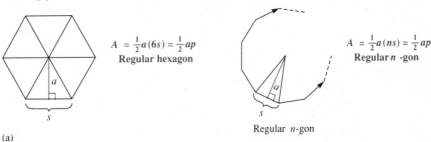

$$A = \frac{1}{2}a(6s) = \frac{1}{2}ap$$
Regular hexagon

(a)

$$A = \frac{1}{2}a(ns) = \frac{1}{2}ap$$
Regular n-gon

Regular n-gon

(b)

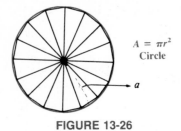

$A = \pi r^2$
Circle

a

FIGURE 13-26

Area of a Circle

The formula for the area of a regular polygon can be used to develop the formula for the area of a circle. The area of a regular polygon inscribed in a circle, as in Figure 13-26, approximates the area of the circle. The area of any inscribed regular n-gon is $\frac{1}{2}ap$, where a is the height of a triangle of the n-gon and p is the perimeter. If the number of sides n is made very large, then the perimeter and the area of the n-gon are close to those of the circle. Also, a is approximately equal to the radius r of the circle, and the perimeter approximates the circumference $2\pi r$. Because the area of the circle is approximately equal to the area of the n-gon, then $\frac{1}{2}ap \doteq \frac{1}{2}r \cdot 2\pi r = \pi r^2$. In fact, the area of the circle is precisely πr^2.

A similar approach to the preceding derivation of the area of a circle was given in 1609 by the astronomer Johann Kepler (1751–1630). The approach shown on the student page from *Addison-Wesley Mathematics*, 1989, Grade 8 is similar to Kepler's.

Area of Circles

A central water filtration plant has a large circular pool with a radius of 22 m. What is the area of the surface of the pool?

To find the area of a circle, we can use a formula. The diagram shows why the formula is reasonable.

A circle is divided into parts.

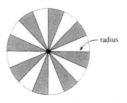

radius

The parts fit together to form a shape like a parallelogram.

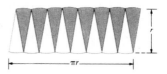

πr

The "parallelogram" has the same area as the circle. The base of the "parallelogram" is $\frac{1}{2}$ the circumference (πr). The height is r.

Area of circle $= \pi r \times r$
$A = \pi r^2$
$A \approx 3.14 \times 22^2$
$A \approx 3.14 \times 484$
$A \approx 1,519.76$

The area of the circular region is about 1,519.76 m².

Area of a Sector

sector A **sector** of a circle is a pie-shaped region of the circle determined by a central angle of the circle. The area of a sector depends on the radius of the circle and the measure of the central angle determining the sector. If the angle has a measure of 90°, as in Figure 13-27(a), the area of the sector is one-fourth the area of the circle, or $\frac{90}{360}\pi r^2$. In any circle, there are 360°, so the area of a sector whose central angle has measure θ degrees is $\frac{\theta}{360}(\pi r^2)$, as shown in Figure 13-27(b).

FIGURE 13-27

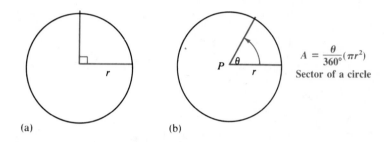

$$A = \frac{\theta}{360°}(\pi r^2)$$

Sector of a circle

(a) (b)

EXAMPLE 13-11 Find the area of each of the sectors shown in Figure 13-28.

FIGURE 13-28

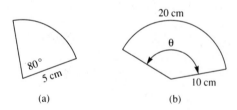

(a) (b)

SOLUTIONS (a) $A = \dfrac{80}{360} \cdot \pi(5\ \text{cm})^2 = \dfrac{50}{9}\pi\ \text{cm}^2$

(b) We need to find θ to find the area of the sector. We know that the length of the arc is 20 cm. Also, the length of the arc is $2\pi r\ \dfrac{\theta}{360}$, or $2\pi \cdot 10 \cdot \dfrac{\theta}{360}$. Thus, $2\pi \cdot 10 \cdot \dfrac{\theta}{360} = 20$ and hence $\dfrac{\theta}{360} = \dfrac{1}{\pi}$. The area A of the sector is $A = \pi r^2\ \dfrac{\theta}{360} = \pi \cdot 10^2 \cdot \dfrac{\theta}{360}$. Consequently, substituting $\dfrac{1}{\pi}$ for $\dfrac{\theta}{360}$ in the given expression for A, we have

$$A = \pi \cdot (10\ \text{cm})^2 \cdot \dfrac{\theta}{360} = \pi \cdot 100\ \text{cm}^2 \cdot \dfrac{1}{\pi} = 100\ \text{cm}^2.$$

PROBLEM SET 13-2

1. Choose the most appropriate metric units (cm², m², or km²) and English units (in.², yd.², mi.²) for measuring each of the following.
   (a) Area of a sheet of notebook paper
   (b) Area of a quarter
   (c) Area of a desktop
   (d) Area of a classroom floor
   (e) Area of a parallel parking space
   (f) Area of an airport runway.

2. Estimate and then measure each of the following, using cm², m², or km².
   (a) Area of a door   (b) Area of a chair seat
   (c) Area of a desktop   (d) Area of a chalkboard

3. Complete the following conversion table.

Item	m²	cm²	mm²
Area of a sheet of paper		588	
Area of a cross section of a crayon			192
Area of a desktop	1.5		
Area of a dollar bill		100	
Area of a postage stamp		5	

4. Explain the difference between a 2-m square and 2 m².

5. Complete the following conversions, using a calculator.
   (a) $4000 \text{ ft.}^2 = $ _____ yd.²
   (b) $10^6 \text{ yd.}^2 = $ _____ mi.²
   (c) $10 \text{ mi.}^2 = $ _____ a. (acres)
   (d) $3 \text{ a. (acres)} = $ _____ ft.²

6. Find the area of $\triangle ABC$ in each of the following triangles.

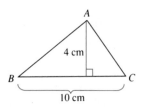

(a)

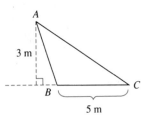

(b)

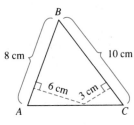

(c)

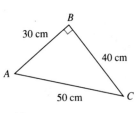

(d)

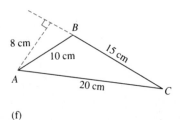

(e)

(f)

7. Find the area of each of the following quadrilaterals.

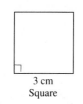

3 cm
Square

(a)

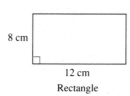

8 cm

12 cm
Rectangle

(b)

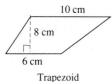

10 cm
8 cm
6 cm
Trapezoid

(c)

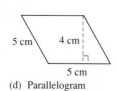

5 cm   4 cm

5 cm
(d) Parallelogram

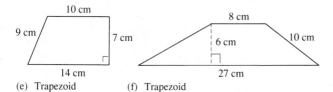

10 cm
9 cm   7 cm
14 cm
(e) Trapezoid

8 cm
6 cm   10 cm
27 cm
(f) Trapezoid

8. Complete each of the following.
 (a) A football field is about 49 m by 100 m or
 _____ m².
 (b) About _____ ares are in two football fields.
 (c) About _____ hectares are in two football fields.

9. In the figure, $\ell \| \overleftrightarrow{AB}$. If the area of $\triangle ABP$ is 10 cm², what are the areas of $\triangle ABQ$, $\triangle ABR$, $\triangle ABS$, $\triangle ABT$, and $\triangle ABU$? Explain your answers.

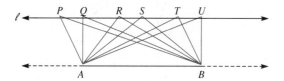

10. (a) A rectangular piece of land is 1300 m by 1500 m. What is the area in square kilometers? What is the area in hectares?
 (b) A rectangular piece of land is 1300 yards by 1500 yards. What is the area in square miles? What is the area in acres? Compare this problem with part (a).

11. Find the area of each regular polygon.

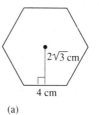

$2\sqrt{3}$ cm

4 cm

(a)

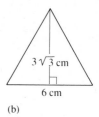

$3\sqrt{3}$ cm

6 cm

(b)

12. Find the areas of each of the following figures if the distance between two adjacent nails in a row or a column is one unit.

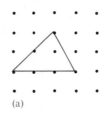

(a)

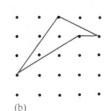

(b)

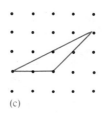

(c)

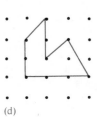

(d)

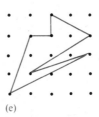

(e)

(f)

13. If all vertices of a polygon are points on square-dot paper, the polygon is called a **lattice polygon.** In 1899, G. Pick discovered a surprising theorem involving I, the number of dots *inside* the polygon, and B, the number of dots that lie *on* the polygon. The theorem states that the area of any lattice polygon is $I + \frac{1}{2}B - 1$. Check that this is true for the polygons in Problem 12.

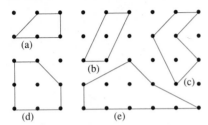

14. For a parallelogram whose sides are 6 cm and 10 cm, which of the following is true?
    (a) The data are insufficient to enable us to determine the area.
    (b) The area equals 60 cm².
    (c) The area is greater than 60 cm².
    (d) The area is less than 60 cm².
15. (a) Find the area of the trapezoid shown.
    ★(b) Show that the area of a trapezoid similar to the one in (a), with bases a and b and with base angles of 45° each is $\dfrac{a^2 - b^2}{4}$.

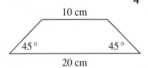

16. If the diagonals of a rhombus are a and b units long, find the area of the rhombus in terms of a and b.
17. Find the area of each of the following. Leave your answers in terms of π.

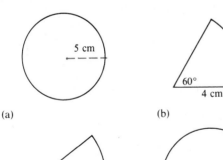

18. (a) If a circle has a circumference of 8π cm, what is its area?
    (b) If a circle with radius r and a square with a side of length s have the same area, express r in terms of s.
19. Find the area of each of the following shaded parts. Assume that all arcs are circular.

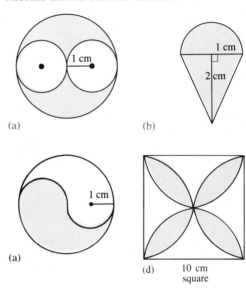

20. Find the cost of carpeting the following rectangular rooms.
    (a) Dimensions: 6.5 m by 4.5 m; cost = $13.85 per square meter
    (b) Dimensions: 15 ft by 11 ft; cost = $30 per square yard
21. Find the area of each of the shaded figures in terms of r.

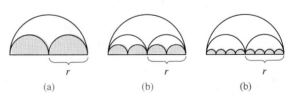

22. Solve for x.

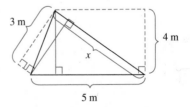

23. A circular flower bed is 6 m in diameter and has a circular sidewalk around it 1 m wide. Find the area of the sidewalk in square meters.

24. Joe uses stick-on square carpet tiles to cover his 3-m by 4-m bathroom. If each tile is 10 cm on a side, how many tiles does he need?

25. A rectangular plot of land is to be seeded with grass. If the plot is 22 m by 28 m and if a 1-kg bag of seed is needed for 85 m² of land, how many bags of seed will it take?

26. Consider the following figures made of five congruent squares, and answer the questions that follow. The figures are constructed in such a way that any two squares share a common side or a common vertex or have no points in common, and each square shares an edge with another. If each square is considered a unit square, then the area of each figure is 5 square units, but the perimeters of the figures are 12, 10, and 12 units, respectively.

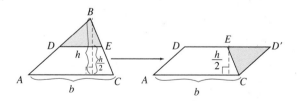

(a) What are the greatest and least perimeters possible of a figure made of unit squares whose area is (i) 5 (ii) 6 (iii) 30? Draw the appropriate figures.

(b) What are the greatest and least possible areas of a figure made of unit squares whose perimeter is (i) 12 units (ii) 26 units? Draw the appropriate figures.

(c) What is the greatest possible perimeter of a figure made of unit squares whose area is n square units?

(d) What is the least possible area of a figure made of unit squares whose perimeter is $2n$ units long?

27. (a) Explain how the drawing can be used to determine a formula for the area of $\triangle ABC$.

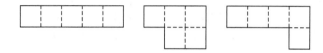

(b) Use paper cutting to reassemble $\triangle ABC$ in (a) into parallelogram $ADD'C$.

28. Find the area of each of the shaded regions.

(a)

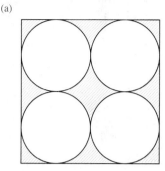

Radius of each circle = 5 cm

(b)

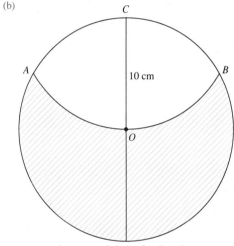

O = center of circle of radius 10 cm
C = center of arc AOB

29. (a) If the ratio of the sides of two squares is 2:3, what is the ratio of the areas? Justify your answer.

(b) If the ratio between the diagonals of two squares is 2:3, what is the ratio of their areas? Justify your answer.

30. (a) If, in two similar triangles, the ratio of the lengths of the corresponding sides is 2:1, what is the ratio of their areas?

(b) Make a conjecture concerning the relationship between the ratio of the areas of two similar triangles and the ratio of the corresponding sides.

(c) Justify your conjecture in (b).

31. (a) The screens of two television sets are similar rectangles. The 20-inch set (the length of the diagonal is 20 inches) costs $400, whereas the 27-inch set with similar features costs $600. If a customer is concerned about the size of the viewing area and is willing to pay the same amount per square foot, which is a better buy? Why?
    (b) What should the length of the diagonal of a TV set be in order for the viewing area to be twice the viewing area of the 20-inch set?

32. The area of a parallelogram can be found by using the concept of a half-turn (a turn by 180°). Consider the parallelogram $ABCD$, and let M and N be the midpoints of $\overline{AB}$ and $\overline{CD}$, respectively. Rotate the shaded triangle with vertex M about M by 180° clockwise, and rotate the shaded triangle with vertex N about N by 180° counterclockwise. What kind of figure do you obtain? Now complete the argument to find the area of the parallelogram.

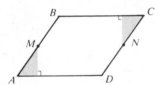

33. Consider the trapezoid $ABCD$. Rotate the trapezoid 180° clockwise about the midpoint M of $\overline{BC}$. Use the figure obtained from the union of the original trapezoid and its image to derive the formula for the area of a trapezoid.

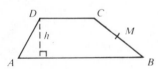

34. The given figure consists of five congruent squares. Find a line through point P that divides the figure into two parts of equal area.

35. A landscape architect wants to divide a circular garden into four congruent regions, each bounded only by arcs. How can this be done?

36. (a) Congruent circles are cut out of a rectangular piece of tin, as shown, to make lids. Find what percent of the tin is wasted.

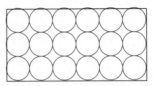

    (b) Suppose that the rectangular piece of tin is the same size as in (a) but smaller congruent circles are cut out. Also suppose that the circles are still tangent to each other and to the sides of the rectangle. What percent of the tin is wasted if the radius of each circle is as follows?
        (i) Half the radius of the circles in (a)
        (ii) One-third the radius of the circles in (a)

★37. In the drawing, quadrilateral $ABCD$ is a parallelogram and P is any point on $\overline{AC}$. Prove that the area of $\triangle BCP$ is equal to the area of $\triangle DPC$.

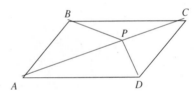

Review Problems

38. Complete each of the following.
    (a) 100 mm = _____ cm
    (b) 10.4 cm = _____ mm
    (c) 350 mm = _____ m
    (d) 0.04 m = _____ mm
    (e) 8 km = _____ m
    (f) 6504 m = _____ km

39. Find the perimeters for each of the following if all arcs shown are semicircles.

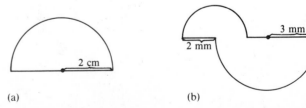

(a)   (b)

LABORATORY ACTIVITY

As van Hiele Level 2 activities, answer the following without using any area formulas.

1. On a geoboard make $\triangle DEF$. Keep the rubber band around D and E fixed and move the vertex F to all the possible locations so that the triangles formed will have the same area as the area of $\triangle DEF$. How do the locations for the third vertex relate to D and E?

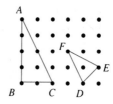

2. On a geoboard, construct, if possible, squares of areas 1, 2, 3, 4, 5, 6, and 7 square units.

3. On a geoboard construct triangles that have areas $\frac{1}{2}$, 1, $1\frac{1}{2}$, 2, ... , until the maximum-size triangle is reached.

B R A I N   T E A S E R

The accompanying rectangle was apparently formed by cutting the square shown along the dotted lines and reassembling the pieces as pictured.

1. What is the area of the square?
2. What is the area of the rectangle?
3. How do you explain the discrepancy?

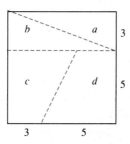

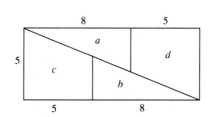

Section 13-3 The Pythagorean Relationship

Pythagoras was one of the most famous geometers of Greek antiquity. One of his most remarkable and useful discoveries is known as the Pythagorean Theorem, which involves a right triangle.

In Figure 13-29 the side c of the triangle opposite the right angle is called the **hypotenuse** of the triangle. The other two sides are called **legs**. The hypotenuse is always the longest side of a right triangle.

hypotenuse / legs

FIGURE 13-29

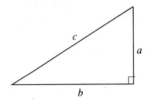

- **T H E O R E M   13-1**

  The Pythagorean Theorem   If a right triangle has legs of lengths a and b and hypotenuse of length c, then $c^2 = a^2 + b^2$.

FIGURE 13-30

Interpreted in terms of area, the Pythagorean Theorem says that the area of a square with the hypotenuse of a right triangle as a side is equal to the sum of the areas of the squares with the legs as sides. This relationship was illustrated on a Greek stamp in 1955, as shown in Figure 13-30, to honor the 2500th anniversary of the founding of the Pythagorean School.

H I S T O R I C A L   N O T E

Pythagoras (ca. 582–507 B.C.), a Greek philosopher and mathematician, was head of a group known as the Pythagoreans. Members of the group regarded Pythagoras as a demigod and attributed all their discoveries to him. The Pythagoreans believed in the transmigration of the soul from one body to another. One of Pythagoras's most unusual discoveries was the dependence of the musical intervals on the ratio of the length of strings at the same tension, the ratio 2:1 giving the octave, 3:2, the fifth, and 4:3, the fourth.

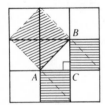

FIGURE 13-31

The Pythagoreans affirmed geometric results on the basis of special cases. As a result, mathematical historians believe that they did not have a proof of the Pythagorean Theorem. It is possible that the Pythagoreans discovered the theorem by looking at a floor tiling consisting of squares like the ones shown in Figure 13-31. Each square can be divided by its diagonal into two congruent isosceles right triangles, so we see that the shaded square constructed with $\overline{AB}$ as a side consists of four triangles each congruent to $\triangle ABC$. Similarly, each of the shaded squares with legs $\overline{BC}$ and $\overline{AC}$ as sides consists of two triangles congruent to $\triangle ABC$. Thus, the area of the larger square is equal to the sum of the areas of the two smaller squares.

The preceding argument does not constitute a proof of the Pythagorean Theorem because it holds only for a right isosceles triangle, not for a right triangle in general. There are hundreds of known proofs for the Pythagorean Theorem today. The classic book *The Pythagorean Proposition*, by E. Loomis, contains many of these proofs.

Many proofs of the Pythagorean Theorem involve constructing a square with area c^2 equal to the areas a^2 and b^2 of two other squares. Let the measures of the legs of a right triangle ABC in Figure 13-32(a) be a and b and let c be the measure of the hypotenuse. We draw a square with sides of length $a + b$ and subdivide it, as shown in Figure 13-32(b). In Figure 13-32(c) another square with side of length $a + b$ is drawn, and each of its sides is divided into two segments of length a and b, as shown.

FIGURE 13-32

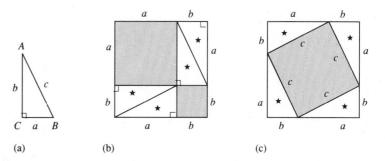

(a)   (b)   (c)

The triangles marked ★ in each of the figures are congruent to $\triangle ABC$. (Why?) Consequently, each of the starred triangles has hypotenuse c and the same area, $\frac{1}{2}ab$. This implies that the length of each side of the shaded quadrilateral in Figure 13-32(c) is c and hence that the figure is a rhombus. In fact, it is possible to show that the figure is a square (see Problem 27 in Problem Set 13-3). Consequently, the area of this square is c^2. To complete the proof of the Pythagorean Theorem, we observe that there are four starred triangles in Figure 13-32(b) and (c). Thus, the sum of the areas of the two shaded squares in Figure 13-32(b) equals the area of the shaded square in Figure 13-32(c). That is, $a^2 + b^2 = c^2$.

A proof of the Pythagorean Theorem using similar triangles is discussed in Problem 23 of Problem Set 13-3. Other proofs of the Pythagorean Theorem are discussed in Problems 24 and 27 of Problem Set 13-3.

EXAMPLE 13-12 For each drawing in Figure 13-33, find x by using the Pythagorean Theorem.

FIGURE 13-33

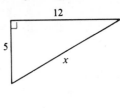

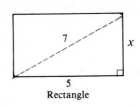

Rectangle

(a)   (b)

SOLUTION (a) By the Pythagorean Theorem,

$$5^2 + 12^2 = x^2$$
$$25 + 144 = x^2$$
$$169 = x^2$$
$$13 = x$$

(b) In the rectangle, the diagonal partitions the rectangle into two right triangles, each with lengths 5 units and width x units. Thus, we have the following.

$$5^2 + x^2 = 7^2$$
$$25 + x^2 = 49$$
$$x^2 = 24$$
$$x = \sqrt{24}, \text{ or approximately } 4.9$$

The Pythagorean Theorem is used in solving many real-life problems, as shown on the following student page from *Addison-Wesley Mathematics*, 1989, Grade 8.

When using the Pythagorean Theorem, we must be certain that we are working with a right triangle. At times, though, the segment whose length we want to find is not a side of any known right triangle. The following examples deal with such situations.

EXAMPLE 13-13 A pole $\overline{BD}$, 28 feet high, is perpendicular to the ground. Two wires $\overline{BC}$ and $\overline{BA}$, each 35 feet long, are attached to the top of the pole and to stakes A and C on the ground, as in Figure 13-34. If points A, D, and C are collinear, how far are the stakes A and C from each other?

FIGURE 13-34

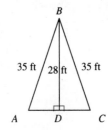

SOLUTION We need to find AC, but $\overline{AC}$ is not a side in any right triangle. However, $AD = DC$ follows from the remark following Theorem 11-3 that a point equidistant from the endpoints of a segment must be on a perpendicular bisector of the segment. Therefore, AC is twice as long as DC. Thus, we want to find DC. Applying the Pythagorean Theorem in $\triangle BDC$, we have $28^2 + (DC)^2 = 35^2$, or $(DC)^2 = 35^2 - 28^2 = 441$. Thus, $DC = \sqrt{441}$, or $DC = 21$ ft., and $AC = 2 \cdot DC = 42$ ft.

Finding the Length of the Hypotenuse

The size of a rectangular display screen is given as the length of the diagonal of the screen. The length of the screen is 24 cm and the width is 18 cm. What is the length of the diagonal?

The diagonal is the hypotenuse of a right triangle whose legs measure 18 cm and 24 cm.

We can use the Pythagorean formula to find the length.

$$a^2 + b^2 = c^2$$
$$18^2 + 24^2 = c^2$$
$$900 = c^2$$
$$\sqrt{900} = \sqrt{c^2}$$
$$30 = c$$

To solve this equation, find the square root of the numbers on each side.

The diagonal is 30 cm long.

EXAMPLE 13-14   In Figure 13-35, find x.

FIGURE 13-35

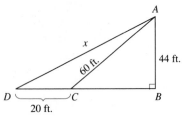

SOLUTION   As shown in Figure 13-35, we need to find x, which is the length of the hypotenuse in the right triangle ABD. In that triangle we know that $AB = 44$ ft., but we do not know the length of the other leg $\overline{DB}$. However, $\overline{DC}$ is part of $\overline{DB}$. Consequently, we need to find the length of $\overline{CB}$, the other part of $\overline{DB}$. $\overline{CB}$ is a leg in the right triangle ABC whose other two sides are given. By applying the Pythagorean Theorem in $\triangle ABC$, we can find CB.

In $\triangle ABC$, $(CB)^2 + 44^2 = 60^2$, or $(CB)^2 = 60^2 - 44^2 = 1664$. Consequently, $CB = \sqrt{1664} \doteq 40.8$ ft. Because $DB = DC + CB$, we have $DB = 20 + 40.8 \doteq 60.8$ ft. Applying the Pythagorean Theorem in $\triangle ABD$, we have

$$x^2 = (DB)^2 + (AB)^2$$
$$x^2 \doteq (60.8)^2 + (44)^2 = 5632.64$$
$$x \doteq 75 \text{ feet}$$

Converse of the Pythagorean Theorem

Given a triangle with sides of lengths a, b, and c such that $a^2 + b^2 = c^2$, must the triangle be a right triangle? This is the case, and we state the following without proof.

● **T H E O R E M**   **13-2**
Converse of the Pythagoran Theorem   If $\triangle ABC$ is a triangle with sides of lengths a, b, and c such that $a^2 + b^2 = c^2$, then $\triangle ABC$ is a right triangle with the right angle opposite the side of length c.

EXAMPLE 13-15   Determine whether the following can be the lengths of the sides of a right triangle.

(a) 51, 68, 85   (b) 2, 3, $\sqrt{13}$ (c) 3, 4, 7

SOLUTION   (a) $51^2 + 68^2 = 7225 = 85^2$, so 51, 68, and 85 can be the lengths of the sides of a right triangle.

(b) $2^2 + 3^2 = 4 + 9 = 13 = (\sqrt{13})^2$, so 2, 3, and $\sqrt{13}$ can be the lengths of the sides of a right triangle.

(c) $3^2 + 4^2 \neq 7^2$, so the measures cannot be the lengths of the sides of a right triangle.

PROBLEM SET 13-3

1. Use the Pythagorean Theorem to find x in each of the following.

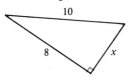

(a)

(b)

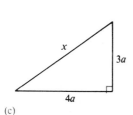

(c)

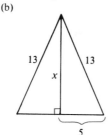

(d)

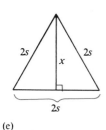

(e)

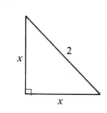

(f)

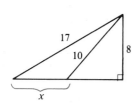

(g)

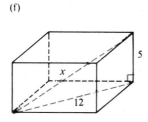

(h)

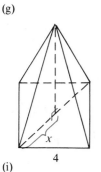

(i)

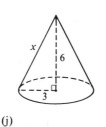

(j)

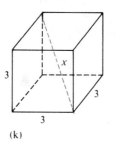

(k)

2. If the hypotenuse of a right triangle is 30 cm long and one of the legs is twice as long as the other, how long are the legs of the triangle?

3. For each of the following, can the given numbers represent lengths of sides of a right triangle?
   (a) 10, 24, 16
   (b) 16, 34, 30
   (c) $\sqrt{2}, \sqrt{2}, 2$
   (d) $2, \sqrt{3}, 1$
   (e) $\sqrt{2}, \sqrt{3}, \sqrt{5}$
   (f) $\dfrac{3}{2}, \dfrac{4}{2}, \dfrac{5}{2}$

4. What is the longest line segment that can be drawn in a right rectangular prism that is 12 cm wide, 15 cm long, and 9 cm high?

5. For each of the following, solve for the unknowns.

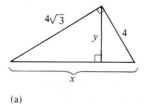

(a)

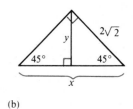

(b)

6. Two cars leave a house at the same time. One car travels 60 km per hour north, while the other car travels 40 km per hour east. After 1 hour, how far apart are the cars?

7. Two airplanes depart from the same place at 2 P.M. One plane flies south at a speed of 376 km per hour, and the other flies west at a speed of 648 km per hour. How far apart are the airplanes at 5:30 P.M.?

8. Starting from point A, a boat sails due south for 6 miles, then due east for 5 miles, and then due south for 4 miles. How far is the boat from A?

9. If the hypotenuse and a leg of one right triangle are congruent to the hypotenuse and a leg of another right triangle, respectively, must the triangles be congruent?

10. A 15-foot ladder is leaning against a wall. The base of the ladder is 3 feet from the wall. How high above the ground is the top of the ladder?

11. Find the area of a regular hexagon inscribed in a circle whose radius is as follows.
    (a) 5 cm
    (b) r cm

12. Find the shaded area enclosed by two semicircles and two tangents to the semicircles, as shown.

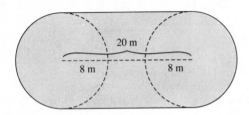

13. Two poles are 25 m and 15 m high. A cable 14 m long joins the tops of the poles. Find the distance between the poles.

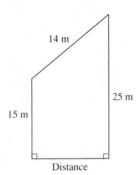

14. Find the area of each of the following.

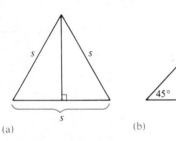

(a)   (b)

15. A builder needs to calculate the dimensions of a regular hexagonal window. If the altitude CD of the window is 1.3 m high, find the width AB (O is the midpoint of $\overline{AB}$.)

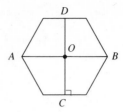

16. The length of the diagonal $\overline{AC}$ of a rhombus $ABCD$ is 20 cm. The distance between $\overline{AB}$ and $\overline{DC}$ is 12 cm. Find the length of the sides of the rhombus and the length of the other diagonal.

17. In $\triangle ABC$, $AC = BC$, $AB = 30$ cm, and AD is the altitude to side BC. If $AD = 24$ cm, find AC.

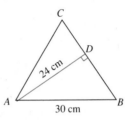

18. (a) Prove that the side opposite the 30° angle in a 30°-60°-90° triangle is half as long as the hypotenuse. (*Hint:* Two such triangles can be placed to make an equilateral triangle.)
    (b) If the hypotenuse in a 30°-60°-90° triangle is c units long, what is the length of the side opposite the 60° angle?

19. If the length of the hypotenuse in a 45°-45°-90° triangle is c, find the length of a leg.

20. Find x in the given figure.

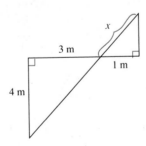

21. Given the following square, use a compass and a straightedge to construct a square whose area is as specified.
    (a) Twice the area of the given square
    (b) Half the area of the given square

22. If possible, draw a square with the given number of square units on a geoboard grid. (You will have to draw your own geoboard grid.)
(a) 5   (b) 7   (c) 8   (d) 14   (e) 15

23. Use the following drawing to prove the Pythagorean Theorem by using corresponding parts of similar triangles $\triangle ACD$, $\triangle CBD$, and $\triangle ABC$. Lengths of sides are indicated by a, b, c, x, and y. (*Hint:* Show that $b^2 = cx$ and $a^2 = cy$.)

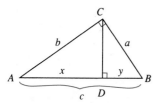

24. Before he was elected president of the United States, James Garfield discovered a proof of the Pythagorean Theorem. He formed a trapezoid like the one that follows and found the area of the trapezoid in two different ways. Can you discover his proof?

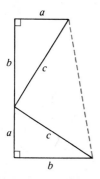

25. Construct semicircles on right triangle ABC with $\overline{AB}$, $\overline{BC}$, and $\overline{AC}$ as diameters. Is the area of the semicircle on the hypotenuse equal to the sum of the areas of the semicircles on the legs?

26. On each side of a right triangle, construct an equilateral triangle. Is the area of the triangle constructed on the hypotenuse always equal to the sum of the areas of the triangles constructed on the legs? Justify your answer.

27. Use the given figure to prove the Pythagorean Theorem by first proving that the quadrilateral with side c is a square; then, compute the area of the square with side $a + b$ in two different ways: (a) as $(a + b)^2$; and (b) as the sum of the areas of the four triangles and the square with side c.

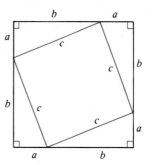

Review Problems

28. Arrange the following in decreasing order: 3.2 m, 322 cm, 0.032 km, 3.020 mm.

29. Find the area of each figure.

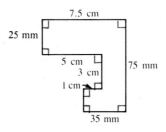

(a)

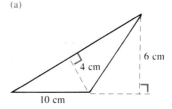

(b)

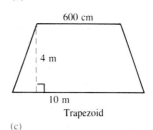

Trapezoid

(c)

30. Complete the following table concerning circles.

	Radius	Diameter	Circumference	Area
(a)	5 cm			
(b)		24 cm		
(c)				17π m²
(d)			20π cm	

31. A wire 10 m long is wrapped around a circular region. If the wire fits exactly, what is the area of the region?

B R A I N   T E A S E R

A spider sitting at A, the midpoint of the edge of the ceiling in the room shown, spies a fly on the floor at C, the midpoint of the edge of the floor. If the spider must walk along the wall, ceiling, or floor, what is the length of the shortest path the spider can travel to reach the fly?

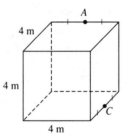

LABORATORY ACTIVITY

As a van Hiele Level 1 activity, consider the following drawings. Without using formulas for areas of figures, check whether the area of the square constructed on the hypotenuse of the right triangle in each case equals the sum of the areas of the squares constructed on the legs of the triangle.

(a)

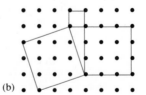

(b)

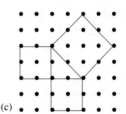

(c)

Section 13-4   Surface Areas of Three-Dimensional Figures

Surface Area of a Prism

The surface area of a polyhedron is the sum of the areas of the faces of the polyhedron. Formulas are available for finding these areas. We develop the formulas for understanding, but most of the examples rely on finding the sum of the areas of the faces of the polyhedra. Cubes are the simplest polyhedra. The surface area of the cube in Figure 13-36(a) is the sum of the areas of the faces of the cube. Because each of the six faces is a square of area 16 cm², the surface area is 6 · (16 cm²), or 96 cm².

FIGURE 13-36

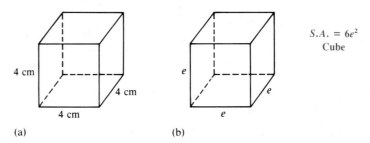

(a)   (b)

$S.A. = 6e^2$
Cube

In general, if the edges of a cube are e units, as in Figure 13-36(b), then each face is a square with area e^2 units. Because there are six faces, the surface area of the cube is given by $S.A. = 6e^2$, where e is the length of a side and $S.A.$ is the surface area.

To find the surface area of other right prisms, we find the sum of the areas of the rectangles that constitute the lateral faces and the areas of the top and bottom. The sum of the areas of the lateral faces is called the **lateral surface area.** Thus, the **surface area** is the sum of the lateral surface area and the area of the bases.

lateral surface area

surface area

Figure 13-37(a) shows a right pentagonal prism, and Figure 13-37(b) shows the figure cut into three pieces. The cuts show the top, the bottom, and the lateral faces. The section formed by the lateral faces is stretched out

FIGURE 13-37

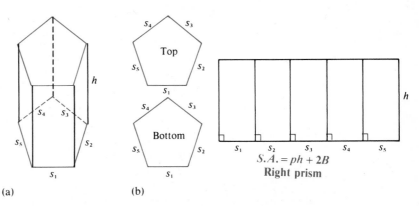

(a)   (b)

$S.A. = ph + 2B$
Right prism

flat. It forms a rectangle whose length is $s_1 + s_2 + s_3 + s_4 + s_5$ and whose width is h. Because $s_1 + s_2 + s_3 + s_4 + s_5$ is the perimeter p of the base of the prism, the lateral surface area is $(s_1 + s_2 + s_3 + s_4 + s_5) \cdot h$, or ph. If B stands for the area of each of the prism's bases, then the surface area $S.A.$ of the right prism is given by the following formula.

$$S.A. = ph + 2B$$

This formula holds for any right prism, regardless of the shape of its bases.

EXAMPLE 13-16   Find the surface area of each of the right prisms in Figure 13-38.

FIGURE 13-38

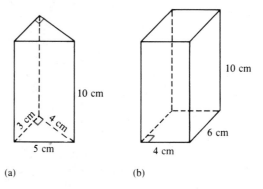

(a)   (b)

SOLUTION   (a) Each base is a right triangle. The area of the bases is $2(\frac{1}{2} \cdot 3 \text{ cm} \cdot 4 \text{ cm})$, or 12 cm². The perimeter of a base is 3 cm + 4 cm + 5 cm, or 12 cm. Hence, the lateral surface area is (12 cm)(10 cm), or 120 cm², and the surface area is 120 cm² + 12 cm², or 132 cm².
(b) The area of the bases is 2(4 cm)(6 cm), or 48 cm². The lateral surface area is 2(4 cm + 6 cm) · 10 cm, or 200 cm², so the surface area of the right prism is 248 cm².

Surface Area of a Cylinder

To find the surface area of the right circular cylinder shown in Figure 13-39, we cut off the bases and slice the lateral surface open by cutting along any line perpendicular to the bases. Such a slice is shown as a dotted segment in Figure 13-39(a); then we unroll the cylinder to form a rectangle, as shown in Figure 13-39(b). To find the total surface area, we need to find the area of the rectangle and the areas of the top and bottom circles. The length of the rectangle is the circumference of the circular base $2\pi r$ and its width is the height of the cylinder h. Hence, the area of the rectangle is $2\pi rh$. The area of each base is πr^2. Because the surface area is the sum of the areas of the two circular bases and the lateral surface area, we have

$$S.A. = 2\pi r^2 + 2\pi rh$$

FIGURE 13-39

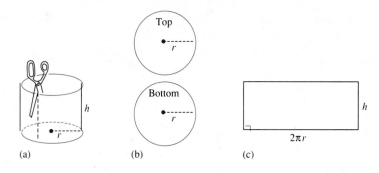

(a)   (b)   (c)

Surface Area of a Pyramid

right regular pyramid

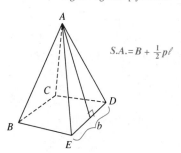

$S.A. = B + \frac{1}{2}p\ell$

Right Square Pyramid

FIGURE 13-40

The surface area of a pyramid is the sum of the lateral surface area of the pyramid and the area of the base. A **right regular pyramid** is a pyramid such that the segments connecting the apex to each vertex of the base are congruent and the base is a regular polygon. The lateral faces of the right regular pyramid pictured in Figure 13-40 are congruent triangles. Each triangle has an altitude of length ℓ called the *slant height*. Since the pyramid is right regular, each side of the base has the same length b. Thus, to find the lateral surface area of a right regular pyramid, we need to find the area of one face and multiply it by the number of faces. Adding the lateral surface area to the area of the base B gives the surface area.

In general, for any right regular pyramid, the surface area is found by adding the area B of the base and the area of the n congruent triangular faces, each with side b and slant height ℓ. The surface area is given by the following formula.

$$S.A. = B + n\left(\frac{1}{2}b\ell\right)$$

Because nb is the perimeter of the base, the formula reduces to the following.

$$S.A. = B + \frac{1}{2}p\ell$$

EXAMPLE 13-17   Find the surface area of the right regular pyramid in Figure 13-41.

FIGURE 13-41

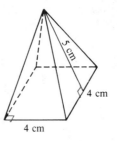

SOLUTION   The surface area consists of the area of the square base plus the area of the four triangular faces. Hence, the surface area is

$$4 \text{ cm} \cdot 4 \text{ cm} + 4 \cdot (\tfrac{1}{2} \cdot 4 \text{ cm} \cdot 5 \text{ cm}) = 16 \text{ cm}^2 + 40 \text{ cm}^2$$
$$= 56 \text{ cm}^2$$

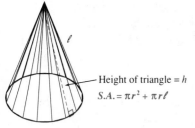

Height of triangle = h

$S.A. = \pi r^2 + \pi r \ell$

FIGURE 13-42

Surface Area of a Cone

It is possible to find a formula for the surface area of a cone by approximating the cone with pyramids. As shown in Figure 13-42, we inscribe in the circular base of the cone a regular polygon with many sides. The polygon can be used as the base of a regular right pyramid. The lateral surface area of the pyramid is close to the lateral surface area of the cone; and the greater the number of faces of the pyramid, the closer the surface area of the pyramid is to that of the cone. We know that the lateral surface of the pyramid is $\tfrac{1}{2}p \cdot h$, where p is the perimeter of the base and h is the height of each triangle. With many sides in the pyramid, the perimeter of its base is close to the perimeter of the circle, $2\pi r$. The height of each triangle of the pyramid is close to the slant height ℓ—a segment connecting the vertex of the cone with a point on the circular base, as shown in Figure 13-42. Consequently, it is reasonable that the lateral surface of the cone becomes $\tfrac{1}{2}p \cdot \ell$, where $p = 2\pi r$. Thus, the lateral surface area is $\tfrac{1}{2} \cdot 2\pi r \cdot \ell$, or $\pi r \ell$. To find the total surface area of the cone, we add πr^2, the area of the base. Thus, $S.A. = \pi r^2 + \pi r \ell$. The surface area of a right circular cone can also be determined by cutting the cone along a slant height ℓ, removing the base, and flattening the lateral surface, as shown in Figure 13-43. Before reading on, try to work on the Laboratory Activity at the end of this section.

The area of the base is the area of a circle with radius r, namely, πr^2. The lateral surface area is the sector of a circle whose radius is ℓ, as shown in Figure 13-43(c). Because the area of a sector with radius ℓ and central angle θ degrees is $\dfrac{\theta}{360} \cdot \pi \ell^2$, the area of the sector can be found if the measure of the central angle θ is known. Thus, we need to find θ in terms of the given quantities r and ℓ.

FIGURE 13-43

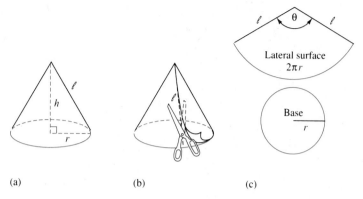

(a)   (b)   (c)

An equation involving θ, r, and ℓ can be obtained by finding the given arc length in two different ways. The length of the arc corresponding to θ is $\dfrac{\theta}{360} \cdot 2\pi\ell$. Also, the length of this arc is $2\pi r$, because it is the circumference of the circular base of the cone. Hence,

$\dfrac{\theta}{360} \cdot 2\pi\ell = 2\pi r$. Therefore,

$\dfrac{\theta}{360} = \dfrac{r}{\ell}$. Consequently, the area of the sector is

$A = \dfrac{\theta}{360} \cdot \pi\ell^2 = \dfrac{r}{\ell} \cdot \pi\ell^2 = \pi r\ell$. Thus, the surface area of a cone is given by

S.A. $= \pi r^2 + \pi r\ell$

EXAMPLE 13-18   Given the cone in Figure 13-44, find the following.

FIGURE 13-44

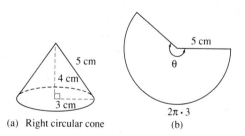

(a) Right circular cone   (b)

(a) The surface area of the cone
(b) The measure of the central angle of the sector that is obtained by cutting the cone along its slant height and flattening the lateral surface

SOLUTION   (a) $S.A. = \pi r^2 + \pi r\ell$
$= \pi(3 \text{ cm})^2 + \pi(3 \text{ cm})(5 \text{ cm})$
$= 9\pi \text{ cm}^2 + 15\pi \text{ cm}^2$
$= 24\pi \text{ cm}^2$

(b) When the cone is cut along its slant height, it unrolls into a sector whose radius is the slant height. The length of the arc in Figure 13-44(b) is the circumference of the circular base of the cone—that is, $2\pi \cdot 3$, or 6π cm.

On the other hand, the length of the arc is $2\pi \cdot 5 \cdot \dfrac{\theta}{360}$. Hence,

$$2\pi \cdot 5 \cdot \frac{\theta}{360} = 6\pi, \text{ and therefore } \theta = \frac{3}{5} \cdot 360, \text{ or } 216°.$$

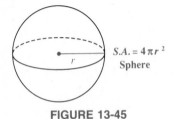

$S.A. = 4\pi r^2$
Sphere

FIGURE 13-45

Surface Area of a Sphere

Finding a formula for the surface area of a sphere is not a simple task when working with elementary mathematics. The formula for the surface area of a sphere is $S.A. = 4\pi r^2$. That is, the surface area of a sphere is four times the area of the great circle pictured in Figure 13-45. What happens to the surface area if r is doubled? Tripled?

LABORATORY ACTIVITY

Create different cones from sectors of a circle. Use a compass to draw a sector of a circle whose diameter is almost as large as the width of a page of paper. Draw two such sectors with the same radii but with different central angles. In one sector make the central angle smaller than 180°, and in the other make it greater than 180°. Then make a cone from each sector by gluing the edges of each sector together. Can you predict which cone will be taller? Can you explain which cone will be taller without performing the experiment?

PROBLEM SET 13-4

1. Find the surface area of each of the following.

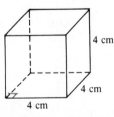

(a) Cube

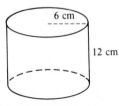

(b) Right circular cylinder

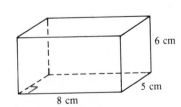

(c) Right rectangular Prism

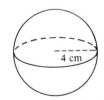

(d) Sphere

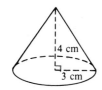

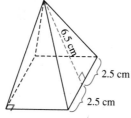

(e) Right circular cone

(f) Right Square Pyramid

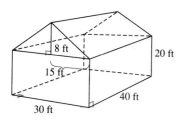

(g)

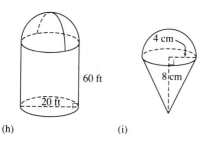

(h)   (i)

2. How many liters of paint are needed to paint the walls of a room that is 6 m long, 4 m wide, and 2.5 m tall if 1 L (liter) of paint covers 20 m²? (Assume there are no doors or windows.)

3. The napkin ring pictured is to be resilvered. How many square millimeters of surface area must be covered?

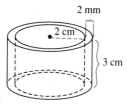

4. Assume that the radius of the Earth is 6370 km and the Earth is a sphere. What is its surface area?

5. Two cubes have sides of length 4 cm and 6 cm, respectively. What is the ratio of their surface areas?

6. Suppose that one cylinder has radius 2 m and height 6 m and another has radius 6 m and height 2 m.
  (a) Which cylinder has the greater lateral surface area?
  (b) Which cylinder has the greater total surface area?

7. The base of a right pyramid is a regular hexagon with sides of length 12 m. The altitude of the pyramid is 9 m. Find the total surface area of the pyramid.

8. (a) What happens to the surface area of a cube if the length of each edge is tripled?
  (b) What is the effect on the lateral surface area of a cylinder if the height is doubled?

9. How does the surface area of a box (including top and bottom) change if:
  (a) each dimension is doubled?
  (b) each dimension is tripled?
  (c) each dimension is multiplied by a factor of k?

10. How does the lateral surface area of a cone change if:
  (a) the slant height is tripled but the radius of the base remains the same?
  (b) the radius of the base is tripled but the slant height remains the same?
  (c) the slant height and the radius of the base are tripled?

11. The sector shown is rolled into a cone so that the dotted edges just touch. Find the following.
  (a) The lateral surface area of the cone
  (b) The total surface area of the cone

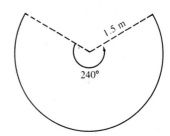

12. The sector shown is rolled into a cone so that the dotted edges just touch. If the area of the sector is 270 cm², find the following.
  (a) The area of the base of the cone
  (b) The height of the cone

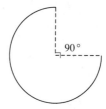

13. A sphere is inscribed in a right cylinder, as shown. Compare the surface area of the sphere with the lateral surface area of the cylinder.

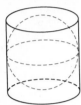

14. Karen is using a lawn mower to cut a rectangular field of grass. She follows the boundary of the field and finds that it takes her 12 rounds to cut one-half of the field and an additional 15 rounds to cut the remainder. If the lawn mower cuts a swath 3 ft. wide, what are the dimensions of the field?

15. Find the surface area of a square pyramid if the area of the base is 100 cm² and the height of the pyramid is 20 cm.

16. Each of the shaded regions shown revolves about the indicated axis. In each case sketch the three-dimensional figure obtained, and find its surface area.

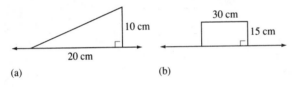

(a)   (b)

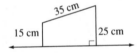

★ (c)

📱 17. The total surface area of a cube is 10,648 cm³. What is the length of each of the following?
(a) One of the sides
(b) A diagonal that is not a diagonal of a face

★18. The surface area of a regular tetrahedron is 400 cm². Find the length of the side of the tetrahedron.

★19. Find the total surface area of the following stand, which was cut from a right circular cone.

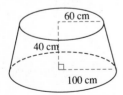

★20. A cylinder is inscribed in a cone, as shown. Find the lateral surface area of the cylinder if the height of the cone is 40 cm, the height of the cylinder 30 cm, and the radius of the base of the cone is 25 cm.

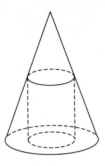

Review Problems

21. Complete each of the following.
(a) 10 m² = _____ cm²
(b) 13,680 cm² = _____ m²
(c) 5 cm² = _____ mm²
(d) 2 km² = _____ m²
(e) 10^6 m² = _____ km²
(f) 10^{12} mm² = _____ m²

22. The sides of a rectangle are 10 cm and 20 cm. Find the length of a diagonal of the rectangle.

23. The length of the side of a rhombus is 30 cm. If the length of one of the diagonals is 40 cm, find the length of the other diagonal.

24. Find the perimeters and the areas of the following figures.

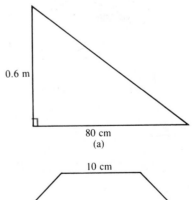

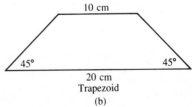

★25. The length of the longer diagonal $\overline{AC}$ of rhombus *ABCD* is 40 cm; *AE* = 24. Find the length of a side of the rhombus and the length of the other diagonal.

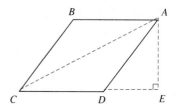

B R A I N   T E A S E R

A manufacturer of paper cups wants to produce paper cups in the form of truncated cones 16 cm high, with one circular base of radius 11 cm and the other of radius 7 cm, as shown. When the base of such a cup is removed and the cup is slit and flattened, the flattened region looks like a part of a circular ring. To design a pattern to make the cup, the manufacturer needs the data required to construct the flattened region. Find these data.

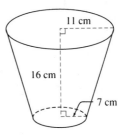

LABORATORY ACTIVITY

1. As a van Hiele Level 1 activity, use four cubes of the same size to build shapes such as the ones shown. In each case find the surface area, using a square face of the cube as a unit of area.

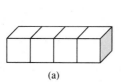

(a)

(b)

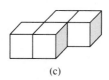

(c)

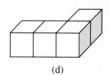

(d)

2. As a van Hiele Level 2 activity, consider the various figures that can be built by using four congruent cubes in such a way that any two cubes in your figure: (a) have no points in common; (b) have an edge in common; or (c) have a whole face in common.
   (i) What figure will have the greatest surface area?
   (ii) What figure will have the least surface area?

Section 13-5   Volume Measure and Volumes

Metric Measure of Volume

Volume describes how much space a three-dimensional figure occupies. The unit of measure for volume must be a shape that will "fill space." Cubes can be closely stacked so that they leave no gaps and fill space. Standard units of volume are based on cubes and are called *cubic units*. The volume of a rectangular right prism can be measured, for example, by determining how many cubes are needed to build it. One way is to count first how many cubes cover the base and then how many layers of these cubes are used to reach the height of the prism, as shown in Figure 13-46(a). There are $8 \cdot 4$, or 32, cubes in the base and there are five such layers. Hence, the volume of the rectangular prism is $8 \cdot 4 \cdot 5$, or 160, cubic units. For any rectangular right prism with dimensions ℓ, w, and h measured in the same linear units, the volume of the prism is given by $V = \ell w h$, as shown in Figure 13-46(b).

FIGURE 13-46

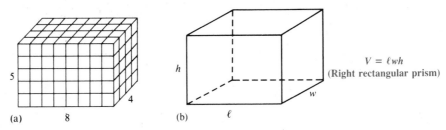

(a)   8   4   5

(b) h w ℓ

$V = \ell w h$
(Right rectangular prism)

cubic foot / cubic centimeter
cubic meter

In the English system of measurement, a commonly used unit of volume is the **cubic foot**. The most commonly used metric units are the **cubic centimeter** and the **cubic meter**. A cubic centimeter is the volume of a cube whose length, width, and height are each one centimeter. One cubic centimeter is denoted by 1 cm³. Similarly, a cubic meter is the volume of a cube whose length, width, and height are each 1 m. One cubic meter is denoted by 1 m³. Other metric units of volume are also symbolized with a raised 3 next to the standard symbol.

Figure 13-47 shows that, since 1 dm = 10 cm, 1 dm³ = (10 cm) $\cdot$ (10 cm) $\cdot$ (10 cm) = 1000 cm³. Similarly, Figure 13-48(a) shows that 1 m³ = 1,000,000 cm³, and Figure 13-48(b) shows that 1 dm³ = 0.001 m³.

FIGURE 13-47

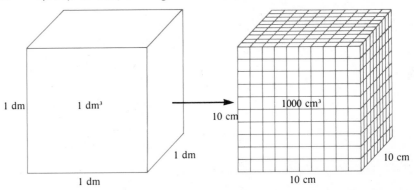

1 dm   1 dm³   1 dm   1 dm

1000 cm³   10 cm   10 cm   10 cm

FIGURE 13-48

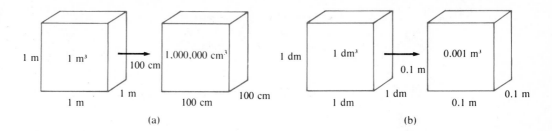

(a)   (b)

Each metric unit of length is 10 times as great as the next smaller unit. Each metric unit of area is 100 times as great as the next smaller unit. Each metric unit of volume is 1000 times as great as the next smaller unit. Hence, to convert from cubic decimeters to cubic centimeters, multiply by 1000; that is, move the decimal point three places to the right. Also, since 1 cm = 0.01 m, then 1 cm³ = (0.01 × 0.01 × 0.01) m³, or 0.000001 m³. Thus, to convert from cubic centimeters to cubic meters, all that is required is to move the decimal point six places to the left.

EXAMPLE 13-19 Convert each of the following.
(a) 5 m³ = _____ cm³   (b) 12,300 mm³ = _____ cm³

SOLUTION (a) 1 m = 100 cm, so 1 m³ = (100 cm)(100 cm)(100 cm), or 1,000,000 cm³. Thus, 5 m³ = (5)(1,000,000 cm³) = 5,000,000 cm³.
(b) 1 mm = 0.1 cm, so 1 mm³ = (0.1 cm)(0.1 cm)(0.1 cm), or 0.001 cm³. Thus, 12,300 mm³ = 12,300(0.001 cm³) = 12.3 cm³.

In the metric system, cubic units may be used for either dry or liquid measure, although units such as liters and milliliters are usually used for capacity measures—that is, for liquids. By definition, a **liter,** symbolized by L, equals, or is the capacity of, a cubic decimeter; that is, 1 L = 1 dm³. (L is not a universally accepted symbol for liter. In the United States, however, L is preferred to either ℓ or l.)

liter

Because 1 L = 1 dm³ and 1 dm³ = 1000 cm³, it follows that 1 L = 1000 cm³ and 1 cm³ = 0.001 L. Prefixes can be used with all base units in the metric system, so 0.001 L = 1 milliliter = 1 mL. Hence, 1 cm³ = 1 mL. These relationships are summarized in Figure 13-49.

FIGURE 13-49

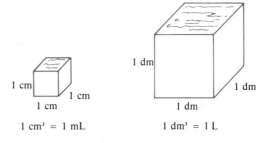

1 cm³ = 1 mL   1 dm³ = 1 L

The metric prefixes used with linear measure can also be used with the liter. Symbols and conversions work just as they did for length. Table 13-6 shows how metric units involving the liter are related.

TABLE 13-6

Unit	Symbol	Relation to Liter	
kiloliter	kL	1000	liters
*hectoliter	hL	100	liters
*dekaliter	daL	10	liters
liter	**L**	**1**	**liter**
*deciliter	dL	0.1	liter
centiliter	cL	0.01	liter
milliliter	mL	0.001	liter

* Not commonly used.

EXAMPLE 13-20   Convert each of the following as indicated.

(a) 27 L = _____ mL   (b) 362 mL = _____ L
(c) 3 mL = _____ cm³   (d) 3 m³ = _____ L

SOLUTION   (a) 1 L = 1000 mL, so 27 L = 27 · 1000 mL = 27,000 mL.
(b) 1 mL = 0.001 L, so 362 mL = 362(0.001 L) = 0.362 L.
(c) 1 mL = 1 cm³, so 3 mL = 3 cm³.
(d) 1 m³ = 1000 dm³ and 1 dm³ = 1 L, so 1 m³ = 1000 L and 3 m³ = 3000 L.

English Measure of Volume

Basic units of volume in the English system are the cubic foot (1 ft.³), the cubic yard (1 yd.³), and the cubic inch (1 in.³). In the United States, 1 gallon = 231 in.³, which is about 3.7853 L, and 1 quart = $\frac{1}{4}$ gallon or 57.749 in.³.

Relationships among the one-dimensional units enable us to convert from one unit of volume to another as shown in the following example.

EXAMPLE 13-21   Convert each of the following, as indicated.

(a) 45 yd.³ = _____ ft.³
(b) 4320 in.³ = _____ yd.³
(c) 10 gal. = _____ ft.³
(d) 3 ft.³ = _____ yd.³

SOLUTION   (a) Because 1 yd.³ = (3 ft.)³ = 27 ft.³, we have 45 yd.³ = 45 · 27 ft.³, or 1215 ft.³.

(b) Because 1 in. $= \frac{1}{36}$ yd., we have 1 in.$^3 = (\frac{1}{36})^3$ yd.^{3} Consequently, 4320 in.$^3 = 4320 \cdot (\frac{1}{36})^3$ yd.$^3 \doteq 0.0926$ yd.^{3}.

(c) Because 1 gal. $= 231$ in.^{3} and 1 in.$^3 = (\frac{1}{12})^3$ ft.^{3}, we have 10 gal. $= 2310$ in.$^3 = 2310(\frac{1}{12})^3$ ft.$^3 \doteq 1.337$ ft.^{3}.

(d) As seen in part (a), 1 ft.$^3 = \frac{1}{27}$ yd.^{3}. Hence 3 ft.$^3 = 3 \cdot \frac{1}{27}$ yd.$^3 = \frac{1}{9}$ yd.^{3}.

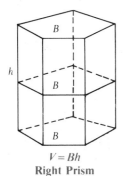

$V = Bh$

Right Prism

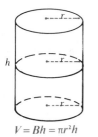

$V = Bh = \pi r^2 h$

Right circular cylinder

FIGURE 13-50

Volume of Right Prisms and Right Cylinders

The volume of a right rectangular prism is given by $V = \ell wh$, where ℓ and w are the length and width of a base, respectively, and h is the height of the prism. Notice that ℓw is the area of a base of the prism. Hence, using B for the area of the base, the formula can be written as $V = Bh$. The same formula holds for any three-dimensional figure *if* all cross sections parallel to the base are congruent to the base. The formulas for volumes of right prisms and right circular cylinders are given in Figure 13-50. The formulas of Figure 13-50 can be intuitively justified by considering three-dimensional figures made of clay. For example, consider the right prism in Figure 13-51(a). Because all the parallel cross sections of the prism are congruent, we should be able to deform the clay model into the right rectangular prism shown in Figure 13-51(b) without changing its altitude or the area of the base. Because the amount of material does not change, the volume of the rectangular prism should be the same as the volume of the original prism. The volume of the rectangular prism is $B_1 h_1$, where B_1 is the area of the rectangular base and h_1 is the height of the rectangular prism. Because $B_1 = B$ and $h_1 = h$, where B and h are the area of the base and the height of the original prism, respectively, it follows that the volume of the original prism is Bh.

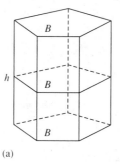

(a)

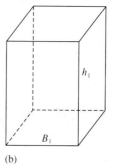

(b)

FIGURE 13-51

EXAMPLE 13-22   Find the volume of each of the figures in Figure 13-52.

FIGURE 13-52

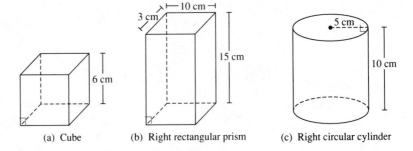

(a) Cube   (b) Right rectangular prism   (c) Right circular cylinder

SOLUTION
(a) $V = Bh = (6 \text{ cm} \cdot 6 \text{ cm}) \cdot 6 \text{ cm} = 216 \text{ cm}^3$
(b) $V = Bh = (10 \text{ cm} \cdot 3 \text{ cm}) \cdot 15 \text{ cm} = 450 \text{ cm}^3$
(c) $V = \pi r^2 h = \pi(5 \text{ cm})^2 \cdot 10 \text{ cm} = 250 \pi \text{ cm}^3$

H I S T O R I C A L   N O T E

Bonaventura Cavalieri (1598–1647), an Italian mathematician and disciple of
Galileo, contributed to the development of geometry, trigonometry, and algebra in
the Renaissance. He became a Jesuit at an early age and later, after reading
Euclid's *Elements*, was inspired to study mathematics. In 1629, Cavalieri became a
professor at Bologna and held that post until his death. Cavalieri is best known for
his principle concerning the volumes of solids.

Cavalieri's Principle

Figure 13-53 shows a right triangular prism that has an equilateral triangle
as a base. This prism can be separated into three pyramids with bases of
equal area and with heights the same as that of the prism. In this special
case, the volume of the right triangular pyramid is one-third the volume of
the triangular prism; that is, $V = \frac{1}{3}Bh$. This can also be demonstrated by
building three paper models of the pyramids and fitting them together into
a prism.

FIGURE 13-53

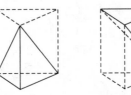

$V = \frac{1}{3}Bh$
Right triangular pyramid

Formulas for many other three-dimensional figures can be derived by using a principle based on a phenomenon described in Figure 13-54. In Figure 13-54(a), a rectangular box has been sliced into thin layers. If the layers are shifted to form the solids in Figure 13-54(b) and (c), the volume of each of the three solids is the same as the volume of the original rectangular box. The principle based on the phenomenon described in Figure 13-54 is referred to as *Cavalieri's Principle*.

FIGURE 13-54

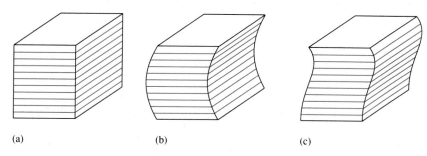

(a)   (b)   (c)

● C A V A L I E R I' S P R I N C I P L E
Two solids with bases in the same plane have equal volumes if every plane parallel to the bases intersects the solids in cross sections of equal area.

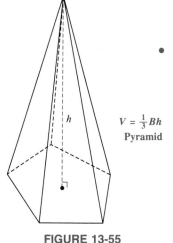

$V = \frac{1}{3}Bh$
Pyramid

Using Cavalieri's Principle, it can be shown that two pyramids that have the same height and the same base areas also have the same volume. Consequently, we have the following

The *volume of any pyramid is $\frac{1}{3}Bh$*, where B is the area of the base and h is the height.

This result is illustrated in Figure 13-55 for a pyramid with a pentagonal base.

FIGURE 13-55

Volume of a Right Circular Cone

To find the volume of a right cone with a circular base, as shown in Figure 13-56, consider the polygonal base of a pyramid with many sides. The base

FIGURE 13-56

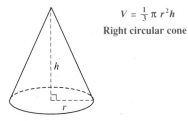

$V = \frac{1}{3}\pi r^2 h$
Right circular cone

approximates a circle, and the volume of the pyramid is approximately the volume of the cone with the circle as a base and the same height as the pyramid. The area of the base is approximately πr^2, where r is the apothem of the polygon. Hence, the formula for the volume of a right circular cone with a circular base is $V = \frac{1}{3}\pi r^2 h$ or $V = \frac{1}{3}Bh$.

EXAMPLE 13-23 Find the volume of each of the figures in Figure 13-57.

FIGURE 13-57

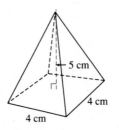

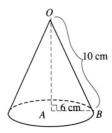

(a) Right square pyramid   (b) Right circular cone

SOLUTION (a) The figure is a pyramid with a square base whose area is (4 cm · 4 cm) and whose height is 5 cm. Hence, $V = \frac{1}{3}Bh = \frac{1}{3}(4 \text{ cm} \cdot 4 \text{ cm})(5 \text{ cm}) = \frac{80}{3}$ cm³.

(b) The base of the cone is a circle of radius 6 cm. Because the volume of the cone is given by $V = \frac{1}{3}\pi r^2 h$, we need to know the height. In the right triangle OAB, $OA = h$ and, by the Pythagorean Theorem, $h^2 + 6^2 = 10^2$. Hence, $h^2 = 100 - 36$, or 64, and $h = 8$ cm. Thus, $V = \frac{1}{3}\pi r^2 h = \frac{1}{3}\pi(6 \text{ cm})^2(8 \text{ cm}) = 96\pi$ cm³.

EXAMPLE 13-24 Figure 13-58 may be assembled into a pyramid. Find its volume.

FIGURE 13-58

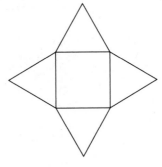

All segments 10 cm

SOLUTION The folded-up pyramid obtained is shown in Figure 13-59. The volume of the pyramid is $V = \frac{1}{3}Bh = \frac{1}{3} \cdot 10^2 h$. We must find h. Notice that h is a leg

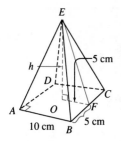

FIGURE 13-59

in the right triangle EOF, where F is the midpoint of CB. We know that $OF = 5$ cm. If we knew EF, we could find h by applying the Pythagorean Theorem to $\triangle EOF$. To find the length of $\overline{EF}$, notice that $\overline{EF}$ is a leg in the right triangle EBF. ($\overline{EF}$ is the perpendicular bisector of $\overline{BC}$ in the equilateral triangle BEC.) In the right triangle EBF, we have $(EB)^2 = (BF)^2 + (EF)^2$. Because $EB = 10$ cm and $BF = 5$ cm, it follows that $10^2 = 5^2 + (EF)^2$, or $EF = \sqrt{75}$ cm $\doteq 8.66$ cm. In $\triangle EOF$, we have $h^2 + 5^2 = (EF)^2$, or $h^2 + 25 = 75$. Thus, $h = \sqrt{50}$ cm $\doteq 7.07$ cm, and $V = \frac{1}{3} \cdot 10^2 \cdot 7.07 \doteq 235.7$ cm³.

Volume of a Sphere

To find the volume of a sphere, imagine that a sphere is composed of a great number of congruent pyramids with apexes at the center of the sphere and that the vertices of the base touch the sphere, as shown in Figure 13-60. If the pyramids have very small bases, then the height of each pyramid is nearly the radius r. Hence, the volume of each pyramid is $\frac{1}{3}Bh$ or $\frac{1}{3}Br$, where B is the area of the base. If there are n pyramids each with base area B, then the total volume of the pyramids is $V = \frac{1}{3}nBr$. Because nB is the total surface area of all the bases of the pyramids and because the sum of the areas of all the bases of the pyramids is very close to the surface area of the sphere, $4\pi r^2$, the volume of the sphere is given by $V = \frac{1}{3}(4\pi r^2)r = \frac{4}{3}\pi r^3$.

FIGURE 13-60

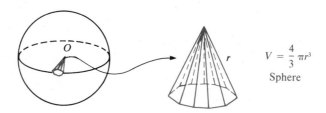

$$V = \frac{4}{3}\pi r^3$$
Sphere

EXAMPLE 13-25   Find the volume of a sphere whose radius is 6 cm.

SOLUTION $V = \dfrac{4}{3}\pi(6 \text{ cm})^3 = \dfrac{4}{3}\pi(216 \text{ cm}^3) = 288\pi \text{ cm}^3$

PROBLEM 2

Half the air is let out of a spherical balloon. If the balloon remains in the shape of a sphere, how does the radius of the smaller balloon compare to the original radius?

Understanding the Problem. In Figure 13-61(b) the volume of the smaller balloon is half the volume of the original balloon in Figure 13-61(a). We are to find a relationship between the radii R and r of the two balloons.

FIGURE 13-61

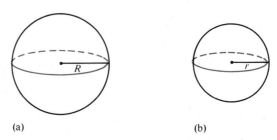

(a)   (b)

Devising a Plan. We can express the volume of each balloon in Figure 13-61 in terms of its radius. Because the volume of the smaller balloon is half the volume of the original balloon, we know that the ratio of their volumes is 1:2, or $\frac{1}{2}$. From that ratio, we should be able to find the ratio between the radii.

Carrying Out the Plan. Let V be the volume of the original balloon, and let v be the volume of the smaller balloon. Using the formula for the volume of a sphere, we obtain the following ratio: $\frac{v}{V} = \frac{\frac{4}{3}\pi r^3}{\frac{4}{3}\pi R^3} = \frac{r^3}{R^3}$. Because $\frac{v}{V} = \frac{1}{2}$, we have $\frac{1}{2} = \frac{r^3}{R^3}$, or $\left(\frac{r}{R}\right)^3 = \frac{1}{2}$. Hence, $\frac{r}{R} = \sqrt[3]{\frac{1}{2}}$, or $\sqrt[3]{0.5}$. Using a calculator with a cube-root function, we find that $r/R \doteq 0.8$, or $r \doteq 0.8R$.

Looking Back. Similar questions could also be asked concerning other solids. For example, we could ask how the sides of two square boxes compare if the volume of one of the boxes is half the volume of the other. We could also generalize the original question by assuming that an arbitrary fraction (or percent) of the air is let out of the balloon.

PROBLEM 3

A manufacturer of metal cans has a large quantity of rectangular metal sheets 20 cm wide by 30 cm long. Without cutting the sheets, the manager wants to make cylindrical pipes with circular cross sections from some of the sheets and box-shaped pipes with square cross sections from the other sheets so that the volume of the box-shaped pipes is greater than the volume of the cylindrical pipes. Is this possible? If so, how should the pipes be made and what are their volumes?

Understanding the Problem. A manufacturer wants to use 20-cm by 30-cm rectangular sheets of metal to make some cylindrical pipes and some box-shaped pipes with square cross sections that have a greater volume than the cylindrical pipes. Is this possible, and if so, how should the pipes be designed and what are their volumes?

Figure 13-62 shows a sheet of metal and two sections of pipe made from it, one cylindrical and the other box-shaped. A model for such pipes can be designed from a piece of paper by bending it into a cylinder or by folding it into a right rectangular prism, as shown.

FIGURE 13-62

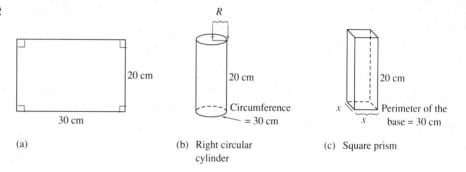

(a)

(b) Right circular cylinder

(c) Square prism

Devising a Plan. If we can compute the volume of the cylinder in Figure 13-62(b) and the volume of the prism in Figure 13-62(c), we can determine which has a greater volume. If the prism has a greater volume, the solution of the problem will be complete. If not, we will need to look for other ways to design the pipes before concluding that a solution is impossible.

To compute the volume of the cylinder, we need to find the area of the base. The area of the circular base is πR^2. To find R, we note that the circumference, of the circle $2\pi R$, is 30 cm. Thus, $R = \dfrac{30}{2\pi} \doteq 4.78$ cm, and the area of the circle is $\pi R^2 = \pi(4.78)^2 \doteq 71.74$ cm². With the given information, we can also find the area of the base of the rectangular box.

Similarly, because the perimeter of the base of the prism is $4x$, we have $4x = 30$, or $x = 7.5$ cm. Thus, the area of the square base is $x^2 = (7.5)^2$, or 56.25 cm².

Carrying Out the Plan. Denoting the volume of the cylindrical pipe by V_1 and the volume of the box-shaped pipe by V_2, we have $V_1 \doteq 71.74 \cdot 20$, or approximately 1434.8 cm³. For the volume of the box-shaped pipe, we have $V_2 \doteq 56.25 \cdot 20$, or 1125 cm². We see that, in our first design for the pipes, the volume of the cylindrical pipe is greater than the volume of the box-shaped pipe, which is not the required outcome.

Are there other ways to design the pipes? Rather than bending the rectangular sheet of metal along the 30-cm side, we could bend it along the 20-cm side to obtain either pipe, as shown in Figure 13-63. Denoting the radius of the cylindrical pipe by r, the side of the box-shaped pipe by y, and their volumes by V_3 and V_4, respectively, we have $V_3 = \pi r^2 \cdot 30 = \pi(20/2\pi)^2 \cdot 30 = (10^2 \cdot 30)/\pi$, or approximately 954.9 cm³. Also, $V_4 = y^2 \cdot 30 = (\frac{20}{4})^2 \cdot 30 = 25 \cdot 30$ or 750 cm³. Because $V_2 = 1125$ cm³ and $V_3 = 945.9$ cm³, we see that the volume of the box-shaped pipe with an altitude of 20 cm [see Figure 13-62(c)] is greater than the volume of the cylindrical pipe with an altitude of 30 cm [see Figure 13-63(b)].

FIGURE 13-63

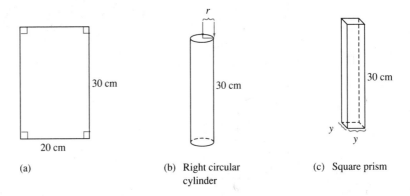

30 cm

20 cm

(a)

r

30 cm

(b) Right circular cylinder

30 cm

y

y

(c) Square prism

Looking Back. We could ask for the volumes of other three-dimensional objects that can be obtained by bending the rectangular sheets of metal. Also, because the lateral surface areas of the four types of pipes were the same but their volumes were different, we might want to investigate whether there are other cylinders and prisms that have the same lateral surface area and the same volume. Also, is it possible to find a circular cylinder with lateral surface area of 600 cm² and smallest possible volume? Similarly, is there a circular cylinder with the given surface area and greatest possible volume?

PROBLEM SET 13-5

1. Complete each of the following.
   (a) $8 \text{ m}^3 = $ _____ dm^3
   (b) $500 \text{ cm}^3 = $ _____ m^3
   (c) $675,000 \text{ m}^3 = $ _____ km^3
   (d) $3 \text{ m}^3 = $ _____ cm^3
   (e) $7000 \text{ mm}^3 = $ _____ cm^3
   (f) $0.002 \text{ m}^3 = $ _____ cm^3
   (g) $400 \text{ in.}^3 = $ _____ yd.^3
   (h) $25 \text{ yd.}^3 = $ _____ ft.^3
   (i) $0.2 \text{ ft.}^3 = $ _____ in.^3
   (j) $1200 \text{ in.}^3 = $ _____ ft.^3

2. Why is a unit sphere, a sphere with radius 1 cm, not a "good" unit of volume measure, even for measuring the volume of another sphere?

3. Find the volume of each of the following.

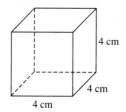

(a) Right rectangular prism

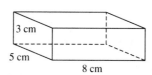

(b) Right rectangular prism

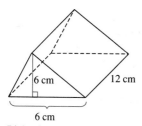

(c) Right triangular prism

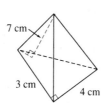

(d) Pyramid with a right triangle as base

(e) Square pyramid

(f) Right circular cone

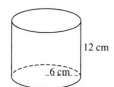

(g) Right circular cylinder

(h) Sphere

4. Find the volume of each of the following.

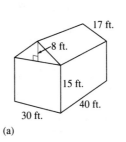

(a)

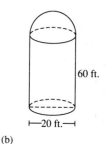

(b)

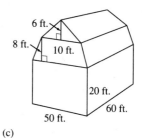

(c)

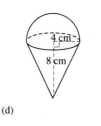

(d)

5. Complete the following chart.

	(a)	(b)	(c)	(d)	(e)	(f)
cm³		500			750	4800
dm³	2					
L			1.5			
mL				5000		

6. Place a decimal point in each of the following to make it an accurate sentence.
   (a) A paper cup holds about 2000 mL.
   (b) A regular soft drink bottle holds about 320 L.
   (c) A quart milk container holds about 10 L.
   (d) A teaspoonful of cough syrup is about 500 mL.

7. What volume of silver is needed to make the napkin ring out of solid silver? Give your answer in cubic millimeters.

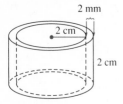

2 mm

2 cm

2 cm

8. Two cubes have sides of lengths 4 cm and 6 cm, respectively. What is the ratio of their volumes?
9. What happens to the volume of a sphere if the radius is doubled?
10. Complete the chart for right rectangular prisms with the given dimensions.

	(a)	(b)	(c)	(d)
Length	20 cm	10 cm	2 dm	15 cm
Width	10 cm	2 dm	1 dm	2 dm
Height	10 cm	3 dm		
Volume in cm³				
Volume in dm³				7.5 dm³
Volume in L			4 L	

11. A right cylindrical tank holds how many liters if it is 6 m long and 13 m in diameter?
12. If the length of the diameter of the Earth is approximately four times the length of the diameter of the moon and both bodies are spheres, what is the ratio of their volumes?
13. A bread pan is 18 cm × 18 cm × 5 cm. How many liters does it hold?
14. An Olympic pool in the shape of a right rectangular prism is 50 m long and 25 m wide. If it is 2 m deep throughout, how many liters of water does it hold?
15. If a faucet is dripping at the rate of 15 drops per minute and there are 20 drops per milliliter, how many liters of water are wasted in a 30-day month?
16. A standard straw is 25 cm long and 4 mm in diameter. How much liquid can be held in the straw at one time?
17. A cross section of a water pipe is a ring whose large circle has a radius of 14.5 cm and whose smaller circle has a radius of 5 cm.
    (a) Find the number of liters of water the pipe can hold if it is 10 m long.
    (b) How long should the pipe be if it is to hold 1,000,000 L of water?

18. A theater decides to change the shape of its popcorn container from a regular box to a right regular pyramid and charge only half as much. If the containers are the same height and the tops are the same size, is this a bargain for the customer?

19. Which is the better buy, a grapefruit 5 cm in radius that costs 22¢ or a grapefruit 6 cm in radius that costs 31¢?
20. Two spherical cantaloupes of the same kind are sold at a fruit and vegetable stand. The circumference of one of the melons is 60 cm, and that of the other is 50 cm. The larger melon is 1½ times as expensive as the smaller. Which melon is a better buy and why?
21. A regular square pyramid is 3 m high and the perimeter of its base is 16 m. Find the volume of the pyramid.
22. A right rectangular prism with base ABCD as the bottom is shown. Suppose that X is drawn so that AX = 3 · AP, where AP is the height of the prism, and X is connected to A, B, C, and D, forming a pyramid. How do the volumes of the pyramid and the prism compare?

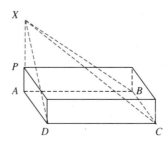

23. A right cylindrical can is to hold exactly 1 L of water. What should the height of the can be if the radius is 12 cm?
24. A box is packed with six pop cans, as shown. What percent of the volume of the interior of the box is not occupied by the pop cans?

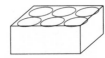

25. An engineer is supposed to design a square-based pyramid whose volume is to be 100 m³.
    (a) Find the dimensions (the length of a side of the square and the altitude) of one such pyramid.
    (b) How many (noncongruent) such pyramids are possible? Why?
26. A square pyramid has a lateral surface area of 2 m². Its height equals the length of the side of the square base. Find the volume of the pyramid.
27. A square sheet of cardboard measuring y cm on a side is to be used to produce an open-top box when the maker cuts off a small square x cm by x cm from each corner and bends up the sides.
    (a) Find the volume of the box if y = 200 cm and x = 20 cm.
    ★(b) Assume that y is known; find the expression for the volume V as a function of x.
★28. If each edge and each side of the base of a right regular pyramid is increased or decreased by the same factor, the new right regular pyramid is said to be similar to the original one. Show that the ratio of the volumes of two square right pyramids equals the cube of the ratio of their corresponding heights.

Review Problems

29. Find the surface areas of the following.

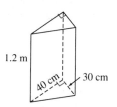

1.2 m

40 cm   30 cm

(a) Right prism

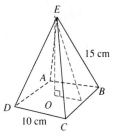

(b) Right square pyramid

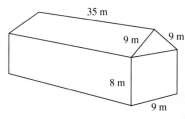

35 m

9 m   9 m

8 m

9 m

(c) Barn (include floor)

30. The diagonal of a rectangle has measure 1.3 m, and a side has measure 120 cm. Find each of the following.
    (a) Perimeter of the rectangle
    (b) Area of the rectangle
31. Find the area of a triangle that has sides of 3 m, 3 m, and 2 m.
32. A poster is to contain 0.25 m² of printed matter, with margins of 12 cm at top and bottom and 6 cm at each side. Find the width of the poster if its height is 74 cm.

LABORATORY ACTIVITY

1. As a van Hiele Level 1 activity, work with 30 congruent cubes. Build the largest cube possible by stacking the cubes. How many of the given cubes did you need to build your cube?
2. As a van Hiele Level 2 activity, use 24 congruent cubes to build solids with the following characteristics.
   (a) The greatest possible surface area
   (b) The least possible surface area

*Section 13-6   Mass and Temperature

Three centuries ago, Isaac Newton pointed out that, in everyday life, the term *weight* is used for what is really mass. He called *mass* a quantity of matter as opposed to *weight,* which is a force exerted by gravitational pull. When an astronaut is in orbit above the Earth, his weight has changed even though his mass remains the same. In common parlance on the Earth, weight and mass are still used interchangeably. In the English system, weight is measured in pounds and ounces. We use the avoirdupois units here. One pound (lb) equals 16 ounces (oz) and 2000 pounds equals 1 English ton.

gram

In the metric system, the base unit for mass is the **gram,** denoted by g. A gram is the mass of 1 cm³ of water. An ordinary paper clip or a thumbtack each has a mass of about 1 g.

As with other base metric units, prefixes are added to gram to obtain other units. For example, a kilogram (kg) is 1000 g. Since 1 cm³ of water has a mass of 1 g, the mass of 1 L of water is 1 kg. A person's mass is measured in kilograms. Two standard loaves of bread have a mass of about 1 kg. A newborn baby has a mass of about 4 kg. Another unit of mass in

metric ton

the metric system is the **metric ton** (t), which is equal to 1000 kg. The metric ton is used to record the masses of objects such as cars and trucks. A small foreign car has a mass of about 1 t.

Table 13-7 lists metric units of mass. Conversions involving metric units of mass are handled in the same way as conversions involving metric units of length. Notice that, in contrast to the English system, the metric units of mass (like other metric units) are defined in terms of each other, using simple relationships.

TABLE 13-7

Unit	Symbol	Relationship to Gram	
ton (metric)	t	1,000,000	grams
kilogram	kg	1000	grams
*hectogram	hg	100	grams
*dekagram	dag	10	grams
gram	**g**	**1**	**gram**
*decigram	dg	0.1	gram
*centigram	cg	0.01	gram
milligram	mg	0.001	gram

* Not commonly used.

EXAMPLE 13-26   Complete each of the following.

(a) 34 g = _____ kg   (b) 6836 kg = _____ t

SOLUTION   (a) 34 g = 34(0.001 kg) = 0.034 kg
(b) 6836 kg = 6836(0.001 t) = 6.836 t

The relationship among the units of volume and mass in the metric system is illustrated in Figure 13-64.

FIGURE 13-64

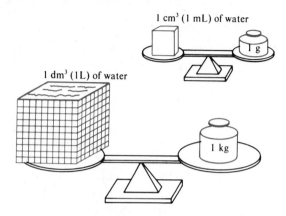

1 cm³ (1 mL) of water

1 g

1 dm³ (1L) of water

1 kg

EXAMPLE 13-27   A waterbed is 180 cm wide, 210 cm long, and 20 cm thick.

(a) How many liters of water can it hold?

(b) What is its mass in kilograms when it is full of water?

SOLUTION   (a) The volume of the waterbed is found by multiplying the length times the width times the height.

$$V = \ell wh$$

$$= 180 \text{ cm} \cdot 210 \text{ cm} \cdot 20 \text{ cm}$$

$$= 756{,}000 \text{ cm}^3, \text{ or } 756{,}000 \text{ mL}$$

Because 1 mL = 0.001 L, the volume is 756 L.

(b) Because 1 L of water has a mass of 1 kg, 756 L of water has a mass of 756 kg.

• R E M A R K

To see one advantage of the metric system, suppose that the bed is 6 ft. by 7 ft. by 9 in. Try to find the volume in gallons and the weight of the water in pounds.

Temperature

degree Kelvin   The base unit of temperature for the metric system is the **degree Kelvin.** However, it is used only for scientific measurements, not for everyday measurements of temperature. For normal temperature measurements in the *degree Celsius*   metric system, the base unit is the **degree Celsius,** named for Anders Celsius, the Swedish scientist who invented the system. The Celsius scale has 100 equal divisions between 0 degrees Celsius (0°C), the freezing point of water, and 100 degrees Celsius (100°C), the boiling point of water. In the English system, the Fahrenheit scale has 180 equal divisions between 32°F, the freezing point of water, and 212°F, the boiling point of water.

Figure 13-65 gives some temperature comparisons of the two scales and further illustrates the relationship between them. Because the Celsius scale has 100 divisions between the freezing point and the boiling point of water, whereas the Fahrenheit scale has 180 divisions, the relationship between the two scales is 100 to 180 or 5 to 9. Hence, for every 5 degrees on the Celsius scale, there are 9 degrees on the Fahrenheit scale, and for each degree on the Fahrenheit scale, there is $\frac{5}{9}$ degree on the Celsius scale. The fact that the ratio between the number of degrees above freezing on the Celsius scale and the number of degrees above freezing on the Fahrenheit scale remains the same and equals $\frac{5}{9}$ enables us to convert temperatures from one system to the other. For example, suppose that we want to convert 50° on the Fahrenheit scale to the corresponding number on the Celsius scale. On the Fahrenheit scale, 50° is 50 − 32, or 18°, above freezing, but on the Celsius scale, it is $\frac{5}{9} \cdot 18$, or 10°, above freezing. Because the freezing temperature on the Celsius scale is 0°, 10° above freezing is 10° Celsius. Thus, 50°F = 10°C. In general, F degrees is $F - 32$ above freezing on the Fahrenheit scale, but only $\frac{5}{9}(F - 32)$ above freezing on the Celsius scale. Thus, we have the relation $C = \frac{5}{9}(F - 32)$. If we solve the equation for F, we obtain $F = \frac{9}{5}C + 32$. Rather than memorize these formulas, we encourage you to reason as shown to convert from one scale to the other.

FIGURE 13-65

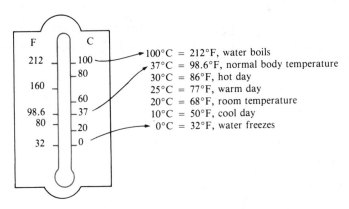

EXAMPLE 13-28 Convert 20°C to degrees Fahrenheit.

SOLUTION For 100 divisions on the Celsius scale, we have 212 − 32, or 180, divisions on the Fahrenheit scale. Hence, for every 1 degree on the Celsius scale, there are $\frac{180}{100}$, or $\frac{9}{5}$, degrees on the Fahrenheit scale. Because 20°C is 20° above freezing, on the Fahrenheit scale it would be $\frac{9}{5} \cdot 20$, or 36, degrees above freezing, or 32 + 36, or 68 degrees. Thus, 20°C = 68°F.

• **R E M A R K**
The Celsius scale is also known as the *centigrade scale,* because it is divided into
100 degrees.

H I S T O R I C A L   N O T E

Gabriel Daniel Fahrenheit (1686–1736) was a German physicist who contributed to
the construction of improved thermometers and introduced the scale bearing his
name. He lived most of his life in England and Holland and made a living
manufacturing meteorological instruments.

Anders Celsius (1701–1744) was a Swedish astronomer. He was a professor
at the University of Uppsala. In 1742 he described the centigrade scale in a paper
before the Swedish Academy of Sciences.

PROBLEM SET 13-6

1. For each of the following, select the appropriate
   metric unit of measure (gram, kilogram, or metric
   ton).
   (a) Car
   (b) Woman
   (c) Can of frozen orange juice
   (d) Elephant
   (e) Jar of mustard
   (f) Bag of peanuts
   (g) Army tank
   (h) Cat
   (i) Dictionary

2. For each of the following, choose the correct unit
   (milligram, gram, or kilogram) to make each sentence reasonable.
   (a) A staple has a mass of about 340 _____.
   (b) A professional football player has a mass of
       about 110 _____.
   (c) A vitamin tablet has a mass of 1100 _____.
   (d) A dime has a mass of 2 _____.
   (e) The recipe said to add 4 _____ of salt.
   (f) One strand of hair has a mass of 2 _____.

3. Complete each of the following.
   (a) 15,000 g = _____ kg
   (b) 8000 kg = _____ t
   (c) 0.036 kg = _____ g
   (d) 72 g = _____ kg
   (e) 4230 mg = _____ g
   (f) 3 g 7 mg = _____ g
   (g) 5 kg 750 g = _____ g
   (h) 5 kg 750 g = _____ kg
   (i) 0.03 t = _____ kg
   (j) 0.03 t = _____ g
   (k) 2.6 lb = _____ oz
   (l) 25 oz = _____ lb
   (m) 50 oz = _____ lb
   (n) 3.8 lb = _____ oz

4. If a paper dollar has a mass of approximately 1 g, is
   it possible to lift $1,000,000 in the following
   denominations?
   (a) $1 bills   (b) $10 bills   (c) $100 bills
   (d) $1000 bills   (e) $10,000 bills

5. A fish tank, which is a right rectangular prism, is
   40 cm by 20 cm by 20 cm. If it is filled with water,
   what is the mass of the water?

6. In a grocery store, one kind of meat costs $5.80 per
   kilogram. How much does 400 g of this meat cost?

7. If a certain spice costs $20 per kilogram, how much
   does 1 g cost?

8. Abel bought a kilogram of Moxwill coffee for $9 and
   Babel bought 400 g of the same brand of coffee for
   $4.60. Who made the better buy?

9. Convert each of the following from degrees Fahrenheit to the nearest integer degree Celsius.
   (a) 10°F   (b) 0°F   (c) 30°F
   (d) 100°F   (e) 212°F   (f) ⁻40°F

10. Answer each of the following.
    (a) The thermometer reads 20°C. Can you go snow
        skiing?
    (b) The thermometer reads 26°C. Will the outdoor
        ice rink be open?
    (c) Your temperature is 37°C. Do you have a fever?
    (d) If your body temperature is 39°C, are you ill?
    (e) It is 40°C. Will you need a sweater at the out-
        door concert?
    (f) The temperature reads 35°C. Should you go
        water skiing?

(g) The temperature reads ⁻10°C. Is it appropriate to go ice fishing?

(h) Your bath water is 16°C. Will you have a hot, warm, or chilly bath?

(i) It's 30°C in the room. Are you uncomfortably hot or cold?

11. Convert each of the following from degrees Celsius to the nearest integer degree Fahrenheit.
   (a) 10°C   (b) 0°C   (c) 30°C
   (d) 100°C   (e) 212°C   (f) ⁻40°C

Review Problems

12. Find the perimeter and the area of the following.

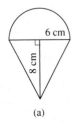

(a)

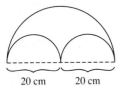

(b)

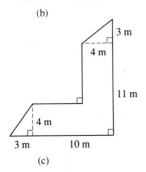

(c)

13. Complete the following.
   (a) 350 mm = _____ cm
   (b) 1600 cm² = _____ m²
   (c) 0.4 m² = _____ mm²
   (d) 5.2 m³ = _____ cm³
   (e) 5.2 m³ = _____ L
   (f) 3500 cm³ = _____ m³

14. Determine whether each of the following is a right triangle.

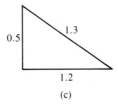

(a)

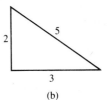

(b)

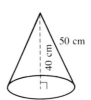

(c)

15. A person walks 5 km north, 3 km east, 1 km north, and then 2 km east. How far is the person from the starting point?

16. Find the volume and the surface area of each of the solids.

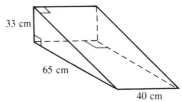

(a) Right circular cone

(b)   Right prism in which the faces are either rectangles or right triangles

LABORATORY ACTIVITY

1. Record the mass of each U.S. coin. Which coin has the greatest mass? Which of the following sets have the same mass?
   (a) A half-dollar vs. two quarters
   (b) A quarter vs. two dimes and a nickel
   (c) A dime vs. two nickels
   (d) A dime vs. ten pennies
   (e) A nickel vs. five pennies
2. Record the temperature of the room on a Celsius thermometer. Pour 200 mL of water into a liter container. Record the temperature of the water. Add 100 mL of ice to the water. Wait one minute and record the temperature of the ice water.

*Section 13-7   Using Logo to Draw Circles

Recall the POLYGON procedure that was developed in Chapter 10 for drawing regular polygons with :N and :SIZE representing the number of sides and the length of a side, respectively. The procedure is as follows.

```
TO POLYGON :N :SIZE
  REPEAT :N [FD :SIZE RT 360/:N]
END
```

The ideas in the POLYGON procedure can be used to demonstrate the mathematical concept that, as the number of sides in a regular polygon increases, the figure approaches a circle. When the turtle is at home with heading 0, the procedure called POLYGONS that follows can be used to draw an equilateral triangle, followed by a square, followed by a regular pentagon, followed by a regular hexagon, and so on, until a regular 20-gon is drawn. The result of executing POLYGONS 3 is shown in Figure 13-66.

FIGURE 13-66

```
TO POLYGONS :N
  FULLSCREEN
  POLYGON :N 20
  IF :N > 20 STOP
  POLYGONS :N + 1
END
```

(*In Apple Logo II, change IF:N>20 STOP to IF :N > 20 [STOP].*)

• R E M A R K

The command FULLSCREEN gives full graphics capability for drawing.

Drawing Turtle-Type Circles

To instruct the turtle to draw a figure that looks like a circle (*turtle-type circle*), we must tell the turtle to move forward a little and turn a little and then repeat this sequence of motions until it comes back to its original position. If the turtle is told to go forward 1 unit and then to turn right 1°, then this sequence of motions repeated 360 times yields a turtle-type circle. The CIRCLE1 procedure from Appendix II along with its output is given in Figure 13-67.

FIGURE 13-67

```
TO CIRCLE1
  REPEAT 360 [FD 1 RT 1]
END
```

CIRCLE 1

The turtle-type circle determined by CIRCLE1 is actually a regular 360-gon (a polygon with 360 sides), but it is a close approximation of a circle and is referred to in Logo as a circle. One way to vary the size of the circle is to vary the amount the turtle moves forward. For example, suppose the turtle moves forward 0.5 unit rather than 1 unit, or—in general—any number of units S. We define a new procedure called VCIRCLE that accepts a variable input :S. Figure 13-68 shows various circles drawn by the VCIRCLE procedure.

FIGURE 13-68

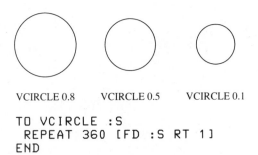

VCIRCLE 0.8   VCIRCLE 0.5   VCIRCLE 0.1

```
TO VCIRCLE :S
  REPEAT 360 [FD :S RT 1]
END
```

Sometimes, it is more useful to draw a circle of a given radius. To write a procedure for drawing a circle of radius R, we utilize the procedure for VCIRCLE and the formula $2\pi r$ for the circumference of a circle. To understand the general case better, we first solve a special case of the problem. Suppose that we want to draw a circle with radius 50. What should the side S of the approximating polygon be? Because the perimeter of the polygon is $360 \cdot S$, and the circumference of a circle with radius 50 is $2\pi \cdot 50$, it follows that $360 \cdot S \doteq 2\pi \cdot 50$. Now, $S \doteq (2\pi \cdot 50)/360$, or 0.873. Thus, VCIRCLE 0.873 will draw a circle with radius approximately 50 units long.

In general, to find a procedure to draw a circle with radius R as an input, we need to find S in terms of R. This can be done as follows.

$$360 \cdot S \doteq 2\pi R$$

$$S \doteq \frac{2\pi R}{360}$$

Hence, a procedure called CIRCLE for drawing a circle with radius R can be written as shown, where π is approximated as 3.1416.

```
TO CIRCLE :R
 VCIRCLE (2*3.1416*:R) / 360
END
```

How can we check that CIRCLE 50 draws a turtle-type circle of radius 50? This can be done by turning the turtle toward the center (after the circle has been completed) and instructing the turtle to go forward 100 units, which is the diameter of a circle with radius 50. If the turtle draws a diameter of the circle, the circle has a radius of 50 units. This check can be accomplished by executing the line

```
RT 90 FD 100 HT
```

• **R E M A R K**
It should be noted that this check is not totally accurate because our turtle-type circle is not a true circle.

Drawing Circles Faster

One way to draw circles faster by using the CIRCLE procedure is to hide the turtle before executing the procedure so that the turtle does not have to be drawn on the screen for each move. You can also speed up construction of the circle by varying the number of repeats. To close the figure, the turtle must complete a 360° trip. To ensure that this happens, the number of times the moves are repeated, multiplied by the number of degrees for each turn, must equal 360. For example, if we decide that the turtle should turn 15° each time, the process should be completed $\frac{360}{15}$, or 24, times because $15° \cdot 24 = 360°$.

In addition, if we wish the size of the faster circle to be approximately the same as that of the original circle, we need to make the perimeter of the polygon approximating the faster circle be the same as the perimeter of the polygon that drew the original approximation by using the CIRCLE procedure. This can be done by adapting the length of each side of the polygon. For example, if the original figure has perimeter 360 units, and the new figure is to have 24 sides and perimeter 360 units, then each side must have length $\frac{360}{24}$, or 15, turtle steps. Consequently, we obtain the following FCIRCLE procedure.

```
TO FCIRCLE
  REPEAT 25 [FD 15 RT 15]
END
```

As an exercise, write a procedure for drawing circles, using variables for both the length of a side and the amount of the turn.

Procedures can also be designed for drawing arcs—that is, continuous parts of a circle. For example, if we wished to draw a semicircle, we could write the following procedure.

```
TO SEMICIRCLE
  REPEAT 180 [FD 1 RT 1]
END
```

As an exercise, develop a procedure called RARC for drawing arcs of variable size.

PROBLEM SET 13-7

1. (a) In the CIRCLE1 procedure in this section, suppose that the instruction RT 1 is changed to RT 5. How does the new figure differ from the original one?
   (b) How does the figure differ if RT 1 is changed to LT 1?
2. Generalize the FCIRCLE procedure to include variable-sized sides and a variable number of repeats.
3. In the VCIRCLE procedure, if the turtle repeats the sequence FD :S RT 1 fewer than 360 times, it will draw an arc of a circle.
   (a) Write a procedure for drawing an arc for which the inputs are the length of a side of an approximating polygon and the number of degrees in the arc.
   (b) Write a procedure for drawing an arc, given the radius of the arc and the number of degrees in the arc.
4. Create your own designs, using the arc procedure developed in Problem 3(b).
5. Design a procedure to fill in a circle—that is, to color in its interior.

6. Write procedures to draw figures similar to each of the following.

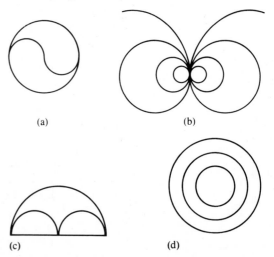

(a)

(b)

(c)

(d)

(e)

7. Write a procedure called SYMBOL for drawing the Olympic symbol in variable sizes.

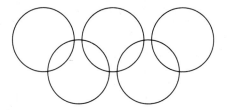

8. Use the procedures developed in Problem 3 to write a procedure to draw variable-sized flowers similar to the one shown.

9. Write a procedure called DIAMCIRC, with radius :R of a circle as an input, that draws the circle and its diameter.

SOLUTION TO THE PRELIMINARY PROBLEM

Understanding the Problem. We can roll a 10-inch by 17-inch rectangular sheet of paper into the circular cylinder in Figure 13-69(a), by rolling the 17-inch side into a circular base, or we can roll it into the circular cylinder in Figure 13-69(b), by rolling the 10-inch-long side into a circular base. We are supposed to determine which of the cylinders has the greater volume.

FIGURE 13-69

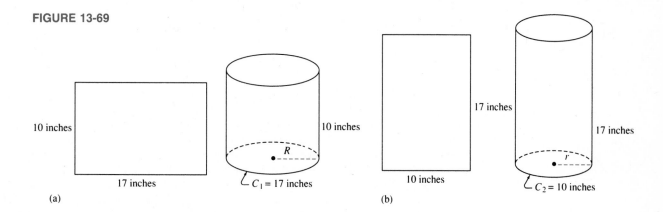

(a)

(b)

Devising a Plan. We know that the volume of a cylinder can be found by multiplying the area of the base by the height of the cylinder. Because we know the heights of the cylinders, we only need to find the area of the bases. The area of each base can be found if the radius of the circular base is known. To find R in Figure 13-69(a), notice that $C_1 = 2\pi R = 17$. Solving this equation, we can find R. Similarly, from Figure 13-69(b), we have $C_2 = 2\pi r = 10$.

Carrying Out the Plan. Solving the equation $2\pi R = 17$, we have $R = \dfrac{17}{2\pi}$. Consequently, the area of the base of the cylinder in Figure 13-69(a) is $\pi R^2 = \pi \cdot \left(\dfrac{17}{2\pi}\right)^2 = \dfrac{289}{4\pi}$ in.^{2} Thus, the volume of the cylinder is $10 \cdot \dfrac{289}{4\pi}$, or approximately 229.98 in.^{3} Similarly, the radius r of the base of the cylinder in Figure 13-69(b) can be found by solving the equation $2\pi r = 10$. Thus, $r = \dfrac{10}{2\pi}$ in. The area of the base of this cylinder is therefore $\pi r^2 = \pi \cdot \left(\dfrac{10}{2\pi}\right)^2 = \dfrac{25}{\pi}$ in.^{2} Thus, the volume of the cylinder is $17 \cdot \dfrac{25}{\pi}$, or approximately 135.28 in.^{3} Consequently, the cylinder in Figure 13-69(a) has the greater volume.

Looking Back. We could have found the greater volume without carrying out all the computations. The volume of the cylinder in Figure 13-69(a) was found to be $10 \cdot \dfrac{289}{4\pi}$, or $\dfrac{2890}{4\pi}$ in.^{2} The volume of the cylinder in Figure 13-69(b) was found to be $\dfrac{17 \cdot 25}{\pi} = \dfrac{17 \cdot 100}{4\pi}$, or $\dfrac{1700}{4\pi}$ in.^{2} Because $\dfrac{2890}{4\pi} > \dfrac{1700}{4\pi}$, the first cylinder has the greater volume.

As another Looking Back activity, notice that the two cylinders in Figure 13-69 have the same lateral surface area (which is $10 \cdot 17$, or 170, square inches) but different volumes. Is there a cylinder whose lateral surface area is 170 in.^{2} but whose volume is greater than either of the volumes we found in the problem?

QUESTIONS FROM THE CLASSROOM

1. A student asks if the units of measure must be the same for each term in order to use the formulas for volumes. How do you respond?

2. In the discussion of the Pythagorean Theorem, squares were constructed on each side of a right triangle. A student asks, "If different similar figures are constructed on each side of the triangle, does the same type of relationship still hold?" How do you reply?

3. A student asks, "Can I find the area of an angle?" How do you respond?

4. A student argues that a square has no area because its interior can be thought of as the union of infinitely many line segments, each of which has no area. How do you react?

5. A student asks whether the volume of a prism is always a lesser number than its surface area. How do you answer?

6. A student asks, "Why should the United States switch to the metric system?" How do you reply?

7. A student claims that, in a triangle with 20° and 40° angles, the side opposite the 40° angle is twice as long as the side opposite the 20° angle. How do you reply?

8. A student interpreted 5 cm³ as shown in the following drawing. What is wrong with this interpretation?

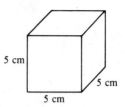

9. To approximate the value of π, a student measures the circumference C of a circle and the diameter d of the circle and finds the ratio C/d. The student wonders whether the ratio will change if she measures in English units rather than in metric units. How do you respond?

10. A student claims that, because are and hectare are measures of area, we should say "square are" and "square hectare." How do you respond?

CHAPTER OUTLINE

I. The English system
  A. Linear measure
     1 ft. = 12 in.
     1 yd. = 3 ft.
     1 mi. = 5280 ft. = 1760 yd.
  B. Area measure
     1. Units commonly used are the **square inch** (in.²), **square yard** (yd.²), and **square foot** (ft.²).
     2. Land can be measured in **acres.**
  C. Volume measure
     Units commonly used are the **cubic inch** (in.³), **cubic foot** (ft.³), **cubic yard** (yd.³), and **gallon.**
  *D. Mass
     Units of mass commonly used are **pound** (lb), **ounce** (oz) (1 ounce = $\frac{1}{16}$ pound), and **ton** (1 ton = 2000 pounds).
II. The metric system
  A. A summary of relationships among prefixes and the base unit of linear measure follows.

Prefix	Unit	Relationship to Base Unit		Symbol
kilo	kilometer	1000	meters	km
*hecto	hectometer	100	meters	hm
*deka	dekameter	10	meters	dam
	meter	**1**	**meter**	**m**
*deci	decimeter	0.1	meter	dm
centi	centimeter	0.01	meter	cm
milli	millimeter	0.001	meter	mm

* Not commonly used.

B. Area measure
   1. Units commonly used are the **square kilometer** (km²), **square meter** (m²), **square centimeter** (cm²), and **square millimeter** (mm²).
   2. Land can be measured using the **are** (100 m²) and the **hectare** (10,000 m²).
C. Volume measure
   1. Units commonly used are the **cubic meter** (m³), **cubic decimeter** (dm³), and **cubic centimeter** (cm³).
   2. $1 \text{ dm}^3 = 1 \text{ L}$ and $1 \text{ cm}^3 = 1 \text{ mL}$.
*D. Mass
   1. Units of mass commonly used are the **milligram** (mg), **gram** (g), **kilogram** (kg), and **metric ton** (t).
   2. 1 L and 1 mL of water have masses of approximately 1 kg and 1 g, respectively.
*E. Temperature
   1. The official unit of metric temperature is the **degree Kelvin,** but the unit commonly used is the **degree Celsius.** In the English system the unit of temperature is the **degree Fahrenheit.**
   2. Basic temperature reference points are the following:
      100°C—boiling point of water
      37°C—normal body temperature
      20°C—comfortable room temperature
      0°C—freezing point of water
   3. $C = \frac{5}{9}(F - 32)$ and $F = \frac{9}{5}C + 32$

III. Distance
   A. **Distance properties.** Given points A, B, and C:
      1. $AB \geqq 0$
      2. $AB = BA$
      3. $AB + BC \geqq AC$
   B. The distance around a two-dimensional figure is called the **perimeter.** The distance C around a circle is called the **circumference.** $C = 2\pi r = \pi d$, where r is the radius of the circle and d is the diameter.

IV. Areas
   A. Formulas for areas
      1. **Square:** $A = s^2$, where s is a side.
      2. **Rectangle:** $A = \ell w$, where ℓ is the length and w is the width.
      3. **Parallelogram:** $A = bh$, where b is the base and h is the height.
      4. **Triangle:** $A = \frac{1}{2}bh$, where b is the base and h is the altitude to that base.
      5. **Trapezoid:** $A = \frac{1}{2}h(b_1 + b_2)$, where b_1 and b_2 are the bases and h is the height.

      6. **Regular polygon:** $A = \frac{1}{2}ap$, where a is the apothem and p is the perimeter.
      7. **Circle:** $A = \pi r^2$, where r is the radius.
      8. **Sector:** $A = \theta\pi r^2/360$, where θ is the measure of the central angle forming the sector and r is the radius of the circle containing the sector.
   B. **The Pythagorean Theorem:** In any right triangle, the square of the length of the hypotenuse is equal to the sum of the squares of the lengths of the legs.
   C. **Converse of the Pythagorean Theorem:** In any triangle ABC with sides of lengths a, b, and c such that $a^2 + b^2 = c^2$, $\triangle ABC$ is a right triangle with the right angle opposite the side of length c.

V. Surface areas and volumes
   A. Formulas for areas
      1. **Right prism:** $S.A. = 2B + ph$, where B is the area of a base, p is the perimeter of the base, and h is the height of the prism.
      2. **Right circular cylinder:** $S.A. = 2\pi r^2 + 2\pi rh$, where r is the radius of the circular base and h is the height of the cylinder.
      3. **Right circular cone:** $S.A. = \pi r^2 + \pi r\ell$, where r is the radius of the circular base and ℓ is the slant height.
      4. **Right regular pyramid:** $S.A. = B + \frac{1}{2}p\ell$, where B is the area of the base, p is the perimeter of the base, and ℓ is the slant height.
      5. **Sphere:** $S.A. = 4\pi r^2$, where r is the radius of the sphere.
   B. Formulas for volumes
      1. **Right prism:** $V = Bh$, where B is the area of the base and h is the height.
         (a) **Right rectangular prism:** $V = \ell wh$, where ℓ is the length, w is the width, and h is the height.
         (b) **Cube:** $V = e^3$, where e is an edge.
      2. **Right circular cylinder:** $V = \pi r^2 h$, where r is the radius of the base and h is the height of the cylinder.
      3. **Pyramid:** $V = \frac{1}{3}Bh$, where B is the area of the base and h is the height of the pyramid.
      4. **Circular cone:** $V = \frac{1}{3}\pi r^2 h$, where r is the radius of the circular base and h is the height.
      5. **Sphere:** $V = \frac{4}{3}\pi r^3$, where r is the radius of the sphere.

CHAPTER TEST

1. Complete the following chart for converting metric measures.

	mm	cm	m	km
(a)				0.05
(b)		320		
(c)	260,000,000			
(d)			190	

2. For each of the following, choose an appropriate metric unit—millimeter, centimeter, meter, or kilometer.
   (a) The thickness of a penny
   (b) The length of a new lead pencil
   (c) The diameter of a dime
   (d) The distance the winner travels in the Indianapolis 500
   (e) The height of a doorknob
   (f) The length of a soccer field

3. For each of the following, describe how you can find the area of the parallelogram.
   (a) Using *DE*   (b) Using *BF*

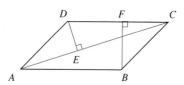

4. What is the area of the shaded region in the figure?

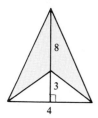

5. What is the area of the shaded region on the geoboard if the unit of measure is 1 cm²?

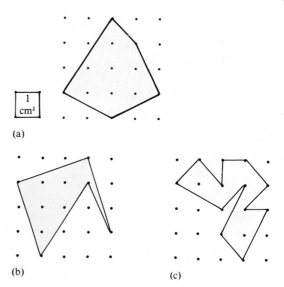

(a)

(b)   (c)

6. Find the area of the kite.

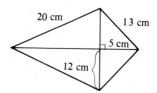

7. Explain how the formula for the area of a trapezoid can be found by using the given pictures.

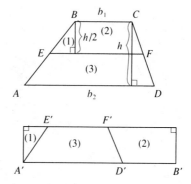

8. Use the figure to find each of the following.
   (a) The area of the hexagon
   (b) The area of the circle

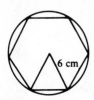

9. Find the area of each shaded region.

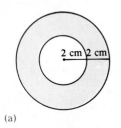

(a)

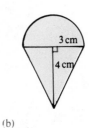

(b)

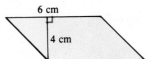

(c)

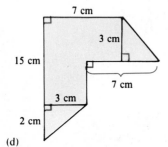

(d)

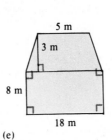

(e)

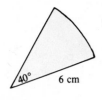

(f)

10. For each of the following, can the measures represent sides of a right triangle? Explain your answers.
    (a) 5 cm, 12 cm, 13 cm
    (b) 40 cm, 60 cm, 104 cm

11. Find the surface area and volume of each of the following.

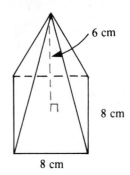

(a) Right square pyramid

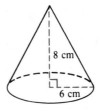

(b) Right circular cone

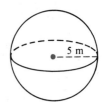

(c) Sphere

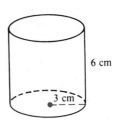

(d) Right circular cylinder

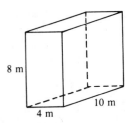

(e) Right rectangular prism

12. In the cone shown, find the following.

12 m

5 m

  (a) The lateral surface area of the cone
  (b) The central angle that corresponds to the arc of the flattened sector

13. Complete each of the following.
  *(a) Very heavy objects have mass that is measured in _____.
  (b) A cube whose length, width, and height are each 1 cm has a volume of _____.
  *(c) If the cube in (b) is filled with water, the mass of the water is _____.
  *(d) Which has a larger volume, 1 L or 1 dm³?
  (e) If a car uses 1 L of gas to go 12 km, the amount of gas needed to go 300 km is _____ L.
  (f) 20 ha = _____ a
  (g) 51.8 L = _____ cm³
  (h) 10 km² = _____ m²
  (i) 50 L = _____ mL
  (j) 5830 mL = _____ L
  (k) 25 m³ = _____ dm³
  (l) 75 dm³ = _____ mL
  *(m) 52,813 g = _____ kg
  *(n) 4800 kg = _____ t

14. Complete the following. (Use a calculator whenever convenient.)
  (a) 50 ft = _____ yd
  (b) 947 yd = _____ mi
  (c) 9800 ft² = _____ yd²
  (d) 3.4 mi² = _____ acres
  (e) 18 yd³ = _____ ft³
  (f) 0.8 ft³ = _____ in³
  (g) 3.8 lb = _____ oz
  (h) 49 oz = _____ lb
  *(i) 28°C = _____ °F
  *(j) 95°F = _____ °C

15. Two cones are defined to be similar if the ratio between their heights equals the ratio between their radii. If two similar cones have heights h_1 and h_2, find the ratio between their volumes in terms of h_1 and h_2.

16. (a) A tank that is a right rectangular prism is 1 m by 2 m by 3 m. If the tank is filled with water, what is the mass of the water?
  (b) Suppose that the tank is exactly half-full of water and then a heavy metal sphere of radius 30 cm is put into the tank. How high is the water now if the height of the tank is 3 m?
  (c) What is the radius of the largest possible metal sphere that can be put into the half-full tank without causing the water to overflow?

*17. For each of the following, fill in the correct unit to make the sentence reasonable.
  (a) Anna filled the gas tank with 80 _____.
  (b) A man has a mass of about 82 _____.
  (c) The textbook has a mass of 978 _____.
  (d) A nickel has a mass of 5 _____.
  (e) A typical adult cat has a mass of about 4 _____.
  (f) A compact car has a mass of about 1.5 _____.
  (g) The amount of coffee in the cup is 180 _____.

*18. For each of the following, decide if the situation is likely or unlikely.
  (a) Carrie's bath water has a temperature of 15°C.
  (b) She found 26°C too warm and lowered the thermostat to 21°C.
  (c) Jim was drinking water with a temperature of ⁻5°C.
  (d) The water in the teakettle has a temperature of 120°C.
  (e) The outside temperature dropped to 5°C, and ice appeared on the lake.

*19. Complete each of the following.
  (a) 2 dm³ of water has a mass of _____ g.
  (b) 1 L of water has a mass of _____ g.
  (c) 3 cm³ of water has a mass of _____ g.
  (d) 4.2 mL of water has a mass of _____ kg.
  (e) 0.2 L of water has a volume of _____ m³.

Coordinate Geometry

PRELIMINARY PROBLEM

A surveyor has three important landmarks A, B, and C, as shown. C is 60 feet from A. The distance from B to the line connecting A and C is 46 feet, and the distance from B to line y is 20 feet. The surveyor wants to put a fourth landmark, D, at a place equidistant from A, B, and C. How far is D from $\overleftrightarrow{AC}$ and y?

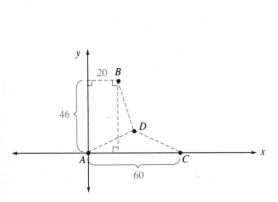

Introduction

In this chapter, we introduce the Cartesian coordinate system (named for René Descartes), which enables us to study geometry by using algebra and to interpret algebraic phenomena geometrically. This is the basis for graphing quantitative information and characterizing geometric figures with algebraic equations. The reason that coordinate geometry is such an important contribution to mathematics and science was expressed eloquently by the great eighteenth century French-Italian mathematician Joseph Louis Lagrange (1736–1813) (see Kline, *Mathematics in Western Culture*):

As long as algebra and geometry proceeded along separate paths, their advance was slow and their applications limited. But when the sciences joined company, they drew from each other's vitality and thence forward marched on at a rapid pace toward perfection.

H I S T O R I C A L   N O T E

René Descartes (1596–1650), a French philosopher and mathematician, invented coordinate geometry. He studied law but never practiced it, instead making lasting contributions to philosophy and science. Perhaps his greatest contribution was to mathematics. His revolutionary work was published in the book *La géométrie* in 1637.

In 1649, Queen Christina of Sweden invited Descartes to come to her court and instruct her. He was apprehensive about going "to live in the land of bears among rocks and ice" but accepted the invitation. The queen fixed 5 o'clock in the morning as the time for her lessons. Descartes, returning one chilly morning from instructing the queen, caught a severe cold and died within a few weeks.

Section 14-1

Coordinate System in a Plane

To set up a Cartesian coordinate system, we place two number lines perpendicular to each other at the point where both have coordinate 0. The intersection point of the two lines is the **origin**. The two lines are usually drawn as shown in Figure 14-1, with the horizontal line called the **x-axis** and the vertical line called the **y-axis**.

origin
x-axis
y-axis

FIGURE 14-1

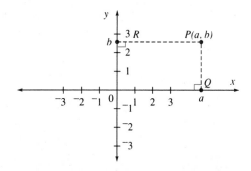

The location of any point P can be described by an ordered pair of numbers, as shown in Figure 14-1. If a perpendicular from P to the x-axis intersects the x-axis at a and a perpendicular from P to the y-axis intersects the y-axis at b, then we say that point P has coordinates (a, b). The first component in the ordered pair (a, b) is the **abscissa,** or **x-coordinate,** of P. The second component is the **ordinate,** or **y-coordinate,** of P.

abscissa / x-coordinate
ordinate / y-coordinate

In Figure 14-2, the x-coordinate of P is $^-3$ and the y-coordinate of P is 2, so P has coordinate $(^-3, 2)$. Similarly, R has an x-coordinate of $^-4$ and a y-coordinate of $^-3$, which can be written as $R(^-4, ^-3)$.

FIGURE 14-2

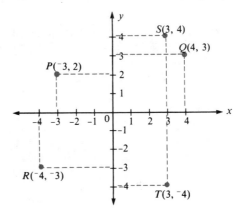

To each point in the plane, there corresponds an ordered pair (a, b). Conversely, to every ordered pair of real numbers, there corresponds a point in the plane. Hence, there is a one-to-one correspondence between all the points in the plane and all the ordered pairs of real numbers. Such a one-to-one correspondence is called a **coordinate system** for the plane.

coordinate system

Together, the x-axis and the y-axis separate the plane into four parts called **quadrants.** Figure 14-3 shows the numbered quadrants. The quadrants do not include points on the axes. Every point on the x-axis has a y-coordinate of zero. Thus, the x-axis can be described as the set of all points (x, y) such that $y = 0$. The set of points on the x-axis is usually denoted by the equation $y = 0$, and we say that the equation of the x-axis is $y = 0$. Similarly, the y-axis can be described as the set of all points (x, y) for which $x = 0$ and y is an arbitrary real number. Thus, $x = 0$ is the equation of the

quadrants

FIGURE 14-3

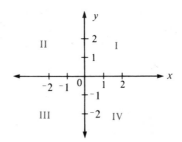

graph

y-axis. If we plot the set of all points that satisfy a given condition, the resulting picture on the Cartesian coordinate system is called the **graph** of the set.

EXAMPLE 14-1 Sketch the graph for each of the following.

(a) $x = 2$ (b) $y = 3$
(c) $x < 2$ and $y = 3$ (d) $x < 2$

SOLUTION (a) The equation $x = 2$ represents the set of all points (x, y) for which $x = 2$ and y is any real number. This set is the line perpendicular to the x-axis at $(2, 0)$ (Figure 14-4). Note that the set does not consist of a single point only.

FIGURE 14-4

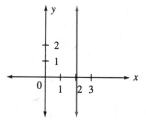

(b) The equation $y = 3$ represents the set of all points (x, y) for which $y = 3$ and x is any real number. This set is the line perpendicular to the y-axis at $(0, 3)$ (Figure 14-5).

FIGURE 14-5

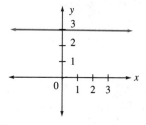

(c) Together, the statements represent the set of all points (x, y) for which $x < 2$ but y is always 3. The set describes a half-line, as shown in Figure 14-6. Note that the hollow dot at $(2, 3)$ indicates that this point is not included in the solution.

FIGURE 14-6

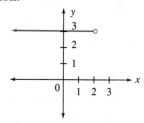

(d) The statement $x < 2$ indicates all points (x, y) for which $x < 2$ and y is any real number—that is, $\{(x, y)|x < 2 \text{ and } y \in R\}$. Because there are no restrictions on the y-coordinates, the coordinates of any point to the left of the line with equation $x = 2$, but not on the line, satisfy the condition. The half-plane in Figure 14-7 is the graph.

FIGURE 14-7

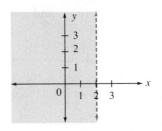

• R E M A R K

Had the inequality in the graph of Example 14-1(d) been $x \leq 2$, then the line $x = 2$ would have been a part of the set and would have been shown as a solid line. The fact that the line is not included is indicated by using the dashed line.

PROBLEM SET 14-1

1. (a) Give the coordinates of each of the points A, B, C, D, E, F, G, and H of the accompanying figure.

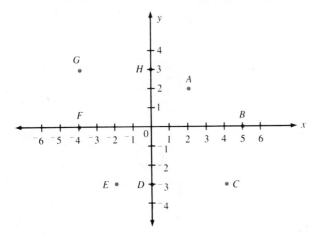

(b) Find the coordinates of another point (not drawn) that is collinear with E, D, and C.

2. Name the quadrant in which each ordered pair is located.
   (a) $(3, 7)$ (b) $(^-5, ^-8)$ (c) $(^-10, 32)$
   (d) $(10, ^-40)$ (e) $(0, 7)$

3. The first quadrant can be described as a set of ordered pairs (x, y) as follows.

   Quadrant I $= \{(x, y)|x > 0 \text{ and } y > 0\}$

   Describe the other quadrants in a similar way.

4. Find the coordinates of two other points collinear with each pair of given points.
   (a) $P(2, 2)$, $Q(4, 2)$
   (b) $P(^-1, 0)$, $Q(^-1, 2)$
   (c) $P(^-3, 0)$, $Q(3, 0)$
   (d) $P(0, ^-2)$, $Q(0, 3)$
   (e) $P(0, 0)$, $Q(0, 1)$
   (f) $P(0, 0)$, $Q(1, 1)$

5. For each of the following, give as much information as possible about x and y.
   (a) The ordered pairs $(^-2, 0)$, $(^-2, 1)$, and (x, y) represent collinear points.
   (b) The ordered pairs $(^-2, 1)$, $(0, 1)$, and (x, y) represent collinear points.
   (c) The ordered pair (x, y) is in the fourth quadrant.

6. Consider the lines through $P(2, 4)$ and perpendicular to the x- and y-axes, respectively. Find both the area and the perimeter of the rectangle formed by these lines and the axes.

7. Plot each of the points $A(^-3, ^-2)$, $B(^-3, 6)$, and $C(4, 6)$, and then find the coordinates of a point D such that quadrilateral $ABCD$ is a rectangle.

8. Plot at least six points, each having the sum of its coordinates equal to 4.

9. Sketch the graphs for each of the following.
    (a) $x = ^-3$
    (b) $y = ^-1$
    (c) $x > ^-3$
    (d) $y > ^-1$
    (e) $x > ^-3$ and $y = 2$
    (f) $y \geq ^-1$ and $x = 0$

10. Find the equations for each of the following.
    (a) The line containing $P(3, 0)$ and perpendicular to the x-axis
    (b) The line containing $P(0, ^-2)$ and parallel to the x-axis
    (c) The line containing $P(^-4, 5)$ and parallel to the x-axis
    (d) The line containing $P(^-4, 5)$ and parallel to the y-axis

11. Use the figure to answer the following questions.

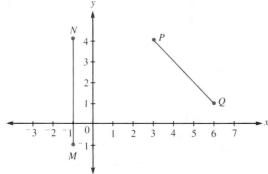

    (a) Give the coordinates of the endpoints of $\overline{PQ}$.
    (b) Give the coordinates of the endpoints of $\overline{MN}$.
    (c) Write the equation of the line parallel to $\overline{MN}$ and containing point P.
    (d) Write the equation of the line perpendicular to $\overline{MN}$ and containing point Q.

12. A *lattice point* is a point whose coordinates are integers. For example, the "dots" in the accompanying figure represent lattice points. The colored dots are the graph of the lattice points that are in the first quadrant or on the coordinate axes and satisfy the equation $x + y = 2$. Find the lattice points in the graph of each of the following.
    (a) $x + y = 5$, and the points are in the first quadrant or on the coordinate axes.
    (b) $x - y = 5$, and the points are in the fourth quadrant or on the coordinate axes.
    (c) $|x + y| = 5$, and the points are in the first or third quadrant or on the coordinate axes.

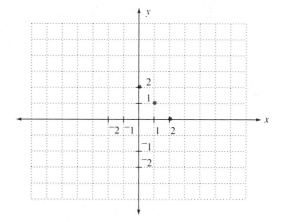

13. Graph all the lattice points satisfying each of the following.
    (a) $y = x + 2$, x and y are integers, and $0 \leq x \leq 4$
    (b) $y = ^-x + 1$, x is an integer, and $^-1 \leq x \leq 3$
    (c) $x^2 + y^2 = 9$, and either x or y is an integer
    (d) $y = x^2$, and $|x| \leq 4$ and x is an integer
    (e) $xy = 5$, and $|x| \leq 4$ and x is an integer

14. Describe algebraically all the points in the following regions.

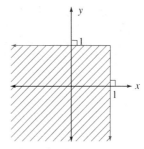

(a)

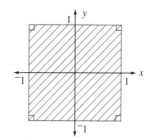

(b)

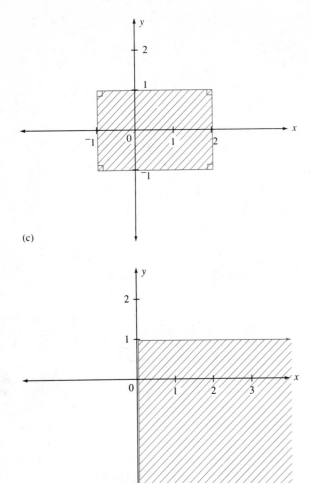

(c)

(d)

15. Use the graph to answer the following questions.

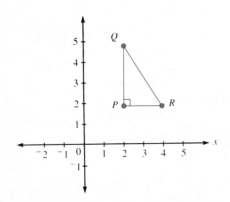

(a) Give the coordinates of the images of points P, Q, and R if $\triangle PQR$ is reflected in the x-axis.

(b) Give the coordinates of the images of points P, Q, and R if $\triangle PQR$ is rotated $90°$ counterclockwise, with the origin as the center of the rotation.

16. Find the coordinates of the images of each of the points $(0, 1)$, $(1, 0)$, $(2, 4)$, $(^-2, 4)$, $(^-2, ^-4)$, and $(2, ^-4)$ under the given transformations.

(a) A reflection in the x-axis

(b) A reflection in the y-axis

(c) A rotation by $90°$ counterclockwise about $(0, 0)$

(d) A half-turn whose center is $(0, 0)$

(e) A translation along the segment $\overline{OA}$ from $O(0, 0)$ to $A(0, ^-4)$

17. Consider $\triangle ABC$, whose vertices are at $A(^-2, 5)$, $B(2, 6)$, and $C(5, 1)$. Find the coordinates of the vertices of the image of the triangle if $\triangle ABC$ is transformed by the following.

(a) A reflection in the x-axis

(b) A reflection in the y-axis

(c) A reflection in the y-axis followed by a reflection in the x-axis

18. (a) Reflect the point $P(2, 4)$ in the y-axis, and then reflect its image in the x-axis. What are the coordinates of the final image point?

(b) If the point $P(a, b)$ is in the first quadrant and is reflected in the y-axis, and then its image is reflected in the x-axis, what are the coordinates of the final image point?

(c) Can the final image points in (a) and (b) be obtained by means of a single transformation?

19. Find the equation of the image of the line $x = 3$ in the following circumstances.

(a) The line is reflected in the x-axis.

(b) The line is reflected in the y-axis.

(c) The line is rotated $90°$ counterclockwise about the origin.

20. Find the images of each point $A(1, 0)$, $B(2, 2)$, $C(3, 1)$, $D(3, ^-1)$, and $E(a, b)$ when it is reflected in the line $\overleftrightarrow{OP}$, where P has the coordinates $(5, 5)$ and O is the origin.

21. Find the coordinates of the image of point $P(a, b)$ when it is rotated $90°$ counterclockwise about the following points.

(a) $(a, 0)$ (b) The origin

LABORATORY ACTIVITY

As van Hiele Level 1 activities, draw each of the following on the grid, and in each case find the coordinates of the vertices.
(a) A rectangle   (b) A parallelogram   (c) A kite

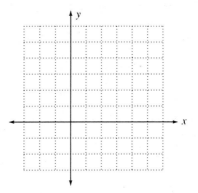

Section 14-2   Equations of Lines

Graphing Lines

In Section 14-1 (Example 14-1), we found the graphs of the equations $x = 2$ and $y = 3$. In general, the graph of the equation $x = a$, where a is some real number, is a line perpendicular to the x-axis through the point with coordinates $(a, 0)$, as shown in Figure 14-8. Similarly, the graph of the equation $y = b$ is a line perpendicular to the y-axis through the point with coordinates $(0, b)$.

FIGURE 14-8

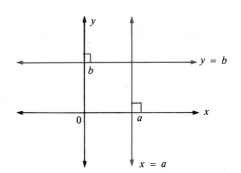

To graph the equation $y = x$, we plot all points whose x- and y-coordinates are equal. For example, $(0, 0)$, $(1, 1)$, $(1.3, 1.3)$, $(4, 4)$, $(4.5, 4.5)$, $(10, 10)$, and $(^-3, ^-3)$ all belong to the graph of line ℓ in Figure 14-9. However, $(1, ^-1)$ and $(2, 4)$ do not belong to the graph. All points represented by the equation $y = x$ lie on line ℓ.

FIGURE 14-9

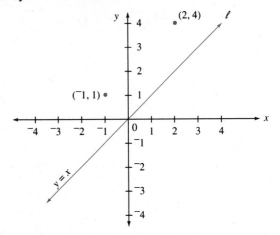

Next, consider the equation $y = 2x$. For any value of x, there is a corresponding value of y. Table 14-1 shows several values of x with corresponding values of y. These five coordinate pairs appear to be on a line, as shown in Figure 14-10, which also reproduces the graph of $y = x$. In fact, it is possible to prove that all points whose coordinates satisfy the equation $y = 2x$ lie on the same straight line.

x	$y = 2x$
0	0
1	2
2	4
-1	-2
-2	-4

TABLE 14-1

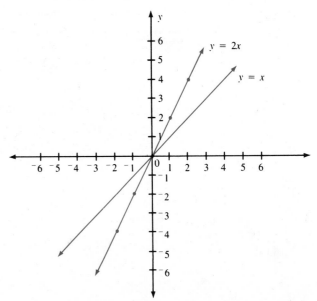

FIGURE 14-10

As Figure 14-10 shows, the graph of $y = 2x$ is *steeper* than the graph of $y = x$. We further explore the notion of steepness by examining the graphs in Figure 14-11.

FIGURE 14-11

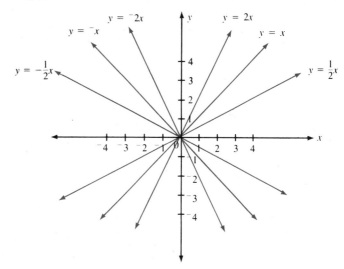

All six lines in Figure 14-11 have equations of the form $y = mx$, where m takes the values 2, 1, $\frac{1}{2}$, $^-\frac{1}{2}$, $^-1$, and $^-2$. The number m is a measure of steepness and is called the **slope** of the line whose equation is $y = mx$. The graph goes up from left to right (increases) if m is positive, and it goes down from left to right (decreases) if m is negative. If m is 0, what happens to the line? What happens when m is very large?

slope

Observe that all six lines in Figure 14-11 pass through the origin. This is true for any line whose equation is $y = mx$. If $x = 0$, then $y = m \cdot 0 = 0$, and (0, 0) is a point on the graph of $y = mx$. Conversely, it is possible to show that any nonvertical line passing through the origin has an equation of the form $y = mx$, for some value of m.

EXAMPLE 14-2   Find the equation of the line that contains (0, 0) and (2, 3).

SOLUTION   The line goes through the origin; therefore, its equation has the form $y = mx$. To find the equation of the line, we must find the value of m. The line contains (2, 3), so we substitute 2 for x and 3 for y in the equation $y = mx$ to obtain $3 = m \cdot 2$, and thus $m = \frac{3}{2}$. Hence, the required equation is $y = \frac{3}{2}x$.

Next, we consider equations of the form $y = mx + b$, where b is a real number. To do this, we examine the graphs of $y = x + 2$ and $y = x$. Given the graph of $y = x$, we can obtain the graph of $y = x + 2$ by "raising" each point on the first graph by two units because, for a certain value of x, the corresponding y value is two units greater. This is shown in Figure 14-12(a). Similarly, to sketch the graph of $y = x - 2$, we first draw the graph of $y = x$ and then lower each point vertically by two units, as shown in Figure 14-12(b).

FIGURE 14-12

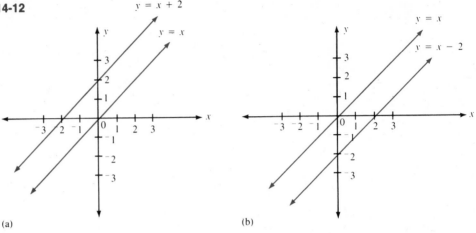

(a)

(b)

The graphs of $y = x + 2$ and $y = x - 2$ are straight lines. Moreover, the lines whose equations are $y = x$, $y = x + 2$, and $y = x - 2$ are parallel. In general, for a given value of m, the graph of $y = mx + b$ is a straight line through $(0, b)$ and parallel to the line whose equation is $y = mx$. Hence, *two nonvertical lines are parallel if their slopes are equal.* The converse of this statement is also true; that is, *if two lines have equal slopes, then they are parallel.* We summarize these two statements in the following property.

● **P R O P E R T Y**
Slopes of Parallel Lines   Two nonvertical lines are parallel if and only if they have equal slopes.

The graph of the line $y = mx + b$, where $b > 0$, can be obtained from the graph of $y = mx$ by sliding $y = mx$ up b units, as shown in Figure 14-13. If $b < 0$, $y = mx$ must be slid down $|b|$ units.

The graph of $y = mx + b$ in Figure 14-13 crosses the y-axis at point $P(0, b)$. The value of y at the point of intersection of any line with the y-axis is called the **y-intercept.** Thus, b is the y-intercept of $y = mx + b$, and this form of the equation of a straight line is called the **slope-intercept form.** Similarly, the value of x at the point of intersection of a line with the x-axis is called the **x-intercept.**

y-intercept

slope-intercept form

x-intercept

FIGURE 14-13

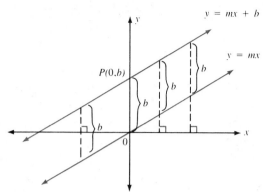

EXAMPLE 14-3 Given the equation $y - 3x = {}^-6$, find each of the following.

(a) The slope of the line
(b) The y-intercept
(c) The x-intercept
(d) Sketch the graph of the equation.

SOLUTION (a) To write the equation in the form $y = mx + b$, we add $3x$ to both sides of the given equation to obtain $y = 3x + ({}^-6)$. Hence, the slope is 3.

(b) The form $y = 3x + ({}^-6)$ shows that $b = {}^-6$, which is the y-intercept. (The y-intercept can also be found directly by substituting $x = 0$ in the equation and finding the corresponding value of y.)

(c) The x-intercept is the x-coordinate of the point where the graph intersects the x-axis. At that point, $y = 0$. Substituting 0 for y in $y = 3x - 6$ gives 2 as the x-intercept.

(d) The y-intercept and the x-intercept are located at $(0, {}^-6)$ and $(2, 0)$, respectively, on the line. We plot these points and draw the line through them to obtain the desired graph in Figure 14-14. Note that any two points of the line can be used to sketch the graph, because any two points determine a line.

FIGURE 14-14

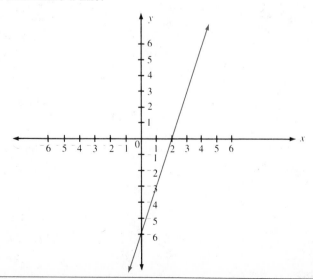

The equation $y = b$ can be written in slope-intercept form as $y = 0 \cdot x + b$. Consequently, its slope is 0 and its y-intercept is b. This should not be surprising; since the line is parallel to the x-axis, its steepness, or slope, should be 0. Any vertical line has equation $x = a$ for some real number a. This equation cannot be written in slope-intercept form. The slope of a vertical line is undefined and will be discussed later in the chapter. In general, *every straight line has an equation of either the form $y = mx + b$ or $x = a$.* Any equation that can be put in one of these forms is called a

linear equation **linear equation.**

• E Q U A T I O N   O F   A   L I N E
Every line has an equation of either the form $y = mx + b$ or $x = a$.

The Slope as Rise/Run

Because a line is determined by any two of its points, it is possible, given the coordinates of two points on a line, to find the equation of the line. For example, given $A(4, 2)$ and $B(1, 6)$, we can find the equation of $\overleftrightarrow{AB}$. Because the line is not perpendicular to the x-axis (why?), it must be of the form $y = mx + b$. Substituting the coordinates of A and B in $y = mx + b$ results in the following equations.

$$2 = m \cdot 4 + b \quad \text{or} \quad 2 = 4m + b$$
$$6 = m \cdot 1 + b \quad \text{or} \quad 6 = m + b$$

To find the equation of the line, we must find the values of m and b. If we solve for b in each of these equations, we obtain $b = 2 - 4m$ and $b = 6 - m$, respectively. Consequently, $2 - 4m = 6 - m$, so $m = -\frac{4}{3}$. Substituting this value of m in either of the equations gives $b = \frac{22}{3}$. Consequently, the equation of the line through A and B is $y = -\frac{4}{3}x + \frac{22}{3}$. The correctness of this equation can be checked by substituting the coordinates of the two given points, $A(4,2)$ and $B(1, 6)$, in the equation.

Using an analogous approach, it is possible to find a general formula for the slope of a line, given two points on the line, $A(x_1, y_1)$ and $B(x_2, y_2)$. If the line is not a vertical line, its equation is given by $y = mx + b$. Substituting the coordinates of A and B into this equation gives the following.

$$y_1 = mx_1 + b \quad \text{and therefore} \quad y_1 - mx_1 = b$$
$$y_2 = mx_2 + b \quad \text{and therefore} \quad y_2 - mx_2 = b$$

By equating these two values for b and solving for m, we identify the formula for slope.

$$y_1 - mx_1 = y_2 - mx_2$$
$$mx_2 - mx_1 = y_2 - y_1$$
$$m(x_2 - x_1) = y_2 - y_1$$
$$m = \frac{y_2 - y_1}{x_2 - x_1}$$

• **S L O P E   F O R M U L A**
Given two points $A(x_1, y_1)$ and $B(x_2, y_2)$ with $x_1 \neq x_2$, the slope m of the line $\overleftrightarrow{AB}$ is given by $m = \dfrac{y_2 - y_1}{x_2 - x_1}$.

By multiplying both the numerator and the denominator on the right side of the slope formula by $^-1$, we obtain

$$m = \frac{y_2 - y_1}{x_2 - x_1} = \frac{(y_2 - y_1)(^-1)}{(x_2 - x_1)(^-1)} = \frac{y_1 - y_2}{x_1 - x_2}$$

This shows that, while it does not matter which point is named (x_1, y_1) and which is named (x_2, y_2), *the order of the coordinates in the subtraction must be consistent.* The slope of the line $\overleftrightarrow{AB}$ is the change in y-coordinates divided by the corresponding change in x-coordinates of any two points on $\overleftrightarrow{AB}$. The difference $x_2 - x_1$ is the **run,** and the difference $y_2 - y_1$ is the **rise.** Thus, the slope is often defined as "rise over run," or $\dfrac{\text{rise}}{\text{run}}$. The slope formula can be interpreted geometrically as shown in Figure 14-15. The ratio $\dfrac{y_2 - y_1}{x_2 - x_1}$ is always the same, regardless of which two points on a given nonvertical line

run / rise

FIGURE 14-15

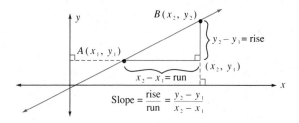

are chosen. This fact is illustrated in Figure 14-16, where right triangles have been constructed and shaded on each line. In each triangle the horizontal side is the run and the vertical side is the rise.

FIGURE 14-16

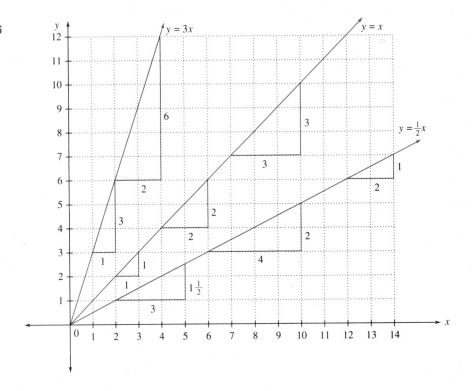

The slope of each line can be calculated as the rise over the run in any of the shaded triangles, with hypotenuse along the given line. To test this fact, notice that

$$\text{for } y = \frac{1}{2}x, \quad m = \frac{\text{Rise}}{\text{Run}} = \frac{1\frac{1}{2}}{3} = \frac{2}{4} = \frac{1}{2}$$

$$\text{for } y = x, \quad m = \frac{\text{Rise}}{\text{Run}} = \frac{1}{1} = \frac{2}{2} = \frac{3}{3}$$

$$\text{for } y = 3x, \quad m = \frac{3}{1} = \frac{6}{2}$$

When a line slopes from the left downward to the right, the slope is negative. This is illustrated in Figure 14-17, where the graph of the line $y = {}^-2x$ is shown. The slope of line $y = {}^-2x$ can be calculated as $\frac{\text{Rise}}{\text{Run}} = \frac{{}^-4}{2} = \frac{{}^-2}{1}$.

FIGURE 14-17

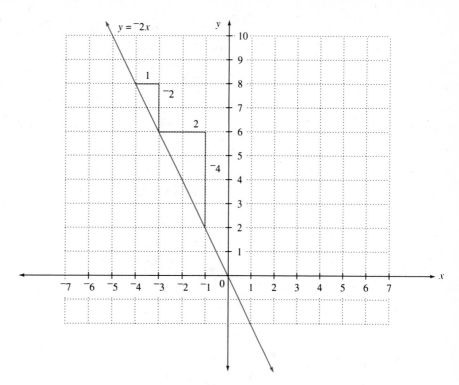

EXAMPLE 14-4   (a) Find the slope of $\overleftrightarrow{AB}$, given $A(3, 1)$ and $B(5, 4)$.

(b) Find the slope and the equation of the line passing through the points $A(^-3, 4)$ and $B(^-1, 0)$.

SOLUTION   (a) $m = \dfrac{4 - 1}{5 - 3} = \dfrac{3}{2}$,   or $\dfrac{1 - 4}{3 - 5} = \dfrac{^-3}{^-2} = \dfrac{3}{2}$

(b) *First method.*

$$m = \frac{4 - 0}{^-3 - (^-1)} = \frac{4}{^-2} = {}^-2$$

The equation of the line can be written in the form $y = mx + b$. Because $m = {}^-2$, it follows that $y = {}^-2x + b$; now the value of b must be found. The required line contains each of the given points, so the coordinates of each point must satisfy the equation. We substitute the coordinates of $B(^-1, 0)$ into $y = {}^-2x + b$ and proceed as follows.

$y = {}^-2x + b$

$0 = {}^-2(^-1) + b$

$0 = 2 + b$

$^-2 = b$

The required equation is $y = {}^-2x + {}^-2$, or $y = {}^-2x - 2$. To check that $y = {}^-2x - 2$ is the required equation, we would have to verify that the coordinates of both A and B satisfy the equation. The verification is left to the reader.

Second method. This approach uses the fact that $\dfrac{\text{Rise}}{\text{Run}}$ is the same for any two points on a line. We found that $m = {}^-2$. Point $P(x, y)$ represents a point on the line shown in Figure 14-18 if and only if the slope determined by P and B (or P and A) equals the slope of the line, which was found to be $^-2$. Using the slope formula, we find that the slope determined by P and B is

$$\frac{y - 0}{x - ({}^-1)} \quad \text{or} \quad \frac{y}{x + 1}$$

FIGURE 14-18

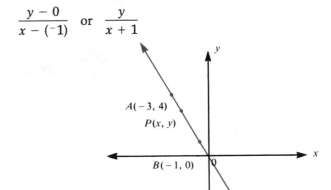

Hence, $P(x, y)$ is on $\overleftrightarrow{AB}$ if and only if

$$\frac{y}{x + 1} = {}^-2$$

$$y = {}^-2(x + 1), \quad \text{or}$$

$$y = {}^-2x - 2$$

Following the second method of solution in the preceding example, we can use the slope formula to find the equation of a line, given any point on the line and the slope of the line. In Figure 14-19, line ℓ has slope m and contains a given point (x_1, y_1). Point (x, y) represents any other point on line ℓ if and only if the slope determined by points (x_1, y_1) and (x, y) is m. We use the slope formula and proceed as follows.

$$\frac{y - y_1}{x - x_1} = m$$

$$y - y_1 = m(x - x_1)$$

FIGURE 14-19

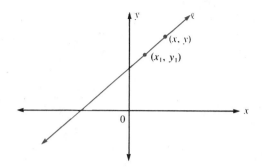

point-slope form   The result is called the **point-slope form** of a line.

● **P O I N T - S L O P E   F O R M   O F   A   L I N E**
The equation of a line with slope m through a given point (x_1, y_1) is $y - y_1 = m(x - x_1)$.

To examine the slope of a vertical line, pick any two points on the line, (x_1, y_1) and (x_2, y_2). Since the line is vertical, $x_1 = x_2$. Consequently,

$$m = \frac{y_2 - y_1}{x_2 - x_1} = \frac{y_2 - y_1}{0}$$

which is not meaningful. Thus, *the slope of a vertical line is undefined.* Consequently, we can also state that *any two lines are parallel if they both have the same slope or if both lines have undefined slope.*

Perpendicular Lines

We have seen that the slopes of two nonvertical lines are equal if and only if the lines are parallel. In addition, vertical lines are parallel, and the slope of each is undefined.

What is the relationship between the slopes of two perpendicular lines if neither of the lines is vertical? We first consider a special case when the lines go through the origin. Suppose that the slopes of the lines ℓ_1 and ℓ_2 shown in Figure 14-20 are m_1 and m_2, respectively. Because the slope of a line is equal to rise over run, the slope of ℓ_1 can also be determined from $\triangle OAB$, in which we choose $OA = 1$. We have $m_1 = \dfrac{\text{Rise}}{\text{Run}} = \dfrac{BA}{1} = BA$.

We now rotate line ℓ_1, along with $\triangle OBA$, 90° counterclockwise about center O. The image of ℓ_1 is ℓ_2. To determine the image of $\triangle OBA$, we need only determine the images of each of the vertices of the triangle. The image of O is O itself. The image of A is A' on the y-axis (why?), and the image

FIGURE 14-20

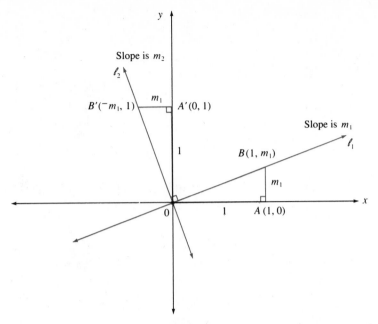

of B is B' on ℓ_2 (why?). Because rotation preserves congruence, $\triangle OB'A' \cong \triangle OBA$; consequently, $\angle A'$ is a right angle, $A'B' = m_1$, and $OA' = 1$. Thus, as shown in Figure 14-20, point B' is at $(-m_1, 1)$. Because the point $(0, 0)$ is also on line ℓ_2, we can use the slope formula to find the slope of ℓ_2 as follows.

$$m_2 = \frac{1 - 0}{-m_1 - 0} = \frac{-1}{m_1}$$

Thus, $m_2 = -1/m_1$, or $m_1 m_2 = -1$.

What is the relationship between the slopes m_1 and m_2 of two perpendicular lines (neither of which is vertical) if the lines do not intersect at the origin? We can always find two lines that pass through the origin and are parallel to each of the given lines. Because parallel lines have equal slopes, the relationship between the slopes of the perpendicular lines is the same as the relationship between the slopes of the perpendicular lines through the origin; that is, $m_1 m_2 = -1$.

It is also possible to prove the converse statement; that is, if the slopes of two lines satisfy the condition $m_1 m_2 = -1$, then the lines are perpendicular. We summarize these results in the following property.

- **P R O P E R T Y**
  Slopes of Perpendicular Lines   Two lines, neither of which is vertical, are perpendicular if and only if their slopes m_1 and m_2 satisfy the condition $m_1 m_2 = -1$. Any vertical line is perpendicular to a line with slope 0.

EXAMPLE 14-5   Find the equation of line ℓ through point $(^-1, 2)$ and perpendicular to the line $y = 3x + 5$.

SOLUTION   To find the equation of the line, we need only know a point on the line and the slope. We have such a point, $(^-1, 2)$, on line ℓ. Suppose that m is the slope of ℓ. Then, because the line $y = 3x + 5$ has slope 3 and is perpendicular to ℓ, we have $m \cdot 3 = ^-1$; therefore, $m = -\frac{1}{3}$. We find the equation of ℓ by using the point-slope form of a line:

$$y - 2 = -\frac{1}{3}(x + 1)$$

This equation can also be written as

$$y = -\frac{1}{3}x + \frac{5}{3}$$

Graphing Inequalities

In applications of mathematics, we often need to graph inequalities as well as equations. Consider, for example, the inequality $y - 3x > ^-6$. This inequality is equivalent to $y > 3x + (^-6)$. A point whose coordinates satisfy $y > 3x + (^-6)$ is above the line represented by $y = 3x + (^-6)$. Consequently, the graph of the inequality is the half-plane above the line given by $y = 3x + (^-6)$. The graph is sketched in Figure 14-21(a). To indicate that the line itself is not included in the graph, the line is dashed.

FIGURE 14-21

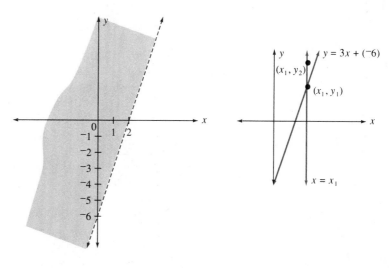

(a)

• R E M A R K
The fact that the graph of $y > 3x + (^-6)$ is the region above the line can be explained by using Figure 14-21(b) as follows. For every point (x_1, y_1) on the line $y = 3x + (^-6)$, we have $y_1 = 3x_1 + (^-6)$. If $y_2 > y_1$, then (x_1, y_2) is on the line $x = x_1$ above the point (x_1, y_1).

The graph of any inequality in one of the forms $y > mx + b$ or $y < mx + b$ is a half-plane either above or below the line $y = mx + b$. Thus, in order to graph an inequality like $y > mx + b$, we first graph the corresponding straight line. Then we check some point not on the line to see if it satisfies the inequality. If it does, the half-plane containing the point is the graph, and if not, the half-plane not including the point is the graph. For example, checking $(0, 0)$ in $y - 3x > {}^-6$ gives $0 - 3 \cdot 0 > {}^-6$, which is a true statement. Thus, the half-plane determined by $y - 3x = {}^-6$ and containing the origin is the graph of the inequality, as pictured in Figure 14-21(a).

EXAMPLE 14-6 Graph the following inequalities on the same coordinate system to determine all points that satisfy both inequalities.

(1) $2x + 3y > 6$

(2) $x - y \le 0$

SOLUTION First, we graph the lines represented by the equations $2x + 3y = 6$ and $x - y = 0$. Next, we must determine the half-planes to be shaded. Substituting $x = 0$ and $y = 0$ in inequality (1) gives $0 > 6$, a false statement, so the required half-plane determined by the first inequality does not contain the point $(0, 0)$. In Figure 14-22, the graph of this inequality is marked with vertical lines. Substituting $x = 0$ and $y = 0$ in inequality (2) gives $0 \le 0$, a true statement. Thus, $(0, 0)$ is part of the required solution. However, $(0, 0)$ is on the line $x - y = 0$, so it is in neither of the half-planes determined by this line. Another point must be checked. Consider, for example, $(1, 2)$. Substituting $x = 1$ and $y = 2$ in inequality (2) gives $^-1 \le 0$, a true statement; hence, $(1, 2)$ is in the half-plane determined by equation (2). In Figure 14-22, the graph of this inequality is marked with horizontal black lines. Hence, the set of common points is the crosshatched, shaded portion of Figure 14-22.

FIGURE 14-22

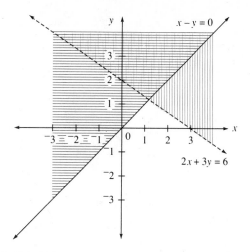

PROBLEM SET 14-2

1. Sketch the graphs of the equations $y = {}^-x$ and $y = {}^-x + 3$ on the same coordinate system.

2. The graph of $y = mx$ is given in the accompanying figure. Sketch the graphs for each of the following on the same figure.
   (a) $y = mx + 3$ (b) $y = mx - 3$

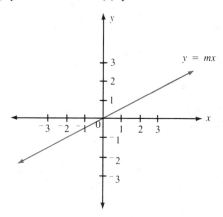

3. Sketch the graphs for each of the following equations or inequalities.
   (a) $y = \dfrac{-3}{4}x + 3$ (b) $y = {}^-3$
   (c) $y \geq 15x - 30$ (d) $x = {}^-2$
   (e) $y = 3x - 1$ (f) $y \leq \dfrac{1}{20}x$

4. Find the x-intercept and y-intercept for the equations in Problem 3, if they exist.

5. In Chapter 13, a relationship between the Fahrenheit and Celsius scales for measuring temperature was discussed. Sketch the graphs of the following.
   (a) The temperature y in degrees Fahrenheit as a function of the temperature x in degrees Celsius, using the formula $y = \frac{9}{5}x + 32$
   (b) The temperature y in degrees Celsius as a function of the temperature x in degrees Fahrenheit, using the formula $y = \frac{5}{9}(x - 32)$
   (c) If the graphs in (a) and (b) are drawn in the same coordinate system, describe their relationship to each other.

6. Write each of the equations in slope-intercept form.
   (a) $3y - x = 0$ (b) $x + y = 3$
   (c) $\dfrac{x}{3} + \dfrac{y}{4} = 1$ (d) $3x - 4y + 7 = 0$
   (e) $x = 3y$ (f) $x - y = 4(x - y)$

7. For each of the following, find the slope, if it exists, of the line determined by the given pair of points.
   (a) $(4, 3)$ and $({}^-5, 0)$
   (b) $({}^-4, 1)$ and $(5, 2)$
   (c) $(\sqrt{5}, 2)$ and $(1, 2)$
   (d) $({}^-3, 81)$ and $({}^-3, 198)$
   (e) $(1.0001, 12)$ and $(1, 10)$
   (f) (a, a) and (b, b)

8. For each of the following, write the equation of the line determined by the given pair of points in slope-intercept form or in the form $x = a$.
   (a) $(^-4, 3)$ and $(1, ^-2)$
   (b) $(0, 0)$ and $(2, 1)$
   (c) $(0, 1)$ and $(2, 1)$
   (d) $(2, 1)$ and $(2, ^-1)$
   (e) $\left(0, \dfrac{^-1}{2}\right)$ and $\left(\dfrac{1}{2}, 0\right)$
   (f) $(^-a, 0)$ and $(a, 0)$, $a \neq 0$

9. Use slopes to determine which of the following pairs of lines are parallel.
   (a) $y = 2x - 1$ and $y = 2x + 7$
   (b) $4y - 3x + 4 = 0$ and $8y - 6x + 1 = 0$
   (c) $y - 2x = 0$ and $4x - 2y = 3$
   (d) $\dfrac{x}{3} + \dfrac{y}{4} = 1$ and $y = \dfrac{4}{3}x$

10. For each of the following, find the equation of a line through $P(^-2, 3)$ and parallel to the line represented by the given equation.
    (a) $y = ^-2x$ (b) $3y + 2x + 1 = 0$
    (c) $x = 0$ (d) $y = ^-1$
    (e) $x = 3$ (f) $y = ^-4$
    (g) $x + y = 2$ (h) $\dfrac{x}{2} + \dfrac{y}{3} = 1$

11. Determine the slope of ℓ in each of the following.

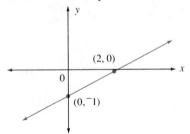

(a)

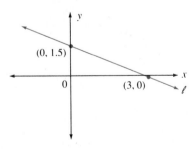

(b)

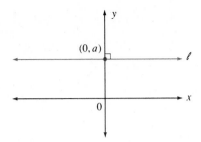

(c)

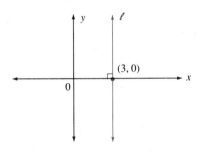

(d)

12. Determine the slopes of lines k, ℓ, and n if the sides of the triangles shown in the figure are parallel to the coordinate axes.

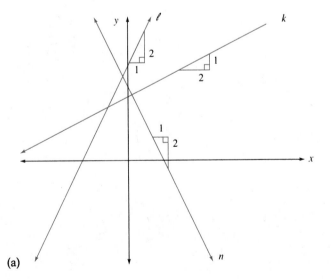

(a)

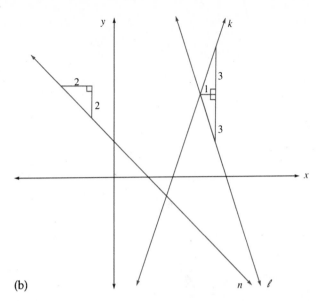

(b)

13. The door on a house was 4 feet above ground level. To allow handicap access, a ramp with a slope of $\frac{1}{10}$ was placed from the ground to the door. How long was the ramp?

14. (a) Let ℓ be a nonvertical line through the origin. Let n be a vertical line through $(1, 0)$. Show that P, the point of intersection of ℓ and n, has coordinates $(1, m)$, where m is the slope of ℓ.
    (b) Let b be a real number and ℓ be a nonvertical line through $(0, b)$. Let P be the point where ℓ intersects the vertical line n through $(1, 0)$. Show that the y-coordinate of P is the sum of b and the slope of ℓ.

15. Use slopes to show that the vertices $A(2, 1)$, $B(3, 5)$, $C(^-5, 1)$, and $D(^-6, ^-3)$ form a parallelogram.

16. Use slopes to show that the points represented by $(0, ^-1)$, $(1, 2)$, and $(^-1, ^-4)$ are collinear.

17. For each of the following, find the equation of the line that passes through the given point and has the given slope.
    (a) $(^-3, 0)$ with slope $\dfrac{^-1}{2}$
    (b) $(1, ^-3)$ with slope $\dfrac{2}{3}$
    (c) $(2, ^-3)$ with slope 0
    (d) $(^-1, ^-5)$ with slope $\dfrac{^-5}{7}$

18. Find the x-intercept and y-intercept of the line whose equation is $\dfrac{x}{a} + \dfrac{y}{b} = 1$, where $a \neq 0$ and $b \neq 0$.

19. Find the equation of the reflection image of the line $y = 3x + 1$ in each of the following.
    (a) The x-axis
    (b) The y-axis
    (c) The line $y = x$

20. Given the points $A(^-1, 1)$, $B(1, 2)$ and $C(^-3, ^-2)$, write an equation for each of the following.
    (a) The line through A perpendicular to $\overleftrightarrow{BC}$
    (b) The line through B perpendicular to $\overleftrightarrow{AC}$

21. Use slopes to determine whether the triangle with the given vertices is a right triangle or not.
    (a) $A(^-2, 3)$, $B(^-3, 5)$, $C(4, 6)$
    (b) $A(3, 1)$, $B(2, 0)$, $C(^-1, 1)$

22. Classify each of the following pairs of lines as parallel, perpendicular, or neither.
    (a) $3y - x = 1$, $2y + 6x - 1 = 0$
    (b) $2y - x - 3 = 0$, $2x - 4y + 16 = 0$
    (c) $x = 3$, $y = 0$
    (d) $x + y = 3$, $x - 2y = 1$

23. Use slopes and the square $OABC$ to verify that the diagonals of a square are perpendicular to each other.

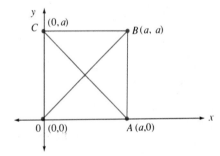

24. Graph each of the following inequalities.
    (a) $x - y + 3 > 0$ (b) $2x > 3y$
    (c) $x - 2y + 1 \leq 0$ (d) $x - 2y + 1 \geq 0$

25. Graph all points that satisfy the following.
    (a) $x - y + 3 > 0$ and $y - 2x - 1 < 0$
    (b) $x > 3$, $y < ^-4$, and $x - y - 3 > 0$
    (c) $x + y + 3 = 0$ and $x - y > 3$

26. Find the equation of the image of the line $y = x$ under the following transformations.
    (a) Reflection in the x-axis
    (b) Reflection in the y-axis
    (c) Rotation of $45°$ counterclockwise about the origin
    (d) Rotation of $90°$ counterclockwise about the origin
    (e) Half-turn with the center at the origin
    (f) Translation in the direction of the x-axis, three units to the right

(g) Translation in the direction of the y-axis, three units up

(h) Sketch the graphs of $y = 2x + 3$ and $y = {}^-2x - 3$ on the same coordinate system. How are the graphs related?

(i) How are the graphs $y = mx + b$ and $y = {}^-mx - b$ related?

27. Find the equation of the image of the line $x - y = 1$ under the following transformations.
    (a) Reflection in the x-axis
    (b) Reflection in the y-axis
    (c) Reflection in the line $y = x$
    (d) Half-turn with the center at the origin

★28. Graph each of the following equations.
    (a) $y = |x|$ (b) $|y| = x$
    (c) $|y| = |x|$ (d) $|x + y| \le 1$
    (e) $|x| + |y| = 1$ (f) $|x| \le |y|$
    (g) $y^2 = x^2$ (h) $xy = 0$

Review Problems

29. Find the equations for each of the following.
    (a) The line containing $({}^-7, {}^-8)$ and parallel to the x-axis
    (b) The line containing $({}^-7, {}^-8)$ and perpendicular to the x-axis

30. Find the coordinates of two other points collinear with the given points.
    (a) $P({}^-2, {}^-2)$, $Q({}^-4, {}^-2)$
    (b) $P({}^-7, {}^-8)$, $Q(3, 4)$

31. Plot each of the points $A(2, 2)$, $B(6, 6)$, and $C(8, {}^-4)$, and then find the coordinates of a point D such that quadrilateral $ABCD$ is a parallelogram.

32. Find the area of the triangle whose vertices are the following.
    (a) $(0, 0)$, $(3, 0)$, $(1, 1)$
    (b) $(0, 0)$, $(6, 3)$, $(10, 0)$
    (c) $(0, 0)$, $(0, {}^-5)$, $(3, 3)$
    (d) $(1, 2)$, $(5, 2)$, $({}^-8, 8)$
    (e) $(0, 0)$, $(1, 1)$, $(7, 1)$

LABORATORY ACTIVITY

As van Hiele Level 2 activities, answer the following.

1. Find the slopes of each of the segments drawn on a geoboard.

2. Use the concept of slope to draw two segments perpendicular to each of the segments in Activity 1.

Section 14-3 Systems of Linear Equations

The mathematical descriptions of many problems involve more than one equation, each involving more than one unknown. To solve such problems, we must find a common solution to the equations, if it exists. For example, finding the solution to a problem may involve finding all x and y values that satisfy both $y = x + 3$ and $y = 2x - 1$. Together, $y = x + 3$ and

system of linear equations $y = 2x - 1$ are an example of a **system of linear equations.** Any solution to the system is an ordered pair (x, y) that satisfies both equations. Systems of linear equations arise in many story problems. Consider the following.

EXAMPLE 14-7 May Chin ordered lunch for herself and several friends by phone without checking prices. Once, she paid $7.00 for 5 soyburgers and 4 orders of fries and another time she paid $6.00 for 4 of each. Set up a system of equations with two unknowns representing the prices of a soyburger and an order of fries, respectively.

SOLUTION Let x be the price in dollars of a soyburger, and let y be the price of an order of fries. Five soyburgers cost $5x$ dollars, and 4 orders of fries cost $4y$ dollars. Because May paid $7.00 for the order, we have $5x + 4y = 7$. Similarly, $4x + 4y = 6$, or $2x + 2y = 3$.

Systems with One Solution

Geometrically, an ordered pair satisfying both equations is a point that belongs to each of the lines. Figure 14-23 shows the graphs of $5x - 2y = 6$ and $x - 4y = -1$. The two lines appear to intersect at $(1, \frac{1}{2})$. Thus, $(1, \frac{1}{2})$ appears to be the solution of the given system of equations. This solution can be checked by substituting 1 for x and $\frac{1}{2}$ for y in each equation. Because $5 \cdot 1 + 2 \cdot \frac{1}{2} = 6$ and $1 - 4 \cdot \frac{1}{2} = {}^-1$, the ordered pair $(1, \frac{1}{2})$ is a solution. Since two distinct lines intersect in only one point, $(1, \frac{1}{2})$ is the only solution to the system.

FIGURE 14-23

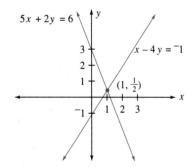

There are certain drawbacks to estimating a solution to a system of equations graphically. The sketch of a graph is often inaccurate, especially if noninteger real numbers are involved in the solution. Moreover, the graphic approach is impractical in solving linear equations with three variables and is impossible when more than three variables are involved. There are various algebraic methods for solving systems of linear equations. Consider, for example, the system $y = x + 3$ and $y = 2x - 1$. Because the solution (x, y) must satisfy each equation, we want x and y in each equation to be the same. Consequently, the expressions $x + 3$ and $2x - 1$ can be equated. The equation $x + 3 = 2x - 1$ has one unknown, x. Solving for x gives $3 + 1 = 2x - x$, and, hence, $4 = x$. Substituting 4 for x in either equation gives $y = 7$. Thus, $(4, 7)$ is the solution to the given system. As before, this solution can be checked by substituting the obtained values for x and y in the original equation. This method for solving a system of linear equations is called the **substitution method.**

substitution method

EXAMPLE 14-8   Solve the following system.

$$3x - 4y = 5$$
$$2x + 5y = 1$$

SOLUTION   First, rewrite each equation, expressing y in terms of x.

$$y = \frac{3x - 5}{4} \quad \text{and} \quad y = \frac{1 - 2x}{5}$$

Then equate the expressions for y, and solve the resulting equation for x.

$$\frac{3x - 5}{4} = \frac{1 - 2x}{5}$$
$$5(3x - 5) = 4(1 - 2x)$$
$$15x - 25 = 4 - 8x$$
$$23x = 29$$
$$x = \frac{29}{23}$$

Substituting $\frac{29}{23}$ for x in $y = \frac{3x - 5}{4}$ gives $y = \frac{-7}{23}$. Hence, $x = \frac{29}{23}$ and $y = \frac{-7}{23}$. This can be checked by substituting the values for x and y in the original equations.

● **R E M A R K**

Sometimes it is more convenient to solve a system of equations by expressing x in terms of y in one of the equations and substituting the obtained expression for x in the other equation.

elimination method

The **elimination method** for solving two equations with two unknowns is based on eliminating one of the variables by adding or subtracting the original or equivalent equations. For example, consider the system

$$x - y = {}^-3$$
$$x + y = 7$$

By adding the two equations, we can eliminate the variable y. The resulting equation can then be solved for x.

$$
\begin{array}{rl}
x - y = & {}^-3 \\
x + y = & 7 \\
\hline
2x = & 4 \\
x = & 2
\end{array}
$$

Substituting 2 for x in the first equation (either equation may be used) gives $2 - y = {}^-3$ and, hence, $y = 5$. Checking this result shows that $x = 2$ and $y = 5$, or (2, 5), is the solution to the system.

Often, another operation is required before equations are added so that an unknown can be eliminated. For example, consider finding the solution of the following system.

$$3x + 2y = 5$$
$$5x - 4y = 3$$

Adding the equations does not eliminate either unknown. However, if the first equation contained $4y$ rather than $2y$, the variable y could be eliminated by adding. To obtain $4y$ in the first equation, we multiply both sides of the equation by 2 to obtain the equivalent equation $6x + 4y = 10$. Adding the equations in the equivalent system gives the following.

$$
\begin{array}{rl}
6x + 4y = & 10 \\
5x - 4y = & 3 \\
\hline
11x = & 13 \\
x = & \dfrac{13}{11}
\end{array}
$$

To find the corresponding value of y, we substitute $\frac{13}{11}$ for x in either of the original equations and solve for y, or we use the elimination method again and solve for y.

An alternate method is to eliminate the x-values from the original system, by multiplying the first equation by 5 and the second by $^-3$ (or the first by $^-5$ and the second by 3). Then we add the two equations, and solve for y.

$$
\begin{array}{rl}
15x + 10y = & 25 \\
{}^-15x + 12y = & {}^-9 \\
\hline
22y = & 16 \\
y = & \dfrac{16}{22}, \quad \text{or} \quad \dfrac{8}{11}
\end{array}
$$

Consequently, $(\frac{13}{11}, \frac{8}{11})$ is the solution of the original system. This solution, as always, should be checked by substitution in the *original* equations.

Solutions to Other Systems

In the upper elementary grades, students learn to graph linear equations. Often, they are also taught the relationship between a pair of linear equations and the intersection of two lines, as the excerpt from *Addison-Wesley Mathematics*, 1989, Grade 8, shows. All examples thus far have had unique solutions. However, other situations may arise. Geometrically, a system of two linear equations can be characterized as follows:

Graphing Pairs of Equations

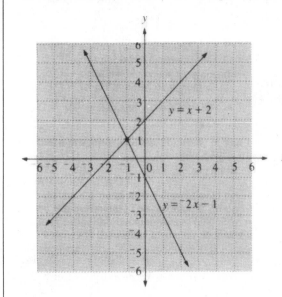

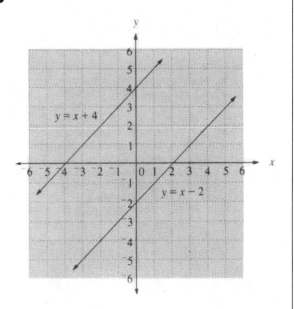

The two lines appear to intersect at Point P with coordinates $(-1, 1)$. To check, substitute $(-1, 1)$ in each equation.

$y = x + 2$	$y = {}^-2x - 1$
$1 = {}^-1 + 2$	$1 = {}^-2 \cdot {}^-1 - 1$
True	True

The graphs of the equations $y = x + 4$ and $y = x - 2$ do not intersect. The two lines are **parallel**.

1. The system has a unique solution if and only if the graphs of the equations intersect in a single point.
2. The system has no solution if and only if the equations represent parallel lines.
3. The system has infinitely many solutions if and only if the equations represent the same line.

Consider the following system.

$$2x - 3y = 1$$
$$^-4x + 6y = 5$$

In an attempt to solve for x, we multiply the first equation by 2 and then add as follows.

$$
\begin{array}{r}
4x - 6y = 2 \\
^-4x + 6y = 5 \\
\hline
0 = 7
\end{array}
$$

A false statement results. Logically, a false result can occur only on the basis of a false assumption or an incorrect procedure. Because our procedure is correct in this case, there must be a false assumption. We assumed that the system has a solution. That assumption caused a false statement; therefore, the assumption itself must be false. Hence, the system has no solution. In other words, the solution set is $\varnothing$. This situation arises if and only if the corresponding lines are parallel.

Next, consider the following system.

$$2x - 3y = 1$$
$$^-4x + 6y = ^-2$$

To solve this system, we multiply the first equation by 2 and add as follows.

$$
\begin{array}{r}
4x - 6y = 2 \\
^-4x + 6y = ^-2 \\
\hline
0 = 0
\end{array}
$$

The resulting statement, $0 = 0$, is always true. Rewriting the equation as $0 \cdot x + 0 \cdot y = 0$ shows that all values of x and y satisfy this equation. The values of x and y that satisfy both $0 \cdot x + 0 \cdot y = 0$ and $2x - 3y = 1$ are those that satisfy $2x - 3y = 1$. Infinitely many such pairs x and y correspond to points on the line $2x - 3y = 1$ and hence to $^-4x + 6y = ^-2$.

One way to check whether a system has infinitely many solutions is to see if each of the original equations represents the same line. In the preceding system, both equations may be written as $y = \frac{2}{3}x - \frac{1}{3}$. Another way to check whether a system has infinitely many solutions is to observe if one equation can be multiplied by some number to obtain the second equation. For example, multiplying the equation $2x - 3y = 1$ by $^-2$ yields the second equation, $^-4x + 6y = ^-2$.

EXAMPLE 14-9 Identify each of the following systems as having a unique solution, no solution, or infinitely many solutions.

(a) $2x - 3y = 5$ 　　 (b) $\dfrac{x}{3} - \dfrac{y}{4} = 1$ 　　　　　 (c) 　$6x - 9y = 5$

　　$\dfrac{1}{2}x - y = 1$ 　　　$3y - 4x + 12 = 0$ 　　　　$^-8x + 12y = 7$

SOLUTION One approach is to attempt to solve each system. Another approach is to write each equation in slope-intercept form and interpret the system geometrically.

(a) *First method.* To eliminate x, multiply the second equation by $^-4$ and add the equations.

$$
\begin{array}{rcr}
2x - 3y &=& 5 \\
^-2x + 4y &=& ^-4 \\
\hline
y &=& 1
\end{array}
$$

Substituting 1 for y in either equation gives $x = 4$. Thus, (4, 1) is the unique solution of the system.

Second method. In slope-intercept form, the first equation is $y = \frac{2}{3}x - \frac{5}{3}$. The second equation is $y = \frac{1}{2}x - 1$. The slopes of the corresponding lines are $\frac{2}{3}$ and $\frac{1}{2}$, respectively. Consequently, the lines are distinct and are not parallel; therefore, they intersect in a single point whose coordinates are the unique solution to the original system.

(b) *First method.* Multiply the first equation by 12, and rewrite the second equation as $^-4x + 3y = ^-12$. Adding the resulting equations gives the following.

$$
\begin{array}{rcr}
4x - 3y &=& 12 \\
^-4x + 3y &=& ^-12 \\
\hline
0 &=& 0
\end{array}
$$

Because every pair (x, y) satisfies $0 \cdot x + 0 \cdot y = 0$, the original system has infinitely many solutions.

Second method. In slope-intercept form, both equations have the form

$$y = \frac{4}{3}x - 4$$

Thus, the two lines are identical, so the system has infinitely many solutions.

(c) *First method.* To eliminate y, multiply the first equation by 4 and the second by 3; then add the resulting equations.

$$
\begin{array}{rcr}
24x - 36y &=& 20 \\
^-24x + 36y &=& 21 \\
\hline
0 &=& 41
\end{array}
$$

No pair of numbers satisfies $0 \cdot x + 0 \cdot y = 41$, so this equation has no solutions; consequently, the original system has no solutions.

Second method. In slope-intercept form, the first equation is $y = \frac{2}{3}x - \frac{5}{9}$. The second equation is $y = \frac{2}{3}x + \frac{7}{12}$. The corresponding lines have the same slope, $\frac{2}{3}$, but different y-intercepts. Consequently, the lines are parallel, and the original system has no solution.

EXAMPLE 14-10 The Park Street Restaurant offers two eggs with sausage for $1.80, or one egg with sausage for $1.35. If there is no break in price for quantity, what is the cost of one egg?

SOLUTION Let x be the cost of one egg and y be the cost of the sausage. The cost of two eggs and sausage is $2x + y$, or $1.80. The cost of one egg and sausage is $x + y$, or $1.35. Thus, the following system is obtained.

$$2x + y = 1.80$$
$$x + y = 1.35$$

Subtracting the equations gives $x = 0.45$. Thus, the cost of one egg is $0.45.

PROBLEM SET 14-3

1. Use the equation $2x - 3y = 5$ for each of the following.
   (a) Find four solutions of the equation.
   (b) Graph all the solutions for which $^-2 \le x \le 2$.
   (c) Graph all the solutions for which $0 \le y \le 2$.

2. Solve each of the following systems, if possible. Indicate whether the system has a unique solution, infinitely many solutions, or no solution.

   (a) $y = 3x - 1$
   $\quad\ y = x + 3$
   (b) $2x - 6y = 7$
   $\quad\ 3x - 9y = 10$
   (c) $3x + 4y = ^-17$
   $\quad\ 2x + 3y = ^-13$
   (d) $8y - 6x = 78$
   $\quad\ 9x - 12y = 12$
   (e) $5x - 18y = 0$
   $\quad\ x - 24y = 0$
   (f) $2x + 3y = 1$
   $\quad\ 3x - y = 1$

3. Solve each of the following systems, if possible. If a solution is not possible, explain why not.

   (a) $y = x + 3$
   $\quad\ 3x - 4y + 1 = 0$
   (b) $\dfrac{x}{3} - \dfrac{y}{4} = 1$
   $\quad\ \dfrac{x}{5} - \dfrac{y}{3} = 2$
   (c) $3x - 4y = ^-x + 3$
   $\quad\ x - 2 = 4(y - 3)$
   (d) $x - y = \dfrac{2}{3}(x + y)$
   $\quad\ x + y = \dfrac{2}{3}(x - y)$

   (e) $\sqrt{2}x - y = 3$
   $\quad\ x - \sqrt{2}y = 1$
   (f) $x - y = \dfrac{x}{3}$
   $\quad\ y - x = \dfrac{3}{4}y + 1$

4. Using the concept of slope, identify whether each of the following systems has a unique solution, infinitely many solutions, or no solution.

   (a) $3x - 4y = 5$
   $\quad\ \dfrac{x}{3} - \dfrac{y}{5} = 1$
   (b) $4y - 3x + 4 = 0$
   $\quad\ 8y - 6x + 40 = 0$
   (c) $3y - 2x = 15$
   $\quad\ \dfrac{2}{3}x - y + 5 = 0$
   (d) $x - y = x + y$
   $\quad\ x = 0$

5. The vertices of a triangle are given by $(0, 0), (10, 0)$, and $(6, 8)$. Show that the segments connecting $(5, 0)$ and $(6, 8)$, $(10, 0)$ and $(3, 4)$, and $(0, 0)$ and $(8, 4)$ intersect at a common point.

6. Two adjacent sides of a parallelogram are on lines with equations $x - 3y + 3 = 0$ and $x + 2y - 2 = 0$. One vertex is at $(0, ^-4)$. Write the equations of the lines containing the other two sides.

7. Find the area of the triangle bounded by the lines $y = 2x + 3$, $x + y = 5$, and $x = 3$.

8. Find the area of $\triangle ABC$ in the figure if the equations of lines ℓ and m are $y = 4x + 2$ and $\dfrac{x}{3} + \dfrac{y}{5} = 1$, respectively, and if $\overline{AB}$ is parallel to the x-axis and A is on the y-axis.

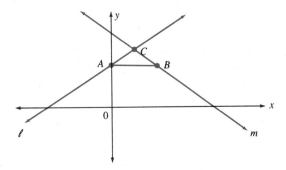

9. Triangle ABC has vertices $A(0, 0)$, $B(2, 5)$, $C(6, 1)$.
   (a) Find the point of intersection P of the lines containing the altitude from A to $\overline{BC}$ and the altitude from B to $\overline{AC}$.
   (b) Show that the third altitude of $\triangle ABC$ goes through the point P.

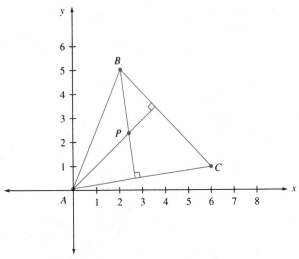

10. The sum of two numbers is $\frac{3}{4}$, and their difference is $\frac{7}{8}$. Find the numbers.
11. The owner of a 5000-gallon oil truck loads the truck with gasoline and kerosene. The profit on each gallon of gasoline is 13¢ and on each gallon of kerosene is 12¢. Find how many gallons of each fuel the owner loaded if the profit was $640.

12. A health-food store has two different kinds of granola—cashew nut granola selling at $1.80 a pound, and golden granola selling at $1.20 a pound. How much of each kind should be mixed to produce a 200-pound mixture selling at $1.60 a pound?
13. A laboratory carries two different solutions of the same acid—a 60% solution, and a 90% solution. How many liters of each solution should be mixed in order to produce 150 L of 80% solution?
14. A physician invests $80,000 in two stocks. At the end of the year, the physician sells the stocks—the first at a 15% profit, and the second at a 20% profit. How much did the physician invest in each stock if the total profit was $15,000?
15. At the end of 10 months, the balance of an account earning simple interest is $2100.
   (a) If, at the end of 18 months, the balance is $2180, how much money was originally in the account?
   (b) What is the rate of interest?
16. If five times the width of a waterbed equals four times its length and its perimeter is 270 inches, what are the length and width of the bed?
17. Josephine's bank contains 27 coins. If all the coins are either dimes or quarters and the value of the coins is $5.25, how many of each kind of coin are there?
18. (a) Solve each of the following systems of equations. What do you notice about the answers?
   (i) $x + 2y = 3$ (ii) $2x + 3y = 4$
        $4x + 5y = 6$ $5x + 6y = 7$
   (iii) $31x + 32y = 33$
         $34x + 35y = 36$
   (b) Write another system similar to those in (a). What solution did you expect? Check your guess.
   (c) Write a general system similar to those in (a). What solution does this system have? Why?
★19. Consider the accompanying figure. Show that the three altitudes of a triangle are concurrent—that is, that they intersect in a single point.

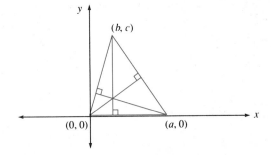

Review Problems

20. Which of the following are not equations of lines?
    (a) $x + y = 3$ (b) $xy = 7$
    (c) $2x + 3y \le 4$ (d) $y = 5$

21. Find the slope and y-intercept of each of the following.

    (a) $6y + 5x = 7$ (b) $\dfrac{2}{3}x + \dfrac{1}{2}y = \dfrac{1}{5}$

    (c) $0.2y - 0.75x - 0.37 = 0$ (d) $y = 4$

22. Write the equations of each of the following.
    (a) A line through $(4, 7)$ and $(^-6, ^-2)$
    (b) A line through $(4, 7)$ parallel to the line
        $y = \frac{5}{3}x + 6$
    (c) A line through $(^-6, ^-8)$ perpendicular to the
        y-axis

23. Graph each of the following.
    (a) $3x + 2y = 14$ (b) $^-x - y = ^-8$
    (c) $2x + 3y \le 4$ (d) $x - 16 \ge ^-8y$

B R A I N   T E A S E R

A school committee meeting began between 3:00 and 4:00 P.M. and ended between 6:00 and 7:00 P.M. The positions of the minute hand and the hour hand of the clock were reversed at the end of the meeting from what they were at the beginning of the meeting. When did the meeting start and end?

LABORATORY ACTIVITY

1. As a van Hiele Level 1 activity, approximate the area of $\triangle OAB$.
2. As a van Hiele Level 2 activity, find the exact area of $\triangle OAB$.

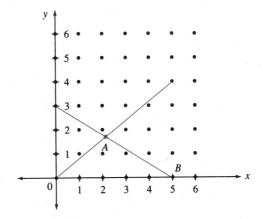

Section 14-4 The Distance and Midpoint Formulas

The Distance Formula

One way to *approximate* the distance between two points in a coordinate plane is to measure it with a ruler that has the same scale as the coordinate axes. Using algebraic techniques, we can calculate the *exact distance* between two points in the plane. First, suppose that the two points are on one of the axes. For example, in Figure 14-24(a), $A(2, 0)$ and $B(5, 0)$ are on the x-axis. The distance between these two points is three units.

$$AB = OB - OA = 5 - 2 = 3$$

FIGURE 14-24

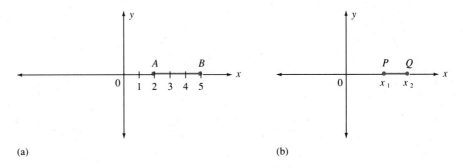

(a)

(b)

In general, if two points P and Q are on the x-axis, as in Figure 14-24(b), with x-coordinates x_1 and x_2, respectively, and $x_2 > x_1$, then $PQ = x_2 - x_1$. In fact, the distance between two points on the x-axis is always the absolute value of the difference between the x coordinates of the points. (Why?)

- **D E F I N I T I O N**
  Given two points $P(x_1, 0)$ and $Q(x_2, 0)$, the distance between them is given by
  $PQ = |x_2 - x_1| = |x_1 - x_2|.$

A similar result holds for any two points on the y-axis.

- **D E F I N I T I O N**
  Given two points $P(0, y_1)$ and $Q(0, y_2)$, the distance between them is given by
  $PQ = |y_2 - y_1| = |y_1 - y_2|.$

Figure 14-25 shows two points in the plane, $C(2, 5)$ and $D(6, 8)$. The distance between C and D can be found by drawing perpendiculars from the points to the x-axis and to the y-axis, respectively, which determines right

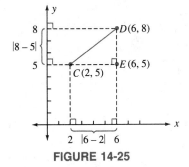

FIGURE 14-25

triangle CDE. The lengths of the legs are found by using horizontal and vertical distances and properties of rectangles.

$$CE = |6 - 2| = 4$$
$$DE = |8 - 5| = 3$$

The distance between C and D can be found by applying the Pythagorean Theorem.

$$CD^2 = DE^2 + CE^2$$
$$= 3^2 + 4^2$$
$$= 25$$
$$CD = \sqrt{25}, \text{ or } 5$$

The method just described can be used to find a formula for the distance between any two points $A(x_1, y_1)$ and $B(x_2, y_2)$. Construct a right triangle with $\overline{AB}$ as one of its sides by drawing a line through A parallel to the x-axis and a line through B parallel to the y-axis, as shown in Figure 14-26. These lines intersect at point C, forming right triangle ABC. Now, apply the Pythagorean Theorem.

FIGURE 14-26

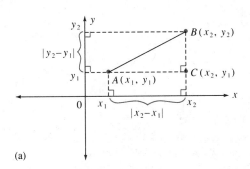

(a)

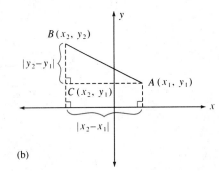

(b)

Figure 14-26 shows that $AC = |x_2 - x_1|$ and $BC = |y_2 - y_1|$. By the Pythagorean Theorem, $(AB)^2 = |x_2 - x_1|^2 + |y_2 - y_1|^2$, and consequently $AB = \sqrt{|x_2 - x_1|^2 + |y_2 - y_1|^2}$. Because $|x_2 - x_1|^2 = (x_2 - x_1)^2$ and $|y_2 - y_1|^2 = (y_2 - y_1)^2$, $AB = \sqrt{(x_2 - x_1)^2 + (y_2 - y_1)^2}$. As shown in Figure 14-26(b), a similar derivation applies to the length of a segment $\overline{AB}$ whose slope is negative. This result is known as the **distance formula.**

distance formula

● **D I S T A N C E   F O R M U L A**
The distance between the points $A(x_1, y_1)$ and $B(x_2, y_2)$ is given by

$$AB = \sqrt{(x_2 - x_1)^2 + (y_2 - y_1)^2}$$

• **R E M A R K**

It makes no difference whether $x_2 - x_1$ or $x_1 - x_2$ is used in the distance formula, because $(x_2 - x_1)^2 = (x_1 - x_2)^2$. The same is true for the y-values.

EXAMPLE 14-11   For each of the following, find the distance between P and Q.

(a) $P(2, 7)$, $Q(3, 5)$
(b) $P(0, 0)$, $Q(3, ^-4)$

SOLUTION   (a) $PQ = \sqrt{(3 - 2)^2 + (5 - 7)^2} = \sqrt{1 + 4} = \sqrt{5}$
(b) $PQ = \sqrt{(0 - 3)^2 + [0 - (^-4)]^2} = \sqrt{9 + 16} = \sqrt{25} = 5$

EXAMPLE 14-12   (a) Show that $A(7, 4)$, $B(^-2, 1)$, and $C(10, ^-5)$ are the vertices of an isosceles triangle.
(b) Show that $\triangle ABC$ in (a) is a right triangle.

SOLUTION   (a) Using the distance formula, find the lengths of the sides.

$$AB = \sqrt{(^-2 - 7)^2 + (1 - 4)^2} = \sqrt{(^-9)^2 + (^-3)^2} = \sqrt{90}$$
$$BC = \sqrt{[10 - (^-2)]^2 + (^-5 - 1)^2} = \sqrt{12^2 + (^-6)^2} = \sqrt{180}$$
$$AC = \sqrt{(10 - 7)^2 + (^-5 - 4)^2} = \sqrt{3^2 + (^-9)^2} = \sqrt{90}$$

Thus, $AB = AC$, so the triangle is isosceles.
(b) Because $(\sqrt{90})^2 + (\sqrt{90})^2 = (\sqrt{180})^2$, $\triangle ABC$ is a right triangle with $\overline{BC}$ as hypotenuse and $\overline{AB}$ and $\overline{AC}$ as legs.

Equation of a Circle

Using the distance formula, we can find the equation of a circle. A circle can be described if we know the location of the center and the length of the radius. Figure 14-27 shows the circle with center $C(5, 4)$ and radius 3 units long.

FIGURE 14-27

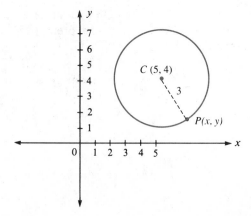

To find the equation of this circle, consider a point $P(x, y)$ on the circle. The distance from P to the center of the circle is 3 units—that is, $CP = 3$. By the distance formula, $\sqrt{(x - 5)^2 + (y - 4)^2} = 3$. Squaring both sides of the equation, we obtain $(x - 5)^2 + (y - 4)^2 = 9$. Thus, the coordinates of any point on the circle satisfy the equation $(x - 5)^2 + (y - 4)^2 = 9$.

To find the equation of any circle with center $C(a, b)$ and radius r, proceed in a similar way. Figure 14-28 shows that any point $P(x, y)$ is on the circle if and only if $PC = r$; that is, P is on the circle if and only if $\sqrt{(x - a)^2 + (y - b)^2} = r$. Squaring both sides results in the *equation of a circle*.

FIGURE 14-28

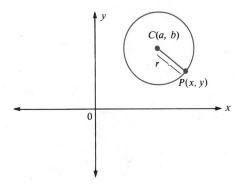

● E Q U A T I O N O F A C I R C L E
The equation of a circle with center (a, b) and radius r is

$$(x - a)^2 + (y - b)^2 = r^2$$

EXAMPLE 14-13

(a) Find the equation of the circle with the center at the origin and radius 4.
(b) Find the equation of the circle with center at $C(^-4, 3)$ and radius 5.
(c) Sketch the graph of $(x + 2)^2 + (y - 3)^2 = 9$.
(d) Write a condition for the set of points in the interior of the circle given in (c).
(e) Find the points of intersection of the circle in (c) and the y-axis.

SOLUTION

(a) The center is at $(0, 0)$ and $r = 4$, so the equation $(x - a)^2 + (y - b)^2 = r^2$ becomes $(x - 0)^2 + (y - 0)^2 = 4^2$, or $x^2 + y^2 = 16$.
(b) The equation is $[x - (^-4)]^2 + (y - 3)^2 = 5^2$, or $(x + 4)^2 + (y - 3)^2 = 25$.
(c) The equation $(x + 2)^2 + (y - 3)^2 = 9$ is in the form $(x - a)^2 + (y - b)^2 = r^2$ if and only if $x - a = x + 2$, $y - b = y - 3$, and $r^2 = 9$. Thus, $a = ^-2$, $b = 3$, and $r = 3$. Hence, the equation is that of a circle with center at $(^-2, 3)$ and $r = 3$. Figure 14-29 shows the graph of the circle.

FIGURE 14-29

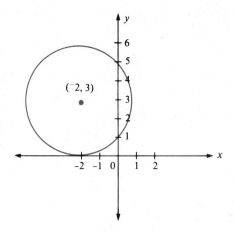

(d) A point (x, y) is in the interior of the circle if and only if the distance between the point and the center of the circle is less than the radius. In this case, $\sqrt{[x - (^-2)]^2 + (y - 3)^2} < 3$, or $(x + 2)^2 + (y - 3)^2 < 9$.

(e) A point on the circle and on the y-axis must satisfy $(x + 2)^2 + (y - 3)^2 = 9$ and $x = 0$. Hence, $(0 + 2)^2 + (y - 3)^2 = 9$, or $(y - 3)^2 = 5$. Hence, $y - 3 = \sqrt{5}$ or $y - 3 = ^-\sqrt{5}$. Consequently, $y = 3 + \sqrt{5}$ or $y = 3 - \sqrt{5}$. The points of intersection are therefore $(0, 3 - \sqrt{5})$ and $(0, 3 + \sqrt{5})$, or approximately $(0, 0.76)$ and $(0, 5.24)$, as shown in Figure 14-29.

EXAMPLE 14-14 Find all points on the y-axis that are 10 units away from $C(8, 3)$.

SOLUTION Suppose that P is a point on the y-axis satisfying the given requirements. Then, P has 0 as its x-coordinate. Thus, the coordinates of P are $(0, y)$. Find y so that $PC = 10$.

$$\sqrt{(0 - 8)^2 + (y - 3)^2} = 10$$

Square both sides of the equation, and solve for y.

$$(0 - 8)^2 + (y - 3)^2 = 100$$
$$64 + (y - 3)^2 = 100$$
$$(y - 3)^2 = 36$$

Thus, $y - 3 = 6$ or $y - 3 = ^-6$, so $y = 9$ or $y = ^-3$. Hence, two points, $P_1(0, 9)$ and $P_2(0, ^-3)$, satisfy the condition.

EXAMPLE 14-15   In Figure 14-30(a), $\overline{AB}$ is a diameter and C is any other point on the circle. For $\triangle ABC$, prove that $\angle C$ is a right angle.

FIGURE 14-30

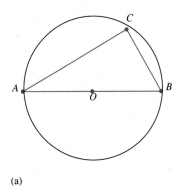

(a)

SOLUTION   We draw a coordinate system with origin through the center O of the circle, as in Figure 14-31. If the radius of the circle is r, then the coordinates of B are $(r, 0)$; the coordinates of A are $(-r, 0)$; and because the point C is an arbitrary point on the circle, we designate its coordinates by (x, y). To prove that $\angle C$ is a right angle, we establish that $\overline{AC}$ is perpendicular to $\overline{BC}$ by showing that the product of the slopes of $\overline{AC}$ and $\overline{BC}$ is $^{-}1$. If m_{AC} and m_{BC} are the slopes of $\overleftrightarrow{AC}$ and $\overleftrightarrow{BC}$, respectively, we have

$$m_{AC} \cdot m_{BC} = \frac{y - 0}{x - (^{-}r)} \cdot \frac{y - 0}{x - r} = \frac{y^2}{(x + r)(x - r)} = \frac{y^2}{x^2 - r^2}$$

FIGURE 14-31

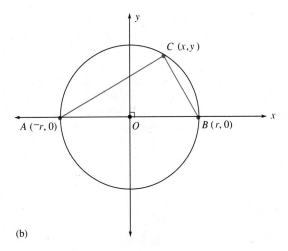

(b)

We need to show now that $\dfrac{y^2}{x^2 - r^2} = {}^{-}1$. So far we have not used the fact that C is on the circle. Because the distance from $C(x, y)$ to $(0, 0)$ is r, we have $\sqrt{(x - 0)^2 + (y - 0)^2} = r$, or $x^2 + y^2 = r^2$, which is the equation of the circle. Consequently, $x^2 - r^2 = {}^{-}y^2$. Substituting ${}^{-}y^2$ for $x^2 - r^2$, we have

$$m_{AC} \cdot m_{BC} = \frac{y^2}{x^2 - r^2} = \frac{y^2}{{}^{-}y^2} = {}^{-}1$$

Consequently, $\overleftrightarrow{AC}$ and $\overleftrightarrow{BC}$ are perpendicular, and therefore, $\angle C$ is a right angle.

The Midpoint Formula

Using the distance formula, we can find the length of a segment if we know the coordinates of its endpoints. In addition, we can use the notion of distance to find the coordinates of the midpoint of a segment. Given two points $A(x_1, y_1)$ and $B(x_2, y_2)$, we can find the coordinates of the midpoint M of the segment $\overline{AB}$ as follows. First, consider a simpler problem. Let $y_1 = y_2 = 0$. Then, the two points $A(x_1, 0)$ and $B(x_2, 0)$ lie on the x-axis, as shown in Figure 14-32 with $x_1 < x_2$.

FIGURE 14-32

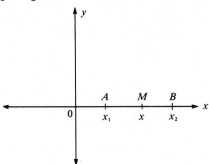

To find the x-coordinate of the midpoint M, use the given information to write an equation for x in terms of x_1 and x_2, and then solve for x. Because M is the midpoint of $\overline{AB}$, $AM = MB$, which implies that $x - x_1 = x_2 - x$; therefore,

$$2x - x_1 = x_2$$
$$2x = x_1 + x_2$$
$$x = \frac{x_1 + x_2}{2}$$

Similarly, for the case in which two points lie on the y-axis, the two points are $A(0, y_1)$ and $B(0, y_2)$, and the y-coordinate of the midpoint is $\dfrac{y_1 + y_2}{2}$.

Now, consider the general case. Let $A(x_1, y_1)$ and $B(x_2, y_2)$ be the endpoints of segment $\overline{AB}$ whose midpoint $M(x, y)$ is shown in Figure 14-33. Because $\overline{AA_1}$, $\overline{MM_1}$, and $\overline{BB_1}$ are parallel and M is the midpoint of $\overline{AB}$, M_1 is the midpoint of $\overline{A_1B_1}$. (Why?) Hence, $x = \dfrac{x_1 + x_2}{2}$. By an analogous argument, $y = \dfrac{y_1 + y_2}{2}$.

FIGURE 14-33

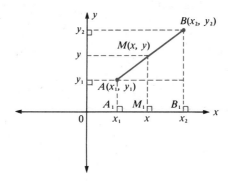

- **M I D P O I N T   F O R M U L A**
  Given $A(x_1, y_1)$ and $B(x_2, y_2)$, the midpoint M of $\overline{AB}$ is

$$M\left(\frac{x_1 + x_2}{2}, \frac{y_1 + y_2}{2}\right)$$

- **R E M A R K**
  To find the midpoint of a line segment, simply find the arithmetic mean of the respective coordinates of the two endpoints.

EXAMPLE 14-16   (a) Find the coordinates of the midpoint of $\overline{AB}$ if A has coordinates $(^-3, 2)$ and B has coordinates $(3, ^-5)$.
   (b) Suppose that M is the midpoint of $\overline{AB}$, A has coordinates $(2, ^-3)$, and M has coordinates $(^-2, 1)$. Find the coordinates of B.

SOLUTION   (a) Let (x, y) be the coordinates of the midpoint of $\overline{AB}$. Then use the midpoint formula.

$$x = \frac{x_1 + x_2}{2} = \frac{^-3 + 3}{2} = 0$$

$$y = \frac{y_1 + y_2}{2} = \frac{2 + (^-5)}{2} = \frac{^-3}{2}$$

Hence, the midpoint has coordinates $\left(0, \dfrac{^-3}{2}\right)$.

(b) Let the coordinates of B be (x, y), as shown in Figure 14-34. The coordinates of the midpoint M are the arithmetic means of the respective coordinates of the endpoints of $\overline{AB}$.

$$-2 = \frac{x + 2}{2} \qquad 1 = \frac{y + (^-3)}{2}$$

$$-4 = x + 2 \qquad 2 = y + (^-3)$$

$$x = {}^-6 \qquad y = 5$$

FIGURE 14-34

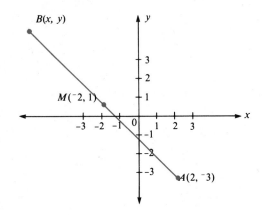

Consequently, $B(^-6, 5)$ is the required point.

EXAMPLE 14-17 Find the equation of the perpendicular bisector ℓ of $\overline{OB}$ if O is the origin and B is at $(2, {}^-4)$, as shown in Figure 14-35.

FIGURE 14-35

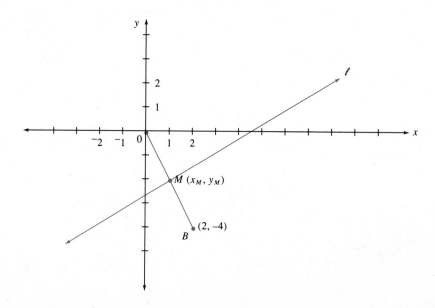

SOLUTION   We can find the coordinates of M, the midpoint of $\overline{OB}$. Then, if we knew the slope of ℓ, we could find the equation of ℓ. First, to find (x_M, y_M), the coordinates of M, we have $x_M = \dfrac{0 + 2}{2} = 1$ and $y_M = \dfrac{0 + (^-4)}{2} = {}^-2$. Thus, M is at $(1, {}^-2)$. Because ℓ is perpendicular to $\overline{OB}$, the slope of ℓ is the negative reciprocal of the slope of $\overline{OB}$, which can be found by using the slope formula, as follows.

$$m_{OB} = \frac{^-4 - 0}{2 - 0} = {}^-2$$

Also,

$$m_\ell = \frac{^-1}{m_{OB}} = \frac{^-1}{^-2} = \frac{1}{2}$$

Using the point slope formula, we have

$$y - (^-2) = \frac{1}{2}(x - 1), \quad \text{or} \quad y = \frac{1}{2}x - \frac{5}{2}$$

PROBLEM 1

Surveyors found the coordinates of three landmarks A, B, and C. They had to determine the coordinates of point D northeast of A so that A, B, C, and D are vertices of a parallelogram. Because point D was not easily accessible, the surveyors calculated the coordinates of D without further measurements. If B is at $(7, 19.3)$, C is at $(17.8, 5.9)$, and A is at $(2.5, 4.7)$, find the coordinates of point D.

Understanding the Problem.   Knowing the points $A(2.5, 4.7)$, $B(7, 19.3)$, and $C(17.8, 5.9)$, we are asked to find the coordinates of point D northeast of A such that A, B, C, and D are vertices of a parallelogram. The approximate location of point D is shown in Figure 14-36.

FIGURE 14-36

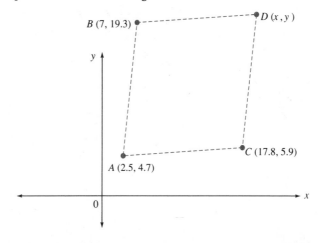

Devising a Plan. We denote the coordinates of D by x and y and look for properties of parallelograms that may help us to determine the values of x and y. We know that, in a parallelogram, the diagonals bisect each other. The point of intersection of the diagonals, denoted by M, is shown in Figure 14-37. The coordinates of M can be found as a midpoint of the diagonal $\overline{BC}$ by using the midpoint formula. $\left(\text{Recall that the midpoint of a segment with endpoints } (x_1, y_1) \text{ and } (x_2, y_2) \text{ is } \left(\dfrac{x_1 + x_2}{2}, \dfrac{y_1 + y_2}{2}\right).\right)$ However, because M is also the midpoint of the diagonal $\overline{AD}$, we can use the midpoint formula again to obtain equations for x and y. Solving each of the equations will give us the values of x and y.

FIGURE 14-37

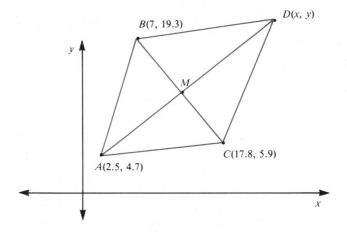

Carrying Out the Plan. Because $M(x_M, y_M)$ is the midpoint of $\overline{BC}$, we have $x_M = \dfrac{7 + 17.8}{2} = 12.4$. Similarly, $y_M = \dfrac{19.3 + 5.9}{2} = 12.6$. Using the fact that M is the midpoint of $\overline{AD}$, we have $12.4 = \dfrac{2.5 + x}{2}$. Thus, $24.8 = 2.5 + x$, or $x = 22.3$. Similarly, $12.6 = \dfrac{4.7 + y}{2}$, or $25.2 = 4.7 + y$, or $y = 20.5$. Consequently, the point D is determined by the ordered pair $(22.3, 20.5)$.

Looking Back. The problem can be extended by not restricting point D to being northeast of A. How many different locations for D are possible if A, B, C, and D are the vertices (not necessarily consecutive) of a parallelogram?

PROBLEM SET 14-4

1. For each of the following, find the length of $\overline{AB}$.
   (a) $A(0, 3)$, $B(0, 7)$ (b) $A(0, {}^-3)$, $B(0, {}^-7)$
   (c) $A(0, 3)$, $B(4, 0)$ (d) $A(0, {}^-3)$, $B({}^-4, 0)$
   (e) $A({}^-1, 2)$, $B(3, {}^-4)$ (f) $A(0, 0)$, $B({}^-4, 3)$
   (g) $A(4, {}^-5)$, $B\left(\dfrac{1}{2}, \dfrac{{}^-7}{4}\right)$ (h) $A(4, 0)$, $B(5.2, {}^-3.7)$
   (i) $A(5, 3)$, $B(5, {}^-2)$ (j) $A(5, 2)$, $B({}^-3, 4)$

2. Find the perimeter of the triangle with vertices at $A(0, 0)$, $B({}^-4, {}^-3)$, and $C({}^-5, 0)$.

3. Show that $(0, 6)$, $({}^-3, 0)$, and $(9, {}^-6)$ are the vertices of a right triangle.

4. Show that the triangle whose vertices are $A({}^-2, {}^-5)$, $B(1, {}^-1)$, and $C(5, 2)$ is isosceles.

5. Find x if the distance between $P(1, 3)$ and $Q(x, 9)$ is 10 units.

6. For each of the following, find the midpoint of the line segment whose endpoints have the given coordinates.
   (a) $({}^-3, 1)$ and $(3, 9)$
   (b) $(4, {}^-3)$ and $(5, {}^-1)$
   (c) $(1.8, {}^-3.7)$ and $(2.2, 1.3)$
   (d) $(1 + a, a - b)$ and $(1 - a, b - a)$

7. One endpoint of a diameter of a circle with center $C({}^-2, 5)$ is given by $(3, {}^-1)$. Find the coordinates of the other endpoint.

8. (a) Find the midpoints of the sides of a triangle whose vertices have the coordinates $(0, 0)$, $({}^-4, 6)$, and $(4, 2)$.
   (b) Find the lengths of the medians of the triangle in (a). (A *median* is a segment connecting the vertex of a triangle to the midpoint of the opposite side.)

9. For each of the following, write the equations of the circle with center C and radius r.
   (a) $C(3, {}^-2)$ and $r = 2$
   (b) $C({}^-3, {}^-4)$ and $r = 5$
   (c) $C({}^-1, 0)$ and $r = 2$
   (d) $C(0, 0)$ and $r = 3$

10. Given the circle whose equation is $x^2 + y^2 = 9$, which of the following points are in its interior, which are in its exterior, and which are on the circle?
    (a) $(3, {}^-3)$ (b) $(2, {}^-2)$
    (c) $(1, 8)$ (d) $(3, 1982)$
    (e) $(5.1234, {}^-3.7894)$ (f) $\left(\dfrac{1}{387}, \dfrac{1}{1983}\right)$
    (g) $\left(\dfrac{{}^-1}{2}, \dfrac{35}{2}\right)$ (h) $(0, 3)$

11. Find the equation of the circle that has its center at the origin and that contains the point with coordinates $({}^-3, 5)$.

12. For each of the following, find the equation of the circle that has its center at $C(4, {}^-3)$ and that passes through the point indicated.
    (a) The origin (b) $(5, {}^-2)$

13. Find the equation of the circle that has a diameter with endpoints at $({}^-8, 2)$ and $(4, {}^-6)$.

14. Graph each of the following, if possible.
    (a) $x^2 + y^2 > 4$ (b) $x^2 + y^2 \le 4$
    (c) $x^2 + y^2 = 9$ (d) $x^2 + y^2 - 4 = 0$
    (e) $x^2 + y^2 + 4 = 0$ (f) $x^2 + y^2 = 4$

15. Find the equation of the circle that passes through the origin and the point $(5, 2)$ and has its center on the x-axis.

16. Is $2x^2 + 2y^2 = 1$ an equation of a circle? If it is, find its center and radius; if it is not, explain why not.

17. (a) Find the coordinates of the point of intersection of any two perpendicular bisectors of two sides of $\triangle OBC$, if O is the origin and the other two vertices are $B(1, 4)$ and $C(5, 0)$.
    (b) Show that the third perpendicular bisector goes through the point you found in (a).
    (c) Use the distance formula to show that the point you found in (a) is equidistant from the vertices of $\triangle OBC$.
    (d) Find the equation of the circle that circumscribes $\triangle OBC$.

18. Find the point on the line $x + y = 3$ that is nearest to the origin.

19. Find the distance from the point $(1, 0)$ to the line $y = 2x$.

20. Find the distance between the line $y = {}^-2x + 1$ and $y = {}^-2x + 3$. The distance between two parallel lines is the distance from any point of one to the other.

21. A point P in space can be determined by giving its location relative to the x-, y-, and z-axes, as shown. For $A(5, 3, 8)$ and $B(7, 6, 4)$, find the following.

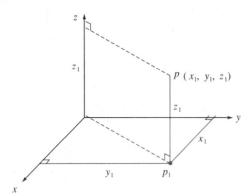

(a) The point of intersection between the line through A parallel to the z-axis and the xy-plane (the plane determined by the x- and y-axes)
(b) The point of intersection between the line through A parallel to the x-axis and the yz-plane
(c) The point of intersection between the line through A parallel to the y-axis and the xy-plane
(d) The distance between the points $(5, 3, 0)$ and $(7, 6, 0)$
(e) The distance between A and $(5, 3, 1)$
(f) The distance between A and $(^-5, 3, 8)$
★(g) The distance between A and the origin
★(h) The distance between A and B
★(i) The distance between the point $P(x_1, y_1, z_1)$ and the origin
★(j) The distance between the points $P(x_1, y_1, z_1)$ and $Q(x_2, y_2, z_2)$

★22. Graph the region enclosed between the curves $x^2 + y^2 = 1$ and $|x| + |y| = 1$.

★23. Three vertices of a parallelogram are given by $(^-1, 4)$, $(3, 8)$, and $(5, 0)$. Find the coordinates of the fourth vertex if it is in the specified quadrant.
(a) Quadrant I   (b) Quadrant II
(c) Quadrant IV

★24. Use the distance formula to show that the points with coordinates $(^-1, 5)$, $(0, 2)$, and $(1, ^-1)$ are collinear.

25. Use coordinates to prove that the midpoint M of the hypotenuse of a right triangle is equidistant from the vertices. (*Hint:* Use the coordinate system shown in the accompanying figure.)

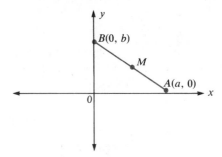

26. The vertices of $\triangle ABC$ are $A(0, 0)$, $B(1, 0)$, and $C(a, b)$. Answer the following.
(a) Write the equations of the three medians of $\triangle ABC$.
★(b) Show that the three medians intersect in one point.
★(c) Show that the point of intersection of the medians divides each median in the ratio 1:2.

★27. Use coordinates to prove that the diagonals of a parallelogram bisect each other.

★28. One day, Linda left home H for school S. Rather than stopping at school, she went on to the corner A, which is twice as far from home as the school and on the same street as her home and the school. Then she headed for the ice cream parlor I. Passing the ice cream parlor, she headed straight for the next corner B, which is on the same street as A and I and twice as far from A as I. Walking toward the park P, she continued beyond it to the next corner C, so that C, P, and B are on the same street and C is twice as far from B as P. At this point, she again headed for the school but continued walking in a straight line twice as far, reaching point D. Then, she headed for the ice cream parlor, but continued in a straight line twice as far to point E. From E, Linda headed for the park but continued in a straight line twice as far to F, where she stopped. The following drawing shows the first part of Linda's walk. What is the location of Linda's final stop?

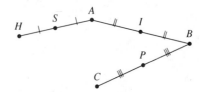

Review Problems

29. Find the equation of the line parallel to the x-axis that contains the point of intersection of the lines with equations $3x + 5y = 7$ and $2x - y = {}^-4$.

30. Solve each of the following systems if possible. If a solution is not possible, explain why not.

    (a) $x + y = 2x - y + 1$

        $3(x + y) = \dfrac{2}{3}(x + y)$

    (b) $2x - 3y = 5$

        $6y - 4x = 0$

31. Find the inequality or inequalities representing each of the following.

    (a) The half-plane determined by $y = \dfrac{3}{4}x + 5$ and containing $(0, 0)$

    (b) The triangular region determined by the line $x + y = {}^-5$, the x-axis, and the y-axis

---

B R A I N   T E A S E R

Among his great-grandfather's papers, José found a parchment describing the location of a hidden treasure. The treasure was buried by a band of pirates on a deserted island that contained an oak tree, a pine tree, and a gallows where the pirates hanged traitors. The map looked like the accompanying figure and gave the following directions.

"Count the steps from the gallows to the oak tree. At the oak, turn 90° to the right. Take the same number of steps and then put a spike in the ground. Next, return to the gallows and walk to the pine tree, counting the number of steps. At the pine tree, turn 90° to the left, take the same number of steps, and then put another spike in the ground. The treasure is buried halfway between the spikes."

José found the island and the two trees but could not find the gallows or the spikes, which had long since rotted. José dug all over the island, but because the island was large, he gave up. Devise a plan to help José find the treasure.

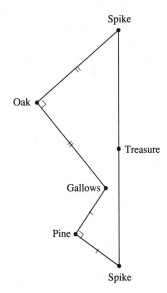

LABORATORY ACTIVITY

1. As a van Hiele Level 1 activity estimate the area of $\triangle ABC$.
2. As van Hiele Level 2 activities, do the following.
   (a) Find the exact area of $\triangle ABC$ (i) by using the distance formula, and (ii) without using the distance formula.
   (b) Draw a triangle that has the same area as $\triangle ABC$ in part (a) but a different perimeter.

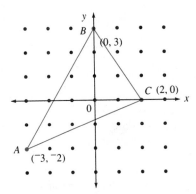

*Section 14-5   Coordinate Geometry and Logo

In Logo, the screen is treated as a Cartesian coordinate system in which each point of the screen is associated with an ordered pair of numbers (x, y). The origin, $(0, 0)$, is at the turtle's home. Figure 14-38 pictures the point $(^-30, 20)$.

FIGURE 14-38

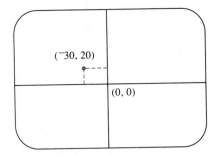

SETX   The primitive **SETX** is used with a number input to move the turtle in a horizontal direction to the position whose x-coordinate is the given input. This command changes neither the turtle's heading nor its y-coordinate.

SETY   **SETY** works in the same way with the *y*-coordinate. For example, if the turtle is at home and we type SETY 50, the turtle moves vertically up to the point where it has 50 as its *y*-coordinate. If we now type SETY ⁻50, the turtle moves down to the point where the *y*-coordinate is ⁻50. SETY does not affect the turtle's heading. Explore at which inputs to SETX and SETY the turtle begins to wrap around the screen. As an example of SETX and SETY, suppose that we start the turtle at home and type the following.

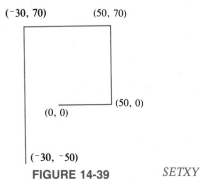

(⁻30, 70)   (50, 70)

(0, 0)   (50, 0)

(⁻30, ⁻50)

FIGURE 14-39

```
SETX 50 SETY 70 SETX -30 SETY -50
```

The turtle's final position has coordinates (⁻30, ⁻50), and the path drawn is shown in Figure 14-39.

To place the turtle at the point with coordinates (⁻30, ⁻50), we could type SETX ⁻30 and then SETY ⁻50. With the SETXY command, the operation

SETXY   can be done in one step. **SETXY** (*SETPOS in Apple Logo II*) takes two inputs; the first is the *x*-coordinate, and the second is the *y*-coordinate. (*In Apple Logo II, the inputs to SETPOS must be made in the form of a list; that is, they must be enclosed in brackets.*) For example, typing SETXY 30 50 (*SETPOS [30 50] in Apple Logo II*) moves the turtle from its present position to the point with coordinates (30, 50) without changing the heading. Do you think that typing SETXY ⁻30 ⁻50 (*SETPOS [⁻30 ⁻50] in Apple Logo II*) will move the turtle to the point with coordinates (⁻30, ⁻50)? Try it. If the experiment did not work, Logo probably treated ⁻30 ⁻50 as a subtraction and thought that there was only one input, namely, ⁻80. Parentheses can be used to overcome this, as in SETXY ⁻30 (⁻50). (*The parentheses are not necessary in Apple Logo II.*)

EXAMPLE 14-18   Write a procedure, using coordinate commands, to draw the parallelogram in Figure 14-40.

FIGURE 14-40

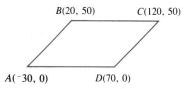

B(20, 50)   *C*(120, 50)

A(⁻30, 0)   *D*(70, 0)

SOLUTION   The solution is given in the following P.GRAM procedure.

```
TO P.GRAM
 PENUP
 SETXY -30 0
 PENDOWN
 SETXY 20 50
 SETXY 120 50
 SETXY 70 0
 SETXY -30 0
END
```

(*In Apple Logo II, SETXY is replaced with SETPOS and the inputs are enclosed in brackets.*)

• R E M A R K

Note that, in P.GRAM, we could have used SETX 120 in place of SETXY 120 50 and SETX ‾30 in place of SETXY ‾30 0 (*or in place of SETPOS [120 50] and SETPOS [‾30 0] in Apple Logo II.*)

Logo coordinate commands can be used for drawing geometric figures. Compare the following two procedures.

```
TO RECTANGLE :WIDTH :LENGTH
  REPEAT 2 [FD :WIDTH RT 90 FD :LENGTH RT 90]
END

TO RECTANGLE1 :WIDTH :LENGTH
  SETXY :WIDTH 0
  SETXY :WIDTH :LENGTH
  SETXY 0 :LENGTH
  SETXY 0 0
END
```

(*In Apple Logo II, when variables are used as inputs, SETXY is replaced with SETPOS LIST; for example, SETPOS LIST :WIDTH :LENGTH.*)

If the turtle starts at home with heading 0, the RECTANGLE and RECTANGLE1 procedures produce identical figures. If the turtle is not at home, the figures drawn by the two procedures are different. Experiment with these procedures to see that this is true, and explain the phenomenon.

We use the coordinate system to investigate several other geometric concepts. Consider how we might write a procedure to draw a line segment connecting two points, given their coordinates (:X1, :Y1) and (:X2, :Y2). To draw the segment, we must pick the pen up, move the turtle to the coordinates of the first point, put the pen down, and have the turtle move to the second point. The procedure called SEGMENT is given in Figure 14-41, along with a figure produced by SEGMENT.

FIGURE 14-41

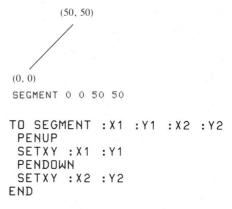

(50, 50)

(0, 0)

```
SEGMENT 0 0 50 50

TO SEGMENT :X1 :Y1 :X2 :Y2
  PENUP
  SETXY :X1 :Y1
  PENDOWN
  SETXY :X2 :Y2
END
```

(*In Apple Logo II, replace SETXY with SETPOS LIST.*)

Now, consider how to write a procedure called COOR.TRI to draw a triangle, given the coordinates of its three vertices. The SEGMENT procedure can be used to draw the three sides. The procedure is given in Figure 14-42, along with an execution of it.

FIGURE 14-42

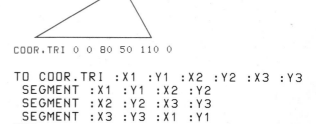

```
COOR.TRI 0 0 80 50 110 0

TO COOR.TRI :X1 :Y1 :X2 :Y2 :X3 :Y3
  SEGMENT :X1 :Y1 :X2 :Y2
  SEGMENT :X2 :Y2 :X3 :Y3
  SEGMENT :X3 :Y3 :X1 :Y1
END
```

Next, we consider how to construct the three medians of the triangles generated by COOR.TRI. Recall that medians are line segments drawn from a vertex of a triangle to the midpoint of the opposite side. If a given segment is horizontal, with coordinates (:X1, 0) and (:X2, 0), as shown in Figure 14-43(a), then the midpoint is determined by using the midpoint formula.

FIGURE 14-43

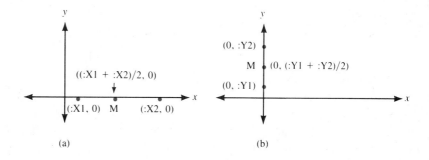

(a)

(b)

Thus, the coordinates of the midpoint are obtained by computing (:X1 + :X2)/2 and retaining 0 as the *y*-coordinate. Similarly, the midpoint of a vertical line with coordinates (0, :Y1) and (0, :Y2), as in Figure 14-43(b), is (0, (:Y1 + :Y2)/2).

If the line is neither horizontal nor vertical, as shown in Figure 14-44, then the midpoint is the arithmetic mean of the *x*- and *y*-coordinates.

FIGURE 14-44

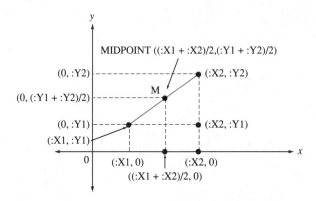

A procedure called MIDPOINT, which moves the turtle to the midpoint of a segment determined by the coordinates of two points, follows.

```
TO MIDPOINT :X1 :Y1 :X2 :Y2
  SETXY (:X1 + :X2)/2 (:Y1 + :Y2)/2
END
```

(*In Apple Logo II, replace SETXY with SETPOS LIST.*)

Once the sides of the triangle are drawn and the midpoints determined, the medians can be drawn by using the TRI.MEDIANS procedure given in Figure 14-45.

FIGURE 14-45

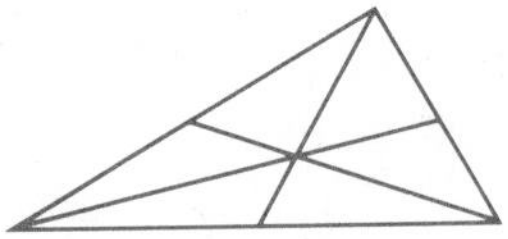

```
TRI.MEDIANS 0 0 80 50 110 0
```

```
TO TRI.MEDIANS :X1 :Y1 :X2 :Y2 :X3 :Y3
  COOR.TRI :X1 :Y1 :X2 :Y2 :X3 :Y3
  SEGMENT :X1 :Y1 (:X2 + :X3)/2 (:Y2 + :Y3)/2
  SEGMENT :X2 :Y2 (:X1 + :X3)/2 (:Y1 + :Y3)/2
  SEGMENT :X3 :Y3 (:X1 + :X2)/2 (:Y1 + :Y2)/2
END
```

medial triangle   A **medial triangle** is a triangle formed by connecting the midpoints of its three sides. A procedure called MEDIAL.TRI for drawing a medial triangle is given in Figure 14-46.

FIGURE 14-46

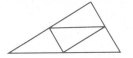

```
MEDIAL.TRI 0 0 80 50 110 0

TO MEDIAL.TRI :X1 :Y1 :X2 :Y2 :X3 :Y3
   COOR.TRI :X1 :Y1 :X2 :Y2 :X3 :Y3
   MIDPOINT :X1 :Y1 :X2 :Y2
   MIDPOINT :X2 :Y2 :X3 :Y3
   MIDPOINT :X3 :Y3 :X1 :Y1
   MIDPOINT :X1 :Y1 :X2 :Y2
END
```

Finding Lengths of Line Segments

It is possible to find the lengths of a line segment by using coordinate commands. Recall that we can find the length of a segment with the distance formula $d = \sqrt{(x_2 - x_1)^2 + (y_2 - y_1)^2}$. We can write a Logo procedure for computing the distance between any two points by using the distance formula and the SQRT primitive. **SQRT** takes one numerical input and outputs the square root of the number. The PRINT (PR) command can be used with SQRT to display the result. For example, PRINT SQRT 2 gives 1.41421. A DISTANCE procedure that prints out the distance between any two points follows.

SQRT

```
TO DISTANCE :X1 :Y1 :X2 :Y2
   PRINT SQRT (:X2 - :X1)*(:X2 - :X1) + (:Y2 - :Y1)
     *(:Y2 - :Y1)
END
```

If we execute DISTANCE ⁻10 20 20 40, where (⁻10, 20) and (20, 40) are the coordinates of the two points, then 36.0555 is displayed on the screen.

The DISTANCE procedure can also be used to compute the distance from a point with given coordinates even if we do not know the exact coordinates of the turtle. Logo has two primitives, XCOR and YCOR, that can be used to determine the coordinates of the turtle. If we type PRINT **XCOR** and press RETURN, the *x*-coordinate of the turtle is displayed. Similarly, PRINT **YCOR** yields the *y*-coordinate of the turtle. With this in mind, we can determine the distance from any point where the turtle is located to the point (5, 10) by executing DISTANCE 5 10 XCOR YCOR.

XCOR
YCOR

The DISTANCE procedure has its limitations. For example, consider writing a procedure to draw a square, given two consecutive vertices of the square. To draw square *ABCD*, where we know the vertices *A*(⁻10, 20) and *B*(0, 40), we need to know the length of segment $\overline{AB}$ and then make each of the other sides the same length. Because the figure is a square, each angle is a right angle. Such a square is pictured in Figure 14-47.

FIGURE 14-47

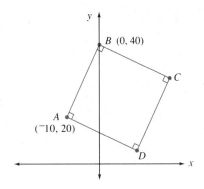

TOWARDS

SETHEADING (SETH)

A procedure called CSQUARE might first lift the pen up and move the turtle to vertex *A*. Now, we want the procedure to draw the square with sides the same length as segment $\overline{AB}$. We can find the length of segment $\overline{AB}$ by using the DISTANCE procedure. Now we know how to make the turtle go to vertex *B*, but without the heading we cannot complete the next leg of the square. Thus, we need to know the heading when the turtle draws segment $\overline{AB}$. Two Logo primitives can be used to determine the heading that will ensure that the turtle passes through vertex *B*. The primitive **TOWARDS** takes two numerical inputs that are interpreted as the *x*- and *y*-coordinates of a point and outputs the heading the turtle would have in going from its present location to the point with the coordinates given as inputs. (*In Apple Logo II, the two numerical inputs are enclosed in brackets.*) The PRINT (PR) command can be used with TOWARDS to display the heading. For example, if the turtle is at home, the PR TOWARDS ⁻10 0 (*in Apple Logo II, PR TOWARDS [10 0]*) yields 270. TOWARDS gives the heading toward some point from the turtle's current position, but it does not actually set the heading. The SETHEADING (SETH) primitive does this. **SETHEADING (SETH)** requires one input and turns the turtle to the heading indicated by the input. SETHEADING does not change the position of the turtle, only its heading. For example, SETHEADING 50 turns the turtle so that it has heading 50.

SETHEADING and TOWARDS can be used to complete the CSQUARE procedure. If the turtle is at (⁻10, 20), we can determine the heading that would be needed for the turtle to pass through (0, 40) by using TOWARDS 0 40 (*in Apple Logo II, TOWARDS [0 40]*). To actually turn the turtle toward (0, 40) to draw the line segment, we use the output from TOWARDS as input to SETHEADING, as in SETHEADING TOWARDS 0 40 (*in Apple Logo II, SETHEADING TOWARDS [0 40]*). Now that the proper heading for drawing the square can be determined, and because all sides of the square are the same length and all angles are 90°, we can write the following CSQUARE procedure.

```
TO CSQUARE
  PU SETXY -10 20 PD
  SETHEADING TOWARDS 0 40
  REPEAT 4 [FD DISTANCE -10 20 0 40 RT 90]
END
```

(In Apple Logo II, replace SETXY ⁻10 20 with SETPOS [⁻10 20] and TOWARDS 0 40 with TOWARDS [0 40].)

OUTPUT (OP)

If CSQUARE is executed, a bug occurs. This is because the value of DISTANCE ⁻10 20 0 40 is printed by DISTANCE and is not kept in the computer's memory to be passed as input to another procedure or another primitive. The primitive OUTPUT (OP) is useful here. **OUTPUT (OP)** takes one input and causes the current procedure to stop and output the result to a calling procedure.

To debug the CSQUARE procedure, we change the DISTANCE procedure to include an OUTPUT statement instead of a PRINT statement. The edited DISTANCE procedure follows.

```
TO DISTANCE :X1 :Y1 :X2 :Y2
  OUTPUT SQRT((:X2 - :X1)*(:X2 - :X1) + (:Y2 - :Y1)
   *(:Y2 - :Y1))
END
```

Now, the distance from (⁻10, 20) to (0, 40) is given by PR DISTANCE ⁻10 20 0 40.

The CSQUARE procedure can be generalized to start with the coordinates of any two points. The generalized procedure, called TWO.POINTS, follows.

```
TO TWO.POINTS :X1 :Y1 :X2 :Y2
  PU SETXY :X1 :Y1 PD
  SETHEADING TOWARDS :X2 :Y2
  REPEAT 4 [FD DISTANCE :X1 :Y1 :X2 :Y2 RT 90]
END
```

(In Apple Logo II, use SETPOS LIST :X1 :Y1 and TOWARDS LIST :X2 :Y2.)

Constructing Triangles with SAS

MAKE

The **MAKE** command can be used to assign a value to a variable. For example, if we execute MAKE "X 5 and then type PRINT :X, which means "Print the value associated with X," then the computer will print 5. The MAKE command can be used inside or outside a procedure. In general, the MAKE command accepts two inputs: the first, preceded by a quotation mark, is the name of the variable; and the second is the value of the variable we are defining. The MAKE command can be used with the other commands introduced in this chapter. For example, we could write a procedure called SAS.TRI to draw a triangle with two sides of length 80 and 50 and an included angle of 30°. To write SAS.TRI procedure to accomplish this, we could tell the turtle to go forward 80 units, the length of the first side, and

SAS.TRI

```
TO SAS.TRI
  FD 80
  MAKE "X XCOR
  MAKE "Y YCOR
  BK 80
  RT 30
  FD 50
  SETXY :X :Y
END
```
(*In Apple Logo II, replace SETXY with SETPOS LIST.*)

FIGURE 14-48

learn the *x*- and *y*-coordinates of its position. We could then back the turtle up 80 units, turn it right 30°, and move it forward 50 units, the length of the second side. To complete the triangle, we could then send the turtle to the coordinates it learned when it drew the first side. The SAS.TRI procedure follows, and the result is shown in Figure 14-48. Compare it to the one found in Chapter 11.

It is left as an exercise to write a variable procedure called SAS with inputs :S1, :A, :S2 for drawing a triangle, given two sides and the included angle.

● **S U M M A R Y   O F   C O M M A N D S**

SETX	Takes one number input and moves the turtle horizontally to the point with that *x*-coordinate. Draws a trail if the pen is down.
SETY	Takes one number input and moves the turtle vertically to the point with that *y*-coordinate. Draws a trail if the pen is down.
SETXY*	Takes two number inputs *A* and *B* and moves the turtle to the point with the given coordinates (*A*, *B*). Draws a trail if the pen is down.
SQRT	Takes one nonnegative number input and yields the square root of that input.
XCOR	Takes no inputs; outputs the turtle's current *x*-coordinate.
YCOR	Takes no inputs; outputs the turtle's current *y*-coordinate.
TOWARDS†	Takes two number inputs, which are interpreted as *x*- and *y*-coordinates of a point, and outputs the heading from the turtle to that point.
SETHEADING (SETH)	Takes one number input and rotates the turtle to point in the direction specified.
OUTPUT (OP)	Takes one input and causes the current procedure to stop and output the result to the calling procedure.
MAKE	Takes two inputs. The first, preceded by a quotation mark, is the name of a variable. The second is the value of the variable.

* In Apple Logo II, SETPOS is used with the list of coordinates as input—for example, SETPOS [20, 30].

† In Apple Logo II, TOWARDS is used with the list of coordinates as input—for example, TOWARDS [20, 30].

PROBLEM SET 14-5

1. Use SETX, SETY, and SETXY (*in Apple Logo II, SETPOS*) to draw the largest rectangle possible on the monitor screen.

2. How are the triangles generated by the MEDIAL.TRI procedure related?

3. Write a procedure called AXES that uses the SETXY (*in Apple Logo II, SETPOS*) primitive to draw the *x*- and *y*-axes with the origin placed at home.

4. If given two vertices of a square, how many different squares can be drawn?

5. Write a procedure called FILL.RECT that uses the SETXY (*in Apple Logo II, SETPOS*) command to fill (color in) a rectangle that has length 50 and width 30. Assume the turtle starts at home with heading 0.

6. Write a procedure called CCIRCLE to draw a circle in which the coordinates of the center of the circle and the radius are inputs. For example, CCIRCLE 10 20 30 should draw a circle that has center (10, 20) and radius 30.

7. Write a procedure called QUAD to draw a quadrilateral if the coordinates of the vertices are input.

8. (a) Write a procedure called MEDIAL.QUAD to draw a medial figure for a quadrilateral if the coordinates of the vertices are inputs.
   (b) Execute your procedure in (a) for several cases, and make a conjecture concerning the quadrilateral formed by the midpoints.

9. Write a procedure called MEDIAL.QUADS with inputs :X1, :Y1, :X2, :Y2, :X3, :Y3, :X4, and :Y4, which are the coordinates of the vertices, and :NUM, which gives the number of medial figures drawn.

10. Write a variable procedure called SAS to draw a triangle, given two sides :S1 and :S2 and the included angle :A.

11. Write a procedure called R.ISOS.TRI to draw a right isosceles triangle of side length given by the input :LEN.

12. Write a procedure to draw a circle that has radius 50 and passes through the point (⁻20, ⁻40).

13. Write a procedure to draw a circle in which the coordinates of the center of the circle and the radius are inputs.

★14. Write a procedure called MEDIAL.TRIS that uses recursion such that :NUM, the number of medial triangles that are to be drawn, is included as input.

SOLUTION TO THE PRELIMINARY PROBLEM

Understanding the Problem. In Figure 14-49, we need to find the coordinates of point D, which is equidistant from points A, B, and C. A point that is equidistant from three noncollinear points is the intersection point of the perpendicular bisectors of the sides of the triangle determined by the three points.

FIGURE 14-49

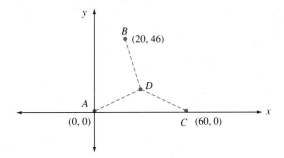

Devising a Plan. Because D shown in Figure 14-49 is equidistant from A, B, and C, it must be on the perpendicular bisectors of $\overline{AB}$, $\overline{BC}$, and $\overline{AC}$. The point D can be found as the intersection of any two of the perpendicular bisectors. That is, we can find the equations of any two of the perpendicular bisectors and solve them simultaneously. Because A, B, and C are known, we can find the equations of the perpendicular bisector k of $\overline{AC}$ and the perpendicular bisector ℓ of $\overline{AB}$, as shown in Figure 14-50. The perpendicular bisector k is a vertical line through the midpoint M of $\overline{AC}$ and has an equation of the form $x = a$. To find the equation of ℓ, we need either two points on ℓ or one point on ℓ and the slope of ℓ. The midpoint N of $\overline{AB}$ is on ℓ, and we know that the slope of ℓ is the negative reciprocal of the slope of $\overleftrightarrow{AB}$, which can be found by using the slope formula.

FIGURE 14-50

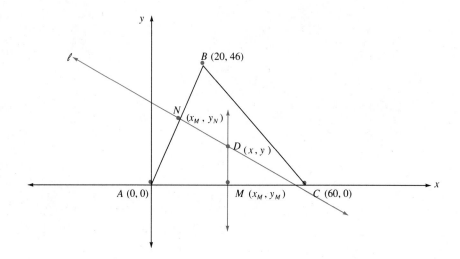

Carrying Out the Plan. Because $x_M = \dfrac{0 + 60}{2} = 30$, the equation of k is $x = 30$. To find the equation of ℓ, we first find the coordinates of N. From the midpoint formula, we have $x_N = \dfrac{0 + 20}{2} = 10$ and $y_N = \dfrac{46 + 0}{2} = 23$.

Next, $m_{AB} = \dfrac{46 - 0}{20 - 0} = \dfrac{23}{10}$. Hence, $m_\ell = \dfrac{-10}{23}$. To find the equation of ℓ, we use the point-slope formula: $y - 23 = \dfrac{-10}{23}(x - 10)$. Solving this equation simultaneously with $x = 30$, we have $y - 23 = \dfrac{-10}{23}(30 - 10)$, or $y = 23 - \dfrac{200}{23} = \dfrac{329}{23} \doteq 14.3$. Thus, point D is 30 feet from line y and approximately 14.3 feet from $\overleftrightarrow{AC}$.

Looking Back. Because D is equidistant from A, B, and C, it is the center of the circle that circumscribes $\triangle ABC$. Knowing the coordinates of D, we could find AD, the radius of the circle, and hence the equation of the circle. The coordinates of D can also be found by using the distance formula and conditions $BD = AD$ and $AD = DC$. These conditions are equivalent to

$(BD)^2 = (AD)^2$ and $(AD)^2 = (DC)^2$. Using the distance formula, we can rewrite these as $(x - 20)^2 + (y - 46)^2 = (x - 0)^2 + (y - 0)^2$ and $(x - 0)^2 + (y - 0)^2 = (x - 60)^2 + (y - 0)^2$.

The solution of the last system is left to the interested reader.

Given any noncollinear points A, B, and C, it is always possible to find a point D equidistant from the given points. Is the same true given any four points whose vertices form a quadrilateral?

QUESTIONS FROM THE CLASSROOM

1. A student asks, "If slope is such an important concept, why is slope of a vertical line undefined?" What is your response?

2. A student argues, "Since 0 is nothing and a horizontal line has slope 0, a horizontal line also has no slope." How do you reply?

3. Trying to find the midpoint M of $\overline{AB}$, where A and B have coordinates $(x_1, 0)$ and $(x_2, 0)$ and $x_2 > x_1$, a student argues as follows. "Since $AB = x_2 - x_1$, half that distance is $\dfrac{x_2 - x_1}{2}$ and, since the midpoint M is halfway between A and B, the x-coordinate of M is $\dfrac{x_2 - x_1}{2}$." How do you respond?

4. A student does not understand why, when solving a system of linear equations, it is necessary to check the solution in the original equations rather than in some simpler equivalent equations. How do you respond?

5. A student claims that the graph of every inequality of the form $ax + by + c > 0$ is the half-plane above the line $ax + by + c = 0$, while the graph of $ax + by + c < 0$ is always below the line. How do you respond?

6. A student claims that the distance formula can be further simplified as follows.

$$d = \sqrt{(x_1 - x_2)^2 + (y_1 - y_2)^2}$$
$$= \sqrt{(x_1 - x_2)^2} + \sqrt{(y_1 - y_2)^2}$$
$$= |x_1 - x_2| + |y_1 - y_2|$$

How do you respond?

7. A student claims that, if lines k and ℓ have slopes m_1 and m_2, respectively, and $m_1 m_2 = 1$, then the line k (the reflection of k in the x-axis) is perpendicular to line ℓ. She wants to know if this is always true, and why. What is your response?

CHAPTER OUTLINE

I. Coordinate system in a plane
 A. Any point in the plane can be described by an ordered pair of real numbers, the first of which is the **x-coordinate** and the second of which is the **y-coordinate.**
 B. Together, the x-axis and y-axis divide the plane into four **quadrants.**
II. Equations of sets of points and notions of slope
 A. The **slope** of a line is a measure of its steepness.
  1. Given (x_1, y_1) and (x_2, y_2) with $x_2 \neq x_1$, the **slope** m of the line through the two points is given by $m = \dfrac{y_2 - y_1}{x_2 - x_1}$.
  2. The slope of a vertical line is not defined.
 B. The equation of any nonvertical line can be written in the following forms.
  1. **Slope intercept form:** $y = mx + b$, where m is the slope and b the y-intercept.

 2. **Point-slope form:** $y - y_1 = m(x - x_1)$, where (x_1, y_1) is a point on the line and m is the slope.
 C. The equation of any vertical line can be written in the form $x = a$.
 D. Two nonvertical lines are **parallel** if and only if they have equal slopes. Vertical lines have no slope and are parallel.
 E. Two lines, neither of which is vertical, are **perpendicular** if and only if the product of their slopes is -1. If one line is vertical and the other has slope 0, the lines are perpendicular.
III. Systems of linear equations
 A. A system of **linear equations** can be solved graphically by drawing the graphs of the equations.
  1. If the equations represent two intersecting lines, the system has a unique solution—that is, the ordered pair corresponding to the point of intersection.

2. If the equations represent two different parallel lines, the system has no solutions.
3. If the two equations represent the same line, the system has infinitely many solutions.
B. A system of linear equations can be solved algebraically by either the **substitution method** or the **elimination method.**

IV. Distance concepts
   A. **Distance Formula:** The **distance** between the points (x_1, y_1) and (x_2, y_2) is given by
   $$d = \sqrt{(x_2 - x_1)^2 + (y_2 - y_1)^2}.$$

B. **Midpoint Formula** Given $A(x_1, y_1)$ and $B(x_2, y_2)$, the coordinates of the **midpoint** M of $\overline{AB}$ are
$$\left(\frac{x_1 + x_2}{2}, \frac{y_1 + y_2}{2} \right)$$

C. The **equation of the circle** with center at (a, b) and radius r is $(x - a)^2 + (y - b)^2 = r^2.$

*V. Coordinate geometry and Logo
The following primitives are used:

SETX	SETY
SETXY	SQRT
XCOR	YCOR
TOWARDS	SETHEADING
OUTPUT	MAKE

CHAPTER TEST

1. Find the perimeter of the triangle with vertices at $A(0, 0)$, $B(^-4, 3)$, and $C(0, 6)$.
2. Show algebraically in at least two different ways that $(4, 2)$, $(0, ^-1)$, and $(^-4, ^-4)$ are collinear points.
3. Sketch the graphs for each of the following.
   (a) $3x - y = 1$ (b) $3x - y \leq 1$
   (c) $2x + 3y + 1 = 0$
4. For each of the following, write the equation of the line determined by the given pair of points.
   (a) $(2, ^-3)$ and $(^-1, 1)$ (b) $(^-3, 0)$ and $(^-3, 2)$
   (c) $(^-2, 3)$ and $(2, 3)$
5. The vertices of $\triangle ABC$ are $A(^-3, 0)$, $B(0, 4)$, and $C(2, 5)$. Find each of the following.
   (a) The equation of the line through C and parallel to $\overleftrightarrow{AB}$.
   (b) The equation of the line through C and parallel to the x-axis.
   (c) The point where the line found in (b) intersects $\overleftrightarrow{AB}$.
6. Find the equation of the line passing through the y-intercept of the line $2x + 3y + 1 = 0$ and perpendicular to that line.
7. Solve each of the following systems, if possible. Indicate whether the system has a unique solution, infinitely many solutions, or no solution.
   (a) $x + 2y = 3$ (b) $\dfrac{x}{2} + \dfrac{y}{3} = 1$
       $2x - y = 9$ $4y - 3x = 2$
   (c) $x - 2y = 1$
       $4y - 2x = 0$
8. A store sells nuts in two types of containers—regular and deluxe. Each regular container contains 1 pound of cashews and 2 pounds of peanuts. Each deluxe container contains 3 pounds of cashews and 1.5

pounds of peanuts. The store sold 170 pounds of cashews and 205 pounds of peanuts. How many containers of each kind were sold?
9. (a) Find the midpoint of the line segment whose endpoints are given by $(^-4, 2)$ and $(6, ^-3)$.
   (b) The midpoint of a segment is given by $(^-5, 4)$ and one of its endpoints is given by $(^-3, 5)$. Find the coordinates of the other endpoint.
10. Graph each of the following.
    (a) $x^2 + y^2 = 16$
    (b) $(x + 1)^2 + (y - 2)^2 = 9$
    (c) $x^2 + y^2 \leq 16$
11. Find the equation of the circle that has its center at $C(^-3, 4)$ and that passes through the origin.
12. Graph each of the following systems.
    (a) $x \geq ^-7$ (b) $y \leq 2x + 3$
        $y \leq 4$ $y \geq x + ^-7$
13. The sum of the numbers of red and black jelly beans on Ronnie's desk is 12. Also, the sum is twice the difference of the numbers of the two colors. How many jelly beans of each color does he have if there are more red than black jelly beans?
14. The freshman class at the university has 225 fewer students enrolled than are in the sophomore class. The number in the sophomore class is only 50 students short of being twice as great as the number in the freshman class. How many students are in each class?
15. In the presidential election of 1932, Franklin D. Roosevelt received 6,563,988 more votes than Herbert Hoover. If one fifth of Roosevelt's votes had been won by Herbert Hoover, then Hoover would have won the election by 2,444,622 votes. How many votes did each receive?

CHAPTER 15

Problem
Solving
Revisited

Introduction

In this chapter, a knowledge of the material in the text is assumed, and we introduce problems that require skills from various chapters. This provides an opportunity to look at problem solving from a broader point of view, one in which the problem solver may not know to which specific topics the problem is related.

In the following examples, problem-solving strategies and the motives for various steps in a solution are discussed. Although not specifically indicated, the examples are solved by following the approach of *Understanding the Problem, Devising a Plan, Carrying Out the Plan, and Looking Back.* Following these examples is a collection of problems, some of which are nontrivial.

EXAMPLE 15-1   In the circle in Figure 15-1, two perpendicular diameters are shown. From a point C on the circle, two segments $\overline{AC}$ and $\overline{CB}$ are drawn so that quadrilateral $ACBO$ is a rectangle. If the diameter of the circle is 10 cm, find the length of $\overline{AB}$.

FIGURE 15-1

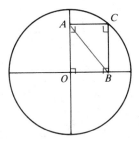

SOLUTION $\overline{AB}$ is the hypotenuse of right triangle AOB. One possible way to find AB is to use the Pythagorean Theorem, from which it follows that $(AB)^2 = (AO)^2 + (OB)^2$. Thus, to find AB, we need to know the lengths of both $\overline{AO}$ and $\overline{OB}$. The lengths of these sides are not given. Moreover, it seems that knowing only the diameter of the circle is not sufficient to determine AO and OB. Thus, using the Pythagorean Theorem does not appear to be a productive strategy.

Our new strategy is to find parts of a triangle by using congruent or similar triangles. Triangle BCA is congruent to $\triangle AOB$. However, there is no more information about $\triangle BCA$ than about $\triangle AOB$. Because Figure 15-1 shows no other triangles, we implore the heuristic of *using a diagram* to derive new information. We need to draw an additional segment to define a new triangle. The newly constructed triangle should have sides of known lengths. Because the length of the diameter is 10 cm and the radius is 5 cm, the most natural choice is $\overline{OC}$, as shown in Figure 15-2. The diagonals of a rectangle are congruent. (In Chapter 11, this was shown by proving $\triangle ABO \cong \triangle COB$.) Thus, $\overline{OC} \cong \overline{AB}$ and $AB = 5$ cm.

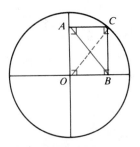

FIGURE 15-2

EXAMPLE 15-2 **835**

The solution to Example 15-1 focused on the goal of finding *AB* and relied on previous experiences in solving such problems by trying the Pythagorean Theorem and using congruent triangles. The Pythagorean Theorem approach was abandoned because of insufficient information. Next, a search for appropriate congruent triangles became the focus. This search became the new goal. In the congruent-triangle approach, we used all possible information from the problem, along with previous definitions and related theorems. The related theorems gave new information that resulted in a solution.

EXAMPLE 15-2   A toy maker decides to design a wooden cube with square holes in each of the cube's faces. The holes extend all the way through the cube, as shown in Figure 15-3. The toy maker wants the length of each side of the square holes to be one-third the length of a side of the cube. If the total surface area of the toy is to be 2 m², how long should the sides of the cube be?

FIGURE 15-3

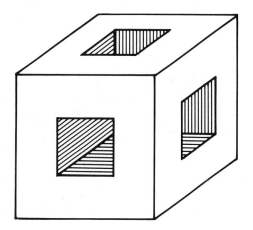

SOLUTION   We designate the length of the side of the cube by x, so the length of a side of one of the holes is $\dfrac{x}{3}$. If we can find the total surface area of the toy in terms of x, then, by setting this expression equal to 2 and solving for x, we will have the required length of a side of the cube.

Because a hole is to be cut through each face of the cube, the area of each face, excluding the area of the hole, is

$$x^2 - \left(\frac{x}{3}\right)^2 \quad \text{or} \quad x^2 - \frac{x^2}{9} \quad \text{or} \quad \frac{8}{9}x^2$$

Because the cube has six faces, the area of these six faces with the areas of the holes excluded is $6 \cdot \frac{8}{9}x^2$, or $\frac{16}{3}x^2$. Due to cutting, there is an "inside cube" (which corresponds to each of the six faces) cut away. Cutting away an inside cube leaves only four faces to be considered for the total surface area. The surface area of the four faces is $4 \cdot \dfrac{x^2}{9}$. Now, the surface area of these six inside cubes is

$$6 \cdot 4 \cdot \frac{x^2}{9}, \quad \text{or} \quad \frac{8}{3} x^2$$

The space in the center of the original cube is empty and has no surface area. Therefore, the total surface area of the toy is $\frac{16}{3} x^2 + \frac{8}{3} x^2$, or $\frac{24}{3} x^2$, or $8x^2$. Consequently,

$$8x^2 = 2$$

$$x^2 = \frac{1}{4}$$

$$x = \frac{1}{2}$$

Thus, the side of the cube should be $\frac{1}{2}$ m, or 50 cm, long.

A related problem is to find the total surface area if cylindrical holes are drilled through each face of a cube.

EXAMPLE 15-3 In a portion of a large city, the streets divide the city into square blocks of equal size, as shown in Figure 15-4. A taxi driver drives daily from point A to P. One day she drove from A to B along $\overline{AB}$ and then from B to P along $\overline{BP}$. If she does not want to cover any distance longer than $AB + BP$, how many possible routes are there from A to P?

FIGURE 15-4

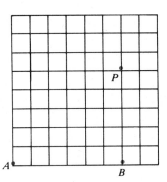

SOLUTION In order to travel the minimum distance, the taxi driver should only go north (upward) and east (to the right). Two routes are shown in Figure 15-5. For each of the routes, the total length of the horizontal segments is AB. Similarly, the total length of the vertical segments is BP. Thus, the length of each of the taxi driver's routes from A to P equals $AB + BP$.

EXAMPLE 15-3   **837**

FIGURE 15-5

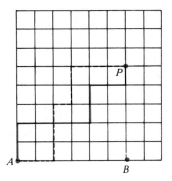

One way to solve the problem is by drawing all possible routes from A to P and counting them. Since that is an enormous task, we try looking for simpler versions of the problem. In Figure 15-6, there is only one possible route from A to C and only one route from A to F. In fact, each of the points on $\overleftrightarrow{AC}$ and $\overleftrightarrow{AF}$ can be reached via only one route.

FIGURE 15-6

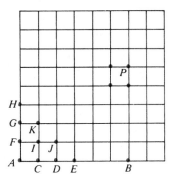

Next, we examine the routes from A to I. Only two are possible, A—F—I and A—C—I. From A to J there are three routes, namely, A—C—D—J, A—C—I—J, and A—F—I—J. Similarly, the number of routes to various other points from A can be counted. Figure 15-7 shows the number of possible routes to various points, starting from A.

FIGURE 15-7

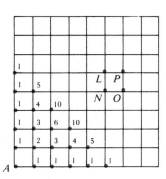

It appears that the number of routes to any given point from A is the sum of the number of routes to each of its two neighboring points, one immediately to the left and the other immediately below. If this pattern continues, it would be easy to work from point to point until we reach point P. The pattern can be justified because each of the routes from N to P in Figure 15-7 can be obtained from the two neighboring points L and O. Any route from A to P must pass through either L or O. The number of routes from A to P that pass through L is the same as the number of routes from A to L because, for each route from A to L, there is one single route to P that passes through L. Similarly, the number of routes from A to P that pass through O is the same as the number of routes from A to O. Thus, the number of routes from A to P is the sum of the routes from A to L and from A to O. Because the pattern in Figure 15-7 continues, there are 462 routes from A to P, as shown in Figure 15-8.

FIGURE 15-8

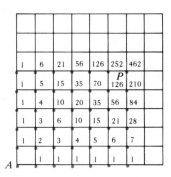

You may wish to investigate this example further by using the concept of combinations discussed in Chapter 8.

A good source of problems for the middle grades is the yearly American Junior High School Mathematics Examination, a Mathematical Association of America activity. These contest problems can be solved using material from normal seventh and eighth grade courses. Students have 40 minutes to work 25 problems. Here are the last four problems from the 1987 exam for you to try. For further information or to find out how students in your school can participate, see the References section in the back of this book.

EXAMPLE 15-3 **839**

3rd AJHSME 1987

22. ABCD is a rectangle, D is the center
    of the circle, and B is on the circle.
    If AD = 4 and CD = 3, then the area of
    the shaded region is between

    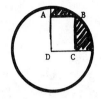

    A) 4 and 5   B) 5 and 6   C) 6 and 7

    D) 7 and 8   E) 8 and 9

23. Assume the adjoining chart shows the 1980
    U.S. population, in millions, for each
    region by ethnic group. To the nearest
    percent, what percent of the U.S. Black
    population lived in the South?

	NE	MW	South	West
White	42	52	57	35
Black	5	5	15	2
Asian	1	1	1	3
Other	1	1	2	4

    A) 20%   B) 25%   C) 40%   D) 56%   E) 80%

24. A multiple choice examination consists of 20 questions.
    The scoring is +5 for each correct answer, –2 for each
    incorrect answer, and 0 for each unanswered question. John's
    score on the examination is 48. What is the maximum number
    of questions he could have answered correctly?

    A) 9   B) 10   C) 11   D) 12   E) 16

25. Ten balls numbered 1 to 10 are in a jar. Jack reaches into the
    jar and randomly removes one of the balls. Then Jill reaches
    into the jar and randomly removes a different ball. The
    probability that the sum of the two numbers on the balls
    removed is even is

    A) $\frac{4}{9}$ B) $\frac{9}{19}$ C) $\frac{1}{2}$ D) $\frac{10}{19}$ E) $\frac{5}{9}$

PROBLEM SET 15-1

Problems 19, 20, 21, 24, 25, 32, and 33 are modifications of the following problems from the Mathematical Association of America's Annual High School Mathematics Examination: 9 (1972); 31 (1970); 15 (1971); 23 (1971); 34 (1970); 32 (1970); and 34 (1968). Also, Problems 17 and 18 are modifications of Problems 190 and 153, respectively, taken from the *Comprehensive School Mathematics Program, Elements of Mathematics, Book B, EM Problem Book*, by CEMREL Inc. (1975).

1. A ball bounces 0.8 of the distance from which it is dropped each time it is dropped. If it is dropped from a height of 6 feet, what is the least number of bounces the ball makes before it rises to a height of less than 1 foot?

2. Jim has saved some silver dollars. He wants to divide them among Tom, Dick, Mary, and Sue so that Tom gets $\frac{1}{2}$ of the total amount, Dick gets $\frac{1}{4}$, Mary gets $\frac{1}{5}$, and Sue gets 9 of the dollars. How many dollars has Jim saved?

3. During the baseball season thus far, Reggie has been at bat 381 times and has a batting average of approximately 0.291—that is, his number of hits divided by 381 is 0.291. If he gets 60 more official times at bat this season, how many hits must he get in order to end the season with a batting average of 0.300 or better?

4. A race track is 400 feet along the straight section and has a semicircle of radius 50 feet at each end. If one horse runs 10 feet from the inside railing at all times and a second horse runs 20 feet from the railing at all times, what is the difference in distance covered by the two horses in one lap of the track?

5. A circular object $\frac{1}{2}$ inch in diameter is dropped on a large grid consisting of squares that measure 3 inches on a side. If the circular object falls within the grid, what is the probability that it will not touch a grid line?

6. Willie can row 4 miles per hour in still water. If it takes him 2 hours to cover a certain distance rowing upstream and only 1 hour to row the same distance downstream, how fast is the current moving?

7. What is the least number of weights that can be used in order to be able to weigh any amount from 1 ounce to 680 ounces on a balance scale?

8. A computer is programmed to scan digits of successive integers. For example, if it scans the integers 1, 2, 3, 4, 5, 6, 7, 8, 9, 10, 11, 12, it has scanned 15 digits. How many digits has the computer scanned if it scans the consecutive integers from 1 through 10,000,000?

9. Find the remainder when $5^{999,999}$ is divided by 7.

10. A box contains ten red balls and five white balls. One ball is drawn at random from the box and is replaced by a ball of the opposite color. Now, if a ball is drawn from the box, what is the probability that it is red?

11. If Tom can beat Dick by 100 m in a 2-km race and Dick can beat Harry by 200 m in a 2-km race, then by how many meters can Tom beat Harry in a 2-km race?

12. Suppose that you have one 5-L container and one 3-L container. How can you take exactly 7 L of water from a well?

13. A single-elimination handball tournament was organized. There were 98 entrants, so in the first round there were 49 matches. In the second round, the 49 players were paired in 24 matches and one player received a bye. In the third round, the 25 players were then paired in 12 matches with one bye. The play and the pairing continued until a champion was determined.
    (a) How many matches were played?
    (b) If n players were entered in the tournament, how many matches would be required?

14. A circular race track for two runners has a 40-m radius for the inside running lane and a 41-m radius for the outside running lane.
    (a) How much of a head start should the outside runner be given?
    (b) How much of a head start should the outside runner be given if the radius of the inside running lane is 80 m and the radius of the outside lane is 81 m?

15. Without using a calculator, find the number of digits in the number $2^{12} \cdot 5^8$.

16. (a) Discover a pattern for the following sequence.
    $$\frac{3}{5}, \frac{7}{9}, \frac{11}{13}, \frac{15}{17}, \frac{19}{21}, \cdots$$
    (b) Find the 1000th fraction in the sequence.
    ★(c) Prove that all the fractions (there are infinitely many) in the sequence are in simplest form.

17. Start with a piece of paper. Cut it into five pieces. Take any one of the pieces and again cut it into five pieces. Then, pick one of these pieces and cut it into five pieces, and so on.
    (a) What numbers of pieces can be obtained in this way?
    (b) What is the number of pieces after the nth experiment?

18. In the figure, $\overline{BC}$ and $\overline{BE}$ represent two positions of a ladder. How wide is $\overline{AD}$ and how long is the ladder if $AC = 12$ m, $ED = 9$ m, $\overline{CB} \cong \overline{BE}$, and $\overline{CB} \perp \overline{BE}$?

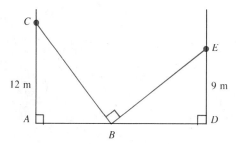

19. Ann and Sue bought identical boxes of stationery. Ann used hers to write 1-sheet letters and Sue used hers to write 3-sheet letters. Ann used all the envelopes and had 50 sheets of paper left, and Sue used all the sheets of paper and had 50 envelopes left. Find the number of sheets of paper in each box.

20. If a number is selected at random from the set of all five-digit numbers in which the sum of the digits equals 43, what is the probability that the number is divisible by 11?

21. An aquarium is in the shape of a right rectangular prism. It has a rectangular face that is 10 inches wide and 8 inches high. When the aquarium is tilted, the water in it just covers an 8- by 10-inch end, but only three-fourths of the rectangular bottom. Find the depth of the water when the aquarium is level on the table.

22. From a wire 10 units long, different shapes are constructed: a square, a rectangle with one side 2 units long, an equilateral triangle, a right isosceles triangle, and a circle.
    (a) Find the area of each shape. Which shape has the greatest area?
    (b) Make a conjecture concerning which figure has the greatest area among all figures with a given perimeter.

23. Susan's executive salary increased each of the past 2 years by 50% over the preceding year. Her present salary is $100,000 per year. To the nearest dollar, how much did she make 2 years ago?

24. Teams A and B play a series of games. The odds of either team's winning any game are even. Team A must win two games and Team B must win three games to win the series. Find the odds in favor of Team A's winning the series.

25. Find the greatest integer such that, when each of the numbers 13,511, 13,903, and 14,589 is divided by this integer, the remainders are the same.

26. Take a two- or three-digit number and create a new number by reversing the digits of the original number. Then, subtract the lesser number from the greater. Observe that the difference is divisible by 9. For example, $561 - 165$ is 396, which is divisible by 9. Is this always true? Justify your answer.

27. What is the angle between the clock hands at 2:15?

28. Given a regular hexagon and a point in its plane, and using only a straightedge and a compass, construct a straight line through the given point that separates the given hexagon into two parts of equal area.

29. Find the sum of all the digits in the integers 1 through 1,000,000,000.

30. Two adjacent sides of a parallelogram are on the lines given by $3x - 2y = 6$ and $5x + 4y = 21$. One vertex is at $(2, \,^-1)$. Without graphing, find the equations of the lines containing the other two sides and the coordinates of the point where the diagonals intersect.

31. Without graphing, find the center and radius of the circle passing through the points with coordinates $(0, 0)$, $(1, \,^-3)$, and $(4, 0)$.

★32. Starting at the same time from diametrically opposite points, Linda and David travel around a circular track at uniform speeds in opposite directions. They meet after David has traveled 100 m and a second time 60 m before Linda completes one lap. Find the circumference of the track.

★33. With 400 members voting, the House of Representatives defeated a bill. A revote, with the same members voting, resulted in passage of the bill by twice the margin by which it was originally defeated. The number voting for the bill on the revote was $\frac{12}{11}$ of the number voting against it originally. How many more members voted for the bill the second time than voted for it the first time?

★34. Lines from the vertices of square $ABCD$ to the midpoints of the sides M, N, O, and P are shown in the following figure.
    (a) Prove that quadrilateral $HGFE$ is a square.
    (b) What is the area of square $HGFE$ if the area of quadrilateral $ABCD$ is 100 cm²? Justify your answer.

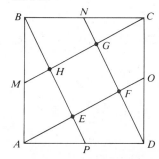

35. The "triangle" pictured below is called **Pascal's triangle,** after the French mathematician Blaise Pascal. Each number in the triangle, except the ones on the "boundary," equals the sum of two immediate neighboring numbers in the preceding row. (Note how the numbers in the triangle compare with those in Figure 15-7.

													Row
						1							(0)
					1		1						(1)
				1		2		1					(2)
			1		3		3		1				(3)
		1		4		6		4		1			(4)
	1		5		10		10		5		1		(5)
1		6		15		20		15		6		1	(6)
1	7	21	35		35	21	7	1					(7)

(a) Continue the triangle by finding two more rows.
(b) Find the sums of the numbers in the first row, the second row, the third row, and the fourth row. Do you notice a pattern? Can you predict the sum of the numbers in the tenth row? Make a general conjecture for the sum of the numbers in the nth row.

(c) Find the "alternate" sum of numbers in each row after row 1; that is,

$$1 - 1$$
$$1 - 2 + 1$$
$$1 - 3 + 3 - 1$$
$$1 - 4 + 6 - 4 + 1$$

(d) Find other patterns among the numbers in Pascal's triangle.

★**36.** Justify your conjecture in Problem 35(b).

★**37.** The king of Ilusia lost a war and was forced to divide his kingdom into a number of smaller countries, no two the same size. The king also had to distribute all 1000 bars of his gold in such a way that each country received 1 bar more than the next smaller country. No bars could be broken. If the king divided his kingdom into the least number of countries possible and divided his gold as described, how many countries were formed and how many bars of gold did each country receive?

An Introduction to BASIC

Introduction

program

Our primary goal in this appendix is to familiarize you with the rudiments of the BASIC language and to provide practice in using some of the commands of BASIC. To communicate with a computer and to tell it how to perform tasks, we write a set of instructions called a **program,** or use programs that other people have written.

BASIC: Variables and Operations

system commands
programming commands

BASIC is a language consisting of words, punctuation, and syntax used in combination to form statements. Some BASIC key words are **system commands,** such as RUN and LIST; other BASIC key words are **programming commands,** such as PRINT, LET, INPUT, REM, END, GOTO, IF-THEN, and FOR-NEXT. Statements are put together, using programming commands, to form a program. Figure AI-1 illustrates two examples of very simple BASIC programs: the first for printing a message and the second for calculating the value of Y for a given value of X, where

$$Y = 5X^4 + \frac{4}{X} - 3$$

In BASIC, numeric variables may be denoted by single letters, by two letters placed next to each other with no spaces between them, by a letter followed by a single digit, or by a letter followed by a number in parentheses.

FIGURE AI-1

```
(a) 10 PRINT "HERE WE GO"
    20 PRINT "LET'S LEARN TO PROGRAM"
    30 END
```

```
(b) 10 INPUT X
    20 LET Y = 5 * X ∧ 4 + 4 / X - 3
    30 PRINT Y
    40 END
```

string variables

In Figure AI-1(b), the variables X and Y are used. A different type of variable, called a **string variable,** is denoted by a letter followed by a dollar sign, for example, A$. A string variable may be used for nonnumeric values such as words or strings of symbols.

Some of the symbols in Figure AI-1(b) that are used in BASIC to represent arithmetic operations are different from usual symbols. Examples are given in Table AI-1.

TABLE AI-1

Operation	Math Symbol	Math Example	BASIC Symbol	BASIC Example
Addition	+	2 + 3	+	2 + 3
Subtraction	−	5 − 2	−	5 − 2
Multiplication	× or ·	5 × 3 or 5 · 3	*	5 * 3
Division	÷	16 ÷ 4	/	16/4
Exponentiation		2^3	∧ or ↑ or **	2 ∧ 3 or 2 ↑ 3 or 2 ** 3

System Commands

line number

RUN

LIST

Each line in the programs in Figure AI-1 is a statement that gives the computer an instruction. Notice that each statement begins with a **line number.** A system command such as RUN does not require a line number. When **RUN** is entered with a program in the internal memory, the computer executes the instructions in the program in the order of the line numbers. In most cases, the numbers 10, 20, 30, . . . or 100, 200, 300, . . . are used for line numbers to leave room for forgotten statements, which may be added later. For example, suppose that after typing line 30 in Figure AI-1(b) (PRINT Y), you realize that you should have had a statement between lines 10 and 20. All that is necessary is to type the new statement preceded by a line number between 10 and 20, such as 15. The new line can be typed at any time when the program is still active. The computer will rearrange all the lines in the correct order and will execute the program in the correct order. To delete errors in a given line, you may retype the line correctly. It should be noted that some computers allow full-screen editing, in which parts of a line may be changed without retyping an entire line. When the system command **LIST** is entered, the program will be displayed with all the line numbers in proper numerical order and all corrections included. LIST can be used at any time to see the complete program that is currently in the computer's memory.

NEW

Another system command that is useful if more than one program is being written is **NEW.** If we type NEW and press the RETURN key, the computer's memory is cleared, and a new program can be written without the danger of having the lines of the new program merged with a program that is already in memory. However, remember that when NEW is typed and the RETURN key is pressed, the old program in the internal memory is lost. If we want the old program saved, it may be stored in memory. The computer manual may be consulted to see how to accomplish this.

Programming Commands

The four BASIC key words that were used in Figure AI-1(b) are INPUT, LET, PRINT, and END. These are called programming commands. In line 10, the key word **INPUT** is followed by the variable X. The INPUT statement causes the computer to stop during the run and print "?". The user must assign a specific numerical value to X in this particular program by typing in that value and pressing RETURN key. After the value is entered, the program will continue. An INPUT statement always consists of the word INPUT and a variable or list of variables separated by commas.

INPUT

LET

In line 20, we see a statement that contains the key word **LET.** A LET statement is used to assign a value to a variable. The LET statement places data in a memory location. In Figure AI-1(b), the variable Y is assigned the value

```
5 * X ∧ 4 + 4 / X - 3
```

and this value is stored in the memory location labeled Y. The statement is composed of a line number, followed by the word LET, followed by a variable that equals a mathematical expression. The command LET is frequently optional. For example, LET X = 17 is simply written as X = 17 on many machines.

PRINT

In line 30, we see the key word **PRINT.** PRINT Y is a direction to the computer to print the value of the variable Y when the program is run. (Other uses of the key word PRINT will be discussed later.)

END

The **END** statement indicates the end of a program. Some systems do not require an END statement, but it is good programming style to use it.

When the program in Figure AI-1(b) is run, the computer acts as the function machine shown in Figure AI-2. When the value of the variable X is input, the machine assigns a value for Y according to the rule $Y = 5X^4 + \dfrac{4}{X} - 3$. Thus, if the input is 2 (that is, X = 2), the output will be $Y = 5 \cdot 2^4 + \dfrac{4}{2} - 3 = 79.$

FIGURE AI-2

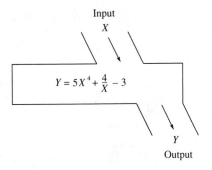

Input
X

$$Y = 5X^4 + \frac{4}{X} - 3$$

Y
Output

To use the program in Figure AI-1(b) to find the value of Y for a given X, such as X = 2, type RUN and then press the RETURN key. (*For the remainder of the chapter, it is assumed that the* RETURN *key is pressed as needed.*) The computer will print a question mark, which indicates that the user should input a value, in our case, 2. The computer then prints the corresponding value of Y, which is 79. The interaction with the computer will look like this (*the boldface characters are typed by the computer*):

RUN
? 2
79

On many computers, the word **READY** is printed when the run is completed. Other machines may indicate this by the word **OK** or a flashing cursor or some other device. These are the computer's way of saying that it is ready for your next instruction. If you wish to input a new number for X into the program, type RUN again and press the RETURN key. Another question mark will appear, and the new number may be input. If we input 180 for X and run the program, the printout appears as follows.

RUN
? 180
5.2488E+09

E-notation

The answer, 5.2488E+09, is represented using **E-notation.** This notation is like scientific notation in that the letter E means "exponent" and indicates the power or exponent on the base ten. The use of E-notation may vary from one brand of computer to another.

1.876E+07 means $1.876 \cdot 10^7$, or 18,760,000

7.9325E−04 means $7.9325 \cdot 10^{-4}$, or 0.00079325

The order of operations that a computer uses is the same as those discussed in previous chapters; that is, exponentiations (if any) are done first; multiplications and divisions are done next, in order from left to right; and additions and subtractions are done last, also in order from left to right unless parentheses indicate otherwise. *When you are in doubt as to how the computer will execute the operations, use parentheses.*

EXAMPLE AI-1 Write (a) through (c) in BASIC notation, and (d) and (e) in base-ten notation.

(a) $b^2 - 4ac$

(b) $\dfrac{3(4 + b)}{c}$

(c) $3 + 4c^3$

(d) 3.4798E + 08

(e) 4.5935E − 05

SOLUTION
(a) B $\wedge$ 2 − 4 $*$ A $*$ C

(b) 3 $*$ (4 + B) / C

(c) 3 + 4 $*$ C $\wedge$ 3

(d) $3.4798 \cdot 10^8$ = 347,980,000

(e) $4.5935 \cdot 10^{-5}$ = 0.000045935

Several BASIC programming commands are used in the following example.

EXAMPLE AI-2 Fair State University is increasing the salaries of its faculty based on performance. A department secretary needs a computer program to check the controller's figures. The program must calculate the next year's salary for each faculty member, given the present salary and the percent of increase of the salary of that faculty member. Write a program for the secretary to calculate each new salary. Try your program for an old salary of $38,479 and a percent of increase of 17%.

SOLUTION If the old salary and the percent of increase are denoted by S and P, respectively, then the new salary N is given by $N = S + S \cdot \dfrac{P}{100}$, or $N = S \cdot \left(1 + \dfrac{P}{100}\right)$. A program for this computation follows.

```
10 REM UNIVERSITY SALARY INCREASE
20 PRINT "ENTER THE OLD SALARY AND THE PERCENT"
30 PRINT "OF INCREASE SEPARATED BY A COMMA."
40 INPUT S, P
50 LET N = S * (1 + P / 100)
60 PRINT "THE NEW SALARY IS $"; N
70 END
```

When the program is run for the given salary and percent of increase, the printout will be as follows.

ENTER THE OLD SALARY AND THE PERCENT
OF INCREASE SEPARATED BY A COMMA.
?38479,17
THE NEW SALARY IS $45020.43

In lines 20 and 30 of Example AI-2, we have used the programming command PRINT. When the program is run, the computer prints everything inside the quotation marks. When a semicolon is placed at the end of a

PRINT statement, the computer continues the next PRINT statement on the same line, one space to the right of the last printed character. (This placement may vary on different machines.) In line 60, PRINT is used with a phrase in quotation marks followed by a semicolon and the letter N. When the semicolon is used, the value of N is printed immediately following the phrase. (You should investigate what happens when a comma is used in place of a semicolon.) Execute the program to determine the output.

REM

A programmer may wish to make a remark or title the program on the very first line. This can be done by using the programming command PRINT or a new programming command, **REM** (for REMARK). If a REM statement is used as in line 10 above the computer will save the line as an explanation of the program for anybody who desires to list the program. The REM statement is ignored during execution and is not printed during a run.

Branching

If-Then Statements

One possible use of the computer in education is in computer-assisted instruction—for example, in designing programs to create drill problems. Suppose we want to design a program that can be used repeatedly to allow students to practice adding two numbers. We want the students to keep working on a problem until they get it correct; then, they will receive a new problem. This can be accomplished through **branching.** One way that branching occurs is when decisions are made in a program through the use of the programming statement **IF-THEN.** (This type of branching is called *conditional branching.*) The general form of an IF-THEN statement is IF (*condition*) THEN (*line number or command*). For example,

branching

IF-THEN

```
30 IF X < 2 THEN 60
```

When the computer executes line 30, it evaluates the condition $X < 2$. If the value of X is less than 2, then the computer branches to the line number following the word THEN, in this case, line 60. If the value of X is not less than 2, the computer executes the next statement listed in numerical order. The condition following the IF part always includes an equality or inequality symbol. However, in BASIC, some of these symbols differ from their mathematical counterparts. The symbols are compared in Table AI-2.

We now attempt to write the two-number drill program mentioned previously. In order for a program to be meaningful to another user, it should be "user friendly"; that is, it should contain instructions telling the user exactly what to do. These instructions can be given by using PRINT statements. The numbers to be added must either be input by the user or generated by the computer's random-number generator. For this program, we choose the second option. However, before doing this, we investigate the computer's random-number generator.

TABLE AI-2

Mathematical Symbol	BASIC Symbol	Meaning
=	=	Equals
<	<	Is less than
≤	< =	Is less than or equal to
>	>	Is greater than
≥	> =	Is greater than or equal to
≠	<>	Is not equal to

RND   The general form of the function is **RND(X),** where **RND** is the name of the function and X is the argument of the function. On some computers, the value of the argument is important; on others, it is not. (On some computers, the argument is not needed at all.) The reader should consult the user's manual for specifics. For this text, we use RND(1).

The RND function causes some computers to select a random (unpredictable) six-digit number between 0 and .999999, such as .893352, .158723, or .931562. Because many programs require the use of random numbers in ranges other than from 0 to 1, we must find a way to select numbers in other ranges. For example, suppose we want the computer to select a nonnegative integer less than 100. If we multiply the RND function by 100, it will generate values between 0 and 99.9999. If we want random-integer values between 0 and 99.9999, we use the INT function, as follows.

```
10 LET N = INT(100 * RND(1))
```

Now, N takes on nonnegative integer values less than 100.

INT   **INT,** called the greatest-integer function, is a BASIC command used in the form of INT(X), where X is the argument. When used in a program, INT(X) will produce the greatest integer less than or equal to X. For example, executing PRINT INT (3.5) produces the computer output **3.**

If we want our two-number addition program to give us addition facts involving numbers between 1 and 10, we use the expression INT(10 ∗ RND(1)) + 1 in our program.

Once the numbers are chosen and added, we must inform the user whether the sum is correct. We must also determine whether the user wishes to continue the practice. IF-THEN and GOTO statements are used to *GOTO*   accomplish this. **GOTO** statements allow the program to branch to another statement instead of following the statements in the order given by the line numbers. (Observe that the GOTO command allows unconditional branching to another line of the program.) These ideas are incorporated in the following program.

```
10 PRINT "THIS PROGRAM PROVIDES ADDITION PRACTICE."
20 LET A = INT (10 * RND(1)) + 1
30 LET B = INT (10 * RND(1)) + 1
40 PRINT "AFTER THE QUESTION MARK, TYPE THE SUM."
50 PRINT A; "+"; B; "=";
```

```
60 INPUT C
70 IF A + B = C THEN 100
80 PRINT "SORRY, TRY AGAIN."
90 GOTO 40
100 PRINT "VERY GOOD, DO YOU WANT TO ADD"
110 PRINT "OTHER NUMBERS?"
120 INPUT D$
130 IF D$ = "YES" THEN 20
140 END
```

Note that there are two IF-THEN statements in the preceding program. When the program is run and line 70 is reached, and if $A + B = C$ is true, then the computer branches to line 100 and continues the run. In line 70, if $A + B = C$ is not true, the computer automatically goes to the next line, line 80, and continues the run.

When the program is run and the computer reaches line 90, the program automatically loops back to line 40, and the run continues. It should be noted that if a student continually misses the addition, the run will never get past line 90. (The program could have been written to ask the student if another try is desired.) On different machines, the procedure to get out of such a loop varies. On many machines, the keys $\boxed{\text{STOP}}$ or $\boxed{\text{BREAK}}$ are used. On some other machines, the user should press the $\boxed{\text{CONTROL}}$ key and the $\boxed{\text{C}}$ key at the same time (called a CONTROL-C, or press the $\boxed{\text{RESET}}$ key or $\boxed{\text{CONTROL}}$ $\boxed{\text{RESET}}$. This may have to be done several times to stop the run, at which time the computer will indicate that it is ready for you to proceed.

Counters

Suppose we want to keep a record of how many drill exercises an individual attempts. This can be done by using a *counter,* which uses either an IF-THEN or a GOTO statement along with a LET statement. A LET statement allows us to set the value of a variable; for example, LET X = 10. BASIC also allows a variable to be defined in terms of itself; for example, LET X = X + 1. The computer does not interpret $X = X + 1$ as an equation, but rather as "replace X with X + 1." This is useful in a program that counts how many exercises were correctly answered or, in general, how many times a certain section of a program has been executed. Consider the following program.

```
10 LET X = 0
20 LET X = X + 1
30 PRINT X
40 IF X < 10 THEN 20
50 END
```

initialized In line 10, X is **initialized,** or set to 0. Line 20 is the counter. When the program is run, the output appears as follows.

1
2
3
⋮
10

To understand this output, notice that in line 10, X equals 0. In line 20, the new value of X becomes 0 + 1, or 1. Hence, at line 30, the value 1 isprinted. Next, the computer executes the instruction in line 40. Because 1 < 10, it branches to line 20. As X now has value 1, the new value of X in line 20 becomes 1 + 1, or 2. Thus, 2 is printed, and so on. After 9 is printed, we are again at line 40. Because 9 < 10, the computer again branches to line 20, and the new value of X becomes 9 + 1, or 10. This value is printed; because 10 < 10 is false, the program continues to line 50 and ends.

We now return to our original addition-drill program. To keep a record of the number of drill exercises attempted, a counter is inserted between lines 30 and 40. A PRINT statement in line 140 outputs the desired record. The revised program is as follows.

```
10  PRINT "THIS PROGRAM PROVIDES ADDITION PRACTICE."
15  LET X = 0
20  LET A = INT (10 * RND(1)) + 1
30  LET B = INT (10 * RND(1)) + 1
35  LET X = X + 1
40  PRINT "AFTER THE QUESTION MARK, TYPE THE SUM."
50  PRINT A;"+";B;"=";
60  INPUT C
70  IF A + B = C THEN 100
80  PRINT "SORRY, TRY AGAIN."
90  GOTO 40
100 PRINT "VERY GOOD, DO YOU WANT TO ADD"
110 PRINT "ANOTHER PAIR OF NUMBERS?"
120 INPUT D$
130 IF D$ = "YES" THEN 20
140 PRINT "THE NUMBER OF EXERCISES WAS " ;X
150 END
```

The program could be edited to allow the computer to tell not only the number of exercises attempted but also the number done correctly.

For-Next Statements

FOR-NEXT

Another method for having the computer count how many times an action is performed is with the use of the key words **FOR-NEXT.** In a BASIC program, FOR-NEXT statements always occur in pairs, with the FOR statement preceding the associated NEXT statement. For example, we could utilize FOR-NEXT statements as shown.

```
20 FOR X = 1 TO 10
 :
 :
120 NEXT X
```

If a program containing the preceding lines is run and line 20 is reached, the computer initializes a counter by assigning the value of 1 to X. At line 120, the computer loops back to line 20, assigns the value 2 to X, again continues to line 120, loops back, and so on, until X = 10. When X is 10 and line 120 is reached, the computer continues on to the next line of the program following line 120. With no other directions in line 20, the computer automatically increments X by 1 each time the loop is passed through. X can
STEP   be incremented for other values by using the word **STEP** and the desired value. For example, replace line 20 with the following.

```
20 FOR X = 1 TO 10 STEP 0.5
```

This line will initialize X with a value of 1 and increase this value by 0.5 each time line 20 is reached. The values of X will be 1, 1.5, 2, 2.5, 3, . . . , 9, 9.5, 10.

STEP can also be used to decrement, rather than increment, the FOR-NEXT loop. For example, consider the following line.

```
20 FOR X = 10 TO 1 STEP -0.5
```

Here, the value of X will be initialized at 10 and will decrease in steps of 0.5 until it reaches X = 1. Thus, the values of X will be 10, 9.5, 9, 8.5, 8, . . . , 1.

FOR-NEXT commands are very useful when you know how many times to go through the loop. The counter and the IF-THEN loop are useful when you are not sure of the number of iterations. A further use of the FOR-NEXT command is given in the following problem.

PROBLEM 1

Professor Anna Litik was asked by the university athletic director to devise a chart for converting the heights of visiting basketball players from inches to centimeters. Help Dr. Litik by writing a program that will print a table giving the conversions incremented by half inches from 65 inches to 84 inches.

Understanding the Problem. The problem is to write a program that will output the number of centimeters that corresponds to a certain number of inches. Furthermore, the numbers of inches are from 65 to 84, inclusive, and the conversions made must be for each half inch. To solve this problem, the conversion factor 1 inch = 2.54 cm is needed. Thus, 2 inches = 2(2.54) cm, or 5.08 cm, and, in general, N inches = N(2.54) cm.

Devising a Plan. We can write a program using FOR-NEXT statements to produce a table for converting heights from inches to centimeters. We let X represent the number of inches starting at 65, increment by 0.5, and end at 84. Between the FOR and NEXT statements, we must print the value of X to represent the equivalent number of centimeters. Because it would be inappropriate to report that a player's height is 196.62 cm, we need to report the heights as integers. We do this by using INT. In our program, we can use INT(X * 2.54) to assign an integer number of centimeters to X inches. However, INT does not round numbers. If we would like to build in a rounding factor, we might consider using INT(X * 2.54 + 0.5). (Why?)

To write the program, we set the first value of X equal to 65 inches. Next, we convert 65 inches to centimeters by multiplying by 2.54 and then choose the greatest integer less than or equal to $65 \cdot 2.54 + 0.5$. We then print X and the obtained integer and loop back for the next value of X, which is 0.5 greater than the last value converted. This procedure continues until all values have been converted. The complete program follows. In line 50, the PRINT statement is used to provide the desired output in a more readable format. When a PRINT statement is typed with no inputs, a blank line is left between the outputs.

```
10 REM THIS PROGRAM WILL PRINT A
20 REM TABLE FOR CONVERTING INCHES
30 REM TO CENTIMETERS
40 PRINT "INCHES", "CENTIMETERS"
50 PRINT
60 FOR X = 65 TO 84 STEP 0.5
70 LET Y = INT(X * 2.54 + 0.5)
80 PRINT X, Y
90 NEXT X
100 END
```

Carrying Out the Plan. A shortened version of the printout obtained when the program is run follows. Notice that the space between the headings and the data was obtained from line 50 in the program.

INCHES	CENTIMETERS
65	165
65.5	166
66	168
66.5	169
67	170
67.5	171
68	173
68.5	174
69	175
69.5	177
⋮	⋮
83.5	212
84	213

Looking Back. This program could be revised to generate other conversion charts. All that would be necessary would be to find the required conversion factors and edit the program accordingly.

Read and Data Statements

READ / DATA   When large blocks of data are used, the key words **READ** and **DATA** are very useful. The formats for the READ and DATA statements are as follows.

READ Variable(s)

DATA Constant(s)

The variables in a READ statement are separated by commas. Similarly, the constants in a DATA statement are separated by commas. A comma should not be used at the end of the data. An example of statements containing the commands READ and DATA follow.

```
10 READ A1, B, B2, Z
50 DATA 9, 6, 2, .5
```

When a program containing READ-DATA statements is run, the computer assigns the constants in the DATA statement to the variables in the READ statement in the order they are listed. A branching command, such as GOTO, is normally used to have the computer loop back to the READ statement so that it will use all DATA when the program is run. It should be noted that several READ statements can be used with one DATA statement as long as there are sufficient data for each of the variables in the READ statement; or, one READ statement may be used with several DATA statements. An example of the use of the READ-DATA commands to solve a problem is given in Problem 2.

PROBLEM 2

Dr. Jubal, an English professor, had five test scores for each of his five graduate students in English. The grades for the students are as follows.

Student # (S)	Grammar (G)	Writing (W)	Drama (D)	Poetry (P)	Novel (N)
1	72	93	86	82	86
2	83	86	95	74	80
3	91	82	76	60	89
4	88	94	72	76	84
5	75	84	98	92	79

Determine averages for Dr. Jubal by writing a program to find the mean for each student.

Understanding the Problem.   In this problem, we are given a list of scores for Dr. Jubal's students on various tests. We are to write a program to calculate the mean for each student, that is, the arithmetic average of the scores for each student. Thus, we need to find the sum of the five scores for each student and divide by 5.

Devising a Plan.   We can write a program to find the mean for each student by using READ-DATA statements. To find the mean for each student, we use a READ statement with the variable S for student number and variables G, W, D, P, and N for grammar, writing, drama, poetry, and novel scores, respectively. For example, for student 1, we want the computer to calculate M = (G + W + D + P + N)/5, or (72 + 93 + 86 + 82 + 86)/5. After the mean is computed for each student, we need a printout that lists students numbers and corresponding means. A sample program to compute the means is as follows.

```
10 REM THIS PROGRAM PRINTS MEANS FOR DR. JUBAL.
20 PRINT "STUDENT #, "MEAN"
30 READ S, G, W, D, P, N
40 LET M = (G + W + D + P + N) / 5
50 PRINT
60 PRINT S, M
70 GOTO 30
80 DATA 1,72,93,86,82,86,2,83,86,95,74,80,3,91,82,76,60,89
90 DATA 4,88,94,72,76,84,5,75,84,98,92,79
100 END
```

●   R E M A R K
Note that not all the data could be listed in one DATA line. The computer will accept data from as many DATA lines as you wish, but the number of DATA items should be a multiple of the number of variables in a READ statement. The DATA statements may be anywhere in the program, but they are usually at the end.

Carrying Out the Plan.   A run for the program would appear as follows.

STUDENT #	MEAN
1	85.8
2	83.6
3	79.6
4	82.8
5	85.6

?OUT OF DATA ERROR IN 30

Now, we have the averages of each of Dr. Jubal's students. Note the message at the end of the output. This message tells us that all the data have been used.

flagging

Looking Back. Various computers may print different messages or no message when all the data are used. To eliminate the message at the end of the printout a method called **flagging** can be used. See a BASIC computer manual for more information about this method.

A FOR-NEXT loop could also be used to signal that all the data for Dr. Jubal's class have been used, as seen in the following modified program.

```
10 REM THIS PROGRAM PRINTS MEANS FOR DR. JUBAL.
20 PRINT "STUDENT #, "MEAN"
30 FOR S = 1 TO 5
40 READ S, G, W, D, P, N
50 LET M = (G + W + D + P + N) / 5
60 PRINT
70 PRINT S, M
80 NEXT S
90 DATA 1,72,93,86,82,86,2,83,86,95,74,80,3,91,82,76,60,89
100 DATA 4,88,94,72,76,84,5,75,84,98,92,79
110 END
```

We now have three methods of getting data into the computer: LET statements, INPUT statements, and READ-DATA statements. One of the primary advantages of READ-DATA statements over INPUT statements is the speed with which the computer is able to accept and use the information. Another advantage is not having to enter information every time the program is run. There is no lag time while the computer waits for the user to input information during the run of the program. However, when using READ-DATA statements, the program itself must be changed to input new data; the use of INPUT allows the user to input new data without altering the program.

PROBLEM 3

In 1980, the number of cars using the Chicago Loop and Inter-Mountain Bypass highways were 220,819,000 and 66,944,000, respectively. If the annual usage growth rates for these two highways were 1.5% and 2.9%, respectively, and if these usage rates were to remain constant, in what year would the number of cars using the Inter-Mountain Bypass equal or surpass the number of cars using the Chicago Loop? How many cars would use each highway in that year?

Understanding the Problem. A useful strategy in problem solving is to compare the given problem to any related problems that have previously been solved. Each number of cars in the current problem plays the role of the principal in a compound-interest problem. Thus, the number of cars using the Chicago Loop is growing according to the formula $220,819,000(1 + .015)^N$, where N is the number of years involved. Similarly, the number of cars using the Inter-Mountain Bypass is growing according to the formula

$$66,944,000(1 + .029)^N$$

Devising a Plan. The program must be written so that the number of cars on each road is computed for different years; in addition, the first time the number of Inter-Mountain cars is greater than or equal to the number of Chicago Loop cars, the computer should print the value of N added to 1980, giving the desired years. The total number of cars for both highways should also be output at this time. The program must have a counter, and it must contain a loop to compute values for different Ns. A program based on this discussion follows.

```
10 REM A TRAFFIC PROBLEM INVOLVING THE CHICAGO LOOP AND IM BYPASS
15 LET N = 0
20 LET N = N + 1
30 LET C = 220819000 * 1.015 ∧ N
40 LET I = 66944000 * 1.029 ∧ N
50 IF I >= C THEN 70
60 GOTO 20
70 PRINT "IN ";N + 1980;", THE NUMBER OF CHICAGO"
80 PRINT "LOOP CARS WILL BE ";C
90 PRINT "IN ";N + 1980;", THE NUMBER OF IM BYPASS"
100 PRINT "CARS WILL BE ";I
110 END
```

Carrying Out the Plan. A run of the preceding program produces the following.

**IN 2068, THE NUMBER OF CHICAGO
LOOP CARS WILL BE 818555517
IN 2068, THE NUMBER OF IM BYPASS
CARS WILL BE 828446826**

Looking Back. An alternative activity might be to modify the program to find the number of cars of both the Chicago Loop and the Inter-Mountain Bypass in the year 2000, assuming the usage rates in the problem remain constant. In what year will the number of cars on the Chicago Loop exceed one-half billion?

SUMMARY OF COMMANDS

RUN	Causes the computer to execute a program.
LIST	Causes the computer to print a listing of a program.
NEW	Clears the computer's memory.
INPUT	Takes one input and causes the computer to pause during execution and output "?" as a prompt for data.
LET	Assigns a value to a variable.
PRINT	Causes the computer to print an input.
END	Indicates the end of a program.
REM	Used to include a remark or reminder.
IF-THEN	Used in the form IF (condition) THEN (line number of condition).
RND(X)	Causes the computer to select a random six-digit number between 0 and .999999.
INT(X)	Outputs the greatest integer less than or equal to X.
GOTO	Used in the form GOTO (line number) for branching.
FOR-NEXT	FOR-NEXT statements occur in pairs in a program, with the FOR statement preceding the NEXT statement.
STEP	Increments values of a variable.
READ-DATA	Used to enter large blocks of data in a program.

PROBLEM SET A1

1. Which of the following are valid variables in BASIC?
   (a) P   (b) M4   (c) 3Z   (d) M
   (e) AB   (f) BA(3)   (g) A4

2. Write each of the following using BASIC notation.

   (a) $X^2 + Y^2 - 3Z$ (b) $\left(\dfrac{24 \cdot 34}{2}\right)^3$

   (c) $a + b - \dfrac{c^2}{d}$ (d) $\dfrac{a + b}{c + d}$

   (e) $\dfrac{15}{a(2b^2 + 5)}$

3. Perform the following calculations in the same order a computer would.
   (a) 3 * 5 - 2 * 6 + 4
   (b) 7 * (6 - 2) / 4
   (c) 3 * (5 + 7) / (3 + 3)
   (d) 3 ∧ 3 / 9
   (e) (2 * (3 - 5)) ∧ 2
   (f) 9 ∧ 2 - 5 ∧ 3

4. Write each of the following as a base-ten number in standard form.
   (a) 3.52E + 07   (b) 1.93E − 05
   (c) −1.233E − 06   (d) −7.402E + 03

5. Predict the output, if any, for each of the following programs. If possible, check your answers on a computer.

   (a) 10 A = 5
       20 B = 10
       30 PRINT A,B
       40 END

   (b) 10 A = 5
       20 B = 10
       30 PRINT "A,B"
       40 END

   (c) 10 A = 5
       20 B = 10
       30 PRINT A, ,B
       40 END

   (d) 10 A = 5
       20 B = 10
       30 PRINT A;B
       40 END

   (e) 10 A = 5
       20 B = 10
           PRINT A,B
       40 END

   (f) 10 A = 5
       20 B = 10
       30 PRINT A
       40 PRINT B
       50 END

(g)
```
10 A = 5
20 B = 10
30 PRINT A;
40 PRINT B
50 END
```
(h)
```
10 A = 5
20 B = 10
30 PRINT "THE VALUE OF A"
35 PRINT "IS ";A;".";
40 PRINT " THE VALUE OF B"
45 PRINT "IS ";B;"."
50 END
```
(i)
```
10 A = 5
20 B = 10
30 PRINT "THE VALUE OF A"
35 PRINT "IS ",A,".";
40 PRINT " THE VALUE OF B"
45 PRINT "IS ";B;"."
50 END
```

6. (a) Write a computer program for calculating the value of Y for a given X, where
$$Y = 13X^5 - \frac{27}{X} + 3.$$

   (b) Use the program in (a) to find the value of Y for: (i) $X = 1.873$; (ii) $X = 7$.

7. (a) Write a program (including a title and directions) for converting degrees Fahrenheit into degrees Celsius, using the formula $C = \frac{5}{9}(F - 32)$.

   (b) Use the program from (a) to convert the following Fahrenheit temperatures to Celsius.

   (i) 212°F   (ii) 98.6°F   (iii) 68°F
   (iv) 32°F   (v) −40°F   (vi) −273°F

8. Write a program for computing the volume of a right rectangular prism given its three dimensions L, W, and H, where V = LWH. Try your program for L = 8, W = 5, and H = 3.

9. $100 is invested in a bank for 25 years at 18% interest compounded annually. (a) Find the balance by using a single PRINT statement. (b) Find the balance by writing a program with an input N, where N is the number of years the money is invested.

10. Determine the output for the following programs and then run the programs on the computer to check your answers.

(a)
```
10 FOR I = 1 TO 15
20 PRINT I,
30 NEXT I
40 END
```
(b)
```
10 FOR I = 1 TO 15
20 PRINT I * 10,
```
```
30 NEXT I
40 END
```
(c)
```
10 FOR X = 1 TO 4 STEP 0.2
20 PRINT X,
30 NEXT X
40 END
```
(d)
```
10 FOR X = 15 TO 1 STEP - 1
20 PRINT X,
30 NEXT X
40 END
```
(e)
```
10 LET X = 100
20 PRINT X,
30 LET X = X - 1
40 IF X < 0 THEN 60
50 GOTO 20
60 END
```
(f)
```
10 LET X = 10
20 LET X = X + 1
30 PRINT X
40 IF X <= 10 THEN 20
50 END
```
(g)
```
10 READ X, Y
20 DATA 2, 3
30 IF X > Y THEN 50
40 PRINT X; " IS LESS THAN ";Y
50 END
```
(h)
```
10 FOR I = 2 TO 5
20 FOR J = 1 TO 3
30 PRINT I; J
40 NEXT J
50 NEXT Y
60 END
```

11. Determine the outputs of each of the following programs. Why are the outputs different?

(a)
```
10 PRINT "HEY YOU OUT THERE"
15 LET K = 0
20 LET K = K + 1
30 IF K > 5 THEN 50
40 GOTO 20
50 END
```
(b)
```
10 LET K = K + 1
20 PRINT "HEY YOU OUT THERE"
30 IF K > 5 THEN 50
40 GOTO 10
50 END
```

12. Rewrite the following program using a FOR-NEXT loops so that the outputs in (a) and (b) are obtained.
```
10 LET N = 1
20 IF N > 20 THEN 60
30 PRINT 2 * N
40 LET N = N + 1
50 GOTO 20
60 END
```

(a) 2
4
6
.
.
.

(b) **2 4 6 8 . . .**

13. Write a program to find the sum of the squares of the first 100 positive integers.

14. Modify the two-number addition program of this section to do two-number multiplications.

15. **SQR** is the BASIC square-root function. It is used in the form SQR(X), where X is the argument. X must be nonnegative. For example, PRINT SQR(16) produces the output **4**. Write and run a program to print a list of numbers from 1 to 10, their square roots, and their squares.

16. Write a program to determine if any positive integer N is a prime number.

17. Write a program to convert degrees Fahrenheit to degrees Celsius, using the formula $C = \dfrac{(F - 32)5}{9}$.
Make the program print Fahrenheit temperatures and corresponding Celsius temperatures from $^-40°F$ to 220°F, in intervals of 10°F.

18. Write a program to calculate the area A and the circumference C of a circle for any radius R that is input. Use $A = \pi R^2$ and $C = 2\pi R$, with $\pi \doteq 3.14159$.

19. Write a program to compute N! where N is any natural number. $(N! = 1 \cdot 2 \cdot 3 \cdot 4 \cdot \ldots \cdot (N - 1) \cdot N.)$

20. Laura won a lottery prize of $50,000. She put the money into a Certificate of Deposit at 15% per year paid annually. Suppose that, just after the interest is paid at the end of the first year, she withdraws $10,000 for a trip. The remainder is reinvested with the same terms. If she repeats this act year after year, write a program to find out how long her money will last.

21. Write a program to verify that
$$1^3 + 2^3 + 3^3 + \cdots + N^3 = (1 + 2 + 3 + \cdots + N)^2$$
is true for the first 10 natural numbers.

22. Write a program to compute the sum of the first 1000 odd natural numbers.

23. Write a program to find them sum
$$1 + \frac{1}{2} + \frac{1}{3} + \frac{1}{4} + \frac{1}{5} + \frac{1}{6} + \cdots + \frac{1}{N}$$
Run the program for N = 100.

24. Plastic Card Company computes its bills on the last day of the month. If a customer pays the bill within the first 10 days of the next month, a 5% discount is given. If the bill is paid within the next 10 days, the face value of the bill is paid. If the bill is paid after the 20th day, a penalty of 2% is added to the original bill computed at the end of the previous month. Write a program to take the customer I.D. number and the amount of the bill and print the amounts to be paid for each of the three options.

25. Write a program to compute and print out the value of the cube and the cube root of the first 20 natural numbers.

26. If you have $1000 invested in a bank at 5% annual interest compounded daily, how long would you have to leave it in the bank to have a balance of $5000?

27. Write a program to generate the first N Fibonacci numbers where N is any natural number. The Fibonacci sequence 1, 1, 2, 3, 5, 8, 13, 21, . . . is obtained by starting with 1, 1 and generating each successive term by summing the two previous terms. Check your program by finding the first ten Fibonacci numbers.

28. In baseball, the number of hits H a player gets divided by the number of times at bat B is called the "batting average." Write a program to have the computer print a player's number and batting average. (The decimal need not be rounded.)

29. Imagine that you are paid 1¢ on the first day, 2¢ on the second day, 4¢ on the third day, 8¢ on the fourth day, and, in general, 2^{n-1} cents on the nth day. Each day's salary is double that of the previous day. Compare the salary on the 15th day with the sum of the salaries for the first 14 days.

30. Write and run a program to find all numbers less than 40 than can be written as a sum of two square numbers.

An Introduction to Logo Turtle Graphics

Introduction

turtle Turtle graphics, implemented using the computer language Logo, are especially suited for studying geometry. Students give instructions to a **"turtle,"** a triangular figure on the display screen.

The following discussion refers to MIT Logo (Terrapin or Krell) run on an Apple or Commodore computer. Most commands also work in Apple Logo II, another version of the language. If commands differ in MIT Logo and Apple Logo II, the changes necessary for Apple Logo II are given in parentheses. If an abbreviation can be used in place of a Logo command, then it will be given in parentheses immediately following the command when it is introduced.

Section AII-1   ## Introducing the Turtle

In Logo, the computer accepts instructions in the nodraw, draw, and edit modes. After Logo is loaded into the computer, the first mode that appears

nodraw mode on the screen is the **nodraw mode.** A question mark, called a *prompt,* and a flashing *cursor* appear on the screen as the computer awaits instructions. To

draw mode
DRAW

NODRAW (ND)

primitives

execute turtle graphic commands, we enter the **draw mode** by typing **DRAW** (*in Apple Logo II, CLEARSCREEN (CS)*) and pressing the RETURN key.

After the DRAW command is executed, we can return to the nodraw mode by executing **NODRAW (ND)** (*in Apple Logo II, TEXTSCREEN*). In the draw mode, the turtle appears in the center of the screen, as shown in Figure AII-1. The turtle's position in the center of the screen is called "home." These built-in words that the computer understands, such as DRAW and NODRAW, are called **primitives.**

FIGURE AII-1

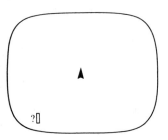

In Figure AII-1, the prompt at the bottom left of the screen indicates that the computer is ready to accept instructions, and the rectangular cursor shows where the next character that is typed will appear. Logo reserves the lines at the bottom of the screen for the user's input and the computer's responses. The remainder of the screen is used for drawing. This division of the screen into a drawing portion and a text portion is referred to as the *split-screen mode.*

Moving the Turtle

FORWARD (FD)
BACK (BK)

To make the turtle change position, we use the primitives **FORWARD (FD)** and **BACK (BK),** *followed by a space* and a numerical input. The numerical input tells the turtle how far to move. For example, after the DRAW command is executed, typing FORWARD 100 and pressing RETURN causes the turtle to move 100 "turtle units" in the direction it is pointing, as shown in Figure AII-2(a). Similarly, the BACK command may be used with a numerical input. For example, BACK 75 causes the turtle to move backwards 75 units. Giving the turtle too great an input causes the turtle to "wrap around" the screen. To explore how the turtle wraps, try FD 250 and observe what happens.

Turning the Turtle

RIGHT (RT)
LEFT (LT)

To make the turtle change direction, we used the commands **RIGHT (RT)** and **LEFT (LT).** The RIGHT and LEFT commands, along with numerical inputs, cause the turtle to turn in place the specified number of degrees. For example, typing RIGHT 90 and pressing RETURN causes the turtle to turn

FIGURE AII-2

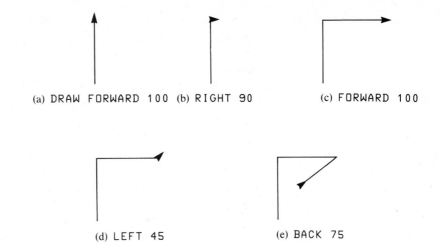

(a) DRAW FORWARD 100 (b) RIGHT 90   (c) FORWARD 100

(d) LEFT 45   (e) BACK 75

90° to the right of the direction it previously pointed. A sequence of moves illustrating these commands is given in Figure AII-2.

Logo accepts a sequence of commands written on one line. For example, Figure AII-2(e) could be drawn by typing the following and pressing RETURN .

```
DRAW FD 100 RT 90 FD 100 LT 45 BK 75
```

(In Apple Logo II, replace DRAW with CLEARSCREEN.)

PENUP(PU)
PENDOWN (PD)
HIDETURTLE (HT)
SHOWTURTLE (ST)

To move the turtle without leaving a trail, we use the command **PENUP (PU).** To make the turtle leave a trail again, type **PENDOWN (PD).** It is possible to hide the turtle by typing **HIDETURTLE (HT).** To make the turtle reappear, type **SHOWTURTLE (ST).**

HOME

To return the turtle to the center of the screen with heading 0, type the command **HOME.** However, a trail to the center of the screen will be drawn from the position the turtle occupied before HOME was typed unless the command PENUP is used before HOME.

To start a new drawing with a clear screen, we type DRAW *(in Apple Logo II, replace DRAW with CLEARSCREEN (CS))*. This returns the turtle to its initial position and direction in the center of the screen and clears the screen. Any time the turtle points straight north (up), we say it has heading 0. A heading of 90 is directly east, 180 is directly south, and 270 is directly west. The screen could be marked as shown in Figure AII-3.

FIGURE AII-3

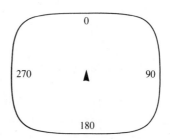

HEADING

PRINT (PR)

To learn the turtle's heading, we use HEADING. **HEADING** needs no inputs; typing HEADING in the draw mode and pressing RETURN causes the computer to output the turtle's heading. To have the computer print only the value of the heading, we use the primitive **PRINT (PR)** along with HEADING, as in PRINT HEADING. For example, if the turtle is at home with heading 0, and we type RT 45 PR HEADING, then 45 will be displayed.

● R E M A R K

PRINT (PR) normally takes one input, causes the input to be printed on the screen, and moves the cursor to the next line. PRINT (PR) may take a word or a list of words as input. For example, PR "TURTLE and PR [TURTLE POWER] are both acceptable.

A summary of commands introduced thus far is shown in Table AII-1.

TABLE AII-1

Command	Abbreviation	Example
DRAW*		
NODRAW†	ND	
FORWARD	FD	FD 50
BACK	BK	BK 60
RIGHT	RT	RT 90
LEFT	LT	LT 45
PENUP	PU	
PENDOWN	PD	
HIDETURTLE	HT	
SHOWTURTLE	ST	
HEADING		PR HEADING
PRINT	PR	PR "LOGO
HOME		

*The command in Apple Logo II is CLEARSCREEN (CS).
†The command in Apple Logo II is TEXTSCREEN (CTRL-T).

● R E M A R K

CTRL-T means press the T key while holding down the CONTROL key.

H I S T O R I C A L   N O T E

The computer language Logo was developed in 1967 at Bolt, Beranek, and Newman, Inc. of Cambridge, Massachusetts, and the Massachusetts Institute of Technology (MIT) by Daniel Bobrow, Wallace Feurzeig, and Seymour Papert. The name "Logo" is derived from the Greek word for "thought." The developers of Logo were influenced by the field of artificial intelligence, the computer language LISP, and the theories of Jean Piaget. The tradition of calling the display creature a turtle can be traced to early experiments involving robot-like creatures referred to as "tortoises." When computer graphics were implemented, the screen creature inherited the turtle terminology.

People studying Logo are encouraged to "play turtle" and act out their commands. For example, to act out drawing a square, we may walk around the square by moving toward 50 units, turning right 90°, moving forward 50 units, turning right 90°, moving forward 50 units, turning right 90°, and finally moving forward 50 units. The sequence of commands for these moves is summarized in Figure AII-4(a), with the resulting square and final position of the turtle shown in Figure AII-4(b).

FIGURE AII-4

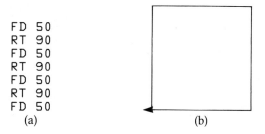

```
FD 50
RT 90
FD 50
RT 90
FD 50
RT 90
FD 50
    (a)                    (b)
```

Notice that the turtle's position in Figure AII-4(b) is the same as its initial position, but its heading is different. When drawing a figure, it is often convenient to have the turtle's final state be the same as its initial state. When a set of commands returns the turtle to its initial position and heading, *state transparent*   we say that the set of commands is **state transparent.**

To return the turtle to its initial state in Figure AII-4(b), we turn it right 90° by adding the line RT 90 at the end of the sequence of commands in Figure AII-4(a). The new sequence of commands is given in Figure AII-5(a), with the resulting square and turtle shown in Figure AII-5(b).

FIGURE AII-5

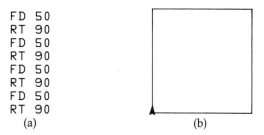

```
FD 50
RT 90
FD 50
RT 90
FD 50
RT 90
FD 50
RT 90
    (a)                    (b)
```

The sequence of commands in Figure AII-5(a) contains the instructions FD 50 and RT 90 repeated four times. Logo allows us to use the REPEAT command to repeat a list of instructions. For example, to draw the square in Figure AII-5(b), we could type the following.

```
REPEAT 4 [FD 50 RT 90]
```

REPEAT   In general, **REPEAT** takes two inputs: a number and a list of commands. The commands in the brackets are repeated the designated number of times. (To obtain brackets on the Apple II Plus computer, the SHIFT M and SHIFT N keys must be used.)

EXAMPLE AII-1   Predict the results of each of the following, indicating the initial and final turtle states. Then, check your answers with a computer. In each case, assume the turtle starts at home with heading 0.

(a) FD 100
     RT 135
     FD 100
     RT 45
     FD 100
     RT 135
     FD 100
     RT 45
(b) REPEAT 2 [FD 100 RT 135 FD 100 RT 45]
(c) REPEAT 8 [FD 50 RT 45]

SOLUTION   Results are depicted in Figure AII-6.

FIGURE AII-6

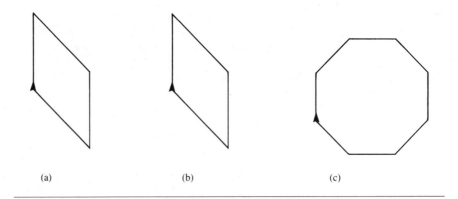

(a)   (b)   (c)

Defining Procedures

The sequence of commands in Figure AII-5(a) instructed the turtle to draw a square. If the screen is cleared, the figure is lost. To redraw the square, the entire sequence of commands must be retyped. Fortunately, with Logo, it is possible to store instructions in the computer's memory by creating a *procedure*   procedure. A **procedure** is a group of one or more instructions to the computer that the computer can store to be used at a later time.

TO   To create a procedure in MIT Logo (Terrapin/Krell or Commodore 64), we type **TO** followed by the name we wish to call the procedure, and press RETURN. (*In Apple Logo II, we type* **EDIT (ED),** *followed by a set of double quotation marks and the procedure name—for example, ED "TRIANGLE.*) *edit mode*   When RETURN is pressed, the computer enters the **edit mode,** or the teaching mode. In this mode, the lines that follow are not executed, but may be stored in memory under the given name. The name must be a sequence of symbols with no spaces, and it may not be the name of a primitive. For example, to create a procedure to draw a square, the following is entered. (To signify the end of a procedure, it is good practice to type END as the last line of the procedure.)

```
TO SQUARE1
 REPEAT 4 [FD 50 RT 90]
END
```

CTRL-C

To define and store a procedure and exit the edit mode, we press **(CTRL-C).** After the procedure has been defined, typing the name of the procedure and pressing ⌷RETURN⌷ causes the computer to immediately execute the instructions in the procedure. In the remainder of this section, we assume that the SQUARE1 procedure just given and all subsequent procedures are stored in the computer's memory and can be reused.

In Logo, it is possible for one procedure to call on another procedure, as shown in Example AII-2. If the SQUARE1 procedure has not been defined on your computer, please define it before working the example.

EXAMPLE AII-2   Predict what figures will be drawn by defining and executing each of the following procedures. Assume the turtle starts at home with heading 0.

(a)
```
TO SQUARE 2
   RT 90
   SQUARE1
END
```

(b)
```
TO SQUARESTACK
   SQUARE1
   RT 90
   SQUARE1
END
```

(c)
```
TO STAIR
   SQUARE1
   RT 180
   SQUARE1
END
```

(d)
```
TO TURNSQUARE
   SQUARE1
   RT 45
   SQUARE1
END
```

SOLUTION   Results are depicted in Figure AII-7.

FIGURE AII-7

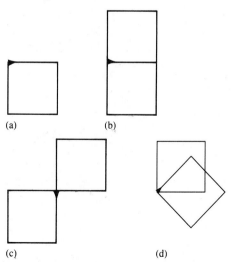

(a)   (b)

(c)   (d)

PROBLEM 1

Write a procedure for drawing a triangle whose sides each have length of 50 turtle steps and whose angles each have measure of 60°.

Understanding the Problem. We are to write a procedure to draw a triangle with all sides of length 50 turtle units and all angles of measure 60°.

Devising a Plan. To write this procedure, it is helpful to sketch a triangle to determine what angle the turtle needs to turn at each vertex of the triangle. Suppose the turtle starts at point A with heading 0 and moves 50 turtle steps to point B, as in Figure AII-8. This can be done by telling the turtle to move FD 50. At point B, the turtle still has heading 0. To walk on $\overrightarrow{BC}$, the turtle may turn 120° to the right. Thus, the next command should be RT 120. The triangle has three sides of equal length, so three turns are necessary to achieve the turtle's initial heading. If we repeat the sequence FD 50 RT 120 three times, this should cause the turtle to walk around the triangle and finish in its original position with its original heading.

FIGURE AII-8

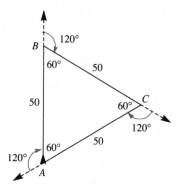

Carrying Out the Plan. A procedure called TRIANGLE1 based on the preceding discussion follows.

```
TO TRIANGLE1
  REPEAT 3 [FD 50 RT 120]
END
```

Looking Back. Executing the TRIANGLE1 procedure yields the desired figure. Additional investigations include writing a procedure to draw the same type of triangle by turning left instead of right or writing a procedure to draw a triangle with one horizontal side. Procedures for drawing other polygons could also be explored.

One of the great advantages of Logo is its ability to use procedures to define new procedures. Consider the following problem.

PROBLEM 2
Write a procedure to draw the "house" in Figure AII-9.

FIGURE AII-9

Understanding the Problem. We are to write a procedure to draw the "house" pictured in Figure AII-9. The top of the house appears to be a triangle similar to the one in Problem 1, and the bottom appears to be a square.

Devising a Plan.   One way to solve the problem is to break down the problem of drawing a house into smaller problems, that of drawing the bottom of the house (the square) and that of drawing the roof (the triangle). The type of programming that starts with a general idea and breaks down the problem *top-down programming* into smaller parts is called **top-down programming.** We have a procedure SQUARE1 for drawing a square of length 50 units, and a procedure TRIANGLE1 for drawing a triangle of length 50 units. If we use these two procedures, then we should be able to draw the house.

Carrying Out the Plan.   If the turtle has heading 0, it may seem that typing SQUARE1 followed by TRIANGLE1 would draw the desired house. The result of this effort is shown in Figure AII-10(a). Why did this not produce the desired figure? The turtle first drew the square in Figure AII-10(a) and returned to its initial position at point *A* with heading 0. Then, typing TRIANGLE1 caused the turtle to draw triangle *ABC* as in Figure AII-8. To draw the roof in proper position, we need the turtle to be at the upper left vertex of the square. This can be achieved by typing FD 50. But, if TRIANGLE1 is typed now, we obtain the shape in Figure AII-10(b), which is still not the desired house.

FIGURE AII-10

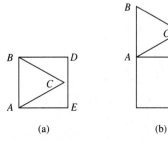

(a)   (b)

After typing SQUARE1 and FD 50, the turtle is at point A with heading 0. To form the roof as in Figure AII-11(a) and to walk on $\overline{AB}$, the turtle needs to turn right by $90° - 60°$, or $30°$. With this heading, typing TRIANGLE1 should cause the turtle to draw the desired roof. The complete procedure, called HOUSE, is shown in Figure AII-11(b).

FIGURE AII-11

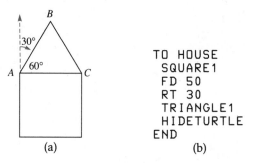

```
TO HOUSE
   SQUARE1
   FD 50
   RT 30
   TRIANGLE1
   HIDETURTLE
END
```

(a)   (b)

Looking Back. If the HOUSE procedure is executed, the desired figure is obtained. Alternate techniques for drawing the figure could also be explored. Houses of other sizes could be drawn and windows and doors could be added.

As seen in Problem 2, trial and error helps the user to get acquainted with the problem and eventually to find the correct solution. This process of rewriting a program that does not do what we want it to do is called *debugging.*

To understand how Logo works when a procedure calls another procedure, a telescoping model of the HOUSE procedure in Problem 2 is given in Figure AII-12.

FIGURE AII-12

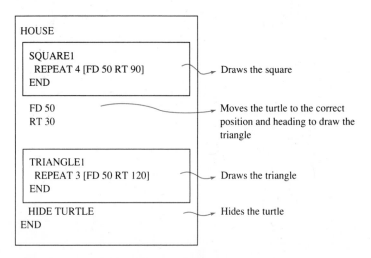

When HOUSE is run, it encounters the call for SQUARE1. At this point, all the lines of SQUARE1 are inserted. After SQUARE1 has been completed, control is returned to the procedure that called it, namely, HOUSE. Now, HOUSE continues where it left off and executes FD 50 RT 30, then calls on the TRIANGLE1 procedure. After TRIANGLE1 has been executed, it returns control to HOUSE, which hides the turtle and encounters its own END statement.

In working through the HOUSE procedure, we went through several steps. A summary of these steps is as follows. These steps might be useful in a variety of problems presented in this text.

1. Sketch your drawing on paper, preferably graph paper, to get an idea of the scale to be used and of how the final picture should look.
2. Divide the drawing into parts that are repeated, that you already know how to draw, or that are smaller parts of the whole. Separate procedures for drawing each individual part are easier to check than a single procedure for the whole drawing.
3. Decide how your individual procedures are going to fit together to form the complete picture. Some procedures may be necessary just to move the turtle to the right position for drawing the individual parts.
4. Write your procedures. One approach is to write individual procedures, make sure they work, and then try to put them all together to form the complete picture. Another approach is to fit the procedures together as they are completed. Either approach is an acceptable problem-solving strategy, and each has advantages in different situations.

We demonstrate how these steps can be used in a problem-solving format in Problem 3.

PROBLEM 3

Write a procedure to draw the figure sketched on the graph paper in Figure AII-13.

FIGURE AII-13

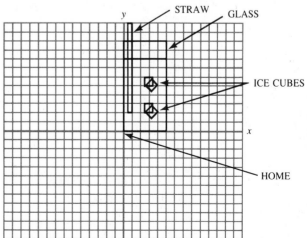

Understanding the Problem. We are to write a procedure to draw a figure similar to the one shown in Figure AII-13. The graph paper gives a scale to draw the various parts.

Devising a Plan. The figure can be broken into three separate parts: the glass, the straw, and the ice cubes. Using top-down programming, a procedure called DRINK to draw this figure might appear as follows.

```
TO DRINK
  GLASS
  ICE.CUBES
  ICE.CUBES
  STRAW
  HT
END
```

To complete the problem, we must write procedures for each portion of the DRINK procedure.

Carrying Out the Plan. First, we design a procedure called GLASS for drawing the glass. If the turtle starts at home with heading 0, one possible procedure and its output are given in Figure AII-14.

FIGURE AII-14
```
TO GLASS
  REPEAT 2 [FD 100 RT 90 FD 50 RT 90]
  FD 80 RT 90
  FD 50 BK 50
  LT 90 BK 80
END
```

Likewise, procedures called STRAW and ICE.CUBES can be designed to draw the other two parts, as shown in Figure AII-15(a) and (b).

FIGURE AII-15
```
TO STRAW
  REPEAT 2 [FD 100 RT 90 FD 5 RT 90]
END

TO ICE.CUBES
  SQUARE3
  RT 45
  SQUARE3
  LT 45
END

TO SQUARE3
  REPEAT 4 [FD 10 RT 90]
END
```

(a)

(b)

If we now execute DRAW (*CS in Apple Logo II*) and attempt to execute the DRINK procedure as defined, the result is as shown in Figure AII-16.

FIGURE AII-16

Here, we encounter a bug. To correct the DRINK procedure to draw the desired figure, we must keep track of the turtle's position and heading. Sometimes, it is convenient to move the turtle to the required positions and headings by using a set of procedures. The following procedures—called SETUP.CUBES1,SETUP.CUBES2, and SETUP.STRAW—move the turtle to the correct position and heading to draw each part.

```
TO SETUP.CUBES1
  PU FD 50 RT 90 FD 25 LT 90 PD
END

TO SETUP.CUBES2
  PU BK 30 PD
END

TO SETUP.STRAW
  PU LT 90 FD 20 RT 90 PD
END
```

If we edit DRINK and add these new procedures, we obtain the procedures and figure shown in Figure AII-17.

FIGURE AII-17

```
TO DRINK
  GLASS
  SETUP.CUBES1
  ICE.CUBES
  SETUP.CUBES2
  ICE.CUBES
  SETUP.STRAW
  STRAW
  HT
END
```

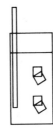

Looking Back. When the DRINK procedure is executed, it yields the desired figure. The procedure could have been written in many different ways. Although various strategies could be used to develop the procedure, we see that the top-down strategy can be very useful. One advantage of the top-down strategy is that it is easier to work with and debug smaller portions of the figure than to try to do the complete figure all at one time.

Writing Procedures with Variables.

The SQUARE1 procedure in this section allowed us to draw only squares of side 50. If we want to draw smaller or larger squares, we must write a new procedure. It would be more convenient if we could write one procedure that would work for a square of any size. This can be accomplished in Logo by using a variable as input, rather than a fixed number such as 50 in FD 50. When we use variable input in Logo, we warn the computer that the "thing" we are going to type is a variable by using a colon before the variable name. For example, a variable input to the SQUARE procedure might be called :SIDE, where :SIDE stands for the length of a side of the square. We define a new SQUARE procedure with variable input :SIDE, and we place the name of the variable in the title line.

```
TO SQUARE :SIDE
 REPEAT 4 [FD :SIDE RT 90]
END
```

If we want the turtle to draw a square of size 40, we type SQUARE 40. Notice that we do not type SQUARE :40 because 40 is not a variable. (In fact, the computer will not understand the instruction SQUARE :40.) Investigate what happens if SQUARE is typed with no inputs.

• R E M A R K

We call the new variable square procedure SQUARE instead of SQUARE1. If we attempt to enter the edit mode to define a new SQUARE1 procedure and the old procedure has not been erased the computer will display the old SQUARE1 procedure on the screen for us to edit. You should consult your Logo manual for directions on how to edit procedures.

A procedure may have more than one input. For example, consider the following equivalent procedures for drawing a rectangle. Two variables are used so that two inputs can be accepted.

```
TO RECTANGLE :HEIGHT :WIDTH
 FD :HEIGHT RT 90
 FD :WIDTH RT 90
 FD :HEIGHT RT 90
 FD :WIDTH RT 90
END

TO RECTANGLE :HEIGHT :WIDTH
 REPEAT 2 [FD :HEIGHT RT 90 FD :WIDTH RT 90]
END
```

Figure AII-18 shows rectangles drawn by either of the RECTANGLE procedures with different inputs for the sides.

FIGURE AII-18

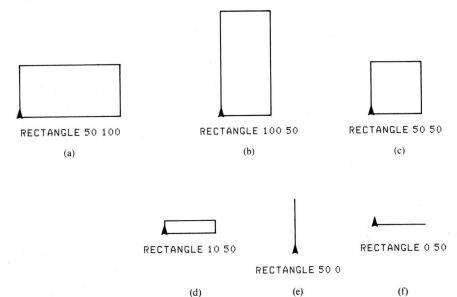

RECTANGLE 50 100

(a)

RECTANGLE 100 50

(b)

RECTANGLE 50 50

(c)

RECTANGLE 10 50

(d)

RECTANGLE 50 0

(e)

RECTANGLE 0 50

(f)

B R A I N   T E A S E R
Write a procedure for drawing the following figure, using a continuous path and without retracing any segment. (Single points may be retraced.)

SUMMARY OF COMMANDS

DRAW*	Needs no input. It sends the turtle home and clears the graphics screen.
NODRAW (ND)†	Needs no input. it exits the graphics mode, clears the screen, and places the cursor in the upper left corner.
FORWARD (FD)	Takes one input. If the input is positive, it moves the turtle forward (in the direction the turtle is facing) the number of turtle units that are input. For example, FD 20 moves the turtle forward 20 units.
BACK (BK)	Takes one input. If the input is positive, it moves the turtle backwards the number of turtle units that are input. For example, BK 40 moves the turtle backwards 40 units.
RIGHT (RT)	Takes one input. If the input is positive, it turns the turtle right from its present heading the number of degrees that are input. For example, RT 90 turns the turtle right 90°.
LEFT (LT)	Takes one input. If the input is positive, it turns the turtle left from its present heading the number of degrees that are input. For example, LT 90 turns the turtle left 90°.
PENUP (PU)	Needs no input. In the graphics mode, it enables the turtle to move without leaving a track.
PENDOWN (PD)	Needs no input. In the graphics mode, it causes the turtle to leave a track.
HIDETURTLE (HT)	Needs no input. It causes the turtle to disappear.
SHOWTURTLE (ST)	Needs no input. it causes the turtle to reappear.
PRINT (PR)	Takes one input. It causes the input to be printed on the screen and moves the cursor to the next line.
HEADING	Needs no input. In the draw mode, it outputs the turtle's heading.
HOME	Needs no input. It returns the turtle to the center of the screen and sets its heading to 0. If the pen is down, it leaves a track from the turtle's present location to the home position.
REPEAT	Takes a number and a list as input. It executes the instructions in the list the designated number of times.
TO‡	Takes the name of a procedure as input and causes Logo to enter the edit mode.

*In Apple Logo II, this command is CLEARSCREEN (SC).
†In Apple Logo II, this command is TEXTSCREEN (CTRL-T).
‡In Apple Logo II, this command is EDIT (ED).

PROBLEM SET AII-1

1. Sketch figures drawn by the turtle, using each of the following sets of instructions. Check your sketches by executing the instructions on a computer. Type DRAW *(CS in Apple Logo II)* after each lettered part.

   (a) FD 50　　(b) FD 50
   　　RT 90　　　　RT 90
   　　FD 50　　　　BK 50
   　　RT 45　　　　RT 60
   　　FD 50　　　　FD 50
   　　RT 135
   　　FD 50

   (c) FD -50 FD 50
   (d) LT -90 BK -50 RT 40 PR HEADING
   (e) RT 360 PR HEADING

2. Experiment with the turtle to find the dimensions of the screen.

3. Predict what the turtle will draw with the following sets of instructions. Check your answers by executing the instructions on the computer.

   SQUARE1 and TRIANGLE1 are defined in the text.

   (a) REPEAT 8 [SQUARE1 RT 45]
   (b) REPEAT 6 [TRIANGLE1 RT 60]
   (c) REPEAT 36 [SQUARE1 RT 10]

4. Write procedures to draw figures similar to each of the following.

Rectangle that is not a square
(a)

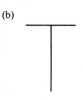

Flag
(b)

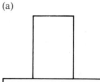

A hat
(c)

The letter *T*
(d)

A rhombus that is not a square
(e)

A square with a smaller square inside
(f)

5. Write a procedure to draw the following.

6. Use any procedures in this section to write new procedures that will draw each of the following figures.

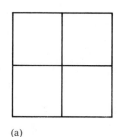

(a)

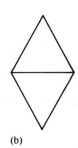

(b)

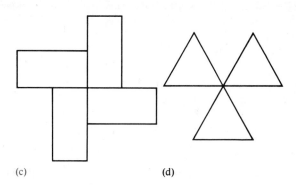

(c)　　　　　　　　(d)

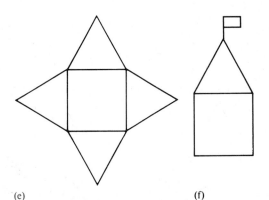

(e)　　　　　　　　(f)

7. Write procedures to draw figures similar to each of the following.

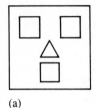

(a)

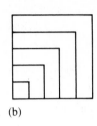

(b)

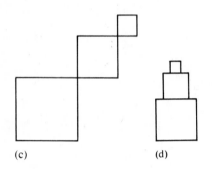

(c)

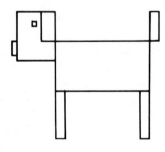

(d)

8. Use top-down programming to write a procedure called DOG to draw a figure similar to the following.

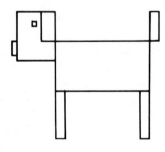

9. Use top-down programming to write a procedure called KITE to draw a figure similar to the following.

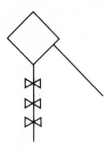

10. Write procedures to draw figures similar to those in Problem 4, but of variable size.

11. Write a procedure called BLADES to draw a figure similar to the following, but of variable size.

12. Write a procedure called RECTANGLES to draw a figure similar to the following, but of variable size.

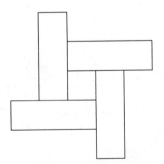

Section AII-2   Using Recursion as a Problem-Solving Tool

recursion

In Section AII-1, we considered procedures that called on other procedures. **Recursion** is the process of a procedure calling on a copy of itself. As a first example of recursion, we write a procedure called CIRC for drawing a "turtle-type" circle. This could be done by having the turtle move forward "a little," then turn right "a little," and continuing this process until a closed figure is obtained. Thus, we could start the procedure with FD 1 RT 1 and then have the turtle start the procedure anew each time the instruction is executed. Such a procedure follows.

```
TO CIRC
  FD 1 RT 1
  CIRC
END
```

To understand how CIRC works and, in general, what happens when a procedure calls itself, we use the telescoping model in Figure AII-19.

FIGURE AII-19

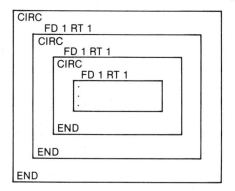

When CIRC is executed, FD 1 RT 1 causes the turtle to move forward 1 unit and then turn right 1°. CIRC then calls a copy of the CIRC procedure, which again executes FD 1 RT 1 and in turn calls another copy of CIRC, and so on. The process continues because we have made CIRC one of the instructions in the CIRC procedure. The END statement is never reached, and the instruction FD 1 RT 1 is executed indefinitely. You may stop the

CTRL-G

execution of the procedure at any time by pressing **CTRL-G.**

tail-end recursion

The repetitive process shown in the CIRC procedure occurs in the type of recursion called **tail-end recursion.** In tail-end recursion, only one recursive call is made within the body of the procedure, and it is the final step before the END statement. Later, we introduce another type of recursion that is

embedded recursion

sometimes called **embedded recursion.**

● **R E M A R K**

When drawing a circle with right turns of 1°, the turtle only has to turn through 360° to complete the circle. A CIRCLE1 procedure could be written using the REPEAT command as follows.

```
TO CIRCLE1
 REPEAT 360 [FD 1 RT 1]
END
```

The CIRCLE1 procedure stops, whereas the CIRC procedure does not.

Recursion is particularly valuable when we do not know how many times to repeat a set of instructions to accomplish some goal. For example, consider the shapes that can be drawn by repeating the instruction "Go forward some fixed distance and turn right some fixed angle." A recursive procedure called POLY that does this is as follows.

```
TO POLY :SIDE :ANGLE
 FD :SIDE RT :ANGLE
 POLY :SIDE :ANGLE
END
```

To execute the POLY procedure, we need two numerical inputs, one for :SIDE and the other for :ANGLE. Figure AII-20 shows shapes drawn by POLY with eight different inputs. The drawings were stopped using CTRL-G.

The POLY procedure draws regular polygons (polygons that have congruent sides and congruent angles), as in Figure AII-20(a), (b), and (c), and also star shapes as in Figure AII-20(d), (e), and (f).

FIGURE AII-20

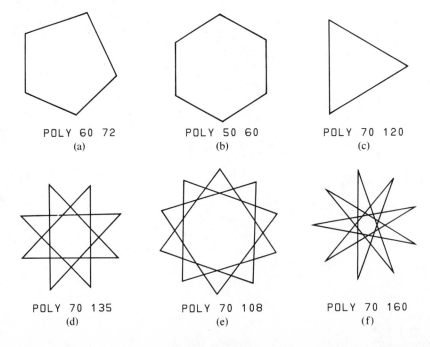

POLY 60 72
(a)

POLY 50 60
(b)

POLY 70 120
(c)

POLY 70 135
(d)

POLY 70 108
(e)

POLY 70 160
(f)

Try other executions of POLY, such as POLY 50 180, POLY 50 181, POLY 60 288, POLY 6000 300, and POLY 7000 135. Try to predict which inputs produce regular polygons and which produce star shapes.

All the figures drawn by the POLY procedure in Figure AII-20 are closed; that is, they can be drawn by starting and stopping at the same point. Will all figures drawn by POLY be closed? We can also ask the following questions:

1. Given the value of :ANGLE in the POLY procedure, is it possible to predict (before the figure is drawn) how many vertices the figure will have?
2. If we wish the POLY procedure to draw a figure with a given number of vertices, can we determine what the correct angle input should be?

With the help of recursion, we can accomplish tasks that cannot be easily done with just the REPEAT command, especially if we do not know how many times to repeat a sequence of instructions. Consider drawing a square-type spiral as shown in Figure AII-21.

FIGURE AII-21

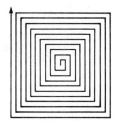

Suppose each side of the figure is 5 units longer than the preceding side. If the turtle starts at home, the figure can be drawn by telling the turtle to move forward a certain length :LEN, turn right 90°, move forward a distance 5 units greater than the previous value of :LEN, and so on. A recursive procedure called SQSPI shows how this can be done.

```
TO SQSPI :LEN
  FD :LEN RT 90
  SQSPI :LEN + 5
END
```

Notice that each time SQSPI calls itself, the length of :LEN is increased by 5 units. When SQSPI is run, the sides grow too large to fit on the screen. Rather than stopping SQSPI with CTRL-G, it is possible to write a "stop" instruction in the procedure. This can be done with the IF and STOP primitives. **IF** is a primitive that tests one of three conditions: equal ($=$), less than ($<$), or greater than ($>$). The IF primitive is used in the following form.

IF

IF *(Condition)*   *(Action to be taken if condition is true)*

The parentheses should not be typed. *(In Apple Logo II, the format is IF (Condition) [Action to be taken if condition is true], where the square brackets must be typed.)*

For example, if we do not want the turtle to draw any segment longer than 100 units, we insert the following instruction.

```
IF :LEN > 100 STOP
```

(In Apple Logo II, IF :LEN > 100 [STOP].) When this line is inserted into a procedure, the IF statement causes the computer to check whether the value of :LEN is greater than 100. If it is, the procedure stops; if not, the next line is executed. The **STOP** primitive causes the current procedure to stop and returns control to the calling procedure, if there is one. An edited form of the SQSPI procedure is as follows.

STOP

```
TO SQSPI :LEN
  IF :LEN > 100 STOP
  FD :LEN RT 90
  SQSPI :LEN + 5
END
```

(In Apple Logo II, replace STOP with [STOP].) The SQSPI procedure can be generalized to draw other spiral-type figures. Investigate the following POLYSPI procedure for various inputs.

```
TO POLYSPI :SIDE :ANGLE
  IF :SIDE > 100 STOP
  FD :SIDE RT :ANGLE
  POLYSPI :SIDE + 5 :ANGLE
END
```

(In Apple Logo II, replace STOP with [STOP].)

What inputs should be given to POLYSPI in order to achieve the same effect as SQSPI? Also, investigate what happens when :ANGLE, rather than :SIDE, is incremented each time the recursive call is made.

Embedded Recursion

Tail-end recursion involves only one recursive call within the body of the procedure, and it is the final step before the END statement. Recursive calls also can be **embedded;** that is, the recursive call is not the last line before the END statement. For example, consider the tail-end recursion in the T.SQUARE procedure and the embedded recursion in the E.SQUARE procedure that follow. Predict the results of executing each of these procedures with input 30; then, execute them to see if you were correct.

embedded recursion

```
TO T.SQUARE :SIDE
  IF :SIDE < 5 STOP
  REPEAT 4 [FD :SIDE RT 90]
  T.SQUARE :SIDE - 10
END
```

```
TO E.SQUARE :SIDE
  IF :SIDE < 5 STOP
  REPEAT 4 [FD :SIDE RT 90]
  E.SQUARE :SIDE - 10
  LT 45 FD :SIDE
END
```

(In Apple Logo II, remember to replace STOP with [STOP].) The T.SQUARE procedure probably did exactly what you expected; however, the E.SQUARE procedure may have surprised you. To see why E.SQUARE behaved the way it did, we use the telescoping model in Figure AII-22.

FIGURE AII-22

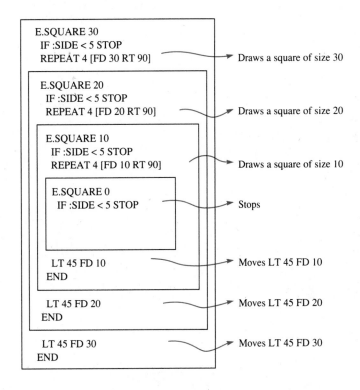

Notice that when :SIDE < 5 in E.SQUARE 0, the STOP command is finally reached. However, STOP stops only the procedure it is in, not the calling procedure. Control is then returned to the previous procedure, and so on.

From our model, we see that recursion works according to the following rules:

1. Executions in Logo programs proceed line by line. When a procedure calls itself, it puts on hold any instructions that are written after the call and inserts a copy of itself at the point where the call occurs. If the called procedure stops, control is returned to the calling procedure at the point

where the call occurred. The remainder of the lines in the calling procedure are then executed.

2. The process in (1) applies to any successive calls.

SUMMARY OF COMMANDS

| IF* | Takes two inputs. The first input must be either true or false. The second input contains instructions that are carried out if and only if the first input is true. |
| STOP | Takes no inputs. Causes the current procedure to stop and returns control to the calling procedure. |

*In Apple Logo II, the second input must be enclosed in brackets, for example, IF :SIDE > 100 [STOP].

PROBLEM SET AII-2

1. Predict the shapes that will be drawn by the following procedures and then check your predictions on the computer. The SQUARE and TRIANGLE procedures are defined as follows, *(In Apple Logo II, replace STOP with [STOP] in (b), (d), (e), and (f).)*

```
TO TRIANGLE :SIDE
  REPEAT 3 [FD :SIDE RT 120]
END
TO SQUARE :SIDE
  REPEAT 4 [FD :SIDE RT 90]
END
```

(a)
```
TO FIGURE :SIDE
   TRIANGLE :SIDE
   RT 10
   FIGURE :SIDE
END
```
(b)
```
TO FIGURE1 :SIDE
   IF :SIDE < 5 STOP
   TRIANGLE :SIDE
   RT 10
   FIGURE1 :SIDE - 5
END
```
(c)
```
TO TOWER :SIDE
   SQUARE :SIDE
   FD :SIDE
   TOWER :SIDE * 0.5
END
```
(d)
```
TO TOWER1 :SIDE
   IF :SIDE < 2 STOP
   SQUARE :SIDE
   FD :SIDE
   TOWER1 :SIDE * 0.5
END
```

(e)
```
TO SQ :SIDE
   IF :SIDE < 2 STOP
   SQUARE :SIDE
   SQ :SIDE - 5
END
```
(f)
```
TO SPIRAL :SIDE
   IF :SIDE > 50 STOP
   FD :SIDE
   RT 30
   SPIRAL :SIDE + 3
END
```

2. Given the following NEWPOLY, POLYSPIRAL, and INSPI procedures, predict the shapes that will be drawn by each and then check your predictions on the computer.

```
TO NEWPOLY :SIDE :ANGLE
  FD :SIDE RT :ANGLE
  FD :SIDE RT :ANGLE * 2
  NEWPOLY :SIDE :ANGLE
END
```

```
TO POLYSPIRAL :SIDE :ANGLE :INC
  FD :SIDE RT :ANGLE
  POLYSPIRAL (:SIDE + :INC) :ANGLE
    :INC
END
```

```
TO INSPI :SIDE :ANGLE :INC
  FD :SIDE RT :ANGLE
  INSPI :SIDE (:ANGLE + :INC) :INC
END
```

(a) NEWPOLY 50 30
(b) NEWPOLY 50 144

(c) `NEWPOLY 50 125`
(d) `POLYSPIRAL 2 85 3`
(e) `POLYSPIRAL 1 119 2`
(f) `POLYSPIRAL 1 100 5`
(g) `INSPI 10 2 20`
(h) `INSPI 2 0 10`
(i) `INSPI 10 5 10`

3. Write recursive procedures to draw figures similar to the following. Use the STOP command in your procedures.

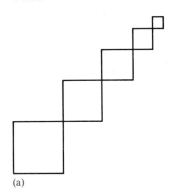

(a)

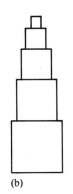

(b)

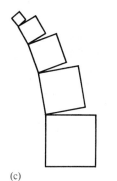

(c)

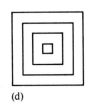

(d)

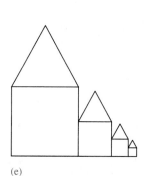

(e)

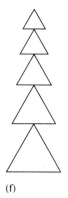

(f)

4. Write a recursive procedure with a STOP command to draw a figure similar to the following.

5. (a) Execute each of the following to see how embedded recursion can be used to "unwind" the turtle. *(Use [STOP] in Apple Logo II.)*

```
TO WOW :X
 IF :X < 5 STOP
 FD :X RT 87
 WOW :X - 2
 LT 87 BK :X
END

TO WOWI :X
 IF :X < 5 STOP
 FD :X RT 118
 WOW1 :X - 2
 LT 118 BK :X
END
```

(b) Write a procedure, using embedded recursion, that "unwinds" like those in (a).

6. (a) Predict what happens when REFLECT 6 is executed. Check your predictions by executing the procedure. *(Use [STOP] in Apple Logo II.)*

```
TO REFLECT :N
 IF :N < 3 STOP
 REPEAT :N [FD 30 RT 360/:N]
 REFLECT :N - 1
 REPEAT :N [ FD 30 RT 360/:N]
END
```

(b) Try REFLECT with various other values of :N.

7. Write a procedure called SPIN.SQ that uses recursion and a STOP command to spin a variable-sized square while "shrinking" its size, as shown.

8. Write a recursive procedure with a STOP statement that draws the following variable size figure made of squares.

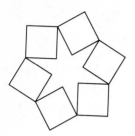

9. Write a procedure utilizing embedded recursion to draw a variable size figure similar to the following:

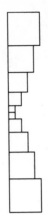

Answers to Selected Problems

CHAPTER 1

Problem Set 1-1

1. (a) $5 \times 6, 6 \times 7, 7 \times 8$ **(c)** 45, 41, 37 **(e)** 26, 37, 50 **(g)** 1, 18, 1 **(i)** 111111, 1111111, 11111111 **(k)** $6 \cdot 2^6, 7 \cdot 2^7, 8 \cdot 2^8$
(m)

 ,

(o) 21, 35, 49 **(q)** 44, 88, 110
2. (a) Arithmetic; 11, 13, 15 **(c)** Geometric; 96, 192, 384 **(e)** Geometric; $5^7, 5^8, 5^9$ **(g)** Geometric; $2^{11}, 2^{13}, 2^{15}$ **(i)** Neither, $6^3, 7^3, 8^3$
3. (a) 12, 14 **(b)** 18, 21
4. (a) 30, 42, 56 **(c)** $n(n + 1) = n^2 + n$
5. (a) $6 + 9 \cdot 5 = 51$
6. (a) $1 + 10 \cdot 4 = 41$
7. 1200 students
9. $1225
11. 19
12. (a) Yes. The difference between terms in the new sequence is the same as in the old sequence. **(b)** Yes. If the fixed number is k, the difference between terms of the second sequence is k times the difference between terms of the first sequence.
14. (a) 1, 5, 12, 22, 35, 51 **(b)** 14,950
16. (a) 299, 447, 644 **(c)** 108, 190, 304
17. (a) 100 **(c)** 100 **(e)** 200
18. The resulting sequence is always an arithmetic sequence.
19. (a) 3, 6, 11, 18, 27 **(c)** 9, 99, 999, 9999, 99999
20. (a) 1, 1, 2, 3, 5, 8, 13, 21, 34, 55, 89, 144 **(c)** 143
21. (a) 199; $2n - 1$ **(b)** $50 \cdot 99$, or 4950; $50(n - 1)$

(c) $3 \cdot 2^{99}$; $3 - 2^{n-1}$ **(d)** 10^{100}; 10^n **(e)** 5^{101}; 5^{n+1} **(f)** 1100; $11n$ **(g)** 2^{199}; 2^{2n-1} **(h)** 405; $9 + 4(n - 1)$, or $4n + 5$ **(i)** 100^3, or 1,000,000; n^3 **(j)** $2 \cdot 3^{99}$; $2 \cdot 3^{n-1}$
22. (a) 11, 15, 19
23. Yes; the common ratio is the same as the ratio of the original sequence.
24. The sequence in (b) becomes greater than the sequence in (a) on the 12th term.

Section 1-2 Time Out

1. None, no dirt in a hole.
2. Fifty-cent piece and a nickel. (One coin is not a fifty-cent piece but the other one is.)
3. 4
4. 3
5. 6 hours (1 cigarette can be made with the butts from the first 5)
6.

7.

3	5	
0	5	(fill $\boxed{5}$)
3	2	(empty $\boxed{5}$ into $\boxed{3}$)
0	2	(empty $\boxed{3}$)
2	0	(pour $\boxed{2}$ into $\boxed{3}$)
2	5	(fill $\boxed{5}$)
3	④	(empty $\boxed{5}$ into $\boxed{3}$)

8. 1 hr 20 min. = 80 min.
9. 25
10. No extra dollar. There is no reason the 2nd column should sum to $50.
11. $63
12. They didn't play each other.
13. None, Noah took animals on the ark, not Adam
14. 68 ft.
15. 5 in.
16. Pour the contents of the 2nd glass into the 5th glass.

Problem Set 1-2

1. Yes; it works with an even or an odd number of numbers.
2. 18
3. $1.19
4. Answers may vary.

6	7	2
1	5	9
8	3	4

5. 325
6. Start both the 7-minute and 11-minute timers. When the 7-minute timer stops, put the egg on. When the 11-minute timer stops, restart it. When it stops this time, the egg is done.
8. 24
10. 12 dogs, 10 boys
12. 16 days
13. 17 rungs
14. (1) Applejack (2) Null Set (3) Fast Jack
(4) Lookout (5) Bent Leg
15. (a) Weigh 4 against 4, pick the heavier side, weigh 2 against 2, and finally, weigh 1 against 1.
17. 310 feet and 230 feet
18. No. To do so, each domino must cover a black and a white square. Because there are only 30 white squares, while there are 32 black squares, this is impossible.
19. (a) 1001 (c) 150
20. (a) 260,610 (c) 20,503
22. Yes; she can use the $8\frac{1}{2}$-inch side twice to get 17 inches and then use the 11-inch side to get back to 6 inches.
23. $13,500
24. 35 moves
25. (a) 21, 24, 27 (b) 243, 2, 729
26. $22 + (n - 1) \cdot 10$ or $10n + 12$
27. 21
28. 903

Problem Set 1-3

1. (a) (i) 541   (ii) $12\overline{)754}$
            $\times 72$
2. (b)
4. Hint: $259 \times 429 = 111,111$
6. 275,000,000
10. $5,256,000
12. 625
14. (a) If the product were abcd, then $a + c = 9$ and $b + d = 9$ (b) If the product were *abcde*, then $c = 9$, $a + d = 9$ and $b + e = 9$
15. $1 \div 30$
17. Play second and make sure that the sum showing when you hand the calculator to your opponent is a multiple of 3.
19. Play first and press 3. After that, make sure that each time you hand your opponent the calculator, it displays 3 more than a multiple of 10.
21. Play second; use a strategy similar to that of problem 20 but use a multiple of 4.
23. (a) 35, 42, 49 (b) 1, 16, 1
24. $20n - 8$
25. 21
26. 9

Chapter Test

1. (a) 15, 21, 28 (c) 400, 200, 100 (e) 17, 20, 23
(g) 5, 25 (i) 125, 216, 343
2. (a) Neither (b) Arithmetic (c) Geometric
(d) Neither (e) Arithmetic (f) Geometric
(g) Geometric (h) Arithmetic (i) Neither
3. (a) $3n + 2$ (b) n^3 (c) 3^n
4. (a) 5, 8, 11, 14, 17 (c) 3, 7, 11, 15, 19
5. (a) 10,100
7. 89 years since there is no year 0.
9. 26
11. 21
12. 128
14. 44,000,000
15. 20
17. 48

CHAPTER 2

Problem Set 2-1

1. (c) is well defined; (a) and (b) are not.
2. (a) $\{m, a, t, h, e, i, c, s\}$ (b) empty set
(c) {January, June, July}, or $\{x \mid x$ is a month which begins with J} (d) $\{21, 22, 23, 24, 25, \ldots\}$, or $\{x \mid x \in N$ and x is greater than 20\}
3. (a) $B = \{x, y, z, w\}$ (b) $3 \notin B$ (c) $\{1, 2\} \subset$ $\{1, 2, 3, 4\}$ (d) $D \not\subseteq E$ (e) $A \not\subset B$

5. Answers may vary.
6. (a) Yes **(b)** No **(c)** Yes
8. (a) $4 \cdot 3 \cdot 2 \cdot 1 = 24$ **(b)** $5 \cdot 4 \cdot 3 \cdot 2 \cdot 1 = 120$
10. $\{\varnothing, \{x\}, \{y\}, \{z\}, \{x, y\}, \{x, z\}, \{y, z\}, \{x, y, z\}\}$
11. $A = C = D$; $E = H$
12. $\overline{A} = \{x | x$ is a college student that does not have a straight-A average$\}$
14. Sets C and D are equal.
16. (a) $\in$ **(b)** $\in$ **(c)** $\notin$ **(d)** $\notin$ **(e)** $\notin$ **(f)** $\notin$ **(g)** $\notin$
(h) $\notin$ **(i)** $\in$ **(j)** $\notin$
18. No; suppose $A = \{1, 2\}$ and $B = \{3\}$. Then $A \not\subseteq B$ and $B \not\subseteq A$.
20. (a) $\{a, b\}$ is equivalent to $\{x, y\}$ a proper subset of $\{x, y, z, w\}$ **(b)** $\{a, b, c\}$ is equivalent to $\{1, 2, 3\}$ a proper subset of $\{1, 2, 3, \ldots, 100\}$ **(c)** is equivalent to itself, a proper subset of $\{1, 2, 3\}$
22. (a) $2^6 = 64$ subsets; $2^6 - 1 = 63$ proper subsets
(b) $2^n - 1$ proper subsets
23. 35

Problem Set 2-2

1. (a) yes **(b)** yes **(c)** yes **(d)** yes **(e)** no **(f)** yes
3. (a) B **(b)** A
4. (a)

(b)

(c)

(d)

5. (a) U **(b)** U **(c)** S **(d)** $\varnothing$ **(e)** S **(f)** U
7. (a) A **(b)** $\varnothing$ **(c)** $\varnothing$ **(d)** $\varnothing$
9. (a) $B - A$, or $B \cap \overline{A}$ **(b)** $A \cap B \cap C$ **(c)** $(A \cap C) - B$, or $(A \cap C) \cap \overline{B}$
10. (a)

(b)

(c)

(d)

12. (a) (i) 5 (ii) 2 **(b)** (i) $n + m$ (ii) the lesser number of m and n
14. (a) No **(b)** No
16. $A = B$
19. 18
22. (a) 20
23. (a) False; let $A = \{a\}$ and $B = \{b\}$ **(b)** False; let $A = B$ **(c)** False; let $A \subseteq B$ **(d)** True **(e)** False; let $A = \{2, 4, 6, 8, \ldots\}$ and $B = \{1, 2, 3, 4, \ldots\}$
(f) False; let $A = \{1, 2\}$ and $B = \{4, 5, 6\}$
25. (a) $\{(x, a), (x, b), (x, c), (y, a), (y, b), (y, c)\}$
(b) $\{(0, a), (0, b), (0, c)\}$ **(c)** $\{(a, x), (a, y), (b, x), (b, y), (c, x), (c, y)\}$ **(d)** $\varnothing$
26. (a) $C = \{a\}$, $D = \{b, c, d, e\}$
27. (a) 3 **(b)** 6 **(c)** 9 **(d)** 20 **(e)** $m \cdot n$
(f) $m \cdot n \cdot p$
29. 5
32. 60
34. 93
36. $\varnothing, \{a\}, \{b\}, \{c\}, \{a, b\}, \{a, c\}, \{b, c\}, \{a, b, c\}$
37. Yes
39. (a) {Massachusetts, Maryland, Mississippi, Minnesota, Missouri, Michigan, Maine, Montana}
(b) $\{x | x$ is a state in the United States starting with the letter M$\}$

Problem Set 2-3

1. Answers may vary. **(a)** The second component is the square of the first component. **(b)** The second component is the husband of the first component. **(c)** The second component is the capital of the first component. **(d)** The second component is the cost of the first component.
3. Answers may vary.
5. (a) no properties, not an equivalence relation
(b) reflexive, symmetric, transitive; an equivalence relation **(c)** reflexive, symmetric, transitive; an equivalence relation **(d)** symmetric; not an equivalence relation **(e)** reflexive, symmetric, transitive; an equivalence relation **(f)** symmetric; not an equivalence relation **(g)** reflexive, symmetric, transitive; an equivalence relation **(h)** transitive; not an equivalence relation
7. (a) {Abe, Anna}, {George}, {Laura}, {Ben, Betty}, {Sue}, {Dax, Doug}, {Zachary}, {Mike, Mary}, {Carolyn}
(b) {Abe, George, Sue, Mike}, {Laura, Anna}, {Ben, Carolyn}, {Betty, Zachary, Mary}, {Dax}, {Doug}
(c) {Abe, Ben, Sue, Dax, Anna}, {George}, {Laura, Betty}, {Zachary, Carolyn}, {Doug, Mike, Mary}
9. (a) $f(x) = 2x$ **(b)** $f(x) = x - 2$
10. (a) No. 1 is paired with 2 elements, a and d.
(b) No. Not every element from $\{1, 2, 3\}$ is paired, namely 2.

11. Yes. Each element in the first set is used and each is associated with only one element in the second set.
13. Answers may vary.
15. (a)

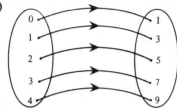

(b) {(0, 1), (1, 3), (2, 5), (3, 7), (4, 9)}
(c)

x	$f(x)$
0	1
1	3
2	5
3	7
4	9

(d)

17. (a) $f(x) = (1/7)x$ **(b)** $g(x) = x + 5$ **(c)** $f(x) = (x - 5)/3$
19. (a) 30 chirps in 15 seconds, or 2 chirps/second
(b) 50 degrees F
21. (a) 4 million **(b)** 4 million **(c)** 9 million
23. (a) Yes **(b)** No
25. No; rich is not well-defined
27. (a) {a, b, c, d} or U **(b)** {a, d} **(c)** $\varnothing$ **(d)** $\varnothing$
(e) $\varnothing$
29. Answers may vary.
30. (a) 6 **(b)** 9

Problem Set 2-4
1. (a) False statement **(b)** Not a statement **(c)** False statement **(d)** Not a statement **(e)** Not a statement
(f) Not a statement **(g)** True statement **(h)** Not a statement **(i)** Not a statement, ambiguous
3. (a) For all natural numbers x, $x + 8 = 11$. **(b)** For no natural numbers x, $x + 0 = x$. **(c)** For no natural numbers x, $x^2 = 4$. **(d)** For all natural numbers x, $x + 1 = x + 2$, or there exists a natural number x such that $x + 1 = x + 2$.

5. (a)

p	$\sim p$	$\sim(\sim p)$
T	F	T
F	T	F

(b)

p	$\sim p$	$p \vee \sim p$	$p \wedge \sim p$
T	F	T	F
F	T	T	F

(c) Yes **(d)** No
7. (a) F **(b)** T **(c)** T **(d)** F **(e)** F **(f)** T **(g)** F
(h) F **(i)** F **(j)** F
9. (a) No **(b)** Yes **(c)** No **(d)** Yes
11. (a) Today is not Wednesday or the month is not June. **(b)** Yesterday I did not eat breakfast or I did not watch television. **(c)** It is not true that both it is raining and it is July.

Problem Set 2-5
1. (a) $p \rightarrow q$ **(b)** $\sim p \rightarrow q$ **(c)** $p \rightarrow \sim q$ **(d)** $p \rightarrow q$
(e) $\sim q \rightarrow \sim p$ **(f)** $q \leftrightarrow p$
3. (a)

p	q	$p \vee q$	$p \rightarrow (p \vee q)$
T	T	T	T
T	F	T	T
F	T	T	T
F	F	F	T

(d)

p	q	$p \rightarrow q$	$\sim(p \rightarrow q)$
T	T	T	F
T	F	F	T
F	T	T	F
F	F	T	F

7. No. Iris can go to the movies or not and the implication is still true.
9. Answers may vary. For example, "If a number is not a multiple of 4, then it is not a multiple of 8.
11. (a) $P \subset Q$
12. (a) p is false. **(b)** False
13. (a) p: Mary's little lamb follows her to school. q: The lamb breaks the rules. r: Mary is sent home. $p \rightarrow (q \cap r)$ **(b)** p: Jack is nimble. q: Jack is quick. r: Jack makes it over the candlestick. $\sim(p \wedge q) \rightarrow \sim r$
(c) p: The apple hit Isaac Newton on the head. q: The laws of gravity were discovered. $\sim p \rightarrow \sim q$
15. (a) Helen is poor. **(b)** Some freshmen are intelligent. **(c)** If I study for the final, then I will look for a teaching job.
16. (a) If a figure is a square, then it is a rectangle.
(b) If a number is an integer, then it is a rational number.

Chapter Test

1. $\{x \mid x$ is a letter of the English alphabet$\}$

3. (a) $\overline{A}$ is the set of people living in Montana who are less than 30 years old. **(b)** $A \cap C$ is the set of people living in Montana who are 30 years or older and own a gun. **(c)** $A \cup B$ is the set of people living in Montana. **(d)** $\overline{C}$ is the set of people living in Montana who do not own a gun. **(e)** $\overline{A \cap C}$ is the set of people living in Montana who do not own a gun. **(f)** $A - C$ is the set of people living in Montana who are 30 years or older and do not own a gun.

5. (a)

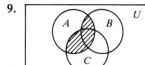

$A \cap (B \cup C)$

7. $2^6 - 1 = 63$

9.

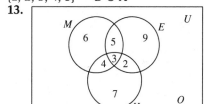

$A \cap (B \cup C) \neq (A \cap B) \cup C$

11. $(A \cap B) \cap C = \{3\} = A \cap (B \cap C); A \cup B = \{1, 2, 3, 4, 5\} = B \cup A$

13.

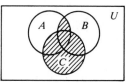

(a) 36 **(b)** 6 **(c)** 5

15. (a) 7 **(b)** 31 **(c)** 37

18. (a) $f(x) = x - 1$ **(b)** $f(x) = (-1/2)x$ **(c)** $f(x) = (-1/2)(x - 1)$ **(d)** $f(x) = (-1/2)x - 1$

19. (a) reflexive, symmetric, transitive **(b)** transitive **(c)** symmetric **(d)** none

21. (a) No women smoke. **(b)** $3 + 5 \neq 8$ **(c)** Some heavy metal rock is not loud. **(d)** Beethoven wrote some non-classical music.

23. (a) equivalent **(b)** not equivalent

25. (a) Joe Czernyu loves Mom and apple pie. **(b)** The Statue of Liberty will eventually rust. **(c)** Albertina will pass Math 100.

CHAPTER 3

Problem Set 3-1

1. (a) $\overline{\overline{\text{MCDXXIV}}}$ **(b)** 46,032 **(c)** ▼▼ **(d)** ∩ ∣ **(e)**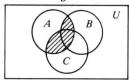

2. (a) MCML; MCMXLVIII **(d)** ≪ ‹▼▼; ≪ ‹

3. (a) Use place value in columns as done in the Hindu-Arabic system. Group the numerals in each column; trade symbols and shift columns if possible.

5. (a) CXXI **(c)** LXXXIX

6. (a) ∩∩∩∩∩ ‖ **(c)** ◁ ‖‖

7. (a) ▼ ‹▼▼; ∩∩∩∩∩∩∩‖ ; LXXII; •••/••

(b) 602; $\frac{999}{999}$‖ ; DCII; •/••/••

(c) 1223; ≪ ≪ ▼▼▼ ; MCCXXIII; •••/••

(d) 667; ‹▼ ▼▼▼▼▼▼; 999999∩∩∩∩∩‖‖‖‖‖; •/‾/‾/••

(e) 106; ▼ ≪≪≪▼▼▼▼▼; 9‖‖‖‖ ; CVI

9. (a) Hundreds **(c)** Thousands

10. (a) 3,004,005 **(c)** 3,560

11. (a) 86 **(b)** 11

12. 811 or 910

13. 4,782,969

14. Assume an eight-digit display without scientific notation. **(a)** 98,765,432 **(c)** 99,999,999

15. (a) Answers vary, e.g. subtract 2020

Problem Set 3-2

1. (a) $k = 2$

2. No. If $k = 0$, we would have $k = 0 + k$, implying $k > k$.

4. (a)

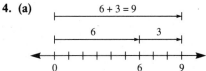

5. (a) 5 **(c)** 0, 1, 2

6. (a) 3 **(c)** a **(e)** 3, 4, 5, 6, 7, 8, 9

7. (a) Yes **(c)** Yes

8. (b) $213 = x + 119$

9. (a) Commutative Property for Addition **(b)** Associative Property for Addition **(c)** Commutative Property for Addition

11. (a) 33, 38, 43 **(b)** 56, 49, 42

14. (a) For example, $5 - 3 \neq 3 - 5$ **(c)** $4 - 0 \neq 0 - 4$ and $0 - 4 \neq 4$

15. (a) $a = b$ **(c)** $a = 0$

16. 0

17. (a)

8	1	6
3	5	7
4	9	2

18.

8	3
4	12

19.

1	5	9
6	7	2
8	3	4

20.

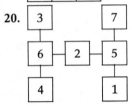

21. (a) Answers may vary **(b)** Yes, for example,

1	2
3	5
4	6

,

1	3
2	5
4	6

, or

1	4
2	5
3	6

22. 28
23. 24¢
25. 45 points
26. 400
30. 26
31. (a) CMLIX **(b)** XXXVIII
32. There are fewer symbols to remember and place value is used.
33. $5 \cdot 10^3 + 2 \cdot 10^2 + 8 \cdot 10^1 + 6 \cdot 1$

Problem Set 3-3
3. (a) Yes **(c)** Yes **(e)** Yes
4. $8 \cdot 3 = (6 + 2) \cdot 3 = 6 \cdot 3 + 2 \cdot 3 = 18 + 6 = 24$
5. (a) Commutative Property for Multiplication
(c) Commutative Property for Addition **(e)** Identity Property for Multiplication **(g)** Distributive Property for Multiplication over Addition **(h)** Distributive Property for Multiplication over Addition
6. (b) 4 **(d)** Any whole number
7. (a) $ac + ad + bc + bd$ **(d)** $x^2 + xy + xz + yx + y^2 + yz$, or $x^2 + 2xy + xz + y^2 + yz$
8. (a) 11 **(c)** 16

9. $a(b + c + d) = a[(b + c) + d] = a(b + c) + ad = (ab + ac) + ad = ab + ac + ad$
10. Only (a).
11. (a) (i) $a^2 + ab + ba + b^2 = a^2 + 2ab + b^2$ **(ii)** 1508 **(b)** $(m + n)(x + y) = (m + n)x + (m + n)y = (mx + nx) + (my + ny) = mx + (nx + my) + ny = mx + (my + nx) + ny = mx + my + nx + ny$
12. (a) 6 **(c)** 4
13. (b)

$$(a + b)(c + d) = ac + ad + bc + bd$$

14. (a) $40 = 8 \cdot 5$ **(c)** $48 = x \cdot 16$ **(e)** $a = b \cdot c$
15. (a) $2 \div 1 \neq 1 \div 2$ **(c)** $8 \div (2 + 2) \neq (8 \div 2) + (8 \div 2)$
17. $(a \cdot b) \div b = a$ if and only if $a \cdot b = b \cdot a$. By the Commutative Property for Multiplication, $a \cdot b = b \cdot a$, for all whole numbers.
20. (a)

□	△
0	34
1	26
2	18
3	10
4	2

(c)

□	△
25	1
1	25

Also, □ = 5 and △ = 5 if □ = △.

21. 1 and 36 2 and 18 3 and 12 4 and 9 6 and 6
23. 30
24. 12
25. (a) Yes **(b)** Yes **(c)** Yes, a **(d)** Yes
26. (a) 3 **(c)** 2 **(e)** 4
27. The answers depend upon the keys available on your calculator.
(a)

$3 = 1 + 9 - 7$	$11 = 7 + 1 + \sqrt{9}$
$4 = 1^7 + \sqrt{9}$	$12 = 19 - 7$
$5 = 7 - \sqrt{9} + 1$	$13 = 91 \div 7$
$6 = 7 - 1^9$	$14 = 7(\sqrt{9} - 1)$
$7 = 7 \cdot 1^9$	$15 = 7 + 9 - 1$
$8 = 7 + 1^9$	$16 = (7 + 9) \cdot 1$
$9 = 1^7 \cdot 9$	$17 = 7 + 9 + 1$
$10 = 1^7 + 9$	$18 = \sqrt{9}(7 - 1)$
	$19 = ?$
	$20 = 7\sqrt{9} - 1$

(c) For example, $22 + 2$.
28. (i) ∩∩∩∩∩∩∩‖‖‖‖   **(ii)** LXXV
(iii) ▼<▼▼▼▼▼   **(iv)** ⋮⋮ (with bar above)
29. $3 \cdot 10^4 + 5 \cdot 10^3 + 2 \cdot 10^2 + 0 \cdot 10^1 + 6$
30. For example, {0, 1}.

31. No. For example, $5 - 2 \neq 2 - 5$.

32.

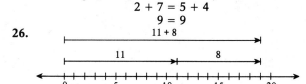

Problem Set 3-4

1. (c) $^1 5 ^2 2 ~ 4$
  $3 ~ 2 ~ 8$
  $\not 5 ~ \not 6 ~ 7^2$
  $+ ~ 1^4 3^2 \not 5 ~_4$
  $\overline{1 ~ 5 ~ 5 ~ 4}$

2. The "scratch marks" represent the normal "carries."

3. The columns separate place value and show that $7 + 8 = 15$ and $20 + 60 = 80$. Finally, $15 + 80 = 95$.

4. (a)   981
        $+421$
        $\overline{1402}$

   (c)   1,069
        2,094
        9,546
        9,003
        $+7,064$
        $\overline{28,776}$

5. (a) 46,414

   (c)   383
        -159
        $\overline{224}$

6. (a) One possibility: 863
                    $+752$
                    $\overline{1615}$

   (b) One possibility: 368
                    $+257$
                    $\overline{625}$

7. If only positive numbers are used: **(a)**   876
                                  -235
                                  $\overline{641}$

   (b)   623
        -587
        $\overline{36}$

9. (a) 34, 39, 44

11. No, not all at dinner. He can have either the steak or the salad.

12. Molly, 55 lbs; Karly, 50 lbs; Samantha, 65 lbs.

13. $124

14. 530 cm

15. (a) (i) No, not clustered (ii) Yes, clustered around 500

17. (a) They all sum to 265. **(b)** They all sum to 265.

19. Answers may vary, for example,   000
                          770
                          000
                          330
                          $+011$
                          $\overline{1111}$

20. $8 + 8 + 8 + 88 + 888$

22. It is doubling the second number in the operation

23. (a) 34; 34; 34 **(b)** 34 **(c)** 34 **(d)** Yes **(e)** Yes

24. $5280 = 5 \cdot 10^3 + 2 \cdot 10^2 + 8 \cdot 10 + 0 \cdot 1$

25. For example, $2 + (3 + 4) = (2 + 3) + 4$
            $2 + 7 = 5 + 4$
            $9 = 9$

26.

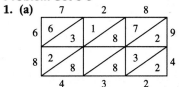

27. 1,000,410

28. (a) $a \cdot (x + 1)$ **(b)** $(3 + a) \cdot (x + y)$

29. 15

Problem Set 3-5

1. (a)

	7	2	8	
6	6／3	1／8	7／2	9
8	2／8	／8	3／2	4
	4	3	2	

2. Diagonals separate place value as placement does in the traditional algorithm.

3. (a)   426
        $\times ~ 783$
        $\overline{1278}$
        3408
        $\underline{2982}$
        $\overline{333558}$

5. (b) 6^{15} **(d)** 10^{12}

6. (a) 2^{100}

7. 86,400; 604,800; 31,536,000 (365 Days)

9. (b) Placement still indicates place value.

10.

→17	×	63		63
8		126		+1008
4		252		1071
2		504		
→ 1		1008		

11. **(a)** Let xy be the number. Then we want $(10x + y) + (10y + x)$ or $11 \cdot (x + y)$ to be close to 50. Therefore the sum we want must be a multiple of 11. 55 is the multiple of 11 closest to 50. Therefore the number could be 14, 23, 32, or 41.

12. **(a)** 21 **(c)** 304

13. **(a)** 22 **(c)** 7

15.
$$6 \cdot 411 = 6 \cdot (4 \cdot 10^2 + 1 \cdot 10 + 1)$$
$$= 6 \cdot (4 \cdot 10^2) + 6 \cdot (1 \cdot 10) + 6 \cdot 1$$
$$= (6 \cdot 4) \cdot 10^2 + (6 \cdot 1) \cdot 10 + 6 \cdot 1$$
$$= 24 \cdot 10^2 + 6 \cdot 10 + 6$$
$$= (2 \cdot 10 + 4) \cdot 10^2 + 6 \cdot 10 + 6$$
$$= (2 \cdot 10) \cdot 10^2 + 4 \cdot 10^2 + 6 \cdot 10 + 6$$
$$= 2 \cdot (10 \cdot 10^2) + 4 \cdot 10^2 + 6 \cdot 10 + 6$$
$$= 2 \cdot 10^3 + 4 \cdot 10^2 + 6 \cdot 10 + 6$$
$$= 2466$$

16.

a	b	$a \cdot b$	$a + b$
67	56	3752	123
32	78	2496	110
15	18	270	33

17. **(a)** 1332 **(b)** Jane, 330 more calories **(c)** Maurice, 96 more calories

18. No, only 2352 calories

19. $60

20. 5

22. **(a)** 77 remainder 7

23. **(a)** 3)876 **(b)** 8)367

24. **(a)** Monthly payments are more expensive. **(b)** $3,700

26. 65,536 bits

27. 3

28. 8 cars

29.

2	11
4	15
0	7
6	19
12	31

31. **(b)** If $ab \cdot cd = ba \cdot dc$ then $ac = bd$

32. 1022

33. **(a)**

763
× 8
6104

(b)

678
× 3
2034

34. **(a)**

762
× 83
63,246

(b)

378
× 26
9,828

35. 7,500,000 cows

36. **(a)**

37
×43
111
1480
1591

39. 19

40. 999999∩∩∩∩∩∩∩IIII

41. 300,260

42. For example, $3 + 0 = 3 = 0 + 3$.

43. **(a)** $x \cdot (a + b + 2)$ **(b)** $(3 + x)(a + b)$

44. 6979

45. 724

Problem Set 3-6

1. **(a)** $(1, 10, 11, 100, 101, 110, 111, 1000, 1001, 1010, 1011, 1100, 1101, 1110, 1111)_{two}$

2. 20

3. $2032_{four} = (2 \cdot 10^3 + 0 \cdot 10^2 + 3 \cdot 10 + 2)_{four} = 2 \cdot 4^3 + 0 \cdot 4^2 + 3 \cdot 4 + 2$

4. **(a)** 111_{two} **(c)** 999_{ten}

5. **(a)** ETE_{twelve}; $EE1_{twelve}$ **(c)** 554_{six}; 1000_{six} **(e)** 444_{five}; 1001_{five}

6. **(a)** There is no numeral 4 in base four. **(c)** There is no numeral T in base three.

7. **(a)** 3212_{five} **(c)** 12110_{four} **(e)** 1431304_{five} **(g)** $9000E0_{twelve}$

8. 100010_{two}

9. **(a)** 117 **(c)** 1331 **(e)** 157 **(g)** 211

10. 72¢; 242_{five}

11. 1 prize of $625, 2 prizes of $125, and 1 of $25.

13. **(a)** 8 weeks, 2 days **(c)** 1 day, 5 hours

14. $E66_{twelve}$; 1662

15. **(a)** 6 **(c)** 9

17. 4; 1, 2, 4, 8; 1, 2, 4, 8, 16

19. **(a)** 121_{five} **(c)** 1010_{five} **(e)** 1001_{two}

21. **(b)** 1 hour 39 minutes 40 seconds

22. **(a)** 2 quarts, 1 pint, 0 cups, or 1 half-gallon, 0 quarts, 1 pint, 0 cups **(c)** 2 quarts, 1 pint, 1 cup

24. **(a)** 3 gross 10 dozen 9 ones

25. **(a)** 22 students on Tuesday; **(b)** 1 gal., 1 half-gallon, 1 qt., 1 pint, and 1 cup

27. There is no numeral 5 in base five; $2_{five} + 3_{five} = 10_{five}$.

28. **(a)**

231_{five}
$+ 22_{five}$
303_{five}

29. (a) 233_{five} **(c)** 2144_{five} **(e)** 67_{eight} **(g)** 110_{two}
30. (a) Nine **(c)** Six
31. 30221_{five}
32. (a) $10040T0_{\text{twelve}}$

Laboratory Activity (p. 175)
1. (a) A computer
2. When a person tells his or her age by listing cards, the person is giving the base two representation for his or her age. The number can then be determined by adding the numbers in the upper left-hand corners of the named cards.

Chapter Test
1. (a) 400,044 **(c)** 1704 **(e)** 1448

2. (a) CMXCIX **(c)** $\dfrac{\bullet}{\bullet\bullet\bullet}$

(e) 1000_{twelve} **(g)** 1241_{nine}
3. (a) 3^{17} **(c)** 3^5
4. (a) Distributive Property for Multiplication over Addition **(c)** Identity Property for Multiplication **(e)** Commutative Property for Multiplication
5. (a) $3 < 13$, since $3 + 10 = 13$
6. $1000 \cdot 438 = 10^3(4 \cdot 10^2 + 8 \cdot 10 + 3)$
$\qquad = 4 \cdot 10^5 + 8 \cdot 10^4 + 3 \cdot 10^3$
$\qquad = 4 \cdot 10^5 + 8 \cdot 10^4 + 3 \cdot 10^3 + 0 \cdot 10^2$
$\qquad\quad + 0 \cdot 10^1 + 0 \cdot 1$
$\qquad = 483,000$
7. (a) 1119
8. (a) 60,074
9. (a) 5 remainder 243 **(c)** 120_{five} remainder 2_{five}
10. (a) $5 \cdot 912 + 243 = 4803$ **(b)** $91 \cdot 11 + 10 = 1011$ **(c)** $23_{\text{five}} \cdot 120_{\text{five}} + 2_{\text{five}} = 3312_{\text{five}}$
(d) $11_{\text{two}} \cdot 11_{\text{two}} + 10_{\text{two}} = 1011_{\text{two}}$
11. (a) tens
12. (a) 9, 10, 11, 12, 13, 14, 15 **(c)** All whole numbers
13. (a)

(c)

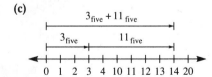

14. (a) $15a$ **(d)** $(x + 5)(3 + y)$
15. (a) 25 **(c)** 72
16. $395
17. $4380
18. 2600

19. $3842
20. Several answers are possible. For example,

$$\begin{array}{r} 296 \\ +541 \\ \hline 837 \end{array} \qquad \begin{array}{r} 569 \\ +214 \\ \hline 783 \end{array}$$

21. 69 miles
22. 40 cans
23. 12 outfits
24.

+	5	7	9
8	13	15	17
11	16	18	20
21	26	28	30

25. 26
26. $2.16
27. $6000 vs. $6400
28. There are 36 bikes and 18 trikes
29. $900E000T_{\text{twelve}}$

CHAPTER 4

Problem Set 4-1
1. (a) $^-2$ **(c)** ^-m **(e)** m
2. (a) 2 **(c)** 0
3. (a) 5 **(c)** $^-5$
4. (a)

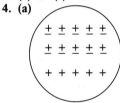

$^+5$ charge

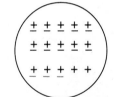

Add 3 negative charges; net result 2 positive charges

(d)

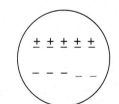

$^-3$ charge on the field

Add 2 negative charges; net result 5 negative charges

5. Black chips represent positive numbers; red chips represent negative numbers.
(a)

Net result: 2 positive chips

(d)

Net result: 5 negative chips

6. (a)

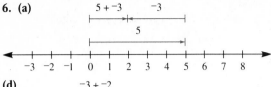

(d)

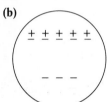

7. (a) 7 **(c)** 0 **(e)** $^-$10 **(g)** 2
8. (a) $^-$17 + 10 = $^-$7 **(c)** 5000 + $^-$100 = 4900
(e) $^-$2 + 7 + 0 + $^-$8 = $^-$3
10.

(b)

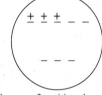

−3 charge on field   Take away 2 positive charges; net
                            result 5 negative charges on the field

11. (a)

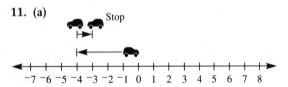

12. (a) $^-$4 − 2 = $^-$6; $^-$4 − 1 = $^-$5; $^-$4 − 0 = $^-$4;
$^-$4 − $^-$1 = $^-$3
13. (a) $^-$9 **(c)** 13
14. (a) $^-$9 **(c)** 1 **(e)** $^-$13
15. (a) Yes
16. (a) $1 + 4x$
17. (a) All negative integers **(c)** All integers less than $^-$1
(e) There are none. **(g)** There are none.
19. (a) I **(c)** $I − \{0\}$ **(e)** $\varnothing$ **(g)** $\{0\}$

21.

		6	4	
2	8	1	7	
		5	3	

23. (a) 59 **(c)** 192
24. (a) 0 **(c)** 1
25. (b) 2 **(d)** The set of all integers greater than or
equal to 0
28. (a) $^-$18 **(c)** $^-$6 **(e)** $^-$11 **(g)** $^-$18
29. (a) True **(c)** True **(e)** False; let $x = ^-1$

Problem Set 4-2
1. $3(^-1) = ^-1 + ^-1 + ^-1 = ^-3$; $2(^-1) = ^-1 + ^-1 = ^-2$; $1(^-1) = ^-1$; $0(^-1) = 0$; $^-1(^-1) = 1$ by
continuing the pattern
3. If you are now at 0 moving west at 4 km/h, you will be at 8 km
west of 0 two hours from now.

4. (a) 12 **(c)** $^-$15 **(e)** 30 **(g)** 0
5. (a) 5 **(c)** $^-$11 **(e)** Impossible; division by 0 is not
defined
6. (a) $^-$10 **(c)** a; $b \neq 0$ or the division is not defined
(e) a; $b \neq 0$ or the division is not defined **(g)** $^-$5
(i) Impossible **(k)** Impossible **(m)** $^-$1
8. $^-$15°C
10. (a) $^-1(^-5 + ^-2) = ^-1 \cdot ^-5 + ^-1 \cdot ^-2$
(c) $^-5(2 + ^-6) = ^-5 \cdot 2 + ^-5 \cdot ^-6$
11. (a) $12/(^-2 + 4) \neq 12/^-2 + 12/4$ since $6 \neq ^-3$
13. (a) $^-$8 **(c)** $^-$1000 **(e)** 1 **(g)** 1
14. (a) 12 **(c)** $^-$5 **(e)** 9 **(g)** $^-$13 **(i)** $^-$32
15. (a) and **(f)** are always negative; **(b)**, **(c)**, **(g)**, and
(h) are always positive.
17. (a) xy **(c)** 0 **(e)** $x + 2y$ **(g)** x
18. (a) $^-$13, $^-$17, $^-$21 **(c)** $^-$9, 3, $^-$1
19. (a) $^-$2 **(c)** 0 **(e)** $^-$36 **(g)** All integers except 0
(i) No solution is possible with integers. **(k)** No
solution is possible with integers. **(m)** All integers
except 0 **(o)** All integers
20. (a) $^-2x + 2$ **(c)** $x^2 − xy$ **(e)** $^-2x − 2y + 2z$
(g) $^-25 − 10x − x^2$ **(i)** $^-x^4 + 3x^2 − 2$
21. (a) $(50 + 2)(50 − 2) = 2496$ **(c)** $x^2 − y^2$
(e) $x^2 − 1$

22. No; it is not of the form $(a - b)(a + b)$.
23. (a) $(3 + 5)x = 8x$ **(c)** $x(y + 1)$ **(e)** $x(x + y)$
(g) $(3y + 2 - z)x$ **(i)** $a(bc + b - 1)$
(k) $(4 - a)(4 + a)$ **(m)** $(2x - 5y)(2x + 5y)$
24. (a) Commutative Property of Multiplication
(c) Associative Property of Multiplication
25. (a) False **(c)** True
26. (a) The sums are 9 times the middle number.
27. (a) The additive inverse of $^-(ab)$ is ab. Also, $(^-a)b$
$+ ab = [(^-a) + a]b = 0 \cdot b = 0$. Thus, the additive
inverse of $(^-a)b$ is also ab. Hence, by the uniqueness of
additive inverses, $(^-a)b = ^-(ab)$.
28. (a) $^-81$ **(c)** $^-2$
29. (a) $^-3$ **(c)** 13 **(e)** $^-3$
31. (a) 5
32. (a) 14 **(c)** $^-4$
33. 400 lb

Problem Set 4-3
1. (a) $^-20, ^-13, ^-5, ^-3, 0, 4$ **(c)** $^-100, ^-20, ^-15, ^-13, 0$
2. (a) $^-5 + 2 = ^-3$ **(c)** $^-10 + 2 = ^-8$
3. (a) $^-18$ **(c)** 18 **(e)** $^-18$ **(g)** $^-7$ **(i)** $^-2$ **(k)** $^-1$
(m) $^-2$
4. (a) True **(c)** True **(e)** True
5. (a) $1, ^-2, 0$ **(c)** $^-6, ^-7$
6. (a) $^-3$ **(c)** 1
7. (a) $n - 6$ or $6 - n$ **(c)** $4n - 7$ **(e)** $n + 10$
(g) $13 - n$
9. Tom is older than 11.
11. Rick has $100; David has $300.
13. Let x be the distance from B to A. Point A is twice
as far from point C as point B is from point A can be
translated as "point A is $2x$ from point C and point B is
x from point A." From this information, we can infer
that the distance from B to C is also x. The distance
from B to C in 5 in. Hence, the distance from A to C is
10 in. An alternate answer is 3 1/3 in.
14. Factory A produces 2800; B produces 1400; C
produces 3100.
16. 524
18. 78, 80, and 82
20. Eldest, $30,000; middle, $24,000; youngest,
$10,000
21. (a) Yes. $x^2 + y^2 \geq 2xy$ if and only if $x^2 - 2xy +$
$y^2 \geq 0$ and $x^2 - 2xy + y^2 = (x - y)^2 \geq 0$. **(b)** $x = y$
23. No; $^-5 < 2$, but $(^-5)^2 > 2^2$.
25. (a) $^-3, ^-2, ^-1, 0, 1$
26. (a) 7 **(c)** $^-3$
27. (a) $^-10$ **(c)** $^-4$ **(e)** $^-21$ **(g)** $^-4$ **(i)** 3 **(k)** 7
(m) 21 **(o)** 15

Chapter 4 Test
1. (a) $^-3$ **(c)** 0 **(e)** $x + ^-y$ **(g)** 32
2. (a) $^-7$ **(c)** 8 **(e)** 8
3. (a) 3 **(c)** Any integer except 0 **(e)** $^-41$
5. (a) $(x - y)(x + y) = (x - y)x + (x - y)y$
$$= x^2 - yx + xy - y^2$$
$$= x^2 - xy + xy - y^2$$
$$= x^2 - y^2$$
6. (a) ^-x **(c)** $3x - 1$ **(e)** 0
7. (a) $x(1 - 3) = ^-2x$ **(c)** $(x - 6)(x + 6)$
(e) $5(1 + x)$
8. (a) $^-2$ **(c)** $1, 2, 3, 4 \ldots$
9. (a) False **(c)** False **(e)** False
10. (a) $2/1 \neq 1/2$ **(c)** $1/2 \notin I$
13. 14 lb
15. 7 nickels and 17 dimes
17. 42 gallons

CHAPTER 5

Problem Set 5-1
1. (a) T **(b)** T **(c)** T **(d)** T **(e)** T **(f)** F
2. (a) $7|(14 + 21)$ or $7|35$ **(b)** $d|(213 - 57 + 57)$,
or $d|213$ **(c)** $d|(a - b + b)$, or $a|a$
4. Yes. $9 \nmid 1379$
6. (a) Theorem 5-3 **(b)** Theorem 5-1(b) **(c)** None
(d) Theorem 5-1(b) **(e)** Theorem 5-3
7. (a) No, since $17|34000$ and $17 \nmid 15$
8. (a) F. $5|(2 + 3)$, but $5 \nmid 2$ and $5 \nmid 3$. **(c)** T. Use
Theorem 5-3. **(j)** F. $3 \nmid 7$ and $3 \nmid 5$, yet $3|(7 + 5) = 12$
(l) F. $9 \nmid 6$, yet $9|6^2$
10. (b) F **(e)** T **(f)** F
12. (a) A number N is divisible by 16 if and only if the
number formed by the last 4 digits is divisible by 16.
(b) A number N is divisible by 25 if and only if the
number formed by the last two digits is divisible by 25.
14. Yes.
16. 85,041
18. (a) No. Suppose that the number is divisible by 10;
then it must be divisible by 5, a contradiction. **(b)** Yes.
For example, $10 \nmid 5$, but $5|5$
19. (a) 747
20. Because each digit, except 0, appears three times, 3
divides the sums of all like digits. Also $3|0$, so that 3
divides the sum of all digits.
21. $a|b$ implies $a \cdot m = b$ for some integer m. $b|c$
implies $b \cdot n = c$ for some integer n. Substituting am for
b, we have $(am)n = c$, or $a(mn) = c$. Therefore, $a|c$.
22. (a) Yes **(d)** Yes

23. (d) Every 6-digit palindrome is in the form $xyzzyx$. The divisibility text for 11 always yields 0 which is divisible by 11. Thus, the palindrome is divisible by 11.
25. $3|6$ and $3|15$, yet $3|286$, so there is no solution.
27. (a) Any integer can be written as $3q$, $3q + 1$, or $3q + 2$ where $q \in I$. If $n = 3q$ then $3|n$. If $n = 3q + 1$ then $n + 1 = 3p + 2$, $n + 2 = 3p + 3$ and hence $3|n + 2$. If $n = 3p + 2$ then $n + 1 = 3q + 3$ and hence $3|n + 1$. **(b)** Among any n consecutive integers there is always one that is divisible by n.
29. Let $N = a_4 \cdot 10^4 + a_3 \cdot 10^3 + a_2 \cdot 10^2 + a_1 \cdot 10^1 + a_0$. Hint:
$9|9$ implies $9|9a_1$
$9|99$ implies $9|99a_2$
$9|999$ implies $9|999a_3$
$9|999$ implies $9|9999a_4$

Problem Set 5-2
1. (a) $504 = 2^3 \cdot 3^2 \cdot 7$ **(b)** $2475 = 3^2 \cdot 5^2 \cdot 11$
(c) $11,250 = 2 \cdot 3^2 \cdot 5^4$
2. (a) Yes **(b)** No **(c)** Yes
3. 73
5. 53, 59, 61, 67, 71, 73, 79, 83, 89, 97, 101, 103, 107, 109, 113, 127, 131, 137, 139, 149, 151, 157, 163, 167, 173, 179, 181, 191, 193, 197, 199
7. (a) $1 \cdot 48$; $2 \cdot 24$; $3 \cdot 16$; $4 \cdot 12$ **(b)** Only one; $1 \cdot 47$
9. (a) 3, 5, 15, or 29 members **(b)** 145 committees of 3; 87 committees of 5; 29 committees of 15; or 15 committees of 29.
11. 2^6, or 64
13. 27,720
15. 3 and 5; 11 and 13; 17 and 19; 29 and 31; 41 and 43; 59 and 61; 71 and 73; 101 and 103; 107 and 109; 137 and 139; 149 and 151; 179 and 181; 191 and 193; 197 and 199
17. No. The student who checked for divisibility by 12 using 2 and 6 is incorrect because $2|n$ and $6|n$ do not imply that $12|n$. They imply only that $6|n$.
22. If we designate a solution as (x, y), then the required solutions are: (1, 60), (2, 30), (3, 20), (4, 15), (5, 12), (6, 10), (10, 6), (12, 5), (15, 4), (20, 3), (30, 2), (60, 1)
23. (a) 1, 2, 4, 8, 16, 32, 64, 128, 256 **(b)** 1, 3, 9, 27, 81, 243
24. (a) 49, 121, 169. These numbers are the squares of prime numbers. **(b)** 81, 625, 2401. These numbers are the primes raised to the 4th power. **(c)** 38, 39, 46. These numbers are the product of 2 primes or the cube of primes.
26. If any prime q in the set $\{2, 3, 5, \ldots, p\}$ divides N, then $q|2 \cdot 3 \cdot 5 \cdot \ldots \cdot p$. Because $q \nmid 1$ by Theorem 5-1(b), $q \nmid (2 \cdot 3 \cdot 5 \cdot \ldots \cdot p + 1)$; that is, $q \nmid N$.
27. (c) $7 \cdot 5^2 \cdot 3^4 \cdot 2^8$ **(d)** $7^3 \cdot 5^6 \cdot 3^{12} \cdot 2^{24}$

29. 111 is composite since $3|111$. Also, 111111 is composite since $3|111111$. Thus whenever n has d digits where $3|d$, n will be composite. We can find infinitely many such n.
32. (a) F **(b)** T **(c)** T **(d)** T
34. Let N be a number such that $12|N$. $12|N$ implies $12m = N$, $3 \cdot 4 \cdot m = N$, $3 \cdot (4 \cdot m) = N$, where $m \in I$. Therefore. $3|N$.

Problem Set 5-3
1. (a) 2; 90 **(b)** 12; 72 **(c)** 4; 312
2. (a) 12; 5544 **(b)** 65; 1690 **(c)** 6; 50,400
3. (a) 4 **(b)** 1
5. (a) 160,280 **(b)** 158,433,320
8. 24
10. 2:30 A.M.
12. (a) ab **(b)** a; a **(c)** a; a^2 **(d)** a; b **(e)** 1; ab
(f) $a|b$ **(g)** $b|a$
14. 15
17. 1, 2, 3, 4, 6, 7, 8, 9, 11, 12, 13, 14, 16, 17, 18, 19, 21, 22, 23, 24.
20. Yes. $d|GCD(a, b)$ and $GCD(a, b)|a$ so $d|a$. Similarly, $d|b$.
22. (a) 83151, 83451, 83751 **(b)** 86691
23. No. $3|3111$
25. $2^3 \cdot 3^2 \cdot 5 \cdot 7 \cdot 11 = 27,270$

Problem Set 5-4
3. (a)

$\oplus$	1	2	3	4	5	6	7
1	2	3	4	5	6	7	1
2	3	4	5	6	7	1	2
3	4	5	6	7	1	2	3
4	5	6	7	1	2	3	4
5	6	7	1	2	3	4	5
6	7	1	2	3	4	5	6
7	1	2	3	4	5	6	7

(b) 6; 4
5. (b) 3 and 11
7. Wednesday
8. (a) 4 **(b)** 0 **(c)** 0 **(d)** 7
11. (a) $24 \equiv 0 \pmod 8$ **(b)** $^-90 \equiv 0 \pmod 3$
(c) $n \equiv 0 \pmod n$
13. (a) 1 **(c)** 10

Chapter Test
1. (a) F **(b)** F **(c)** T **(d)** F **(e)** F
3. (a) 83,160 is divisible by 2, 3, 4, 5, 6, 7, 8, 9, 11.
(b) 83,193 is divisible by 3 and 11.
5. (a) 2, 5, 8 **(b)** 1, 4, 7 **(c)** 17, 46, 75
7. The number must be divisible by both 8 and 3. Since $3|4152$ and $8|4152$, then $24|4152$.
9. (a) $2^4 \cdot 5^3 \cdot 7^4 \cdot 13 \cdot 29$ **(b)** $278 \cdot 279$, or 77,562
11. 1, 2, 3, 4, 6, 8, 9, 12, 16, 18, 24, 36, 48, 72, 144

13. 15 minutes
15. 9:30 A.M.
17. (a) 1 (b) 4 (c) 3

CHAPTER 6

Problem Set 6-1
1. (a) The solution to $8x = 7$ is (7/8). (b) Jane ate seven eighths of Jill's candy. (c) The ratio of boys to girls is seven to eight.
3. (a) 2/3 (b) 4/6 (c) 6/9 (d) 8/12. The diagram illustrates the Fundamental Law of Fractions
5. (a) 3/8 (b) 1/2 (c) 1/6 (d) 1/3
7. (a) 52/31 (b) 3/5 (c) −5/7
9. (a) undefined (b) undefined (c) 0 (d) cannot be simplified (e) cannot be simplified (f) 2/3 (g) 5/3
10. (a) 1 (b) $2x/9y$ (e) $1/(3 + b)$ (f) $a/(3a + b)$
12. Only the fractions in (c), (e), and (f) are equal.
13. (b) $^-36$ (c) x is any rational number except 0.
15. (a) T (b) T (c) F (d) F (e) T

Problem Set 6-2
2. (a) $\dfrac{-11}{16}$ (b) $\dfrac{-4}{12}$, or $\dfrac{-1}{3}$
3. (a) $\dfrac{-31}{20}$ (b) $\dfrac{58}{35}$ (c) $\dfrac{-19}{40}$ (d) $\dfrac{5y - 3x}{xy}$
4. (b) $\dfrac{-23}{21}$ (c) $\dfrac{-6y + 6x - 1}{4xy}$
5. (a) $18\dfrac{2}{3}$ (c) $-\left(2\dfrac{93}{100}\right)$
7. (a) $\dfrac{7}{12}$ (b) $\dfrac{49}{12}$ (c) $\dfrac{71}{24}$ (d) $\dfrac{-23}{3}$ (e) $\dfrac{43}{2^4 \cdot 3^4}$
(f) $\dfrac{472}{45}$
12. (a) 2 (b) 3/4 (c) 1/3 (d) 0
14. (a) No
16. (a) $\dfrac{d - a}{bc}$ (b) $\dfrac{12a + 2b}{a^2 - b^2}$ (c) $\dfrac{a^3bd - bc^2}{adc}$
18. (a) $\dfrac{3 + 3}{3} \neq \dfrac{3}{3} + 3$ (b) $\dfrac{4}{2 + 2} \neq \dfrac{4}{2} + \dfrac{4}{2}$
(c) $\dfrac{ab + c}{a} \neq \dfrac{áb + c}{á}$
20. She saves 1/20
22. $6\dfrac{7}{12}$ yards

24. $1\dfrac{7}{8}$ cups
26. $2\dfrac{1}{6}$ hours
27. $2\dfrac{5}{6}$ yards
30. (a) $\dfrac{1}{2} + \dfrac{3}{4} = \dfrac{5}{4} \in Q$
(c) $\dfrac{1}{2} = \dfrac{2}{4}, \dfrac{1}{2} + \dfrac{1}{4} = \dfrac{3}{4}$, and $\dfrac{2}{4} + \dfrac{1}{4} = \dfrac{3}{4}$
32. (a) $1\dfrac{1}{2}, 1\dfrac{3}{4}, 2$; arithmetic, $\dfrac{1}{2} - \dfrac{1}{4} = \dfrac{3}{4} - \dfrac{1}{2} =$
$1 - \dfrac{3}{4} = \dfrac{5}{4} - 1$ (b) $\dfrac{6}{7}, \dfrac{7}{8}, \dfrac{8}{9}$; not arithmetic; $\dfrac{2}{3} - \dfrac{1}{2} \neq \dfrac{3}{4}$
$-\dfrac{2}{3}$
34. $1, \dfrac{7}{6}, \dfrac{8}{6}, \dfrac{9}{6}, \dfrac{10}{6}, \dfrac{11}{6}, 2$
36. (a) $f(0) = -2$ (b) $f(-2) = 0$ (c) $f(-5) = \dfrac{1}{2}$
38. (a) $\dfrac{2}{3}$ (b) $\dfrac{13}{17}$ (c) $\dfrac{25}{49}$ (d) $\dfrac{a}{1}$, or a (e) Reduced

Problem Set 6-3
1. (a) $\dfrac{1}{4} \cdot \dfrac{1}{3} = \dfrac{1}{12}$ (b) $\dfrac{2}{4} \cdot \dfrac{3}{5} = \dfrac{6}{20}$
2. (a)
3. (a) $\dfrac{3}{4}$ (b) $\dfrac{3}{8}$ (c) $\dfrac{-5a}{3b}$
5. (a) $10\dfrac{1}{2}$
6. (a) -3 (b) $\dfrac{5}{3}$
7. (a) 27 (b) $\dfrac{8}{7}$ (c) $\dfrac{-6}{7}$ (d) $\dfrac{y}{x}$ (e) $\dfrac{27}{64}$ (f) $\dfrac{1}{12}$
8. (a) $\dfrac{11}{5}$ (b) $\dfrac{77}{12}$ (c) $\dfrac{22}{3}$ (j) $\dfrac{5}{x}$
9. (a) 20 (b) 16
11. (a) Less than 1 (b) Less than 1 (c) Greater than 2

12. (a) 48⁻ **(b)** 12⁺

15. (a) $\dfrac{21}{8}$ **(b)** $\dfrac{3}{35}$ **(c)** -28 **(d)** $\dfrac{-56}{5}$

17. 400

19. (a) 39 uniforms **(b)** $\dfrac{1}{4}$ yards left

22. 29/36

26. 1/4

28. \$225

30. 7 ounces

32. (a) $n(n+1) + \left(\dfrac{1}{2}\right)^2$

34. (a) (i) $\dfrac{-4}{5}$ **(ii)** $\dfrac{-26}{17}$ **(iii)** $\dfrac{-14}{33}$ **(b) (i)** $\dfrac{-4}{3}$ **(ii)** $\dfrac{-30}{7}$

(iii) $\dfrac{-3}{10}$ **(c)** $\dfrac{5}{4}$

36. $c = 0$ or $a = b$, where $b \neq 0$.

37. (a) $2S = 2\left(\dfrac{1}{2} + \dfrac{1}{2^2} + \cdots + \dfrac{1}{2^{64}}\right) = 1 + \dfrac{1}{2} + \dfrac{1}{2^2} +$

$\cdots + \dfrac{1}{2^{63}}$ **(b)** Note that $2S = 1 + S - \dfrac{1}{2^{64}}$. Hence,

$2S - S = 1 + S - \dfrac{1}{2^{64}} - S = 1 - \dfrac{1}{2^{64}}$. **(c)** $1 - \dfrac{1}{2^n}$

39. (a) $1\dfrac{49}{99}$ **(b)** $25 \cdot \left(2\dfrac{49}{99}\right)$

41. 120 students

42. (a) $\dfrac{16}{15x}$

Problem Set 6-4

1. (a) > **(b)** > **(c)** < **(d)** < **(e)** = **(f)** =

3. (c) $\dfrac{-1}{5}, \dfrac{-19}{36}, \dfrac{-17}{30}$

4. (a) $x \leq \dfrac{27}{16}$ **(b)** $x < \dfrac{17}{5}$

6. (a) $399\dfrac{80}{81}$ **(b)** $180\dfrac{89}{90}$ **(c)** $3\dfrac{699}{820}$

9. (a) about 180 **(d)** about 6

12. $\dfrac{a}{b} < 1$ and $\dfrac{c}{d} > 0$ imply $\dfrac{a}{b} \cdot \dfrac{c}{d} < 1 \cdot \dfrac{c}{d}$ or $\dfrac{a}{b} \cdot \dfrac{c}{d} < \dfrac{c}{d}$

14. We need to show that $\dfrac{n}{n+1} < \dfrac{n+1}{n+2}$. This inequality is equivalent to $n^2 + 2n < n^2 + 2n + 1$, or $0 < 1$.

17. Answers may vary. The following are possible answers. **(b)** $\dfrac{-22}{27}, \dfrac{-23}{27}$

19. (a) 28 **(b)** -301

21. We are considering $\dfrac{a}{b}$ and $\dfrac{a+x}{b+x}$ when $a < b$.

$\dfrac{a}{b} < \dfrac{a+x}{b+x}$ because $ab + ax < ab + bx$.

22. (d) 1 (provided that $|x| \neq |y|$)

23. $6\dfrac{7}{18}$ hours

24. (d) -3

26. (a) 3 and 4

Problem Set 6-5

1. $\dfrac{3}{2}$

3. (a) 30 **(b)** $-3\dfrac{1}{3}$ **(c)** $23\dfrac{1}{3}$ **(d)** $10\dfrac{1}{2}$

5. 2469

7. 270 miles

9. 72 minutes for 30 inches

11. 500 ft. by 900 ft.

13. \$77 and \$99

15. $9\dfrac{9}{14}$ days

17. (a) $2:5$. Because the ratio is $2:3$, there are $2x$ boys and $3x$ girls, hence the ratio of boys to all the students is $2x/(2x + 3x) = 2/5$.

19. $13\dfrac{1}{3}$ hours

20. $\dfrac{a}{b} = \dfrac{c}{d}$ implies $ad = bc$, which is equivalent to

$d = \dfrac{bc}{a}$; then, $\dfrac{d}{c} = \dfrac{b}{a}$.

22. (a) $\dfrac{1}{2}$

24. $\dfrac{37}{125}$ of a mile

26. (a) $x \geq \dfrac{3}{2}$ **(d)** $x \leq \dfrac{-56}{5}$

Problem Set 6-6

1. (a) $\dfrac{1}{3^{13}}$ **(d)** 5^{19} **(f)** a^5

2. (a) $\left(\dfrac{1}{2}\right)^{10}$ **(b)** $\left(\dfrac{1}{2}\right)^3$ **(c)** $\left(\dfrac{2}{3}\right)^9$

3. (a) False $2^3 \cdot 2^4 \neq (2 \cdot 2)^{3+4}$ **(b)** False $2^3 \cdot 2^4 \neq$
$(2 \cdot 2)^{3\cdot4}$ **(c)** False $2^3 \cdot 2^3 \neq (2 \cdot 2)^{2\cdot3}$ **(d)** False $a^0 = 1$
if $a \neq 0$ **(e)** False $(2 + 3)^2 \neq 2^2 + 3^2$ **(f)** False
$(2 + 3)^{-2} \neq \dfrac{1}{2^2} + \dfrac{1}{3^2}$ **(g)** False $a^{mn} = (a^m)^n \neq a^m \cdot a^n$

(h) True $\left(\dfrac{a}{b}\right)^{-1} = \dfrac{1}{\left(\dfrac{a}{b}\right)} = \dfrac{b}{a}$

4. (a) 5 **(b)** 6 or -6 **(c)** -2
5. 10^{11}; 10^5
6. (a) $x \leq 4$
7. (a) $\dfrac{1 - x^2}{x}$ **(b)** $\dfrac{x^2y^2 - 1}{y^2}$ **(c)** $6x^2 + 4x$

8. (f) $\left(\dfrac{3}{4}\right)^{100}$

9. (a) 10^{10} **(b)** $10^{10} \cdot (6/5)^2$
11. (a) 3/4 **(b)** 24 **(c)** 3/128 **(d)** $n = -7$
13. (a) 32^{50} because $32^{50} = (2^5)^{50} = 2^{250}$ and
$4^{100} = 2^{200}$
14. 216

16. (a) $\dfrac{2}{7}$ **(b)** $\dfrac{40}{3}$ **(c)** $\dfrac{1}{3^4}$ **(h)** $\dfrac{x}{x + y}$

17. (a) $\dfrac{-4}{3}$ **(b)** $\dfrac{-9}{10}$ **(c)** $\dfrac{60}{13}$

18. $1\dfrac{1}{5}$ days

20. $\dfrac{-6}{7}, \dfrac{-3}{4}, \dfrac{-2}{3}, \dfrac{-1}{2}, 0, \dfrac{7}{9}, \dfrac{4}{5}, \dfrac{6}{7}, \dfrac{9}{7}$

Chapter Test
1. (a)

3. (a) $\dfrac{6}{7}$ **(b)** $\dfrac{ax}{b}$ **(c)** $\dfrac{0}{1}$

5. (a) $\dfrac{11}{10}$ **(b)** $\dfrac{13}{175}$ **(c)** $\dfrac{10}{13}$ **(d)** $\dfrac{25}{24}$ **(e)** $\dfrac{50}{9}$ **(f)** $\dfrac{-26}{27}$

7. $-2\dfrac{1}{3}, -1\dfrac{7}{8}, 0, (71/140)^{300}, 69/140, 1/2, 71/140,$
$(74/73)^{300}$

8. (a) 6 **(b)** $\dfrac{5}{4}$ **(c)** $\dfrac{-1}{4}$

9. (a) $x \leq \dfrac{42}{25}$ **(c)** $x = \dfrac{8}{9}$

12. (a) $\dfrac{1}{2^{11}}$ **(b)** $\dfrac{1}{5^{20}}$ **(c)** $\left(\dfrac{3}{2}\right)^{28}$, or $\dfrac{3^{28}}{2^{28}}$ **(d)** 3^{18}

14. (a) 15 **(b)** 15 **(c)** 4
16. \$70

CHAPTER 7

Problem Set 7-1
1. (a) $0 \cdot 10^0 + 0 \cdot 10^{-1} + 2 \cdot 10^{-2} + 3 \cdot 10^{-3}$
(c) $3 \cdot 10^2 + 1 \cdot 10 + 2 \cdot 10^0 + 0 \cdot 10^{-1} + 1 \cdot 10^{-2} +$
$0 \cdot 10^{-3} + 3 \cdot 10^{-4}$
2. (a) 4356.78 **(c)** 40,000.03
3. (a) 536.0076 **(c)** 0.000436
4. (a) 436/1000 **(c)** $^-$316,027/1000 **(e)** $^-$43/10
6. (a) 0.8 **(b)** 3.05 **(c)** 0.5 **(d)** 0.03125 **(e)** 0.01152
(f) 0.2128 **(h)** 0.08
7. (a) 39.202 **(c)** $^-$390.6313 **(e)** $^-$10.4
8. (a) 17.702 **(c)** 0.0272
10. 0.8
11. Lining up the decimal points acts as using place
value.
12. (a) 463,000,000 **(c)** 4,630,000,000 **(e)** 463,000
13. (a) 0.000463 **(c)** 0.00463
15. (a), (c), and (f)
17. 1.679 points
20. 62.298 lb
22. \$8.00
23. (a) 5.4, 6.3, 7.2 **(c)** 0.0625, 0.03125, 0.015625
26. (a) 91,000,000.1106 **(c)** 154,815,802.09496
28. No
30. The number of digits in the terminating decimal is
the greater of m or n.

Problem Set 7-2
1. (a) $0.\overline{4}$ **(c)** $0.\overline{27}$ **(e)** $0.02\overline{6}$ **(g)** $0.8\overline{3}$
3. (a) The sum is always 999. **(c)** It appears that the
sum will be a power of 10 less 1. **(d)** No
4. (a) $0.\overline{076923}$ **(c)** $0.\overline{157894736842105263}$
5. (a) 221/90 **(c)** 243/99 **(e)** 243/9900 **(g)** 4/9
(i) 5/9 **(k)** $^-$232/99
6. (a) $3.2\overline{3}, 3.\overline{23}, 3.23, 3.\overline{22}, 3.2$
8. (a) 3.25 **(c)** 0.01515
10. (a) 200 **(c)** 204 **(e)** 203.65
12. (a) Okay, it only totals \$2.17
13. \$37
15. 28,000 years
16. (a) $3.325 \cdot 10^3$ **(c)** $1.3 \cdot 10^{-4}$
17. (a) 0.0000000032 **(c)** 0.42
18. (a) $1.27 \cdot 10^7$ **(c)** $5 \cdot 10^7$
19. (b) 19,900
20. (a) $4.8 \cdot 10^{28}$ **(c)** $2 \cdot 10^2$
22. Because $1/99 = 0.0101010101 \ldots$, then $51/99 =$
$51(1/99) = 51 \cdot 0.01010101 \ldots = 0.51515151 \ldots$
However, $x/99$ behaves differently if $x > 99$.
23. (b) $6/7 = 0.\overline{857142}, 7/8 = 0.875, 8/9 = 0.\overline{8}$
24. (a) $0.44\overline{6355}$; 6 **(b)** $1.3\overline{5775}$; yes; 4

26. $22,761.95
28. (a) 1672/100 **(c)** ⁻507/100

Problem Set 7-3

1. (a) 789% **(c)** 19,310% **(e)** 83.3̄% or 83 1/3%
(g) 12.5% **(i)** 62.5% **(k)** 80%
2. (e) 0.136̄ **(g)** 0.003̄
5. (a) 2.04 **(c)** 60 **(e)** 300%
7. $16,960
9. $437.50
11. 20%
13. Approximately 18.4%
15. 100%
17. $5.10
19. $336
21. $3200
23. 16.6̄%
25. Approximately $82,644.63
27. $440
29. $187.50
31. (a) $3.30 **(c)** $1.90
33. (a) Approximately 4.9%, 34.6%, and 60.5%
(c) Approximately 8.2%, 40.8%, and 51%
34. (a) $d + 1$
35. 97 days
37. 0.2̄

Problem Set 7-4

1. (a) 2, 3%, 4, $125.50
  (c) 5, 0.83̄%, 60, $645.30
3. $24.46
5. Approximately $32,040.82
7. $4416.34
9. $81,628.82
11. The Pay More Bank has a better rate.
13. Approximately $2.53
17. Approximately 12.78%

Problem Set 7-5

1. Answers may vary. One answer is
0.232233222333 . . .
3. 0.9̄, 0.99̄8, 0.9̄8, 0.98̄8, 0.9, 0.89̄8
4. (a), (d), (e), and (f) represent irrational numbers
5. (a) 15 **(c)** 13 **(e)** Impossible
6. (a) 4.12 **(c)** 4.58 **(e)** 4.51
7. (a) False, $\sqrt{2} + 0$ **(c)** False: $\sqrt{2} \cdot \sqrt{2}$

9. Answers may vary. For example, $\sqrt{2}$, $\sqrt{3}$, and $\sqrt{5}$
11. No; 22/7 is a rational number that can be represented by the repeating decimal 3.142857‾.
13. (a) R **(c)** Q **(e)** R
14. (a) $x \le 8/3$

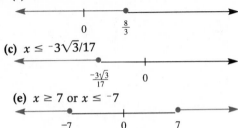

(c) $x \le {}^{-}3\sqrt{3}/17$

(e) $x \ge 7$ or $x \le {}^{-}7$

15. (a) N, I, Q, R **(c)** R **(e)** ∅
16. (a) 64 **(c)** ⁻64 **(e)** All real numbers greater than 0
19. Suppose $\sqrt{3}$ is rational. $\sqrt{3} = a/b$ where a and b are integers and $b \ne 0$. Therefore, $3 = a^2/b^2$, or $3b^2 = a^2$. a^2 has an even number of 3's in its prime factorization but $3b^2$ has an odd number of 3's in its prime factorization and this is impossible. Thus, $\sqrt{3}$ is irrational.
21. (a) m is a perfect square. **(b)** Use the result of Problem 20.
23. 3/12500
25. 8/33
27. $20,274

Problem Set 7-6

1. (a) $6\sqrt{5}$ **(c)** $11\sqrt{3}$ **(e)** 13/14
2. (a) ⁻3 **(c)** 2 **(e)** ⁻3
3. (a) $2\sqrt{3} + 3\sqrt{2} + 6\sqrt{5}$ **(c)** $30 + 12\sqrt{6}$
(e) $17\sqrt{2}$
4. (a) 4 **(c)** 32 **(e)** 1/256 **(g)** 1/4 **(i)** 4 **(k)** 10
(m) 16 **(o)** 4
6. (a) Sometimes **(c)** Always **(e)** Always
7. 21
8. (a) 2^{10} **(c)** 2^{12}
10. (a) $\sqrt{3}$ **(c)** $\sqrt{12} + \sqrt{14}$
12. (a) 4 **(c)** ⁻4/7
14. (a) n is odd

Chapter 7 Test

1. (a) ⁻0.693 **(c)** 0.2284 **(e)** ⁻0.097
2. (a) $3 \cdot 10 + 2 \cdot 1 + 0 \cdot 10^{-1} + 1 \cdot 10^{-2} + 2 \cdot 10^{-3}$

3. A fraction in simplest form, a/b, can be written as a terminating decimal if and only if the prime factorization of the denominator contains no primes other than 2 or 5.
5. (a) $0.\overline{571428}$ **(c)** $0.\overline{6}$
6. (a) 7/25 **(c)** 94/45
7. (a) $307.6\overline{3}$ **(c)** 308
8. (a) $x \leq 3.\overline{3}$ **(c)** 20,000 **(e)** 34
9. (a) 25% **(c)** $56.\overline{6}$
10. (a) 12.5% **(c)** 627% **(e)** 150%
11. (a) 0.60 **(c)** 1
12. (a) No; $-\sqrt{2} + \sqrt{2}$ is not an irrational number.
(c) No; $\sqrt{2} \cdot \sqrt{2}$ is not an irrational number.
14. (a) $4.26 \cdot 10^5$ **(c)** $3.2 \cdot 10$
17. $9280
19. 88.6%
21. It makes no difference.
23. $15,000
25. (a) $11\sqrt{2}$ **(c)** $6\sqrt{10}$
26. (a) $1/2^{11}$ **(c)** $(3/2)^{28}$

CHAPTER 8

Problem Set 8-1
1. (a) $\{1, 2, 3, 4\}$ **(c)** $S = \{(1, \text{Red}), (1, \text{Blue}), (2, \text{Red}), (2, \text{Blue}), (3, \text{Red}), (3, \text{Blue}), (4, \text{Red}), (4, \text{Blue})\}$
(e) $S = \{(1, 1), (1, 2), (1, 3), (1, 4), (2, 1), (2, 2), (2, 3), (2, 4), (3, 1), (3, 2), (3, 3), (3, 4), (4, 1), (4, 2), (4, 3), (4, 4)\}$
2. (a) $S = \{0, 1, 2, 3, 4, 5, 6, 7, 8, 9\}$ **(c)** $B = \{1, 3, 5, 7, 9\}$
3. (b) $P(A) = \dfrac{5}{10}$, or $\dfrac{1}{2}$ **(c)** $P(B) = \dfrac{5}{10}$, or $\dfrac{1}{2}$
(d) $P(C) = \dfrac{9}{10}$
4. (a) $P(\text{Red}) = \dfrac{26}{52}$, or $\dfrac{1}{2}$ **(c)** $P(\text{Red or a 10}) = \dfrac{28}{52}$ or $\dfrac{7}{13}$ **(e)** $P(\text{Not a queen}) = \dfrac{48}{52}$, or $\dfrac{12}{13}$ **(g)** $P(\text{Face card and a club}) = \dfrac{3}{52}$
5. (a) $P(\text{Brown}) = \dfrac{4}{12}$, or $\dfrac{1}{3}$ **(c)** $P(\text{Red}) = \dfrac{0}{12} = 0$
6. $P(\text{Vowel}) = \dfrac{5}{26}$; $P(\text{Consonant}) = 1 - \dfrac{5}{26} = \dfrac{21}{26}$
7. (a) $P(\text{Win on first roll}) = \dfrac{8}{36}$, or $\dfrac{2}{9}$ **(c)** $P(\text{Neither winning nor losing on first roll}) = \dfrac{24}{36}$, or $\dfrac{2}{3}$ **(e)** $P(1) = 0$.

8. 70%
9. (a) $P(\text{Black}) = \dfrac{18}{38}$, or $\dfrac{9}{19}$ **(c)** $P(\text{not 1–12}) = \dfrac{26}{38}$, or $\dfrac{13}{19}$
10. 10
11. (a) No **(c)** Yes **(e)** No **(g)** No
12. $\dfrac{45}{150}$ or $\dfrac{3}{10}$
13. (a) $\dfrac{1}{2}$ **(c)** $\dfrac{3}{4}$
14. 0.7
15. No, the sum can't be greater than 1
16. (a) $\dfrac{45}{80}$ **(c)** $\dfrac{60}{80}$
17. $\dfrac{1}{24}$

Problem Set 8-2
1. (a) $\dfrac{1}{216}$ **(b)** $\dfrac{1}{120}$
2. (b) $\dfrac{1}{64}$ **(d)** $\dfrac{21}{108}$, or $\dfrac{7}{36}$
3. $\dfrac{1}{30}$
4. (a) $P(SOS) = \dfrac{1}{3}$ using box 1 and $P(SOS) = \dfrac{1}{5}$ using box 2, so choose box 1. **(b)** $P(SOS) = \dfrac{4}{27}$ with both boxes
5. (a) $\dfrac{64}{75}$ **(b)** $\dfrac{11}{75}$
6. She should play Billie-Bobby-Billie; then the probability of winning two in a row is $\dfrac{3}{5}$.
7. (a) $P(\infty) = \dfrac{1}{5}$ **(c)** $P(\text{at most one black}) = \dfrac{11}{15}$
8. $P(\text{at least 3 H}) = \dfrac{5}{16}$
10. (a) $\dfrac{1}{4}$ **(c)** $\dfrac{1}{8}$
11. (a) $P(\text{3 plums}) = \dfrac{25}{8000}$, or $\dfrac{1}{320}$ **(c)** $P(\text{3 lemons}) = 0$
12. $\dfrac{1}{32}$
13. 1
15. $\dfrac{1}{256}$

17. Approximately 0.986

18. (a) $\dfrac{1}{25}$ **(c)** $\dfrac{16}{25}$

20. 0.7

21. 0.08$\overline{3}$

23. 0.4

24. (a) A is the best choice followed by B and then C.

(b) No. C is now the best choice. $P(C$ winning$) = \dfrac{35}{99}$,

$P(B$ winning$) = \dfrac{34}{99}$, $P(A$ winning$) = \dfrac{30}{99}$.

25. The probabilities of Abe's winning the game are summarized in the table below. Of the 12 possible games, only 8 result in choices with equally likely probabilities.

Abe's choice

		HH	HT	TH	TT
	HH	—	.50	.75	.50
Your choice	HT	.50	—	.50	.25
	TH	.25	.50	—	.50
	TT	.50	.75	.50	—

26. (a) (v) **(b)** (iii) **(c)** (ii) **(d)** (i) **(e)** (iv)

27. (a) $\dfrac{1}{30}$ **(b)** 0 **(c)** $\dfrac{19}{30}$

Problem Set 8-3

1. (a) $\dfrac{6}{18}$ or $\dfrac{1}{3}$ **(b)** $\dfrac{2}{11}$

2. $\dfrac{1}{4}$

4. $\dfrac{3}{51}$

6. 0.0005

7. $\dfrac{1}{4}$

8. $\dfrac{4500}{10,000}$, or $\dfrac{9}{20}$

9. (a) $\dfrac{3}{12}$ or $\dfrac{1}{4}$ **(c)** $\dfrac{216}{1320}$ or $\dfrac{9}{55}$

10. $\dfrac{69}{3000}$ or $\dfrac{23}{1000}$

11. (a) $\dfrac{38}{100}$ or $\dfrac{19}{50}$ **(c)** $\dfrac{25}{36}$

12. $\dfrac{10}{30}$ or $\dfrac{1}{3}$

13. (a) Let the numbers 1, 2, 3, 4, 5, and 6 represent the numbers of the die and ignore the numbers 0, 7, 8, 9.

14. 1200 fish

16. Pick a starting spot in the table and count the number of digits it takes before all the numbers 1 through 9 are obtained. Repeat this experiment many times and find the average number of coupons.

20. (a) 7 **(b)** Answers may vary

21. Answers vary, e.g., use a random digit table. Let the digits 1–8 represent a win and the digits 0 and 9 represent losses. Mark off blocks of 3. If only the digits 1–8 appear, then this represents 3 wins in a row.

23. Let the 10 ducks be represented by the digits 0, 1, 2, 3, . . . , 8, 9. Then pick a starting point in the table and mark off 10 digits to simulate which ducks the hunters shoot at. Count how many of the digits 0 through 9 are not in the 10 digits and this represents the ducks that escaped. Do this experiment many times and take the average to determine an answer. See how close your simulation comes to the theoretical probability of 3.49.

Problem Set 8-4

1. 12 to 40, or 3 to 10; 40 to 12, or 10 to 3

3. 15 to 1

4. (a) $\dfrac{1}{2}$ **(c)** 1023 to 1

5. $\dfrac{5}{8}$

6. 1 to 1

7. 4 to 6 or 2 to 3

9. $0.25

10. $3.50

11. $3.00

12. 3 hours

14. $10,000

15. (a) Al gets $75, Betsy gets $25. **(c)** Al gets approximately $89, Betsy gets approximately $11.

Problem Set 8-5

1. 224

3. 32

5. 1352; 35,152

7. (a) T **(b)** F **(c)** F **(d)** F **(e)** T **(f)** T **(g)** T

9. 15

10. (a) 12 **(c)** 3360 **(e)** 3780

11. (a) 24,360 **(b)** 4,060

14. $\dfrac{1}{120}$

15. 45

16. 1,000

18. (a) 6 **(b)** 36

19. 72

21. (a) $\dfrac{1}{13}$ **(b)** $\dfrac{8}{65}$

22. (a) 10 **(b)** 1 **(c)** 1 **(d)** 3

24. 3480

25. 1260

27. (a) $\dfrac{1}{4}$ **(b)** $\dfrac{1}{52}$ **(c)** $\dfrac{48}{52}$, or $\dfrac{12}{13}$ **(d)** $\dfrac{3}{4}$ **(e)** $\dfrac{1}{2}$ **(f)** $\dfrac{1}{52}$

(g) $\dfrac{4}{13}$ **(h)** 1

28. (a) $\dfrac{15}{19}$ **(b)** $\dfrac{56}{361}$ **(c)** $\dfrac{28}{171}$

Chapter Test

1. (a) S = {Sunday, Monday, Tuesday, Wednesday, Thursday, Friday, Saturday} **(b)** E = {Tuesday, Thursday} **(c)** $P(T) = \dfrac{2}{7}$

2. (a) $P(A) = 0$ **(b)** $P(A) = 1$ **(c)** $0 \le P(A) \le 1$ **(d)** $P(\overline{A}) = 1 - P(A)$

3. (a) $P(\text{Black}) = \dfrac{5}{12}$ **(c)** $P(\text{Neither red nor white}) = \dfrac{5}{12}$ **(e)** $P(\text{Black and white}) = 0$

5. (a) $P(3W) = \dfrac{64}{729}$ **(b)** $P(3W) = \dfrac{24}{504}$, or $\dfrac{1}{21}$

7. $P(L) = \dfrac{6}{25}$

9. $\dfrac{7}{45}$

10. $\dfrac{4}{48}$, or $\dfrac{1}{12}$

12. $\dfrac{3}{8}$

13. 30¢

15. 900

17. 24

20. $\dfrac{2}{20}$, or $\dfrac{1}{10}$

21. (a) 60 **(c)** $\dfrac{1}{60}$

23. $\dfrac{2}{5}$

24. 0.027

25. (a) $n!$ **(b)** n

26. $\dfrac{63}{80}$

27. $\dfrac{6}{27}$ or $\dfrac{2}{9}$

28. (a) For example, let the digits 1, 2, 3, 4, 5, 6, represent the numbers on the die, disregard 0, 7, 8 and 9. **(c)** For example, let the digits 1, 2, 3 represent Red, 4, 5, 6 represent white, and 7, 8, 9 represent Blue. Disregard the number 0.

29. $P(A) = \dfrac{14}{48}$, $P(B) = \dfrac{20}{48}$, $P(C) = \dfrac{14}{48}$

30. $\dfrac{8}{20}$ or $\dfrac{2}{5}$

CHAPTER 9

Problem Set 9-1

1. (a) 72, 74, 81, 81, 82, 85, 87, 88, 92, 94, 97, 98, 103, 123, 125 **(b)** 72 lbs. **(c)** 125 lbs.

2.

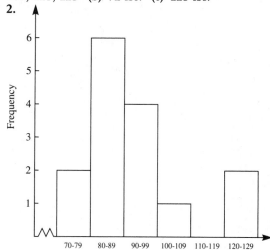

Weights of Students in East Junior
High Algebra I Class

4.

Home Run Leaders
1976–88

	National League		American League	
	9 8 7 7 7 6 1	2	2	
	9 8 8 0 0	3	2 2 9 9	
		4	0 0 1 2 3 5 6 9	
		2	5	

1 | 3 | represents 31 home runs | 3 | 2 represents 32 home runs

5.

Average Ages of Airplanes
as of July 1, 1988

	Major U.S. Airlines		Selected Foreign Airlines
		7	7
		8	2 7 8
5	9	1 6 9
8 3 1	10	0 3
	11	
1	12	
	13	0
9 6	14	
5 3 1	15	

5 | 9 | represents 531 9.5 years | 8 | 2 represents 8.2 years

7. (a)

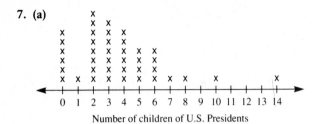

Number of children of U.S. Presidents

(c) 2

8.

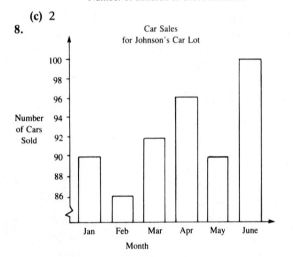

10. (b)

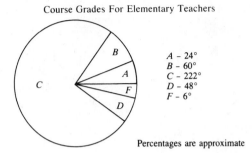

Course Grades For Elementary Teachers

A – 24°
B – 60°
C – 222°
D – 48°
F – 6°

Percentages are approximate

11. (a) Fall Text Book Costs

```
1
* | 6
2 | 3 3
* | .
3 | 0 3
* | 5 7 7 9 9
4 | 0 1 2 2
* | 5 8 9
5 | 0 0 1 3    2 | 3  represents
* | 8                  $23
6 | 0 2 2
```

(c) (d) Frequency polygon and histogram on same graph.

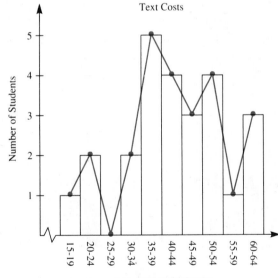

15. The line graph is more helpful, since we can approximate the point midway between 8:00 and 12:00 noon and then draw a vertical line upward until it hits the line graph. An approximation for the 10:00 temperature can then be obtained from the vertical axis.

Problem Set 9-2
1. (a) Mean = 6.625, median = 7.5, mode = 8
(c) Mean ≐ 19.9, median = 18, modes = 18 and 22
(e) Mean = 5.83, median = 5, mode = 5
2. (a) The mean, median and mode are all 80.
4. 150 pounds
6. (a) $\bar{x}$ = 18.4 years **(d)** The mean in (b) is equal to the mean in (a) plus 5 years. The mean in (c) is equal to the mean in (a) plus 10 years or the mean in (b) plus 5 years.
7. Mean = $22,700, median = $20,000, mode = $20,000
8. Mode
9. Approximately 2.59
10. 215.45 pounds
12. $1880
14. s ≐ 7.3 cm
16. (a) s = 0 **(b)** Yes
17. (a) Approximately 76.81 **(e)** Approximately 12.52
18. 91
19. 96, 90, and 90
23.
(a)

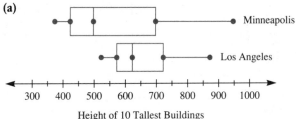

Height of 10 Tallest Buildings
in Minneapolis and Los Angeles

(b) There are no outliers
24. (a) (i) Increase by $1000 (ii) Increase by $1000 (iii) Increase by $1000 (iv) Increase by $1000 (v) Stays the same **(b)** (i) Increase by 5% (ii) Increase by 5%
25. (a) (i) $\bar{x}$ = 5, m = 5 (ii) $\bar{x}$ = 100, m = 100 (iii) $\bar{x}$ = 307, m = 307 **(b)** The mean and median of an arithmetic sequence are the same.
27. (a)   History Test Scores

```
5 | 5
6 | 4 8
7 | 2 3 3 4 6 7 9
8 | 0 2 5 5 5 6 7 8 8 9
9 | 0 0 3 4 6          7 | 2  represents a
                              score of 72
```

(c)

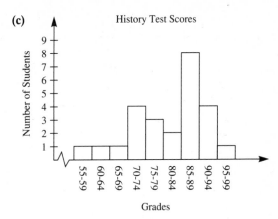

History Test Scores

(e) Approximately 115°

Problem Set 9-3
1. (a) 1020 **(c)** 1.5
2. 97.5%
3. 0.68
4. (a) verbal; 0.6; quantitative, 0.8$\bar{3}$; logical reasoning, 1 **(b)** (i) Logical reasoning (ii) verbal (iii) Holly has a composite score of 0.8$\bar{1}$.
5. (b) P_{16} = 53
6. They are the same.
9. 1.4%
10. Nathan, Jill has a percentile rank of 40.
12. 90
14. 50
15. 1600
16. (a) 74.17 **(e)** 15.43
17. 27.74
18. 76.$\bar{6}$

Problem Set 9-4
3. She could have taken a different number of quizzes during the first part of the quarter than the second part.
4. When the radius of a circle is doubled, the area is quadrupled, which is misleading since the population has only doubled.
5. The horizontal axis does not have uniformly-sized intervals and both the horizontal axis and the graph are not labeled.
7. There were more scores above the mean than below, but the mean was affected more by low scores.
10. The three-dimensional drawing distorts the graph. The result of doubling the radius and the height of the can are to increase the volume by a factor of 8.

Chapter Test
1. If the average is 2.41 children, then the *mean* is being used. If the average is 2.5, then the *mean* or the median might have been used.

2. 23

3. (a) Mean = 30, median = 30, mode = 10

5.

Miss Rider's Class
Masses in Kilograms

(a)

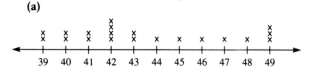

(b)   Miss Rider's Class
Masses in Kilograms

```
3 |
* | 9 9
4 | 0 0 1 1 2 2 2 2 3 3 4
* | 5 6 7 8 9 9 9        4 | 0 represents
                              40 kg
```

6. (a)   Test Grades

Class	Tally	Frequency
61–70	⊬ I	6
71–80	⊬ ⊬ I	11
81–90	⊬ II	7
91–100	⊬ I	6
		30

(b) and **(c)** are shown on the same graph.

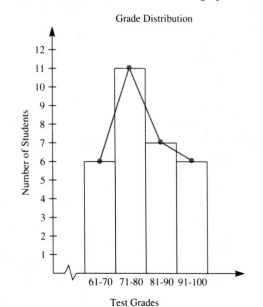

Grade Distribution

Test Grades

7.

Wagetum
Expenditures

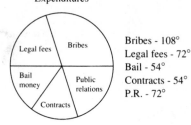

Bribes - 108°
Legal fees - 72°
Bail - 54°
Contracts - 54°
P.R. - 72°

8. The widths of the bars are not uniform and the graph has no title.

10. 150 mph

11. (a)   Life Expectancy
for Males and Females

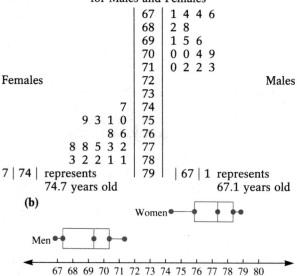

```
              | 67 | 1 4 4 6
              | 68 | 2 8
              | 69 | 1 5 6
              | 70 | 0 0 4 9
              | 71 | 0 2 2 3
Females       | 72 |              Males
              | 73 |
          7   | 74 |
      9 3 1 0 | 75 |
          8 6 | 76 |
    8 8 5 3 2 | 77 |
    3 2 2 1 1 | 78 |
7 | 74 | represents | 79 | | 67 | 1 represents
    74.7 years old           67.1 years old
```

(b)

```
                      Women ●—●  ●  ●●
        Men ●—●  ●  ●
```

67 68 69 70 71 72 73 74 75 76 77 78 79 80

13. (a) 360 **(b)** none **(c)** 350 **(d)** $S \doteq 108.21$

14.

(c)   * ●—●●●—● *

40   50   60   70   80   90   100

(e) 30%

15. (a) 25 **(b)** 475

17. (a) 525

18. 1.6

CHAPTER 10

Problem Set 10-1

1. (a) {C} (c) {C} (e) $\overleftrightarrow{CE}$ (g) $\overrightarrow{BA}$
3. (a) ∅ (c) {C} (e) {A} (g) Answers vary.
(i) Plane *BCD*
4. (a) True (c) False (e) True (g) False (i) False
(k) True
7. (a) None (b) One
9.　　(b) 15°7′48″
11. (a) Approximately 44°
13. (a) 4 (b) 6 (c) 8 (d) $2(n - 1)$
15. (a)

Number of Intersection Points

	0	1	2	3	4	5
2	⟷	✕	Not Possible	Not Possible	Not Possible	Not Possible
3	⟷	✳	⟷	✕	Not Possible	Not Possible
4	⟷	✳	Not Possible	⟷	✳	Not Possible
5	⟷	✳	Not Possible	Not Possible	⟷	✕
6	⟷	✳	Not Possible	Not Possible	Not Possible	⟷

Number of Lines

(b) $n(n - 1)/2$

17. (a) No; if ∠*BDC* were a right angle, then both $\overleftrightarrow{BD}$ and $\overleftrightarrow{BC}$ would be perpendicular to $\overleftrightarrow{DC}$ and thus be parallel. (b) No; the angle formed by $\overrightarrow{PD}$ and $\overrightarrow{PC}$ must have measure less than a right angle. Otherwise, $\overrightarrow{DP}$ would be parallel to either $\overleftrightarrow{DC}$ or $\overleftrightarrow{PC}$. This is impossible (c) Yes; use the definition of perpendicular planes.

21. Suppose α ‖ β, and γ intersects α in $\overleftrightarrow{AB}$, and γ intersect β in $\overleftrightarrow{CD}$. If $\overleftrightarrow{AB}$ ∩ $\overleftrightarrow{CD}$ is point *Q*, then *Q* is a point of both plane α and plane β. This cannot happen so $\overleftrightarrow{AB}$ ‖ $\overleftrightarrow{CD}$.

22. Answers may vary.
```
(a) TO ANGLE :SIZE
    FD 100 BK 100
    RT :SIZE FD 100
    BK 100 LT :SIZE
    END
(c) TO PERPENDICULAR :LENGTH1
        :LENGTH2
    FD :LENGTH1 BK :LENGTH1/2
    RT 90 FD :LENGTH2
    BK :LENGTH2 LT 90
    BK :LENGTH1/2
    END
```

Problem Set 10-2

1. (a) 1, 2, 3, 6, 7, 8, 9, 11, 12 (c) 1, 2, 7, 8, 9, 11
(e) 7, 8
2. (a)

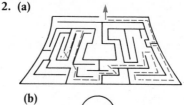

(b)

3. (a) Outside
5. (a) {E, G} (c) $\overrightarrow{EH} \cup \overrightarrow{GK}$
7. (a) and (c) are convex; (b) and (d) are concave.
9. (d), (e) and (f) are impossible because each angle of an equilateral triangle has measure 60°.
10. (a) 35 (c) 4850

13. 14
15. (a) False. To be isosceles, the triangle may have only 2 congruent sides, not necessarily 3. (c) True
(e) True (g) True (i) True (k) False. All squares are rectangles. (m) True (o) False. See (n).
17. (a) Answers may vary.
```
    TO SQUARE :SIDE
      REPEAT 4 [FD :SIDE RT 90]
    END
```
(b) Answers may vary.
```
    TO RECTANGLE :WIDTH :LENGTH
      REPEAT 2 [FD :WIDTH RT 90 FD
        :LENGTH RT 90]
    END
```
18. (b) $n(n - 1)/2$
21. (a) {C} (c) $\overline{AB}$, $\overline{AC}$, and $\overline{AD}$
22. (a) False. A ray has only one endpoint. (c) False. Skew lines cannot be contained in the single plane.
(e) True
23.

　　$\overline{}$　　$\overline{}$　$\overline{}$
　　A　　　　B　　C　　　　　D

Problem Set 10-3

5. 14 pairs
7. (a) 60° **(c)** 60°
8. (a) Yes; a pair of corresponding angles are 50° each.
(c) Yes; a pair of alternate interior angles are 40° each.
9. (a) No. Two or more obtuse angles will produce a sum of more than 180°. **(c)** No. The sum of the measures of the three angles would be more than 180°.
10. (a) 70° **(c)** 65°
11. (a) $x = 40°$ and $y = 50°$
13. 90°
15. (a) 360° **(b)** 360°
17. (a) 20 **(b)** 150°
18. (b) The sum of the measures of the angles in all n triangles is $180n$ degrees. Subtracting the measures of all nonoverlapping angles whose vertex is P, we obtain $180n - 360° = (n - 2)180°$.
19. (b) There are $n - 2$ triangles which can be drawn from any vertex of the n-gon. Hence, there are $(n - 2)180$ degrees in the sum of the angle measures of the interior angles of any convex polygon.
20. (a) True **(c)** False **(e)** False
21. (a) Equal
(b) $m(\angle 4) = 180° - m(\angle 3)$ (Straight angle)
$= 180° - [180° - m(\angle 1) - m(\angle 2)]$
$= m(\angle 1) + m(\angle 2)$
23. Theorem 10-1(a) Supplements of the same angle, or congruent angles, are congruent.
Proof: **(a)** Let both $\angle 2$ and $\angle 3$ be supplements of $\angle 1$.
$m(\angle 2) + m(\angle 1) = 180$
$m(\angle 3) + m(\angle 1) = 180$
$m(\angle 2) + m(\angle 1) = m(\angle 3) + m(\angle 1)$
$m(\angle 2) = m(\angle 3)$
$\angle 2 \cong \angle 3$
(b) Let $\angle 3$ be the supplement of $\angle 1$, and $\angle 4$ be the supplement of $\angle 2$, and $\angle 1 \cong \angle 2$.
$m(\angle 3) + m(\angle 1) = 180$
$m(\angle 4) + m(\angle 2) = 180$
$m(\angle 3) + m(\angle 1) = m(\angle 4) + m(\angle 2)$
$\angle 1 \cong \angle 2$ implies $m(\angle 1) = m(\angle 2)$
$m(\angle 3) + m(\angle 2) = m(\angle 4) + m(\angle 2)$
$m(\angle 3) = m(\angle 4)$
$\angle 3 \cong \angle 4$
Theorem 10-1(b) Complements of the same angle, or congruent angles, are congruent.
Proof: Proof is similar to the above.

25. If two lines are perpendicular to the same line, then congruent corresponding angles of 90° each are formed, and hence the lines are parallel.

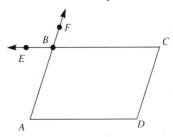

(a) $m(\angle A) = m(\angle FBC)$ (corresponding angles)
$m(\angle FBE) + m(\angle FBC) = 180°$ (supplementary angles)
$m(\angle FBE) = m(\angle ABC)$ (vertical angles)
Thus,
$m(\angle ABC) + m(\angle A) = 180°$ (substitution)
(b) $m(\angle A) = m(\angle ABE)$ (alternate interior angles)
$m(\angle ABE) = m(\angle C)$ (corresponding angles)
Hence,
$m(\angle A) = m(\angle C)$. Likewise $m(\angle B) = m(\angle D)$.
27. Let $ABCD$ be a quadrilateral with $m(\angle 1) = m(\angle 3)$ and $m(\angle 2) = m(\angle 4)$.

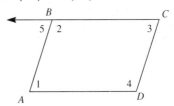

We are given that $m(\angle 1) = m(\angle 3)$ and $m(\angle 2) = m(\angle 4)$. Also, we know $m(\angle 1) + m(\angle 2) + m(\angle 3) + m(\angle 4) = 360°$. Substituting, we have $m(\angle 1) + m(\angle 2) + m(\angle 1) + m(\angle 2) = 360°$. Thus $2m(\angle 1) + 2m(\angle 2) = 360°$, or $2[m(\angle 1) + m(\angle 2)] = 360°$, and so $m(\angle 1) + m(\angle 2) = 180°$. Because $m(\angle 5) + m(\angle 2) = 180°$, then $m(\angle 1) + m(\angle 2) = m(\angle 5) + m(\angle 2)$. Subtracting $m(\angle 2)$ from both sides, we have $m(\angle 1) = m(\angle 5)$. Now, because alternate interior angles are congruent, we have $\overleftrightarrow{AD} \parallel \overleftrightarrow{BC}$. Similarly, it can be shown that $\overleftrightarrow{AB} \parallel \overleftrightarrow{DC}$.
28. 83.5° or 83°30′

29. Answers may vary.
  (a) TO PARALLELOGRAM :L :W :A
       REPEAT 2[FD :L RT 180-:A FD
         :W RT :A]
     END
  (b) TO RECTANGLE :L :W
       PARALLELOGRAM :L :W 90
     END
  (c) TO RHOMBUS :L :A
       PARALLELOGRAM :L :L :A
     END

31. No, the union of two rays will always extend infinitely in at least one direction.
35. Sketches may vary, but the possibilities are the empty set, a single point, a segment, a quadrilateral, a pentagon, and a hexagon. There are various types of quadrilaterals possible.
37.
            (b) All sides are the same length and all angles are right angles. **(c)** Impossible because all squares are parallelograms.

Problem Set 10-4
1. (a) Quadrilateral pyramid **(b)** Quadrilateral prism; possibly a trapezoidal prism **(c)** Pentagonal pyramid
4. (a) 5 **(b)** 4 **(c)** 4
5. (a) True **(c)** True **(e)** False **(g)** False
8. Drawings may vary, but the statement is true.
10. (a)

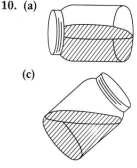

(c)

11. (b) (4)
12. (a)

(c)

(e)

15. Pyramid   Prism
  (a) $n + 1$ $n + 2$
  (b) $n + 1$ $2n$
  (c) $2n$ $3n$
  (d) $(n + 1) + (n + 1) - 2n = 2$
       $(n + 2) + 2n - 3n = 2$
18. (a) Yes **(b)** Yes **(c)** No
19. (a) Yes; It is also a rectangle because the opposite sides are parallel and congruent and plane ABE is perpendicular to plane ADE making $\angle ABF$ a right angle. A parallelogram with a right angle is a rectangle.
(b) Planes ABG, BFE, GFE, FEC, BCD, and GCD
(c) Yes; If $\overleftrightarrow{CD}$ intersects the plane ABF, it must intersect it along $\overleftrightarrow{AB}$, since $\overleftrightarrow{CD}$ is in the plane determined by ABC and any point common to both planes is on $\overleftrightarrow{AB}$. This is a contradiction because $\overleftrightarrow{AB}$ and $\overleftrightarrow{CD}$ are parallel.
21. 140°
23. (a) Right **(b)** The sum of the measures of complementary angles is 90°; hence the measures of the third angle must be 90°, and the triangle is a right triangle.
25. Parallelogram

Problem Set 10-5

1. (a), (b), (c), (e), (g), (h), and **(j)** are traversable.

(a)

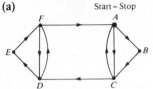

Path:
ABCACDEFDFA; any
point can be a starting
point.

(c)

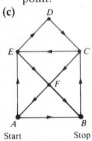

Start   Stop

Path:
ABCFAEDCEFB;
only points *A* and *B*
can be starting points.

(e)

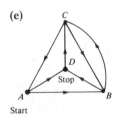

Path: *ABCBDCAD*;
only points *A* and *D*
can be starting
points.

(g)

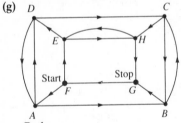

Path:
FADABCBGFEDCHEHG;
only points *F* and *G*
can be starting
points.

5. Yes. See figure.

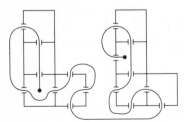

7.

Network	R	V	A	V − A + F
(a)	6	6	10	2
(b)	7	4	9	2
(c)	6	6	10	2
(d)	4	4	6	2
(e)	5	4	7	2
(f)	8	8	14	2
(g)	9	8	15	2
(h)	6	4	8	2
(i)	7	7	12	2
(j)	8	12	18	2

9. (a) Yes **(c)** Yes **(e)** Yes

Problem Set 10-6

1. (a) TO RECTANGLE :LENGTH :WIDTH
　　　　PARALLELOGRAM :LENGTH :WIDTH
　　　　　90
　　　END
(b) TO RHOMBUS :SIDE :ANGLE
　　　　PARALLELOGRAM :SIDE :SIDE
　　　　　:ANGLE
　　　END
3. TO CUBE :SIDE
　　REPEAT 3 [RHOMBUS :SIDE 60 RIGHT 120]
　END
4. (a) 60° **(c)** 45°
6. No; the methods of this section yield an equilateral
triangle if a 6-pointed star is attempted.
7. Answers may vary.
(a) TO HEXSTACK :SIDE
　　　REPEAT 3 [LEFT 30 HEXAGON
　　　　:SIDE FD :SIDE RT 60 FD
　　　　:SIDE LT 60]
　　END
　　TO HEXAGON :SIDE
　　　REPEAT 6 [FD :SIDE RIGHT 60]
　　END
(b) TO HONEYCOMB :SIDE
　　　REPEAT 3 [HEXAGON :SIDE RT 120]
　　END
8. Answers may vary.
　TO THIRTY
　　FD 100 BK 100 RT 30
　　FD 100 BK 100 LT 30
　END

10. Answers may vary.

```
TO COUNT.ANGLES :NUMBER
  IF :NUMBER = 1 OUTPUT 0 STOP
  OUTPUT :NUMBER - 1 +
    COUNT.ANGLES :NUMBER - 1
END
```

(In Apple Logo II, replace IF :NUMBER = 1 OUTPUT 0 STOP *with* IF :NUMBER = 1 [OUTPUT 0 STOP].*)*

Chapter 10 Test

2. (a) $\overleftrightarrow{AB}$, $\overleftrightarrow{BC}$ and $\overleftrightarrow{AC}$ **(c)** $\overline{AB}$ **(e)** $\overline{AB}$

3. (b) Planes *APQ* and *BPQ* **(d)** No. $\overleftrightarrow{PQ}$ and $\overleftrightarrow{AB}$ are skew lines so that no single plane contains them.

6. (a) No. The sum of the measures of two obtuse angles is greater than 180°, which is the sum of the measures of the angles of any triangle.

7. 18°, 36°, 126°.

8. (b) 90

9. (b) Euler's formula holds.

11. Answers may vary, but the possibilities are a point, a segment, a triangle, or a quadrilateral.

13. 35°8′35″

15. 8

17. (a) (i), (ii), and (iv) are traversable.

(b) (i)

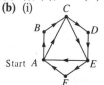

Path: *ABCDEFACEA*; any point can be used as a starting point.

(ii)

Path: *ABCDAEDBE*; points *A* and *E* are possible starting points.

(iv)

Path: *ACDEACDEABC*; points *A* or *C* are possible starting points.

19. Answers may vary.

```
TO ISOS :LEG :ANGLE
  FD :LEG
  RT 180 - :ANGLE
  FD :LEG
  RT 90 + :ANGLE/2
END
```

CHAPTER 11

Problem Set 11-1

1. (a) $BC > AC$ **(b)** $m(\angle A) > m(\angle B)$ **(c)** The side of greater length is opposite the angle of greater measure.

2. (c) Right **(d)** No triangle is possible.

4. 22

5. (a) Yes; *SAS* **(c)** No

7. (a) $\triangle AEC \cong \triangle ADB$ by *SAS* **(c)** $\triangle BDA \cong \triangle BEC$ by *SAS*

9. The lengths of the wires must be the same because they are congruent parts of congruent triangles formed.

13. (a) $\triangle ABC \cong \triangle ABC$; $\triangle ACB \cong \triangle ABC$; $\triangle BAC \cong \triangle ABC$; $\triangle BCA \cong \triangle ABC$; $\triangle CAB \cong \triangle ABC$; $\triangle CBA \cong \triangle ABC$ **(b)** Consider $\triangle ACB \cong \triangle ABC$. Because $\triangle ABC$ is equilateral, it is also isosceles. We also know that the base angles of an isosceles triangle are congruent. Suppose $\angle A \cong \angle B$. Then by the triangle congruence, we have $\angle B \cong \angle C$. Hence $\angle A \cong \angle B \cong \angle C$, and the triangle is equiangular.

15. (a) *F* is the midpoint of both diagonals. **(b)** We can show $\triangle ABD \cong \triangle CBD$ by *SSS* and, then $\angle BDC \cong \angle BDA$ by *CPCTC*. $\triangle AFD \cong \triangle CFD$ by *SAS*, so $\overline{AF} \cong \overline{FC}$, thus *F* is the midpoint of $\overline{AC}$. A similar argument will show $\overline{BF} \cong \overline{FD}$. **(c)** 90° **(d)** From part (b), $\angle AFD \cong \angle DFC$ by *CPCTC*, but are also supplementary. Hence, $m(\angle AFD) = 90°$. A similar argument is used for $\angle BFA$ and $\angle BFC$.

17. (a) The angles formed by the diagonals of a rhombus are right angles. **(b)** First show that $\triangle ABO \cong \triangle CDO$ and conclude that $\overline{AO} \cong \overline{OC}$. Then show that $\triangle ABO \cong \triangle CBO$ by *SSS*. Hence, conclude that $\angle AOB \cong \angle COB$ and consequently that each angle is a right angle.

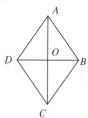

19. $\triangle BAC \cong \triangle CAB$; *SAS*. $\angle ABC \cong \angle ACB$ by *CPCTC*

23. (a) A triangle is constructed because the computer does not know the difference in an angle measure and a compass heading. **(b)** In reality, no because no triangle has one angle with measure 190°. **(c)** Add the following:

```
IF NOT (:ANGLE < 180) PRINT [NO
TRIANGLE IS POSSIBLE.] STOP
```

(In Apple Logo II, use the following line:
IF NOT (:ANGLE < 180) [PRINT [NO
TRIANGLE IS POSSIBLE.] STOP].*)*

Problem Set 11-2

2. (a) No; By *ASA*, the triangle is unique. **(b)** No; By *AAS*, the triangle is unique. **(c)** No; By *ASA*, the triangle is unique. **(d)** Yes; *AAA* does not determine a unique triangle.

3. (a) Yes; *ASA* **(d)** No

5. The triangles are all congruent. This can be proved in a variety of ways. One can determine the measures of all the angles and use *ASA*.

6. (a) Parallelogram **(c)** None **(e)** Rhombus **(g)** Parallelogram

7. (a) True **(c)** True **(e)** True **(g)** True **(i)** False; A square can be a trapezoid.

9. (a) $\overline{OP} \cong \overline{QO}$ **(b)** $\angle PDO \cong \angle QBO$; alternate interior angles formed by the transversal $\overleftrightarrow{DB}$ and parallel lines $\overleftrightarrow{DC}$ and $\overleftrightarrow{AB}$. $\angle DPO \cong \angle BQO$ because $\overleftrightarrow{PQ}$ is a transversal of $\overleftrightarrow{CD}$ and $\overleftrightarrow{AB}$. $\overline{DO} \cong \overline{BO}$; diagonals of a parallelogram bisect each other. $\triangle POD \cong \triangle QOB$; *AAS*. $\overline{PO} \cong \overline{QO}$; *CPCTC*.

11. (a) They are congruent. **(b)** Show that $\triangle ABC \cong \triangle BCD \cong \triangle CDE \cong \triangle DEA \cong \triangle EAB$.

13. (c) Parallelogram **(d)** Suppose *ADCB* in part (a) is a parallelogram. Use *SAS* to show that $\triangle EDH \cong \triangle GBF$ and conclude that $\overline{EH} \cong \overline{GF}$. Similarly, show that $\triangle ECF \cong \triangle GAH$ and hence that $\overline{EF} \cong \overline{GH}$. Next use *SSS* to prove that $\triangle EFG \cong \triangle GHE$. Now conclude that $\angle GEH \cong \angle EGF$ and consequently that $\overline{FG} \parallel \overline{EH}$. Similarly, show that $\overline{EF} \parallel \overline{HG}$.

15. (a) Use *ASA* to prove that $\triangle ABF \cong \triangle CDF$ and consequently that $\overline{BF} \cong \overline{FD}$ and $\overline{AF} \cong \overline{FC}$. **(b)** Show that $\triangle ABD \cong \triangle DCA$ and conclude that $\overline{BD} \cong \overline{CA}$.

17. (a) The length of one side of each square must be equal. **(b)** The lengths of the sides of two perpendicular sides of the rectangles. **(c)** Answers vary. One solution is the lengths of two adjacent sides of the parallelograms and the angles between them.

19. (a) Answers may vary.
```
TO RHOMBUS :SIDE :ANGLE
   REPEAT 2 [FD :SIDE RT (180-
      :ANGLE) FD :SIDE RT :ANGLE]
END
```
(b) They are congruent.
(c)
```
TO SQ.RHOM :SIDE
   RHOMBUS :SIDE 90
END
```
22. (a) Yes; *SAS* **(c)** No

Problem Set 11-3

5. (d) The lines containing the altitudes meet at a point inside the triangle. **(e)** The lines containing the altitudes meet at the vertex of the right angle. **(f)** The lines containing the altitudes meet outside the triangle.

6. (a) The perpendicular bisectors meet at a point inside the triangle. **(b)** The perpendicular bisectors meet at the midpoint of the hypotenuse of the right triangle. **(c)** The perpendicular bisectors meet at a point outside the triangle.

7. Draw triangle *ABC*. The intersection of the perpendicular bisectors of the sides of this triangle should be the point to locate the airport.

12. (a) $\overleftrightarrow{PQ}$ is the perpendicular bisector of $\overline{AB}$. **(b)** *Q* is on the perpendicular bisector of $\overline{AB}$ because $\overline{AQ} \cong \overline{QB}$. Similarly, *P* is on the perpendicular bisector of $\overline{AB}$. Because a unique line contains two points, the perpendicular bisector contains $\overleftrightarrow{PQ}$.

13. (b) Construct two perpendicular segments bisecting each other and congruent to the given diagonal. **(d)** Without the angle between the sides being given, there is no unique parallelogram. **(h)** The kite would not be unique without knowing lengths of some sides. **(j)** Consider $\triangle ABC$ and the angle bisector $\overleftrightarrow{CD}$ Since $\overline{AC} \cong \overline{BC}$, then $\overleftrightarrow{CD} \perp \overline{AB}$. It is possible to construct $\triangle ADC$, since *AD* is half as long as the base and $m(\angle DAC) = 90° - \frac{1}{2}m(\angle ACB)$.

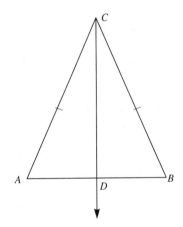

17. Answers may vary.
```
TO ALTITUDES
   REPEAT 3 [RT 30 FD 60 RT 90 FD
      110 BK 130 FD 20 LT 90 FD 60
      RT 90]
END
```
19. (a) Yes; *SAS* **(c)** Yes; *SSS*

20. $\triangle ABC \cong \triangle DEC$ by *ASA*. ($\overline{BC} \cong \overline{CE}$, $\angle ACD \cong \angle ECD$ as vertical angles, and $\angle B \cong \angle E$ as alternate interior angles formed by the parallels $\overline{AB}$ and $\overline{ED}$ and the transversal $\overleftrightarrow{EB}$.) $\overline{AC} \cong \overline{DC}$ by *CPCTC*.

Problem Set 11-4
1. The diameter is the longest chord of a circle.
3. Right triangle
4. (a) 90° (b) 90° (c) 90° (d) An angle whose vertex is on a circle and whose sides intersect the circle in two points (determining a diameter) is a right angle. (e) In the drawing below, $\triangle AOC$ and $\triangle BOC$ are isosceles. (Why?) $\angle OAC \cong \angle OCA$ and $\angle OCB \cong \angle OBC$; base angles of an isosceles triangle are congruent. Therefore, $m(\angle OAC) + m(\angle OCA) + m(\angle OCB) + m(\angle OBC) = 2m(\angle OAC) + 2m(\angle OBC) = 180°$. Thus, $m(\angle OAC) + m(\angle OBC) = 90°$. Hence $m(\angle ACB) = 90°$.

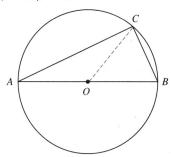

9. Hint: First inscribe a square in the given circle.
11. Hint: The center of the circle is at the intersection point of the diagonals.
13. Hint: Draw a perpendicular from O to ℓ to obtain the radius of the circle.
15. (e) $m(\angle 1) = m(\angle 2) = m(\angle 3)$
17. Given that $\overline{AB} \cong \overline{CD}$ (see the figure), prove that $\overline{OM} \cong \overline{ON}$. First prove that $\overline{AM} \cong \overline{MB}$ and $\overline{CN} \cong \overline{ND}$. Then show that $\triangle ABO \cong \triangle COD$. Hence, conclude that $\angle A \cong \angle C$. Now prove that $\triangle AMO \cong \triangle CNO$ (by SAS). Consequently $\overline{OM} \cong \overline{ON}$.

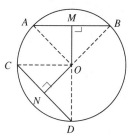

20. Answers may vary.
```
TO DIAMETER
  REPEAT 360 [FD 1 RT 1]
  RT 90 FD 100
END
```
21. $\overline{AB}$
23. The triangles are congruent by AAS. Sometimes this result is called Hypotenuse-Acute Angle or HA.

Problem Set 11-5

3. This illustration is one possibility.
(a)

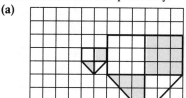

(c)

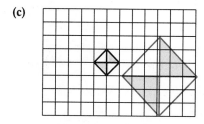

5. (c) The triangles are similar if the corresponding sides are proportional.
7. Answers may vary. (a) Two rectangles, one of which is a square and the other is not. (b) Two rhombuses, one of which is a square and the other is not but the sides are all the same length.
9. (b) (i) 2/3 (ii) 1/2 (iii) 3/4 (iv) 3/4

11. (a) 9 (d) 26/3

14. (a) (1) $\triangle ABC \sim \triangle ACD$ by AA since $\angle ADC$ and $\angle ACB$ are right angles, and $\angle A$ is common to both. (2) $\triangle ABC \sim \triangle CBD$ by AA since $\angle CDB$ and $\angle ACB$ are right angles and $\angle B$ is common to both. (3) Using (1) and (2), $\triangle ACD \sim \triangle CBD$ by the transitive property.
(b) (1) $AC/AB = CD/BC = AD/AC$ (2) $BC/BA = CD/AC = BD/BC$ (3) $AC/CB = CD/BD = AD/CD$

17. 15 m

19. (a) $\triangle ABC \sim \triangle BDC$ **(b)** $m(\angle ABC) = m(\angle ACB)$; base angles of an isosceles triangle are congruent and have the same measure.

$$m(\angle ABC) + m(\angle ACB) + 36° = 180°$$
$$2m(\angle ABC) = 144°$$
$$m(\angle ABC) = 72°$$
$$\tfrac{1}{2}m(\angle ABC) = m(\angle DBC) = 36°$$
$$\triangle ABC \sim \triangle BDC \text{ by AA}$$

21. (a) $\angle C \cong \angle ADG$ because both are right angles. $\angle CGF$ and $\angle AGD$ are complementary, as are $\angle AGD$ and $\angle GAD$. Thus $\angle CGF \cong \angle GAD$ and $\triangle GCF \sim \triangle ADG$ by AA.

23. Answers may vary.

   (a)
```
TO RECTANGLE :LEN :WID
   REPEAT 2 [FD :LEN RT 90 FD
      :WID RT 90]
   END
   TO SIM.RECT :LEN :WID
   RECTANGLE :LEN*2 :WID*2
   END
```
   (b)
```
TO SIM.RECTANGLE :LEN :WID
   :SCALE
   RECTANGLE :LEN*:SCALE
      :WID*:SCALE
   END
```
   (c)
```
TO PARALLELOGRAM :LEN :WID
   :ANGLE
   REPEAT 2 [FD :LEN RT 180-
      :ANGLE FD :WID RT :ANGLE]
   END
   TO SIM.PAR :LEN :WID :ANGLE
      :SCALE
   PARALLELOGRAM :LEN*:SCALE
      :WID*:SCALE :ANGLE
   END
```

25. No; the image is two-dimensional while the original person is three-dimensional.

Problem Set 11-6

Answers for the entire section may vary. Procedures are written only as possible answers.

2.
```
TO RTISOS :HYPOT
   DRAW
   FD :HYPOT RT 135
   CHECK
   END
```
(In Apple Logo II, replace DRAW with CLEARSCREEN.)

```
TO CHECK
   FORWARD 1
   SETHEADING TOWARDS 00
   IF ABS (HEADING - 225) < 2
      HOME STOP
   SETHEADING -135
   CHECK
   END
```
(In Apple Logo II, replace SETHEADING TOWARDS 00 with SETHEADING TOWARDS [0 0] and IF ABS (HEADING-225)<2 HOME STOP with IF ABS (HEADING-225<2) [HOME STOP].)
```
TO ABS :VALUE
   IF :VALUE<0 OUTPUT-:VALUE ELSE
      OUTPUT :VALUE
   END
```
(In Apple Logo II, replace IF :VALUE<0 OUTPUT -:VALUE ELSE OUTPUT :VALUE with IF :VALUE <0 [OUTPUT -:VALUE] [OUTPUT :VALUE].)

3.
```
TO TRI30 :HYPOT
   DRAW
   FD :HYPOT/2 RT 120
   FD :HYPOT RT 120
   HOME
   END
```
(In Apple Logo II, replace DRAW with CLEARSCREEN.)

4.
```
TO STAR :SIDE
   HEXAGON :SIDE
   REPEAT 6 [LT 60 FD :SIDE RT 120
      FD :SIDE]
   END
   TO HEXAGON :SIDE
   REPEAT 6 [FD :SIDE RT 60]
   END
```

Chapter 11 Test

4. (a) $x = 8$; $y = 5$ **(b)** $x = 6$

7. Hint: Find the intersection of the perpendicular bisector of $\overline{AB}$ and line ℓ.

9. (a) False; A chord has its endpoints on the circle. **(b)** False; A diameter intersects a circle in two points, and a tangent intersects it in only one point. **(c)** True **(d)** True **(e)** True

11. (a) (iii) and (iv) **(b)** Any regular convex polygon can be inscribed in a circle.

13. 256/5 m

CHAPTER 12

Problem Set 12-1
1. (a) A translation
2. (a)

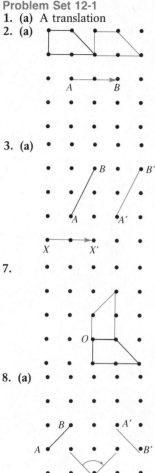

3. (a)

7.

8. (a)

10. Hint: Find the image of the center, *M*, and one point on the circumference of the circle. Use these to find the image of the circle.
13. Hint: Find the midpoint of $\overline{PP'}$. This is the center of the half-turn.
14. Hint: Find the image *m'*, of line *m* under a half-turn with center *P*. This intersection of *m'* and line *l* is point *A*.
15. (c) No
16. Hint: Find the image, circle *O'*, of circle *O* under a half-turn with point *P* as center. The intersection of circle *O'* and circle *Q* will determine point *B* if it exists. (It may be possible to find two points on circle *Q* such that either may be point *B*.)

17. Hint: Pick any point, *P*, on the smaller circle. Rotate the middle circle 60 degrees using point *P* as the center. The intersection of the image of the middle circle and the larger circle will determine a vertex of the required triangle.
19.
```
TO ROTATE :A :SIDE
   SQUARE :SIDE
   RIGHT :A
   SQUARE :SIDE
END
TO SQUARE :SIDE
   REPEAT 4[FORWARD :SIDE RIGHT
     90]
END
```
20. (a)
```
TO TURN.CIRCLE :A
   CIRCLE
   LEFT :A
   CIRCLE
END
TO CIRCLE
   REPEAT 360[FORWARD 1 RT 1]
END
```
To produce the desired transformation, execute
`TURN.CIRCLE 180.`

Problem Set 12-2
1. (a)

3. (b) Yes. Find *A'* and *C'*, the images of *A* and *C*. Label the point of intersection of $\overline{AB}$ and line *l* as point *P*; label the point of intersection of $\overline{BC}$ and line *l* as point *Q*. Draw $\overleftrightarrow{A'P}$ and $\overleftrightarrow{C'Q}$. The intersection of these lines is *B'*.
5. (a) Yes, there are infinitely many such lines all of which contain the center of the circle. **(c)** Yes, the reflecting line is the line containing the ray. **(e)** Yes, there are two such lines: the perpendicular bisectors of the pairs of parallel sides. **(g)** Yes, there is one such line in a general isosceles triangle: the line that is the perpendicular bisector of the side that is not congruent to the other two. **(i)** There are none. **(k)** Yes, there is one such line; the line that is the perpendicular bisector of the chord determined by the endpoints of the arc. **(m)** Yes, there are two, the diagonals. **(o)** Yes, there are *n* such lines.

9. The images are congruent. No; unless m and ℓ are the same line.
11. The images are congruent, but not the same.
13. **(a)** The images are the same. **(b)** Yes
14. 1 to 2 is a rotation: 1 to 3 is a rotation; 1 to 4 is a translation; 1 to 5 is a rotation; 1 to 6 is a translation; 1 to 7 is a translation.

18. **(a)** ⁻150 degree rotation about the turtle's starting point. **(c)** 45 degree rotation and slide.
19. **(b)** The drawing produced in FIG2 is a reflection of the drawing produced by FIG1 through a horizontal line that contains the starting point of the turtle.
20. **(c)** A reflection in a vertical line through the turtle's home. **(d)** A half-turn with the turtle's home as center.
23. Half-turn about the center of the letter O
24. **(a)** Infinitely many with the center of the circle as the center of the rotations

Problem Set 12-3

2. **(a)** A translation determined by slide arrow $\overrightarrow{NM}$.
(c) A rotation of 45 degrees with center A in a clockwise direction. **(e)** A reflection in line n.
3. **(a)** A half-turn with center the point of intersection of the perpendicular lines. **(c)** A rotation of 50 degrees counterclockwise with the same center as the given rotations. **(e)** A translation of 5 cm along the same line but in the direction of the 10 cm translation. **(g)** A single reflection in a line concurrent with the other three lines.
5. **(c)** C is the midpoint of the segment connecting the images.
6. **(a)** Point P
7. Straight up; the transformation is a translation, the composition of two half-turns where the centers are each of the quarters.
9. **(a)** Yes **(c)** No
10. **(a)** (2,1) **(c)** (7,4)
11.

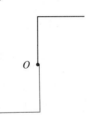

Problem Set 12-4
1. **(a)** Line, rotational and point symmetry **(c)** Line symmetry
3. **(a)**

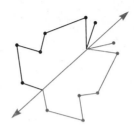

4. **(a)** (i) 4 (iii) 2
5. **(a)** 1 vertical **(c)** None **(e)** 5 lines
6. Sketches may vary. **(a)** Any scalene triangle
(c) Not possible
8. **(a)** Yes, a figure with point symmetry has 180 degree rotational symmetry. **(c)** Yes, figures may vary.
(e) Yes, see part (a).
9. **(a)**

O

10. **(a)** 7 **(c)** 7
12. TO TURN.SYM :S :N :A
  REPEAT :N[SQUARE :S RIGHT :A]
  END
  TO SQUARE :S
  REPEAT 4[FORWARD :S RIGHT 90]
  END
  (a) Execute TURN.SYM 50 6 60
  (c) Execute TURN.SYM 50 2 180
  (e) Execute TURN.SYM 50 6 300
13. TO TURN.SY :S :N :A
  REPEAT :N[EQTRI :S RIGHT :A]
  END
  TO EQTRI :S
  REPEAT 3[FORWARD :S RIGHT 120]
  END
  (b) Execute TURN.SY 50 3 120
  (d) Execute TURN.SY 50 6 300

Problem Set 12-5

1. (a)

2. (b) Yes
3. (a), (c), and **(d)** tessellate the plane.
4. (a) The dual is also a tessellation of squares.
6. (a)
```
TO TESSELSQUARE
  PENUP BACK 70 PENDOWN
  REPEAT 9[SQUARE 20 FORWARD
  20]
  PENUP BACK 180 RIGHT 90
  FORWARD 20 LEFT 90 PENDOWN
  REPEAT 9[SQUARE 20 FORWARD
  20]
END
TO SQUARE :SIDE
  REPEAT 4[FORWARD :SIDE RIGHT
  90]
END
```
(c)
```
TO TESSELHEX
  PENUP BACK 70 LEFT 90 PENDOWN
  REPEAT 4[HEXAGON 20 RIGHT
  120 FORWARD 20 LEFT 60
  HEXAGON 20 FORWARD 20 LEFT
  60]
END
TO HEXAGON :SIDE
  REPEAT 6[FORWARD :SIDE RIGHT
  60]
END
```

Problem Set 12-6

1.
```
TO WALL3 :XPT :YPT :SIDE
  DRAW
  SETUP :XPT :YPT
  WALLPAPER3 :YPT :SIDE
END
```
(In Apple Logo II, replace DRAW with CLEARSCREEN.)

```
TO SETUP :XPT :YPT
  PENUP
  SETXY :XPT :YPT
  PENDOWN
END
```
(In Apple Logo II, replace SETXY :XPT :YPT with SETPOS (LIST :XPT :YPT).)

```
TO WALLPAPER3 :YPT :SIDE
  TRISTRIP :SIDE
  PENUP
  SETUP (:XPT+:SIDE*(SORT 3)/2) :YPT
  PENDOWN
  WALLPAPER3 :YPT :SIDE
END
TO TRISTRIP :SIDE
  IF XCOR+:SIDE>120 TOPLEVEL
  IF (ANYOF (XCOR<-120)
  (XCOR+:SIDE*(SQRT 3)/2>120)
  (YCOR<-100)(YCOR+:SIDE>100))
  STOP
  TRIANGLE :SIDE
  FORWARD :SIDE
  RIGHT 60
  TRIANGLE :SIDE
  LEFT 60
  TRISTRIP :SIDE
END
```
(In Apple Logo II, replace IF XCOR+:SIDE >120 TOPLEVEL with IF XCOR+:SIDE>120 [THROW "TOPLEVEL]. Also replace IF (ANYOF (XCOR<-120) (XCOR+:SIDE(SQRT 3)/2>120) (YCOR<-100) (YCOR+:SIDE>100)) STOP with IF (OR (XCOR<-120) (XCOR+:SIDE*(SQRT 3)/2>120) (YCOR <-100) (YCOR+:SIDE>100)) [THROW "TOPLEVEL].)*

```
TO TRIANGLE :SIDE
  REPEAT 3[FORWARD :SIDE RIGHT
  120]
END
```

2. The conditions are to keep the turtle from drawing off the screen. It forces the boundaries to be as follows: $-120 < x < 120$ and $-100 < y < 100$.

5. Yes; once the figures fit between two parallel lines, then one could make a rubber stamp of the parallel lines and the drawings between them and stamp them all across the plane.

7. ```
TO WALL6 :XPT :YPT :SIDE
  DRAW
  SETUP :XPT :YPT
  WALLPAPER6 :YPT :SIDE
END
```

*(In Apple Logo II, replace DRAW with CLEARSCREEN.)*

```
TO SETUP :XPT :YPT
  PENUP
  SETXY :XPT :YPT
  PENDOWN
END
```

(In Apple Logo II, replace SETXY :XPT :YPT with SETPOS (LIST :XPT :YPT).)

```
 TO WALLPAPER6 :YPT :SIDE
 CHEVRONSTRIP :SIDE
 PENUP
 SETUP (XCOR+:SIDE) :YPT
 PENDOWN
 WALLPAPER6 :YPT :SIDE
END
TO CHEVRONSTRIP :SIDE
 IF XCOR+:SIDE>120 TOPLEVEL
 IF (ANYOF (XCOR-:SIDE<-120)
  (XCOR+:SIDE>120)
  (YCOR-:SIDE*(SQRT 2)/2<-100)
  (YCOR+:SIDE>100)) STOP
 CHEVRON :SIDE
 FORWARD :SIDE
 CHEVRONSTRIP :SIDE
END
```

(In Apple Logo II, replace IF XCOR+:SIDE >120 TOPLEVEL , with IF XCOR+:SIDE>120 [THROW "TOPLEVEL], and replace IF (ANYOF (XCOR-:SIDE<-120) (XCOR+:SIDE>120) (YCOR-:SIDE(SQRT 2)/2<-100) (YCOR+:SIDE>100)) STOP with IF (OR (XCOR-:SIDE<-120) (XCOR+:SIDE>120) (YCOR-:SIDE*(SQRT 2)/2<-100) (YCOR+:SIDE>100)) [STOP].)*

```
 TO CHEVRON :SIDE
  FORWARD :SIDE RIGHT 135
  FORWARD :SIDE*(SQRT 2)/2 LEFT 90
  FORWARD :SIDE*(SQRT 2)/2
   RIGHT 135
  FORWARD :SIDE RIGHT 45
  FORWARD :SIDE*(SQRT 2)/2
   RIGHT 90
  FORWARD :SIDE*(SQRT 2)/2
   RIGHT 45
 END
```

Chapter 12 Test

1. **(a)**

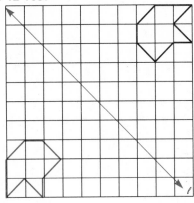

(c)

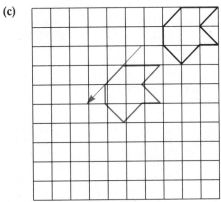

3. **(a)** 4 **(c)** 1 **(e)** 2
4. **(a)** Line and rotational **(c)** Line
5. **(a)** Infinitely many **(c)** 3
6. **(a)** Reflection **(c)** Glide reflection
8. This answer depends totally upon how the letters are made, but generally we have the following: *c* has line symmetry; *i* has line symmetry; *o* has line, rotational, and point symmetry; *s* has rotational and point symmetry; *t* has line symmetry; *v* has line symmetry; *w* has line symmetry; *x* has line, rotational, and point symmetry; *z* has rotational and point symmetry.
10. Hint: Construct the perpendicular bisector of $\overline{AB}$.
11. Hint: $\overline{BC}$ formed by the midpoints of $\overline{A'B'}$ and $\overline{A'C'}$.

CHAPTER 13

Problem Set 13-1
7. **(a)** 0.35; 3500 **(b)** 163; 1630 **(c)** 0.035; 3.5
(d) 0.1; 10 **(e)** 200; 2000
```

8. (a) 10.00 **(b)** 0.77 **(c)** 10.0 **(d)** 15.5 **(e)** 195.0
(f) 8.1 **(g)** 40.0
10. (a) 1724 **(b)** 106 **(c)** 316
12. (a) 1.0 **(b)** 0.17 **(c)** 0.262 **(d)** 3000 **(e)** 0.03
(f) 170 **(g)** 3500 **(h)** 0.359 **(i)** 0.1 **(j)** 64.7 **(k)** 1
(l) 5000 **(m)** 5130
14. (b) and **(c)**
16. (a) answers vary **(b)** 8
18. (a) 6π cm **(b)** 6π cm **(c)** 4 cm **(d)** $6\pi^2$ cm
20. πr
22. (a) $2:1$ **(b)** The ratio of the perimeters of two
similar triangles is the same as the ratio of
corresponding sides.
24. (a) 3096 **(b)** 1032 **(c)** March 4.04

Problem Set 13-2

3.

m²	cm²	mm²
0.0588	588	58,800
0.000192	1.92	192
1.5	15,000	1,500,000
0.01	100	10,000
0.0005	5	500

5. (a) 444.4 **(b)** 0.32 **(c)** 6400 **(d)** 130680
6. (a) 20 cm² **(b)** 900 cm² or 0.09 m² **(c)** 7.5 m²
7. (a) 9 cm² **(b)** 96 cm² **(c)** 64 cm²
8. (a) 4900 m² **(b)** 98 **(c)** 0.98
10. (a) 1.95 km², 195 ha **(b)** 1,950,000 square yards;
approximately 0.63 square miles; approximately 403
acres. The comparable problem in (a) is much easier
since the conversions in (b) from square yards to square
miles and then to acres involve complicated conversion
factors.
12. (a) 3 **(b)** 2 **(c)** 2 **(d)** 5 **(e)** 6 **(f)** 4.5

16. $\dfrac{ab}{2}$

18. (a) 16π cm² **(b)** $r = \dfrac{s}{\sqrt{\pi}}$

19. (a) 2π cm² **(b)** $\left(2 + \dfrac{\pi}{2}\right)$ cm²

21. (a) $\dfrac{1}{4}\pi r^2$ **(b)** $\dfrac{1}{8}\pi r^2$ **(c)** $\dfrac{1}{16}\pi r^2$

23. 7π m²
24. 1200

28. (a) $400 - 100\pi$ cm² **(b)** $\dfrac{100}{3}\pi + 50\sqrt{3}$ cm²

29. (a) $4:9$. Justification: $\dfrac{A_1}{A_2} = \dfrac{s_1^2}{s_2^2}$, and $\dfrac{s_1}{s_2} = \dfrac{2}{3}$, hence

$\dfrac{A_1}{A_2} = \left(\dfrac{2}{3}\right)^2 = \dfrac{4}{9}$. **(b)** $4:9$ (Hint: $A = d^2/2$, where d is
the length of a diagonal.)

31. (a) The 27-in. set is the better buy. The ratio of the
areas of similar rectangles is the square of the ratio of
the sides. In this case, $(20/27)^2 = 0.548$, so the 20-in.
set has an area which is about 55% the area of the
27-in. set, yet, you pay 66% the price of the larger set.
(b) 28.3 in.
34. P should be connected to the point that is 2 units
above P and $1\frac{1}{2}$ units to the right of P.
36. (a) 21.46% **(b)** (i) same as in (a). (ii) same as
in (a).
38. (a) 10 **(b)** 104 **(c)** 0.35 **(d)** 40 **(e)** 8000

Problem Set 13-3

1. (c) 5a
3. (a) No **(b)** Yes **(c)** Yes
4. $\sqrt{450}$, or $15\sqrt{2}$ cm
6. $\sqrt{5200}$ km, or $20\sqrt{13}$ km, or approximately
72.1 km
8. $\sqrt{125}$ mi. or about 11.2 mi.
10. $\sqrt{216}$ feet, or $6\sqrt{6}$ feet, or about 14.7 feet.
12. $(320 + 64\pi)$ m²
14. (a) $\dfrac{\sqrt{3}s^2}{4}$ **(b)** $\dfrac{s^2}{2}$

16. 12.5 cm; 15 cm
18. (a)

Draw $\triangle DCB \cong \triangle ABC$. Since all the interior angles in
$\triangle ABD$ are 60°, the triangle is equilateral. Hence, $AB =$
$BD = AD$. Since $AC = CD$, it follows that $AC = \dfrac{1}{2}AD$,
and hence $AC = \dfrac{1}{2}AB$. **(b)** $\dfrac{\sqrt{3}c}{2}$

20. $\dfrac{5}{3}$m

23. $\triangle ACD \sim \triangle ABC$. Thus, $\dfrac{b}{x} = \dfrac{c}{b}$ implies $b^2 = cx$.

$\triangle BCD \sim \triangle BAC$. Thus, $\dfrac{a}{y} = \dfrac{c}{a}$ implies $a^2 = cy$.

Consequently, $a^2 + b^2 = cx + cy = c(x + y) = c^2$.
25. Yes
28. 0.032 km, 322 cm, 3.2 m, 3.020 cm
29. (a) 3325 mm², or 33.25 cm² **(b)** 30 cm²
(c) 32 m²
30. (a) 10 cm; 10π cm; 25π cm² **(b)** 12 cm; 24π cm;
144π cm² **(c)** $\sqrt{17}$ m; $2\sqrt{17}$ m; $2\pi\sqrt{17}$ m
(d) 10 cm; 20 cm; 100π cm²

Problem Set 13-4

1. (a) 96 cm² **(b)** 216π cm² **(c)** 236 cm²
(d) 64π cm² **(e)** 24π cm² **(f)** 90 cm²

3. 2688π mm²

5. $\dfrac{16}{36}$, or $\dfrac{4}{9}$

6. (a) They are the same. **(b)** The one with radius 6 m.

8. (a) The area is nine times the original. **(b)** It is doubled.

10. (a) It is tripled. **(b)** It is tripled. **(c)** It is nine times the original area.

13. Let the radius of the sphere be r and the height of the cylinder h. The area of the sphere is $4\pi r^2$. The lateral surface area of the cylinder is $2\pi rh$. Since $h = 2r$, $2\pi rh = 2\pi r \cdot 2r = 4\pi r^2$.

15. $(100\sqrt{17} + 100)$ cm² or approximately 512.3 cm²

18. 15.2 cm

20. 375π cm²

21. (a) 100,000 **(b)** 1.368 **(c)** 500 **(d)** 2,000,000 **(e)** 1 **(f)** 1,000,000

23. $20\sqrt{5}$ cm

25. The length of the side is 25 cm. The length of the diagonal $\overline{AD}$ is 30 cm.

Problem Set 13-5

1. (a) 8000 **(b)** 0.0005 **(c)** 0.000675 **(d)** 3,000,000 **(e)** 7

3. (a) 64 cm³ **(b)** 120 cm³ **(c)** 216 cm³ **(d)** 14 cm³ **(e)** 50 cm³

5.

	(a)	(b)	(c)	(d)	(e)	(f)
cm³	2000	500	1500	5000	750	4800
dm³	2	0.5	1.5	5	0.750	4.8
L	2	0.5	1.5	5	0.750	4.8
mL	2000	500	1500	5000	750	4800

7. 1680π mm³

9. It is multiplied by 8.

11. $253{,}500\pi$ L

13. 1.62 L

15. 32.4 L

17. (a) 25π L **(b)** 127.32 km

18. No, the customer pays $\dfrac{1}{2}$ as much for $\dfrac{1}{3}$ of the popcorn.

20. The larger melon is the better buy. The volume of the larger melon is 1.728 times the volume of the smaller, but is only $1\dfrac{1}{2}$ times as expensive.

22. They are the same.

24. Approximately 21.5%

26. $\dfrac{2}{3}\sqrt{\dfrac{2}{5\sqrt{5}}}$ m² $\doteq$ 0.28 m²

28. Let two square pyramids have sides and heights of s, h, and s_1 and h_1. If pyramids are similar, then

$$\frac{s}{s_1} = \frac{h}{h_1} = r. \text{ Hence } \frac{V}{V_1} = \frac{\frac{1}{3}s^2 h}{\frac{1}{3}s_1^2 h_1} = \left(\frac{s}{s_1}\right)^2 \cdot \frac{h}{h_1} =$$

$r^2 \cdot r = r^3$

30. (a) 340 cm **(b)** 6000 cm²

32. 62 cm

Problem Set 13-6

1. (a) Tons or kilograms **(b)** Kilograms **(c)** Grams **(d)** Tons **(e)** Grams **(f)** Grams **(g)** Tons **(h)** Kilograms or grams **(i)** Kilograms or grams

3. (a) 15 **(b)** 8 **(c)** 36 **(d)** 0.072 **(e)** 4.230 **(f)** 3.007 **(g)** 5750 **(h)** 5.750 **(i)** 30 **(j)** 30,000 **(k)** 41.6 **(l)** 1.56 **(m)** 3.1 **(n)** 60.8

5. 16,000 g, or 16 kg

7. $0.02

9. (a) $^{-}12°$C **(b)** $^{-}18°$C **(c)** $^{-}1°$C **(d)** 38°C **(e)** 100°C **(f)** $^{-}40°$C

11. (a) 50°F **(b)** 32°F **(c)** 86°F **(d)** 212°F **(e)** 414°F **(f)** $^{-}40°$F

13. (a) 35 **(b)** 0.16 **(c)** 400,000 **(d)** 5,200,000 **(e)** 5,200 **(f)** 0.0035

15. $\sqrt{61}$ km

Problem Set 13-7

1. (a) It draws a circle five times The circumference is $\dfrac{1}{5}$ of the circumference of CIRCLE1.

3. (a)
```
TO ARC :S :D
  REPEAT :D [FD :S RT 1]
END
```

7.
```
TO SYMBOL :R
  PU LT 90 FD 140 RT 90 PD
  REPEAT 3 [CIRCLE :R PU RT 90 FD
  9*:R/4 LT 90 PD]
  PU LT 90 FD :R * 45/8 LT 90
  REPEAT 2 [CIRCLE :R PU RT 90 FD
  9*:R/4 LT 90 PD]
  HIDETURTLE
END
TO CIRCLE :R
  HT
  VCIRCLE 0.01745 * :R
  ST
END
TO VCIRCLE :S
  REPEAT 360 [FD :S RT 1]
END
```

```
9. TO DIAMCIRC :R
     REPEAT 360 [FD :R *0.0A745 RT 1]
     RT 90
     FD 2*:R
     END
```

Chapter Test

1. (a) 50,000; 5000; 50 **(b)** 3200; 3.2; 0.0032
(c) 26,000,000; 260,000; 260 **(d)** 190,000; 19,000;
0.19
3. (a) Find the area of $\triangle ADC$ and double it;
$A = 2(\frac{1}{2} \cdot DE \cdot AC)$. **(b)** $A = b \cdot h = DC \cdot FB$
7. The area of the trapezoid is equal to the area of the
rectangle constructed from its component parts. The
area of the rectangle is $\frac{h}{2}(b_1 + b_2)$, which is the
formula for the area of a trapezoid.
9. (a) 12π cm² **(b)** $(12 + 4.5\pi)$ cm² **(c)** 24 cm²
10. (a) Yes, $13^2 = 12^2 + 5^2$
11. (a) S.A. $= 32(2 + \sqrt{13})$ cm², V $= 128$ cm³
(b) S.A. $= 96\pi$ cm², V $= 96\pi$ cm³ **(c)** S.A. $=$
100π m², V $= \dfrac{500}{3}\pi$ m³
13. (a) Metric tons **(b)** 1 cm³, or 1 mL **(c)** 1 g
(d) Same volume **(e)** 25
14. (a) 16.7 **(b)** 0.54 **(c)** 1089 **(d)** 2176
16. (a) 6000 kg **(b)** 5.7 cm
19. (a) 2000 **(b)** 1000 **(c)** 3 **(d)** 0.0042 **(e)** 0.0002

CHAPTER 14

Problem Set 14-1

1. (a) $A(2, 2)$; $B(5, 0)$; $C(4, {}^-3)$; $D(0, {}^-3)$; $E({}^-2, {}^-3)$;
$F({}^-4, 0)$; $G({}^-4, 3)$; $H(0, 3)$ **(b)** $(2, {}^-3)$; answers may
vary.
3. Quadrant II $= \{(x, y) | x < 0 \text{ and } y > 0\}$ Quadrant
III $= \{(x, y) | x < 0 \text{ and } y < 0\}$ Quadrant IV $=$
$\{(x, y) | x > 0 \text{ and } y < 0\}$
5. (a) $x = {}^-2$; y is any real number.
7. D has coordinates $(4, {}^-2)$.
9. (a) **(b)**

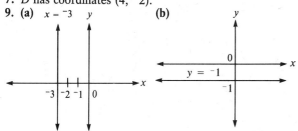

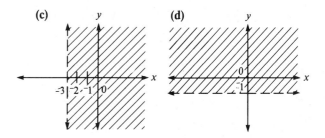

11. (a) $P(3, 4)$; $Q(6, 1)$ **(b)** $N({}^-1, 4)$; $M({}^-1, {}^-1)$
(c) $x = 3$ **(d)** $y = 1$
12. (a)

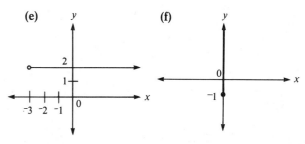

13. (a)

15. (a) $P'(2, {}^-2)$; $Q'(2, {}^-5)$, $R'(4, {}^-2)$ **(b)** $P'({}^-2, 2)$;
$Q'({}^-5, 2)$; $R'({}^-2, 4)$
16. (a) $(0, {}^-1)$, $(1, 0)$, $(2, {}^-4)$, $({}^-2, {}^-4)$, $({}^-2, 4)$, $(2, 4)$
(b) $(0, 1)$, $({}^-1, 0)$, $({}^-2, 4)$, $(2, 4)$, $(2, {}^-4)$, $({}^-2, {}^-4)$
(c) $({}^-1, 0)$, $(0, 1)$, $({}^-4, 2)$, $({}^-4, {}^-2)$, $(4, {}^-2)$, $(4, 2)$
(d) $(0, {}^-1)$, $({}^-1, 0)$, $({}^-2, {}^-4)$, $(2, {}^-4)$, $(2, 4)$, $({}^-2, 4)$
(e) $(0, {}^-3)$, $(1, {}^-4)$, $(2, 0)$, $({}^-2, 0)$, $({}^-2, {}^-8)$, $(2, {}^-8)$

18. (a) $(^-2, ^-4)$ **(b)** $(^-a, ^-b)$ **(c)** Yes; a half-turn about $(0, 0)$.

Problem Set 14-2

1.

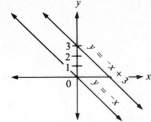

3. (a)

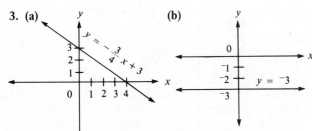

(b)

(c)

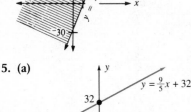

5. (a)

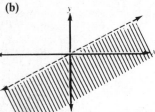

$$y = \frac{9}{5}x + 32$$

32

100

7. (a) $\frac{1}{3}$ **(b)** $\frac{1}{9}$ **(c)** 0 **(d)** No slope **(e)** 20,000
(f) 1 if $a \neq b$

9. (a) Parallel **(b)** Parallel **(c)** Parallel **(d)** Not parallel

10. (a) $y = ^-2x - 1$ **(b)** $y = \frac{^-2}{3}x + \frac{5}{3}$ **(c)** $x = ^-2$

12. (a) $m_l = \frac{2}{1} = 2$ $m_k = \frac{1}{2}$ = $m_n = \frac{^-2}{1} = ^-2$

14. (a) The equation of ℓ is $y = mx$; the equation of n is $x = 1$. The point of intersection can be found by substituting 1 for x in $y = mx$. Thus, $y = m \cdot 1 = m$, so the point of intersection of ℓ and m is $(1, m)$.
(b) The equation for ℓ is $y = mx + b$; the equation for n is $x = 1$. Substituting 1 for x in $y = mx + b$ yields $y = m \cdot 1 + b$, or $y = m + b$. Thus the y-coordinate of P is $m + b$.
16. Let A, B, and C have coordinates $(0, ^-1)$, $(1, 2)$, and $(^-1, ^-4)$, respectively. The slope of $\overline{AB}$ is 3; the slope of $\overline{BC}$ is 3. Hence, A, B, and C are collinear.

17. (a) $y = \frac{^-1}{2}x - \frac{3}{2}$ **(b)** $y = \frac{2}{3}x - \frac{11}{3}$
19. (a) $y = ^-3x - 1$
20. (a) $y = -x$ **(b)** $y - 2 = (-2/3)(x - 1)$
22. (a) perpendicular **(b)** parallel **(c)** perpendicular **(d)** neither
24. (a)

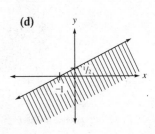

(b)

(c)

(d)

26. (a) $y = ^-x$ **(b)** $y = ^-x$ **(c)** $x = 0$ **(d)** $y = ^-x$
(e) $y = x$ **(f)** $y = x - 3$ **(g)** $y = x + 3$ **(h)** one is the reflection of the other in the x-axis **(i)** same as (h)

28. (a)

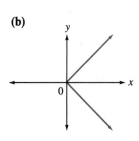

(b)

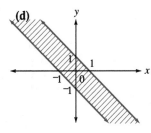

(c)

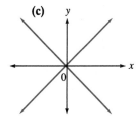

(d)

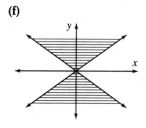

(e)

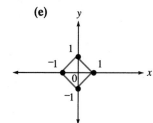

(f)

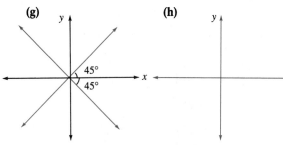

(g)

(h)

29. (a) $y = {}^-8$ **(b)** $x = {}^-7$
31. There are three possible locations for D: $(4, -8)$, $(12, 0)$ or $(0, 12)$.

Problem Set 14-3
1. (a) $\left(0, \dfrac{-5}{3}\right)$; $\left(\dfrac{5}{2}, 0\right)$; $(1, {}^-1)$; $\left(2, \dfrac{-1}{3}\right)$. Answers may vary.

(b)

(c)

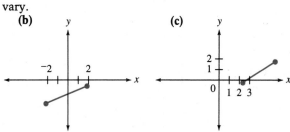

2. (a) $(2, 5)$, unique solution **(b)** No solution
(c) $(1, {}^-5)$, unique solution
3. (a) $({}^-11, {}^-8)$ **(b)** $\left(\dfrac{-30}{11}, \dfrac{-84}{11}\right)$ **(c)** $\left(\dfrac{13}{3}, \dfrac{43}{12}\right)$
4. (a) Unique solution **(b)** No solution **(c)** Same line; infinitely many solutions **(d)** Unique solution
6. $y = \dfrac{-1}{2}x - 4$ and $y = \dfrac{1}{3}x - 4$.
8. $\dfrac{162}{85}$ sq. units
10. $\dfrac{55}{72}$ and $\dfrac{-1}{72}$
12. $133\dfrac{1}{3}$ pounds of cashew nut granola and $66\dfrac{2}{3}$ pounds of golden granola.
14. \$20,000 and \$60,000, respectively.
16. Width 60 inches; length 75 inches.
18. (a) The answers are all $({}^-1, 2)$.
(b) $13x + 14y = 15$
$16x + 17y = 18$ The solution is $({}^-1, 2)$.
20. (b) and **(c)** are not equations of lines.
22. (a) $y = \dfrac{9}{10}x + \dfrac{17}{5}$ **(b)** $y = \dfrac{5}{3}x + \dfrac{1}{3}$

Problem Set 14-4
1. (a) 4 **(b)** 4 **(c)** 5 **(d)** 5 **(e)** $\sqrt{52}$, or $2\sqrt{13}$
3. The sides have lengths $\sqrt{45}$, $\sqrt{180}$, and $\sqrt{225}$. Since $(\sqrt{45})^2 + (\sqrt{180})^2 = (\sqrt{225})^2$, the triangle is a right triangle.

5. $x = 9$ or $x = {}^-7$

7. $({}^-7, 11)$

9. (a) $(x - 3)^2 + (y + 2)^2 = 4$ **(b)** $(x + 3)^2 + (y + 4)^2 = 25$

11. $x^2 + y^2 = 34$

13. $(x + 2)^2 + (y + 2)^2 = 52$

14. (a)   **(b)**

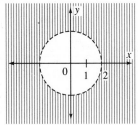 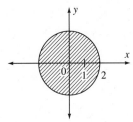

(c)

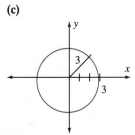

18. $(3/2, 3/2)$

20. $\dfrac{2}{5}\sqrt{5}$

21. (a) $(5, 3)$ **(b)** $(3, 8)$ **(c)** no point of intersection **(d)** $\sqrt{13}$ **(e)** 7 **(f)** 10

23. (a) $(9, 4)$ **(b)** $({}^-3, 12)$ **(c)** $(1, {}^-4)$

25. M has coordinates $\left(\dfrac{a}{2}, \dfrac{b}{2}\right)$.

$$BM = \sqrt{\left(\frac{a}{2}\right)^2 + \left(\frac{b}{2} - b\right)^2} = \sqrt{\frac{a^2}{4} + \frac{b^2}{4}}$$

$$AM = \sqrt{\left(\frac{a}{2} - a\right)^2 + \left(\frac{b}{2} - 0\right)^2} = \sqrt{\frac{a^2}{4} + \frac{b^2}{4}}$$

26. (a) The median from C: $y = \dfrac{2b}{2a - 1}\left(x - \dfrac{1}{2}\right)$

The median from B: $y = \dfrac{b}{a - 2}(x - 1)$

The median from A: $y = \dfrac{b}{a + 1}x$

(b) Solve any two equations and check that the solution satisfies the third equation. The medians intersect at $\left(\dfrac{a + 1}{3}, \dfrac{b}{3}\right)$. **(c)** Use the distance formula to find the ratios.

29. $y = 2$

31. (a) $y < \dfrac{3}{4}x + 5$ **(b)** $x + y + 5 \geq 0$ and $x \leq 0$ and $y \leq 0$

Problem Set 14-5

1. This answer will vary depending on the version of Logo used.

3.
```
TO AXES
  SETXY 0 120
  SETXY 0 (-120)
  SETXY 0 0
  SETXY 130 0
  SETXY -130 0
  SETXY 0 0
END
```
(In Apple Logo use `SETPOS` *instead of* `SETXY`*)*

5.
```
TO FILL.RECT
  REPEAT 50 [SETY 30 SETY 0 RT 90
  FD 1 LT 90]
END
```

7.
```
TO QUAD :X1 :Y1 :X2 :Y2 :X3 :Y3
  :X4 :Y4
  PU SETXY :X1 :Y1 PD
  SETXY :X2 :Y2
  SETXY :X3 :Y3
  SETXY :X4 :Y4
  SETXY :X1 :Y1
END
```

9. Use the QUAD procedure from problem 7 and the following.
```
TO MEDIAL.QUADS :NUM :X1 :Y1 :X2
  :Y2 :X3 :Y3 :X4 :Y4
  IF :NUM=0 STOP
  QUAD :X1 :Y1 :X2 :Y2 :X3 :Y3 :X4
  :Y4
  MEDIAL.QUADS :NUM-1 (:X1 +
  :X2)/2 (:Y1 + :Y2)/2 (:X2 +
  :X3)/2 (:Y2 + :Y3)/2 (:X3 +
  :X4)/2 (:Y3 + :Y4)/2(:X4 +
  :X1)/2 (:Y4 + :Y1)/2
END
```

11.
```
TO R.ISOS.TRI :LEN
  FD :LEN
  RT 90
  FD :LEN
  RT 135
  FD (SQRT 2) * :LEN
END
```

13.
```
TO GENCIRC :X :Y :R
  PU
  SETXY :X :Y
  FD :R RT 90 PD
  REPEAT 360 [FD 3.141*:R/180 RT
  1]
END
```

Chapter Test
1. 16
3. (a)

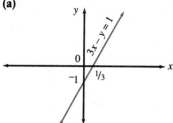

(b)

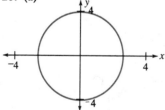

4. (a) $y = \dfrac{-4}{3} x - \dfrac{1}{3}$

6. $y = \dfrac{3}{2} x - \dfrac{1}{3}$

8. 80 regular and 30 deluxe.
10. (a)

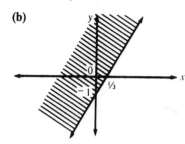

(b)

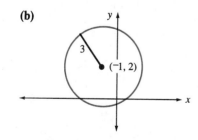

(c)

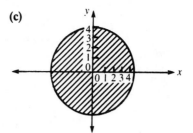

11. $(x + 3)^2 + (y - 4)^2 = 25$
14. 275 freshmen and 500 sophomores
15. Hoover, 15,957,537; Roosevelt, 22,521,525

APPENDIX I

Problem Set A1
1.
2. (a) $X \wedge 2 + Y \wedge 2 - 3*Z$ (c) $A + B - C \wedge 2/D$
   (e) $15/(A*(2*B \wedge 2 + 5))$
3. (a) 7 (c) 6 (e) 16
4. (a) 35,200,000 (c) $^-0.000001233$
6. (a)
```
5 REM WE INPUT THE VALUE OF
    THE VARIABLE X
10 INPUT X
20 LET Y = 13*X ^ 5 - 27/X + 3
30 PRINT "WHEN X = ";X;", Y =
    "; Y
40 END
```
   (b) (i)
```
RUN
? 1.873
WHEN X = 1.873, Y = 288.247015
```
   (ii)
```
RUN
? 7
WHEN X = 7, Y = 218490.143
```
9. (a)
```
PRINT 100*1.18 ^ 25
6266.8628
```
   (b)
```
5 REM N IS THE NUMBER OF YEARS
    THE MONEY IS INVESTED
10 INPUT N
15 REM B IS THE BALANCE
20 LET B = 100*1.18 ^ N
30 PRINT "AFTER ";N;" YEARS,
    THE BALANCE IS $";B
40 END
```
12. (a)
```
10 FOR N = 1 TO 20
10 PRINT 2*N
30 NEXT N
40 END
```

14.
```
10 PRINT "THIS PROGRAM IS TO
   PRACTICE MULTIPLYING."
20 PRINT "TYPE THE TWO NUMBERS
   TO BE MULTIPLIED";
21 PRINT "SEPARATED BY A COMMA."
25 REM A AND B REPRESENT THE
   NUMBERS TO BE MULTIPLIED
26 REM X INITIALIZES A COUNTER
27 REM C REPRESENTS THE PRODUCT
   OF A AND B
28 LET X = 0
30 INPUT A,B
35 LET X = X + 1
40 PRINT "AFTER THE QUESTION
   MARK, TYPE THE PRODUCT."
50 PRINT A;"*";B;"=";
60 INPUT C
70 IF A*B > C THEN 100
80 PRINT "SORRY, TRY AGAIN."
90 GOTO 40
100 PRINT "VERY GOOD. DO YOU
    WANT TO MULTIPLY OTHER
    NUMBERS?"
110 INPUT D$
120 IF D$ = "YES" THEN 20
130 PRINT "THE NUMBER OF
    ATTEMPTED EXERCISES WAS ";X
140 END
```

15.
```
5 REM THIS PROGRAM COMPUTES
  SQUARES AND SQUARE ROOTS
8 REM N REPRESENTS A NATURAL
  NUMBER
10 PRINT "NUMBER","SQUARE
   ROOT","SQUARE"
20 FOR N = 1 TO 10
30 PRINT N,SQR(N),N^2
40 NEXT N
50 END
```

17.
```
10 REM THIS PROGRAM CONVERTS
   DEGREES FAHRENHEIT
20 REM TO DEGREES CELSIUS
25 REM F REPRESENTS A NUMBER OF
   DEGREES FAHRENHEIT
26 REM C REPRESENTS A NUMBER OF
   DEGREES CELSIUS
30 PRINT "DEGREE FAHRENHEIT",
   "DEGREE CELSIUS"
40 FOR F = -40 TO 220 STEP 10
50 LET C = 5/9*(F - 32)
60 PRINT F,,C
70 NEXT F
80 END
```

19.
```
10 REM THIS PROGRAM CALCULATES N!
15 REM N IS A NATURAL NUMBER
16 REM T IS USED TO ACCUMULATE
   PRODUCTS
17 REM A IS USED AS A COUNTER
20 PRINT "WHAT IS THE VALUE OF N";
30 INPUT N
40 LET T = 1
50 FOR A = 1 TO N
60 LET T = T*A
70 NEXT A
80 PRINT "N","N!"
90 PRINT N,T
100 END
```

20.
```
10 REM LAURA'S LOTTERY
11 REM P IS THE PRIZE
12 REM A IS THE AMOUNT
   ACCUMULATED
13 REM N IS A COUNTER
14 REM P IS THE DIFFERENCE IN A
   AND $10000
15 LET N = 0
20 LET P = 50000
30 LET A = P*(1 + .15)
40 LET N = N + 1
50 LET P = A - 10000
60 IF P <= 0 THEN 80
70 GOTO 30
80 PRINT "YOU'RE OUT OF MONEY."
90 PRINT "IT LASTED ";N - 1;"
   YEARS."
100 END
```

```
YOU'RE OUT OF MONEY.
IT LASTED 9 YEARS.
```

23.
```
10 REM HARMONIC SERIES
11 REM K IS A COUNTER
12 LET K = 0
13 REM Y ACCUMULATES THE SUM
14 LET Y = 0
20 PRINT "HOW MANY TERMS DO YOU
   WANT";
30 INPUT N
40 LET K = K + 1
50 LET Y = Y + 1/K
60 IF k >= N THEN 80
70 GOTO 40
80 PRINT "THE VALUE OF THE FIRST
   ";N;" TERMS OF THE ";
90 PRINT "HARMONIC SERIES IS ";Y
100 END
```

```
HOW MANY TERMS DO YOU WANT? 100
THE VALUE OF THE FIRST 100 TERMS
OF THE HARMONIC SERIES IS
5.187377
```

26.
```
10 REM THIS PROGRAM PRINTS
   INTEREST COMPOUNDED DAILY
15 REM N IS A COUNTER
16 REM B IS THE AMOUNT
   ACCUMULATED
17 LET N = 0
20 LET N = N + 1
30 LET B = 1000*(1 + 5/36500)^N
40 IF B > 5000 THEN 60
50 GOTO 20
60 PRINT "AFTER ";N;" DAYS, THE
   BALANCE EXCEEDS $5000."
70 END
```

```
AFTER 11750 DAYS, THE BALANCE
EXCEEDS $5000.
```

28.
```
10 REM THIS PROGRAM OUTPUTS
   BATTING AVERAGES
11 REM K COUNTS THE PLAYERS
12 REM A IS THE BATTING AVERAGE
13 REM R IS THE BATTING AVERAGE
   IN THOUSANDTHS
15 LET K = 0
20 PRINT "HOW MANY PLAYERS ARE
   THERE";
30 INPUT N
40 PRINT "PLAYER #","# OF
   BATS","# OF HITS","BATTING
   AVERAGE"
50 LET K = K + 1
60 PRINT "AFTER THE QUESTION
   MARK, TYPE THE # OF AT BATS,"
70 PRINT "THE # OF HITS OF
   PLAYER ";K;" SEPARATED BY
   COMMAS."
80 INPUT B,H
90 LET A = H/B
100 LET R = INT(1000*A)
105 LET R = R/1000
110 PRINT K,B,H,R
120 IF K < N THEN 50
130 END
```

30.
```
10 REM SUM OF TWO SQUARES
11 REM X AND Y REPRESENT
   POSSIBLE NUMBERS
12 REM Z IS THE SUM OF X^2 AND
   Y^2
```

```
20 FOR X = 1 TO 6
30 FOR Y = 1 TO 6
40 LET Z = X^2 + Y^2
50 IF X >= Y THEN 70
60 IF Z < 40 THEN 100
70 NEXT Y
80 NEXT X
90 GOTO 120
100 PRINT Z;"=" ;X;"^2 +";Y;"^2"
110 GOTO 70
120 END
```

```
5 = 1^2 + 2^2
10 = 1^2 + 3^2
17 = 1^2 + 4^2
26 = 1^2 + 5^2
37 = 1^2 + 6^2
13 = 2^2 + 3^2
20 = 2^2 + 4^2
29 = 2^2 + 5^2
25 = 3^2 + 4^2
34 = 3^2 + 5^2
```

APPENDIX II

Problem Set AII-1

1. (a)

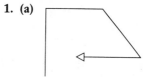

(c)

(e) 0

3. (a)

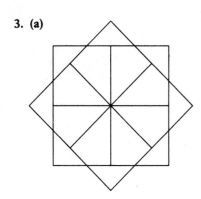

(c)

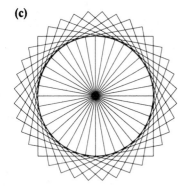

4. Answers may vary.

(a) TO RECT
```
  REPEAT 2[FORWARD 30 RIGHT 90
    FORWARD 60 RIGHT 90]
END
```

(c) TO HAT
```
  REPEAT 2 [FORWARD 20 RIGHT 90
    FORWARD 30 RIGHT 90]
  PENUP LEFT 90 FORWARD 30
  PENDOWN
  REPEAT 2[LEFT 90 FORWARD 6
    LEFT 90 FORWARD 90]
END
```

(e) TO RHOMBUS
```
  RIGHT 20 FORWARD 40
  RIGHT 70 FORWARD 80
  RIGHT 110 FORWARD 40
  RIGHT 70 FORWARD 80
END
```

6. Answers may vary
```
  TO SQUARE1
    REPEAT 4[FORWARD 50 RIGHT 90]
  END
```

```
TO TRIANGLE1
  REPEAT 3[FORWARD 50 RIGHT 120]
END
```

(a) TO SQUARE.PILE
```
    REPEAT 4[SQUARE1 RIGHT 90]
    END
```

(c) TO RECT1
```
    REPEAT 2[FORWARD 60 RIGHT 90
      FORWARD 30 RIGHT 90]
    END
    TO RECL.SWIRL
      REPEAT 4[RECT1 LEFT 90]
    END
```

(e) TO STAR
```
    RIGHT 30
    REPEAT 4[TRIANGLE1 RIGHT 60
      FORWARD 50 RIGHT 30]
    END
```

7. Answers may vary.

(a) TO SQUARE.FACE
```
    SQUARE 60
    FORWARD 5 PENUP RIGHT 90
    FORWARD 25
    LEFT 90 PENDOWN
    SQUARE 10 PENUP FORWARD 18
    PENDOWN RIGHT 30
    TRIANGLE 10
    PENUP LEFT 30 FORWARD 15 LEFT
      90 FORWARD 10
    RIGHT 90 PENDOWN
    SQUARE 10 PENUP RIGHT 90
    FORWARD 20 LEFT 90 PENDOWN
    SQUARE 10
END
TO SQUARE :S
  REPEAT 4[FORWARD :S RIGHT 90]
END
TO TRIANGLE :S
  REPEAT 3[FORWARD :S RIGHT
    120]
END
```

(c) TO TAIL :S
```
    SQUARE :S
    FORWARD :S RIGHT 90 FORWARD
      :S LEFT 90
    SQUARE :S/2
    FORWARD :S/2 RIGHT 90 FORWARD
      :S/2 LEFT 90
    SQUARE :S/4
END
```

9.  ```
    TO KITE
      LEFT 45
      REPEAT 4[FORWARD 40 RIGHT 90]
      RIGHT 45
      REPEAT 3[BACK 20 K.TAIL RIGHT
      120]
      BACK 20 FORWARD 80 RIGHT 45
       FORWARD 30
      RIGHT 90 FORWARD 80
    END
      TO K.TAIL
       RIGHT 60
       REPEAT 3[FORWARD 10 RIGHT
         120]
       LEFT 180
       REPEAT 3[FORWARD 10 LEFT 120]
      END
    ```

10. (a) ```
    TO RECT :L :W
      REPEAT 2[FORWARD :L RIGHT 90
       FORWARD :W RIGHT 90]
    END
    ```
    (c) ```
    TO HAT :S
      RECT :S :S/2
      PENUP LEFT 90 FORWARD :S/2
      PENDOWN
      REPEAT 2[LEFT 90 FORWARD
      :S/10 LEFT 90 FORWARD
      :S+:S/2]
    END
    ```
    (e) ```
    TO RHOMBUS :S :A
      REPEAT 2[FORWARD :S RIGHT
      (180-:A) FORWARD :S RIGHT
      :A]
    END
    ```

11. ```
    TO BLADES :S
     REPEAT 12[FORWARD :S
      PARALLELOGRAM :S*3/2 :S 30
      RIGHT 30]
    END
    TO PARALLELOGRAM :S1 :S2 :A
     REPEAT 2[FORWARD :S1 RIGHT :A
      FORWARD :S2 RIGHT (180-:A)]
    END
    ```

Problem Set AII-2

3. Answers may vary.
   (a) ```
   TO STRETCH :S
       IF :S<5 STOP
       SQUARE :S
       FORWARD :S RIGHT 90
       FORWARD :S LEFT 90
       STRETCH :S-10
       END
   ```
   *(In Apple Logo II, replace IF :S<5 STOP with IF :S<5 [STOP].)*

(c) ```
   TO PISA :S :A
     IF :S<5 STOP
     SQUARE :S
     FORWARD :S LEFT :A
     PISA :S*0.75 :A
   END
   ```
   (In Apple Logo II, replace IF :S<5 STOP with IF :S<5 [STOP].)

(e) ```
   TO ROW.HOUSE :S
   IF :S<5 STOP
     HOUSE :S
     SETUP :S
     ROW.HOUSE :S/2
   END
   ```
   *(In Apple Logo II, replace IF :S<5 STOP with IF :S<5 [STOP].)*
   ```
   TO HOUSE :S
     SQUARE :S
     FORWARD :S
     RIGHT 30 TRIANGLE :S
     LEFT 30
   END
   TO SETUP :S
     BACK :S RIGHT 90
     FORWARD :S LEFT 90
   END
   ```

4. ```
   TO NEST.TRI :S
    IF :S<10 STOP
    RIGHT 30 TRIANGLE :S
    FD :S/2 RIGHT 30
    NEST.TRI :S/2
   END
   ```
   (In Apple Logo II, replace IF :S<10 STOP with IF :S<10 [STOP].)
   ```
   TO TRIANGLE :S
    REPEAT 3[FORWARD :S RIGHT 120]
   END
   ```

7. Answers may vary.
   ```
   TO SPIN.SQ :S
    IF :S<5 STOP
    SQUARE :S
    RIGHT 20
    SPIN.SQ :S-5
   END
   ```
   (In Apple Logo II, replace IF :S<5 STOP with IF :S<5 [STOP].)
   ```
   TO SQUARE :S
    REPEAT 4[FORWARD :S RIGHT 90]
   END
   ```
   ```

9. Answers may vary.

```
TO SQ.TOWER :S
 IF :S<5 STOP
 SQUARE :S FORWARD :S
 SQ.TOWER :S/2
 SQUARE :S FORWARD :S
END
```

(In Apple Logo II, replace IF :S<5 STOP *with* IF :S<5 [STOP].)

```
TO SQUARE :S
 REPEAT 4[FORWARD :S RIGHT 90]
END
```

REFERENCES

Billstein, R. "Checkerboard Mathematics." *Mathematics Teacher*. 86 (December 1975): 640–646.

Billstein, R., S. Libeskind, and J. Lott. *Logo: MIT Logo for the Apple*. Menlo Park, CA: Benjamin/Cummings Publishing Company, 1985.

Billstein, R., S. Libeskind, and J. Lott. *Apple Logo: Programming and Problem Solving*. Menlo Park, CA: Benjamin/Cumming Publishing Company, 1986.

Comprehensive School Mathematics Program. *Elements of Mathematics, Book O, Intuitive Background*. St. Ann, MO: CEMREL, 1973.

Engel, A. *A Short Course in Probability*. St. Louis, MO: Comprehensive School Mathematics Project, 1970.

Gardner, M. "The Paradox of the Nontransitive Dice and the Elusive Principle of Indifference," *Scientific American* 223 (December 1970): 110–114.

Halmos, P. "The Heart of Mathematics." *American Mathematical Monthly*. 87 (July 1980): 519–524.

Hoffer, A. "Making a Better Beer Glass." *The Mathematics Teacher*. 75 (May 1982): 378–379.

Hoffer, A. *van Hiele-Based Research*. In R. Lesh and M. Landau. (eds.), *Acquisition of Mathematics Concepts and Processes*. New York, NY: Academic Press, 1983.

Huff, D. *How to Lie with Statistics*. New York, NY: Norton, 1954.

Kline, M. *Mathematics in Western Culture*. New York, NY: Oxford, 1953.

Lindquist, M., and M. Dana. "The Neglected Decimeter." *Arithmetic Teacher*. 24 (October 1977): 10–17.

Loomis, E. *The Pythagorean Proposition*. Washington, D.C.: National Council of Teachers of Mathematics, 1972.

Lott, J. "Escher-like Logo-type Tessellations." *Logo Exchange* 6 (November 1987): 7–11.

Mathematical Association of America. American Junior High School Mathematics Examination. Write for information to: Executive Director of the American Mathematics Competitions, Professor Walter E. Mientka, Department of Mathematics and Statistics, University of Nebraska, Lincoln, NB. 68588–0322.

National Council of Teachers of Mathematics. *Curriculum and Evaluation Standards for School Mathematics*. Reston, VA.: National Council of Teachers of Mathematics, 1989.

Pawley, R. "5-Con Triangles." *The Mathematics Teacher*. 60 (May 1967): 438–443.

Phillips, J., and R. Zwoyer. *Motion Geometry*. New York, NY: Harper and Row Publishers, 1976.

Polya, G. *How To Solve It*. Princeton, N.J.: Princeton University Press, 1957.

Ranucci, E., and J. Teeters. *Creating Escher-type Drawings*. Palo Alto, CA: Creative Publications, 1977.

Tukey, J. *Exploring Data Analysis*. Menlo Park, CA: Addison-Wesley, 1977.

Index

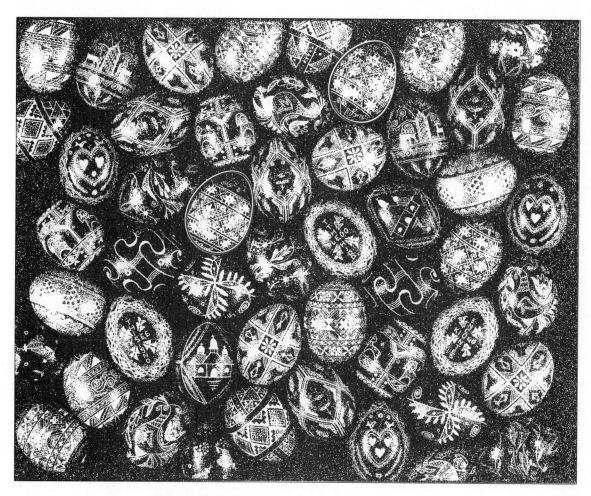

Cover Puzzle Answer

The eggs outlined above are the two identical eggs.